MU SHI SHI

8, 9, and 10

Yuki Urushibara

Translated and adapted by
William Flanagan

Lettered by
North Market Street Graphics

Ballantine Books * New York

A Del Rey Manga/Kodansha Trade Paperback Original

Mushishi volume 8 copyright © 2007 Yuki Urushibara
Mushishi volume 9 copyright © 2008 Yuki Urushibara
Mushishi volume 10 copyright © 2008 Yuki Urushibara
English translation copyright © 2010 Yuki Urushibara

All rights reserved.

Published in the United States by Del Rey, an imprint of The Random House Publishing Group, a division of Random House, Inc., New York.

DEL REY is a registered trademark and the Del Rey colophon is a trademark of Random House, Inc.

Publication rights arranged through Kodansha Ltd.

First published in Japan in 2007 and 2008 by Kodansha Ltd., Tokyo

ISBN 978-0-345-50560-6

Printed in the United States of America

www.delreymanga.com

9 8 7 6 5 4 3 2 1

Translator/adaptor: William Flanagan
Lettering: North Market Street Graphics

A Message from the Author

One New Year's Day, my grandmother watched a high school soccer game and said in a very serious voice, "It's good for kids that age to be out having fun." At that age, apparently, she had been put to work in apprentice-level jobs. It's very true that in the intervening years everything has changed. But my grandmother and her generation were there before the changes, and they're connected to us. I wonder what will become of my generation. Perhaps now is the only time we'll be able to have a sense of that fact.

—Yuki Urushibara

蟲師
むしし
師
Mushishi
8

Yuki Urushibara

Contents

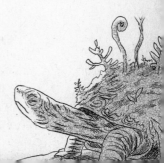

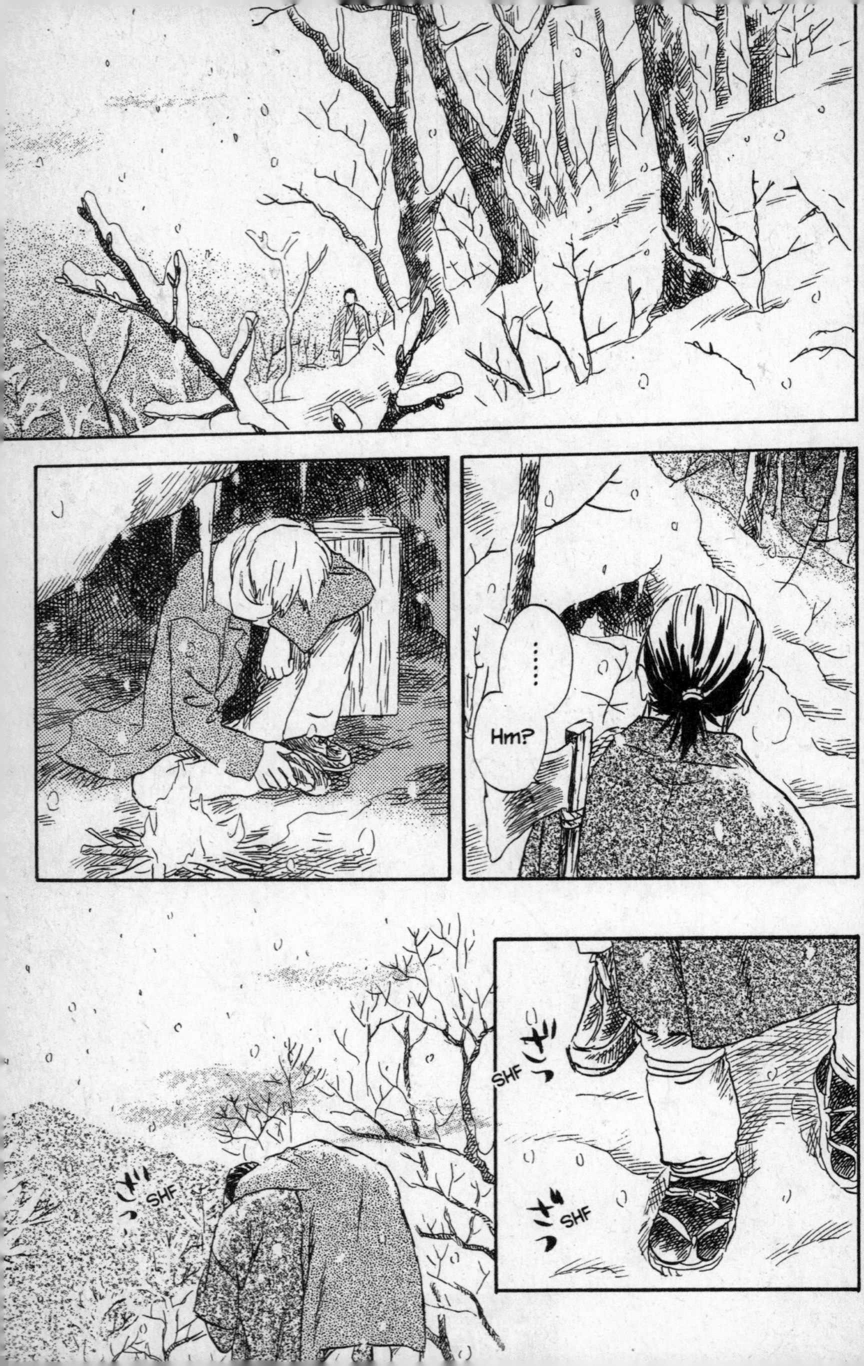
……
Hm?
ザッ SHF
ザッ SHF
ザッ SHF

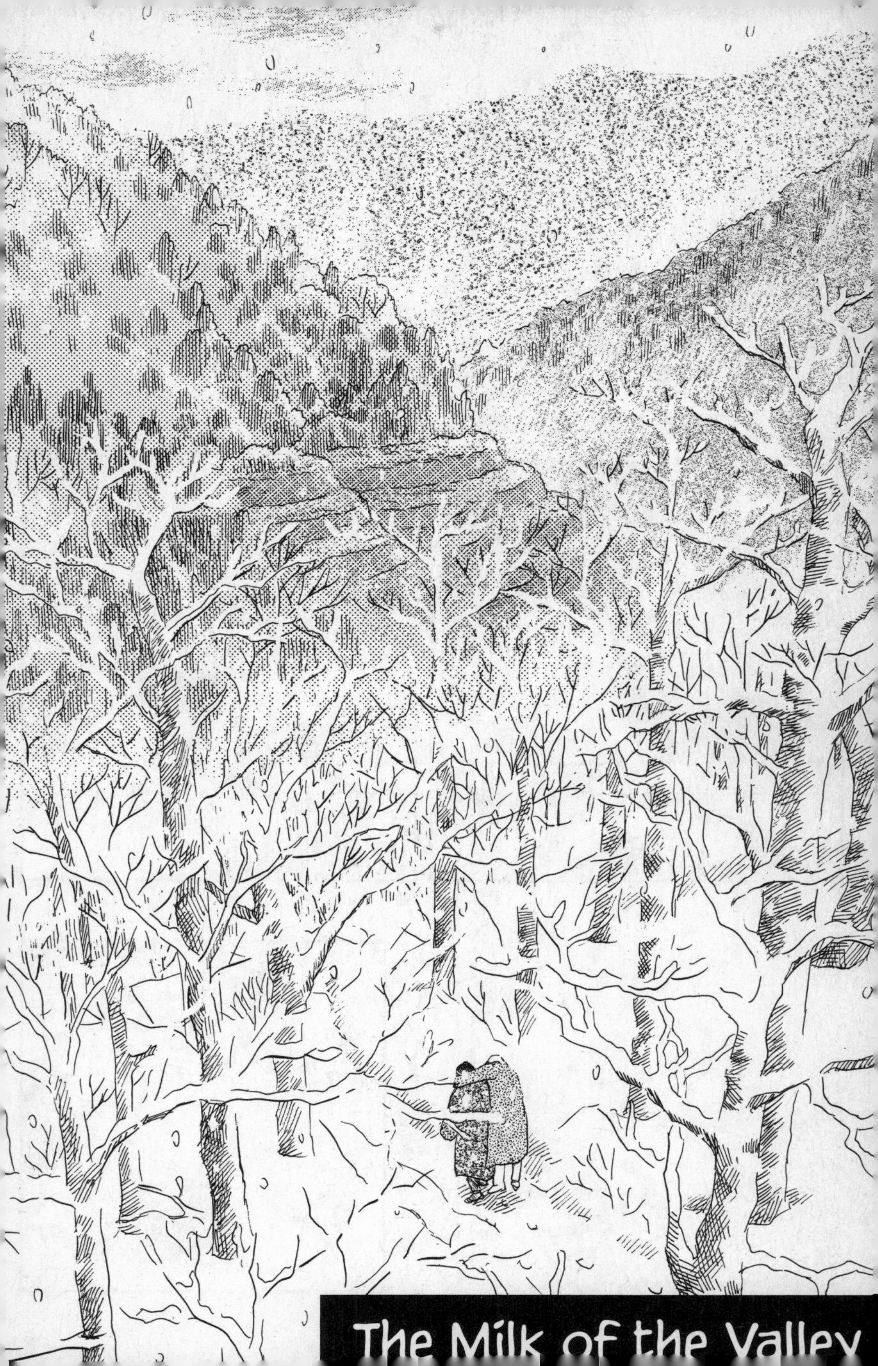

The Milk of the Valley

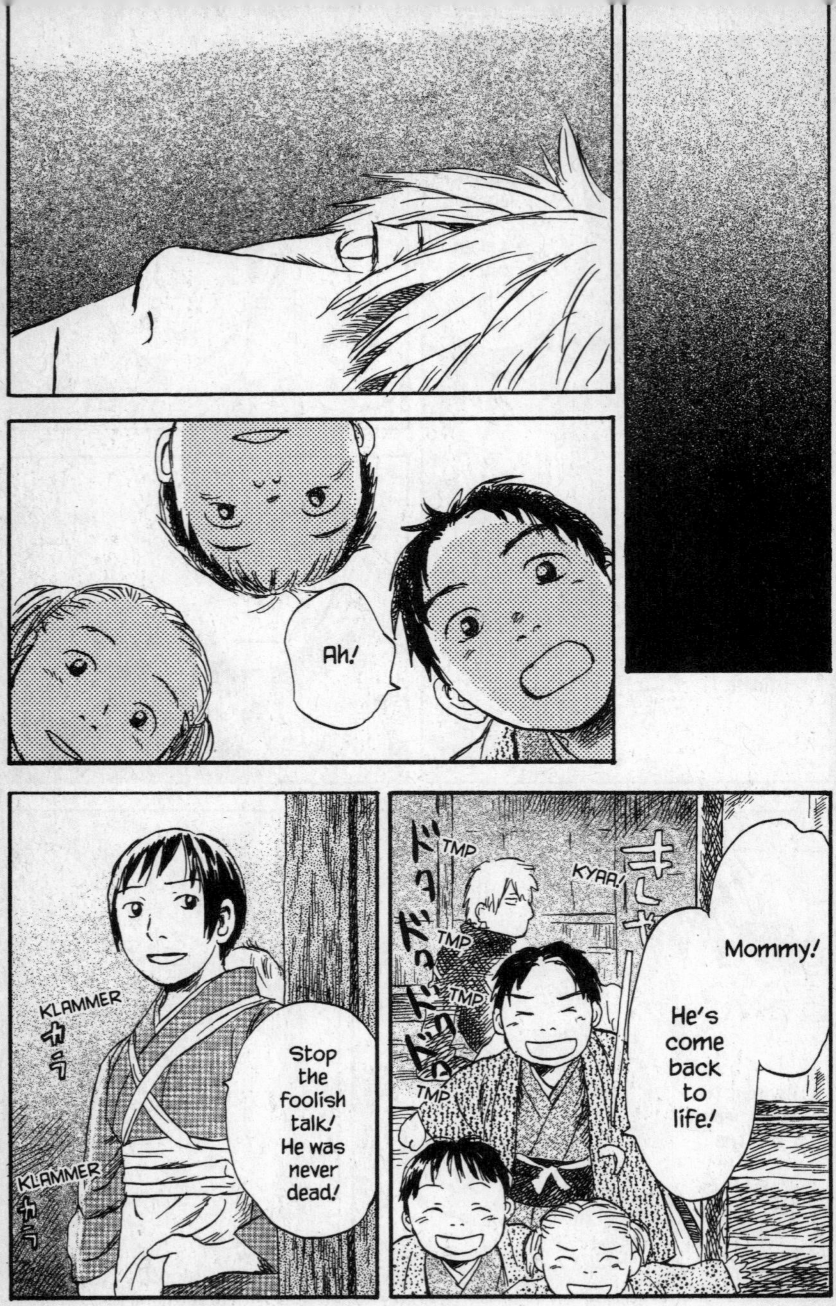
Ah!
Mommy! He's come back to life!
TMP
KYAA!
TMP
TMP
TMP
Stop the foolish talk! He was never dead!
KLAMMER
KLAMMER

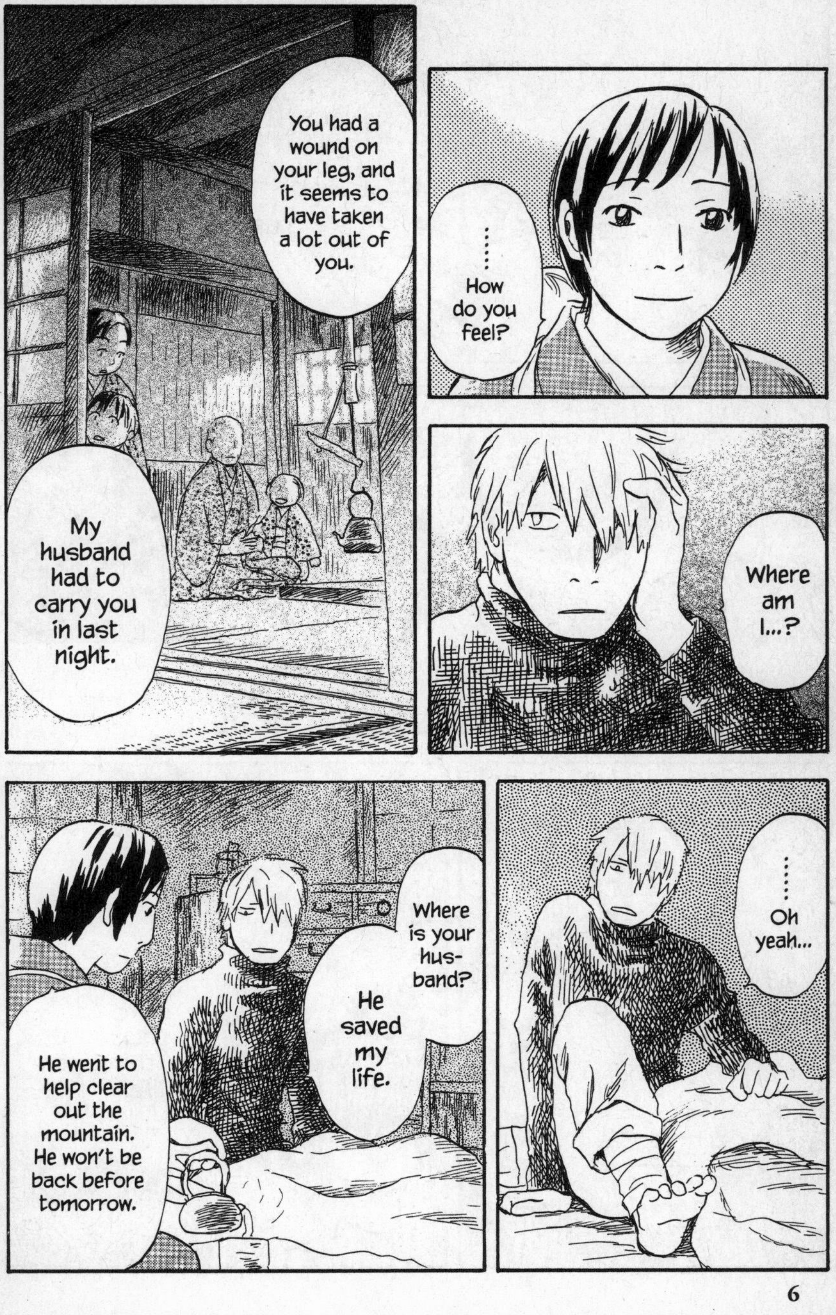
.....
How do you feel?
Where am I...?
You had a wound on your leg, and it seems to have taken a lot out of you.
My husband had to carry you in last night.
.....
Oh yeah...
Where is your hus-band?
He saved my life.
He went to help clear out the mountain. He won't be back before tomorrow.

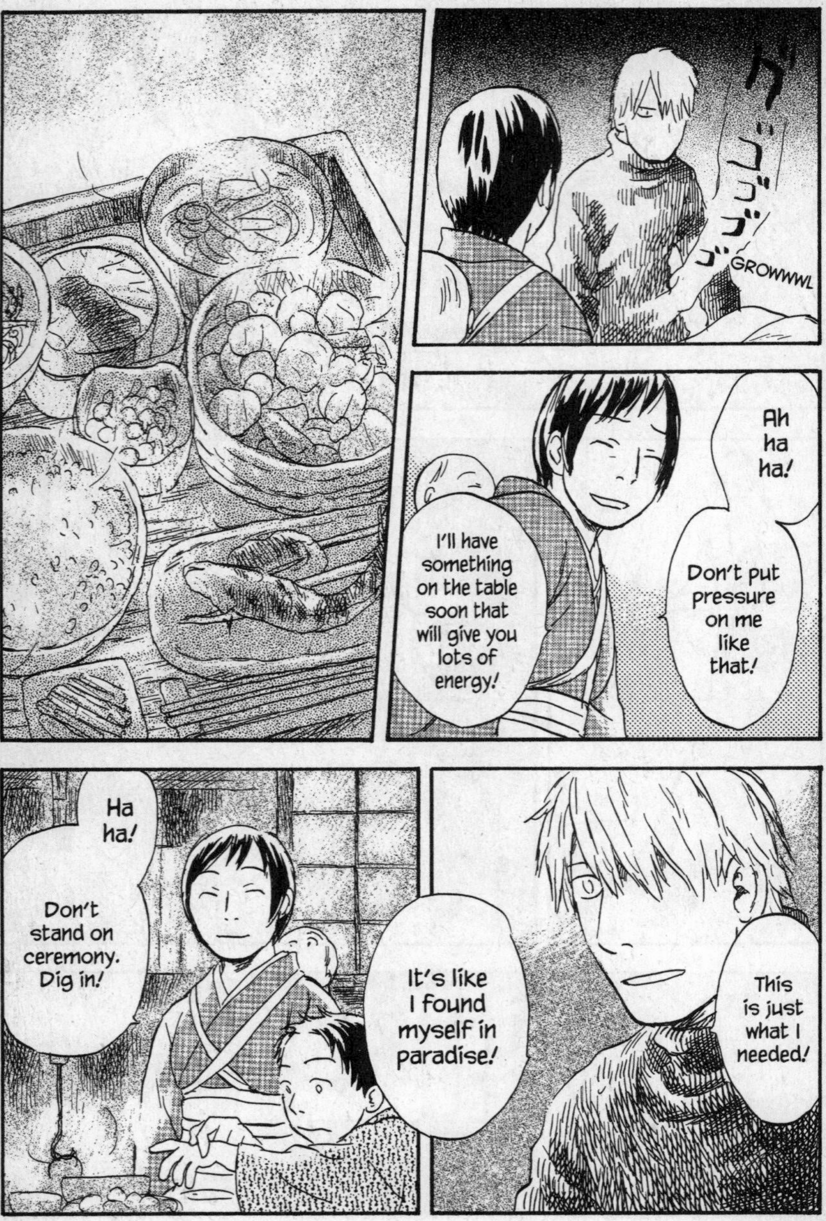
グッゴゴゴゴ
GROWWWL
Ah ha ha!
Don't put pressure on me like that!
I'll have something on the table soon that will give you lots of energy!
This is just what I needed!
It's like I found myself in paradise!
Ha ha!
Don't stand on ceremony. Dig in!

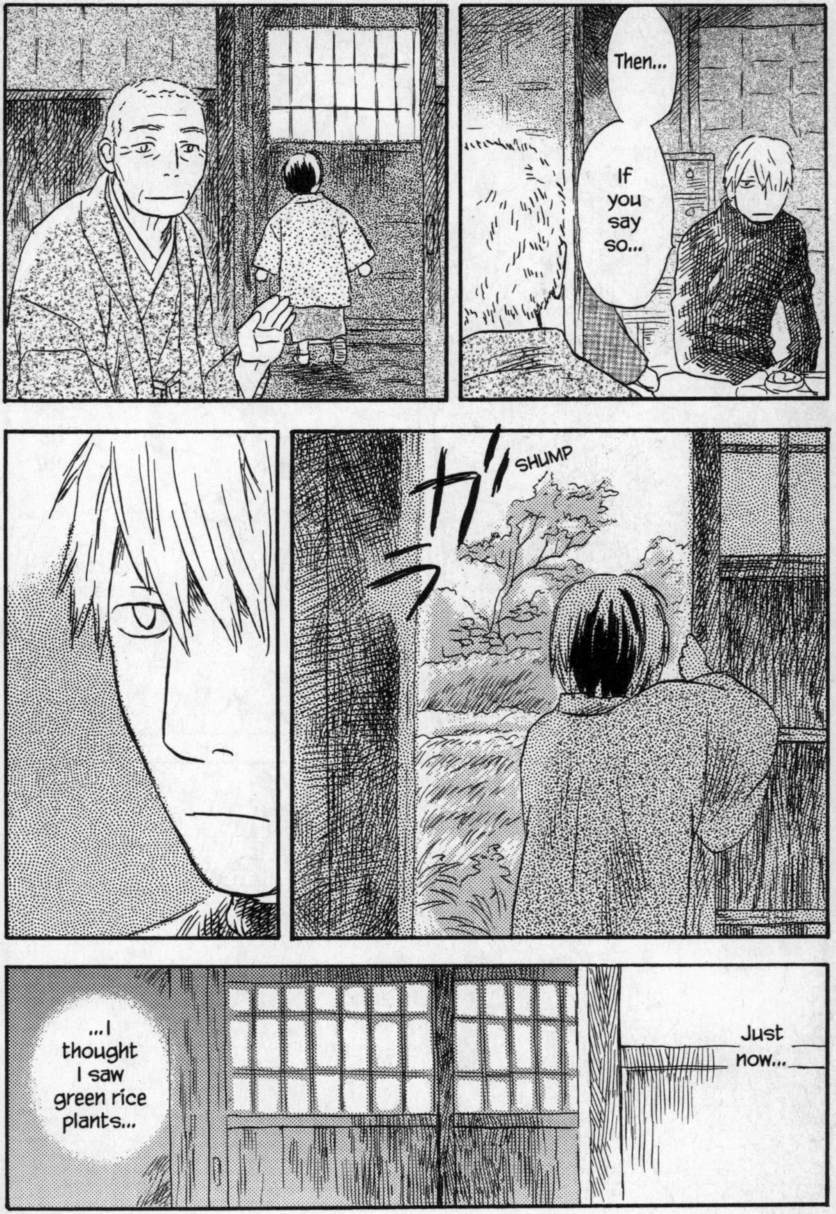
Then...
If you say so...
SHUMP
Just now...
...I thought I saw green rice plants...

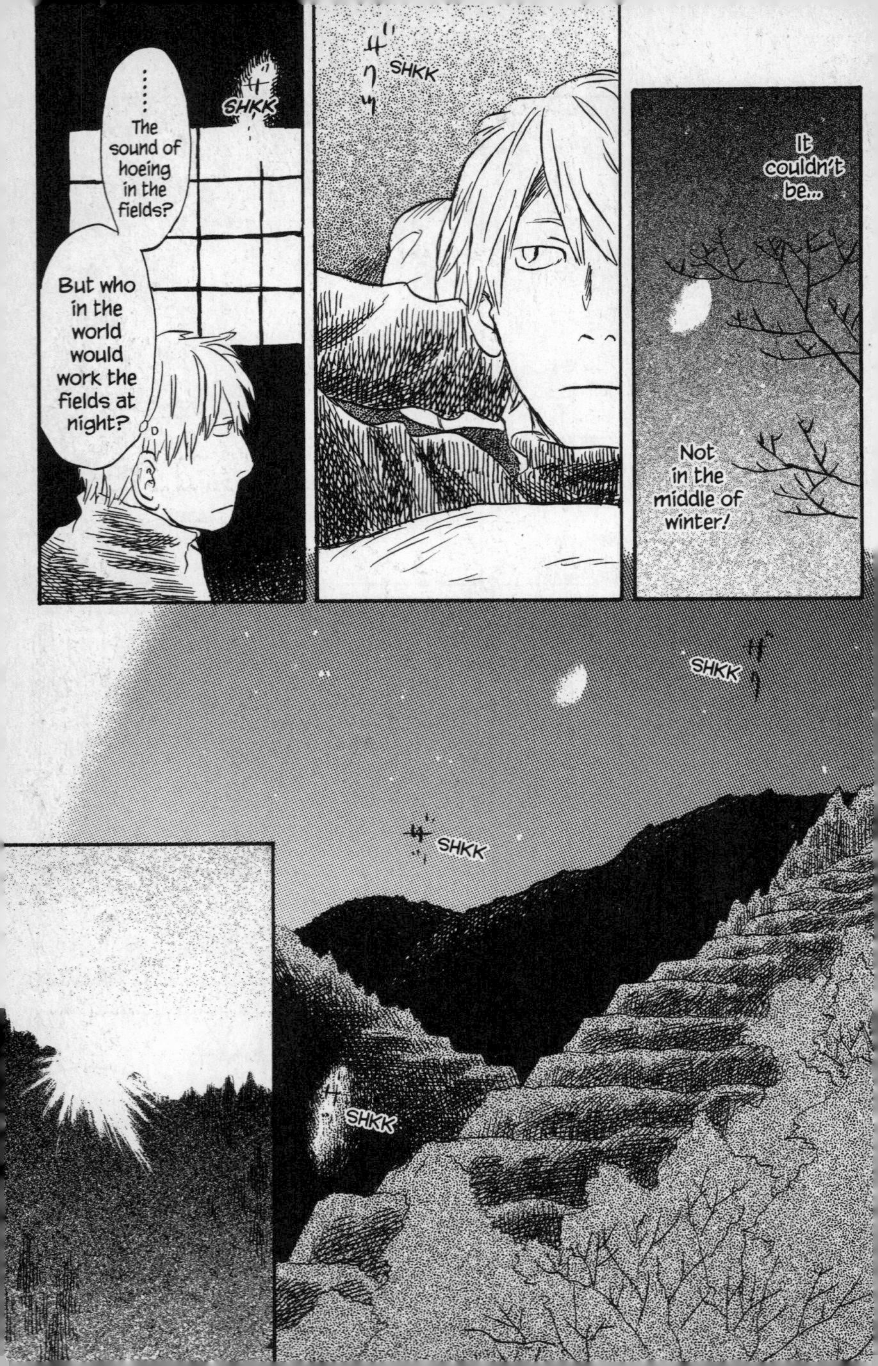

It couldn't be...
Not in the middle of winter!
SHKK
......
The sound of hoeing in the fields?
But who in the world would work the fields at night?
SHKK
SHKK
SHKK
SHKK

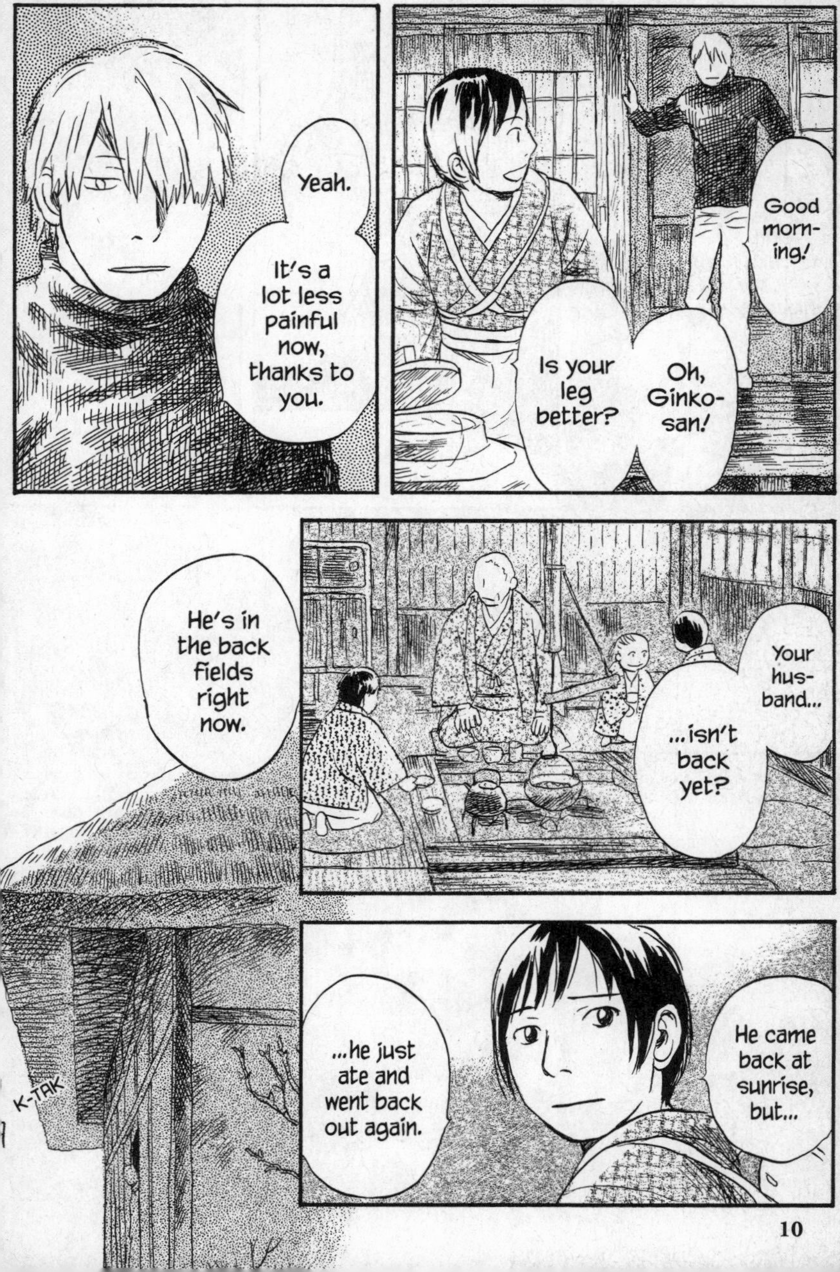
Good morning!
Oh, Ginko-san!
Is your leg better?
Yeah.
It's a lot less painful now, thanks to you.
Your husband...
...isn't back yet?
He's in the back fields right now.
He came back at sunrise, but...
...he just ate and went back out again.
K-TAK

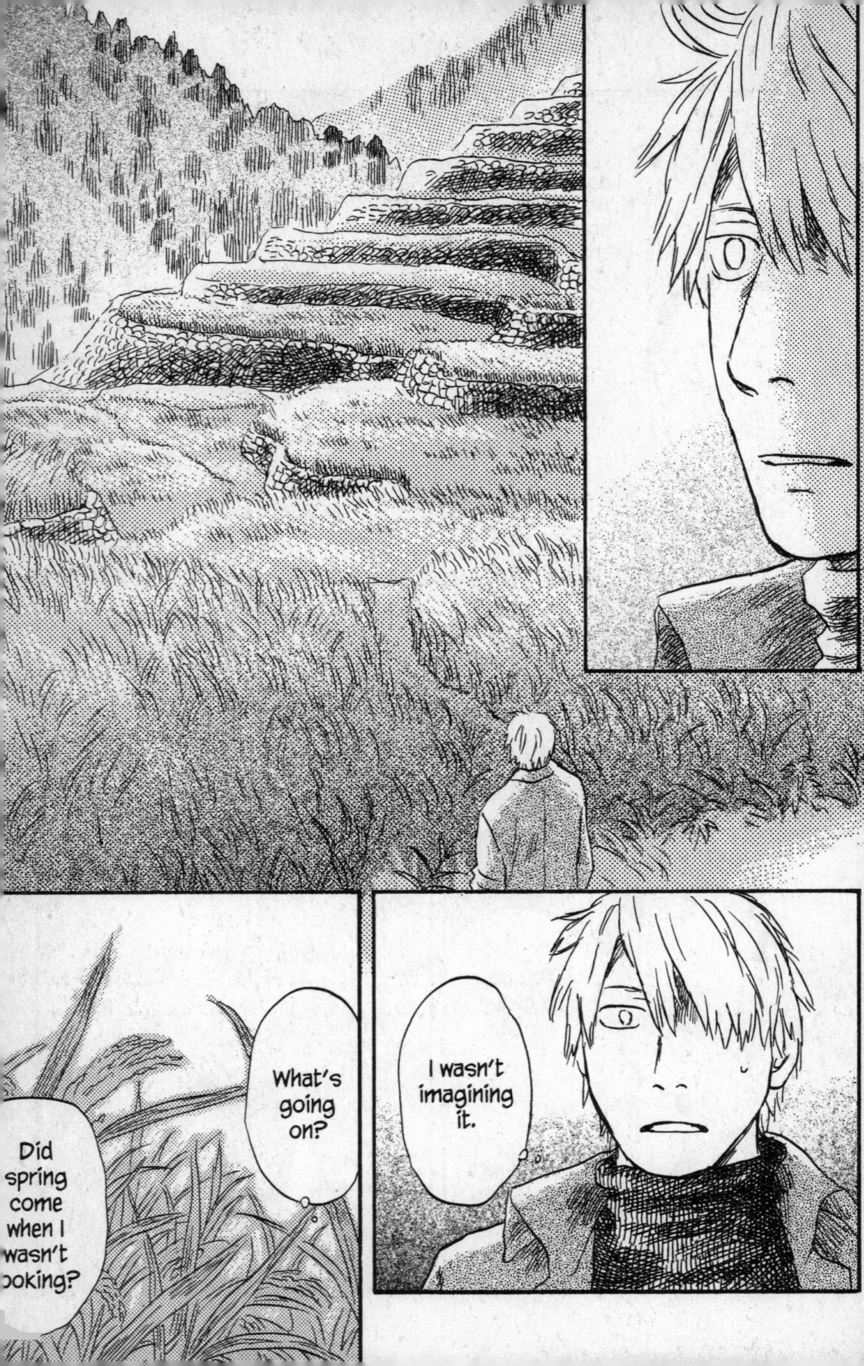
I wasn't imagining it.
What's going on?
Did spring come when I wasn't ooking?

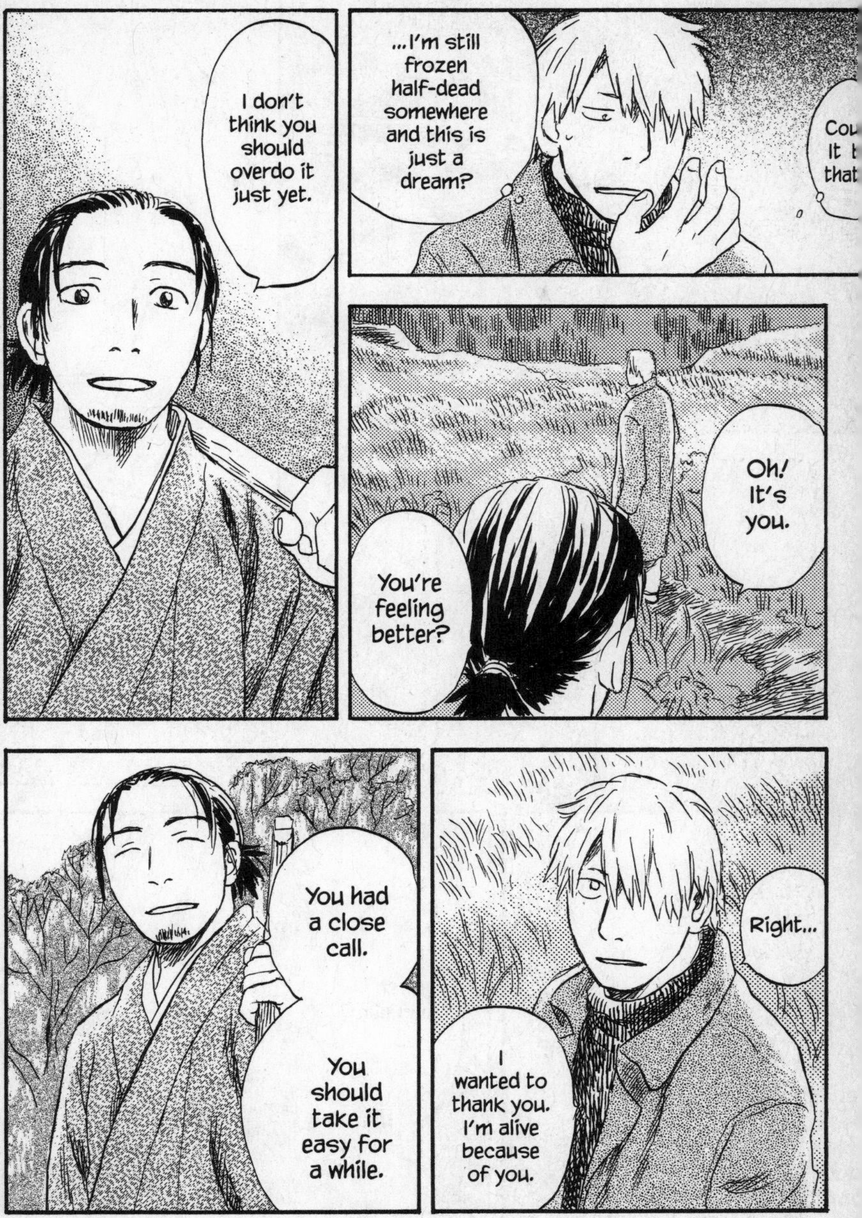
...I'm still frozen half-dead somewhere and this is just a dream?
Oh! It's you.
You're feeling better?
I don't think you should overdo it just yet.
Right...
I wanted to thank you. I'm alive because of you.
You had a close call.
You should take it easy for a while.

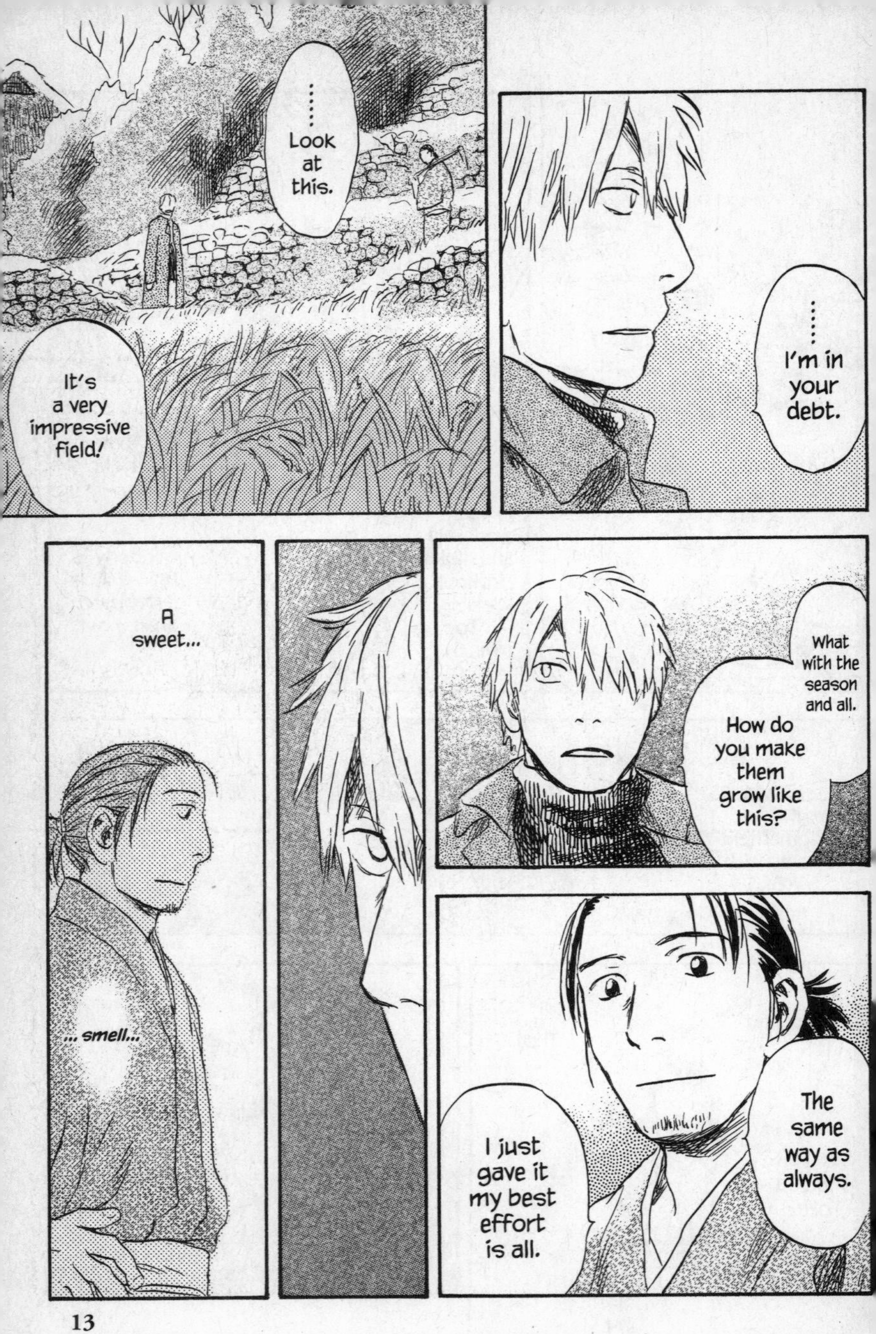
......
I'm in your debt.
......
Look at this.
It's a very impressive field!
What with the season and all.
How do you make them grow like this?
The same way as always.
I just gave it my best effort is all.
A sweet...
... smell...

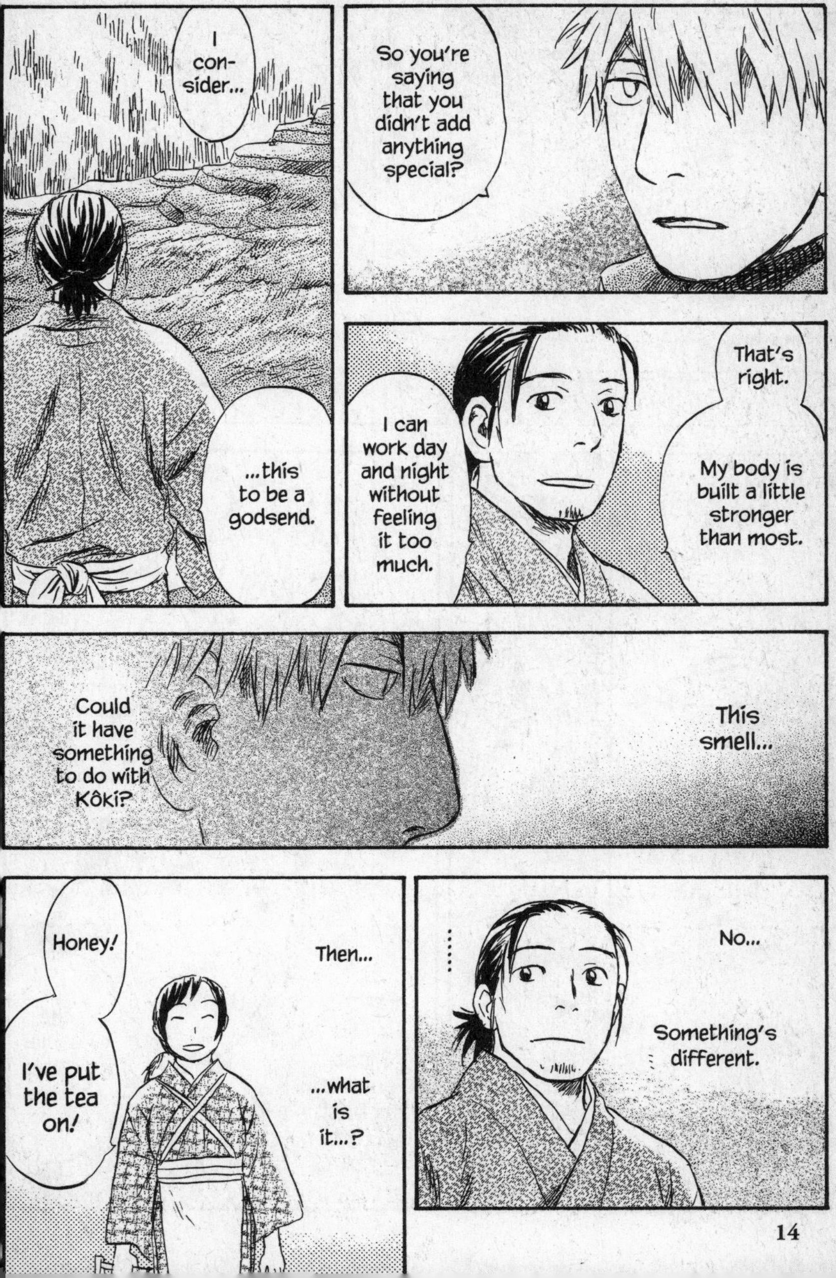
So you're saying that you didn't add anything special?
That's right.
My body is built a little stronger than most.
I can work day and night without feeling it too much.
I consider...
...this to be a godsend.
This smell...
Could it have something to do with Kôki?
No...
Something's different.
......
Then...
...what is it...?
Honey!
I've put the tea on!

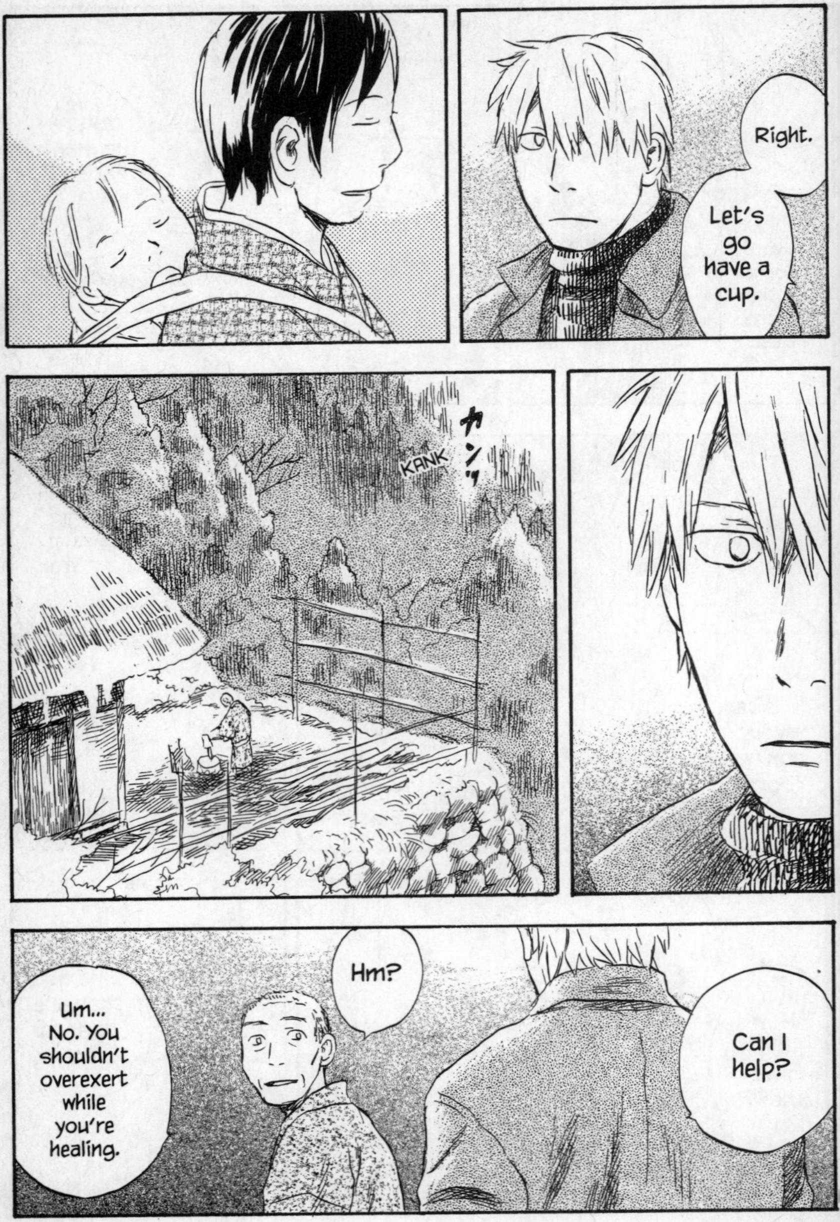

Right.
Let's go have a cup.
KANK
カンッ
Can I help?
Hm?
Um... No. You shouldn't overexert while you're healing.

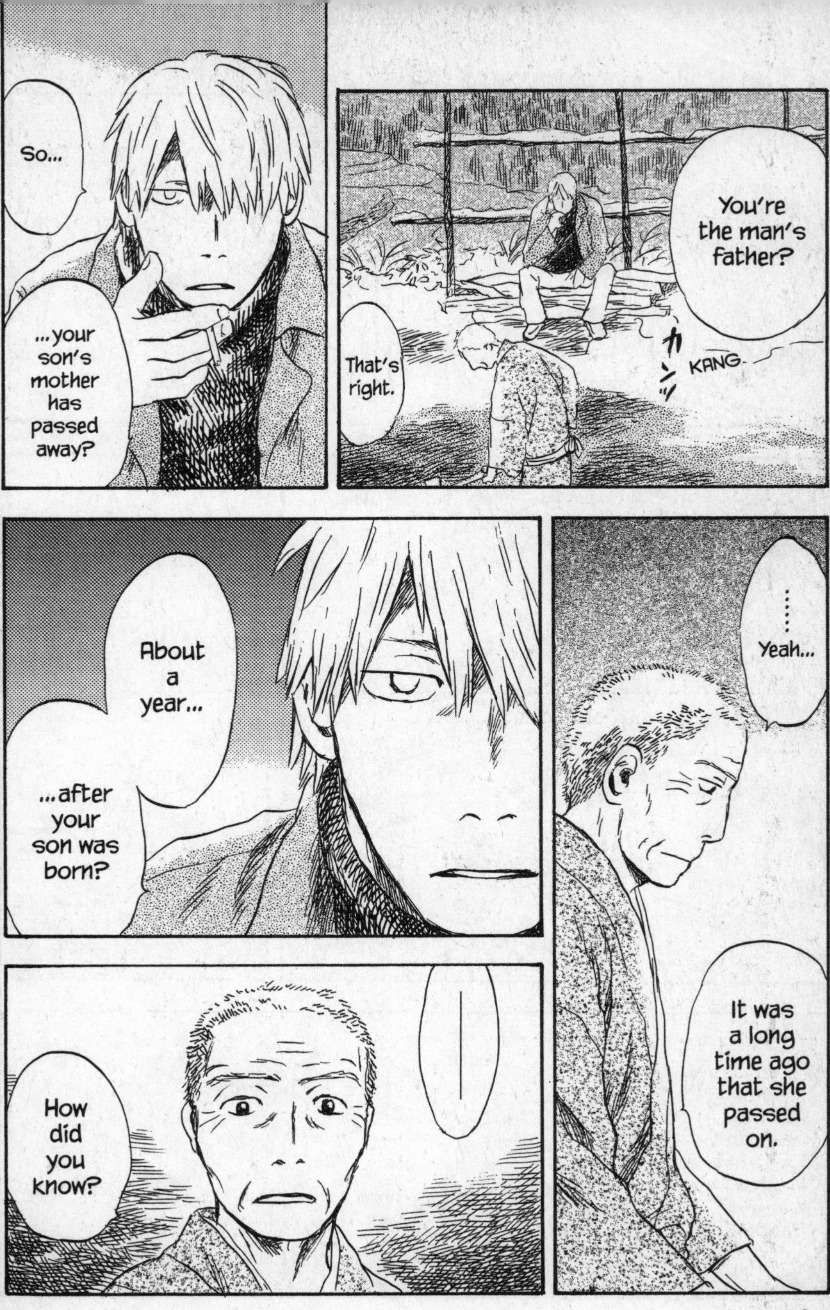
You're the man's father?
カンッ
KANG
That's right.
So...
...your son's mother has passed away?
......
Yeah...
It was a long time ago that she passed on.
About a year...
...after your son was born?
—
How did you know?

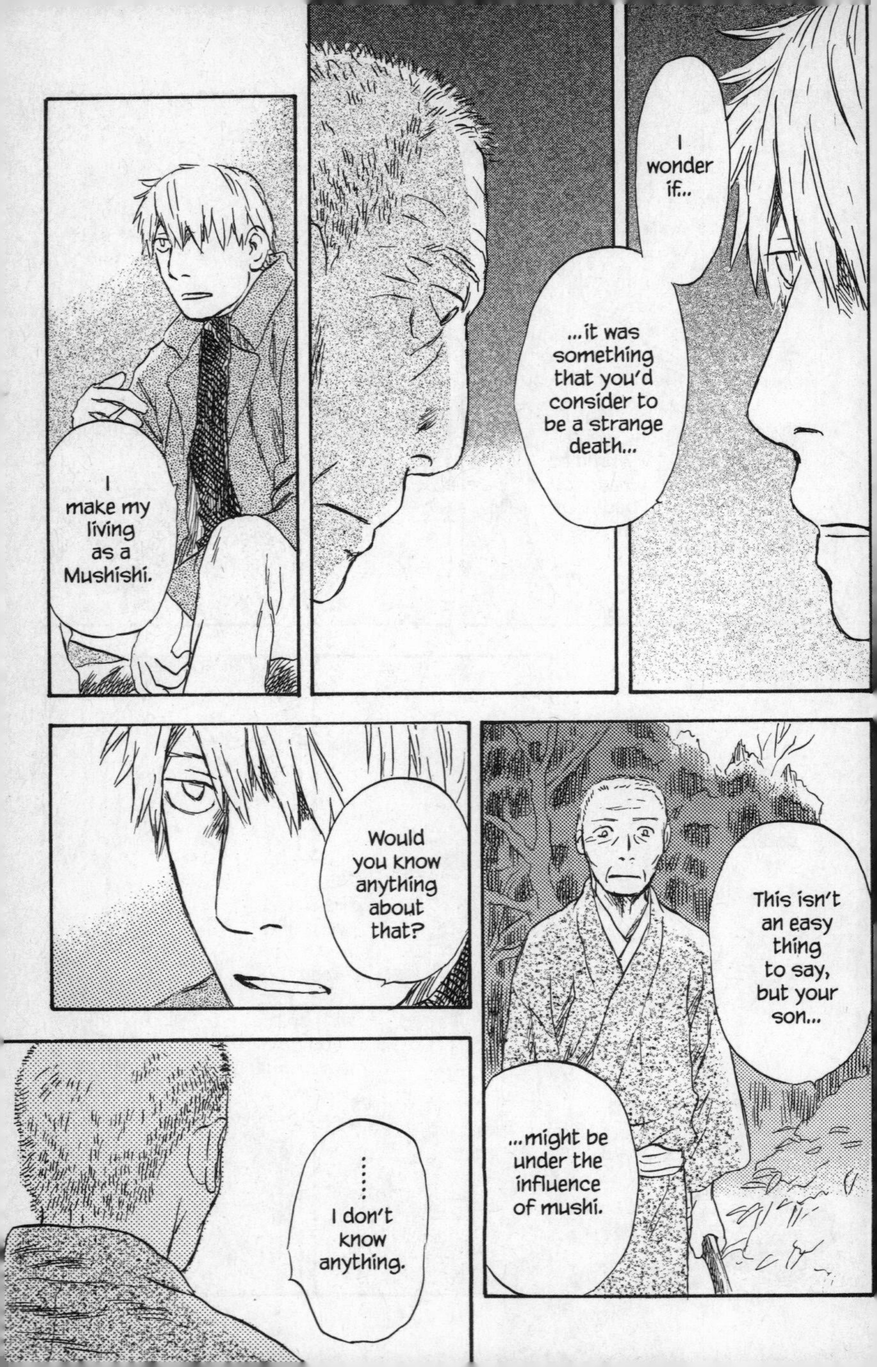
I wonder if...
...it was something that you'd consider to be a strange death...
I make my living as a Mushishi.
This isn't an easy thing to say, but your son...
...might be under the influence of mushi.
Would you know anything about that?
......
I don't know anything.

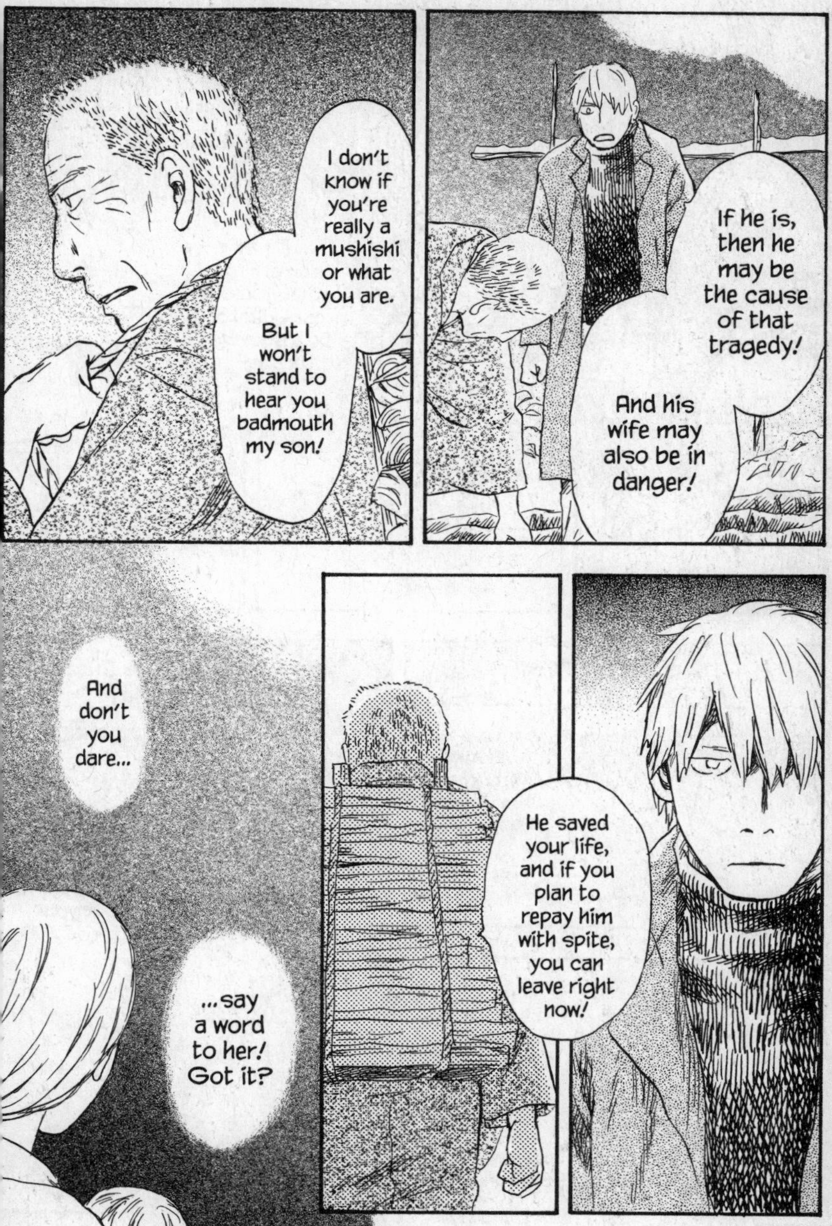
If he is, then he may be the cause of that tragedy!
And his wife may also be in danger!
I don't know if you're really a mushishi or what you are.
But I won't stand to hear you badmouth my son!
He saved your life, and if you plan to repay him with spite, you can leave right now!
And don't you dare...
...say a word to her! Got it?

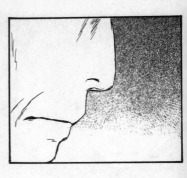

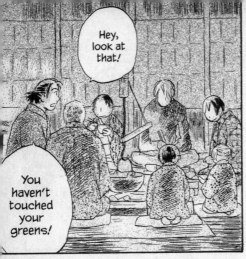

Hey, look at that!

You haven't touched your greens!

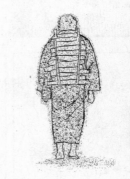

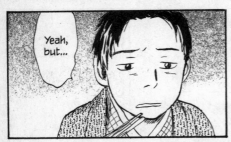

Yeah, but...

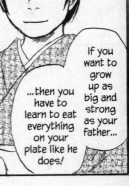

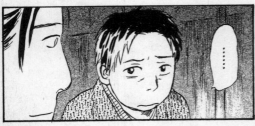

.....

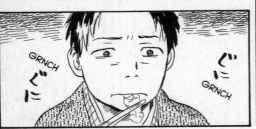

GRNCH

GRNCH

If you want to grow up as big and strong as your father...

...then you have to learn to eat everything on your plate like he does!

19

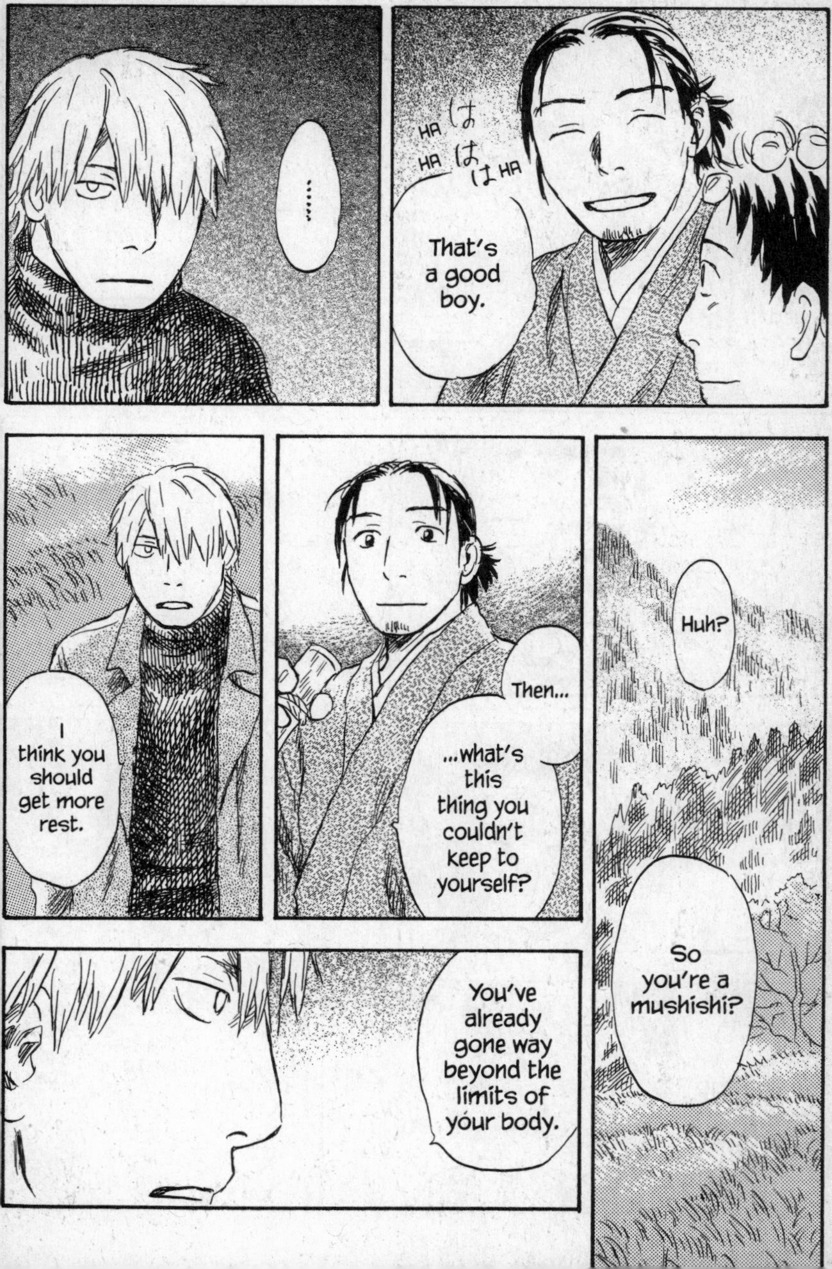
HA は HA は は HA
That's a good boy.
......
Huh?
So you're a mushishi?
Then...
...what's this thing you couldn't keep to yourself?
I think you should get more rest.
You've already gone way beyond the limits of your body.

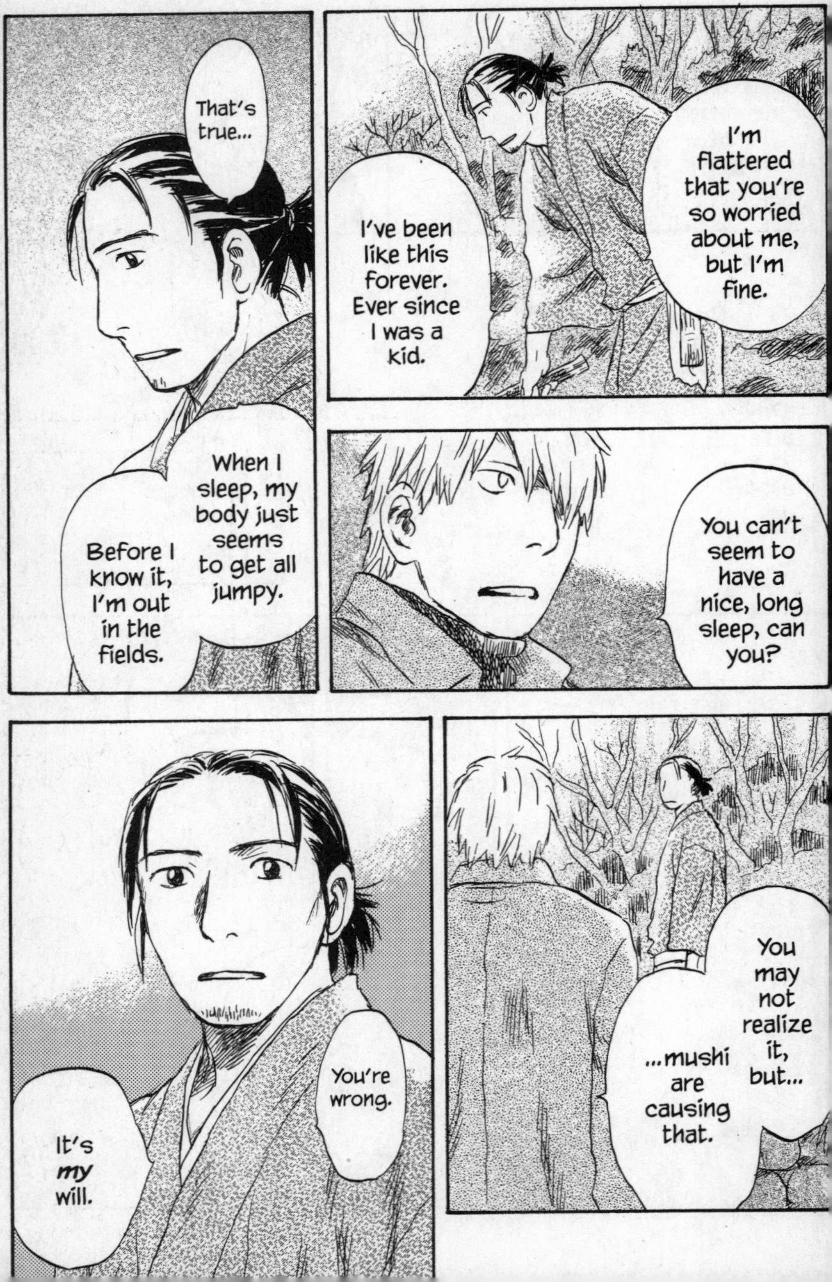
I'm flattered that you're so worried about me, but I'm fine.
I've been like this forever. Ever since I was a kid.
You can't seem to have a nice, long sleep, can you?
That's true...
When I sleep, my body just seems to get all jumpy.
Before I know it, I'm out in the fields.
You may not realize it, but...
...mushi are causing that.
You're wrong.
It's *my* will.

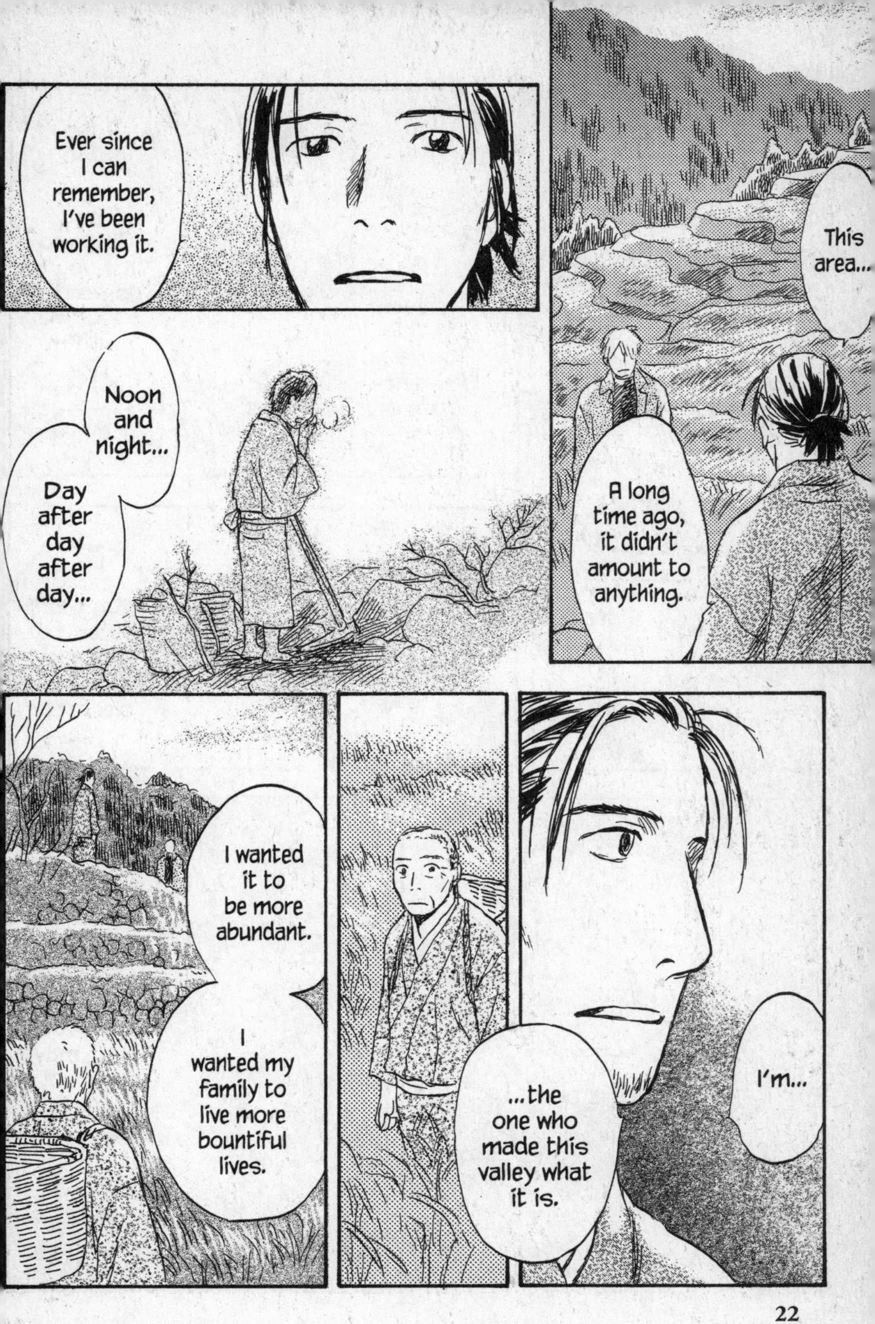
This area...
A long time ago, it didn't amount to anything.
Ever since I can remember, I've been working it.
Noon and night...
Day after day after day...
I'm...
...the one who made this valley what it is.
I wanted it to be more abundant.
I wanted my family to live more bountiful lives.

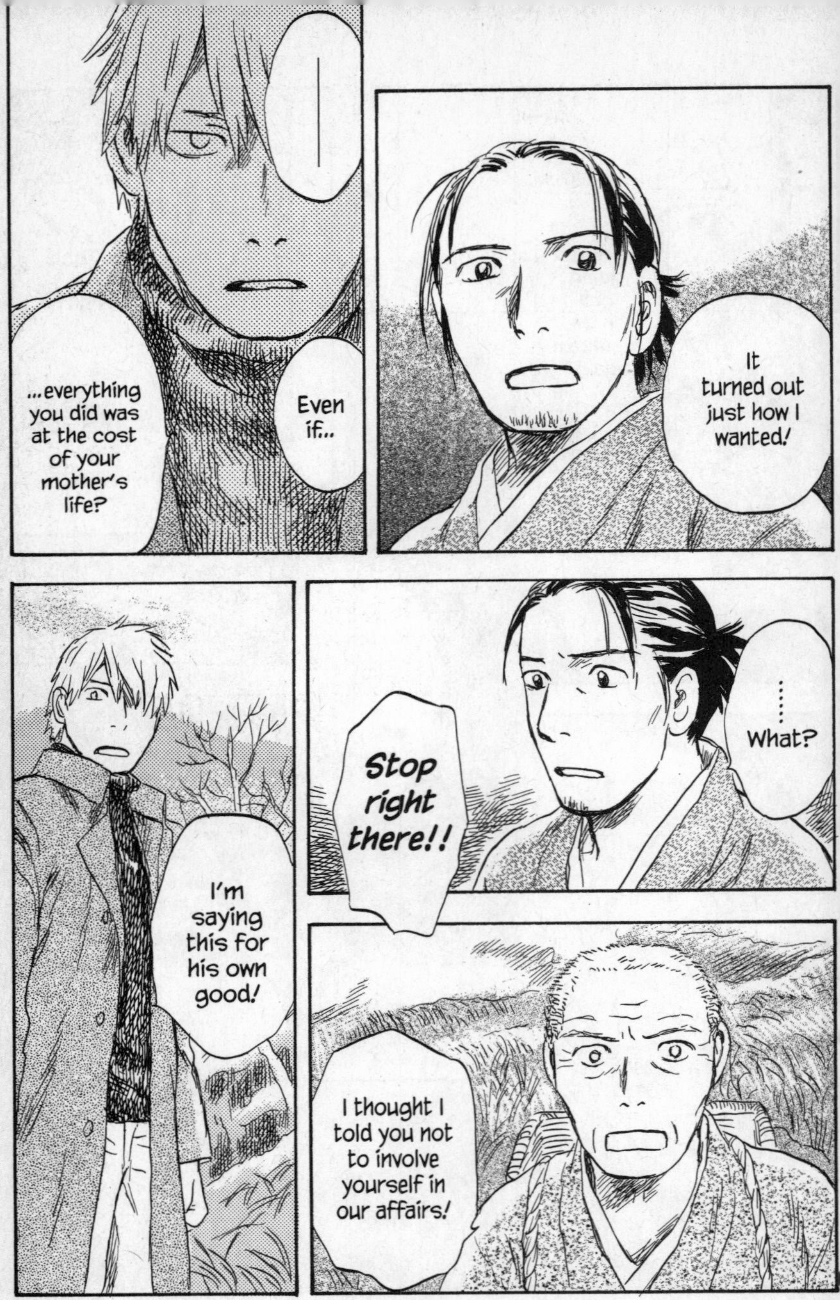
It turned out just how I wanted!
—
Even if...
...everything you did was at the cost of your mother's life?
......What?
Stop right there!!
I thought I told you not to involve yourself in our affairs!
I'm saying this for his own good!

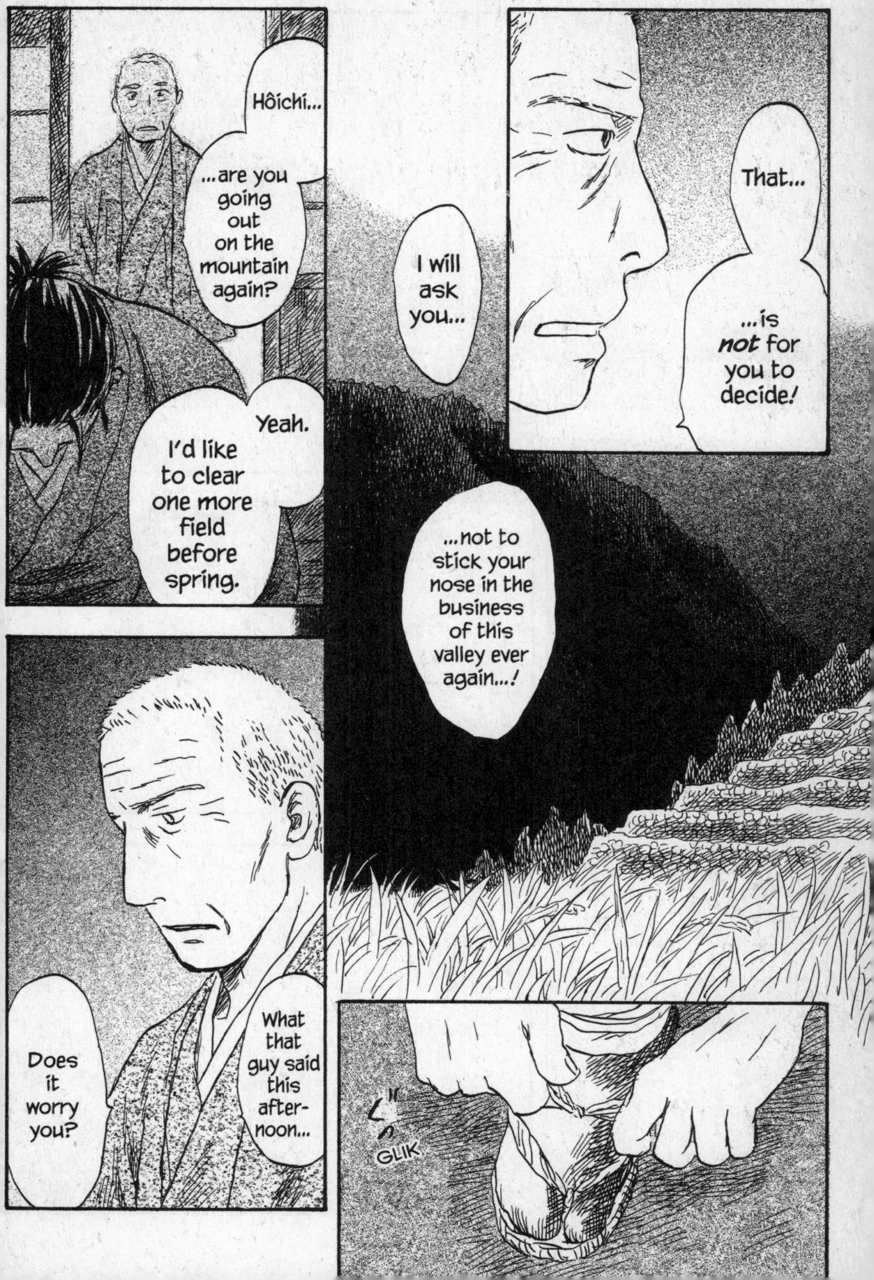
That...
...is *not* for you to decide!
I will ask you...
...not to stick your nose in the business of this valley ever again...!
GLIK
Hôichi...
...are you going out on the mountain again?
Yeah. I'd like to clear one more field before spring.
What that guy said this afternoon...
Does it worry you?

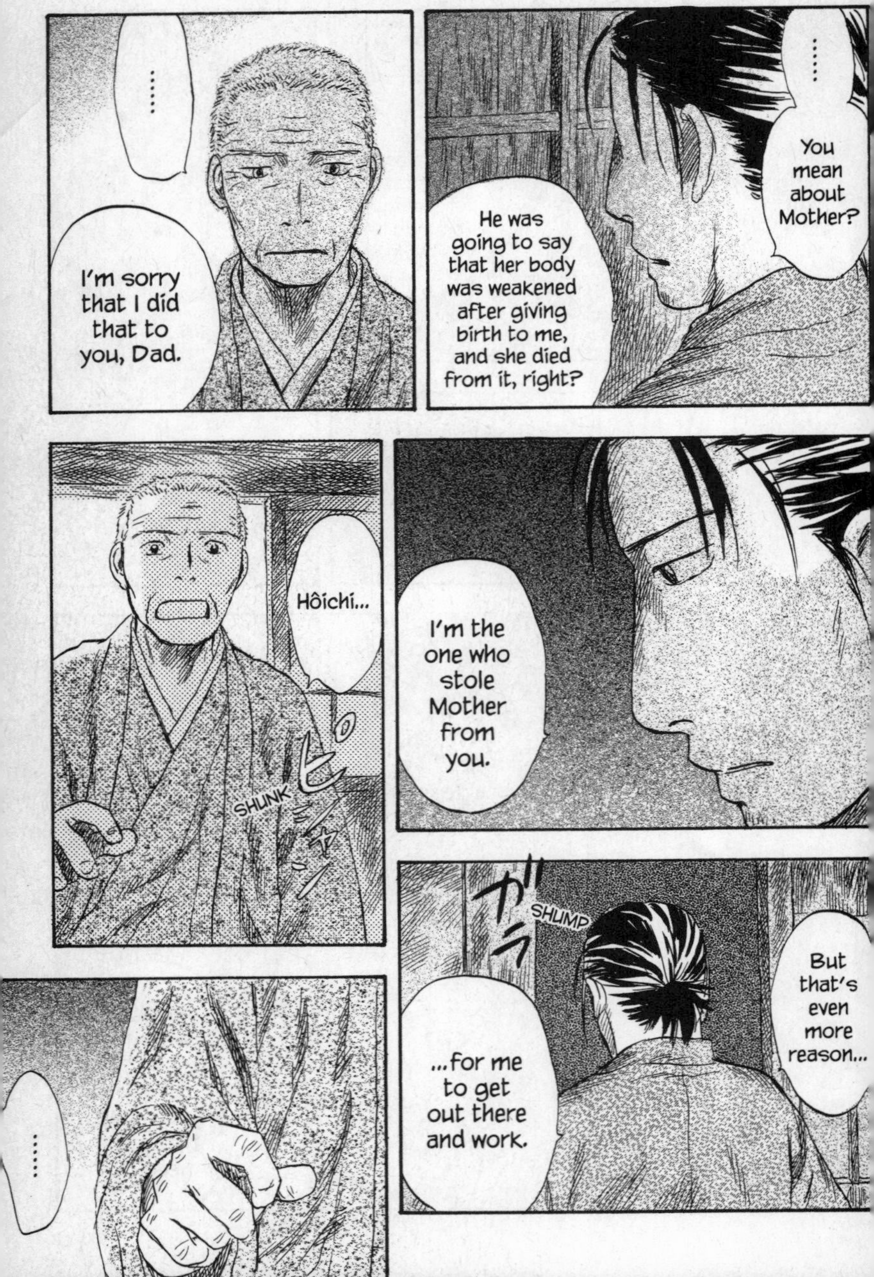
......
You mean about Mother?
He was going to say that her body was weakened after giving birth to me, and she died from it, right?
......
I'm sorry that I did that to you, Dad.
I'm the one who stole Mother from you.
Hôichi...
SHUNK
SHUMP
But that's even more reason...
...for me to get out there and work.
......

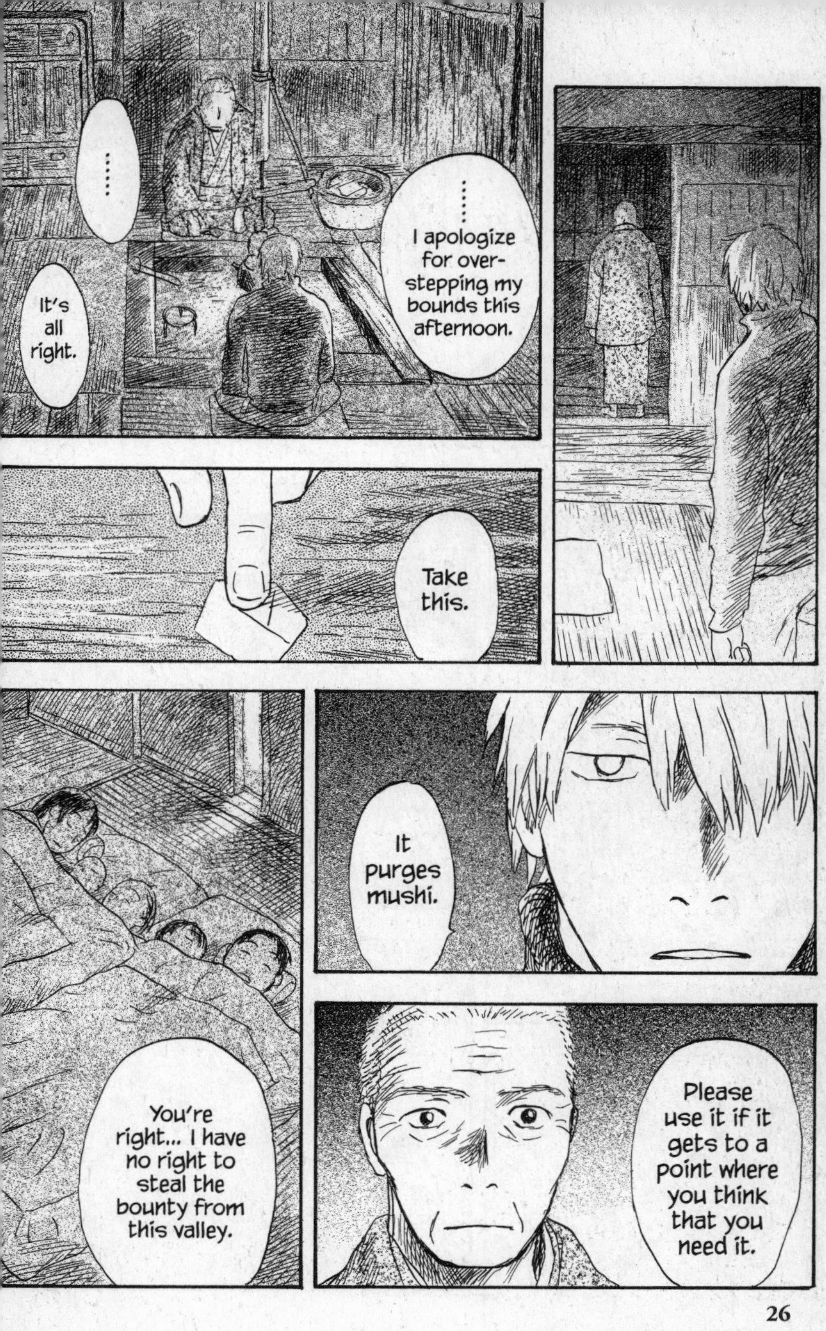

...... I apologize for over-stepping my bounds this afternoon.
......
It's all right.
Take this.
It purges mushi.
Please use it if it gets to a point where you think that you need it.
You're right... I have no right to steal the bounty from this valley.

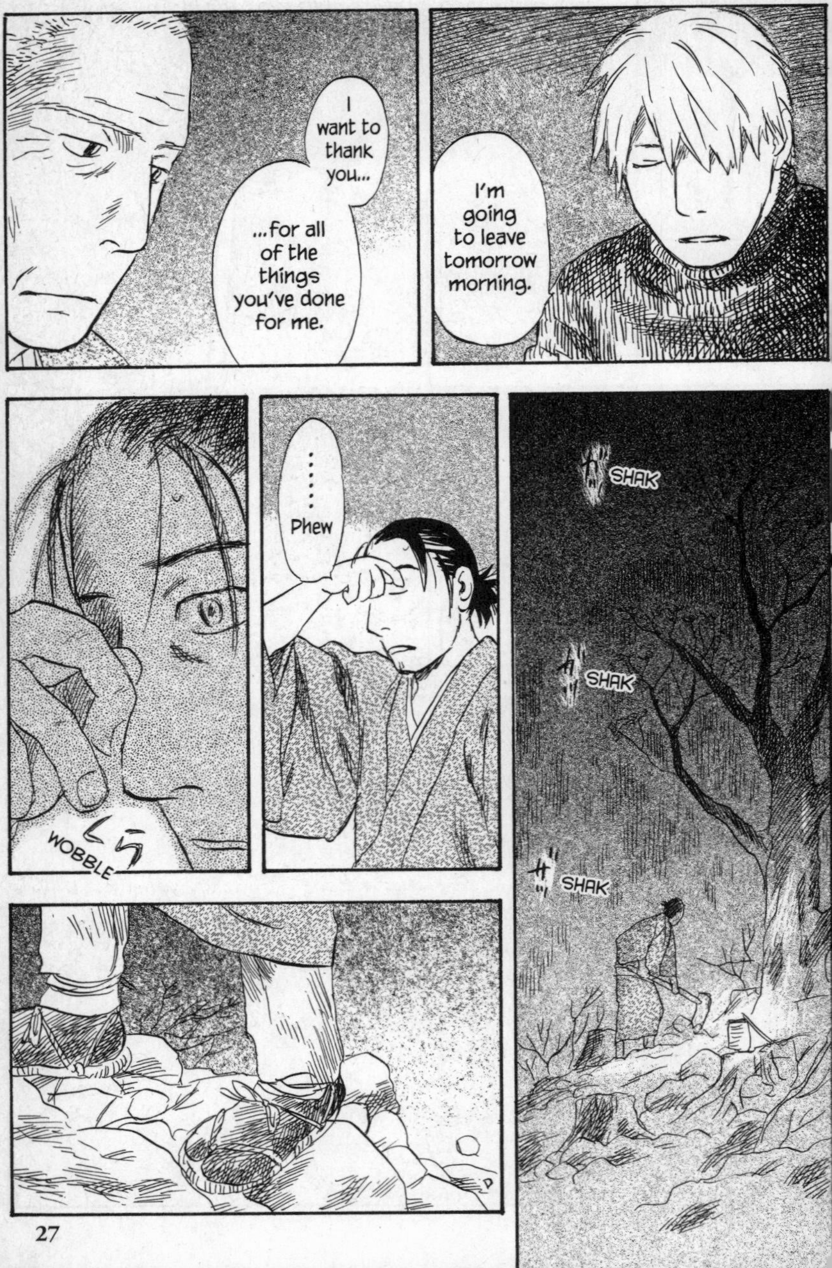

I'm going to leave tomorrow morning.
I want to thank you...
...for all of the things you've done for me.
SHAK
SHAK
SHAK
...... Phew
WOBBLE

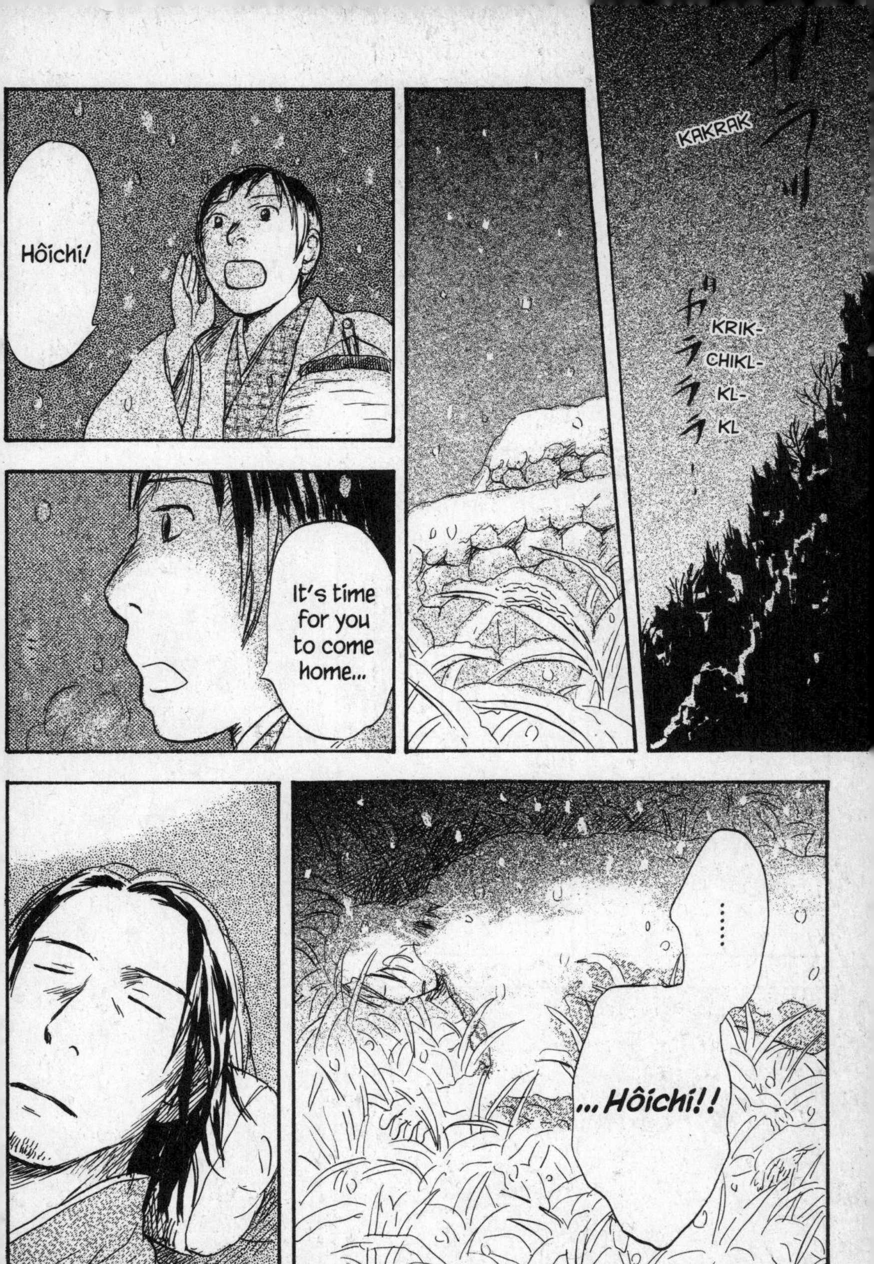
KAKRAK
KRIK-
CHIKL-
KL-
KL
Hôichi!
It's time for you to come home...
......
...Hôichi!!

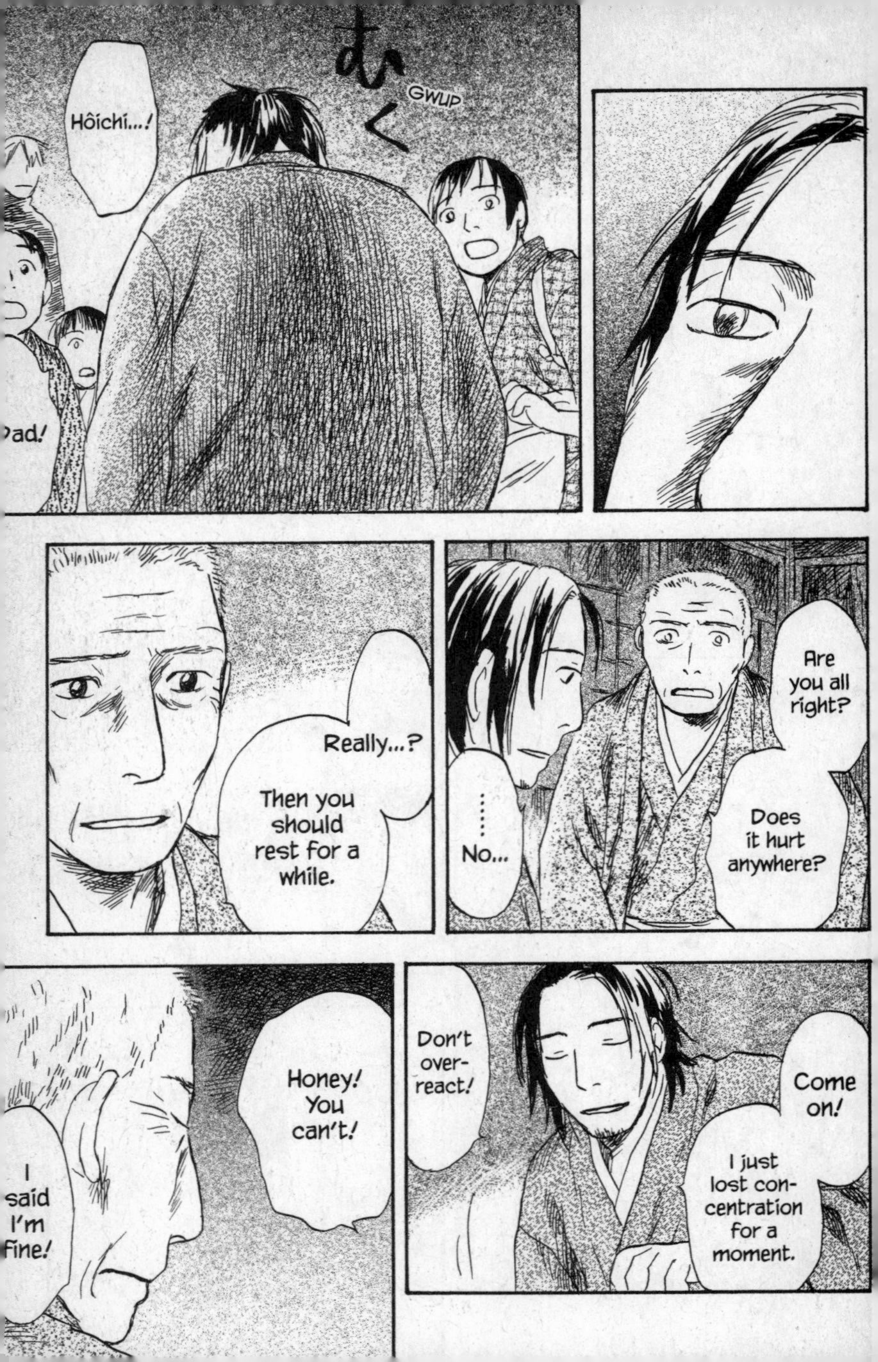
むく
GWUP
Hôichi...!
Dad!
Are you all right?
Does it hurt anywhere?
...... No...
Really...?
Then you should rest for a while.
Come on!
I just lost concentration for a moment.
Don't over-react!
Honey! You can't!
I said I'm fine!

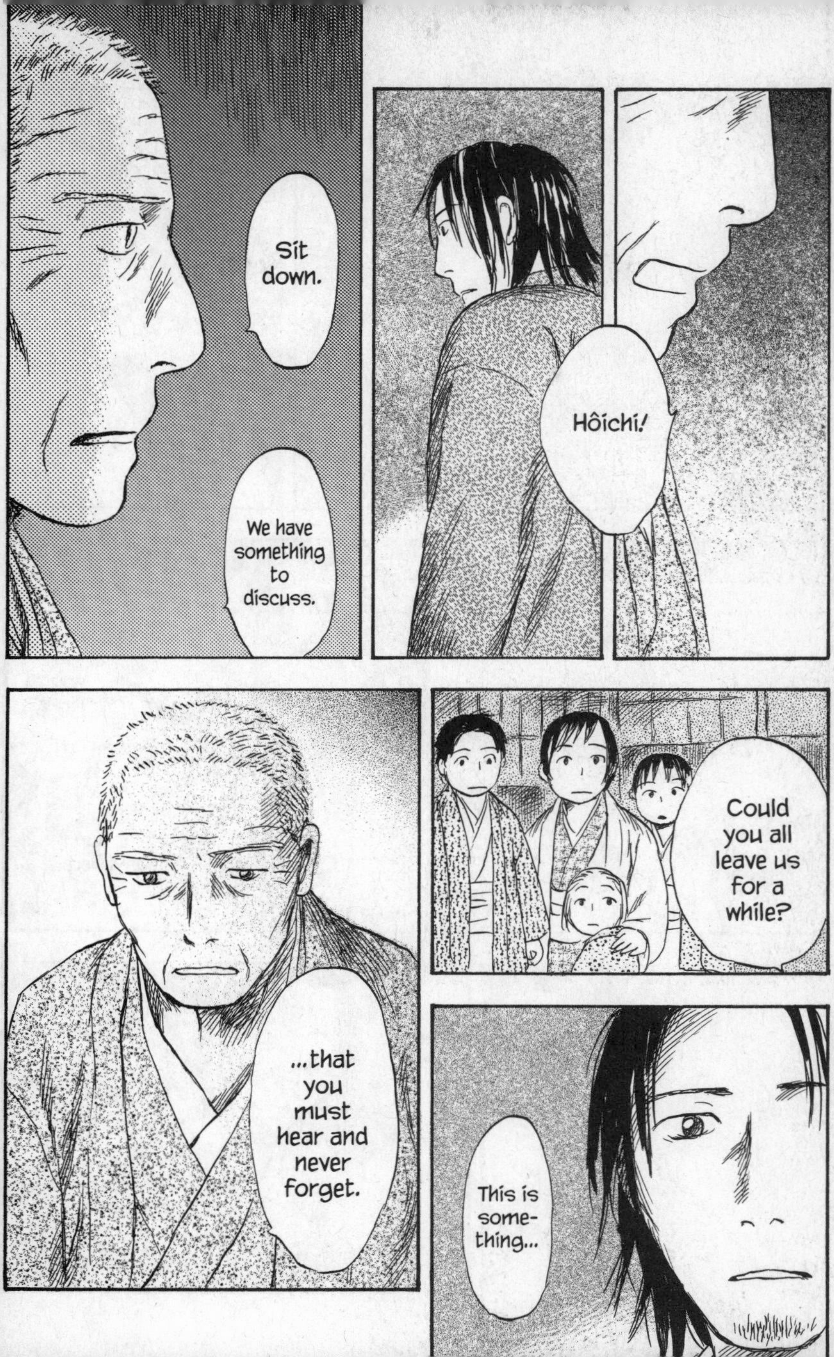
Hôichi!
Sit down.
We have something to discuss.
Could you all leave us for a while?
This is something...
...that you must hear and never forget.

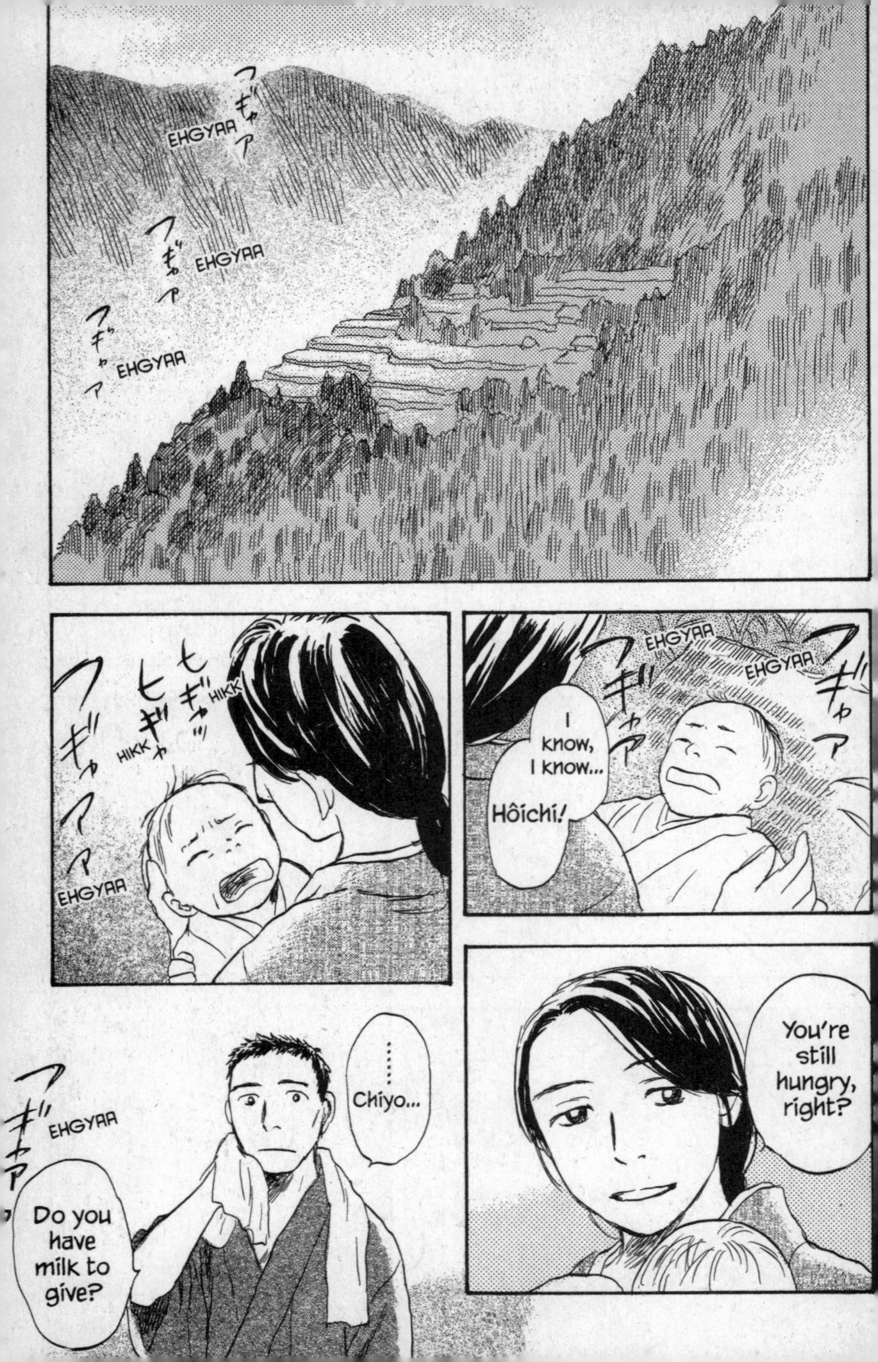
EHGYAA
EHGYAA
EHGYAA
EHGYAA
EHGYAA
I know, I know...
Hôichi!
HIKK
HIKK
EHGYAA
You're still hungry, right?
......Chiyo...
EHGYAA
Do you have milk to give?

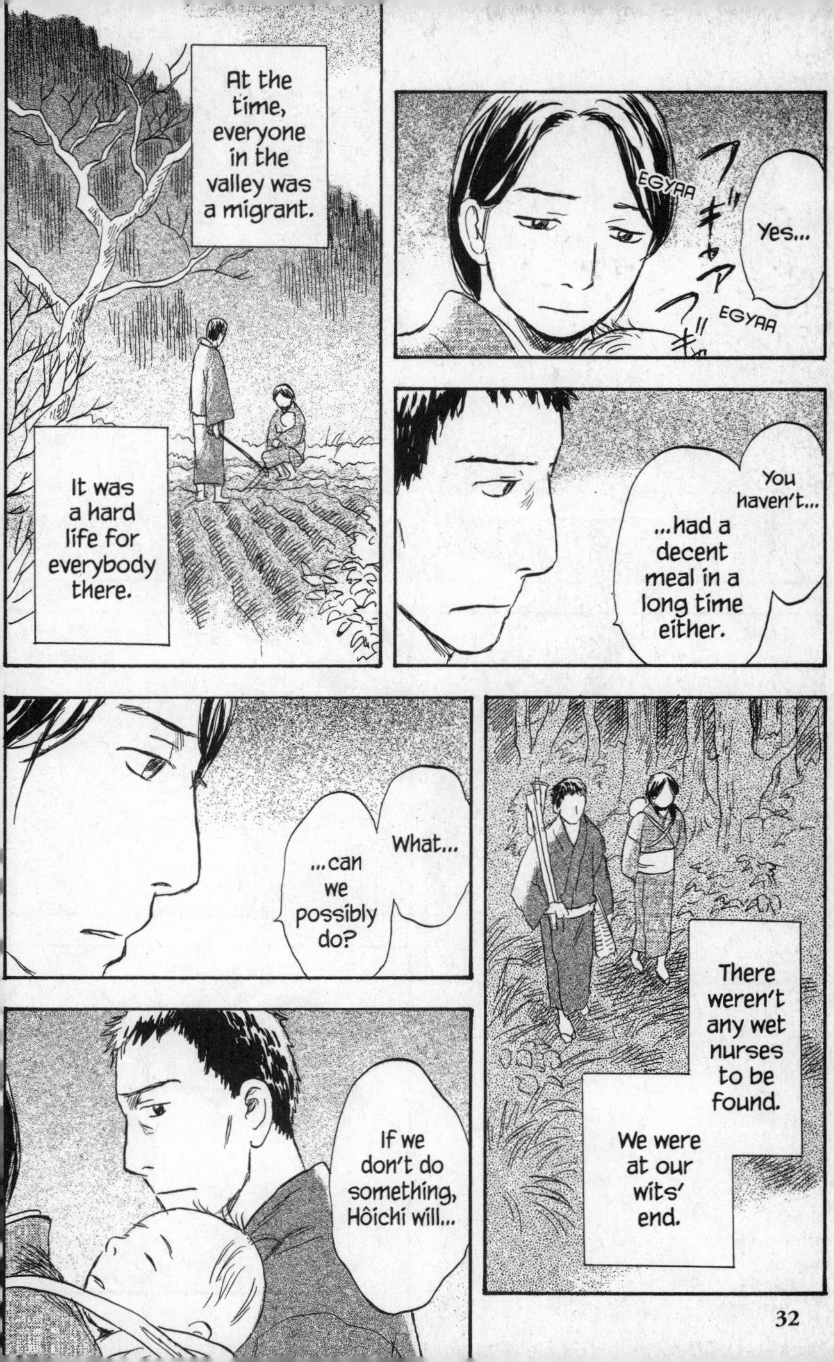
Yes...
EGYAA
EGYAA
You haven't...
...had a decent meal in a long time either.
At the time, everyone in the valley was a migrant.
It was a hard life for everybody there.
There weren't any wet nurses to be found.
We were at our wits' end.
What...
...can we possibly do?
If we don't do something, Hôichi will...

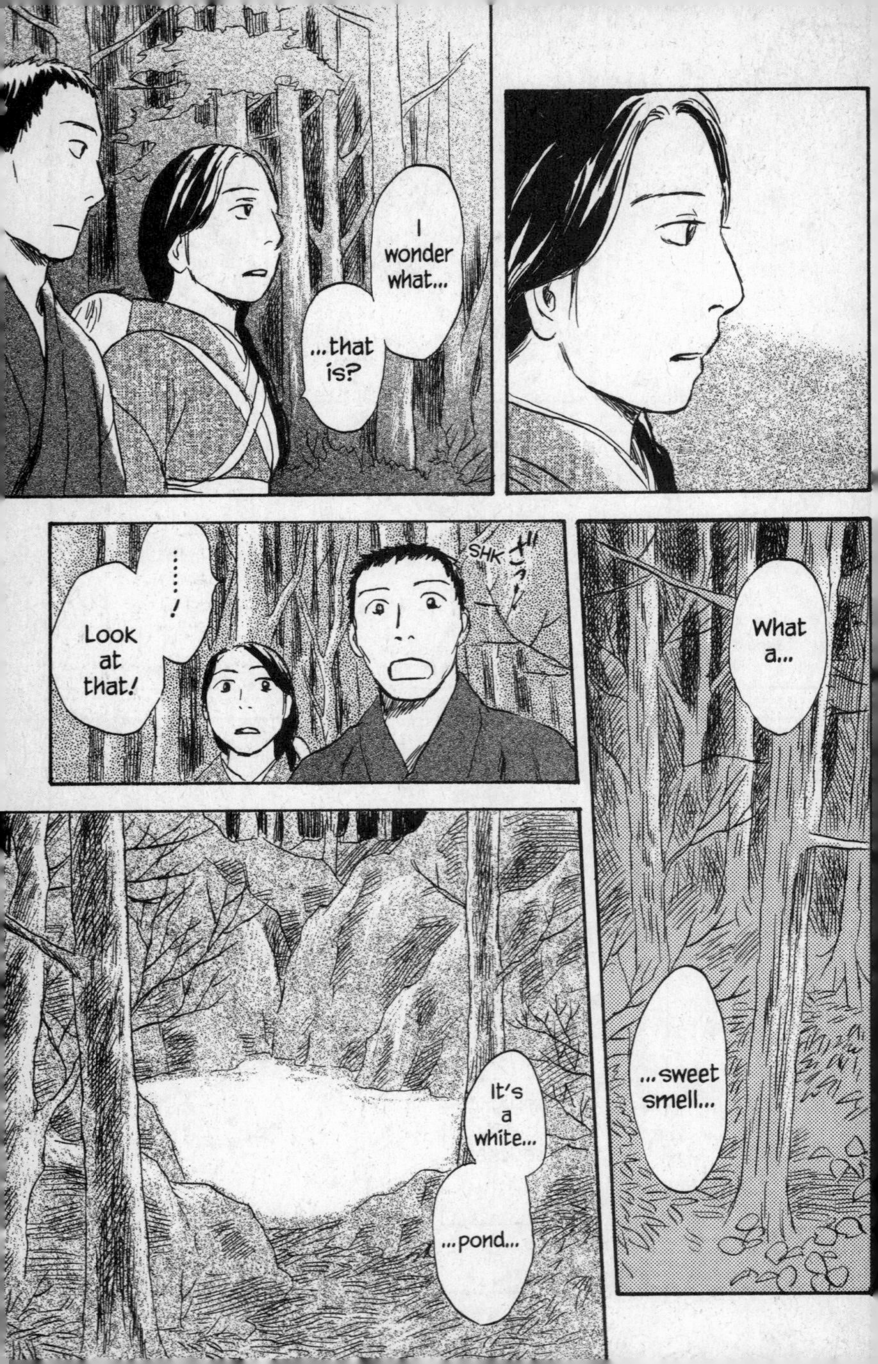
I wonder what...
...that is?
What a...
...sweet smell...
SHK
......!
Look at that!
It's a white...
...pond...

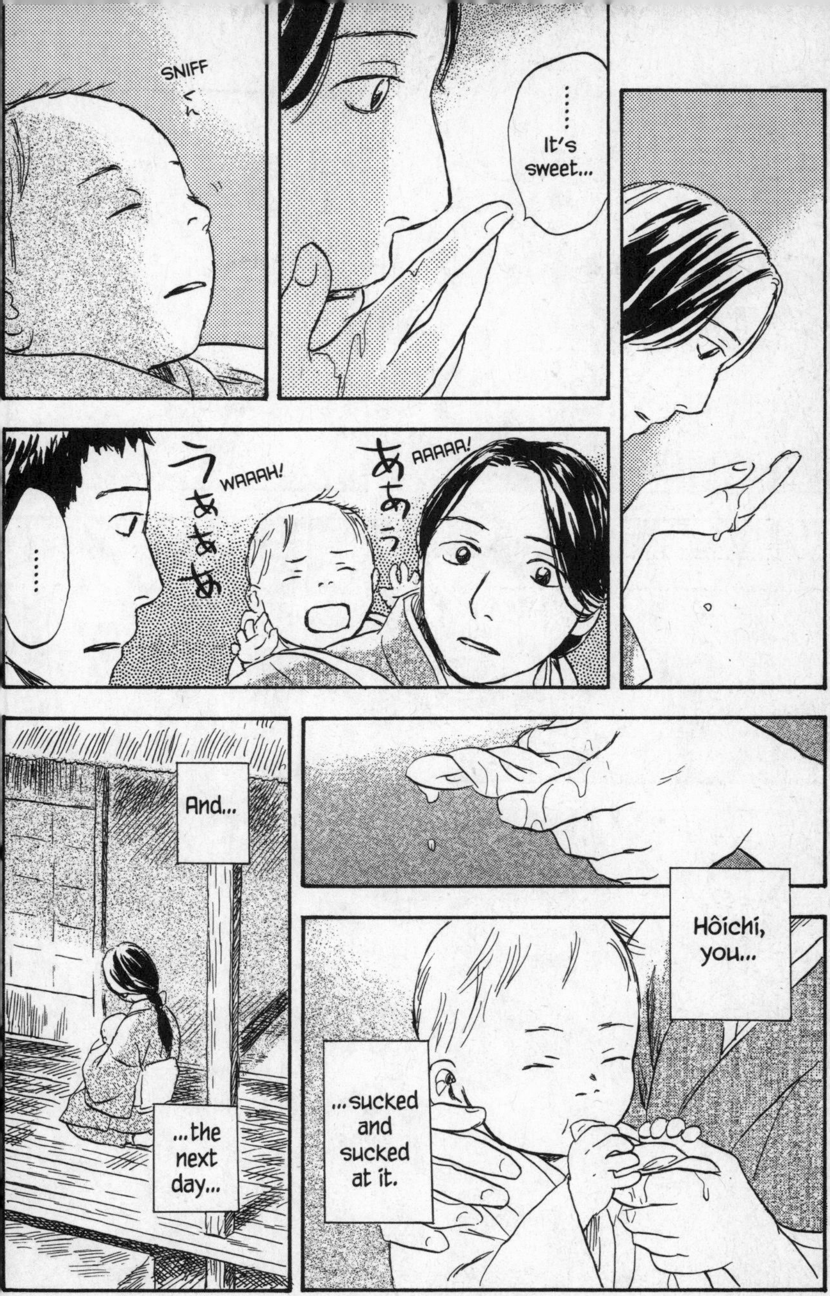

......
It's sweet...
SNIFF
くん
AAAAA!
あぁぅ
WAAAAH!
うあああ
......
Hôichi, you...
...sucked and sucked at it.
And...
...the next day...

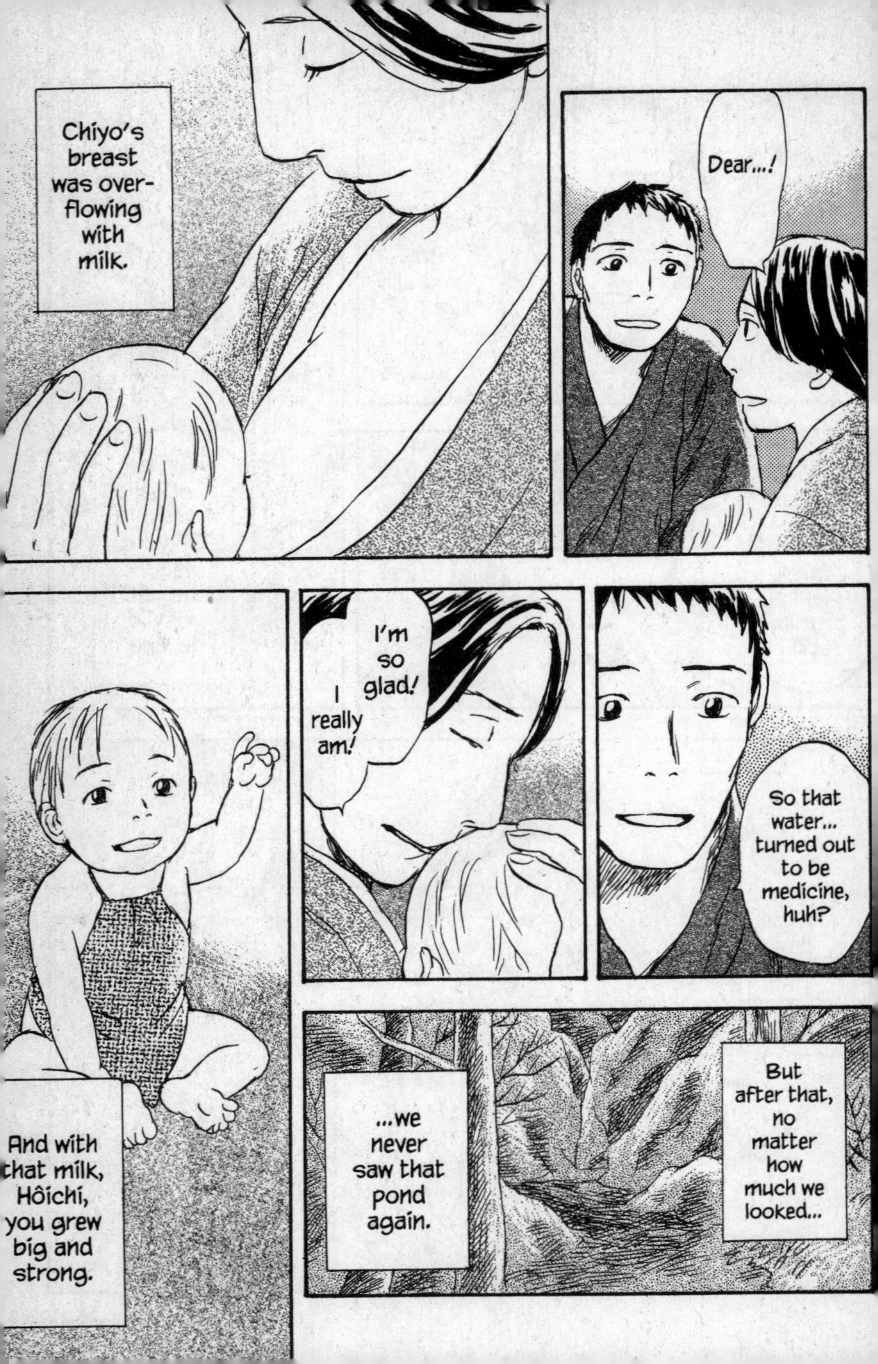
Dear...!
Chiyo's breast was over-flowing with milk.
So that water... turned out to be medicine, huh?
I'm so glad!
I really am!
But after that, no matter how much we looked...
...we never saw that pond again.
And with that milk, Hôichi, you grew big and strong.

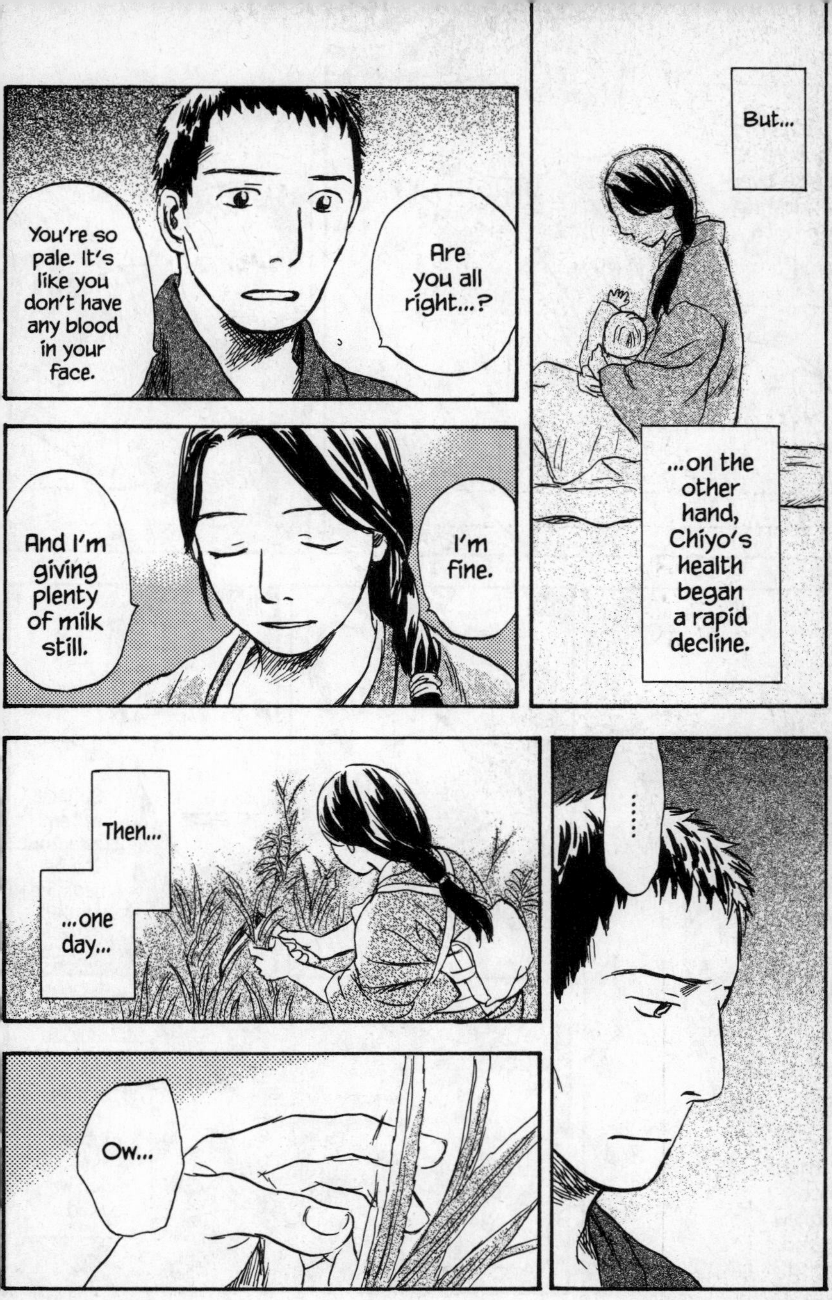
But...
...on the other hand, Chiyo's health began a rapid decline.
Are you all right...?
You're so pale. It's like you don't have any blood in your face.
I'm fine.
And I'm giving plenty of milk still.
......
Then...
...one day...
Ow...

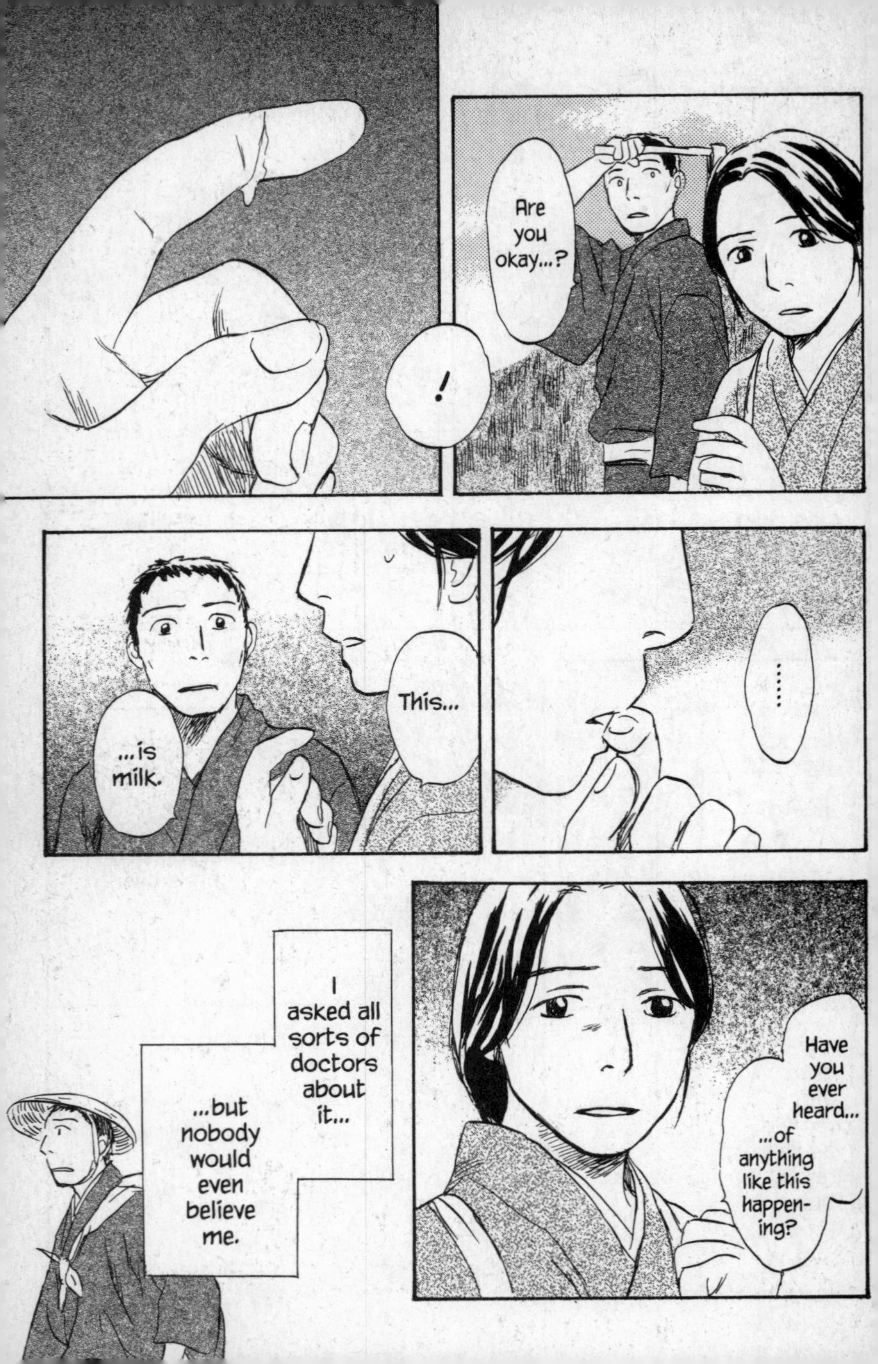
Are you okay...?
!
......
This...
...is milk.
Have you ever heard...
...of anything like this happening?
I asked all sorts of doctors about it...
...but nobody would even believe me.

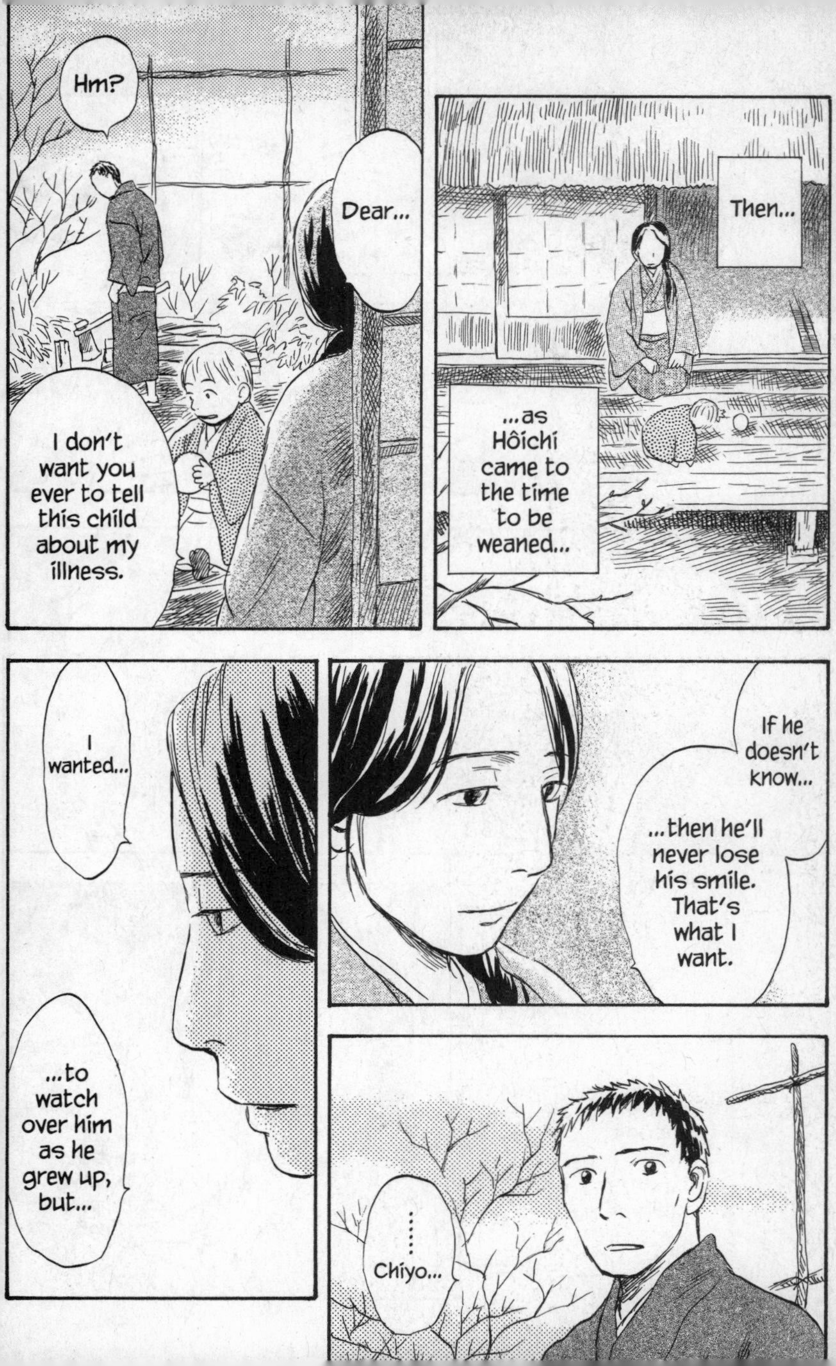
Then...
...as Hôichi came to the time to be weaned...
Dear...
Hm?
I don't want you ever to tell this child about my illness.
If he doesn't know...
...then he'll never lose his smile. That's what I want.
......
Chiyo...
I wanted...
...to watch over him as he grew up, but...

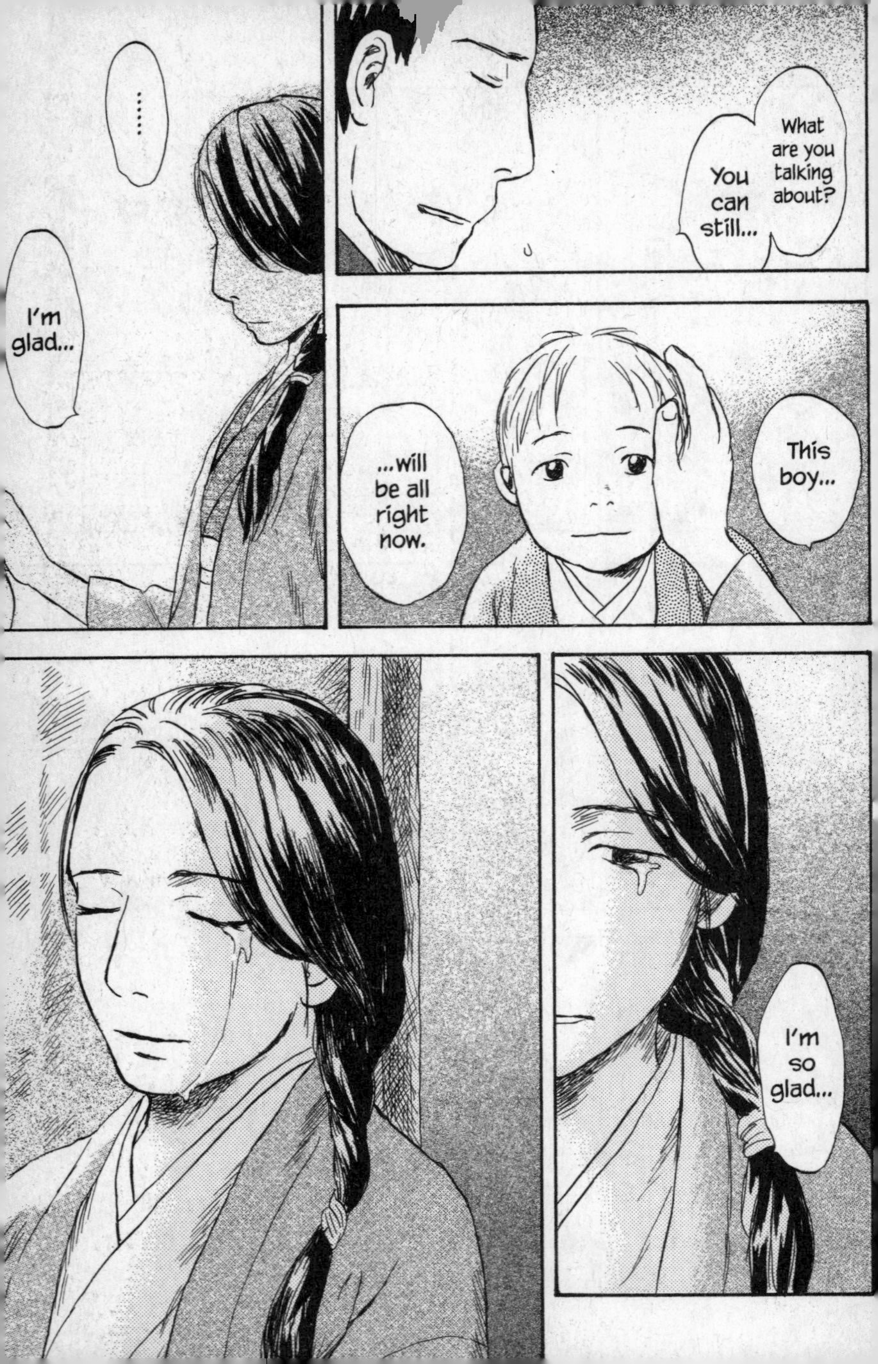
What are you talking about?
You can still...
This boy...
...will be all right now.
......
I'm glad...
I'm so glad...

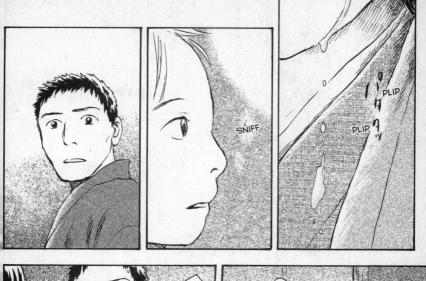

SNIFF

PLIP

PLIP

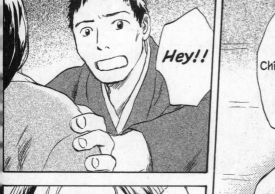

Hey!!

Chiyo...

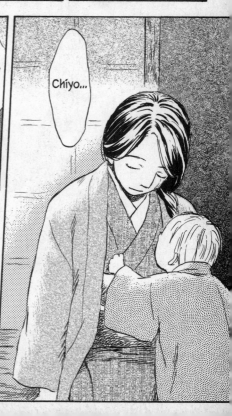

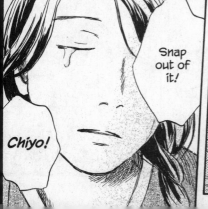

Snap out of it!

Chiyo!

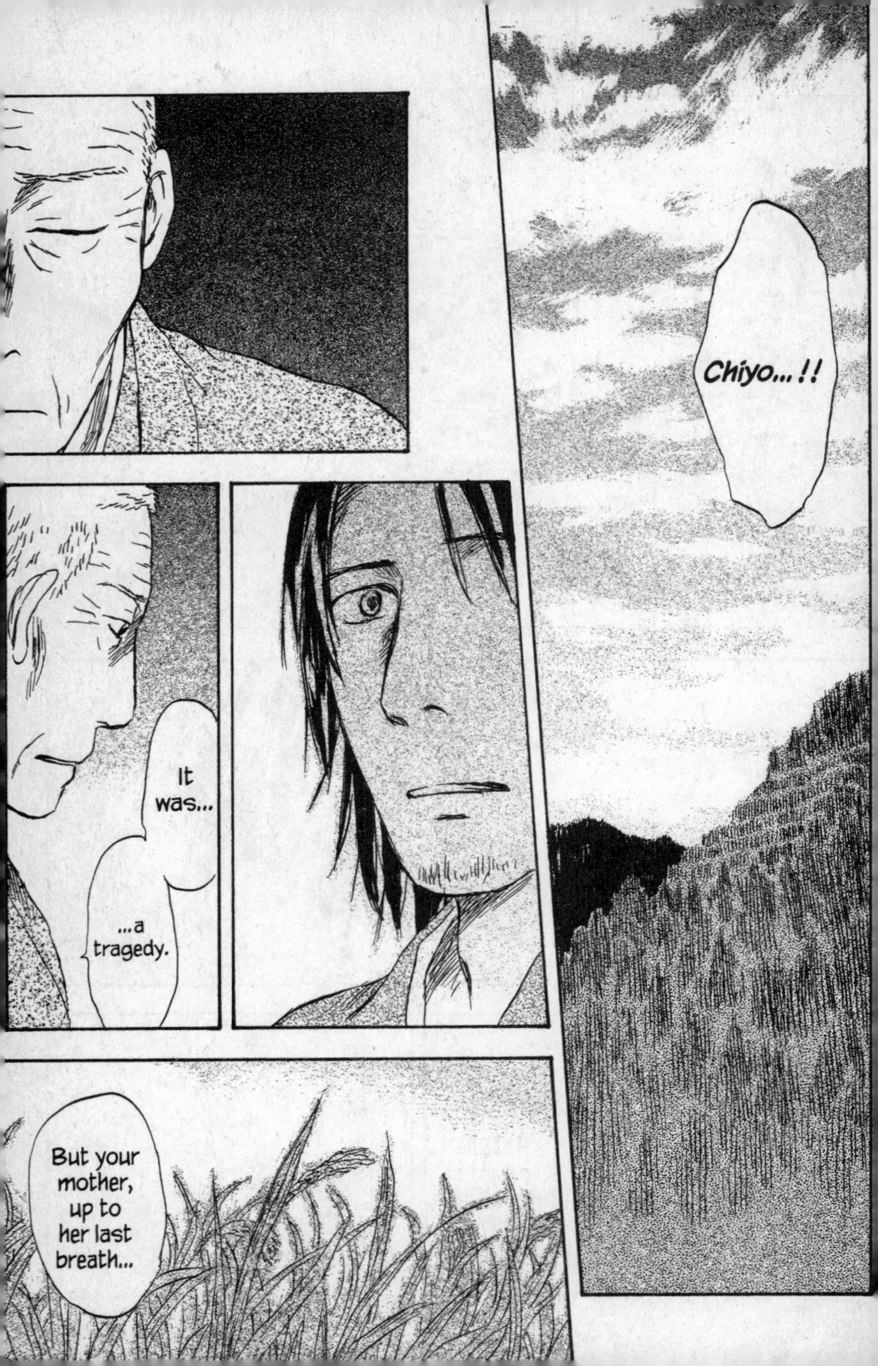
Chiyo...!!
It was...
...a tragedy.
But your mother, up to her last breath...

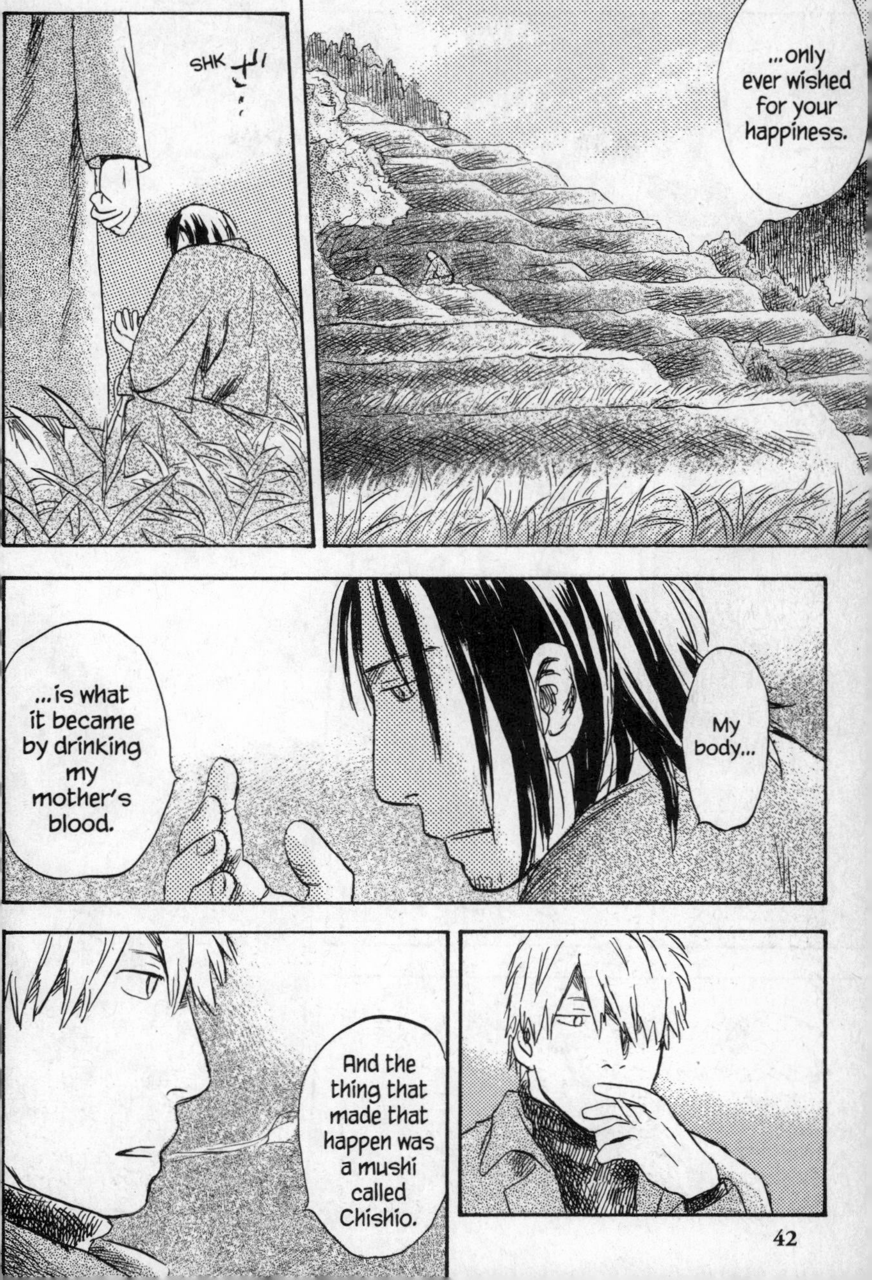
...only ever wished for your happiness.
SHK
My body...
...is what it became by drinking my mother's blood.
And the thing that made that happen was a mushi called Chishio.

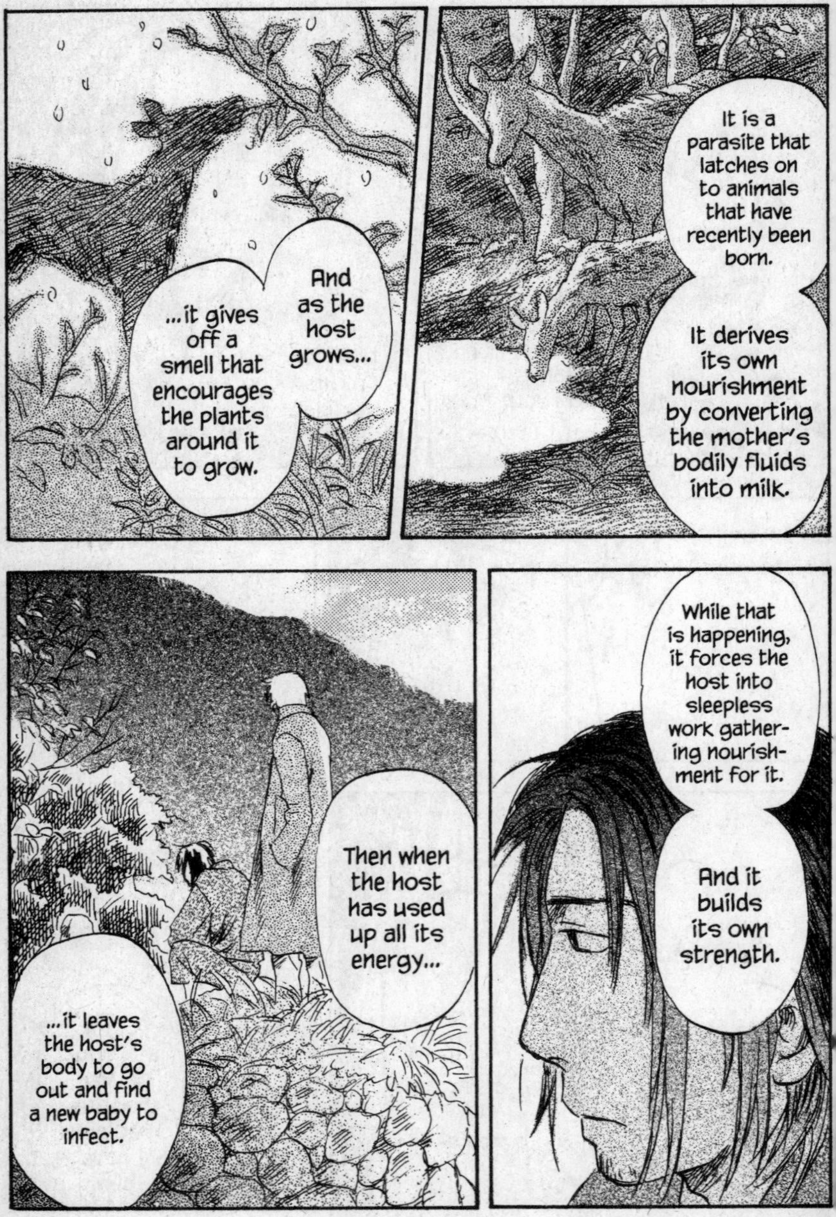
It is a parasite that latches on to animals that have recently been born.
It derives its own nourishment by converting the mother's bodily fluids into milk.
And as the host grows...
...it gives off a smell that encourages the plants around it to grow.
While that is happening, it forces the host into sleepless work gather-ing nourish-ment for it.
And it builds its own strength.
Then when the host has used up all its energy...
...it leaves the host's body to go out and find a new baby to infect.

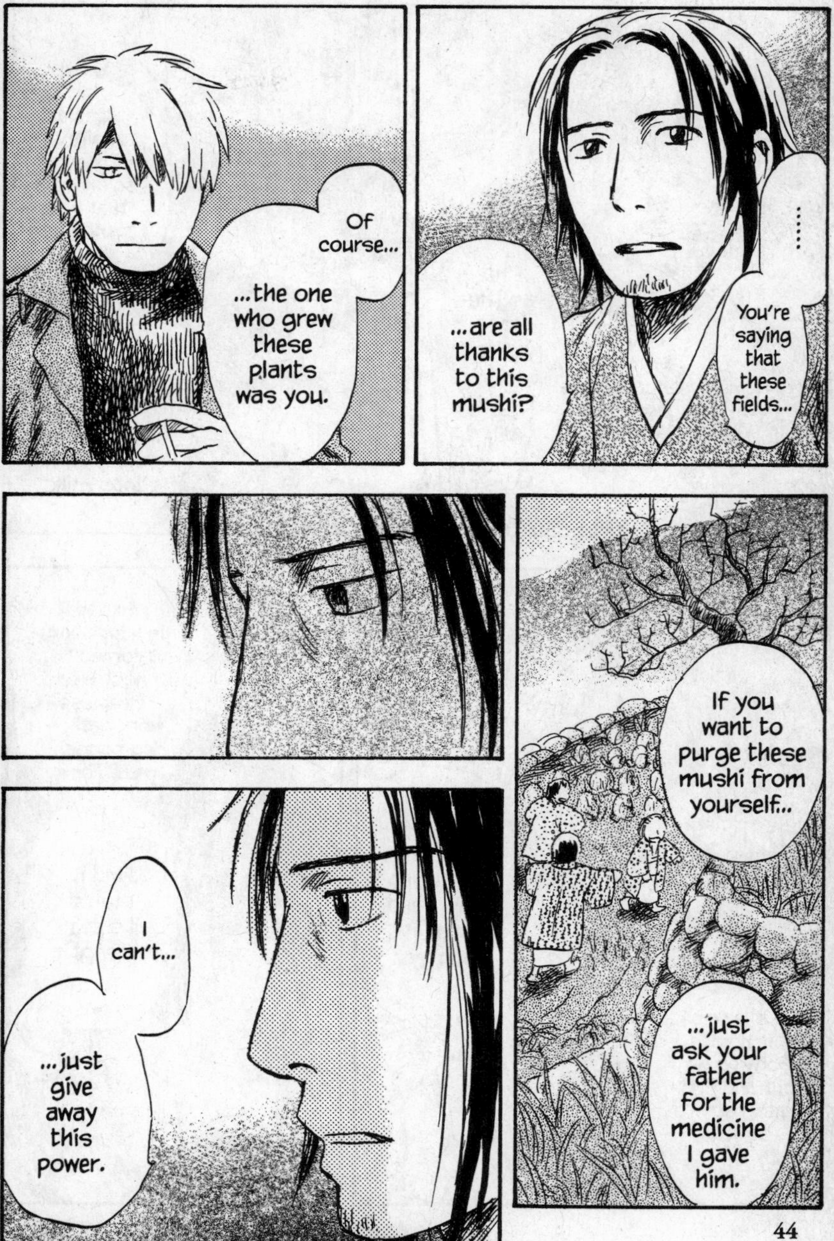
......
You're saying that these fields...
...are all thanks to this mushi?
Of course...
...the one who grew these plants was you.
If you want to purge these mushi from yourself...
...just ask your father for the medicine I gave him.
I can't...
...just give away this power.

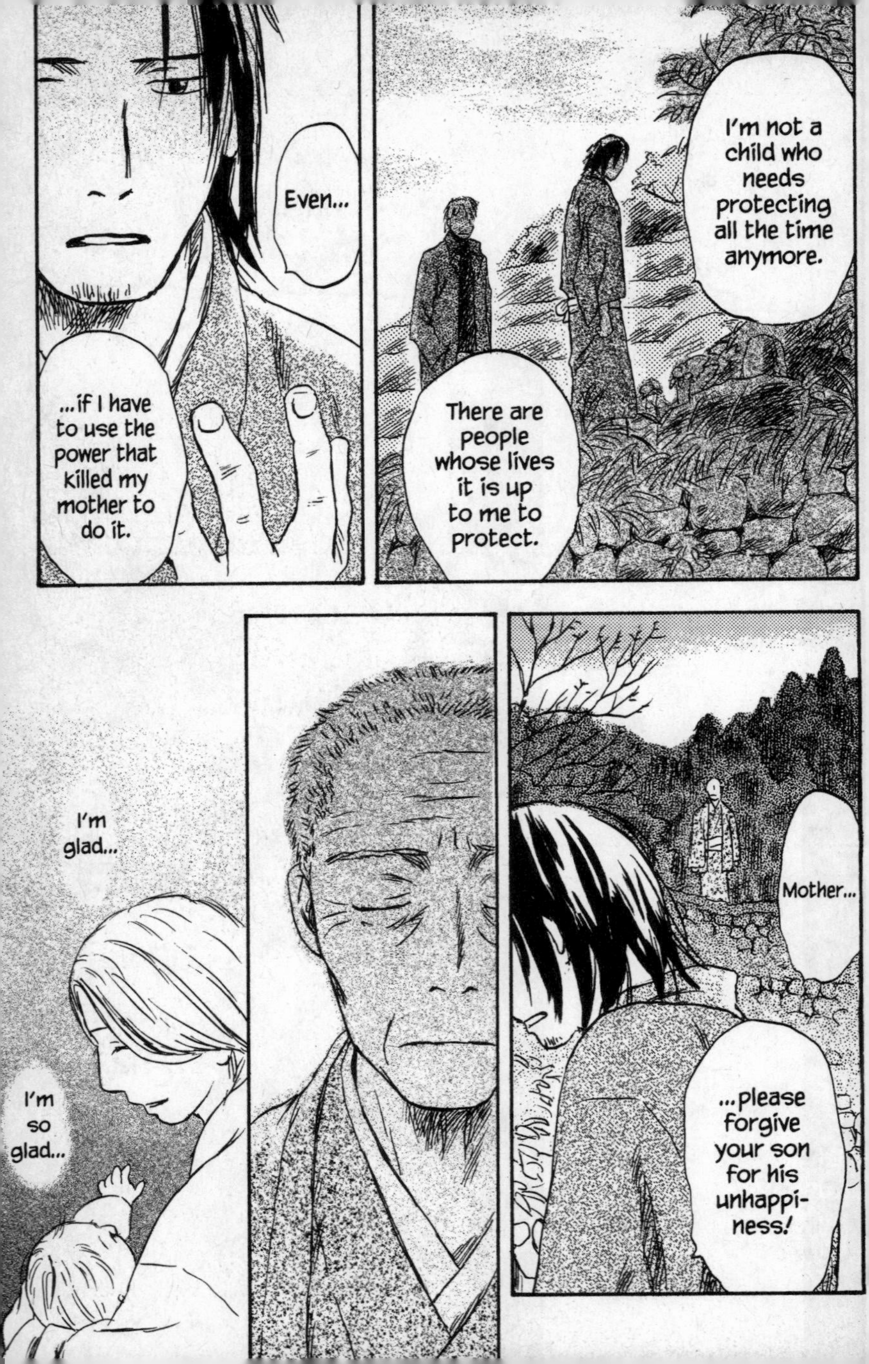
I'm not a child who needs protecting all the time anymore.
There are people whose lives it is up to me to protect.
Even...
...if I have to use the power that killed my mother to do it.
Mother...
...please forgive your son for his unhappi-ness!
I'm glad...
I'm so glad...

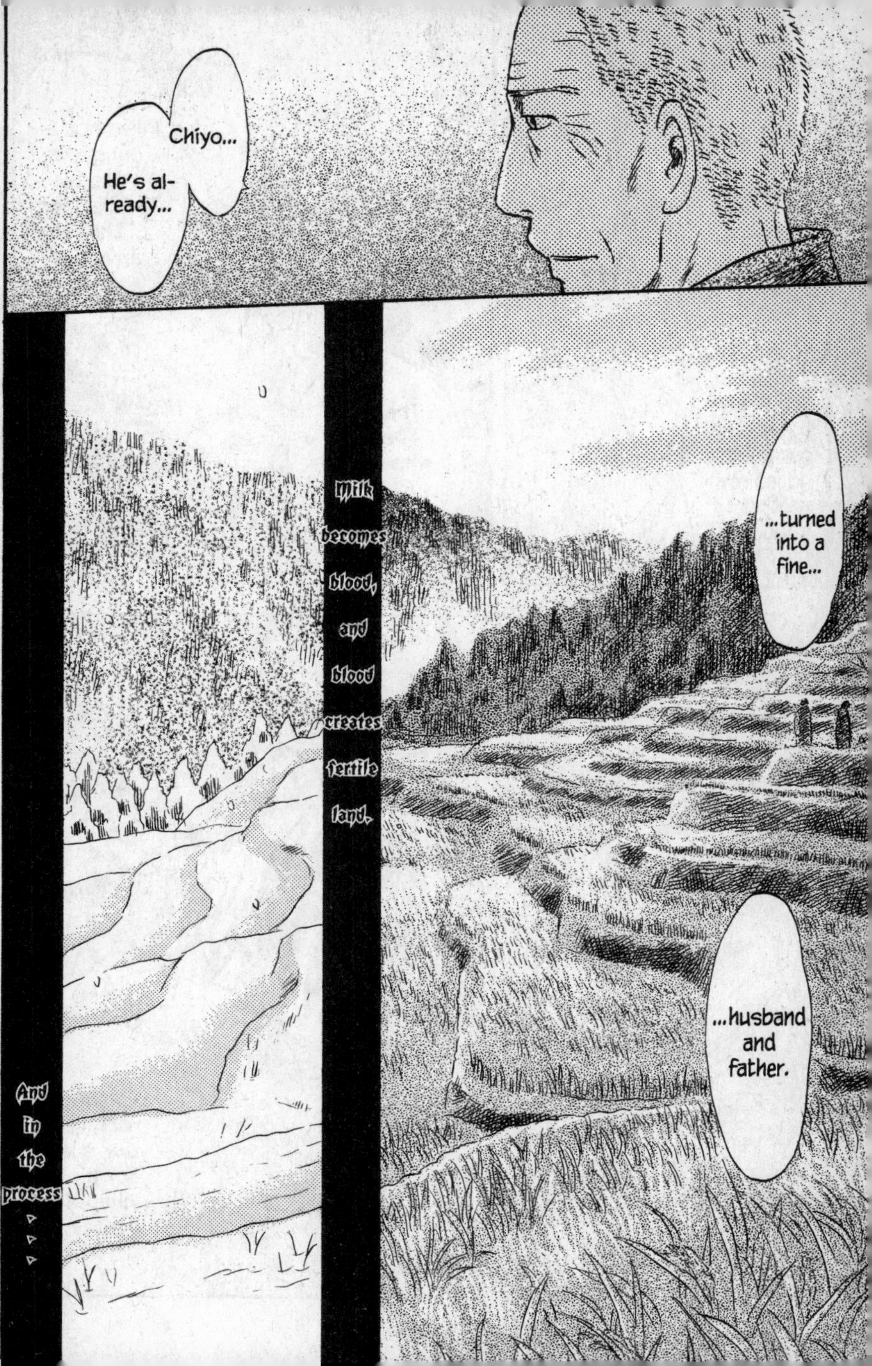
Chiyo... He's al-ready...
...turned into a fine...
...husband and father.
Milk becomes blood, and blood creates fertile land.
And in the process...

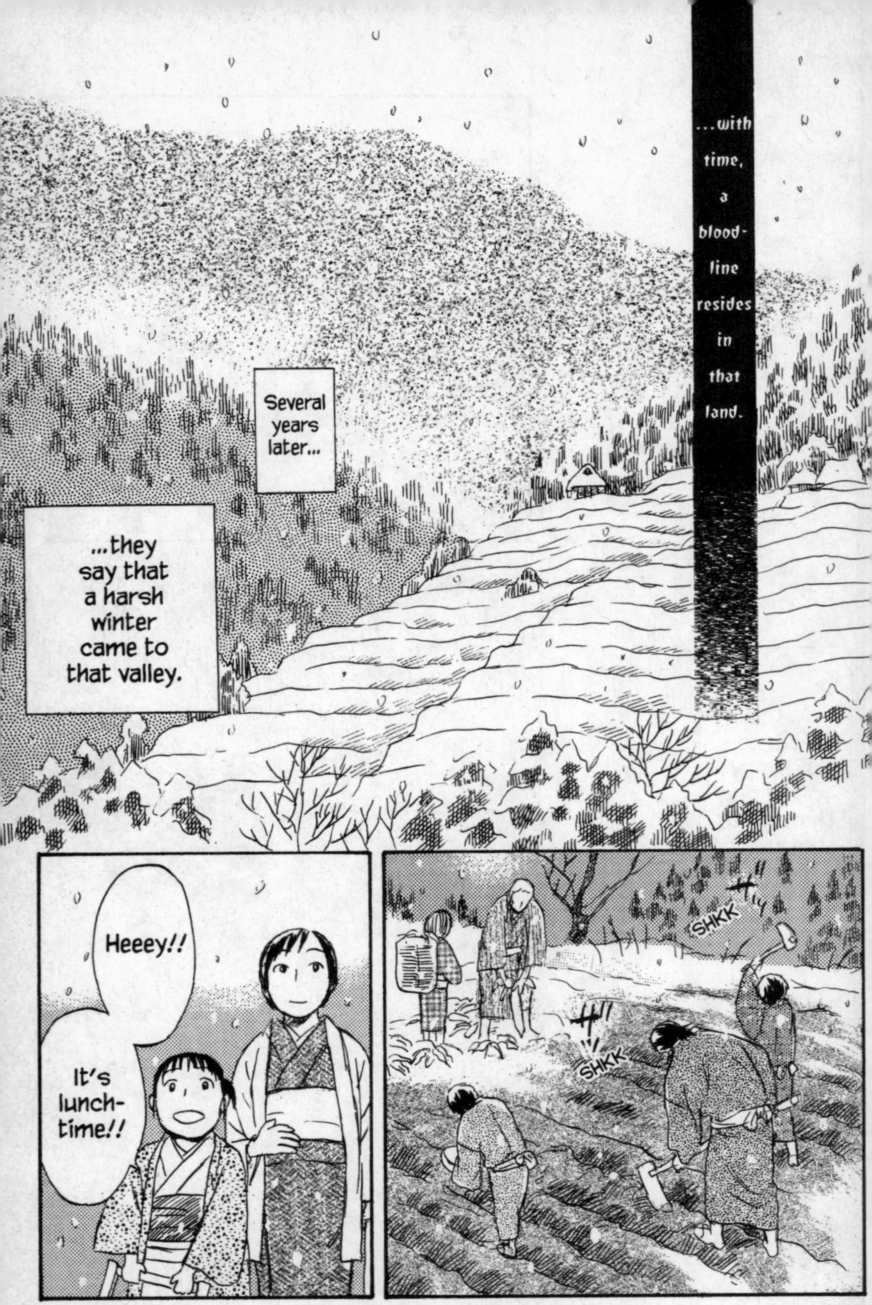
...with time, a blood-line resides in that land.
Several years later...
...they say that a harsh winter came to that valley.
SHKK
SHKK
Heeey!!
It's lunch-time!!

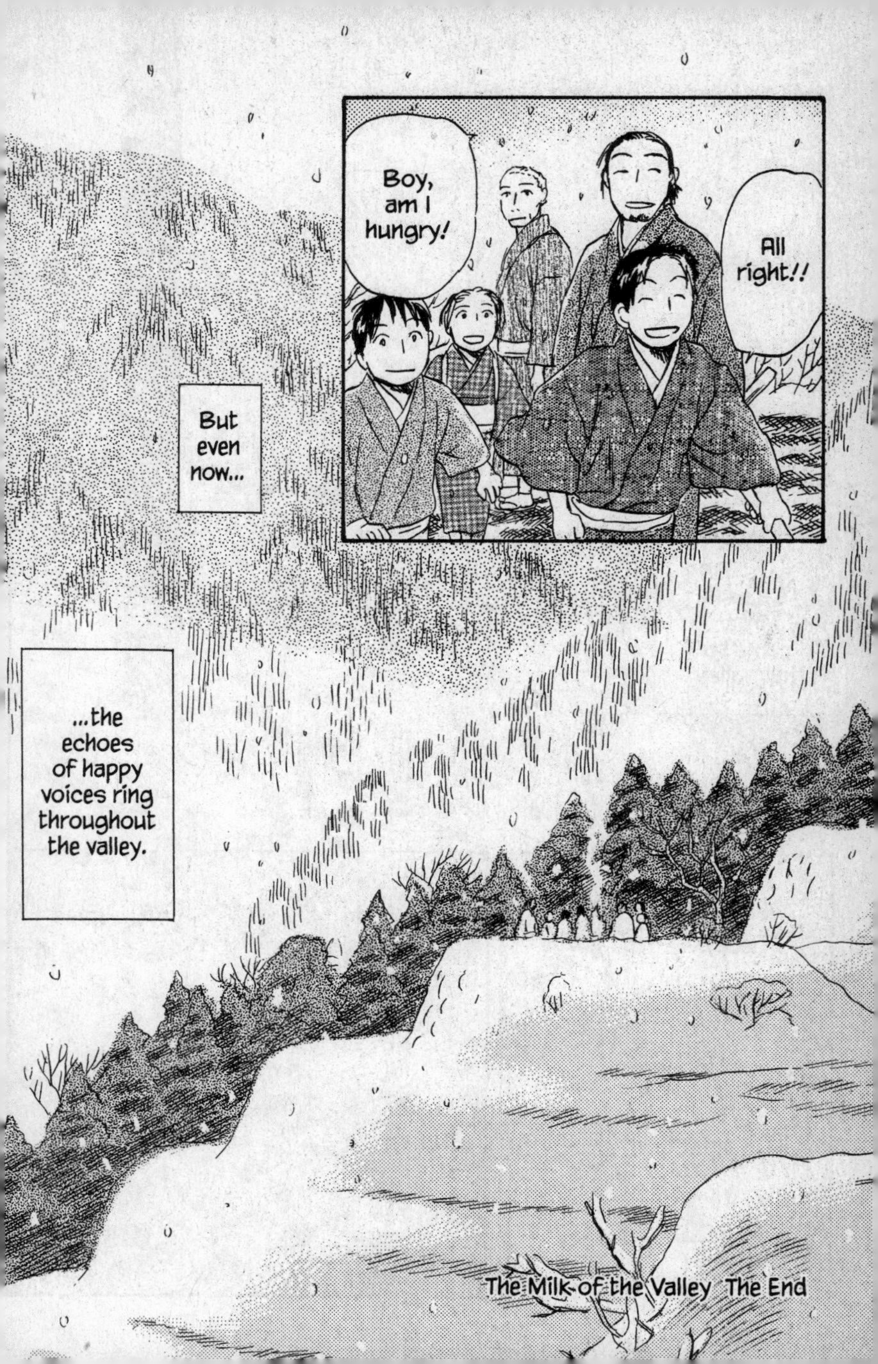
All right!!
Boy, am I hungry!
But even now...
...the echoes of happy voices ring throughout the valley.
The Milk of the Valley The End

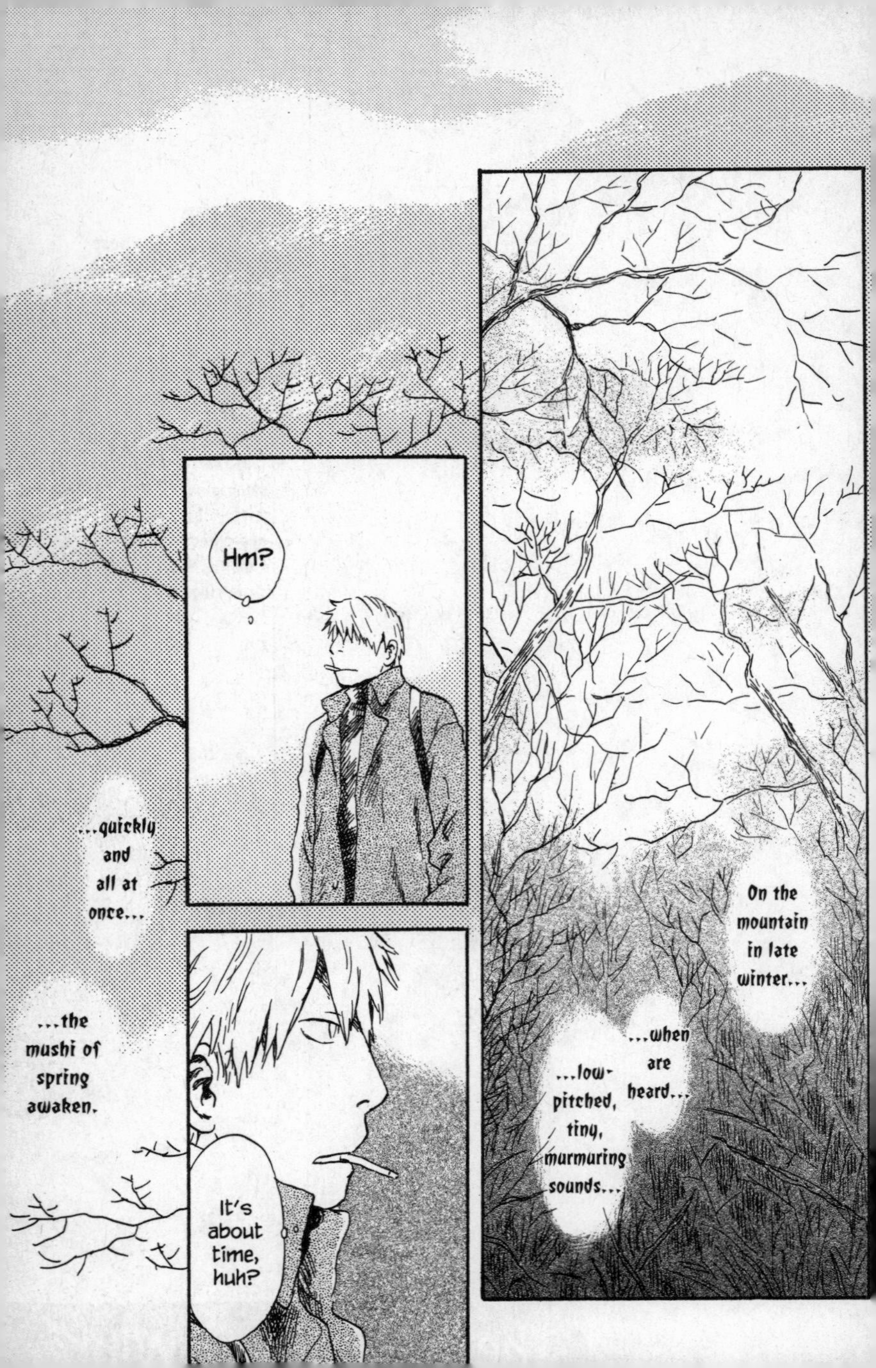
On the mountain in late winter...
...when are heard...
...low-pitched, tiny, murmuring sounds...
Hm?
...quickly and all at once...
...the mushi of spring awaken.
It's about time, huh?

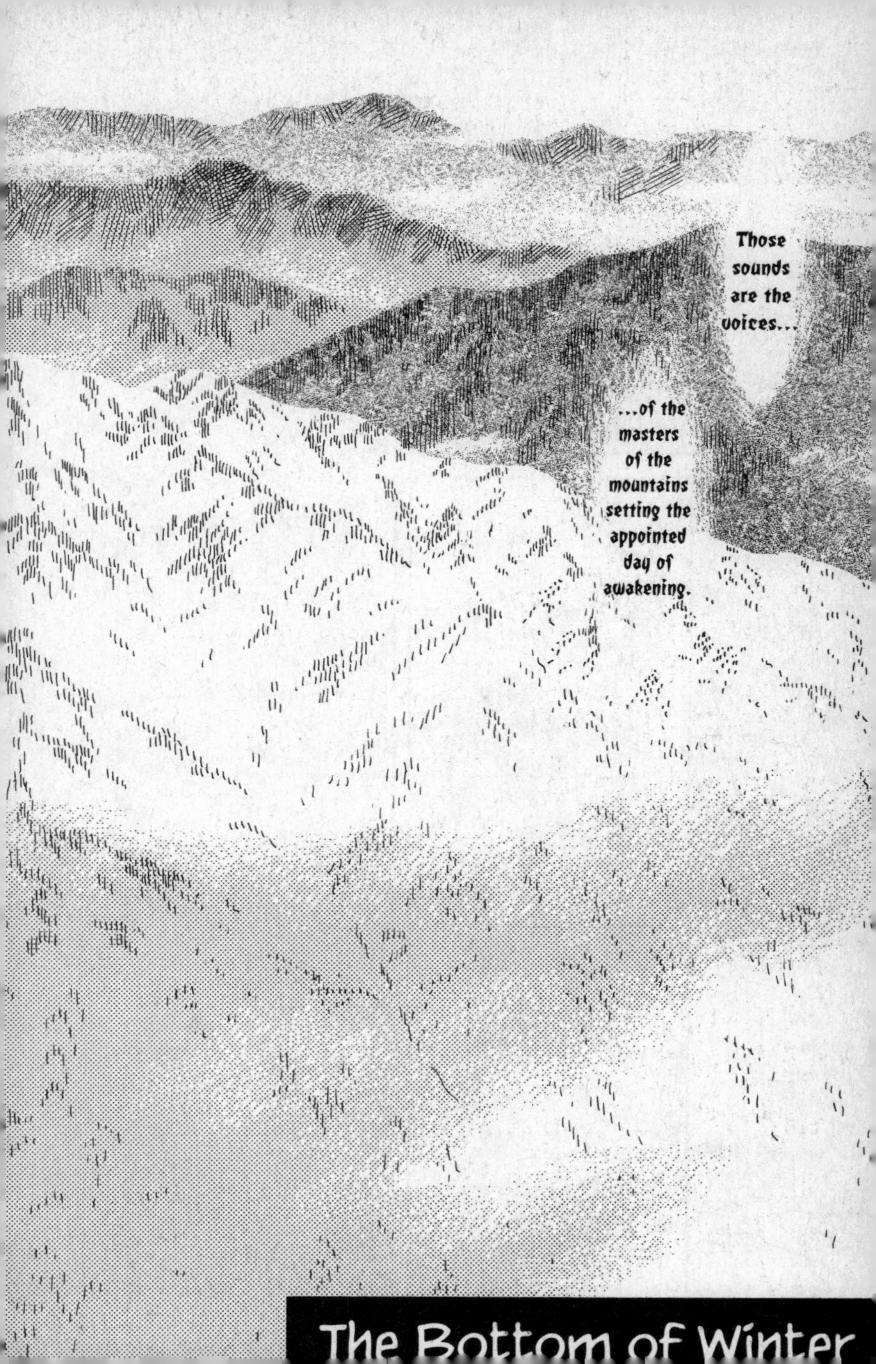
Those sounds are the voices...
...of the masters of the mountains setting the appointed day of awakening.
The Bottom of Winter

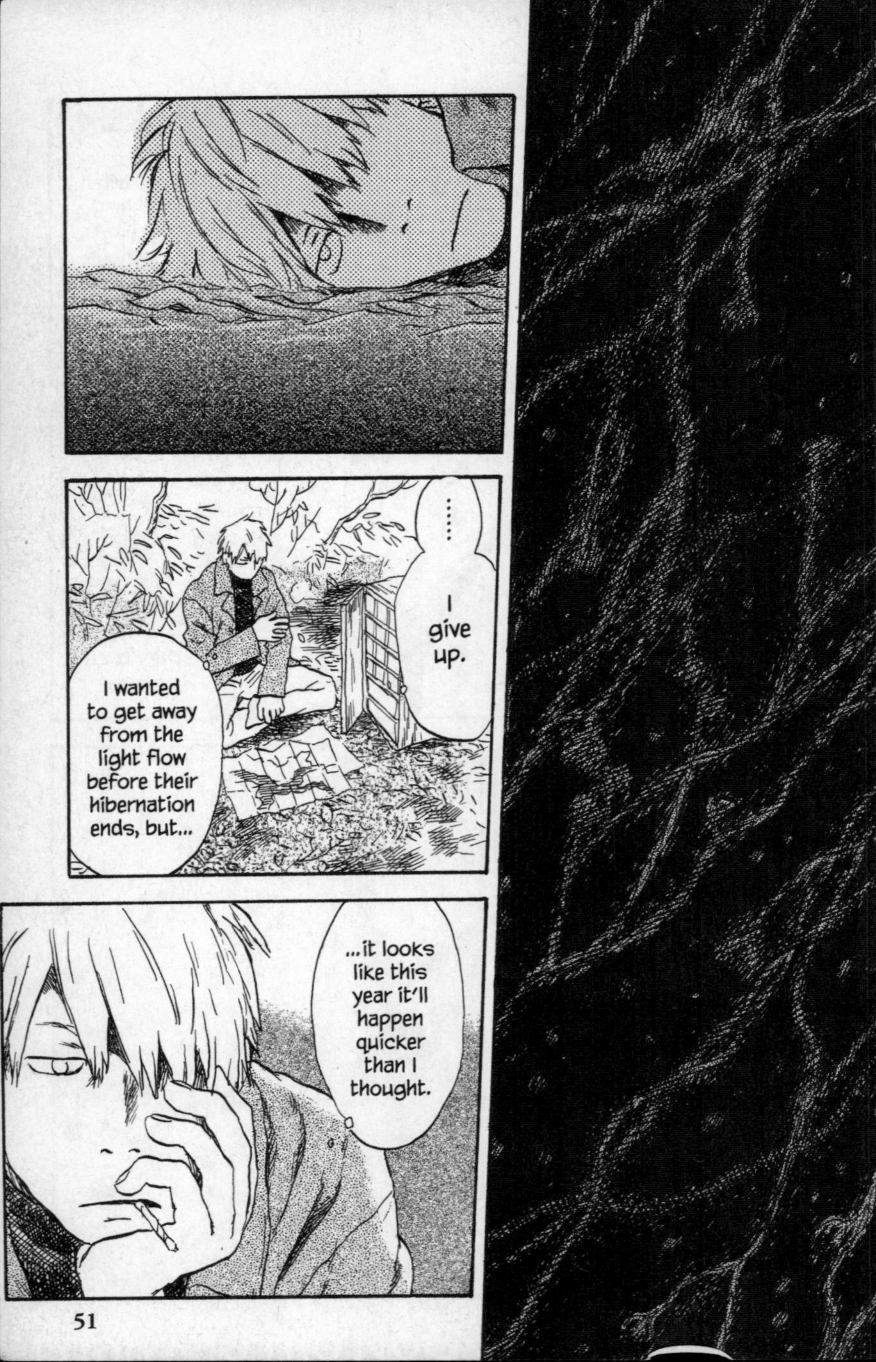

......
I give up.
I wanted to get away from the light flow before their hibernation ends, but...
...it looks like this year it'll happen quicker than I thought.

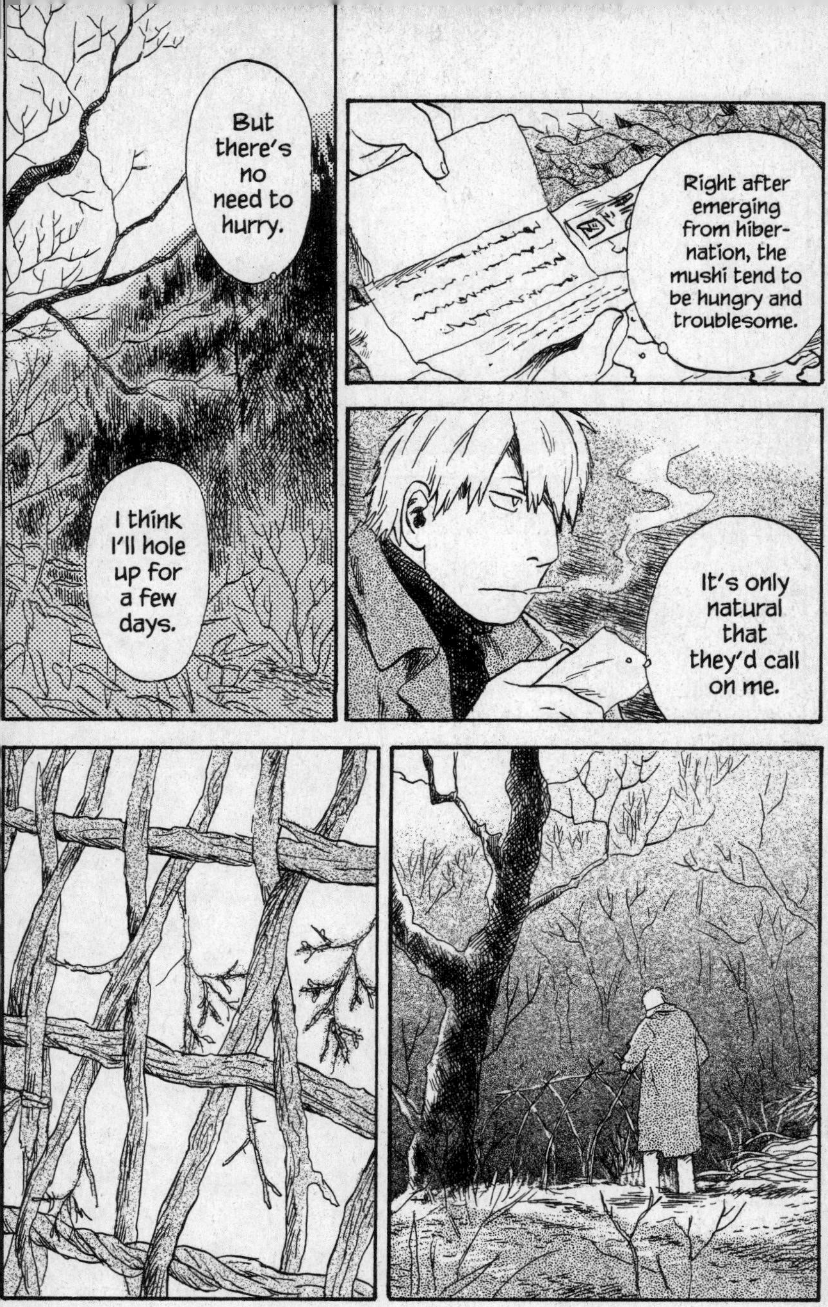
Right after emerging from hiber-nation, the mushi tend to be hungry and troublesome.
It's only natural that they'd call on me.
But there's no need to hurry.
I think I'll hole up for a few days.

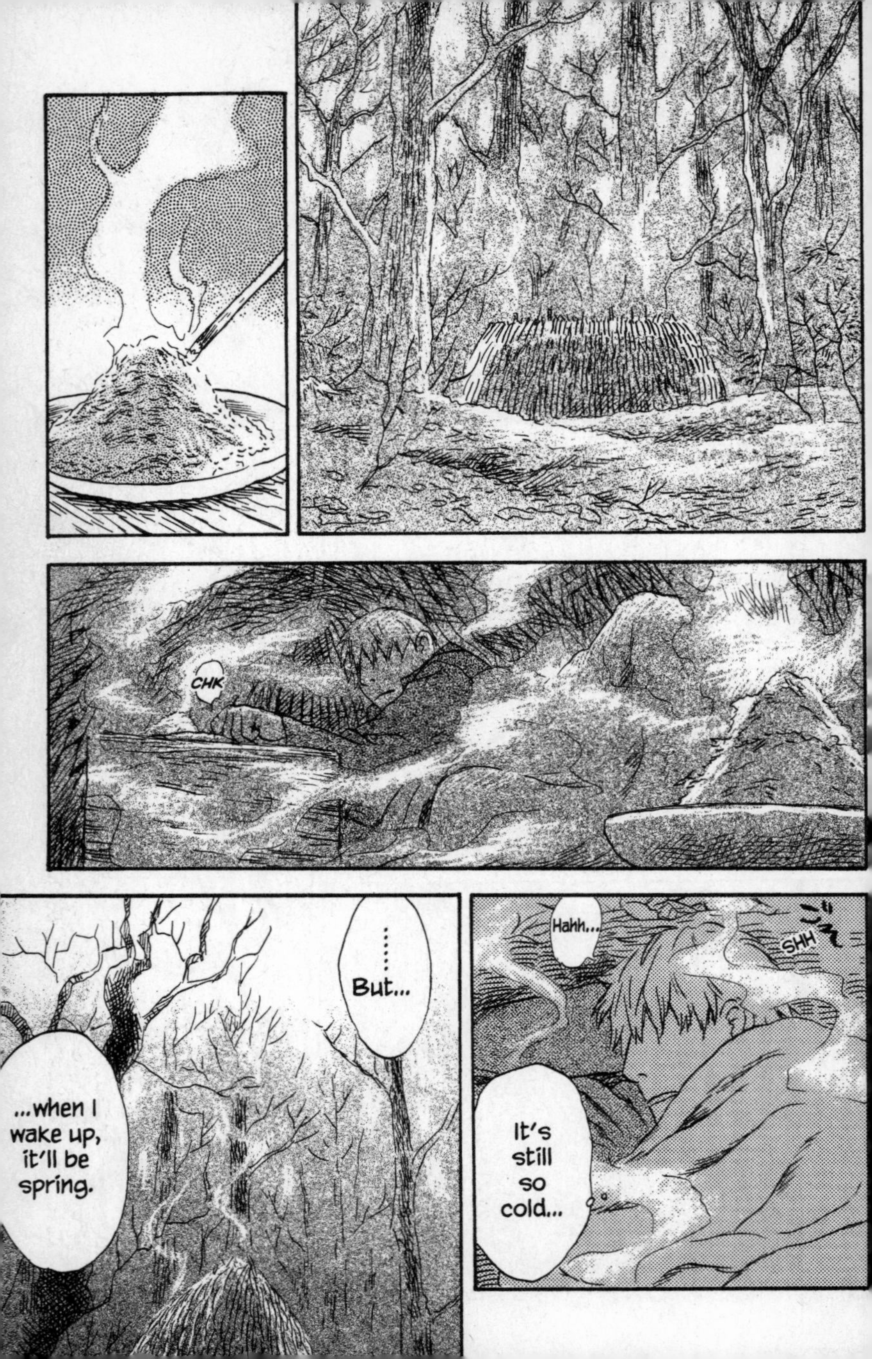
CHK
Hahh...
SHH
It's still so cold...
...... But...
...when I wake up, it'll be spring.

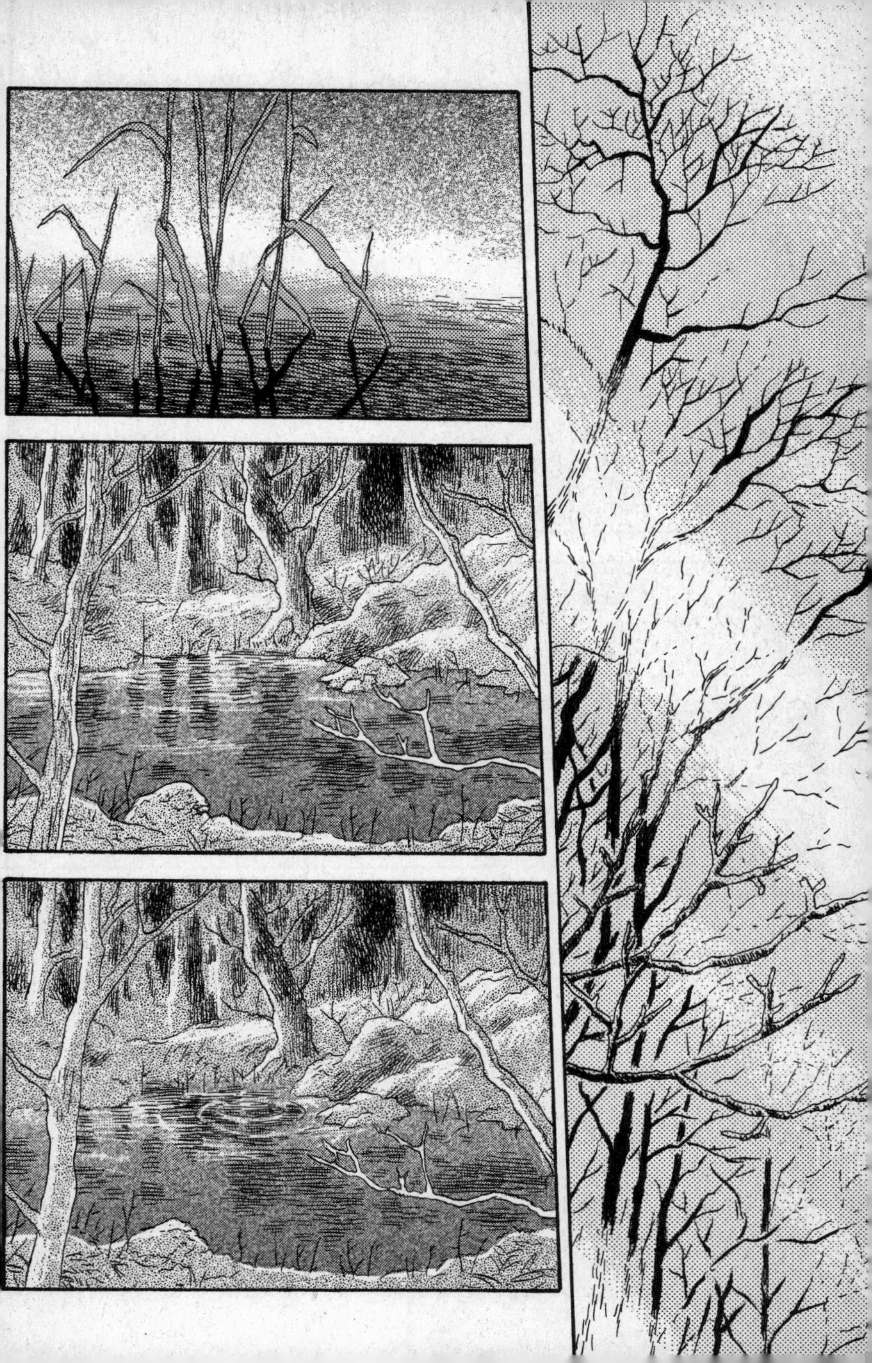

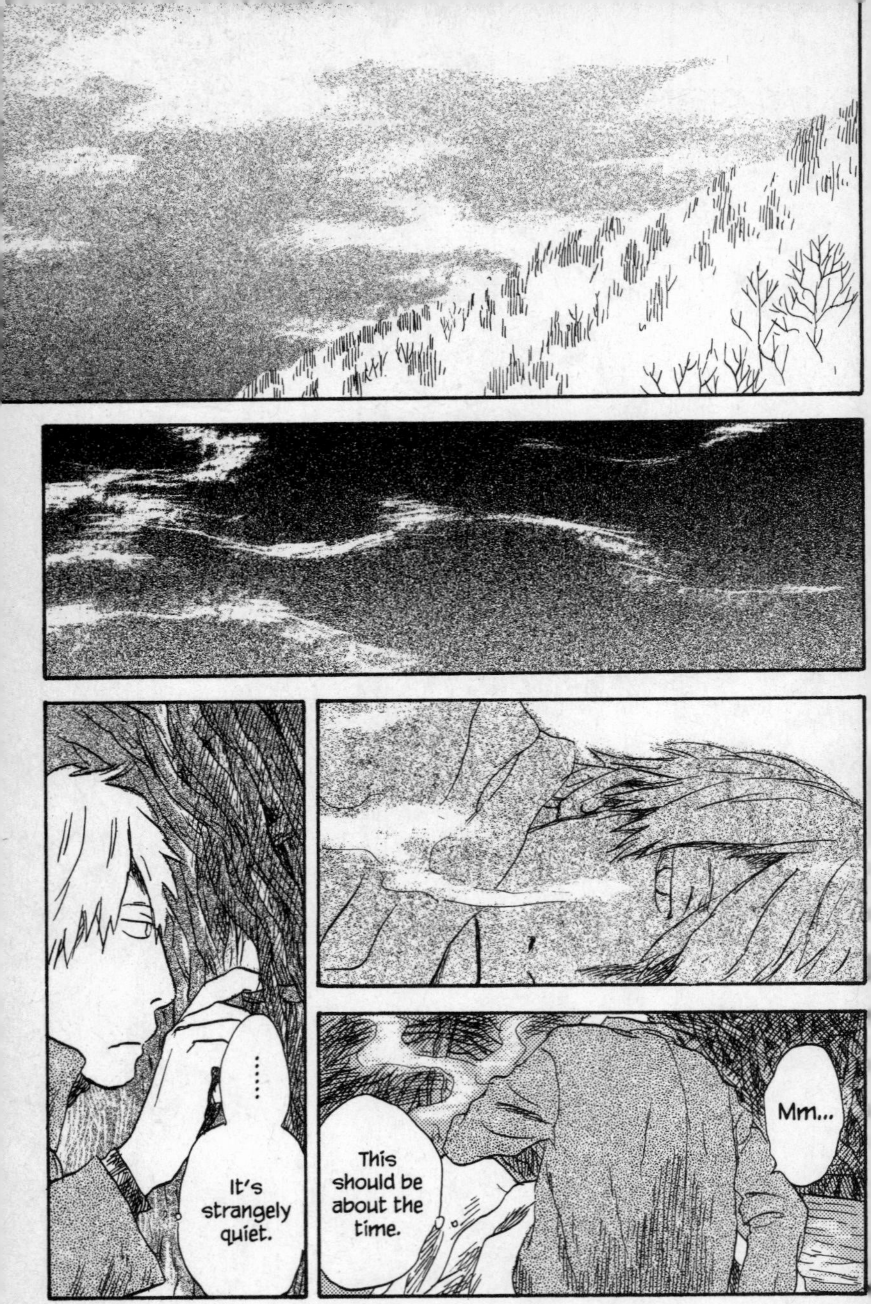
Mm...
This should be about the time.
......
It's strangely quiet.

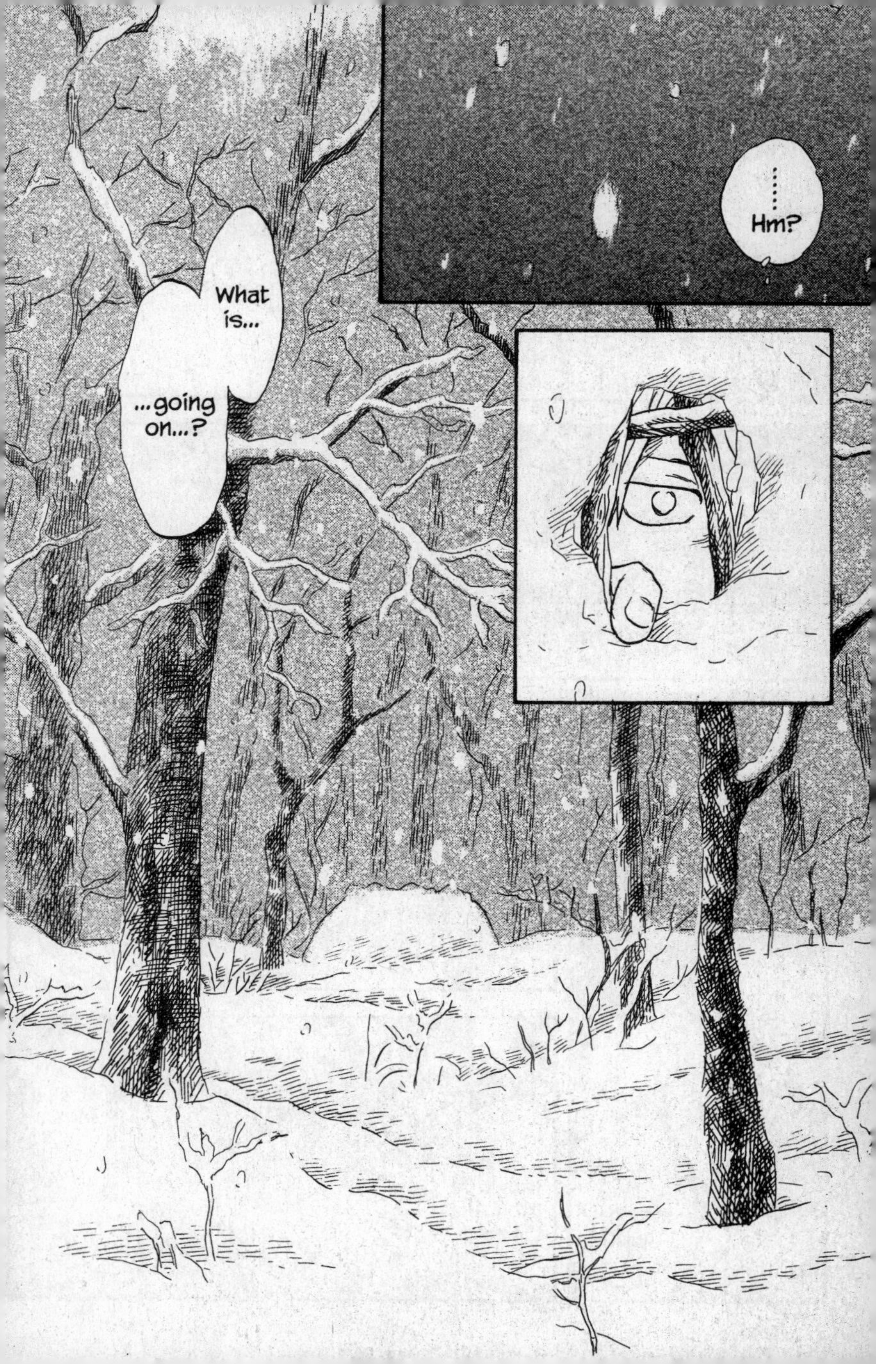
......Hm?
What is... ...going on...?

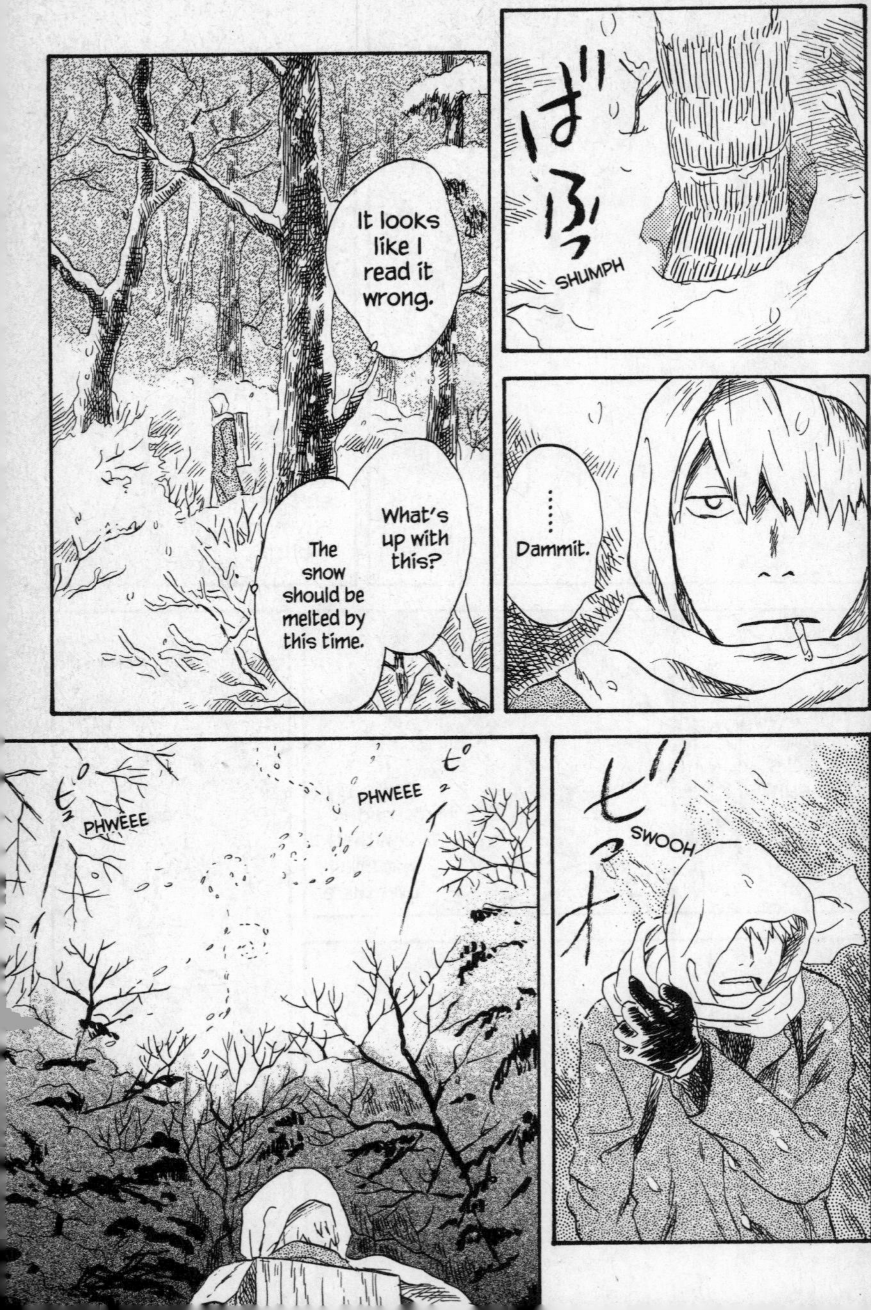

ばふっ
SHUMPH
……
Dammit.
It looks like I read it wrong.
What's up with this?
The snow should be melted by this time.
ビュオ
SWOOH
ピュ
PHWEEE
ピュ
PHWEEE

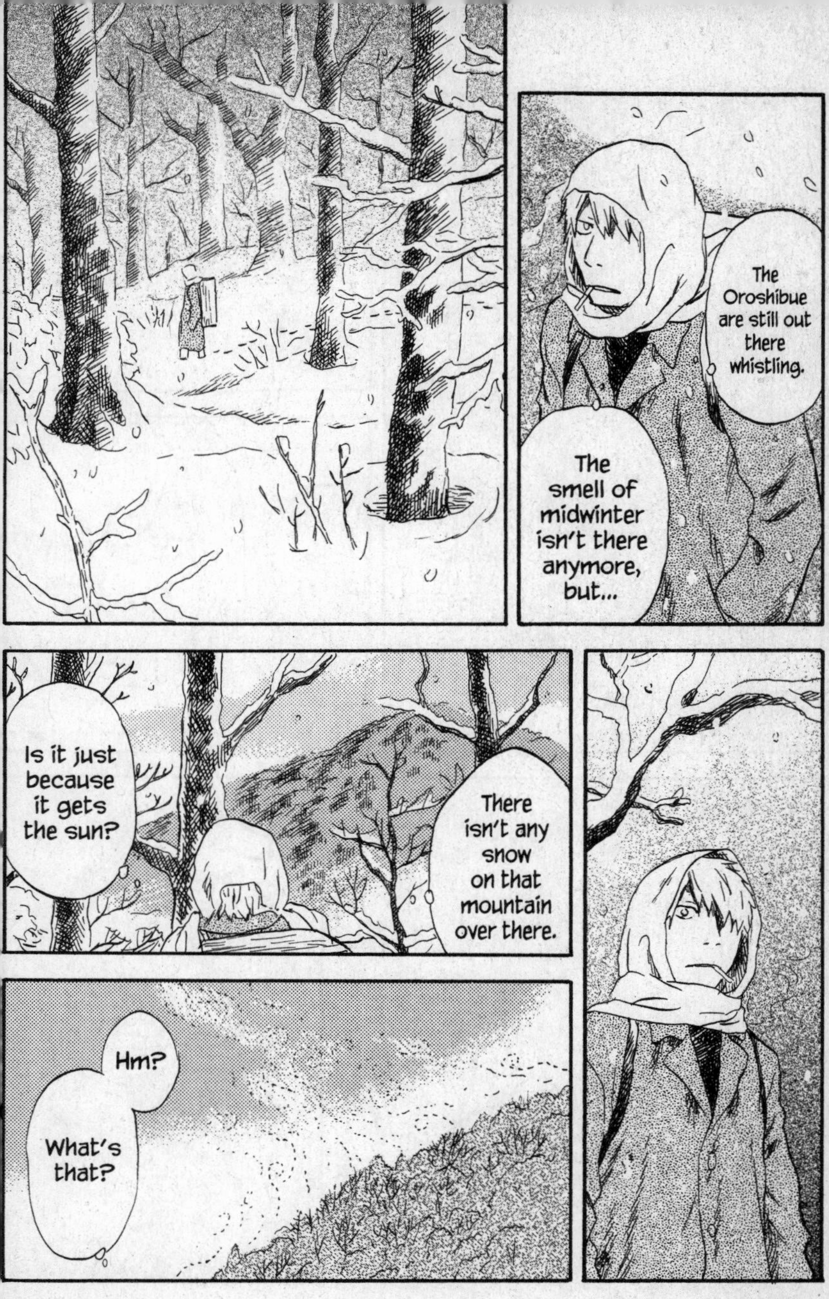

The Oroshibue are still out there whistling.
The smell of midwinter isn't there anymore, but...
There isn't any snow on that mountain over there.
Is it just because it gets the sun?
Hm?
What's that?

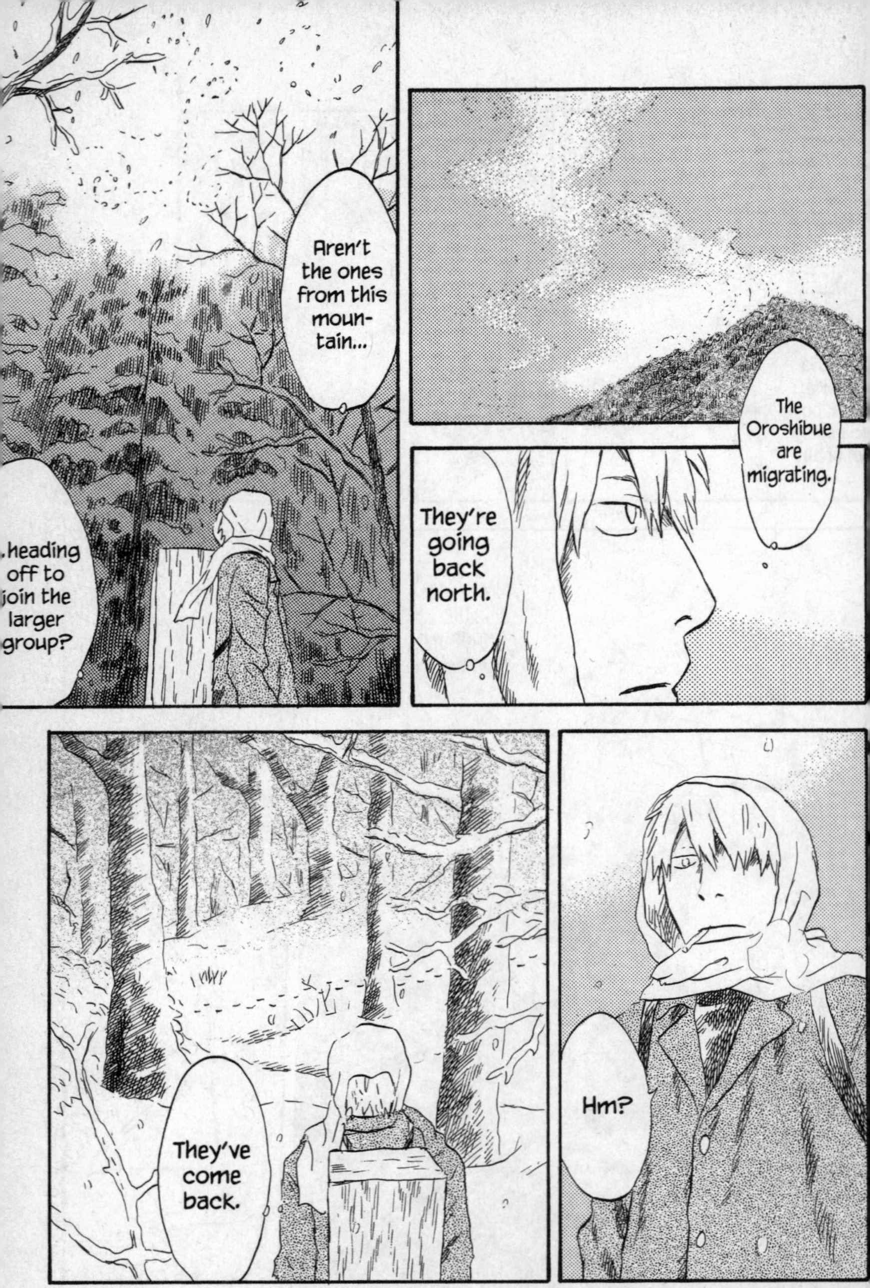
The Oroshibue are migrating.
They're going back north.
Aren't the ones from this moun-tain...
...heading off to join the larger group?
Hm?
They've come back.

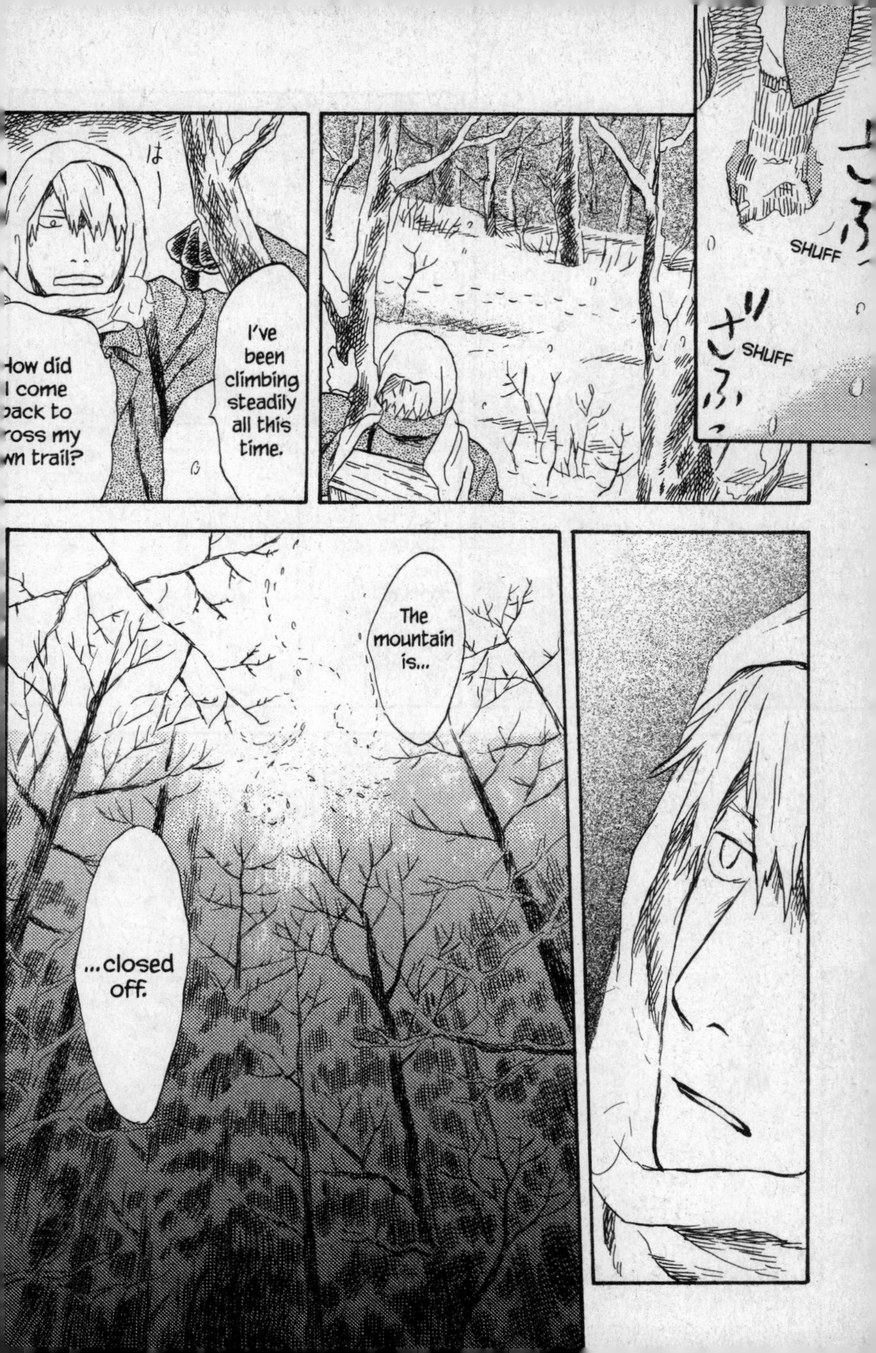
さふっ
SHUFF
ざふっ
SHUFF
I've been climbing steadily all this time.
はー
How did I come ack to ross my wn trail?
The mountain is...
...closed off.

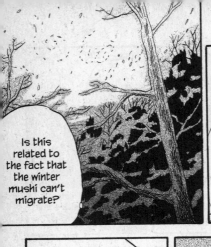

I don't remember anything unusual happening when I came to this mountain.
I don't get it.
Is this related to the fact that the winter mushi can't migrate?
I wonder...
...what's hap-pened here...?
SHF ざっ
Maybe I should go see the master.
ザッ SHF
There's no... voice.
There's no trace of Mugura either.

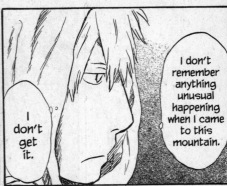

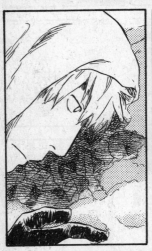

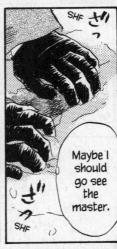

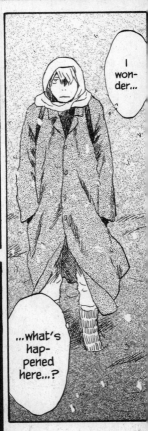

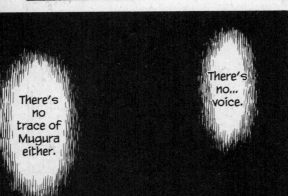

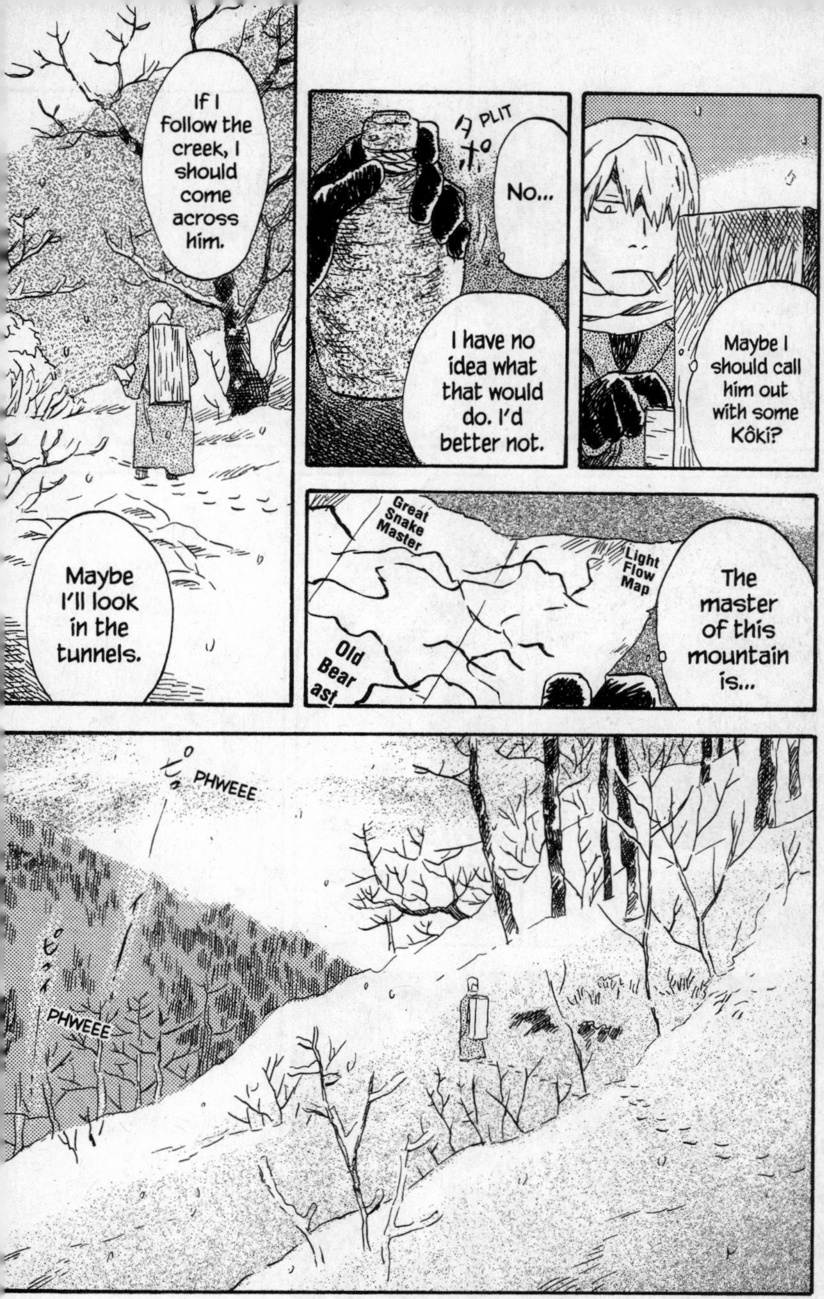
Maybe I should call him out with some Kôki?
PLIT
No...
I have no idea what that would do. I'd better not.
The master of this mountain is...
Great Snake Master
Light Flow Map
Old Bear ast
If I follow the creek, I should come across him.
Maybe I'll look in the tunnels.
PHWEEE
PHWEEE

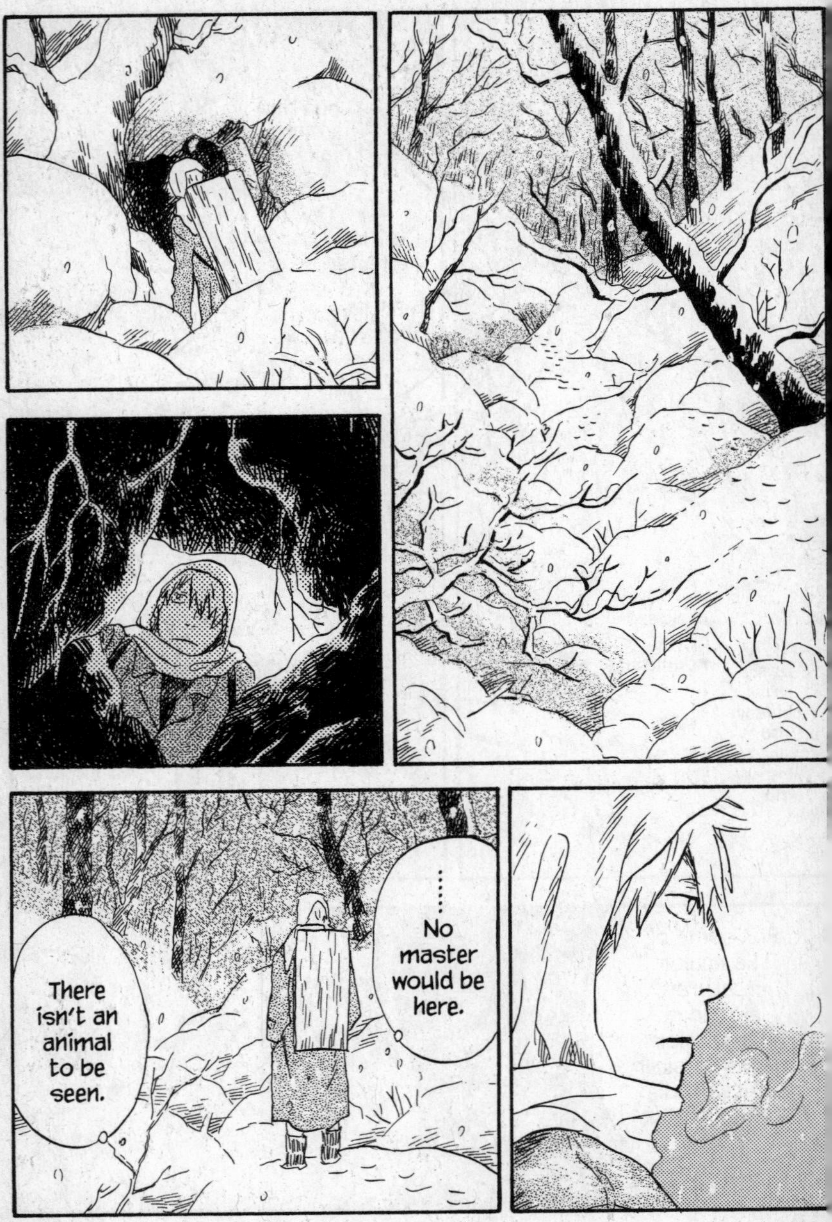
...... No master would be here.
There isn't an animal to be seen.

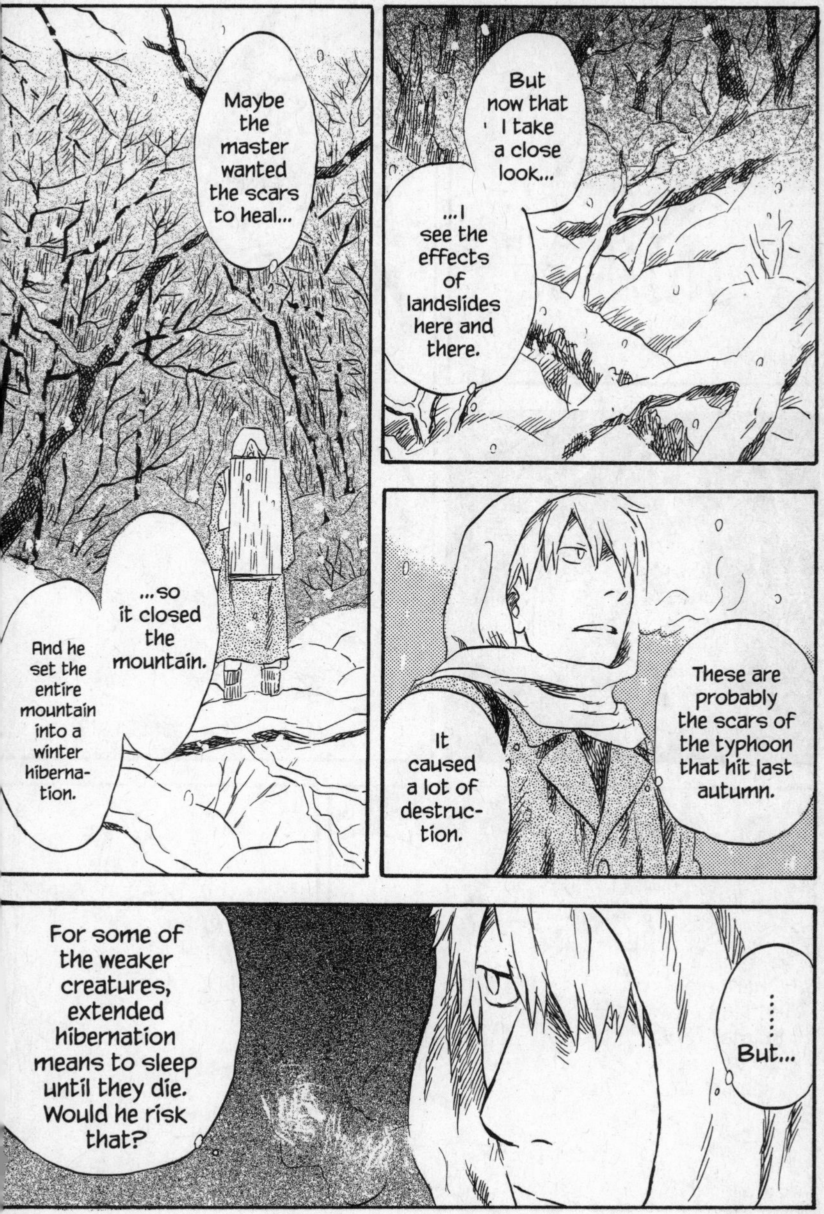
But now that I take a close look...
...I see the effects of landslides here and there.
These are probably the scars of the typhoon that hit last autumn.
It caused a lot of destruction.
Maybe the master wanted the scars to heal...
...so it closed the mountain.
And he set the entire mountain into a winter hiberna-tion.
......But...
For some of the weaker creatures, extended hibernation means to sleep until they die. Would he risk that?

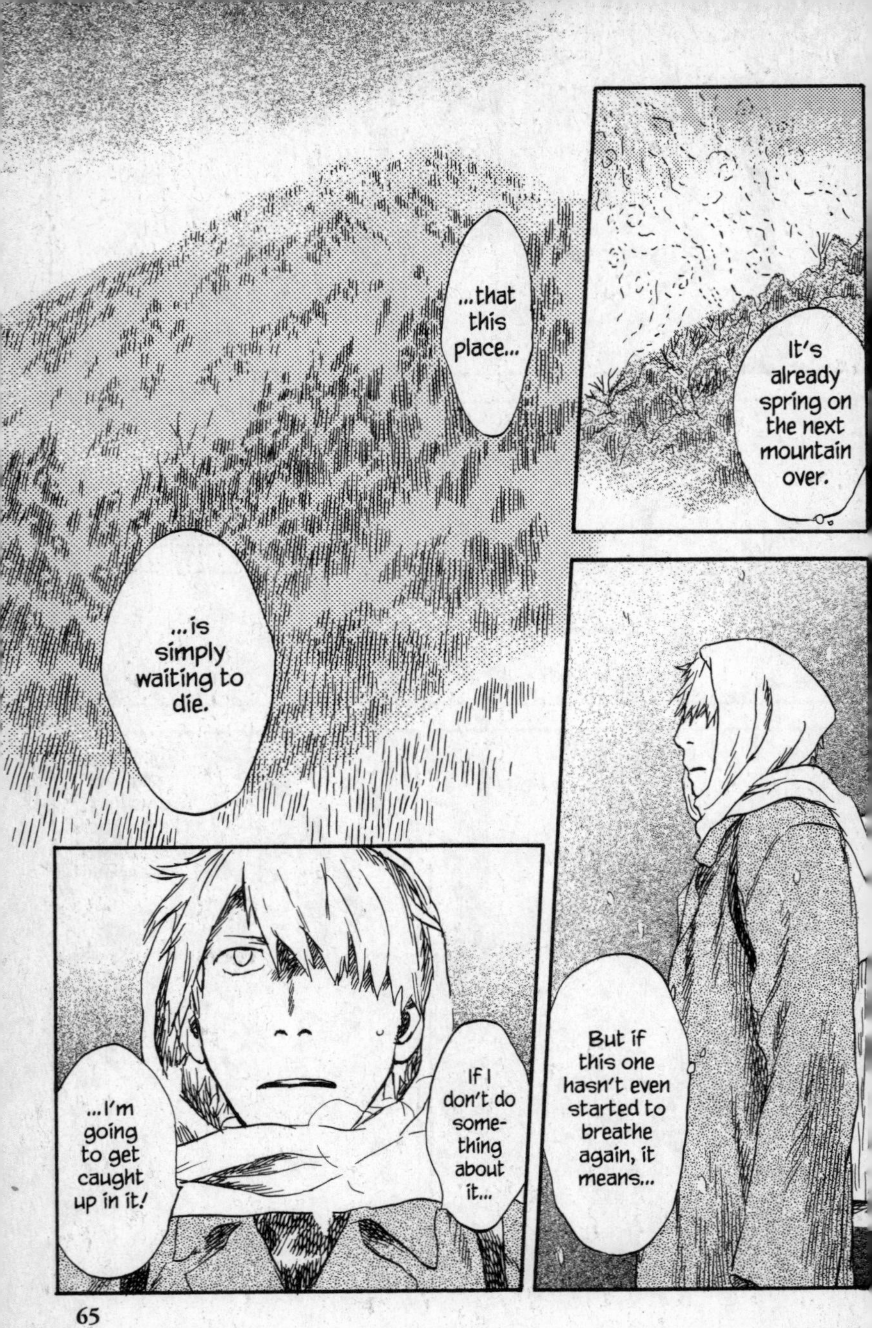
It's already spring on the next mountain over.
But if this one hasn't even started to breathe again, it means...
...that this place...
...is simply waiting to die.
If I don't do some-thing about it...
...I'm going to get caught up in it!

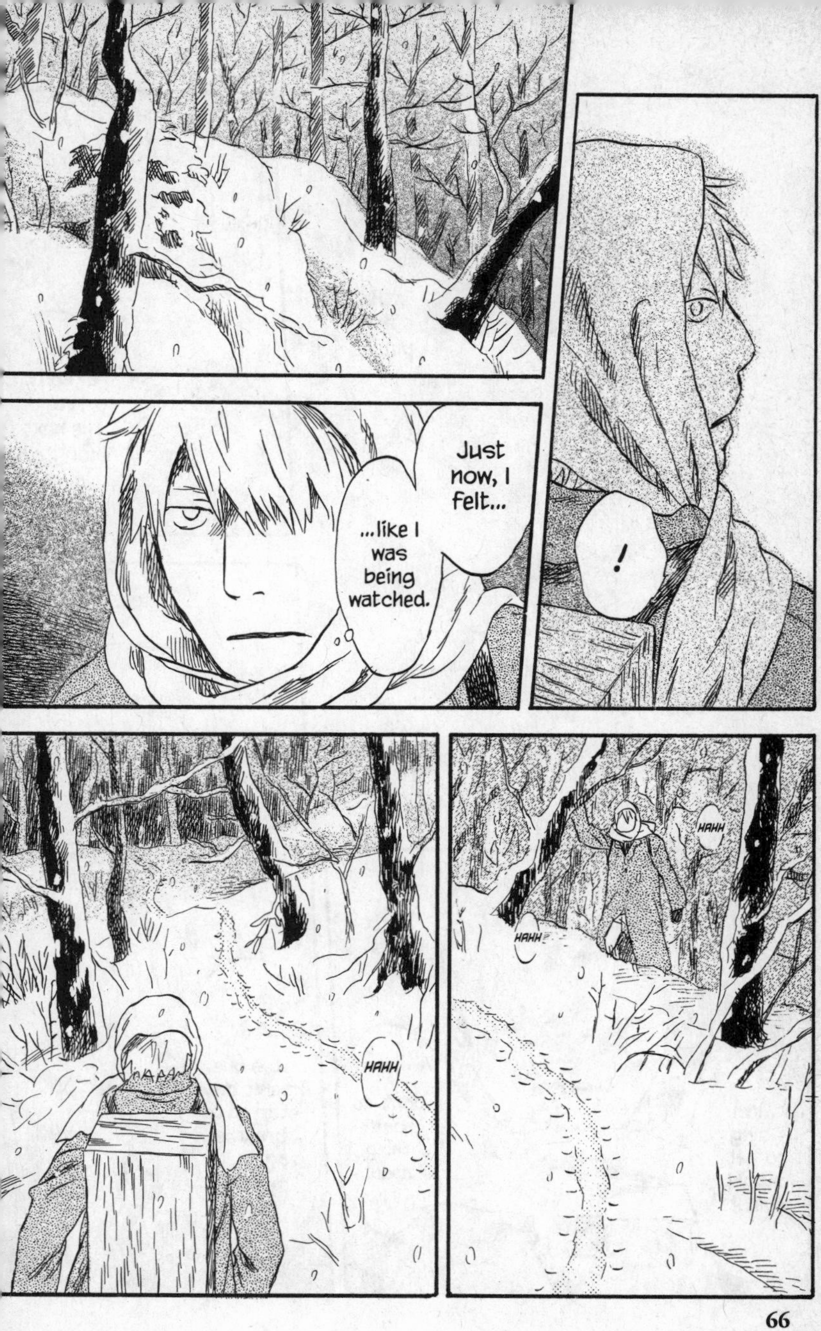
!
Just now, I felt...
...like I was being watched.
HAHH
HAHH
HAHH

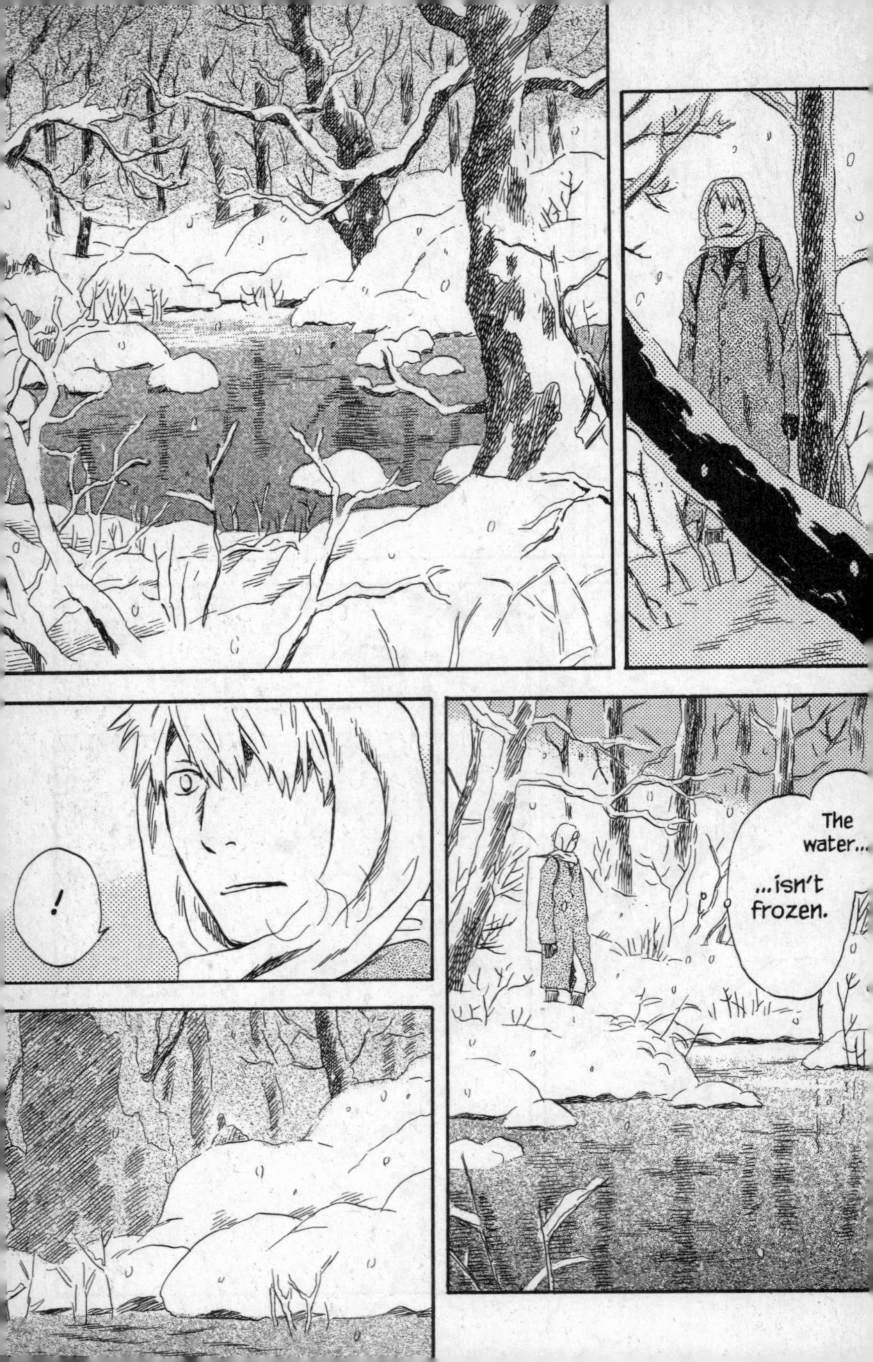
The water...
...isn't frozen.
!

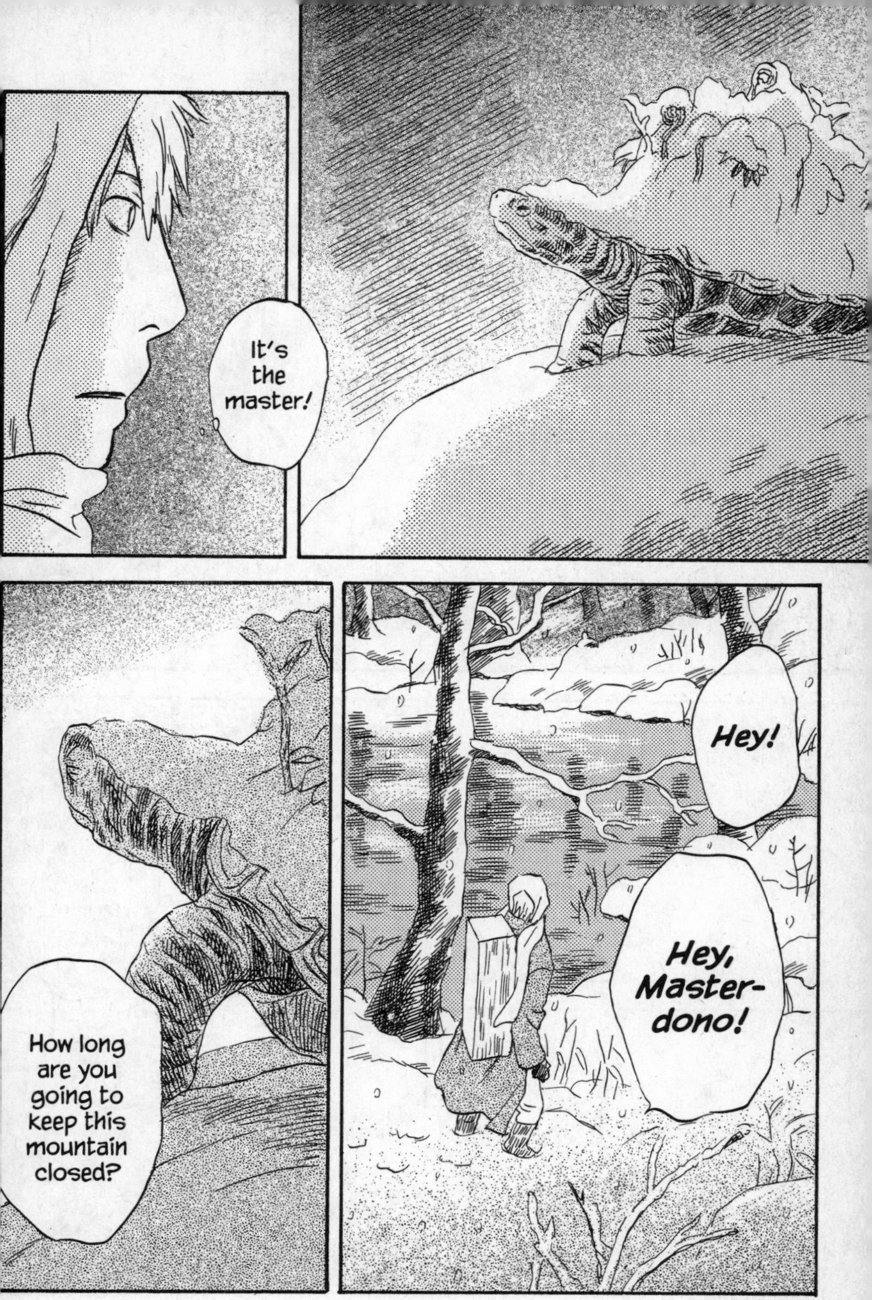
It's the master!
Hey!
Hey, Master-dono!
How long are you going to keep this mountain closed?

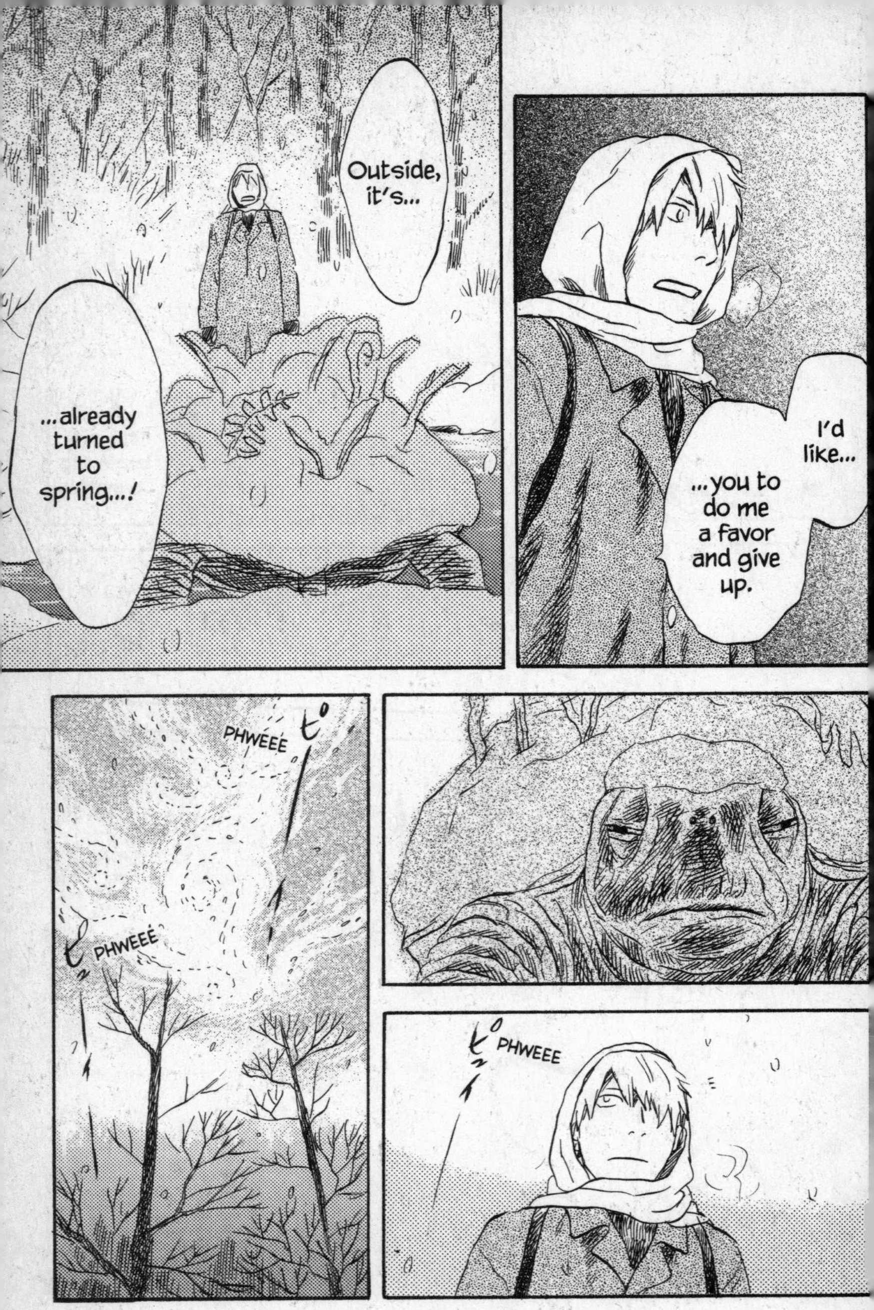

I'd like...
...you to do me a favor and give up.
Outside, it's...
...already turned to spring...!
PHWEEE
PHWEEE
PHWEEE

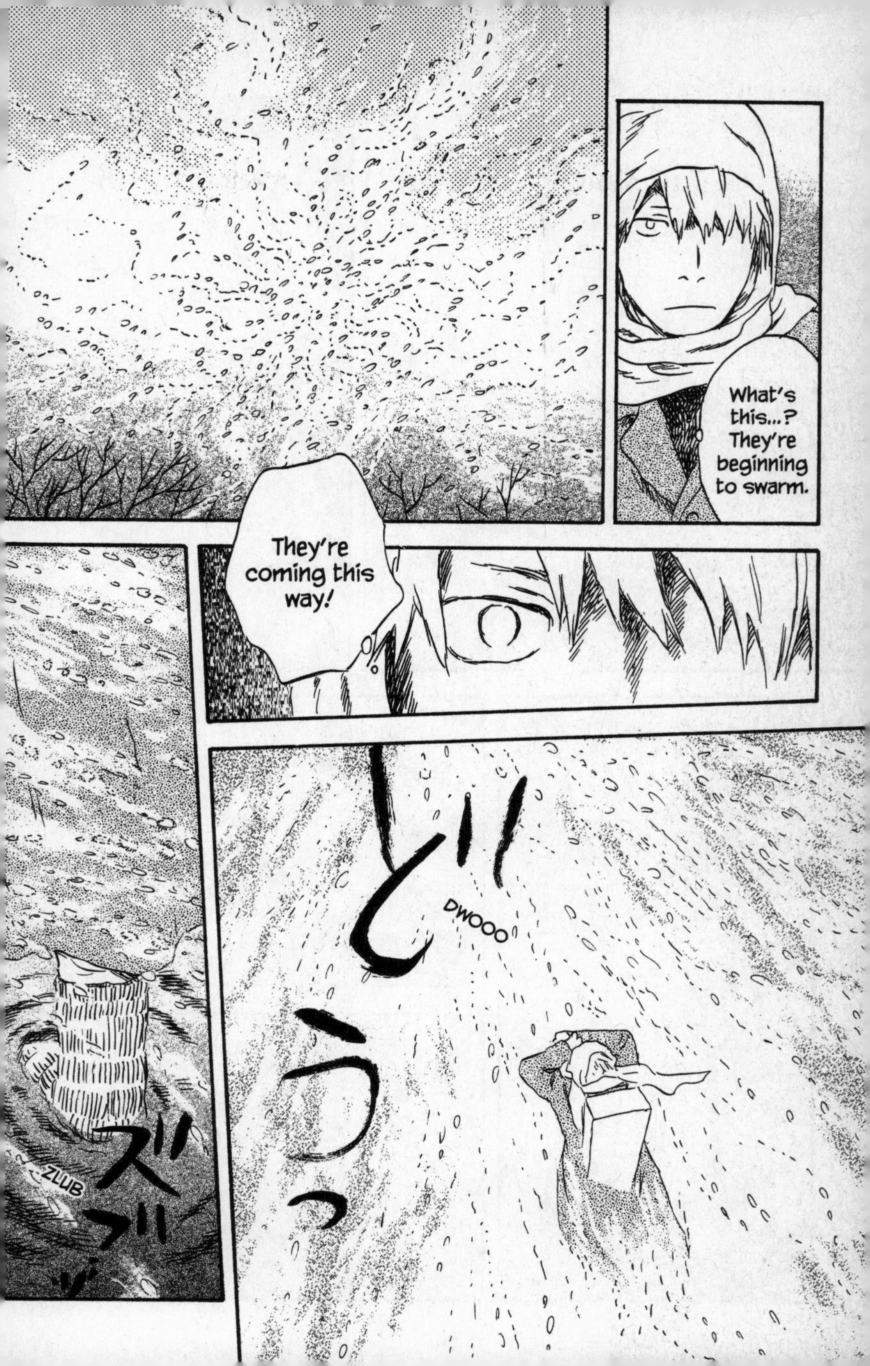
What's this...? They're beginning to swarm.
They're coming this way!
DWOOO
ZLUB

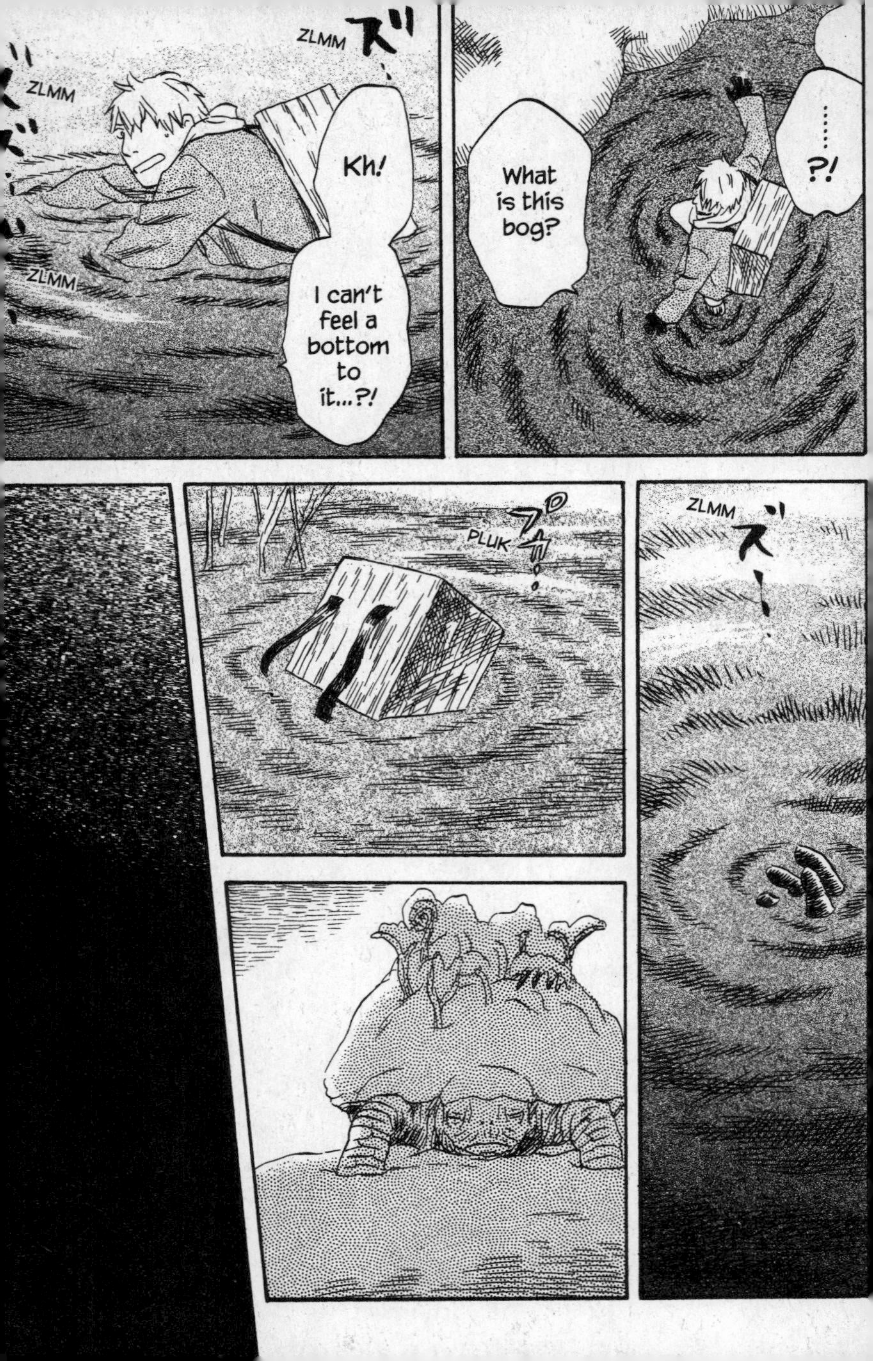
......
?!
What is this bog?
ZLMM
Kh!
I can't feel a bottom to it...?!
ZLMM
ZLMM
ZLMM
PLUK

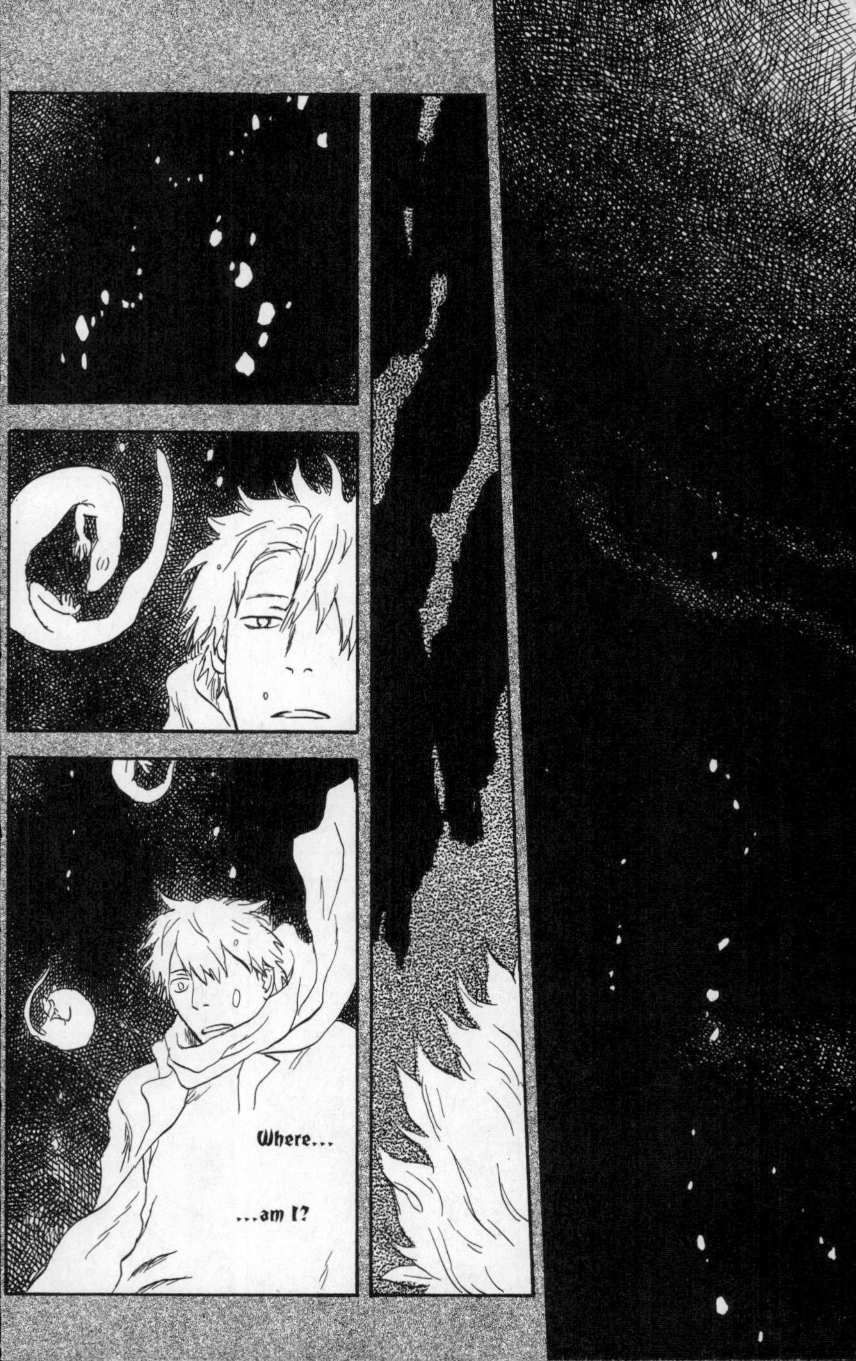
Where...
...am I?

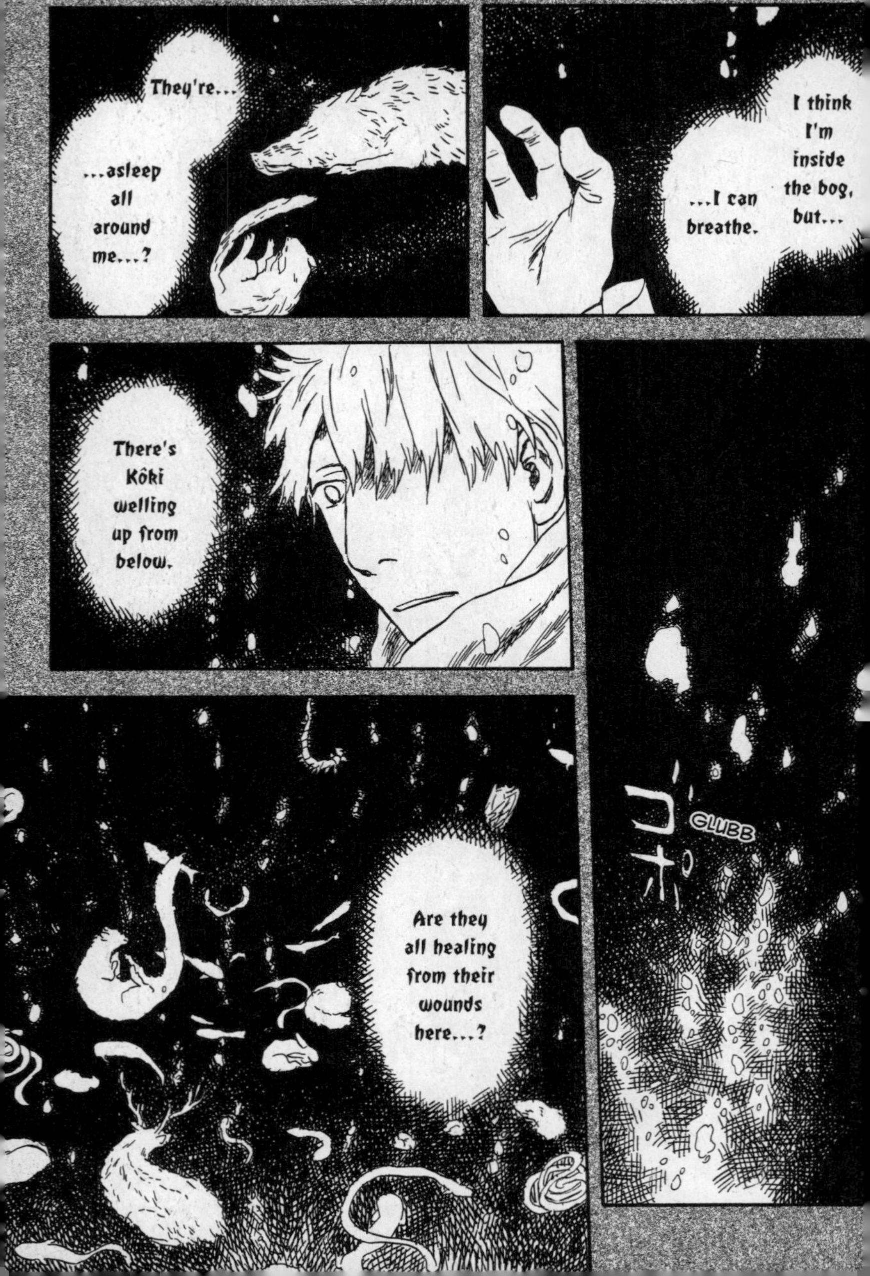
I think I'm inside the bog, but...
...I can breathe.
They're...
...asleep all around me...?
コポ
GLUBB
There's Kôki welling up from below.
Are they all healing from their wounds here...?

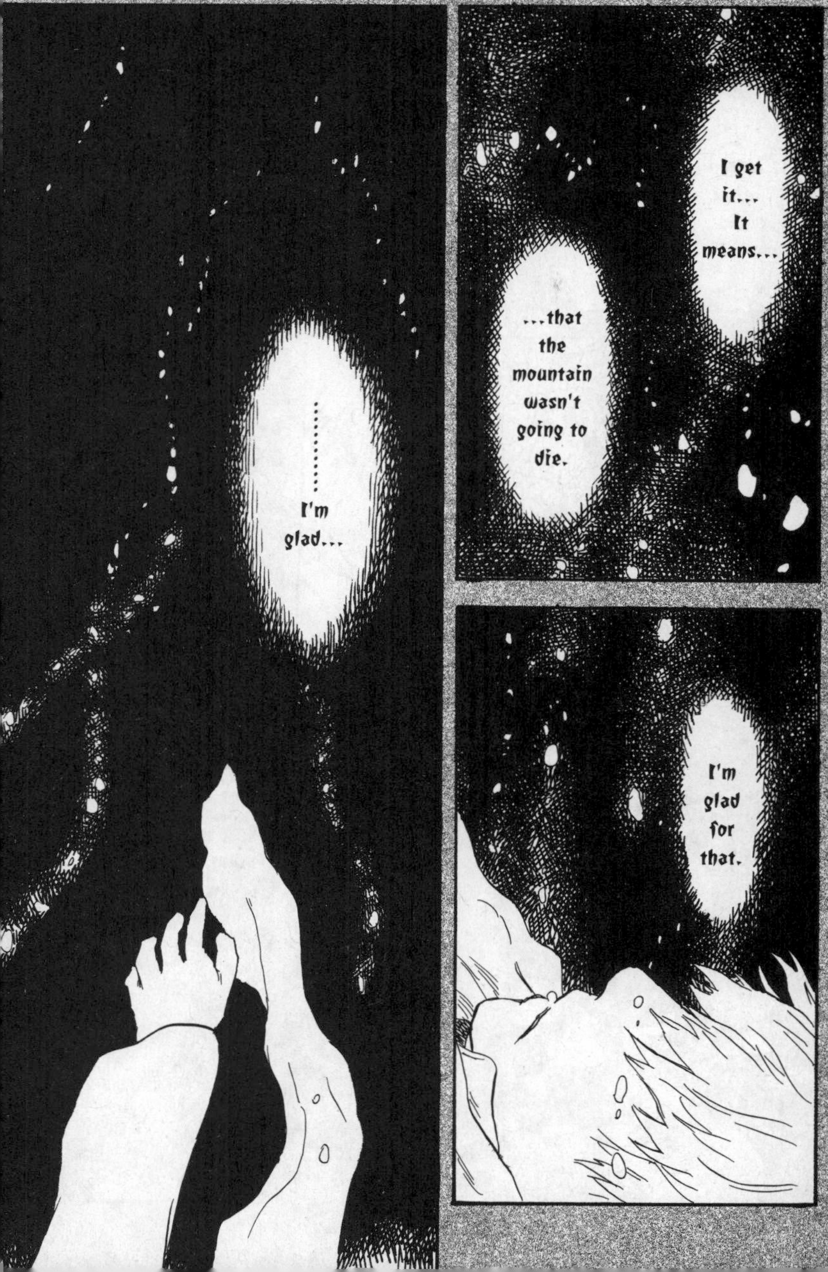
I get it... It means...
...that the mountain wasn't going to die.
I'm glad for that.
......
I'm glad...

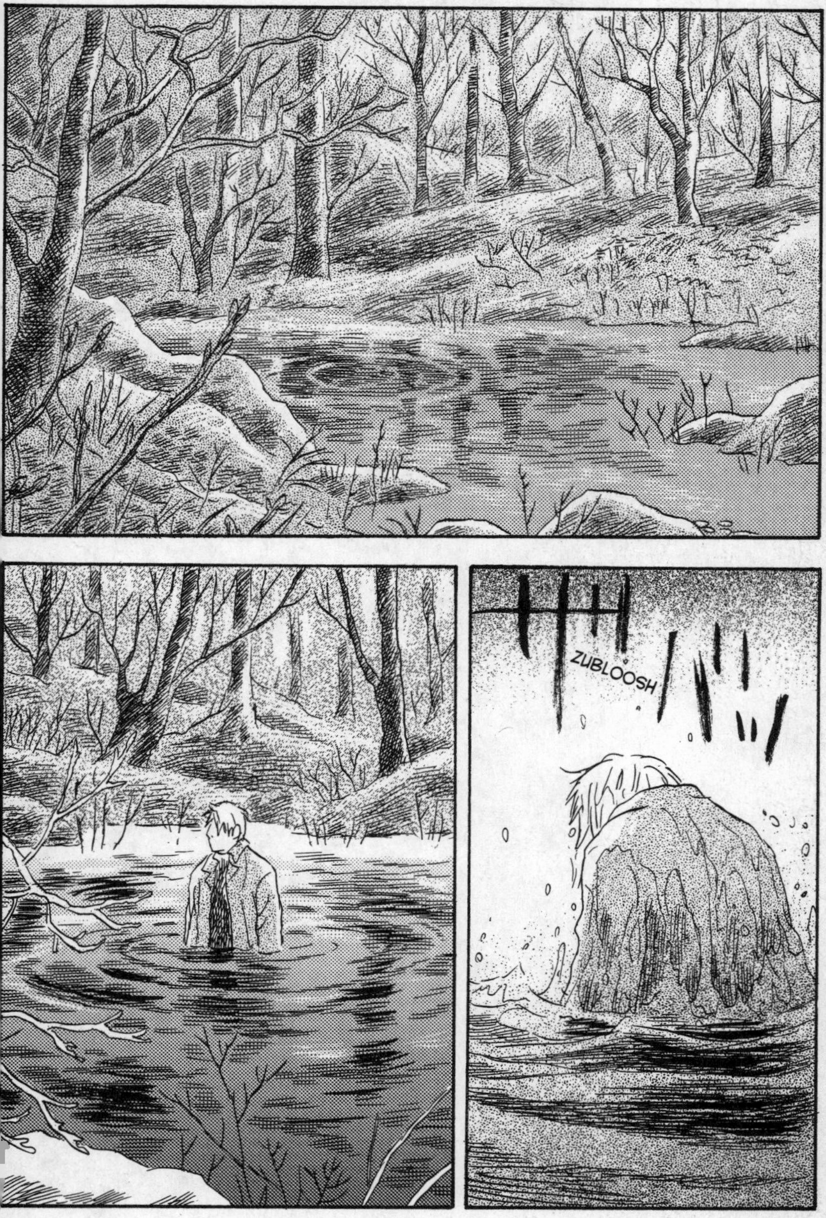
ZUBLOOSH

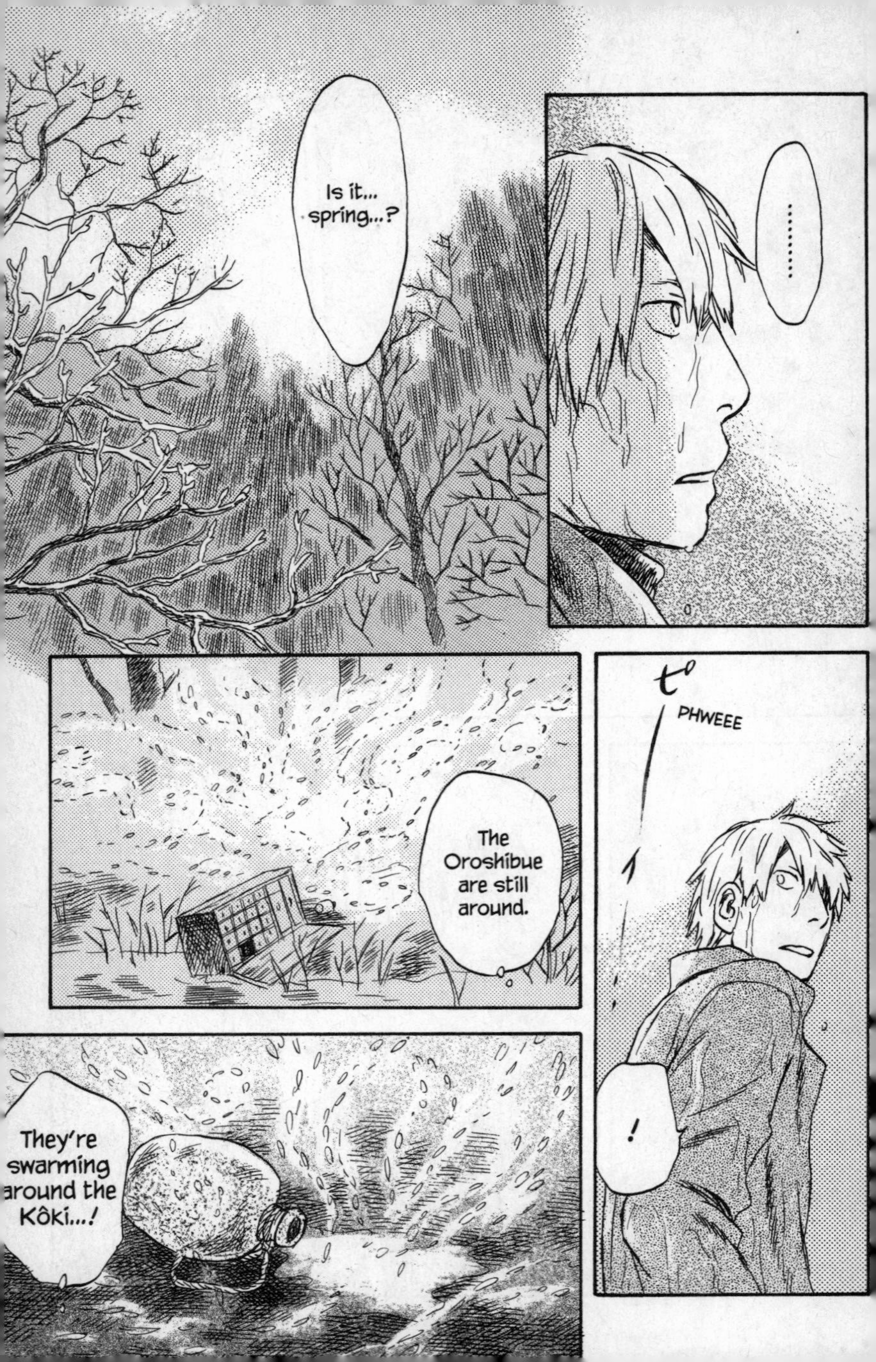
......
Is it... spring...?
PHWEEE
!
The Oroshibue are still around.
They're swarming around the Kôki...!

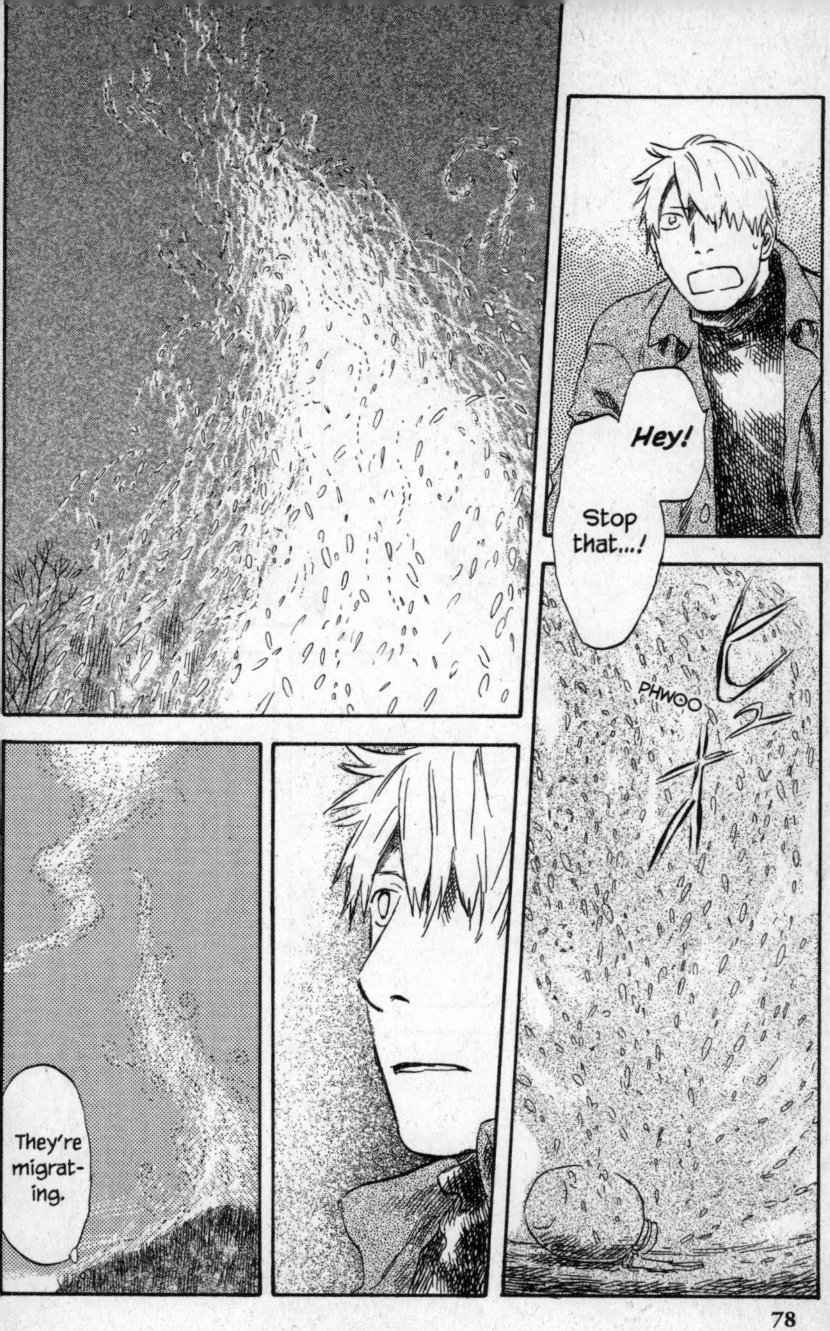
Hey!
Stop that...!
PHWOO
They're migrat-ing.

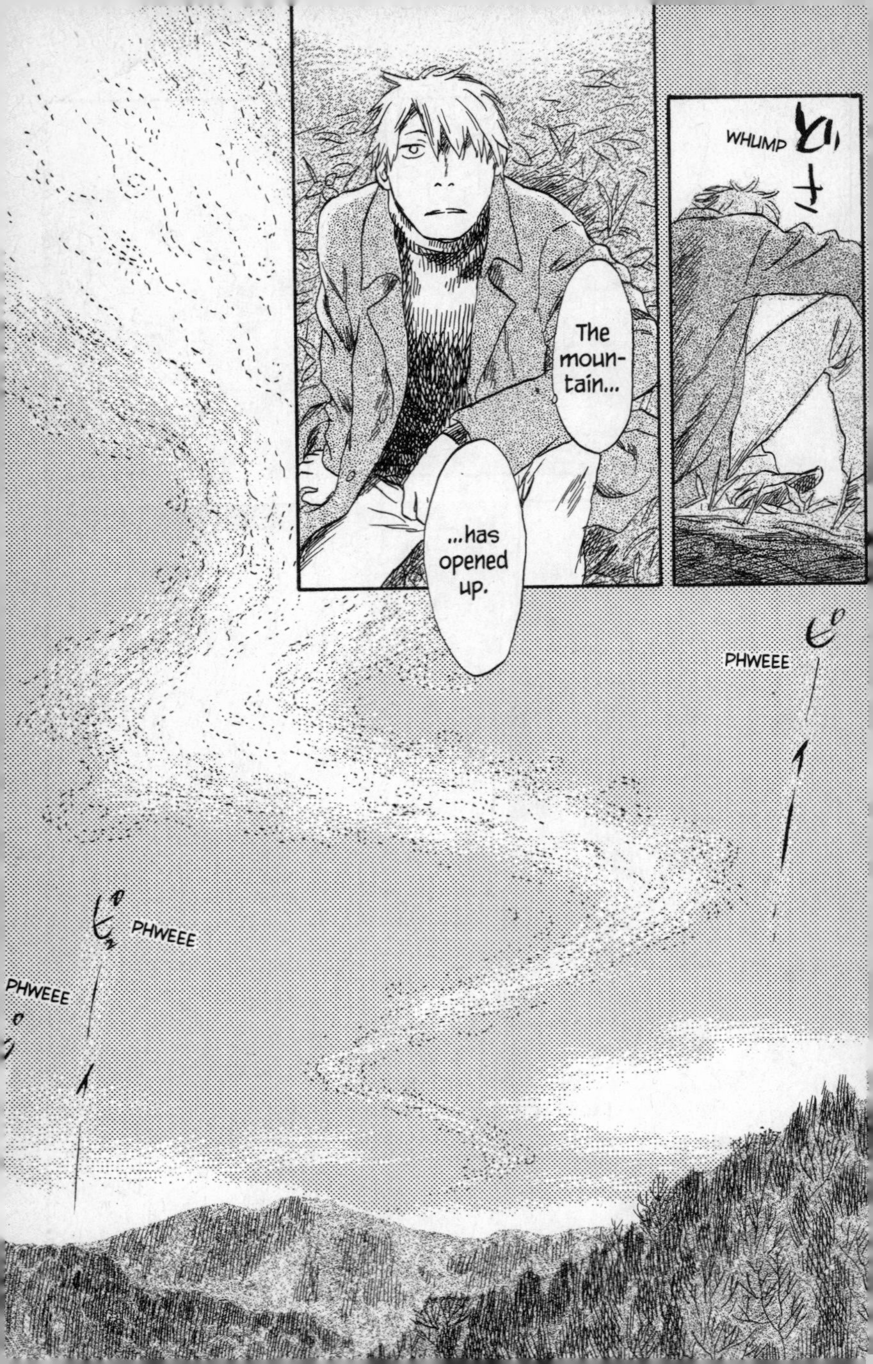

WHUMP
どさ
The mountain...
...has opened up.
PHWEEE
PHWEEE
PHWEEE

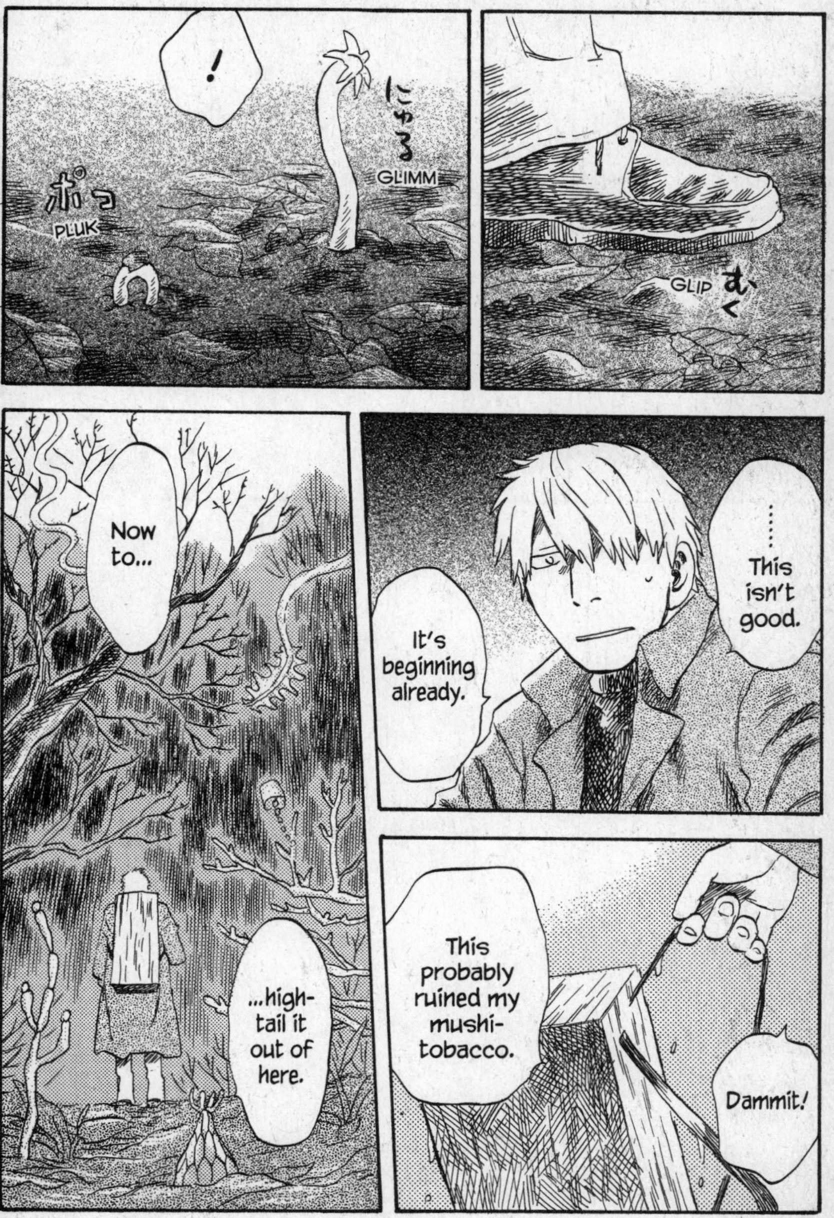
むく
GLIP
!
にゅる
GLIMM
ポコ
PLUK
......
This isn't good.
It's beginning already.
This probably ruined my mushi-tobacco.
Dammit!
Now to...
...high-tail it out of here.

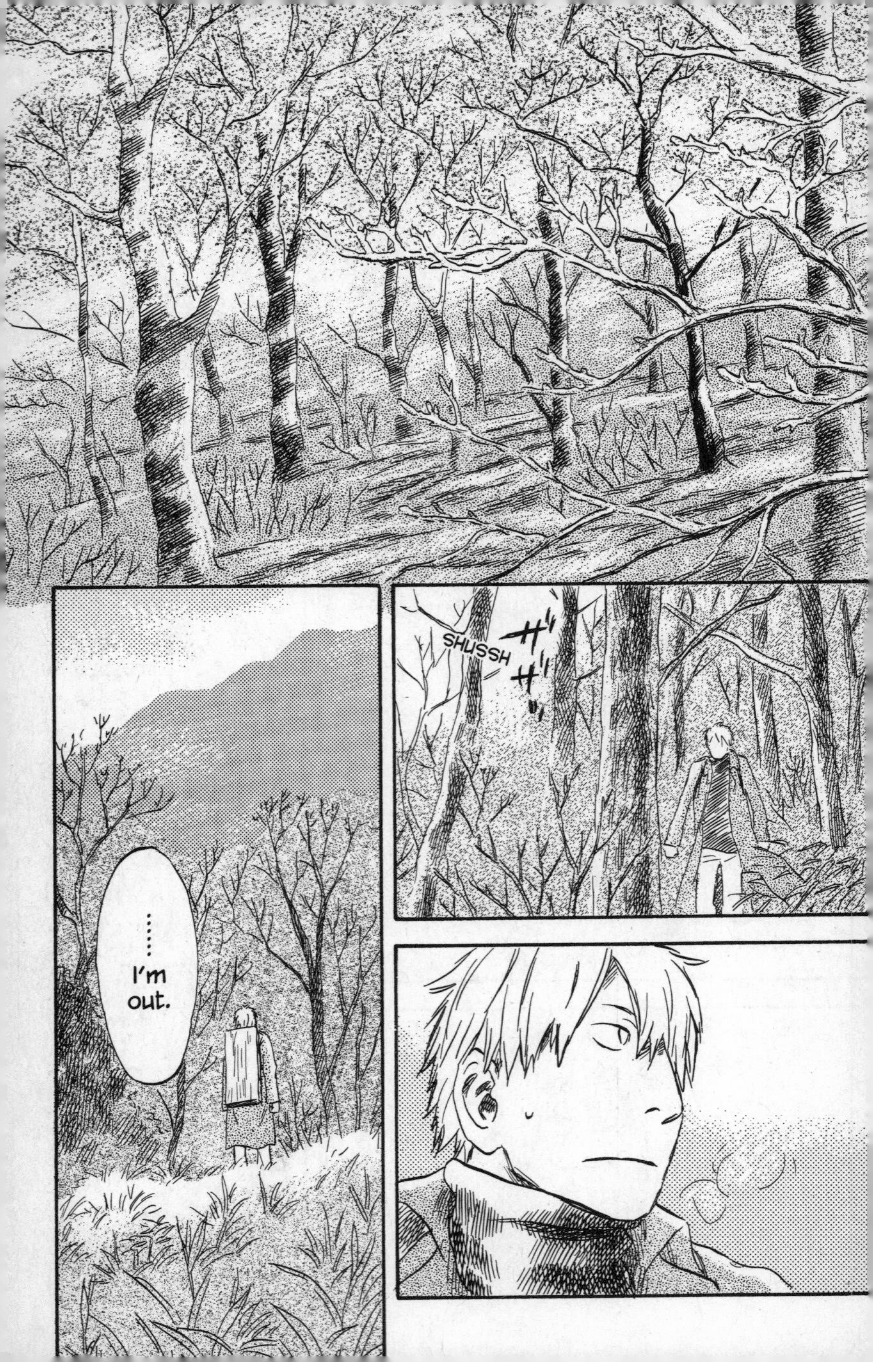
SHUSSH
…… I'm out.

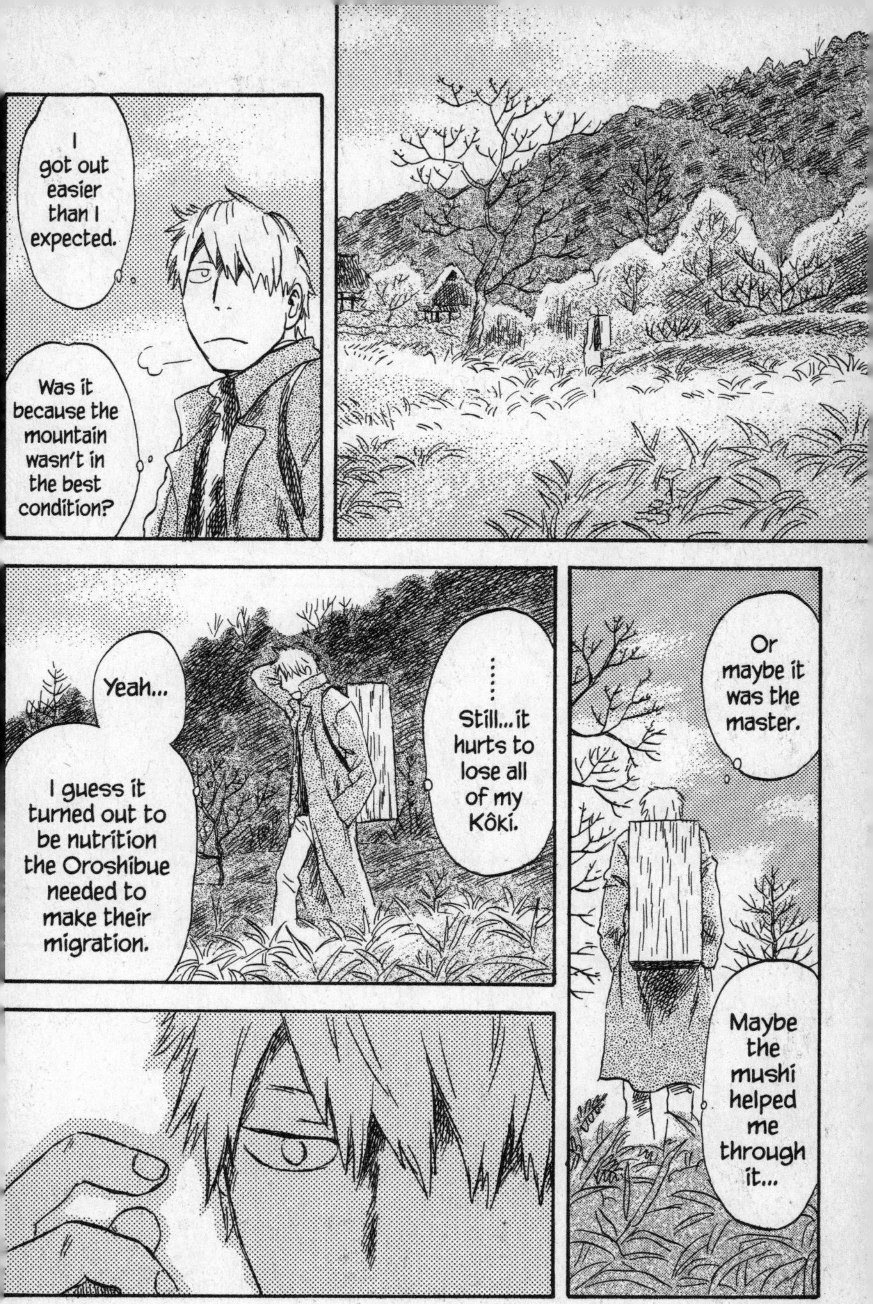
I got out easier than I expected.
Was it because the mountain wasn't in the best condition?
Or maybe it was the master.
Maybe the mushi helped me through it...
......Still...it hurts to lose all of my Kôki.
Yeah...
I guess it turned out to be nutrition the Oroshibue needed to make their migration.

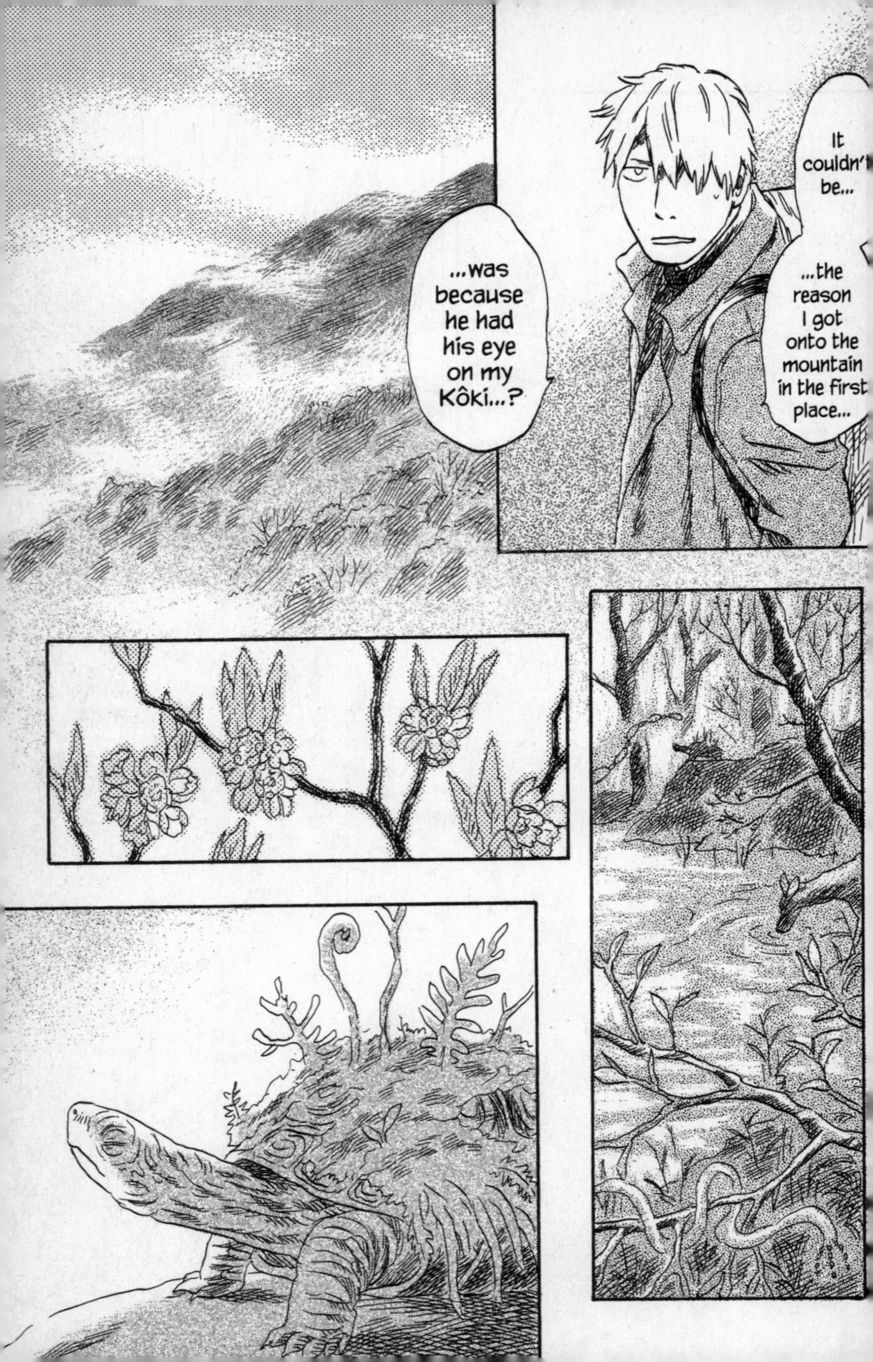
It couldn't be...
...the reason I got onto the mountain in the first place...
...was because he had his eye on my Kôki...?

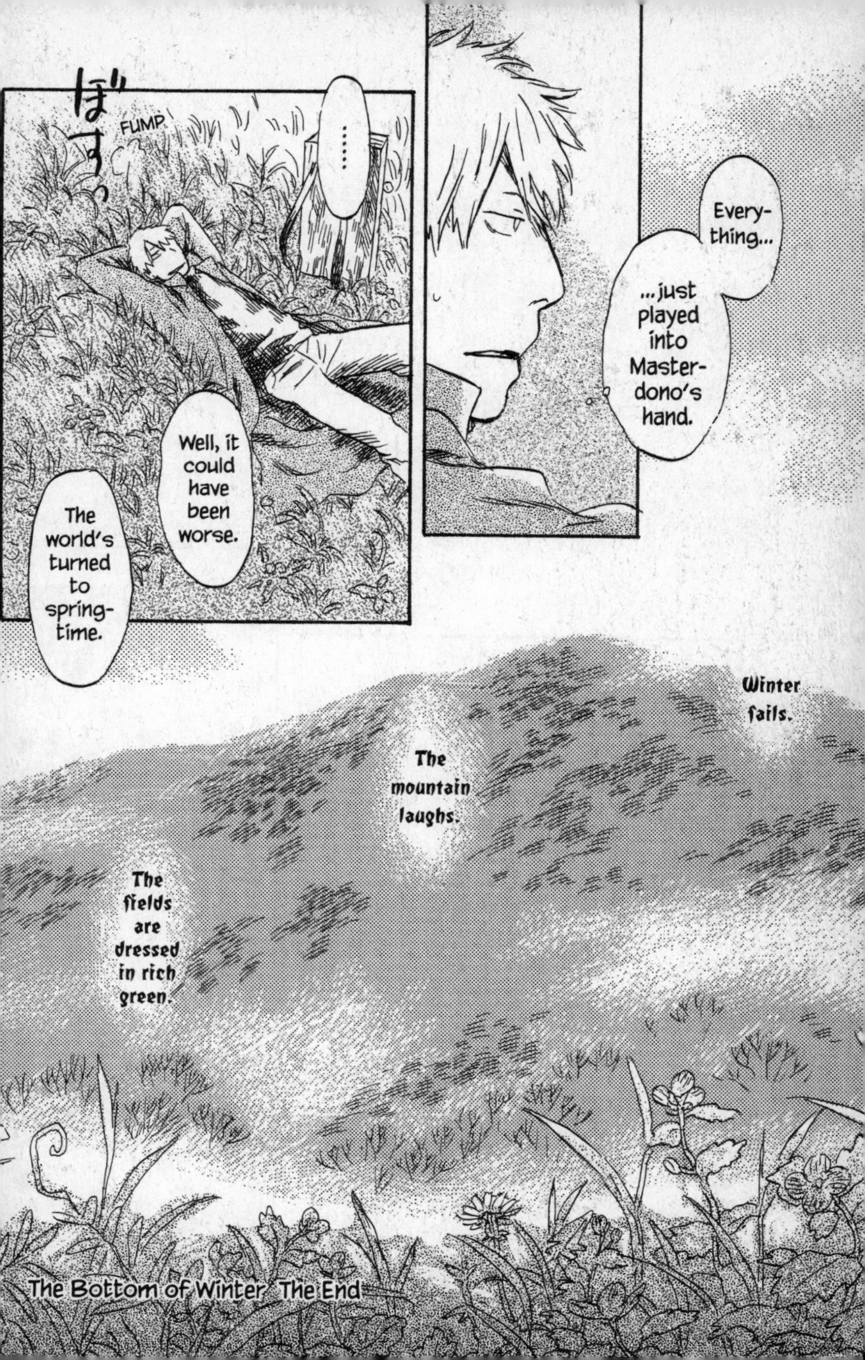
Every-thing...
...just played into Master-dono's hand.
......
ぼすっ
FUMP
Well, it could have been worse.
The world's turned to spring-time.
Winter fails.
The mountain laughs.
The fields are dressed in rich green.
The Bottom of Winter The End

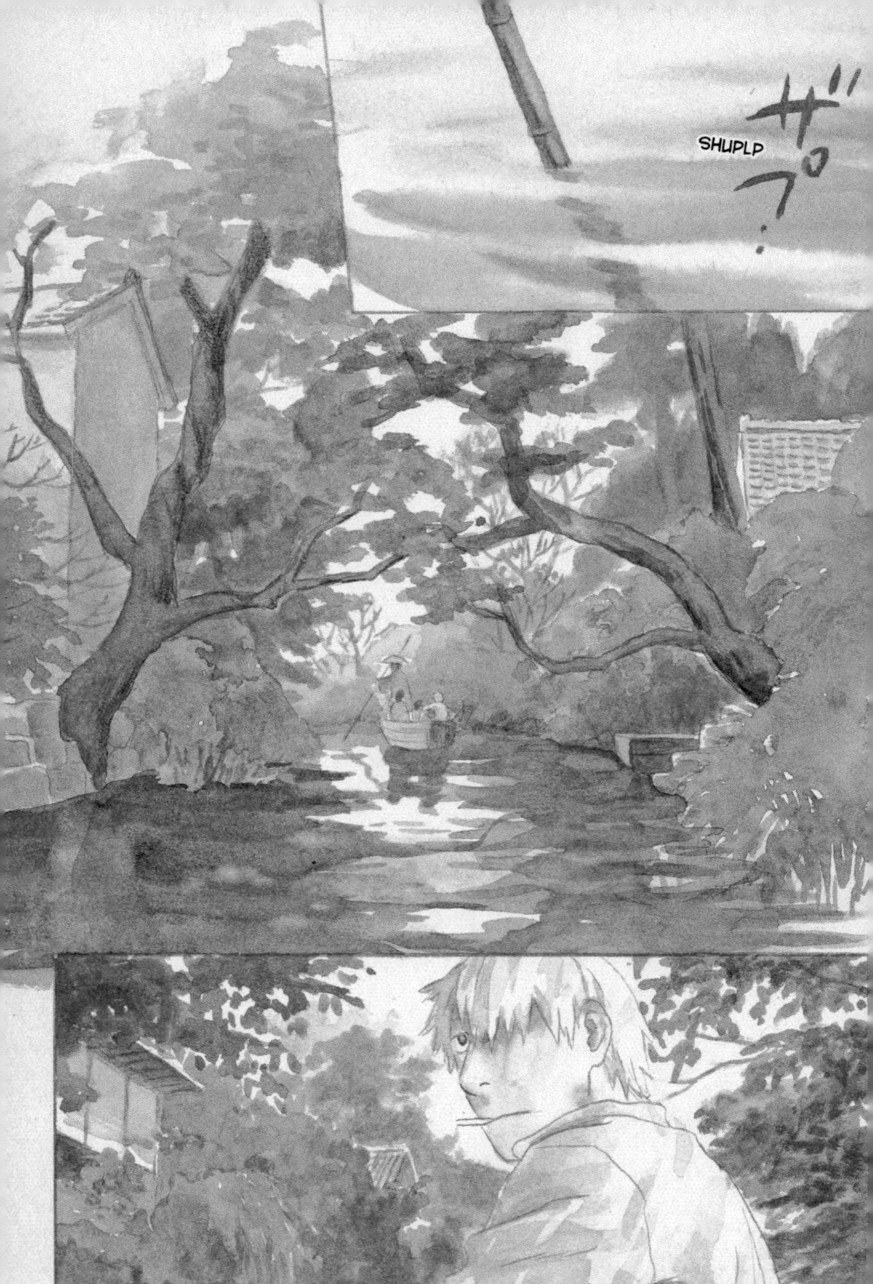
ザブ…
SHUPLP

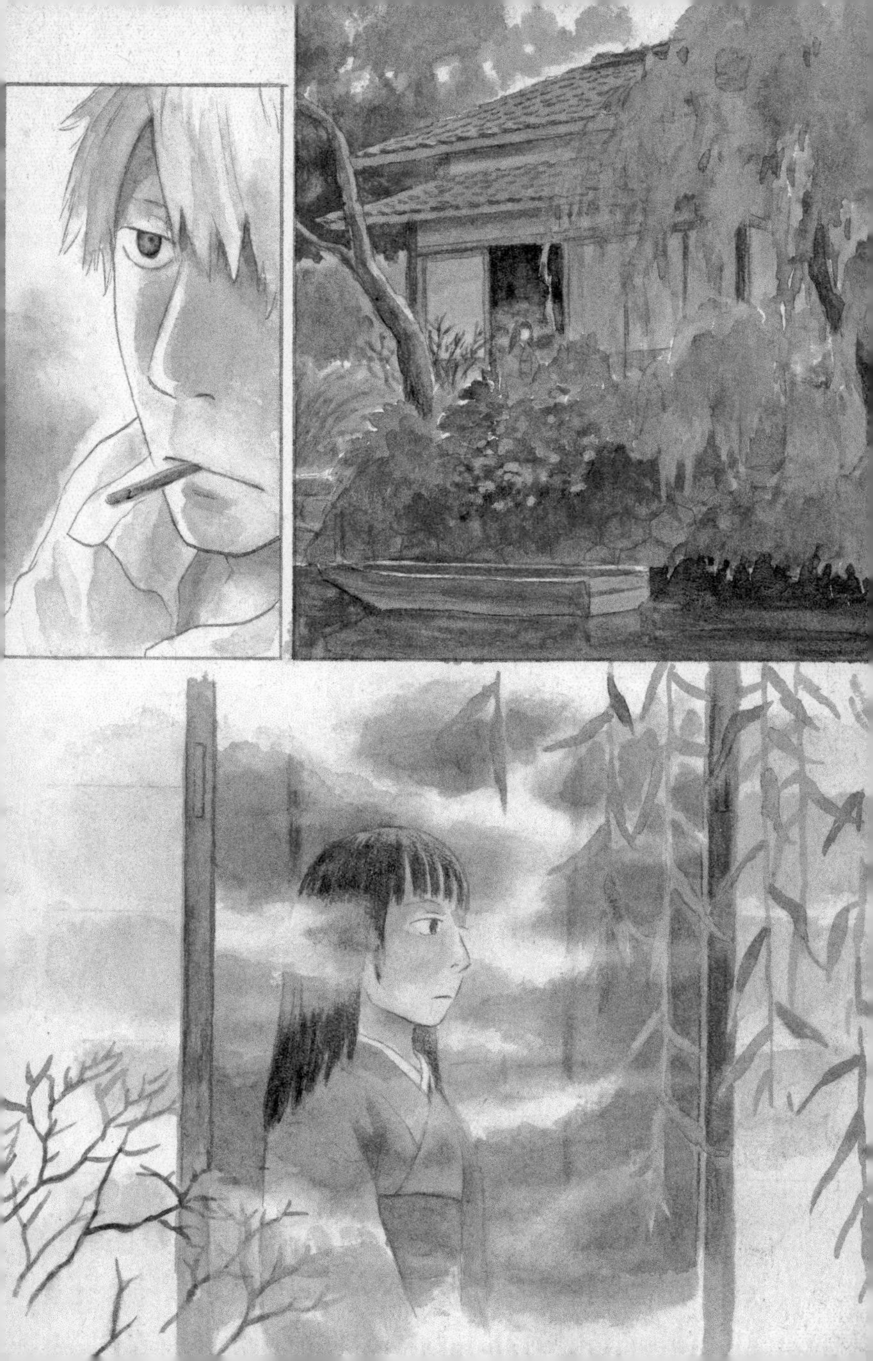

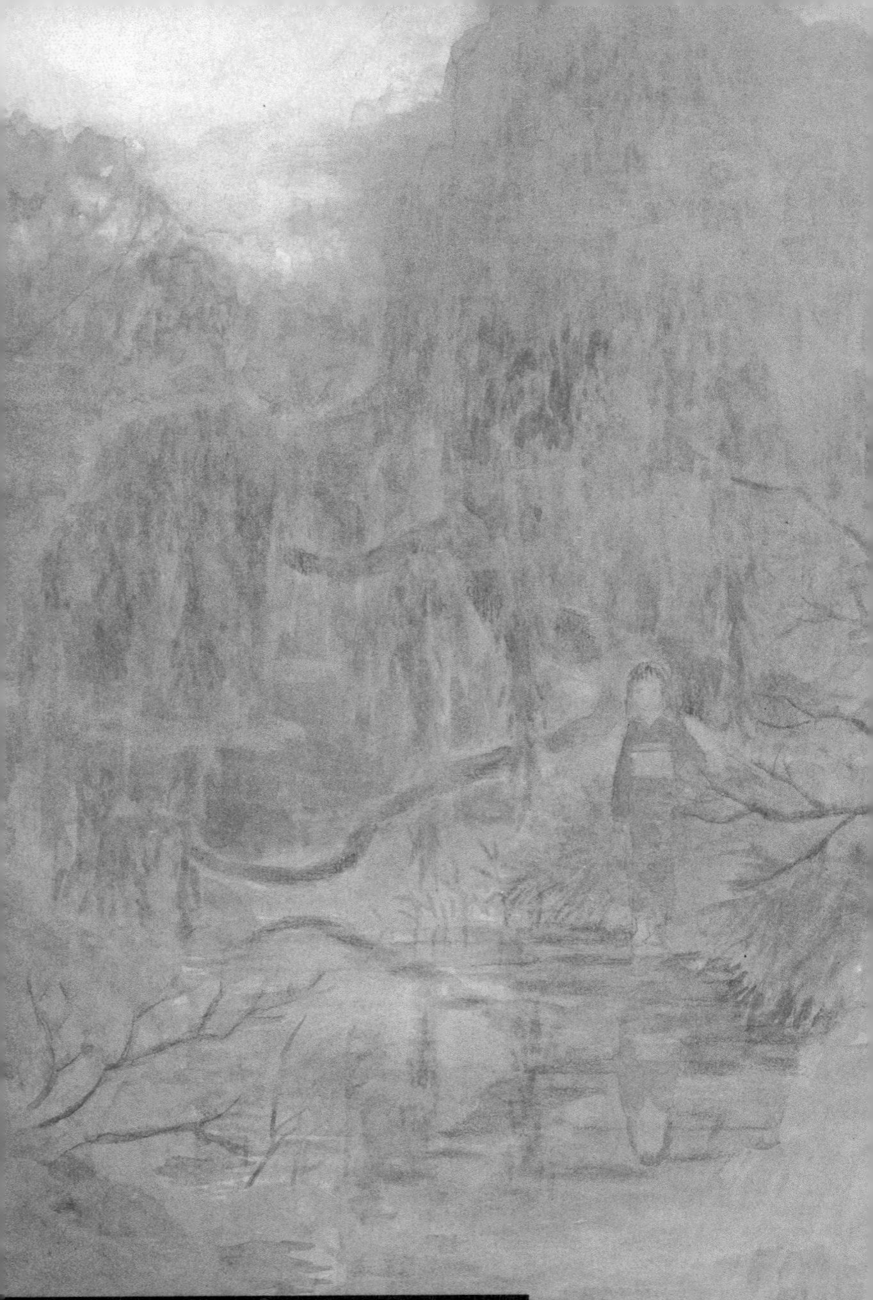

The Hidden Channel

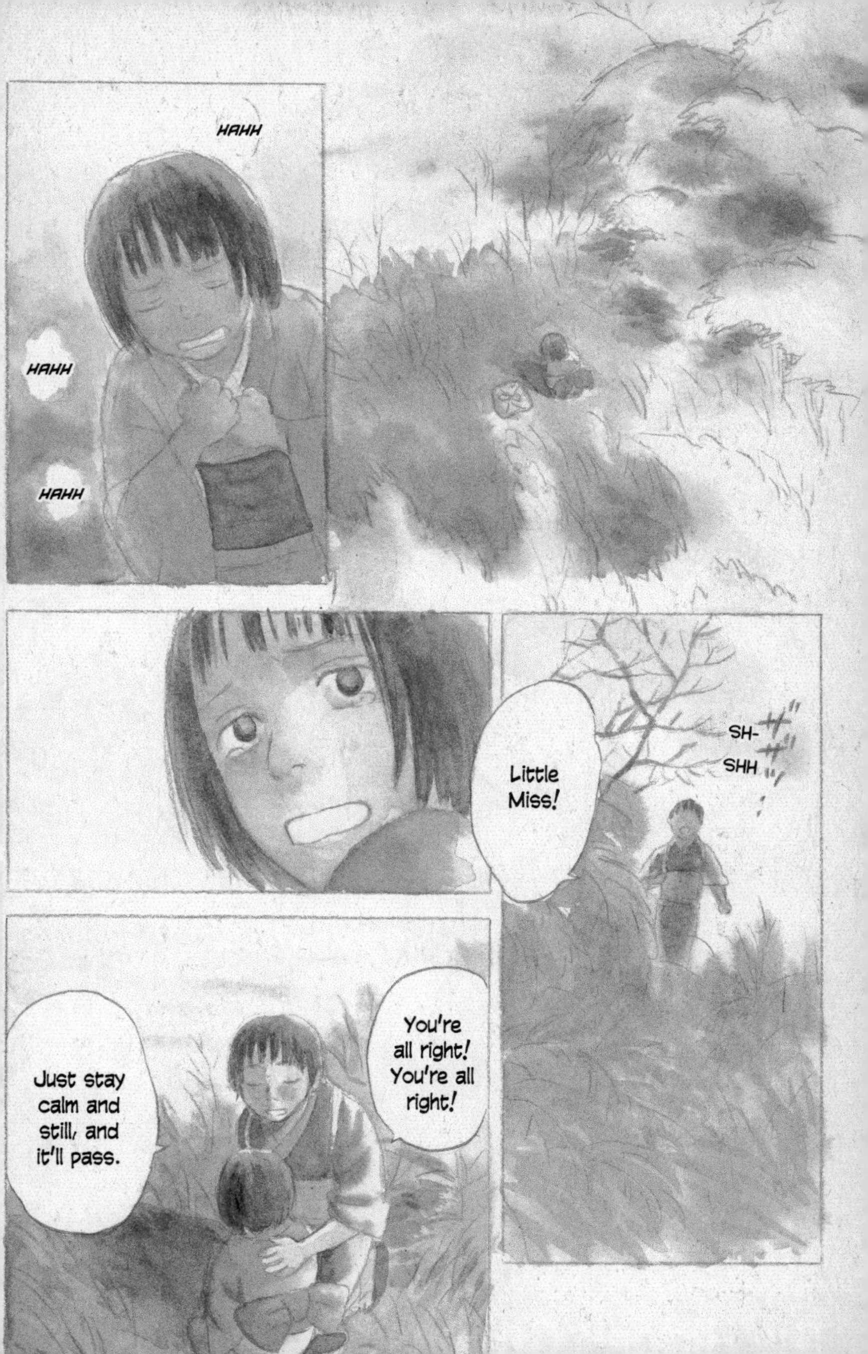
HAHH
HAHH
HAHH
SH- SHH
Little Miss!
You're all right! You're all right!
Just stay calm and still, and it'll pass.

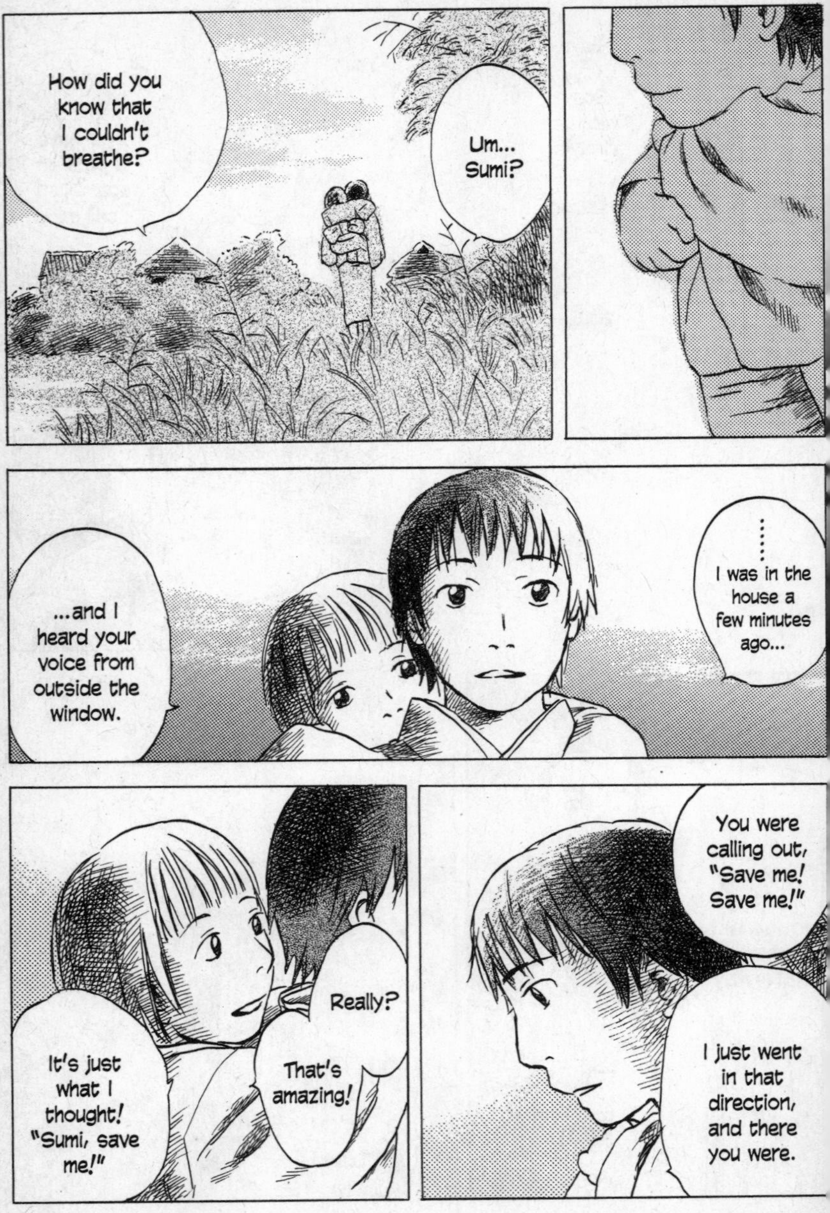
Um...
Sumi?
How did you know that I couldn't breathe?
......
I was in the house a few minutes ago...
...and I heard your voice from outside the window.
You were calling out, "Save me! Save me!"
I just went in that direction, and there you were.
Really?
That's amazing!
It's just what I thought! "Sumi, save me!"

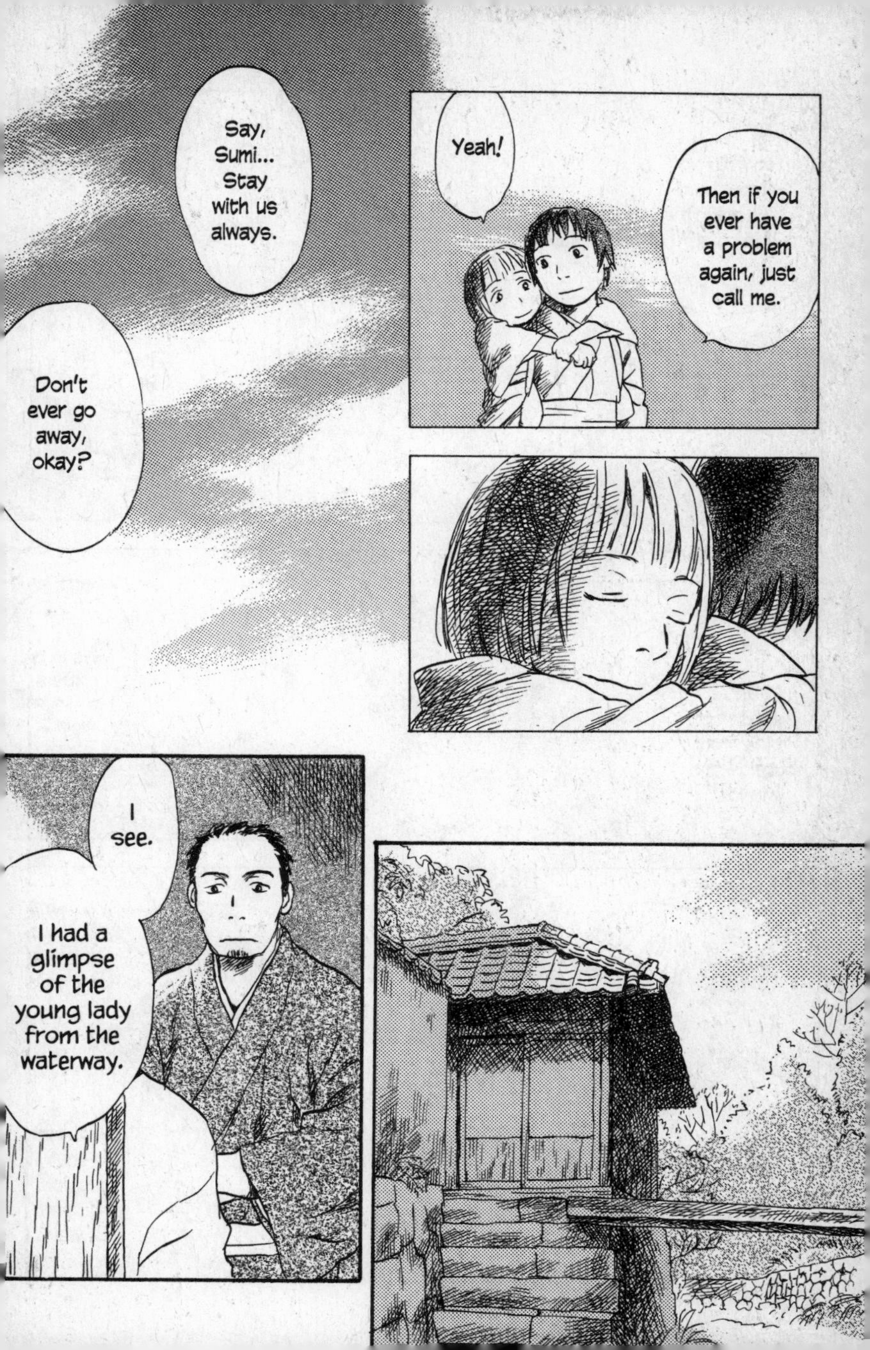
Then if you ever have a problem again, just call me.
Yeah!
Say, Sumi... Stay with us always.
Don't ever go away, okay?
I see.
I had a glimpse of the young lady from the waterway.

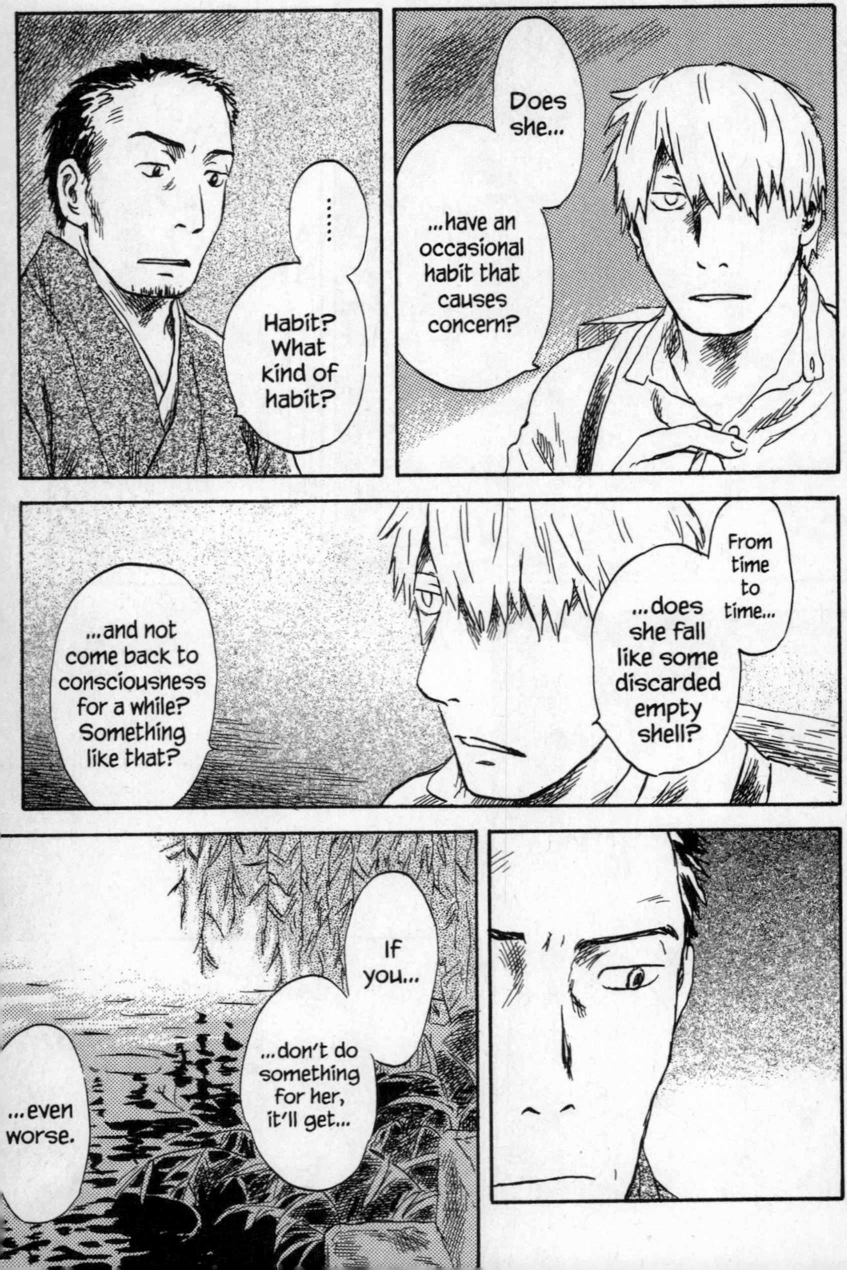
Does she...
...have an occasional habit that causes concern?
......
Habit? What kind of habit?
From time to time...
...does she fall like some discarded empty shell?
...and not come back to consciousness for a while? Something like that?
If you...
...don't do something for her, it'll get...
...even worse.

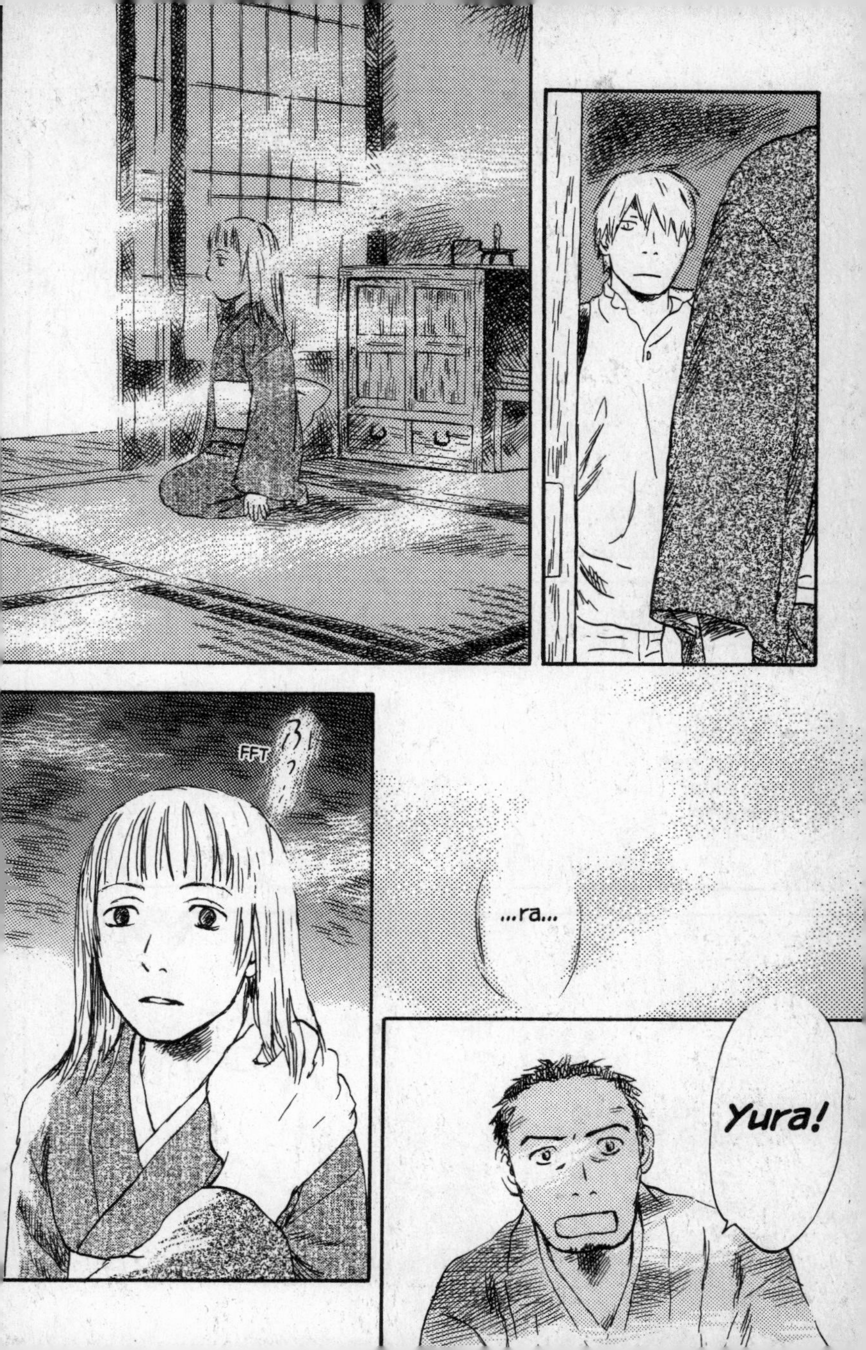
...ra...
Yura!
FFT

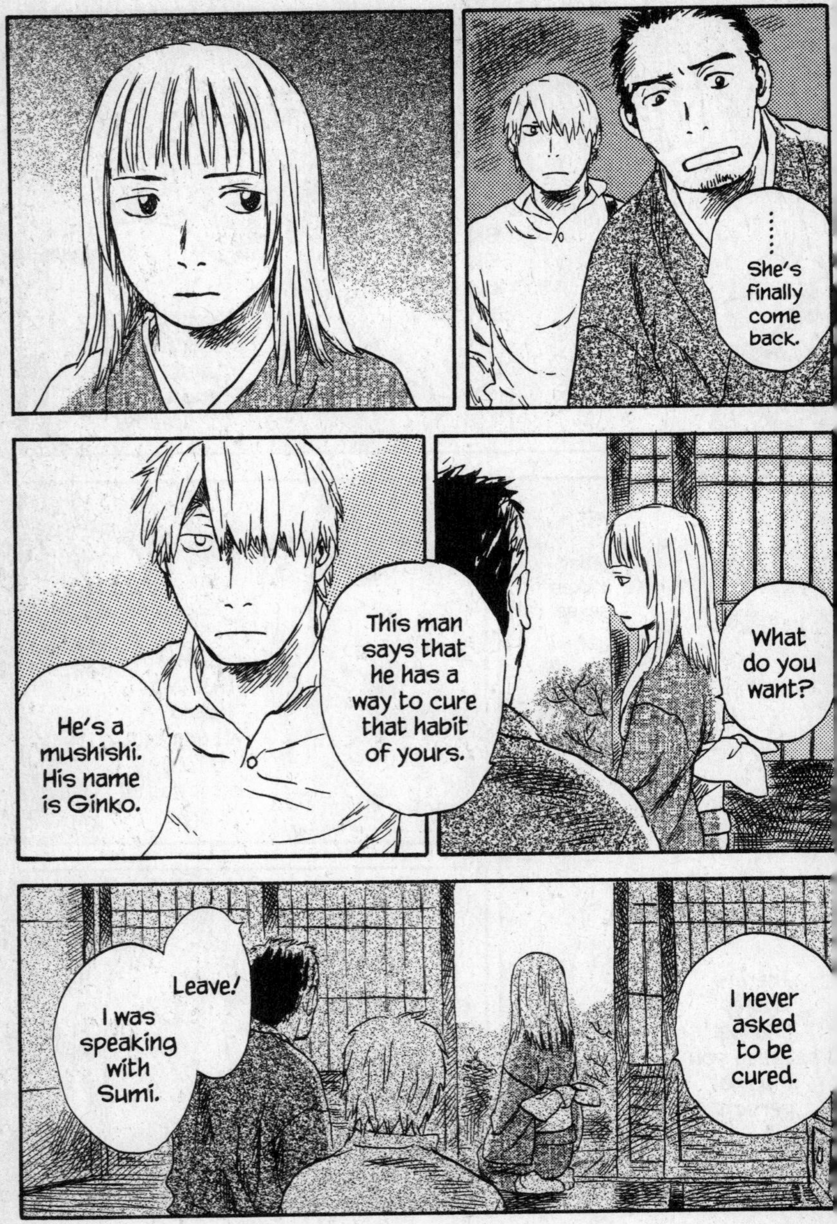
......
She's finally come back.
What do you want?
This man says that he has a way to cure that habit of yours.
He's a mushishi. His name is Ginko.
I never asked to be cured.
Leave!
I was speaking with Sumi.

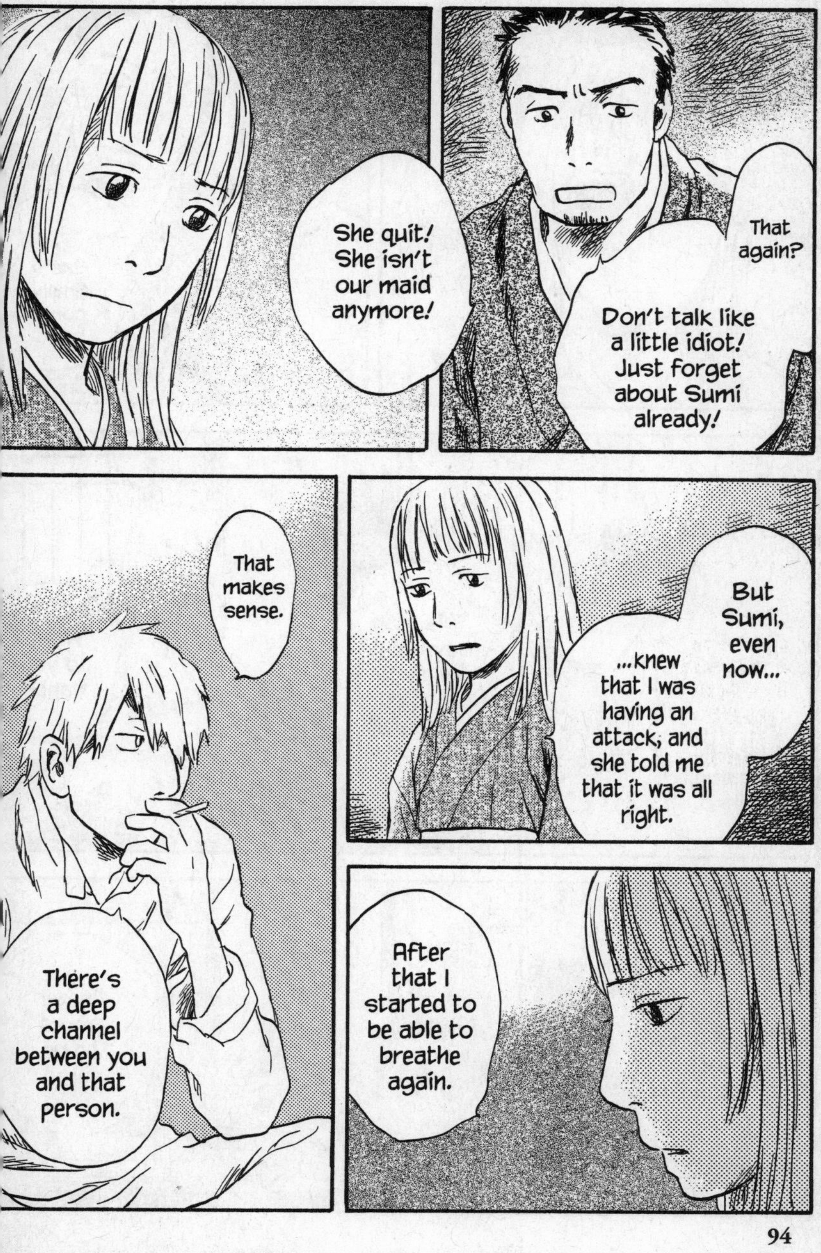
That again?
Don't talk like a little idiot! Just forget about Sumi already!
She quit! She isn't our maid anymore!
But Sumi, even now...
...knew that I was having an attack, and she told me that it was all right.
After that I started to be able to breathe again.
That makes sense.
There's a deep channel between you and that person.

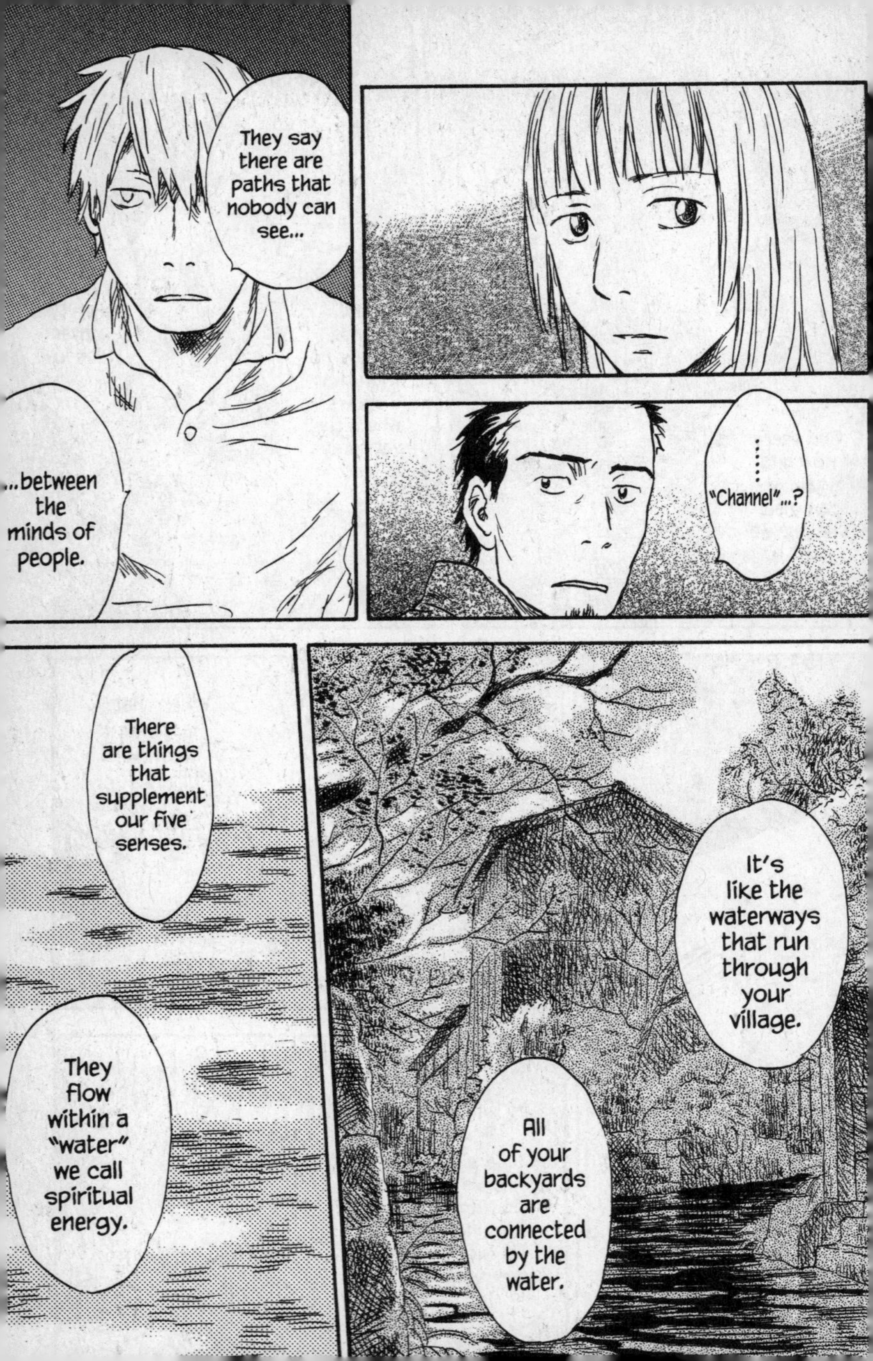
......
"Channel"...?
They say there are paths that nobody can see...
...between the minds of people.
It's like the waterways that run through your village.
All of your backyards are connected by the water.
There are things that supplement our five senses.
They flow within a "water" we call spiritual energy.

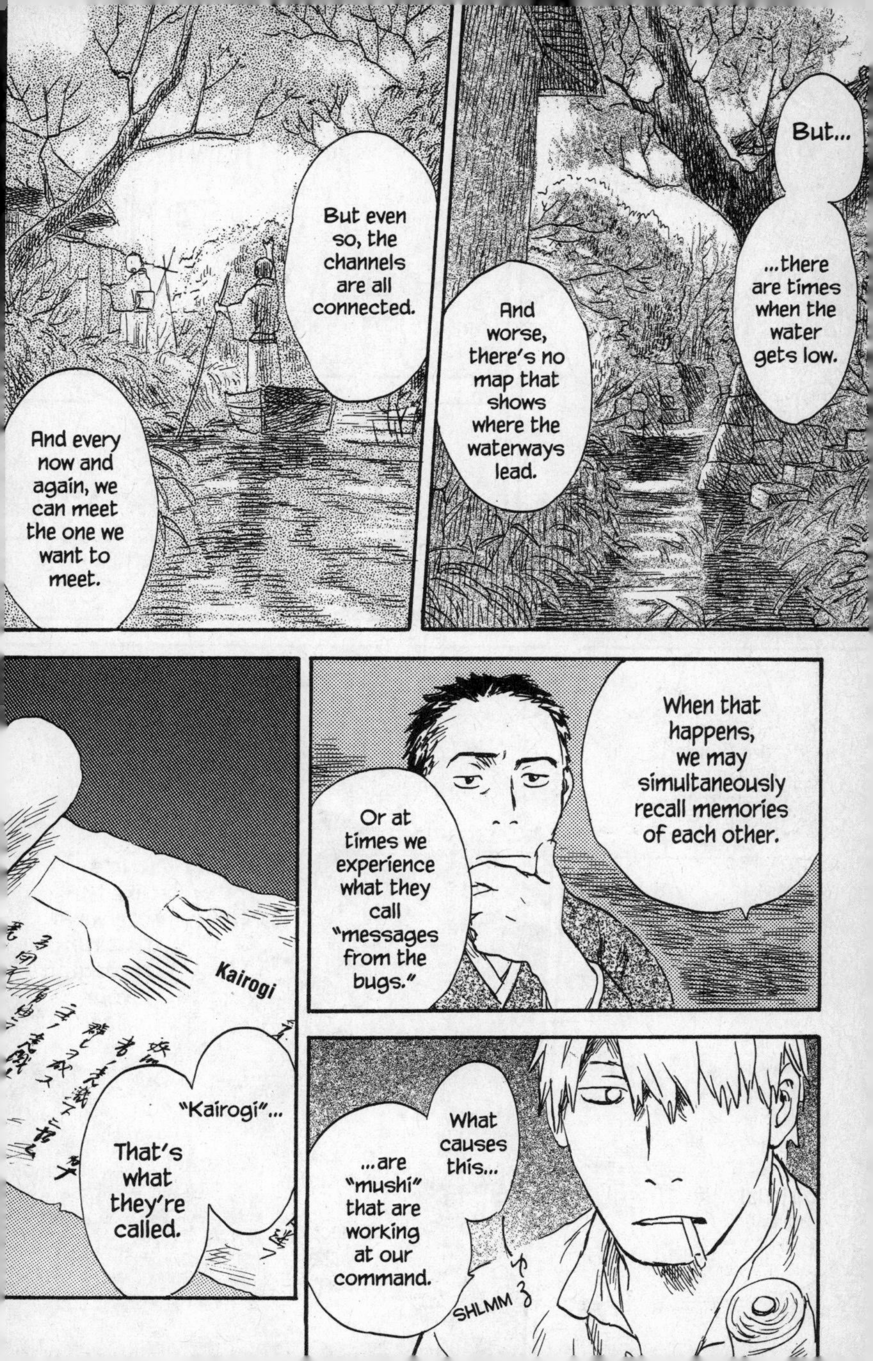
But...
...there are times when the water gets low.
And worse, there's no map that shows where the waterways lead.
But even so, the channels are all connected.
And every now and again, we can meet the one we want to meet.
When that happens, we may simultaneously recall memories of each other.
Or at times we experience what they call "messages from the bugs."
What causes this...
...are "mushi" that are working at our command.
SHLMM
Kairogi
"Kairogi"...
That's what they're called.

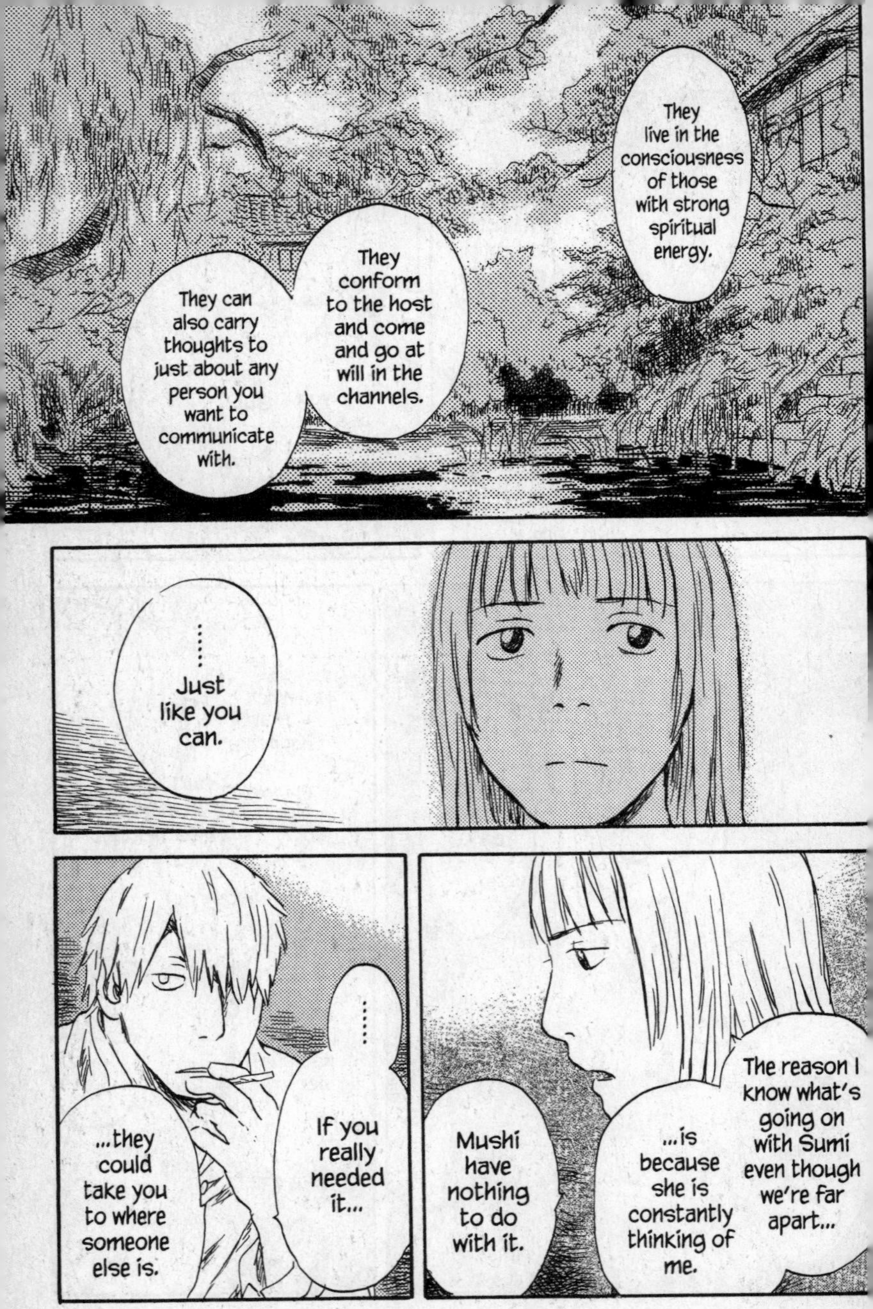
They live in the consciousness of those with strong spiritual energy.
They conform to the host and come and go at will in the channels.
They can also carry thoughts to just about any person you want to communicate with.
...... Just like you can.
The reason I know what's going on with Sumi even though we're far apart...
...is because she is constantly thinking of me.
Mushi have nothing to do with it.
......
If you really needed it...
...they could take you to where someone else is.

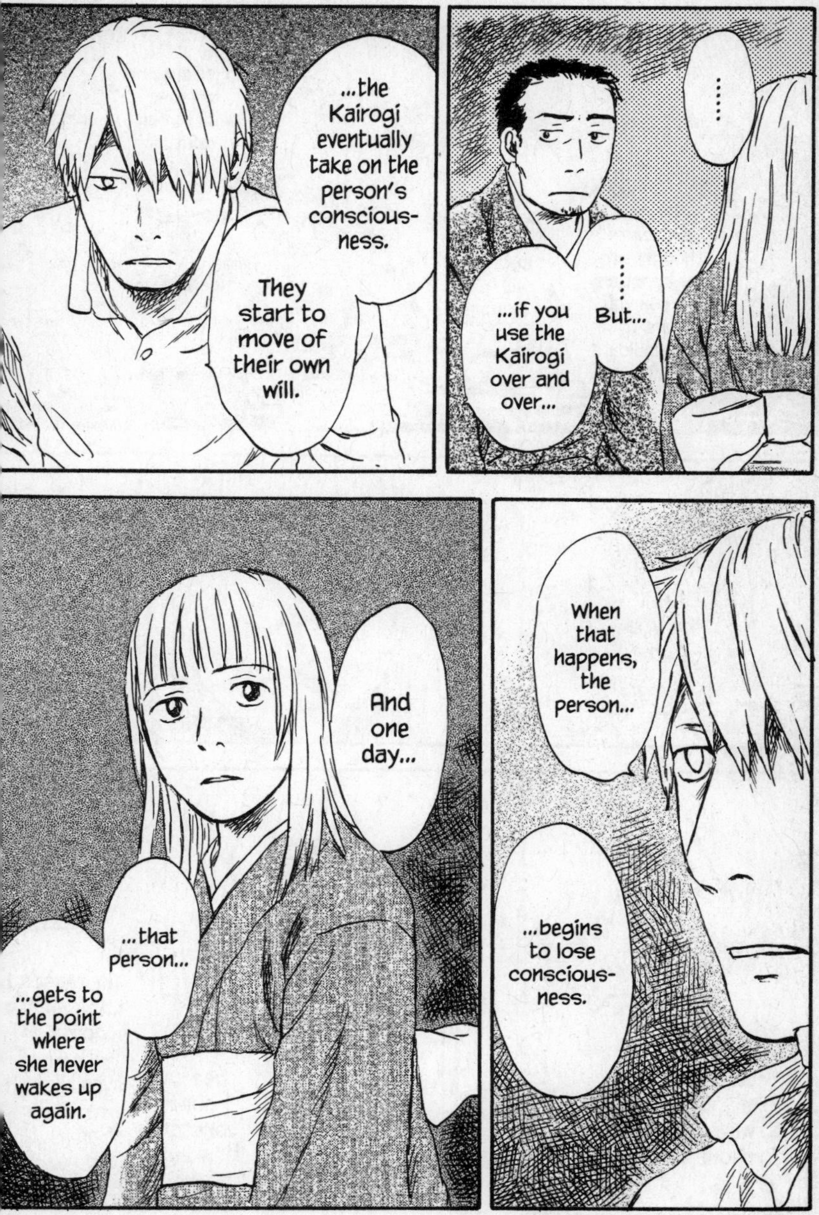
......
...... But...
...if you use the Kairogi over and over...
...the Kairogi eventually take on the person's conscious-ness.
They start to move of their own will.
When that happens, the person...
...begins to lose conscious-ness.
And one day...
...that person...
...gets to the point where she never wakes up again.

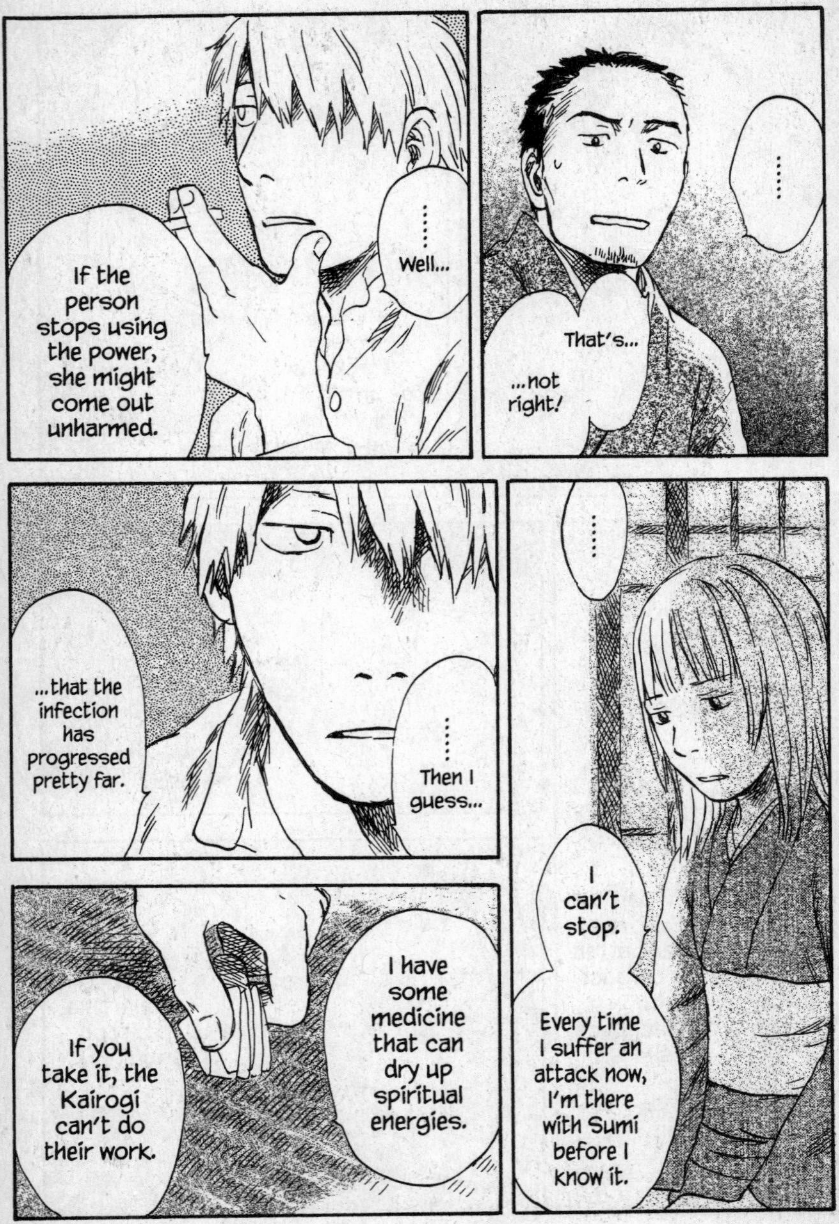
……
That's...
...not right!
……
Well...
If the person stops using the power, she might come out unharmed.
……
I can't stop.
Every time I suffer an attack now, I'm there with Sumi before I know it.
……
Then I guess...
...that the infection has progressed pretty far.
I have some medicine that can dry up spiritual energies.
If you take it, the Kairogi can't do their work.

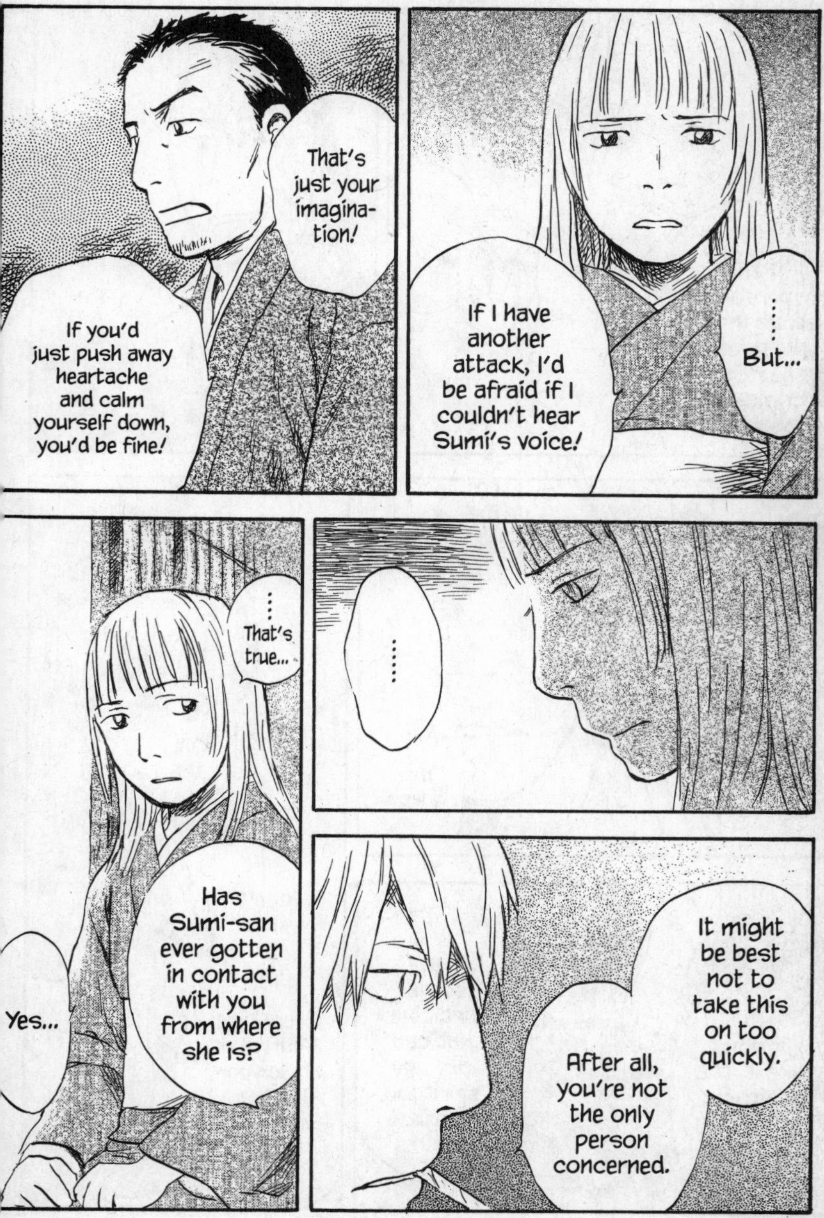

...... But...
If I have another attack, I'd be afraid if I couldn't hear Sumi's voice!
That's just your imagination!
If you'd just push away heartache and calm yourself down, you'd be fine!
......
It might be best not to take this on too quickly.
After all, you're not the only person concerned.
...... That's true...
Has Sumi-san ever gotten in contact with you from where she is?
Yes...

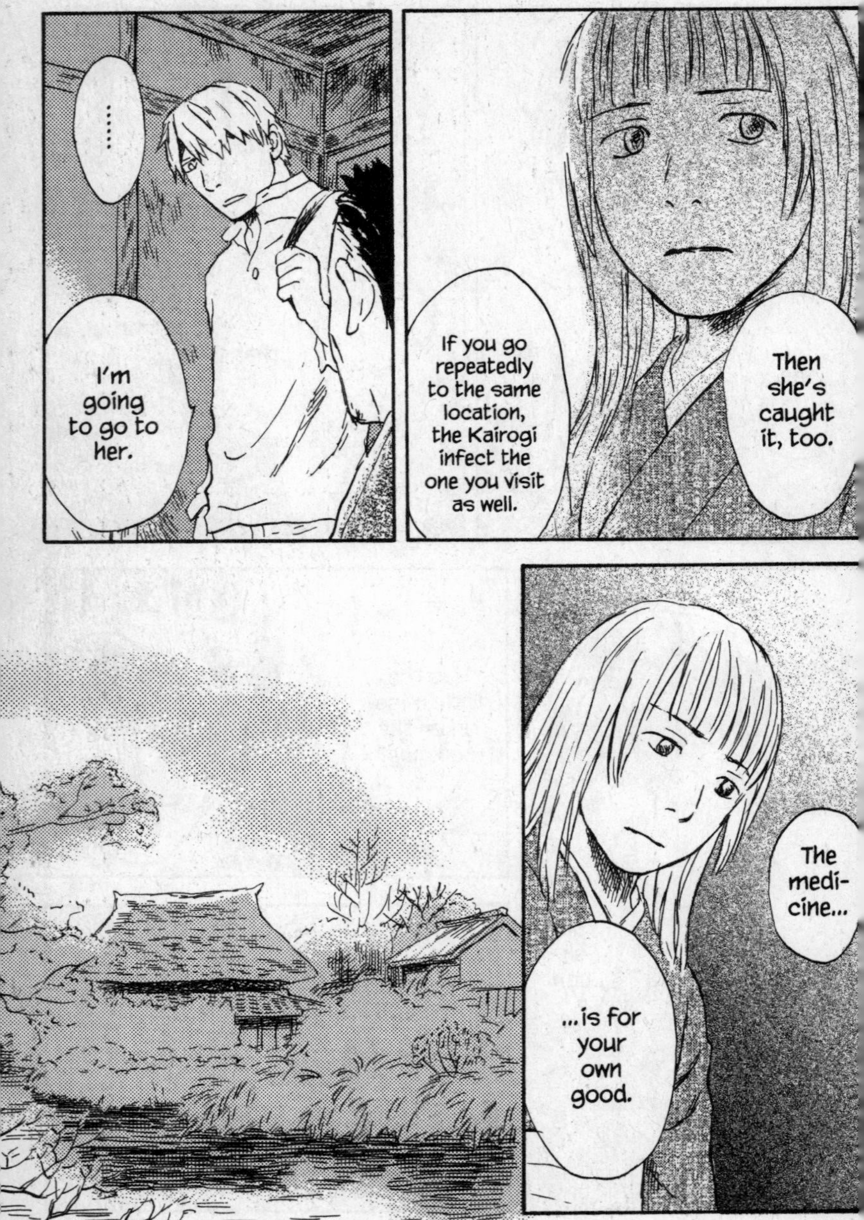
Then she's caught it, too.
If you go repeatedly to the same location, the Kairogi infect the one you visit as well.
……
I'm going to go to her.
The medicine...
...is for your own good.

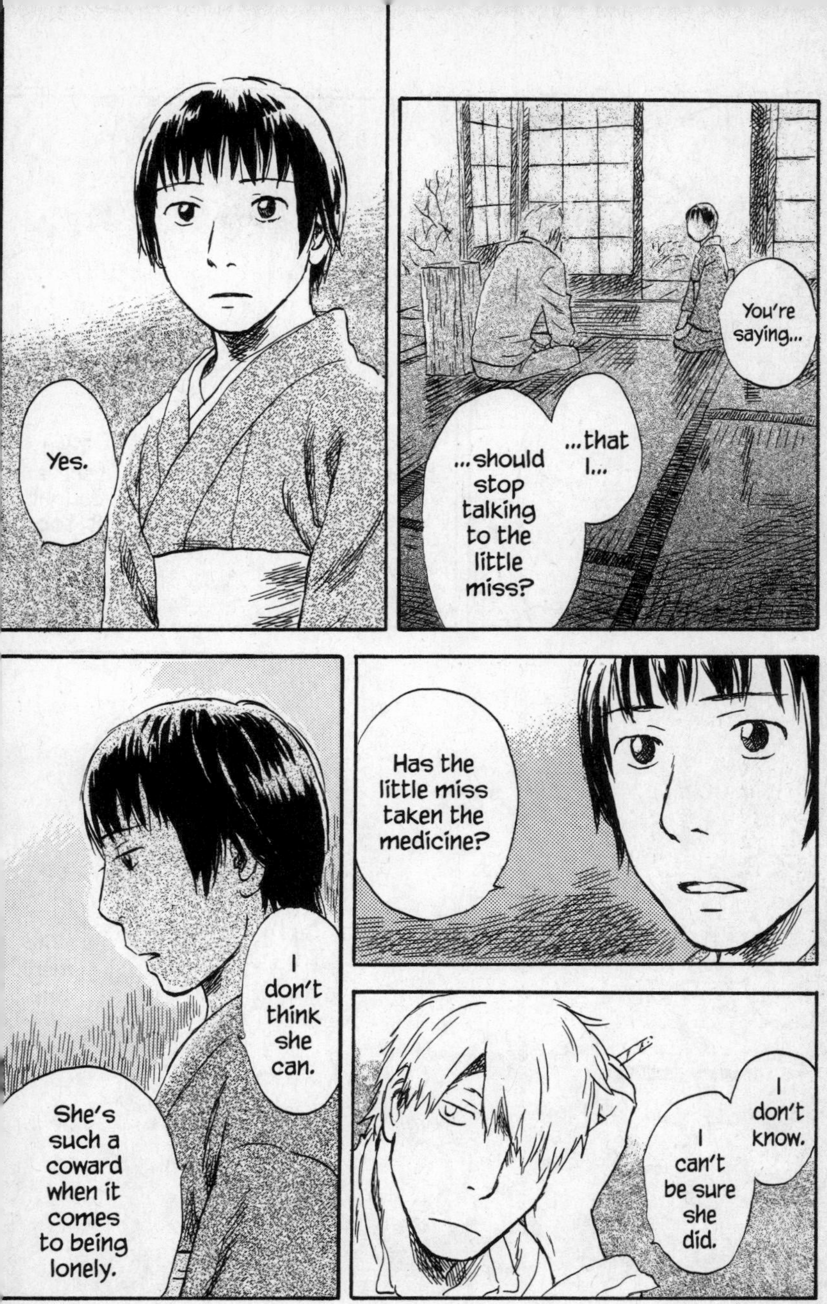
You're saying...
...that I...
...should stop talking to the little miss?
Yes.
Has the little miss taken the medicine?
I don't know.
I can't be sure she did.
I don't think she can.
She's such a coward when it comes to being lonely.

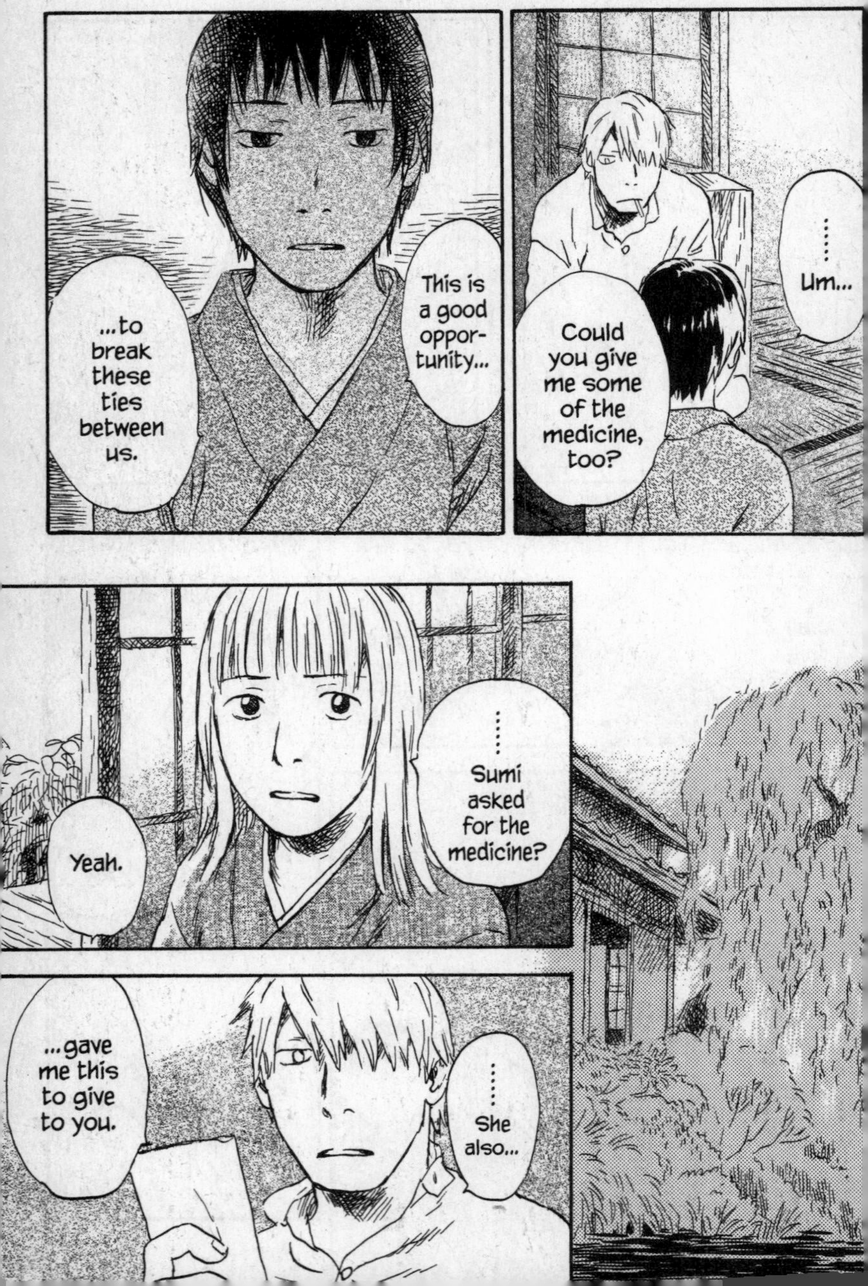
......Um...
Could you give me some of the medicine, too?
This is a good opportunity...
...to break these ties between us.
......Sumi asked for the medicine?
Yeah.
......She also...
...gave me this to give to you.

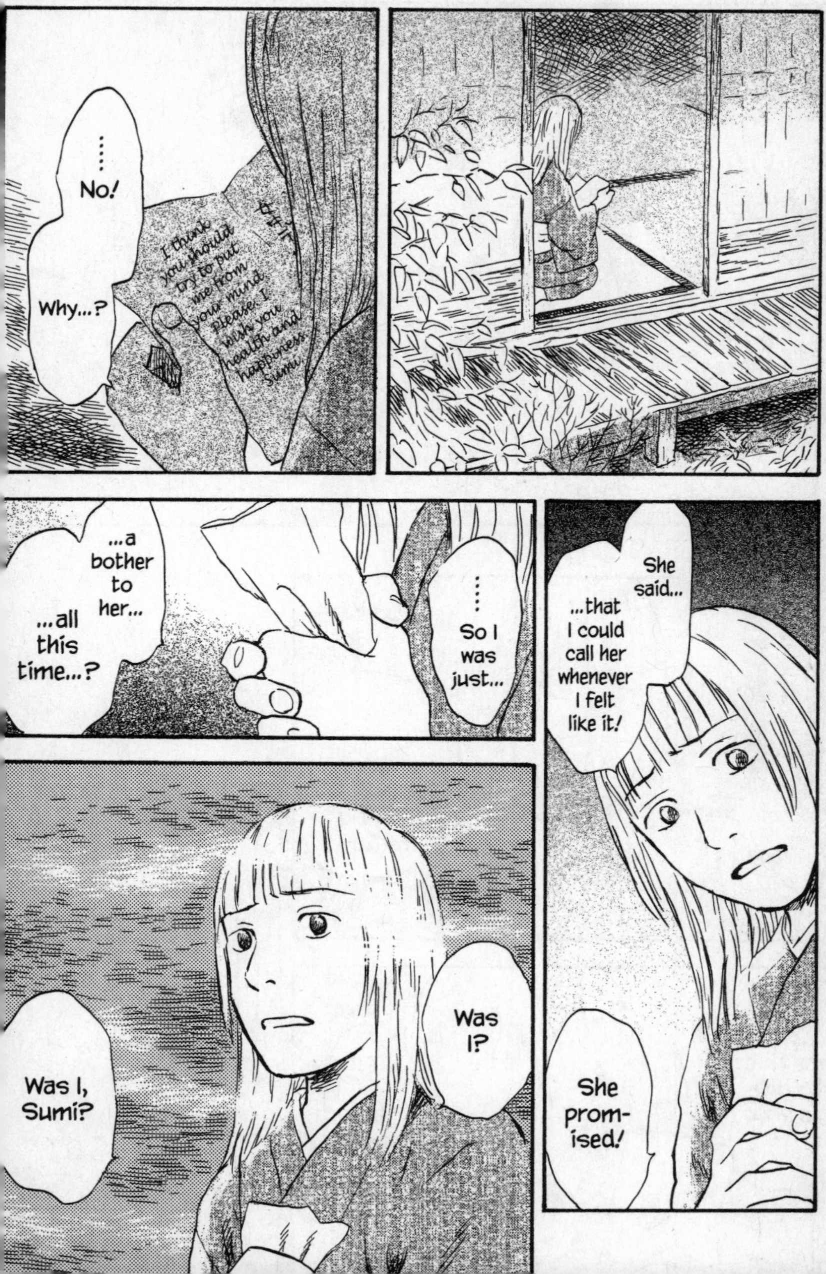
……
No!
Why...?
I think you should try to put me from your mind. Please. I wish you health and happiness. Sumi
She said...
...that I could call her whenever I felt like it!
She promised!
……
So I was just...
...a bother to her...
...all this time...?
Was I?
Was I, Sumi?

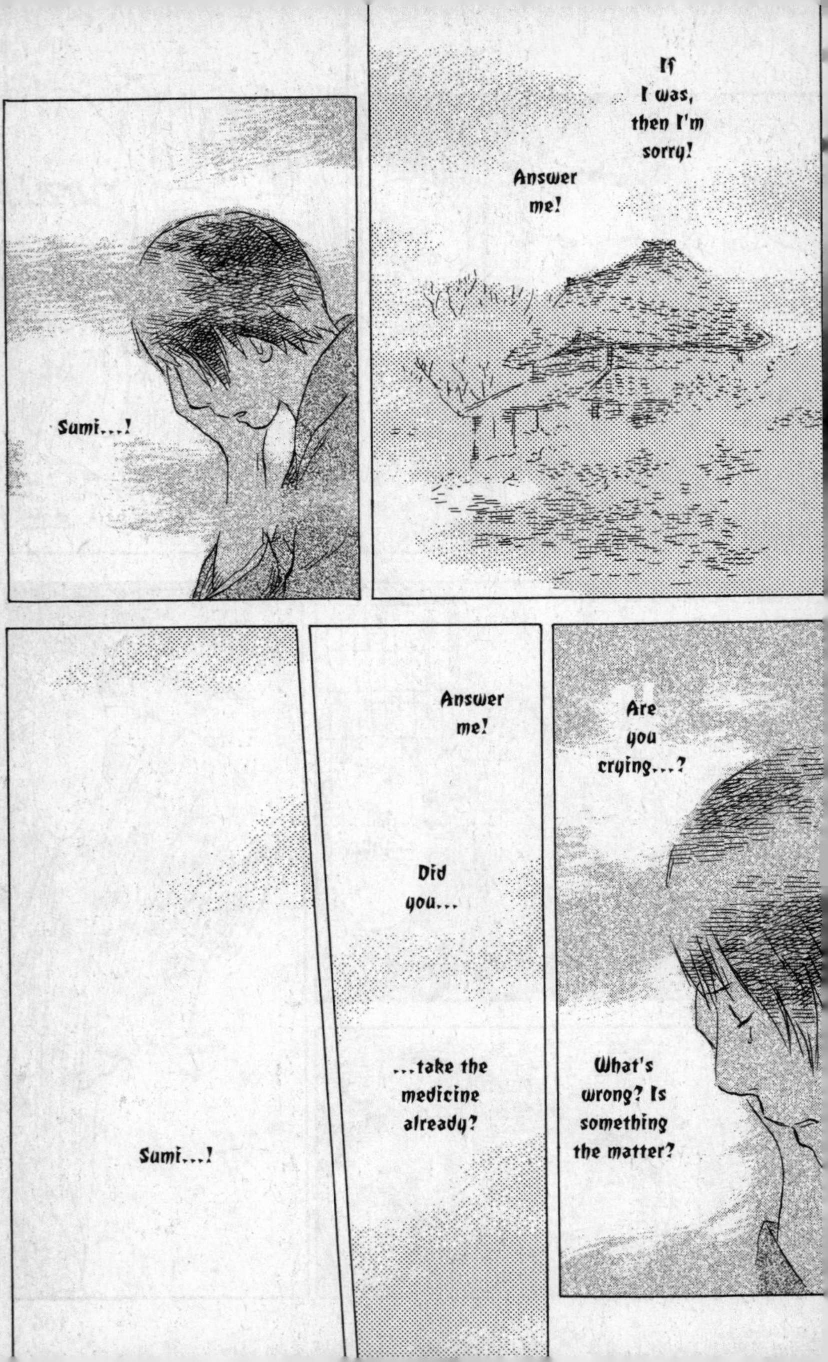
If I was, then I'm sorry!
Answer me!
Sumi...!
Are you crying...?
What's wrong? Is something the matter?
Answer me!
Did you...
...take the medicine already?
Sumi...!

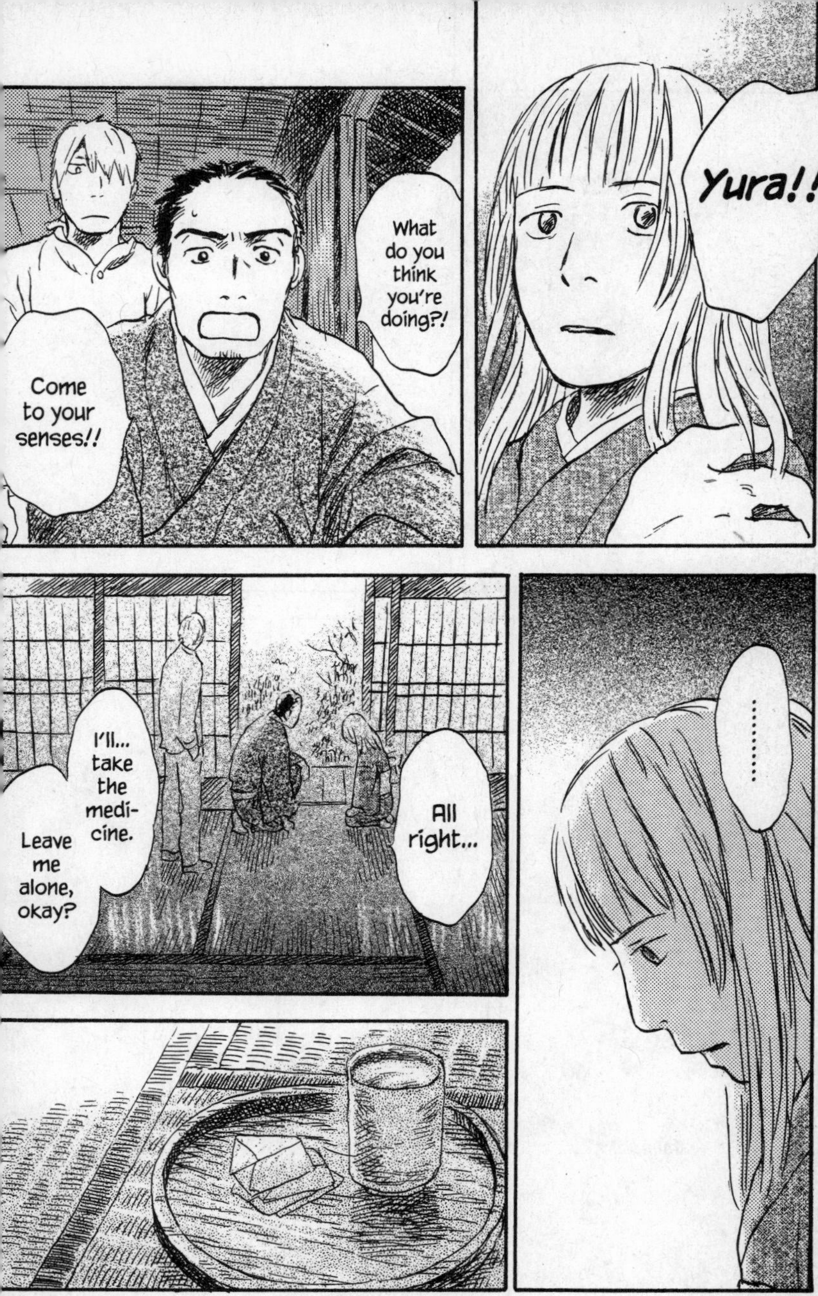
Yura!!
What do you think you're doing?!
Come to your senses!!
......
All right...
I'll... take the medicine.
Leave me alone, okay?

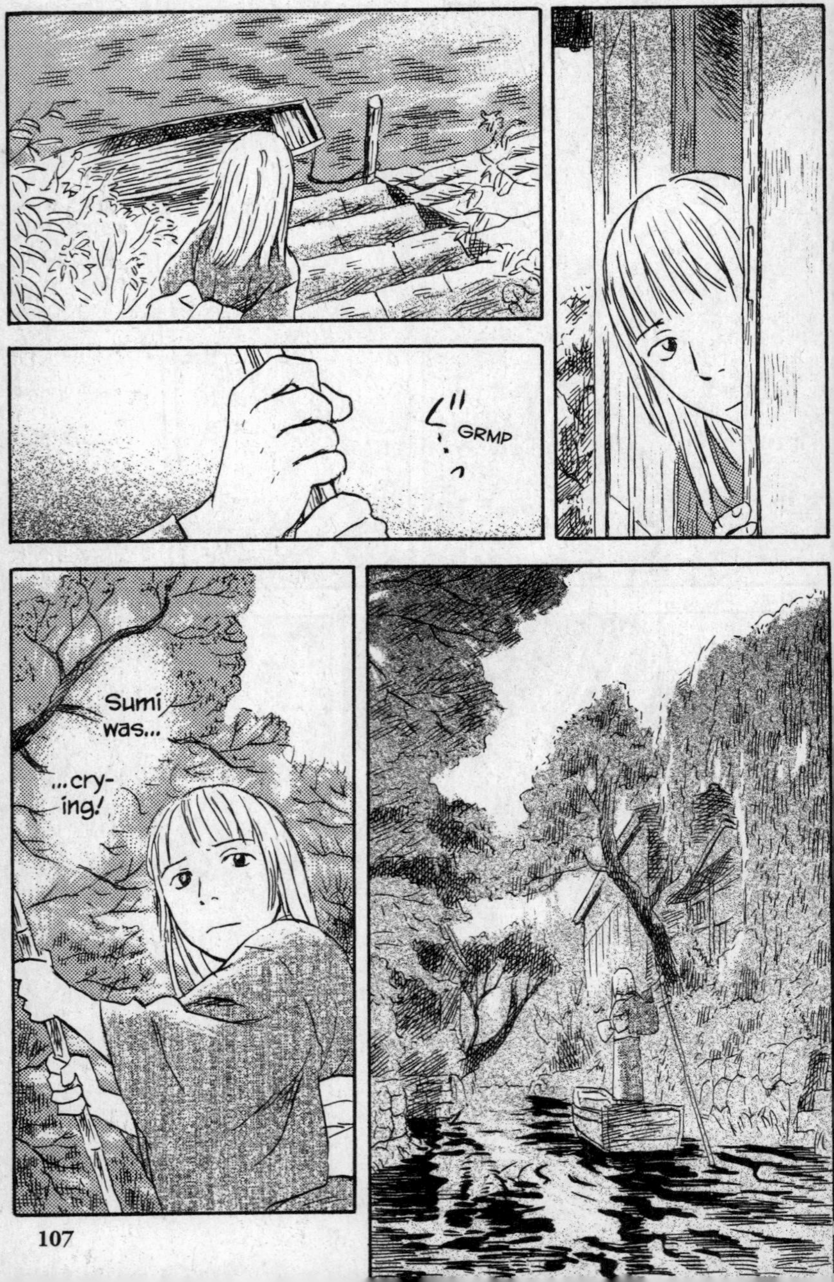
GRMP
Sumi was...
...cry-
ing!

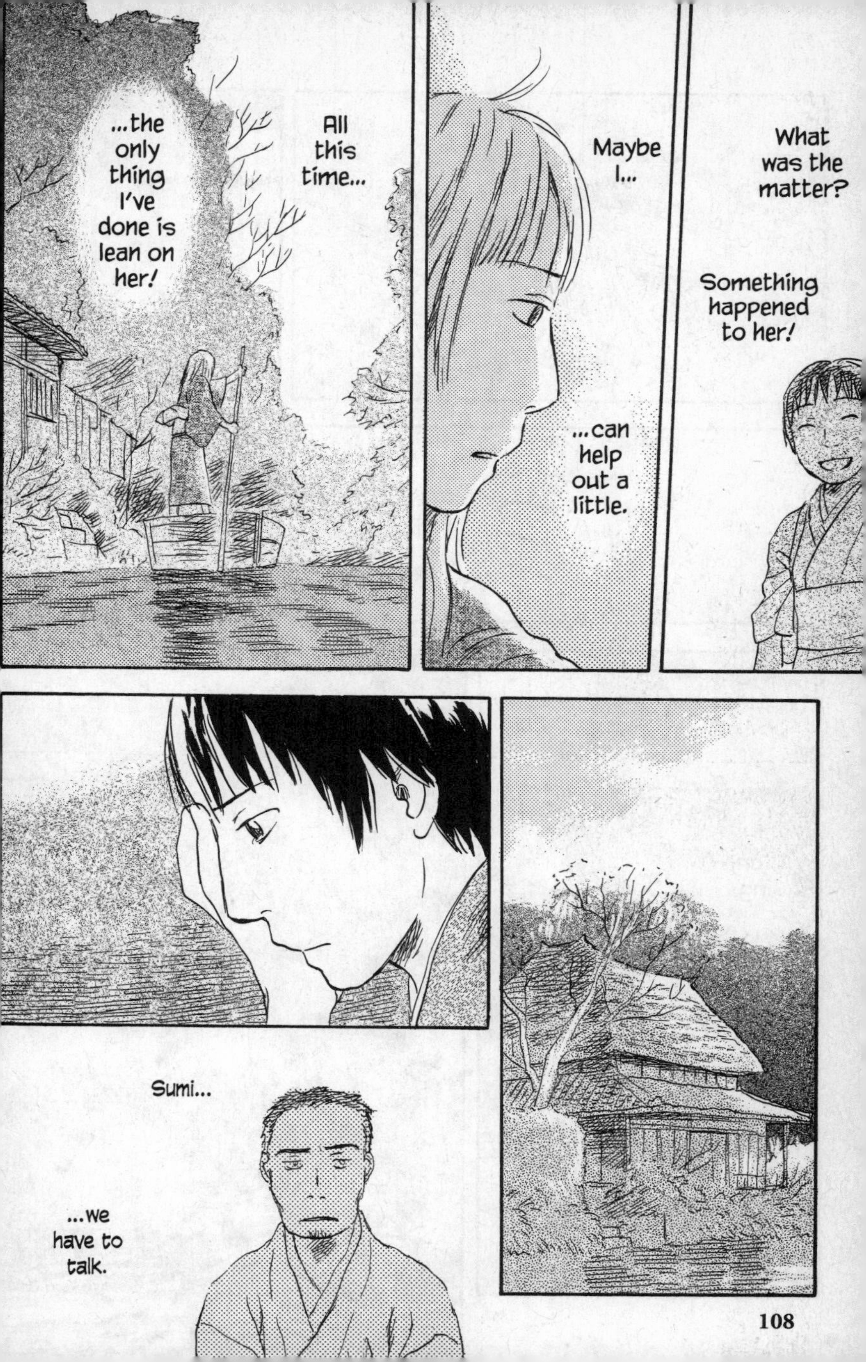
What was the matter?
Something happened to her!
Maybe I...
...can help out a little.
All this time...
...the only thing I've done is lean on her!
Sumi...
...we have to talk.

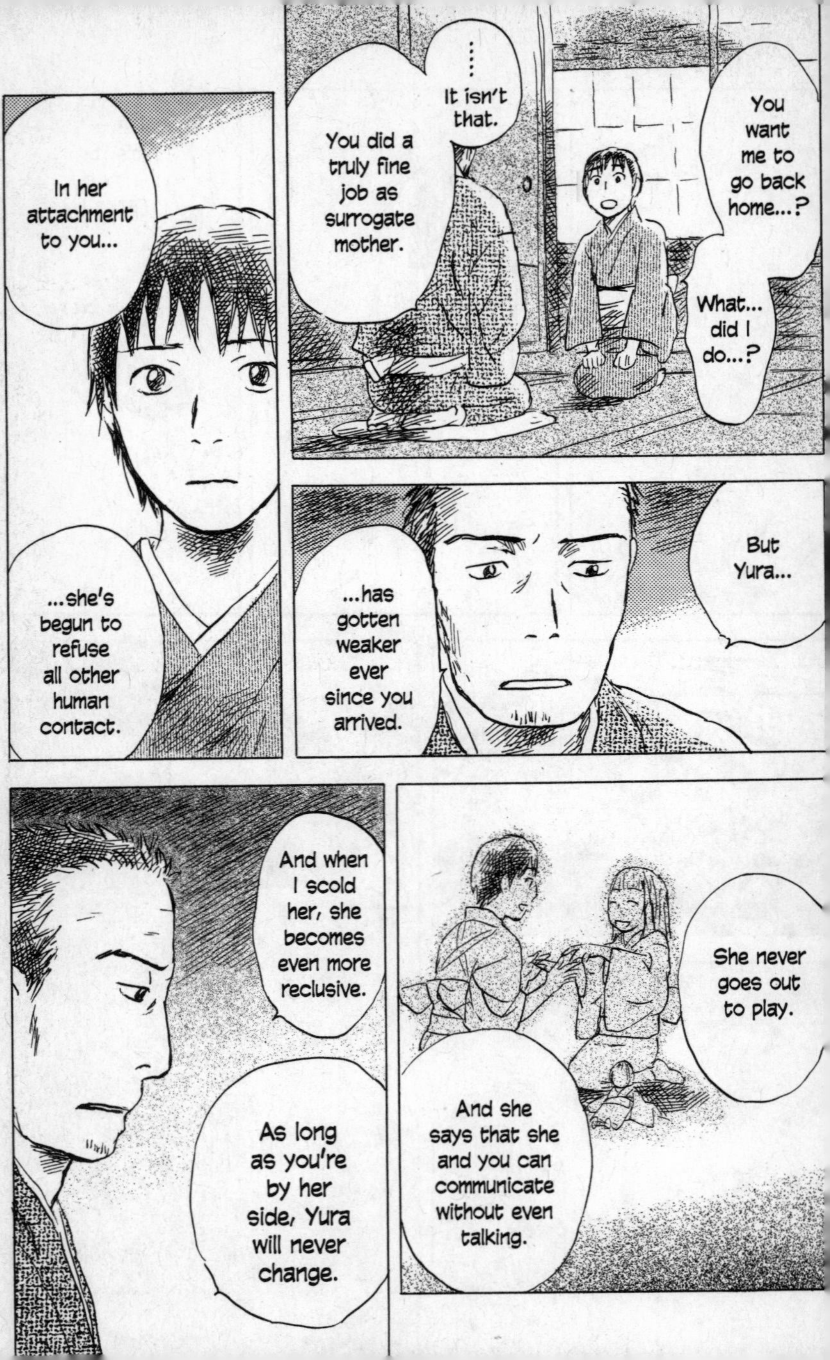
You want me to go back home...?
What... did I do...?
......
It isn't that.
You did a truly fine job as surrogate mother.
But Yura...
...has gotten weaker ever since you arrived.
In her attachment to you...
...she's begun to refuse all other human contact.
She never goes out to play.
And she says that she and you can communicate without even talking.
And when I scold her, she becomes even more reclusive.
As long as you're by her side, Yura will never change.

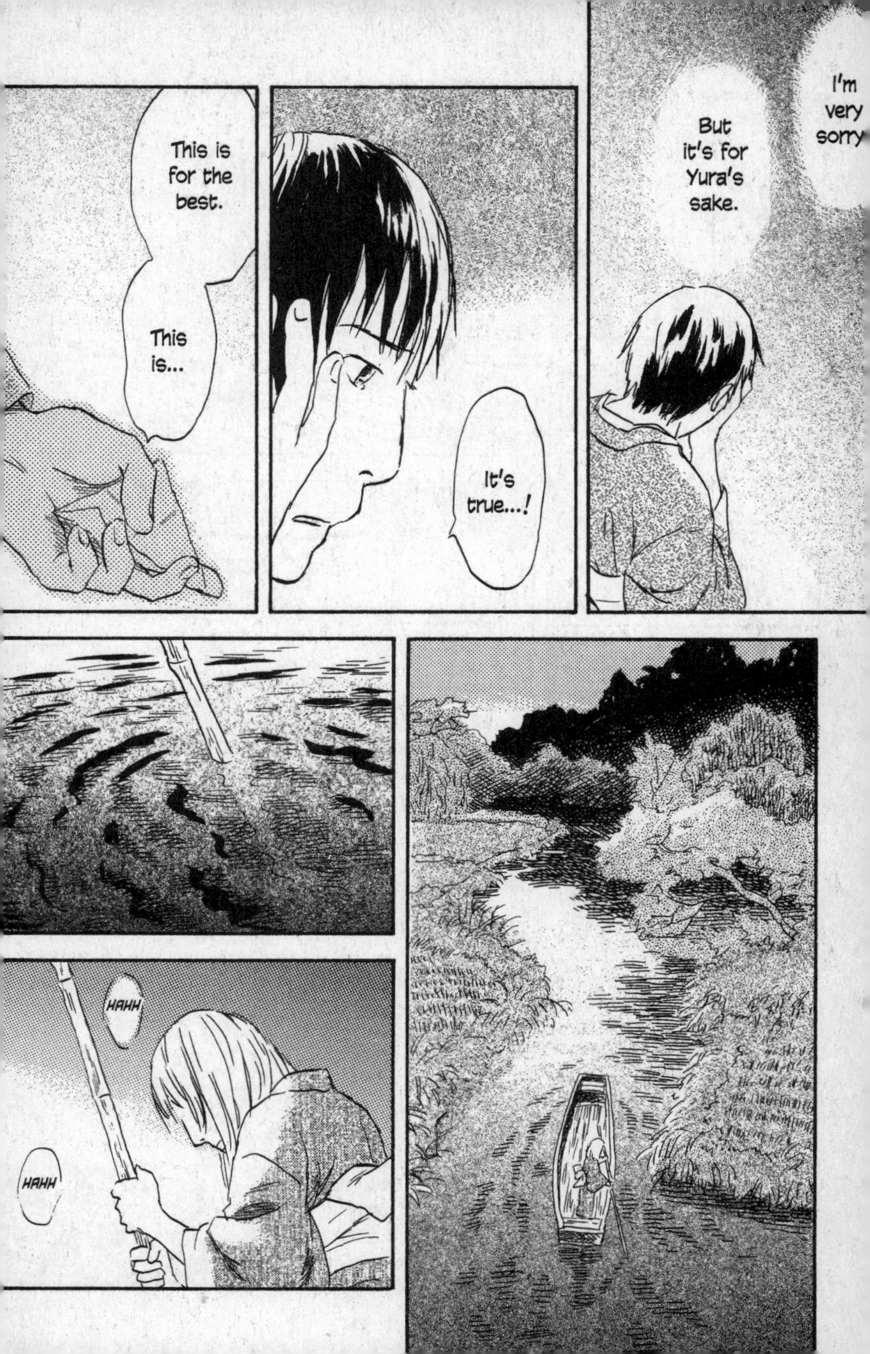
I'm very sorry
But it's for Yura's sake.
It's true...!
This is for the best.
This is...
HAHH
HAHH

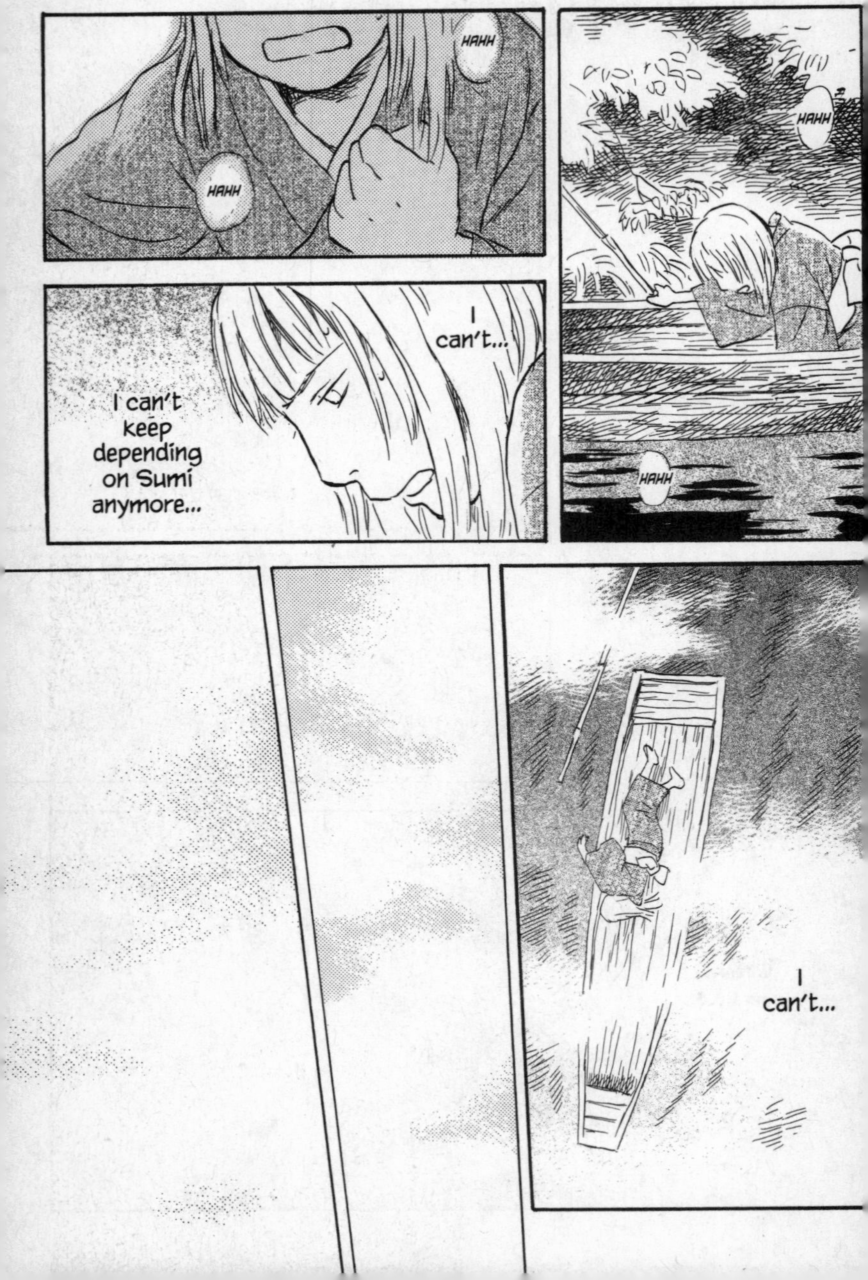
HAHH
HAHH
HAHH
HAHH
I can't...
I can't keep depending on Sumi anymore...
I can't...

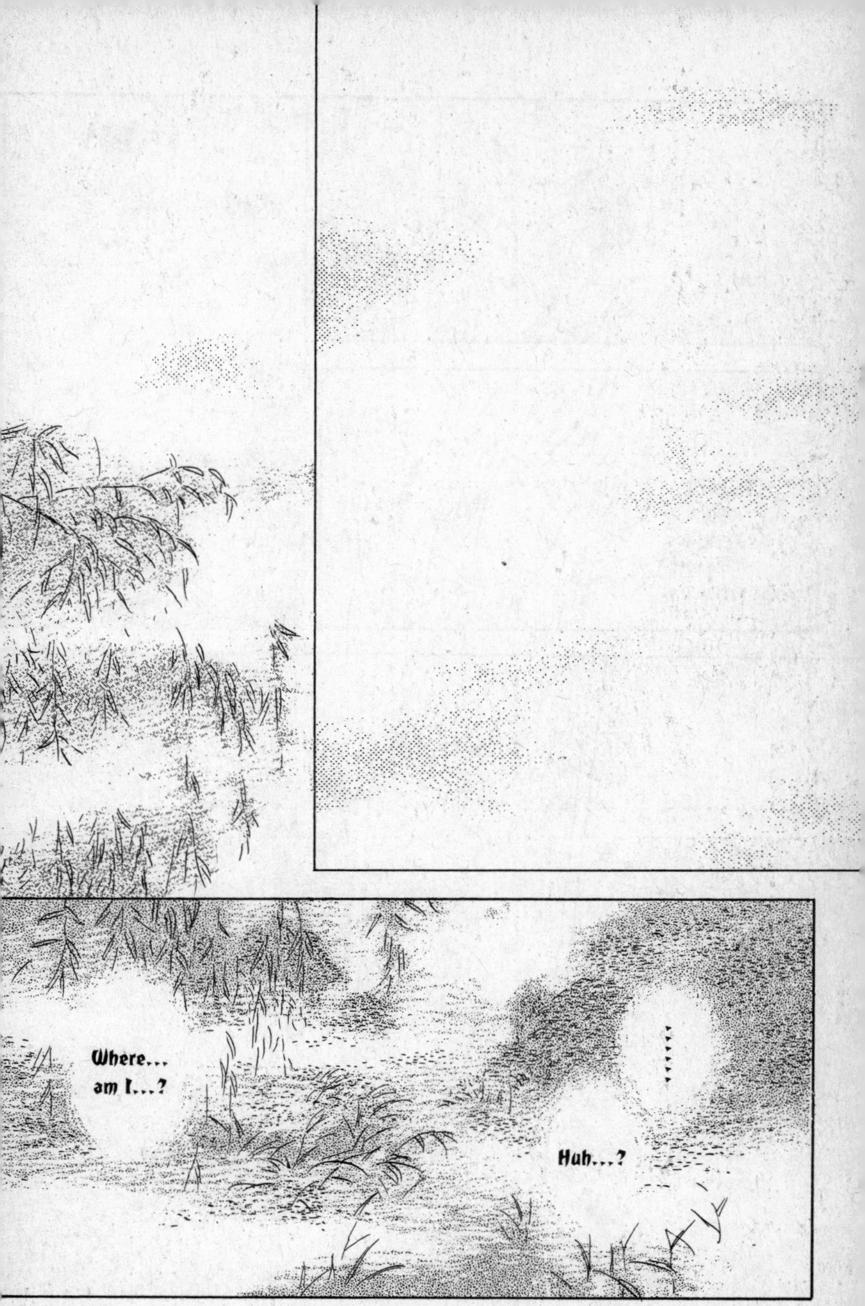
......
Huh...?
Where... am I...?

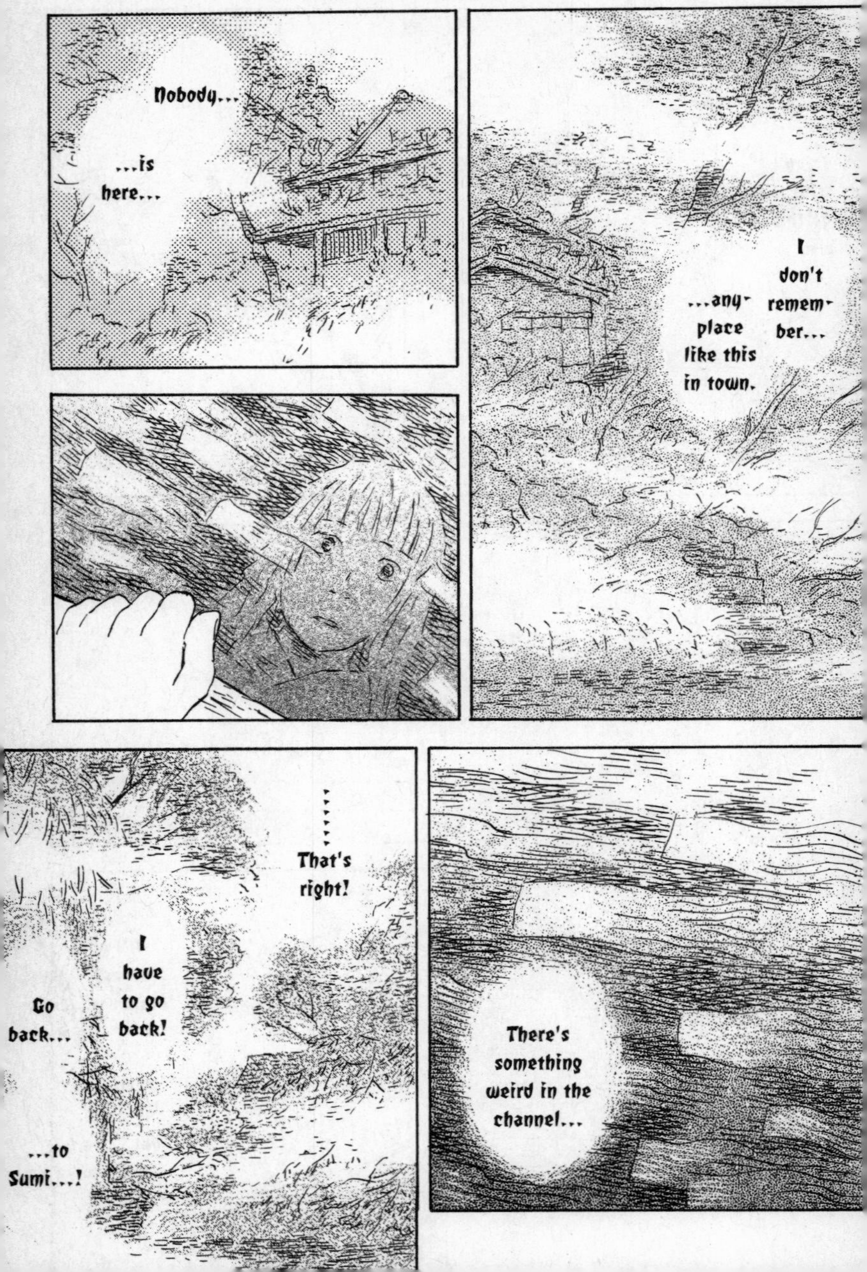
I don't remember...
...anyplace like this in town.
Nobody...
...is here...
There's something weird in the channel...
......That's right!
I have to go back!
Go back...
...to Sumi...!

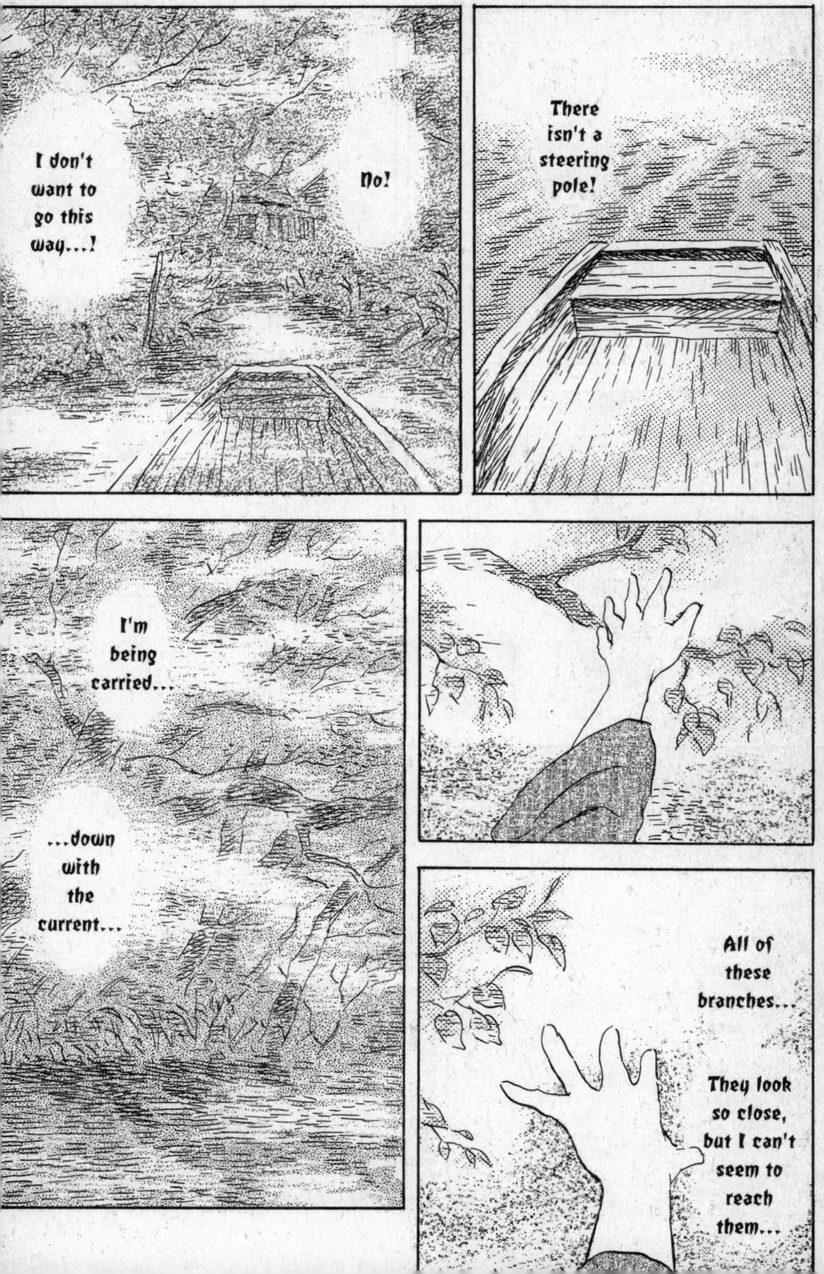
There isn't a steering pole!
No!
I don't want to go this way...!
All of these branches...
They look so close, but I can't seem to reach them...
I'm being carried...
...down with the current...

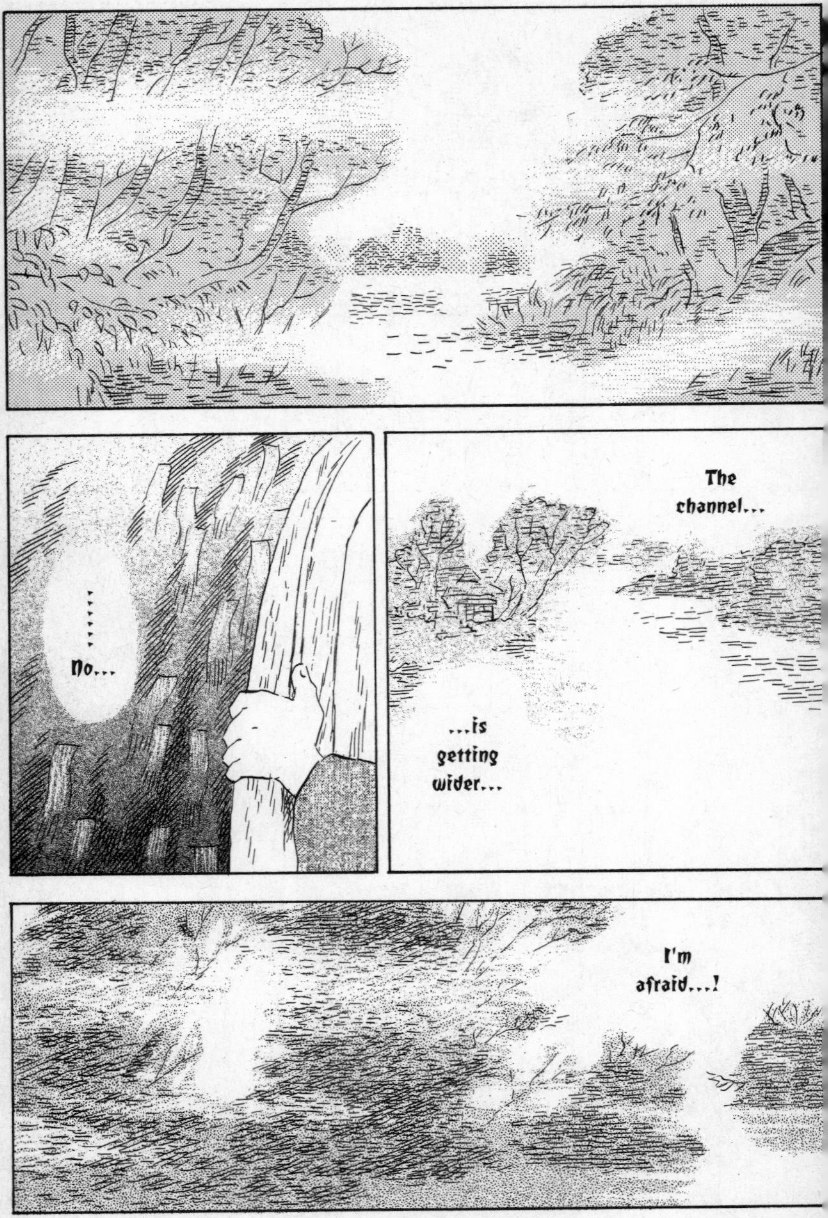
The channel...
...is getting wider...
......
No...
I'm afraid...!

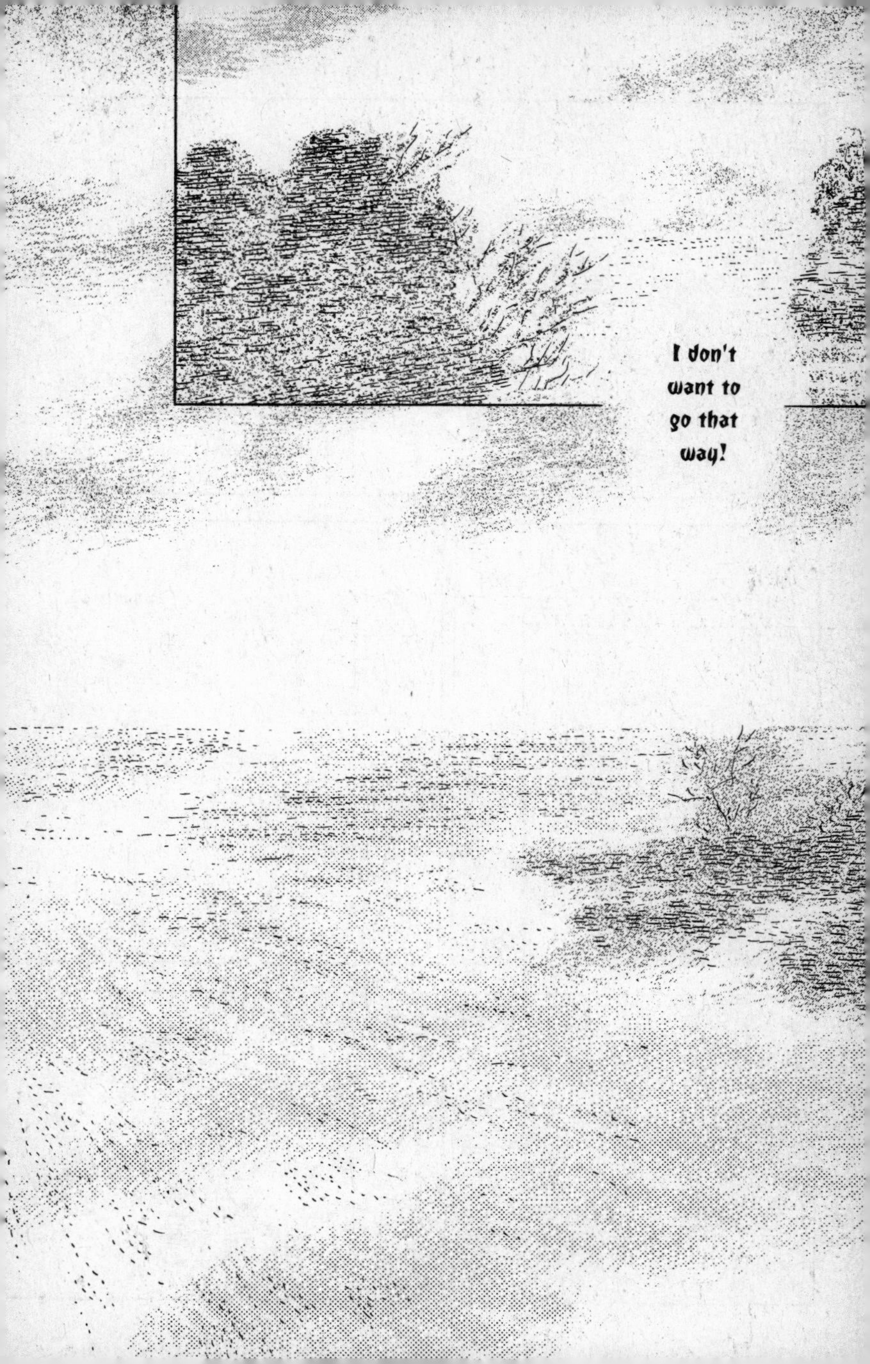
I don't want to go that way!

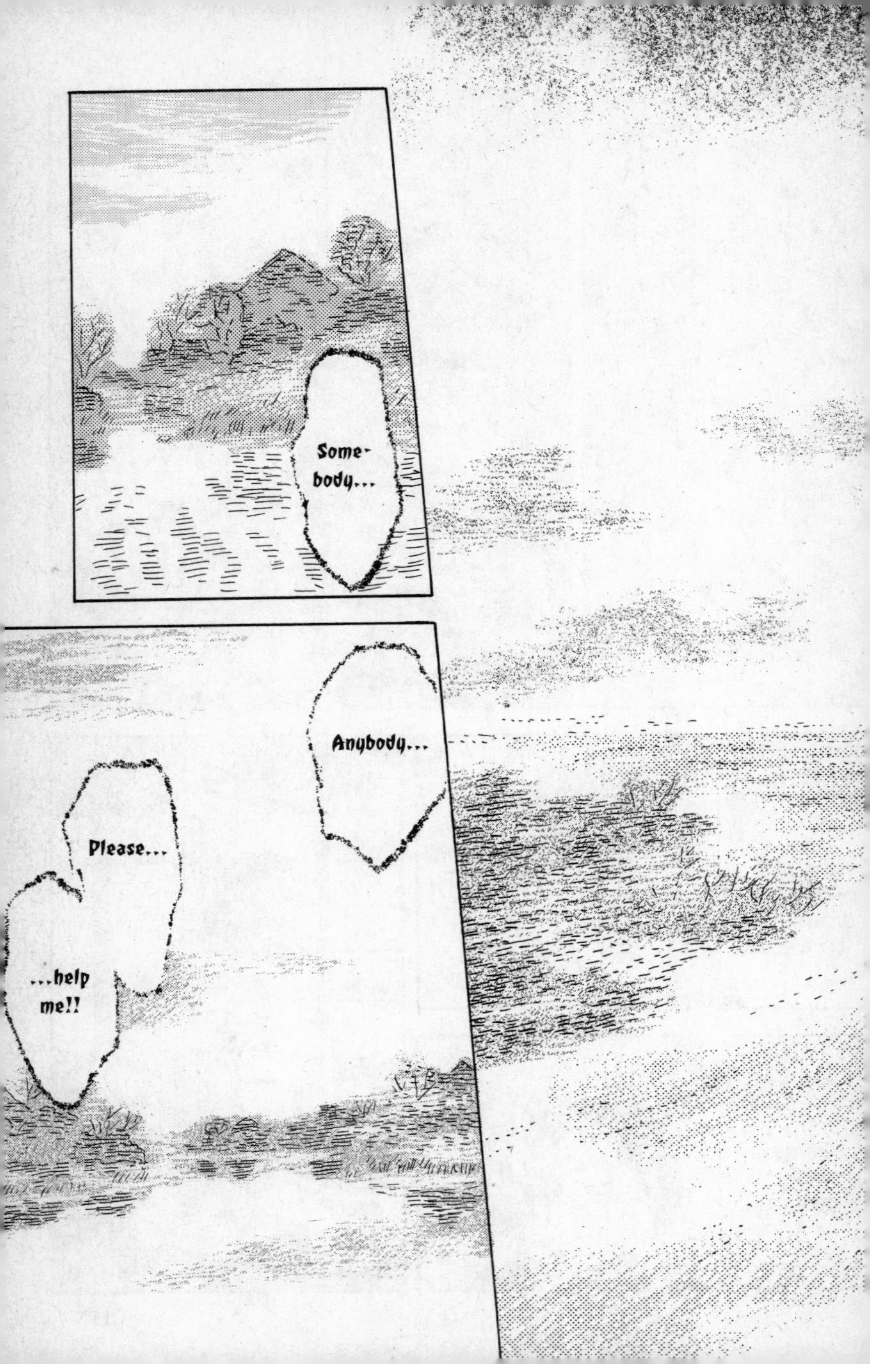
Some-
body...
Anybody...
Please...
...help
me!!

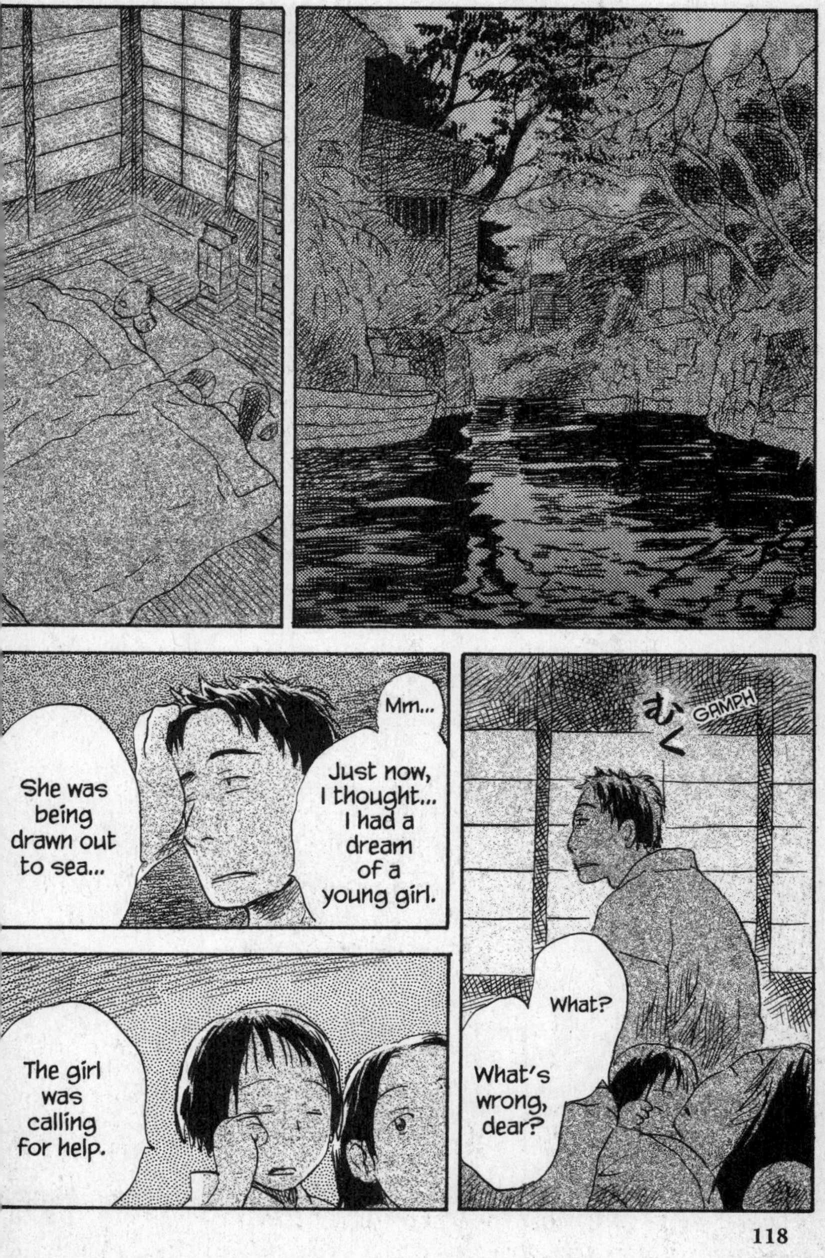
むく
GAMPH
What?
What's wrong, dear?
Mm...
Just now, I thought... I had a dream of a young girl.
She was being drawn out to sea...
The girl was calling for help.

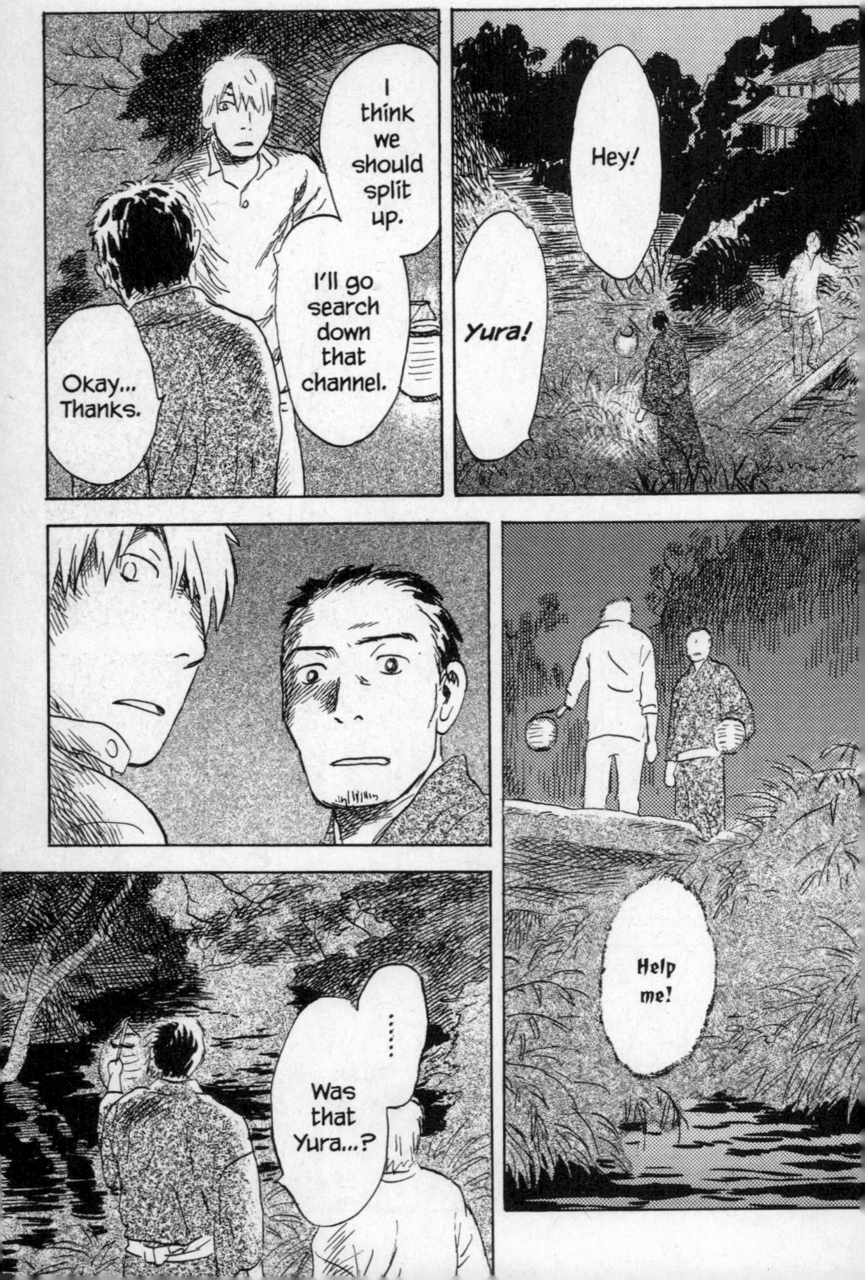
Hey!
Yura!
I think we should split up.
I'll go search down that channel.
Okay... Thanks.
Help me!
......
Was that Yura...?

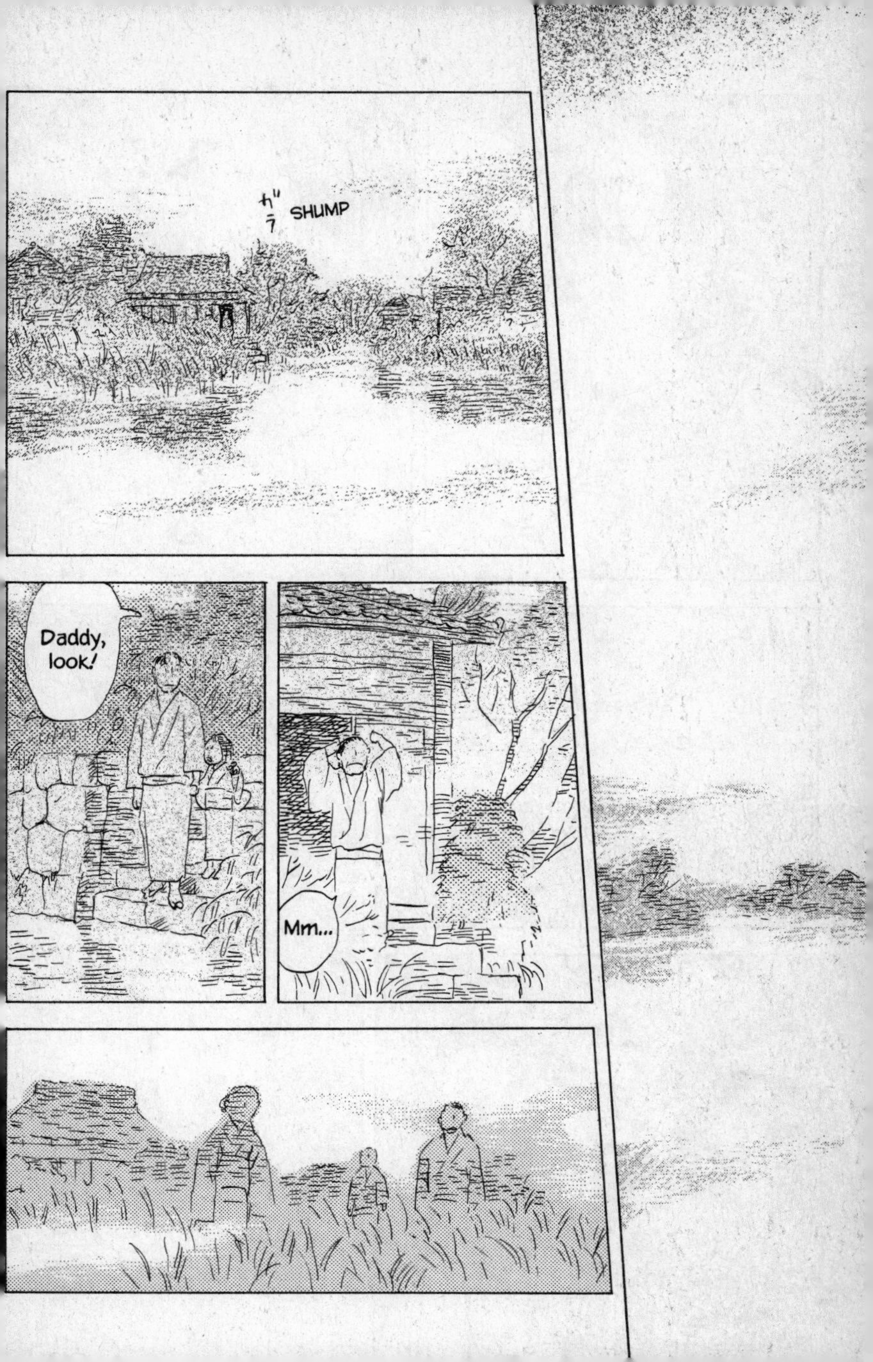
ガラ
SHUMP
Mm...
Daddy, look!

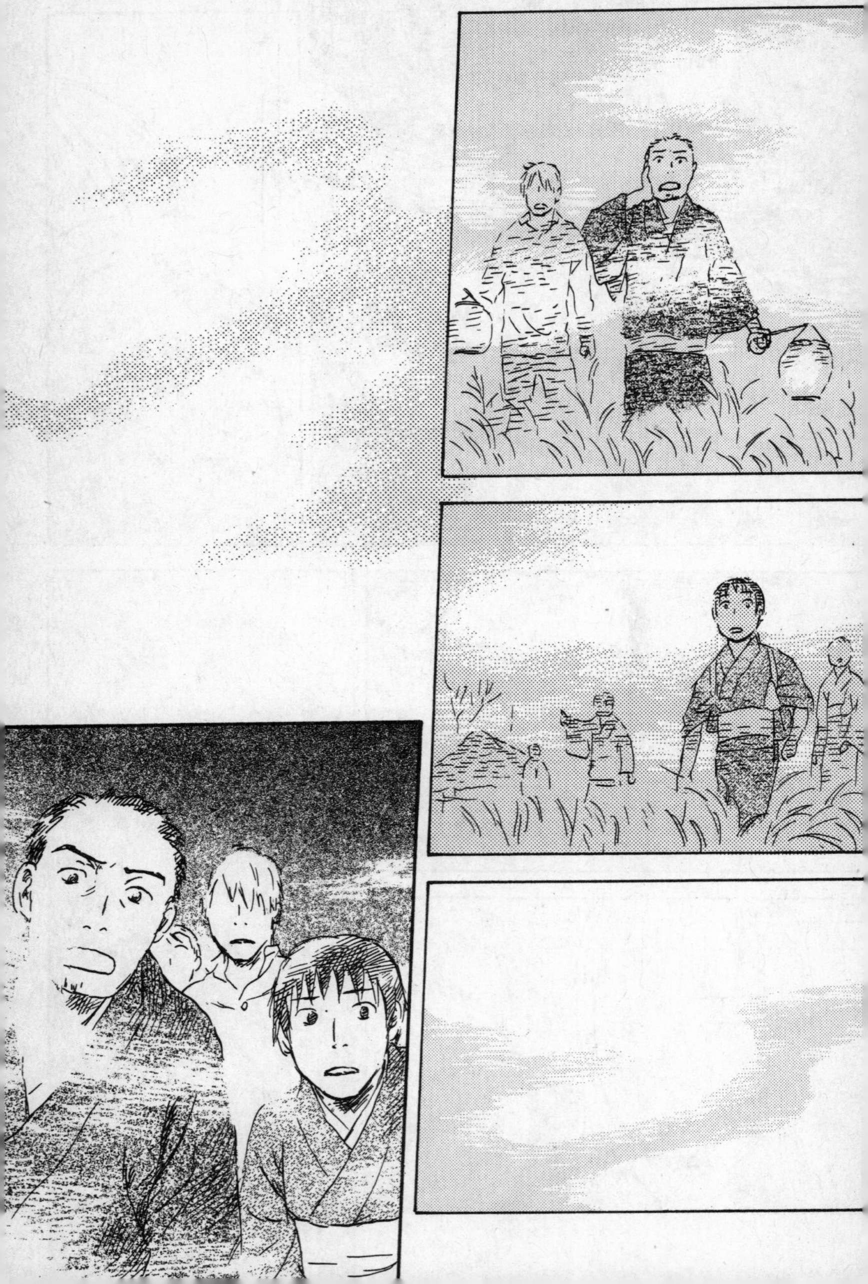

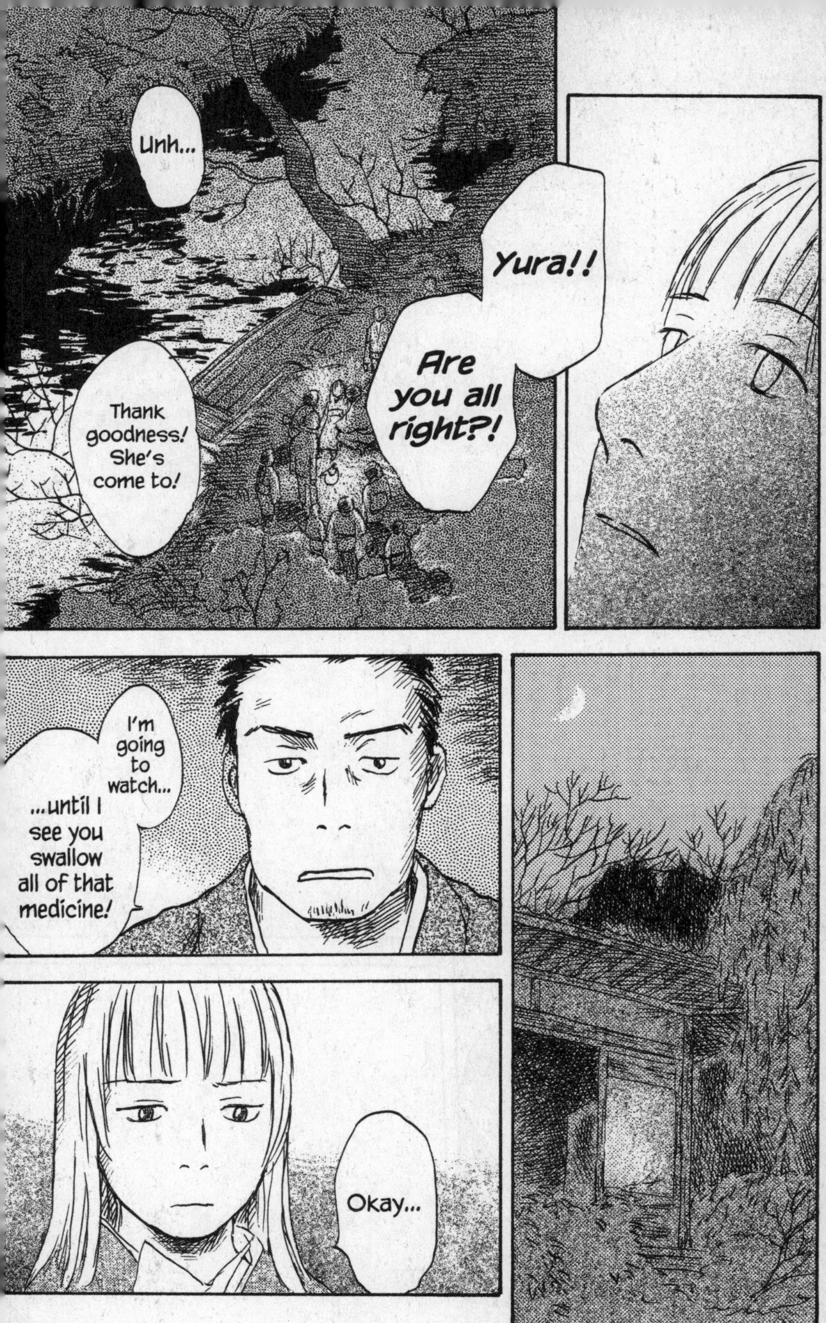
Yura!!
Are you all right?!
Unh...
Thank goodness! She's come to!
I'm going to watch...
...until I see you swallow all of that medicine!
Okay...

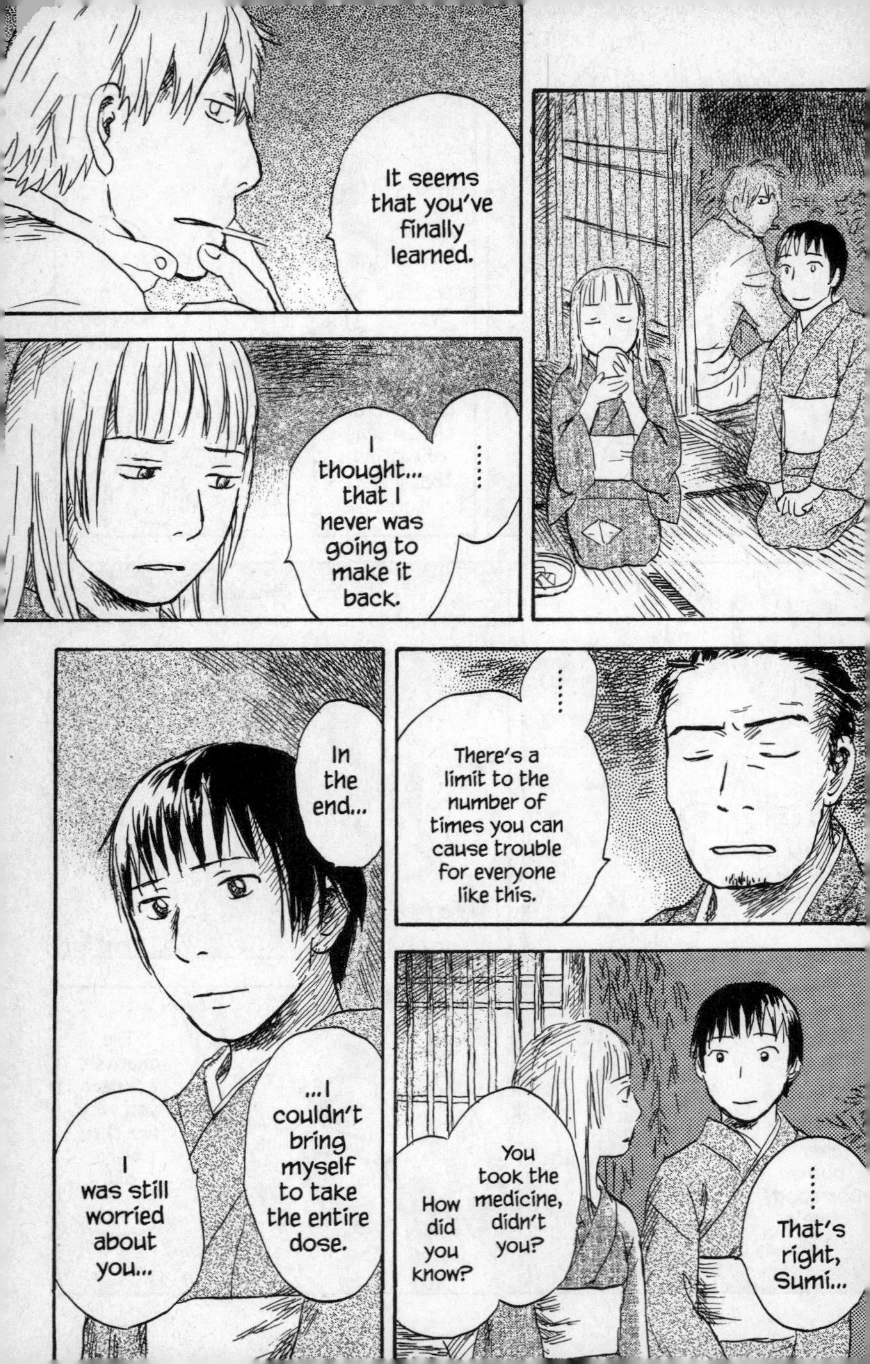
It seems that you've finally learned.
......
I thought... that I never was going to make it back.
......
There's a limit to the number of times you can cause trouble for everyone like this.
......
That's right, Sumi...
You took the medicine, didn't you?
How did you know?
In the end...
...I couldn't bring myself to take the entire dose.
I was still worried about you...

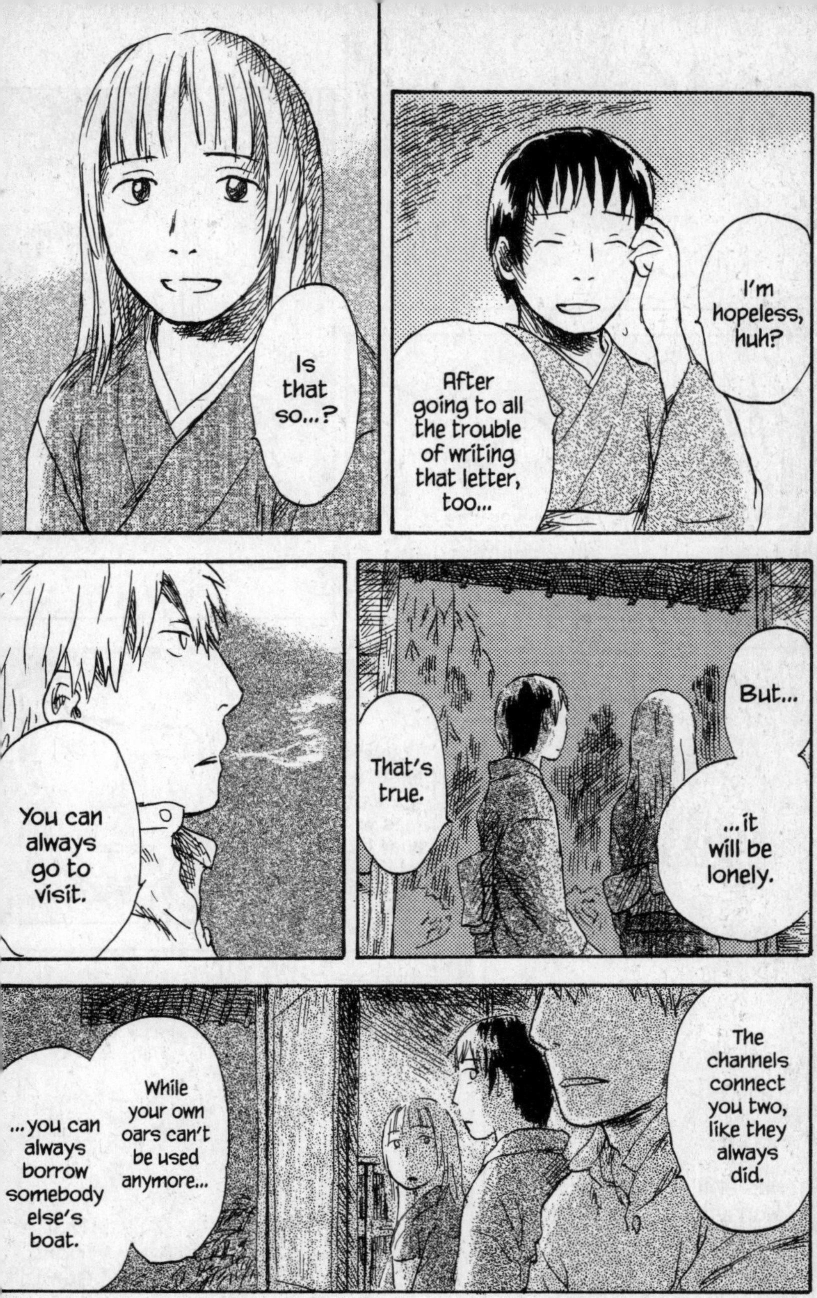
I'm hopeless, huh?
After going to all the trouble of writing that letter, too...
Is that so...?
But...
...it will be lonely.
That's true.
You can always go to visit.
The channels connect you two, like they always did.
While your own oars can't be used anymore...
...you can always borrow somebody else's boat.

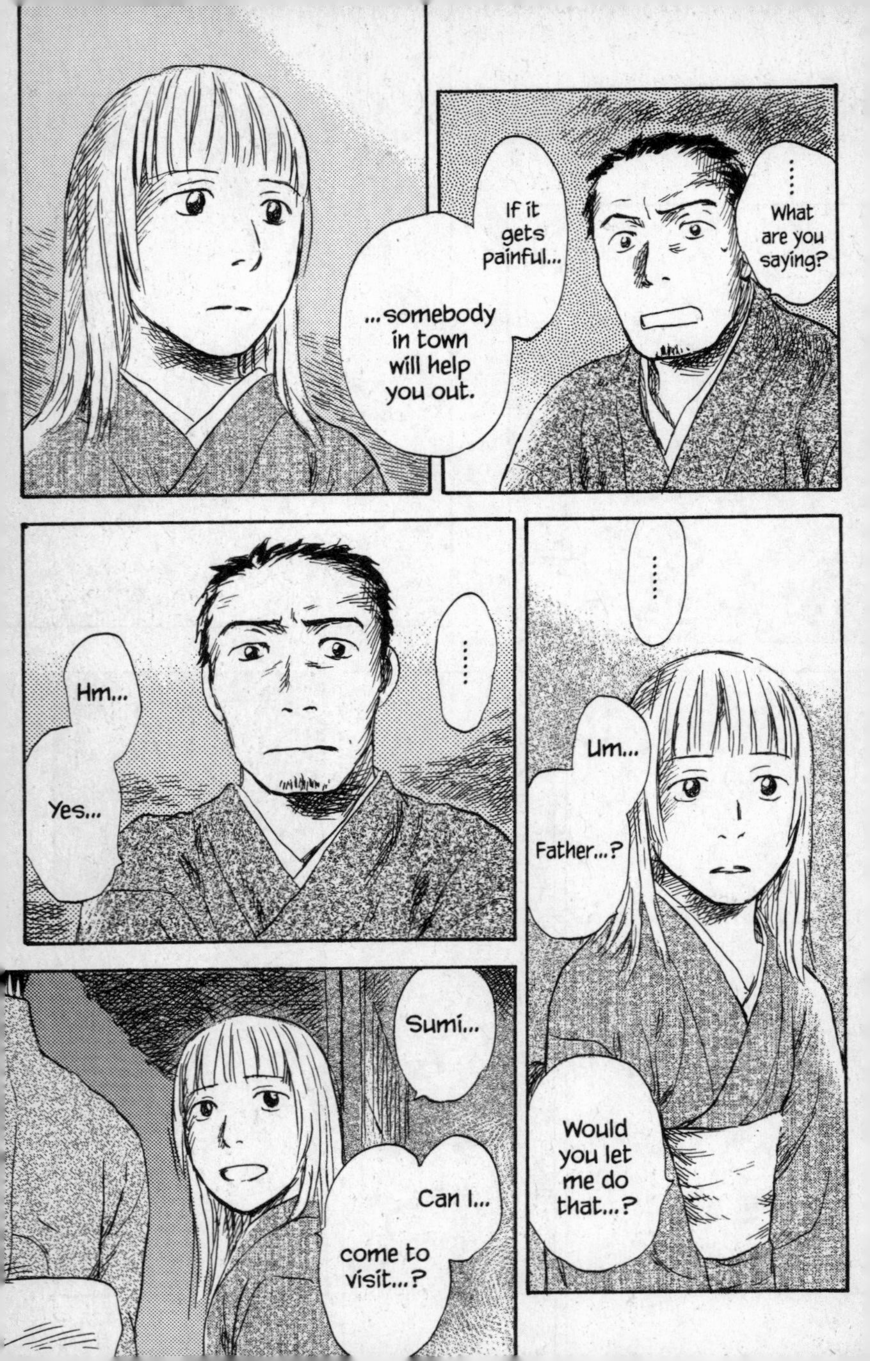

……
What are you saying?
If it gets painful...
...somebody in town will help you out.
……
Um...
Father...?
Would you let me do that...?
……
Hm...
Yes...
Sumi...
Can I...
come to visit...?

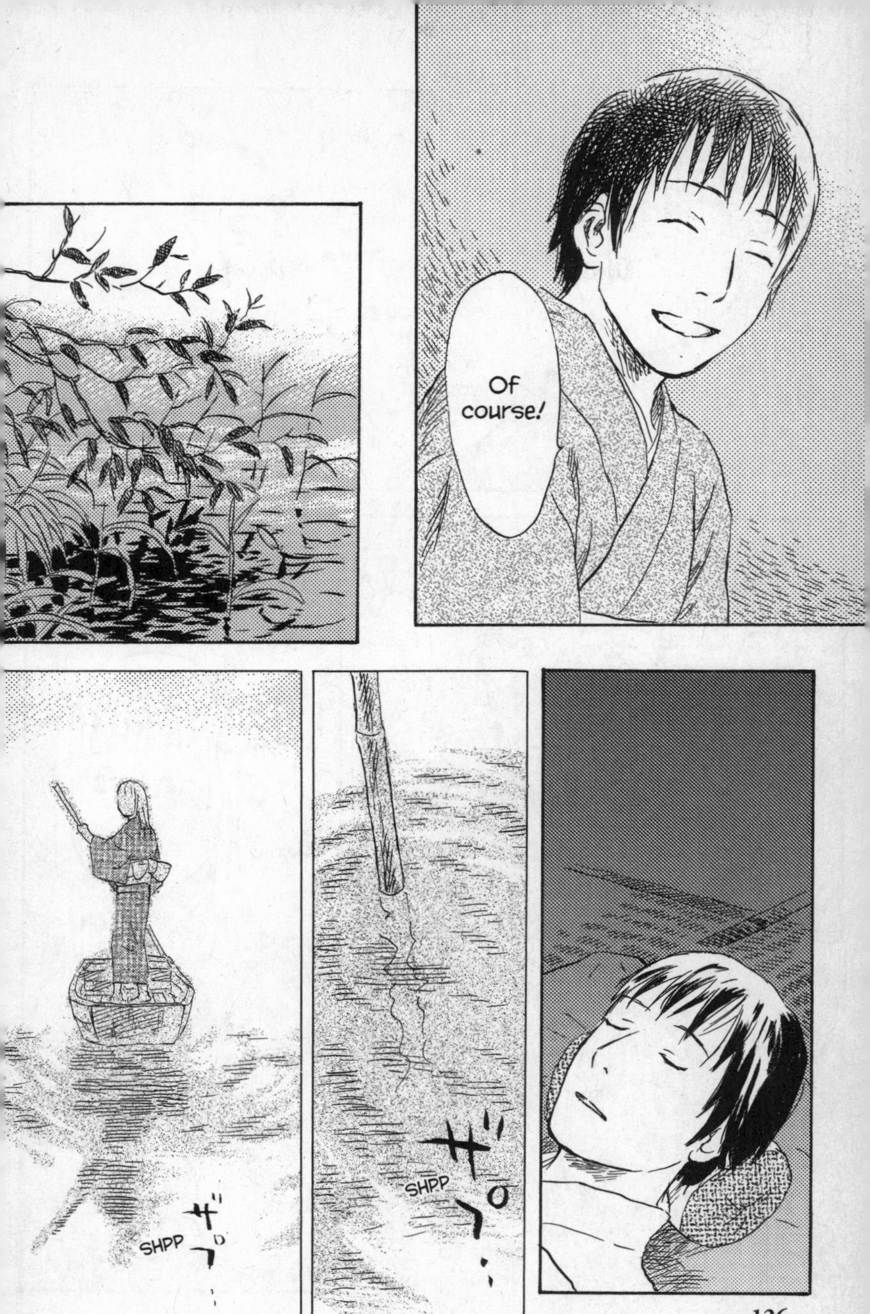
Of course!
SHPP
SHPP

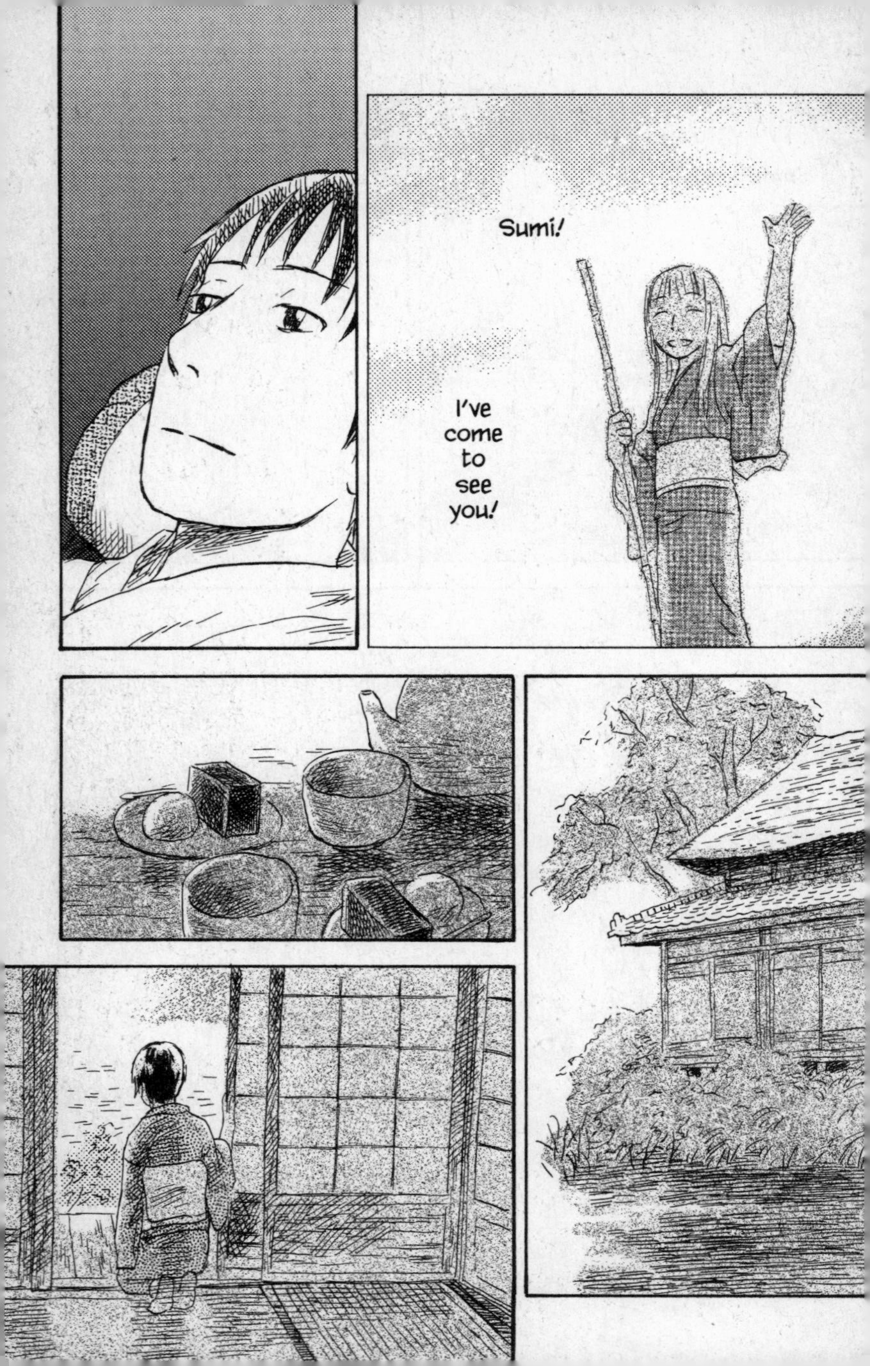
Sumi!
I've come to see you!

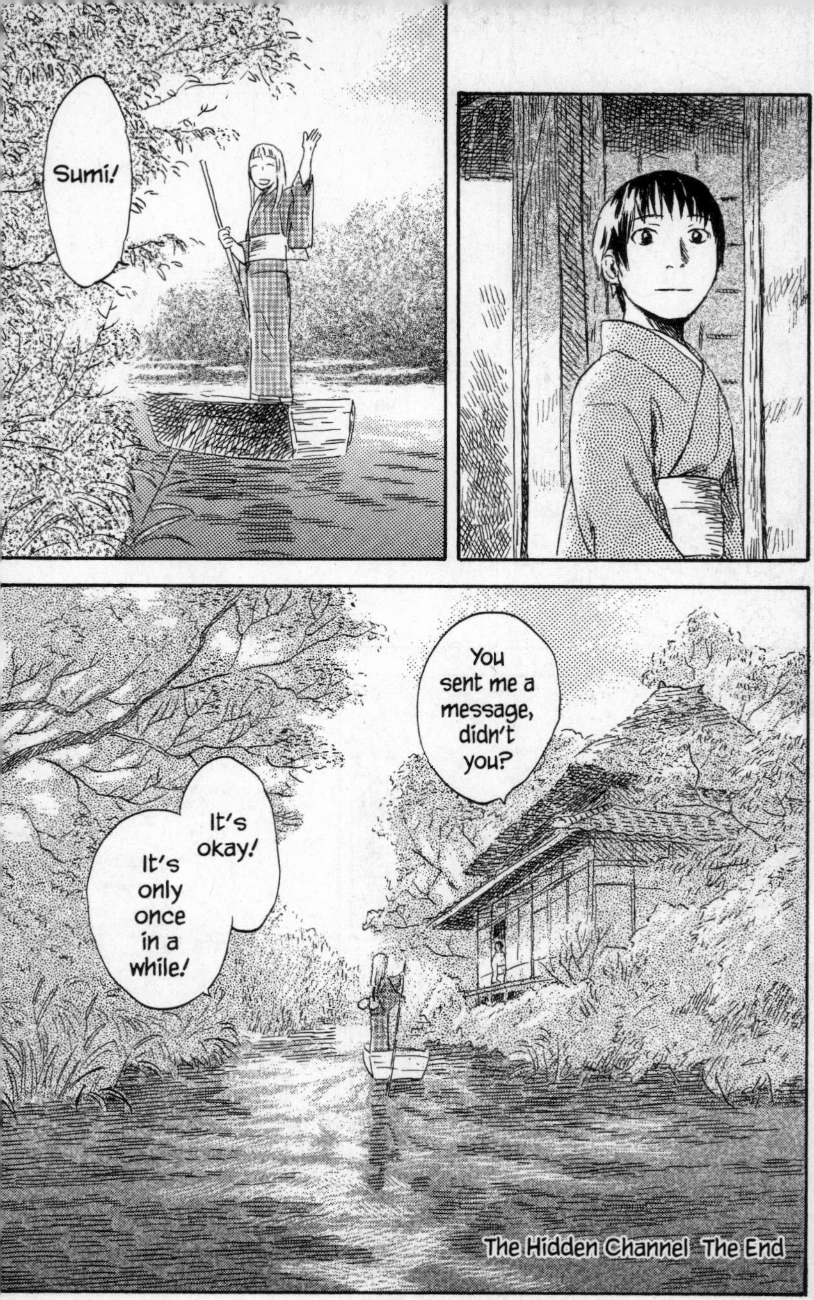
Sumi!
You sent me a message, didn't you?
It's okay!
It's only once in a while!
The Hidden Channel The End

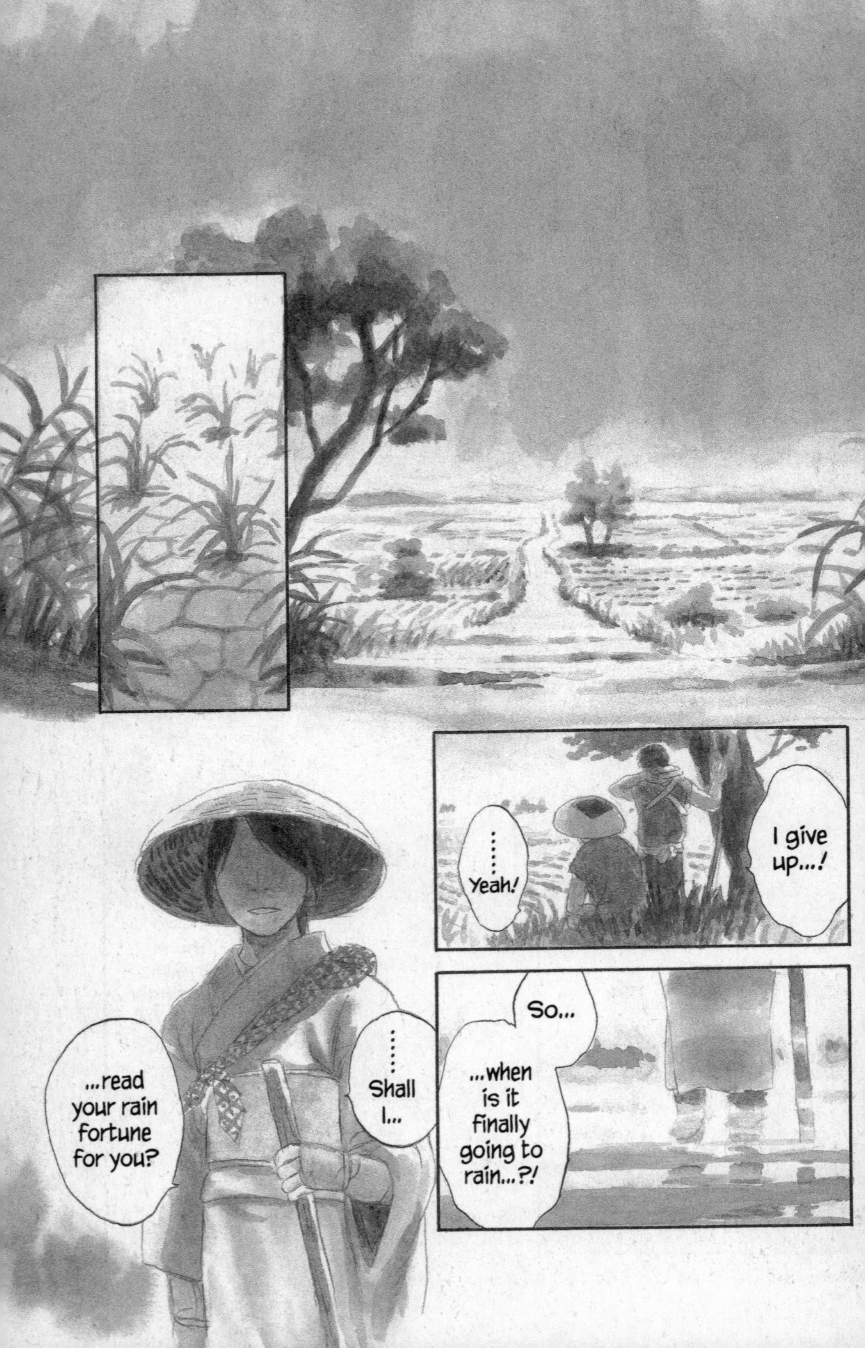
I give up...!
......
Yeah!
So...
...when is it finally going to rain...?!
......
Shall I...
...read your rain fortune for you?

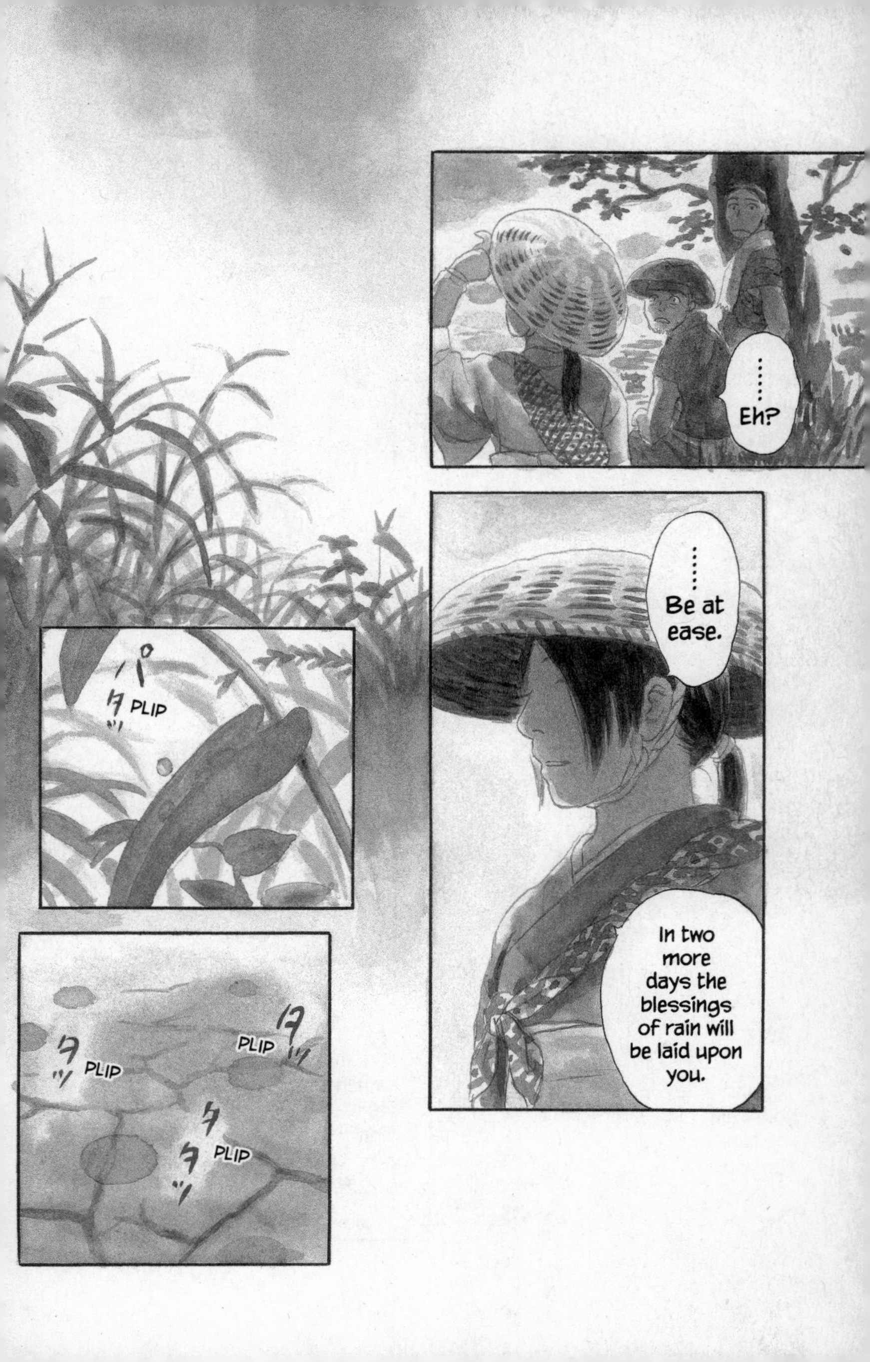
......Eh?
......Be at ease.
In two more days the blessings of rain will be laid upon you.
パタッ PLIP
タッ PLIP
タッ PLIP
タタッ PLIP

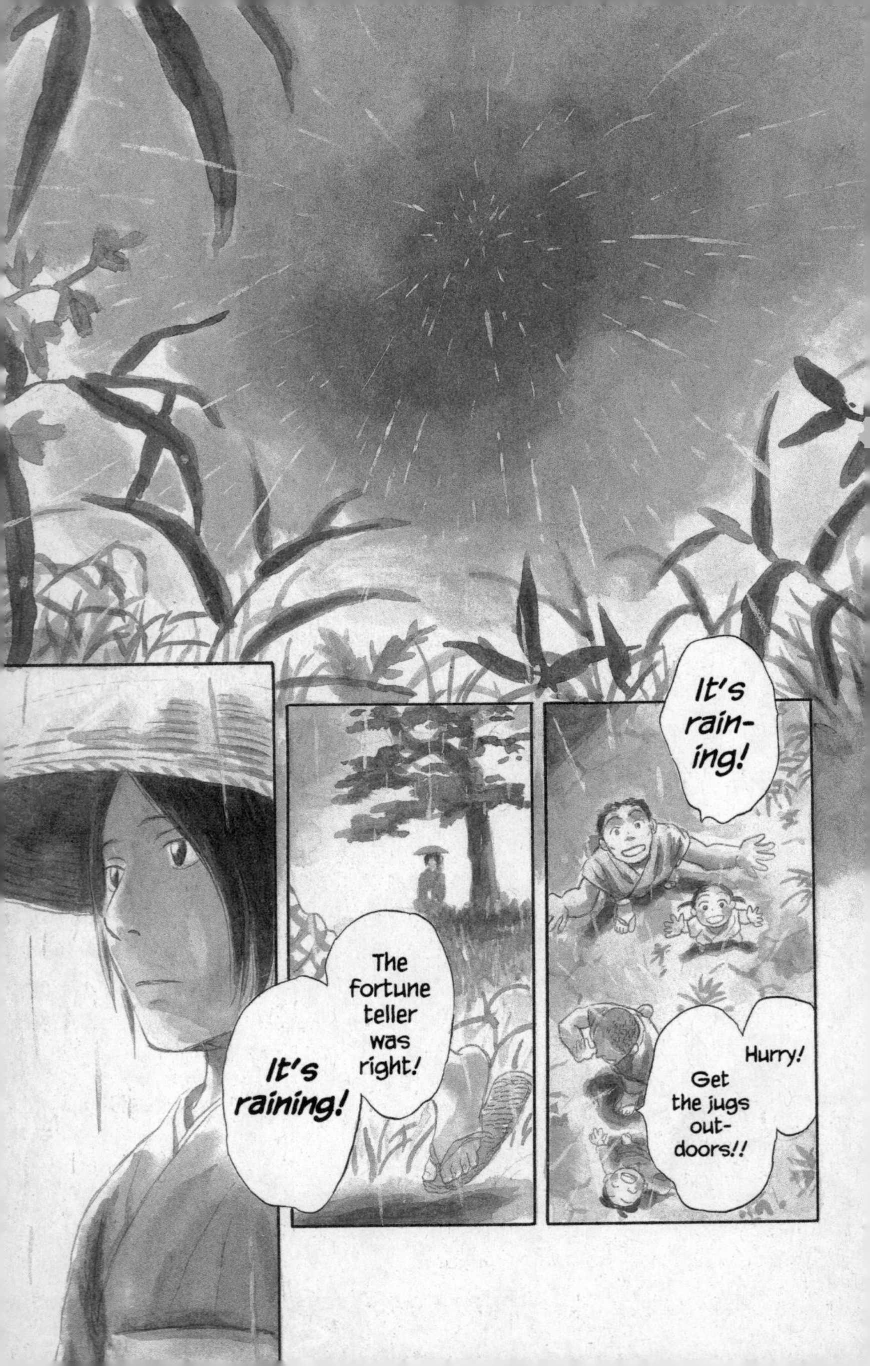
It's raining!
Hurry! Get the jugs outdoors!!
The fortune teller was right!
It's raining!

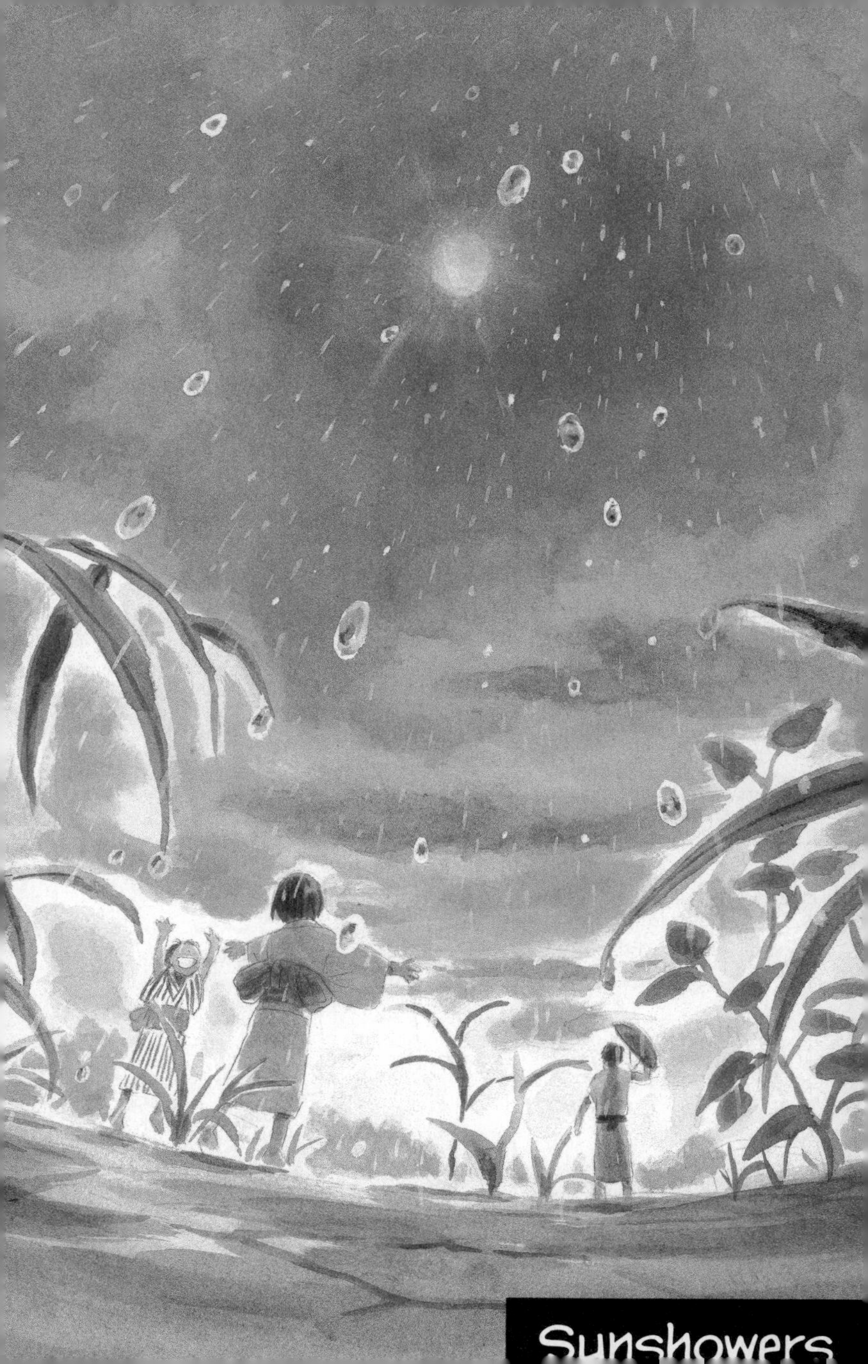

Sunshowers

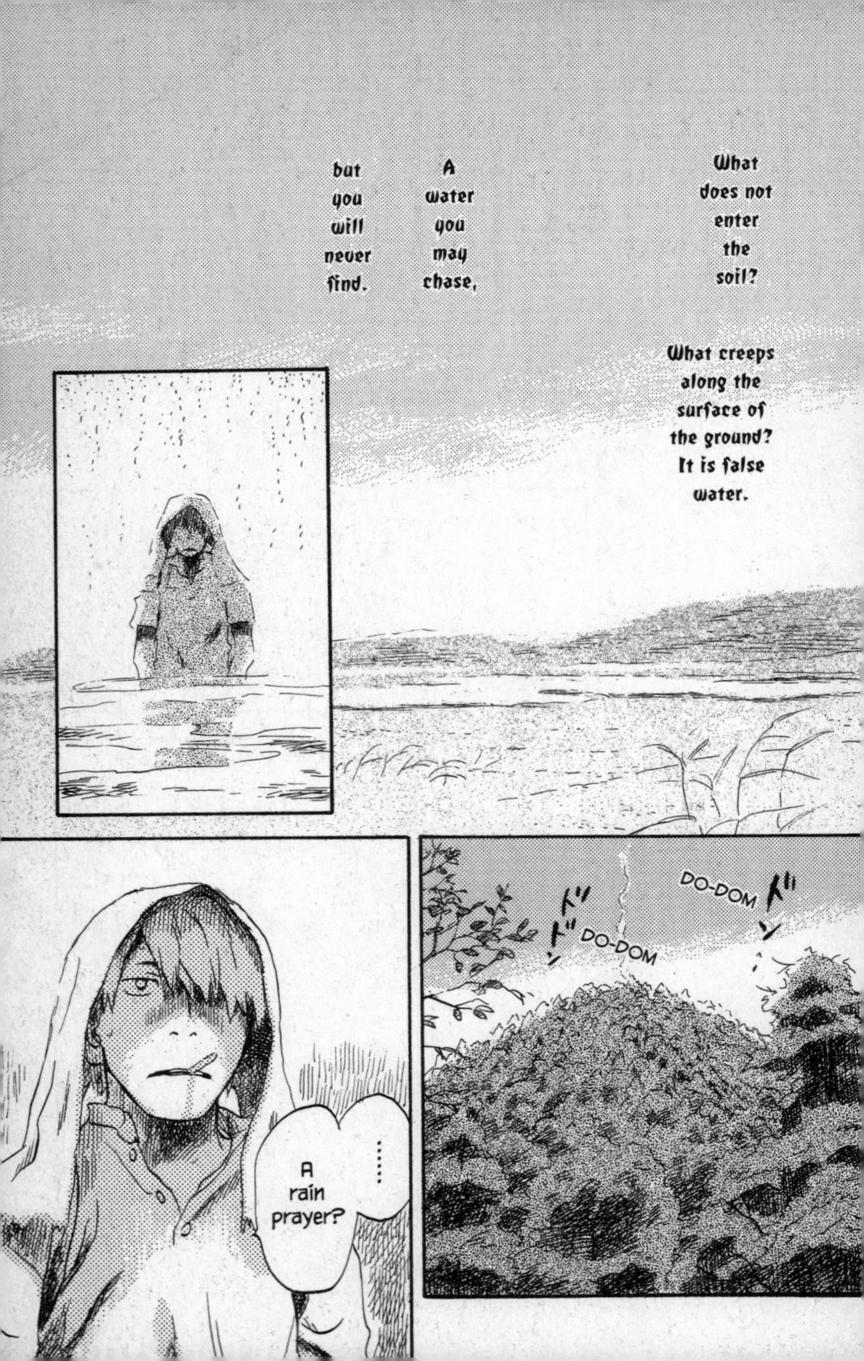
What does not enter the soil?
What creeps along the surface of the ground? It is false water.
A water you may chase,
but you will never find.
DO-DOM
DO-DOM
......
A rain prayer?

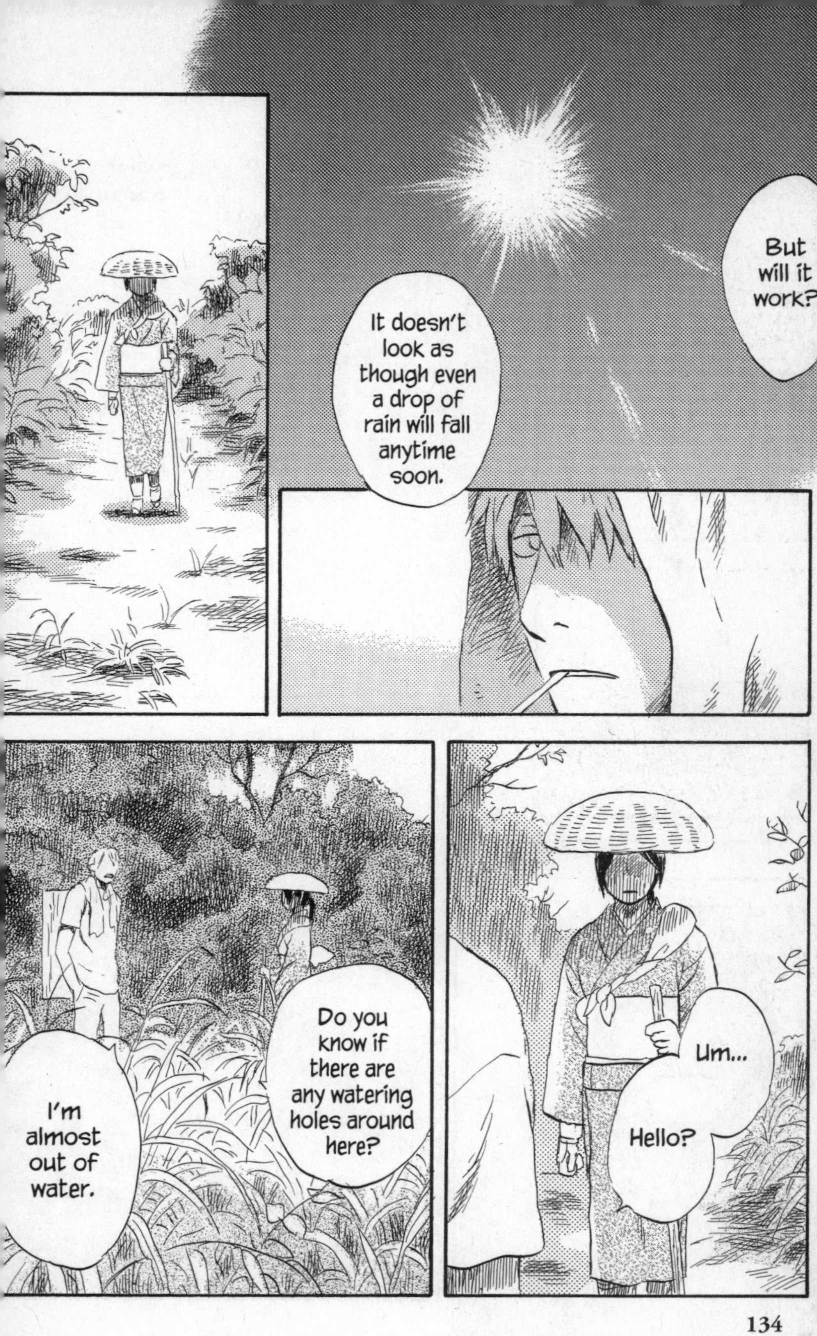
But will it work?
It doesn't look as though even a drop of rain will fall anytime soon.
Um...
Hello?
Do you know if there are any watering holes around here?
I'm almost out of water.

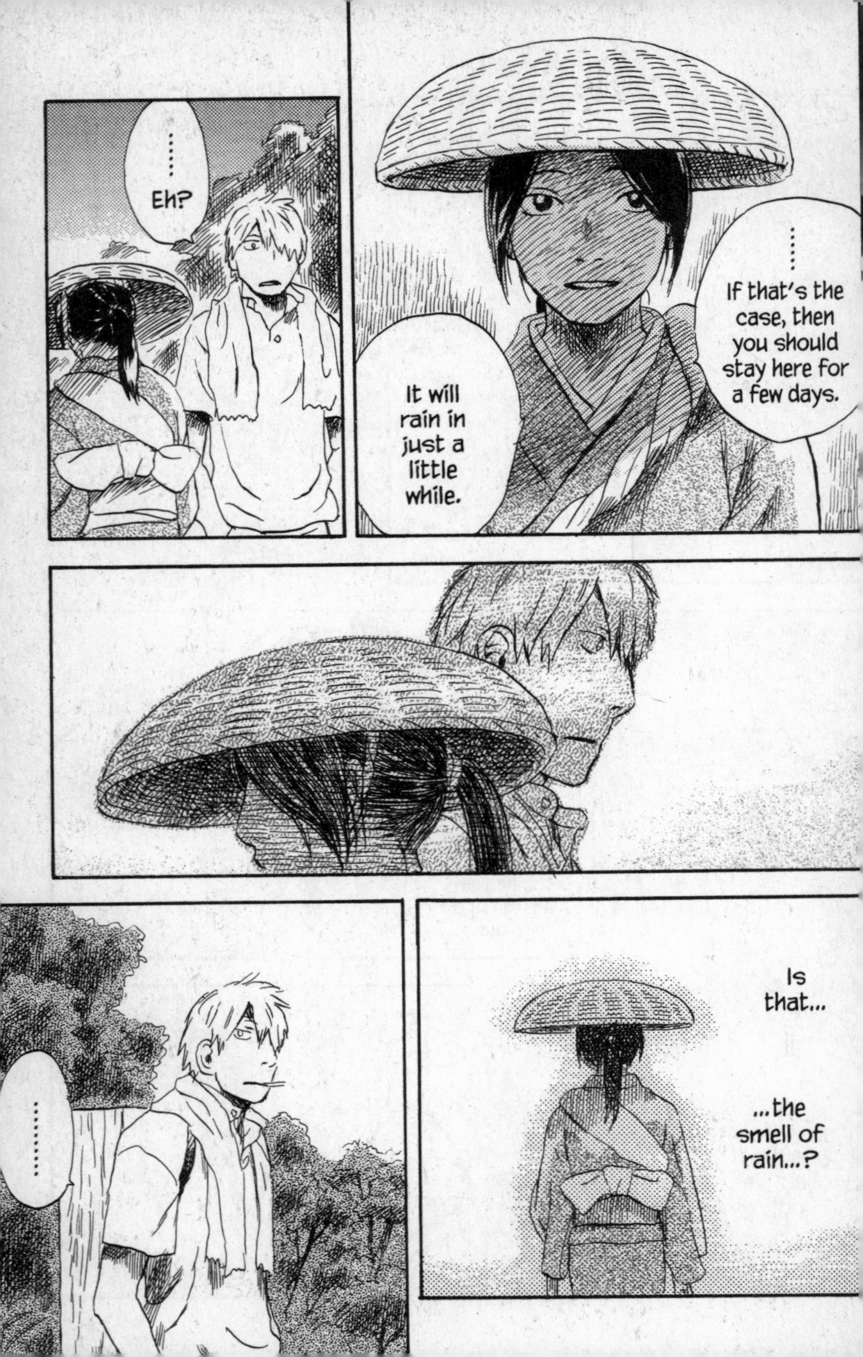

......
If that's the case, then you should stay here for a few days.
It will rain in just a little while.
......
Eh?
Is that...
...the smell of rain...?
....

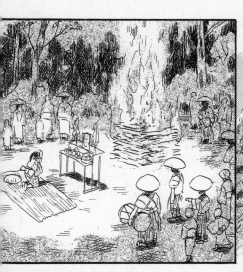

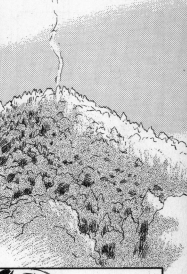

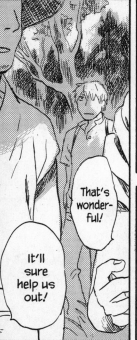

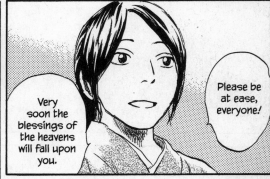

Please be at ease, everyone!

Very soon the blessings of the heavens will fall upon you.

That's wonder-ful!

It'll sure help us out!

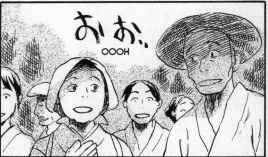

おお、
OOOH

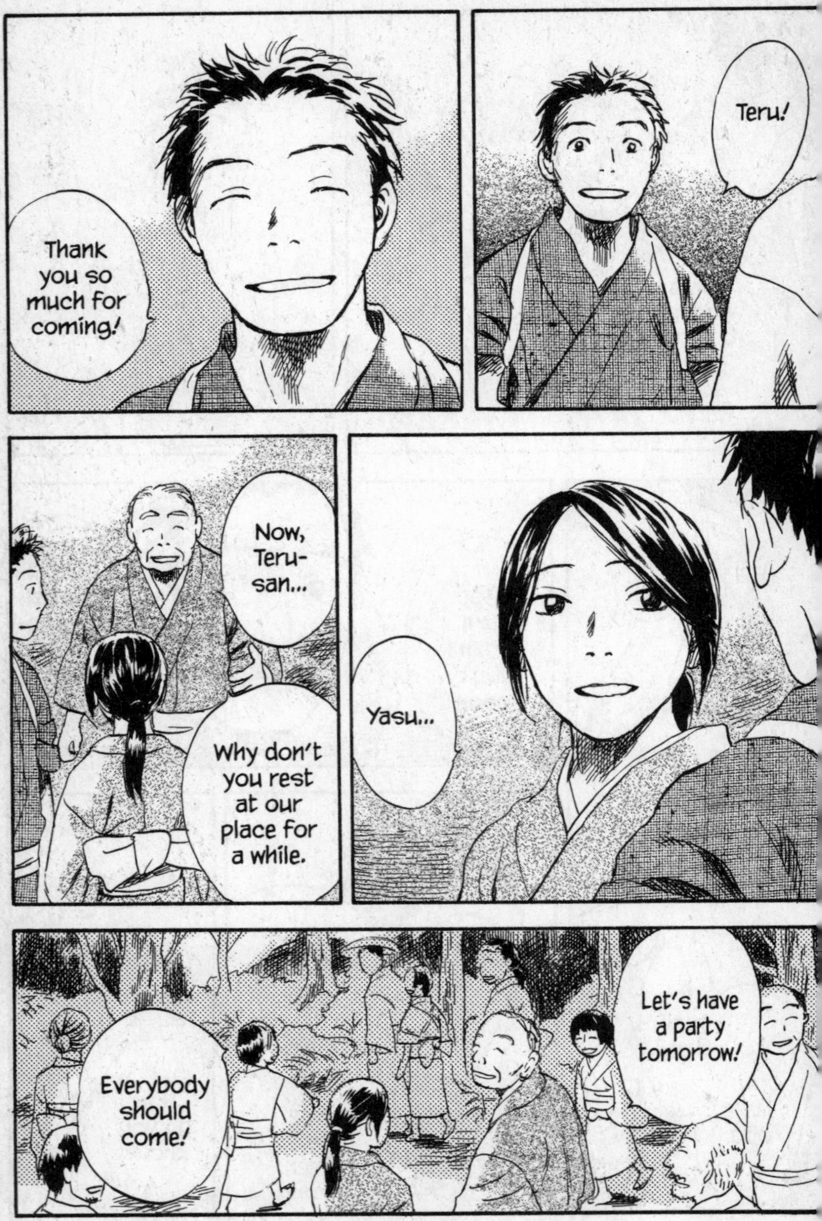
Teru!
Thank you so much for coming!
Yasu...
Now, Teru-san...
Why don't you rest at our place for a while.
Let's have a party tomorrow!
Everybody should come!

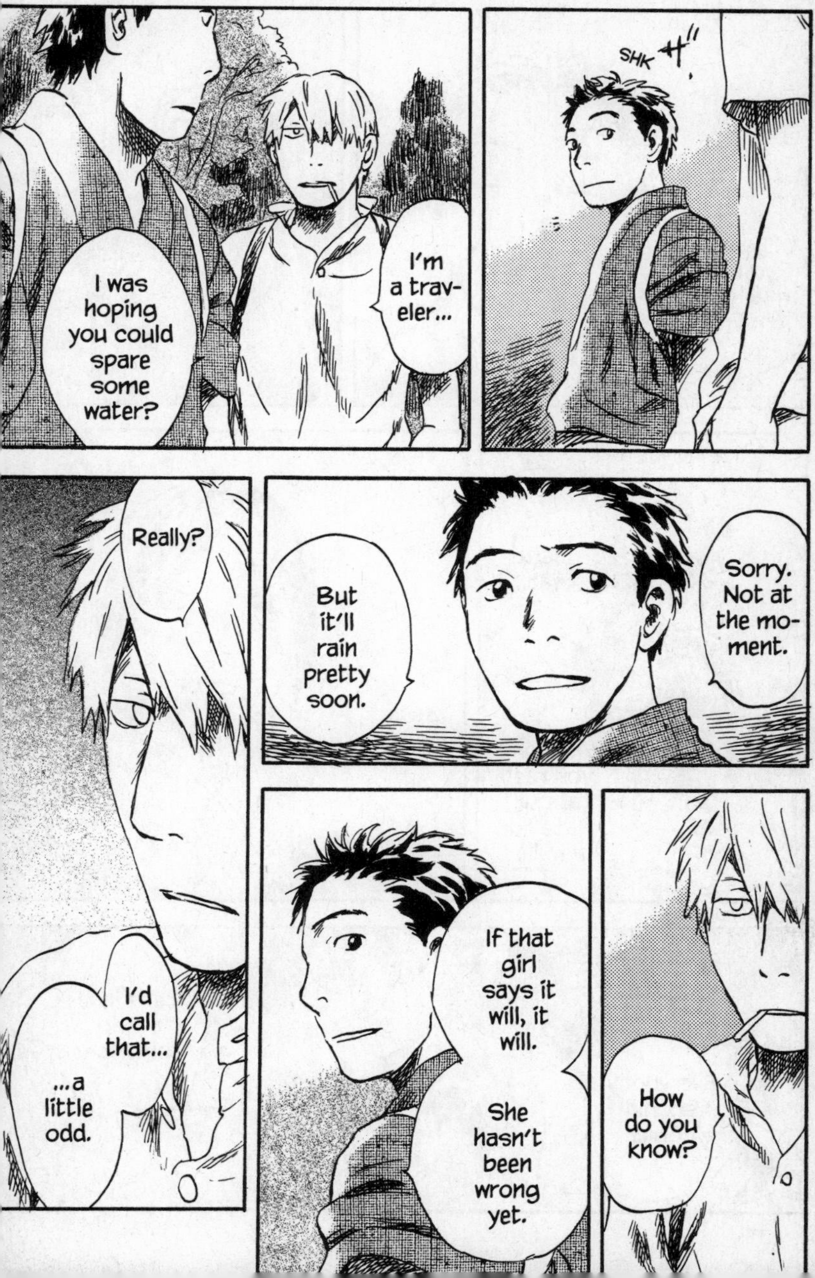
SHK
I'm a trav-eler...
I was hoping you could spare some water?
Sorry. Not at the mo-ment.
But it'll rain pretty soon.
How do you know?
If that girl says it will, it will.
She hasn't been wrong yet.
Really?
I'd call that...
...a little odd.

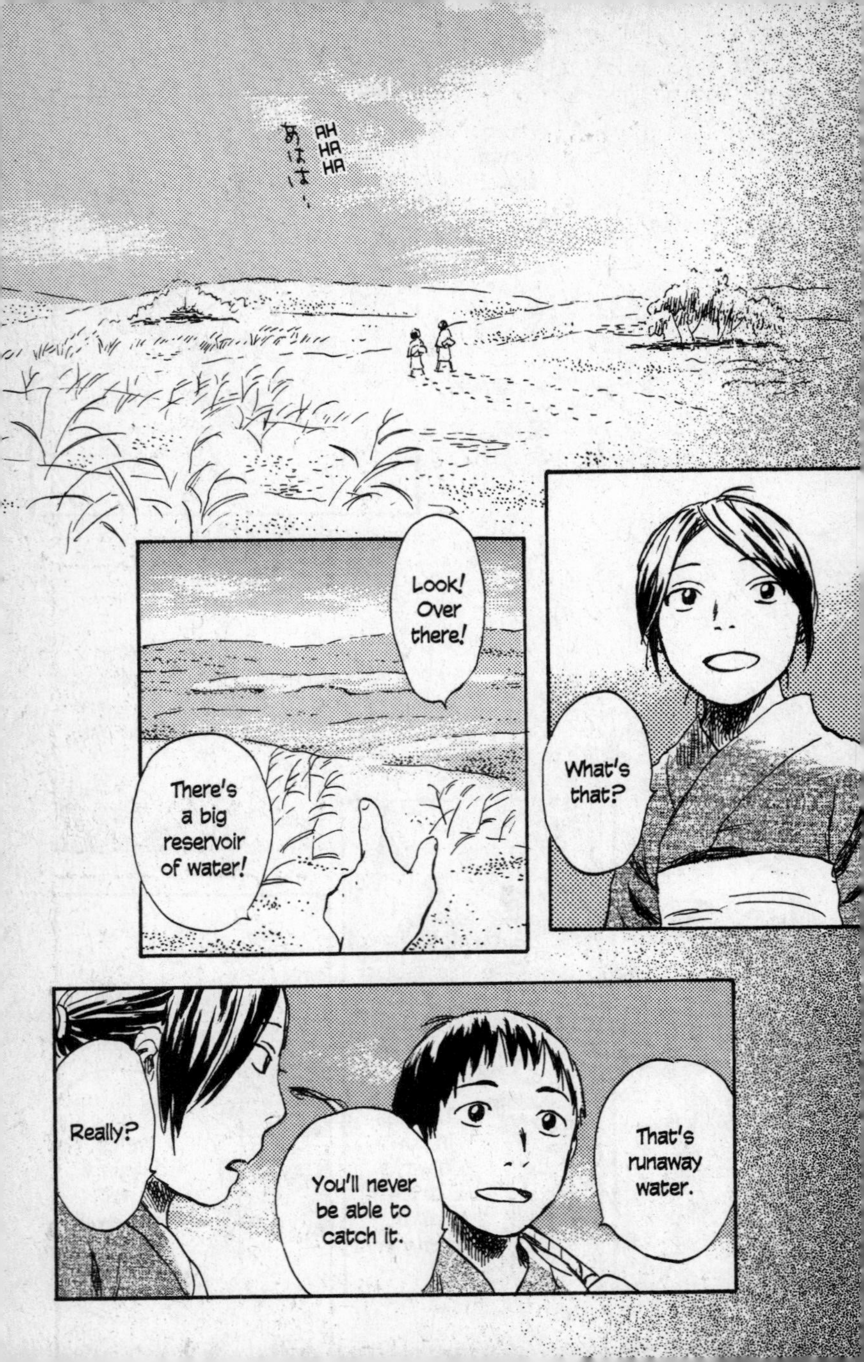
AH HA HA
あはは…
What's that?
Look! Over there!
There's a big reservoir of water!
That's runaway water.
You'll never be able to catch it.
Really?

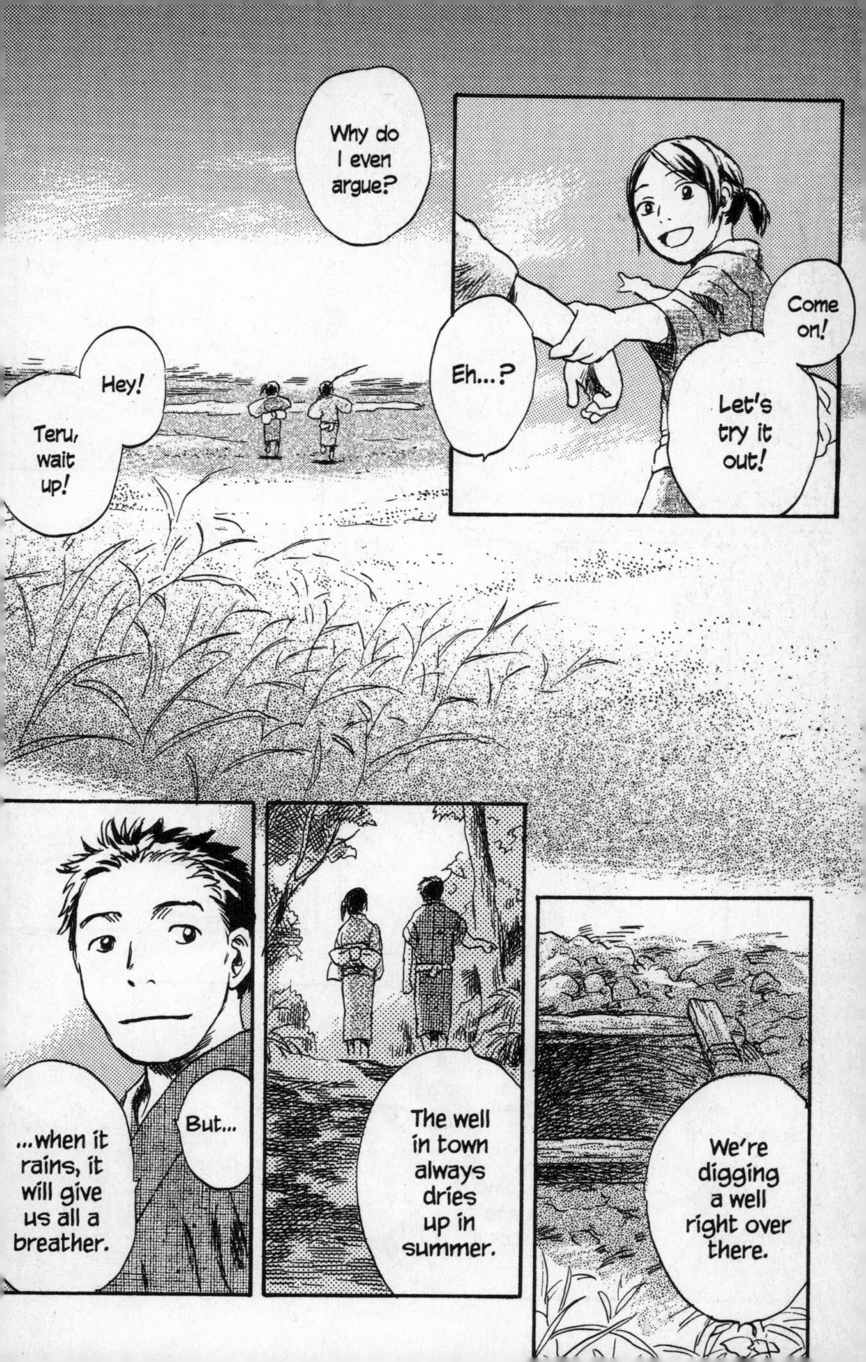
Come on!
Let's try it out!
Eh...?
Why do I even argue?
Hey!
Teru, wait up!
We're digging a well right over there.
The well in town always dries up in summer.
But...
...when it rains, it will give us all a breather.

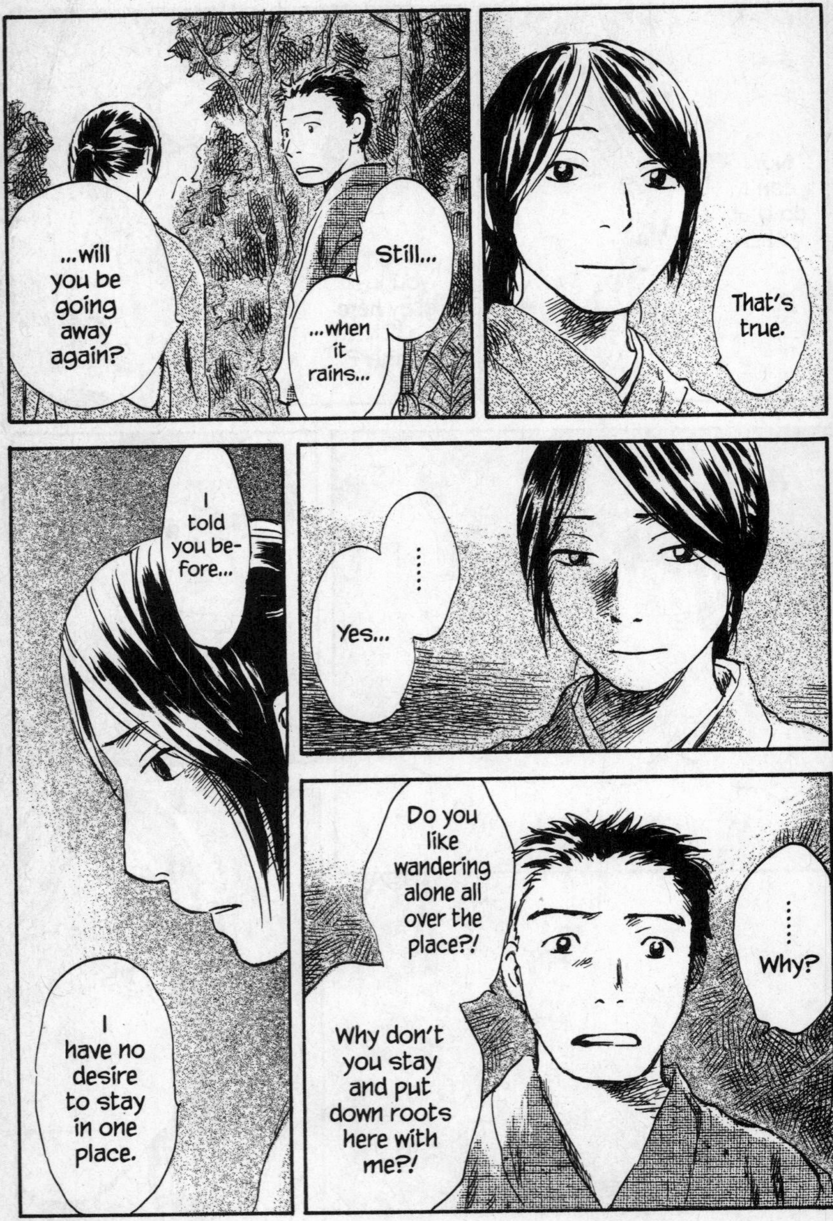
That's true.
Still...
...when it rains...
...will you be going away again?
......
Yes...
......
Why?
Do you like wandering alone all over the place?!
Why don't you stay and put down roots here with me?!
I told you be-fore...
I have no desire to stay in one place.

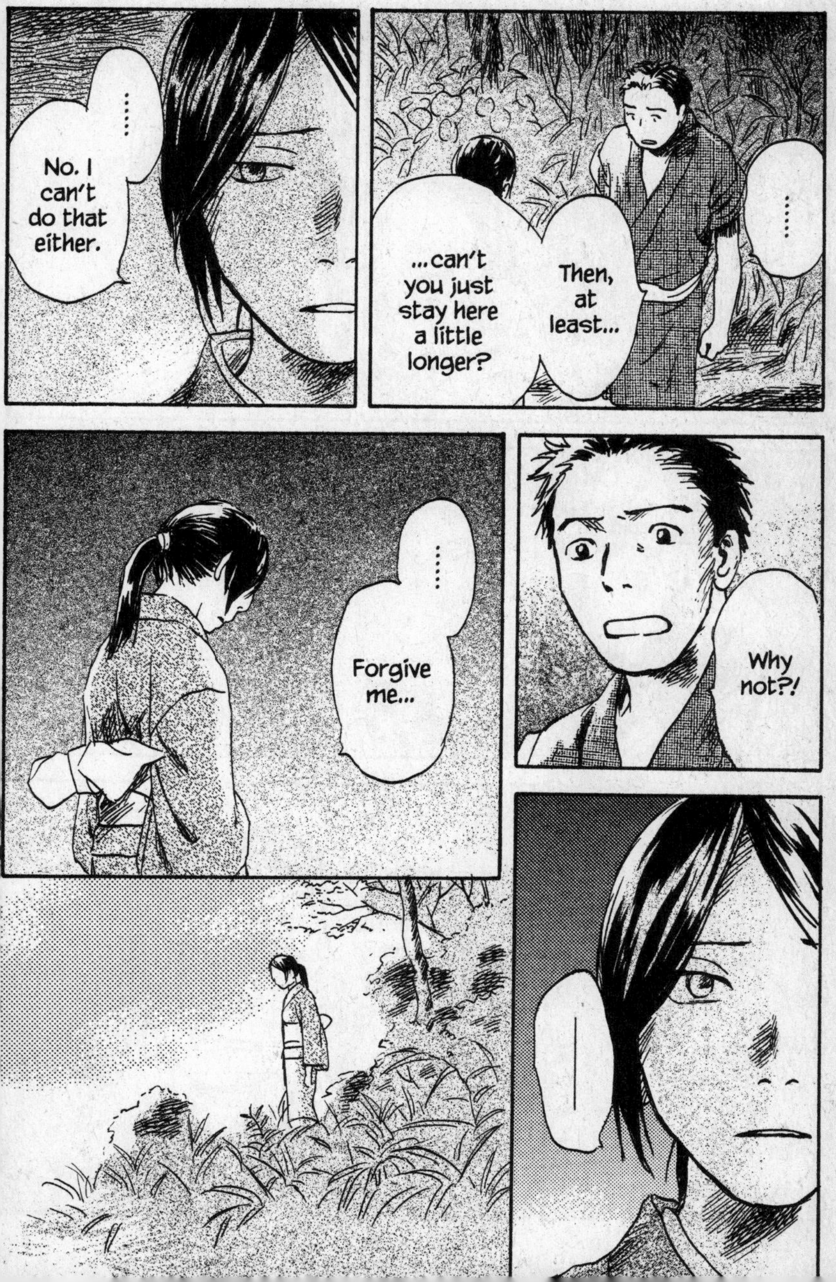
......
Then, at least...
...can't you just stay here a little longer?
......
No. I can't do that either.
Why not?!
......
Forgive me...

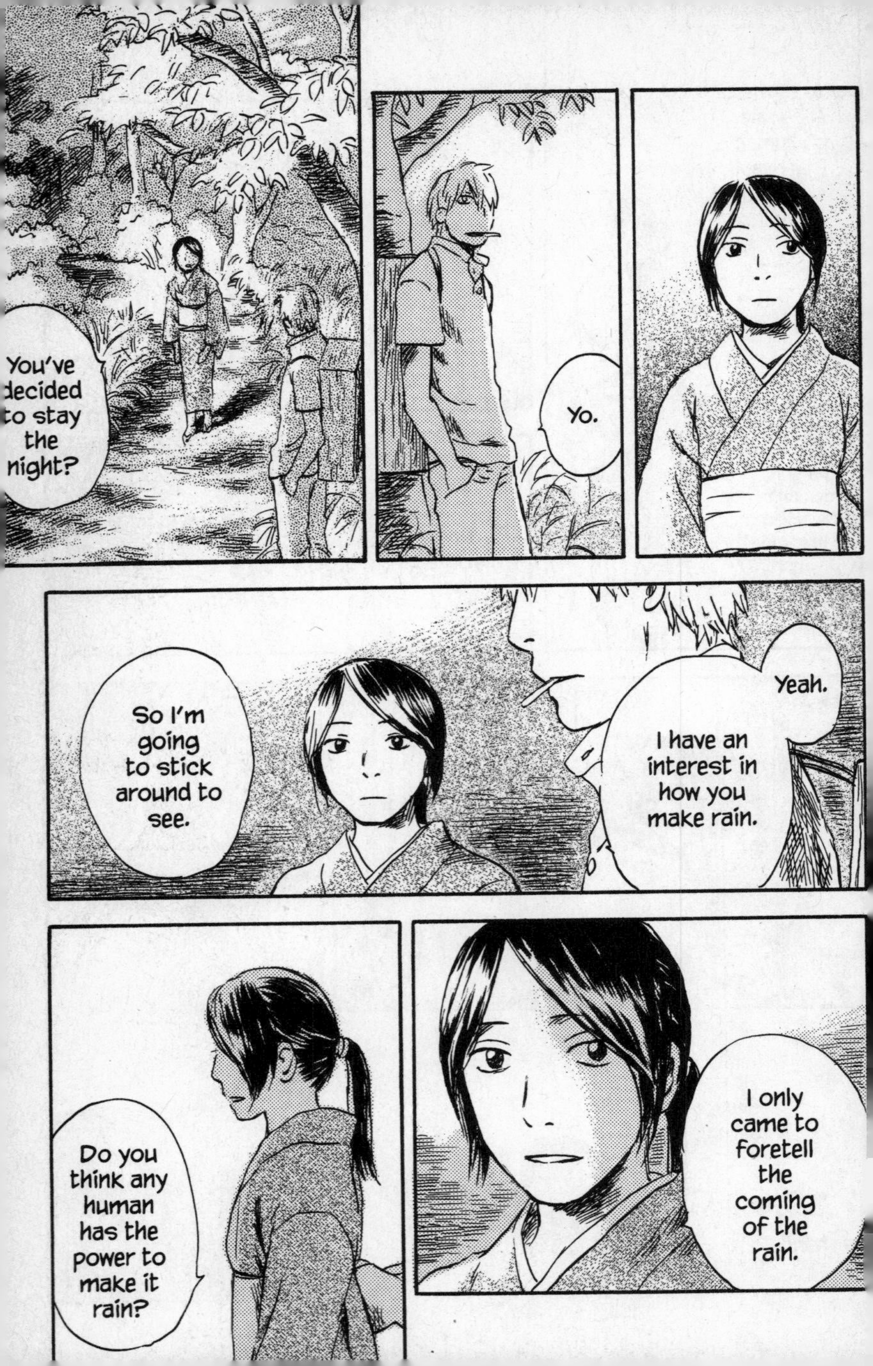
Yo.
You've decided to stay the night?
Yeah.
I have an interest in how you make rain.
So I'm going to stick around to see.
I only came to foretell the coming of the rain.
Do you think any human has the power to make it rain?

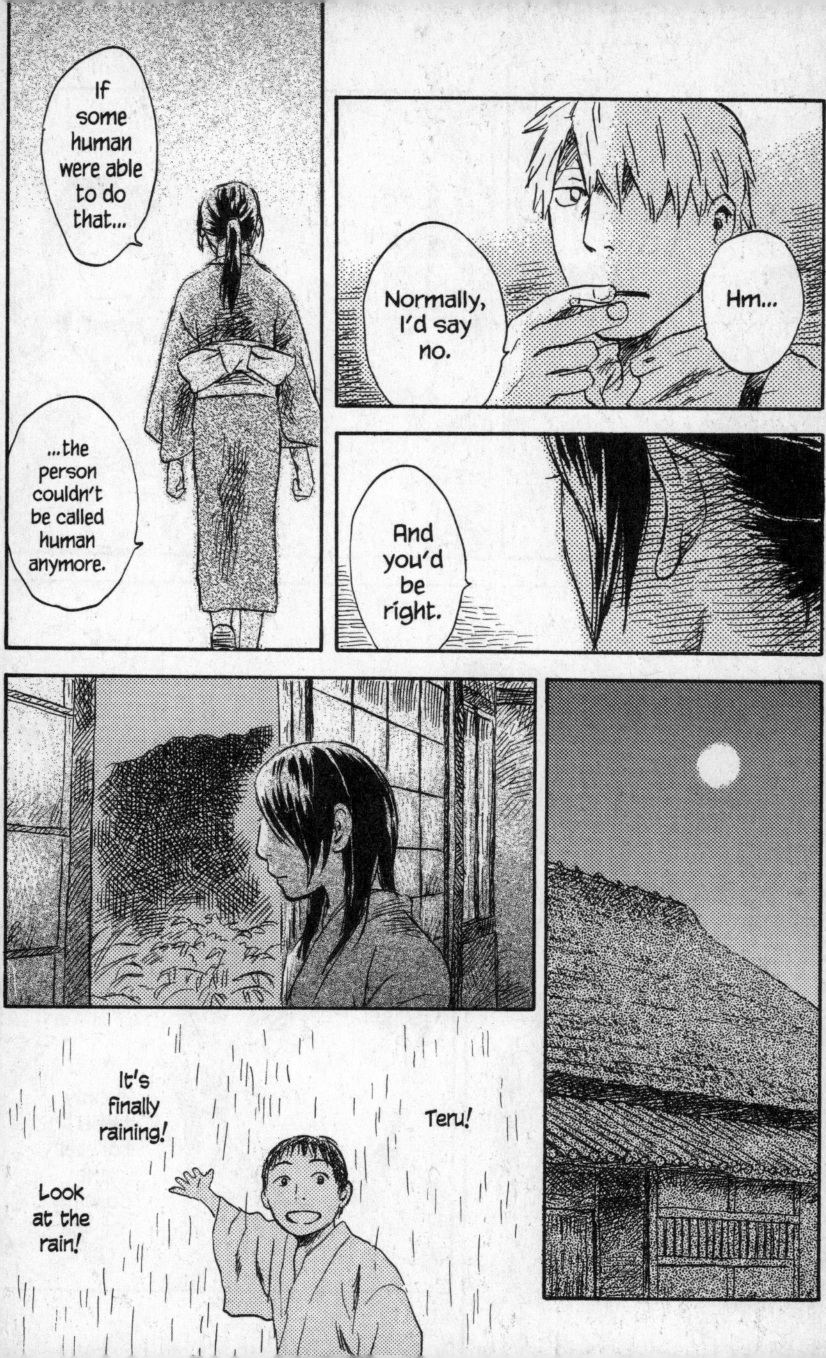
Hm...
Normally, I'd say no.
And you'd be right.
If some human were able to do that...
...the person couldn't be called human anymore.
Teru!
It's finally raining!
Look at the rain!

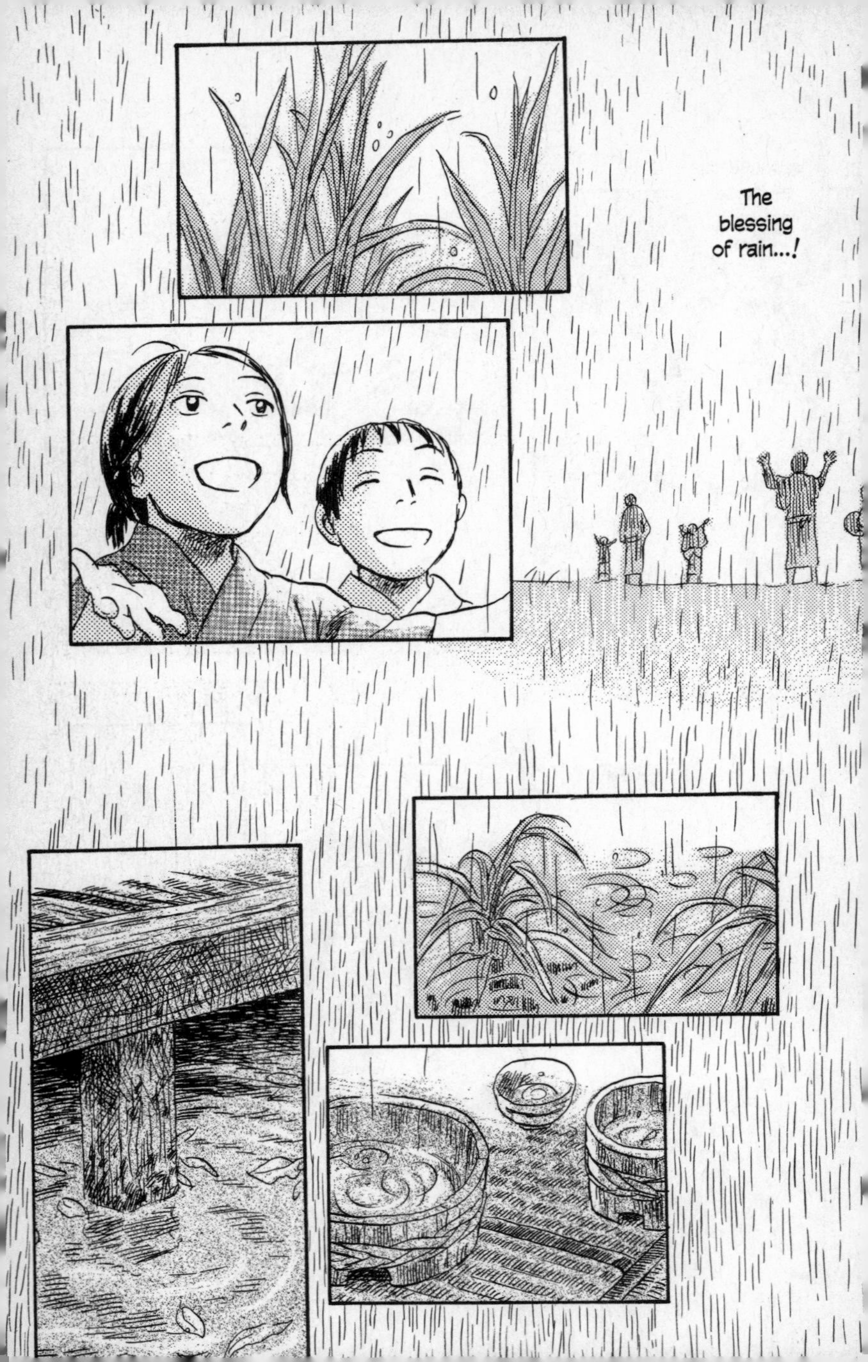
The blessing of rain...!

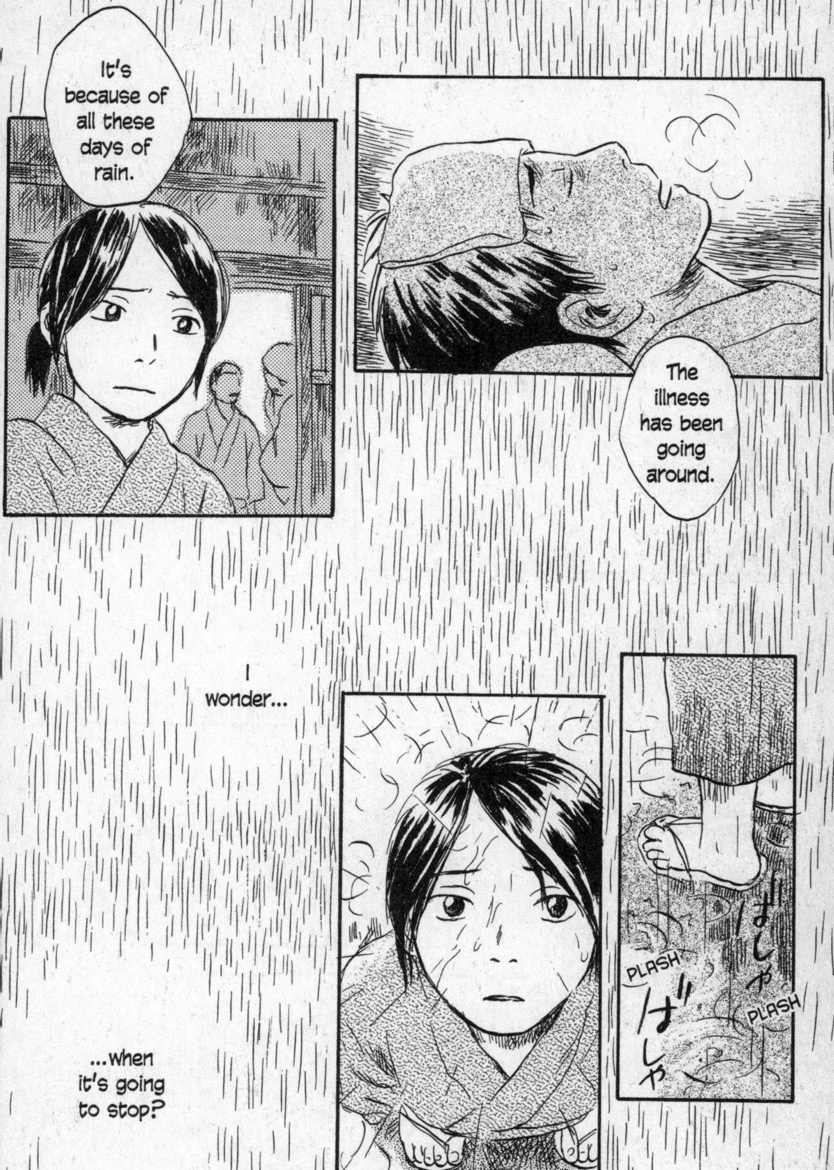
The illness has been going around.
It's because of all these days of rain.
ばしゃ
PLASH
ばしゃ
PLASH
I wonder...
...when it's going to stop?

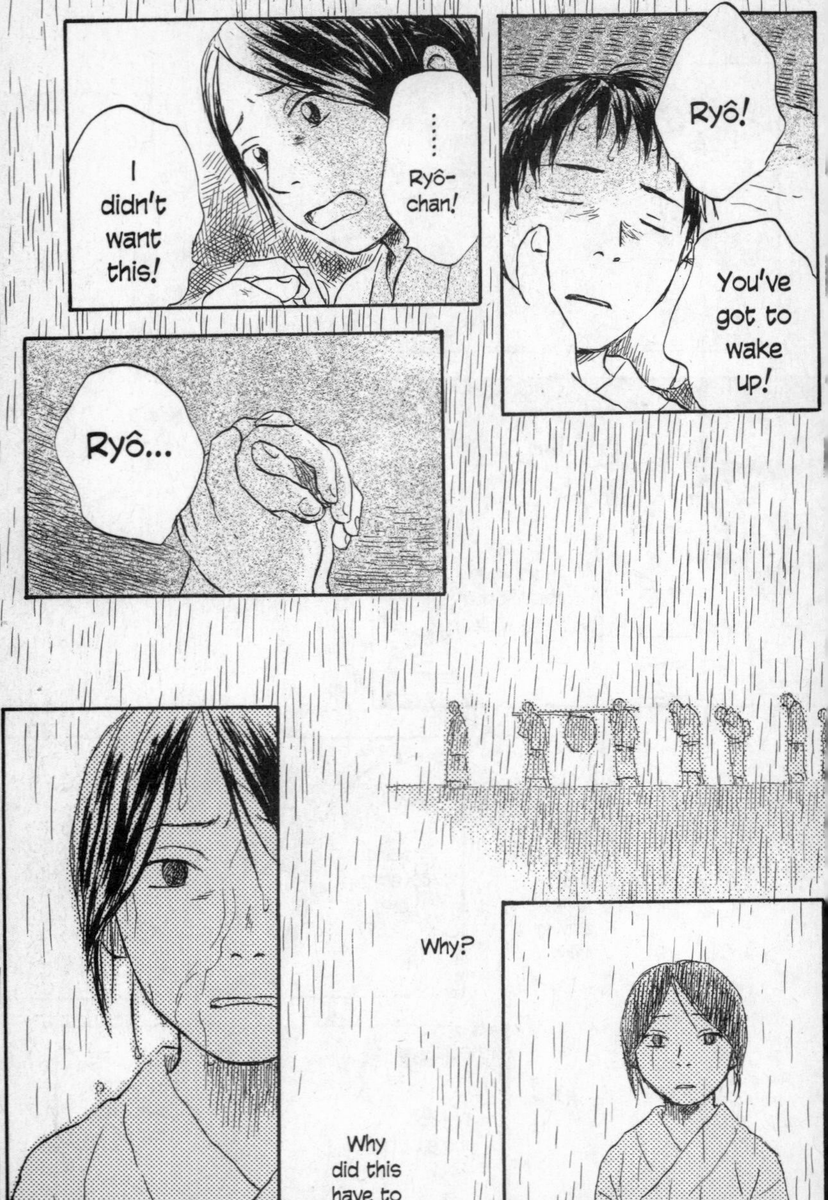
Ryô!
You've got to wake up!
...... Ryô-chan!
I didn't want this!
Ryô...
Why?
Why did this have to happen?

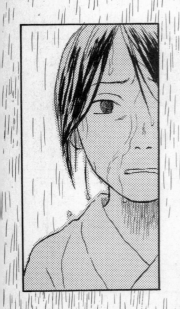

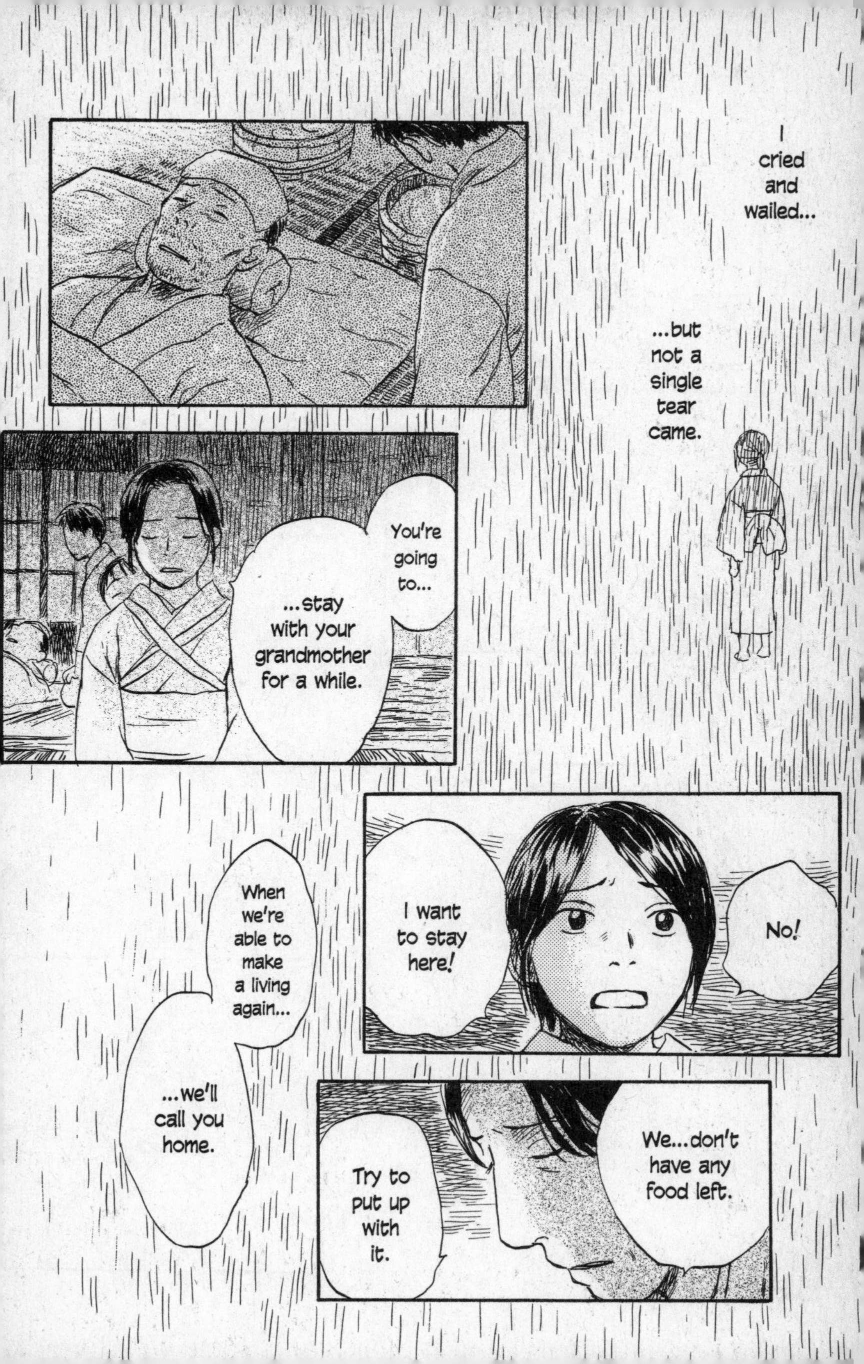
I cried and wailed...
...but not a single tear came.
You're going to...
...stay with your grandmother for a while.
No!
I want to stay here!
We...don't have any food left.
Try to put up with it.
When we're able to make a living again...
...we'll call you home.

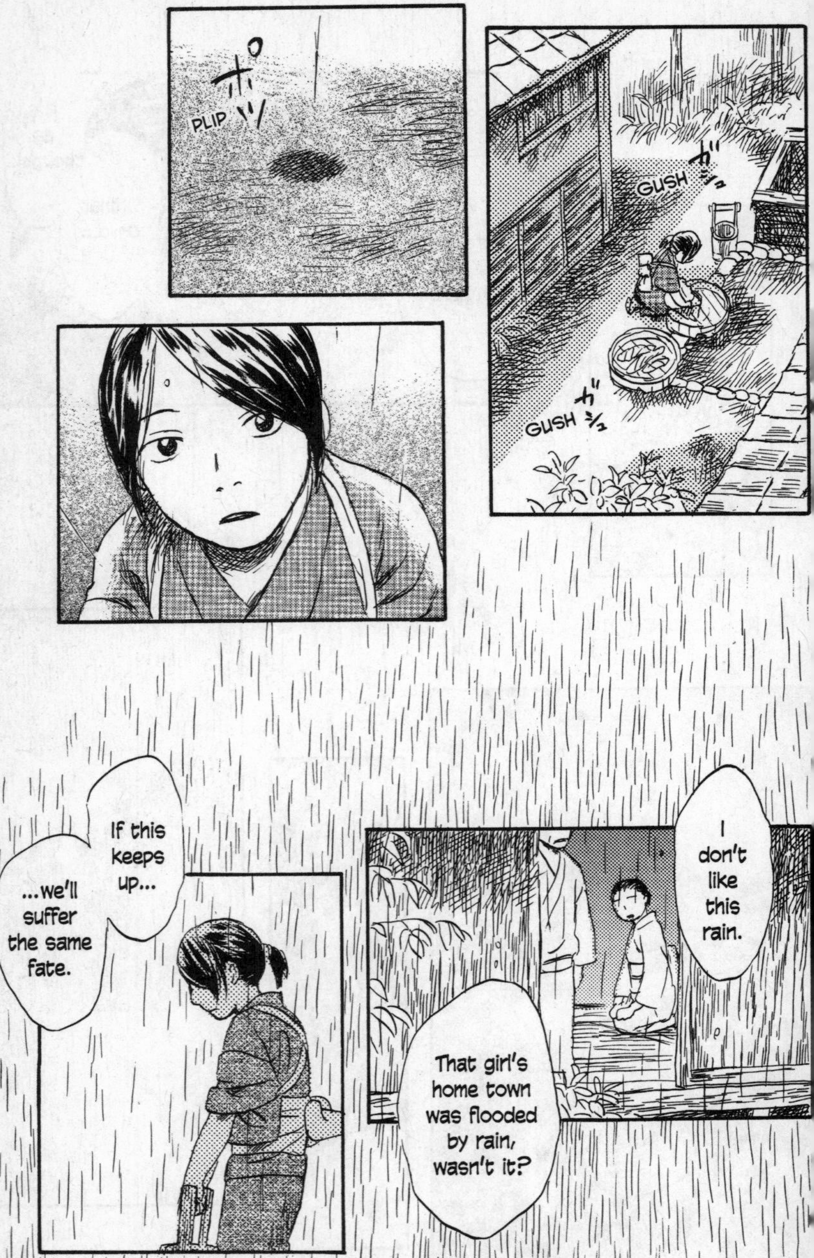
GUSH
GUSH
PLIP
I don't like this rain.
That girl's home town was flooded by rain, wasn't it?
If this keeps up...
...we'll suffer the same fate.

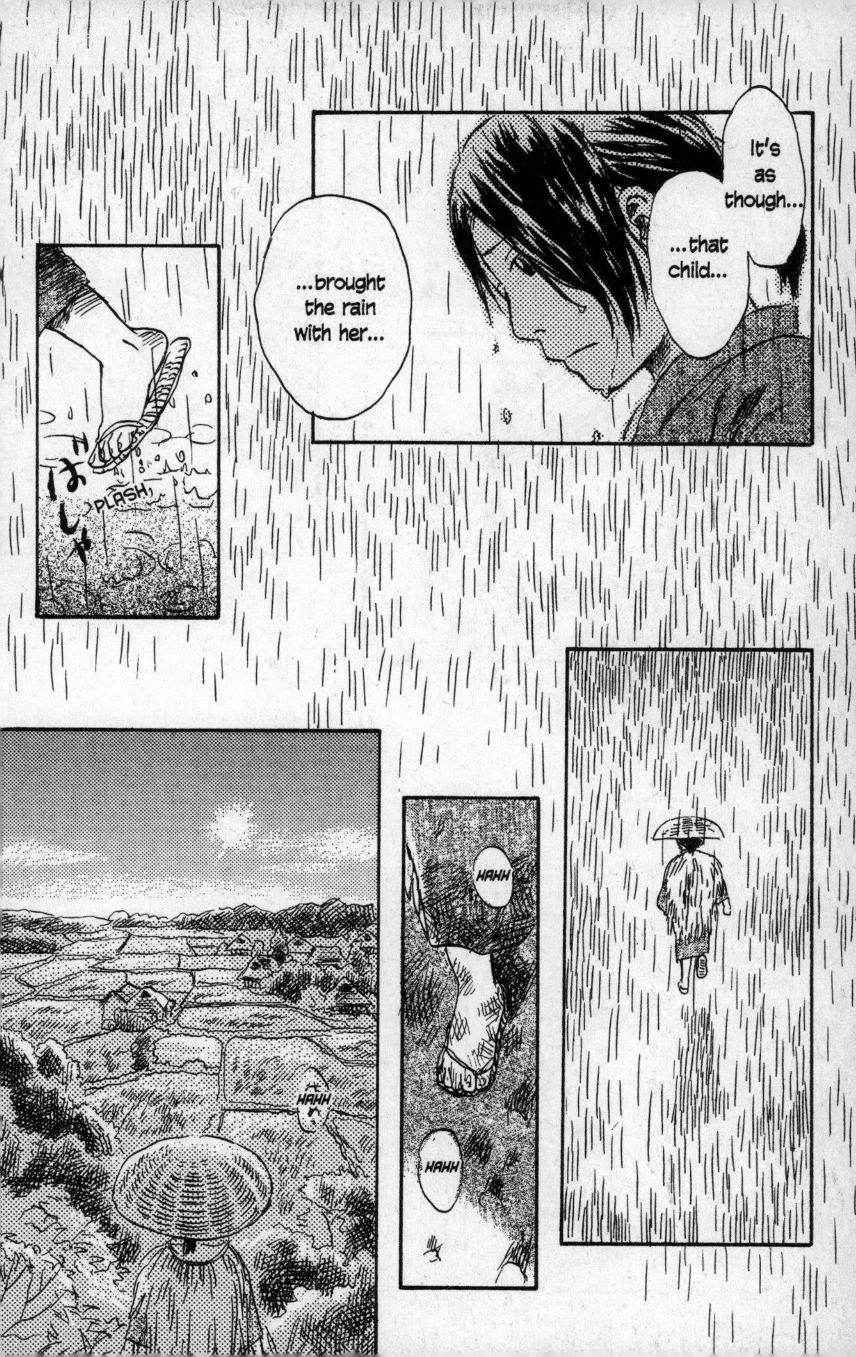
It's as though...
...that child...
...brought the rain with her...
PLASH
HAHH
HAHH
HAHH

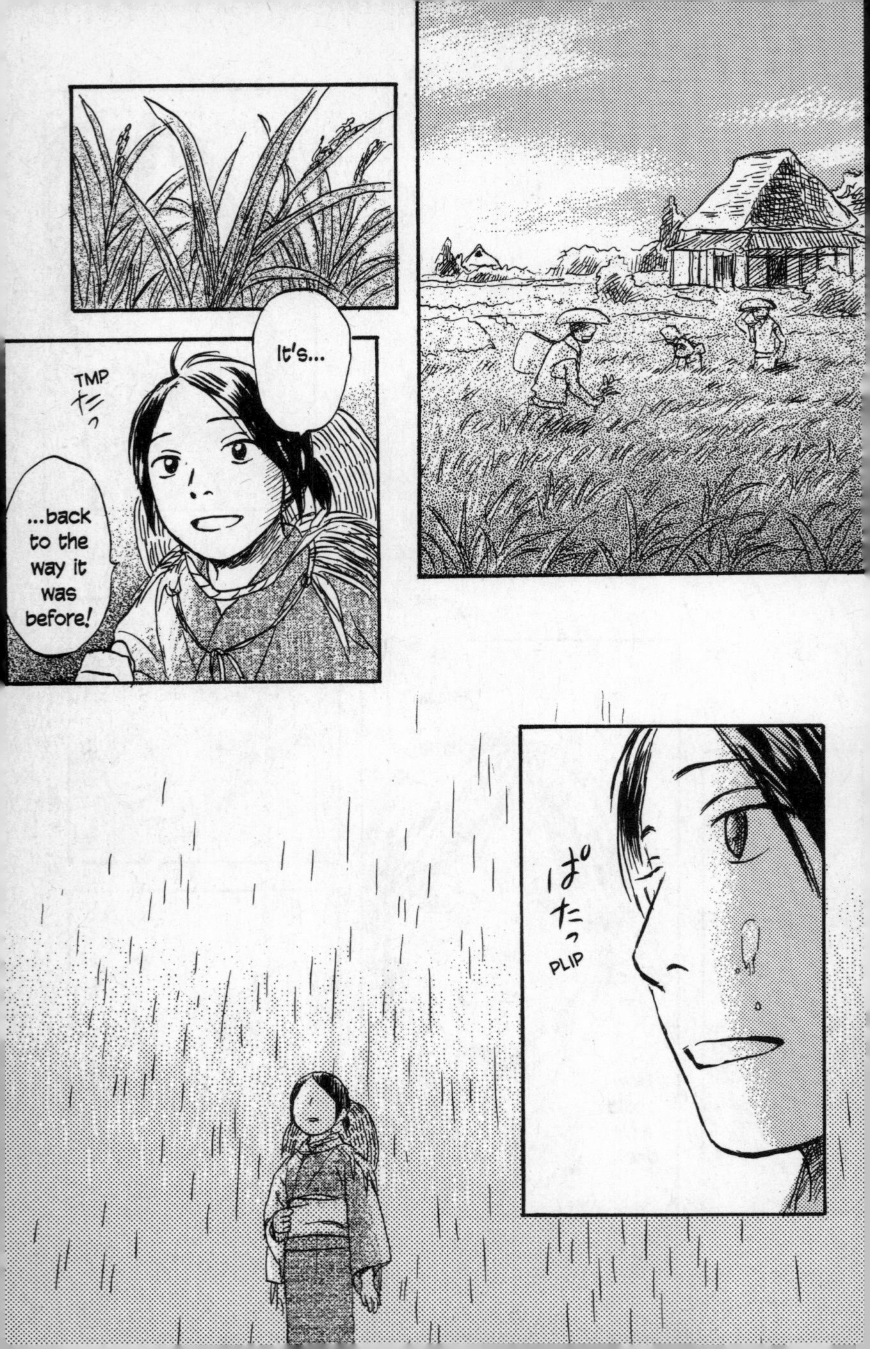
TMP
たっ
It's...
...back to the way it was before!
ぱたっ
PLIP

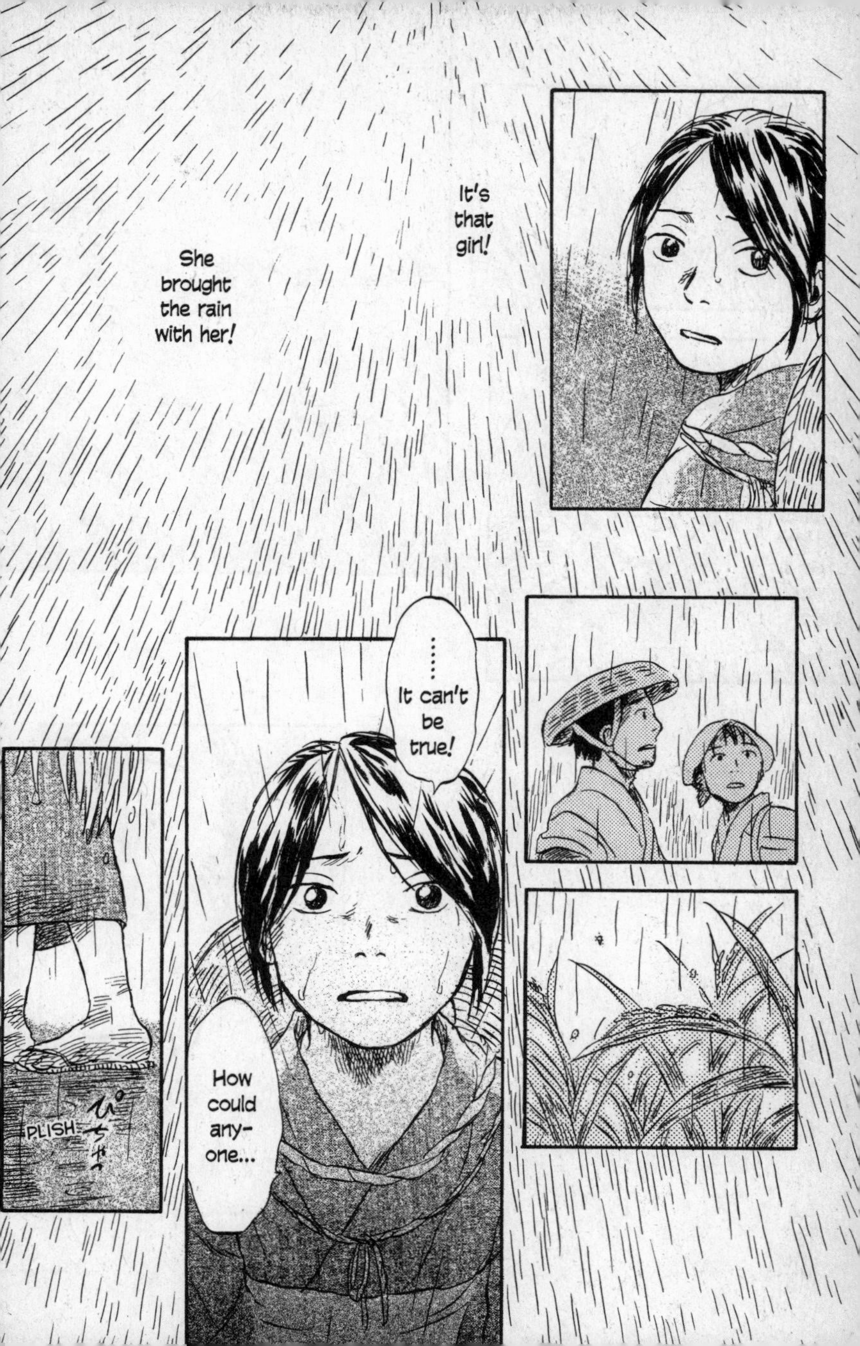
It's that girl!
She brought the rain with her!
...... It can't be true!
How could any-one...
PLISH

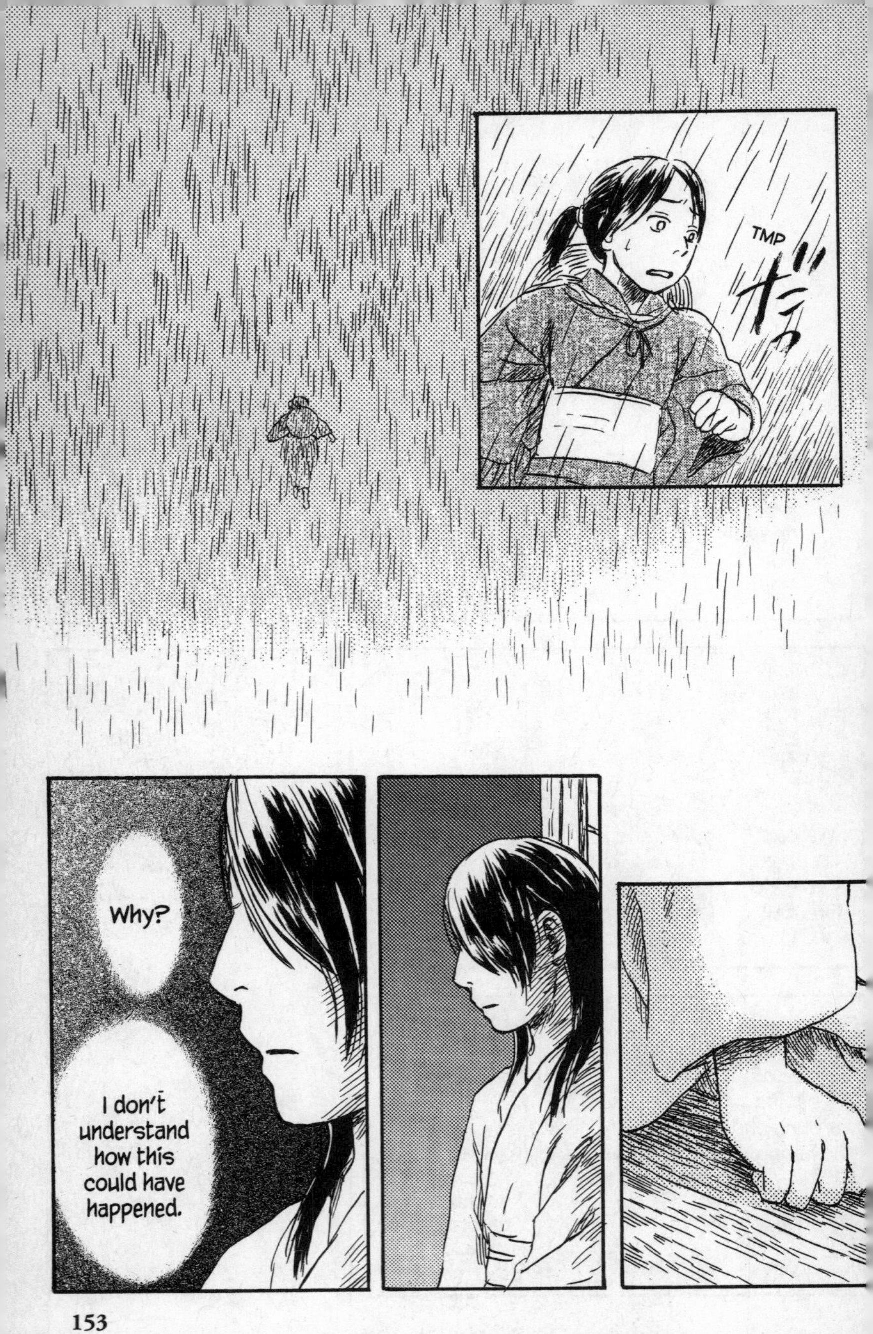
TMP
Why?
I don't understand how this could have happened.

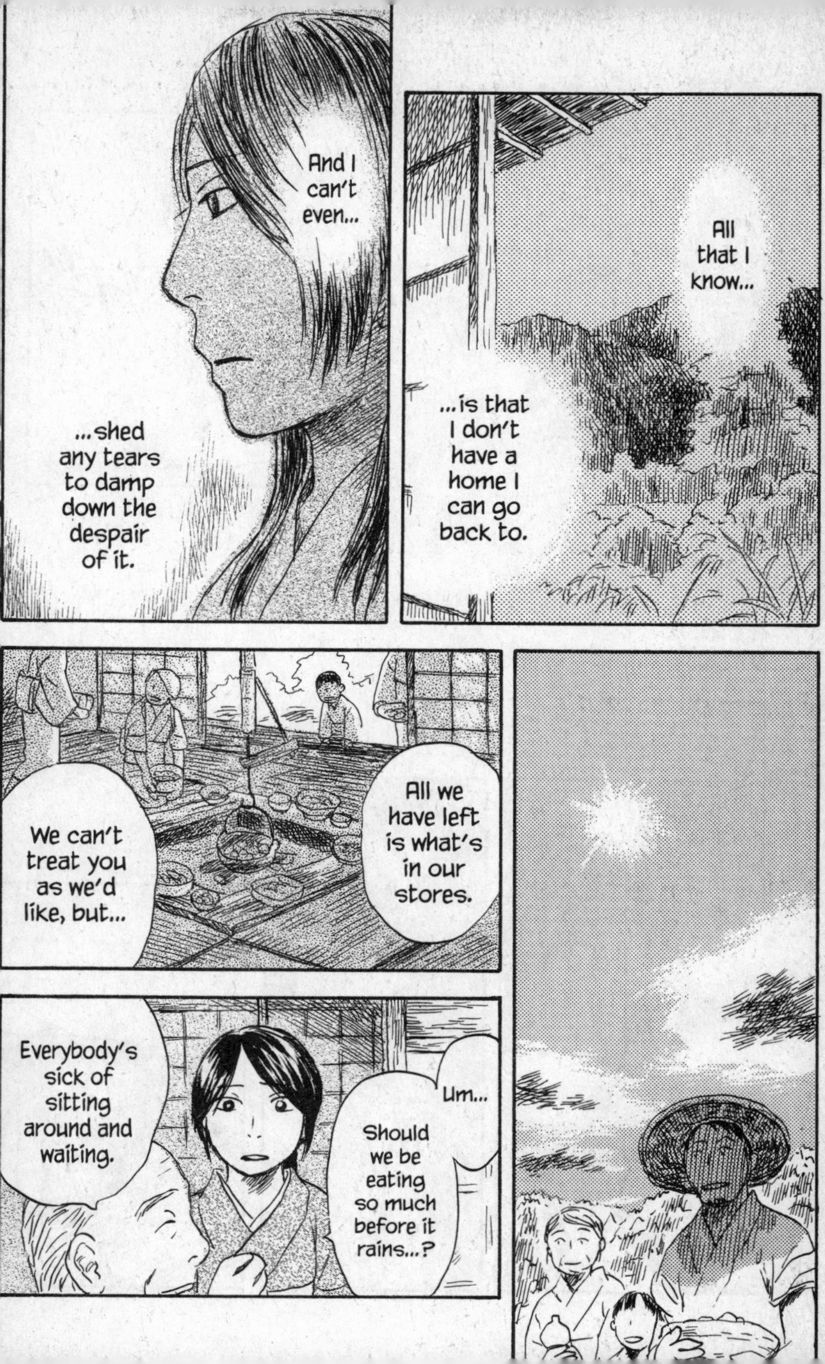
All that I know...
...is that I don't have a home I can go back to.
And I can't even...
...shed any tears to damp down the despair of it.
All we have left is what's in our stores.
We can't treat you as we'd like, but...
Um...
Should we be eating so much before it rains...?
Everybody's sick of sitting around and waiting.

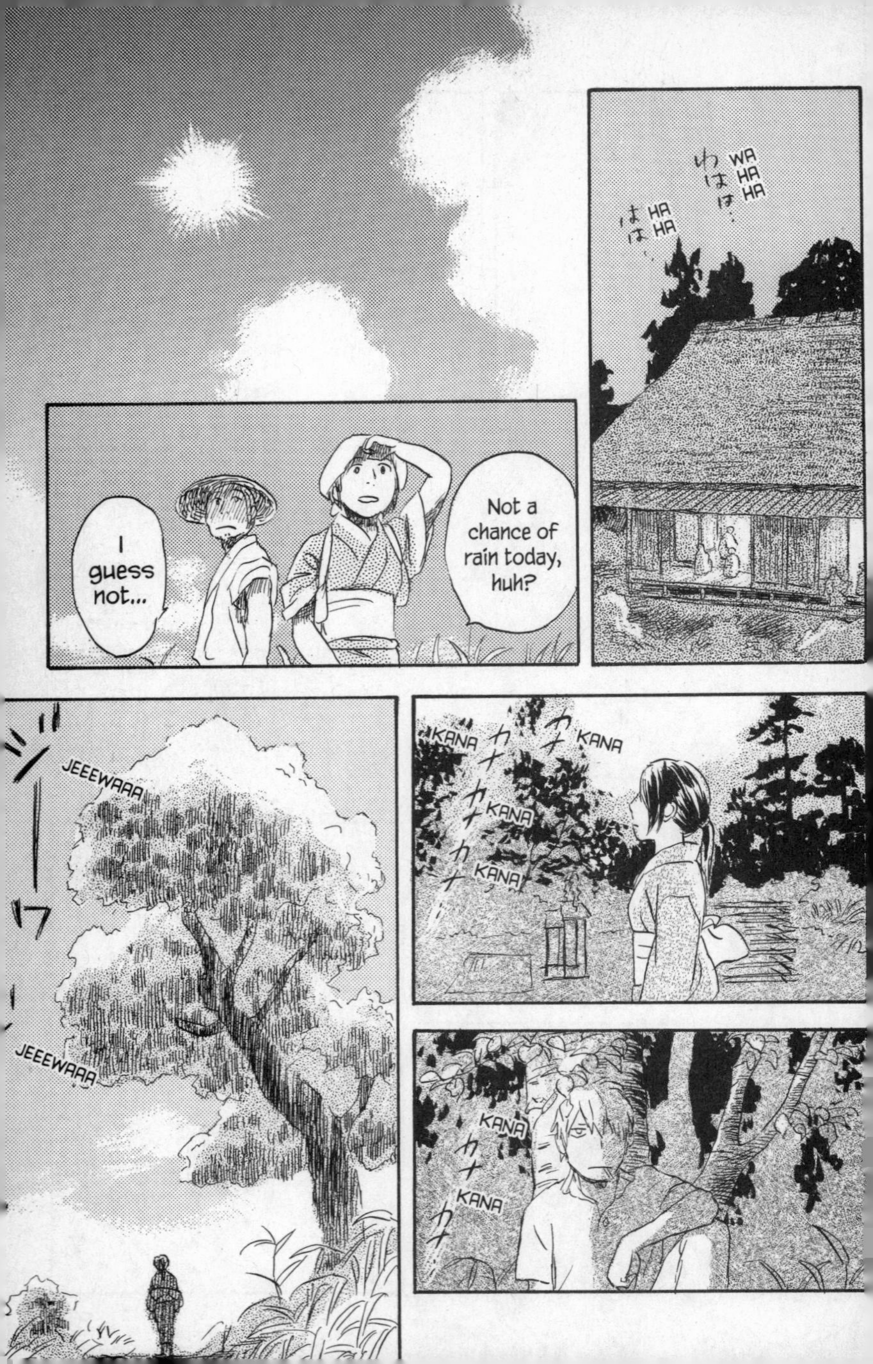
わはは
WA HA HA
はは
HA HA
Not a chance of rain today, huh?
I guess not...
KANA
KANA
KANA
KANA
KANA
KANA
JEEEWAAA
JEEEWAAA

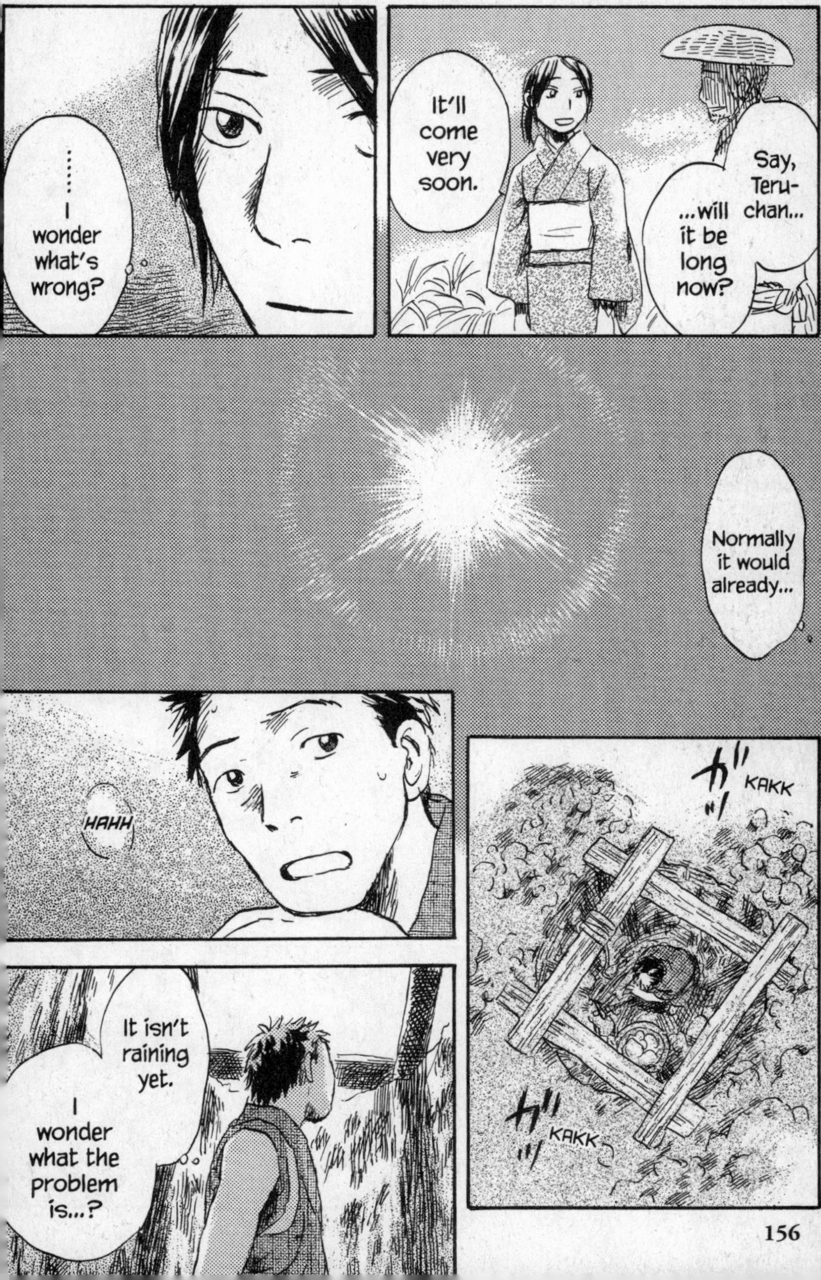

Say, Teru-chan...
...will it be long now?
It'll come very soon.
...... I wonder what's wrong?
Normally it would already...
KAKK
KAKK
HAHH
It isn't raining yet.
I wonder what the problem is...?

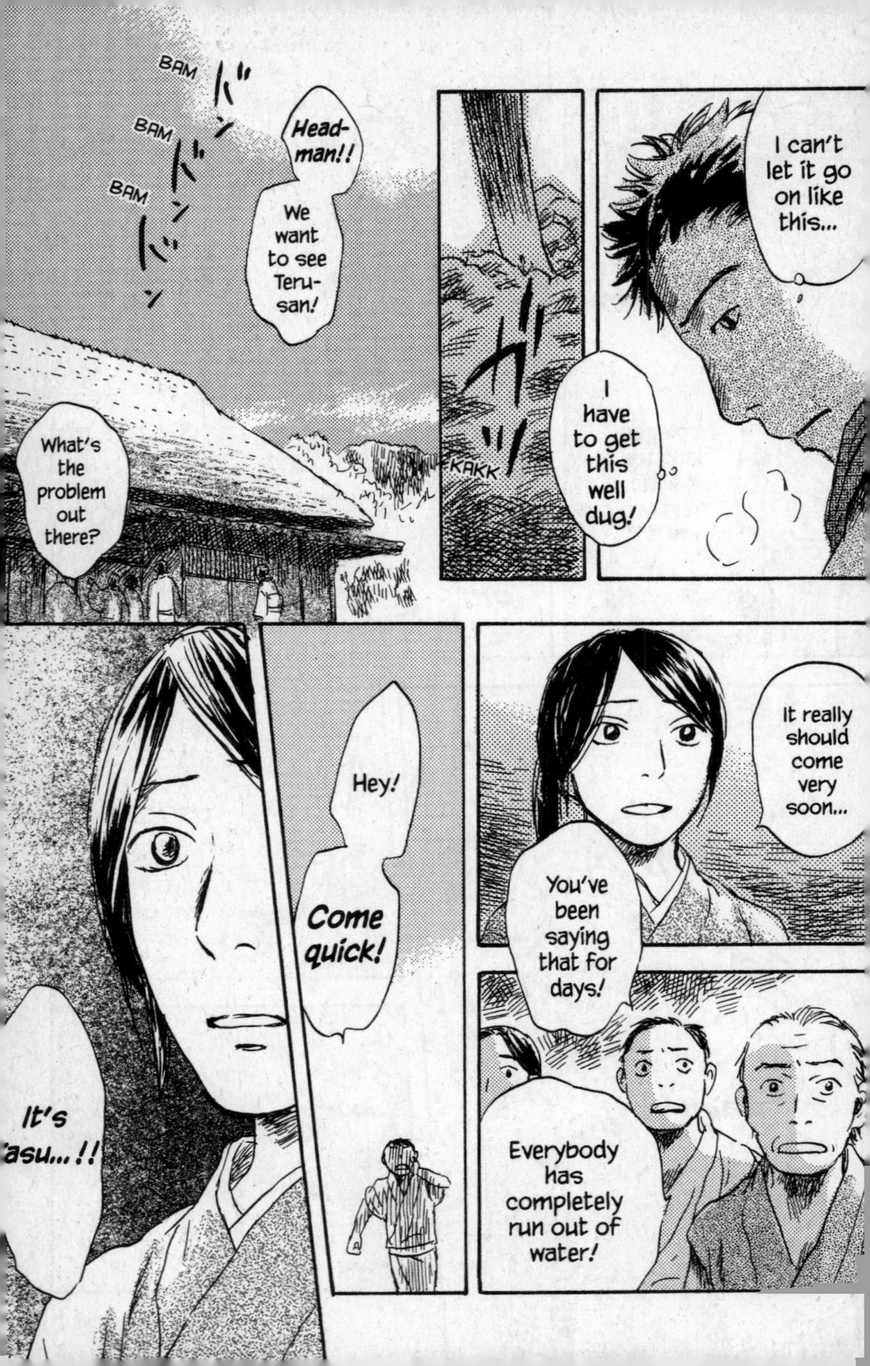
I can't let it go on like this...
I have to get this well dug!
KAKK
BAM
BAM
BAM
Head-man!!
We want to see Teru-san!
What's the problem out there?
It really should come very soon...
You've been saying that for days!
Everybody has completely run out of water!
Hey!
Come quick!
It's
asu...!!

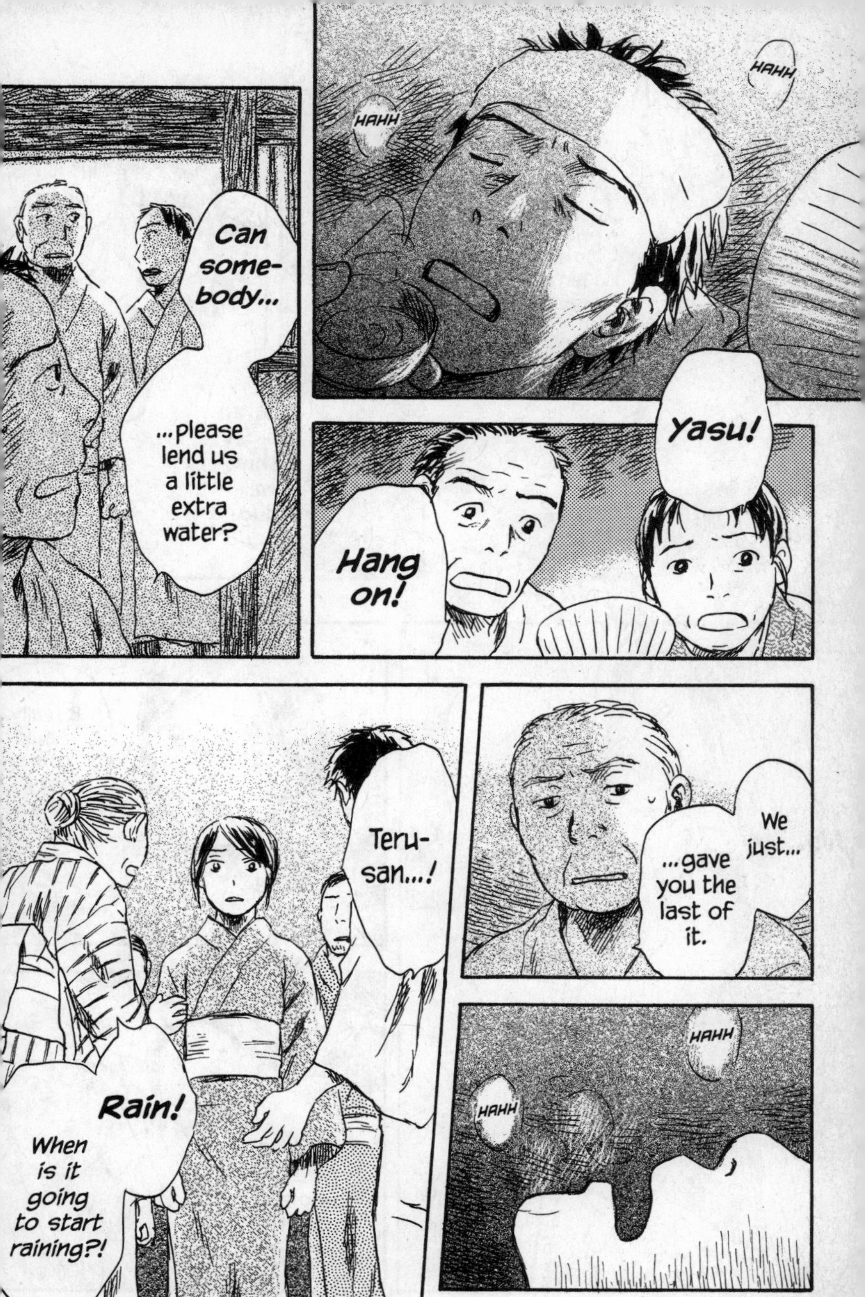
HAHH
HAHH
Yasu!
Hang on!
Can somebody...
...please lend us a little extra water?
We just...
...gave you the last of it.
HAHH
HAHH
Teru-san...!
Rain!
When is it going to start raining?!

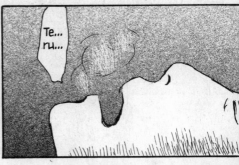

Te...
ru...

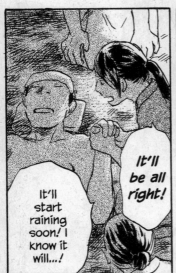

It'll
be all
right!

It'll
start
raining
soon! I
know it
will...!

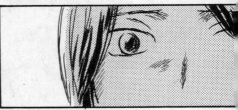

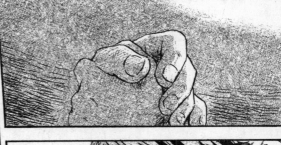

No...!!

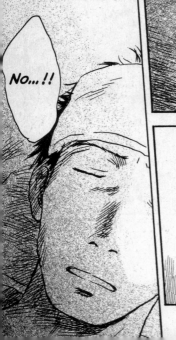

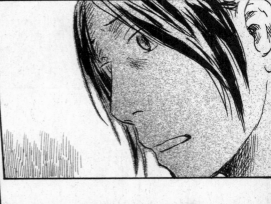

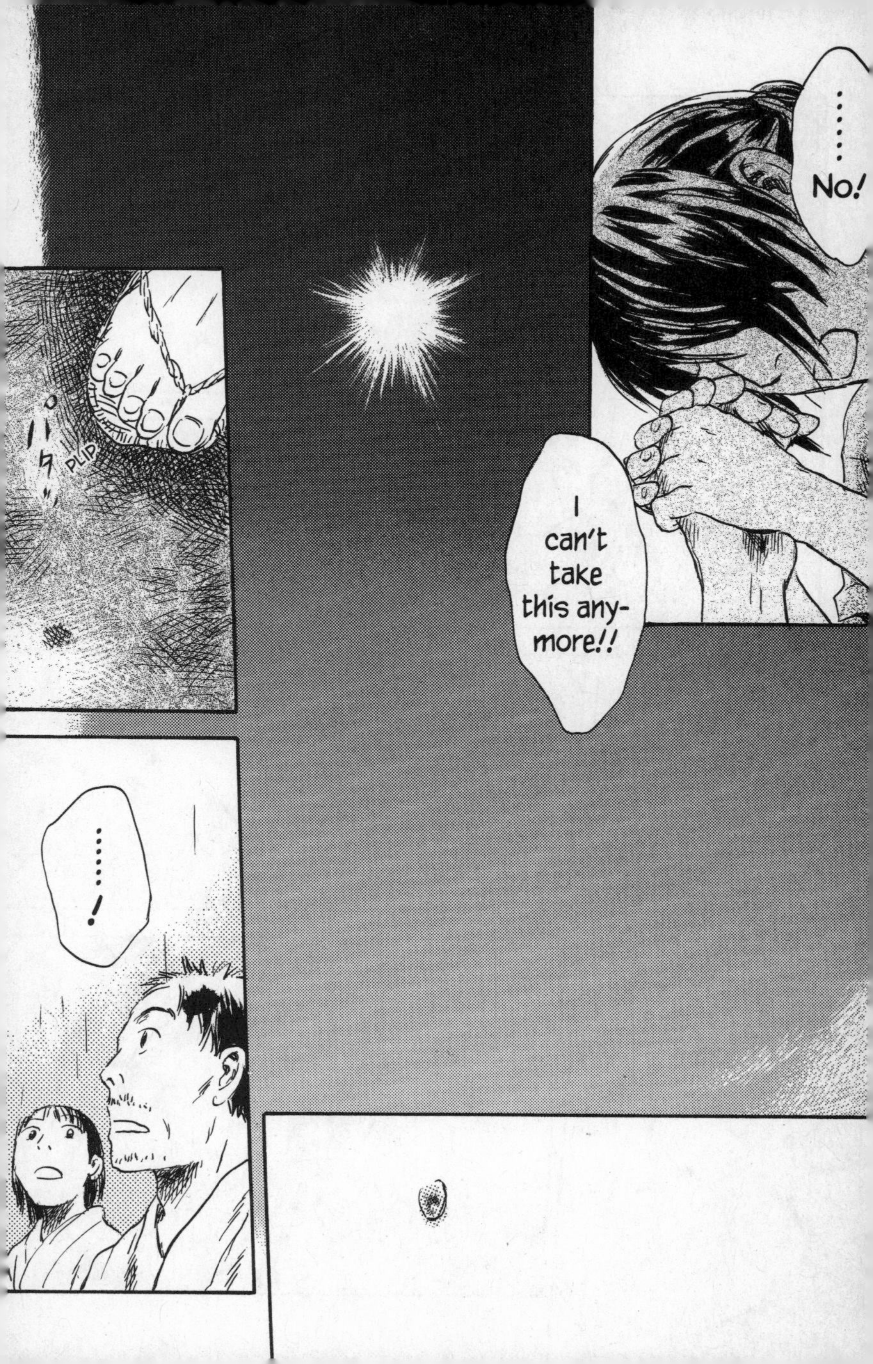
......No!
I can't take this anymore!!
PLIP
......!

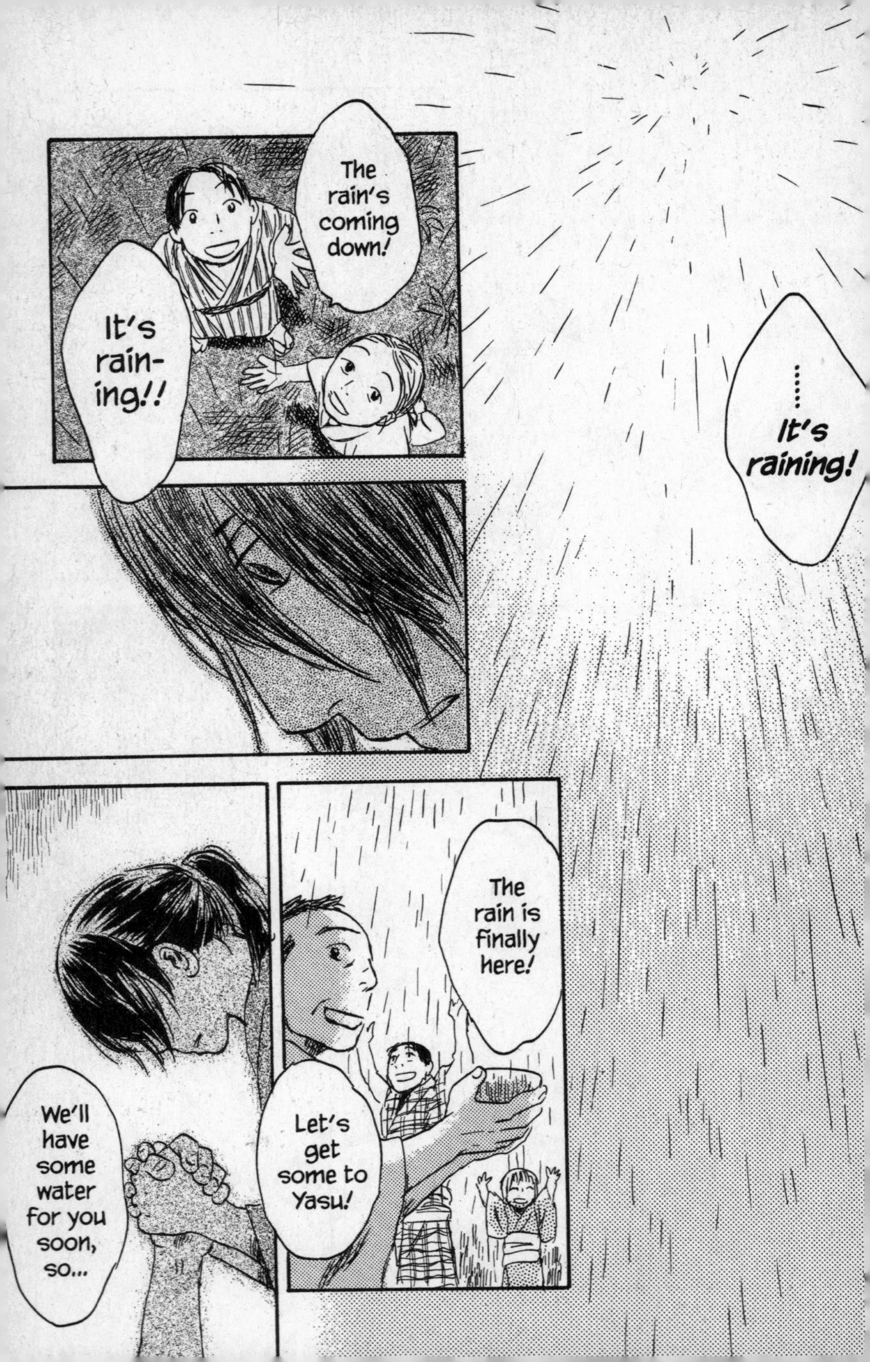
……It's raining!
The rain's coming down!
It's raining!!
The rain is finally here!
Let's get some to Yasu!
We'll have some water for you soon, so...

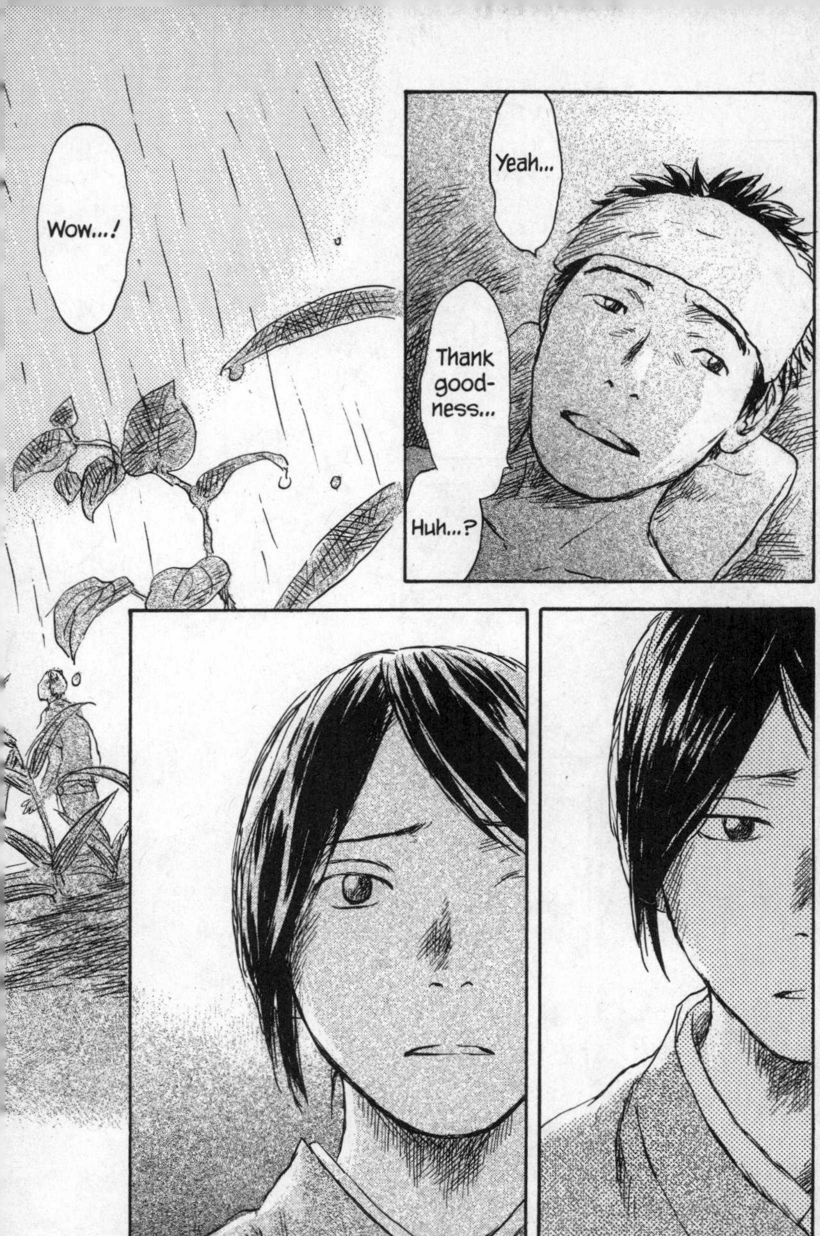
Yeah...
Thank good-ness...
Huh...?
Wow...!

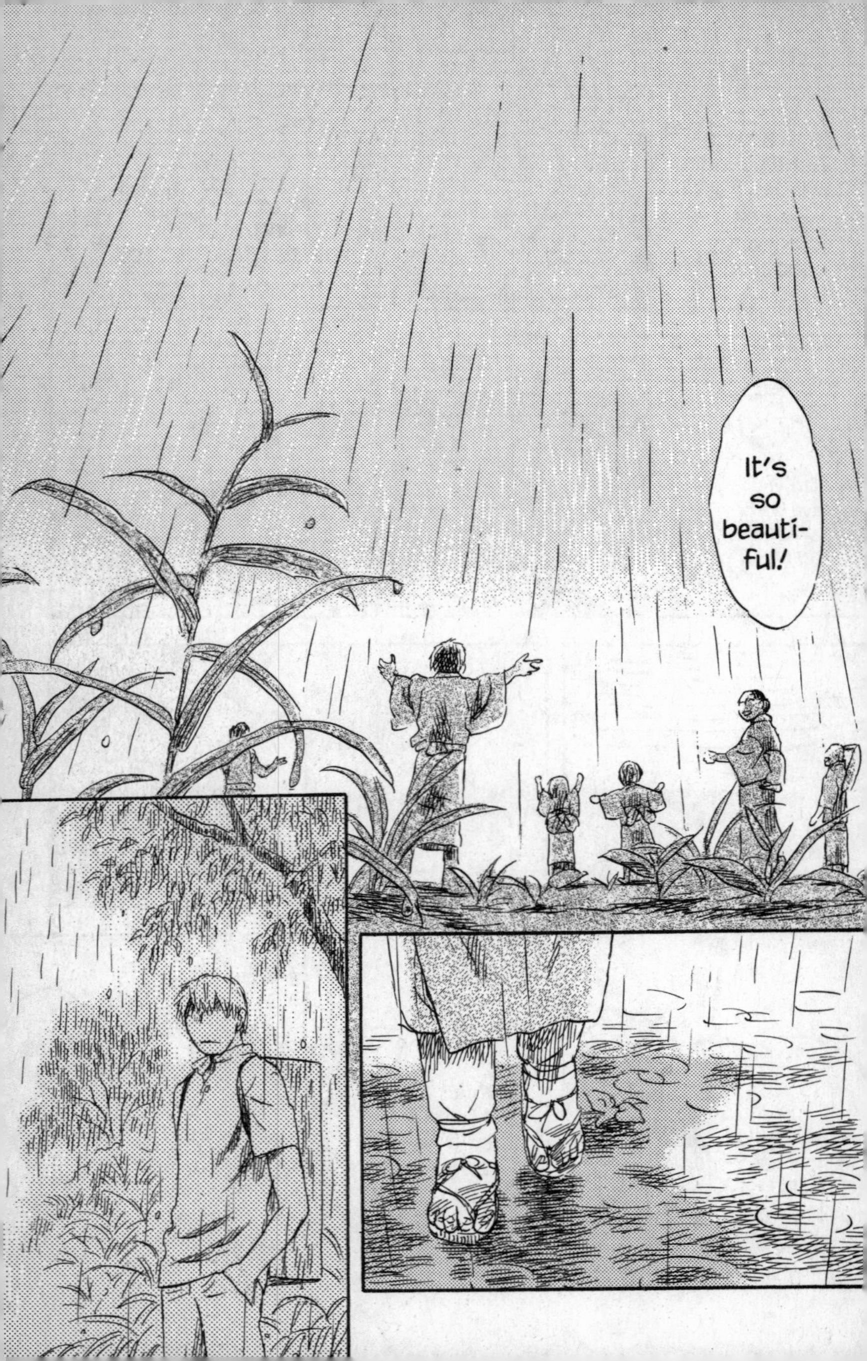
It's so beautiful!

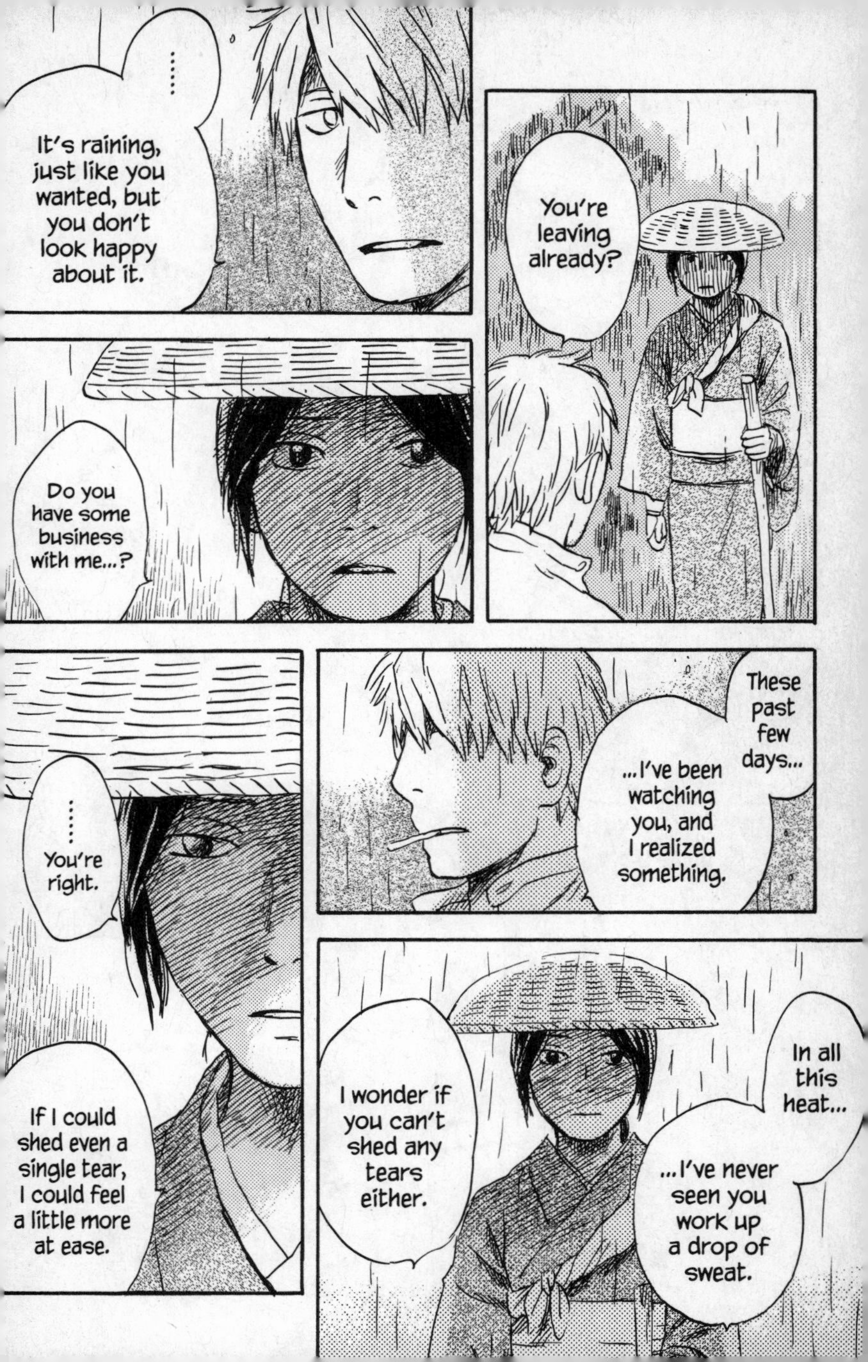
You're leaving already?
......
It's raining, just like you wanted, but you don't look happy about it.
Do you have some business with me...?
These past few days...
...I've been watching you, and I realized something.
In all this heat...
...I've never seen you work up a drop of sweat.
I wonder if you can't shed any tears either.
...... You're right.
If I could shed even a single tear, I could feel a little more at ease.

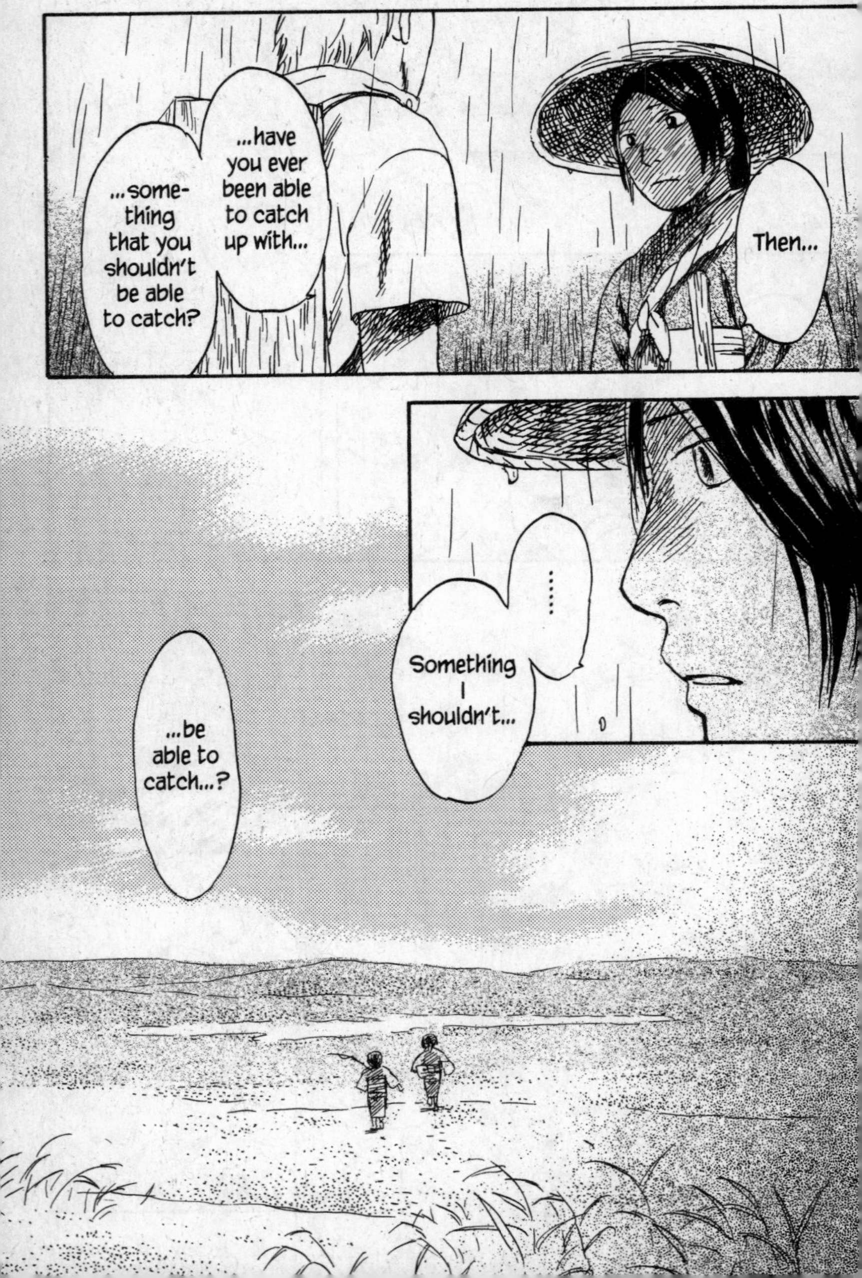
Then...
...have you ever been able to catch up with...
...some-thing that you shouldn't be able to catch?
......
Something I shouldn't...
...be able to catch...?

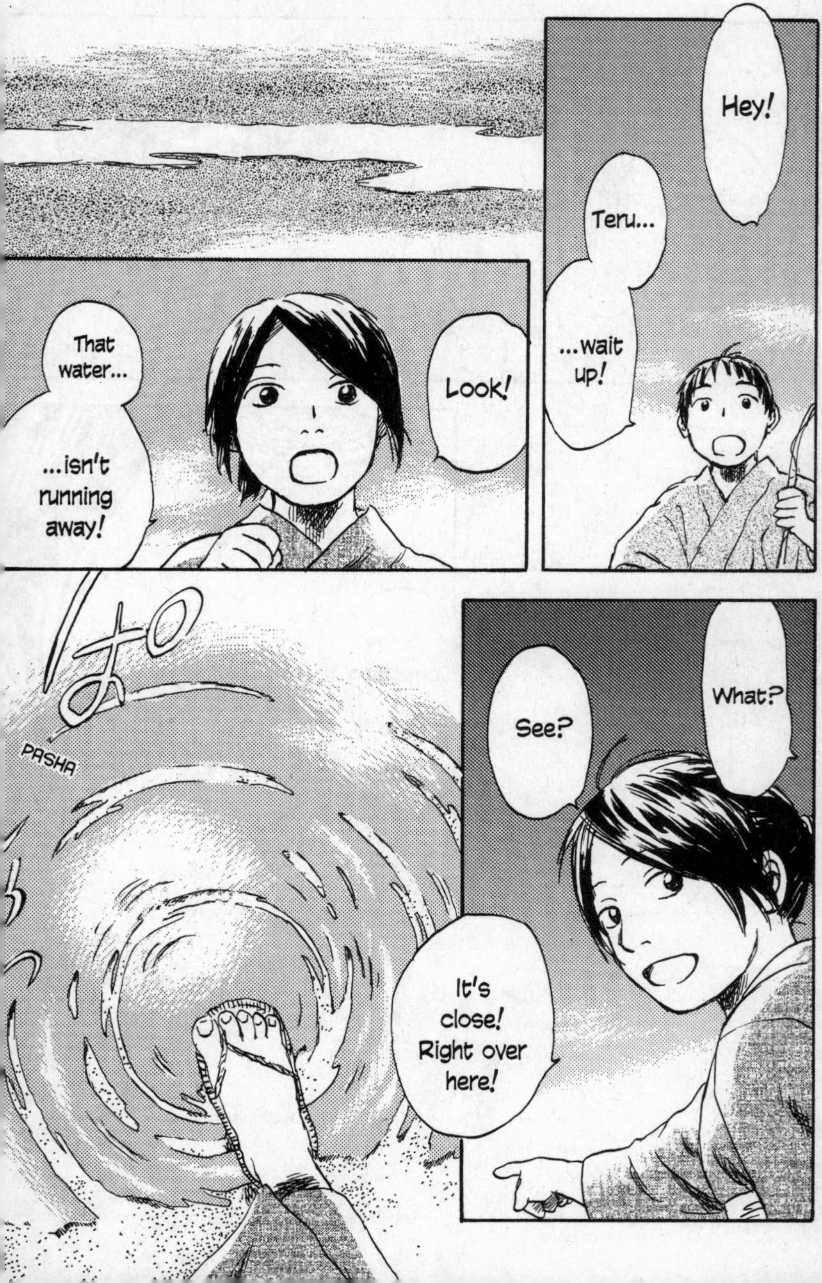
Hey!
Teru...
...wait up!
Look!
That water...
...isn't running away!
What?
See?
It's close! Right over here!
PASHA

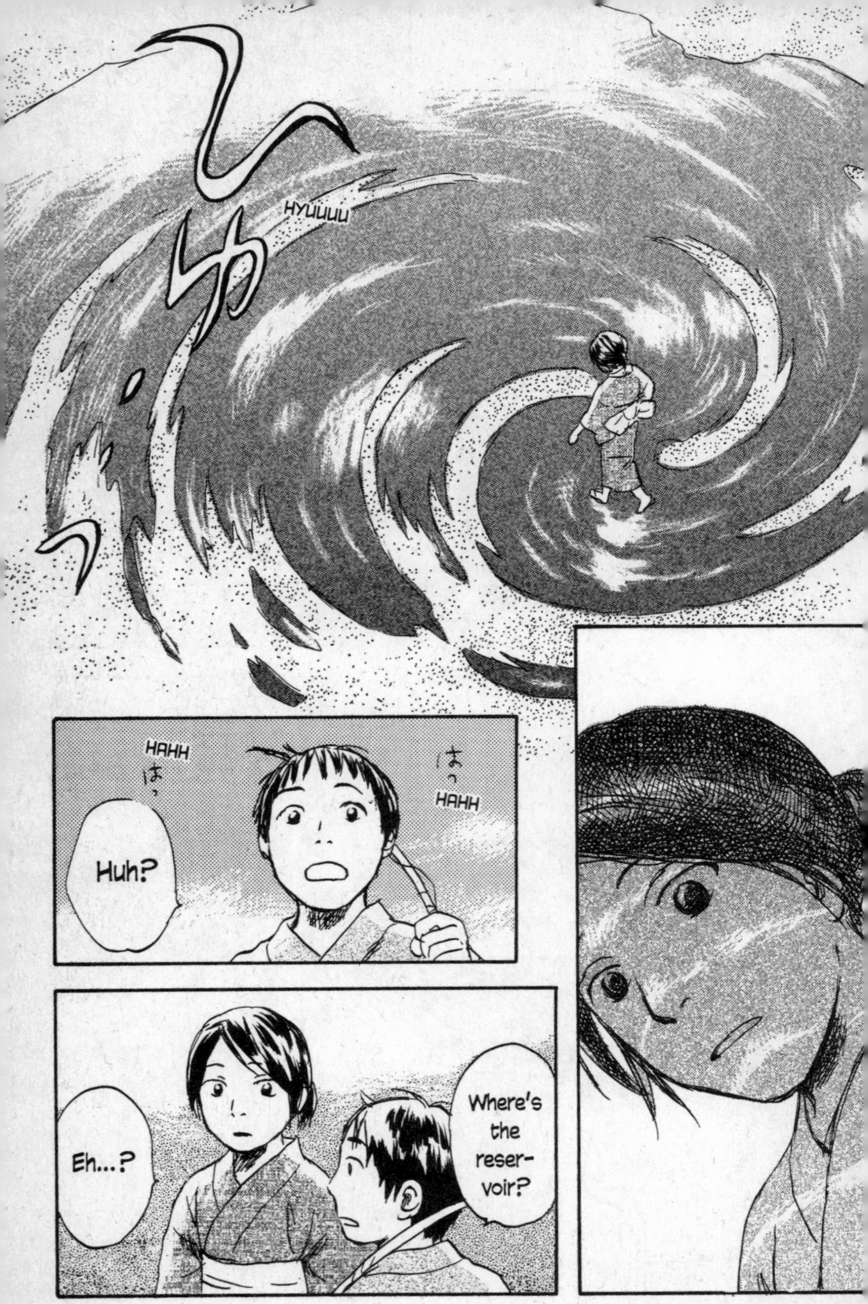
ひゅっ
HYUUUU
はっ
HAHH
HAHH
は、
Huh?
Where's the reser-voir?
Eh...?

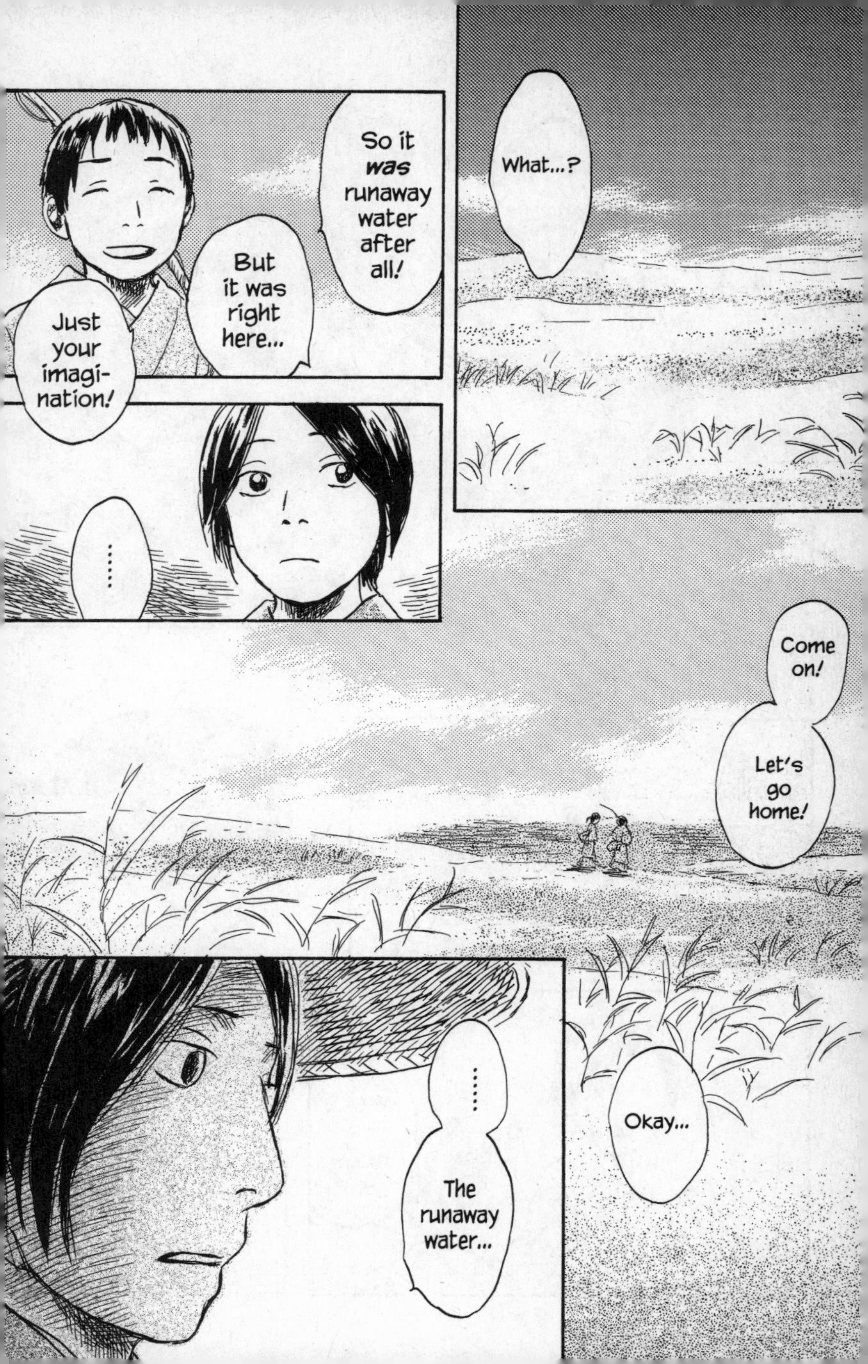
What...?
So it *was* runaway water after all!
But it was right here...
Just your imagination!
......
Come on!
Let's go home!
Okay...
......
The runaway water...

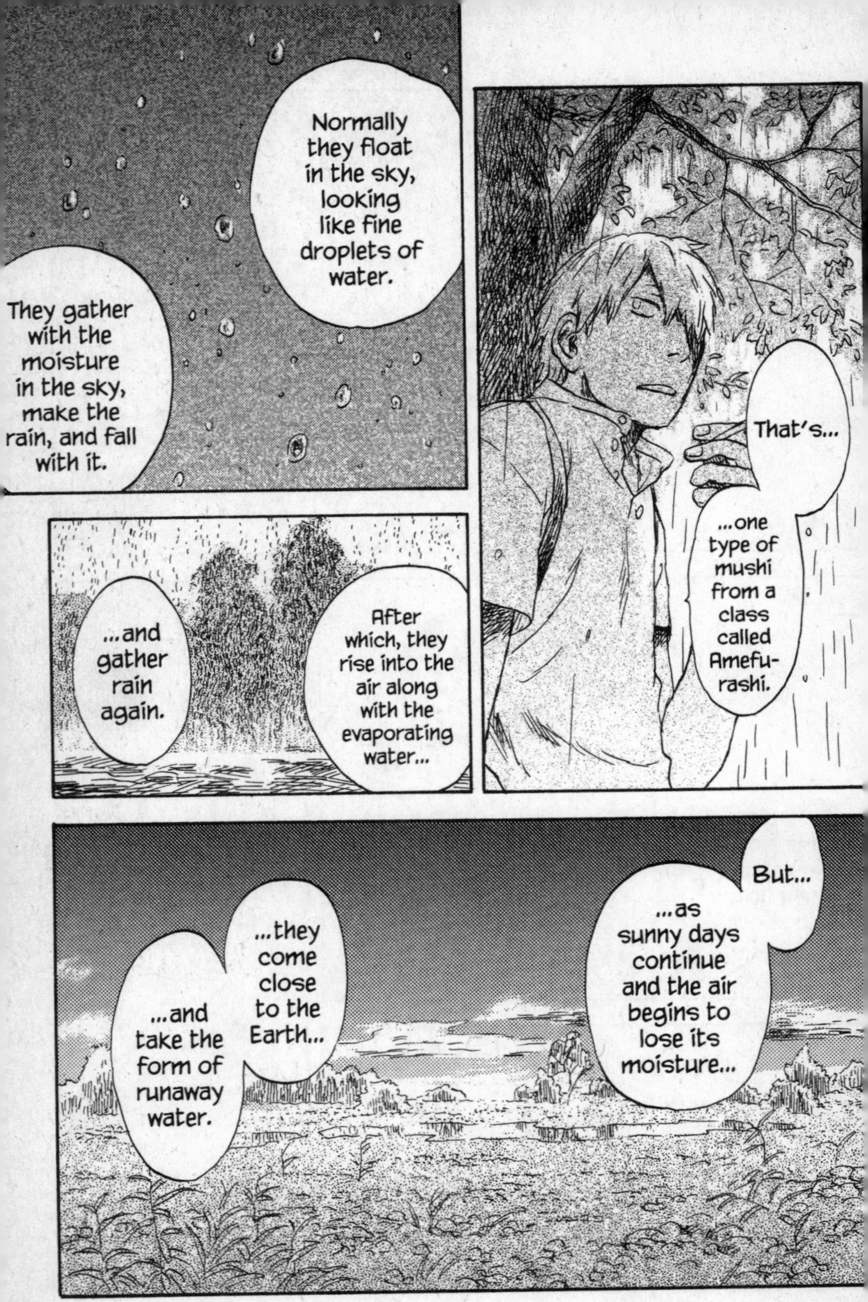
That's...
...one type of mushi from a class called Amefu-rashi.
Normally they float in the sky, looking like fine droplets of water.
They gather with the moisture in the sky, make the rain, and fall with it.
After which, they rise into the air along with the evaporating water...
...and gather rain again.
But...
...as sunny days continue and the air begins to lose its moisture...
...they come close to the Earth...
...and take the form of runaway water.

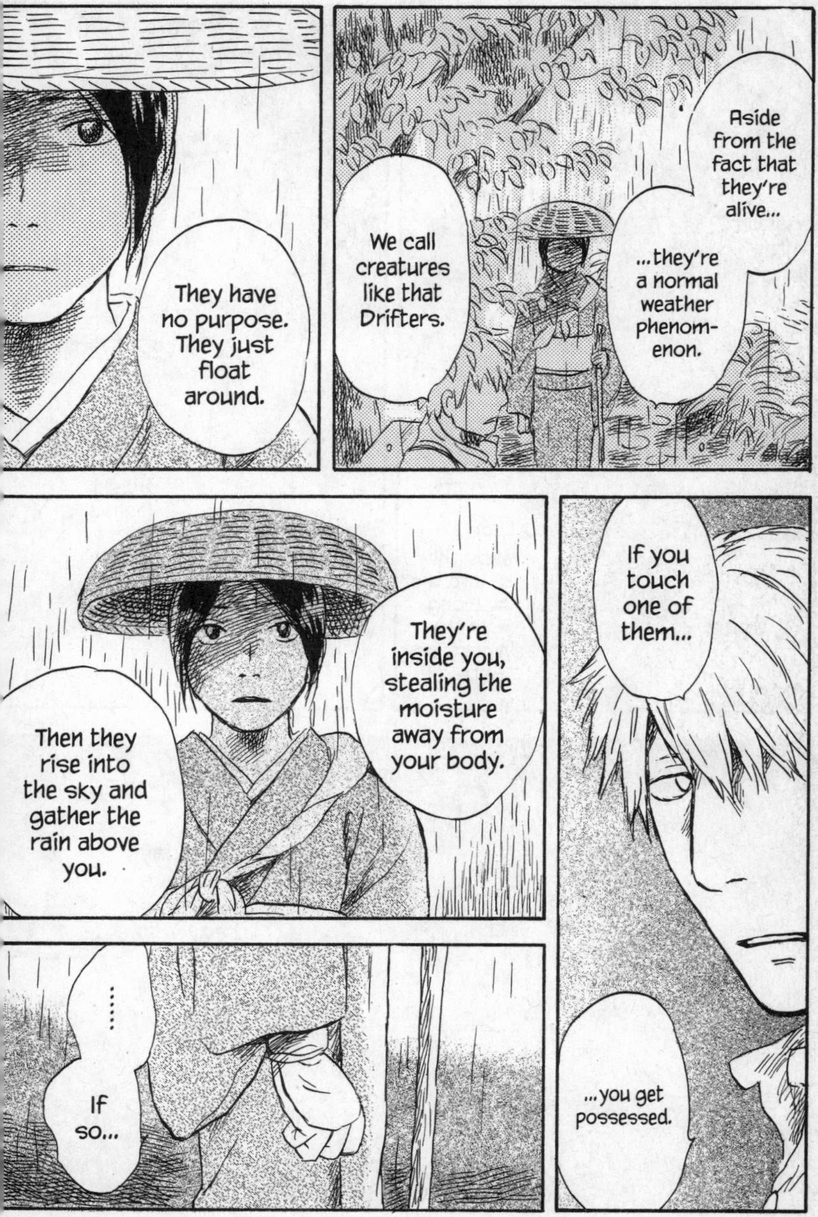
Aside from the fact that they're alive...
...they're a normal weather phenom-enon.
We call creatures like that Drifters.
They have no purpose. They just float around.
If you touch one of them...
...you get possessed.
They're inside you, stealing the moisture away from your body.
Then they rise into the sky and gather the rain above you.
......
If so...

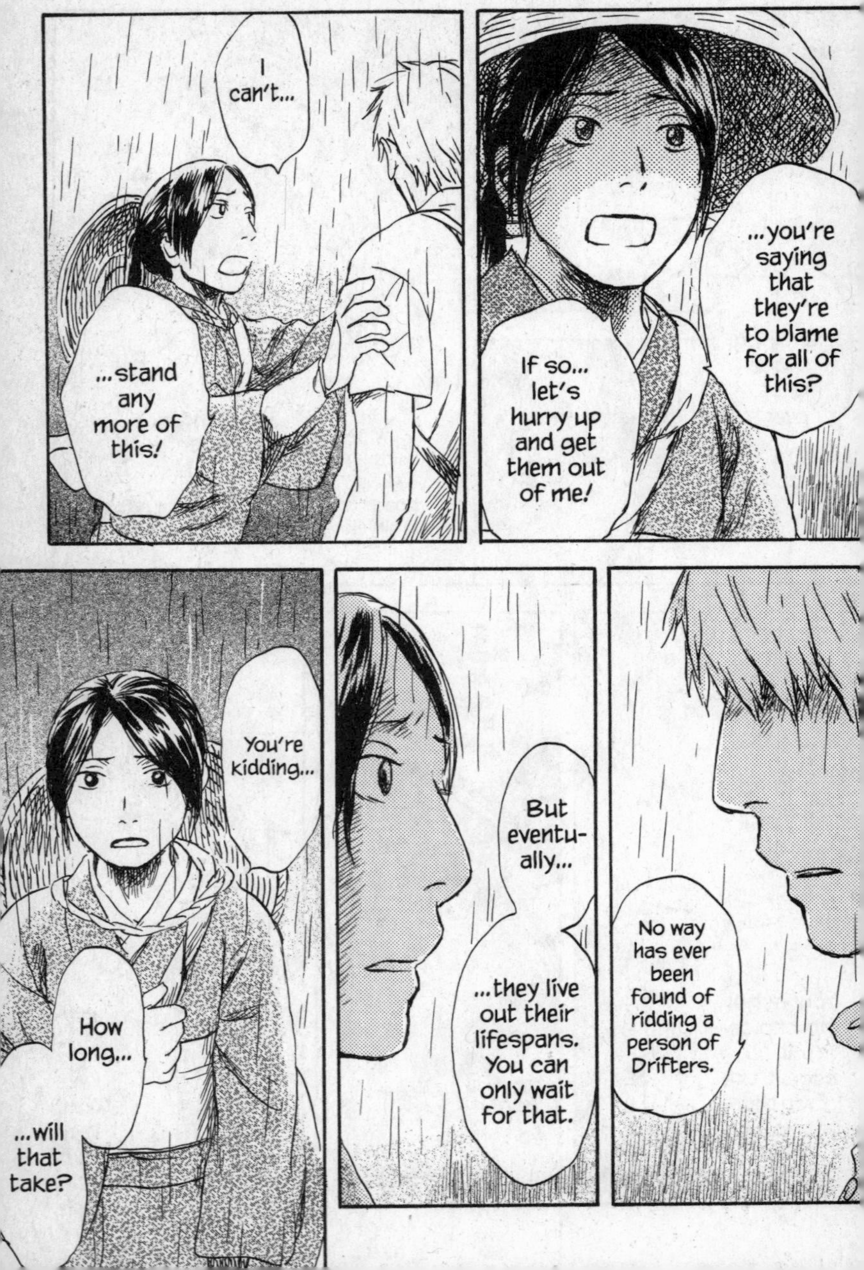
...you're saying that they're to blame for all of this?
If so... let's hurry up and get them out of me!
I can't...
...stand any more of this!
No way has ever been found of ridding a person of Drifters.
But eventu-ally...
...they live out their lifespans. You can only wait for that.
You're kidding...
How long...
...will that take?

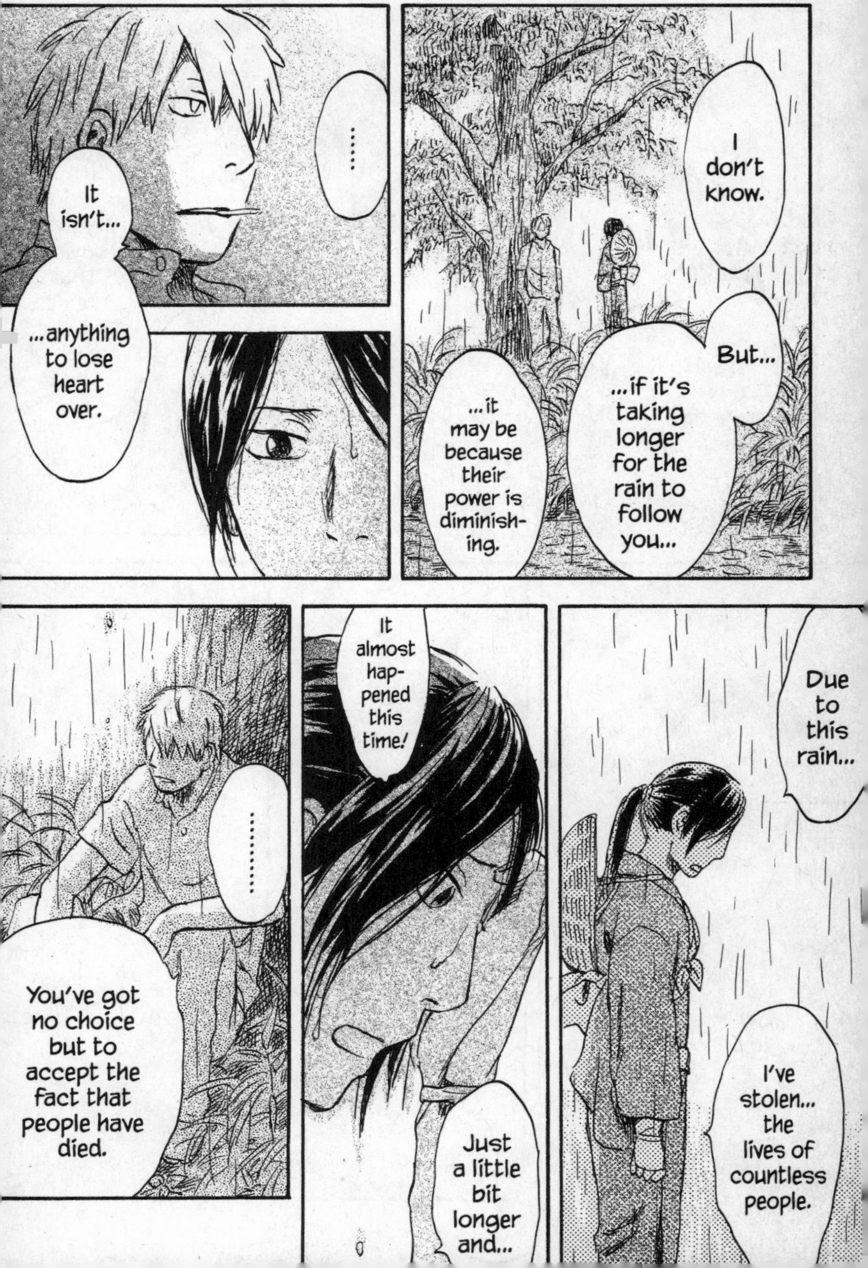
I don't know.
But...
...if it's taking longer for the rain to follow you...
...it may be because their power is diminish-ing.
......
It isn't...
...anything to lose heart over.
Due to this rain...
I've stolen... the lives of countless people.
It almost hap-pened this time!
Just a little bit longer and...
....
You've got no choice but to accept the fact that people have died.

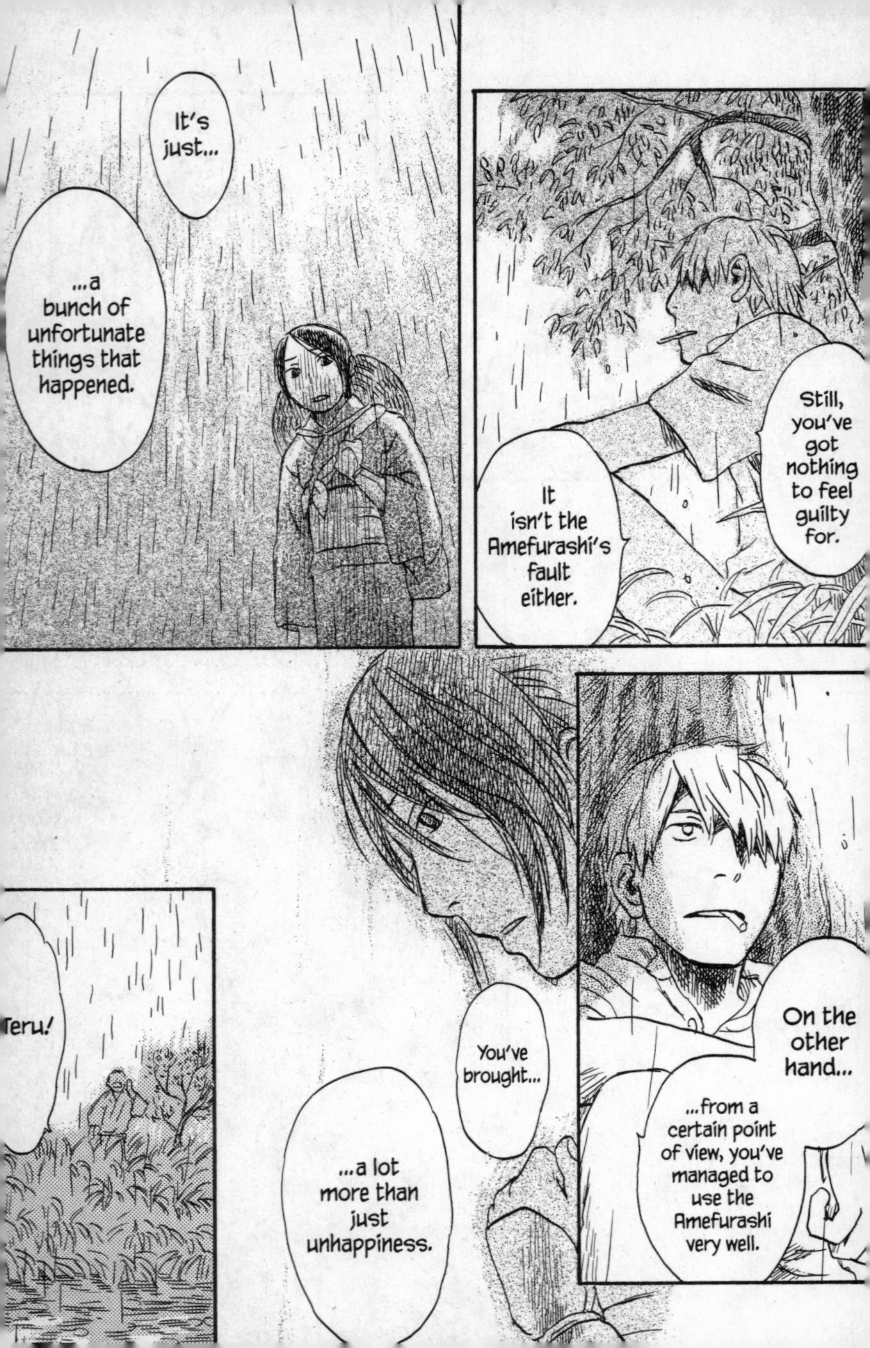
Still, you've got nothing to feel guilty for.
It isn't the Amefurashi's fault either.
It's just...
...a bunch of unfortunate things that happened.
On the other hand...
...from a certain point of view, you've managed to use the Amefurashi very well.
You've brought...
...a lot more than just unhappiness.
Teru!

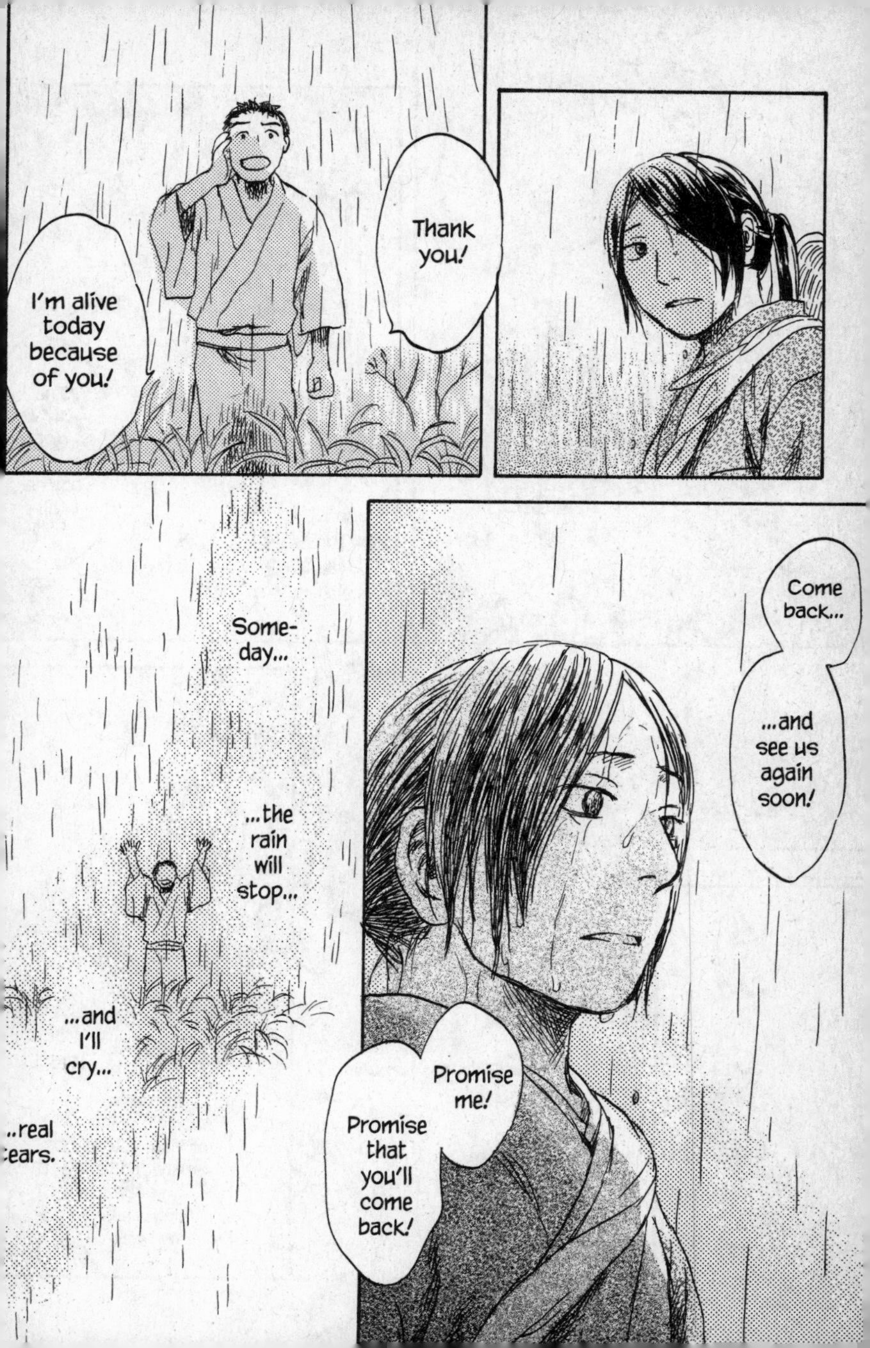

Thank you!
I'm alive today because of you!
Come back...
...and see us again soon!
Promise me!
Promise that you'll come back!
Some-day...
...the rain will stop...
...and I'll cry...
..real ears.

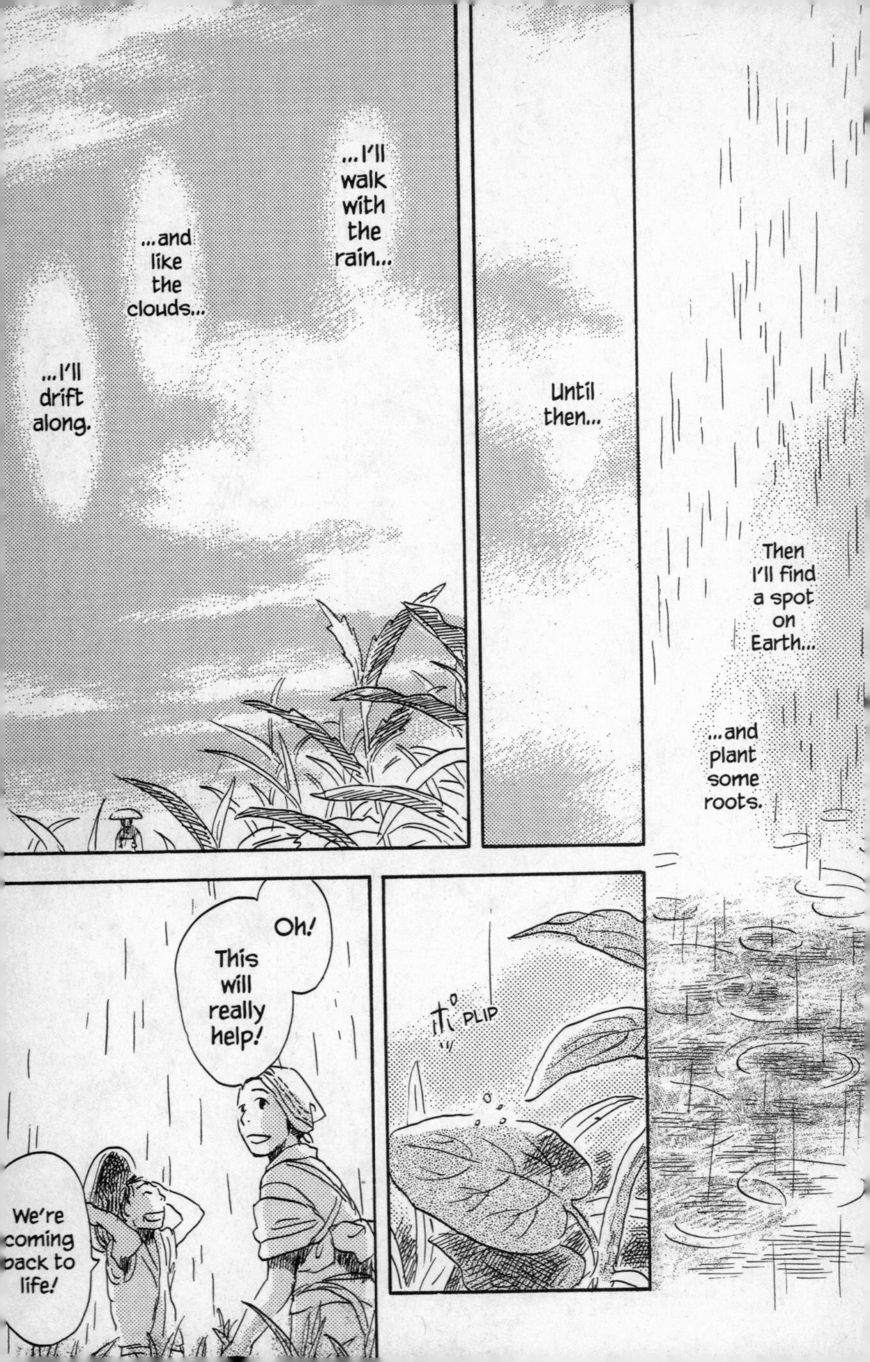
Then I'll find a spot on Earth...
...and plant some roots.
Until then...
...I'll walk with the rain...
...and like the clouds...
...I'll drift along.
PLIP
Oh! This will really help!
We're coming back to life!

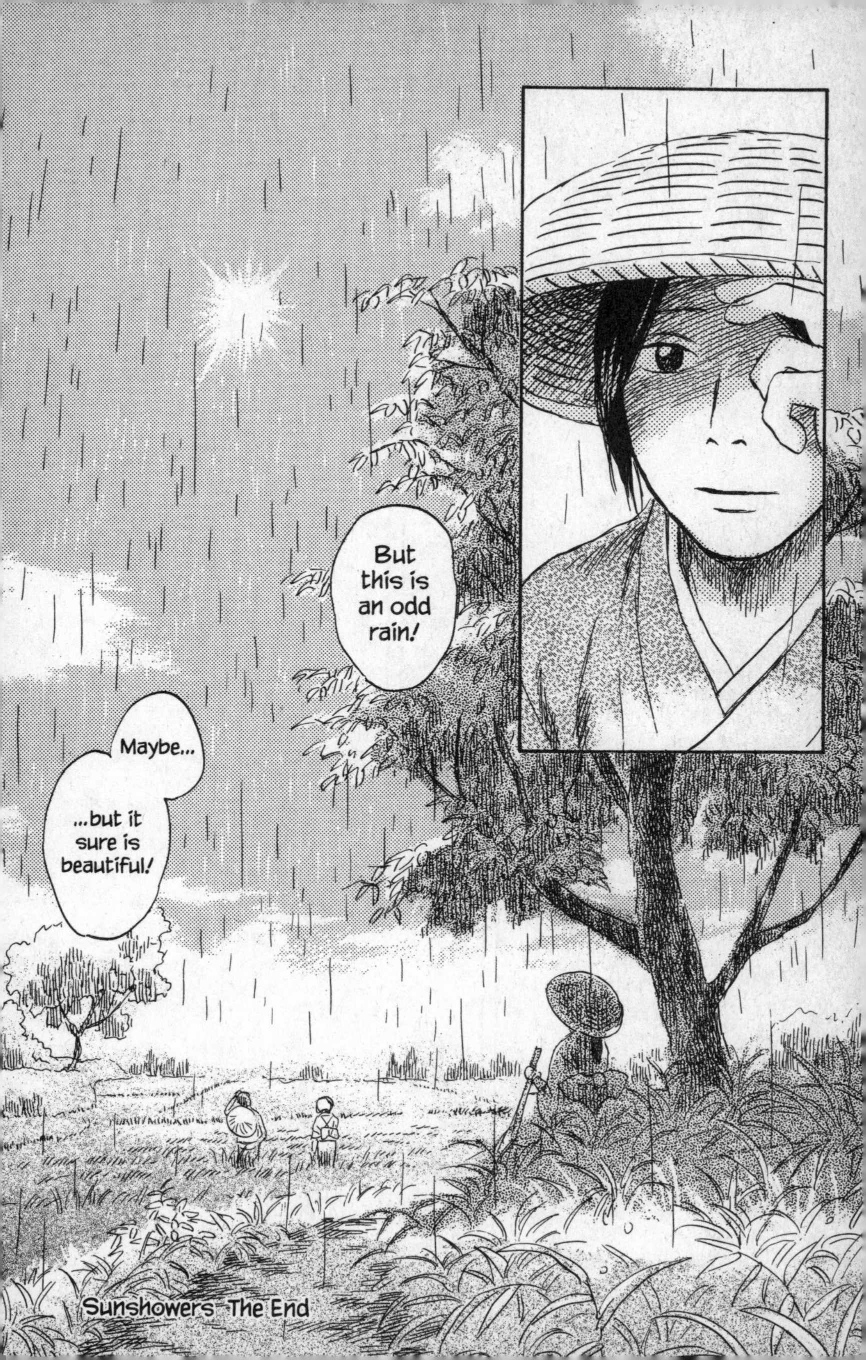
But this is an odd rain!
Maybe...
...but it sure is beautiful!
Sunshowers The End

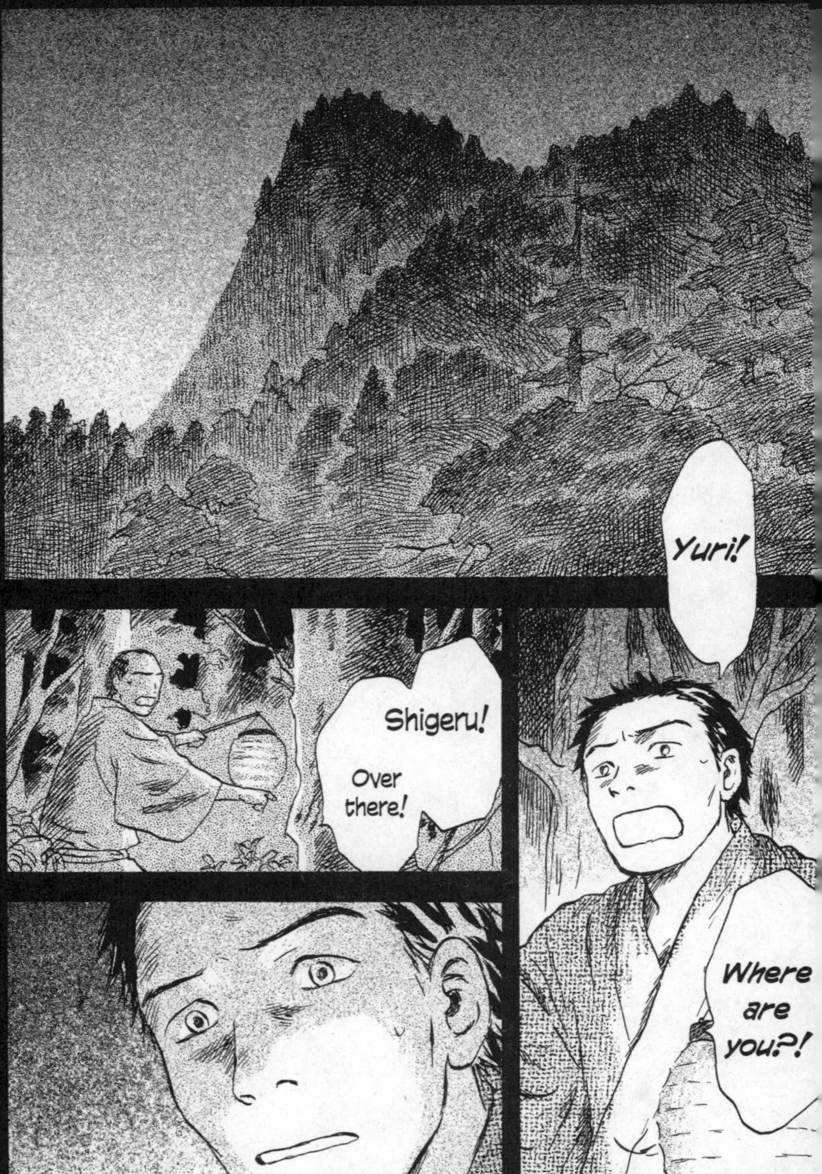
Yuri!
Where are you?!
Shigeru!
Over there!

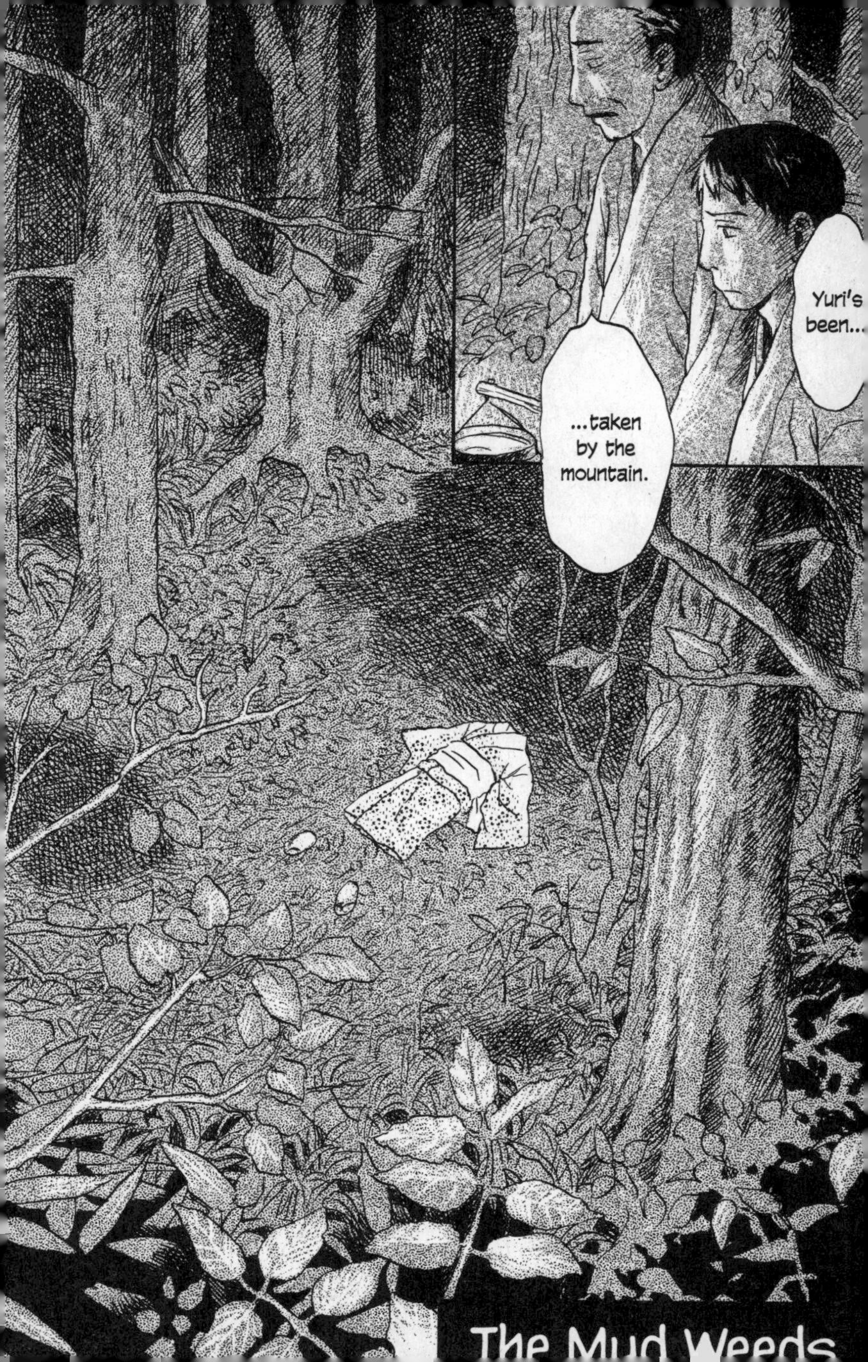
Yuri's been...
...taken by the mountain.
The Mud Weeds

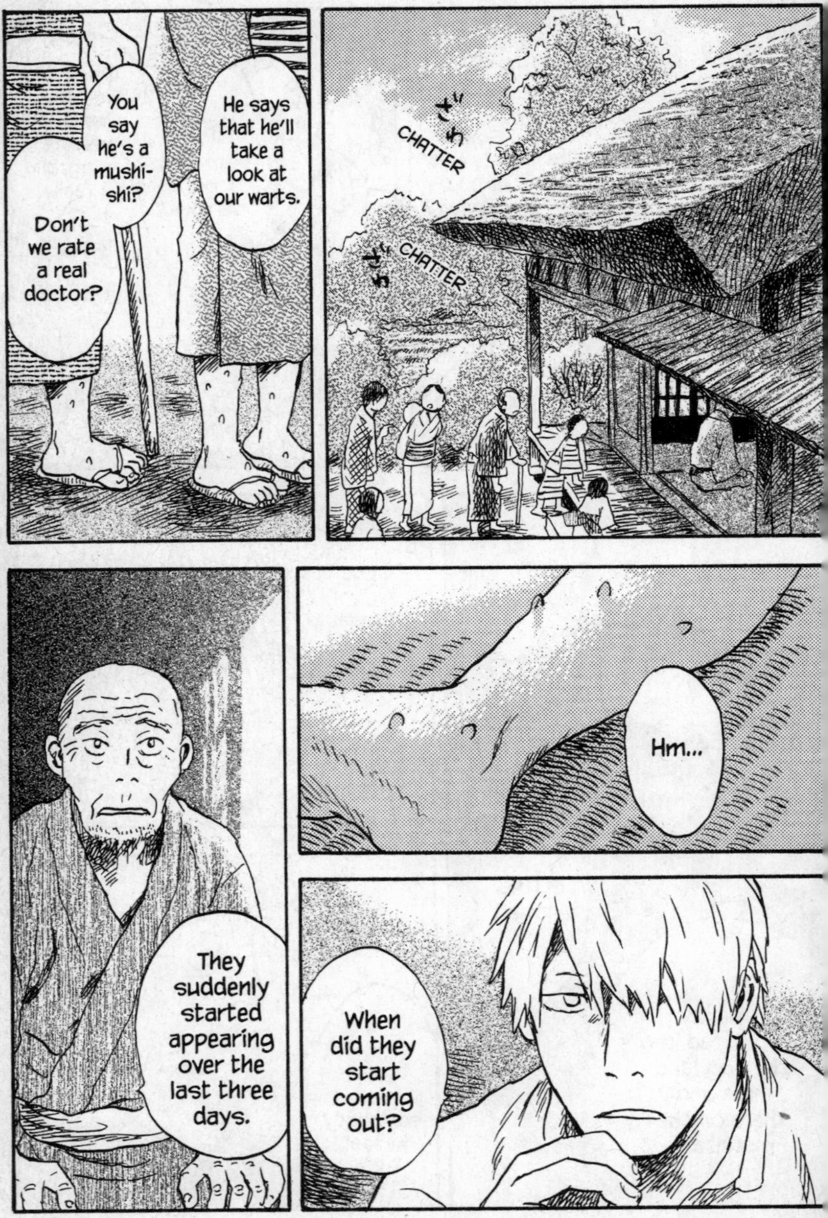
ざわ
CHATTER
ざわ
CHATTER
He says that he'll take a look at our warts.
You say he's a mushi-shi?
Don't we rate a real doctor?
Hm...
When did they start coming out?
They suddenly started appearing over the last three days.

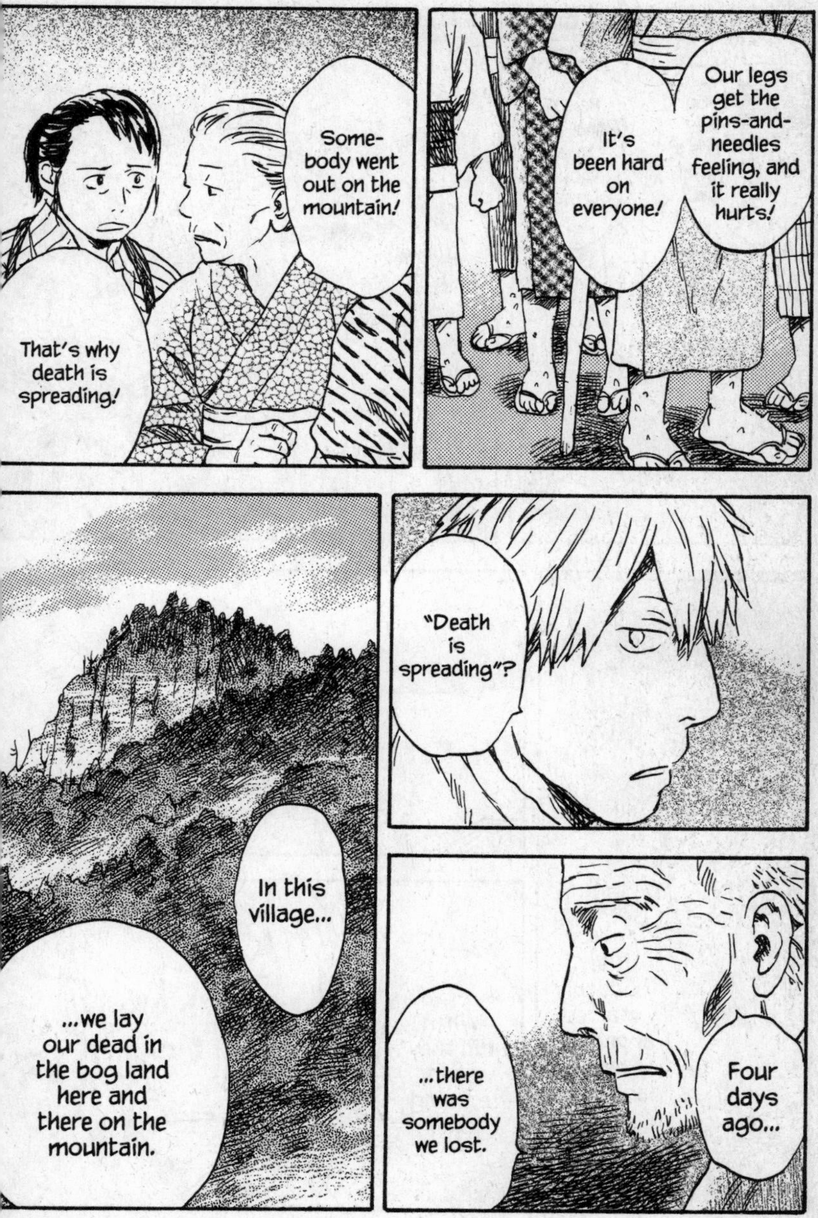
Our legs get the pins-and-needles feeling, and it really hurts!
It's been hard on everyone!
Some-body went out on the mountain!
That's why death is spreading!
"Death is spreading"?
Four days ago...
...there was somebody we lost.
In this village...
...we lay our dead in the bog land here and there on the mountain.

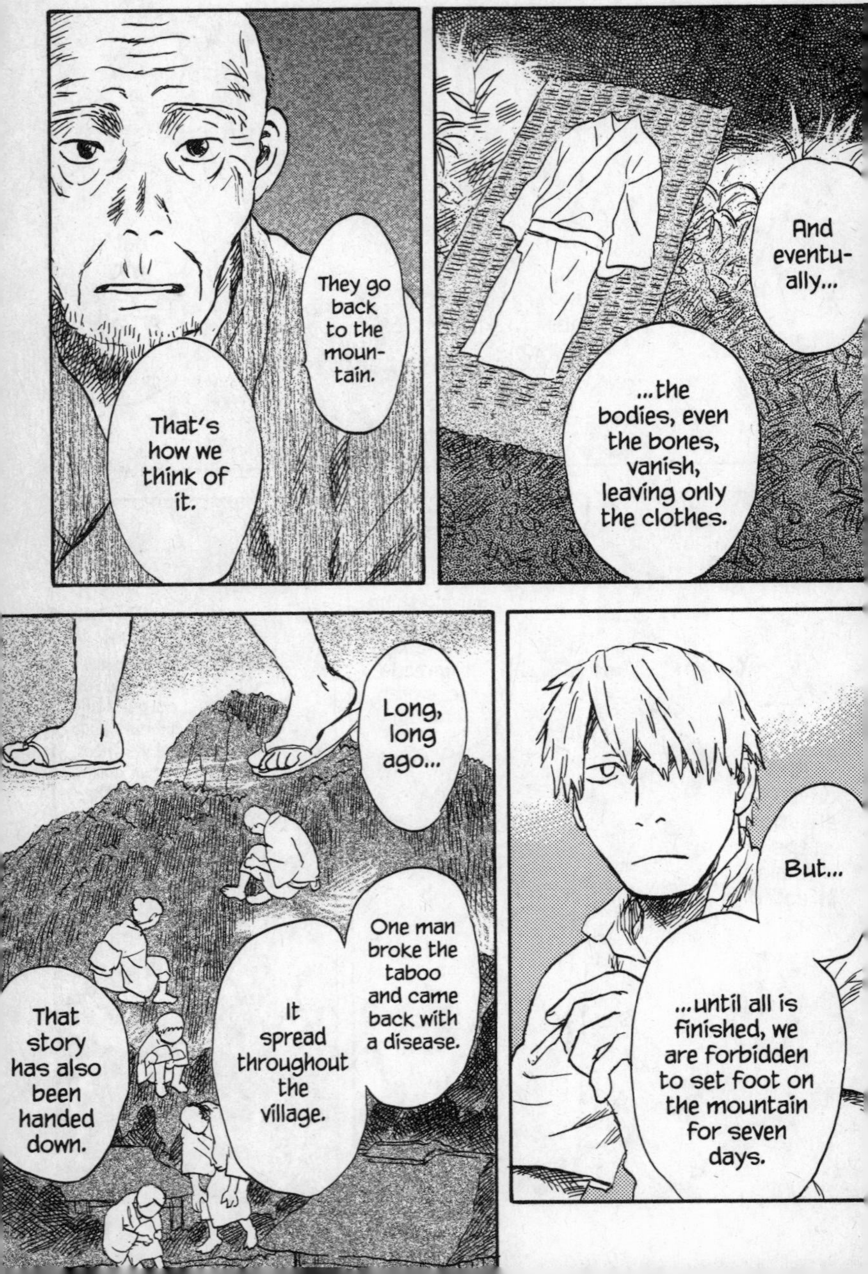
And eventu-ally...
...the bodies, even the bones, vanish, leaving only the clothes.
They go back to the moun-tain.
That's how we think of it.
But...
...until all is finished, we are forbidden to set foot on the mountain for seven days.
Long, long ago...
One man broke the taboo and came back with a disease.
It spread throughout the village.
That story has also been handed down.

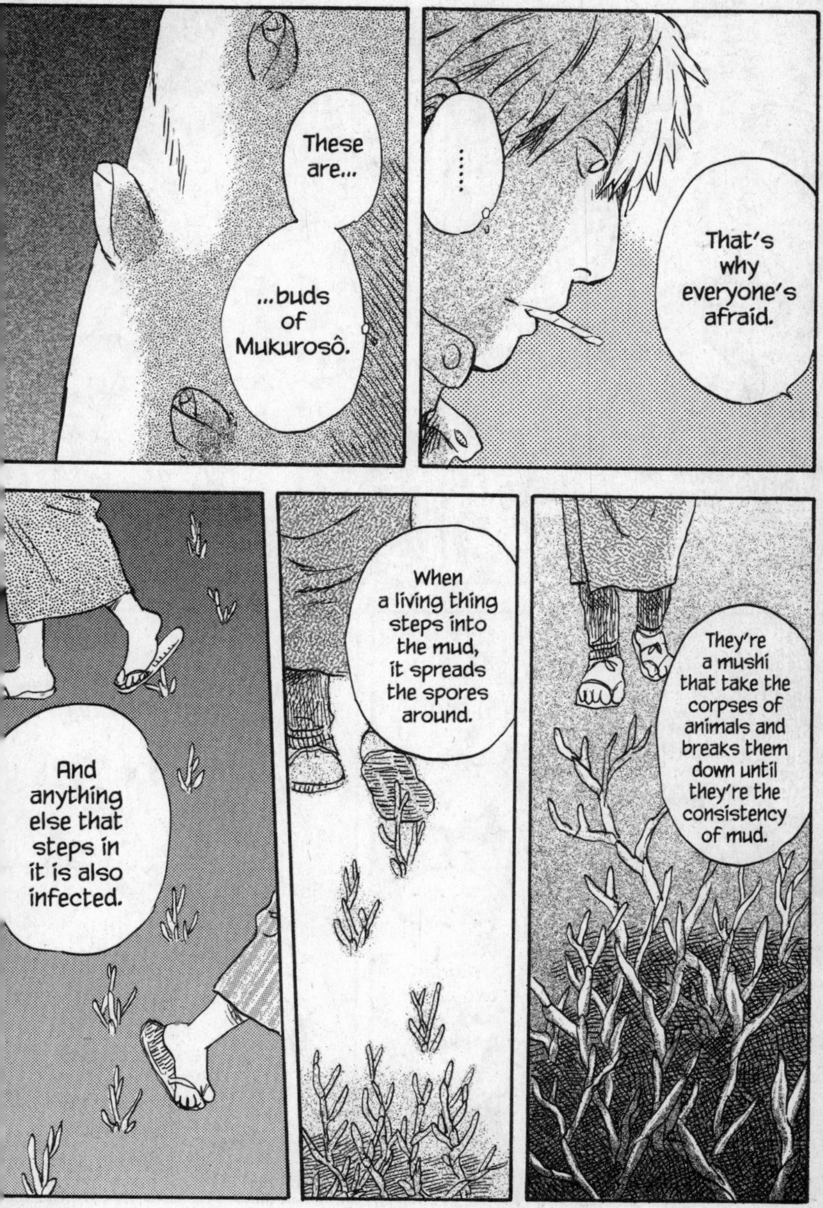

......
That's why everyone's afraid.
These are...
...buds of Mukurosô.
They're a mushi that take the corpses of animals and breaks them down until they're the consistency of mud.
When a living thing steps into the mud, it spreads the spores around.
And anything else that steps in it is also infected.

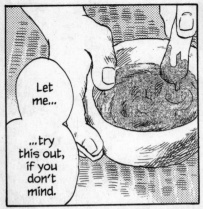

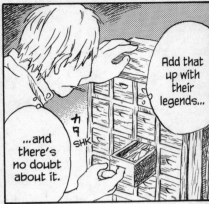

Add that up with their legends...
カタ
SHK
...and there's no doubt about it.
Let me...
...try this out, if you don't mind.
ぽろっ
GLPP
......
It came off!
おおっ
OOOH
My wart came off!

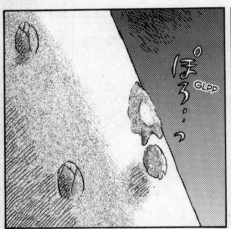

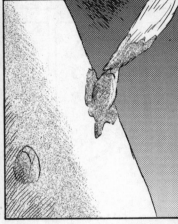

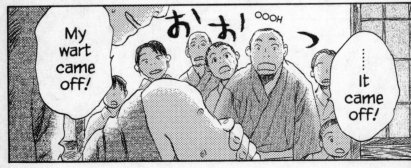

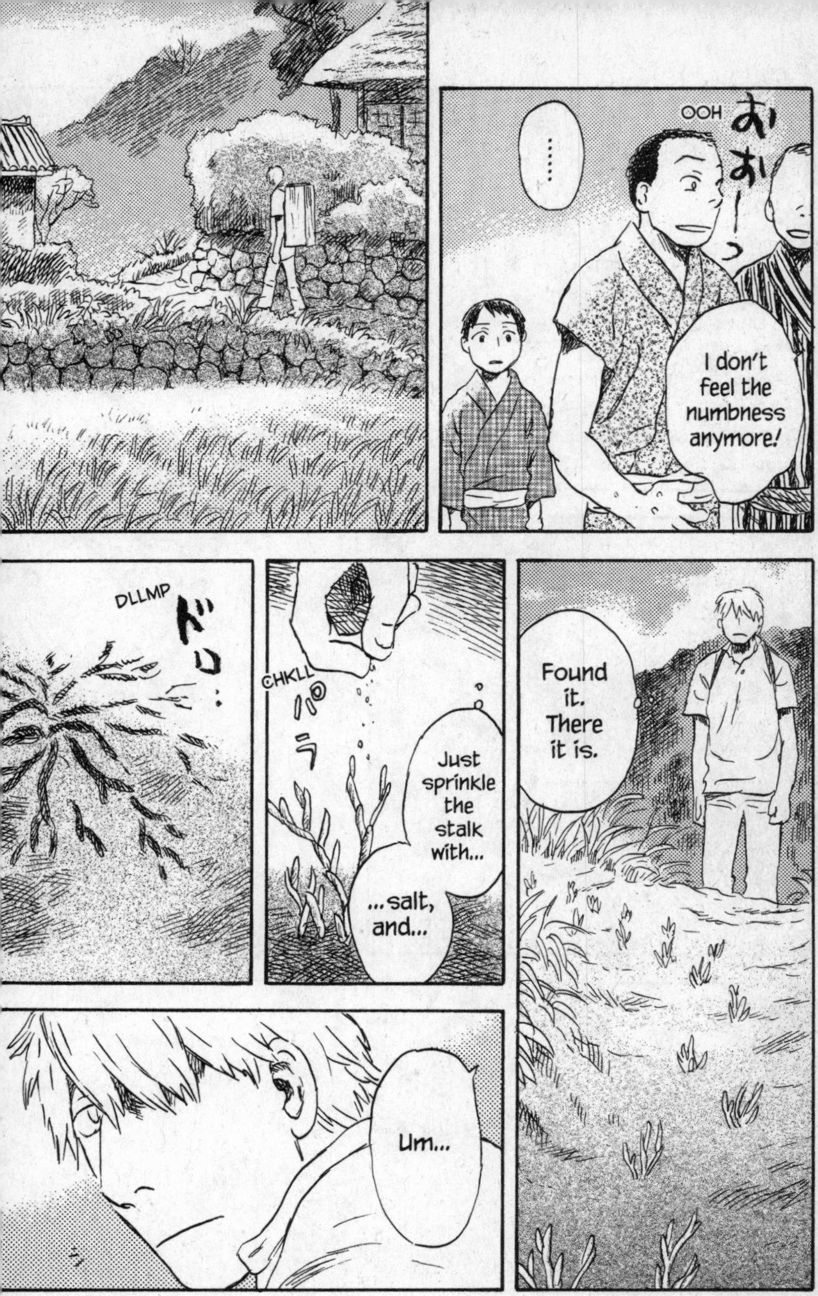
OOH
おおーっ
......
I don't feel the numbness anymore!
Found it. There it is.
CHKLL
パラ
Just sprinkle the stalk with...
...salt, and...
DLLMP
ドロ..
Um...

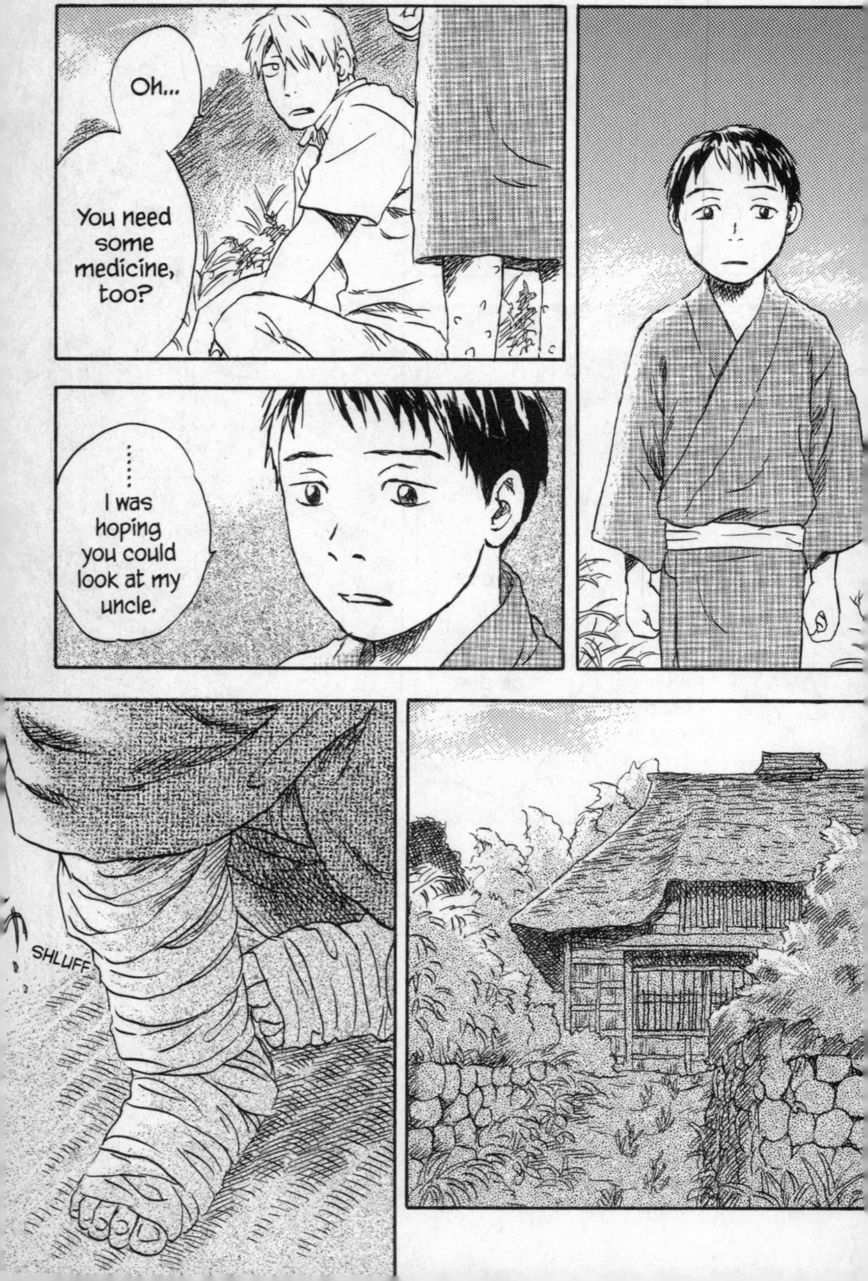
Oh...
You need some medicine, too?
...... I was hoping you could look at my uncle.
SHLUFF

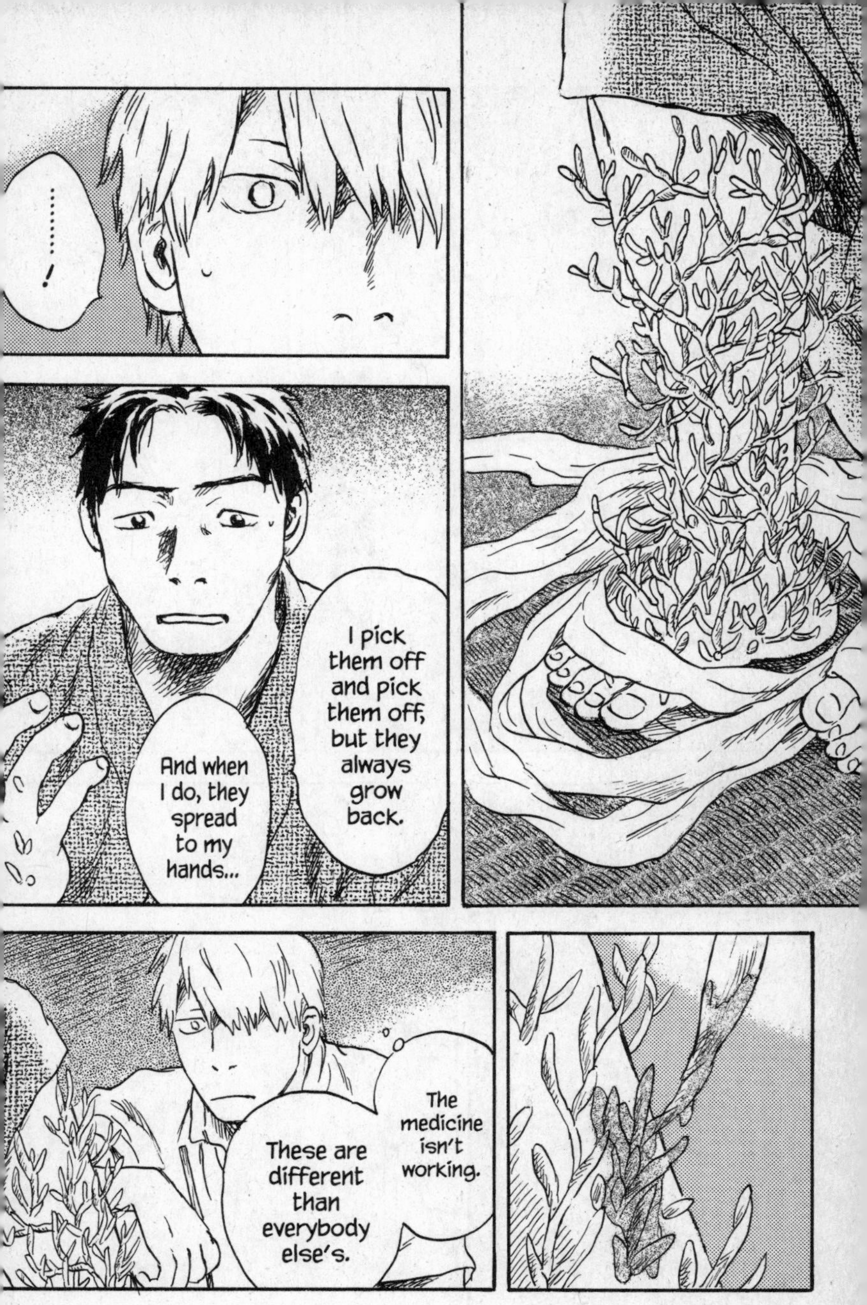
……!
I pick them off and pick them off, but they always grow back.
And when I do, they spread to my hands…
The medicine isn't working.
These are different than everybody else's.

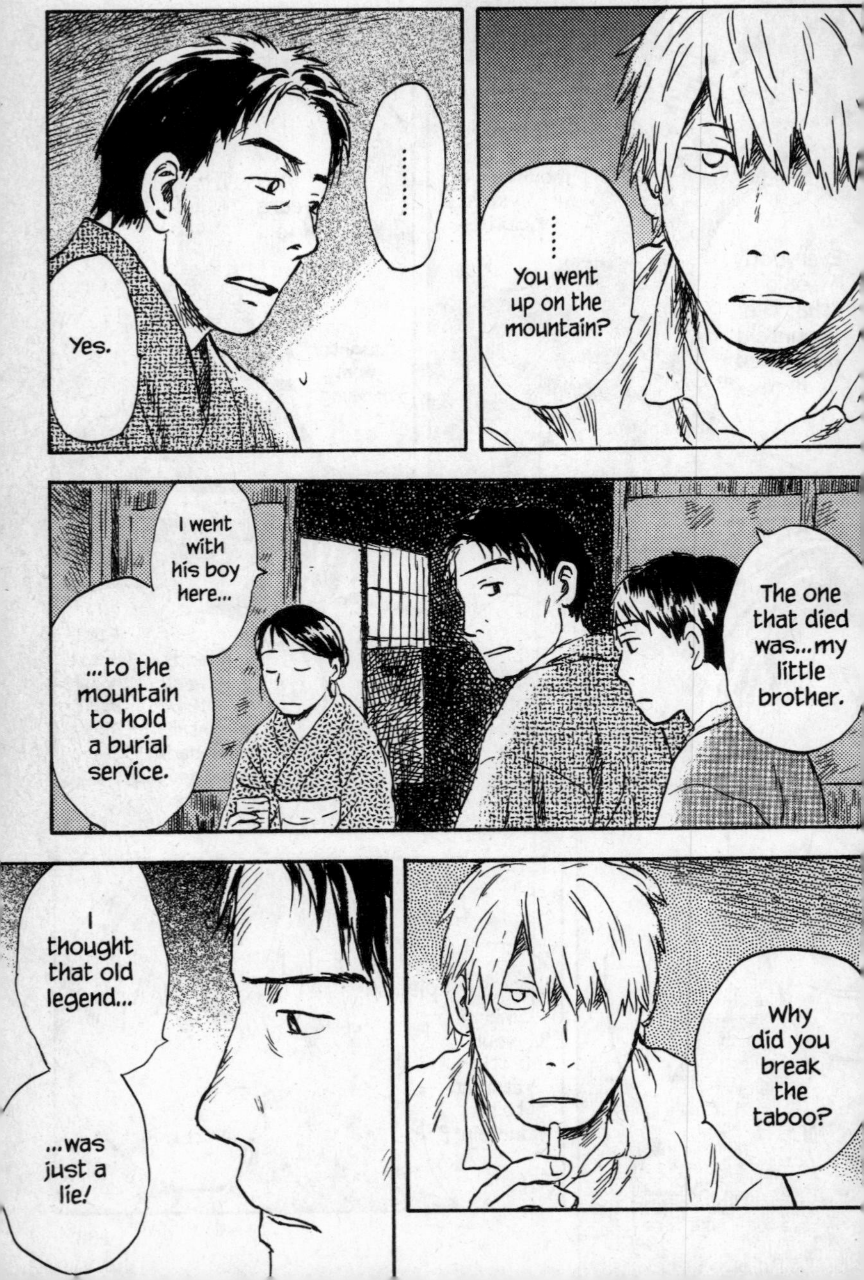
......
You went up on the mountain?
......
Yes.
The one that died was...my little brother.
I went with his boy here...
...to the mountain to hold a burial service.
Why did you break the taboo?
I thought that old legend...
...was just a lie!

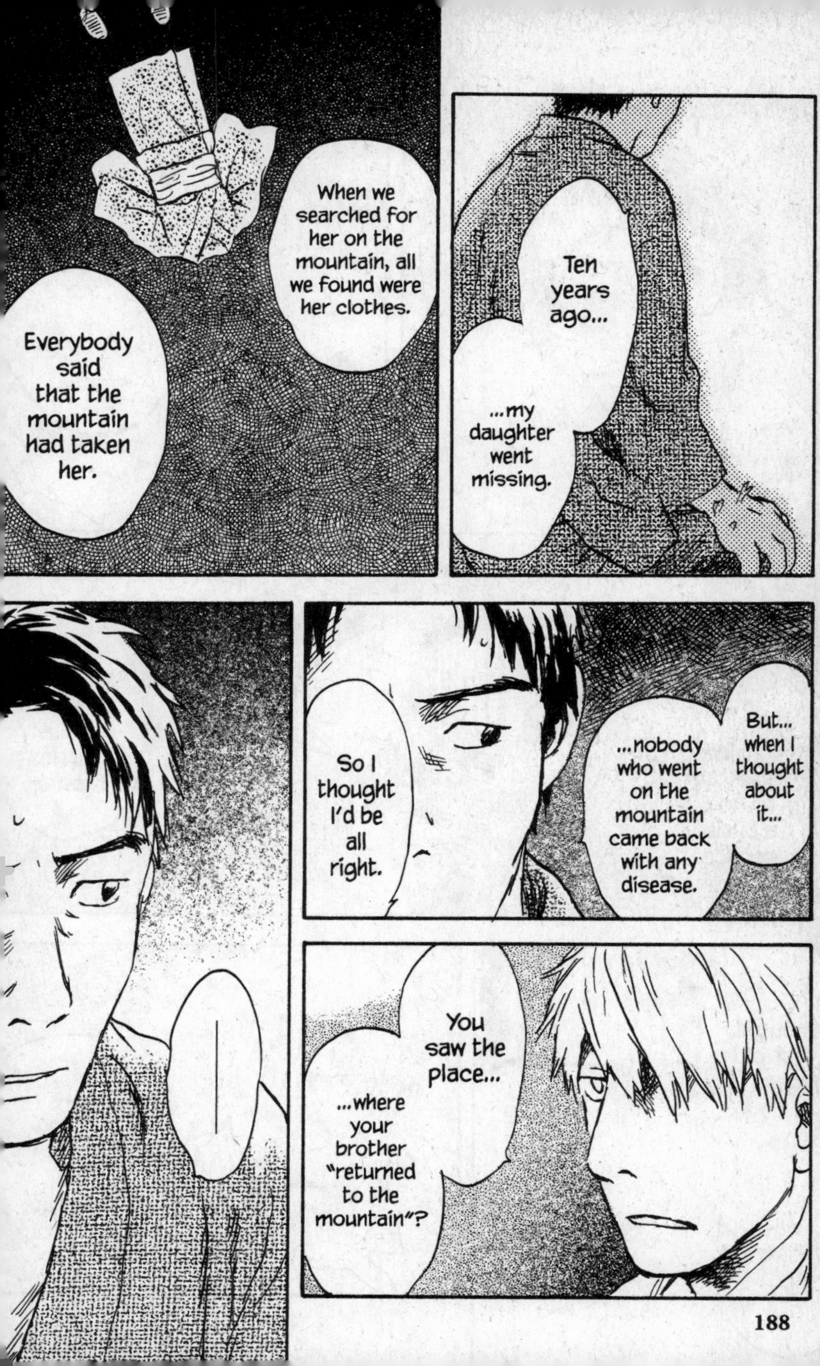
Ten years ago...
...my daughter went missing.
When we searched for her on the mountain, all we found were her clothes.
Everybody said that the mountain had taken her.
But... when I thought about it...
...nobody who went on the mountain came back with any disease.
So I thought I'd be all right.
You saw the place...
...where your brother "returned to the mountain"?

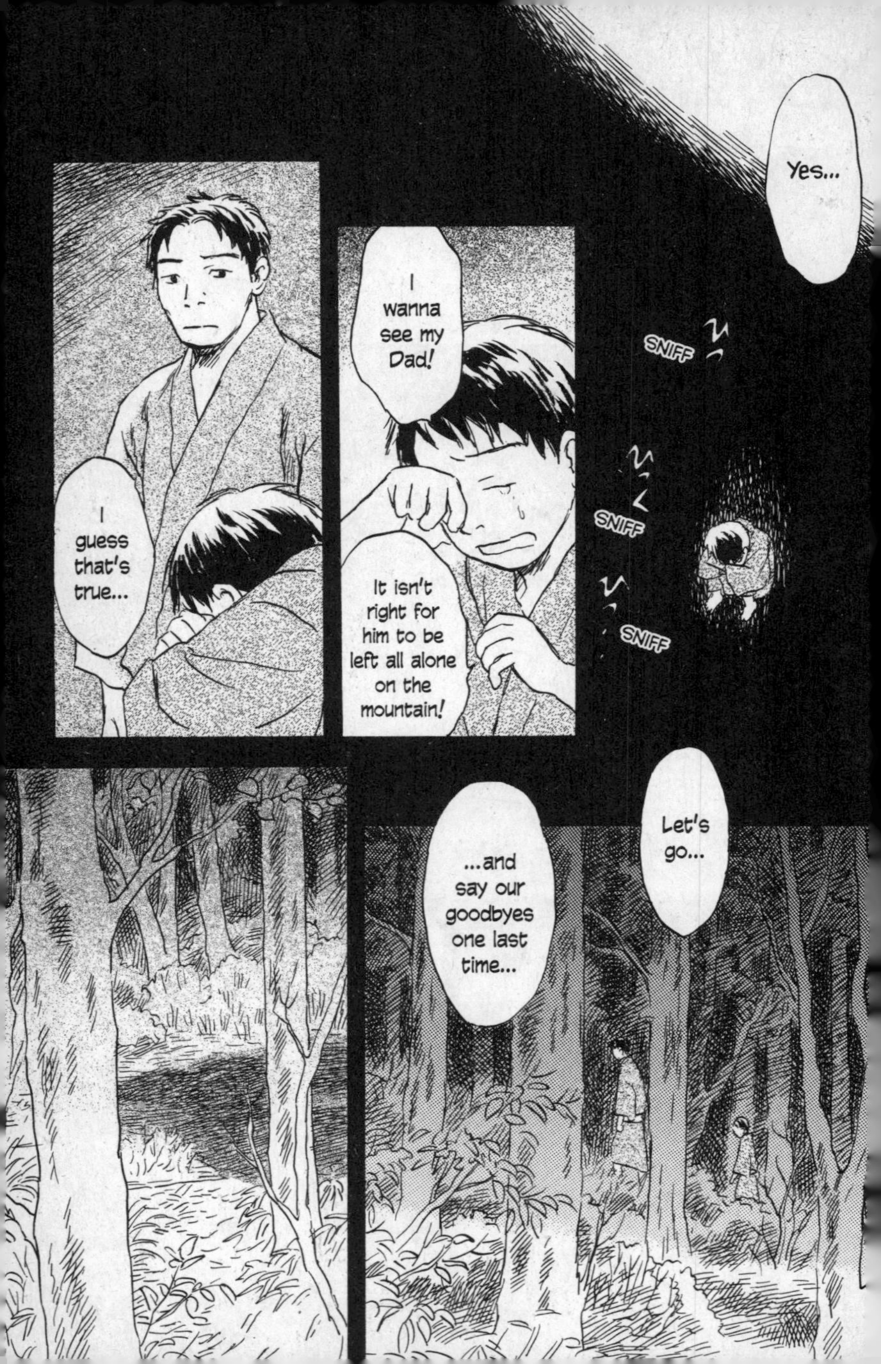
Yes...
SNIFF
SNIFF
SNIFF
I wanna see my Dad!
It isn't right for him to be left all alone on the mountain!
I guess that's true...
Let's go...
...and say our goodbyes one last time...

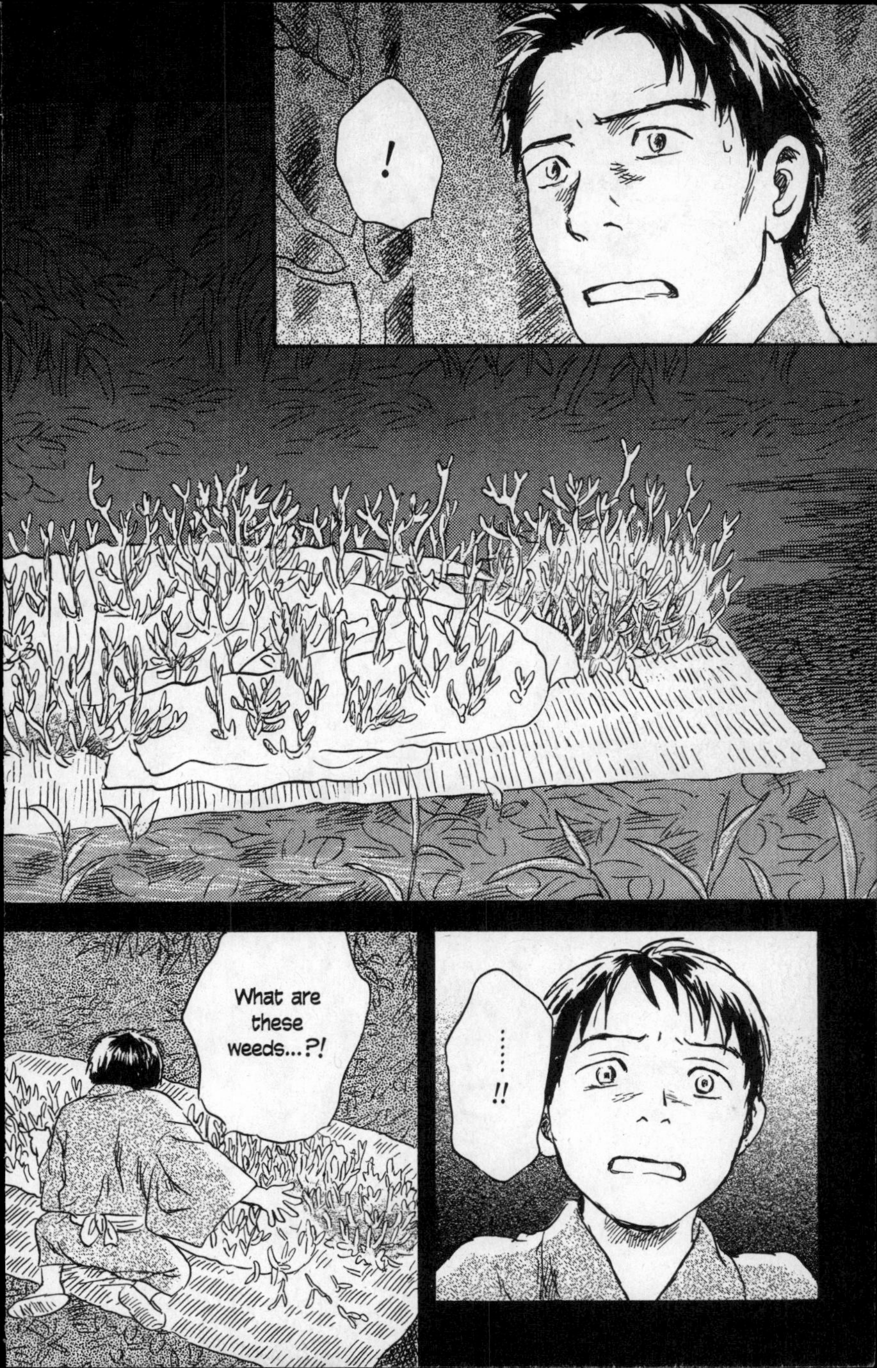
!
......!!
What are these weeds...?!

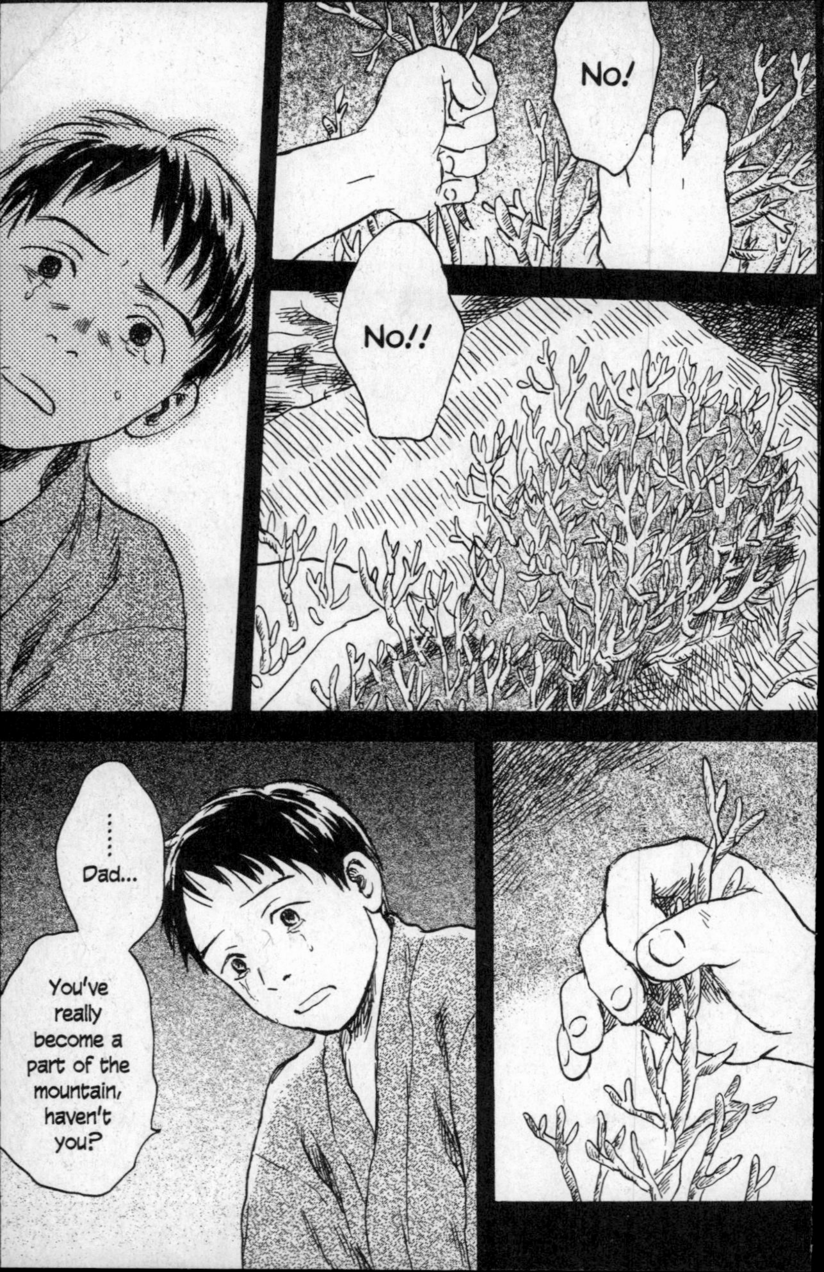
No!
No!!
......
Dad...
You've really become a part of the mountain, haven't you?

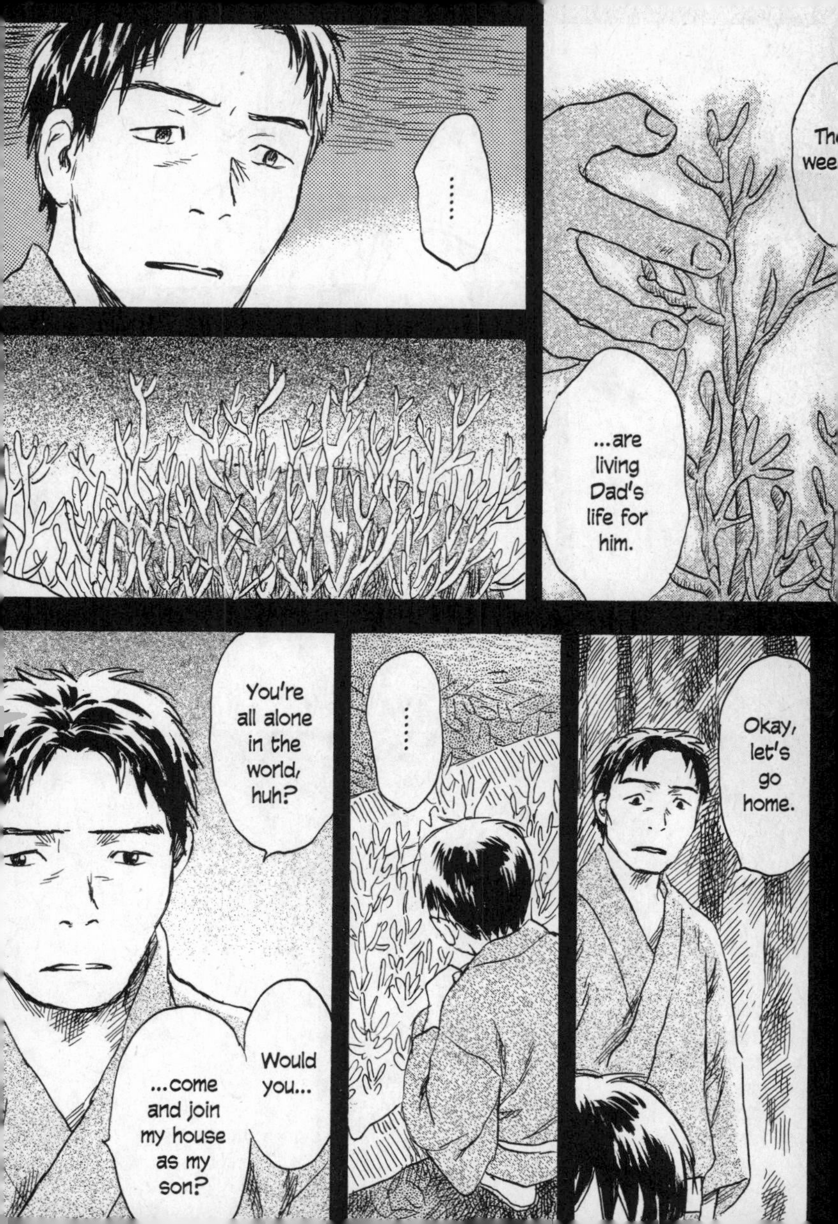
Th wee
...are living Dad's life for him.
......
Okay, let's go home.
......
You're all alone in the world, huh?
Would you...
...come and join my house as my son?

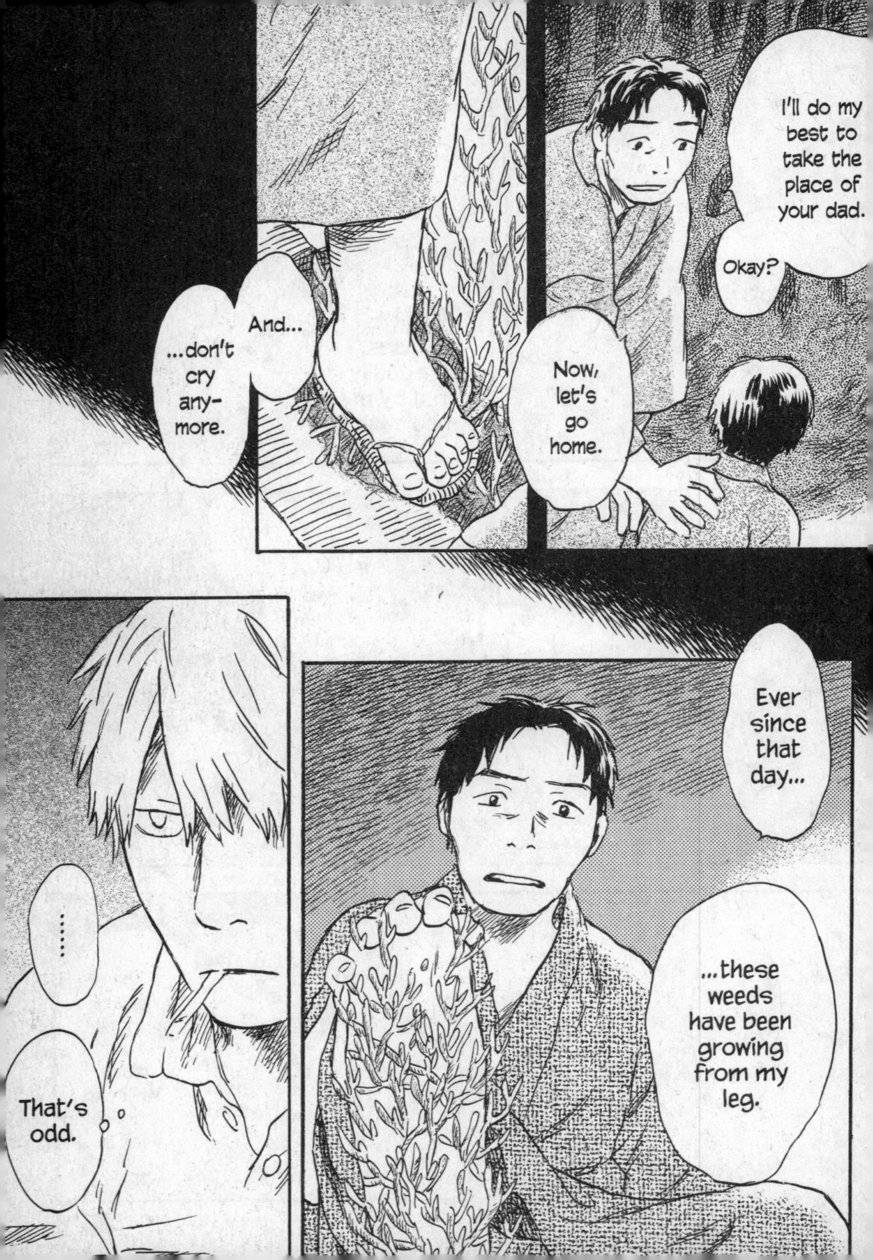
I'll do my best to take the place of your dad.
Okay?
Now, let's go home.
And...
...don't cry any-more.
Ever since that day...
...these weeds have been growing from my leg.
......
That's odd.

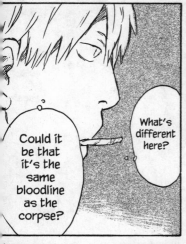

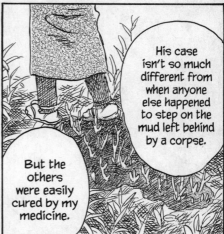

His case isn't so much different from when anyone else happened to step on the mud left behind by a corpse.
But the others were easily cured by my medicine.
What's different here?
Could it be that it's the same bloodline as the corpse?
No...
If it were, the man's nephew would be in the same condition.
There must be some other cause.
They went on purpose to a place where a corpse lay...
...and stepped in the mud...
......

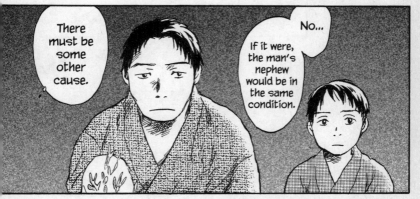

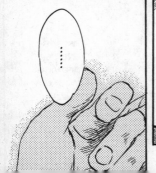

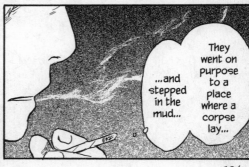

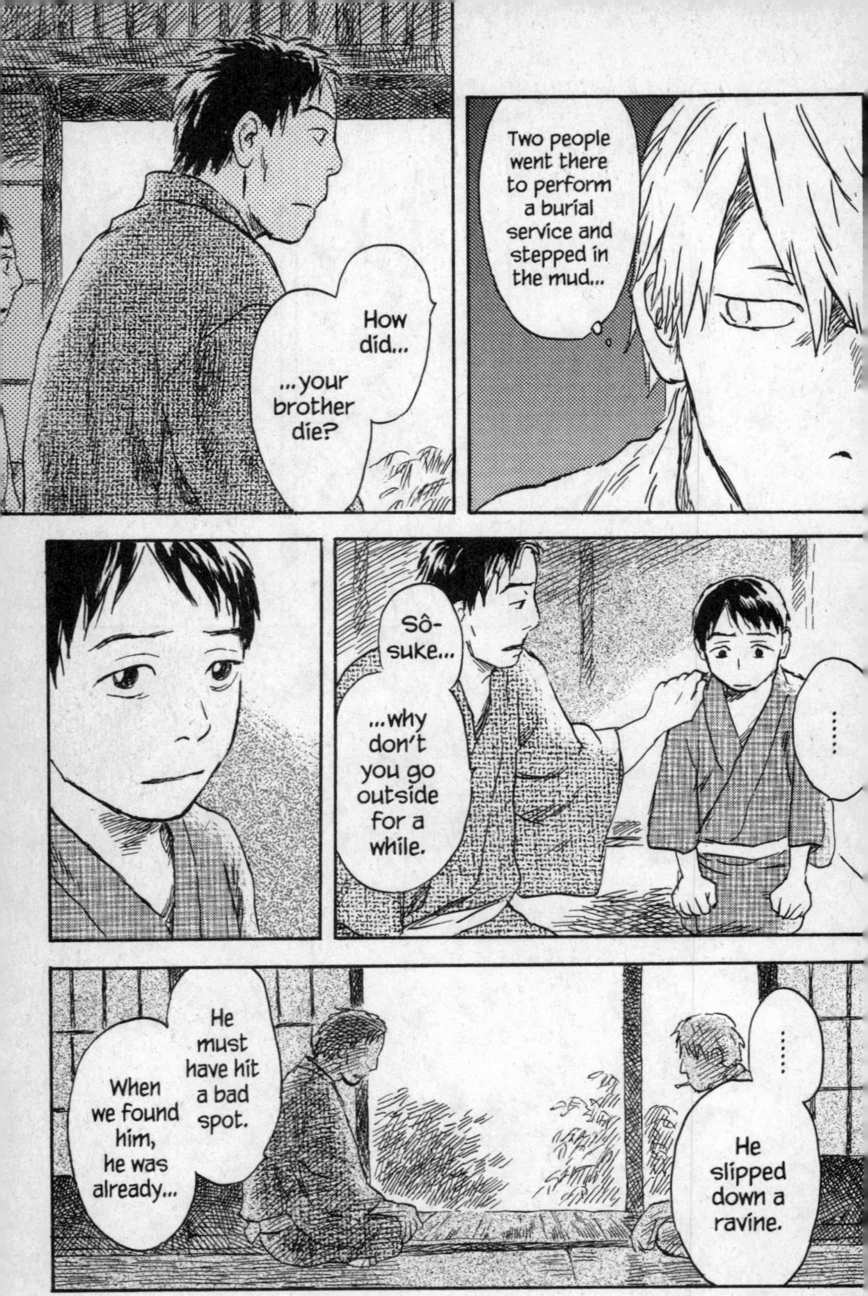
Two people went there to perform a burial service and stepped in the mud...
How did...
...your brother die?
......
Sô-suke...
...why don't you go outside for a while.
......
He slipped down a ravine.
He must have hit a bad spot.
When we found him, he was already...

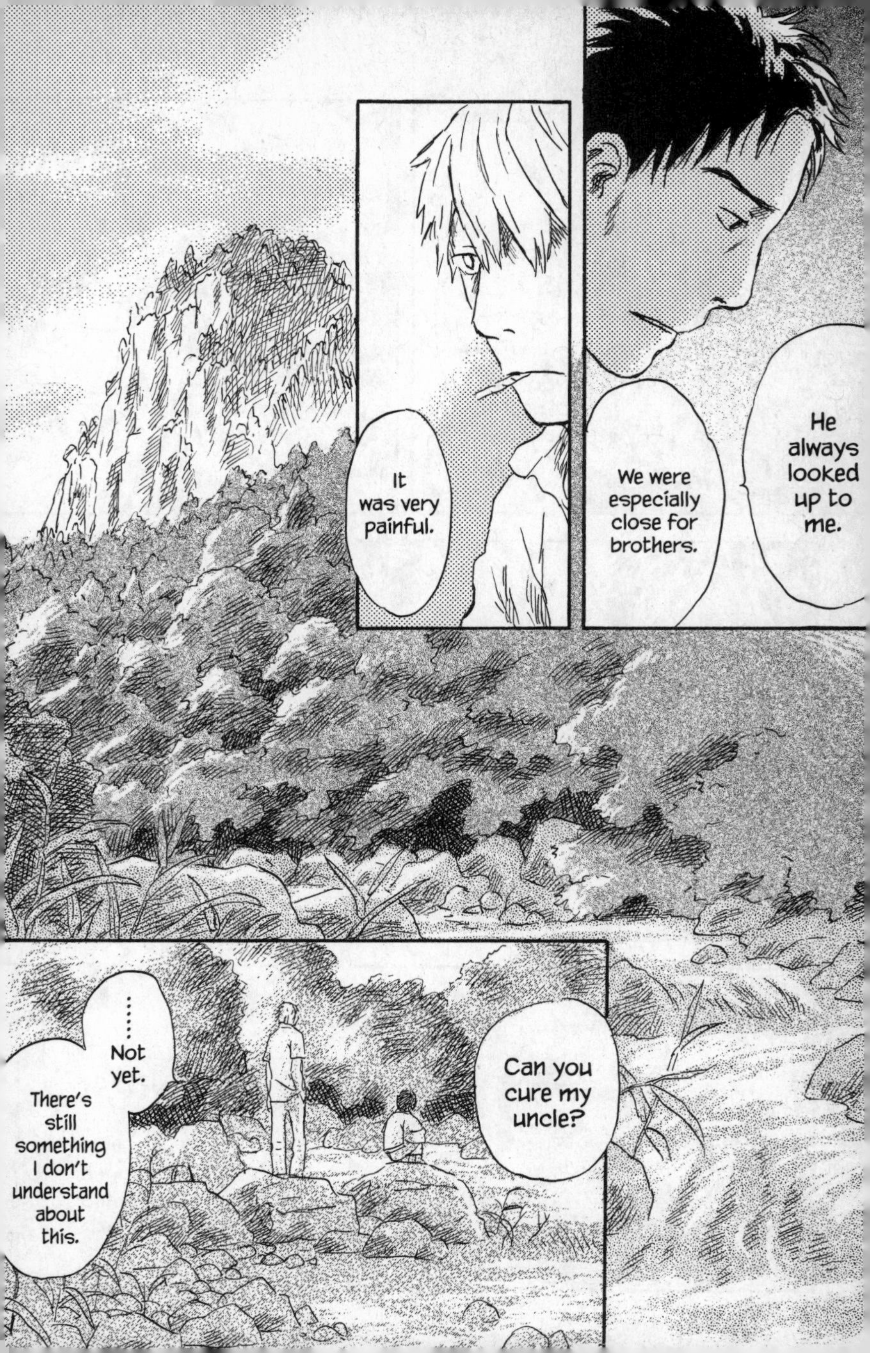

He always looked up to me.
We were especially close for brothers.
It was very painful.
Can you cure my uncle?
...... Not yet.
There's still something I don't understand about this.

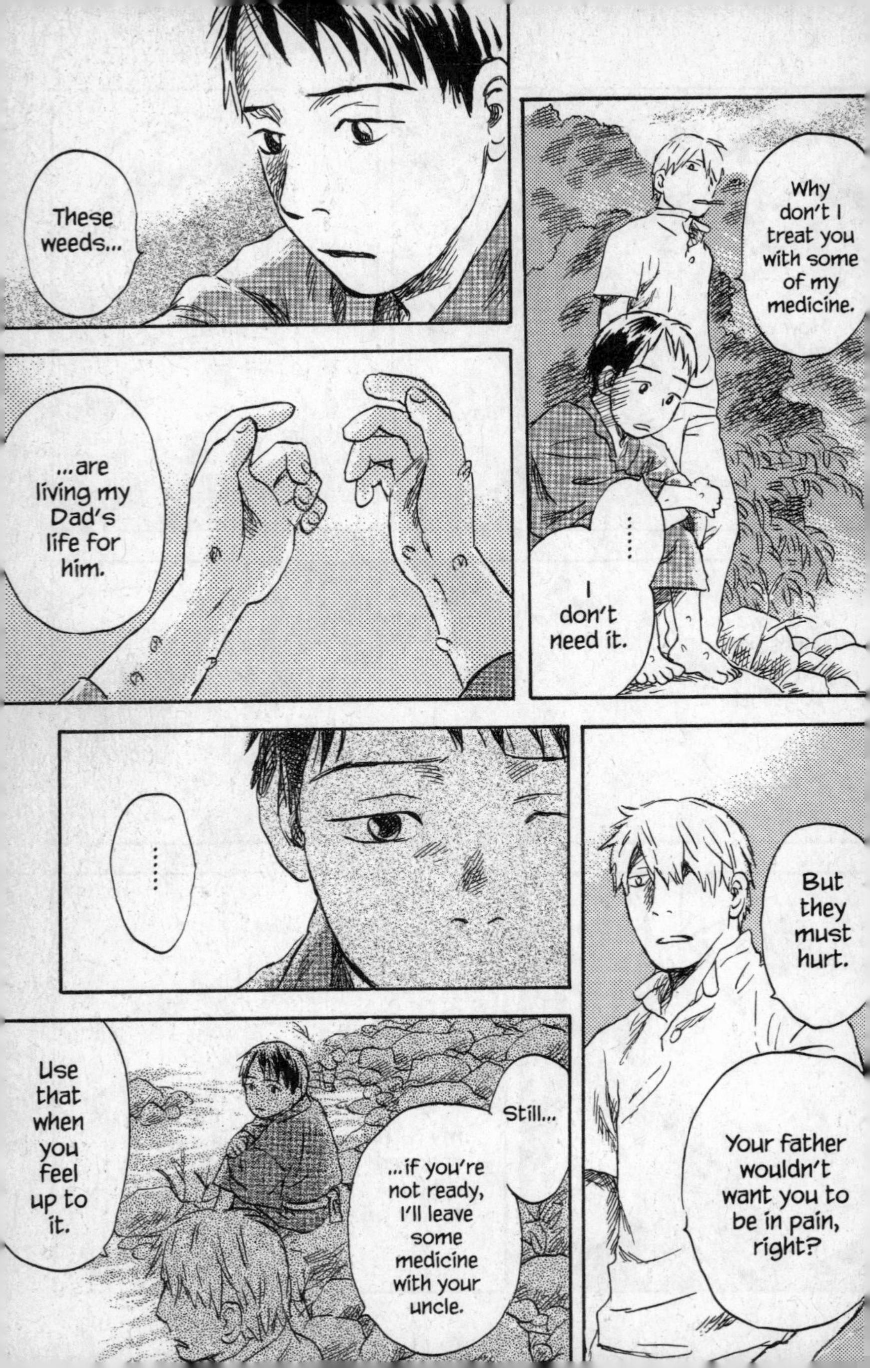
Why don't I treat you with some of my medicine.
......
I don't need it.
These weeds...
...are living my Dad's life for him.
But they must hurt.
Your father wouldn't want you to be in pain, right?
......
Still...
...if you're not ready, I'll leave some medicine with your uncle.
Use that when you feel up to it.

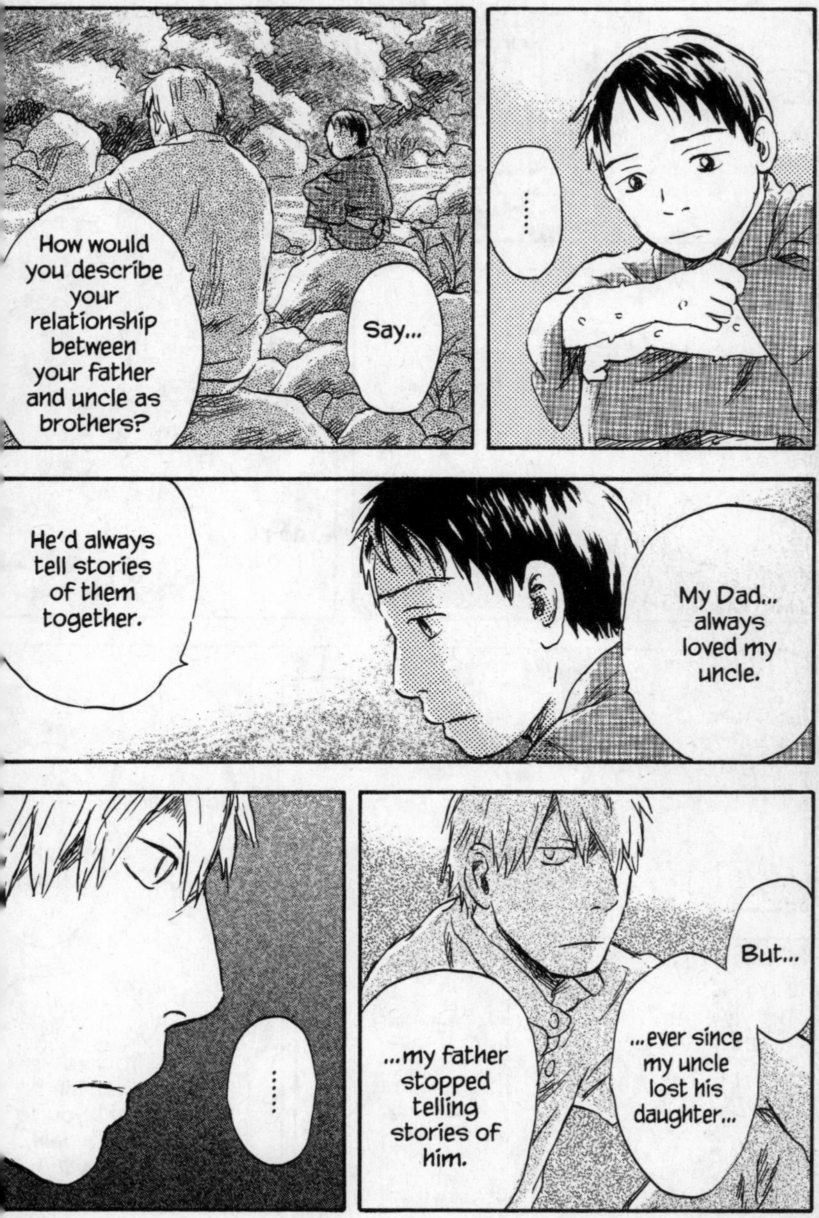
......
Say...
How would you describe your relationship between your father and uncle as brothers?
My Dad... always loved my uncle.
He'd always tell stories of them together.
But...
...ever since my uncle lost his daughter...
...my father stopped telling stories of him.
......

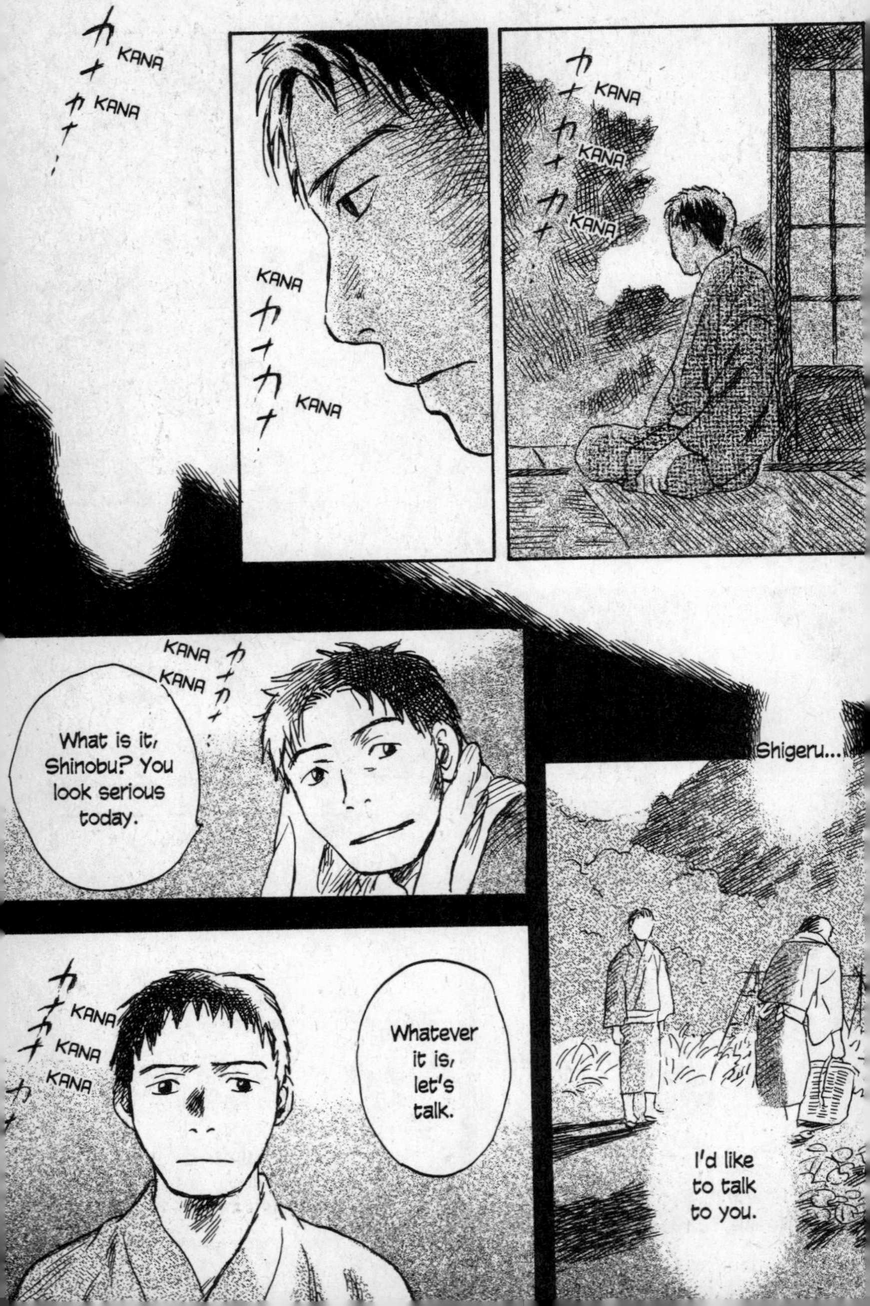
カナカナカナ
KANA
KANA
KANA
KANA
カナカナ
KANA
カナカナ…
KANA
KANA
Shigeru...
I'd like to talk to you.
KANA
KANA
カナカナ…
What is it, Shinobu? You look serious today.
KANA
KANA
KANA
カナカナカ
Whatever it is, let's talk.

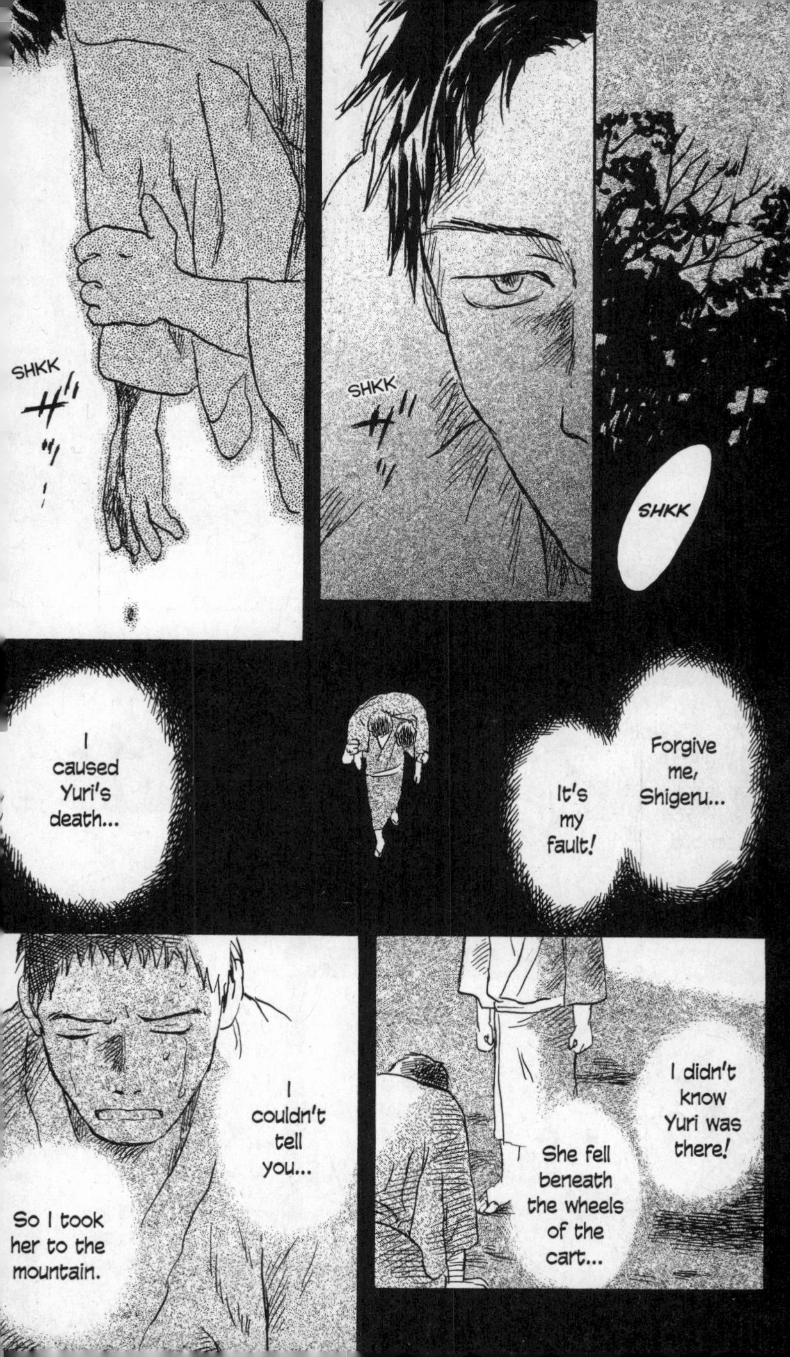
SHKK
SHKK
SHKK
Forgive me, Shigeru...
It's my fault!
I caused Yuri's death...
I didn't know Yuri was there!
She fell beneath the wheels of the cart...
I couldn't tell you...
So I took her to the mountain.

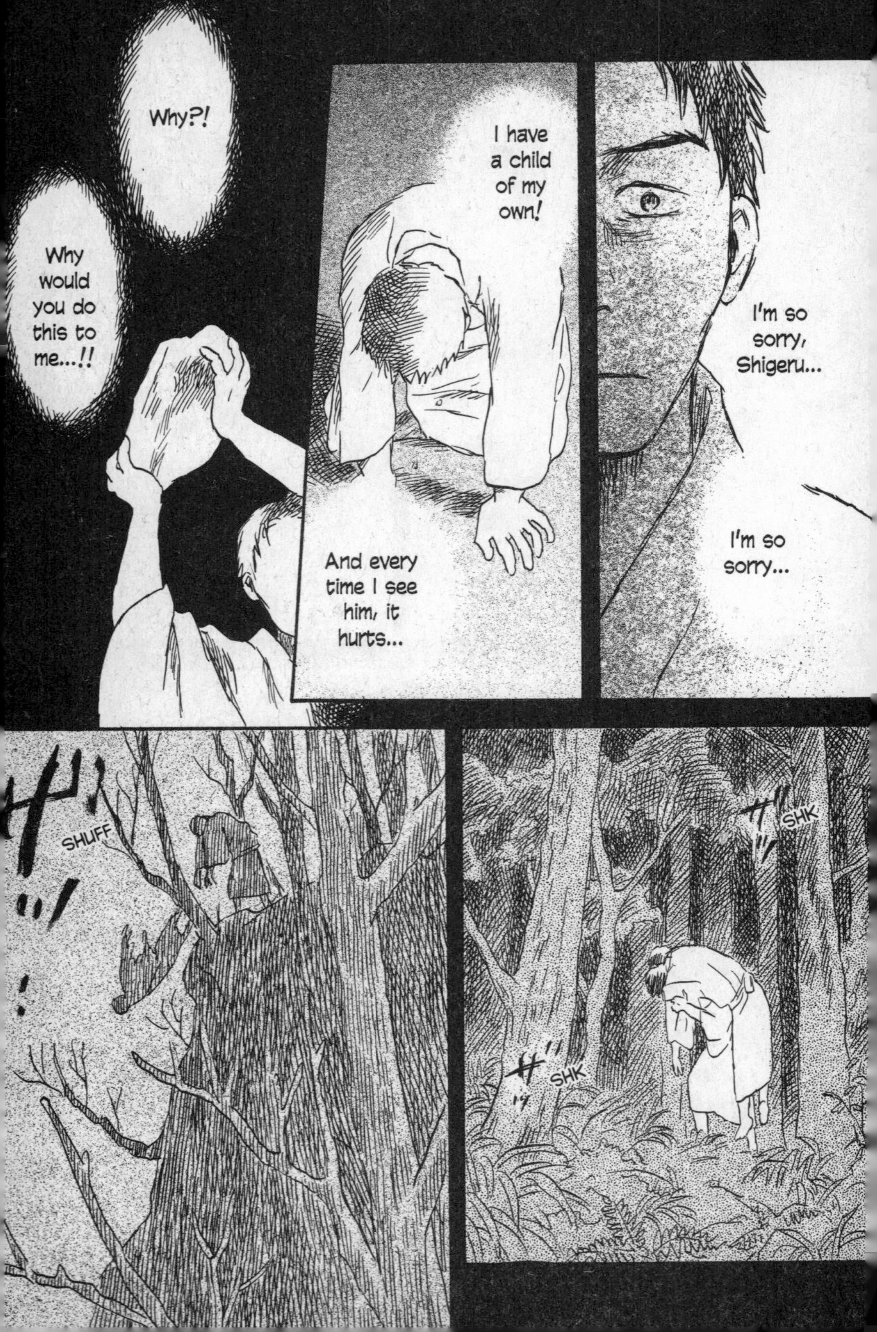
I'm so sorry, Shigeru...
I'm so sorry...
I have a child of my own!
And every time I see him, it hurts...
Why?!
Why would you do this to me...!!
SHK
SHK
SHUFF

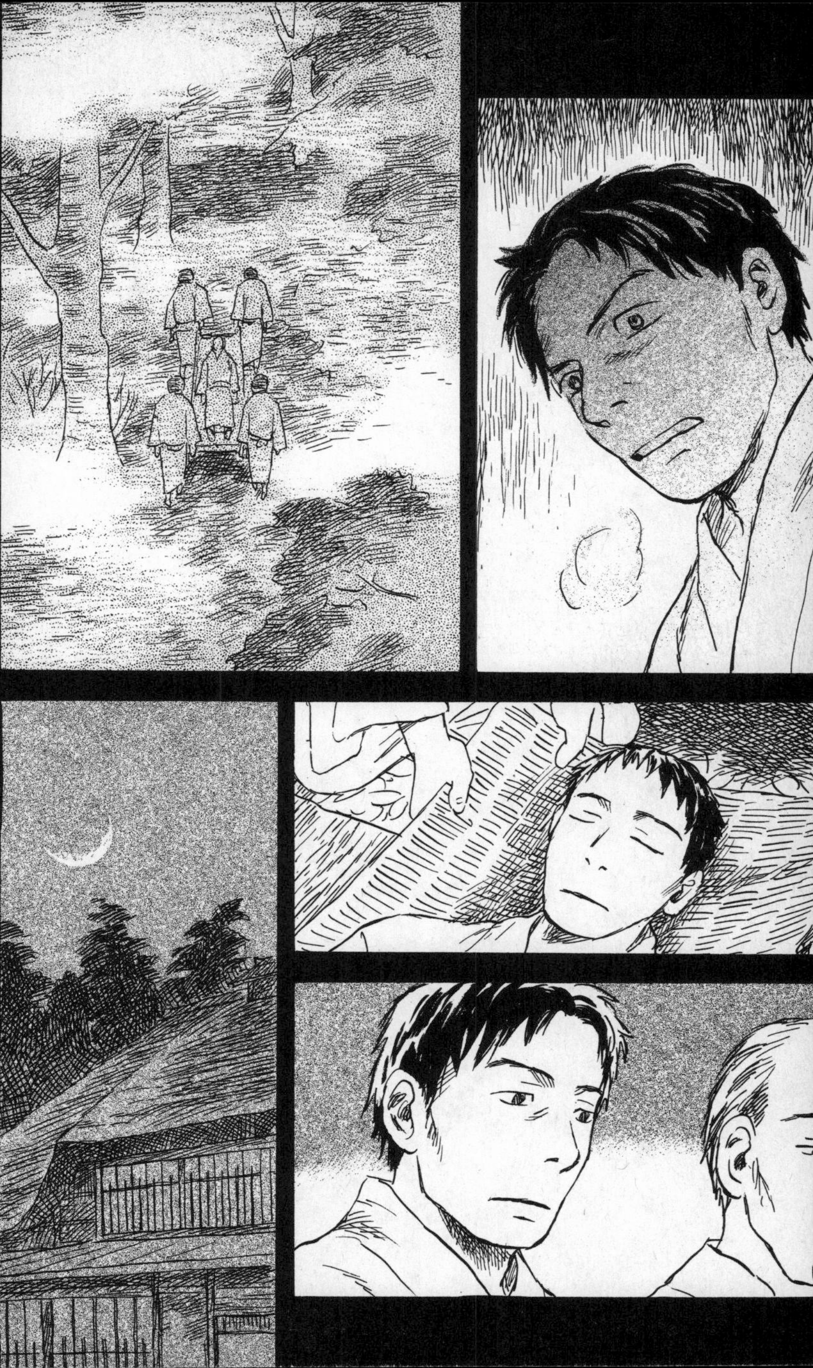

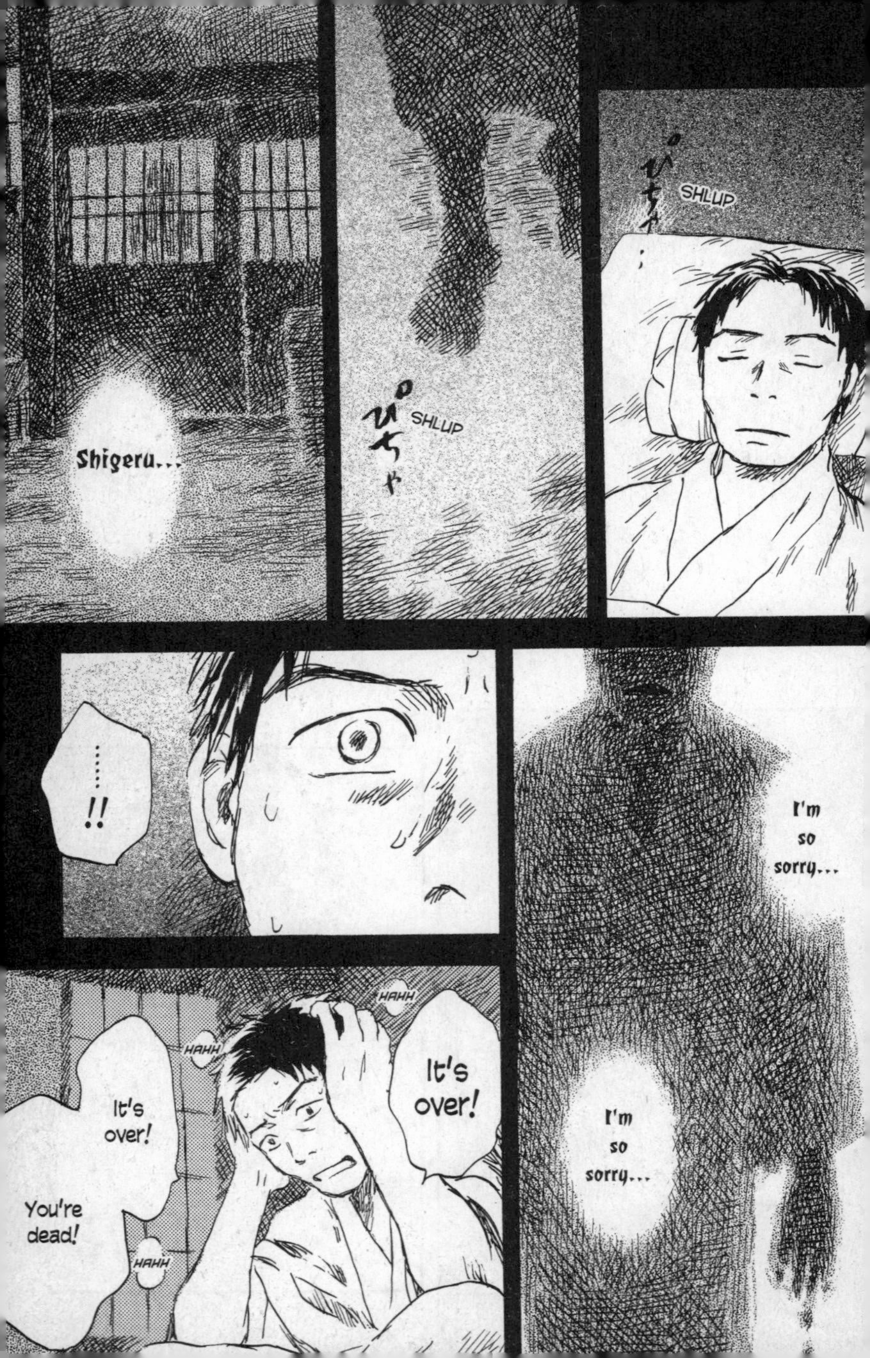

ぴちゃ
SHLUP
ぴちゃ
SHLUP
Shigeru...
I'm so sorry...
I'm so sorry...
......!!
HAHH
It's over!
HAHH
It's over!
You're dead!
HAHH

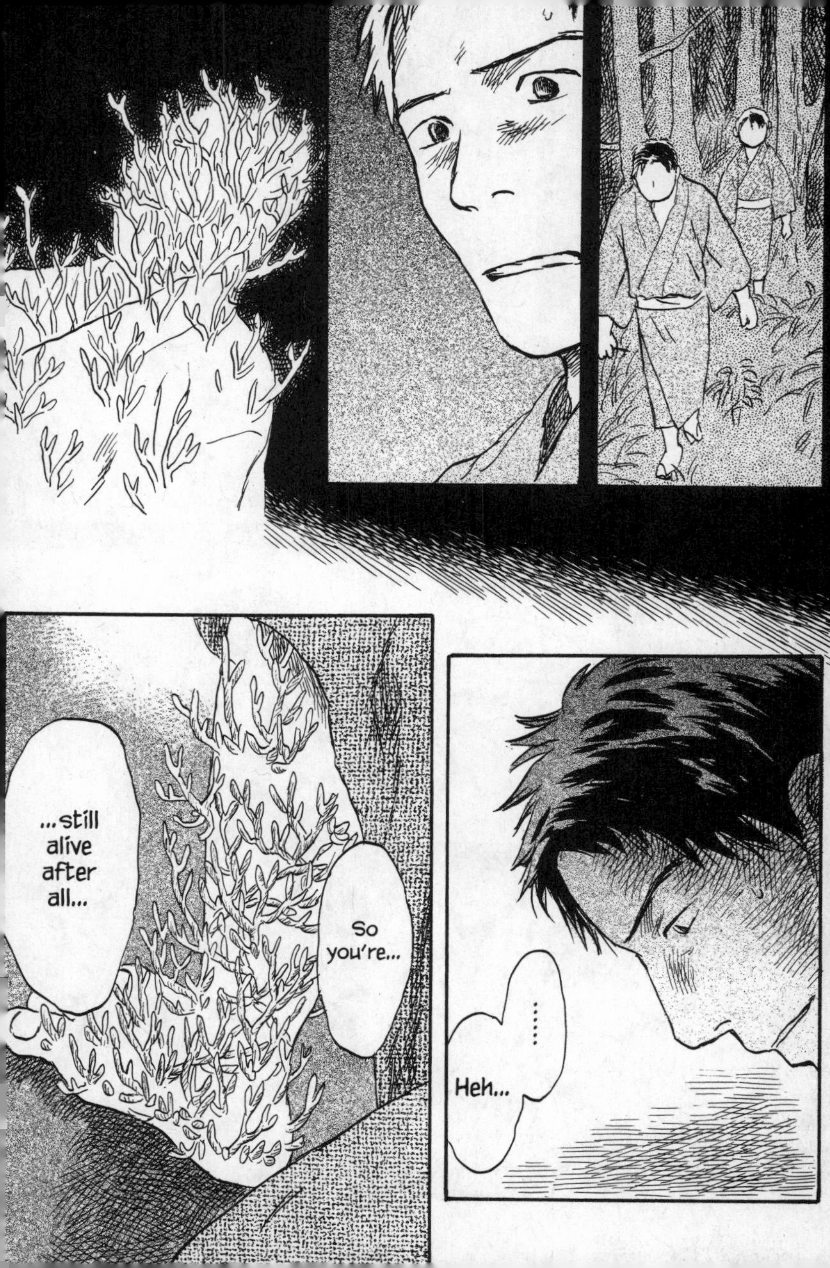
......
Heh...
So you're...
...still alive after all...

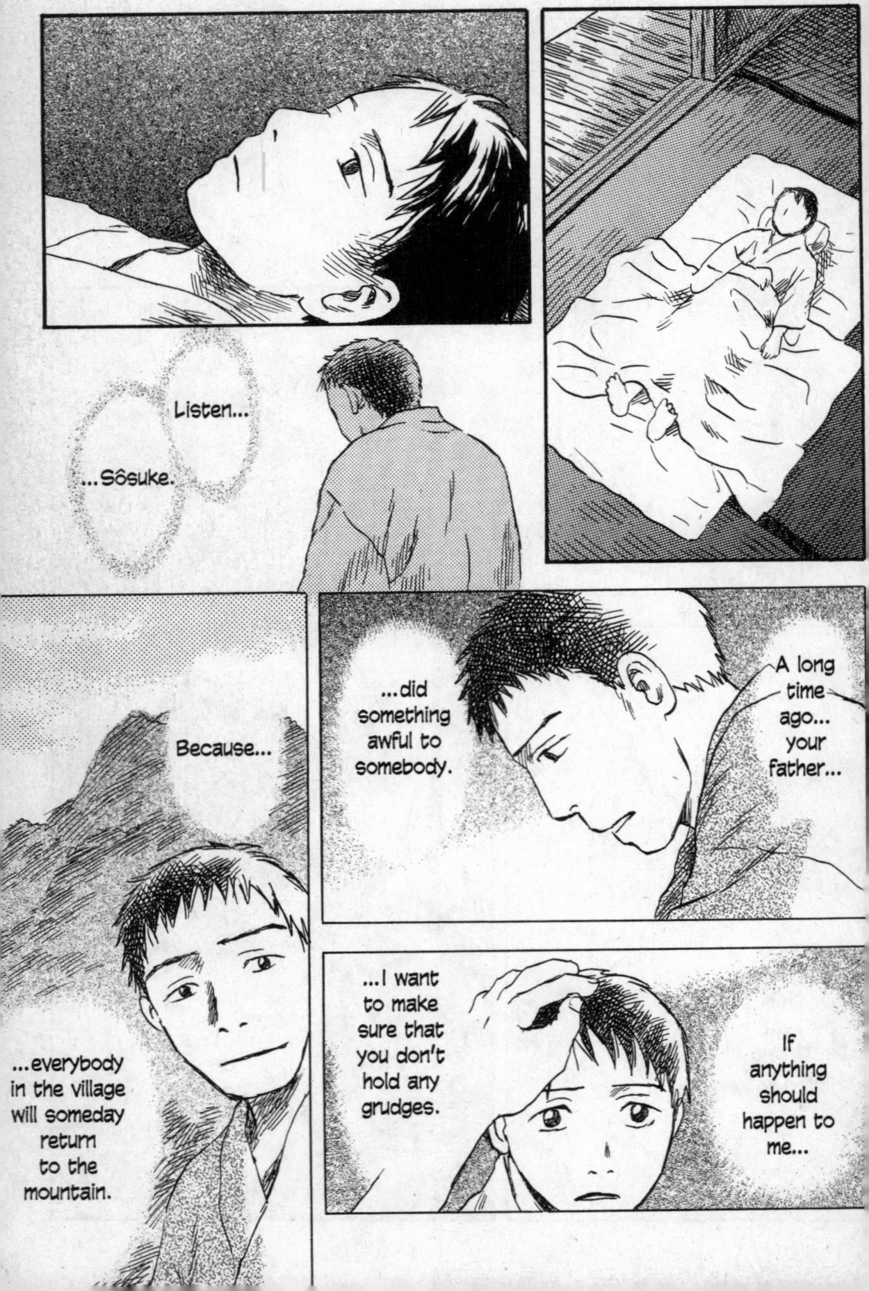
Listen...
...Sôsuke.
A long time ago... your father...
...did something awful to somebody.
If anything should happen to me...
...I want to make sure that you don't hold any grudges.
Because...
...everybody in the village will someday return to the mountain.

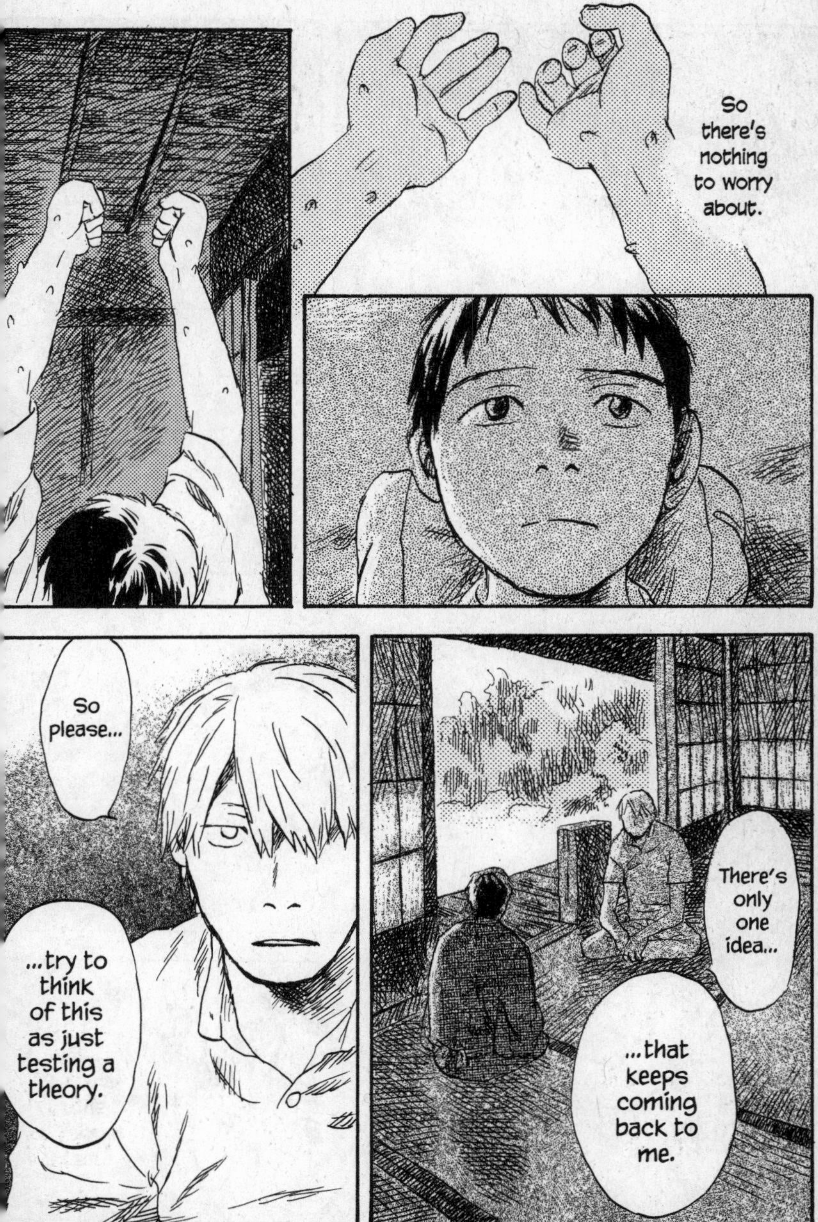
So there's nothing to worry about.
There's only one idea...
...that keeps coming back to me.
So please...
...try to think of this as just testing a theory.

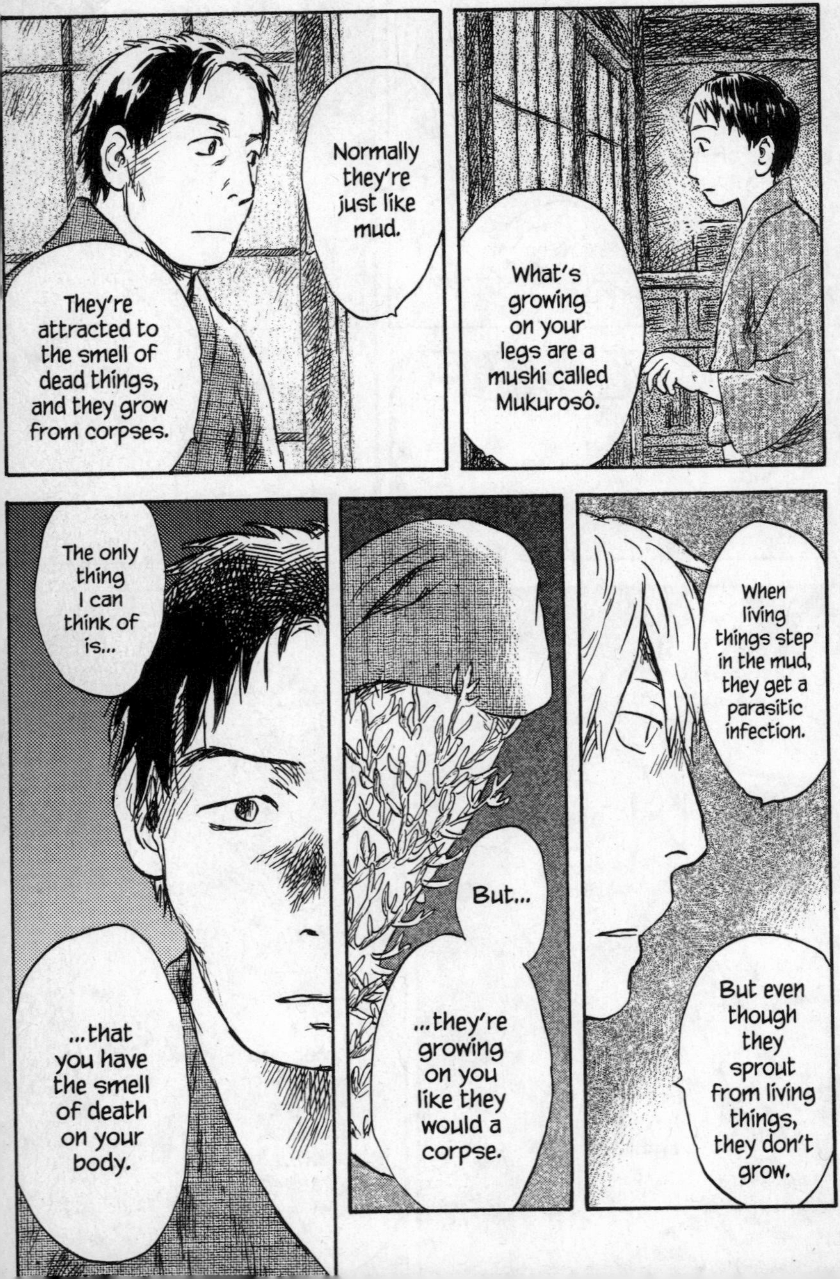
What's growing on your legs are a mushi called Mukurosô.
Normally they're just like mud.
They're attracted to the smell of dead things, and they grow from corpses.
When living things step in the mud, they get a parasitic infection.
But even though they sprout from living things, they don't grow.
But...
...they're growing on you like they would a corpse.
The only thing I can think of is...
...that you have the smell of death on your body.

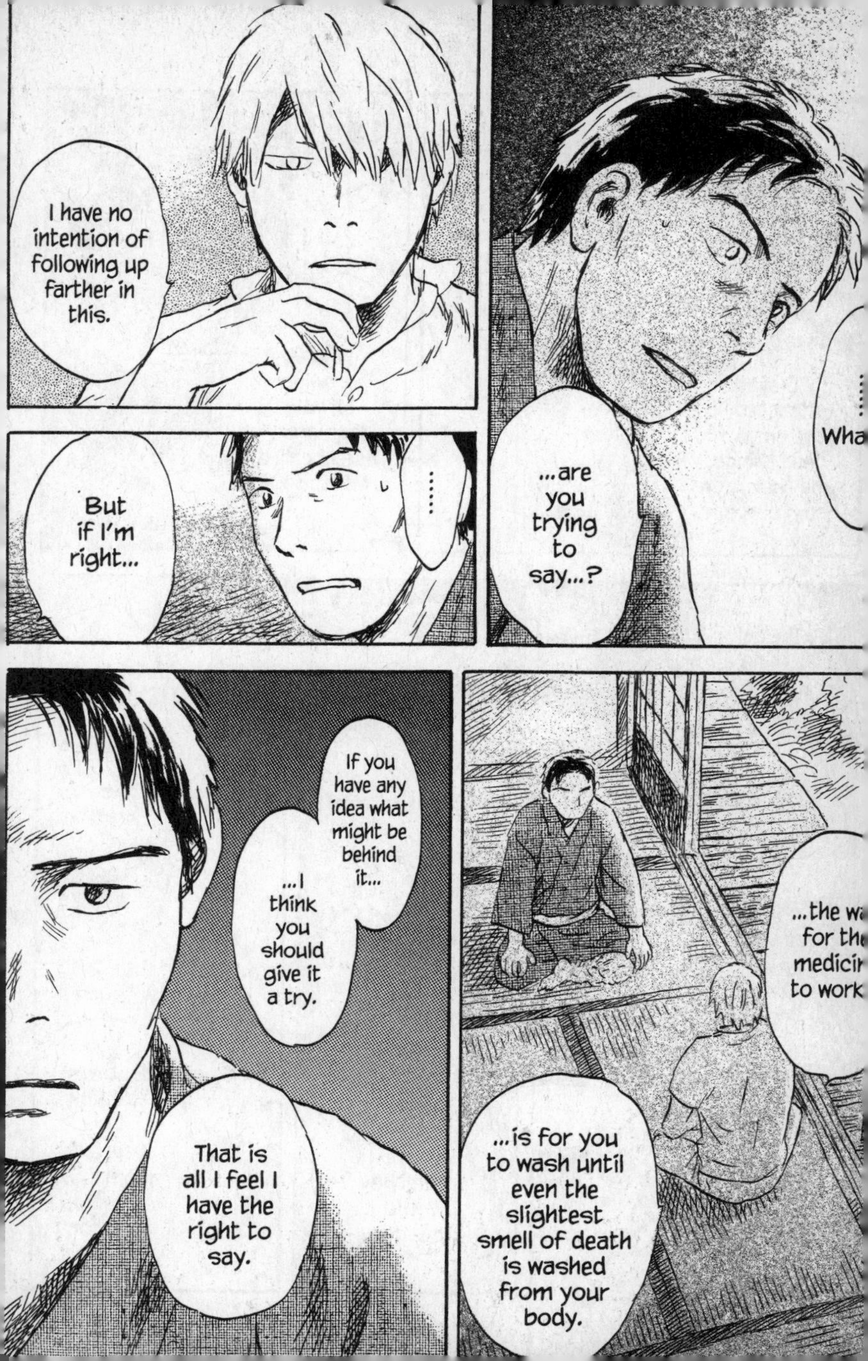

……
Wha
...are you trying to say...?
I have no intention of following up farther in this.
But if I'm right...
……
...the wa for the medicir to work
...is for you to wash until even the slightest smell of death is washed from your body.
If you have any idea what might be behind it...
...I think you should give it a try.
That is all I feel I have the right to say.

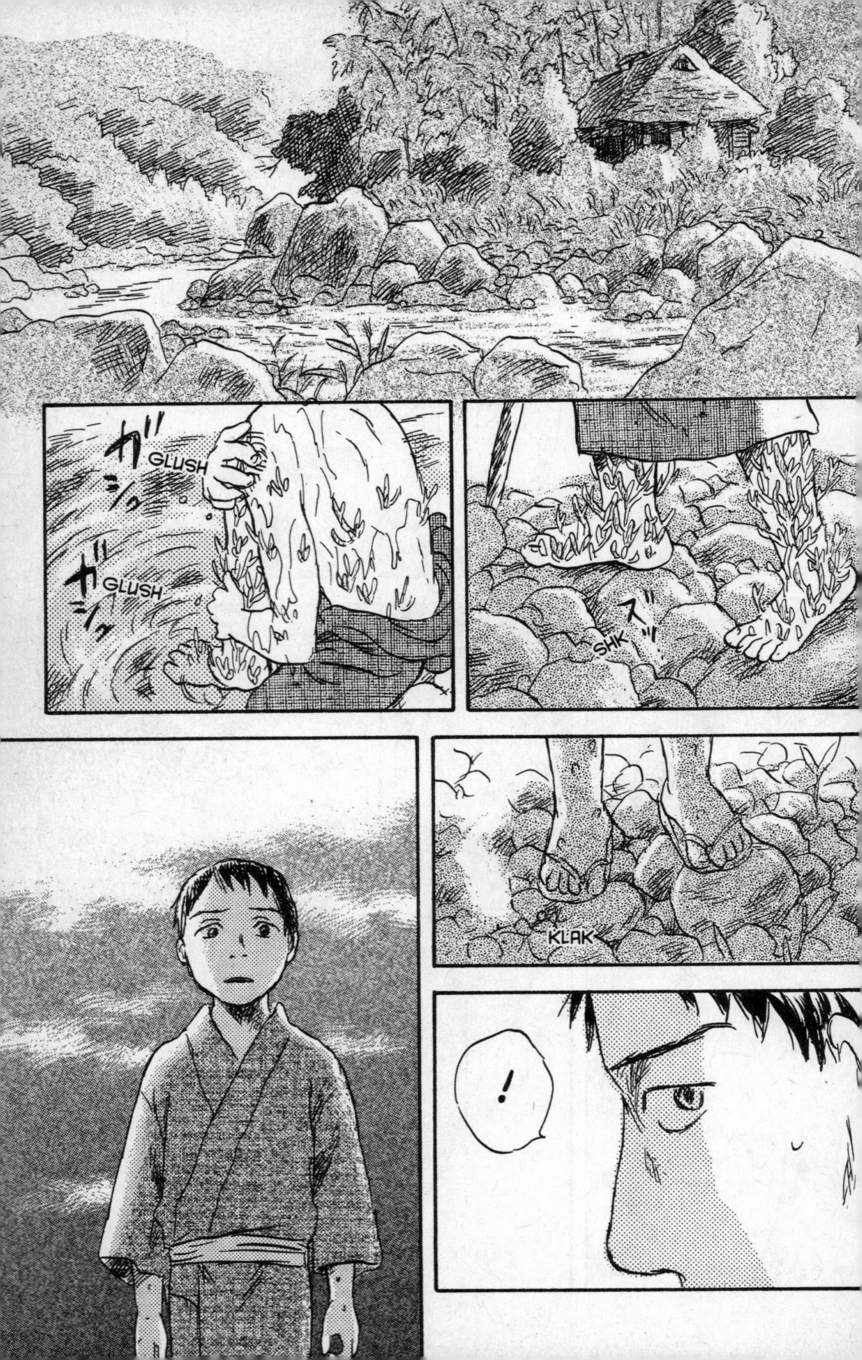
SHK
GLUSH
GLUSH
KLAK
!

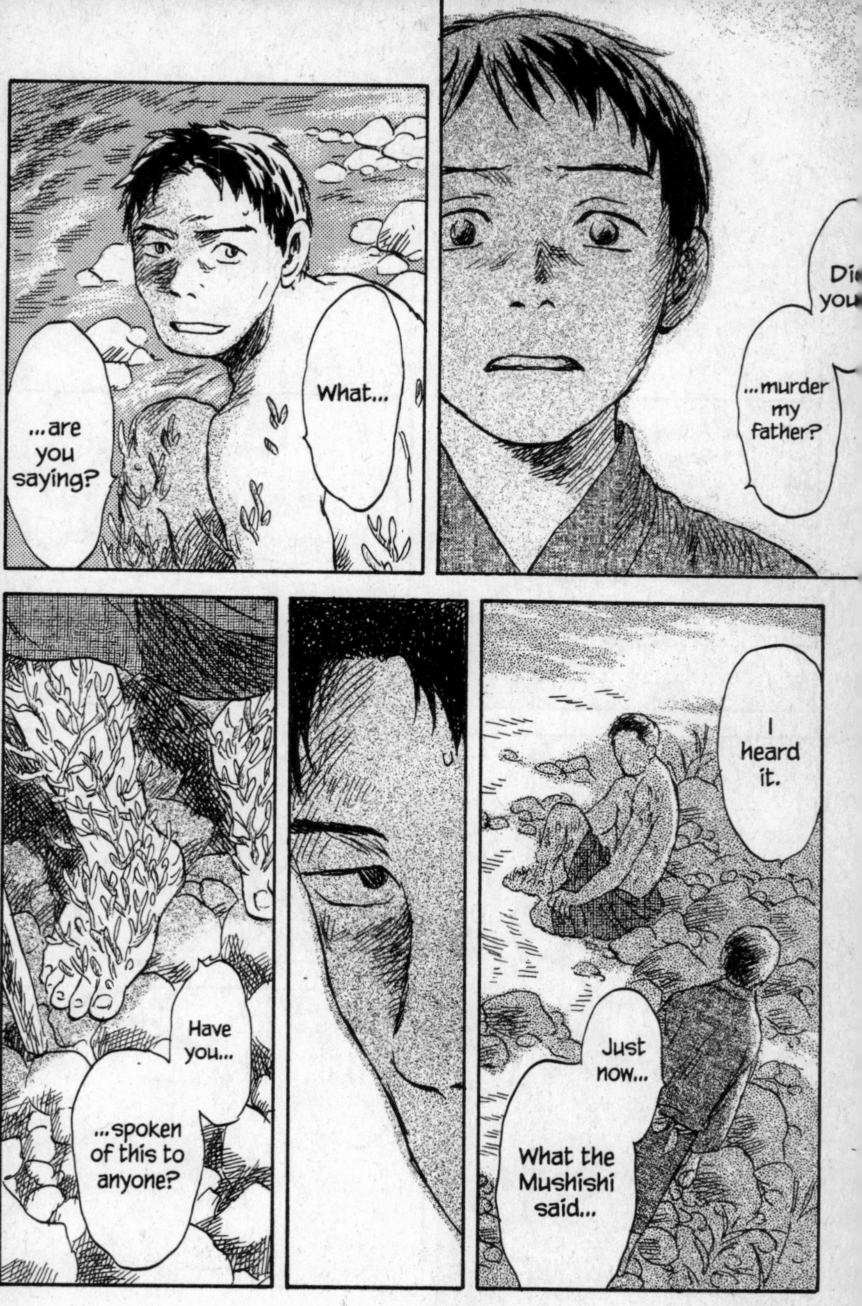
Di you
...murder my father?
What...
...are you saying?
I heard it.
Just now...
What the Mushishi said...
Have you...
...spoken of this to anyone?

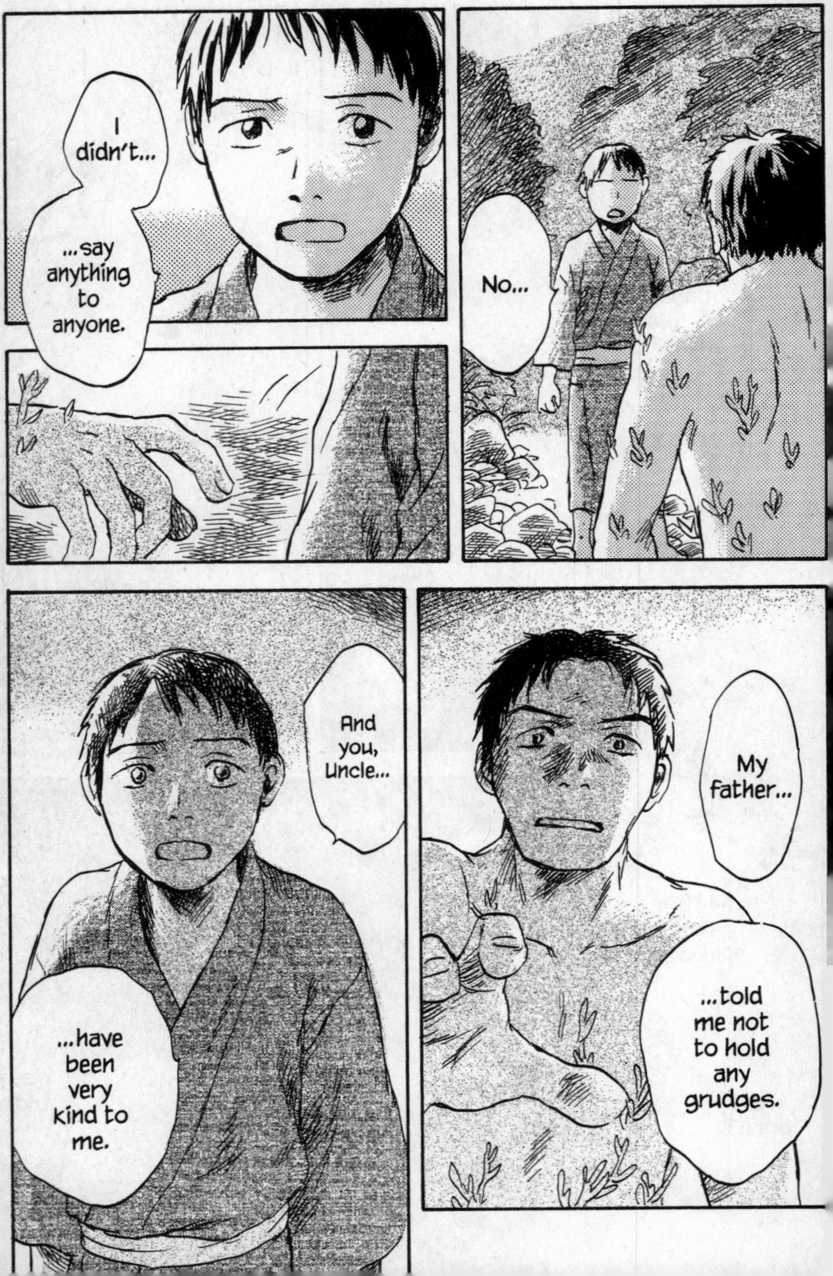
No...
I didn't...
...say anything to anyone.
My father...
...told me not to hold any grudges.
And you, Uncle...
...have been very kind to me.

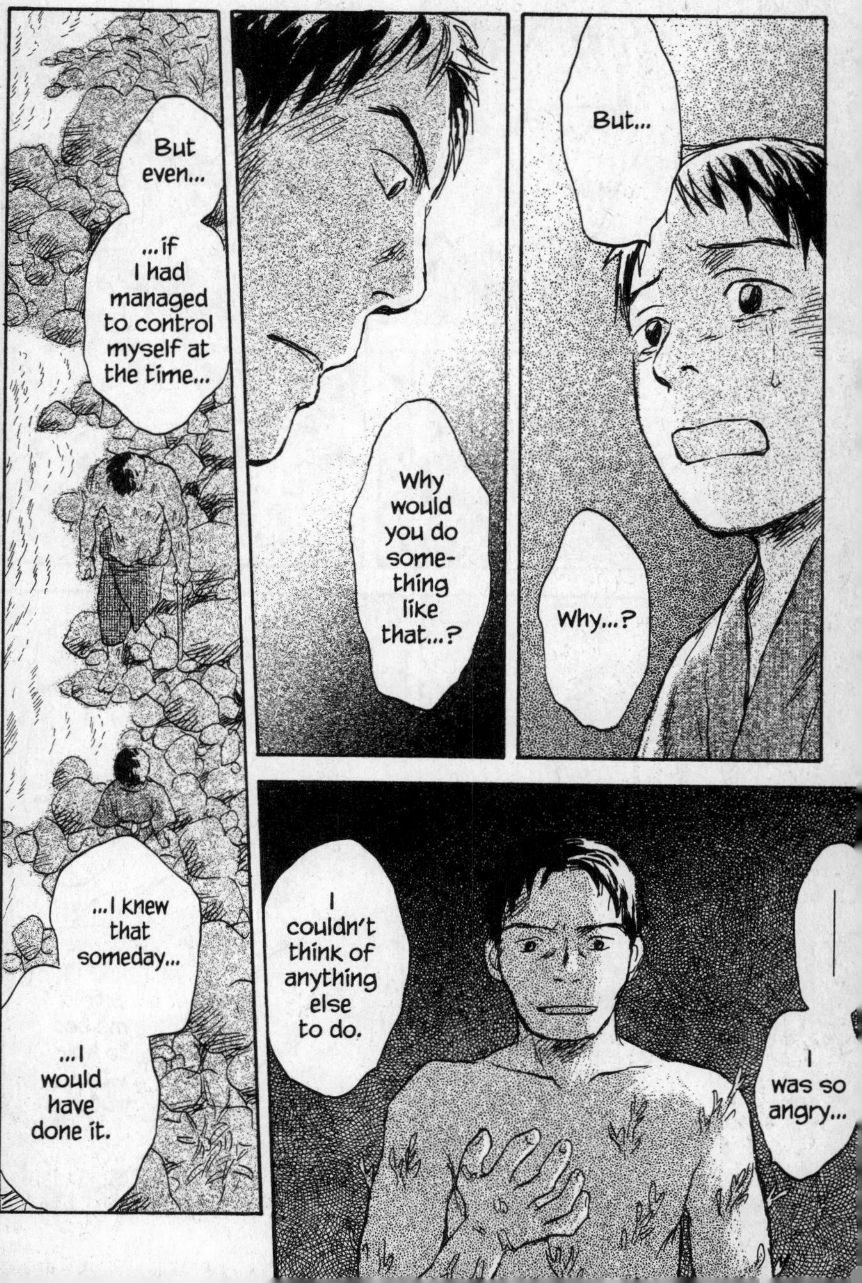
But...
Why...?
Why would you do something like that...?
I was so angry...
I couldn't think of anything else to do.
But even...
...if I had managed to control myself at the time...
...I knew that someday...
...I would have done it.

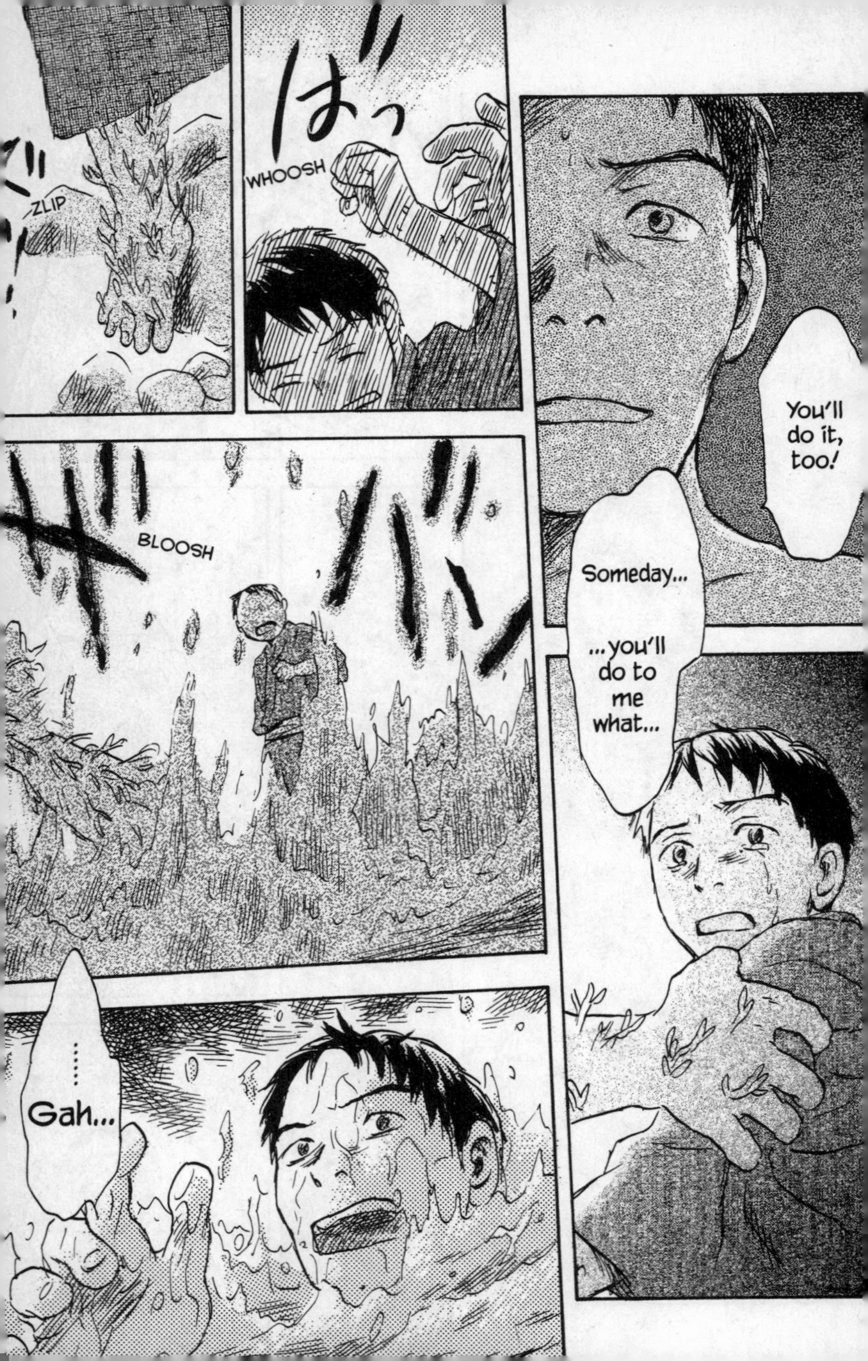
You'll do it, too!
Someday...
...you'll do to me what...
ばっ
WHOOSH
ZLIP
BLOOSH
Gah...

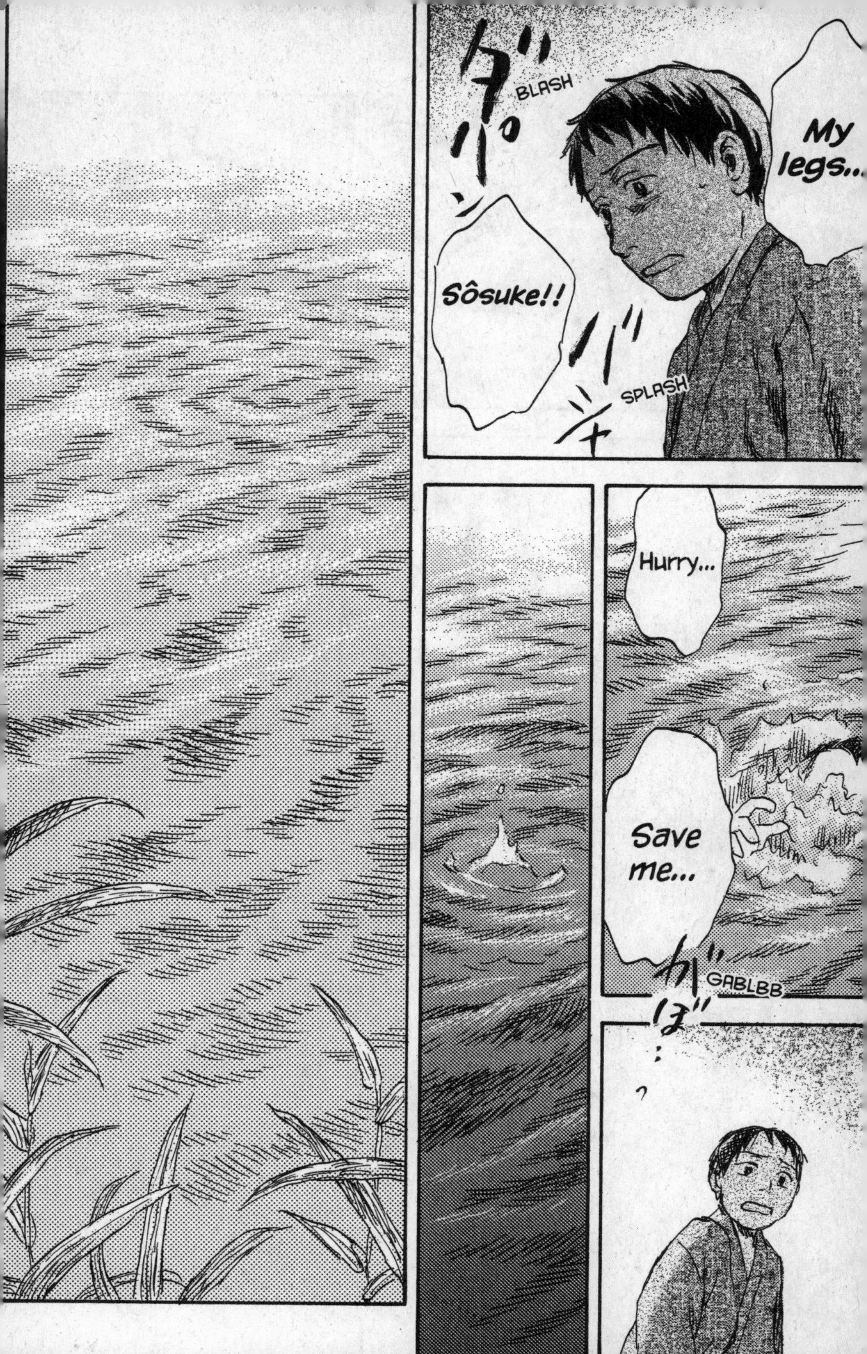
My legs...
BLASH
Sôsuke!!
SPLASH
Hurry...
Save me...
GABLBB

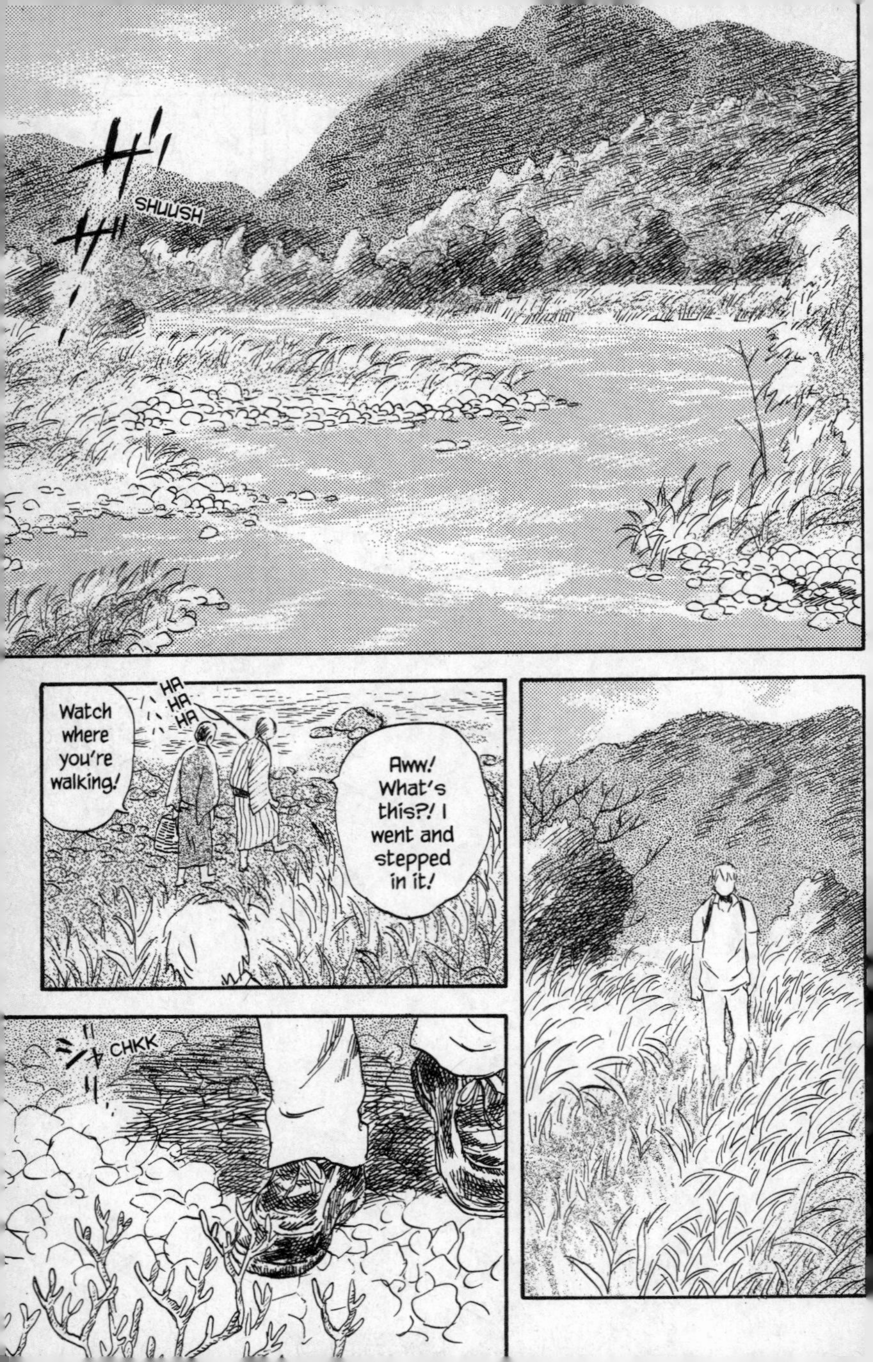
SHUUSH
Aww! What's this?! I went and stepped in it!
HA HA HA
Watch where you're walking!
CHKK

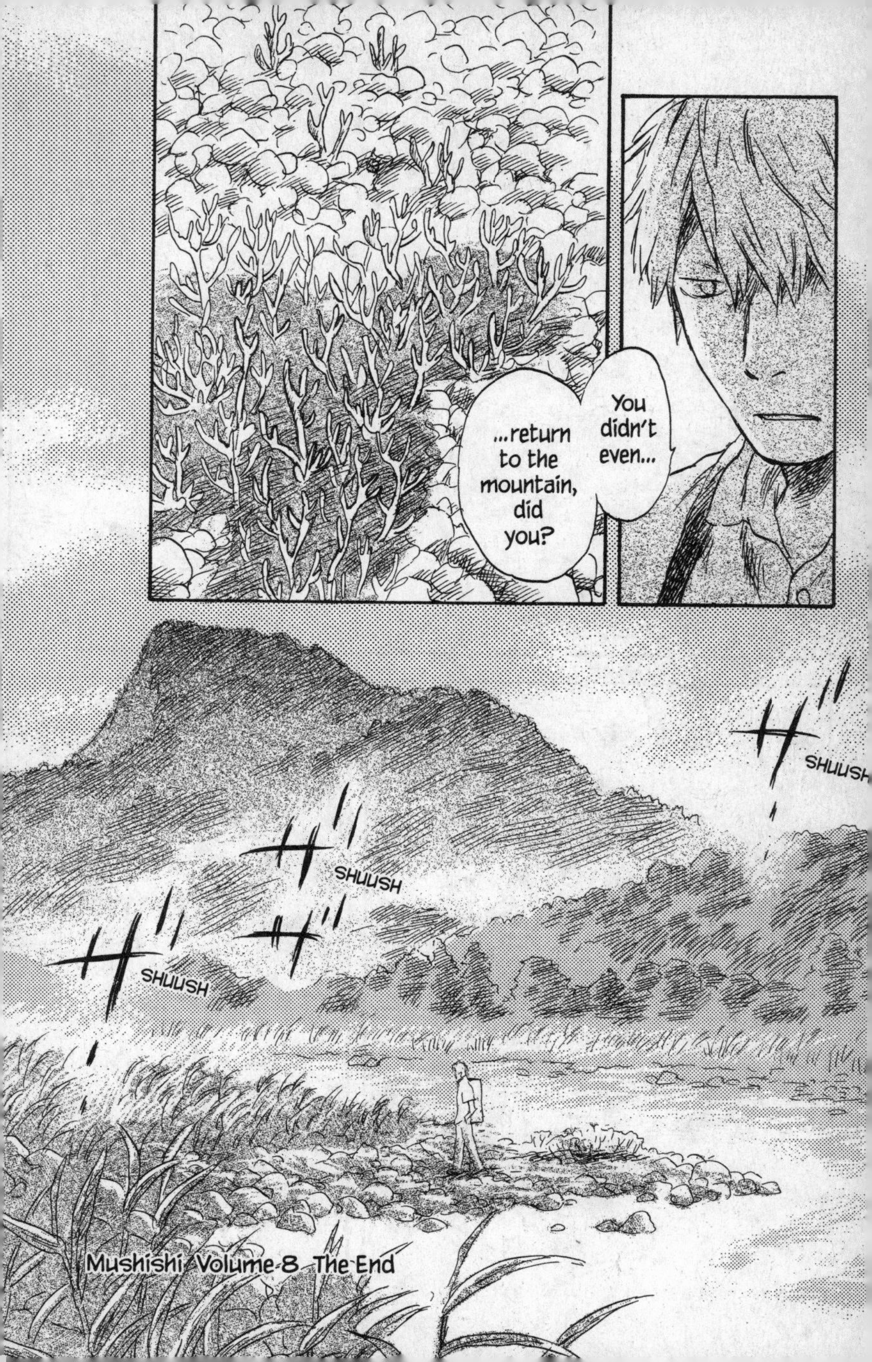
You didn't even...
...return to the mountain, did you?
SHUUSH
SHUUSH
SHUUSH
Mushishi Volume 8 The End

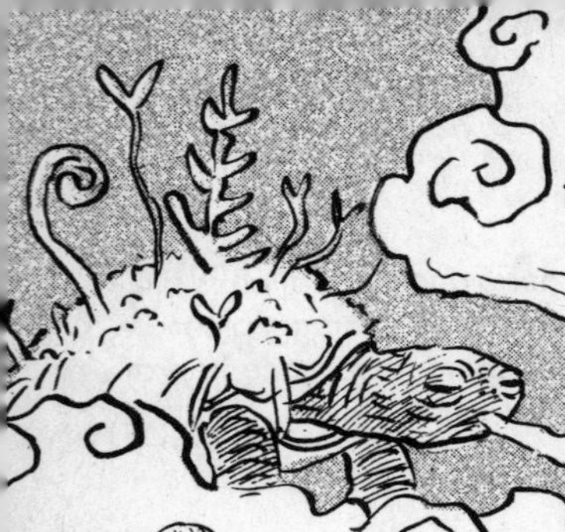

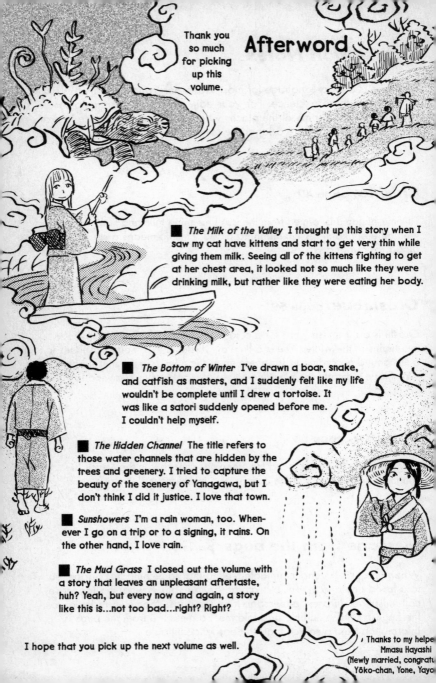

Thank you so much for picking up this volume.

Afterword

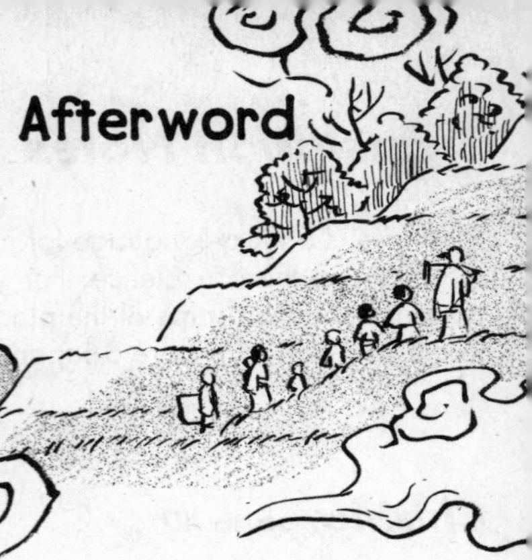

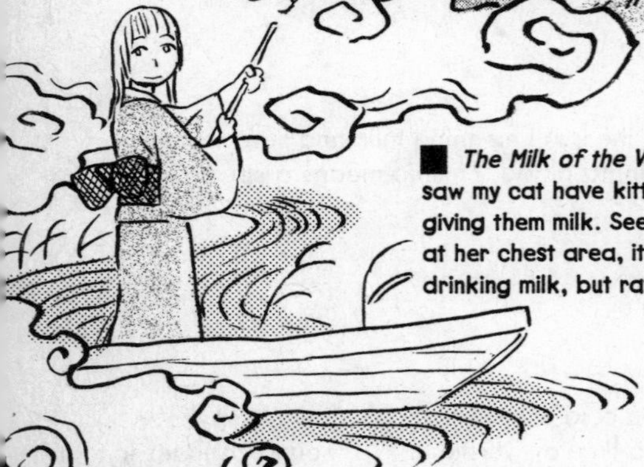

■ *The Milk of the Valley* I thought up this story when I saw my cat have kittens and start to get very thin while giving them milk. Seeing all of the kittens fighting to get at her chest area, it looked not so much like they were drinking milk, but rather like they were eating her body.

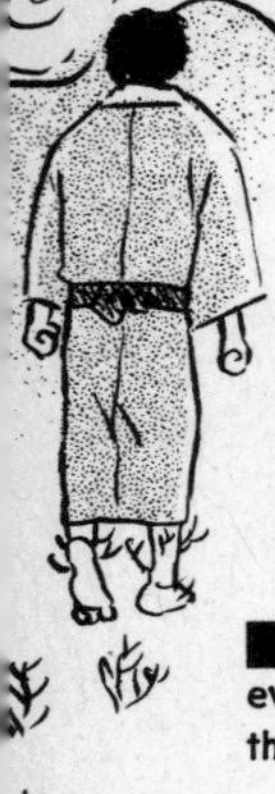

■ *The Bottom of Winter* I've drawn a boar, snake, and catfish as masters, and I suddenly felt like my life wouldn't be complete until I drew a tortoise. It was like a satori suddenly opened before me. I couldn't help myself.

■ *The Hidden Channel* The title refers to those water channels that are hidden by the trees and greenery. I tried to capture the beauty of the scenery of Yanagawa, but I don't think I did it justice. I love that town.

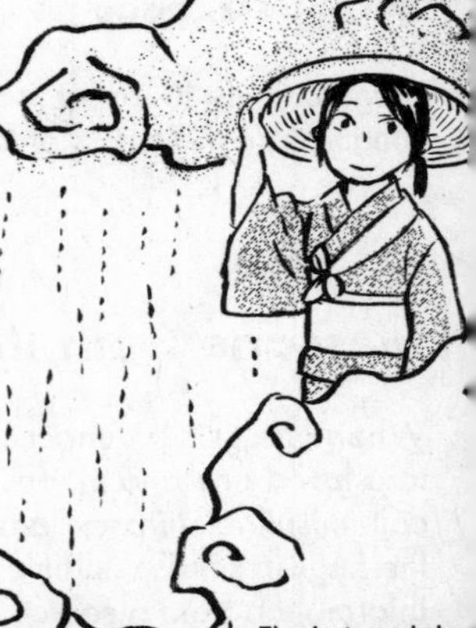

■ *Sunshowers* I'm a rain woman, too. Whenever I go on a trip or to a signing, it rains. On the other hand, I love rain.

■ *The Mud Grass* I closed out the volume with a story that leaves an unpleasant aftertaste, huh? Yeah, but every now and again, a story like this is...not too bad...right? Right?

I hope that you pick up the next volume as well.

Thanks to my helpe
Mmasu Hayashi
(Newly married, congratu
Yōko-chan, Yone, Yayo

Translation Notes

Japanese is a tricky language for most Westerners, and translation is often more an art than a science. For your edification and reading pleasure, here are notes on some of the places where we could have gone in a different direction, or where a Japanese cultural reference is used.

Chishio, page 42

This mushi name is formed from the kanji meaning milk and tide. Written with different kanji for *chi* meaning blood, *chishio* means a spurt of blood, as out of a wound.

Oroshibue, page 59

Oroshi is a Japanese word for a cold wind that blows down from the mountains in the winter. *Fue* is a flute or whistle (the "f" sound changes to a "b" sound according to Japanese linguistic rules). So the mushi name *Oroshibue* indicates the whistling sound of a cold mountain wind in winter.

Mugura, page 61

Mugura is the Japanese word for creeping vines, but in the Mushishi world *Mugura* are indicators of the actions of a mushi master of a mountain.

Message from the bugs, page 96

When one gets an unaccountable feeling that something has happened to a loved one and it turns out later to be true, this is what the Japanese call *mushi no shirase*, "a message from the bugs." Somewhat similar to the English phrase "a little bird told me," a message from the bugs is information from a source that isn't easily identifiable.

Kairogi, page 96

Most *mushi* names in *Mushishi* are a combination of normal, well-known kanji combined to make an easily understandable word. *Kairogi* is an exception. In Japanese, *kairo* means waterway, so that makes sense, but I can only guess what the *gi* part of the name is supposed to mean. Also, the single kanji for the name is not commonly used in Japanese. It can be found among the Chinese character lists, but it seems to be scarce even there. The character is made up of two parts: one meaning small and another which means boat. Again, this is understandable, but to combine the meanings into one kanji (instead of forming a compound of two kanji) is unusual for Urushibara-sensei.

Amefurashi, page 169

The kanji for *ame* means rain, and the kanji for *furashi* means to fall.

Drifters, page 170

The Japanese term *nagaremono* has many meanings in Japanese. One is a thing that goes with the flow. Vagabond is another meaning found in the dictionary, as is drifter. Migrant tribes are also called *nagaremono*.

Mukurosô, page 182

Mukuro is a slightly archaic word for corpse, and *sô* is one of the words for grass. So *Mukurosô* is another perfectly understandable mushi name.

Yanagawa, page 217

The town that is the basis for the third chapter in this volume is Yanagawa in the southern part of Fukuoka prefecture (located on the southern island of Kyushu). Its canals—originally irrigation canals, but they were widened and maintained—have become a prime attraction for tourists from all over Japan.

219

蟲師
むしし

Mushishi

9

Yuki Urushibara

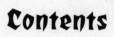

Contents

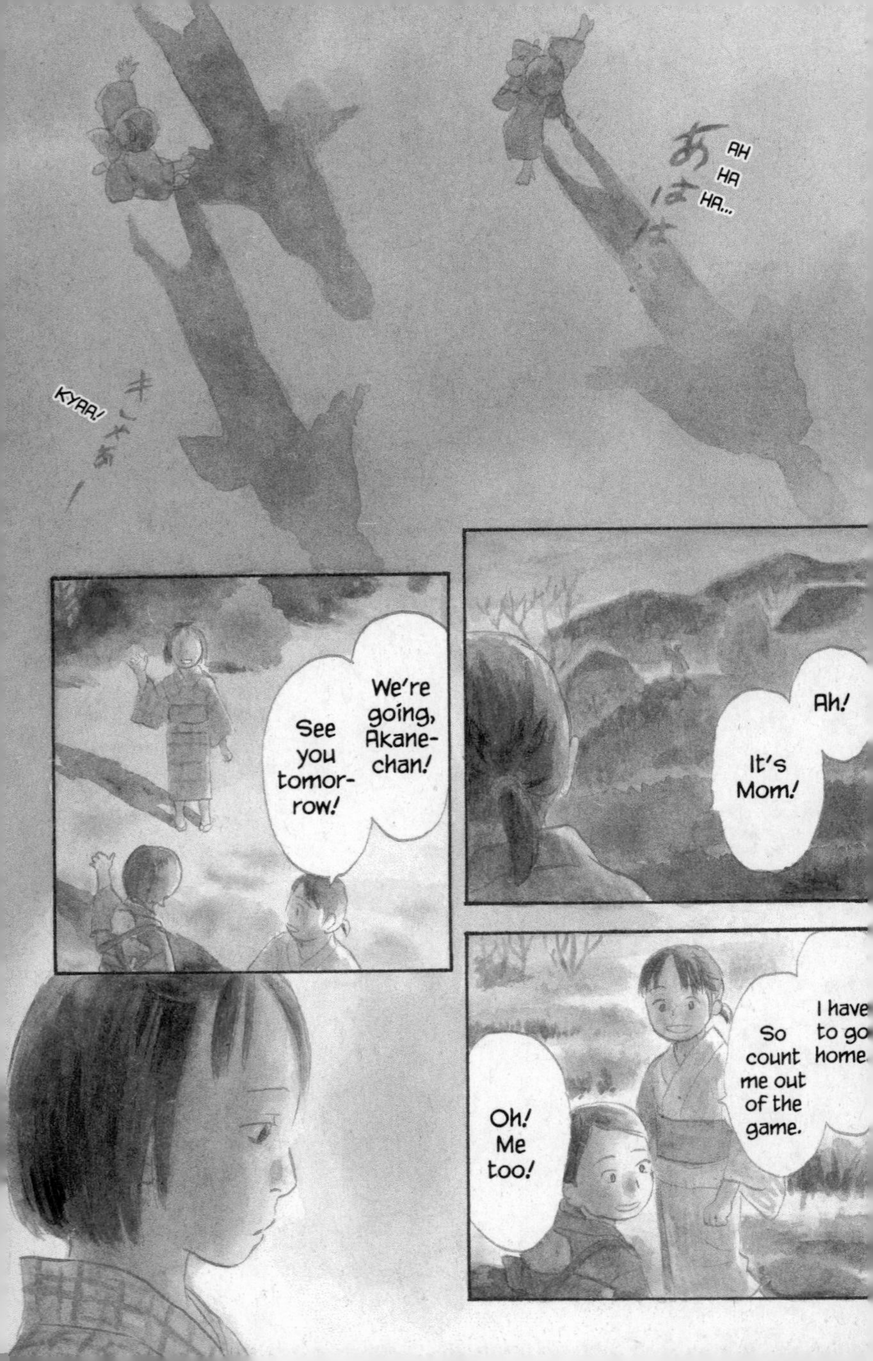
あはは
AH HA HA...
きゃあ!
KYAA!
Ah! It's Mom!
We're going, Akane-chan! See you tomorrow!
I have to go home. So count me out of the game.
Oh! Me too!

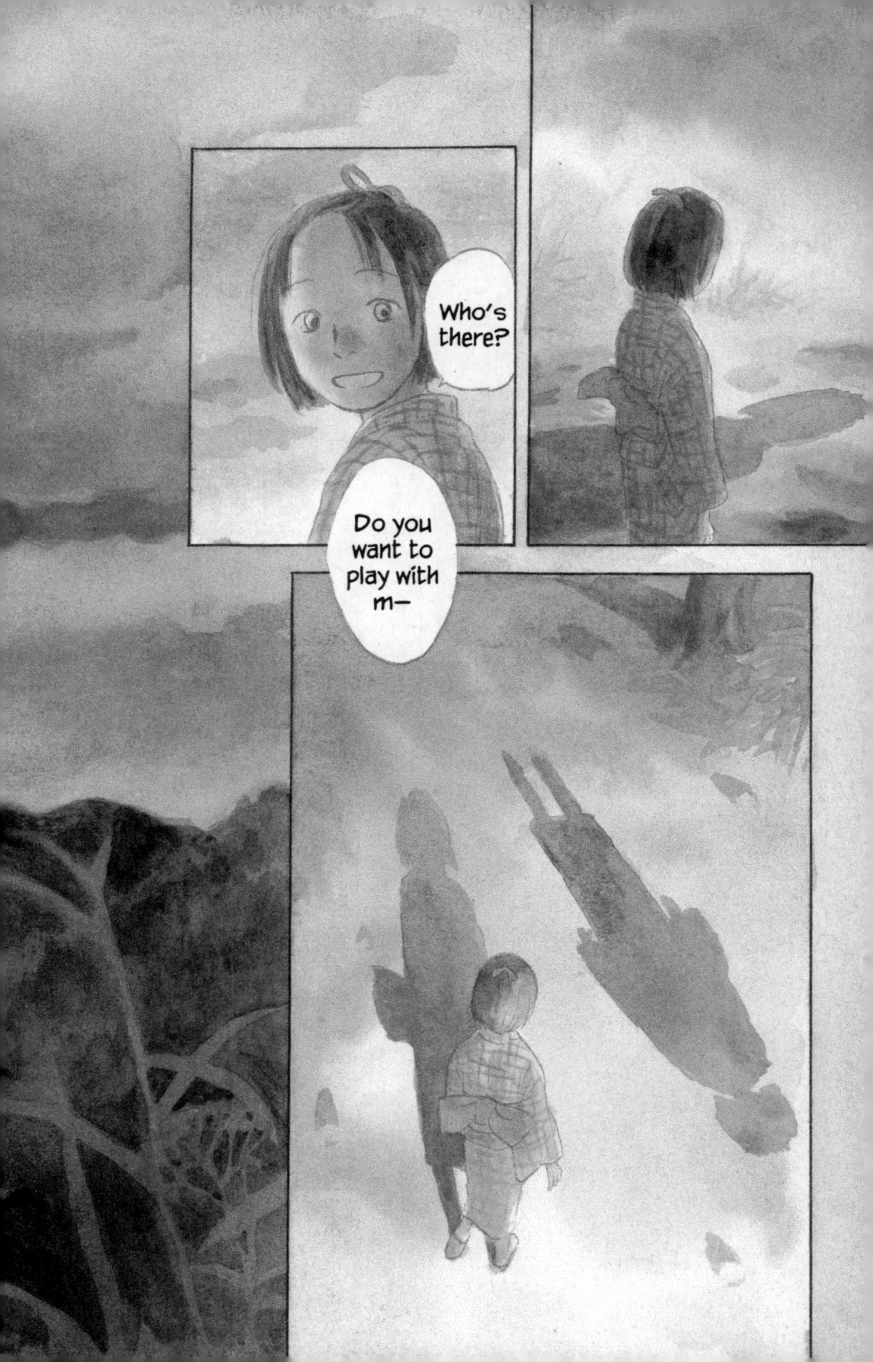
Who's there?
Do you want to play with m–

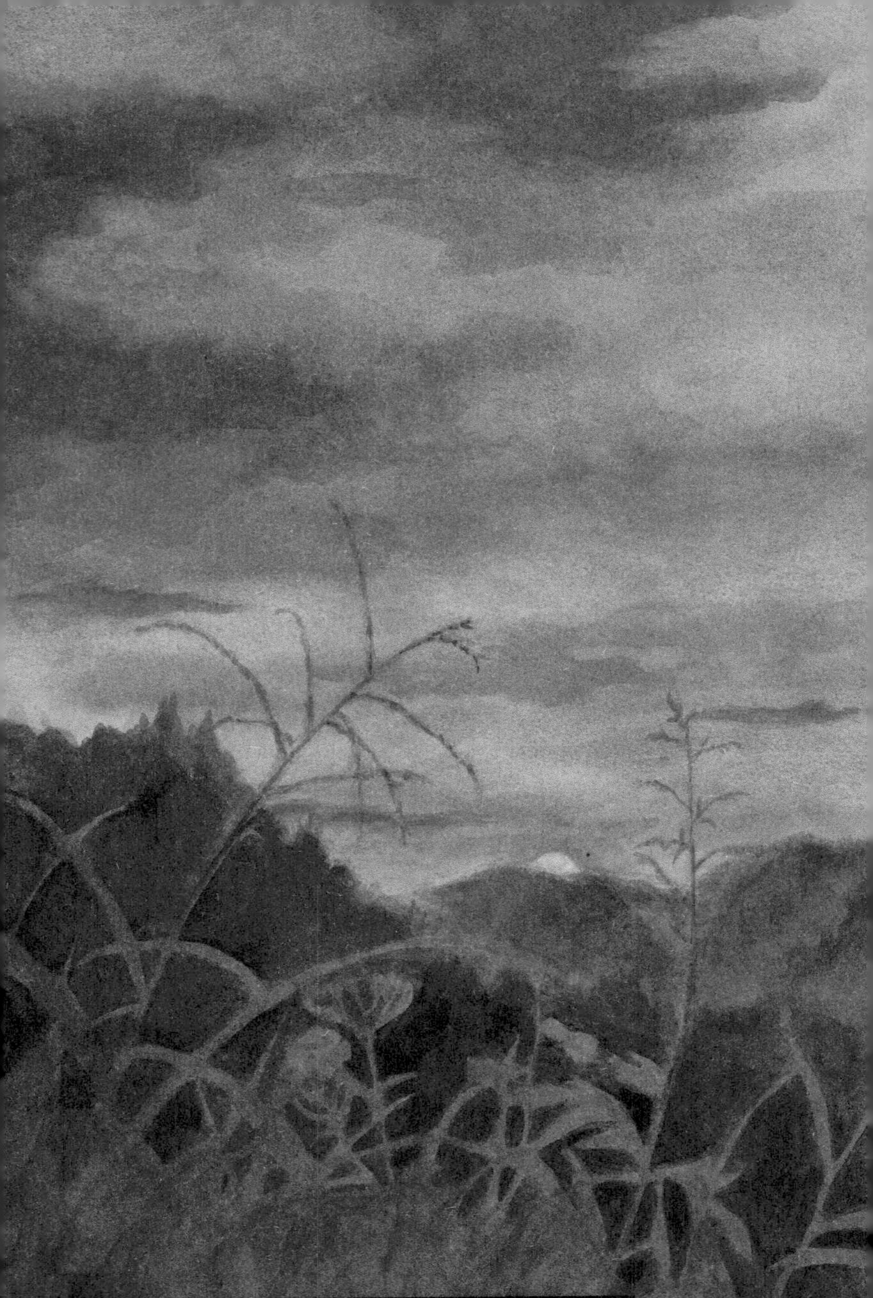

The Final Bit of Crimson

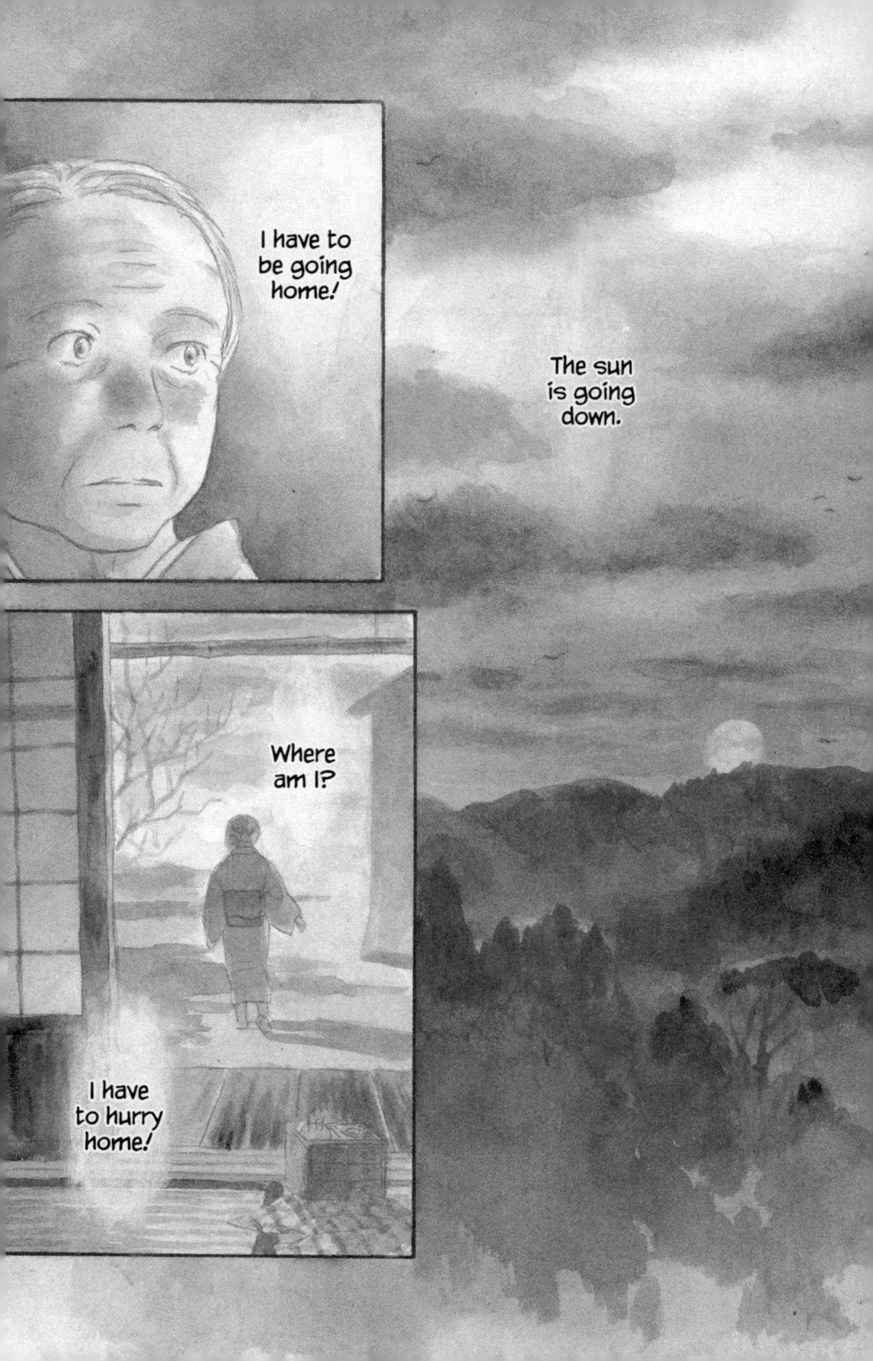
The sun is going down.
I have to be going home!
Where am I?
I have to hurry home!

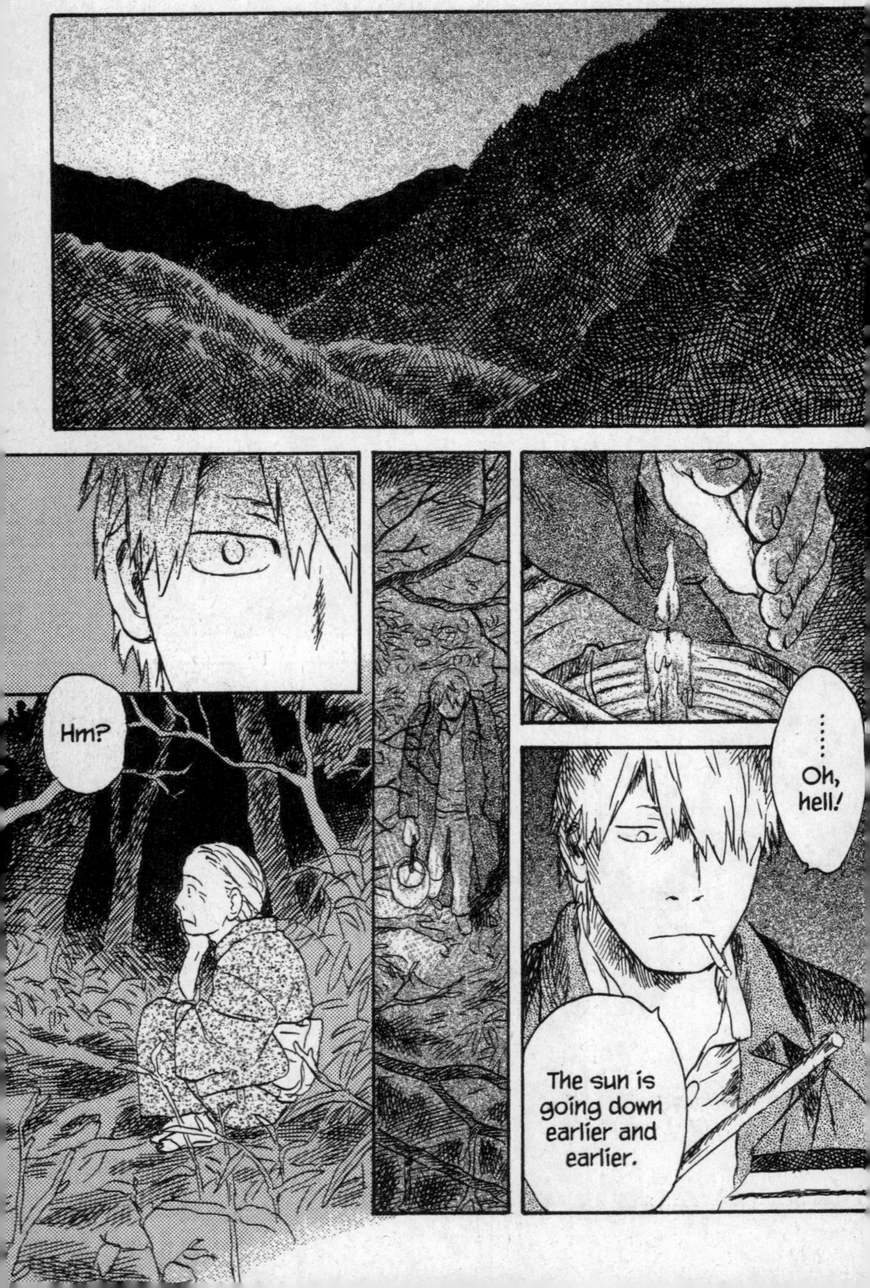
......Oh, hell!
The sun is going down earlier and earlier.
Hm?

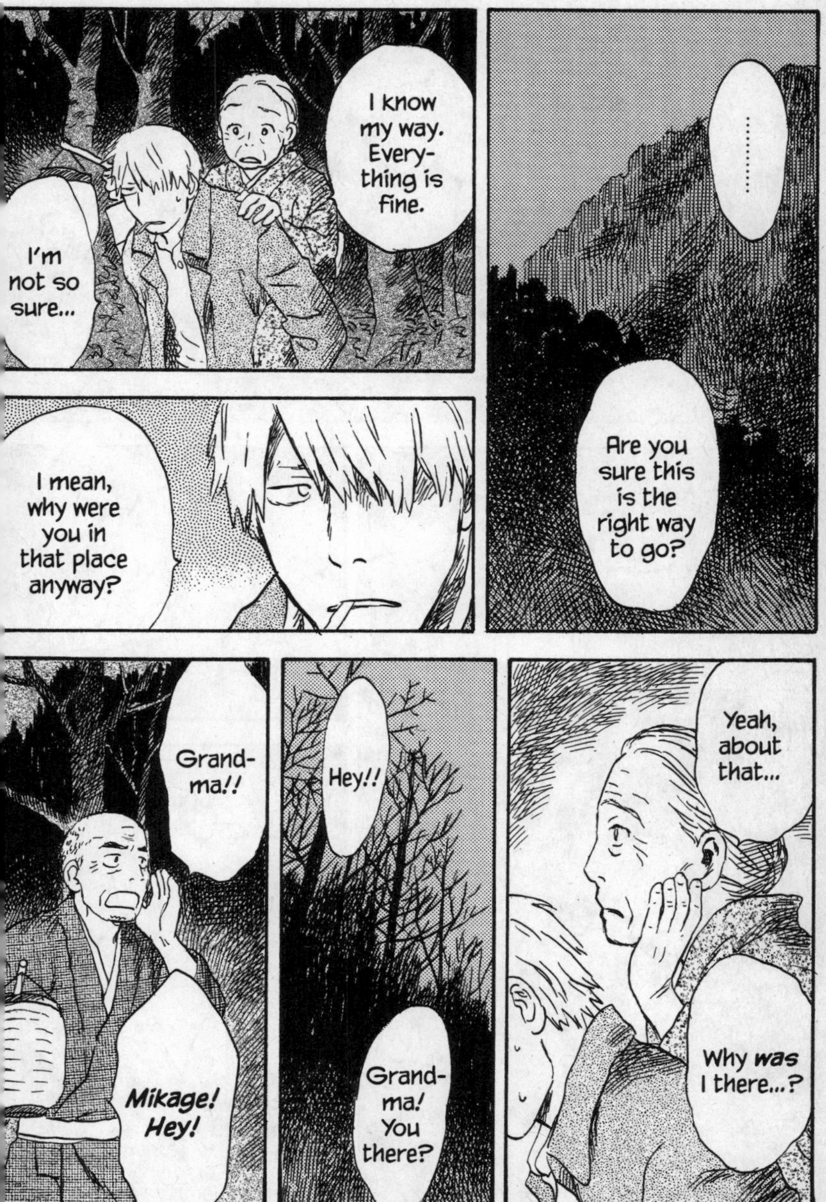
……
Are you sure this is the right way to go?
I know my way. Every-thing is fine.
I'm not so sure...
I mean, why were you in that place anyway?
Yeah, about that...
Why *was* I there...?
Hey!!
Grand-ma! You there?
Grand-ma!!
Mikage! Hey!

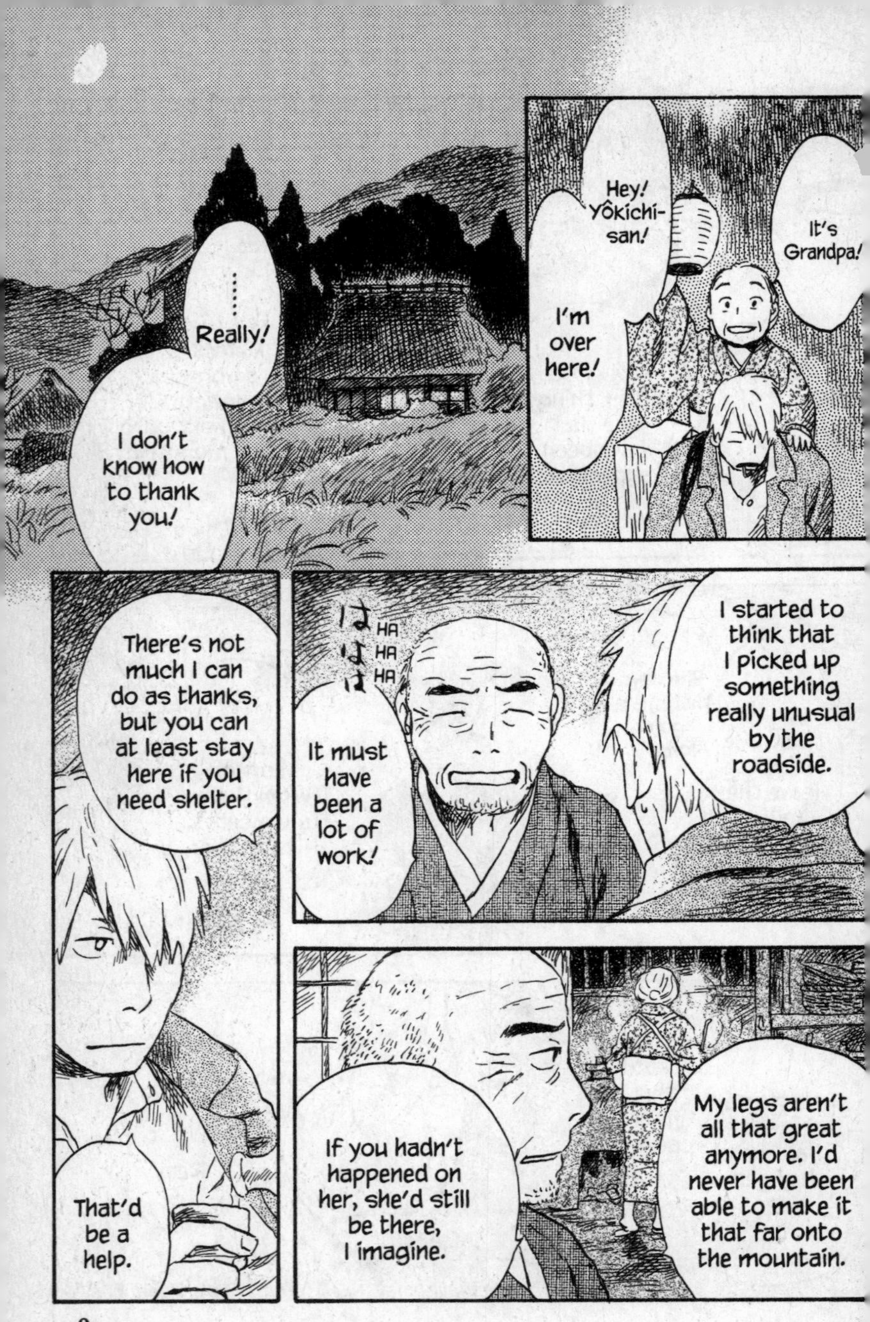
It's Grandpa!
Hey! Yôkichi-san!
I'm over here!
......
Really!
I don't know how to thank you!
I started to think that I picked up something really unusual by the roadside.
ははは HA HA HA
It must have been a lot of work!
My legs aren't all that great anymore. I'd never have been able to make it that far onto the mountain.
If you hadn't happened on her, she'd still be there, I imagine.
There's not much I can do as thanks, but you can at least stay here if you need shelter.
That'd be a help.

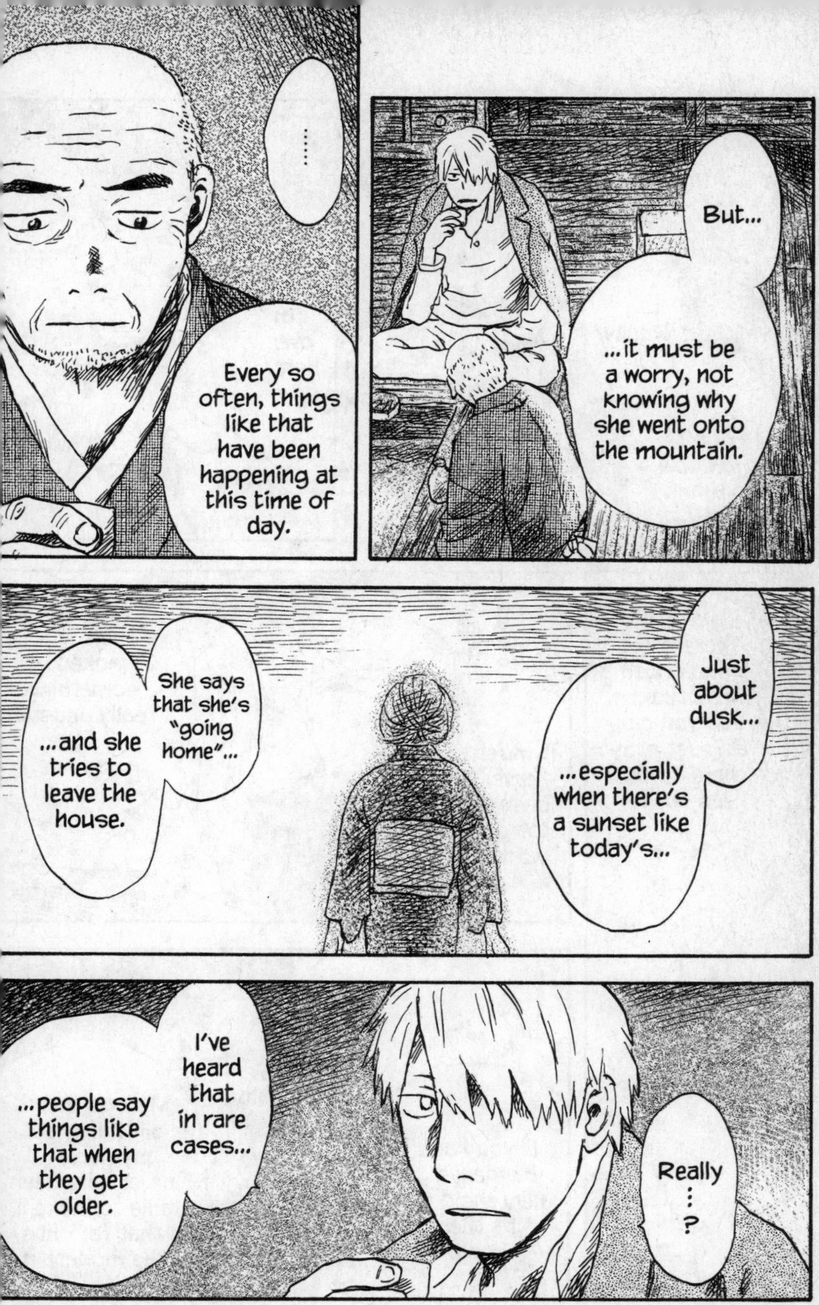
But...
...it must be a worry, not knowing why she went onto the mountain.
......
Every so often, things like that have been happening at this time of day.
Just about dusk...
...especially when there's a sunset like today's...
She says that she's "going home"...
...and she tries to leave the house.
Really...?
I've heard that in rare cases...
...people say things like that when they get older.

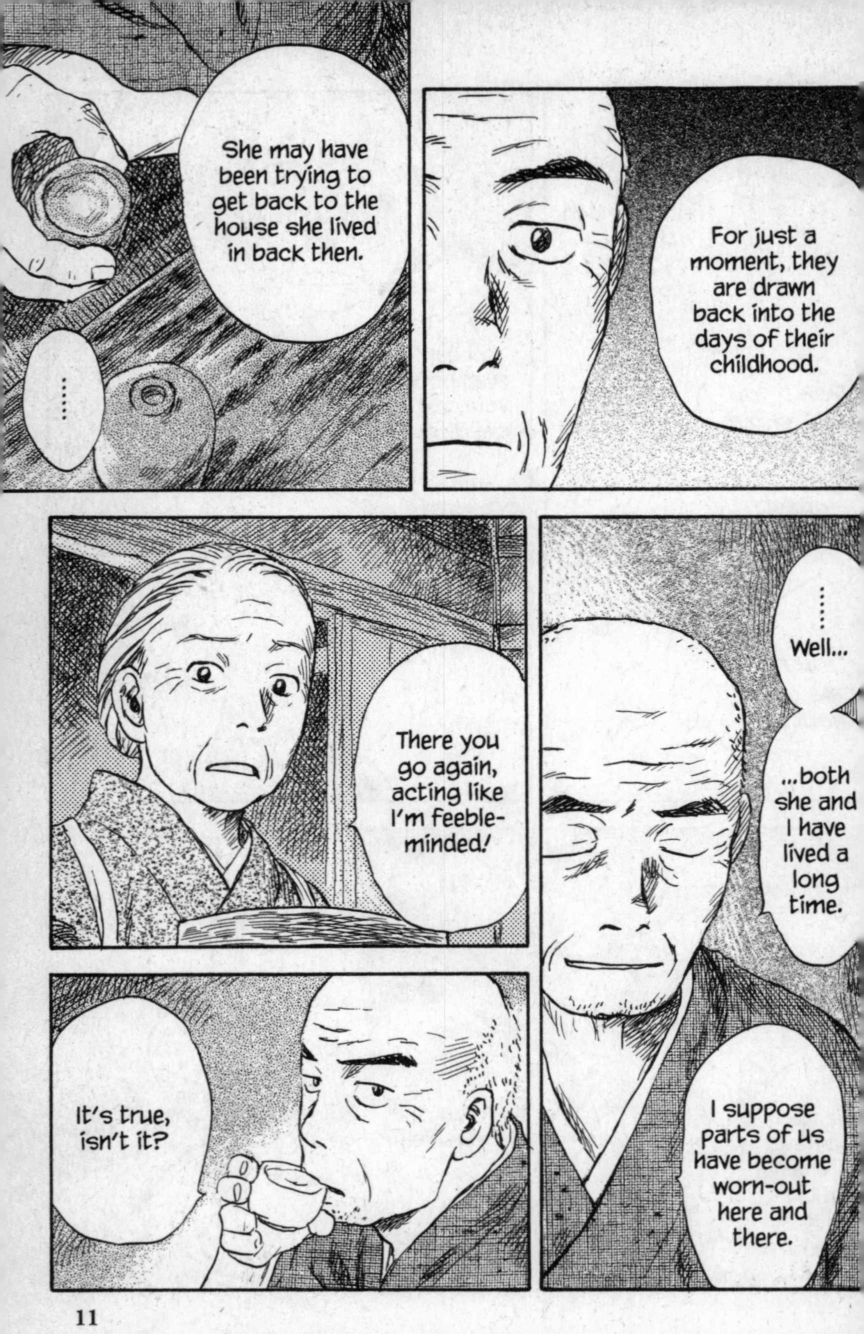
For just a moment, they are drawn back into the days of their childhood.
She may have been trying to get back to the house she lived in back then.
……
……
Well...
...both she and I have lived a long time.
I suppose parts of us have become worn-out here and there.
There you go again, acting like I'm feeble-minded!
It's true, isn't it?

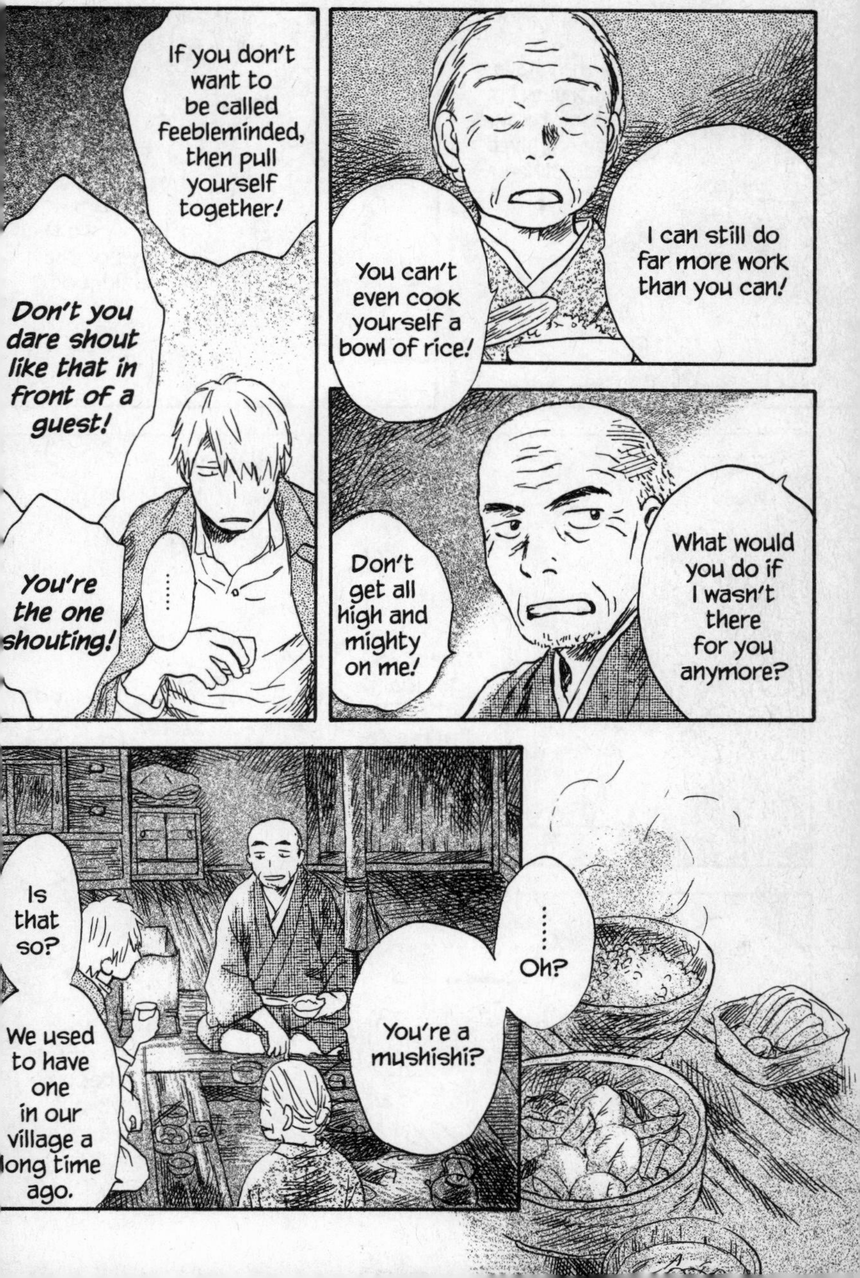
I can still do far more work than you can!
You can't even cook yourself a bowl of rice!
What would you do if I wasn't there for you anymore?
Don't get all high and mighty on me!
If you don't want to be called feebleminded, then pull yourself together!
Don't you dare shout like that in front of a guest!
......
You're the one shouting!
......
Oh?
You're a mushishi?
Is that so?
We used to have one in our village a long time ago.

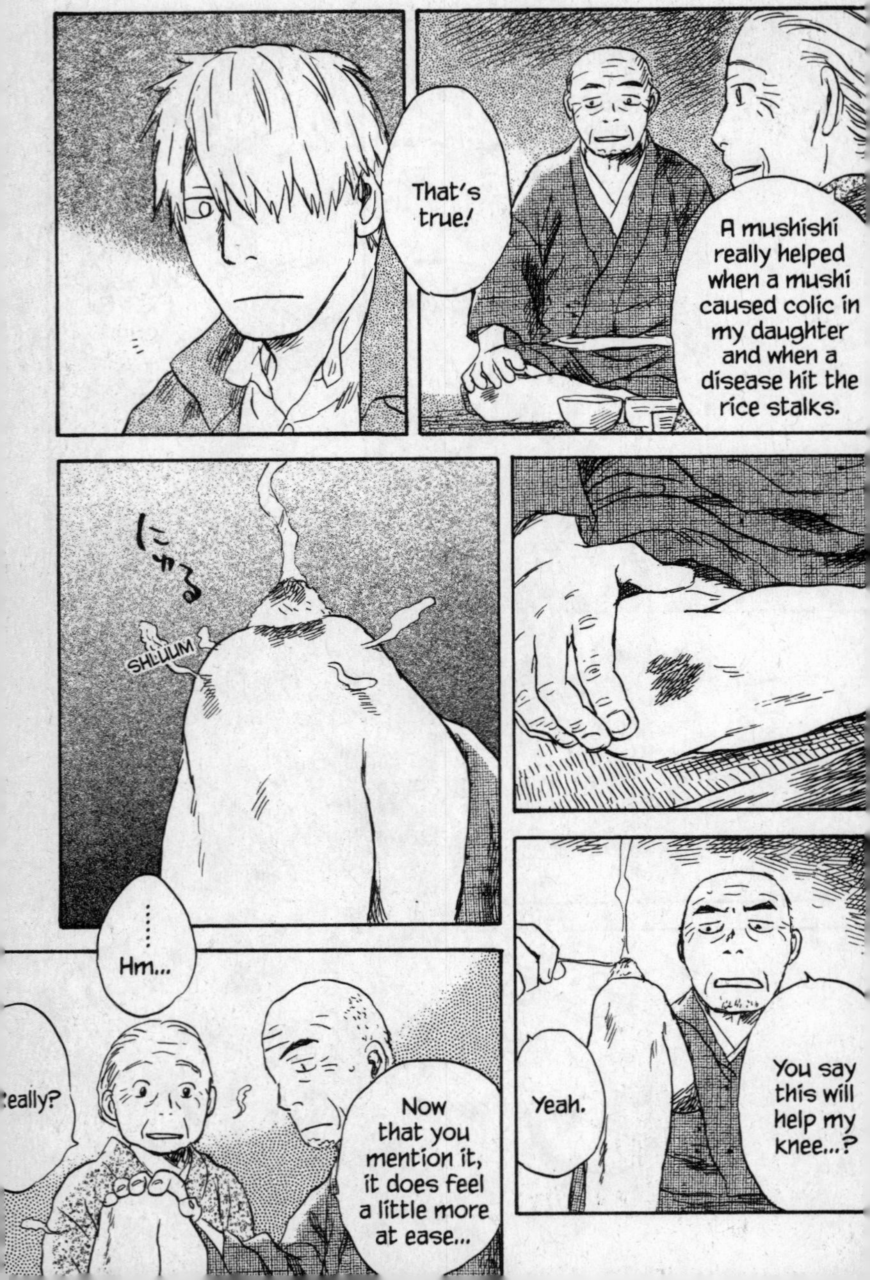

A mushishi really helped when a mushi caused colic in my daughter and when a disease hit the rice stalks.
That's true!
にゅる
SHLUUM
You say this will help my knee...?
Yeah.
……
Hm...
Now that you mention it, it does feel a little more at ease...
eally?

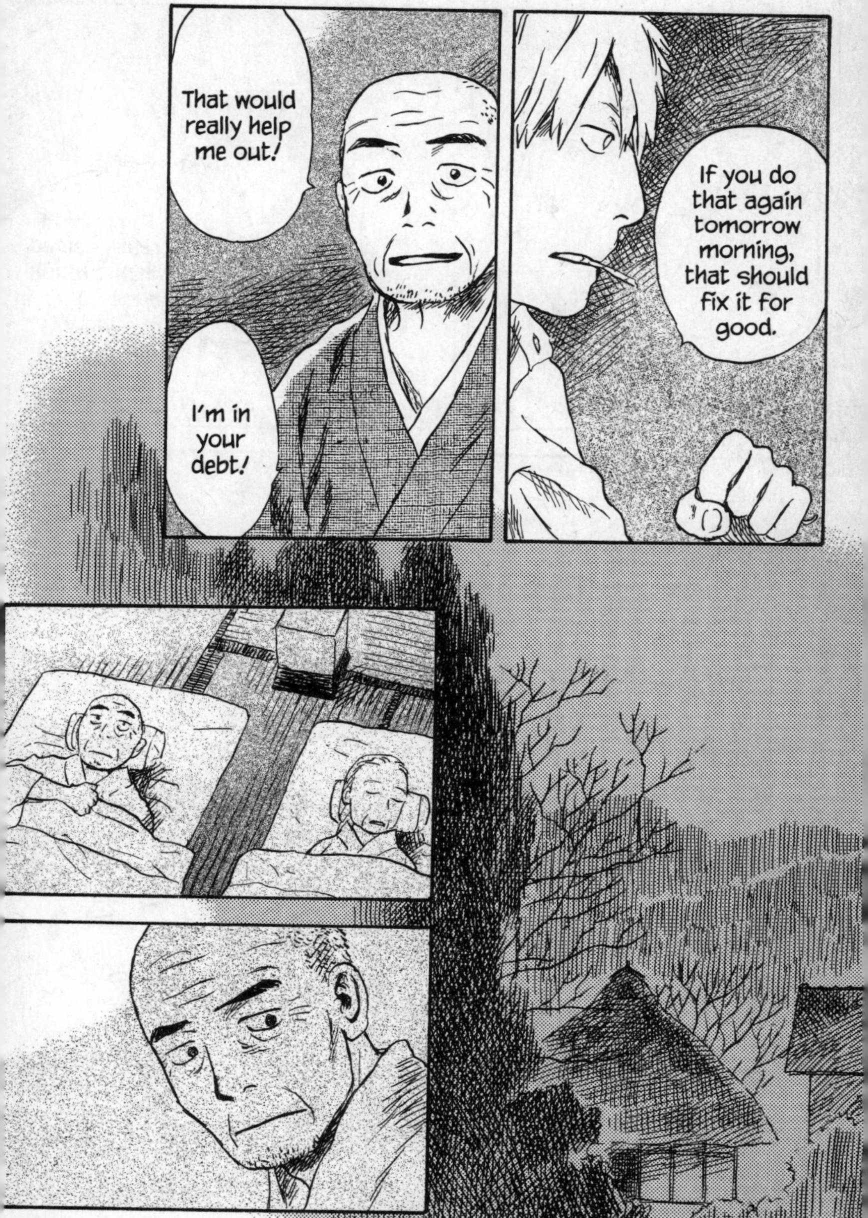
If you do that again tomorrow morning, that should fix it for good.
That would really help me out!
I'm in your debt!

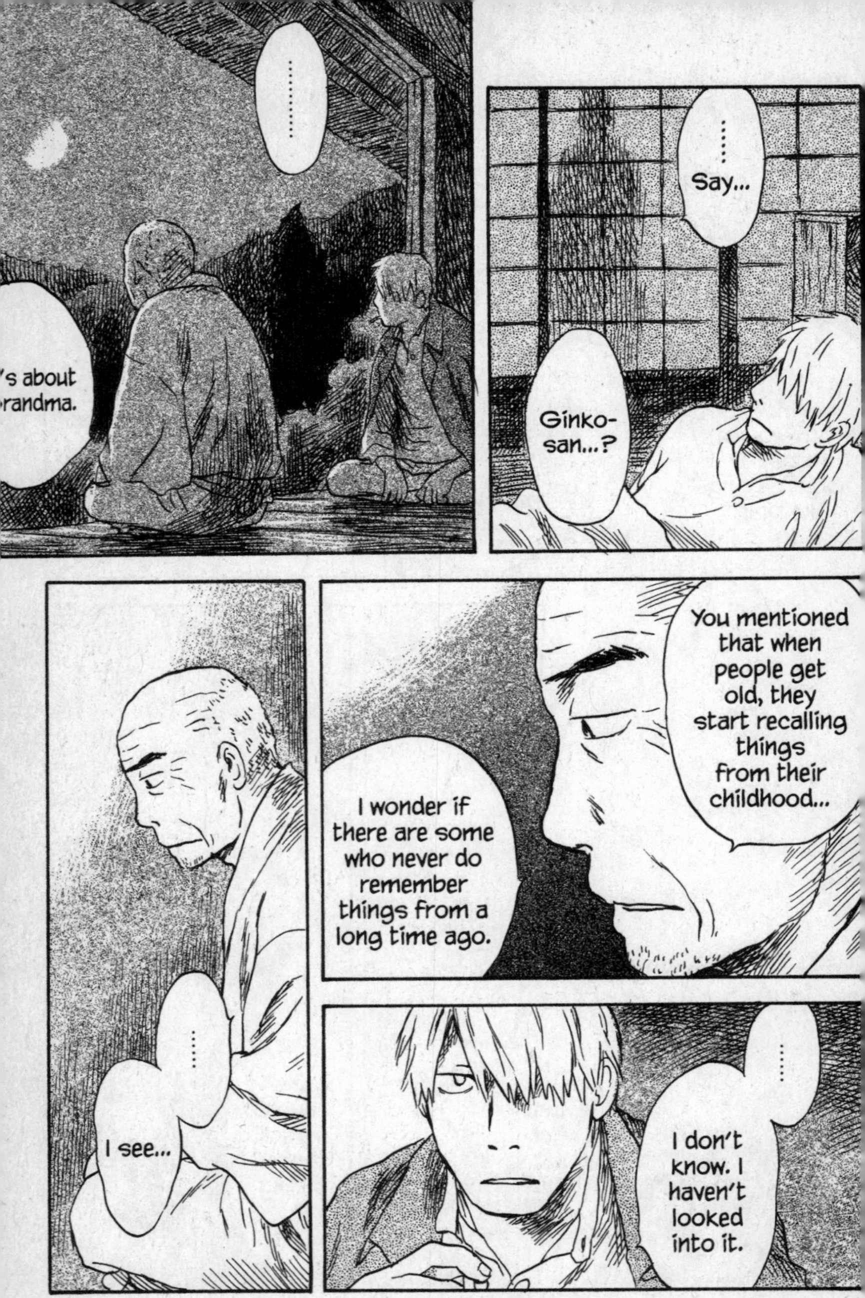
......
Say...
Ginko-san...?
....
's about randma.
You mentioned that when people get old, they start recalling things from their childhood...
I wonder if there are some who never do remember things from a long time ago.
......
I don't know. I haven't looked into it.
......
I see...

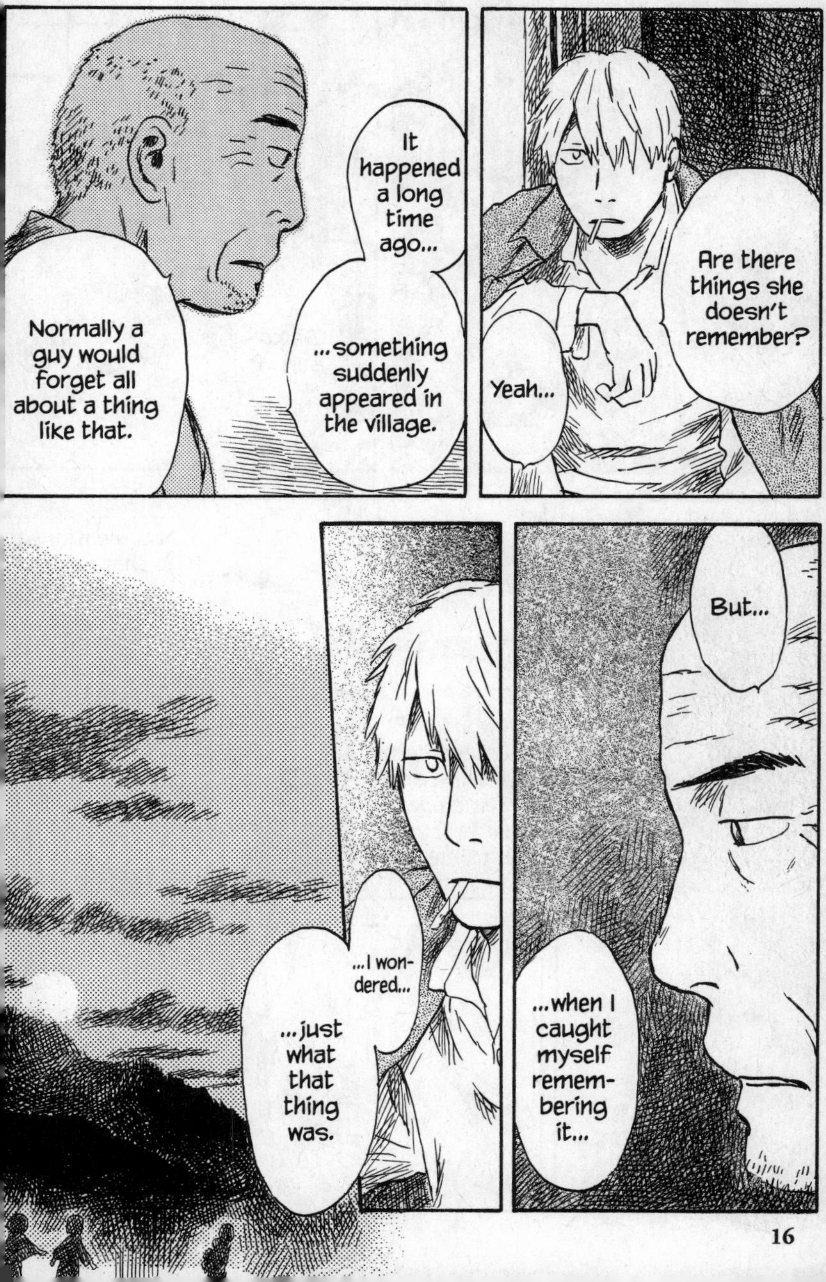
Are there things she doesn't remember?
Yeah...
It happened a long time ago...
...something suddenly appeared in the village.
Normally a guy would forget all about a thing like that.
But...
...when I caught myself remem-bering it...
...I won-dered...
...just what that thing was.

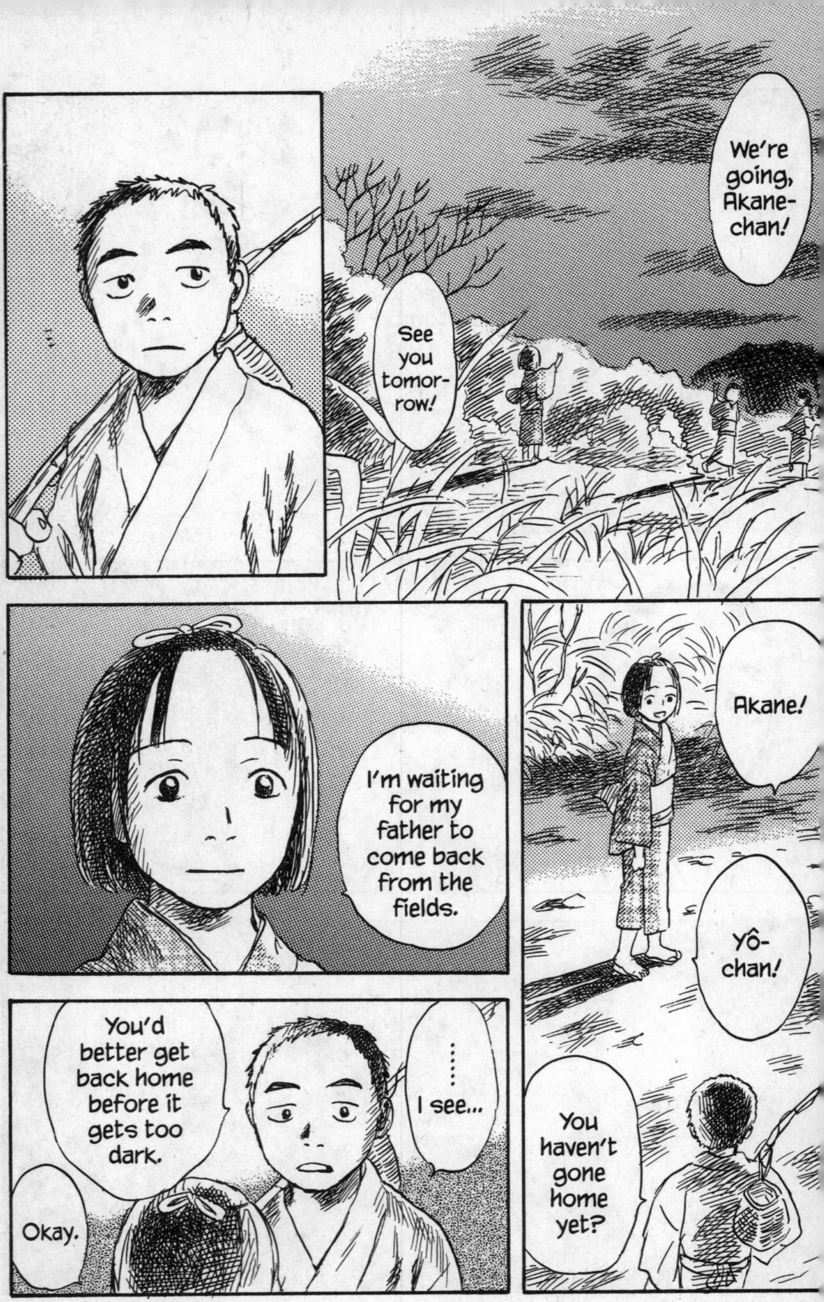
We're going, Akane-chan!
See you tomorrow!
Akane!
Yô-chan!
You haven't gone home yet?
I'm waiting for my father to come back from the fields.
...... I see...
You'd better get back home before it gets too dark.
Okay.

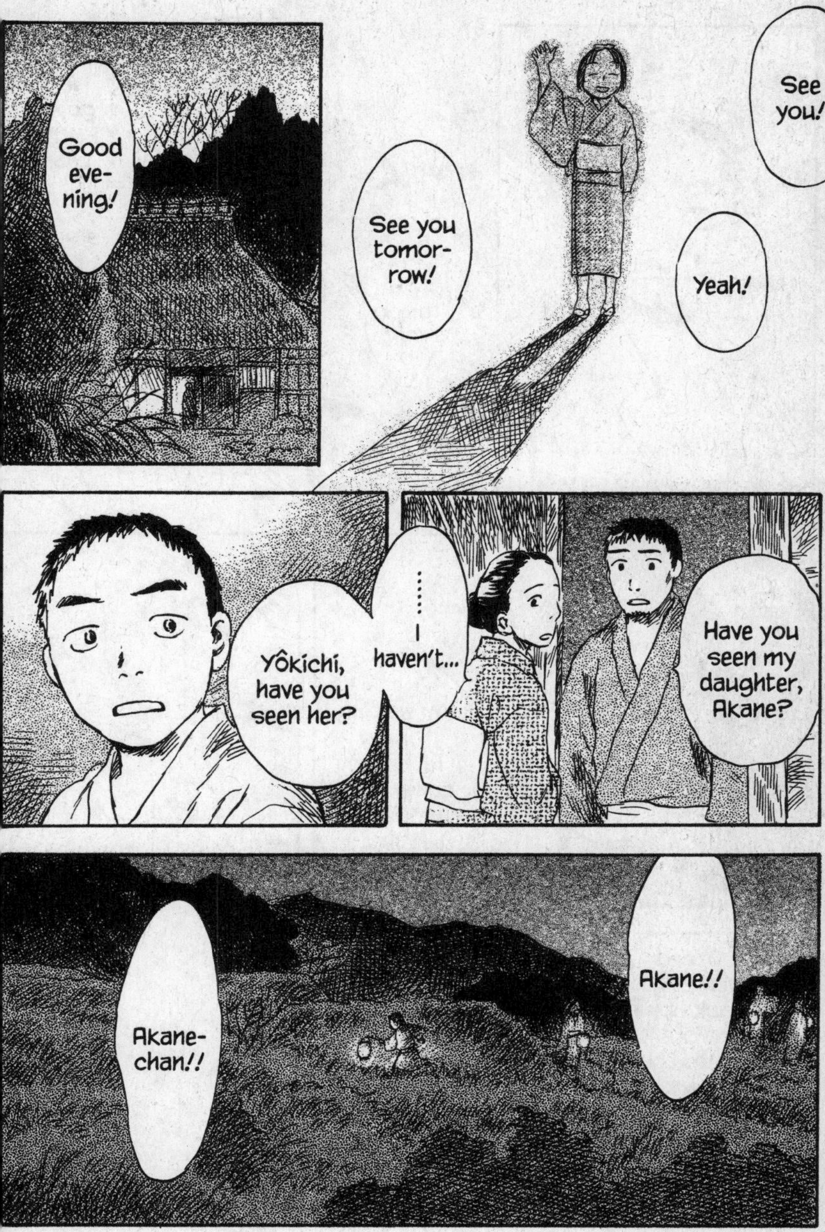
See you!
Yeah!
See you tomorrow!
Good evening!
Have you seen my daughter, Akane?
......
I haven't...
Yôkichi, have you seen her?
Akane!!
Akane-chan!!

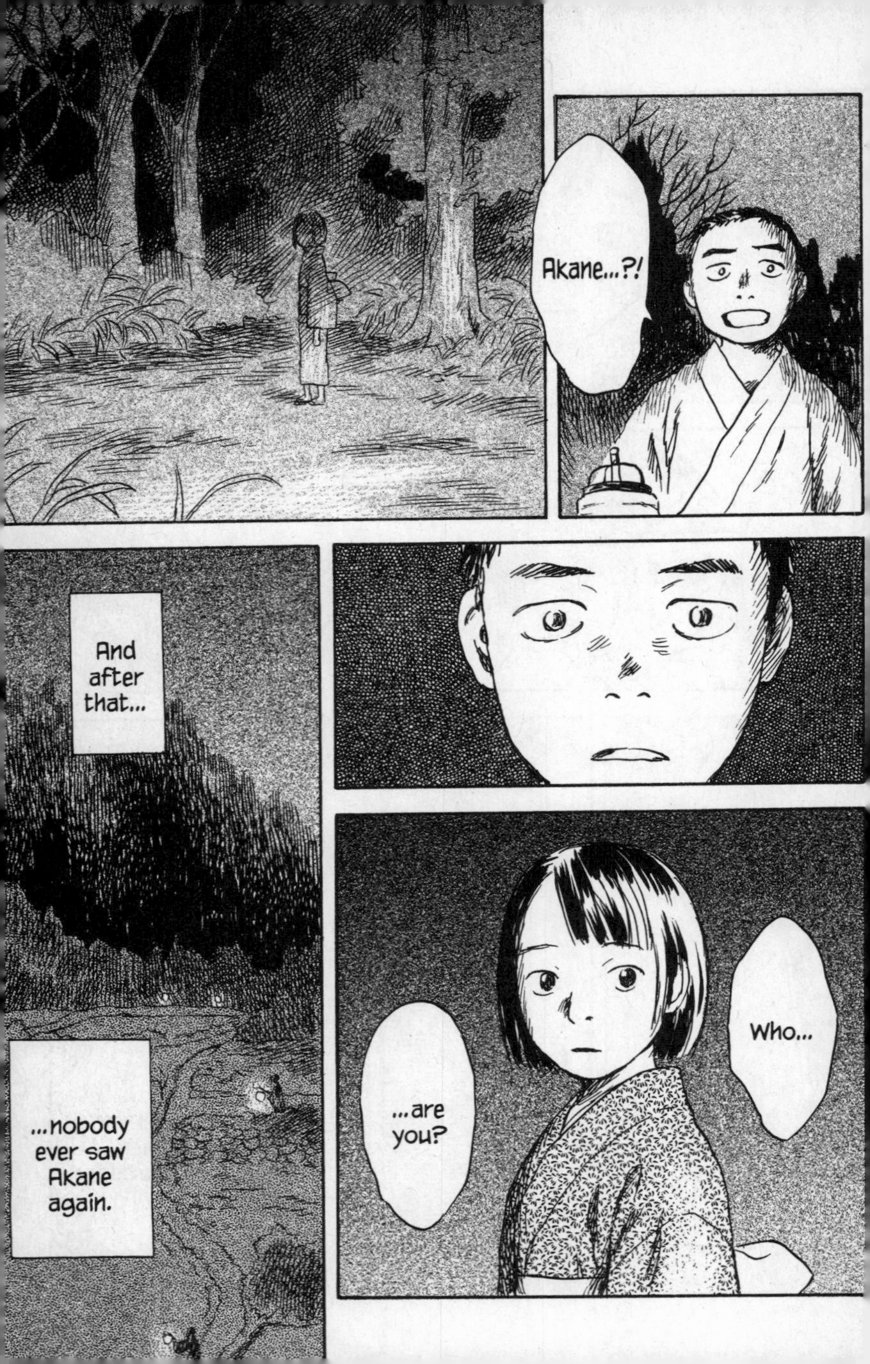
Akane...?!
Who...
...are you?
And after that...
...nobody ever saw Akane again.

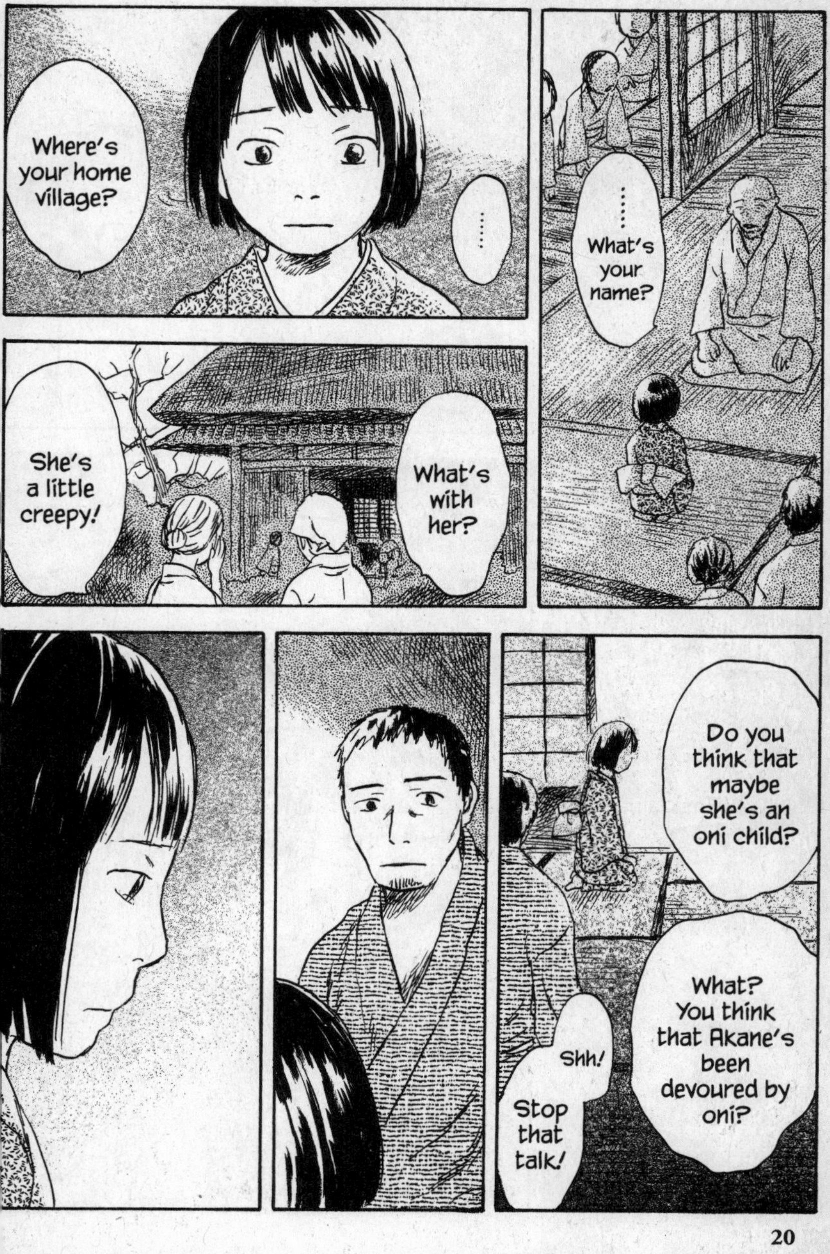
......
What's your name?
......
Where's your home village?
What's with her?
She's a little creepy!
Do you think that maybe she's an oni child?
What? You think that Akane's been devoured by oni?
Shh!
Stop that talk!

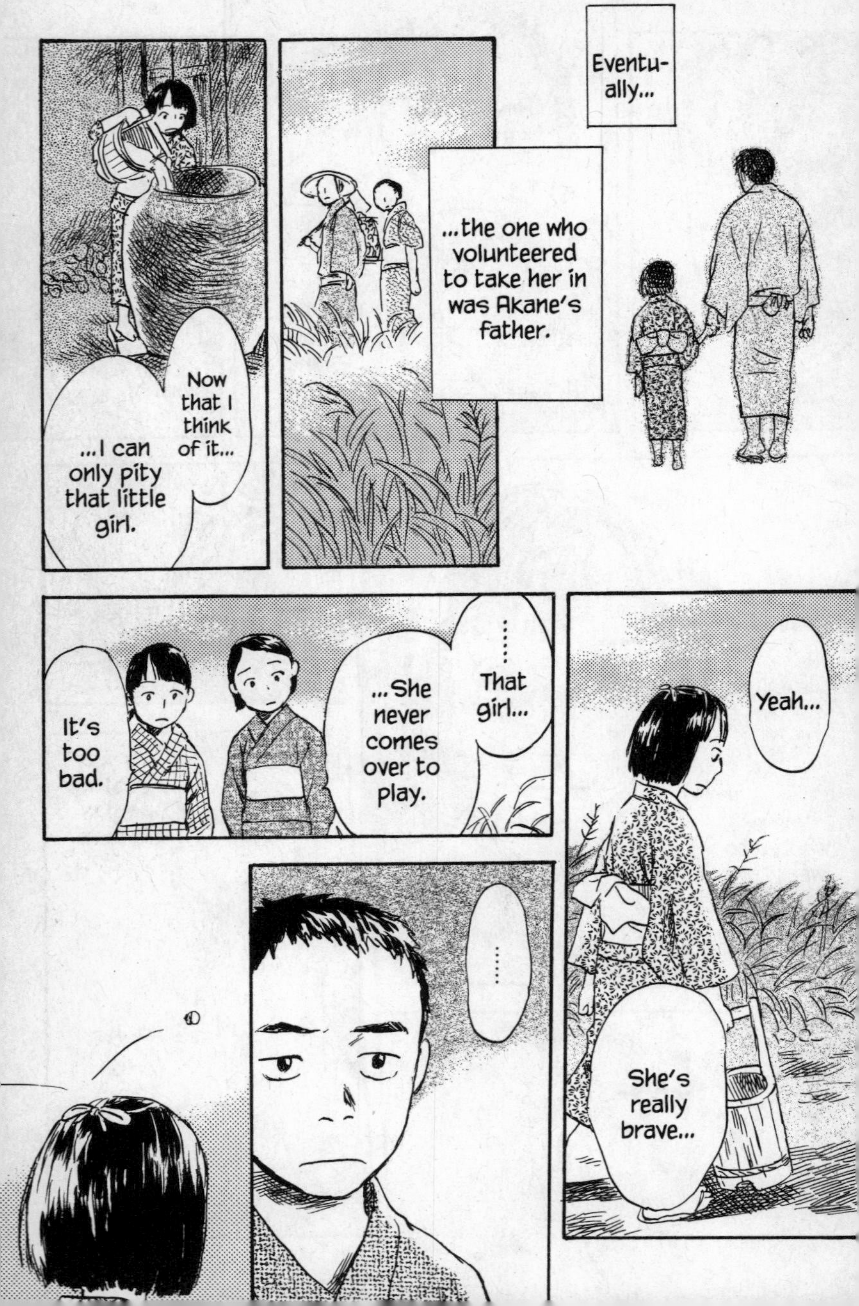
Eventu-ally...
...the one who volunteered to take her in was Akane's father.
Now that I think of it...
...I can only pity that little girl.
Yeah...
She's really brave...
......
That girl...
...She never comes over to play.
It's too bad.
......

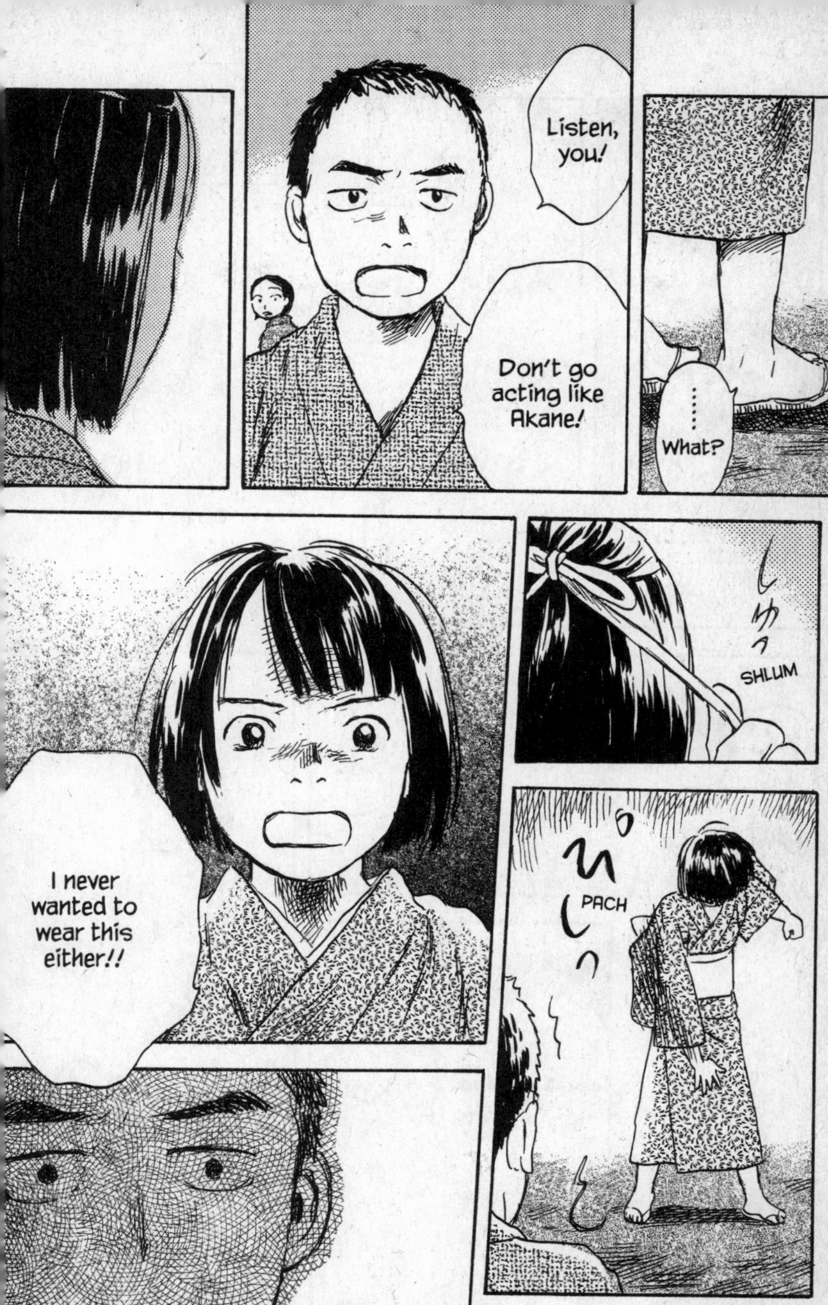

...... What?
Listen, you!
Don't go acting like Akane!
SHLUM
PACH
I never wanted to wear this either!!

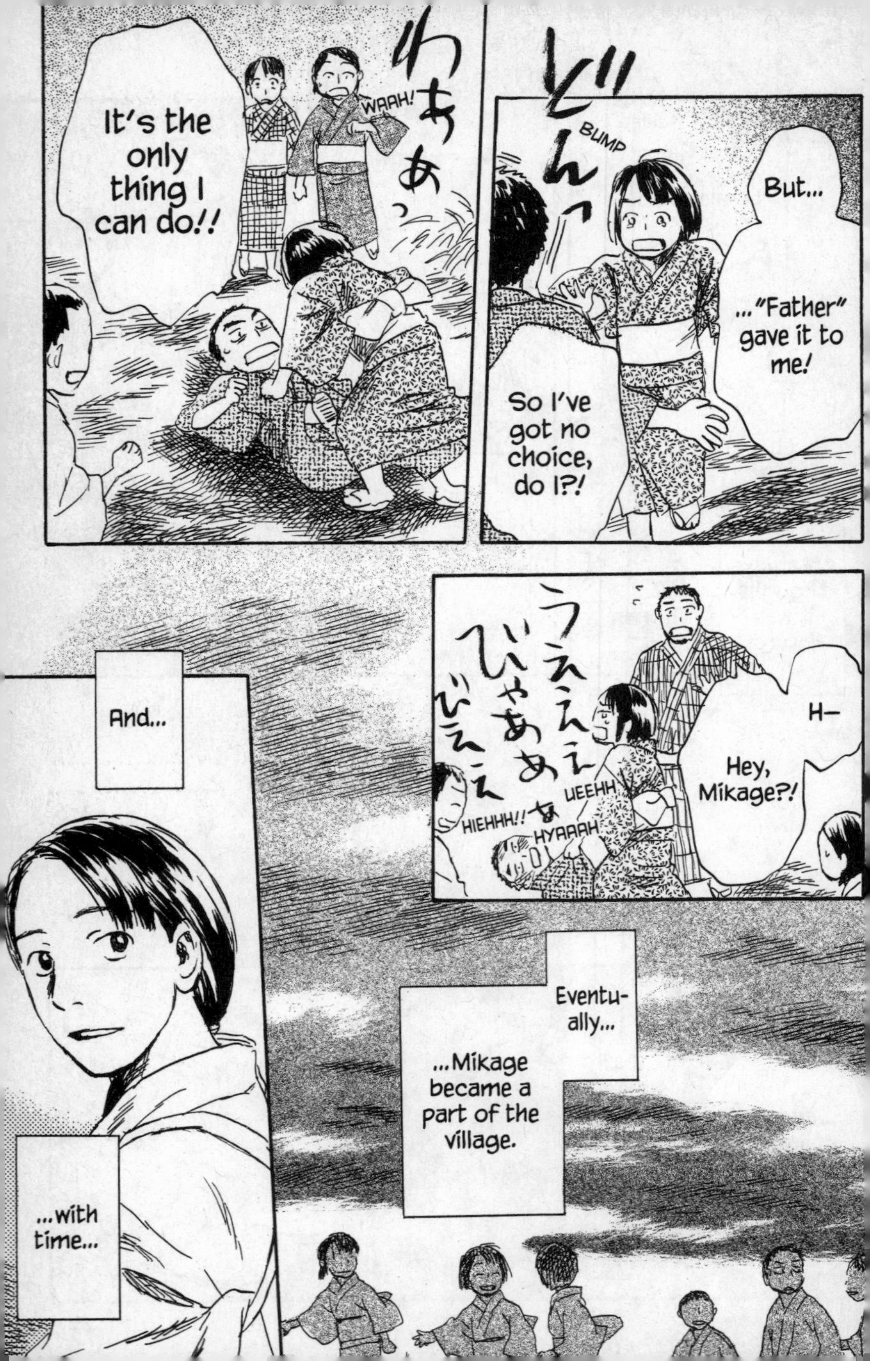
どんっ
BUMP
But...
..."Father" gave it to me!
So I've got no choice, do I?!
わあっ
WAAH!
It's the only thing I can do!!
H—
Hey, Mikage?!
UEEHH
HYAAAH
HIEHHH!!
Eventu-ally...
...Mikage became a part of the village.
And...
...with time...

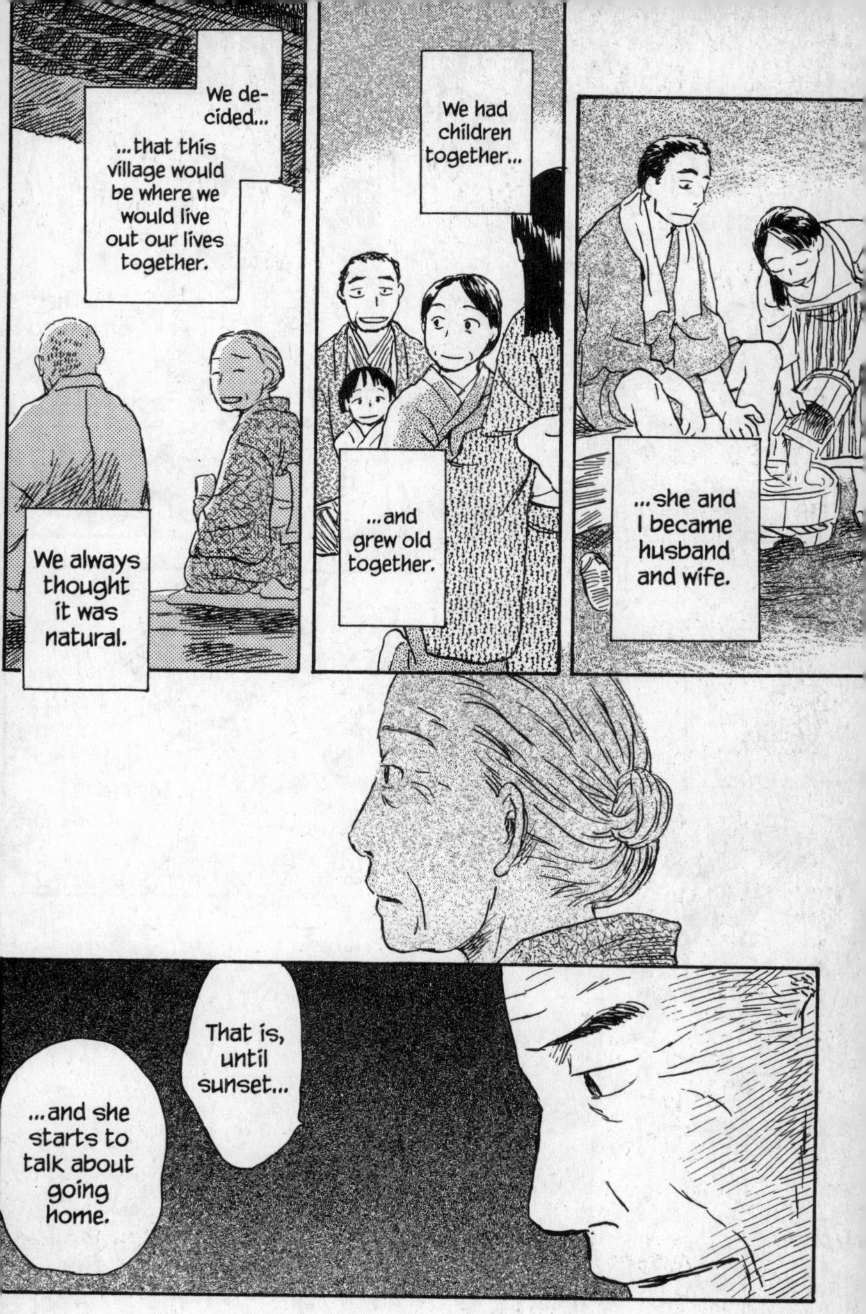
...she and I became husband and wife.
We had children together...
...and grew old together.
We decided...
...that this village would be where we would live out our lives together.
We always thought it was natural.
That is, until sunset...
...and she starts to talk about going home.

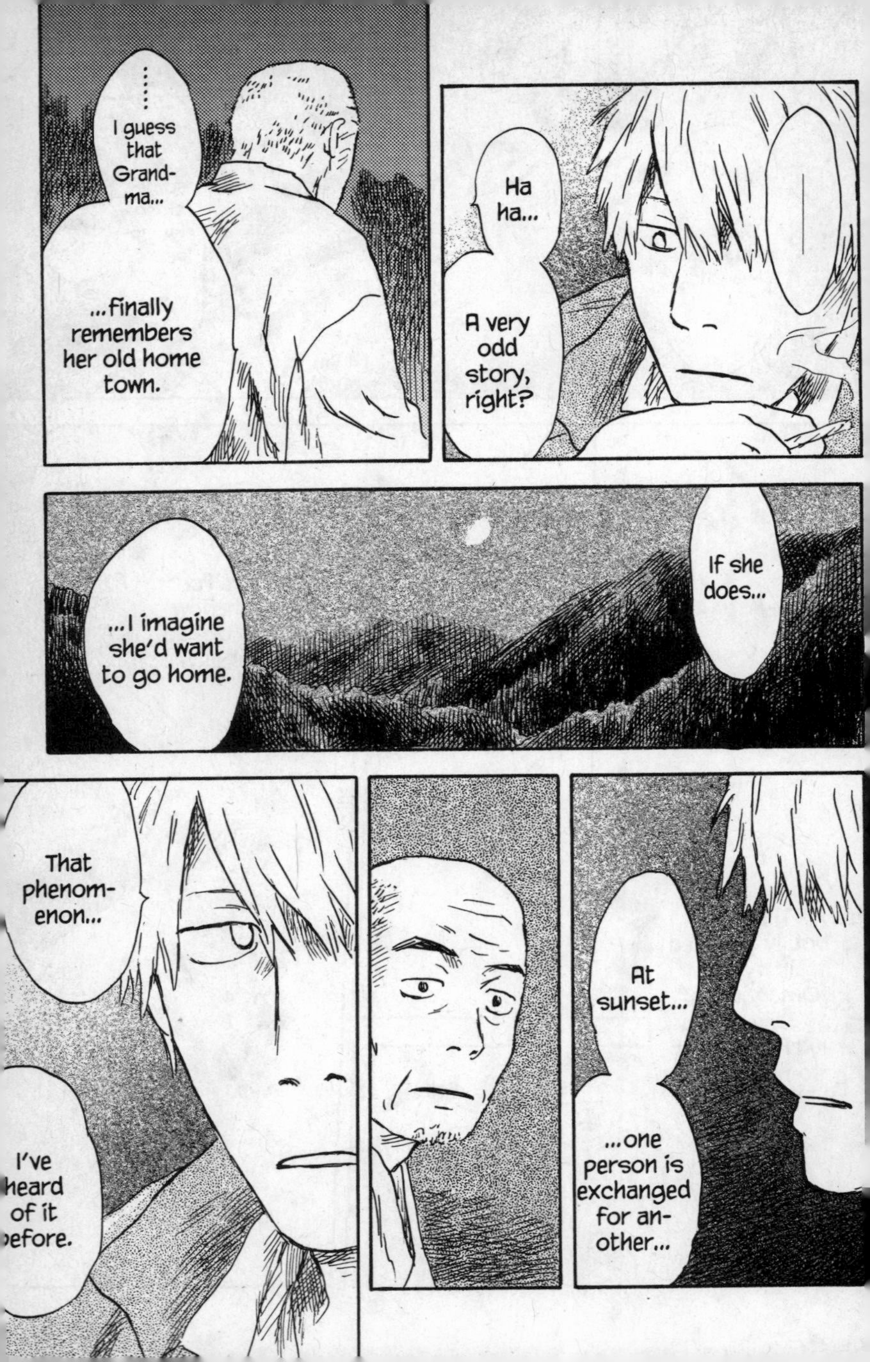
Ha ha...
A very odd story, right?
......
I guess that Grand-ma...
...finally remembers her old home town.
If she does...
...I imagine she'd want to go home.
At sunset...
...one person is exchanged for an-other...
That phenom-enon...
I've heard of it before.

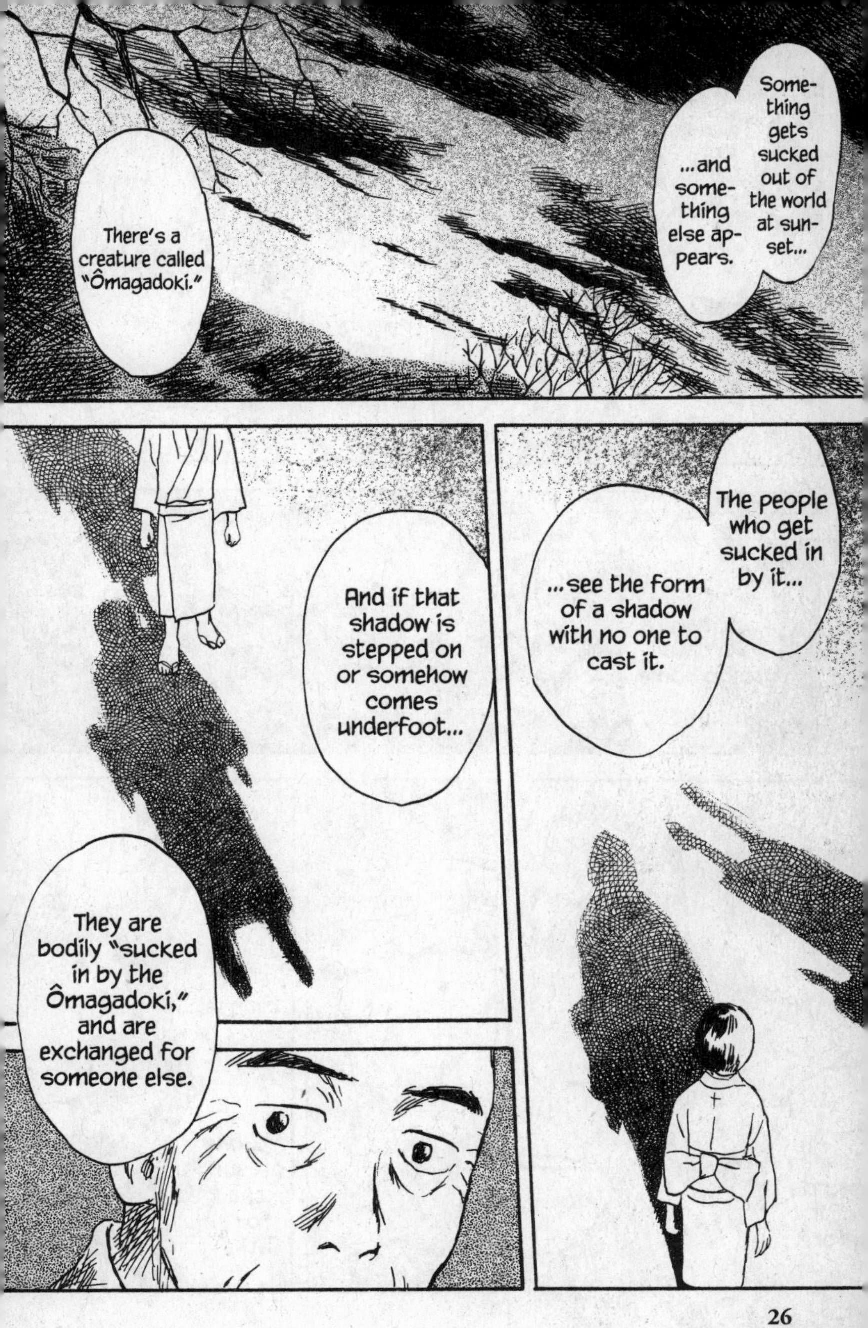
Something gets sucked out of the world at sunset...
...and something else appears.
There's a creature called "Ômagadoki."
The people who get sucked in by it...
...see the form of a shadow with no one to cast it.
And if that shadow is stepped on or somehow comes underfoot...
They are bodily "sucked in by the Ômagadoki," and are exchanged for someone else.

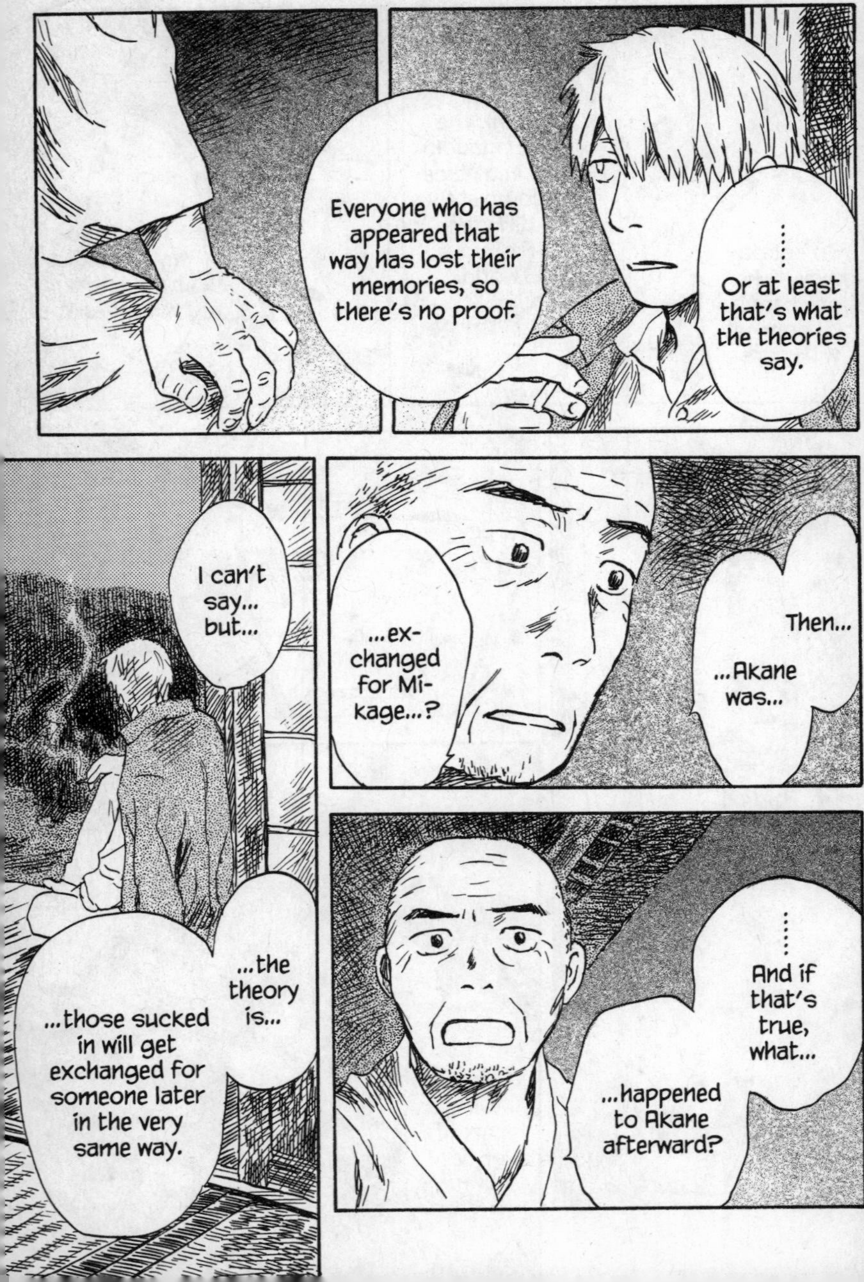
......
Or at least that's what the theories say.
Everyone who has appeared that way has lost their memories, so there's no proof.
Then...
...Akane was...
...ex-changed for Mi-kage...?
......
And if that's true, what...
...happened to Akane afterward?
I can't say... but...
...the theory is...
...those sucked in will get exchanged for someone later in the very same way.

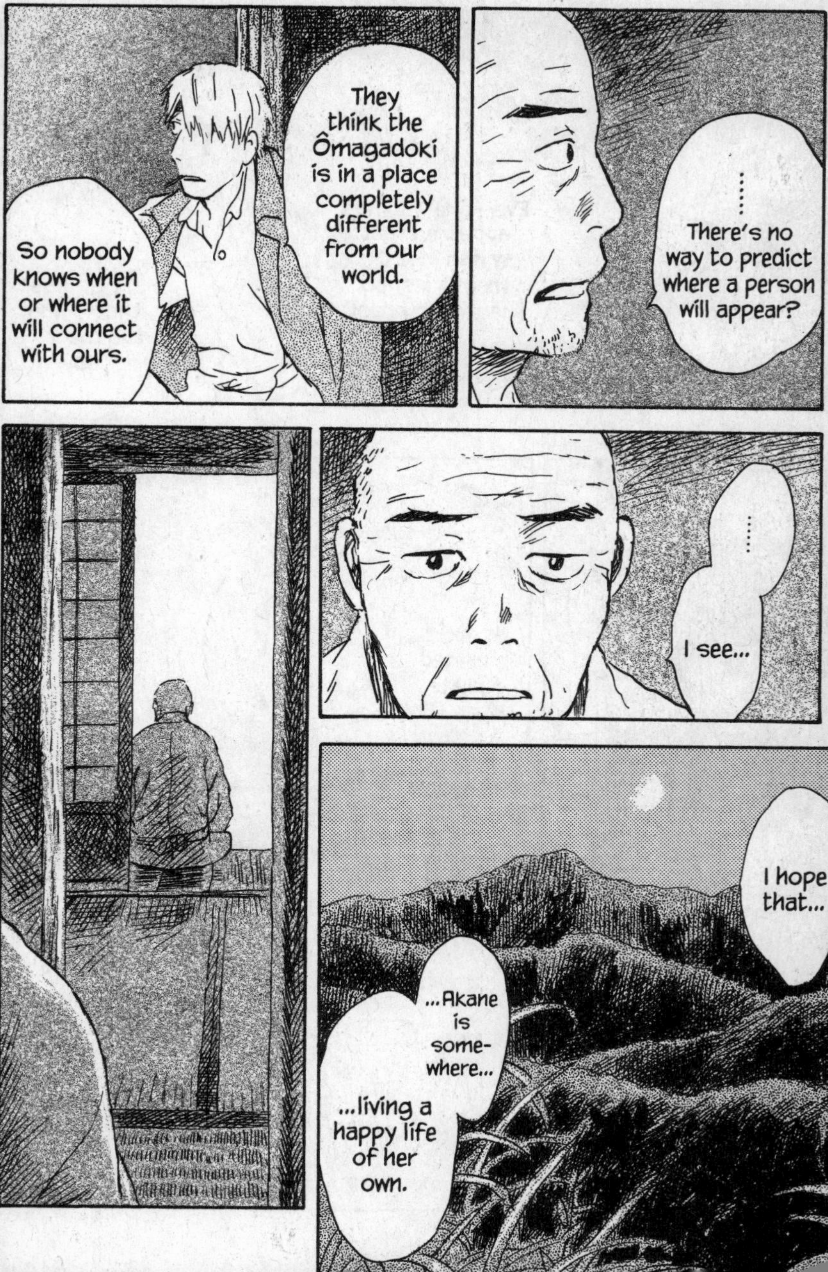
They think the Ômagadoki is in a place completely different from our world.
So nobody knows when or where it will connect with ours.
......
There's no way to predict where a person will appear?
......
I see...
I hope that...
...Akane is somewhere...
...living a happy life of her own.

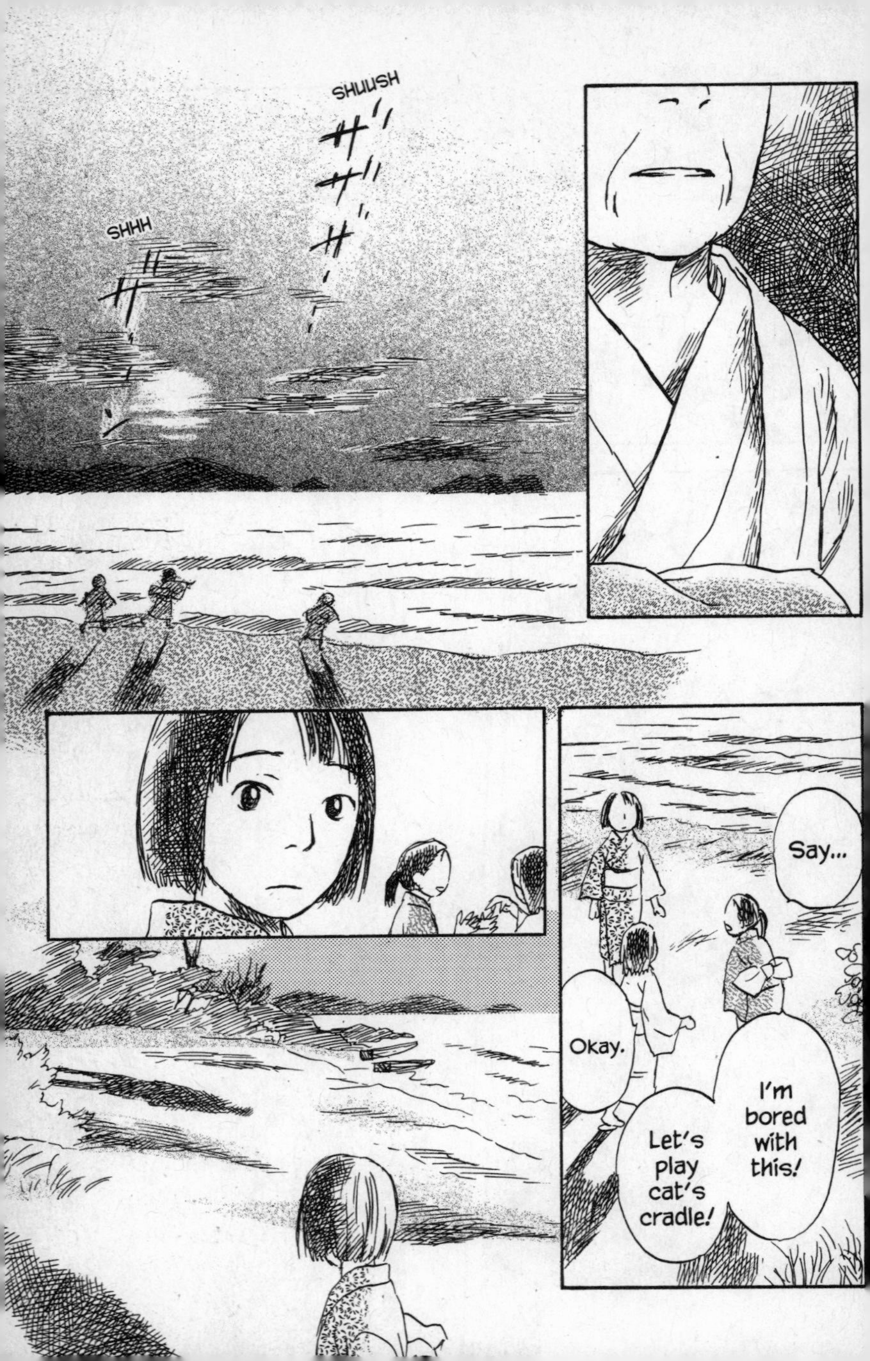
SHUUSH
SHHH
Say...
I'm bored with this!
Let's play cat's cradle!
Okay.

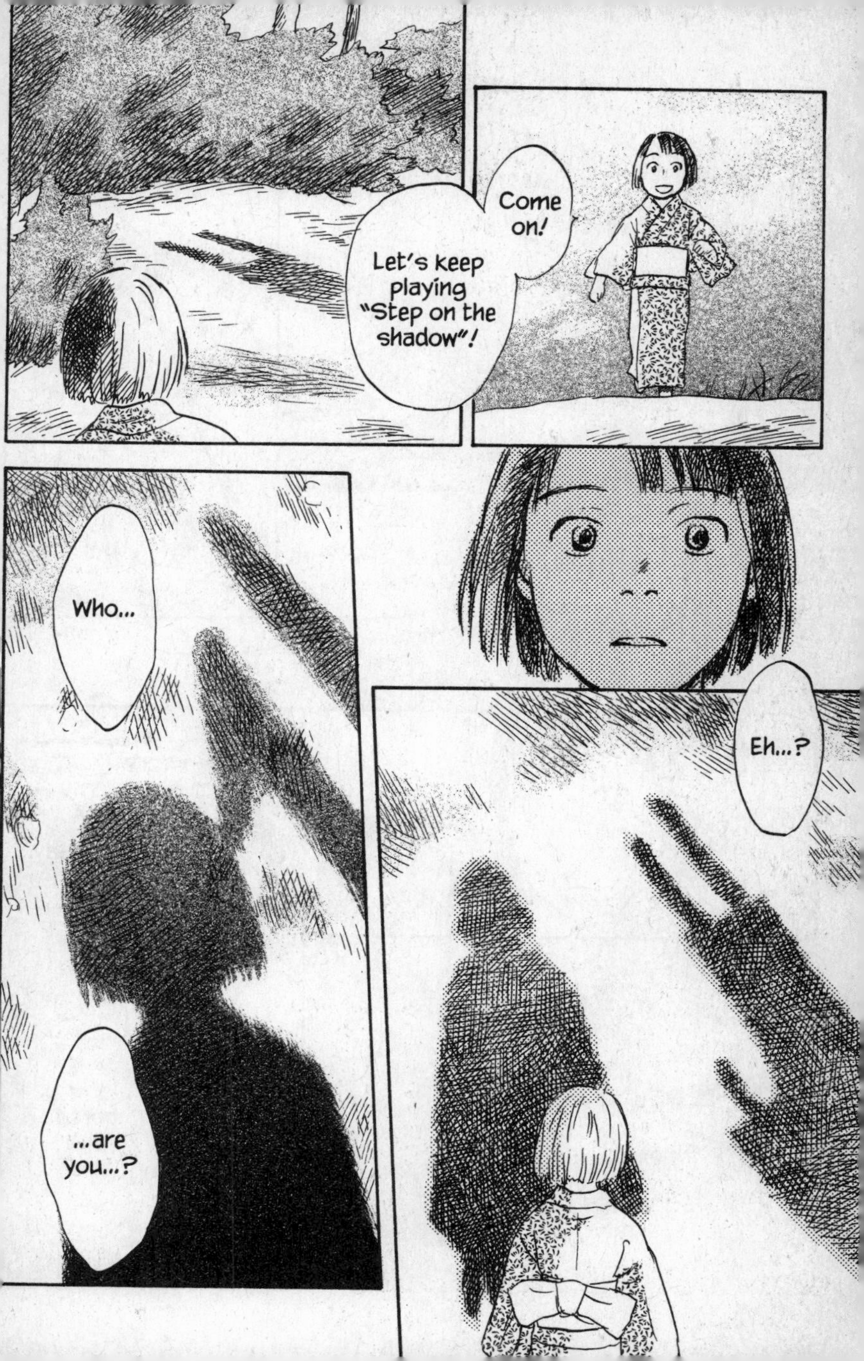
Come on!
Let's keep playing "Step on the shadow"!
Eh...?
Who...
...are you...?

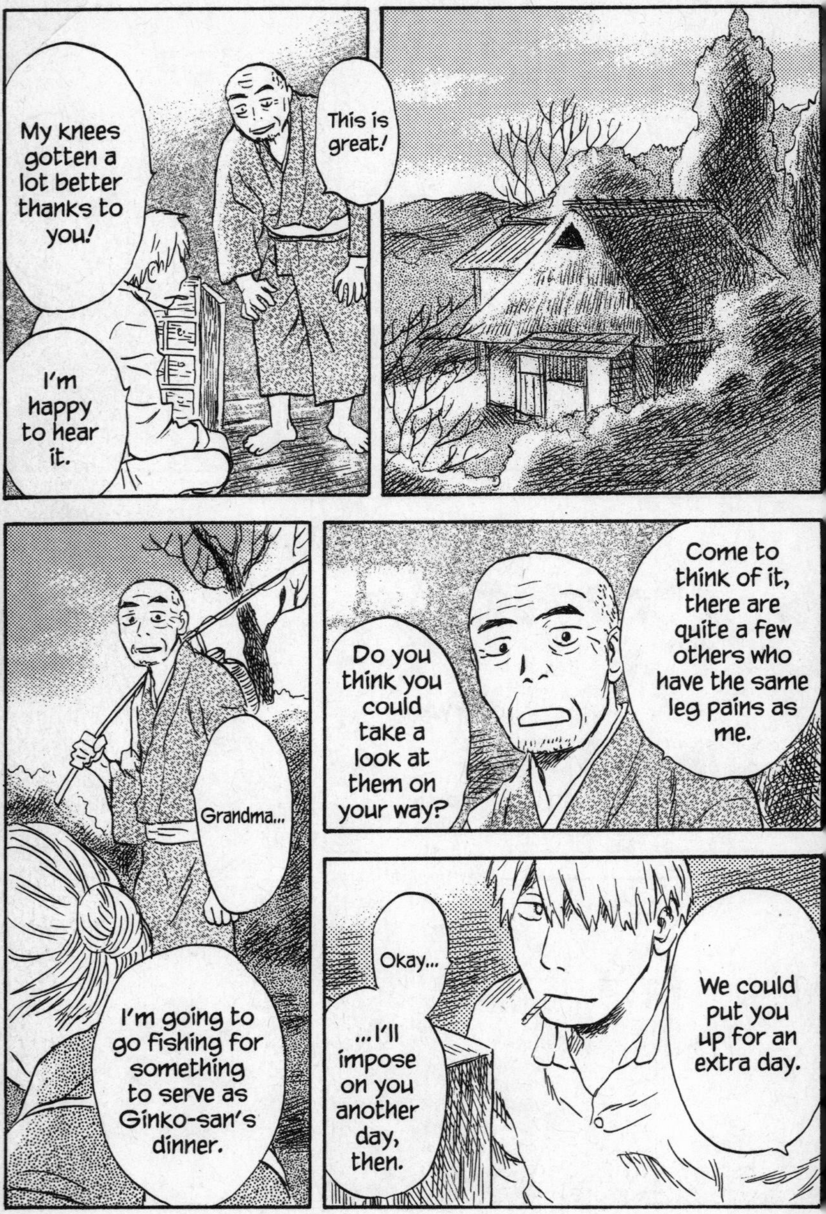
This is great!
My knees gotten a lot better thanks to you!
I'm happy to hear it.
Come to think of it, there are quite a few others who have the same leg pains as me.
Do you think you could take a look at them on your way?
We could put you up for an extra day.
Okay...
...I'll impose on you another day, then.
Grandma...
I'm going to go fishing for something to serve as Ginko-san's dinner.

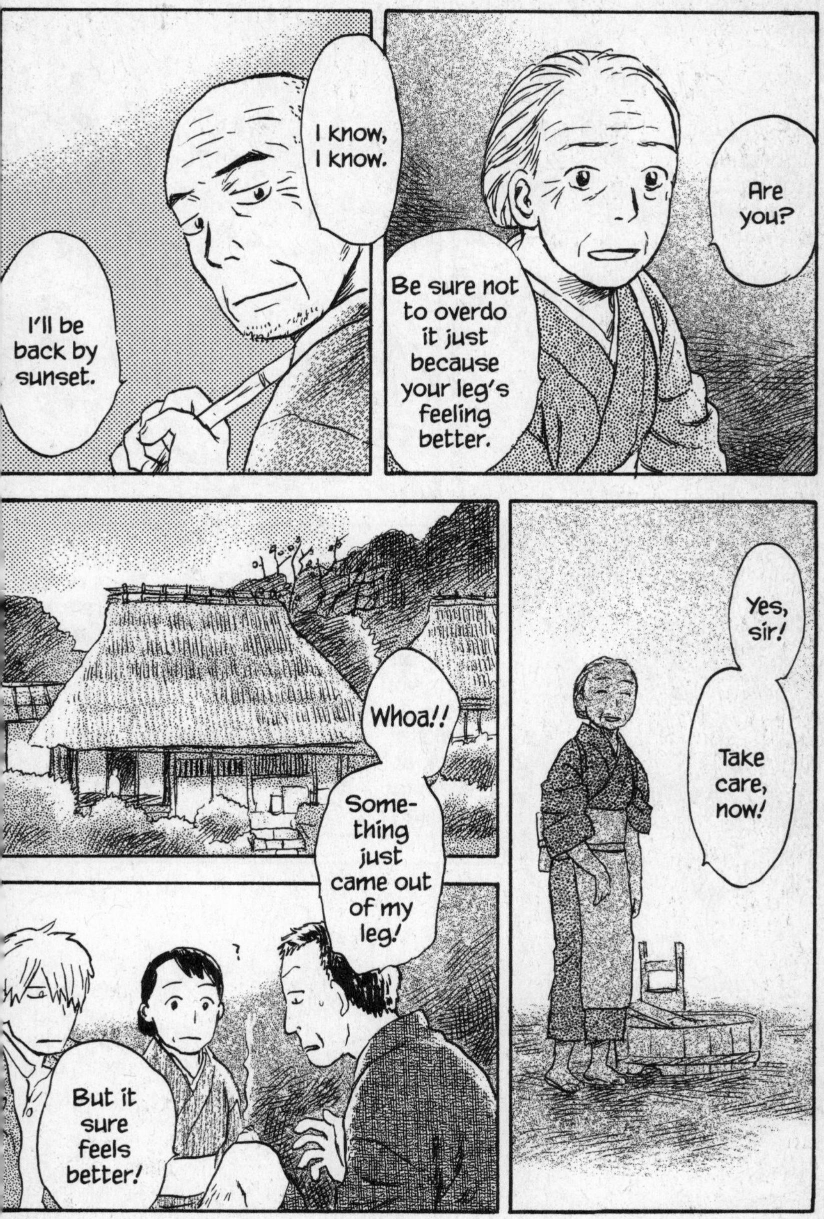
Are you?
Be sure not to overdo it just because your leg's feeling better.
I know, I know.
I'll be back by sunset.
Yes, sir!
Take care, now!
Whoa!!
Some-thing just came out of my leg!
?
But it sure feels better!

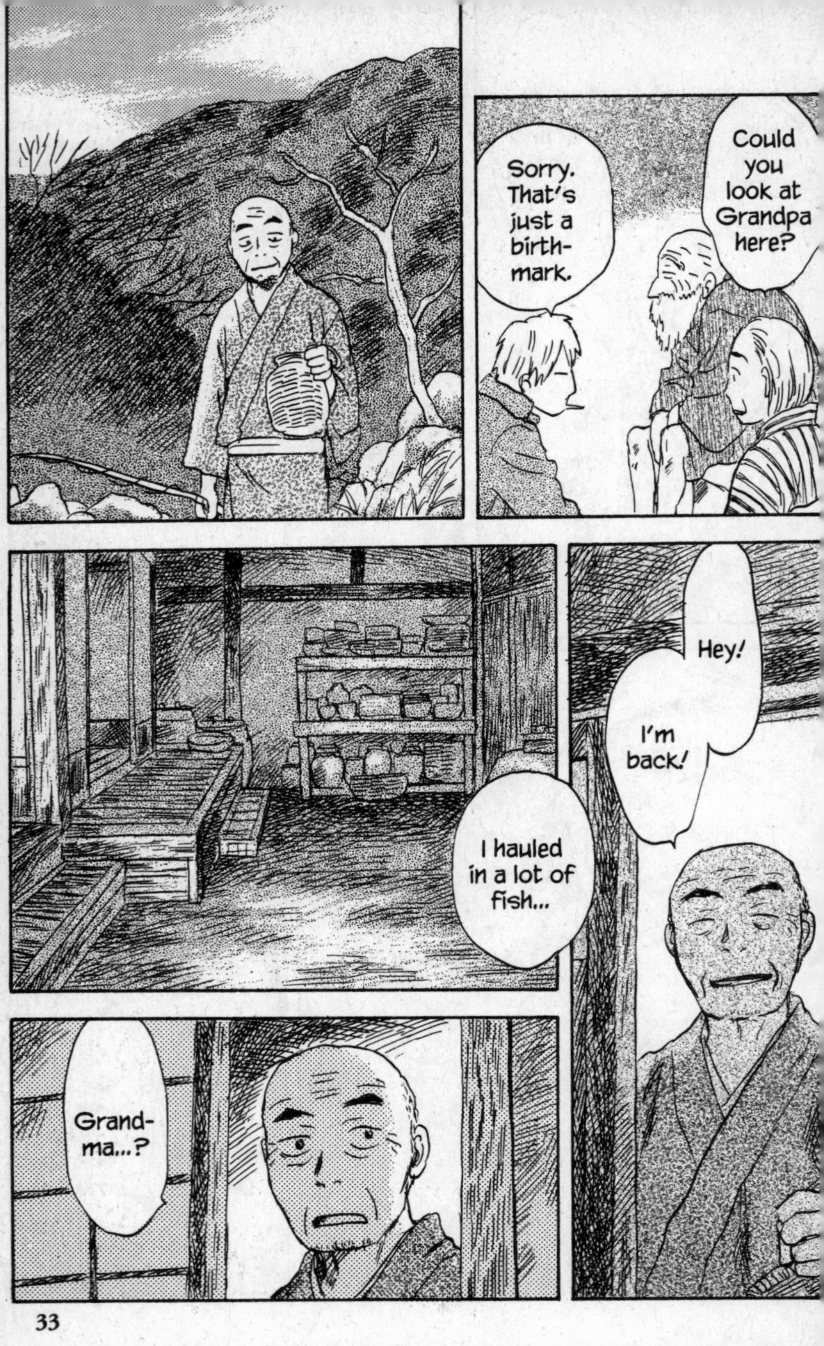
Could you look at Grandpa here?
Sorry. That's just a birth-mark.
Hey!
I'm back!
I hauled in a lot of fish...
Grand-ma...?

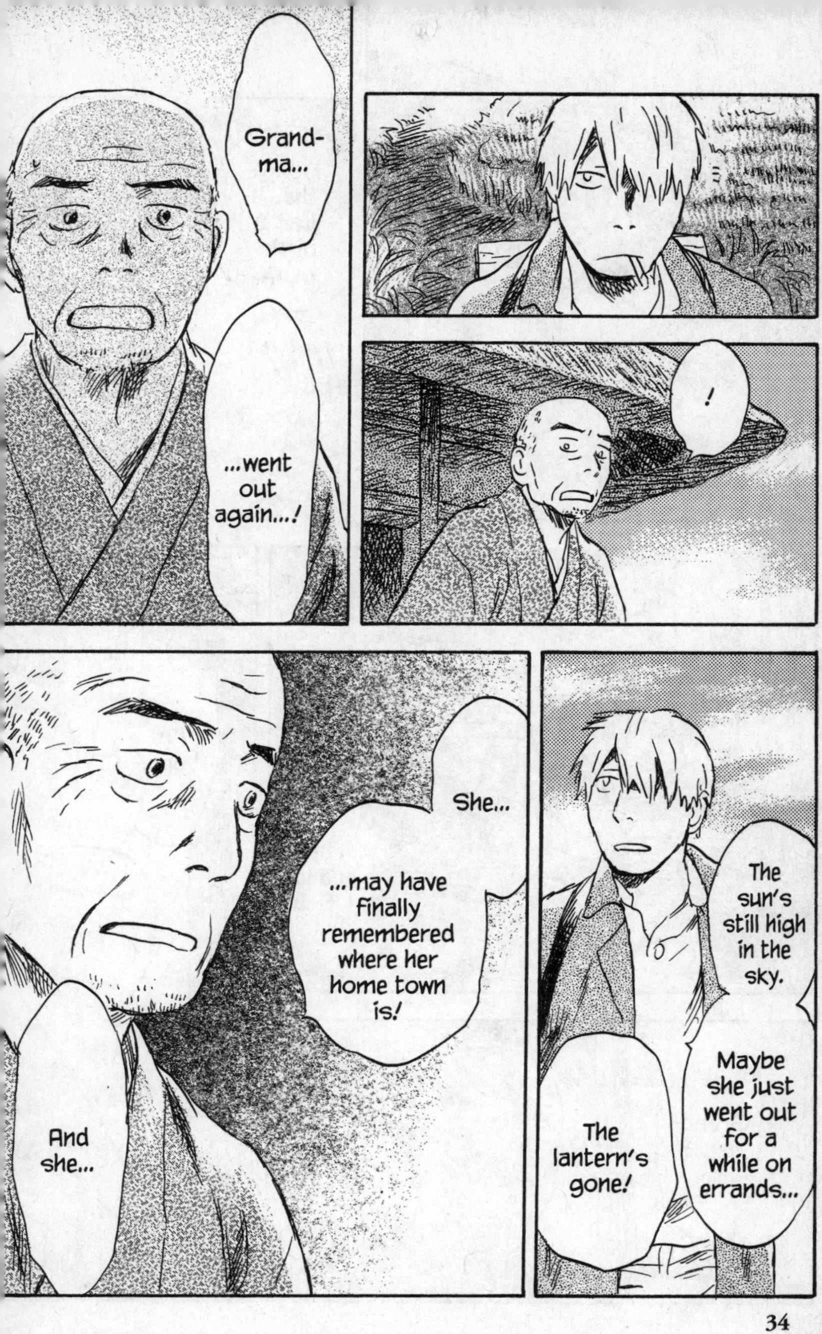
!
Grand-ma...
...went out again...!
The sun's still high in the sky.
Maybe she just went out for a while on errands...
The lantern's gone!
She...
...may have finally remembered where her home town is!
And she...

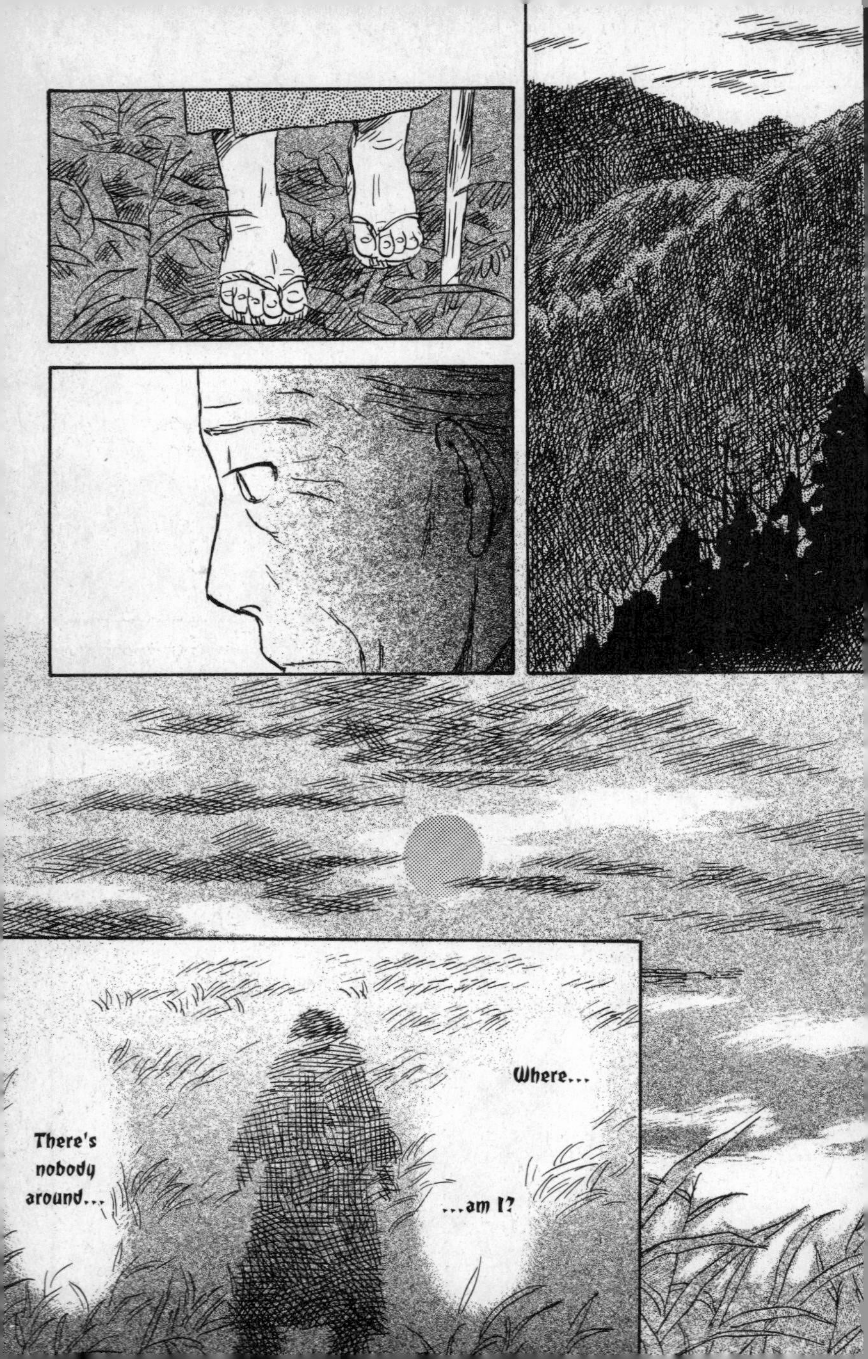
Where...
...am I?
There's nobody around...

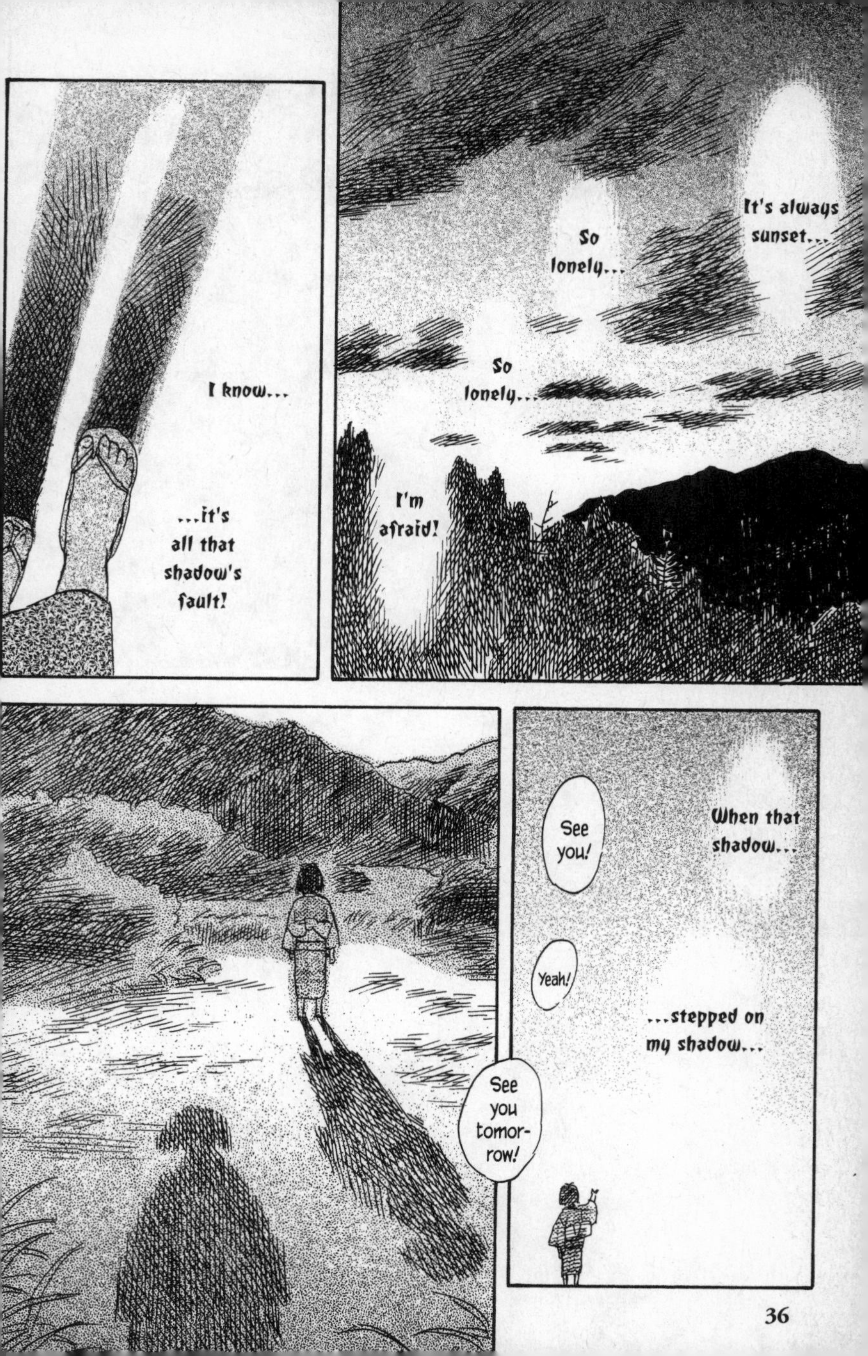
It's always sunset...
So lonely...
So lonely...
I'm afraid!
I know...
...it's all that shadow's fault!
When that shadow...
See you!
Yeah!
...stepped on my shadow...
See you tomorrow!

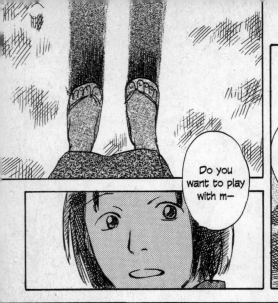

Do you want to play with m—

Who's there?

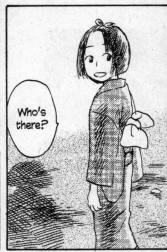

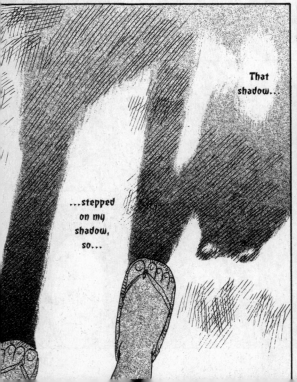

That shadow...

...stepped on my shadow, so...

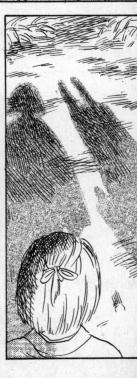

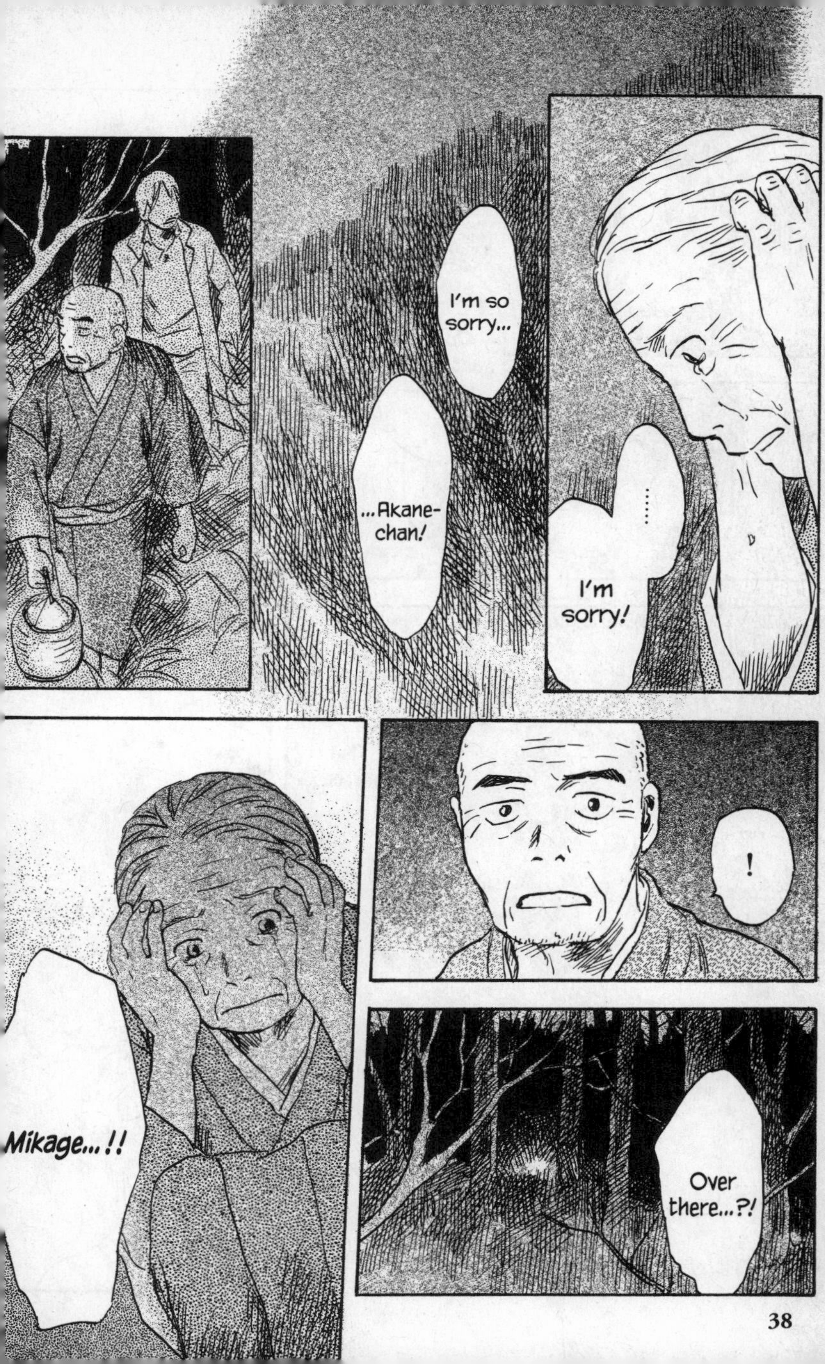
......
I'm sorry!
I'm so sorry...
...Akane-chan!
!
Over there...?!
Mikage...!!

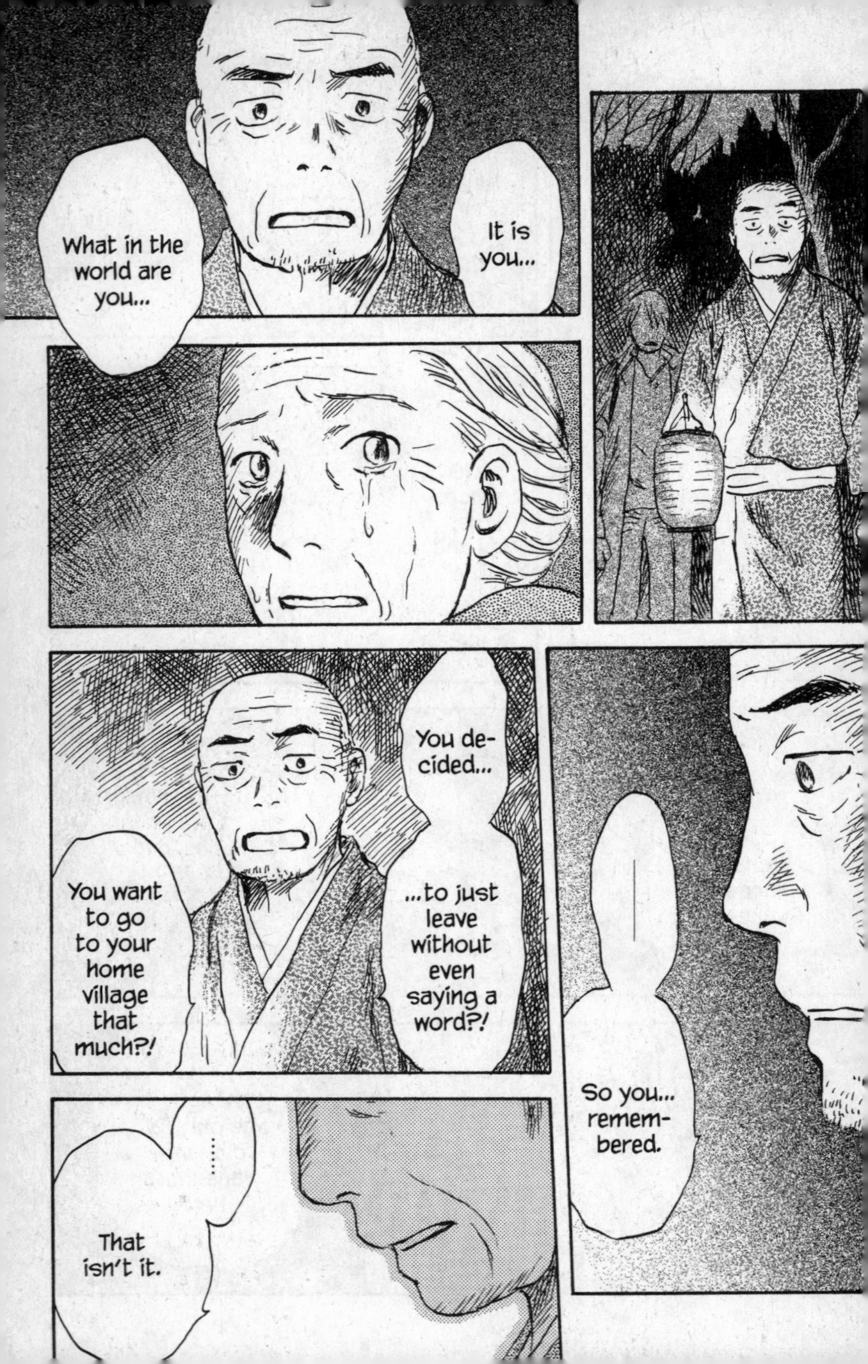
It is you...
What in the world are you...
So you... remembered.
You decided...
...to just leave without even saying a word?!
You want to go to your home village that much?!
......
That isn't it.

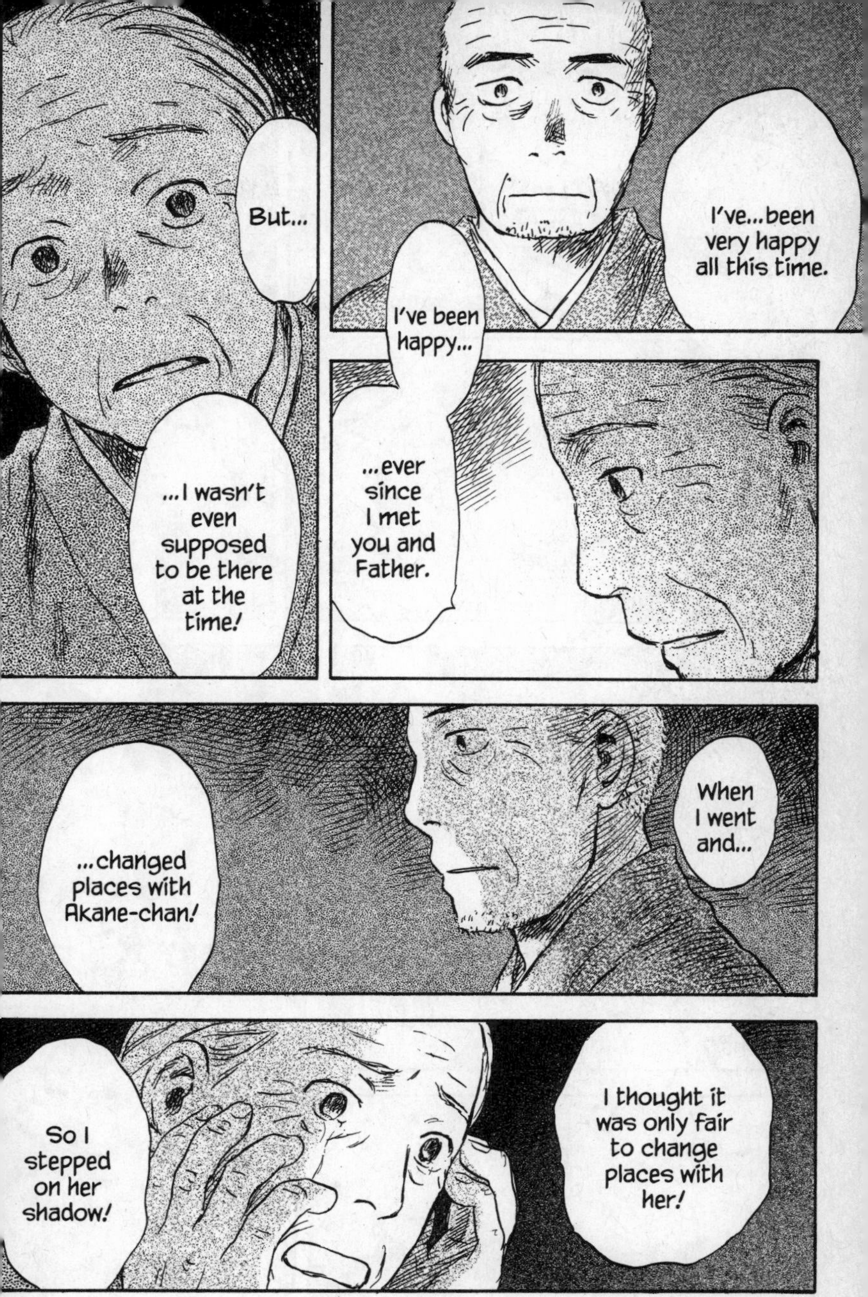
I've...been very happy all this time.
I've been happy...
...ever since I met you and Father.
But...
...I wasn't even supposed to be there at the time!
When I went and...
...changed places with Akane-chan!
I thought it was only fair to change places with her!
So I stepped on her shadow!

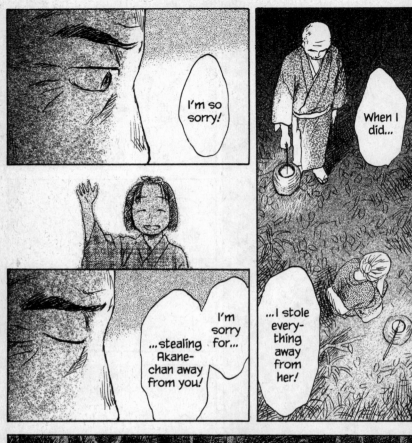

I'm so sorry!

When I did...

I'm sorry for...

...stealing Akane-chan away from you!

...I stole everything away from her!

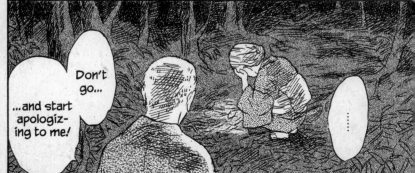

Don't go...

...and start apologizing to me!

......

41

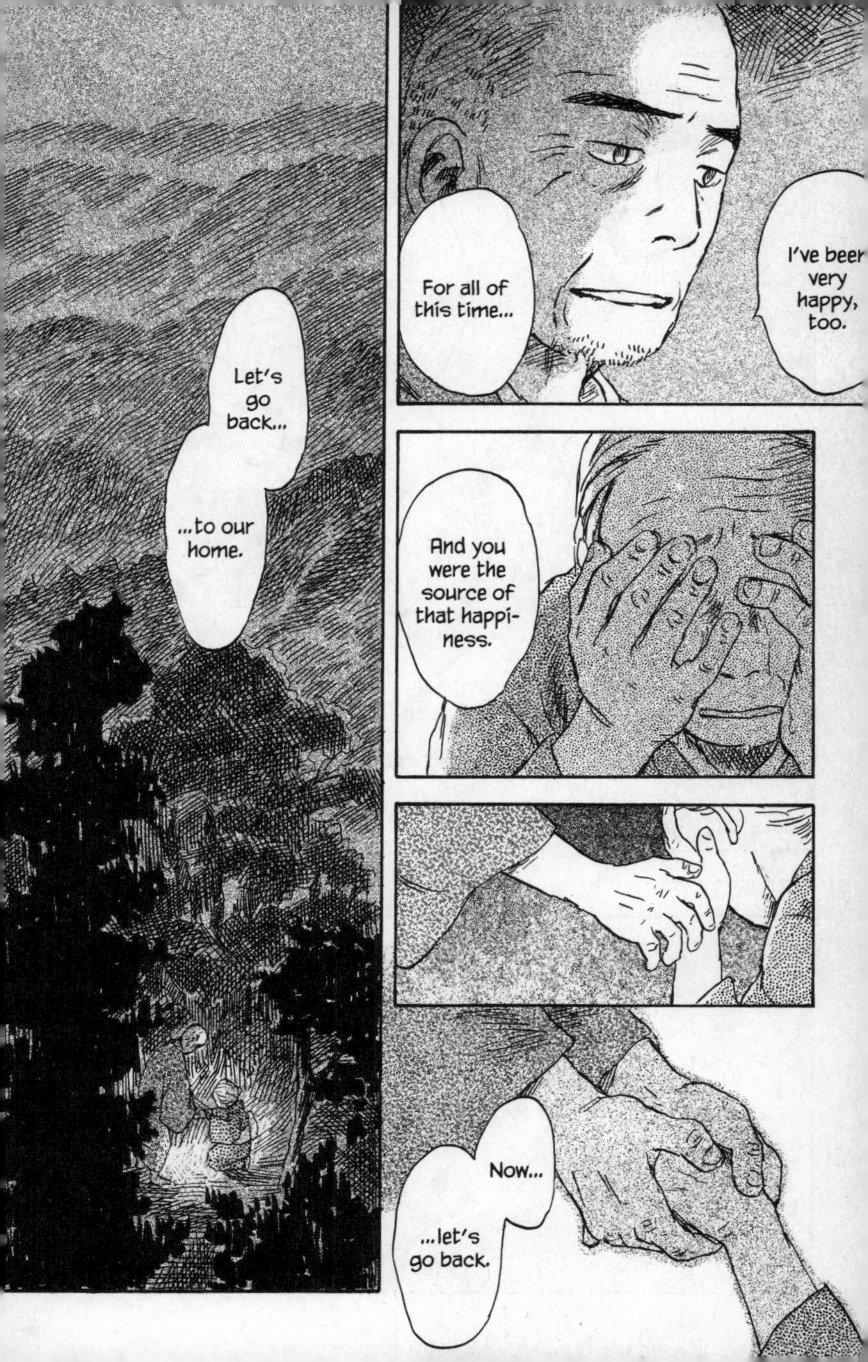
I've been very happy, too.
For all of this time...
And you were the source of that happiness.
Now...
...let's go back.
Let's go back...
...to our home.

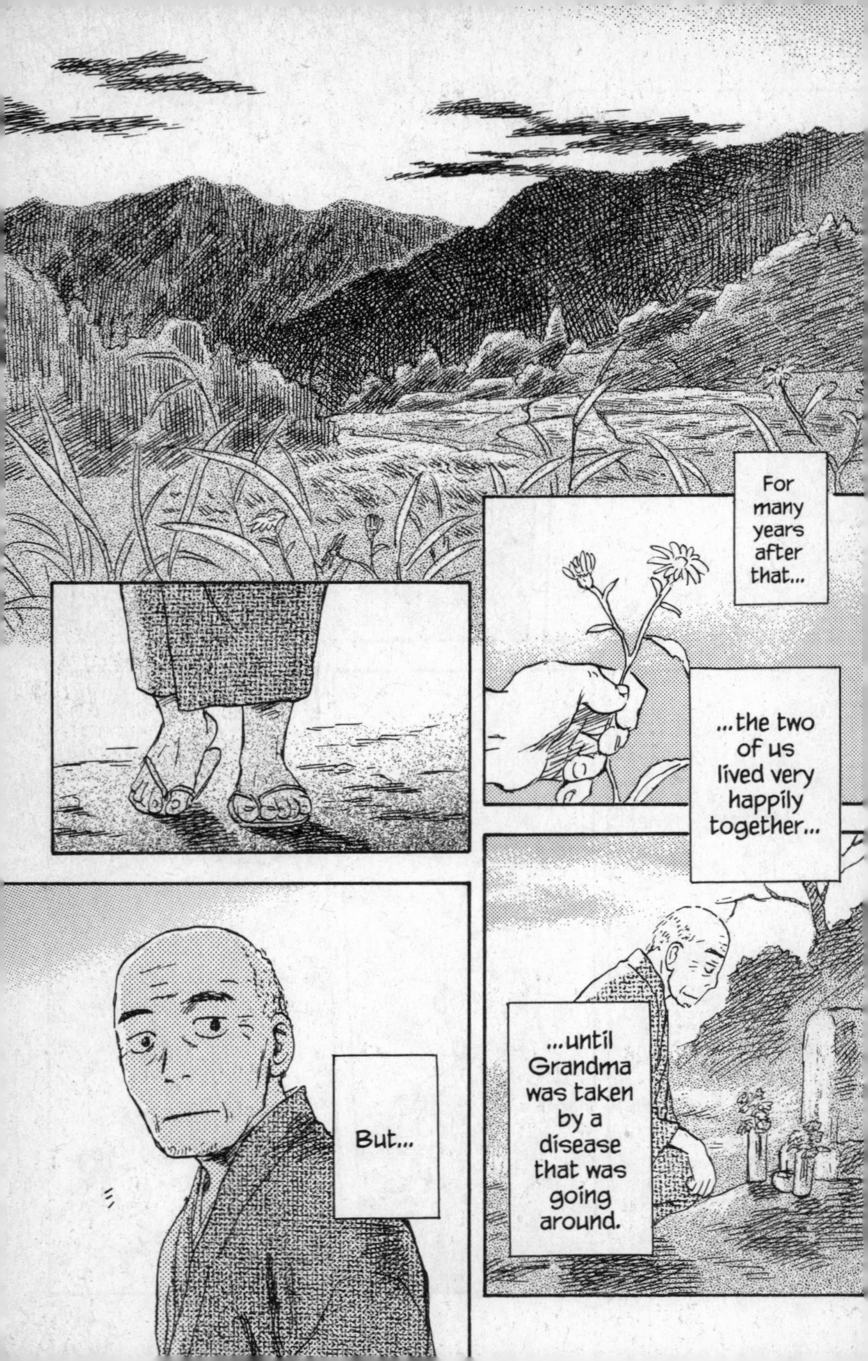
For many years after that...
...the two of us lived very happily together...
...until Grandma was taken by a disease that was going around.
But...

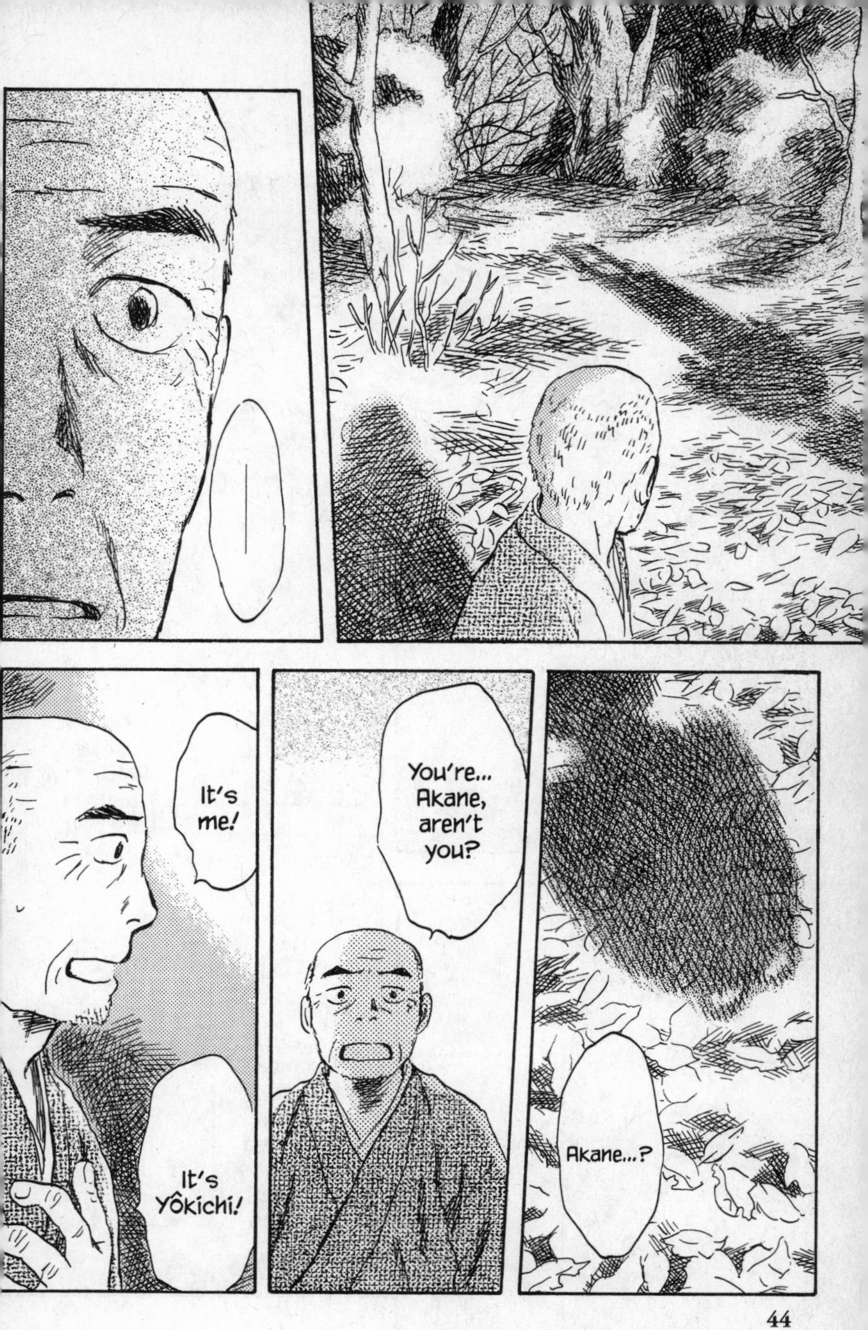
Akane...?
You're... Akane, aren't you?
It's me!
It's Yôkichi!

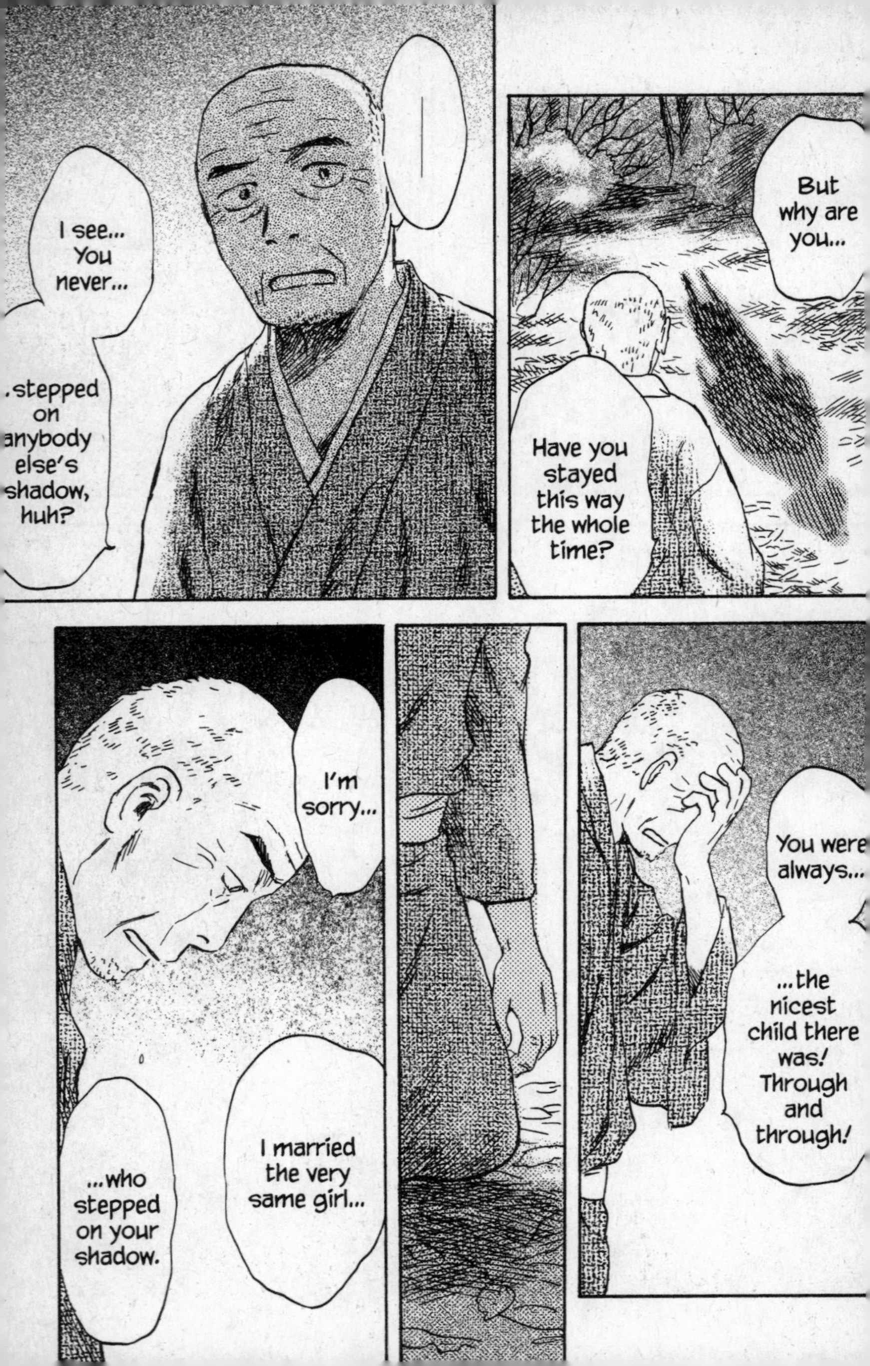
I see... You never...
...stepped on anybody else's shadow, huh?
But why are you...
Have you stayed this way the whole time?
I'm sorry...
I married the very same girl...
...who stepped on your shadow.
You were always...
...the nicest child there was! Through and through!

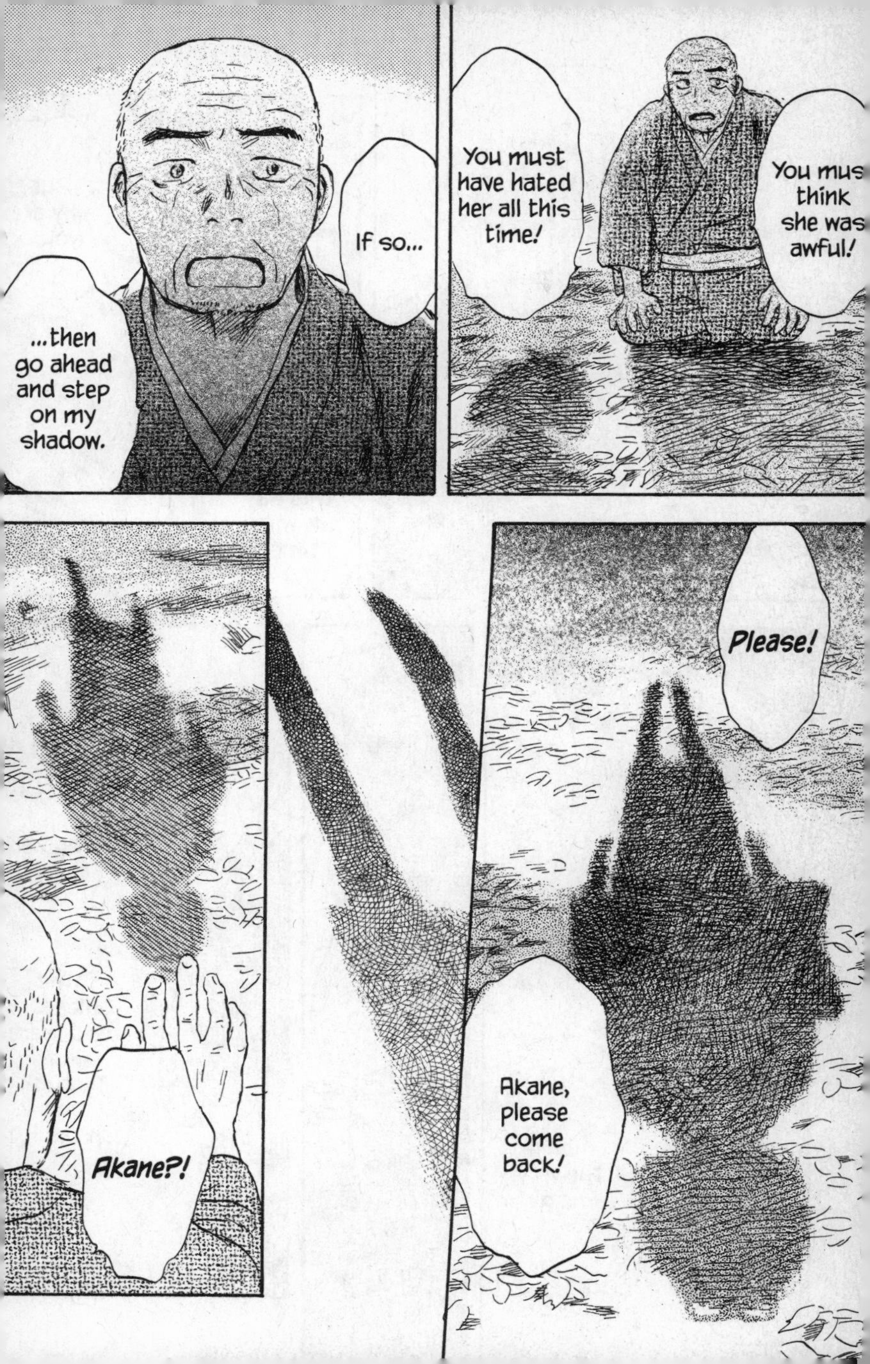
You mus think she was awful!
You must have hated her all this time!
If so...
...then go ahead and step on my shadow.
Please!
Akane, please come back!
Akane?!

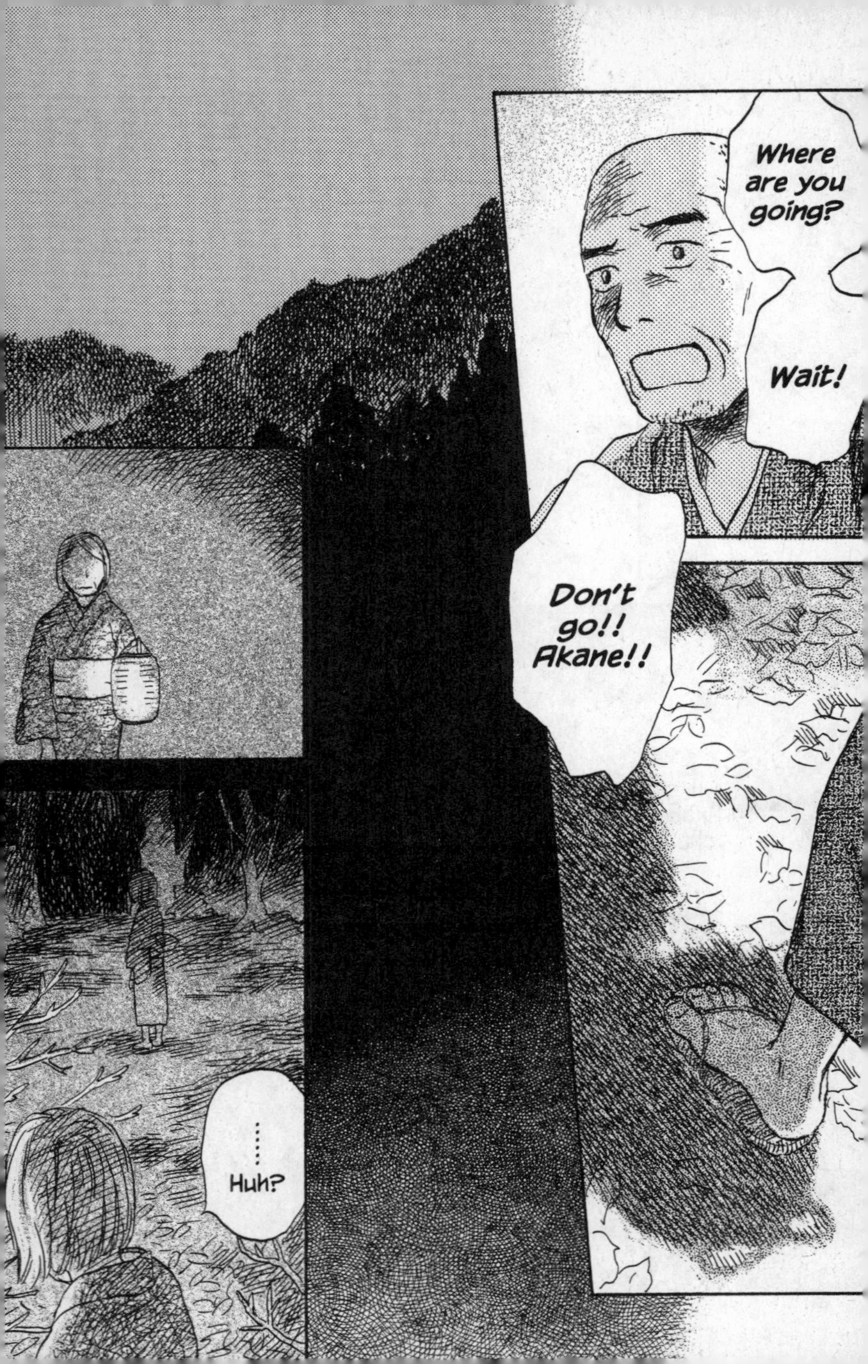
Where are you going?
Wait!
Don't go!! Akane!!
...... Huh?

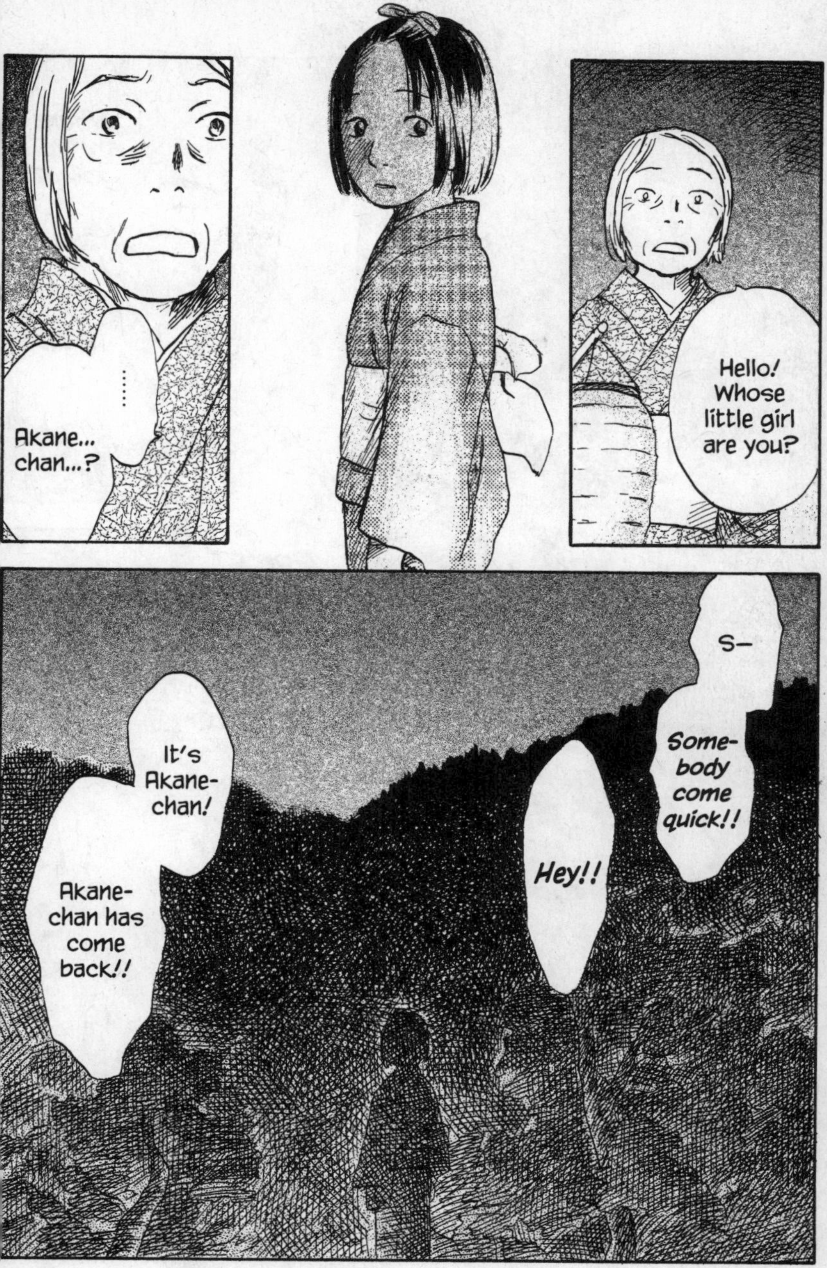
Hello! Whose little girl are you?
......
Akane... chan...?
S—
Some-body come quick!!
Hey!!
It's Akane-chan!
Akane-chan has come back!!

The Final Bit of Crimson The End

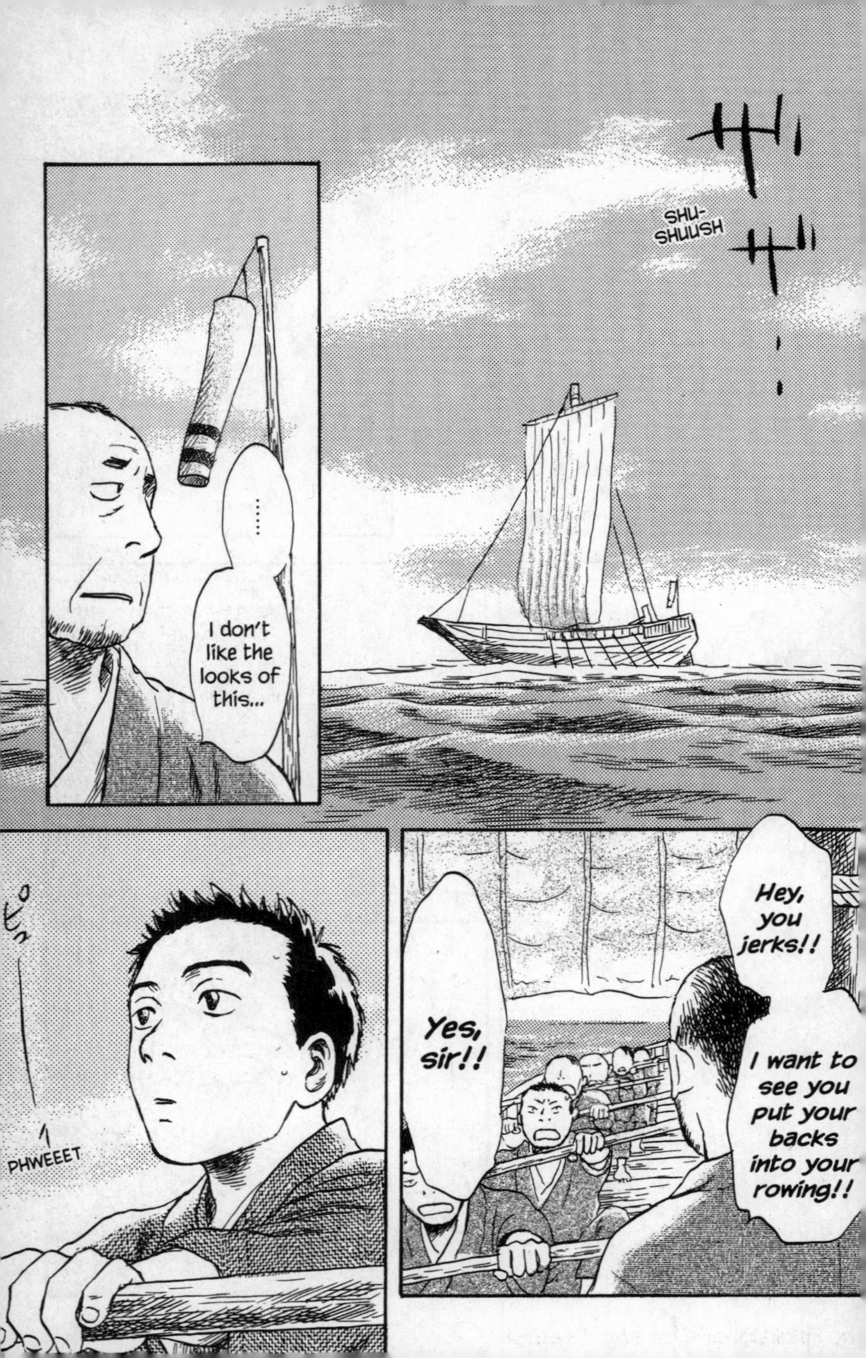
SHU-SHUUSH
......
I don't like the looks of this...
Hey, you jerks!!
I want to see you put your backs into your rowing!!
Yes, sir!!
PHWEEET

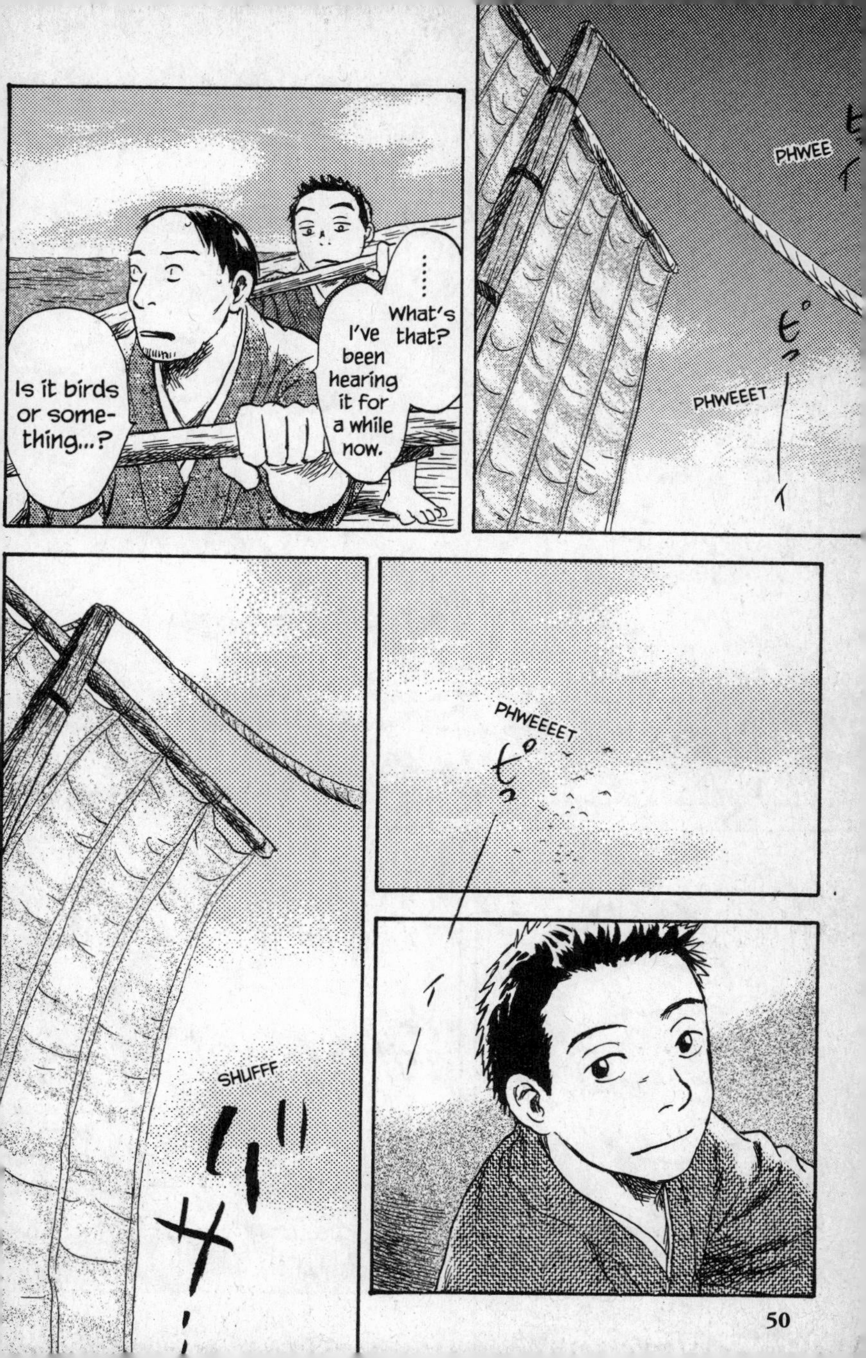
PHWEE
PHWEEET
......
What's that? I've been hearing it for a while now.
Is it birds or some-thing...?
PHWEEEET
SHUFFF

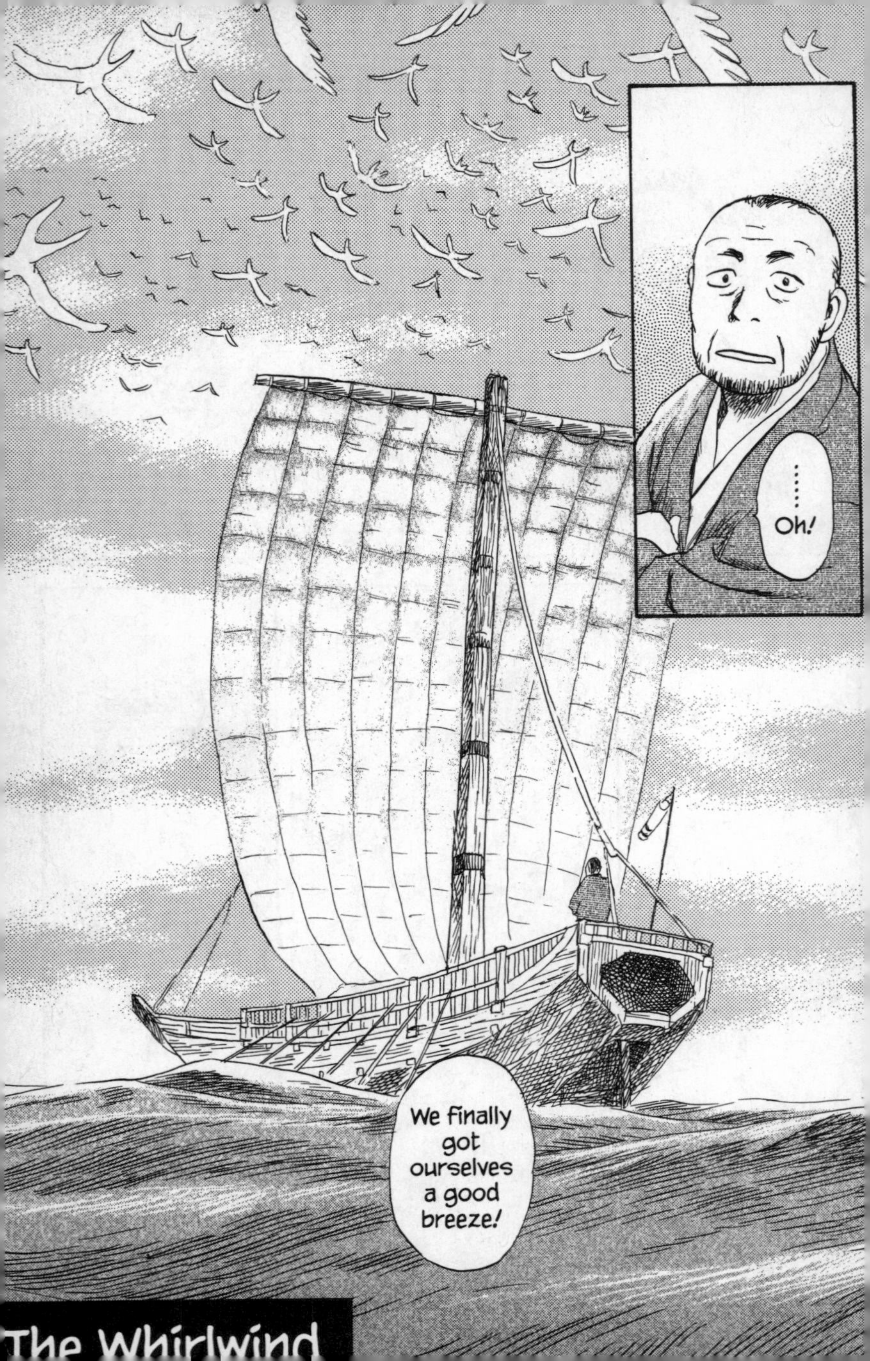
......Oh!
We finally got ourselves a good breeze!

The Whirlwind

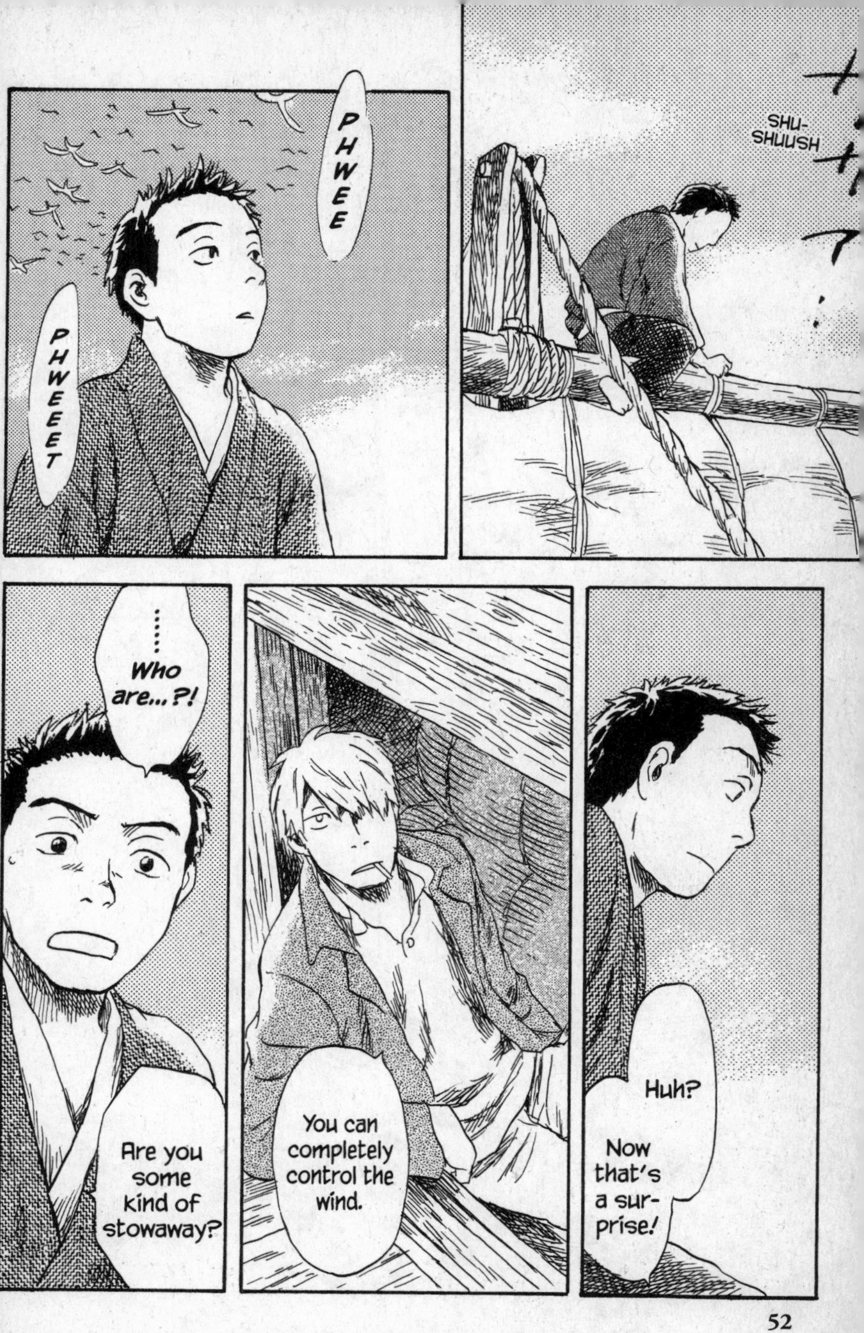
SHU-SHUUSH
PHWEE
PHWEEET
Huh?
Now that's a sur-prise!
You can completely control the wind.
...... Who are...?!
Are you some kind of stowaway?

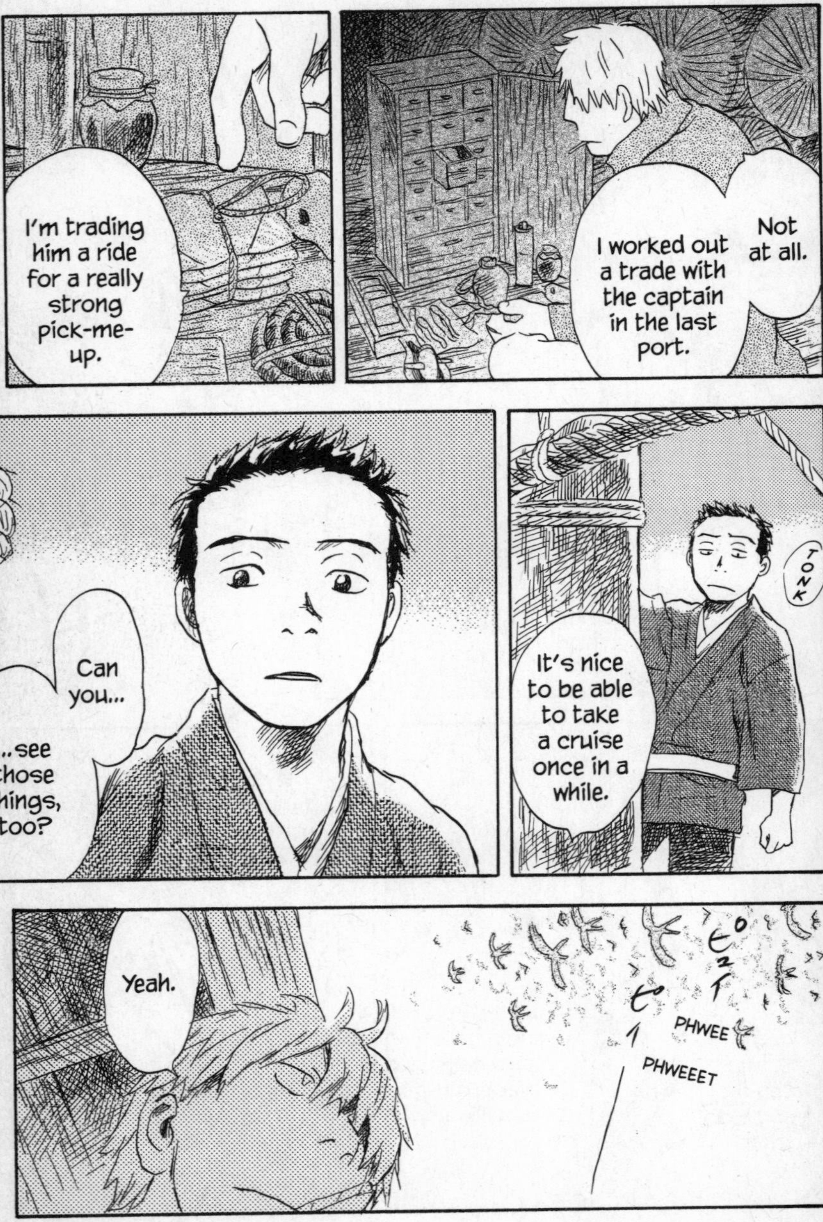
Not at all.
I worked out a trade with the captain in the last port.
I'm trading him a ride for a really strong pick-me-up.
TONK
It's nice to be able to take a cruise once in a while.
Can you...
...see those things, too?
PHWEE
PHWEEET
Yeah.

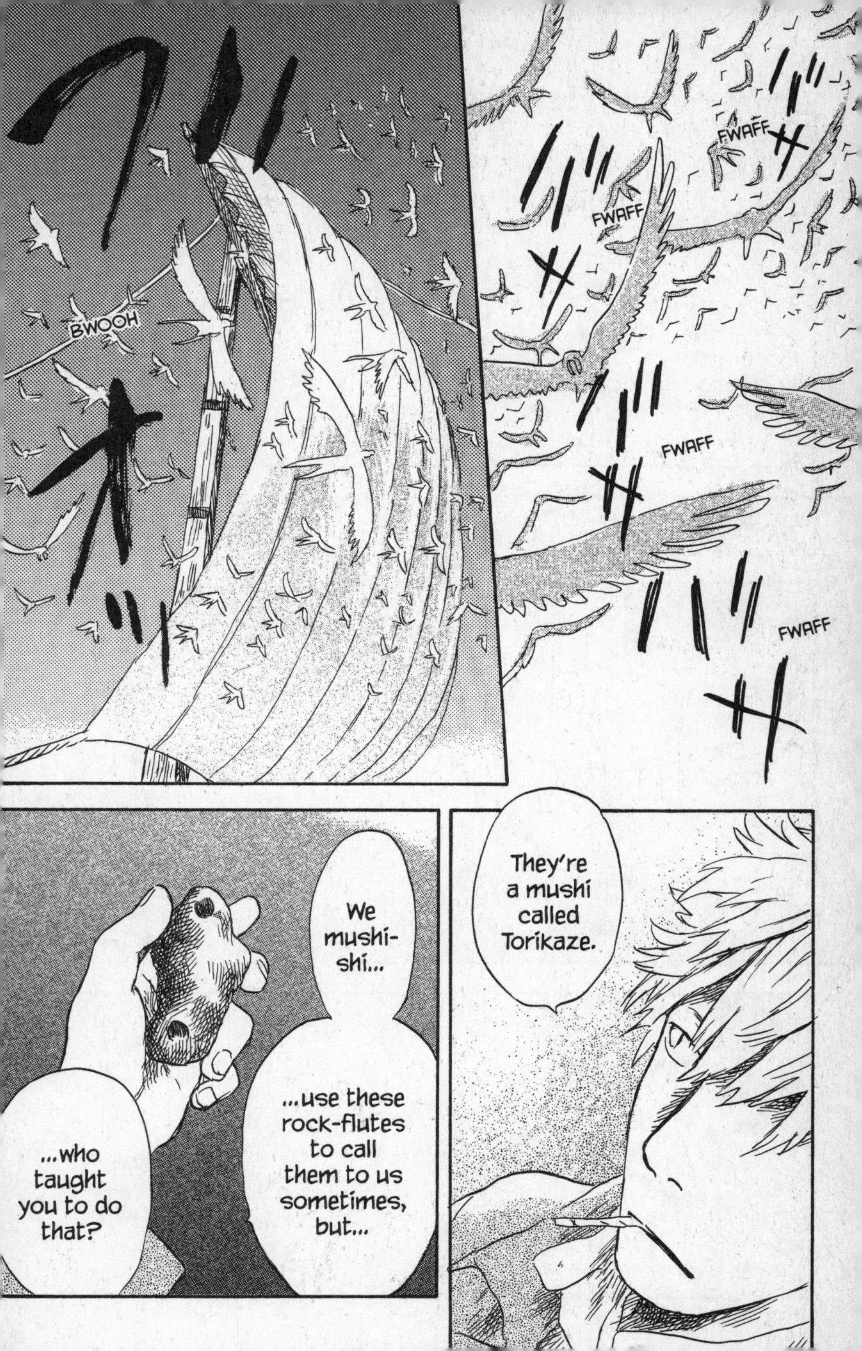
FWAFF
FWAFF
FWAFF
FWAFF
BWOOH
They're a mushi called Torikaze.
We mushi-shi...
...use these rock-flutes to call them to us sometimes, but...
...who taught you to do that?

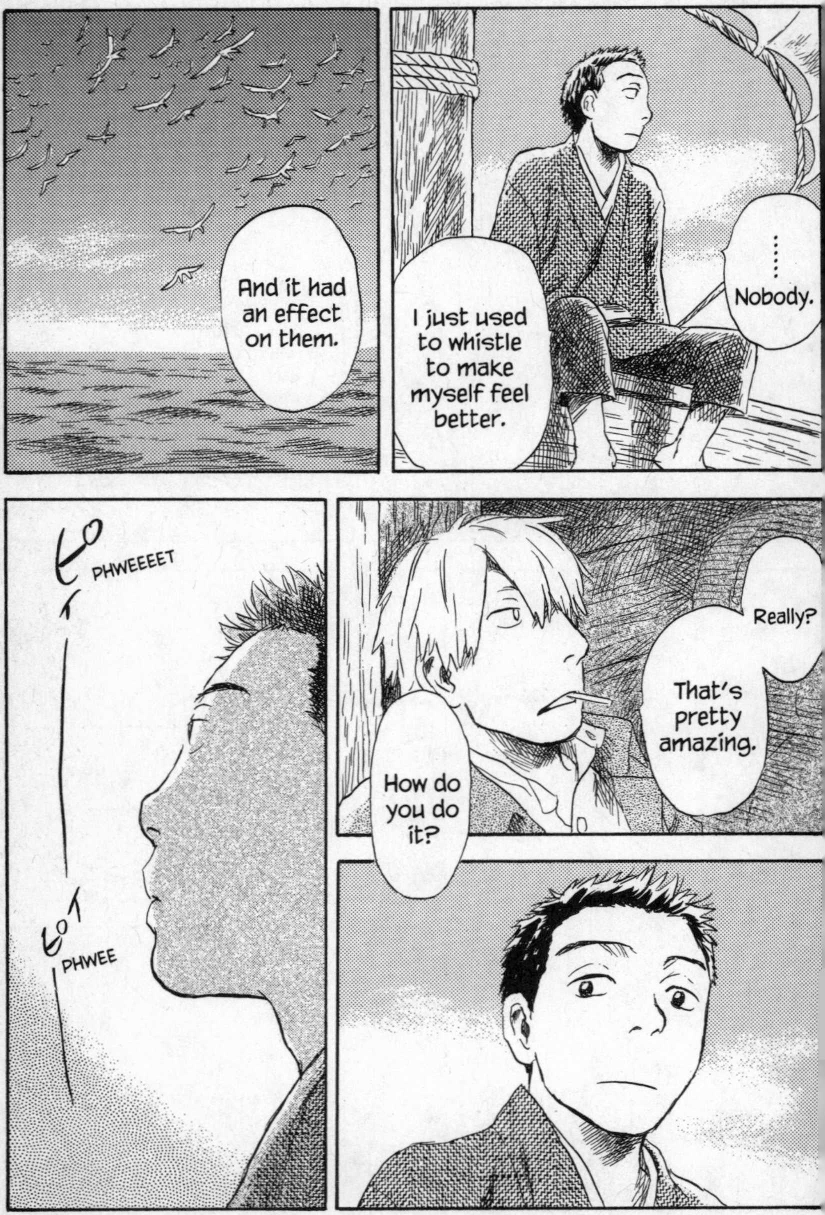

......Nobody.
I just used to whistle to make myself feel better.
And it had an effect on them.
Really?
That's pretty amazing.
How do you do it?
PHWEEEET
PHWEE

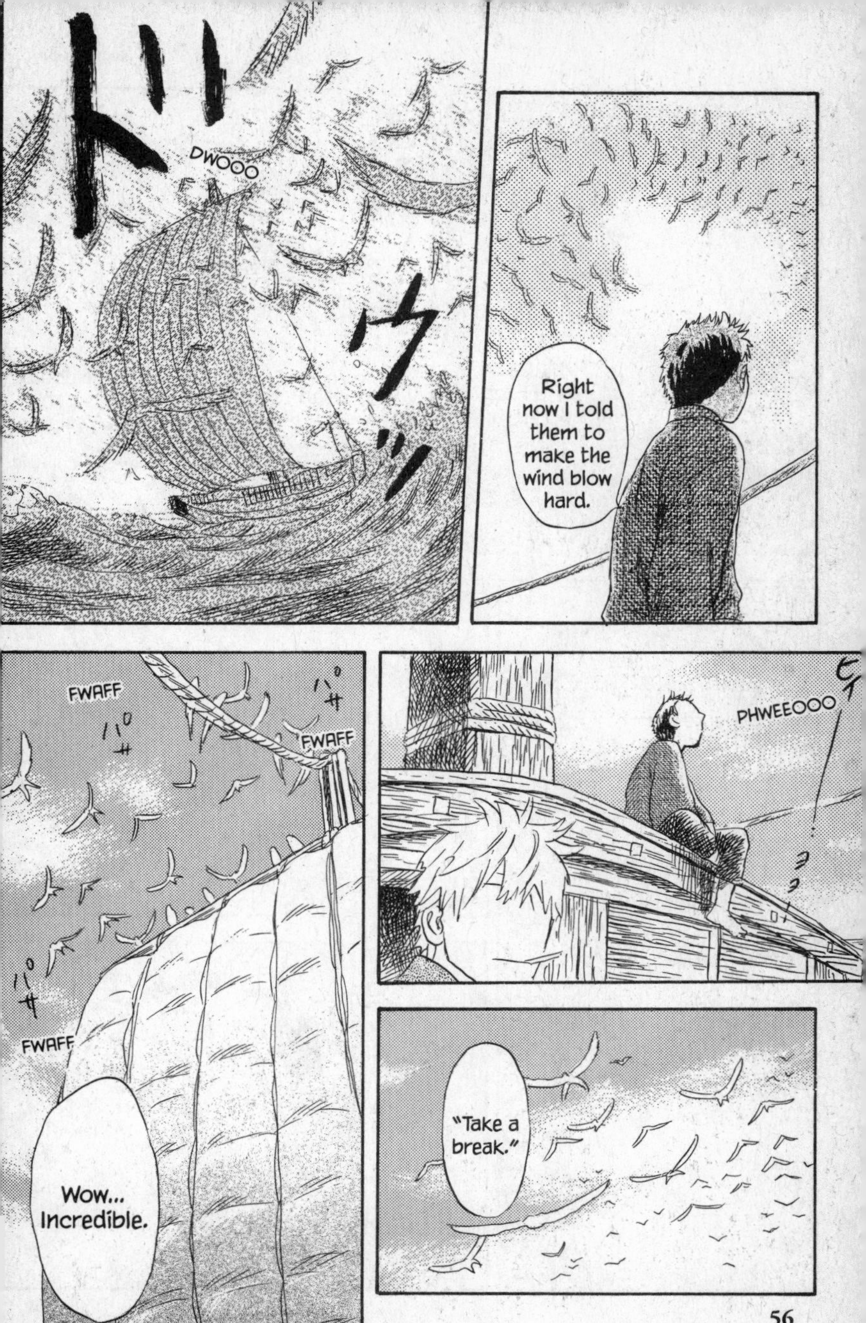
Right now I told them to make the wind blow hard.
ドッ
DWOOO
PHWEEOOO
"Take a break."
FWAFF
FWAFF
FWAFF
Wow... Incredible.

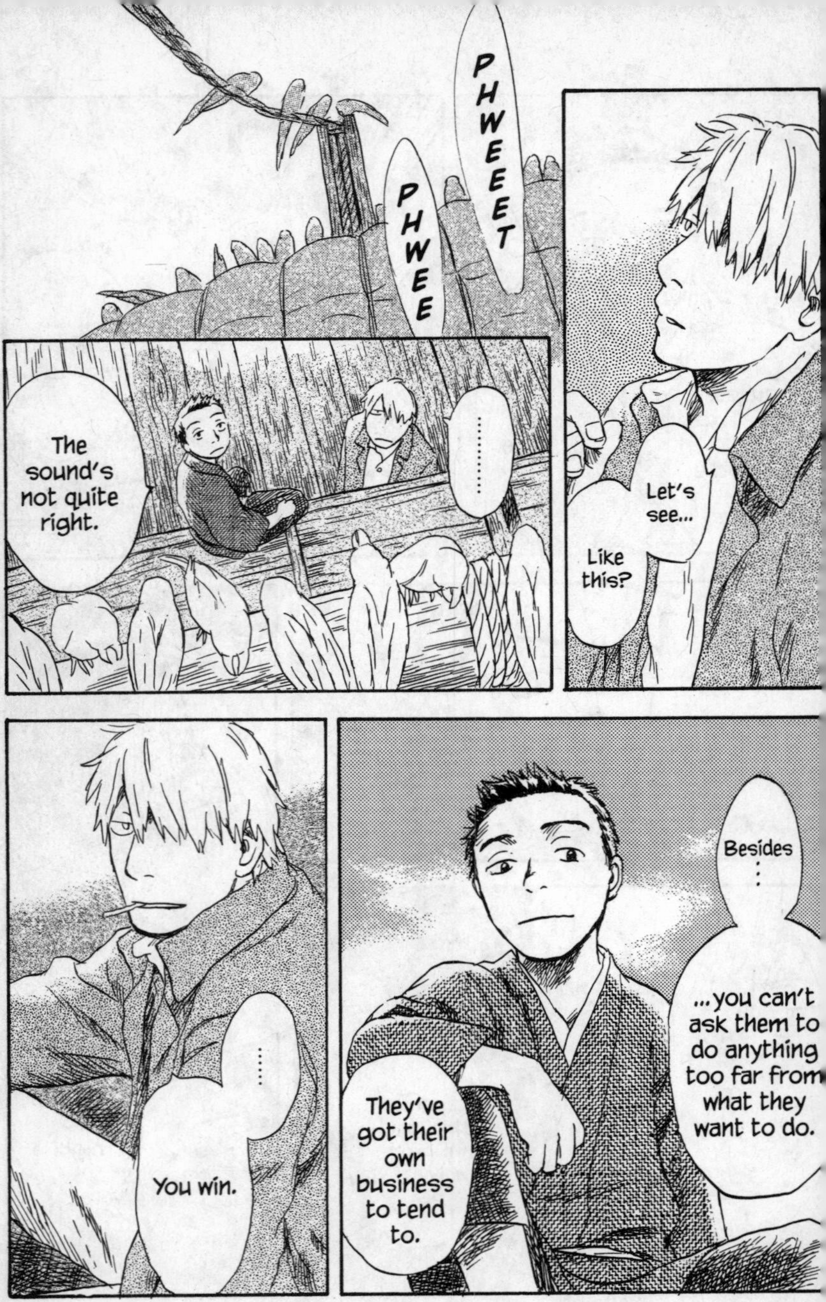
Let's see...
Like this?
PHWEEEET
PHWEE
......
The sound's not quite right.
Besides...
...you can't ask them to do anything too far from what they want to do.
They've got their own business to tend to.
......
You win.

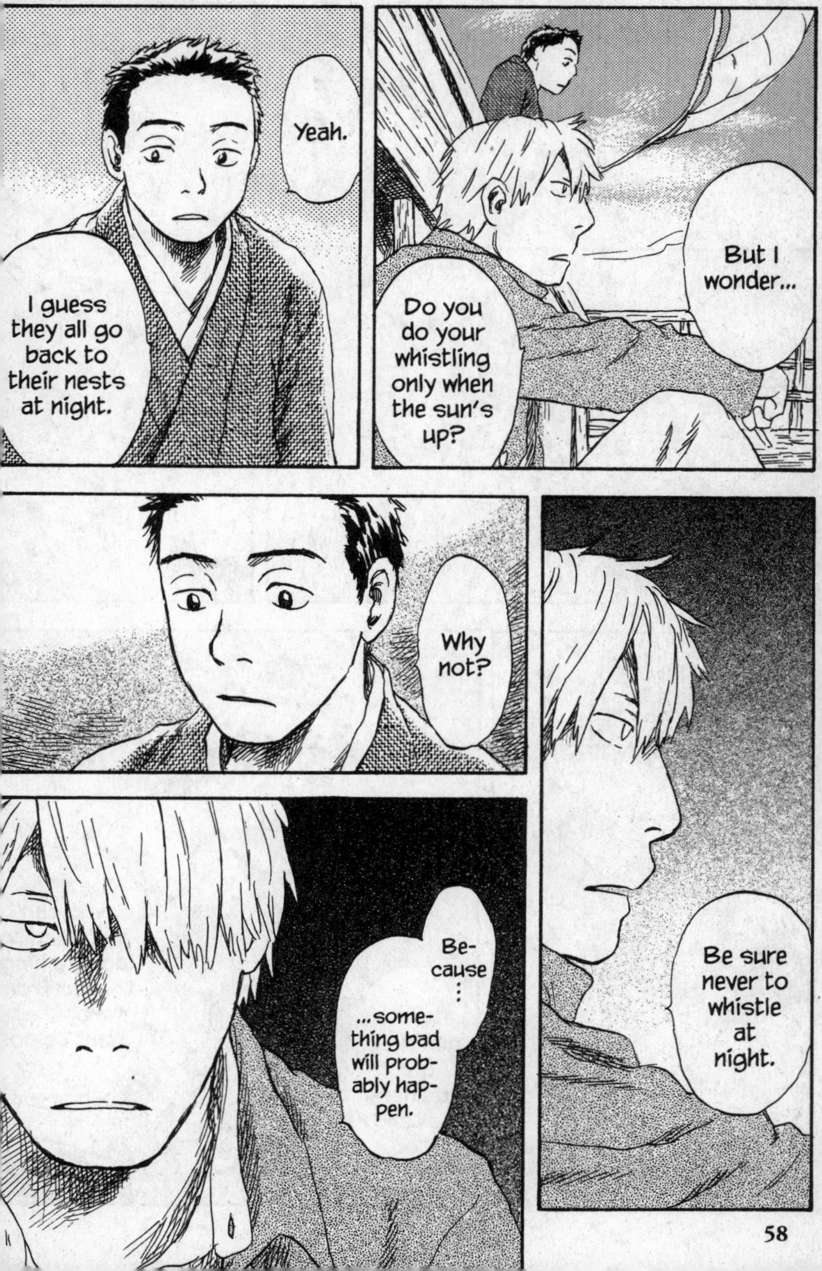
But I wonder...
Do you do your whistling only when the sun's up?
Yeah.
I guess they all go back to their nests at night.
Be sure never to whistle at night.
Why not?
Be-cause...
...some-thing bad will prob-ably hap-pen.

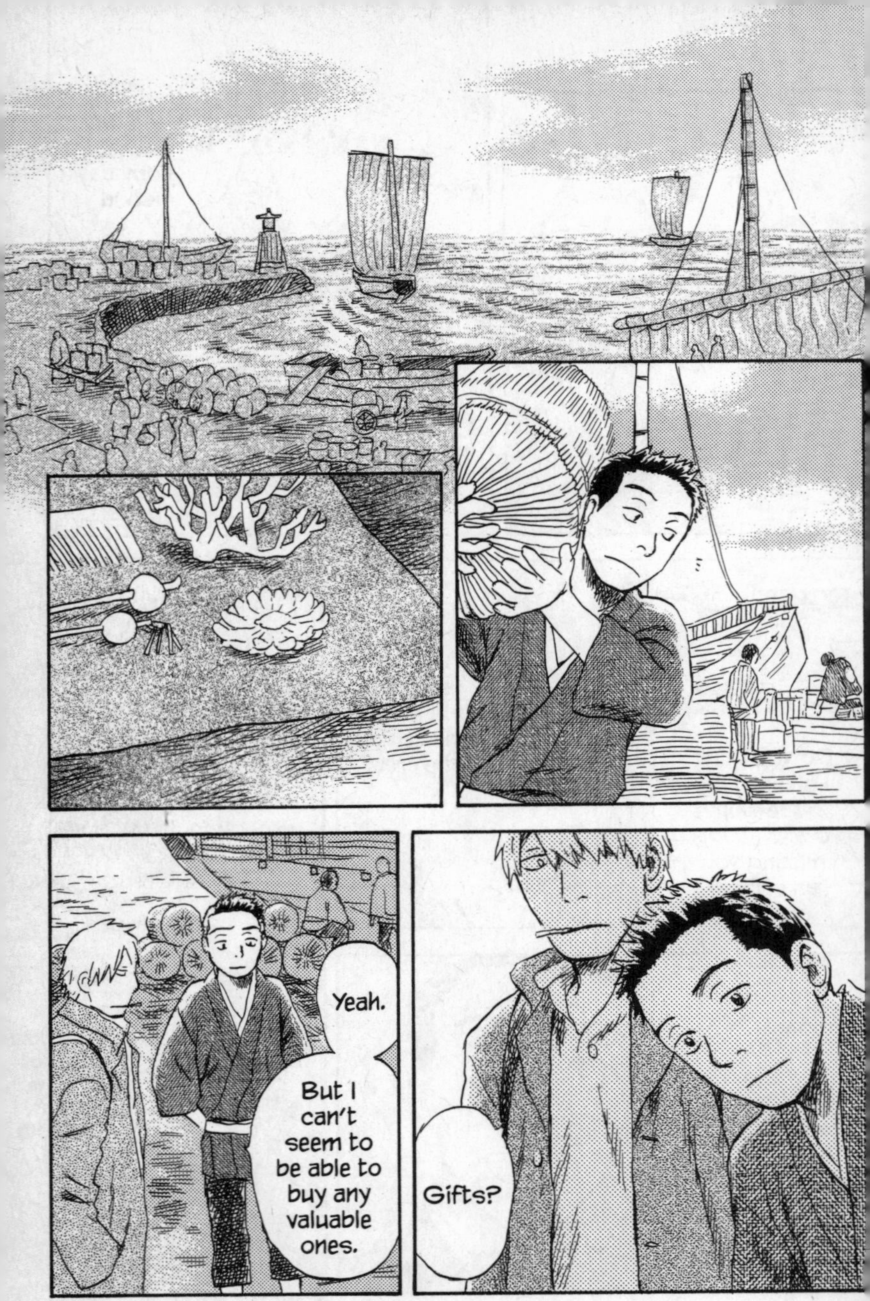
Gifts?
Yeah.
But I can't seem to be able to buy any valuable ones.

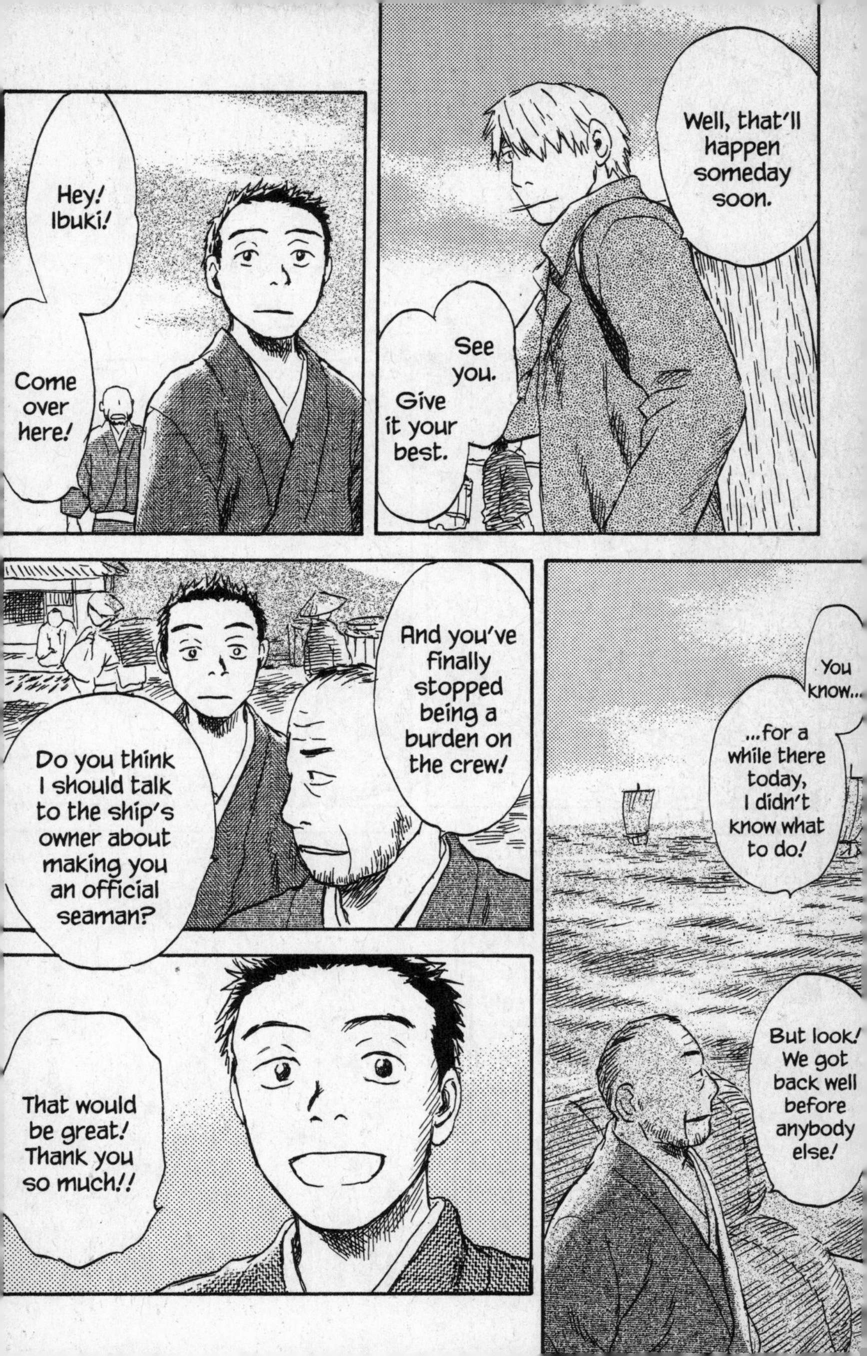

Well, that'll happen someday soon.
See you. Give it your best.
Hey! Ibuki!
Come over here!
You know...
...for a while there today, I didn't know what to do!
But look! We got back well before anybody else!
And you've finally stopped being a burden on the crew!
Do you think I should talk to the ship's owner about making you an official seaman?
That would be great! Thank you so much!!

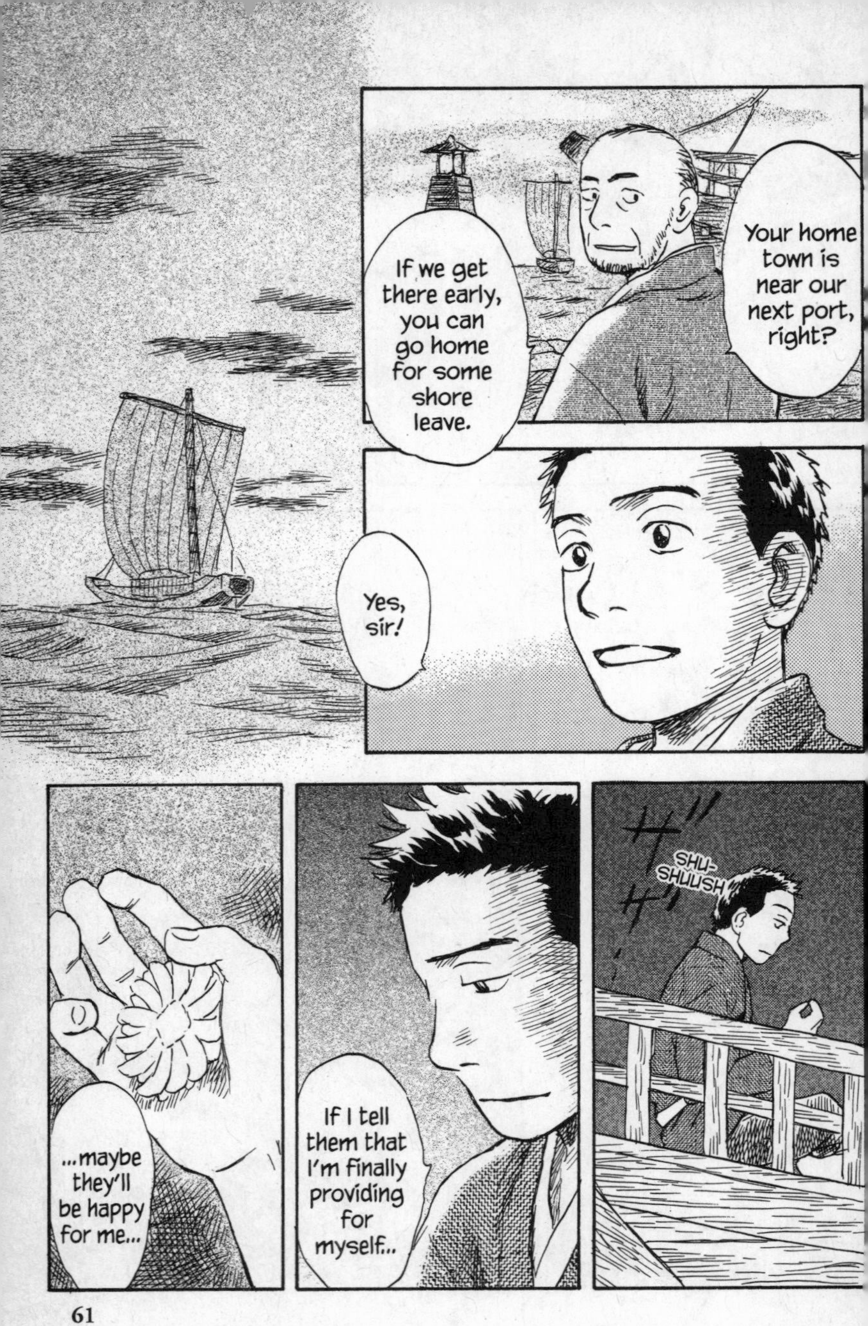
Your home town is near our next port, right?
If we get there early, you can go home for some shore leave.
Yes, sir!
SHU-SHUUSH
If I tell them that I'm finally providing for myself...
...maybe they'll be happy for me...

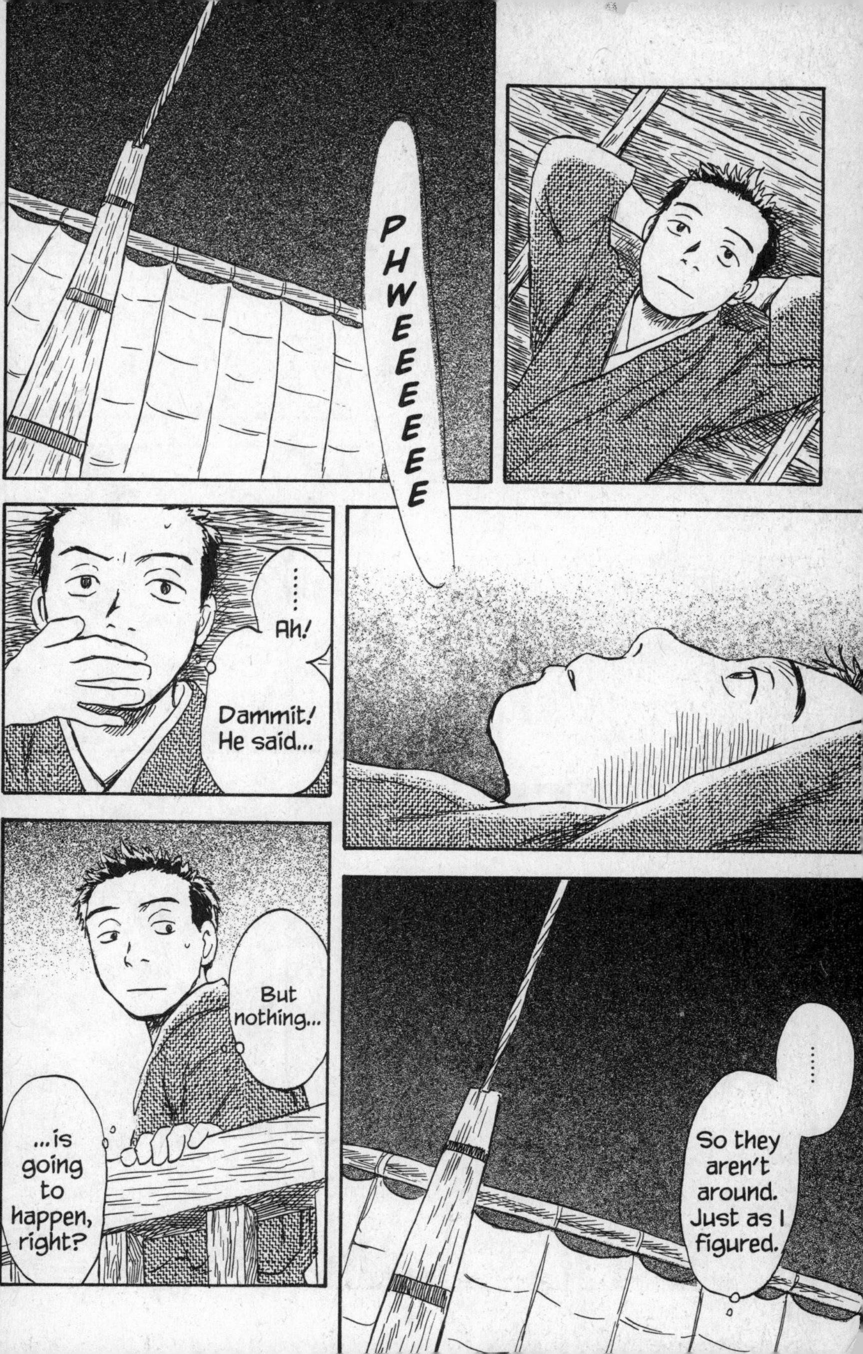
PHWEEEEEEE
...... Ah!
Dammit! He said...
......
So they aren't around. Just as I figured.
But nothing...
...is going to happen, right?

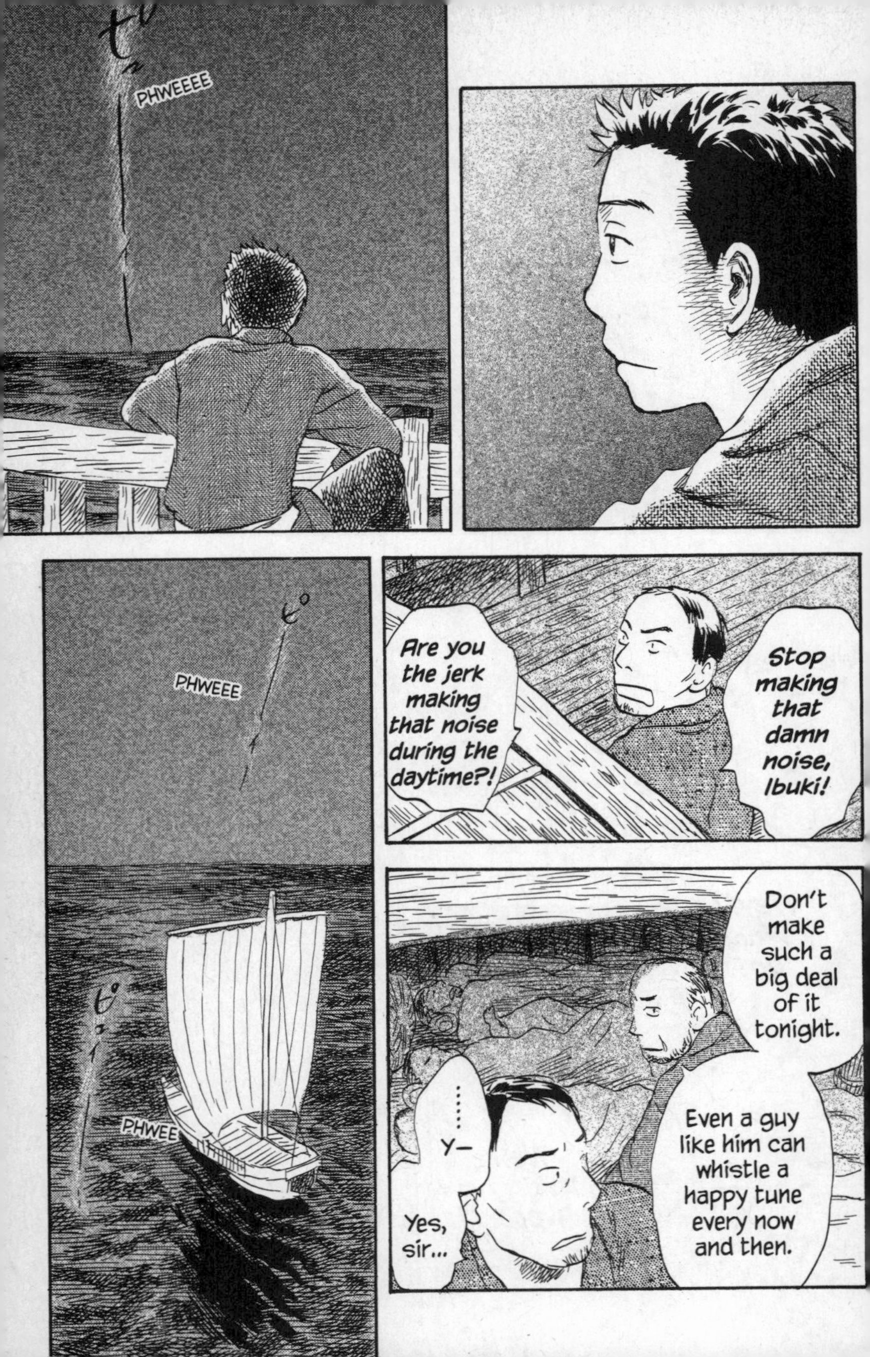
PHWEEEE
Stop making that damn noise, Ibuki!
Are you the jerk making that noise during the daytime?!
Don't make such a big deal of it tonight.
Even a guy like him can whistle a happy tune every now and then.
......Y—
Yes, sir...
PHWEEE
PHWEE

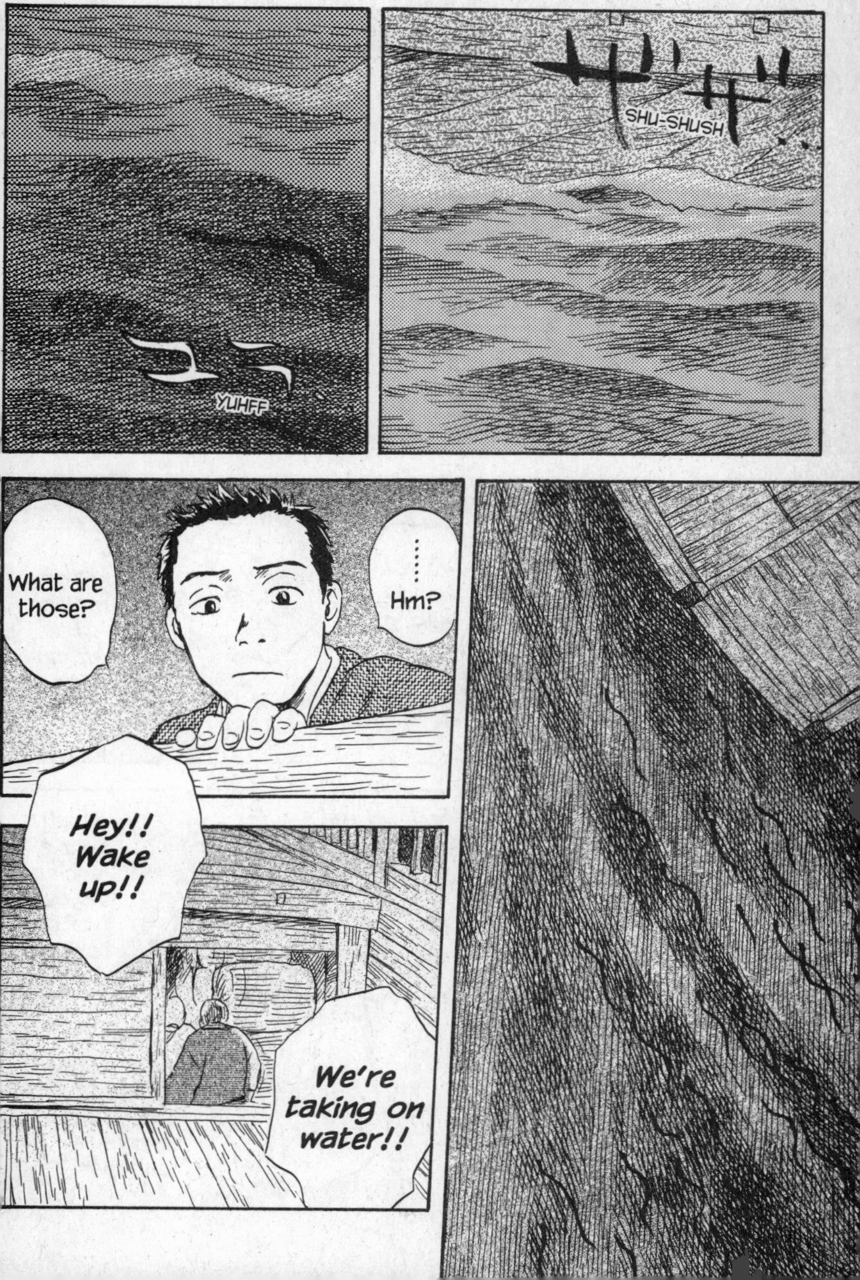
SHU-SHUSH
YUHFF
...... Hm?
What are those?
Hey!! Wake up!!
We're taking on water!!

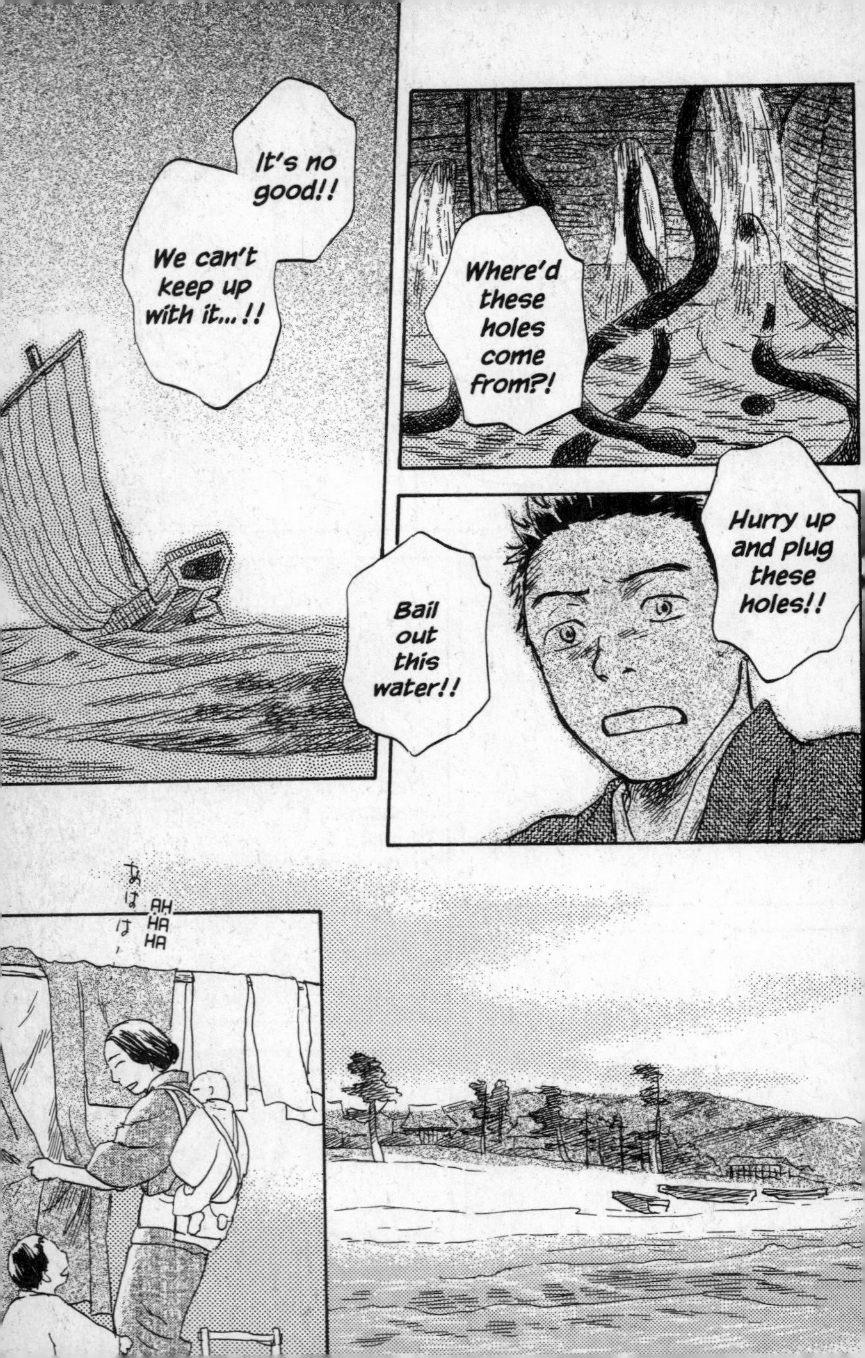
Where'd these holes come from?!
Hurry up and plug these holes!!
Bail out this water!!
It's no good!!
We can't keep up with it...!!
あはは
AH HA HA

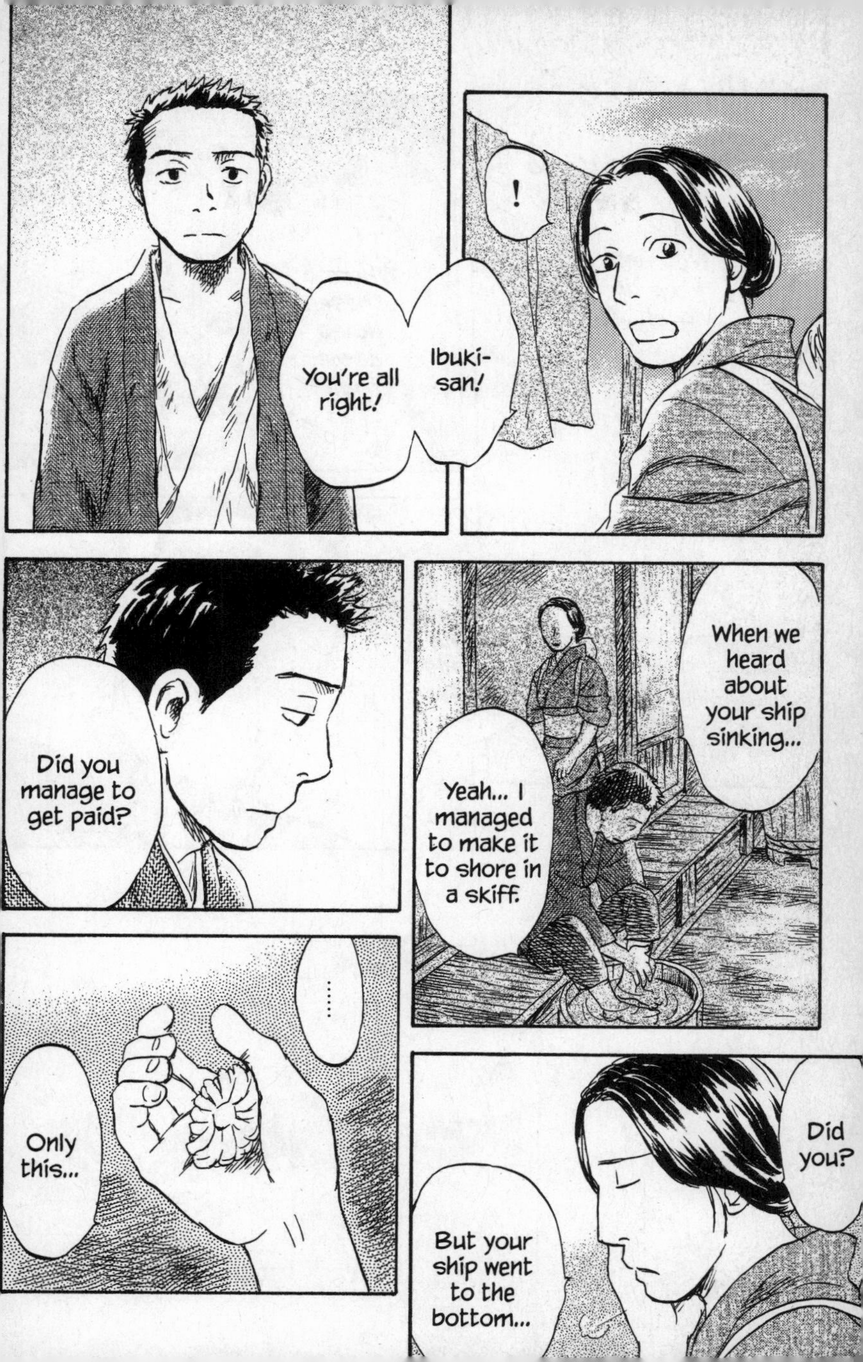
!
Ibuki-san!
You're all right!
When we heard about your ship sinking...
Yeah... I managed to make it to shore in a skiff.
Did you manage to get paid?
Did you?
But your ship went to the bottom...
......
Only this...

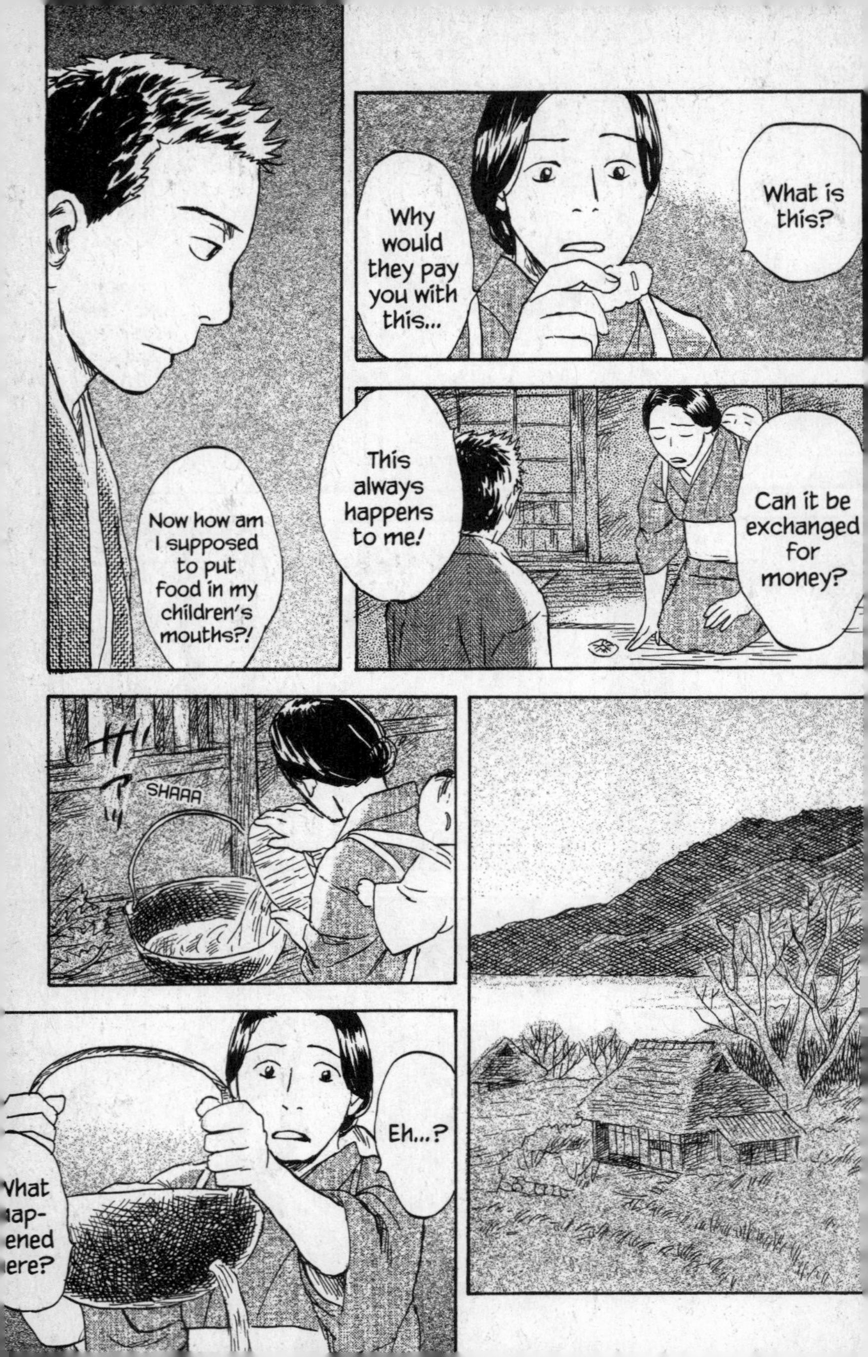
What is this?
Why would they pay you with this...
Can it be exchanged for money?
This always happens to me!
Now how am I supposed to put food in my children's mouths?!
SHAAA
Eh...?
Vhat ap- ened ere?

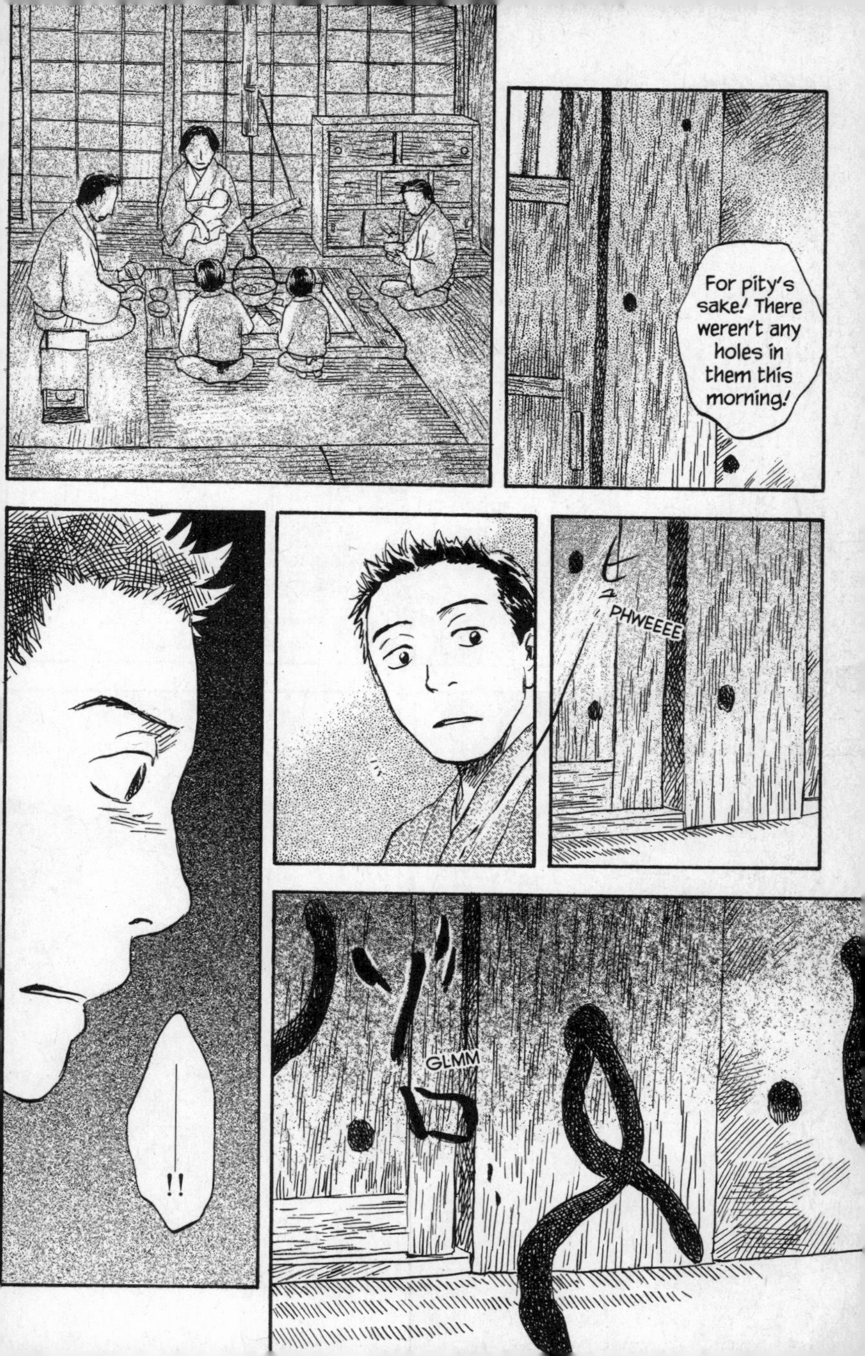
For pity's sake! There weren't any holes in them this morning!
PHWEEEE
!!
GLMM

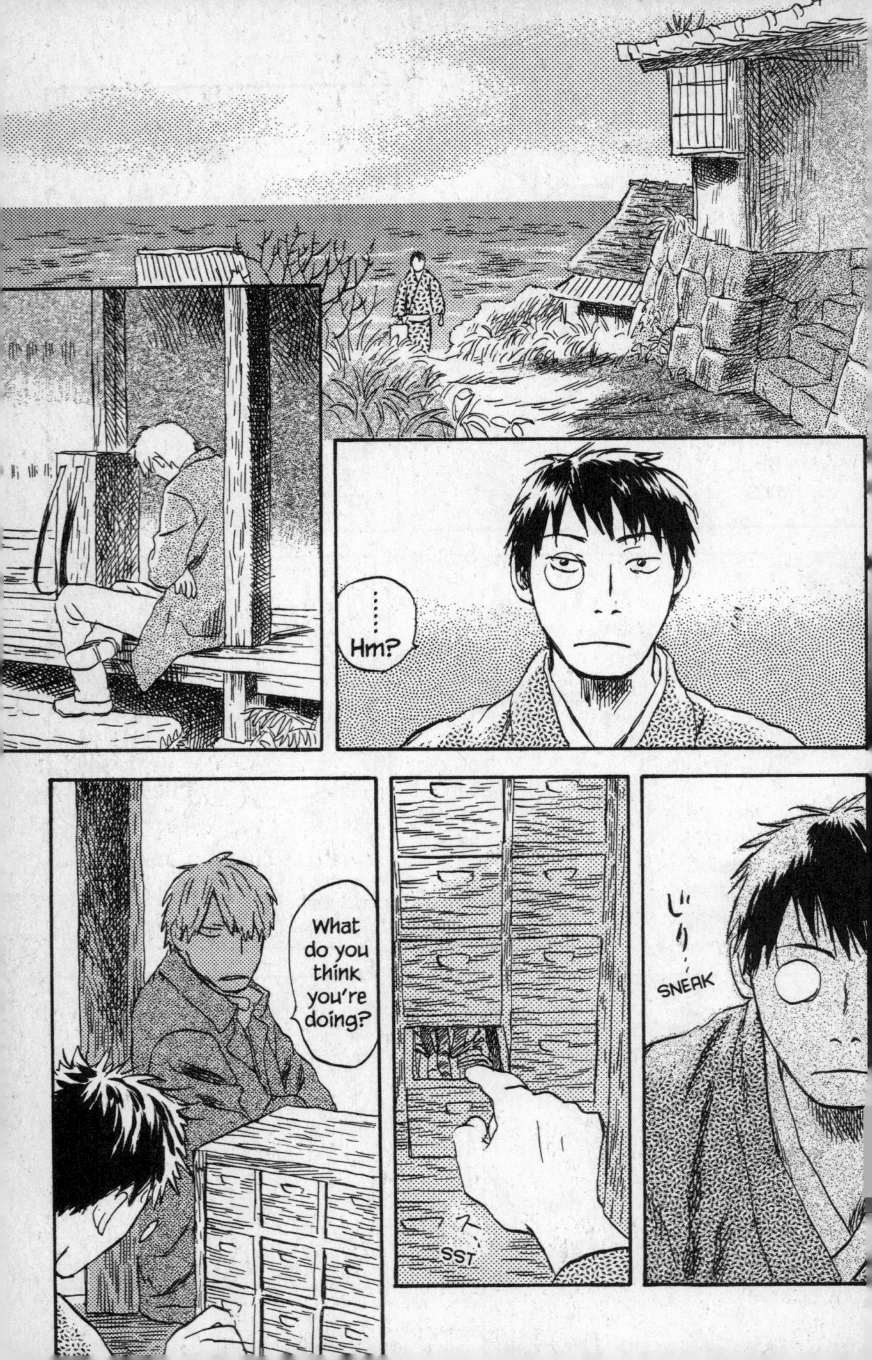
......
Hm?
じり
SNEAK
SST
What do you think you're doing?

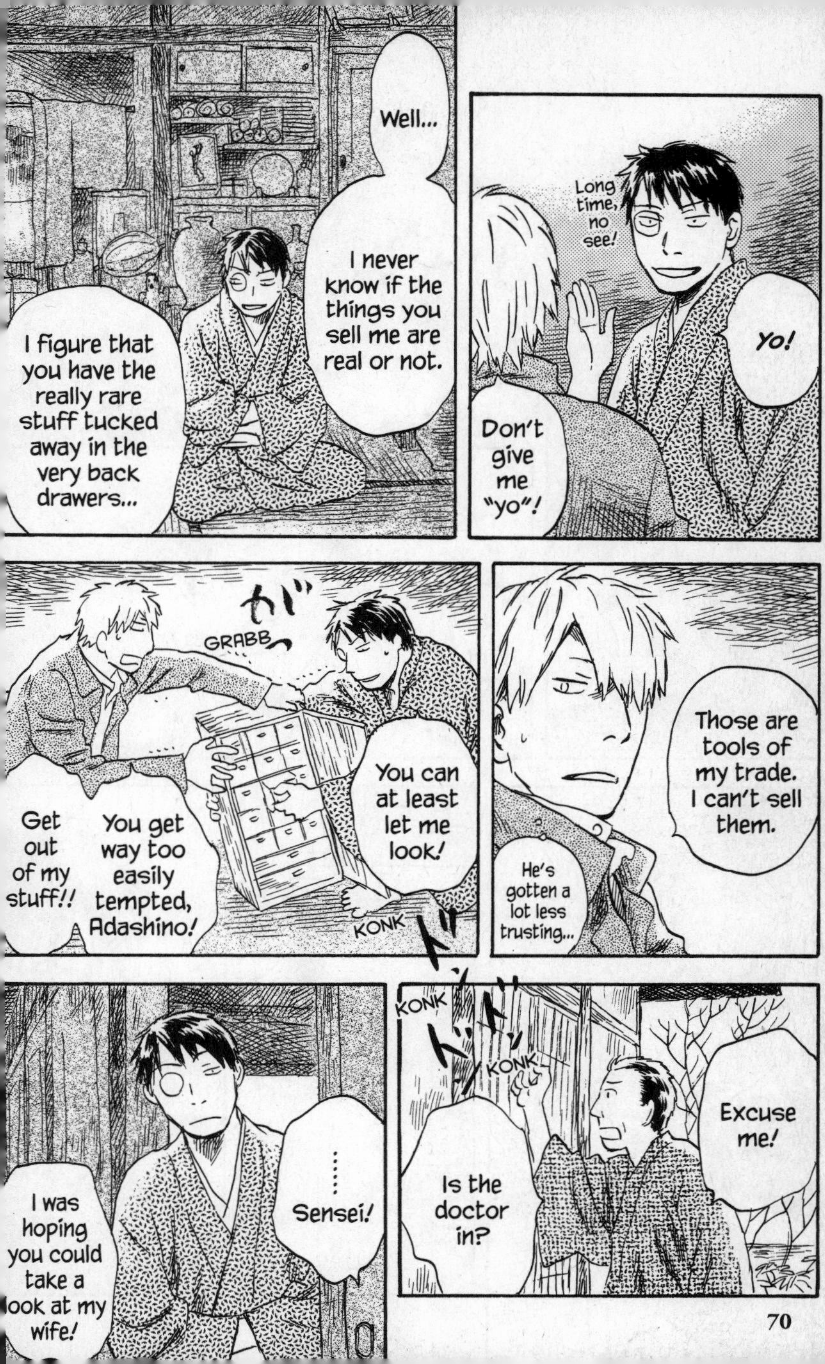
Long time, no see!
Yo!
Don't give me "yo"!
Well...
I never know if the things you sell me are real or not.
I figure that you have the really rare stuff tucked away in the very back drawers...
Those are tools of my trade. I can't sell them.
He's gotten a lot less trusting...
が
GRABB
You can at least let me look!
You get way too easily tempted, Adashino!
Get out of my stuff!!
KONK
KONK
KONK
Excuse me!
Is the doctor in?
......
Sensei!
I was hoping you could take a look at my wife!

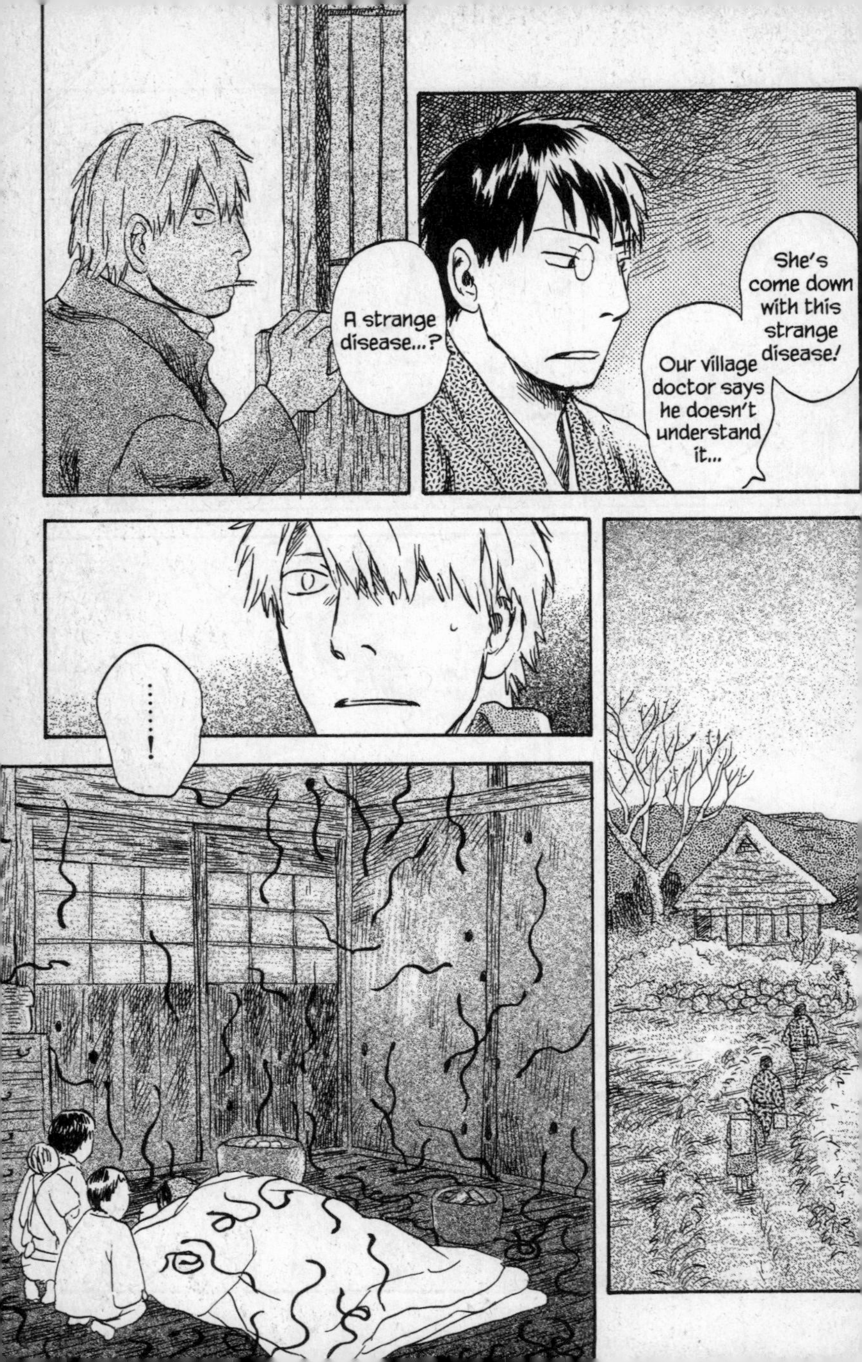
She's come down with this strange disease!
Our village doctor says he doesn't understand it...
A strange disease...?
......!

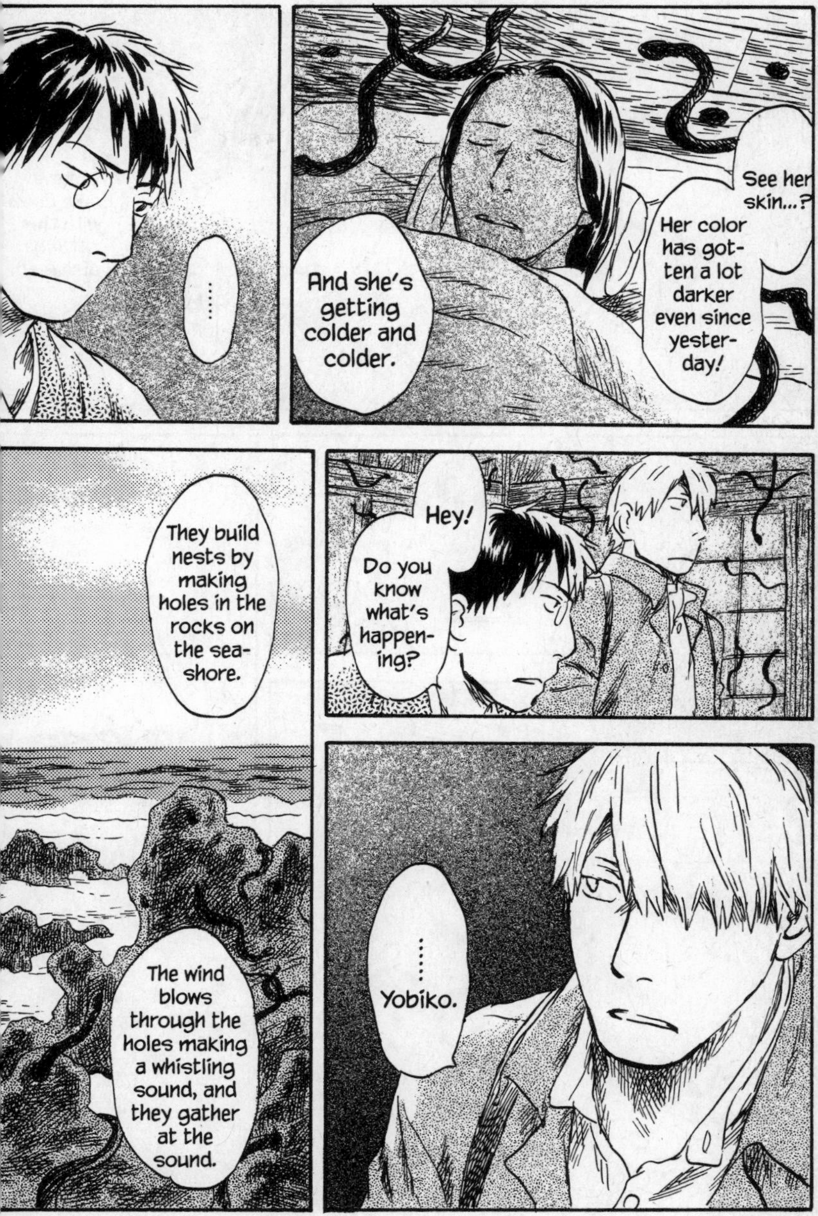

See her skin...?
Her color has gotten a lot darker even since yesterday!
And she's getting colder and colder.
......
Hey!
Do you know what's happening?
They build nests by making holes in the rocks on the seashore.
...... Yobiko.
The wind blows through the holes making a whistling sound, and they gather at the sound.

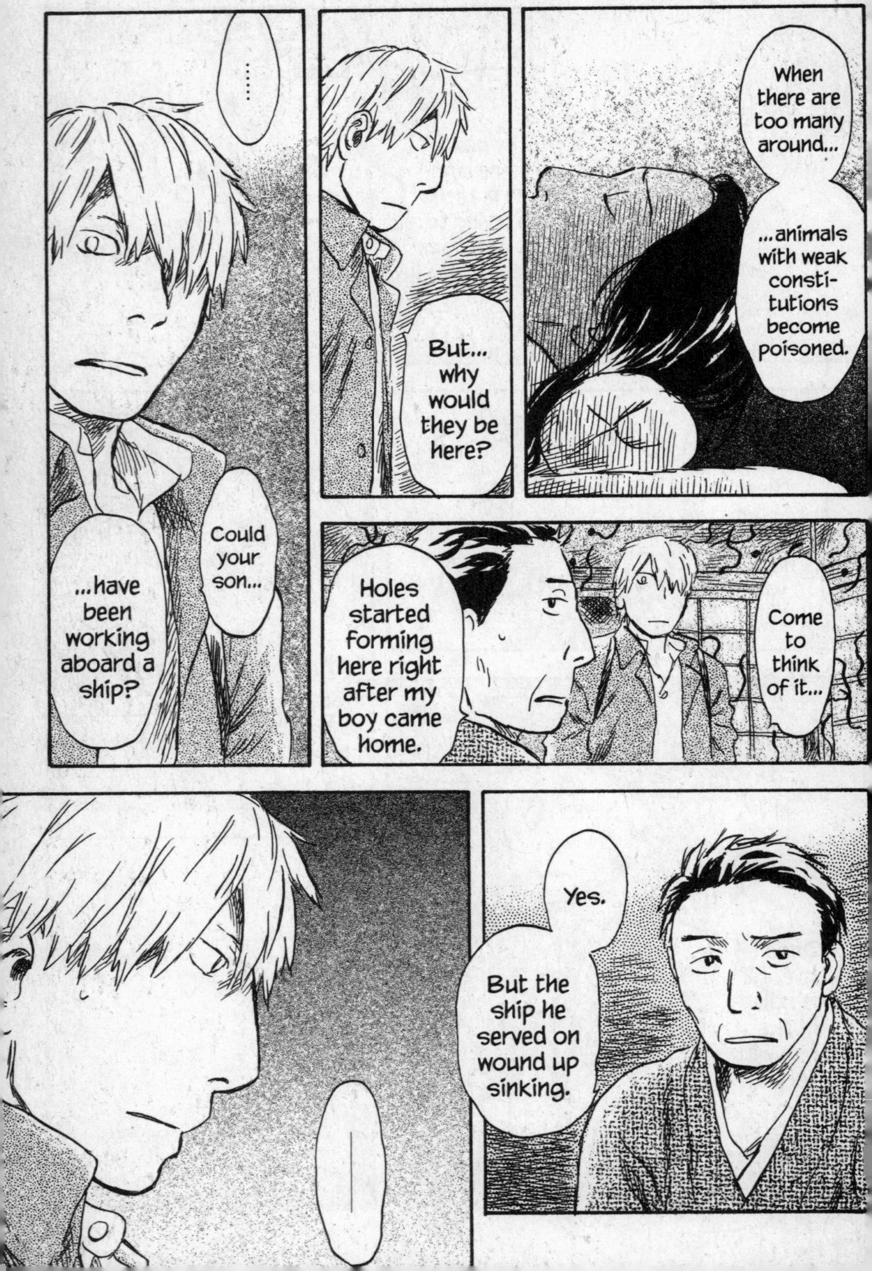

When there are too many around...
...animals with weak constitutions become poisoned.
But... why would they be here?
Come to think of it...
Holes started forming here right after my boy came home.
......
Could your son...
...have been working aboard a ship?
Yes.
But the ship he served on wound up sinking.
—

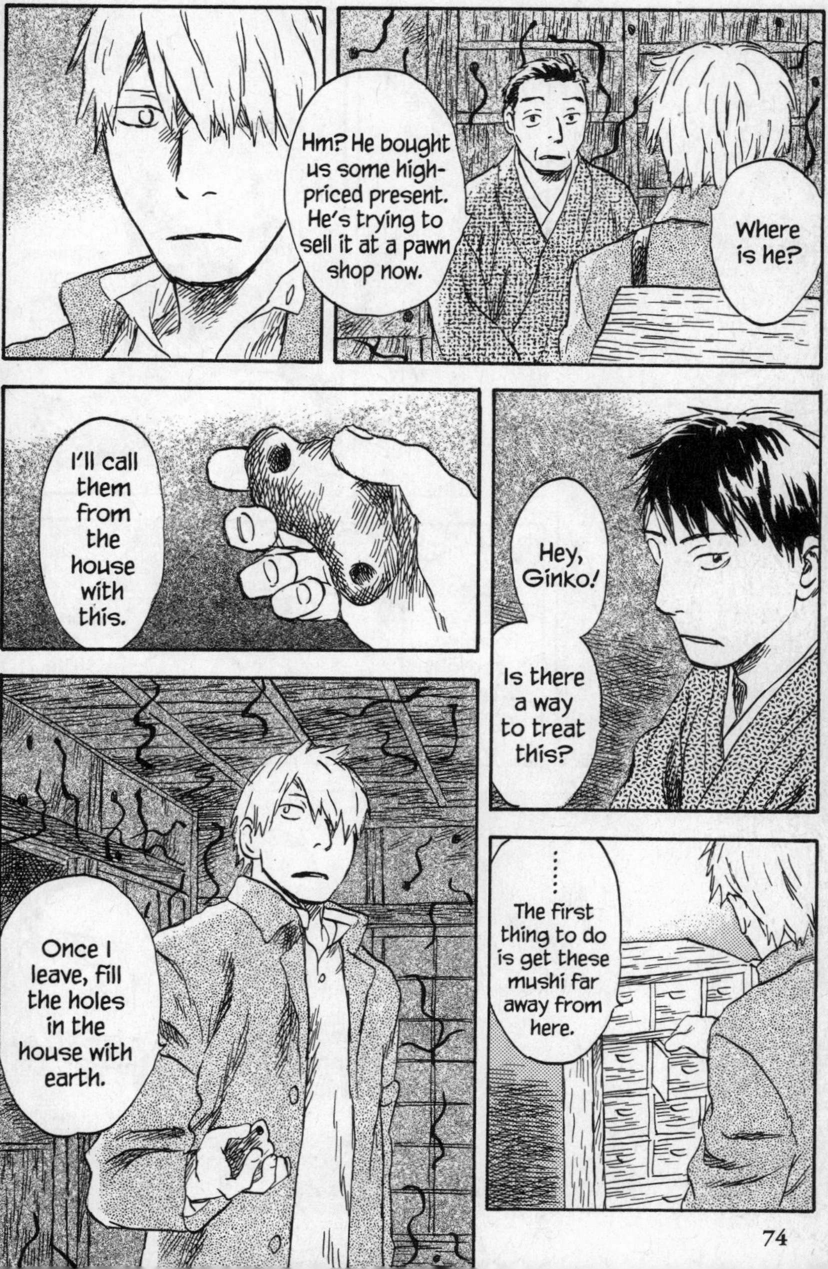
Where is he?
Hm? He bought us some high-priced present. He's trying to sell it at a pawn shop now.
Hey, Ginko!
Is there a way to treat this?
I'll call them from the house with this.
……
The first thing to do is get these mushi far away from here.
Once I leave, fill the holes in the house with earth.

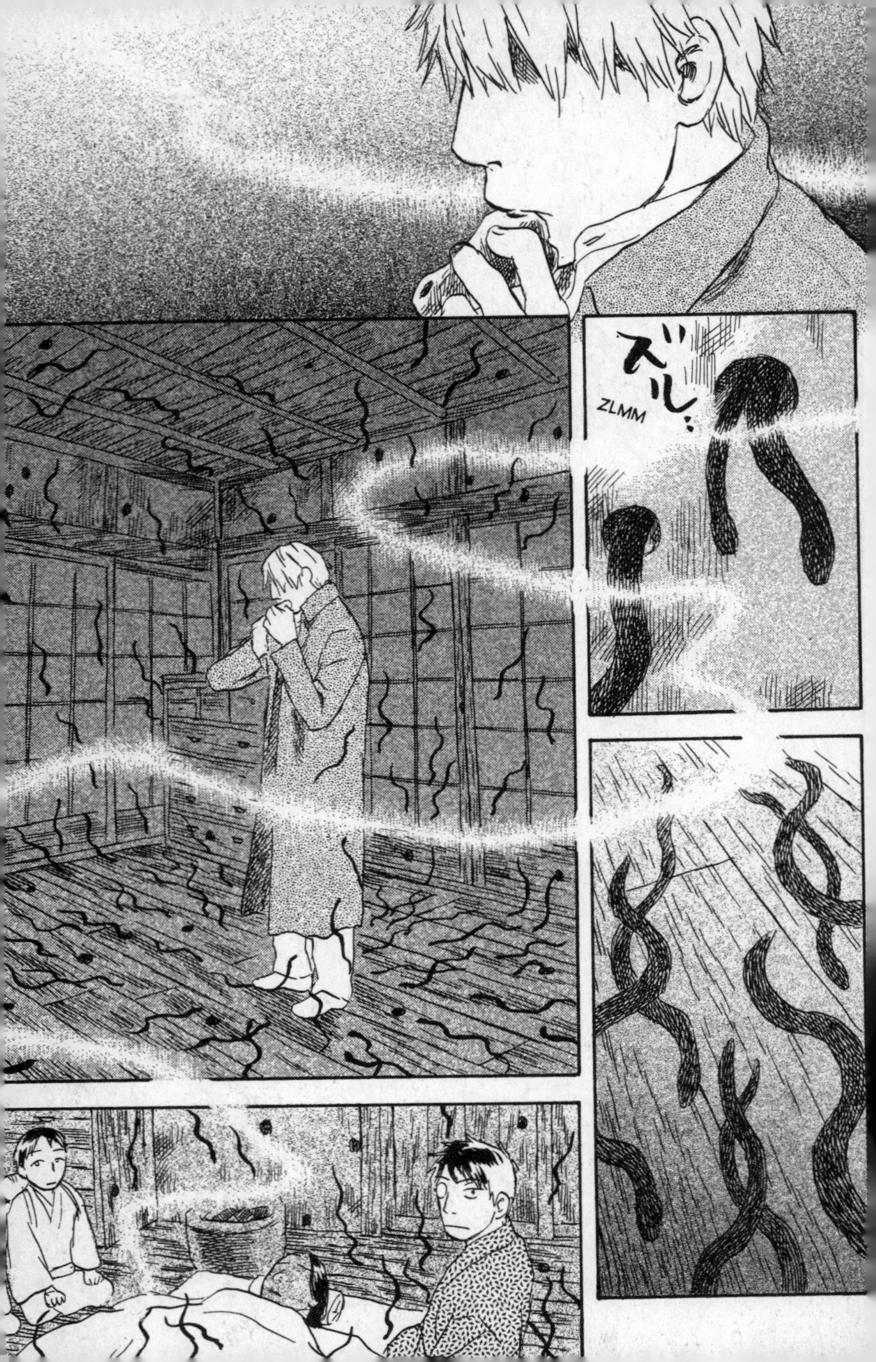
ズル…
ZLMM

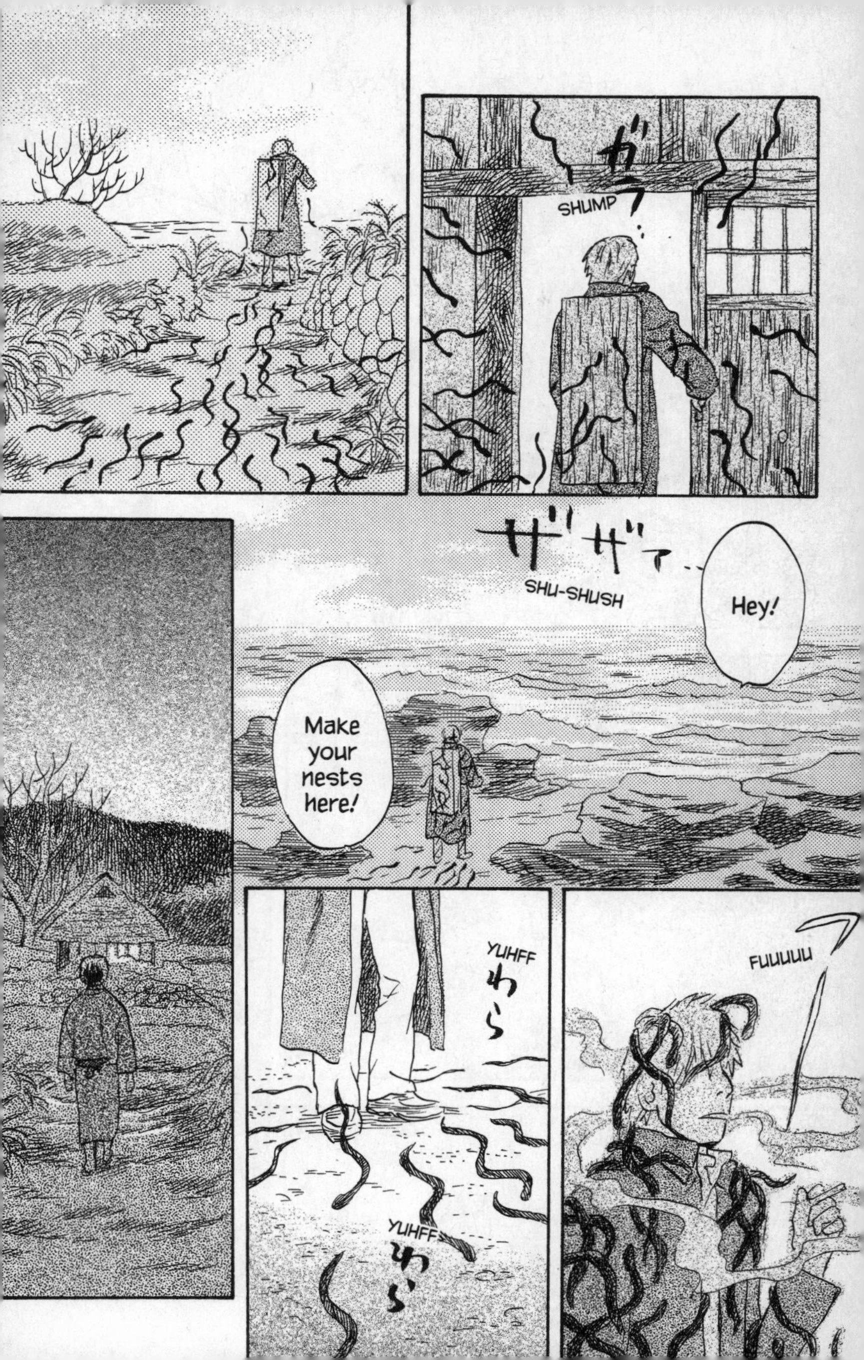
ガラ
SHUMP
ザザァ…
SHU-SHUSH
Hey!
Make your nests here!
FUUUUU
わら
YUHFF
わら
YUHFF

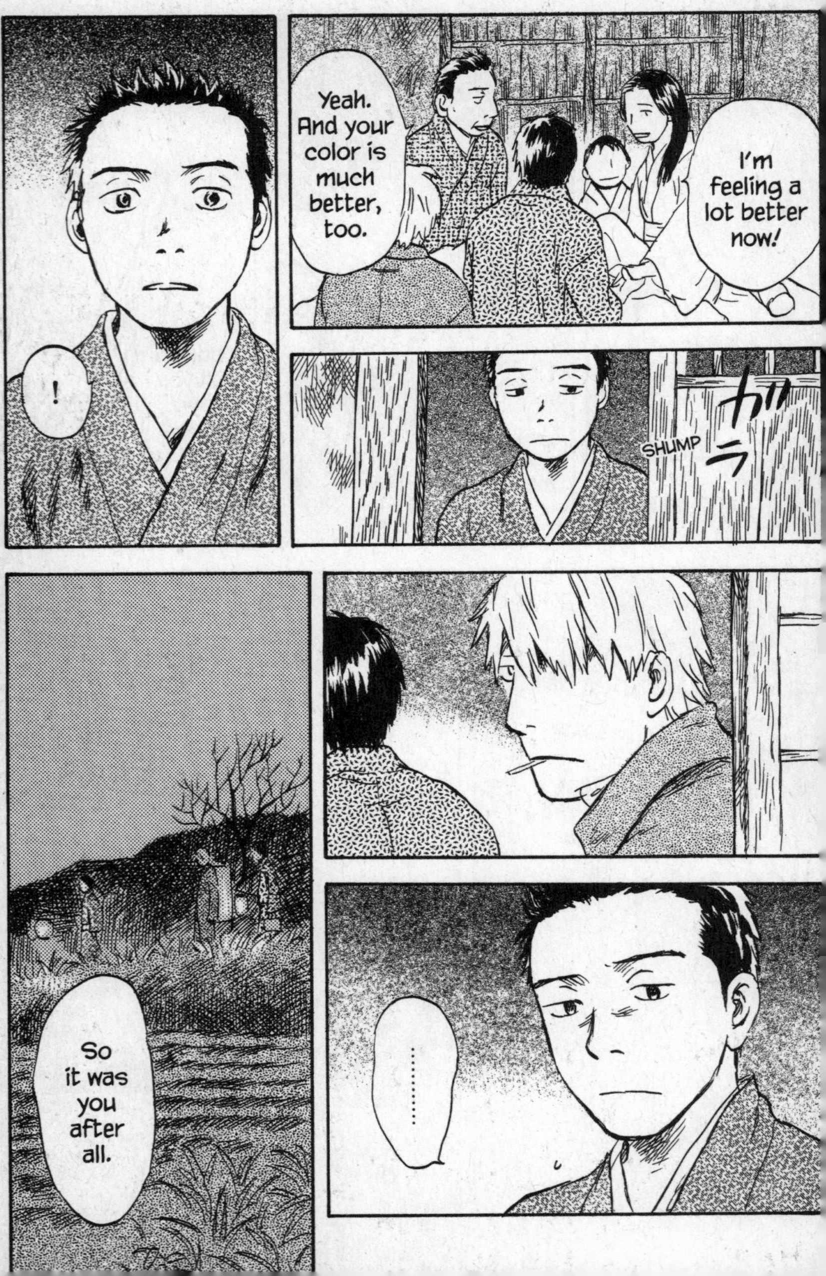
I'm feeling a lot better now!
Yeah. And your color is much better, too.
SHUMP
ガラ
!
……
So it was you after all.

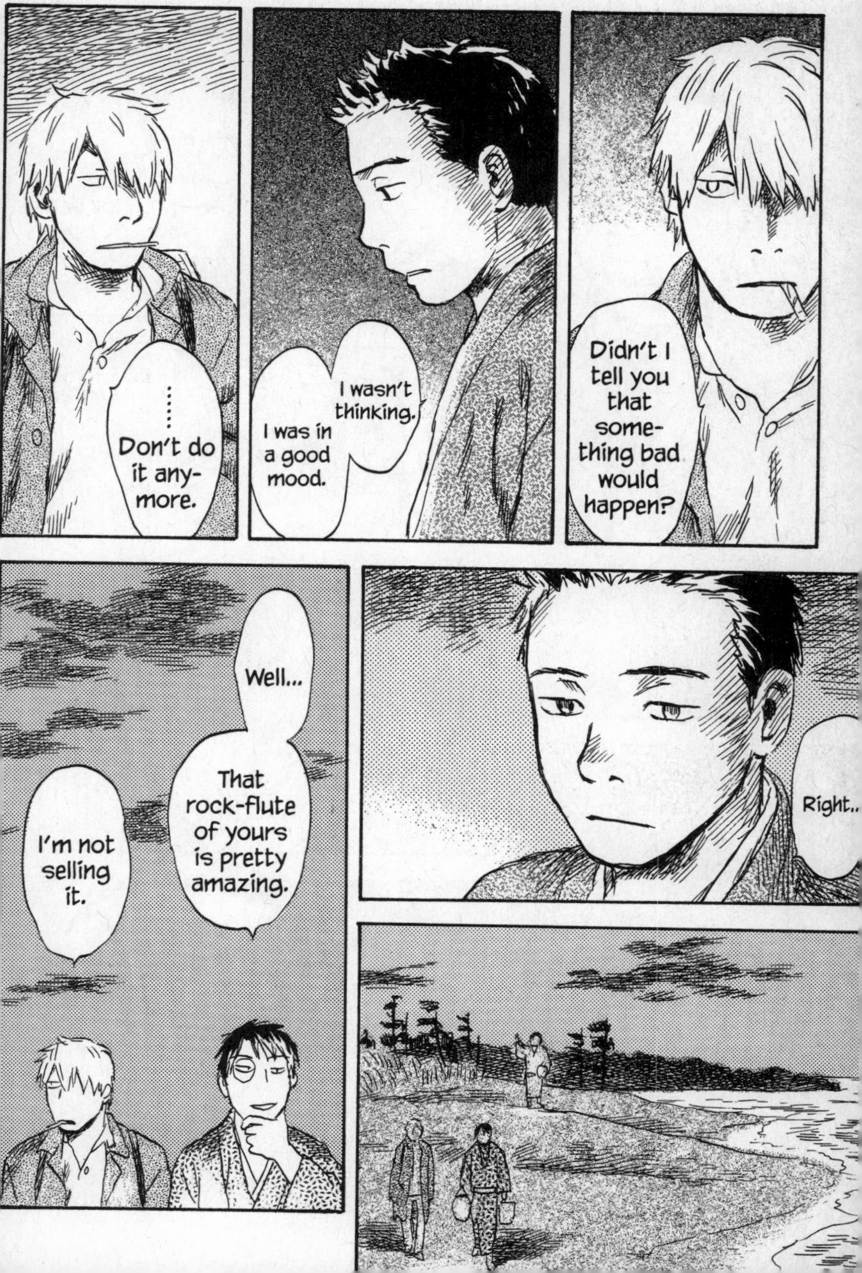
Didn't I tell you that something bad would happen?
I wasn't thinking.
I was in a good mood.
...... Don't do it anymore.
Right..
Well...
That rock-flute of yours is pretty amazing.
I'm not selling it.

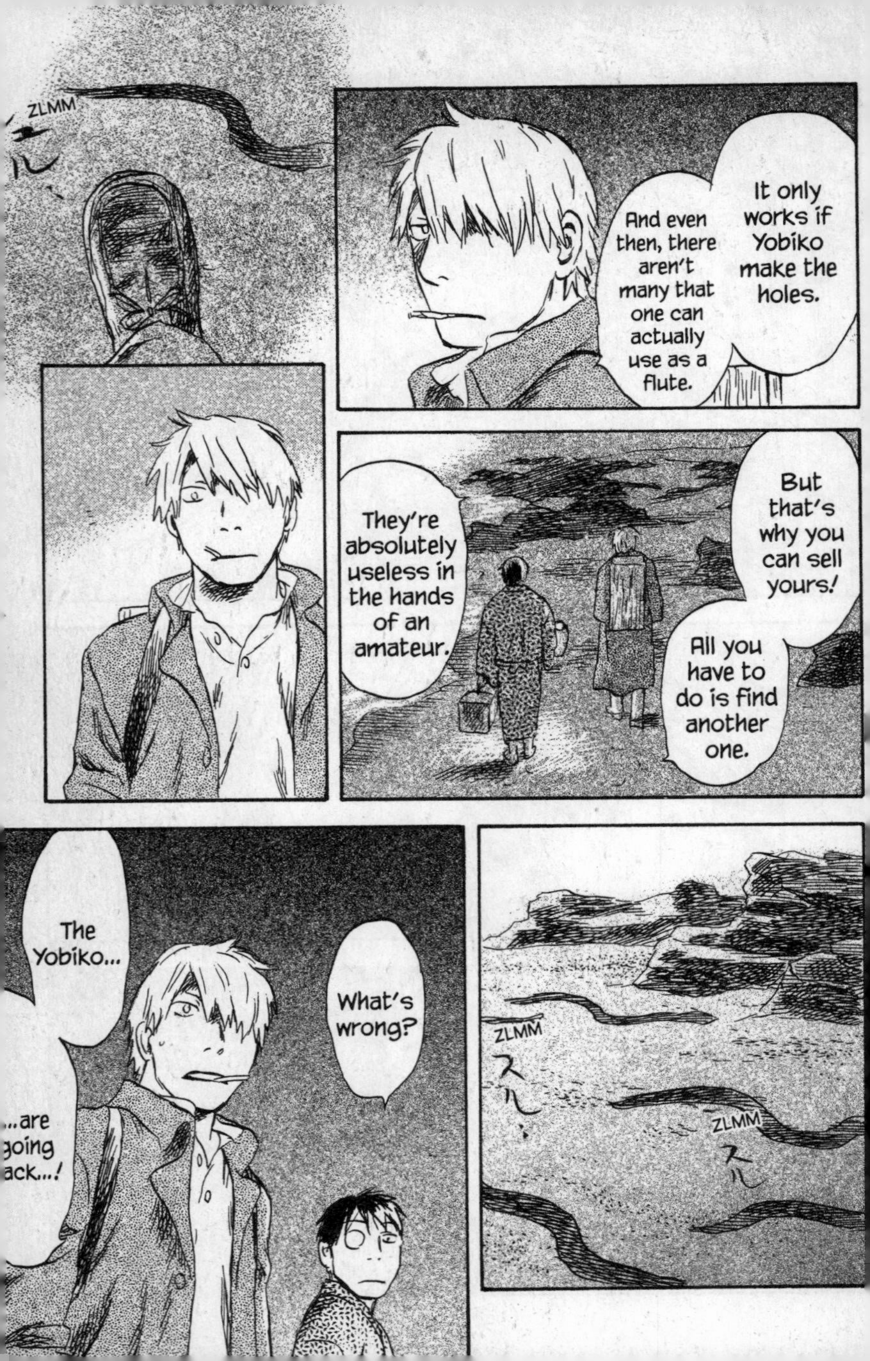
It only works if Yobiko make the holes.
And even then, there aren't many that one can actually use as a flute.
ZLMM
But that's why you can sell yours!
All you have to do is find another one.
They're absolutely useless in the hands of an amateur.
ZLMM
ZLMM
What's wrong?
The Yobiko...
...are going ack...!

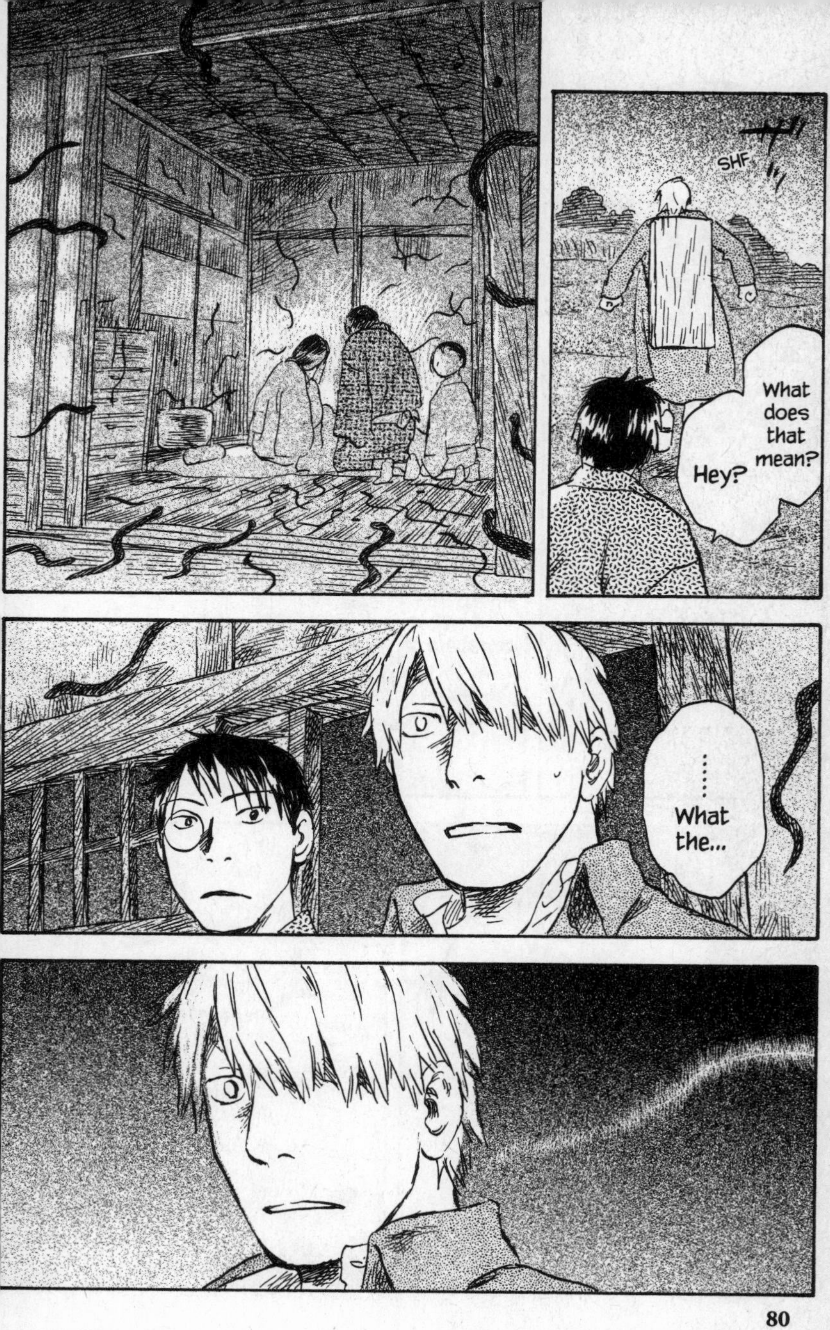
SHF
What does that mean?
Hey?
...... What the...

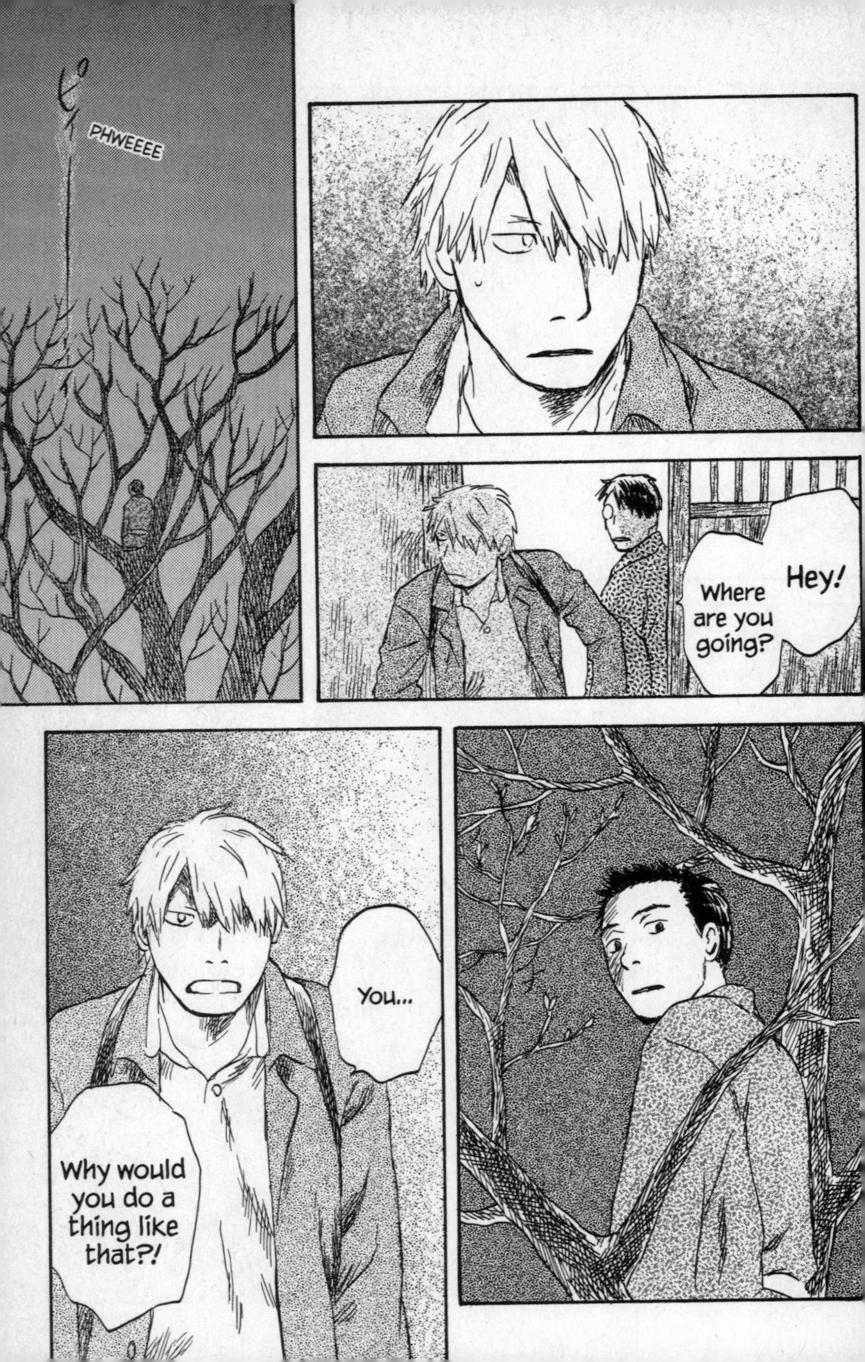
Hey!
Where are you going?
ピィ
PHWEEEE
You...
Why would you do a thing like that?!

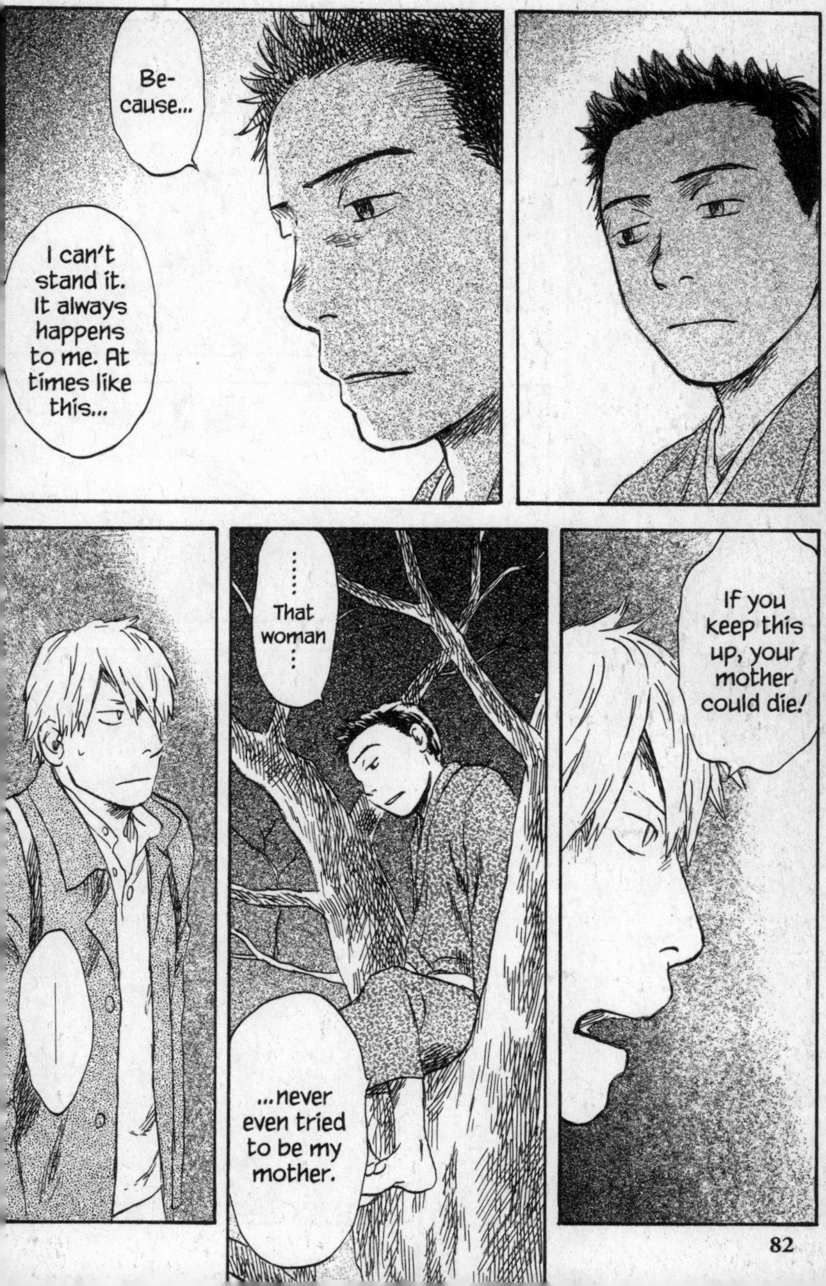
Be-cause...
I can't stand it. It always happens to me. At times like this...
If you keep this up, your mother could die!
...... That woman ......
...never even tried to be my mother.

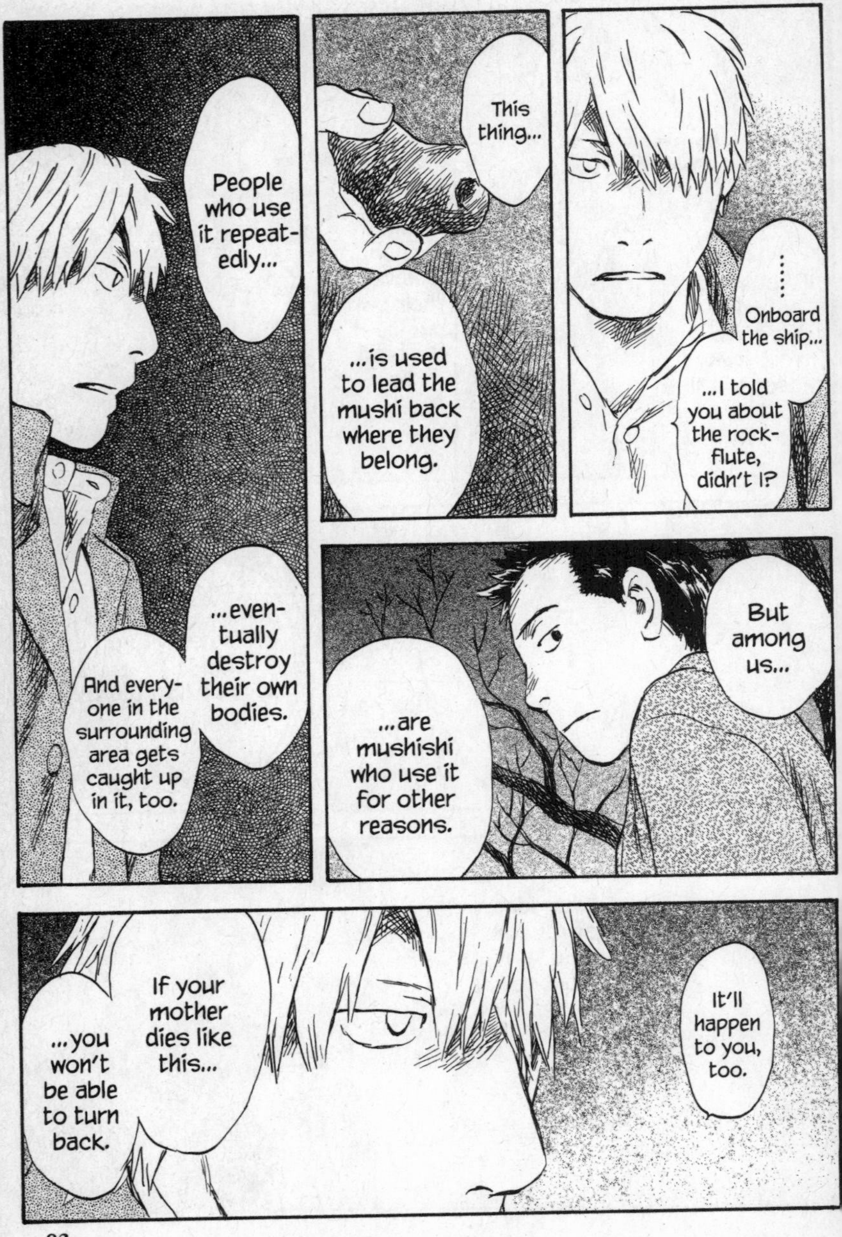
......
Onboard the ship...
...I told you about the rock-flute, didn't I?
This thing...
...is used to lead the mushi back where they belong.
But among us...
...are mushishi who use it for other reasons.
People who use it repeatedly...
...eventually destroy their own bodies.
And everyone in the surrounding area gets caught up in it, too.
It'll happen to you, too.
If your mother dies like this...
...you won't be able to turn back.

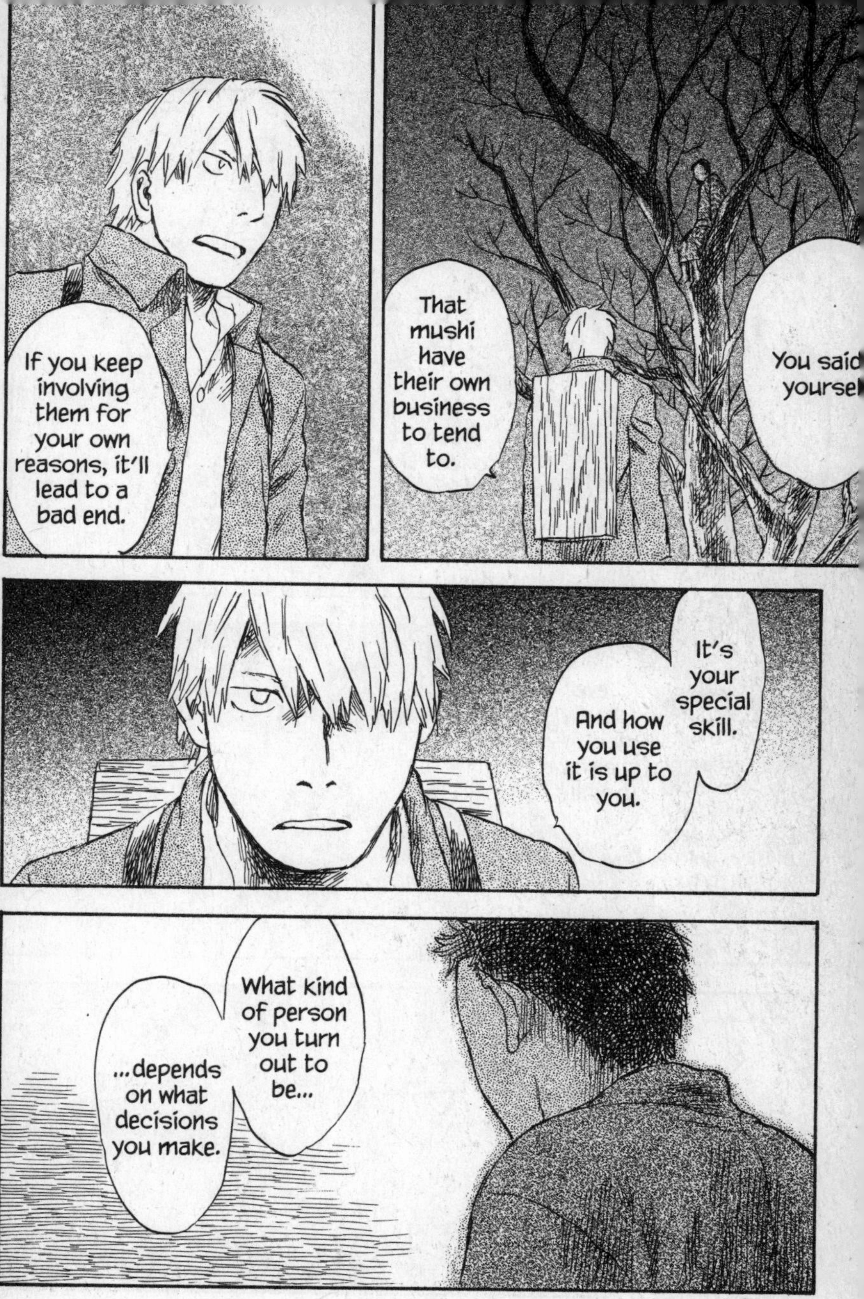
You said yoursel
That mushi have their own business to tend to.
If you keep involving them for your own reasons, it'll lead to a bad end.
It's your special skill.
And how you use it is up to you.
What kind of person you turn out to be...
...depends on what decisions you make.

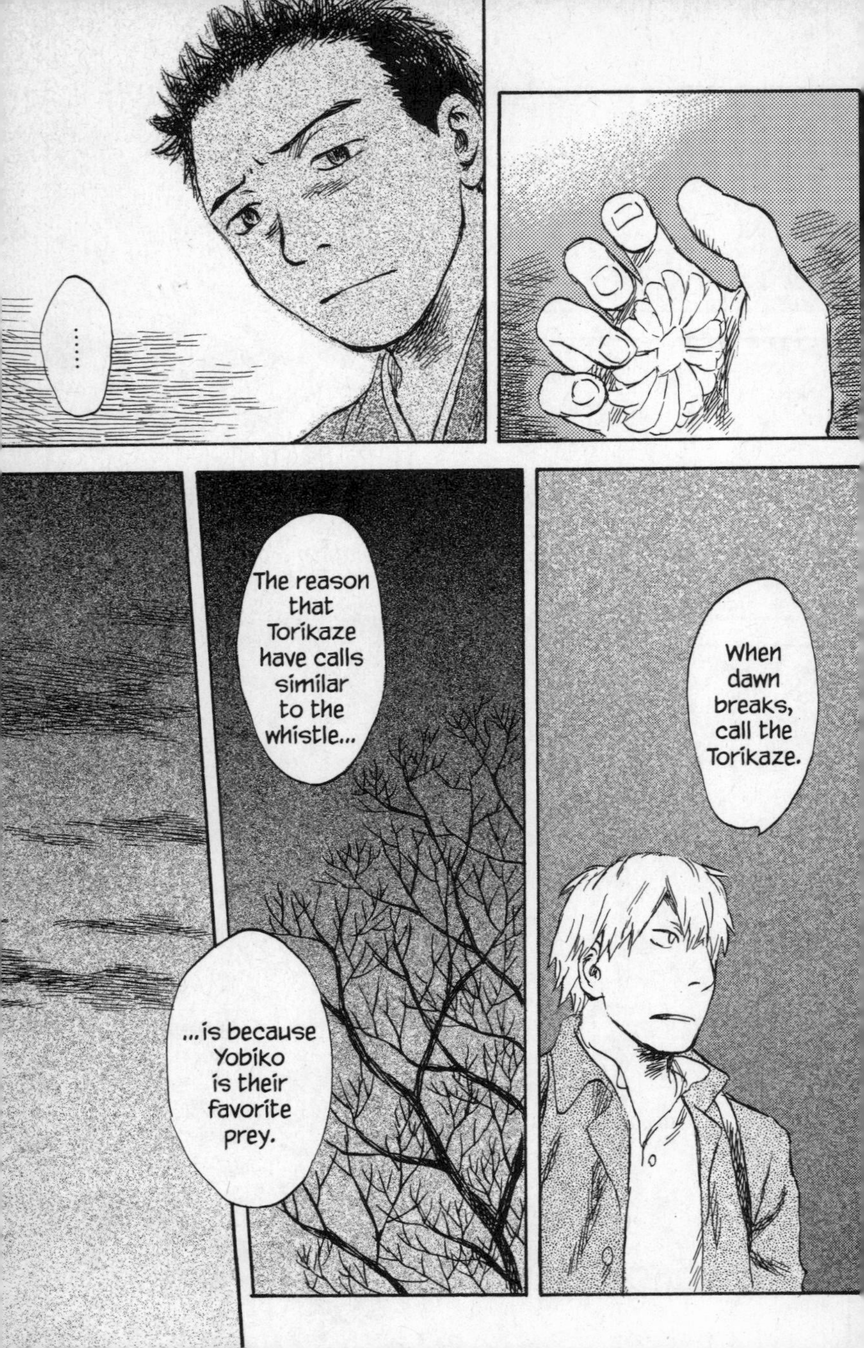
……
When dawn breaks, call the Torikaze.
The reason that Torikaze have calls similar to the whistle…
…is because Yobiko is their favorite prey.

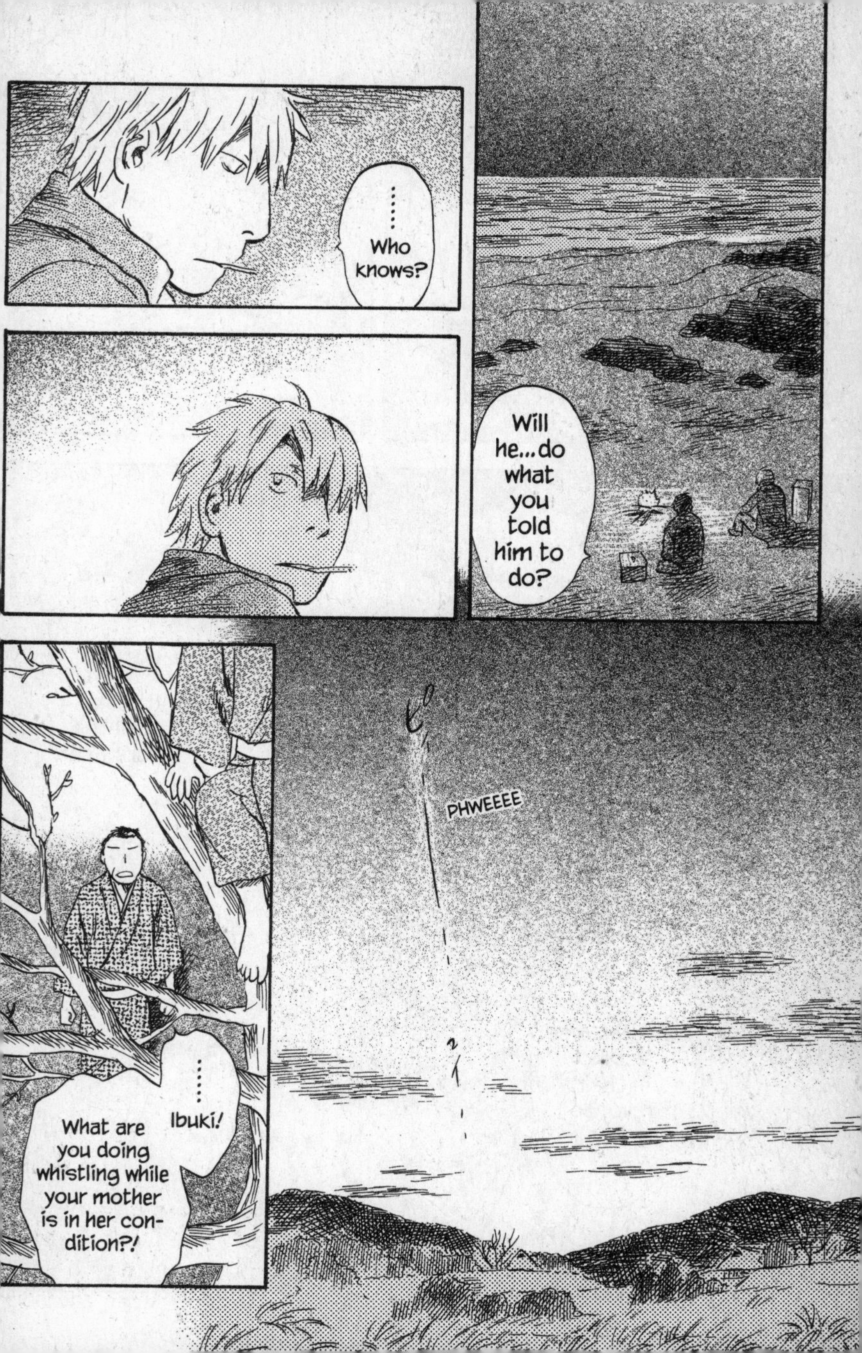
Will he...do what you told him to do?
...... Who knows?
PHWEEEE
...... Ibuki!
What are you doing whistling while your mother is in her condition?!

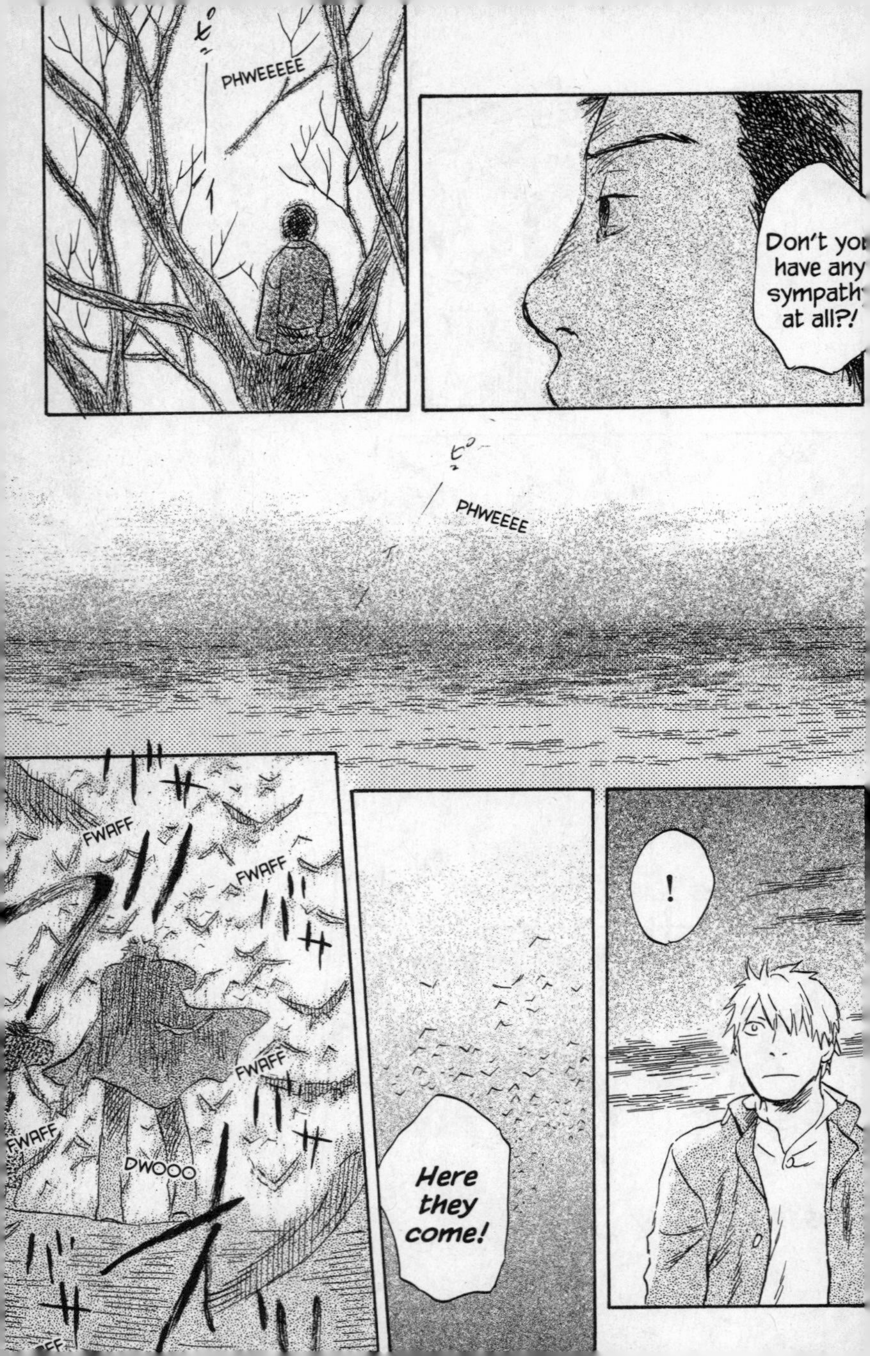

Don't you have any sympath at all?!
PHWEEEEE
PHWEEEE
!
Here they come!
FWAFF
FWAFF
FWAFF
FWAFF
DWOOO

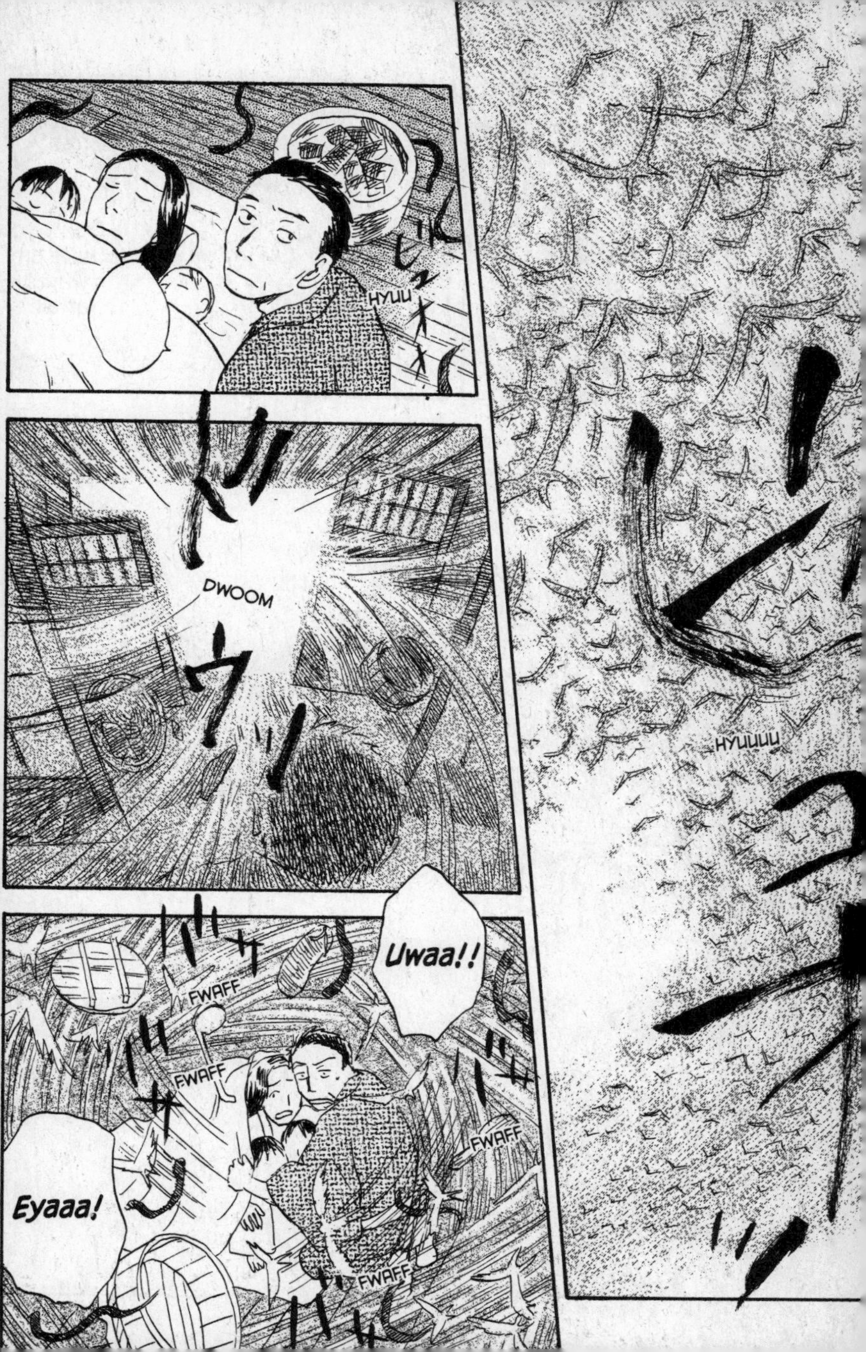
HYUUUU
HYUU
DWOOM
Uwaa!!
FWAFF
FWAFF
FWAFF
FWAFF
Eyaaa!

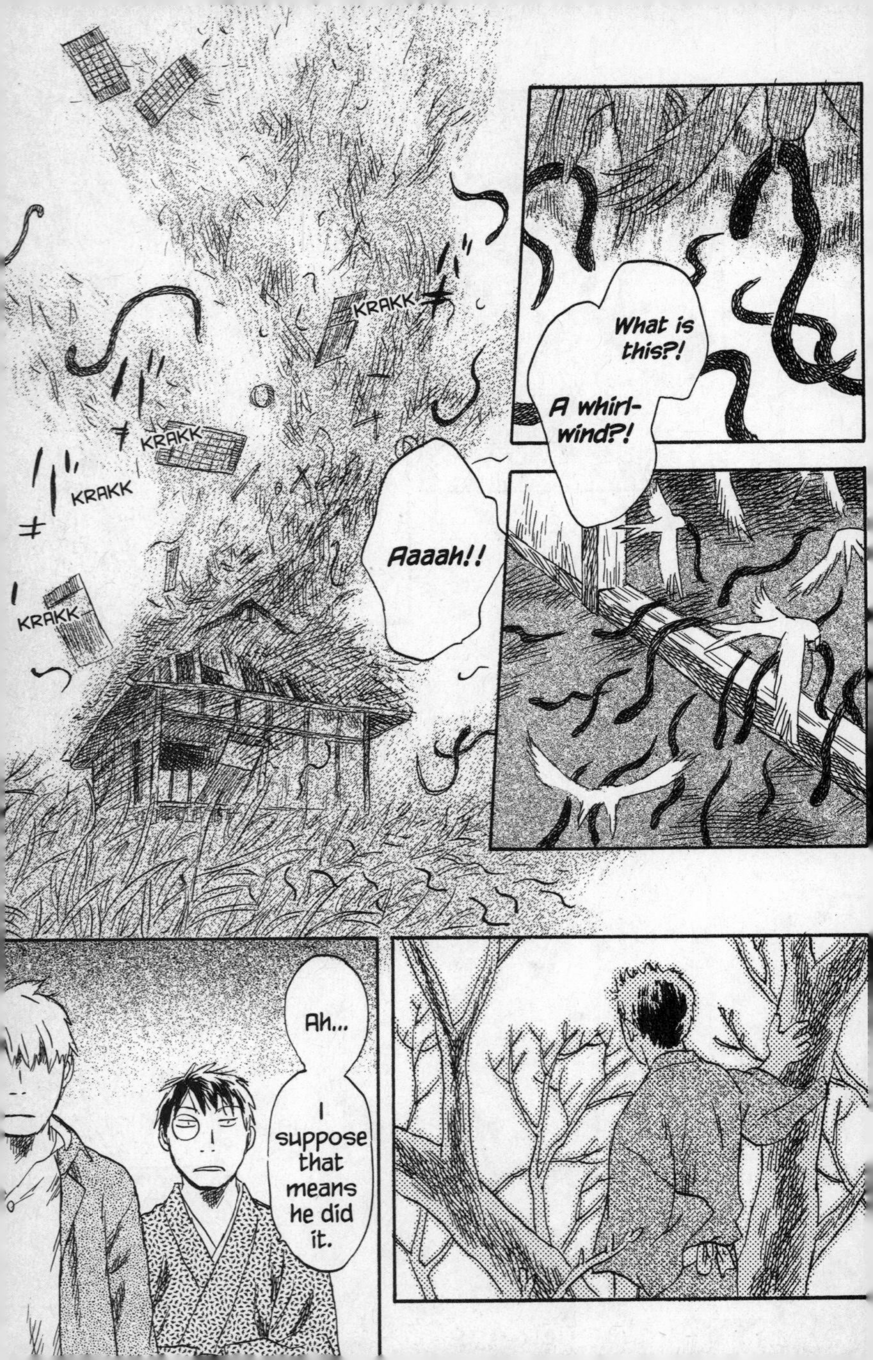
What is this?!
A whirl-wind?!
Aaaah!!
KRAKK
KRAKK
KRAKK
KRAKK
Ah...
I suppose that means he did it.

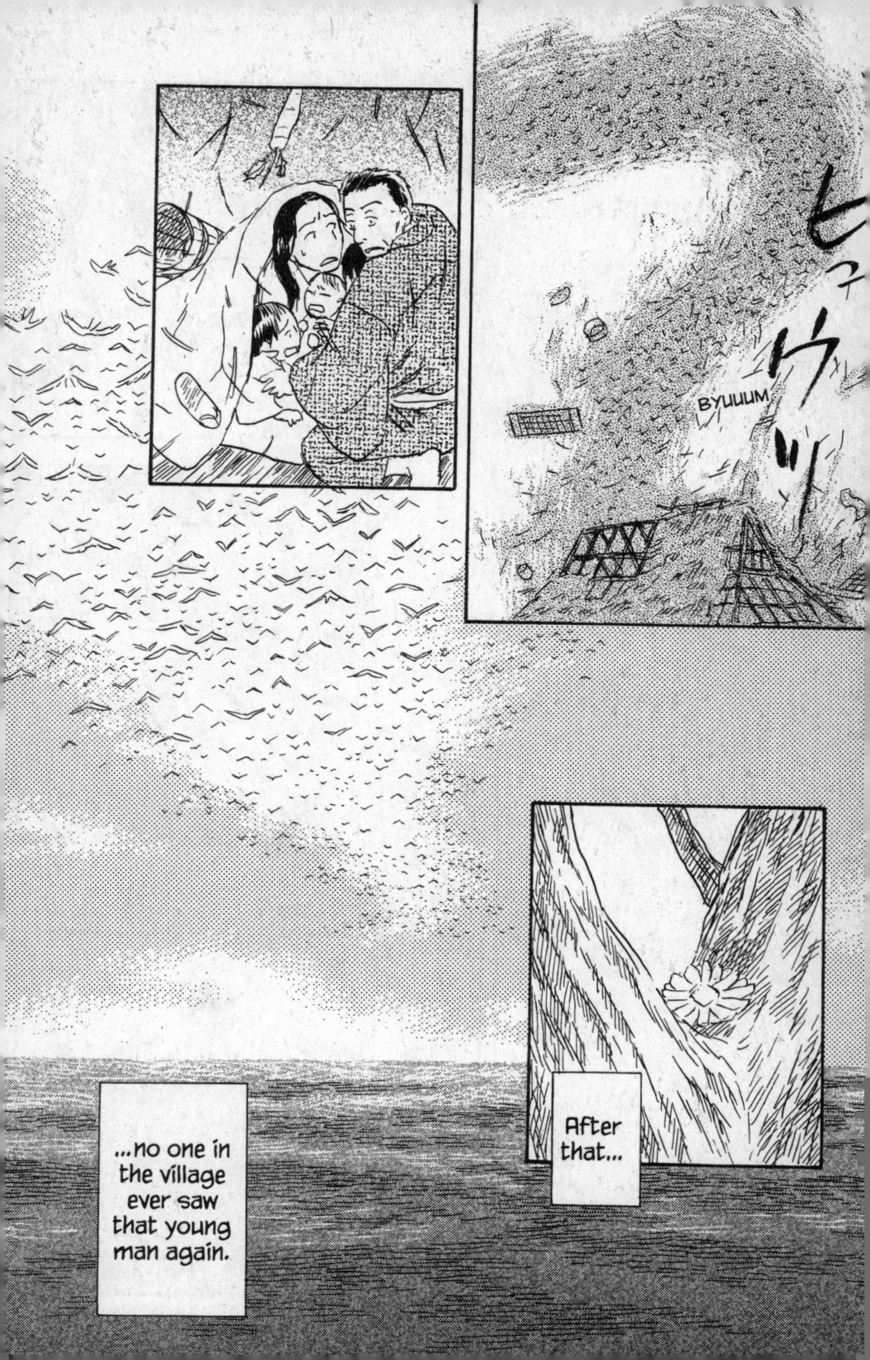
BYUUUM
After that...
...no one in the village ever saw that young man again.

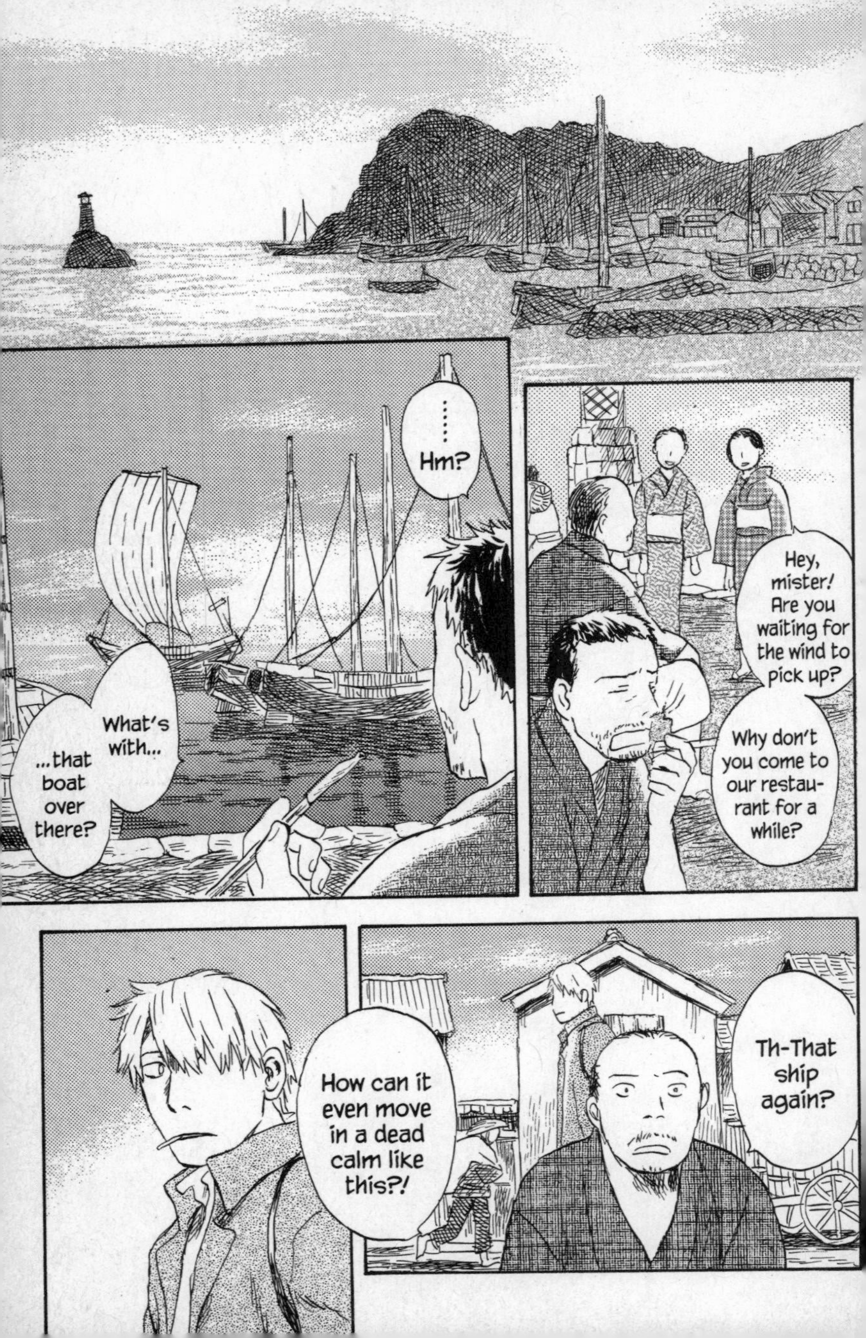
Hey, mister! Are you waiting for the wind to pick up?
Why don't you come to our restau-rant for a while?
...... Hm?
What's with...
...that boat over there?
Th-That ship again?
How can it even move in a dead calm like this?!

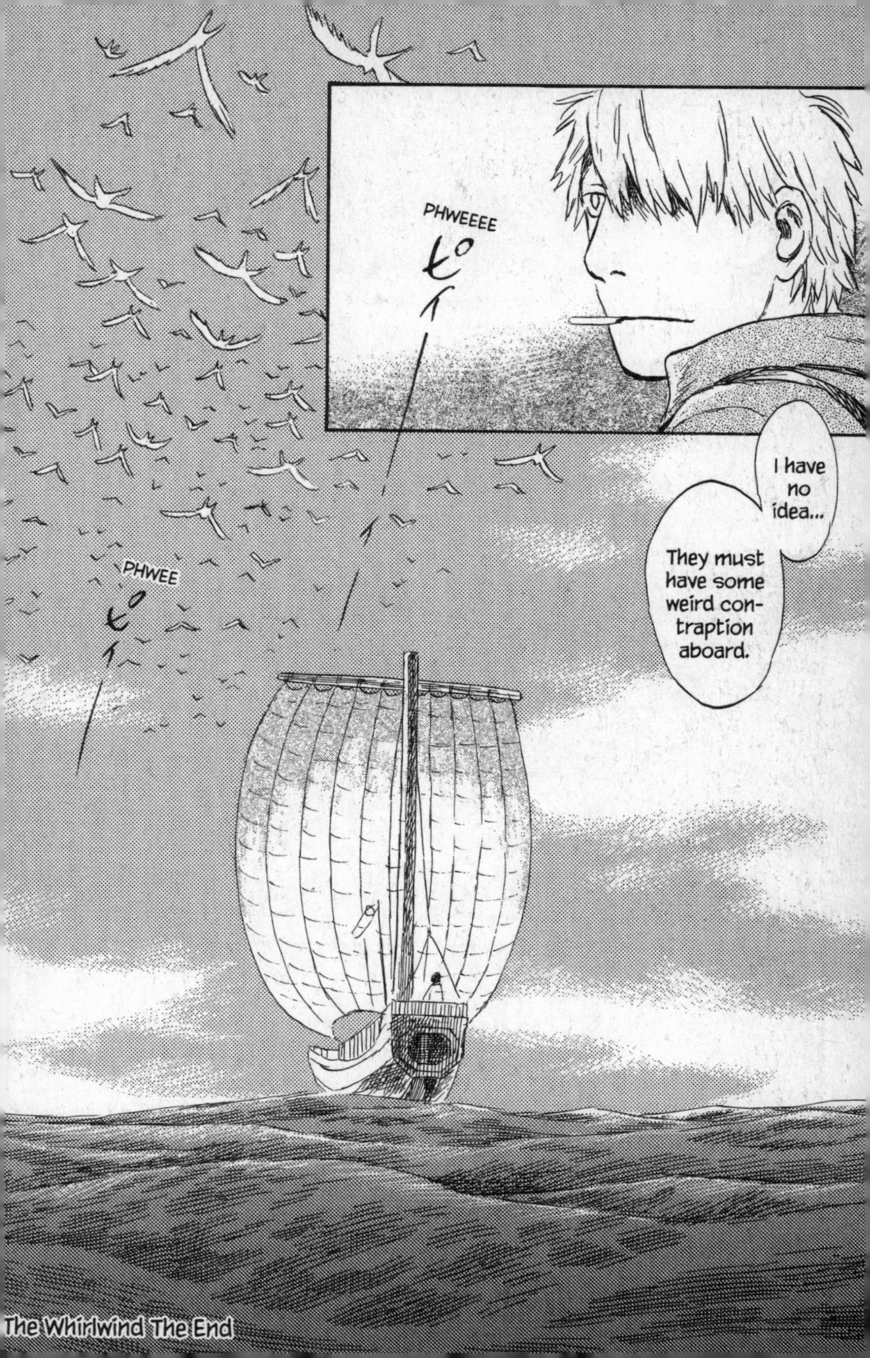
PHWEEEE
I have no idea...
They must have some weird contraption aboard.
PHWEE
The Whirlwind The End

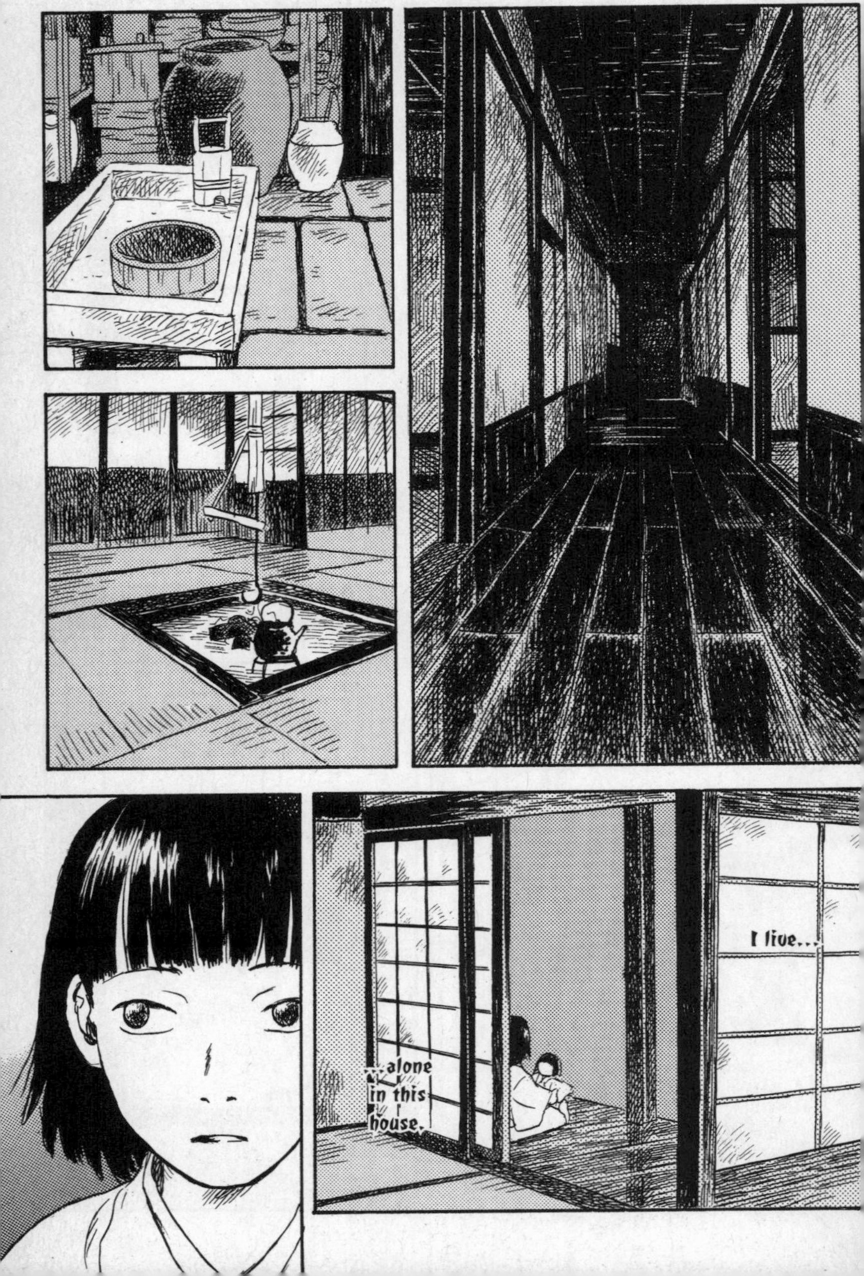
I live...
...alone in this house.

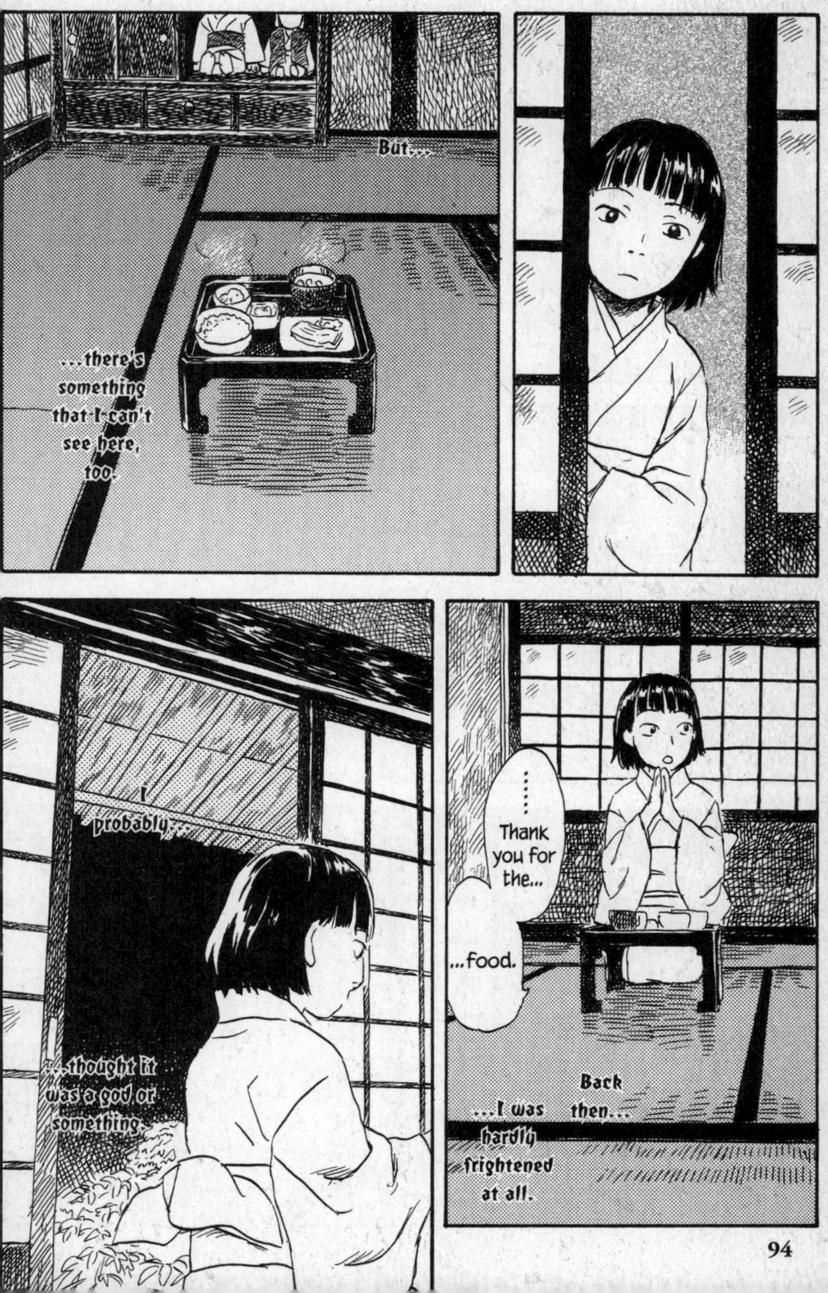

But...
...there's something that I can't see here, too.
...... Thank you for the...
...food.
Back then...
...I was hardly frightened at all.
I probably...
...thought it was a god or something.

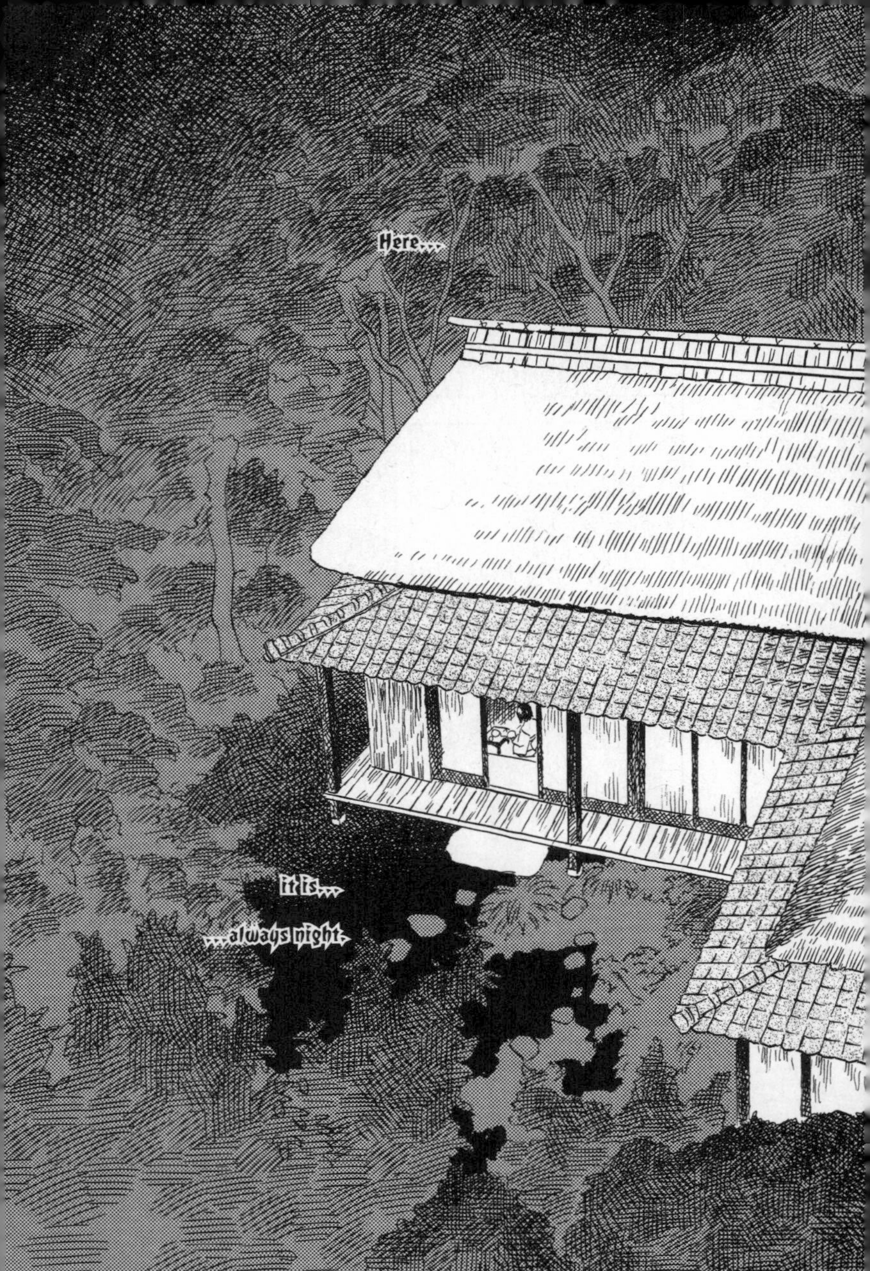
Here...
it is...
...always night.

Stars in the Jar of the Sky

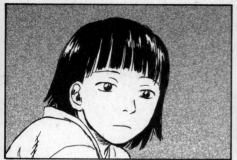

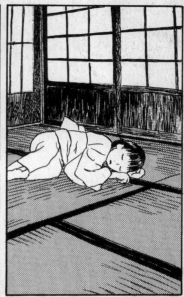

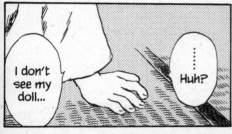

I don't see my doll...

.....

Huh?

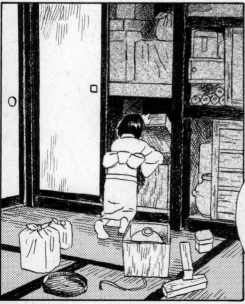

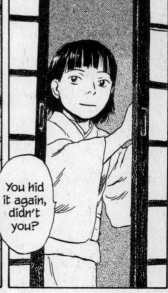

You hid it again, didn't you?

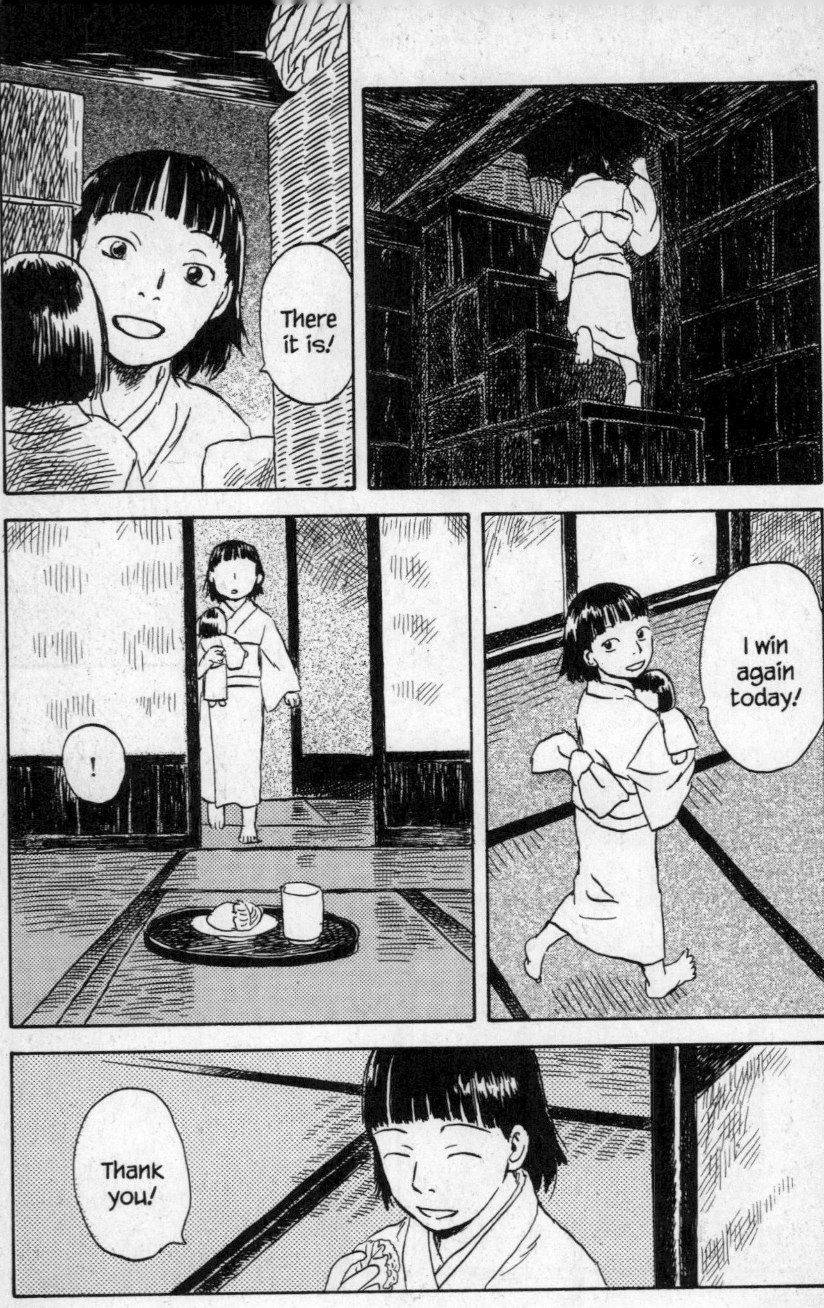
There it is!
I win again today!
!
Thank you!

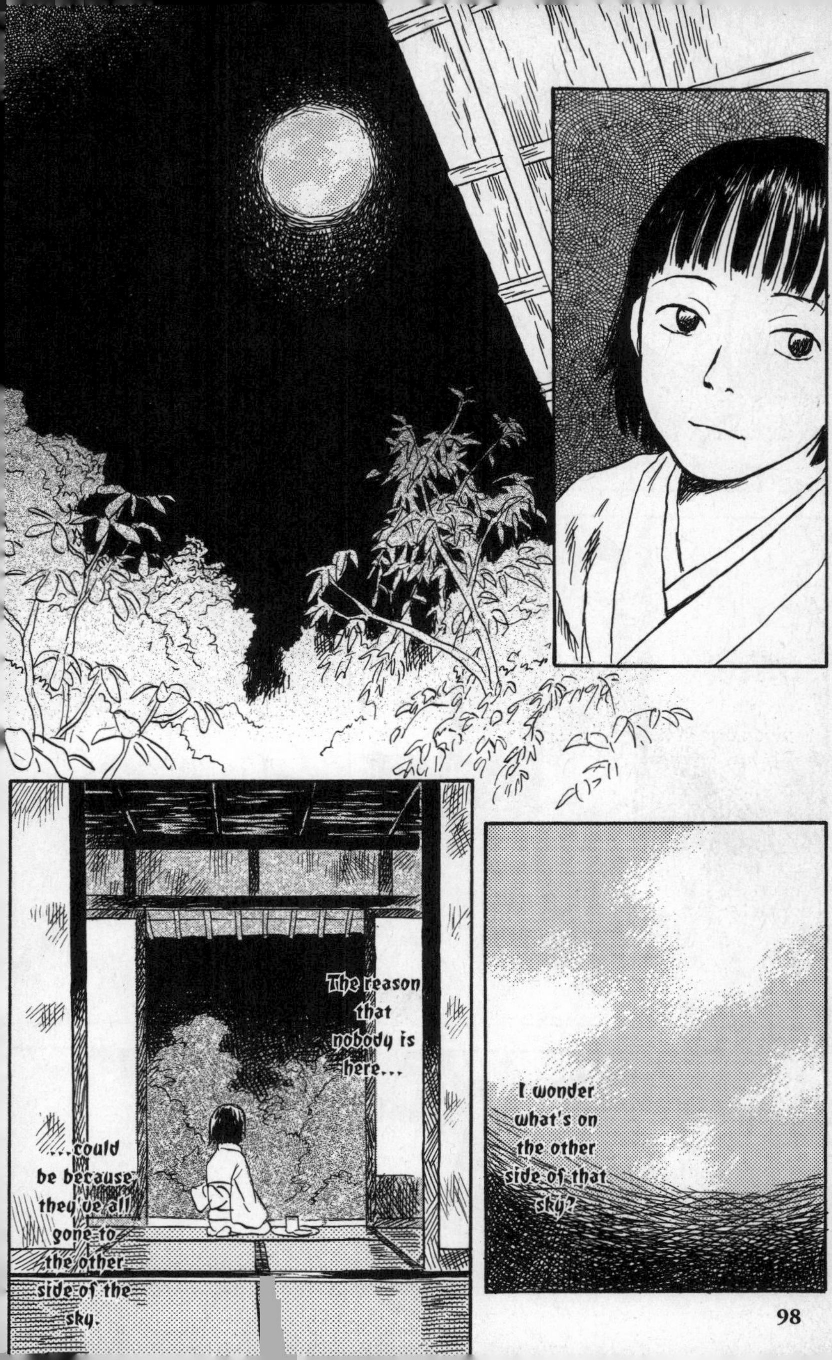
I wonder what's on the other side of that sky?
The reason that nobody is here...
...could be because they've all gone to the other side of the sky.

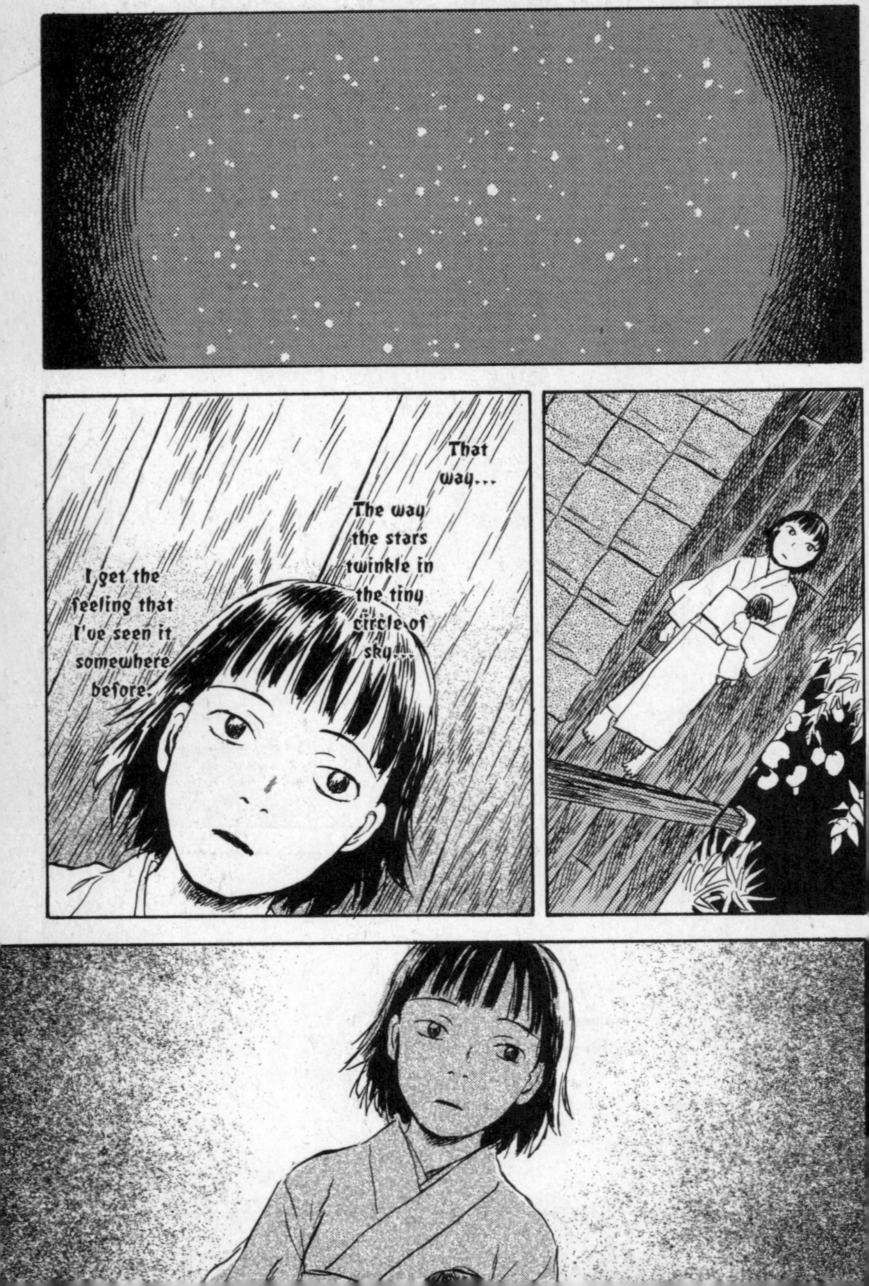
That way...
The way the stars twinkle in the tiny circle of sky...
I get the feeling that I've seen it somewhere before.

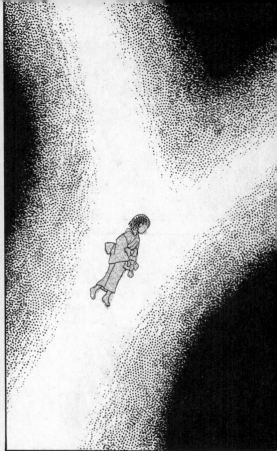

But here...

...everything is so beautiful.

Such a pleasant feeling.

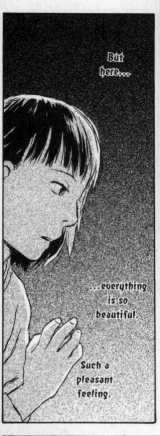

...to remember anything...

becomes too much of a bother.

Just trying.

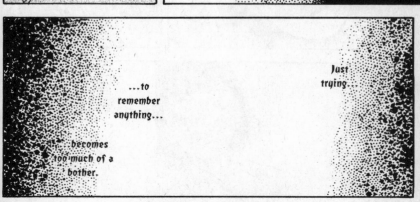

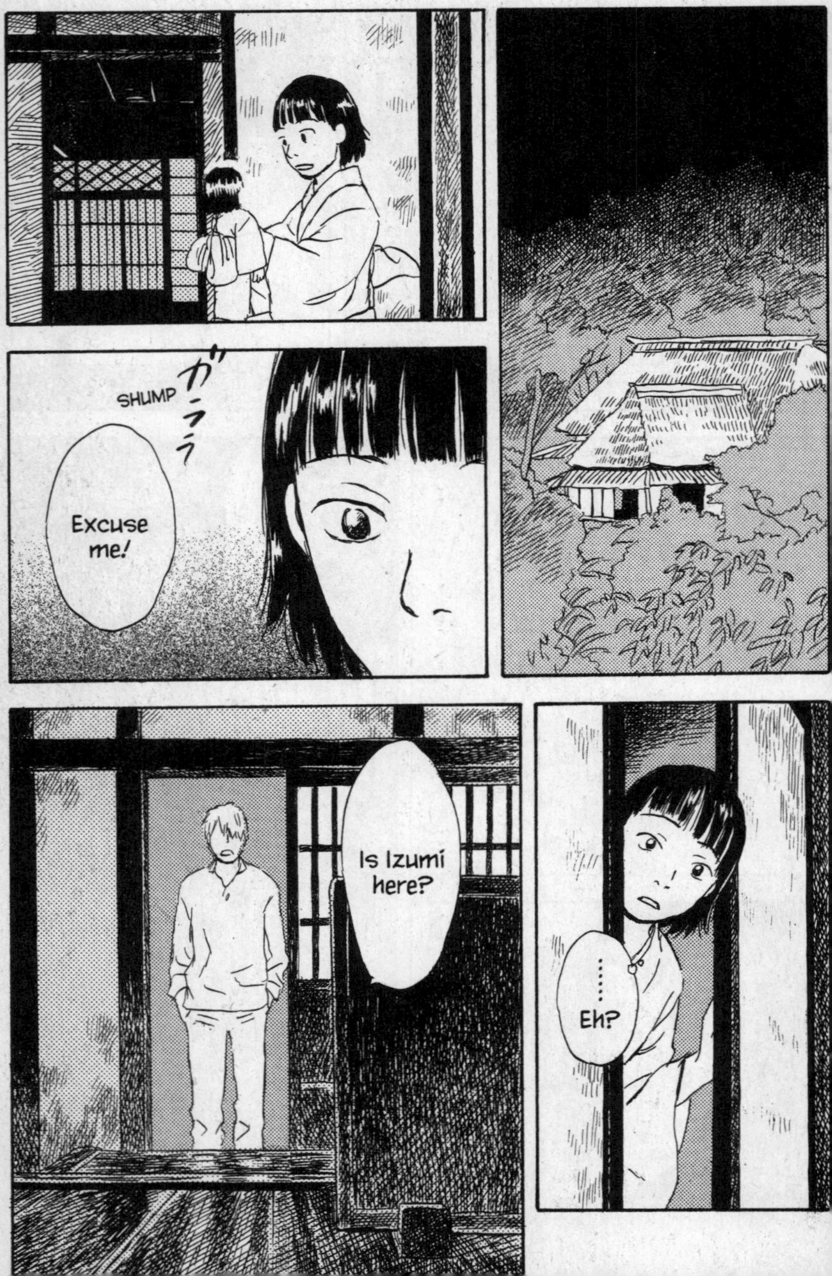
ガララ
SHUMP
Excuse me!
...... Eh?
Is Izumi here?

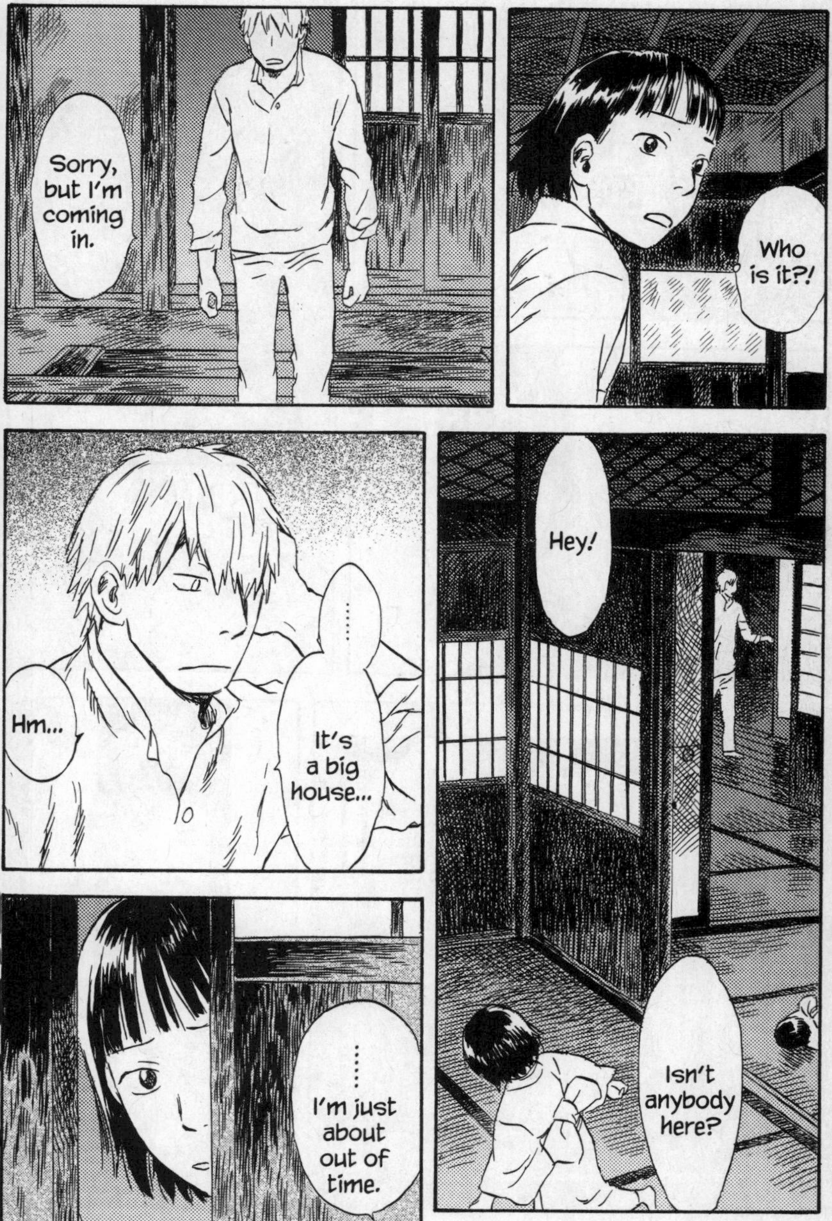
Who is it?!
Sorry, but I'm coming in.
Hey!
Isn't anybody here?
......
It's a big house...
Hm...
......
I'm just about out of time.

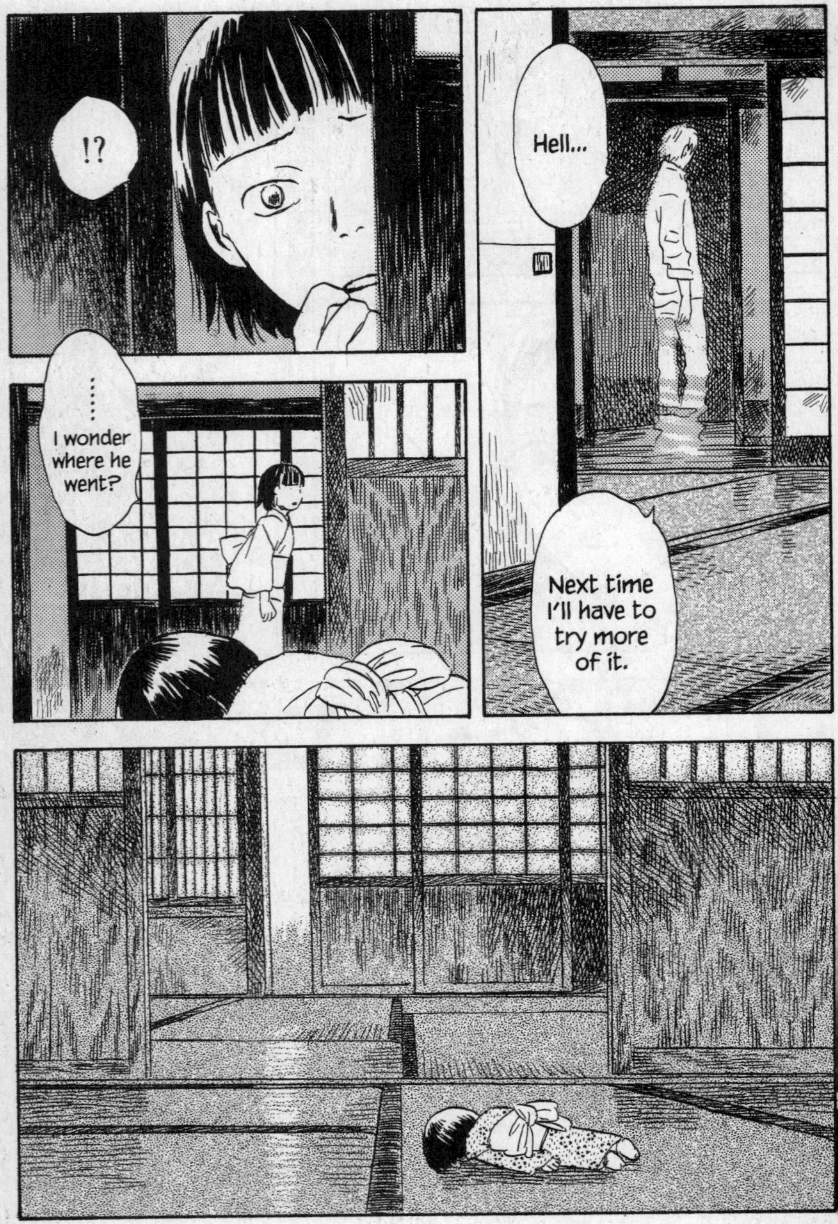
Hell...
Next time I'll have to try more of it.
!?
...... I wonder where he went?

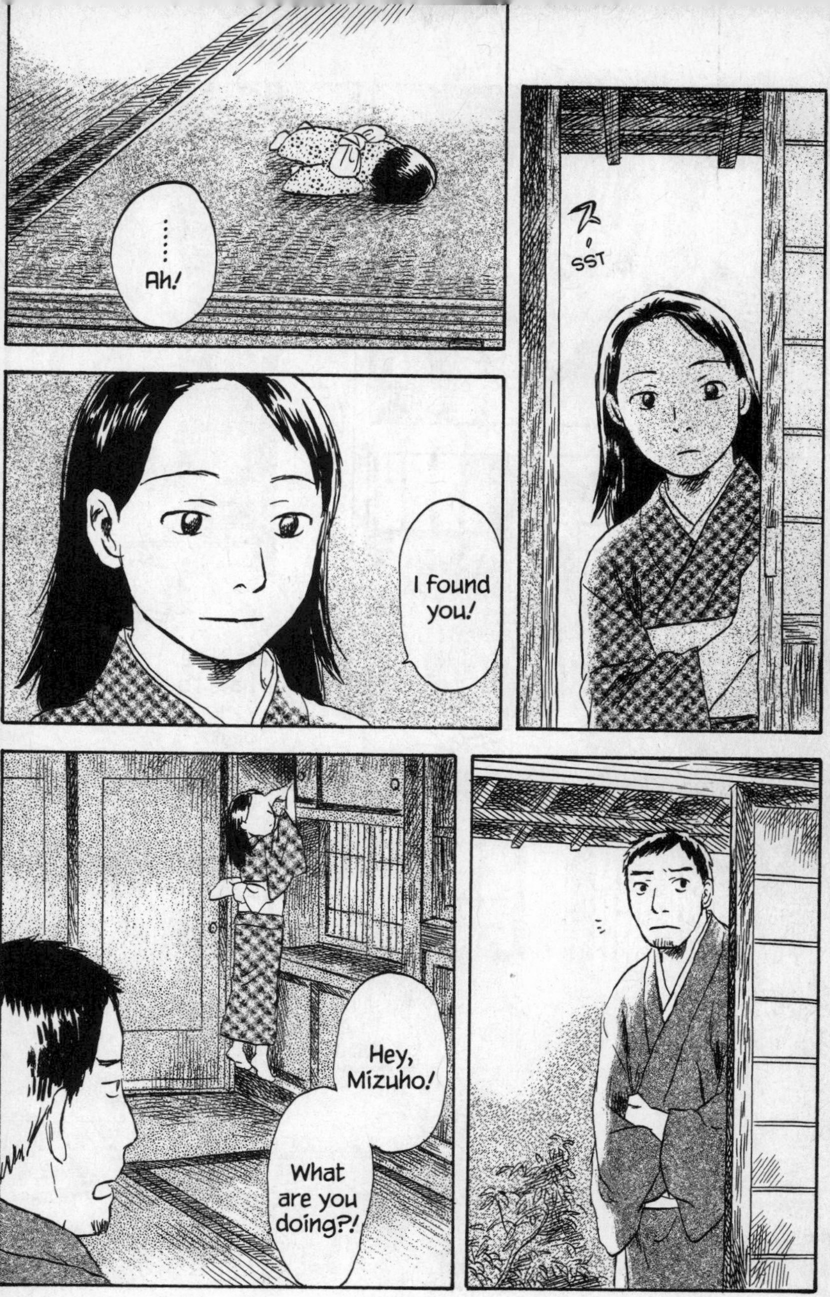

ス
SST
……Ah!
I found you!
Hey, Mizuho!
What are you doing?!

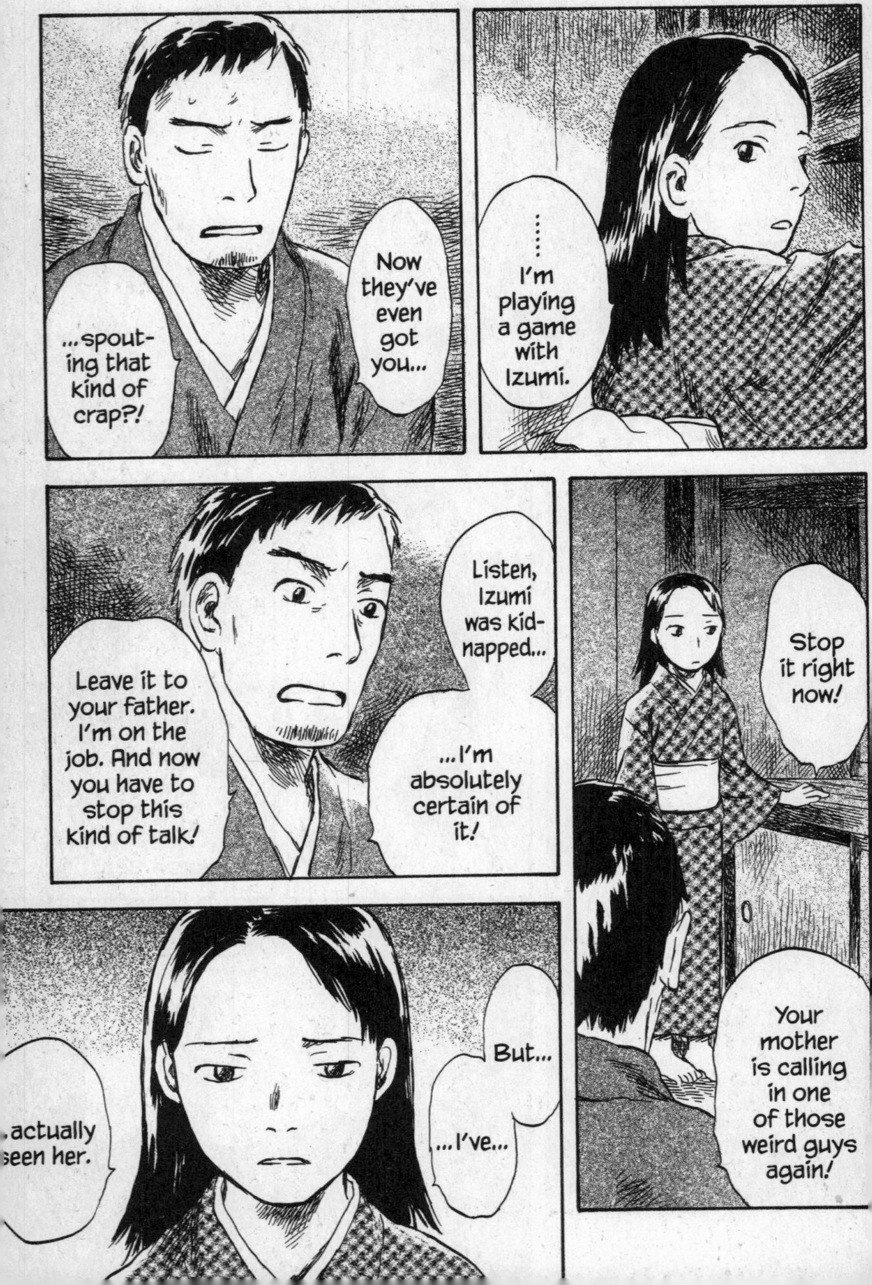
……
I'm playing a game with Izumi.
Now they've even got you...
...spouting that kind of crap?!
Stop it right now!
Your mother is calling in one of those weird guys again!
Listen, Izumi was kid-napped...
...I'm absolutely certain of it!
Leave it to your father. I'm on the job. And now you have to stop this kind of talk!
But...
...I've...
actually seen her.

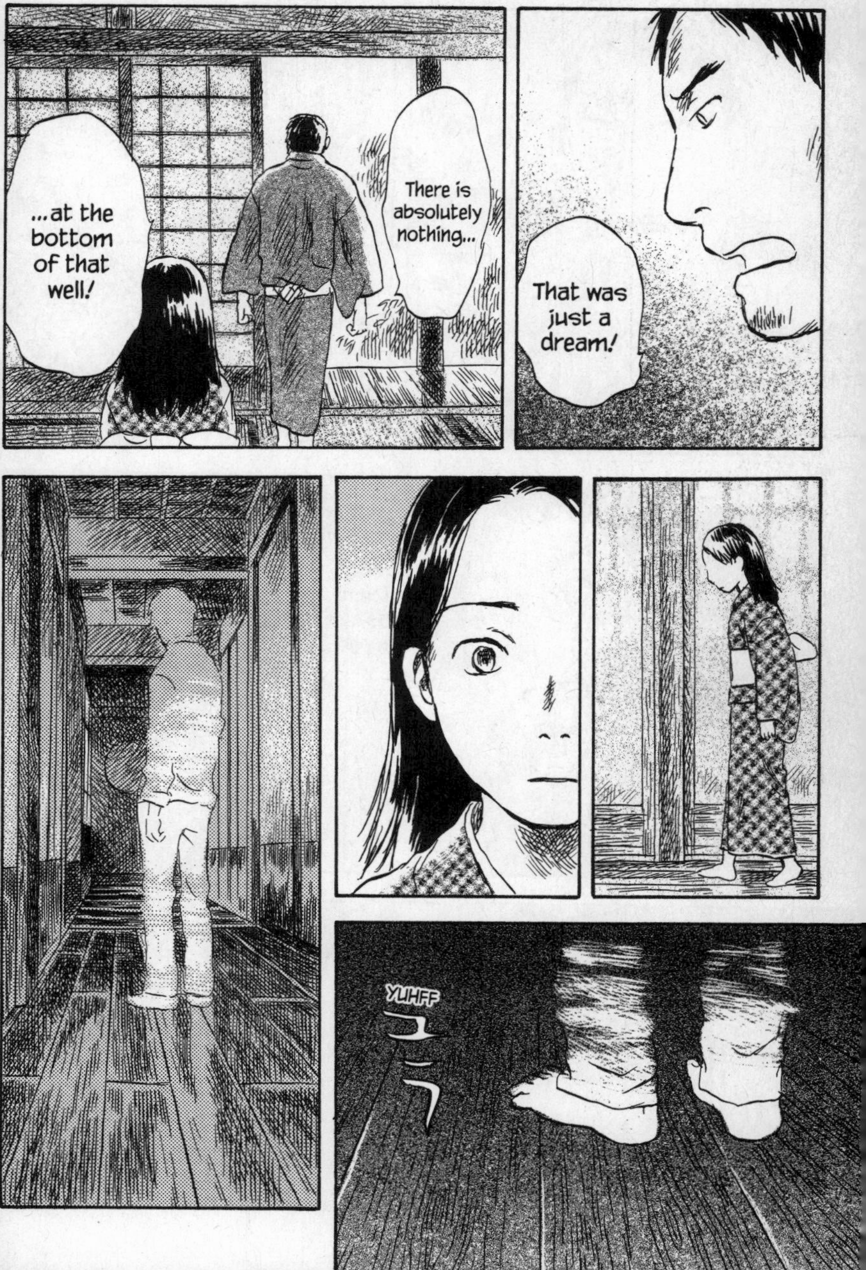
That was just a dream!
There is absolutely nothing...
...at the bottom of that well!
YUHFF

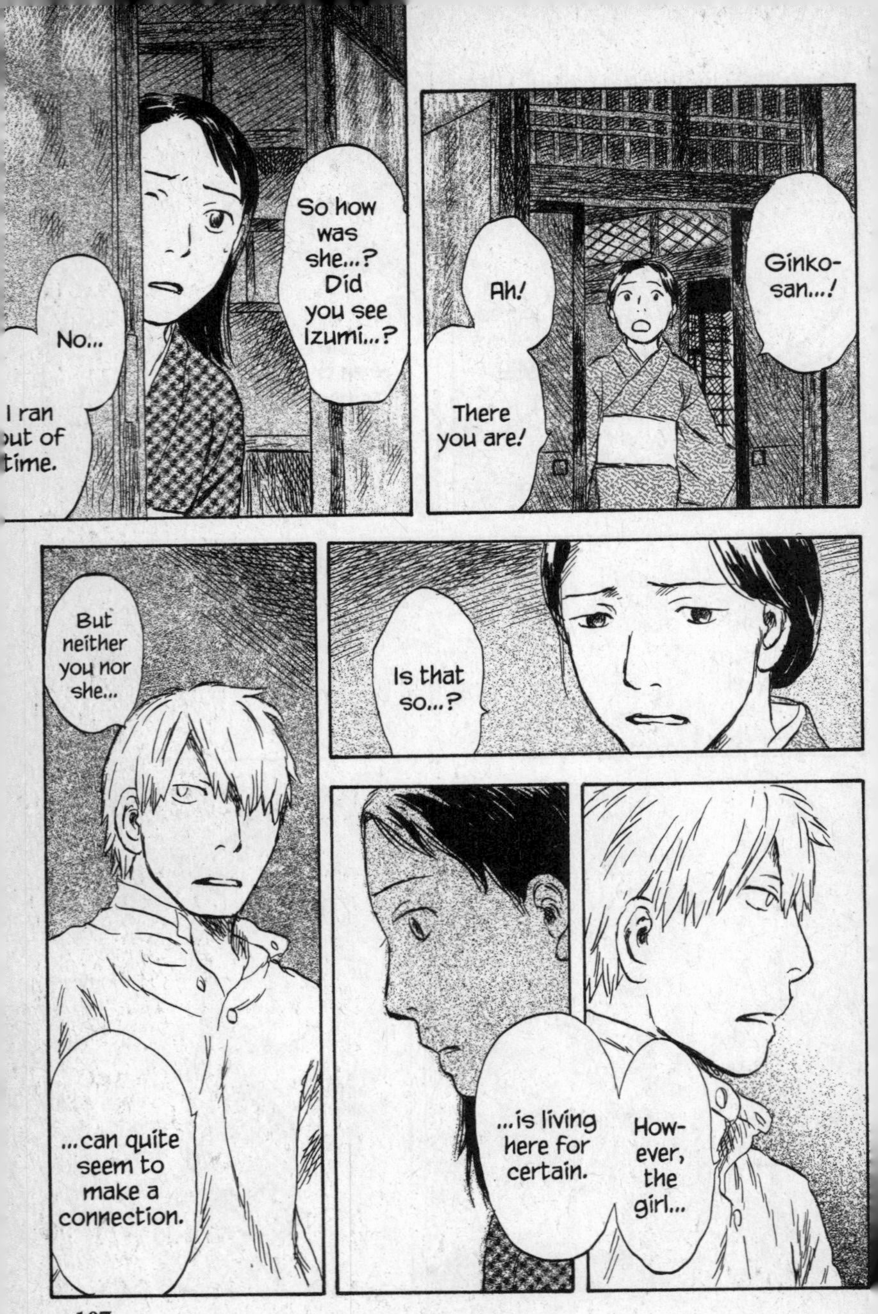
Ginko-san...!
Ah!
There you are!
So how was she...? Did you see Izumi...?
No...
I ran out of time.
Is that so...?
However, the girl...
...is living here for certain.
But neither you nor she...
...can quite seem to make a connection.

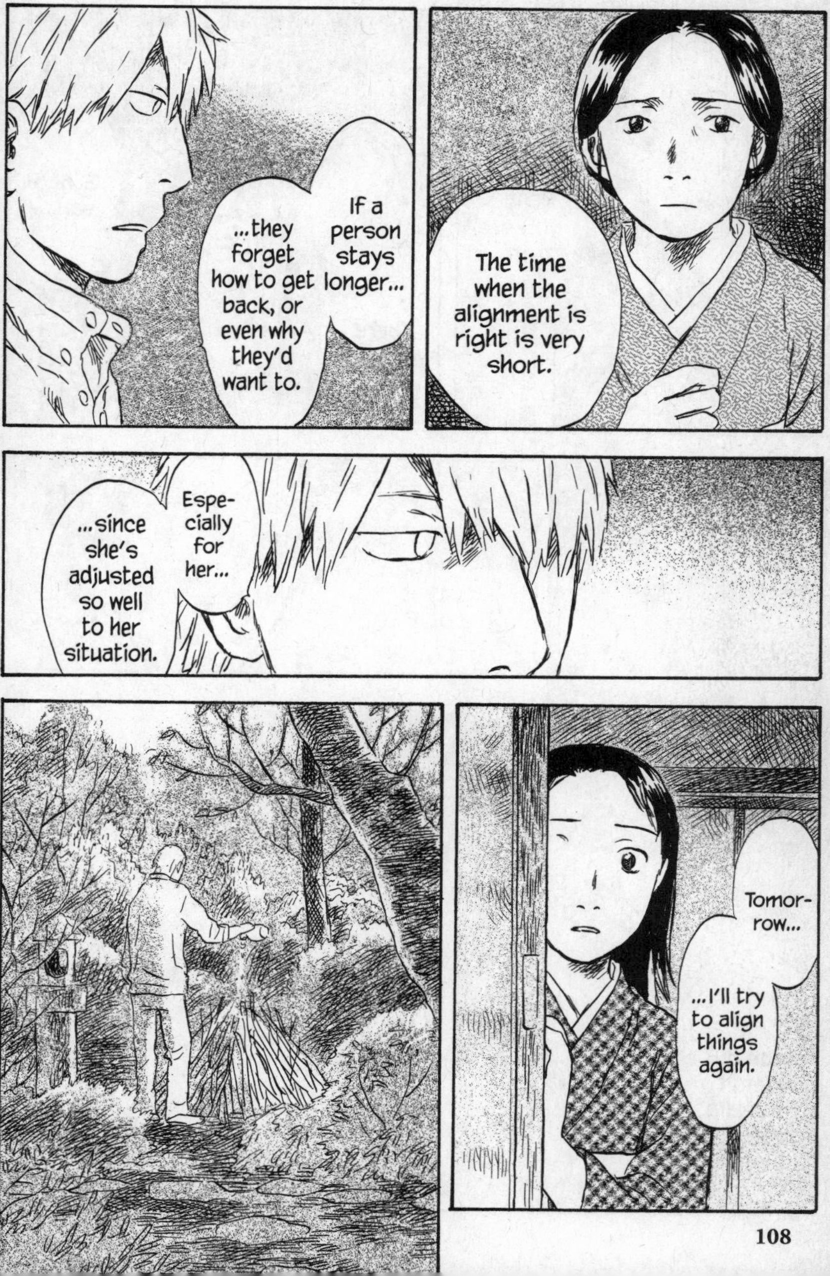
The time when the alignment is right is very short.
If a person stays longer...
...they forget how to get back, or even why they'd want to.
Espe-cially for her...
...since she's adjusted so well to her situation.
Tomor-row...
...I'll try to align things again.

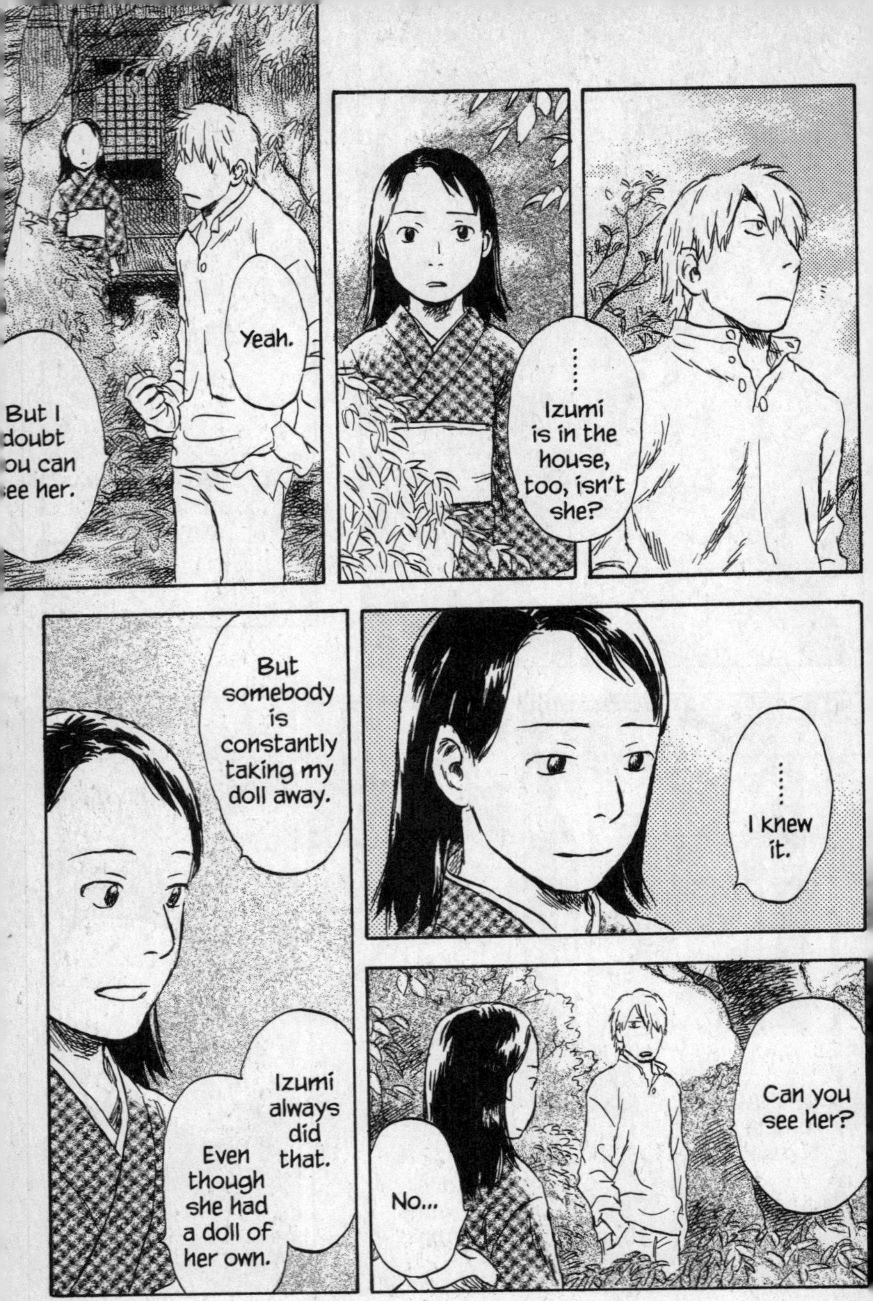

...... Izumi is in the house, too, isn't she?
Yeah.
But I doubt ou can ee her.
...... I knew it.
Can you see her?
No...
But somebody is constantly taking my doll away.
Izumi always did that.
Even though she had a doll of her own.

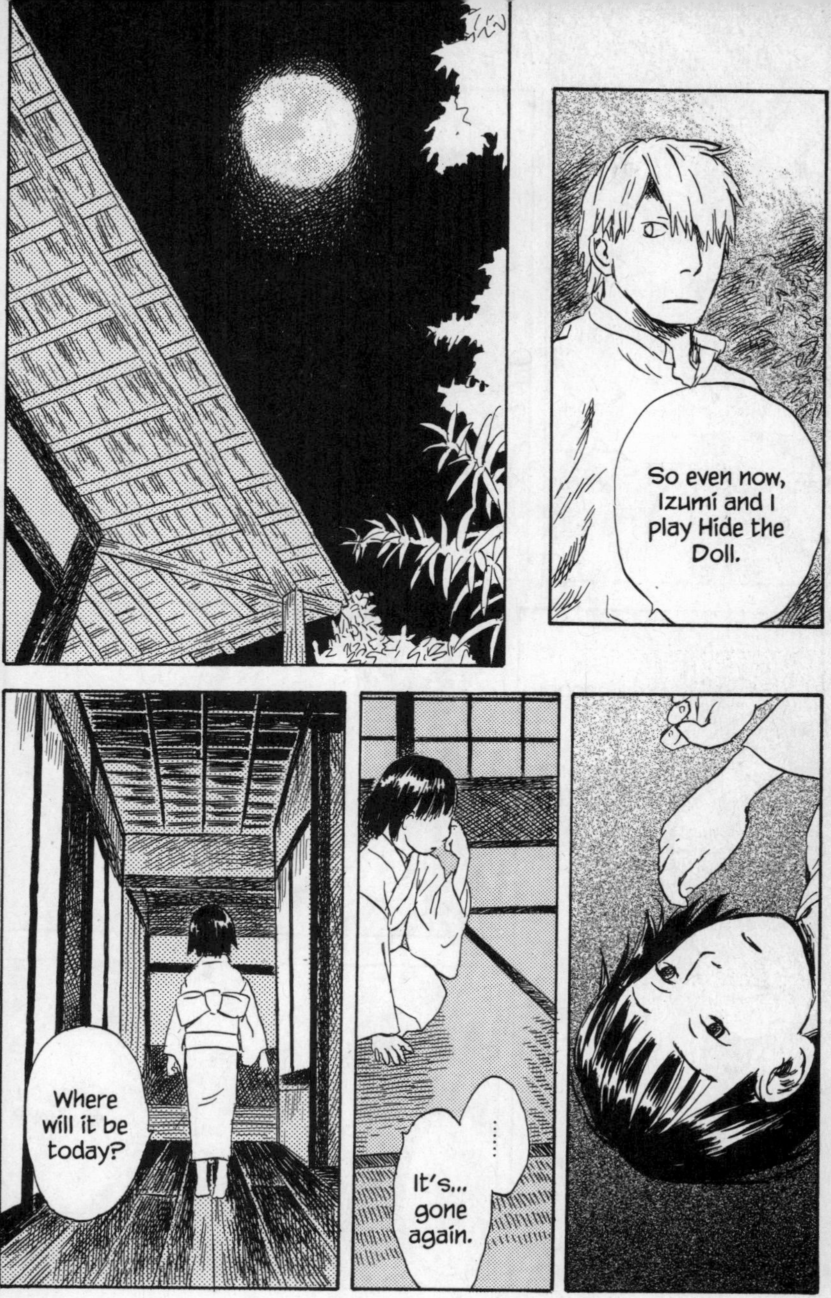
So even now, Izumi and I play Hide the Doll.
......
It's... gone again.
Where will it be today?

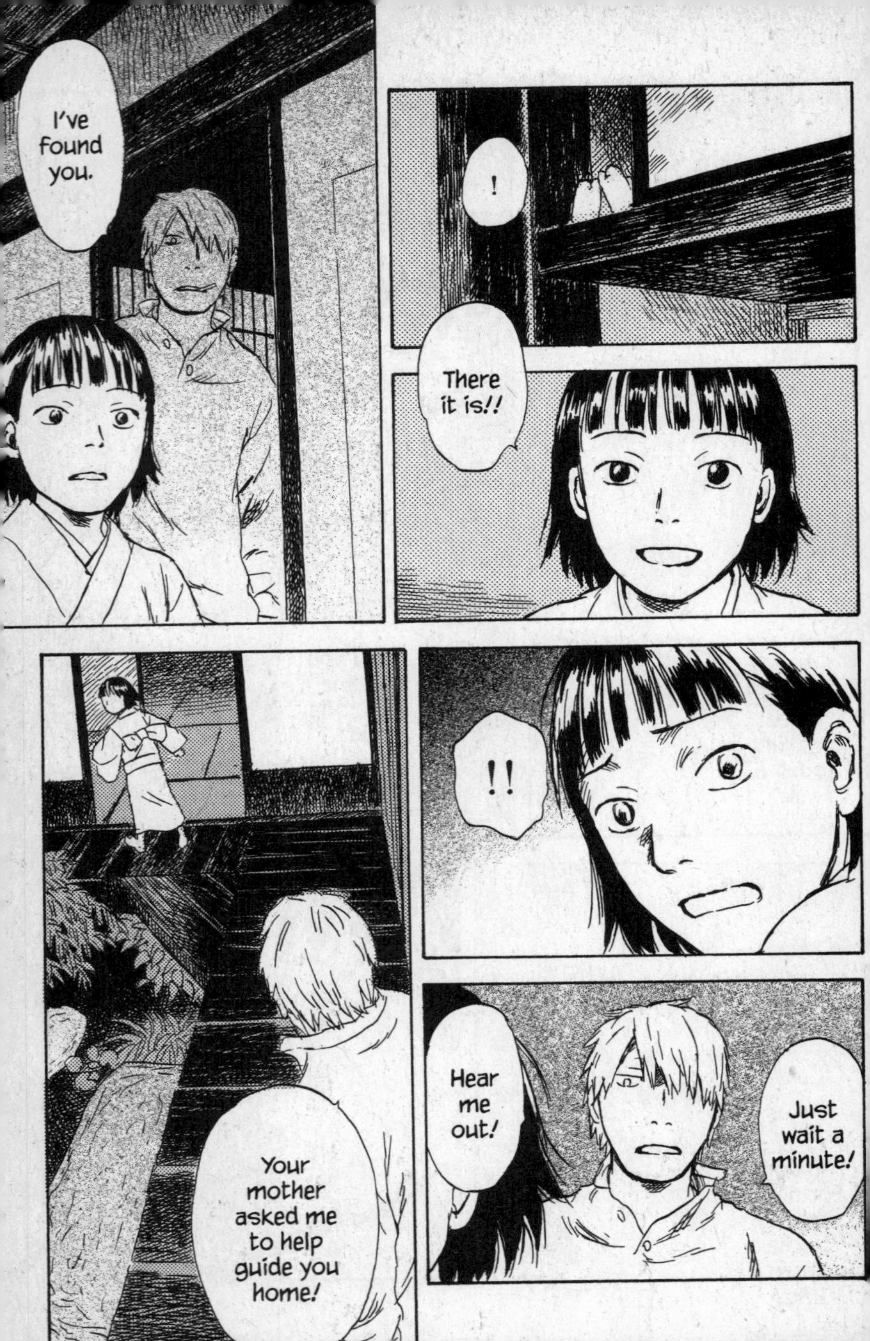
!
There it is!!
I've found you.
!!
Just wait a minute!
Hear me out!
Your mother asked me to help guide you home!

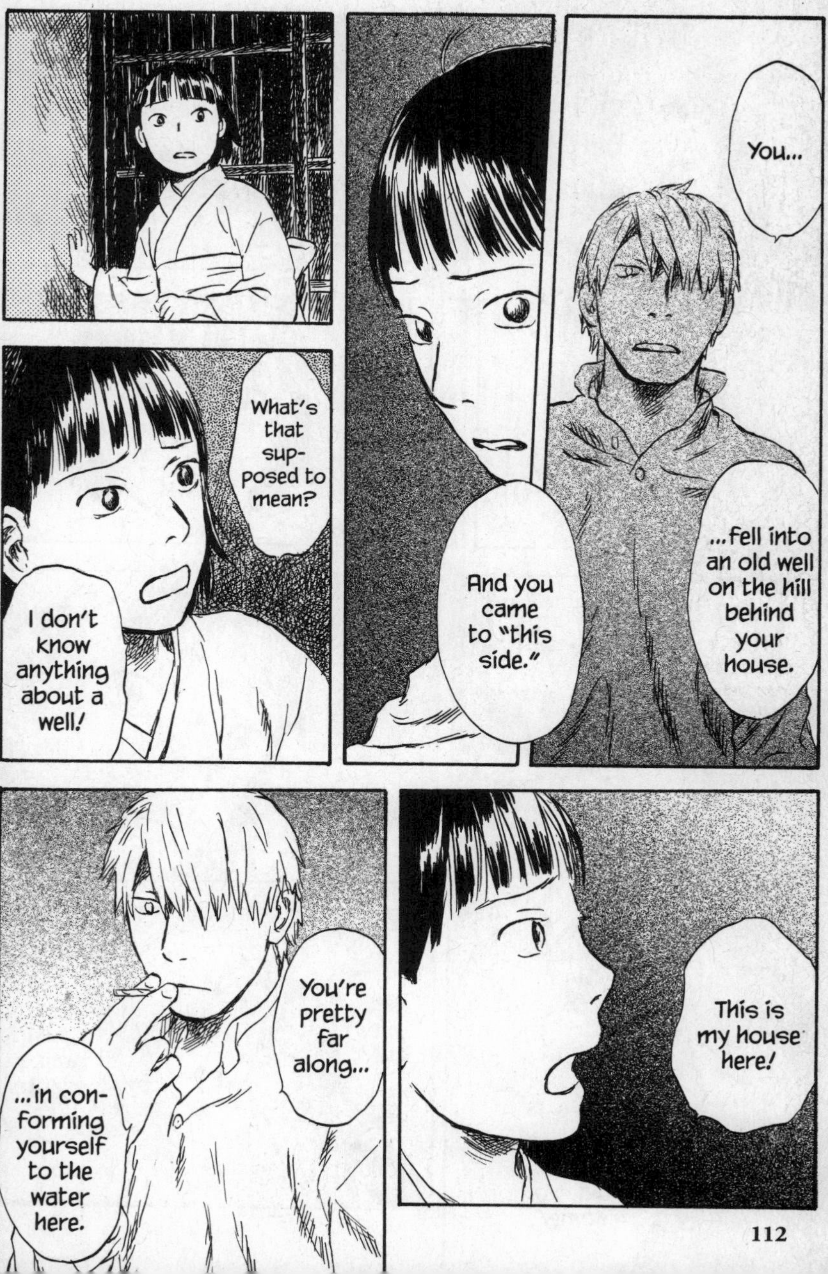
You...
...fell into an old well on the hill behind your house.
And you came to "this side."
What's that sup-posed to mean?
I don't know anything about a well!
This is my house here!
You're pretty far along...
...in con-forming yourself to the water here.

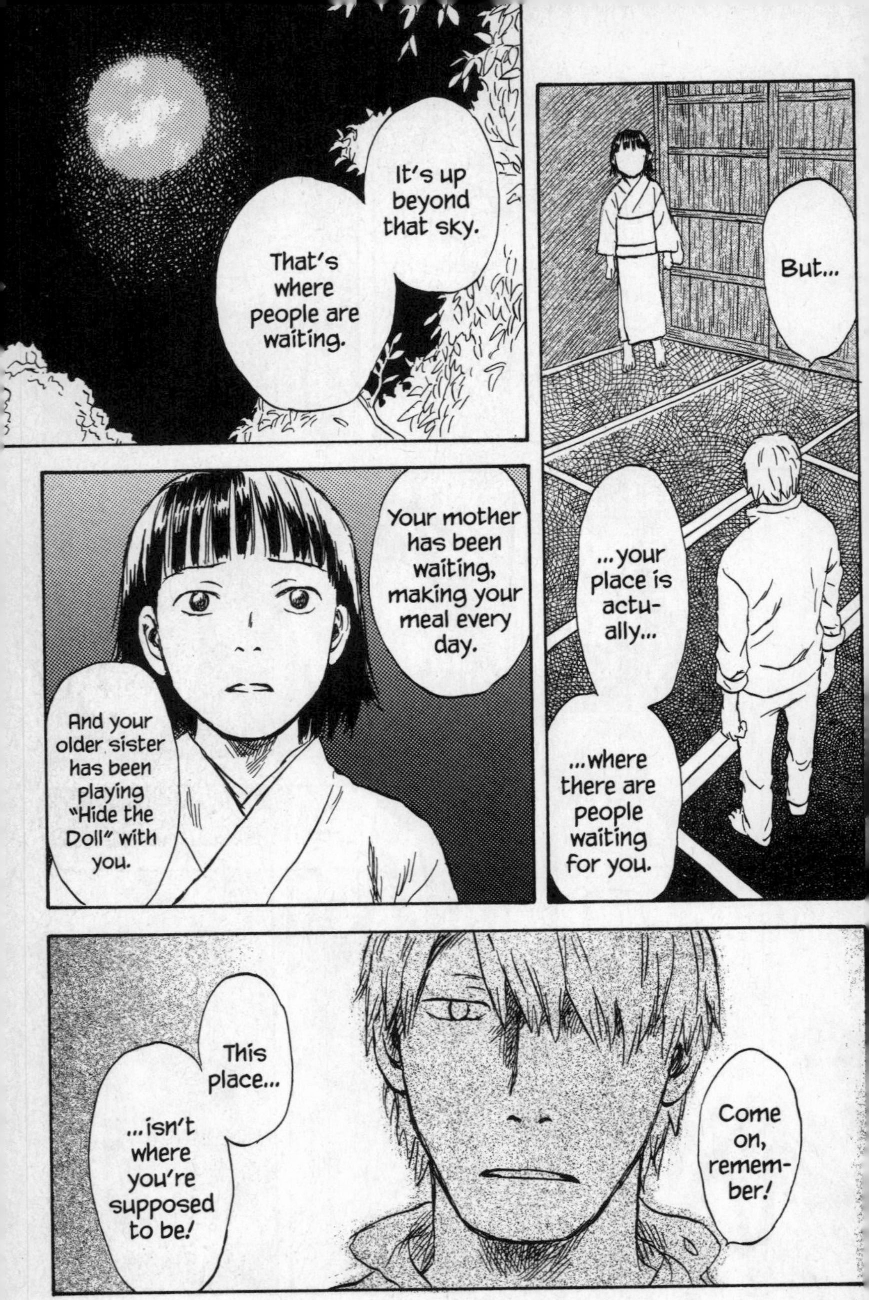
But...
...your place is actually...
...where there are people waiting for you.
It's up beyond that sky.
That's where people are waiting.
Your mother has been waiting, making your meal every day.
And your older sister has been playing "Hide the Doll" with you.
Come on, remember!
This place...
...isn't where you're supposed to be!

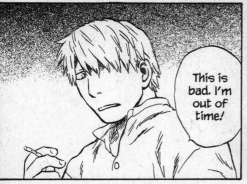

This is bad. I'm out of time!

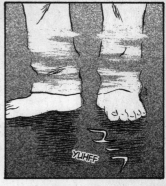

YUHFF

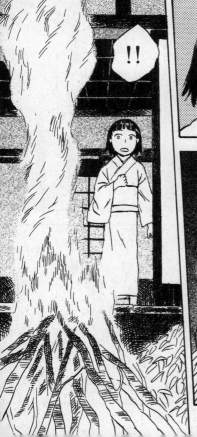

!!

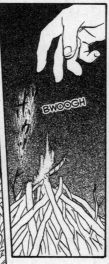

I'll have to do it whether you like it or not.

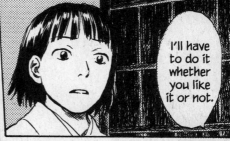

BWOOCH

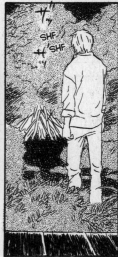

SHF
SHF

114

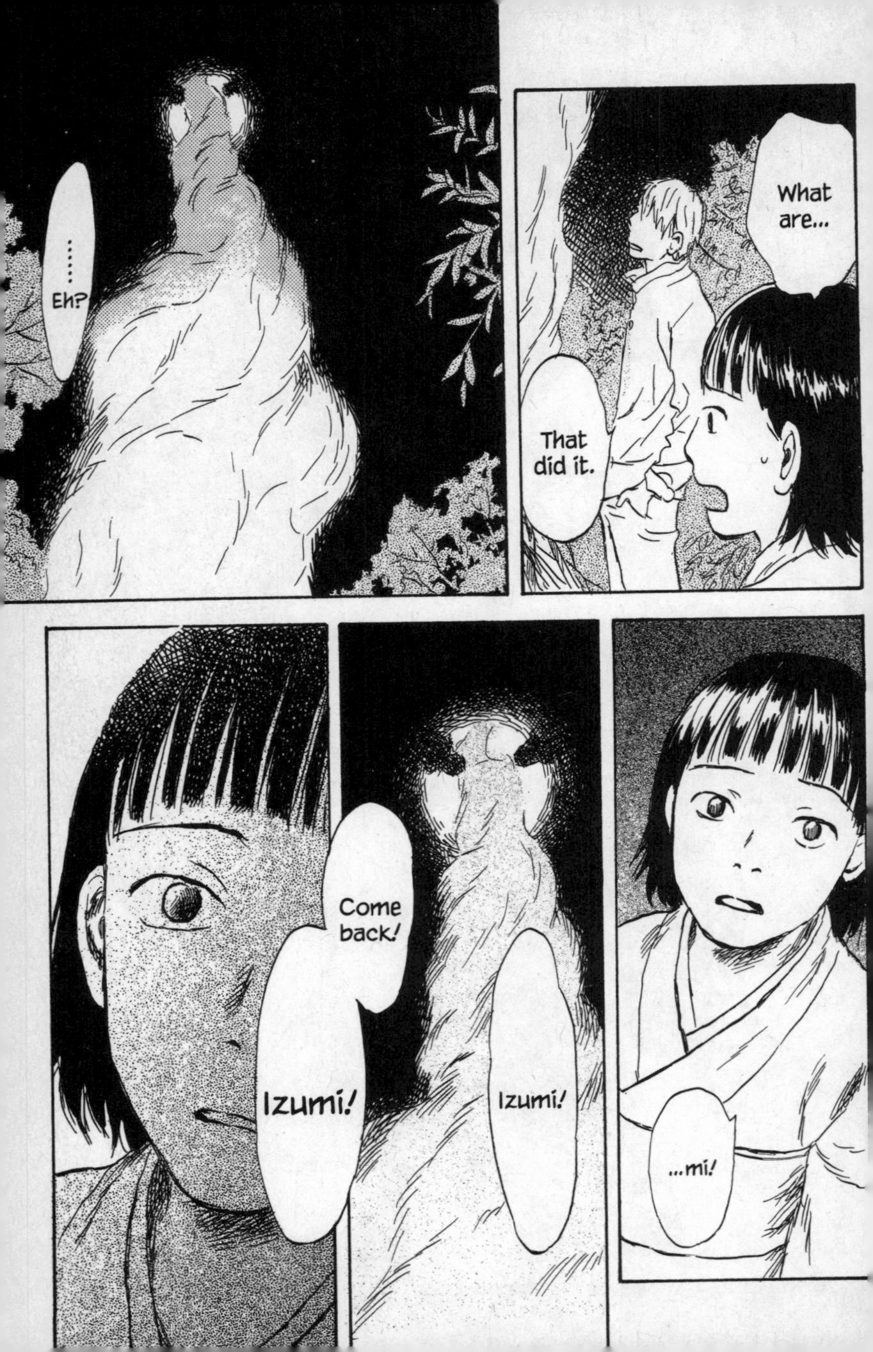
What are...
That did it.
...... Eh?
...mi!
Izumi!
Come back!
Izumi!

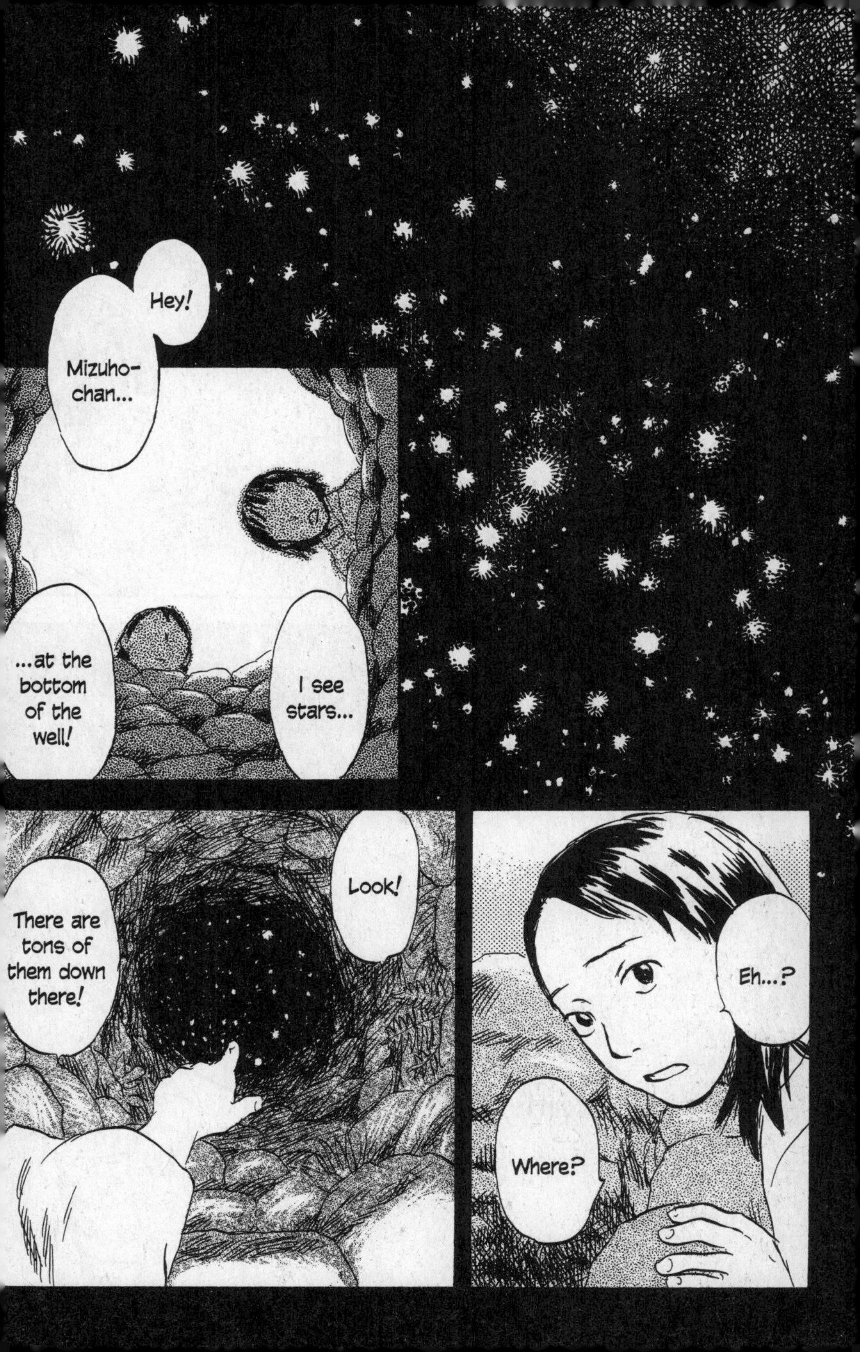
Hey!
Mizuho-chan...
I see stars...
...at the bottom of the well!
Eh...?
Where?
Look!
There are tons of them down there!

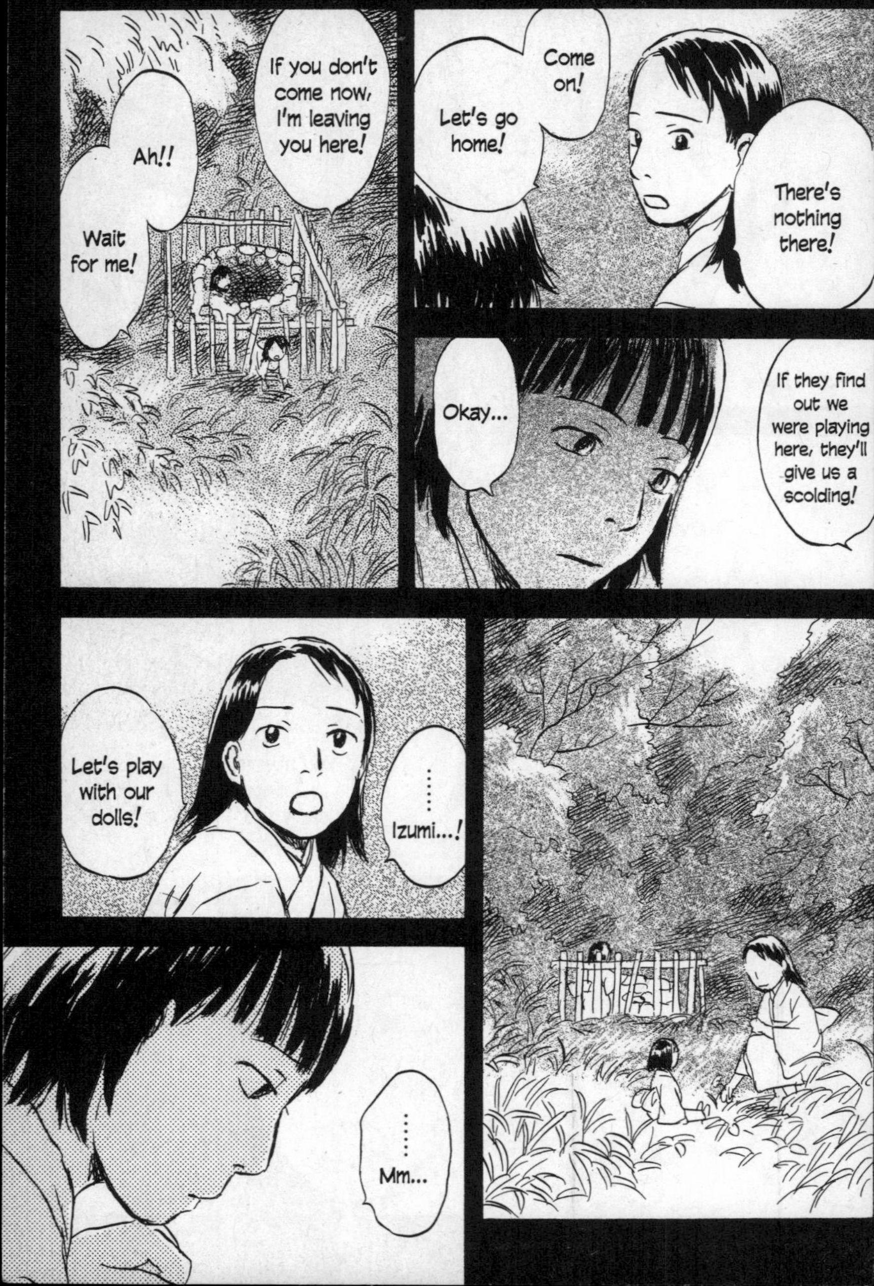
There's nothing there!
Come on!
Let's go home!
If they find out we were playing here, they'll give us a scolding!
Okay...
If you don't come now, I'm leaving you here!
Ah!!
Wait for me!
......Izumi...!
Let's play with our dolls!
......Mm...

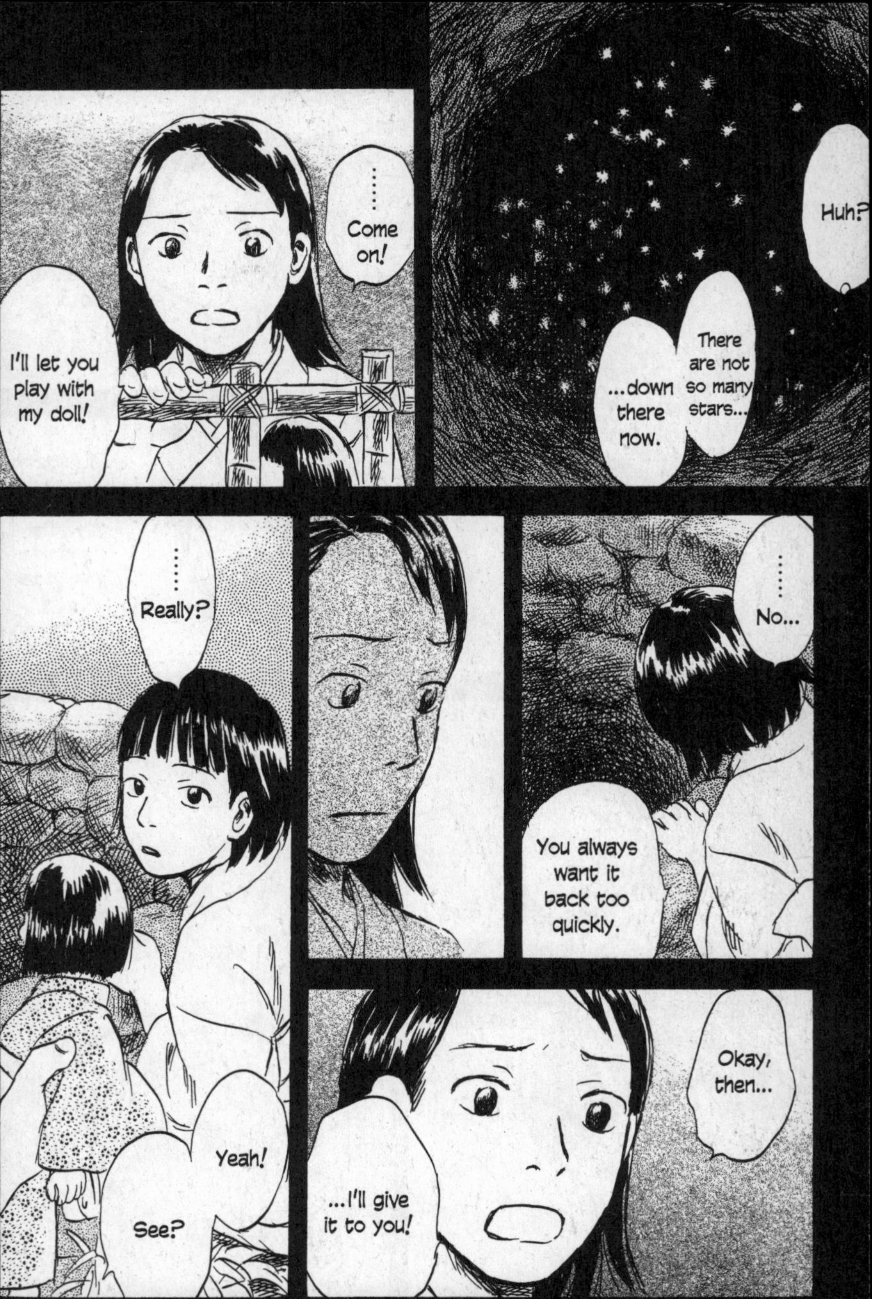
Huh?
There are not so many stars...
...down there now.
......
Come on!
I'll let you play with my doll!
......
No...
You always want it back too quickly.
Okay, then...
...I'll give it to you!
......
Really?
Yeah!
See?

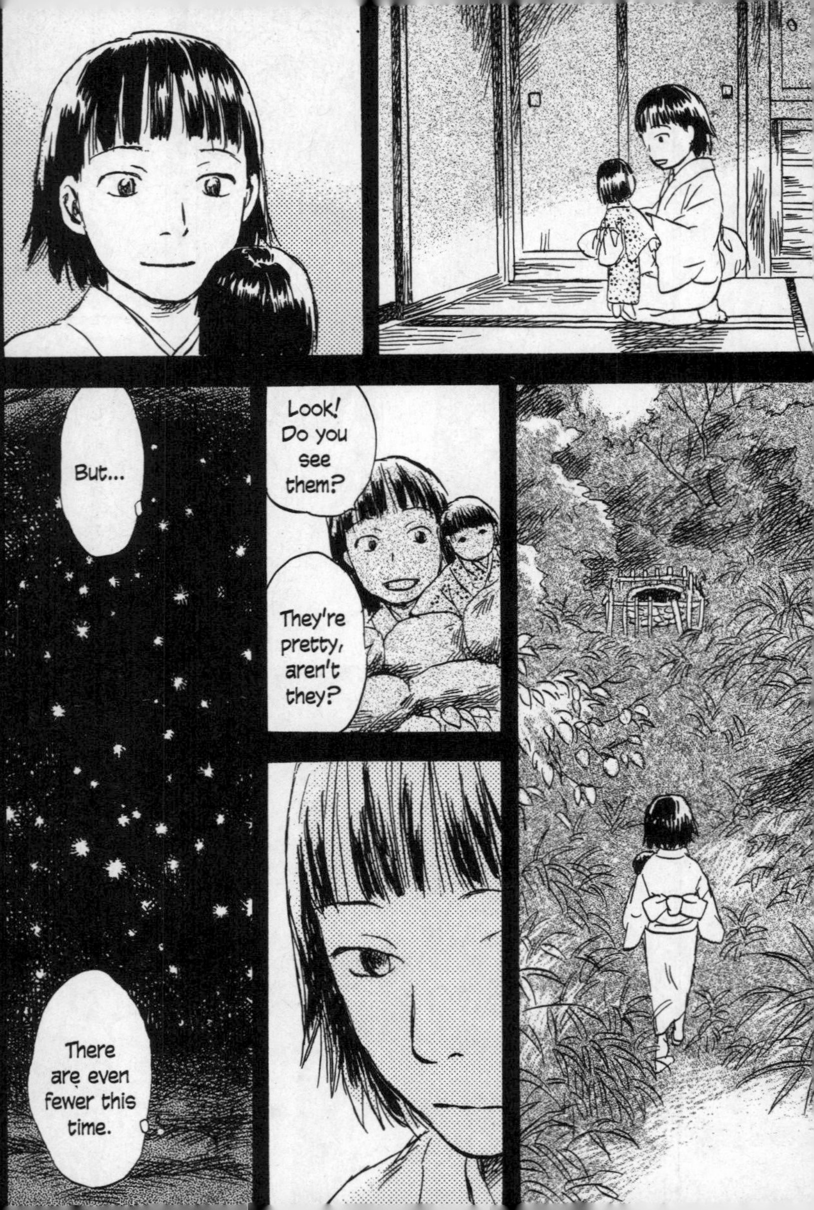
Look! Do you see them?
They're pretty, aren't they?
But...
There are even fewer this time.

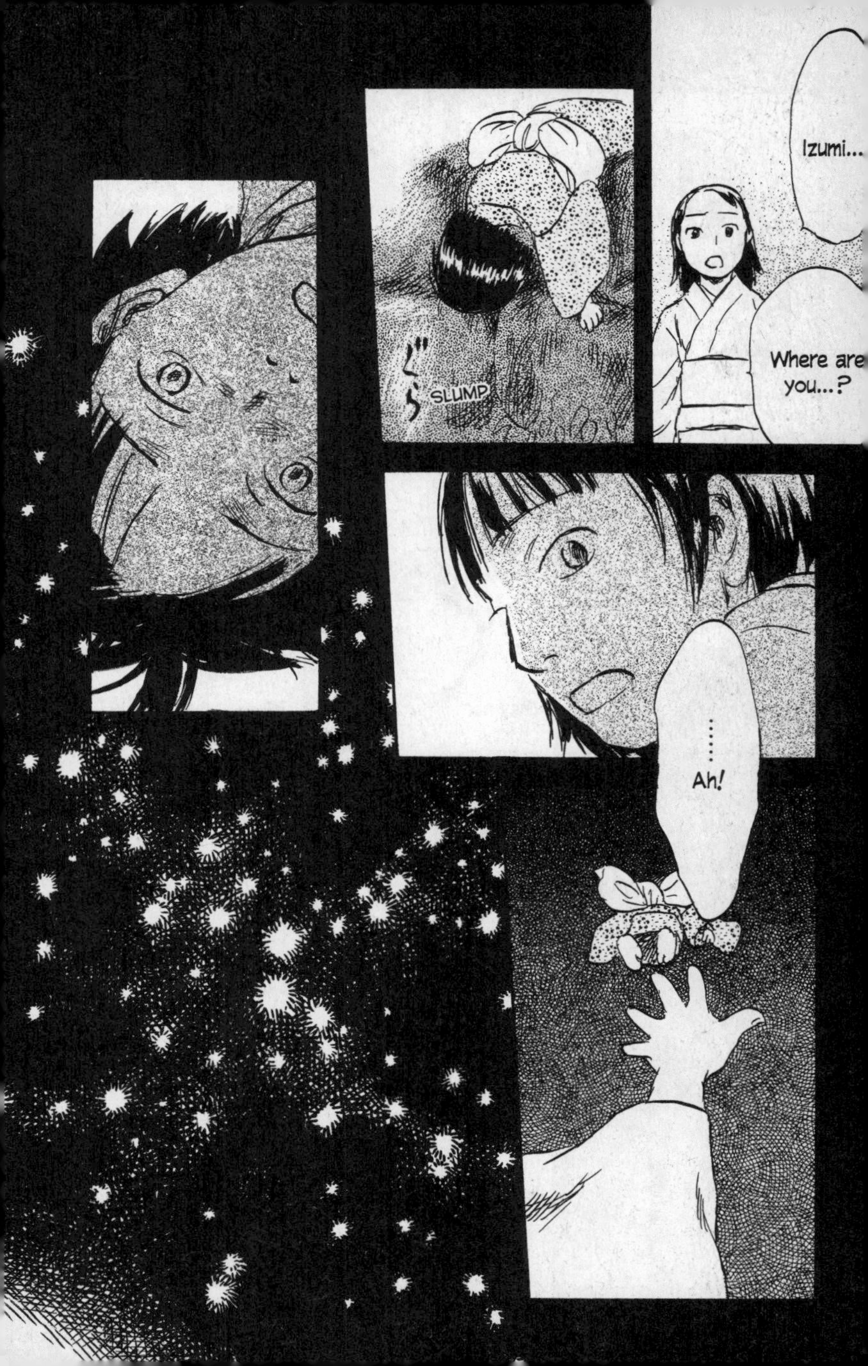
Izumi...
Where are you...?
ぐら
SLUMP
......Ah!

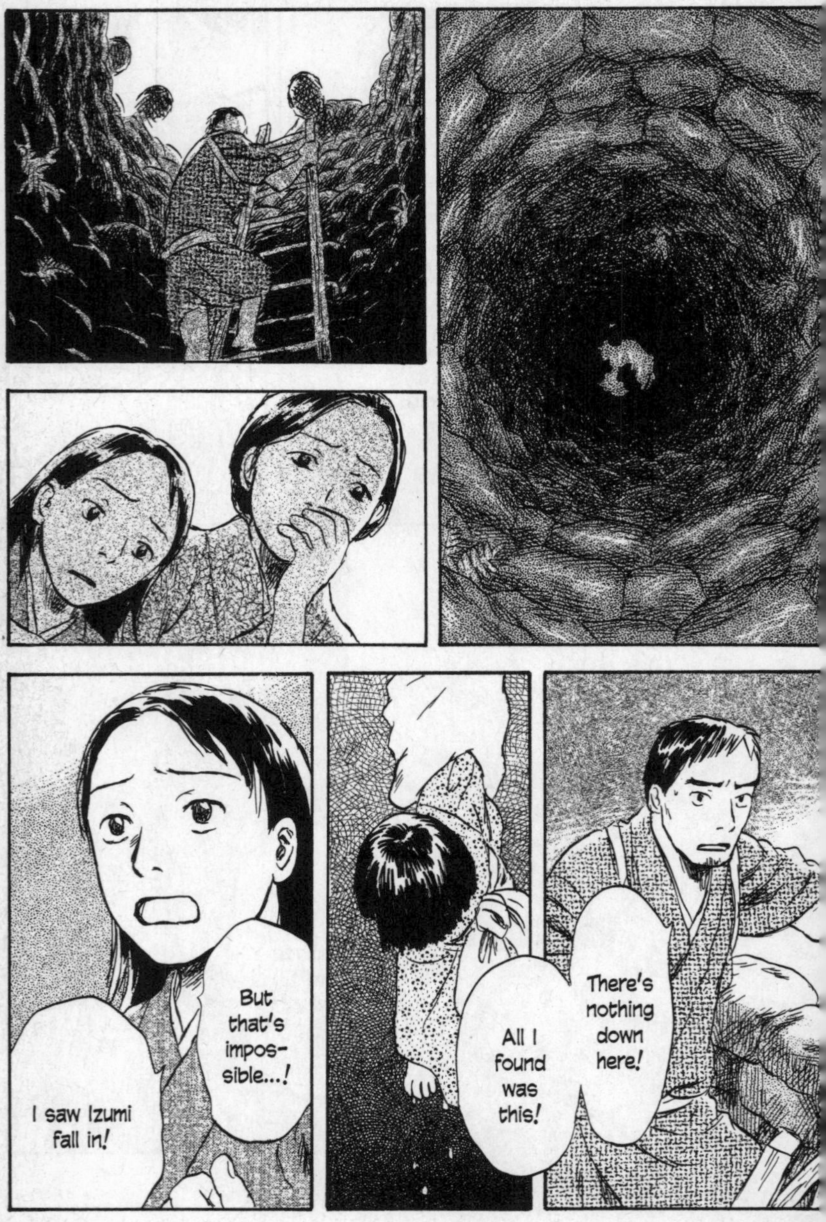
There's nothing down here!
All I found was this!
But that's impos-sible...!
I saw Izumi fall in!

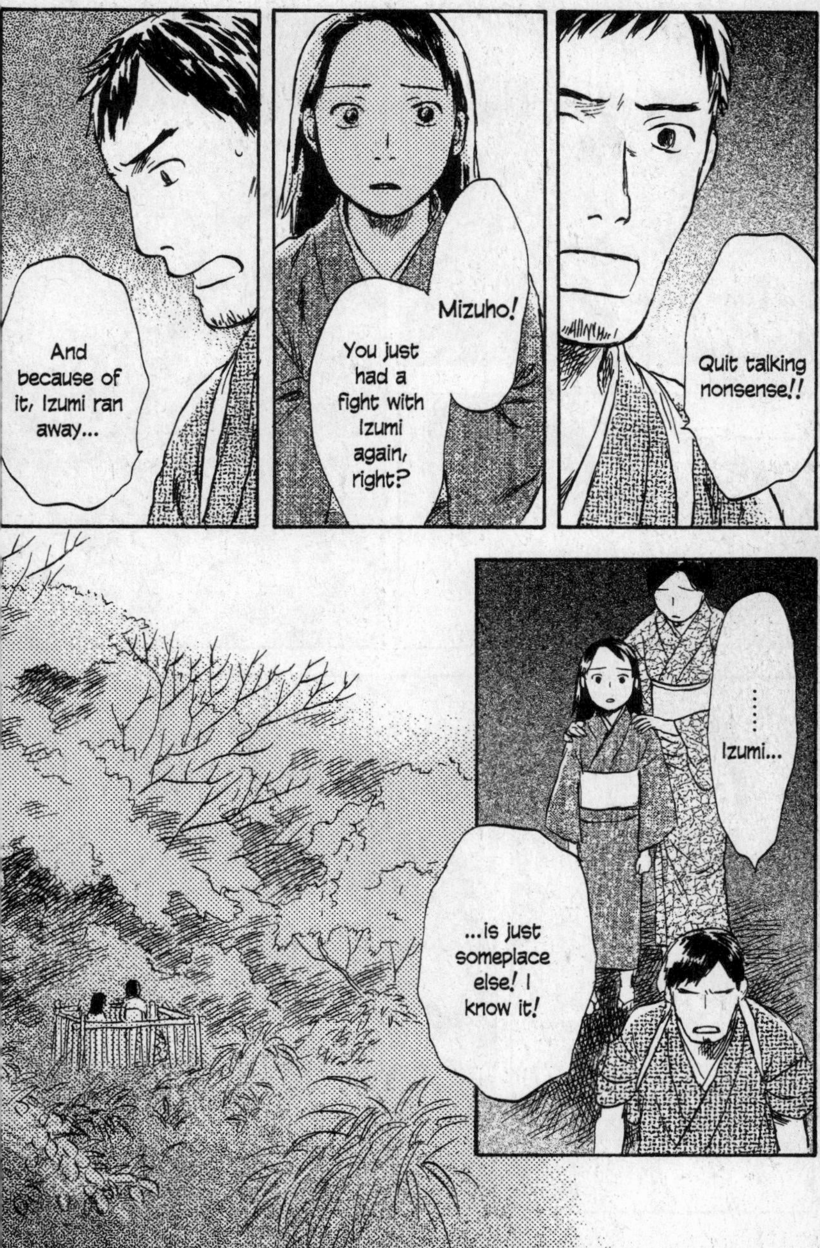
Quit talking nonsense!!
Mizuho!
You just had a fight with Izumi again, right?
And because of it, Izumi ran away...
......Izumi...
...is just someplace else! I know it!

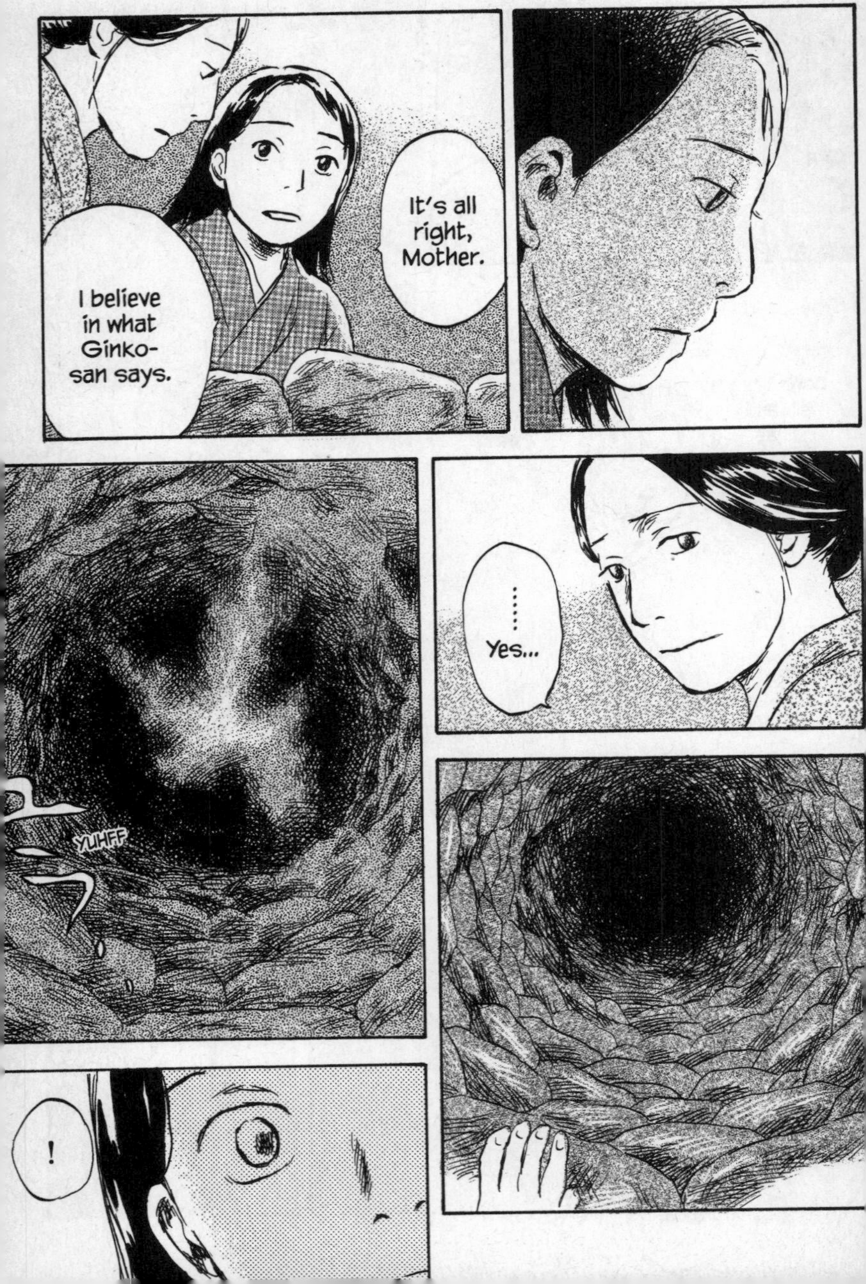
It's all right, Mother.
I believe in what Ginko-san says.
...... Yes...
YUHFF
!

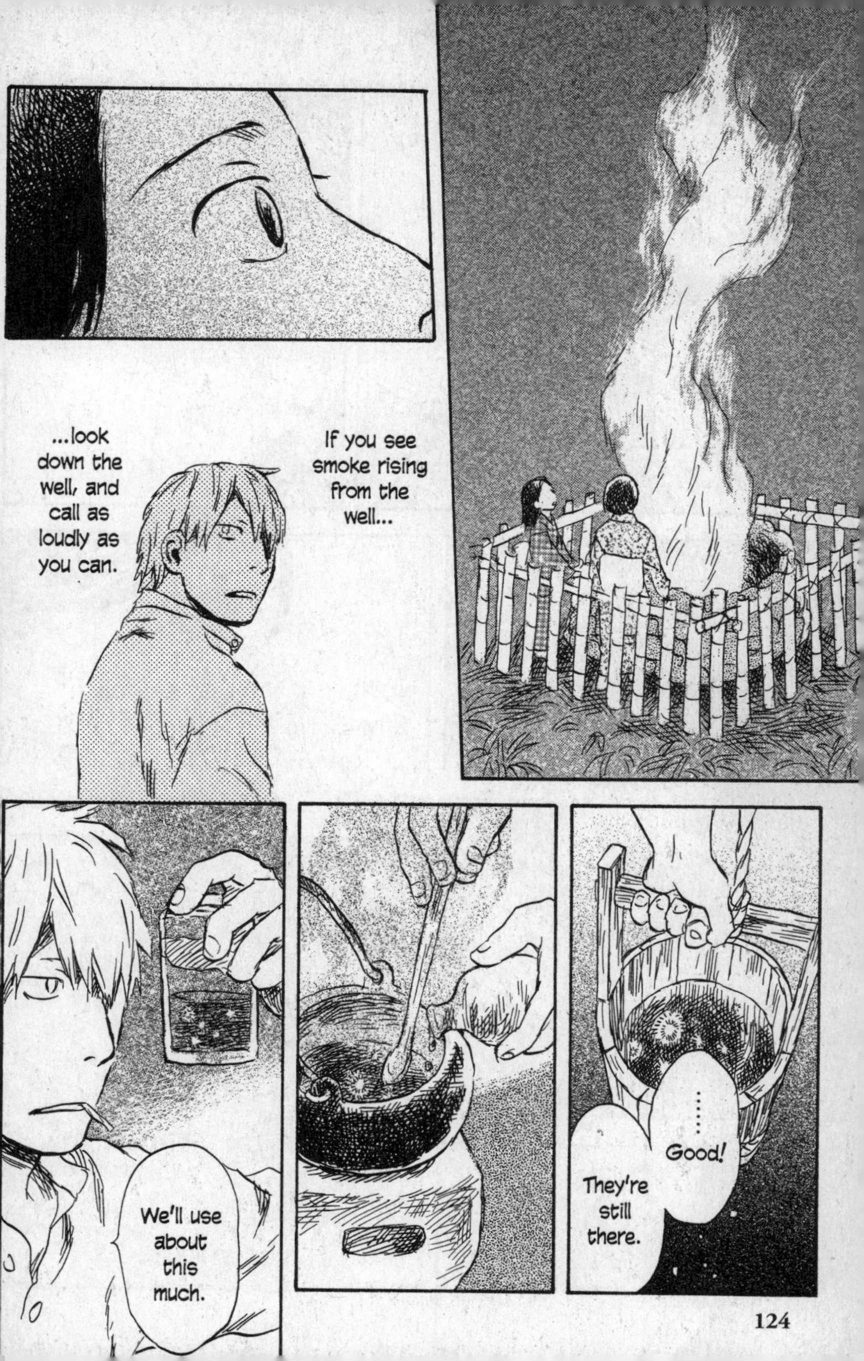
If you see smoke rising from the well...
...look down the well, and call as loudly as you can.
...... Good!
They're still there.
We'll use about this much.

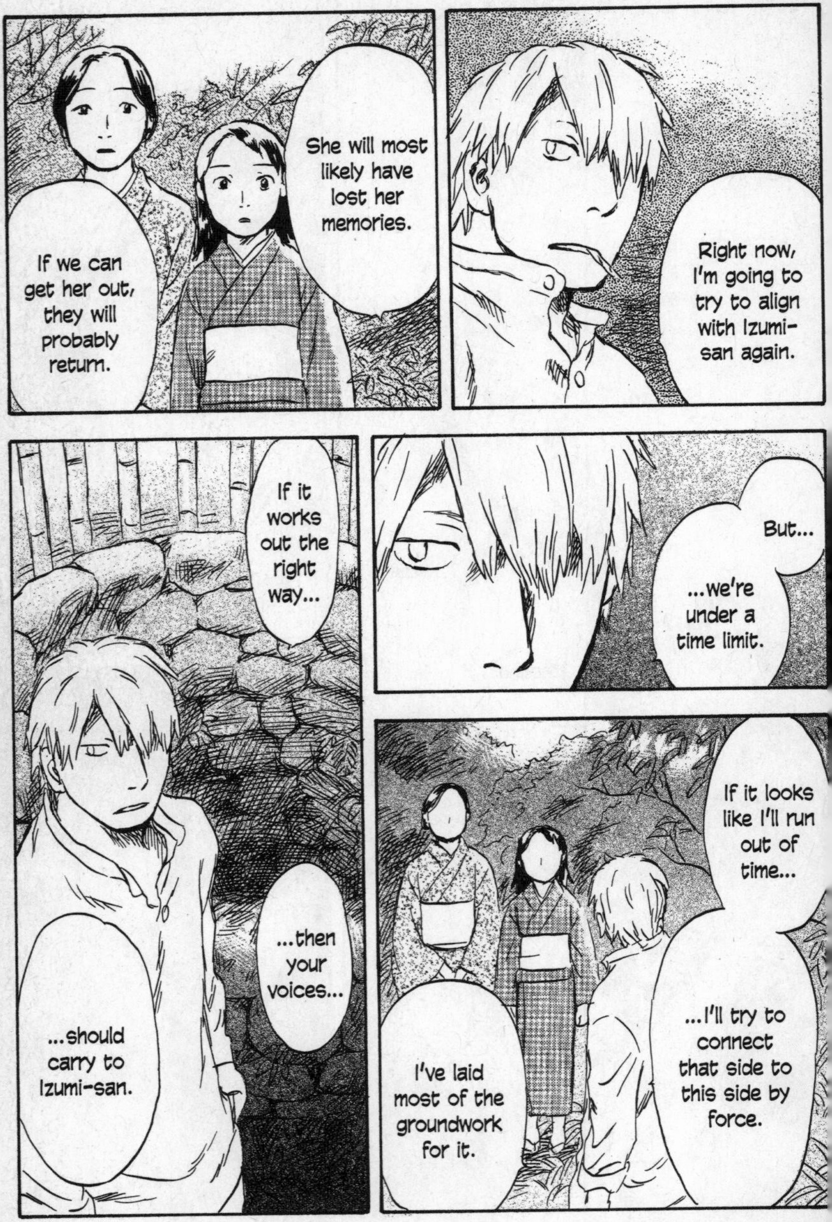
Right now, I'm going to try to align with Izumi-san again.
She will most likely have lost her memories.
If we can get her out, they will probably return.
But...
...we're under a time limit.
If it looks like I'll run out of time...
...I'll try to connect that side to this side by force.
I've laid most of the groundwork for it.
If it works out the right way...
...then your voices...
...should carry to Izumi-san.

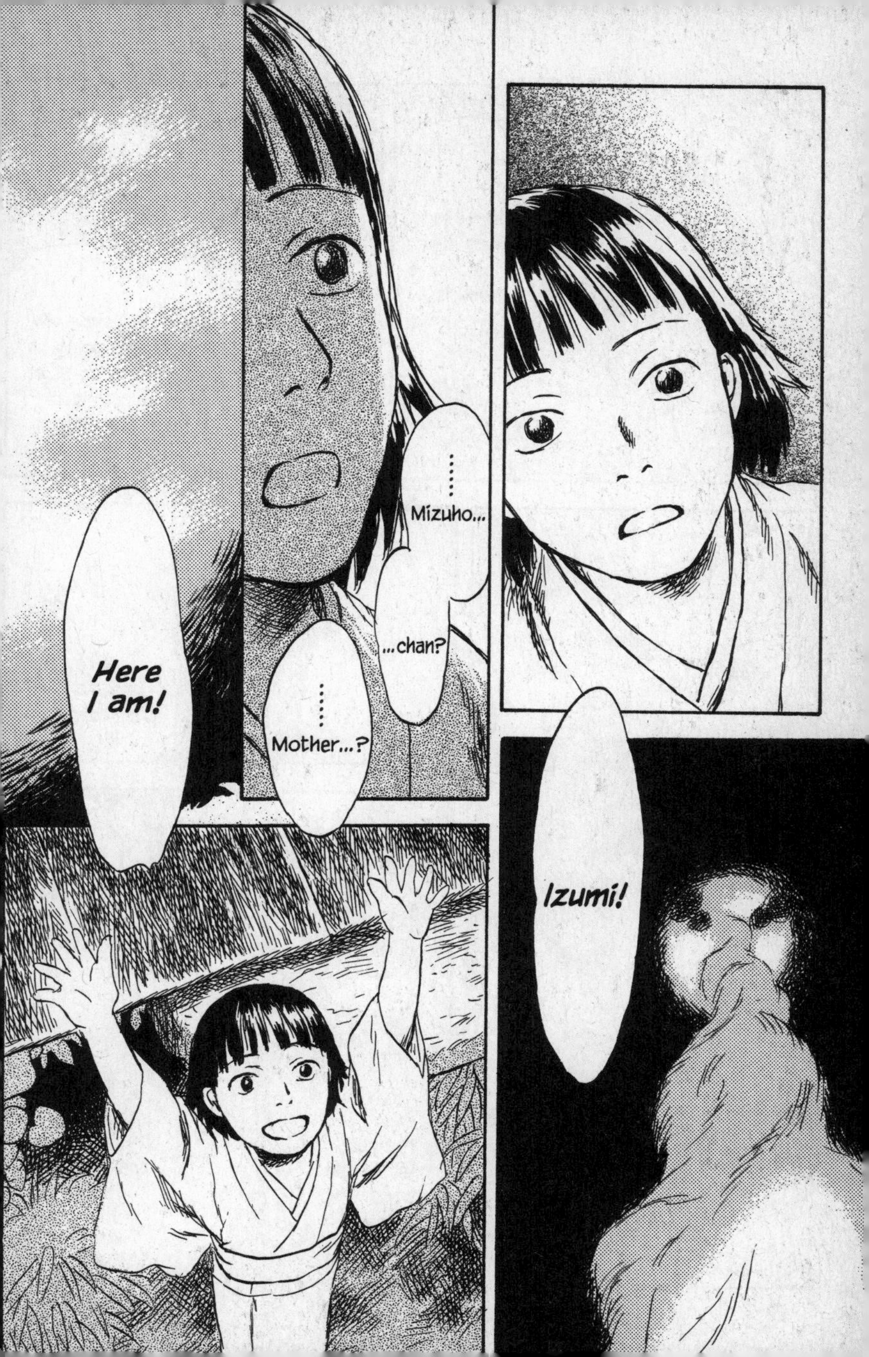
...
Mizuho...
...chan?
...
Mother...?
Here I am!
Izumi!

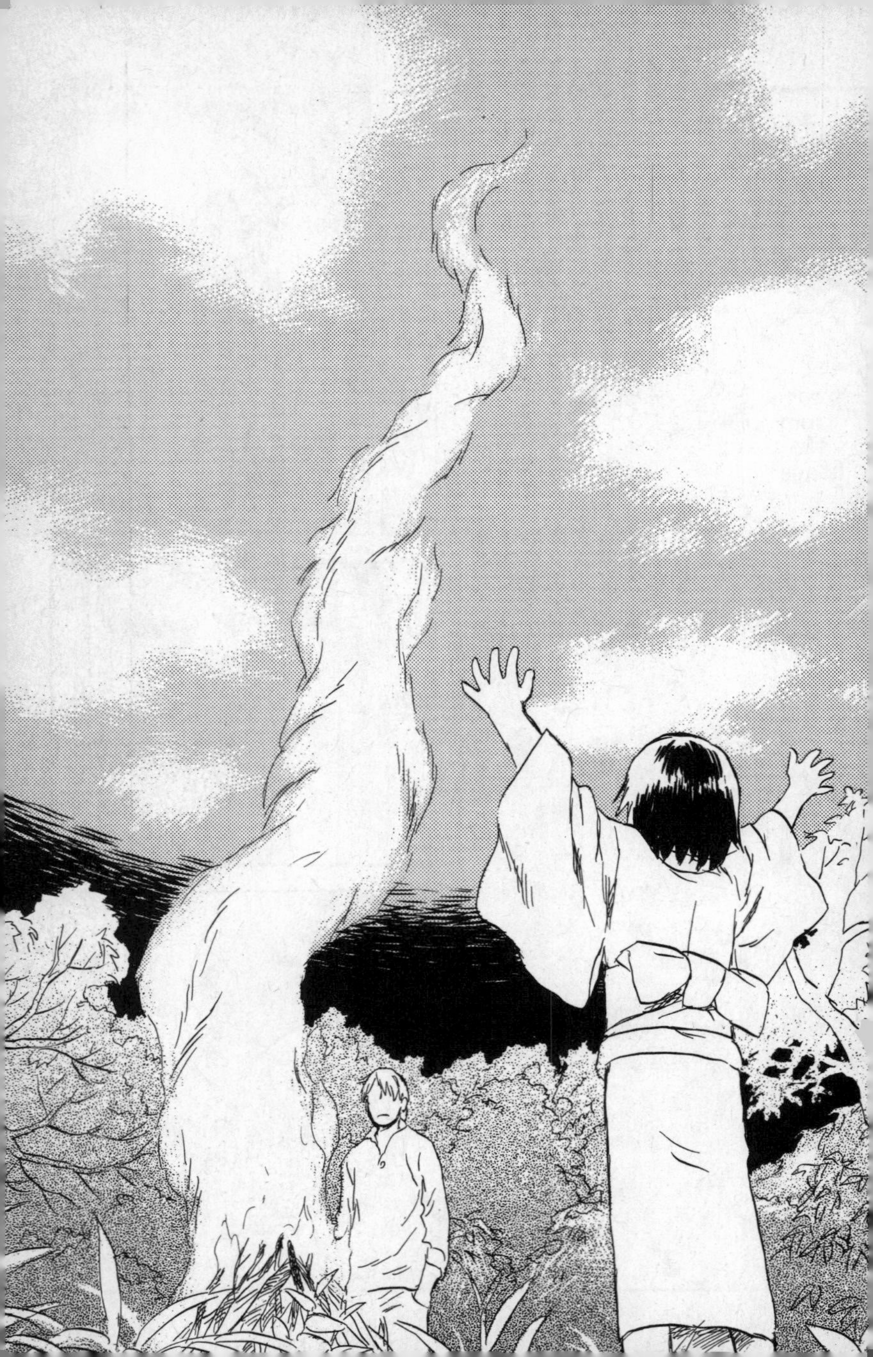

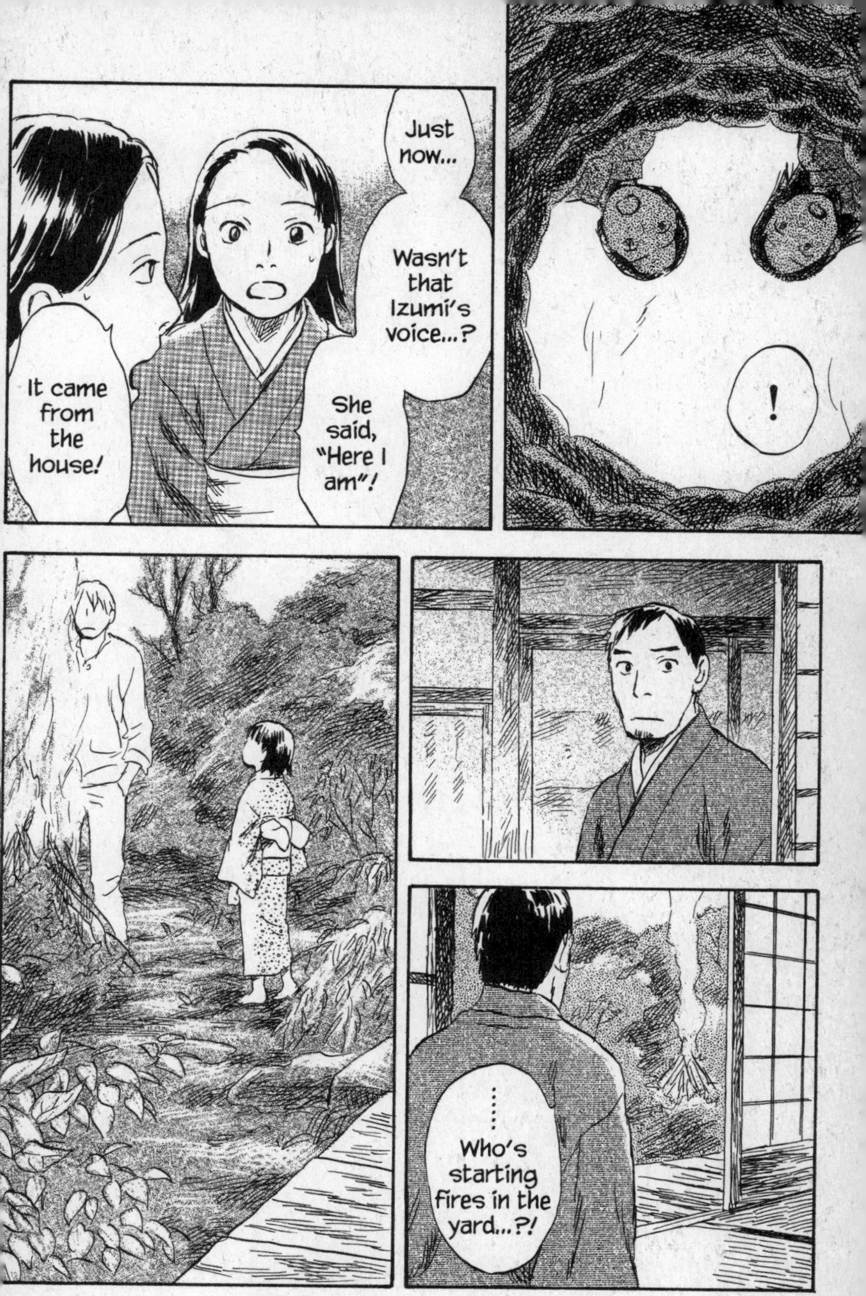
!
Just now...
Wasn't that Izumi's voice...?
She said, "Here I am"!
It came from the house!
......
Who's starting fires in the yard...?!

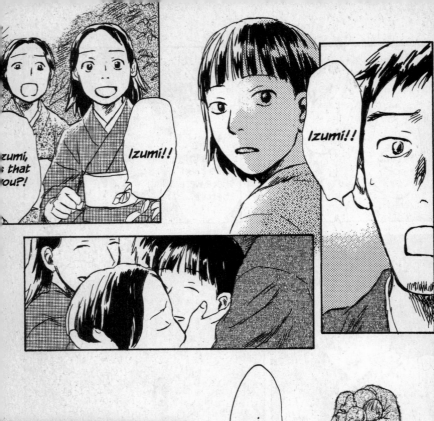

zumi,
s that
ou?!

Izumi!!

Izumi!!

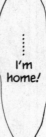

......
I'm
home!

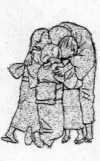

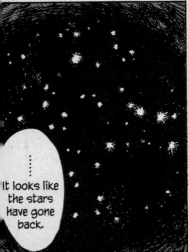

......
It looks like
the stars
have gone
back.

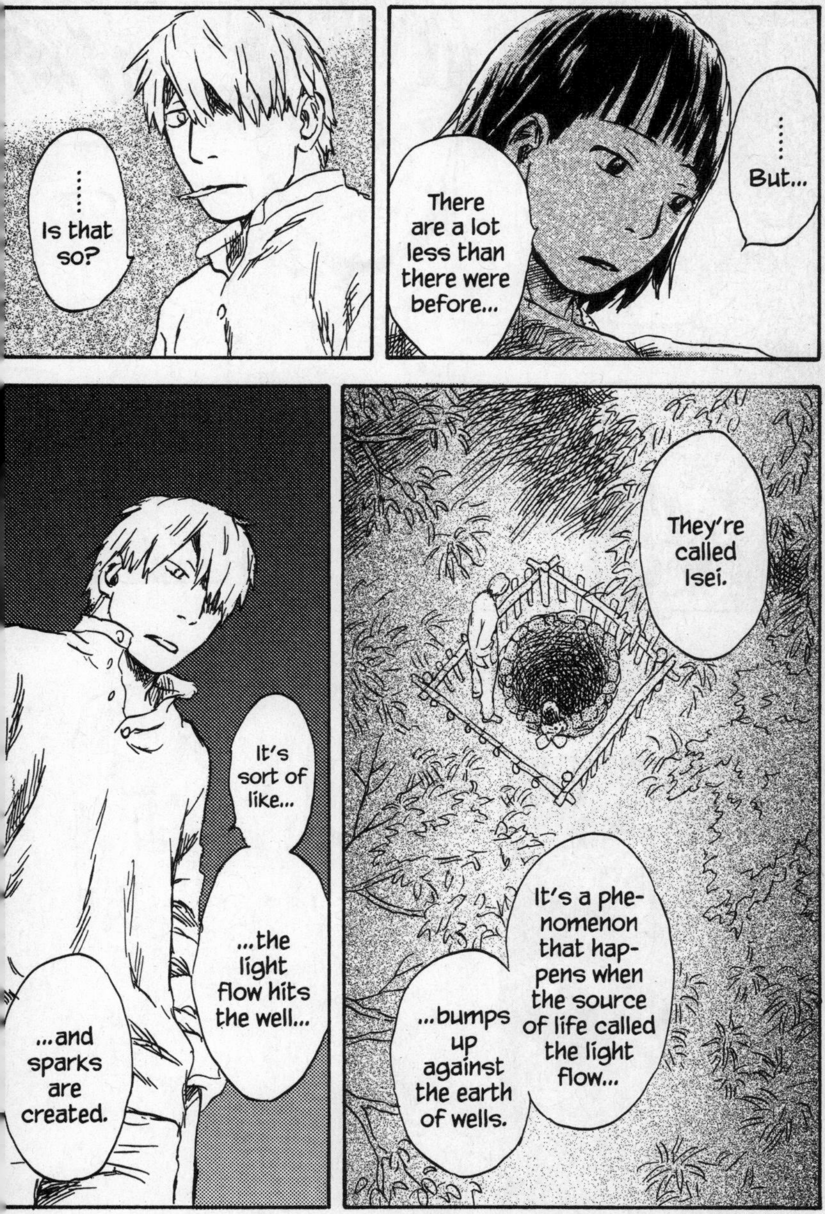
......But...
There are a lot less than there were before...
......Is that so?
They're called Isei.
It's a phenomenon that happens when the source of life called the light flow...
...bumps up against the earth of wells.
It's sort of like...
...the light flow hits the well...
...and sparks are created.

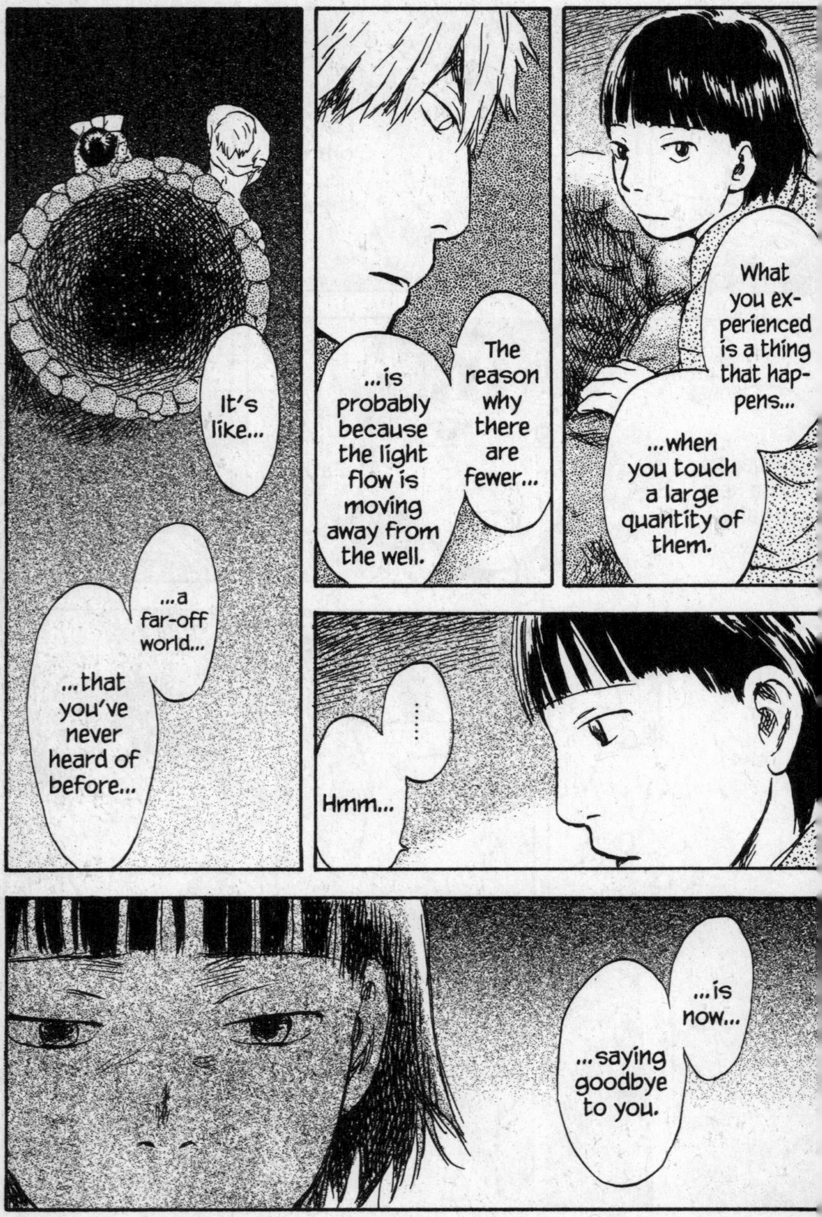

What you experienced is a thing that happens...
...when you touch a large quantity of them.
The reason why there are fewer...
...is probably because the light flow is moving away from the well.
......
Hmm...
It's like...
...a far-off world...
...that you've never heard of before...
...is now...
...saying goodbye to you.

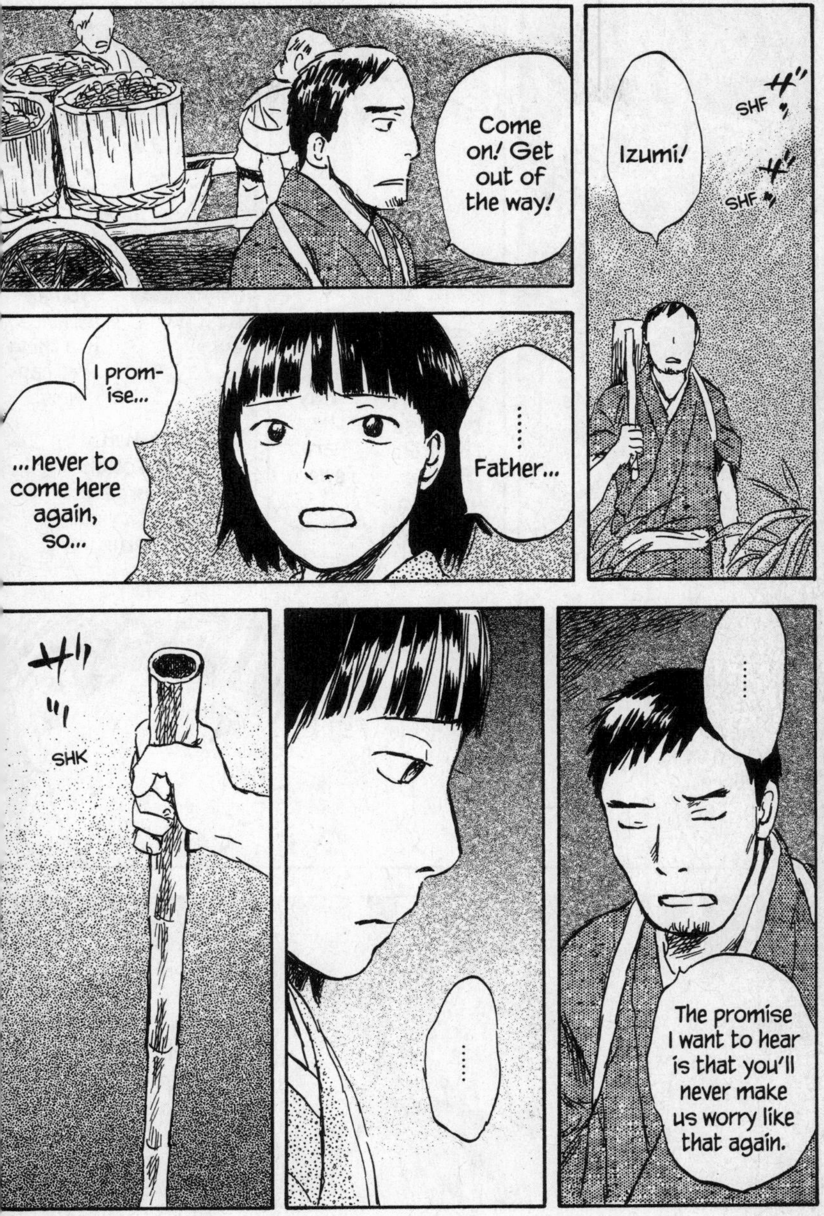
Izumi!
SHF
SHF
Come on! Get out of the way!
......
Father...
I promise...
...never to come here again, so...
......
The promise I want to hear is that you'll never make us worry like that again.
......
SHK

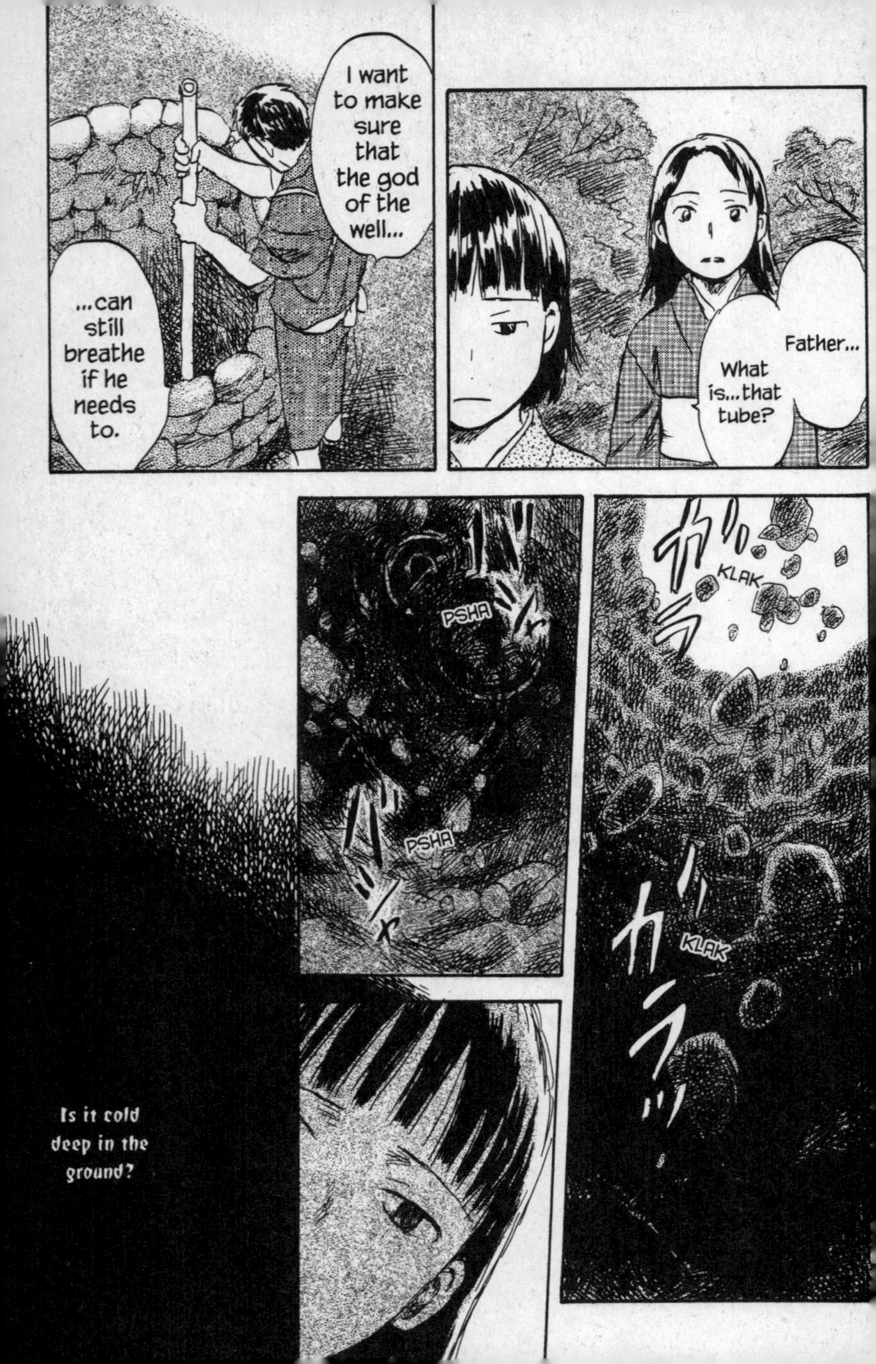
Father...
What is...that tube?
I want to make sure that the god of the well...
...can still breathe if he needs to.
KLAK
KLAK
PSHA
PSHA
Is it cold deep in the ground?

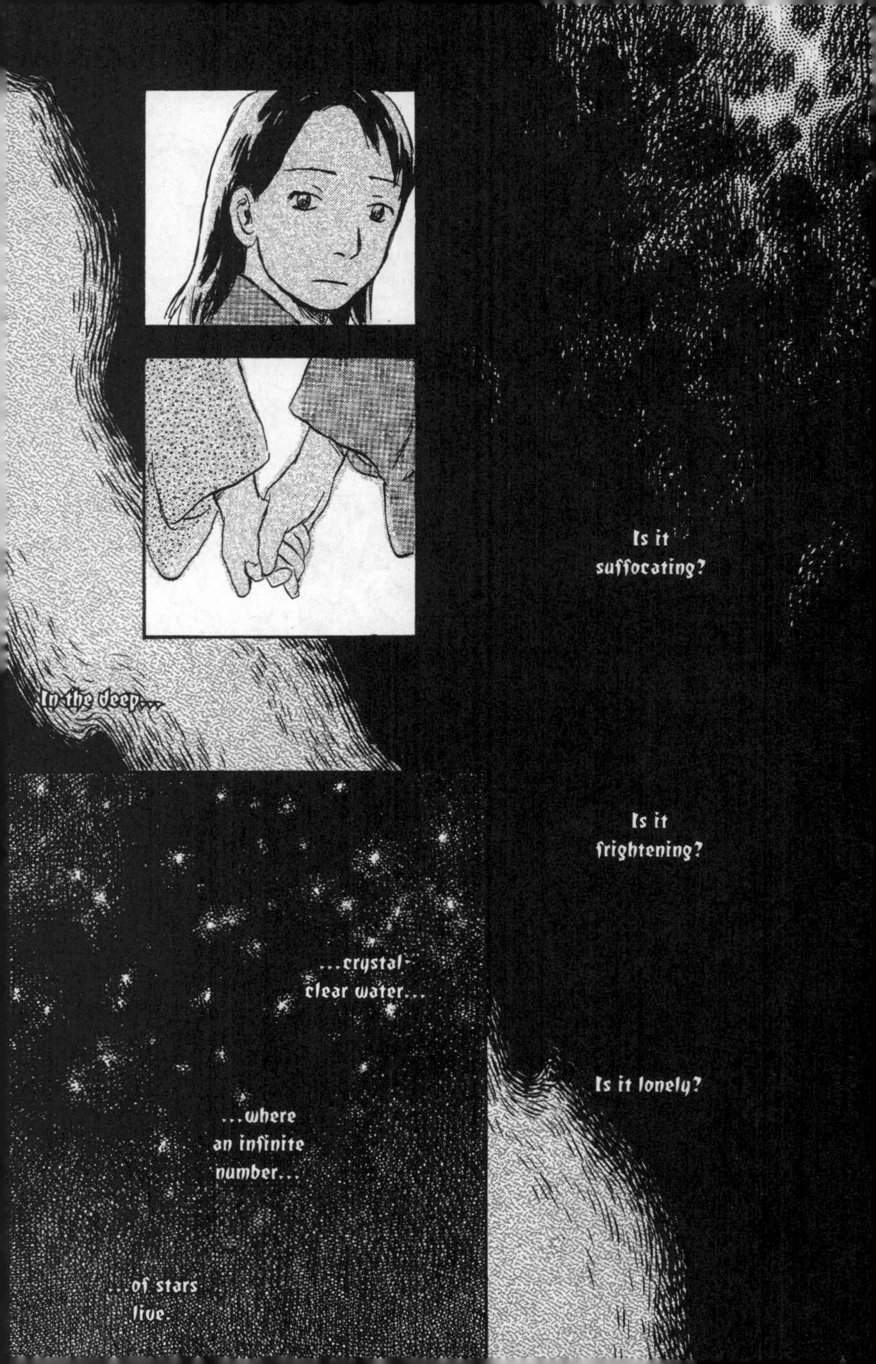
Is it suffocating?
Is it frightening?
Is it lonely?
In the deep...
...crystal-clear water...
...where an infinite number...
...of stars live.

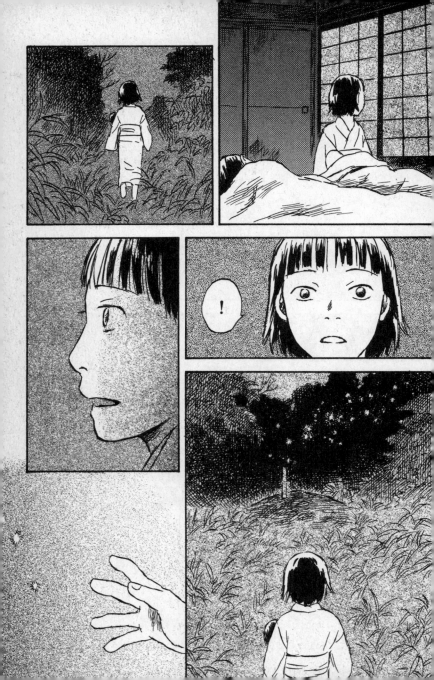

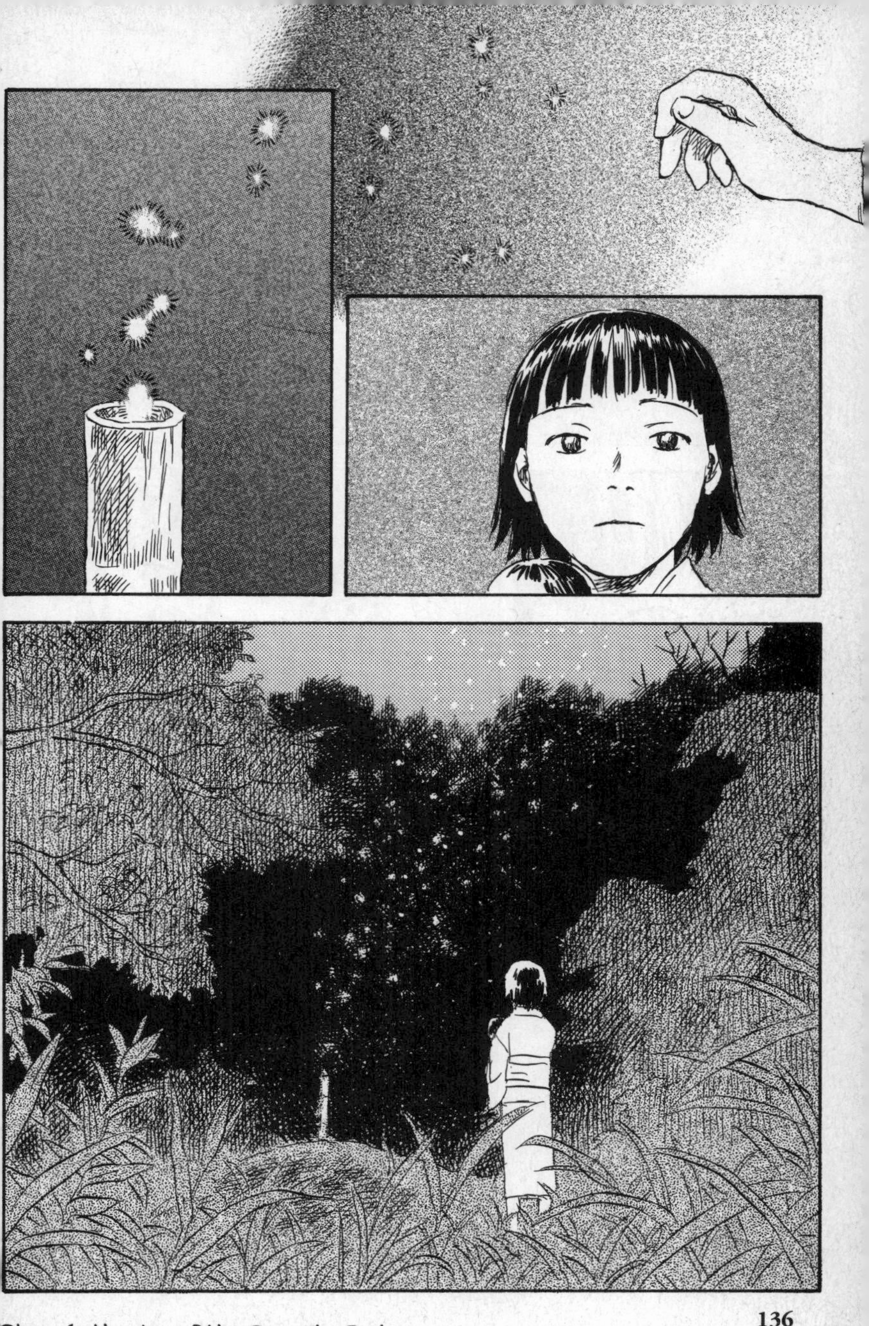

Stars in the Jar of the Sky The End

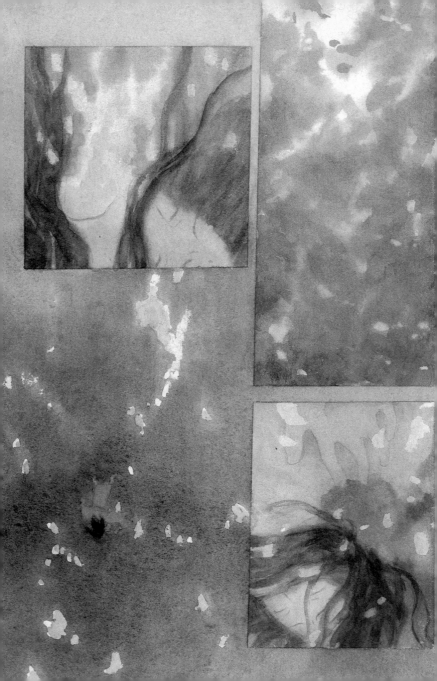

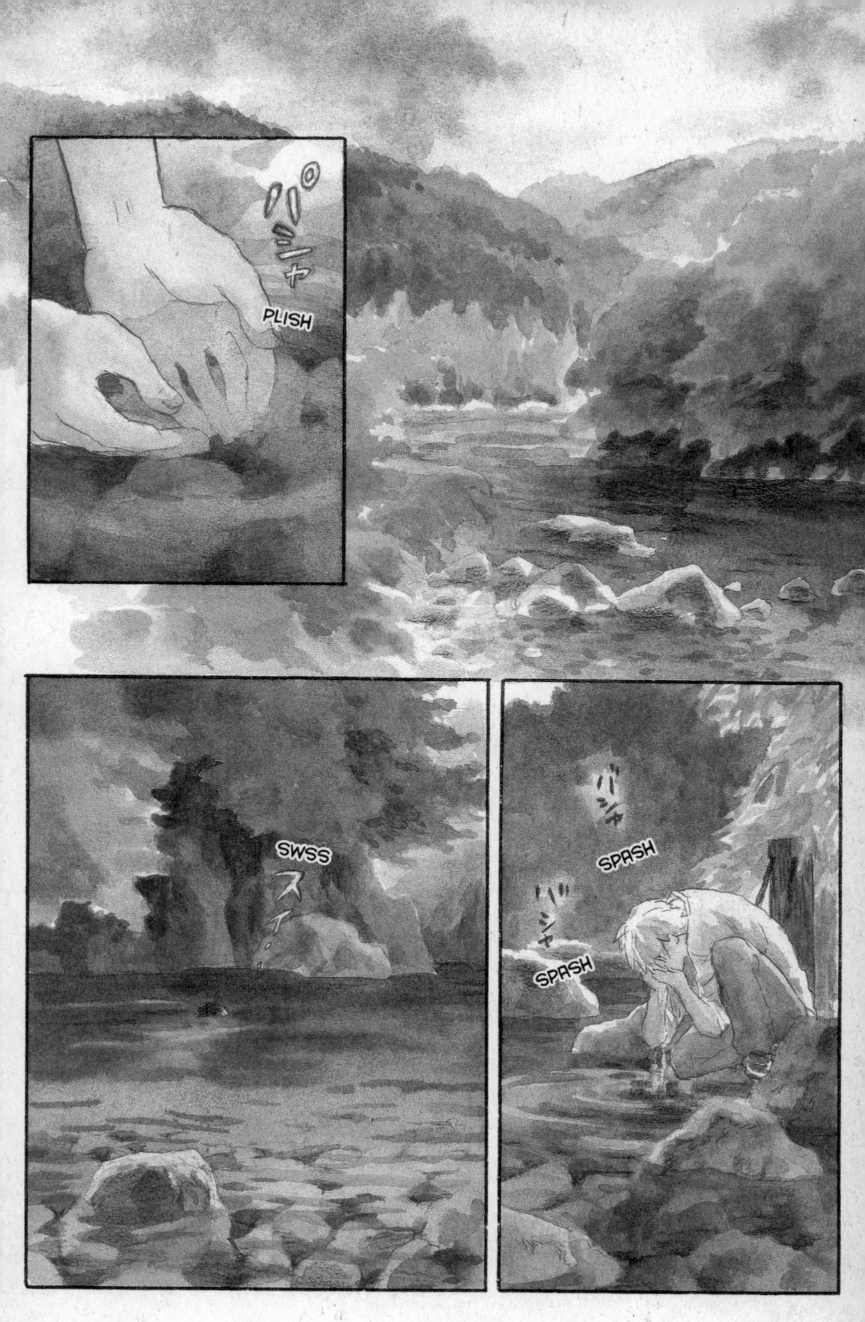
パシャ
PLISH
バシャ
SPASH
バシャ
SPASH
SWSS
スィ。

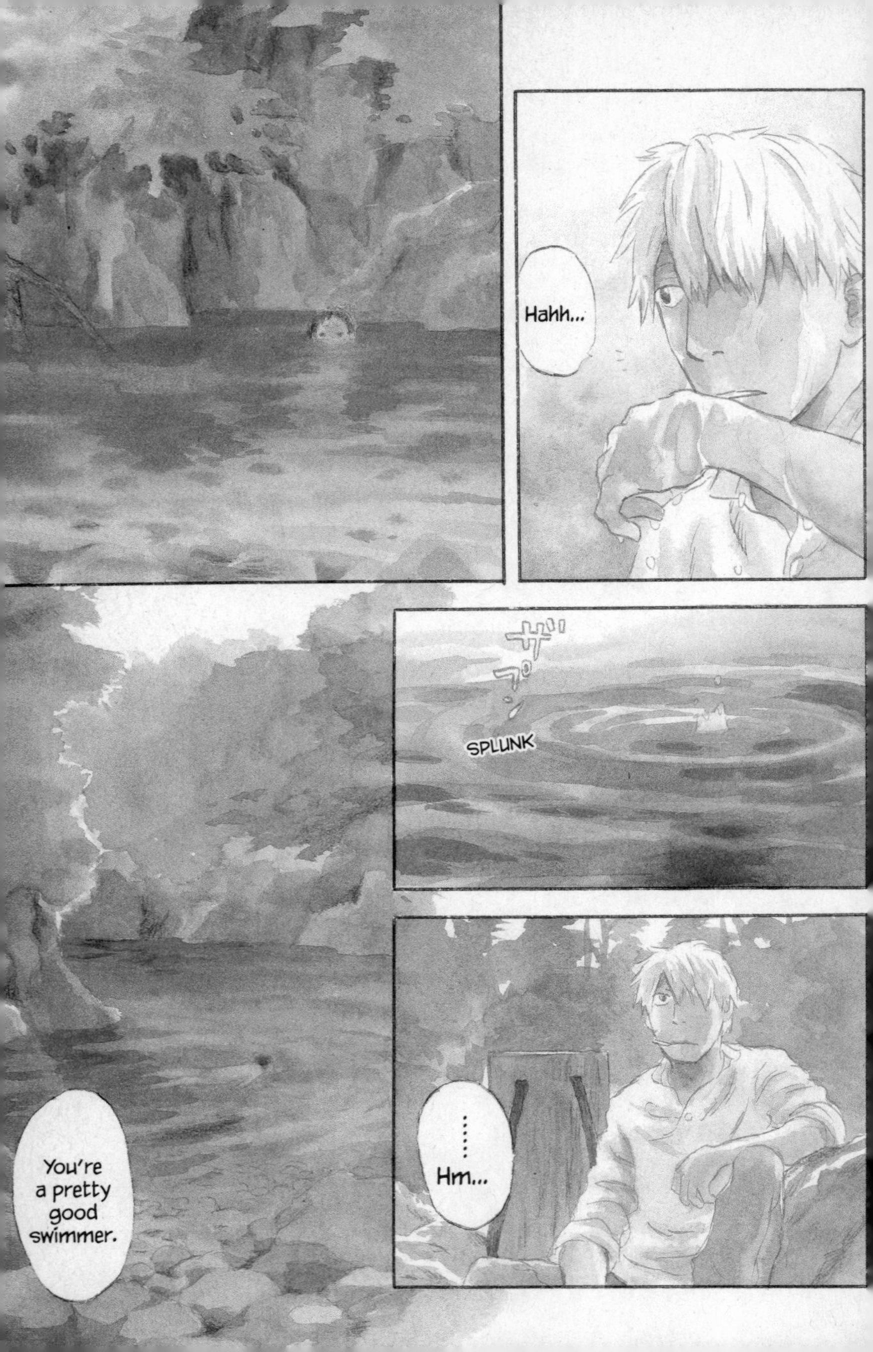
Hahh...
ザプ
SPLUNK
...... Hm...
You're a pretty good swimmer.

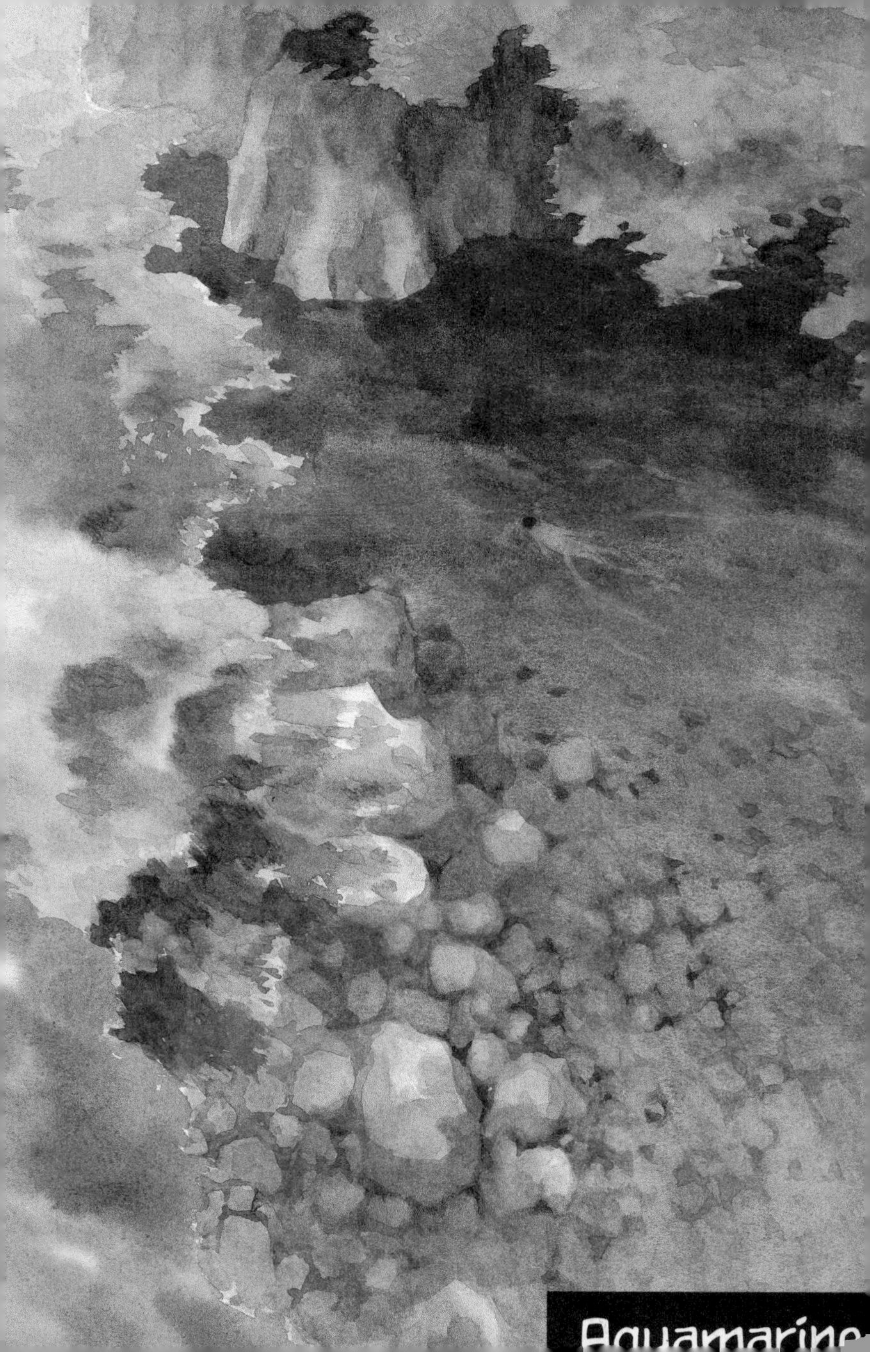

Aquamarine

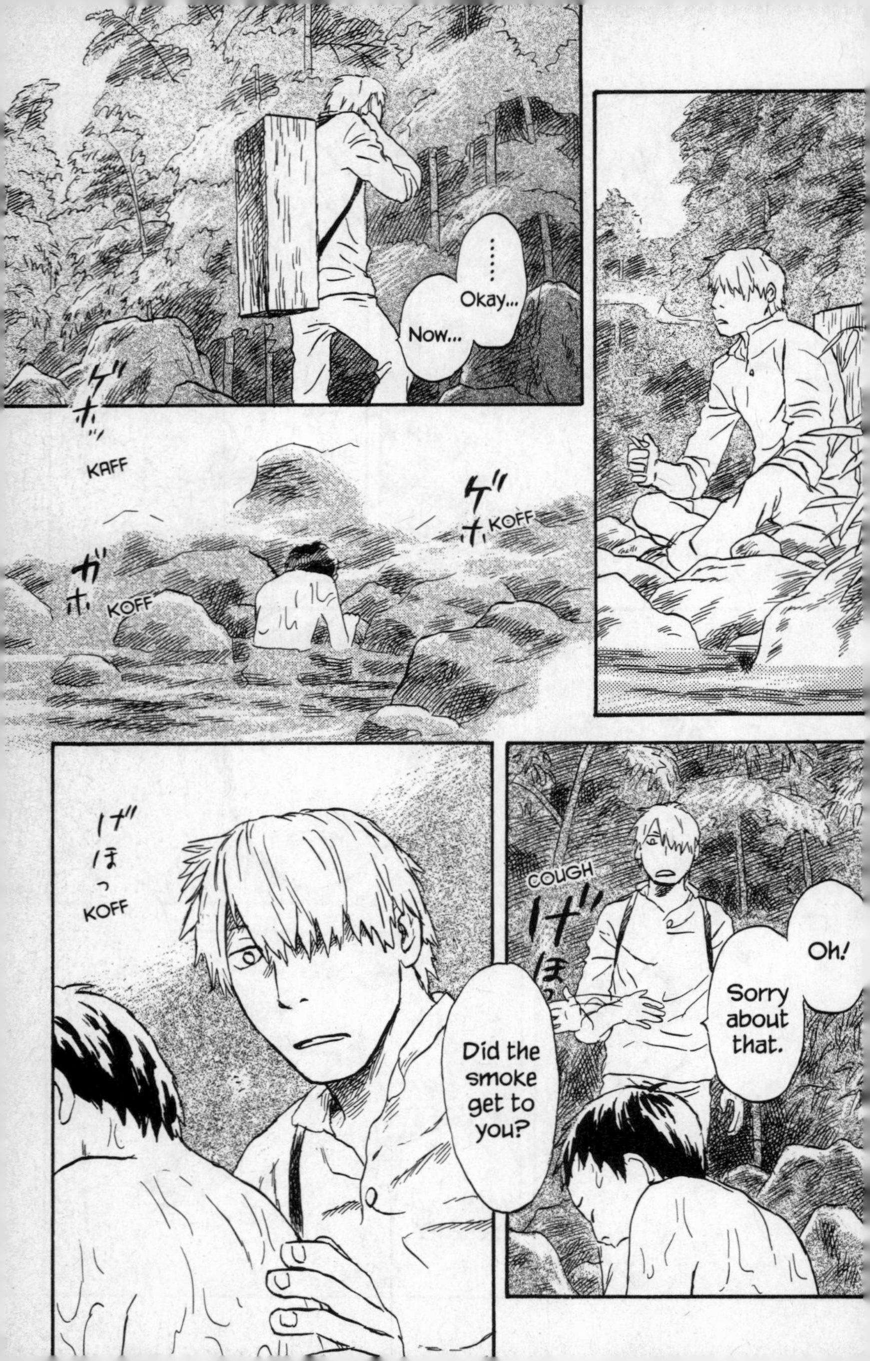
......
Okay...
Now...
ゲホ
KOFF
ガホ
KOFF
ゲホッ
KAFF
COUGH
げほっ
Oh!
Sorry about that.
げほっ
KOFF
Did the smoke get to you?

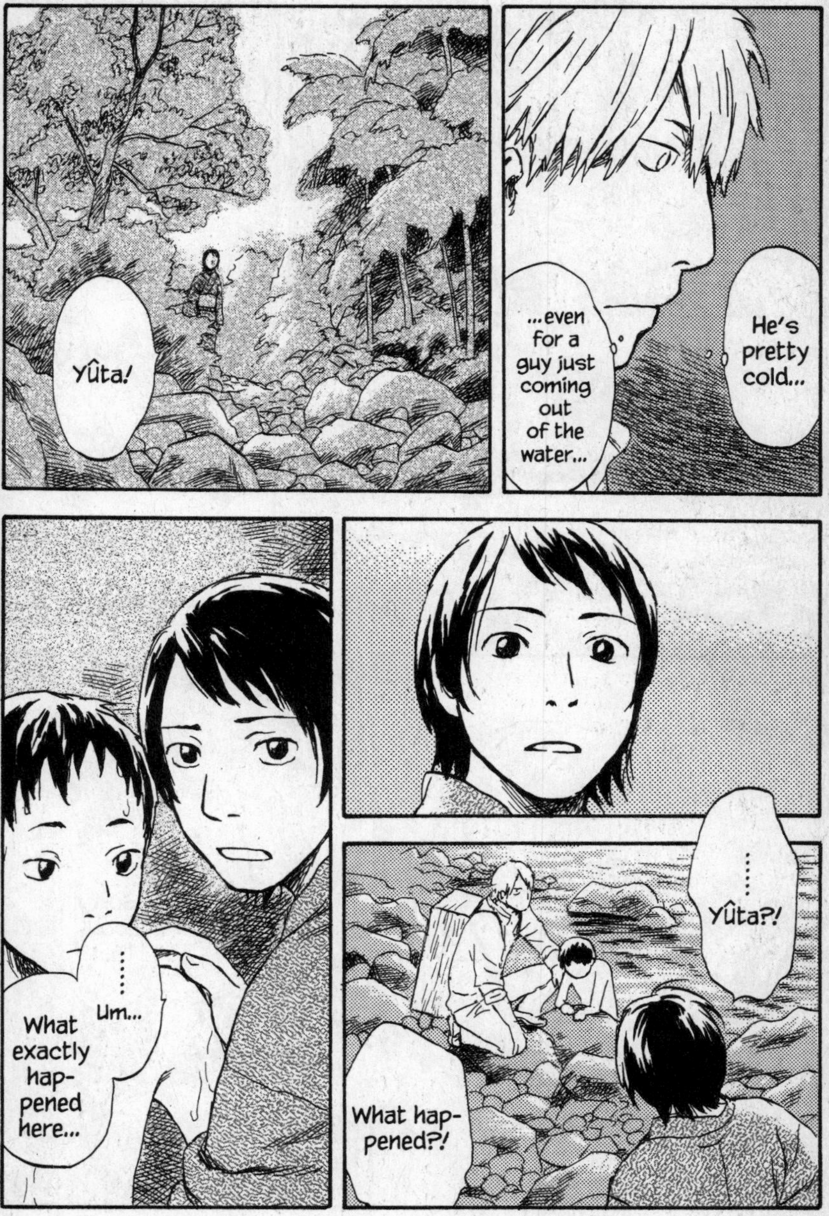
He's pretty cold...
...even for a guy just coming out of the water...
Yûta!
...... Yûta?!
What hap-pened?!
...... um...
What exactly hap-pened here...

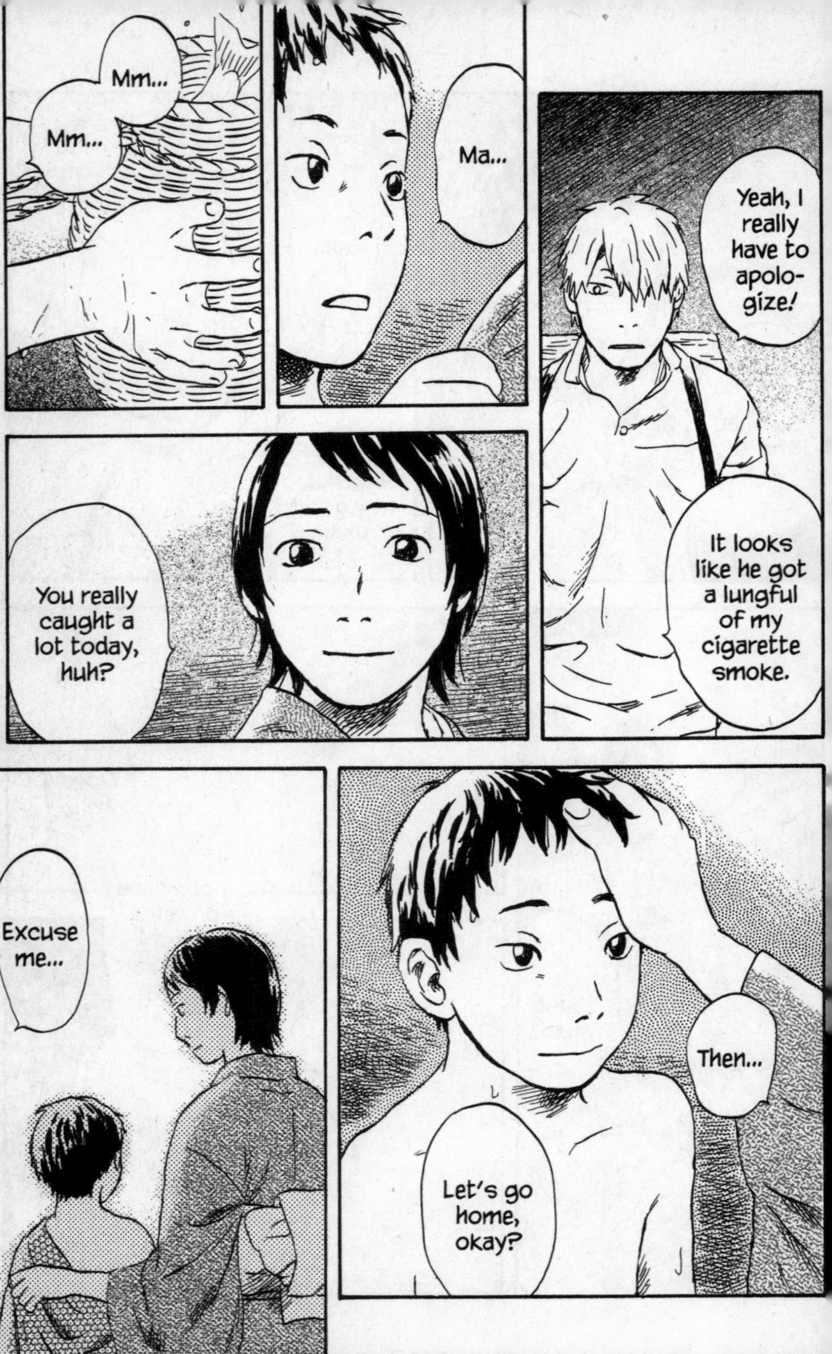

Yeah, I really have to apologize!
It looks like he got a lungful of my cigarette smoke.
Ma...
Mm...
Mm...
You really caught a lot today, huh?
Then...
Let's go home, okay?
Excuse me...

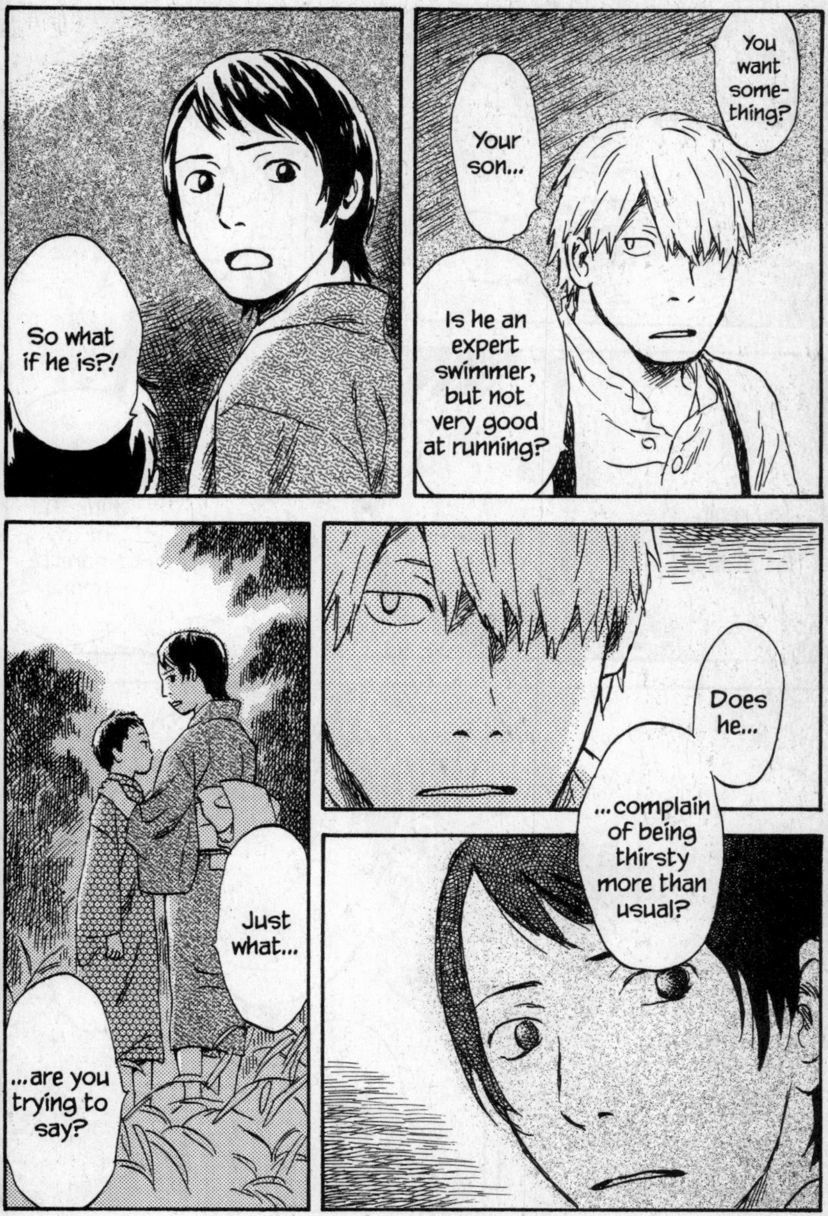
You want something?
Your son...
Is he an expert swimmer, but not very good at running?
So what if he is?!
Does he...
...complain of being thirsty more than usual?
Just what...
...are you trying to say?

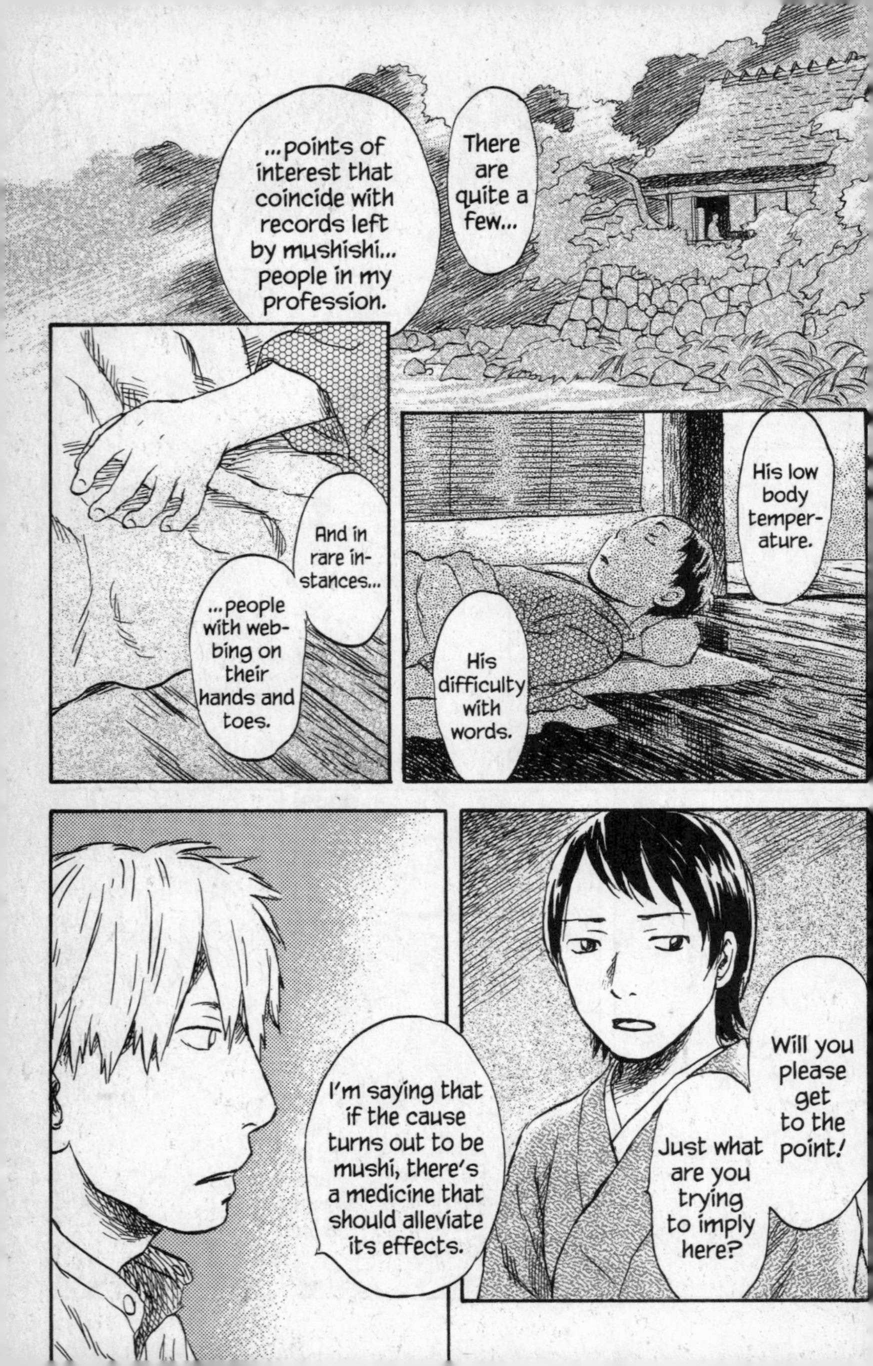
There are quite a few...
...points of interest that coincide with records left by mushishi... people in my profession.
His low body temper-ature.
His difficulty with words.
And in rare in-stances...
...people with web-bing on their hands and toes.
Will you please get to the point!
Just what are you trying to imply here?
I'm saying that if the cause turns out to be mushi, there's a medicine that should alleviate its effects.

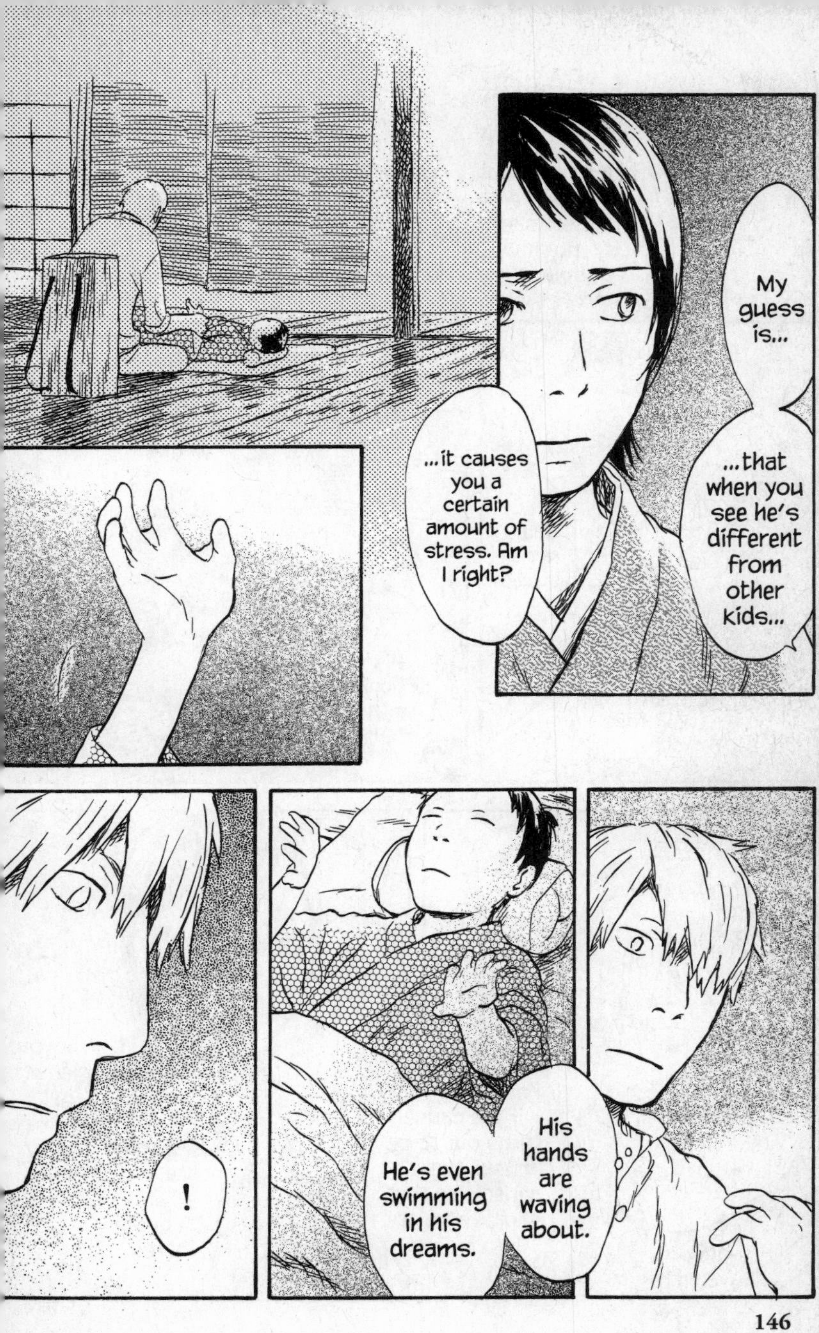
My guess is...
...that when you see he's different from other kids...
...it causes you a certain amount of stress. Am I right?
His hands are waving about.
He's even swimming in his dreams.
!

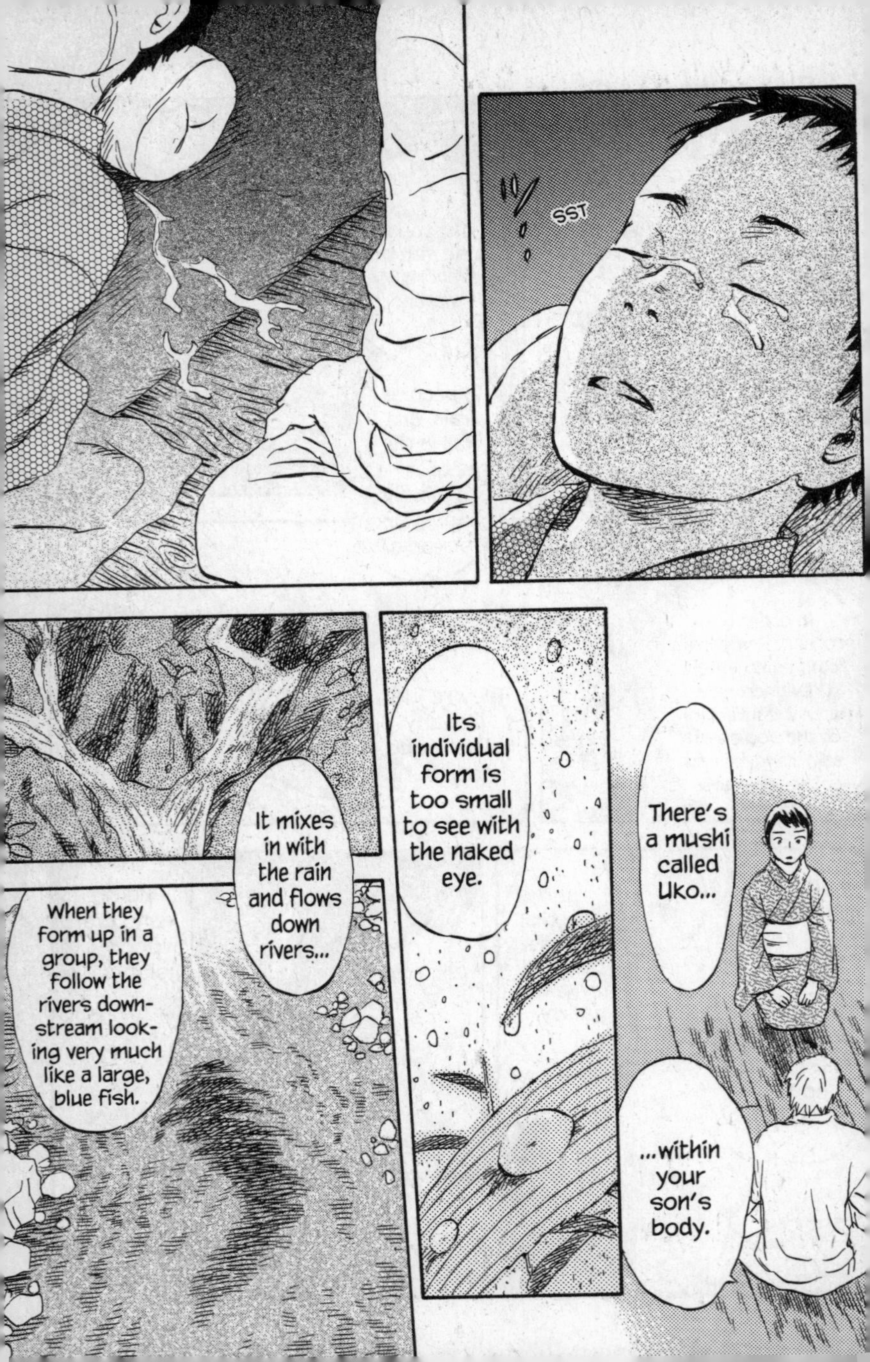
SST
There's a mushi called Uko...
...within your son's body.
Its individual form is too small to see with the naked eye.
It mixes in with the rain and flows down rivers...
When they form up in a group, they follow the rivers down-stream look-ing very much like a large, blue fish.

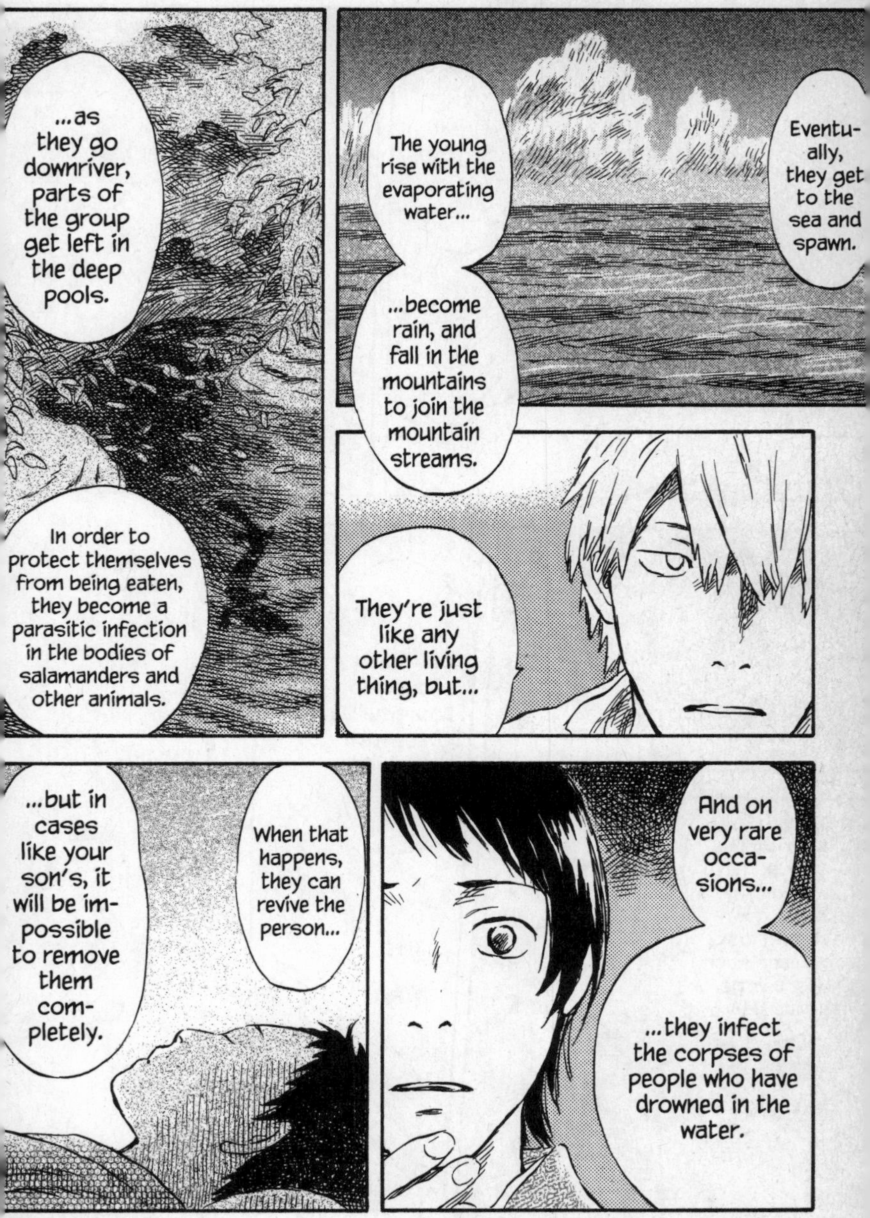
Eventu-ally, they get to the sea and spawn.
The young rise with the evaporating water...
...become rain, and fall in the mountains to join the mountain streams.
They're just like any other living thing, but...
...as they go downriver, parts of the group get left in the deep pools.
In order to protect themselves from being eaten, they become a parasitic infection in the bodies of salamanders and other animals.
And on very rare occa-sions...
...they infect the corpses of people who have drowned in the water.
When that happens, they can revive the person...
...but in cases like your son's, it will be im-possible to remove them com-pletely.

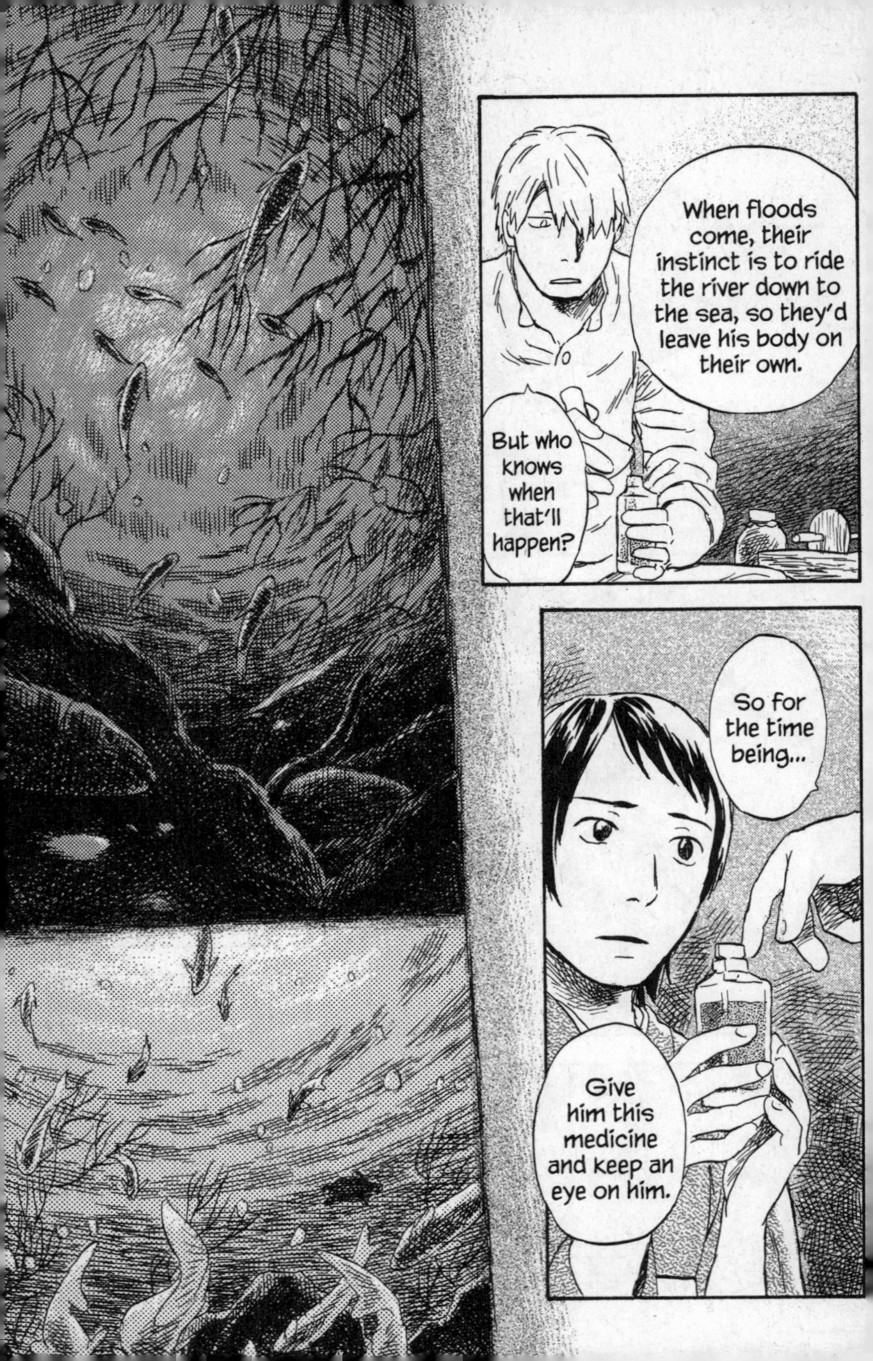
When floods come, their instinct is to ride the river down to the sea, so they'd leave his body on their own.
But who knows when that'll happen?
So for the time being...
Give him this medicine and keep an eye on him.

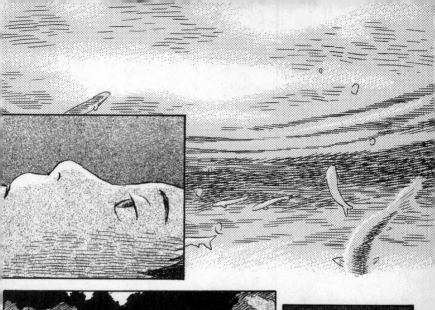

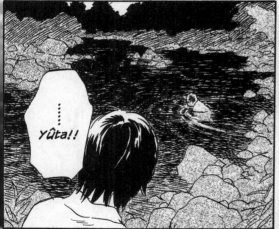

......
Yûta!!

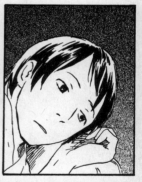

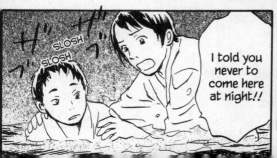

ブ"
SLOSH
ブ"
SLOSH

I told you never to come here at night!!

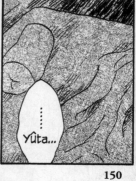

......
Yûta...

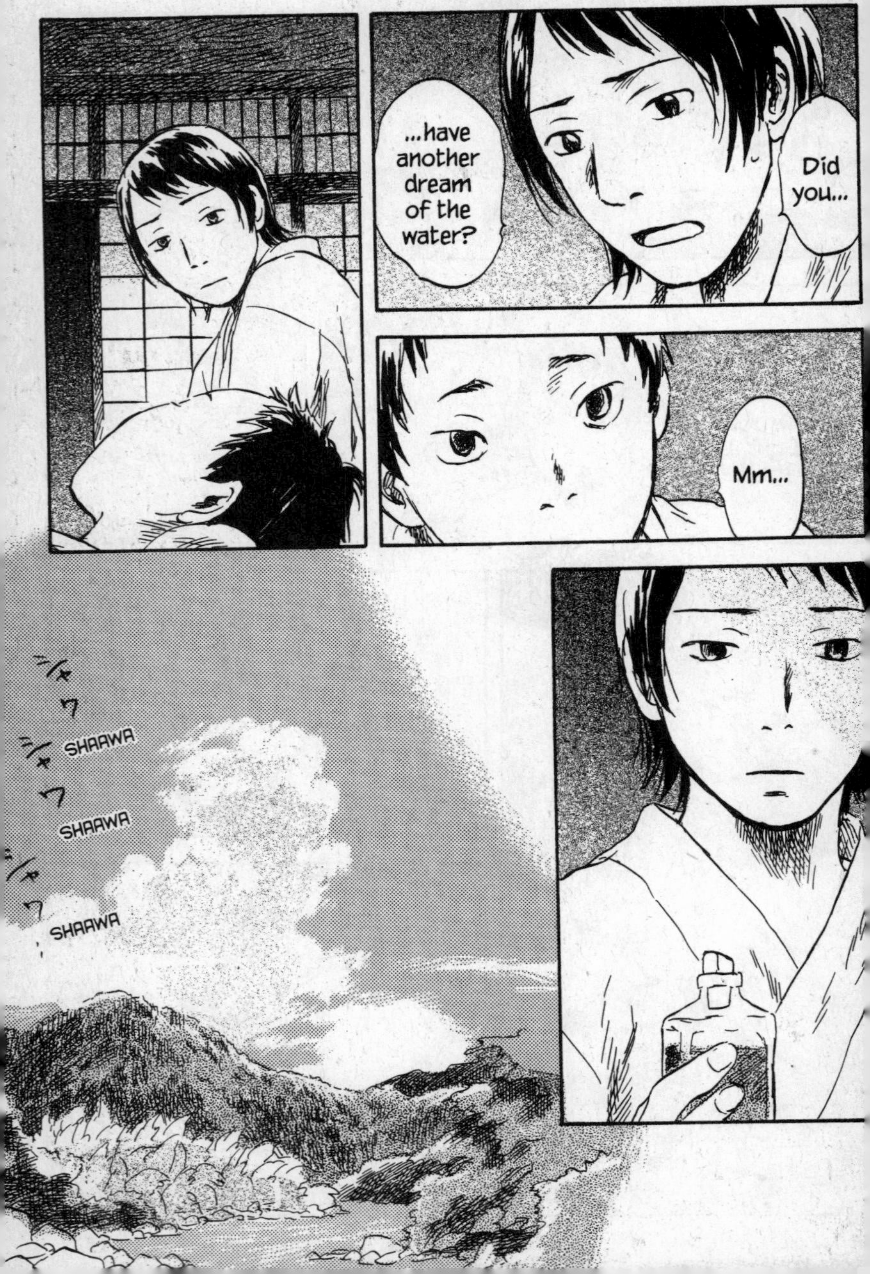
Did you...
...have another dream of the water?
Mm...
SHAAWA
SHAAWA
SHAAWA

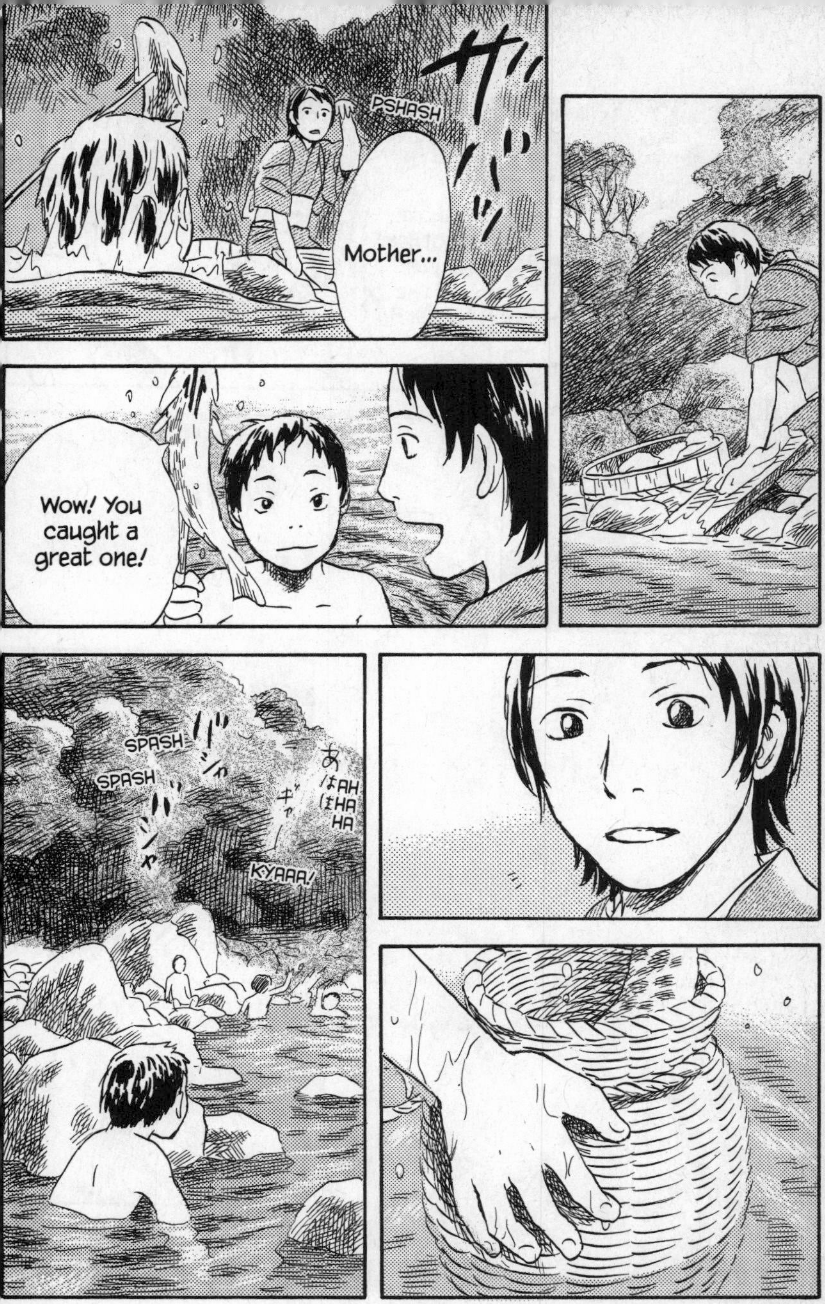
PSHASH
Mother...
Wow! You caught a great one!
SPASH
SPASH
AH HA HA
KYAAA!

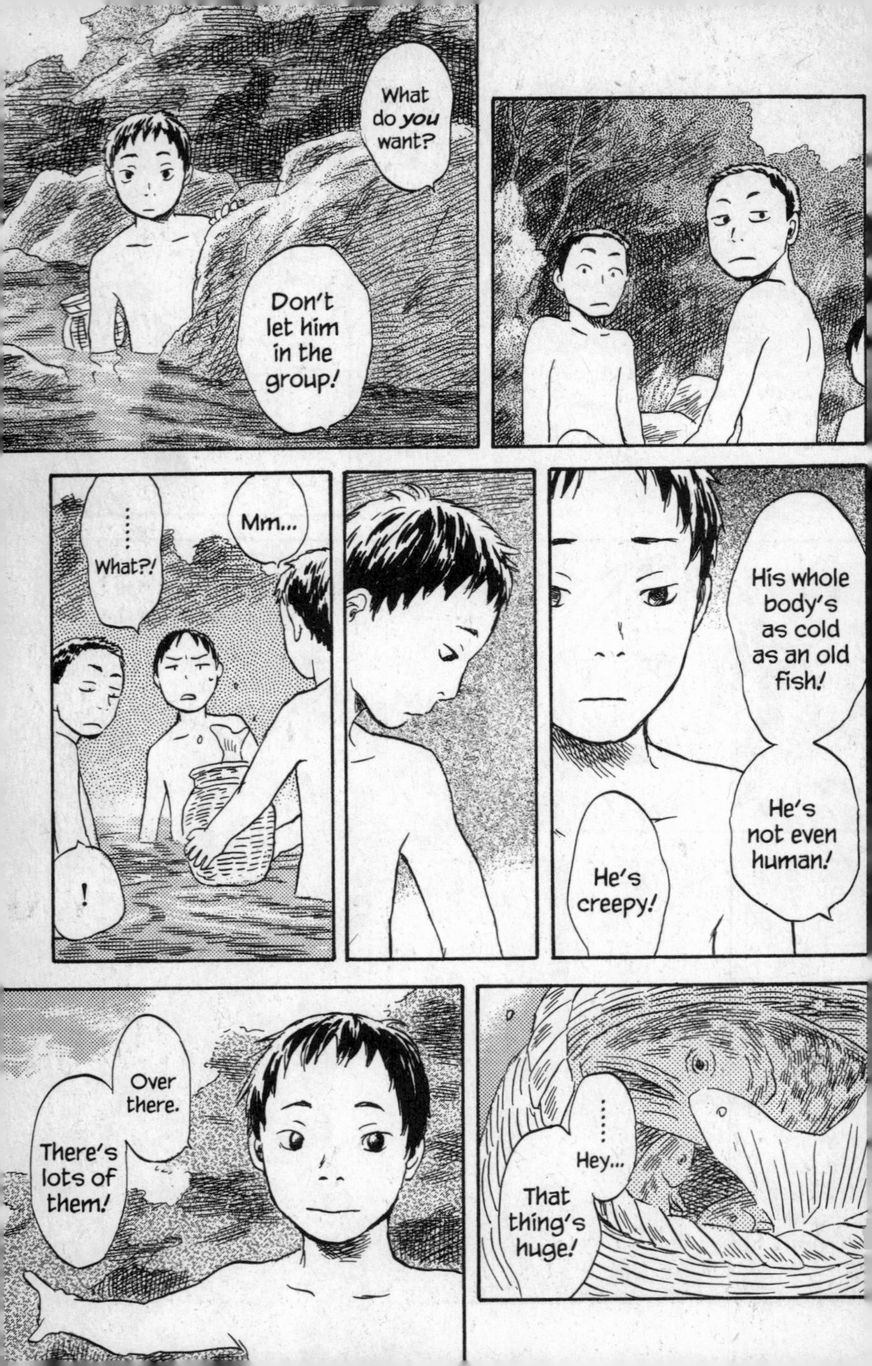
What do *you* want?
Don't let him in the group!
His whole body's as cold as an old fish!
He's not even human!
He's creepy!
Mm...
...... What?!
!
...... Hey...
That thing's huge!
Over there.
There's lots of them!

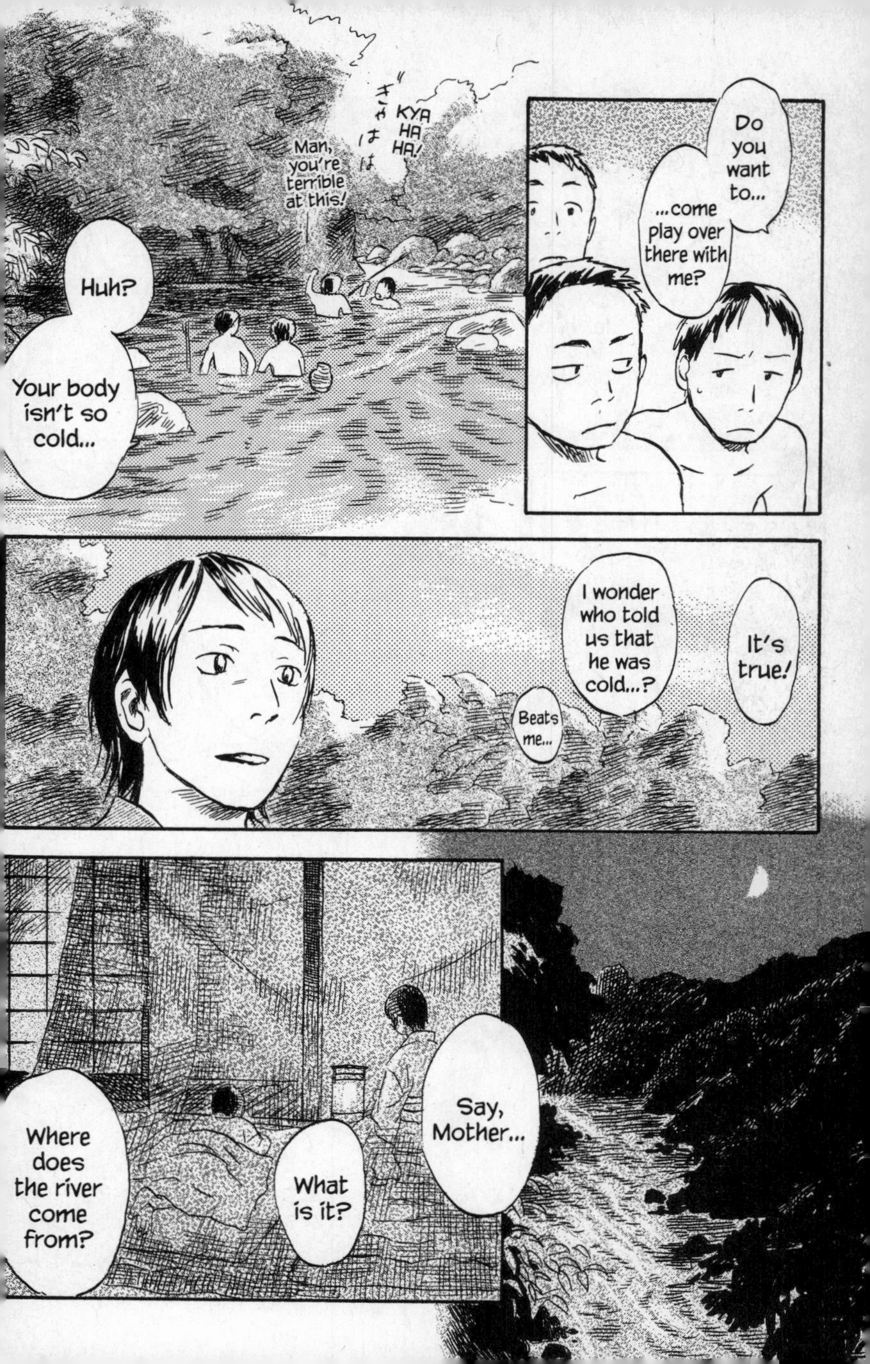
Do you want to...
...come play over there with me?
ぎゃはは
KYA HA HA!
Man, you're terrible at this!
Huh?
Your body isn't so cold...
It's true!
I wonder who told us that he was cold...?
Beats me...
Say, Mother...
What is it?
Where does the river come from?

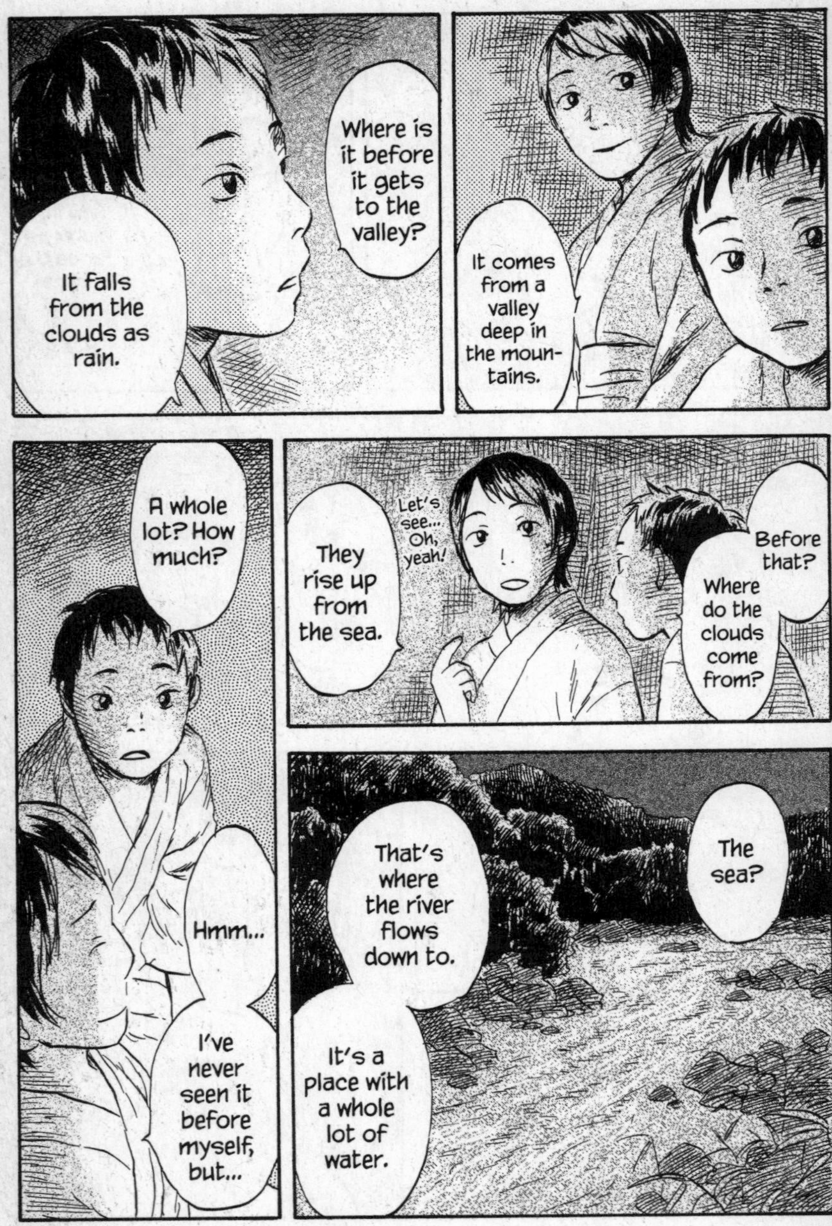
It comes from a valley deep in the moun-tains.
Where is it before it gets to the valley?
It falls from the clouds as rain.
Before that?
Where do the clouds come from?
Let's see... Oh, yeah!
They rise up from the sea.
The sea?
That's where the river flows down to.
It's a place with a whole lot of water.
A whole lot? How much?
Hmm...
I've never seen it before myself, but...

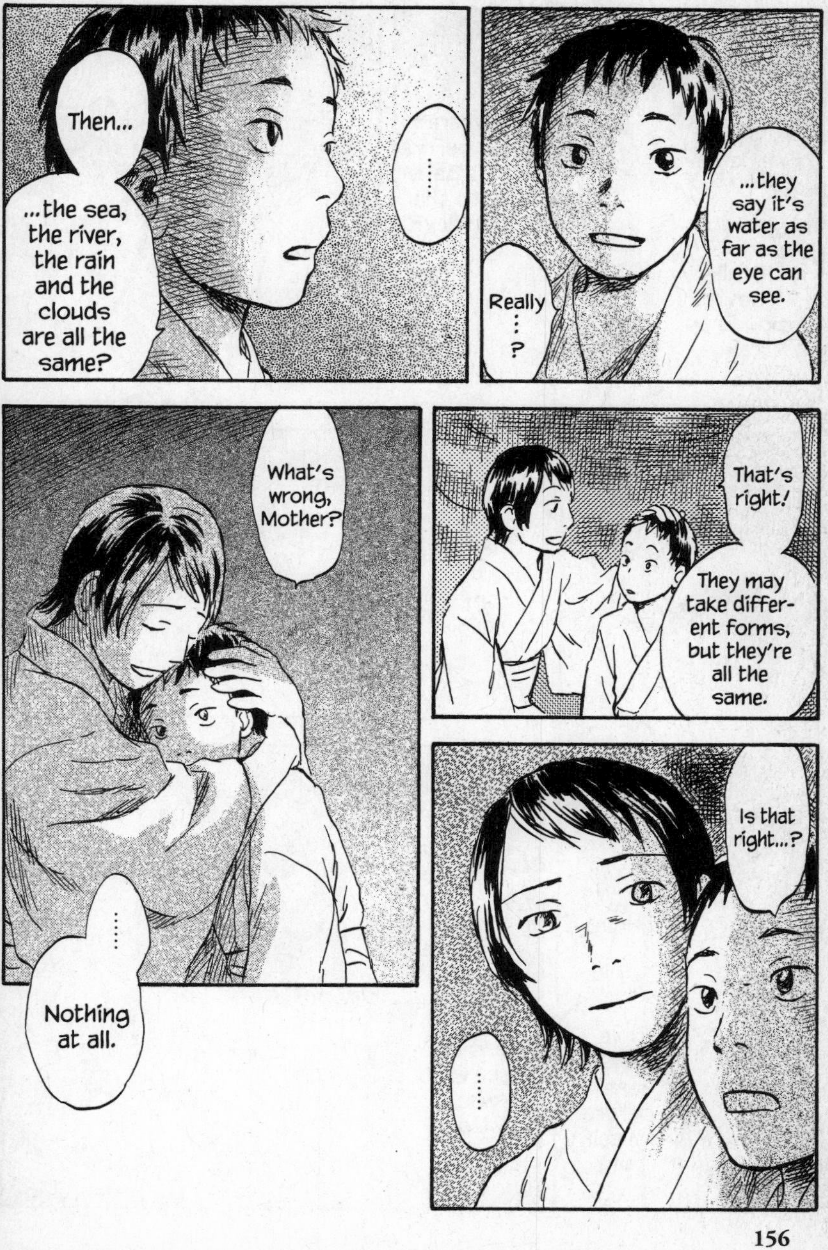
...they say it's water as far as the eye can see.
Really...?
......
Then...
...the sea, the river, the rain and the clouds are all the same?
That's right!
They may take different forms, but they're all the same.
Is that right...?
......
What's wrong, Mother?
......
Nothing at all.

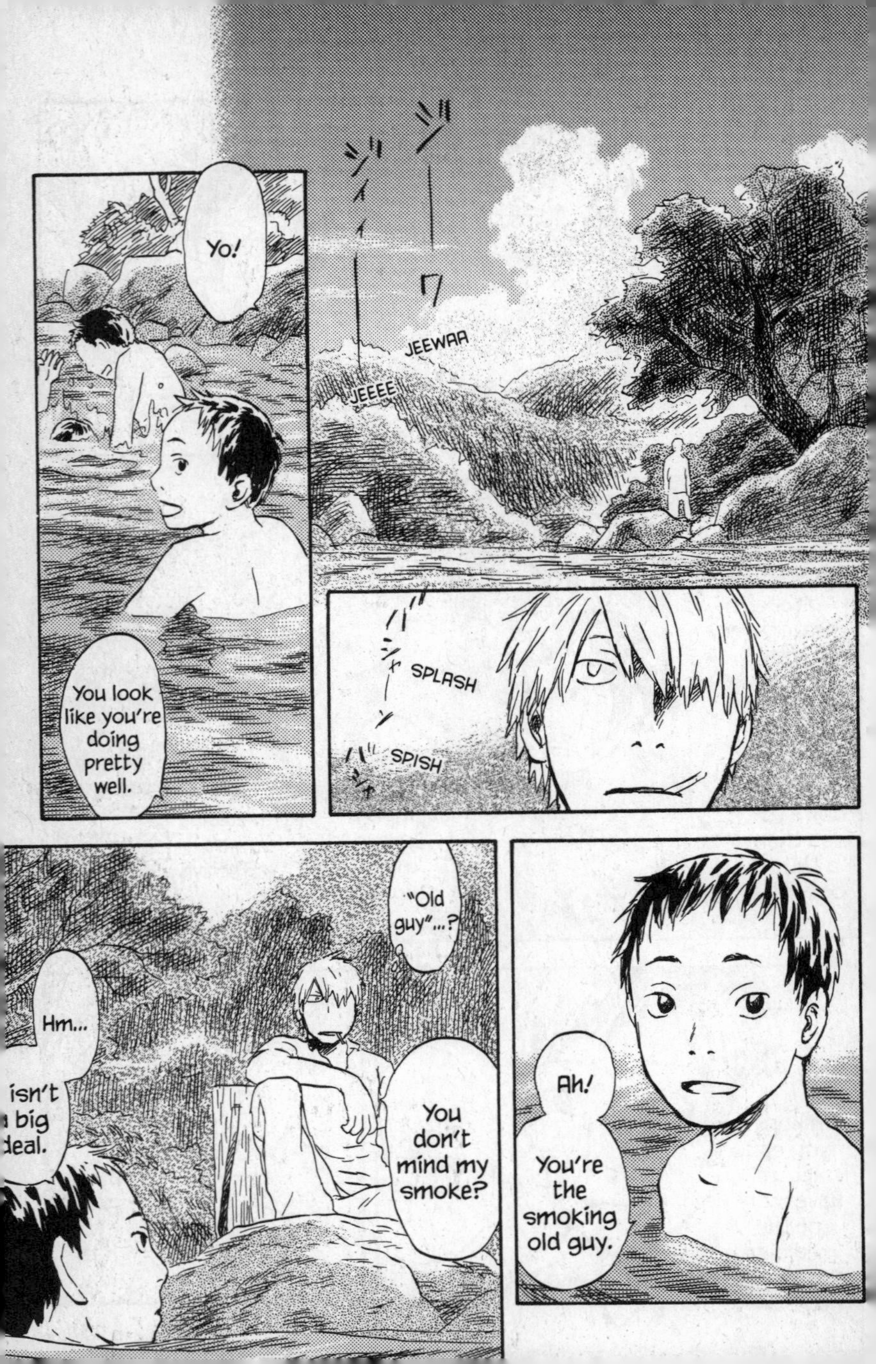
JEEWAA
JEEEE
SPLASH
SPISH
Yo!
You look like you're doing pretty well.
Ah!
You're the smoking old guy.
"Old guy"...?
You don't mind my smoke?
Hm...
isn't big deal.

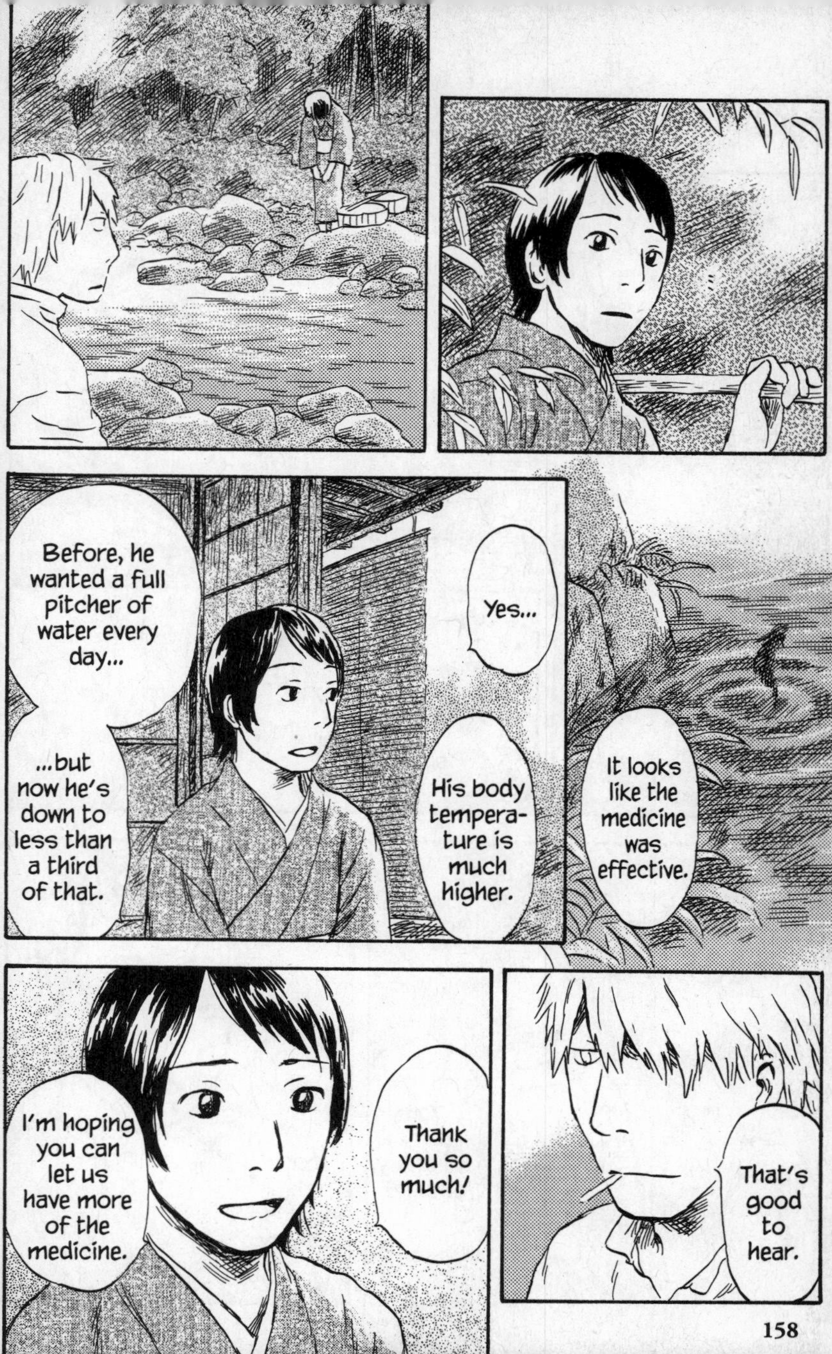
It looks like the medicine was effective.
Yes...
His body temperature is much higher.
Before, he wanted a full pitcher of water every day...
...but now he's down to less than a third of that.
That's good to hear.
Thank you so much!
I'm hoping you can let us have more of the medicine.

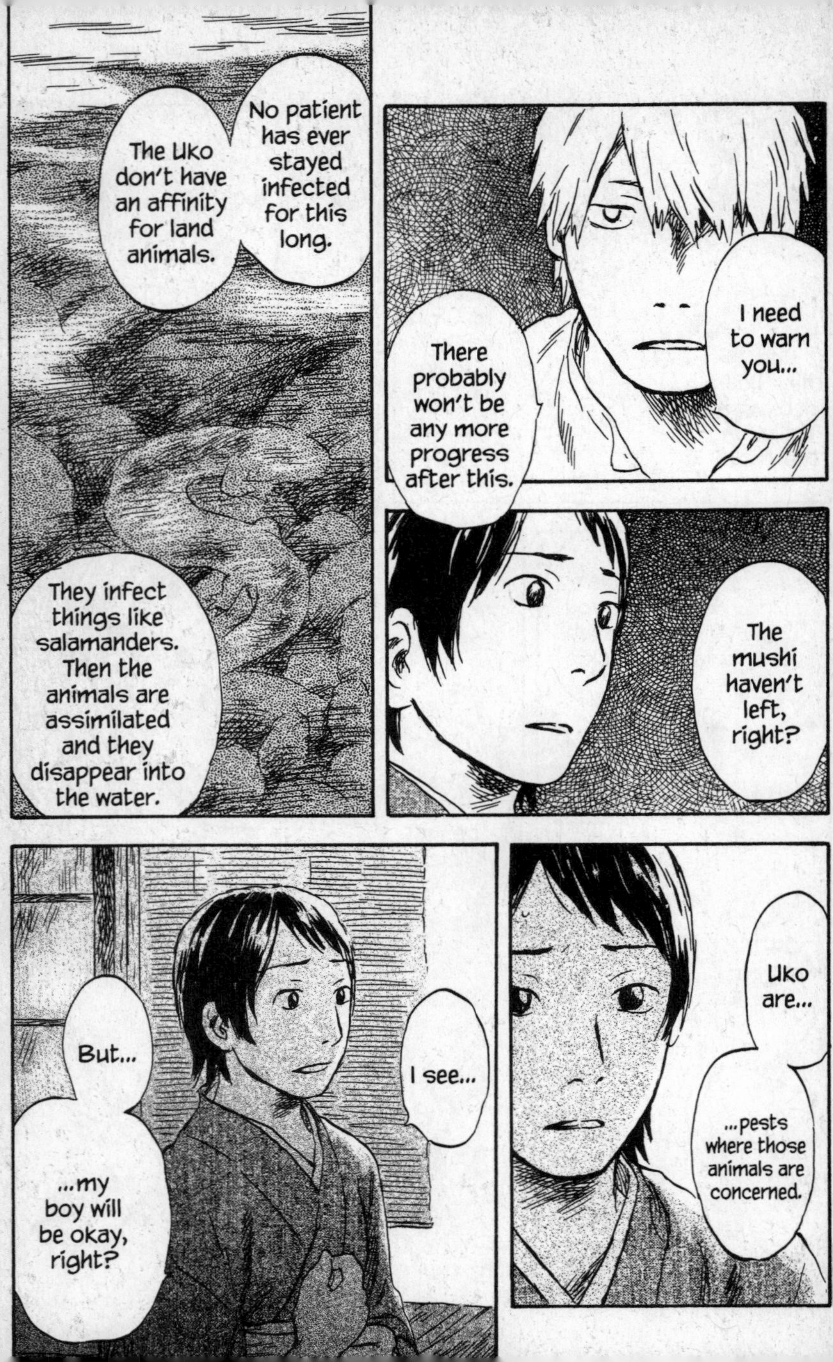
I need to warn you...
There probably won't be any more progress after this.
The mushi haven't left, right?
No patient has ever stayed infected for this long.
The Uko don't have an affinity for land animals.
They infect things like salamanders. Then the animals are assimilated and they disappear into the water.
Uko are...
...pests where those animals are concerned.
I see...
But...
...my boy will be okay, right?

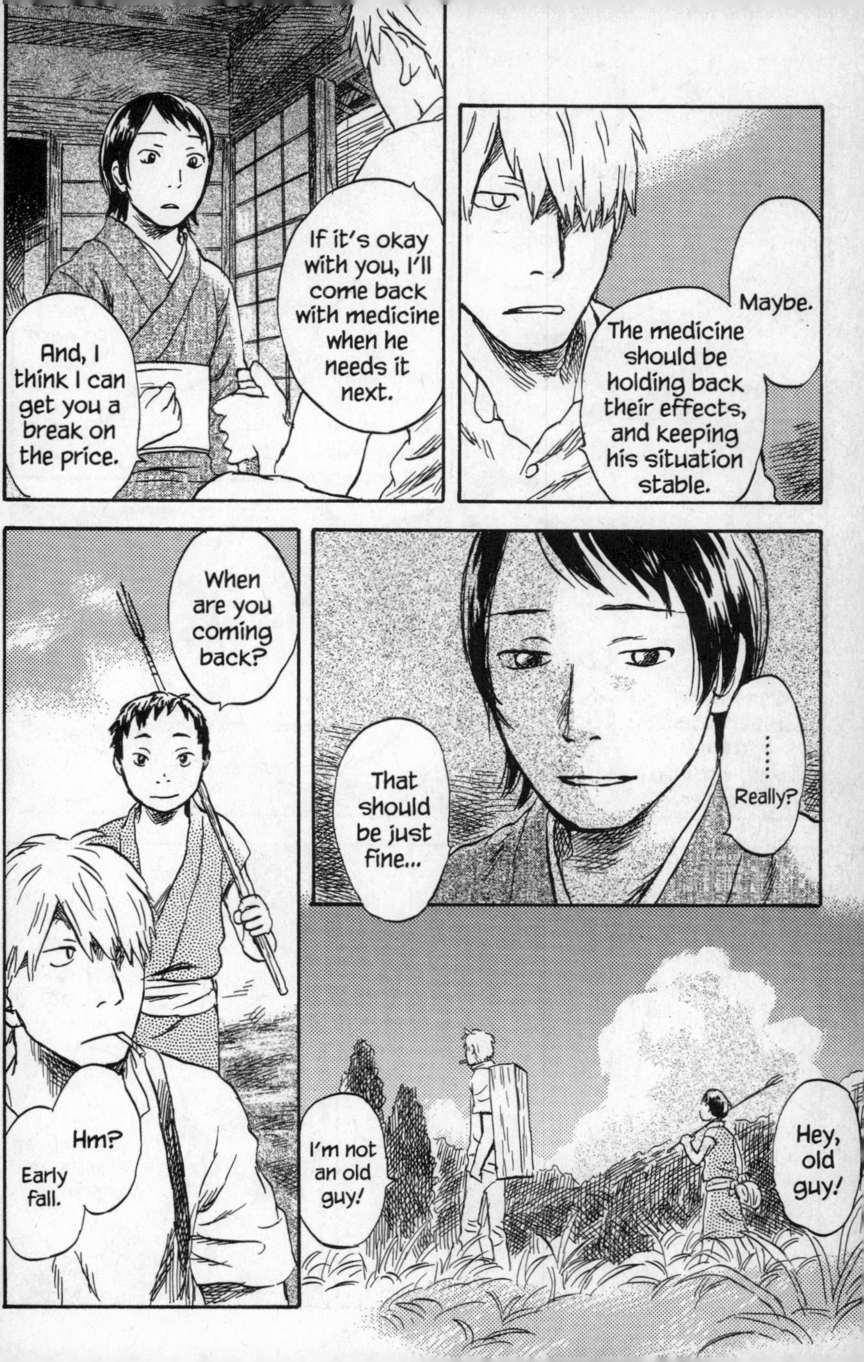
Maybe.
The medicine should be holding back their effects, and keeping his situation stable.
If it's okay with you, I'll come back with medicine when he needs it next.
And, I think I can get you a break on the price.
……
Really?
That should be just fine...
Hey, old guy!
I'm not an old guy!
When are you coming back?
Hm?
Early fall.

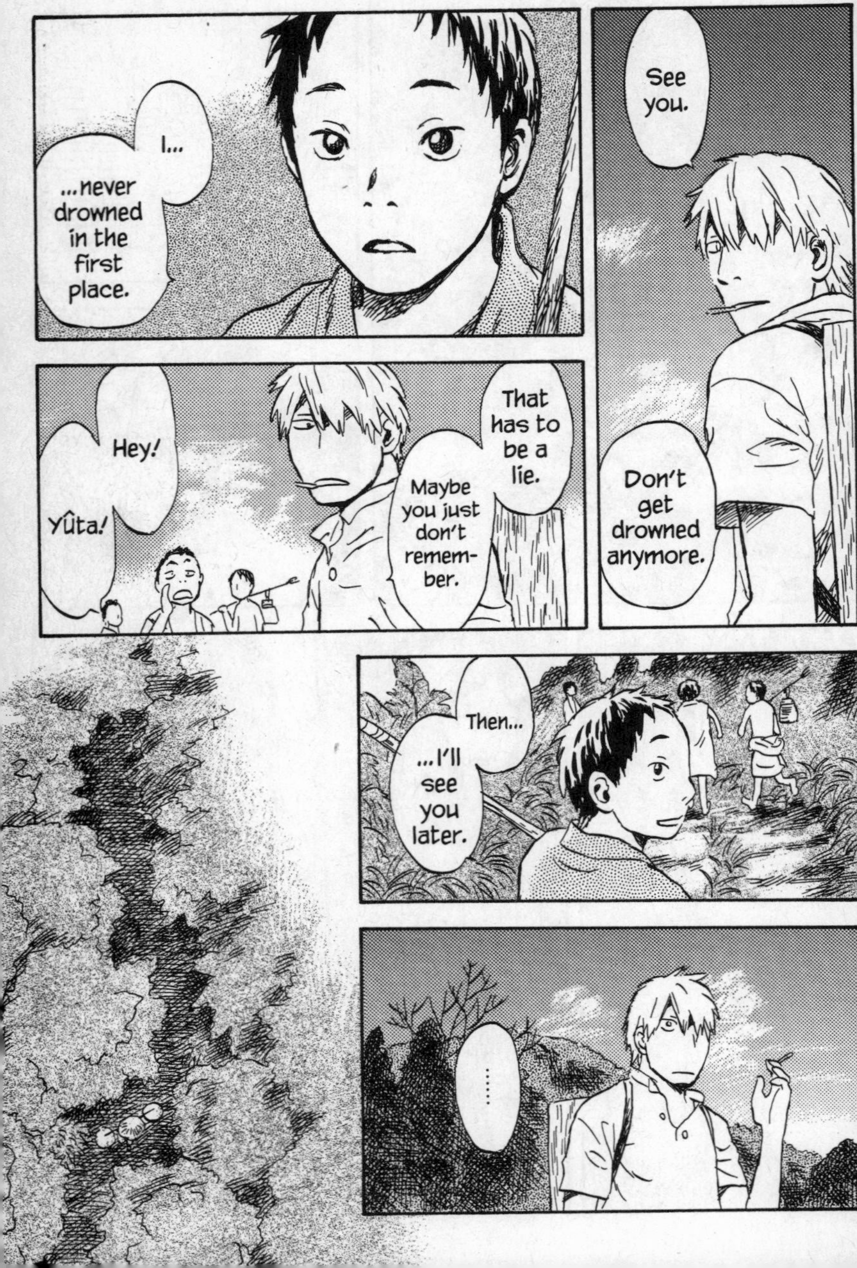
See you.
Don't get drowned anymore.
I...
...never drowned in the first place.
That has to be a lie.
Maybe you just don't remember.
Hey!
Yûta!
Then...
...I'll see you later.
......

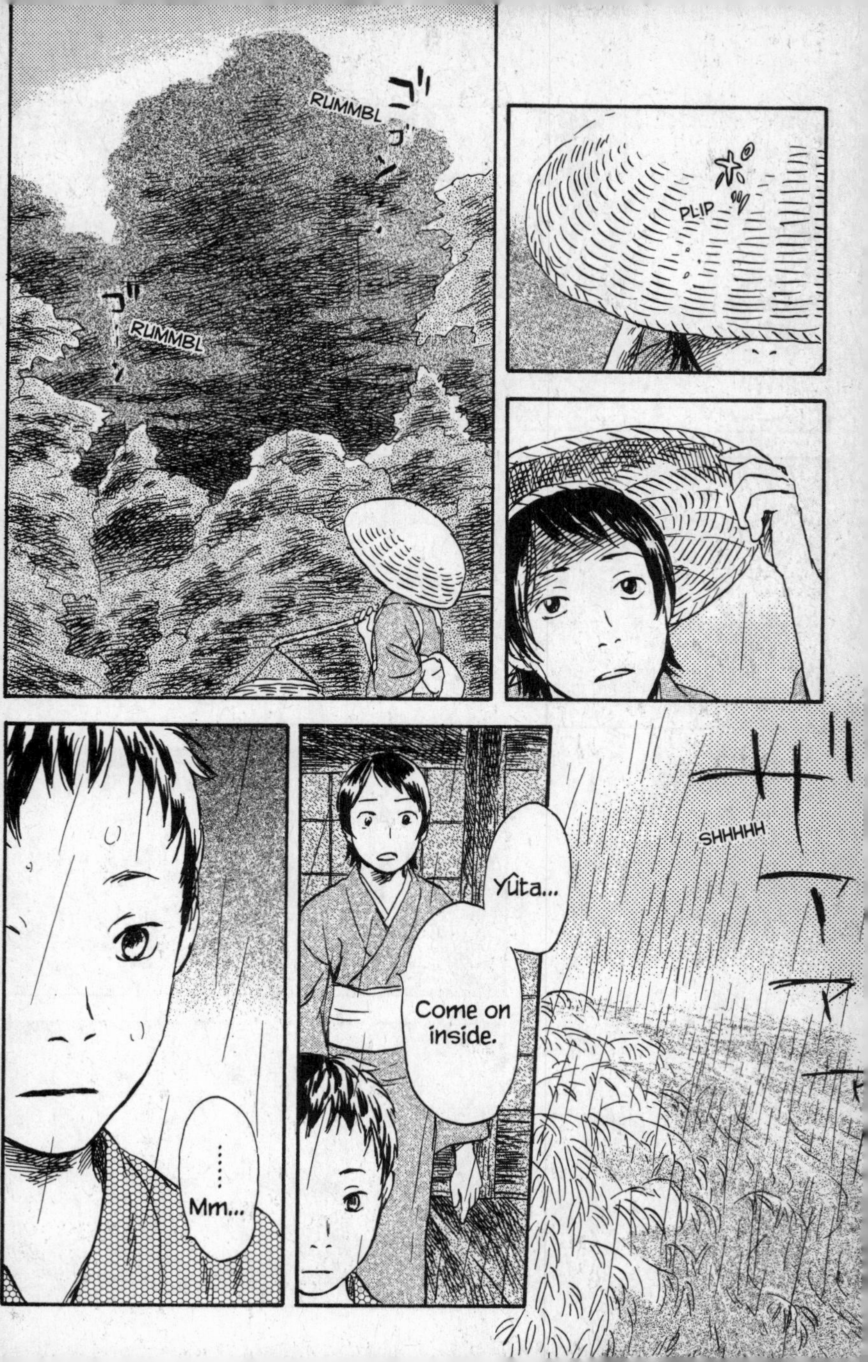
PLIP
RUMMBL
RUMMBL
SHHHHH
Yûta...
Come on inside.
......
Mm...

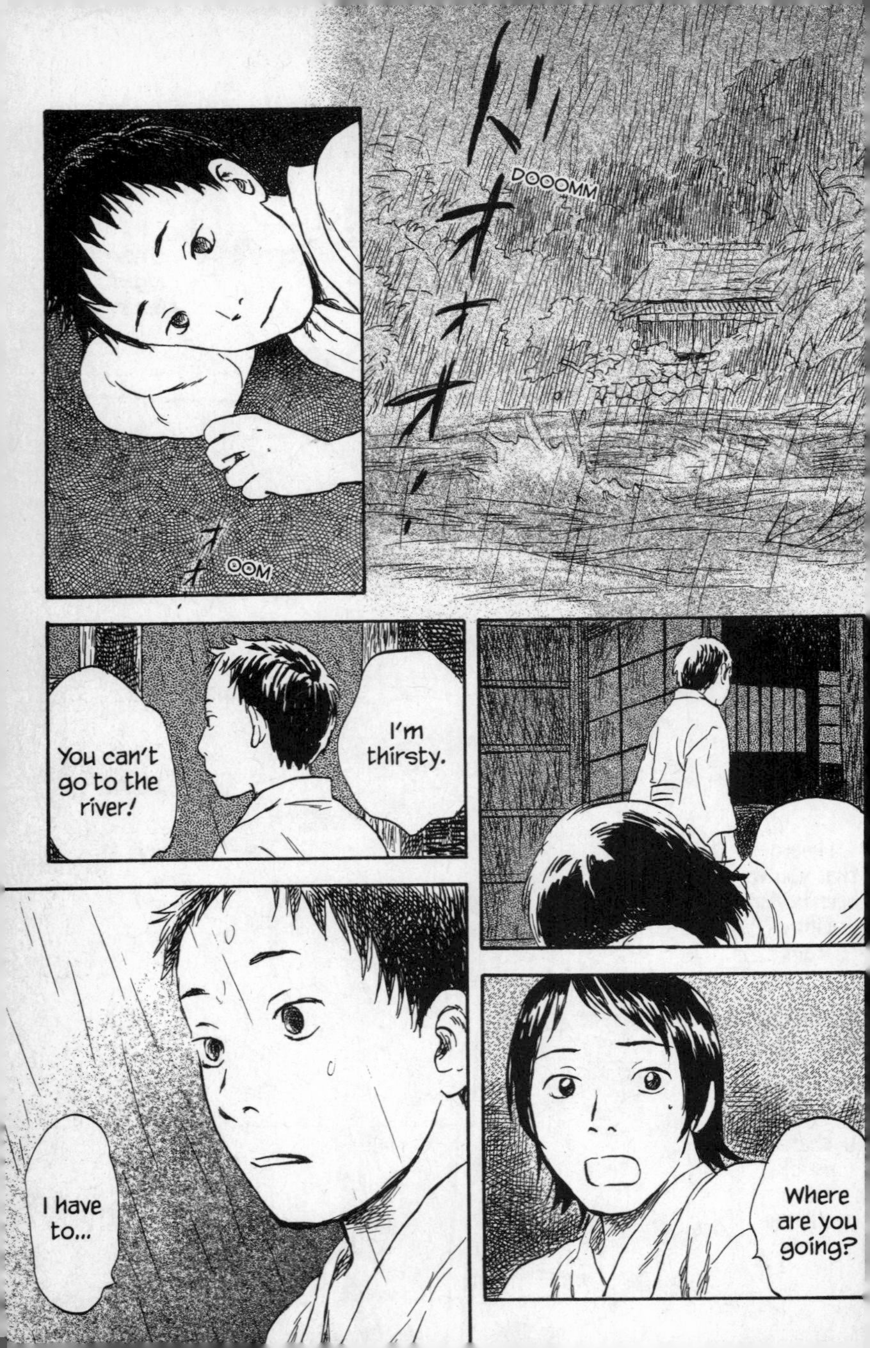
DOOOMM
OOM
I'm thirsty.
You can't go to the river!
Where are you going?
I have to...

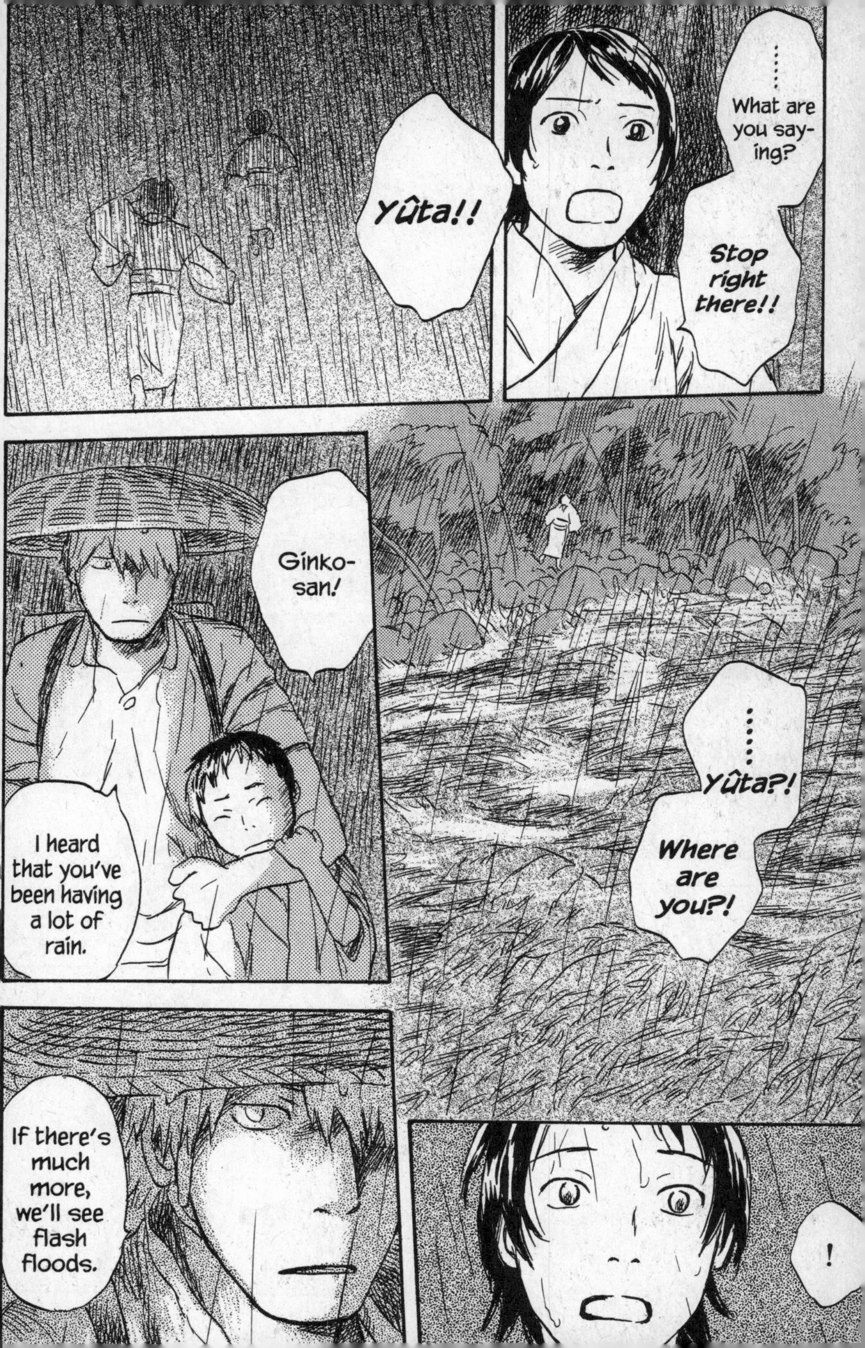
......What are you saying?
Stop right there!!
Yûta!!
......Yûta?!
Where are you?!
Ginko-san!
I heard that you've been having a lot of rain.
!
If there's much more, we'll see flash floods.

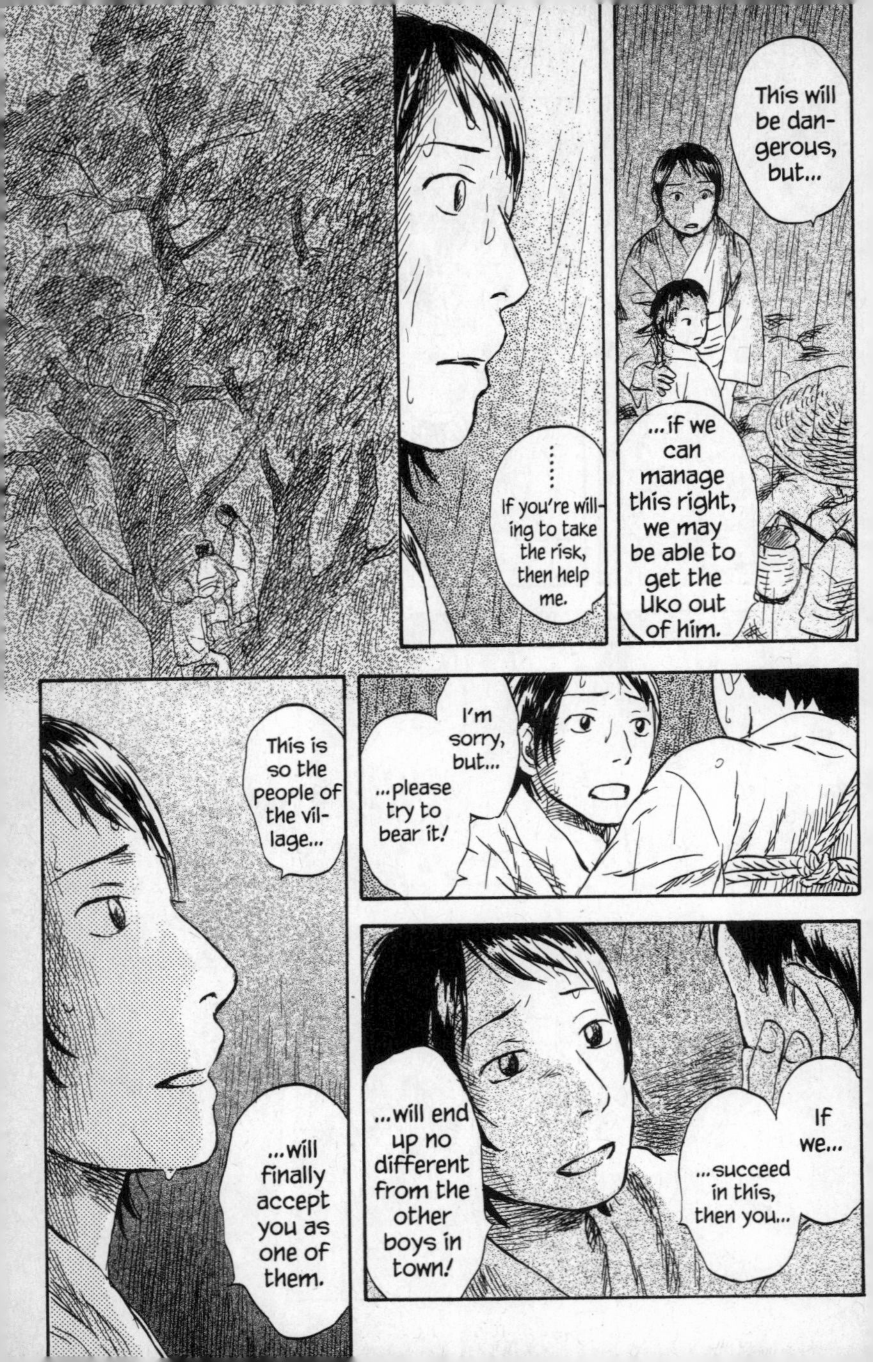
This will be dan-gerous, but...
...if we can manage this right, we may be able to get the Uko out of him.
......
If you're will-ing to take the risk, then help me.
I'm sorry, but...
...please try to bear it!
If we...
...succeed in this, then you...
...will end up no different from the other boys in town!
This is so the people of the vil-lage...
...will finally accept you as one of them.

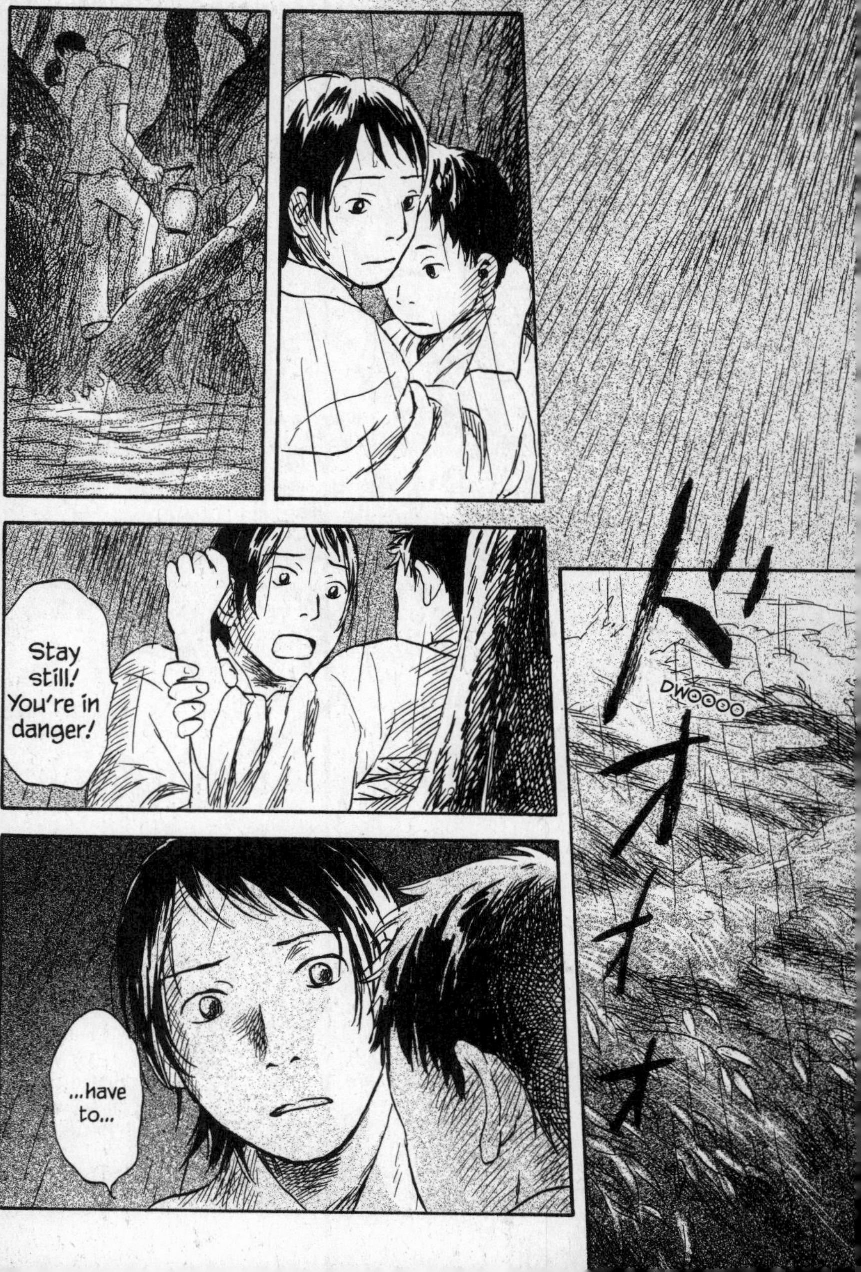
DWOOOO
Stay still! You're in danger!
...have to...

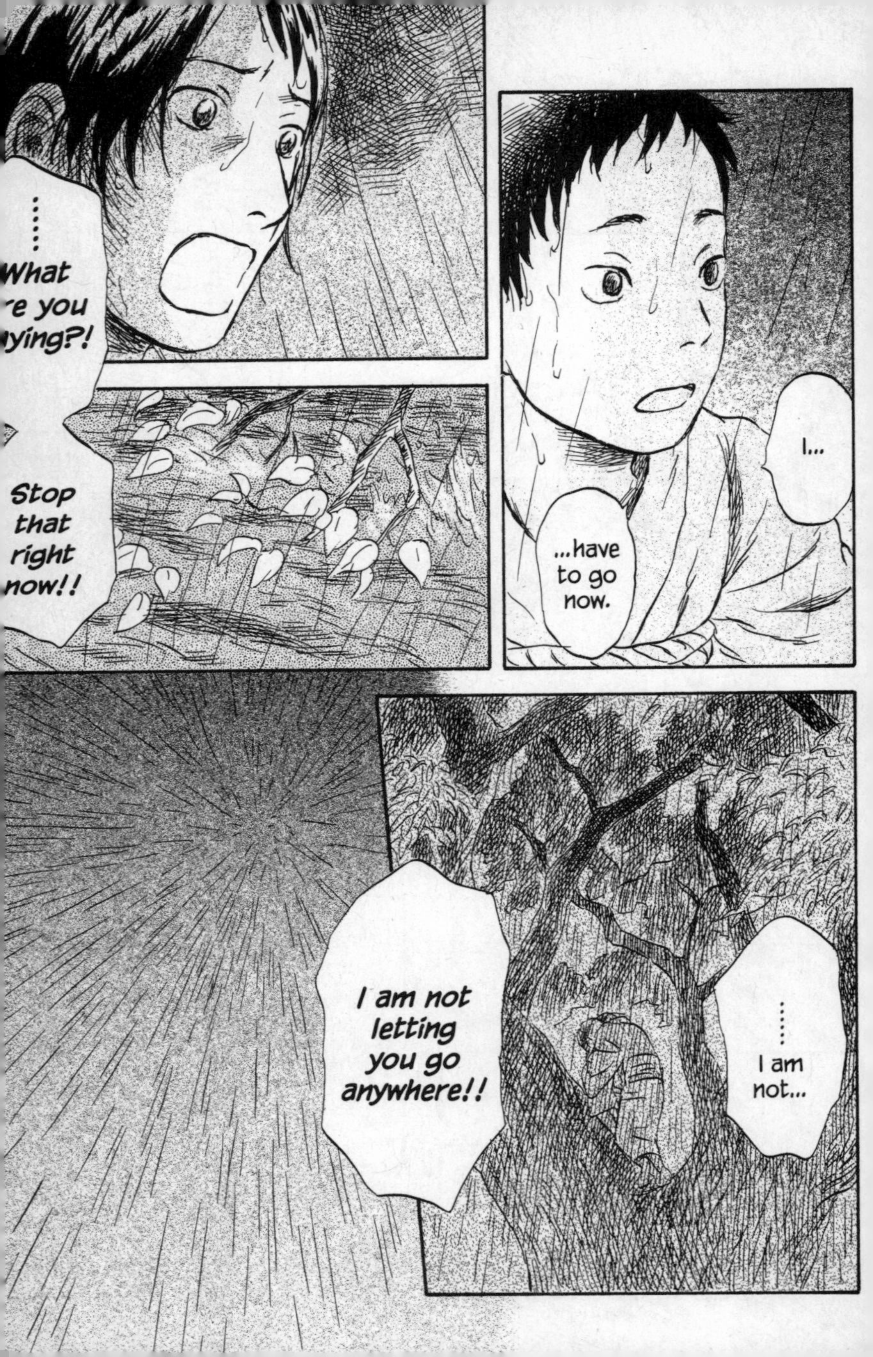
I...
...have to go now.
......What e you ying?!
Stop that right now!!
...... I am not...
I am not letting you go anywhere!!

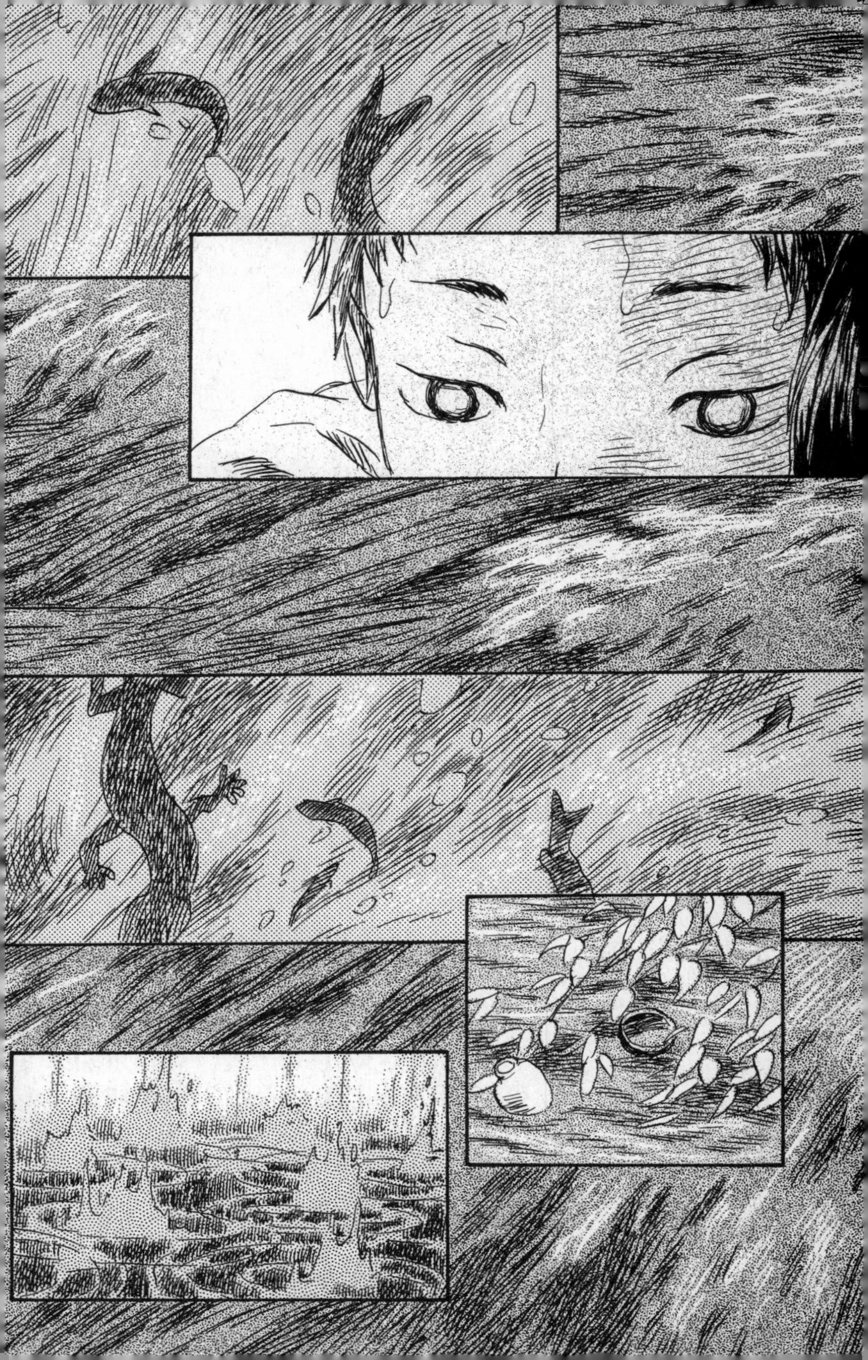

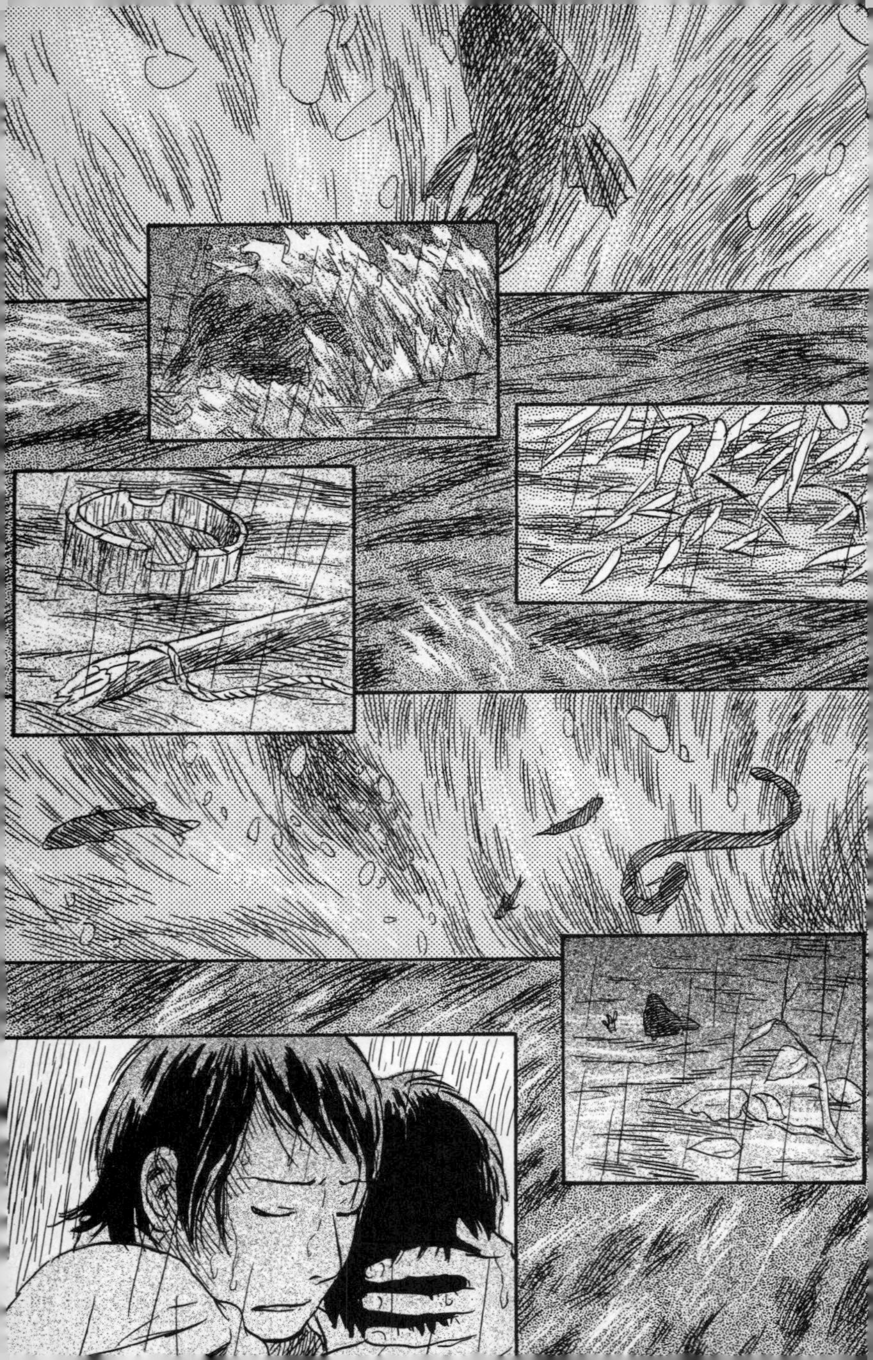

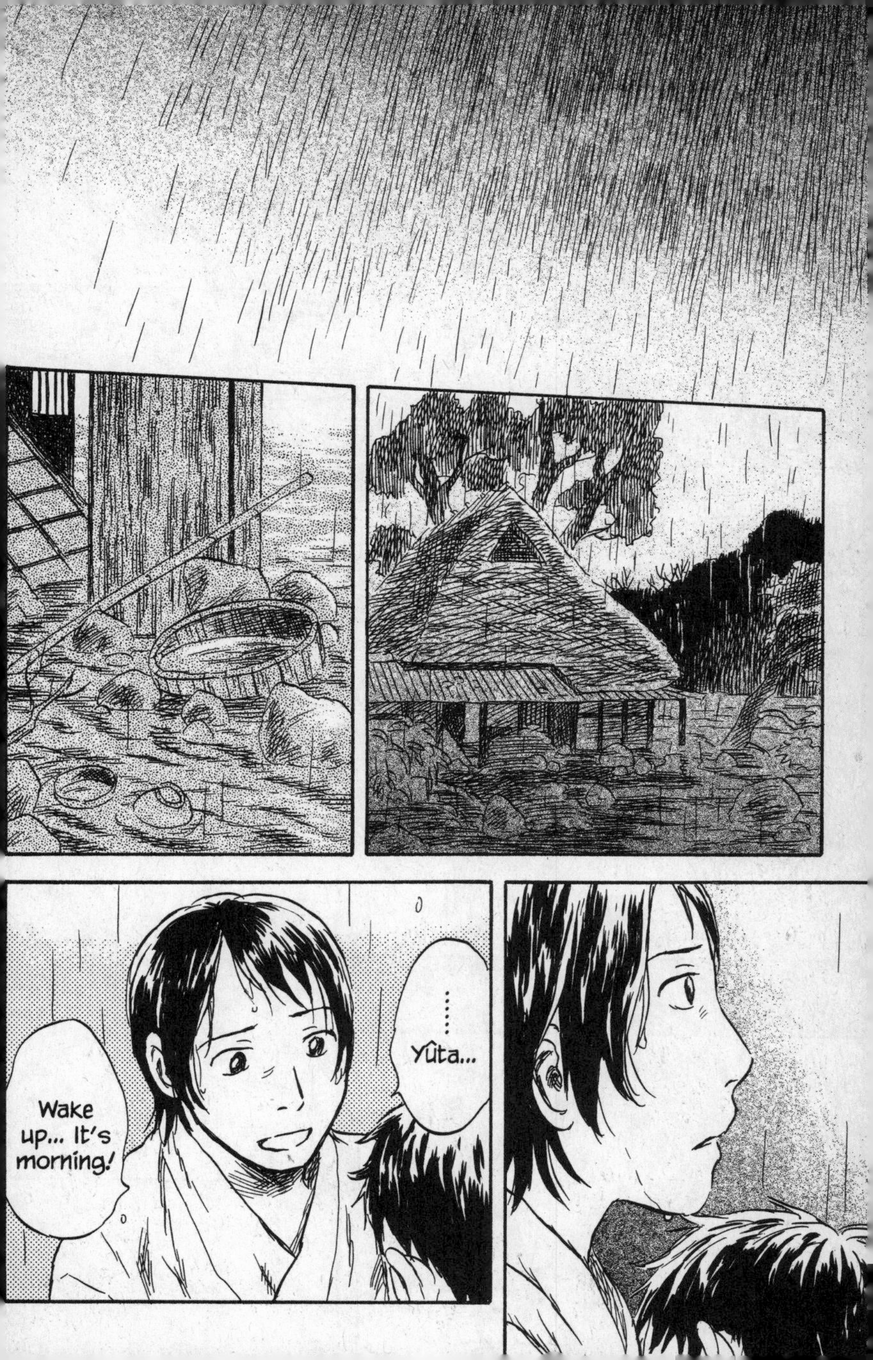
......
Yûta...
Wake up... It's morning!

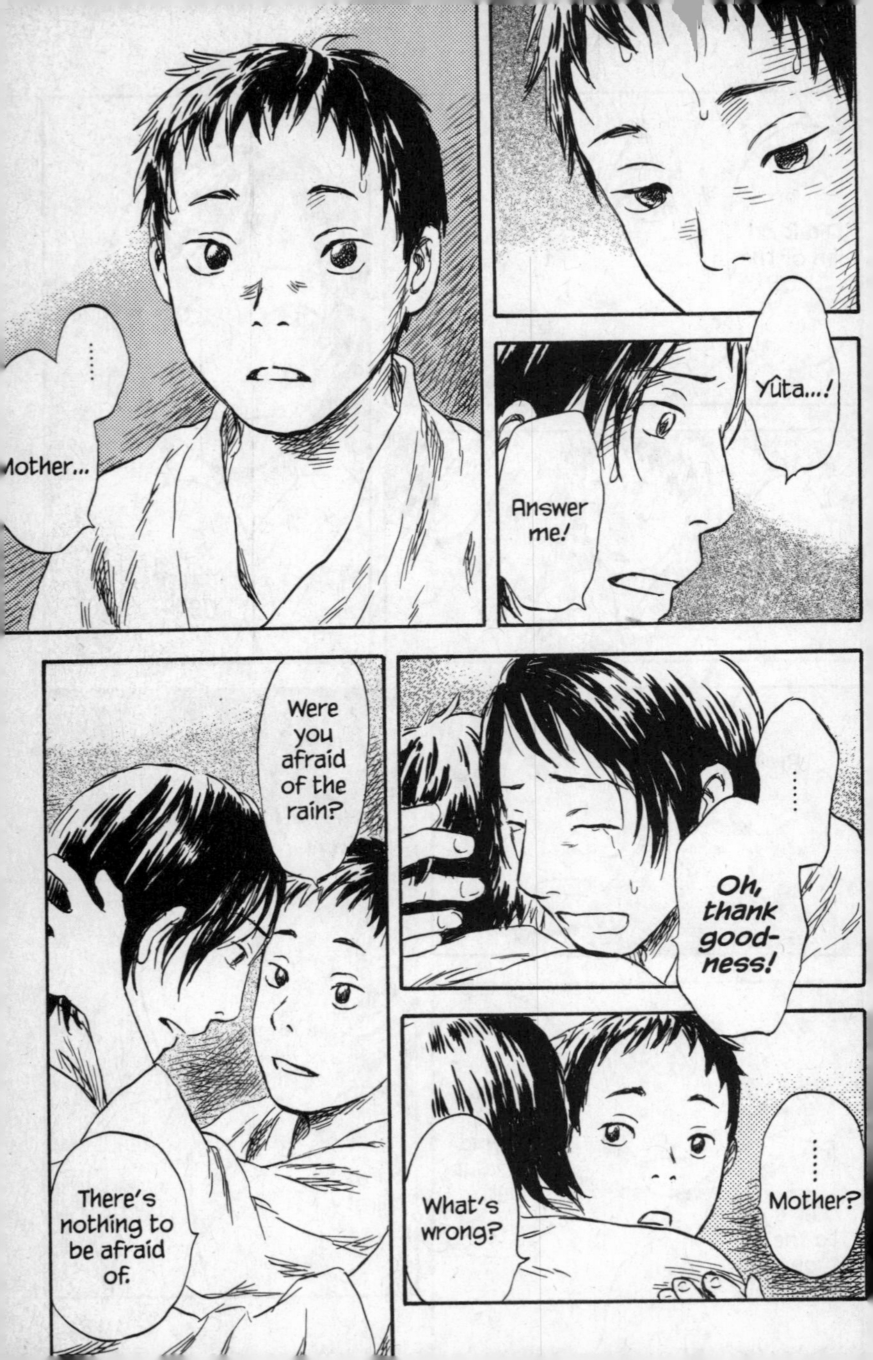
Yûta...!
Answer me!
......
Mother...
......
Oh, thank goodness!
...... Mother?
What's wrong?
Were you afraid of the rain?
There's nothing to be afraid of.

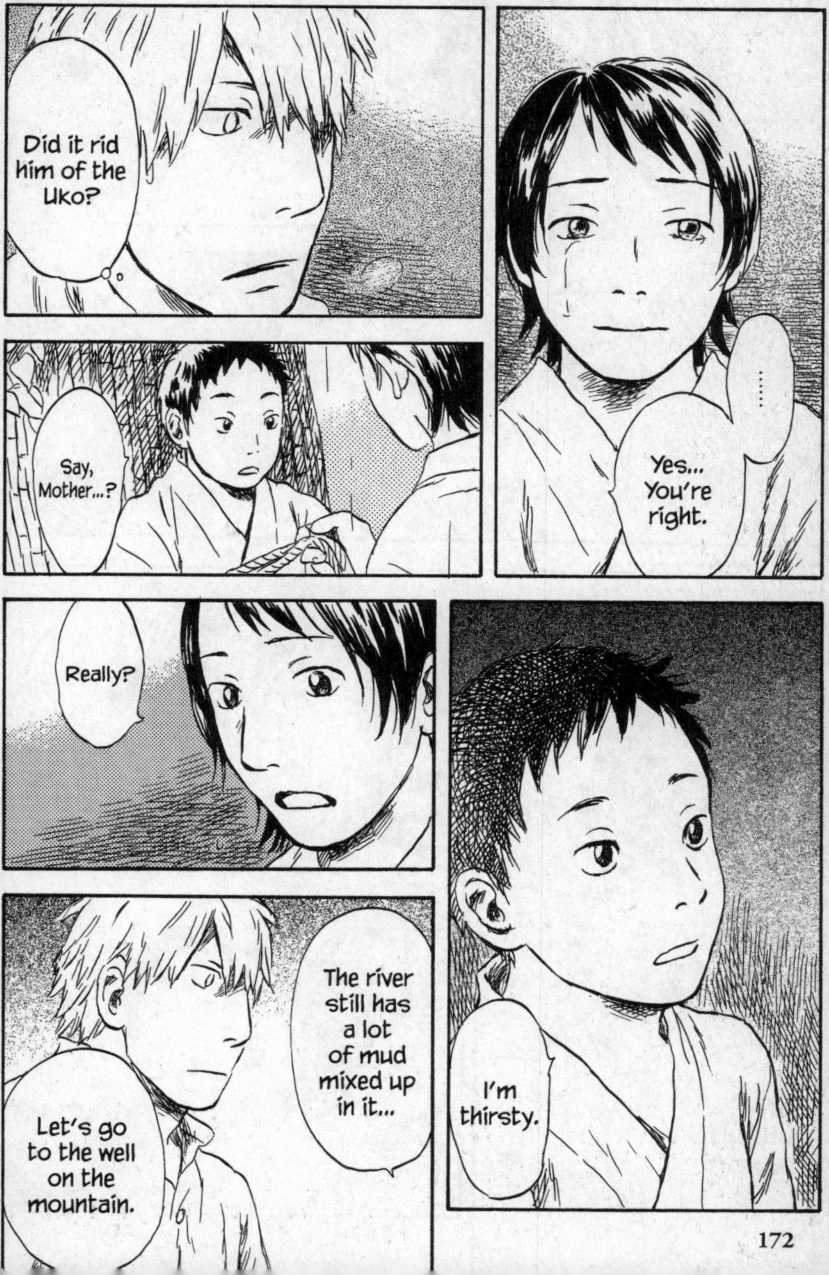
......
Yes... You're right.
Did it rid him of the Uko?
Say, Mother...?
I'm thirsty.
Really?
The river still has a lot of mud mixed up in it...
Let's go to the well on the mountain.

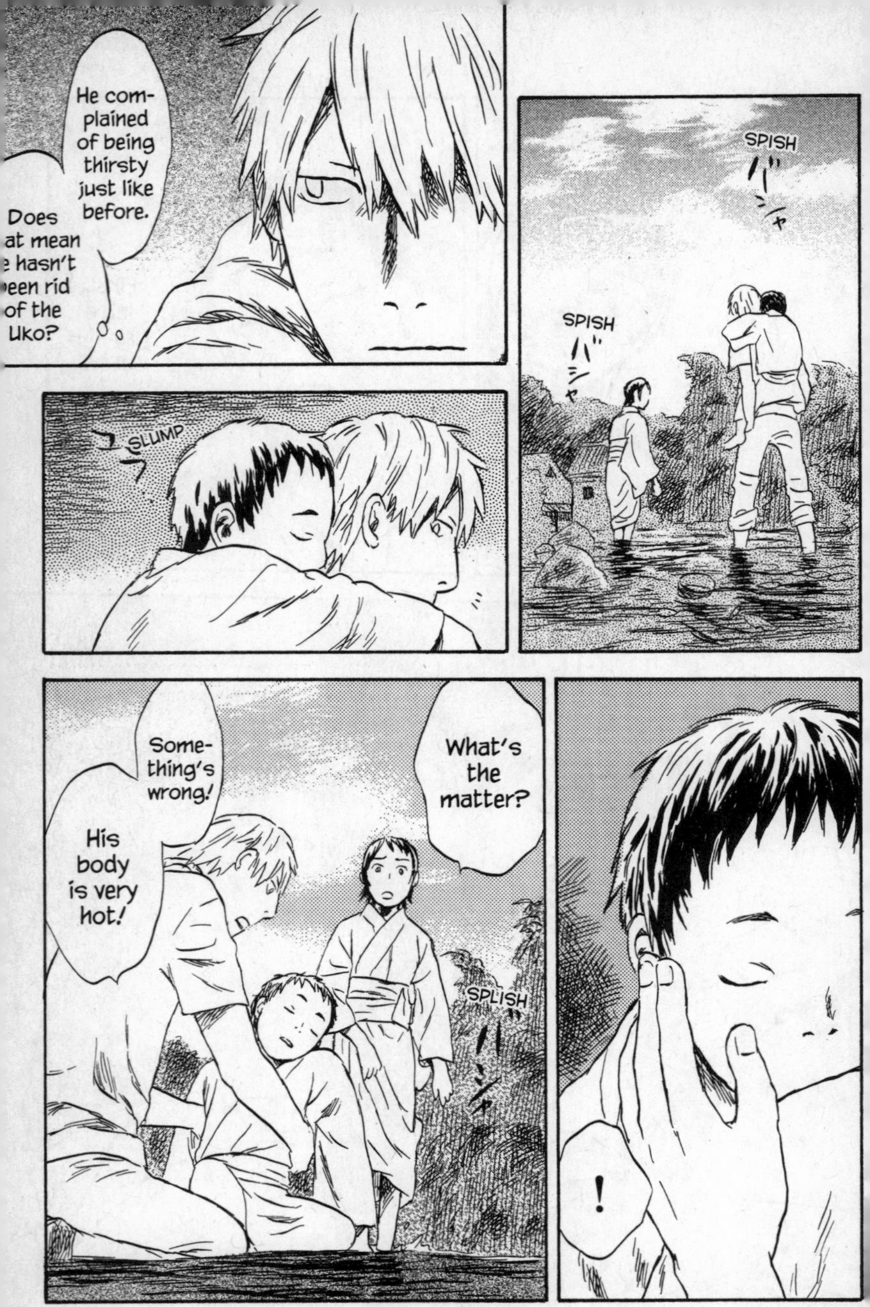
He complained of being thirsty just like before.
Does at mean e hasn't een rid of the Uko?
SPISH
バシャ
SPISH
バシャ
SLUMP
!
What's the matter?
Something's wrong!
His body is very hot!
SPLISH
バシャ

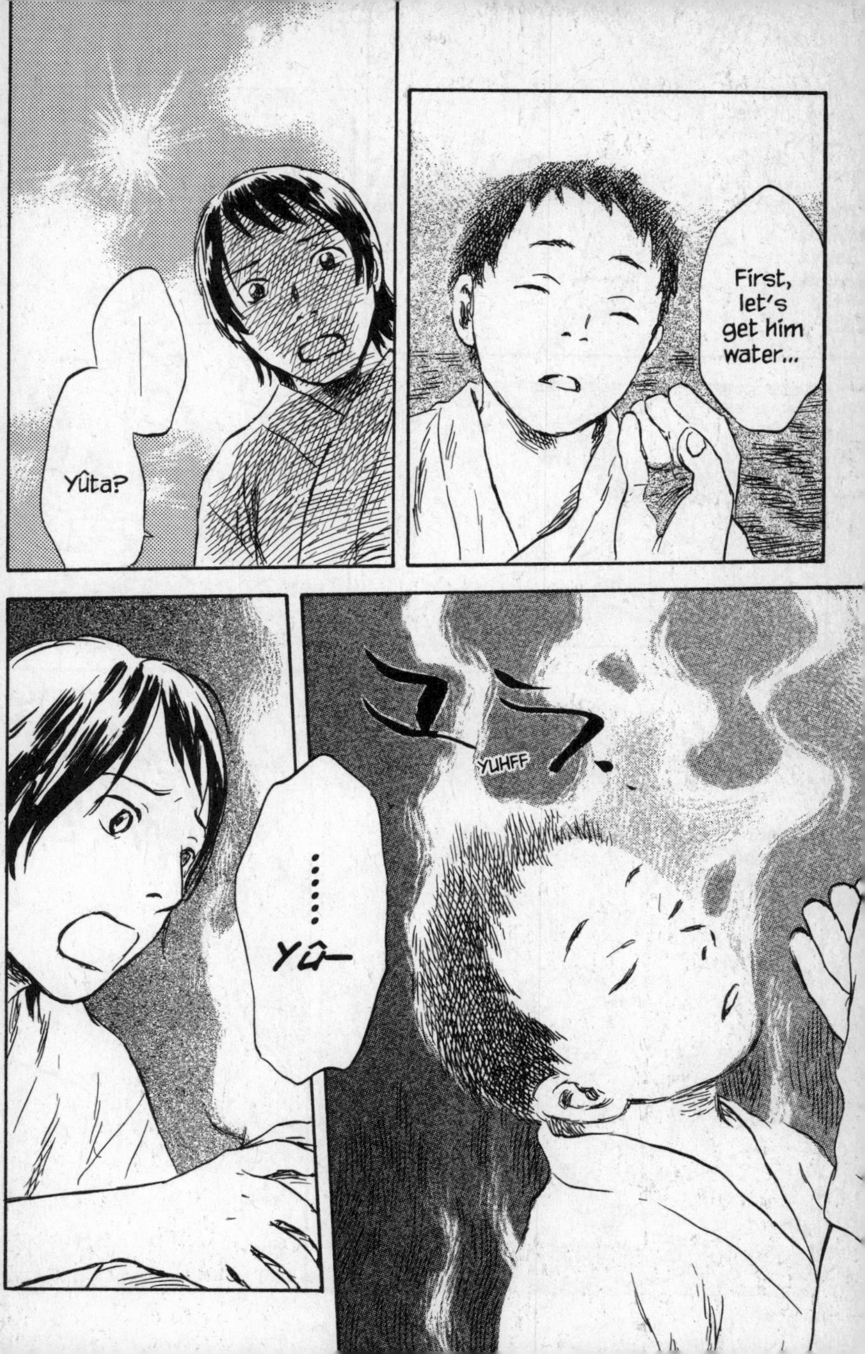
First, let's get him water...
—
Yûta?
YUHFF
...... Yû—

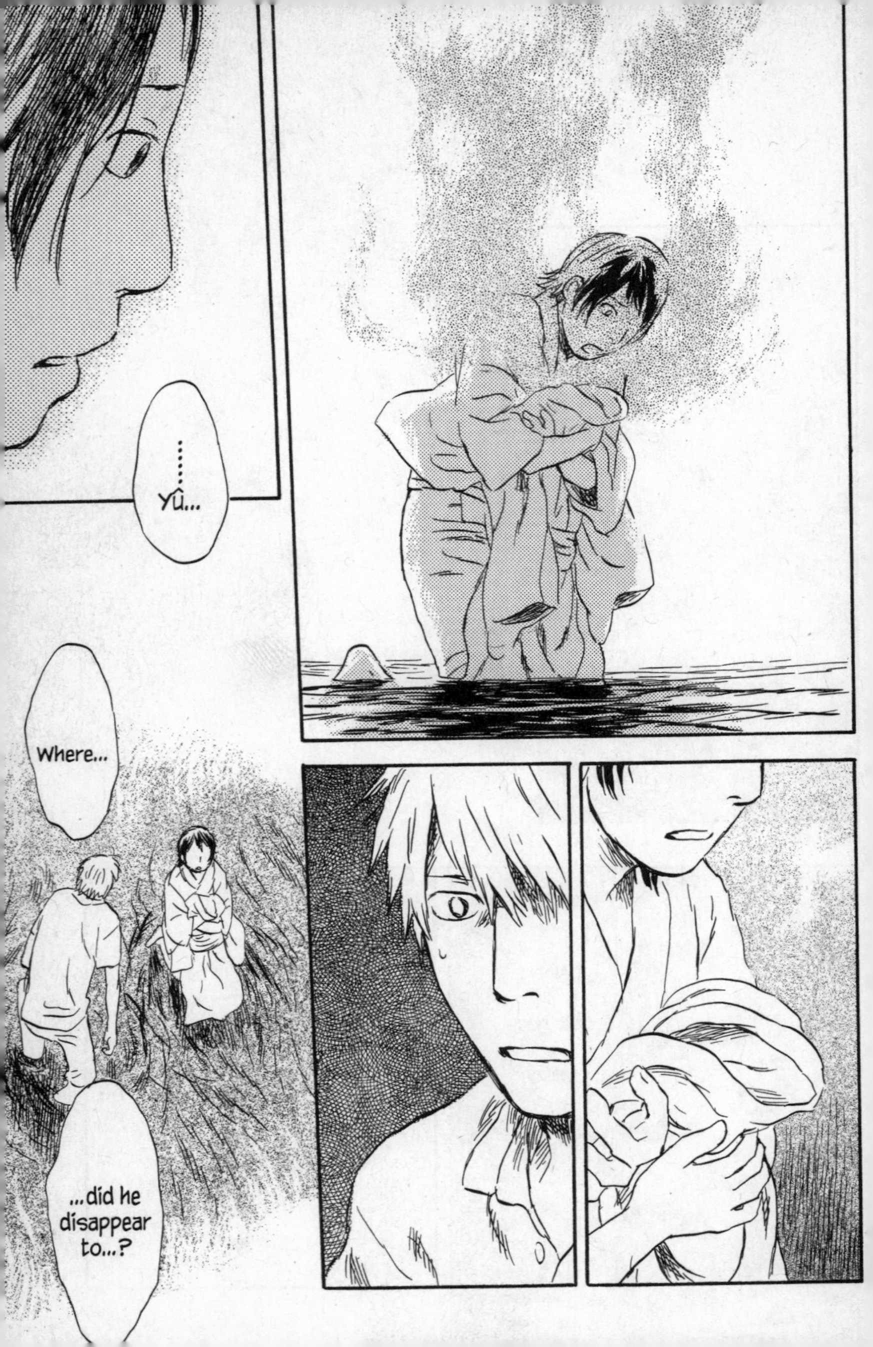
......Yû...
Where...
...did he disappear to...?

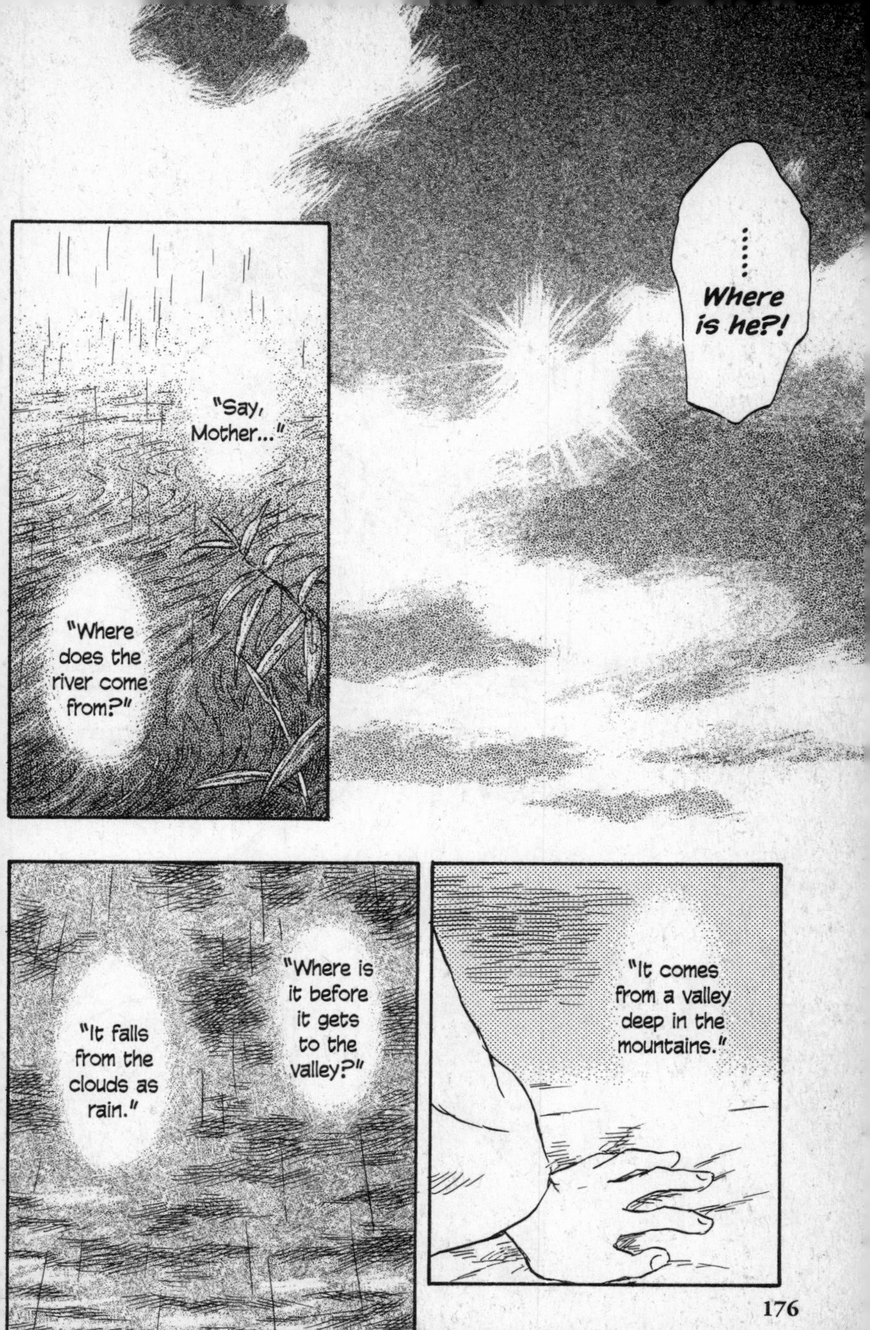
……
Where is he?!
"Say, Mother..."
"Where does the river come from?"
"It comes from a valley deep in the mountains."
"Where is it before it gets to the valley?"
"It falls from the clouds as rain."

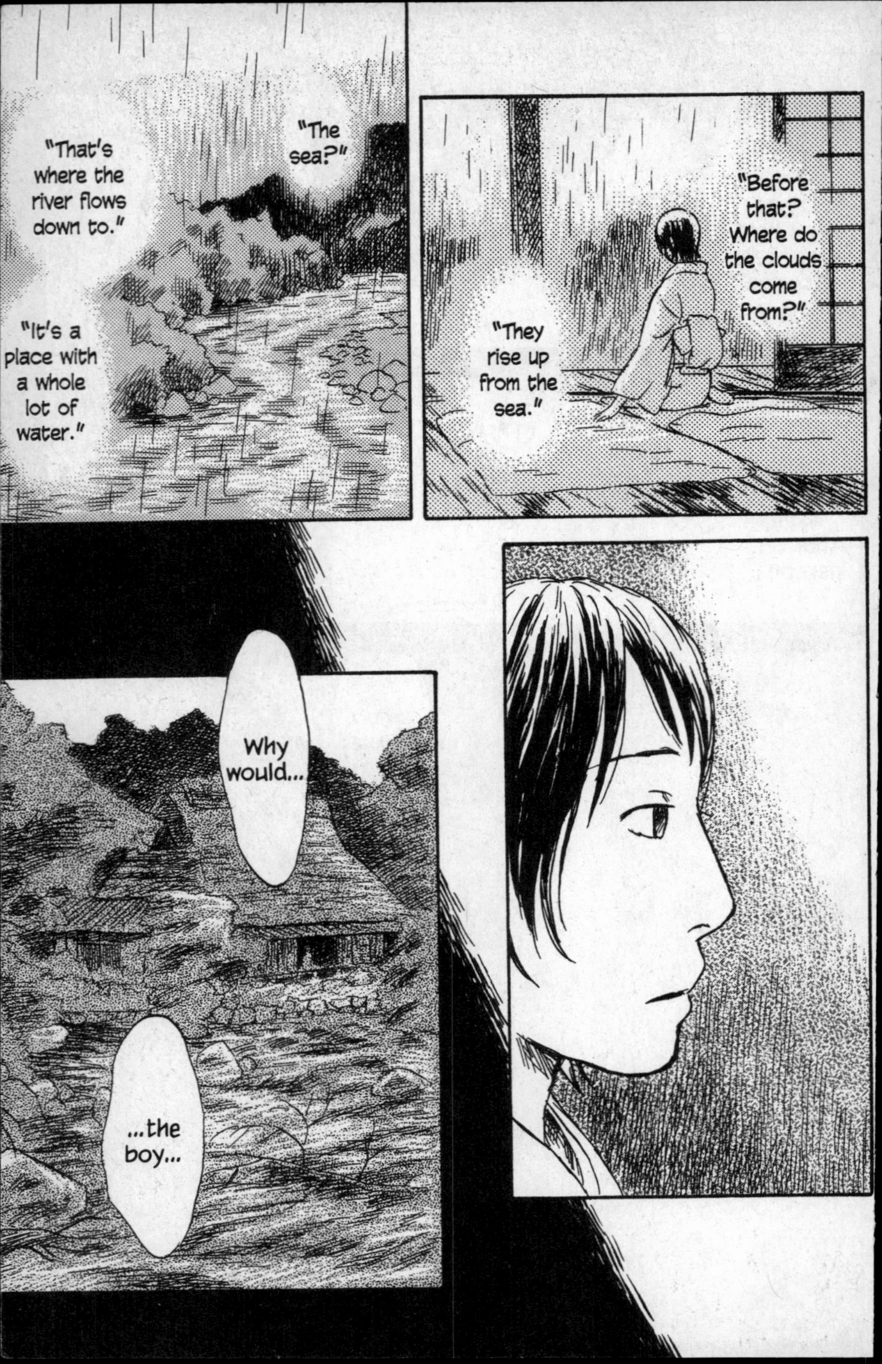
"Before that? Where do the clouds come from?"
"They rise up from the sea."
"The sea?"
"That's where the river flows down to."
"It's a place with a whole lot of water."
Why would...
...the boy...

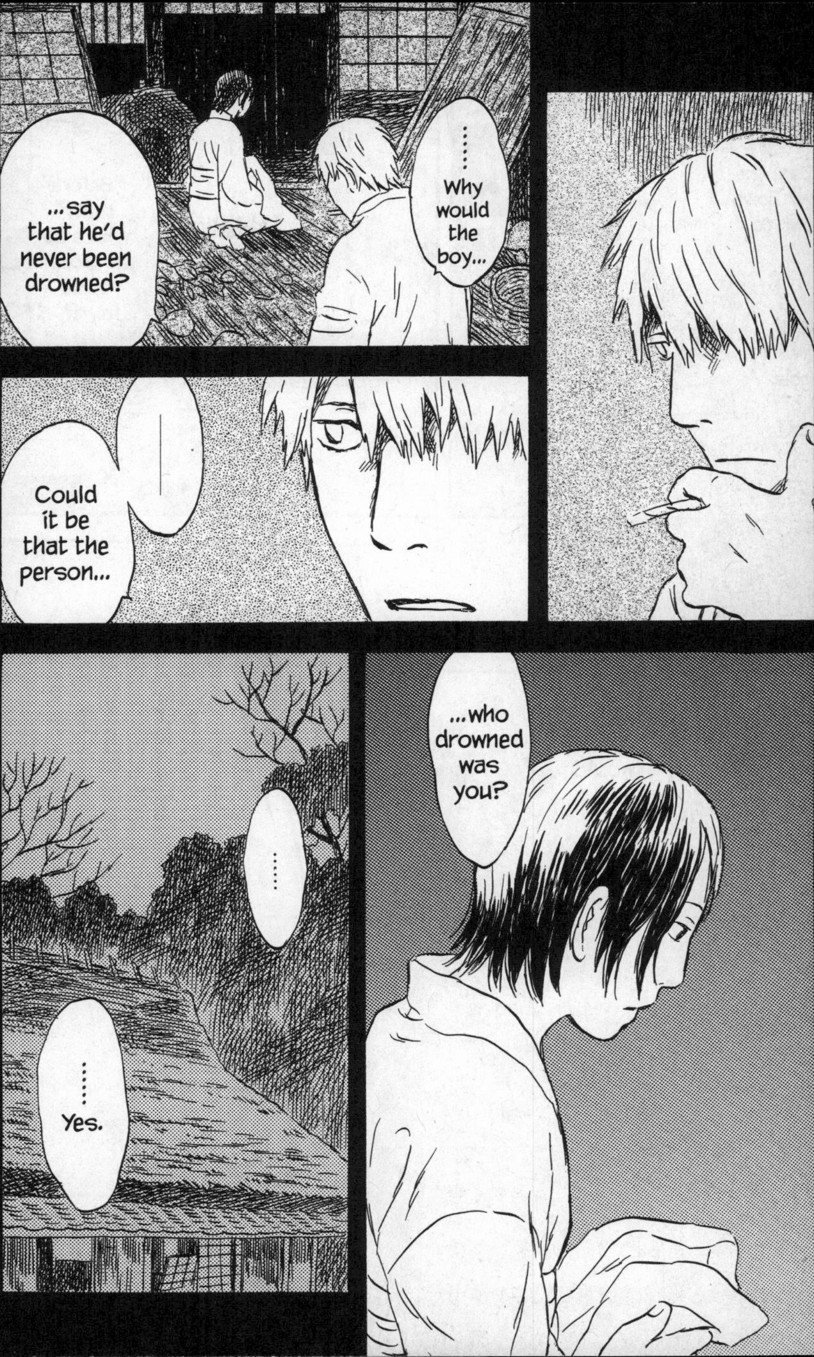

......
Why would the boy...
...say that he'd never been drowned?
—
Could it be that the person...
...who drowned was you?
......
...... Yes.

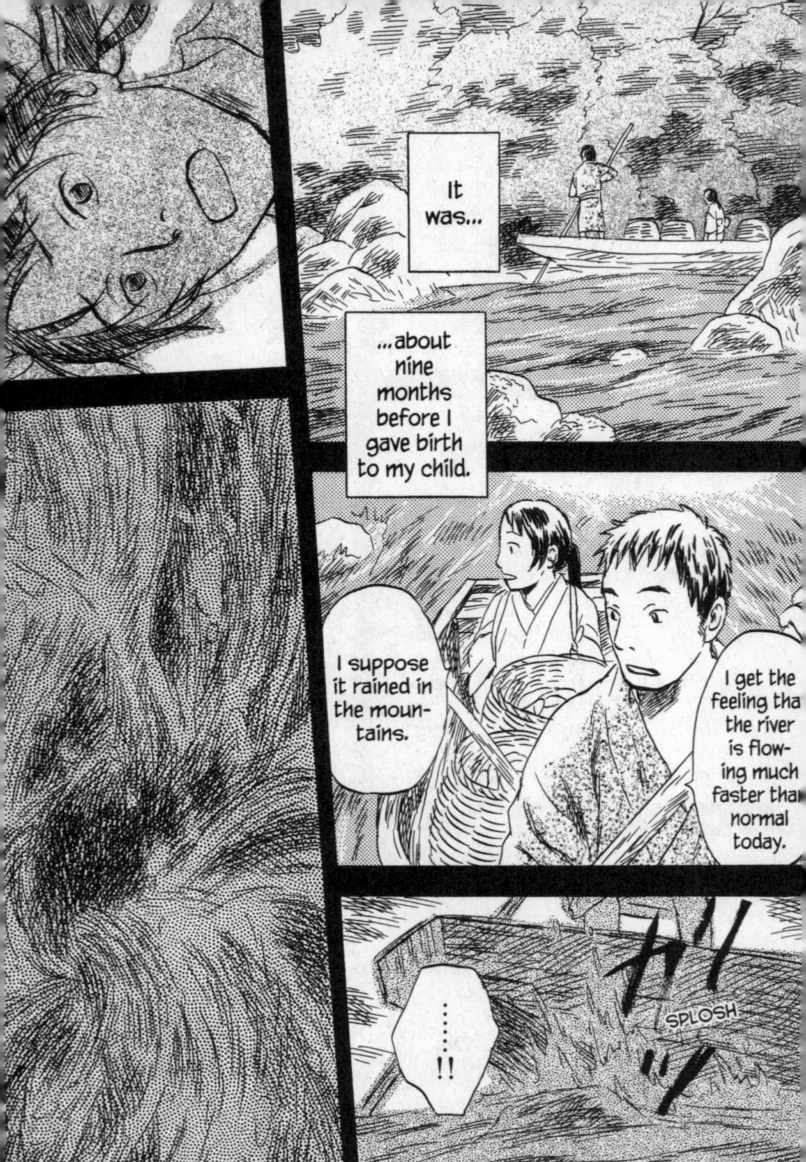
It was...
...about nine months before I gave birth to my child.
I get the feeling tha the river is flowing much faster thai normal today.
I suppose it rained in the mountains.
SPLOSH
......!!

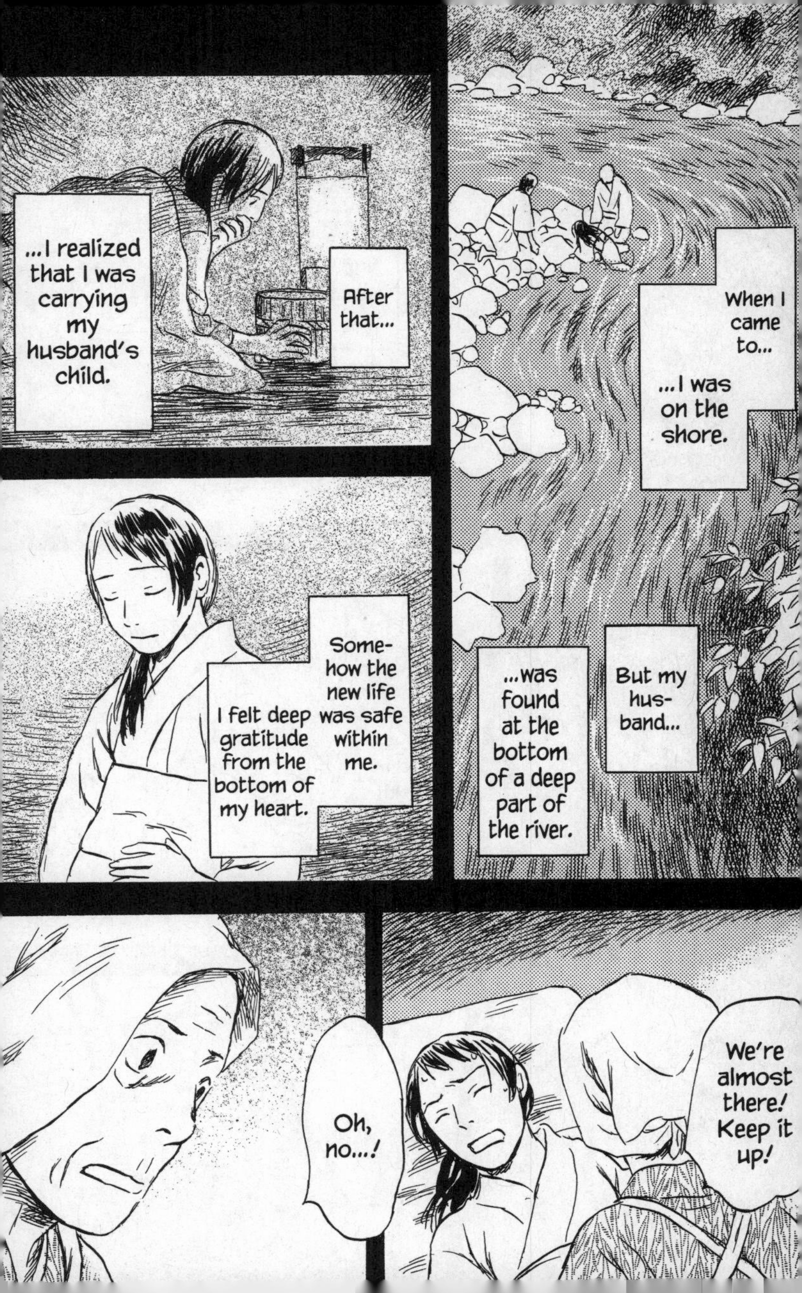
When I came to...
...I was on the shore.
But my husband...
...was found at the bottom of a deep part of the river.
After that...
...I realized that I was carrying my husband's child.
Somehow the new life was safe within me.
I felt deep gratitude from the bottom of my heart.
We're almost there! Keep it up!
Oh, no...!

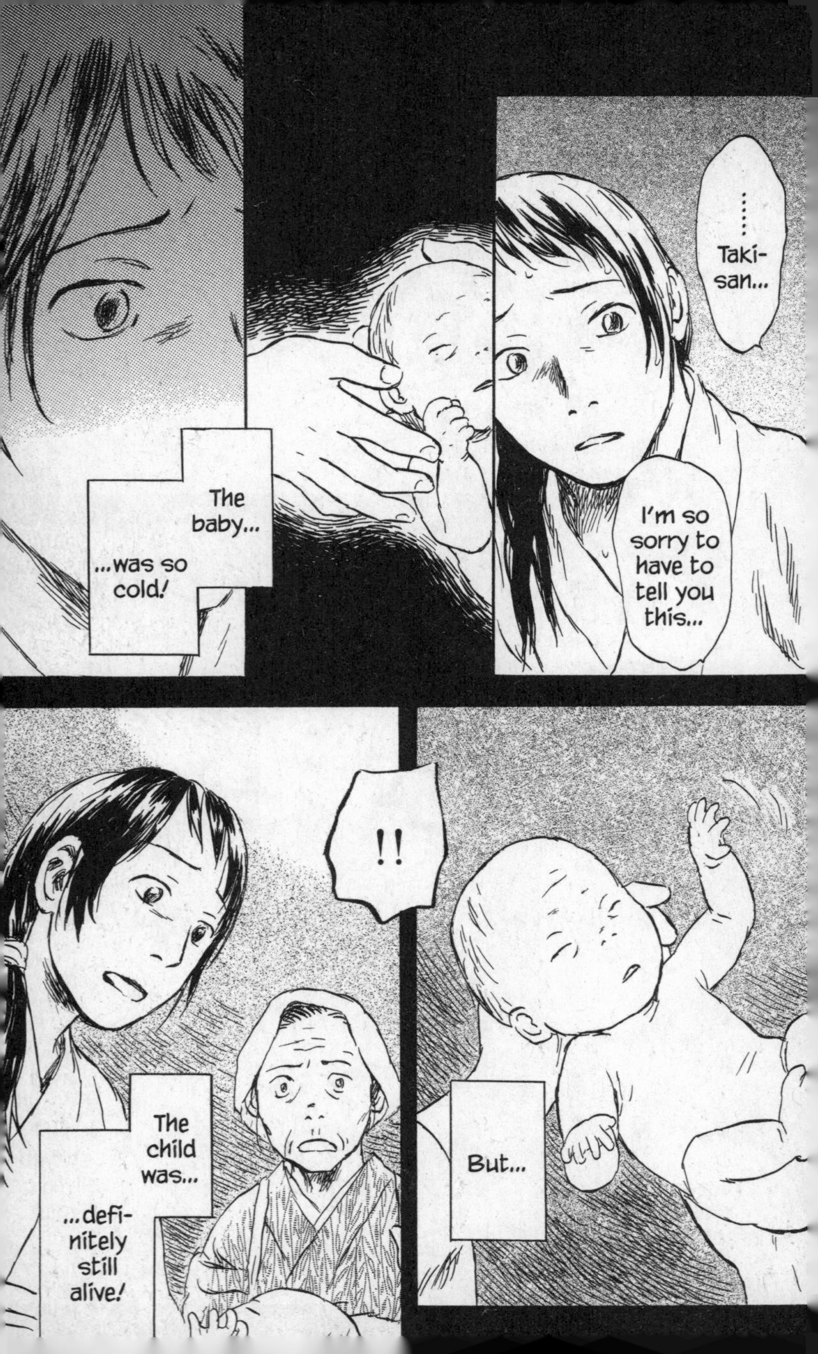
……
Taki-san...
I'm so sorry to have to tell you this...
The baby...
...was so cold!
But...
!!
The child was...
...defi-nitely still alive!

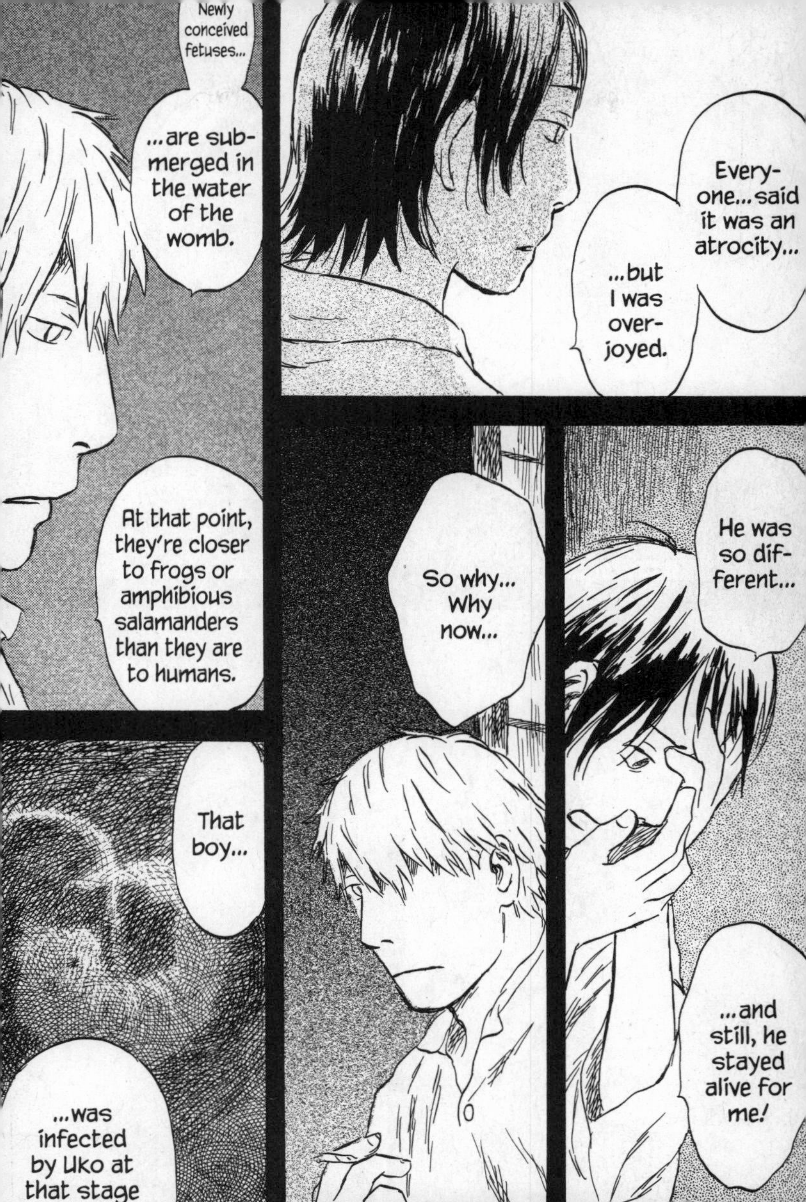
Every-one...said it was an atrocity...
...but I was over-joyed.
Newly conceived fetuses...
...are sub-merged in the water of the womb.
At that point, they're closer to frogs or amphibious salamanders than they are to humans.
He was so dif-ferent...
...and still, he stayed alive for me!
So why... Why now...
That boy...
...was infected by Uko at that stage

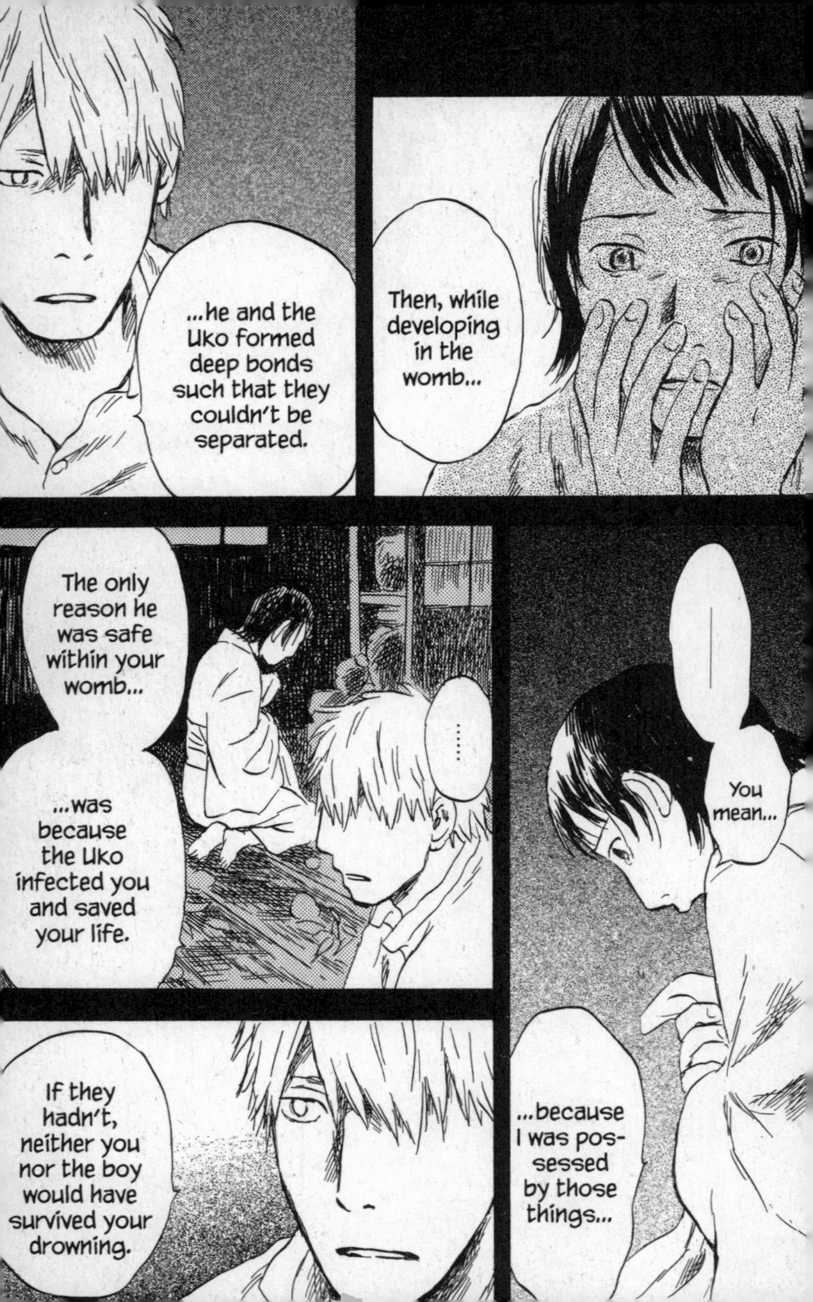
Then, while developing in the womb...
...he and the Uko formed deep bonds such that they couldn't be separated.
—
You mean...
...because I was possessed by those things...
The only reason he was safe within your womb...
......
...was because the Uko infected you and saved your life.
If they hadn't, neither you nor the boy would have survived your drowning.

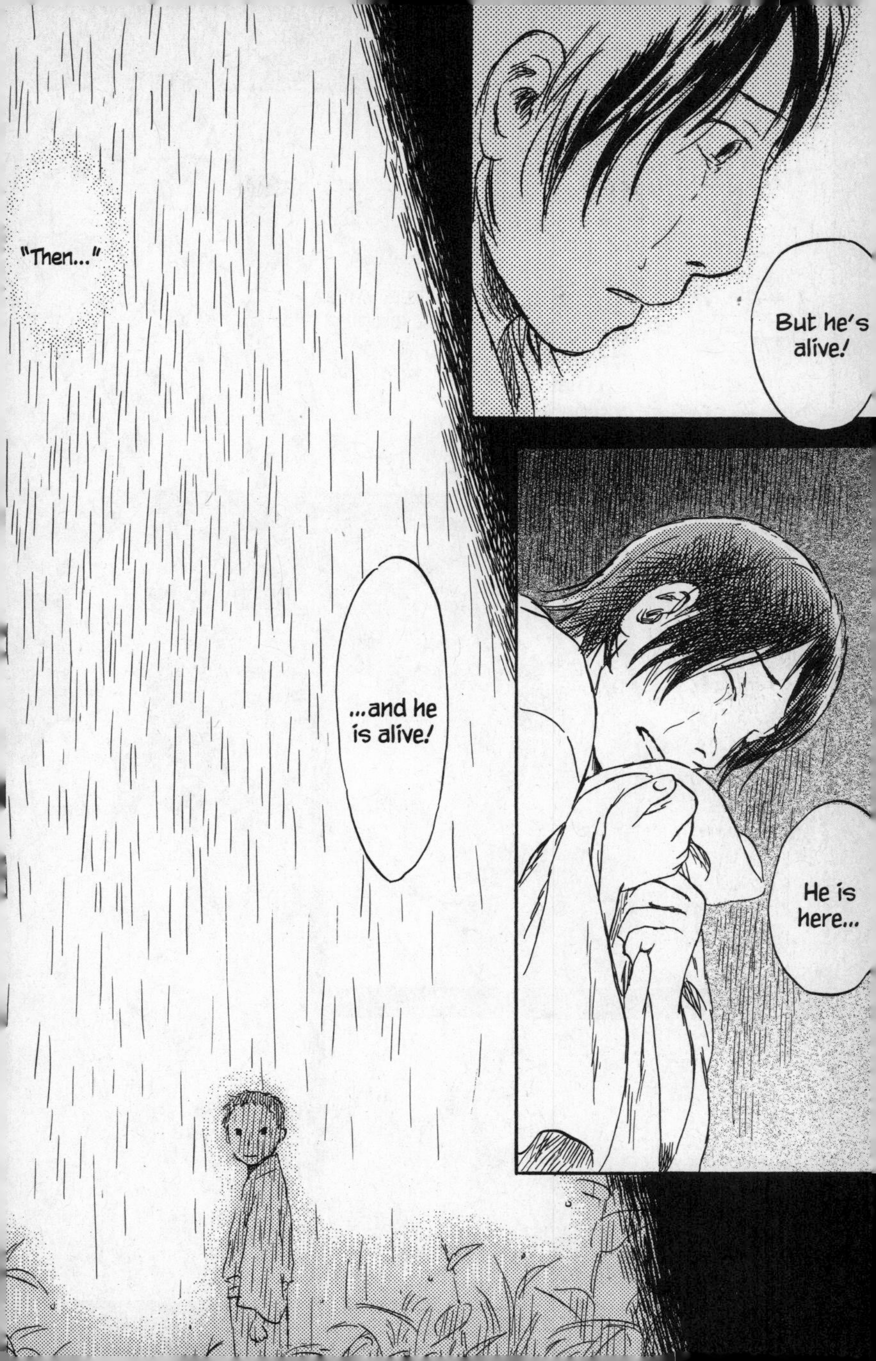
But he's alive!
He is here...
...and he is alive!
"Then..."

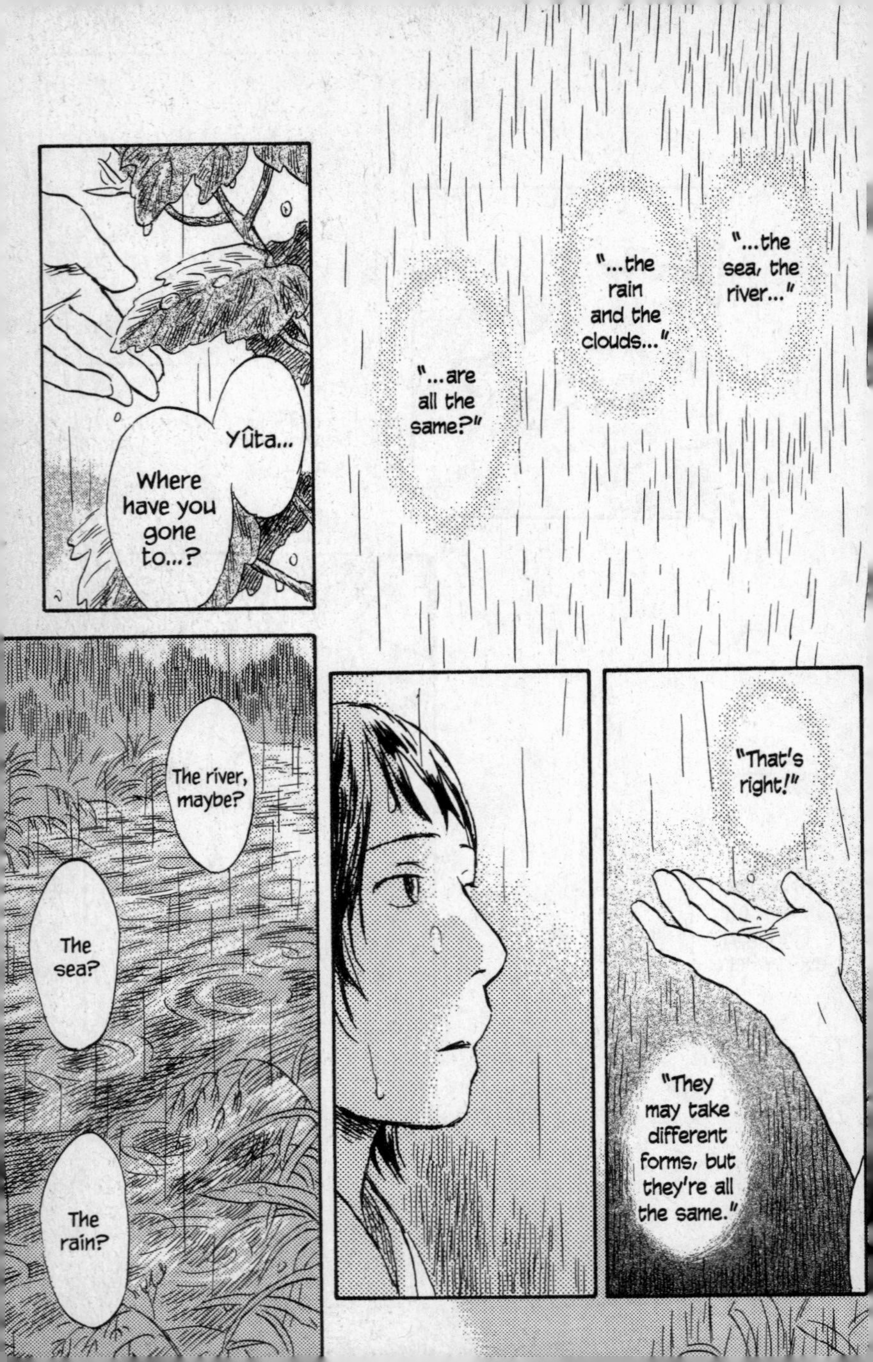
"...the sea, the river..."
"...the rain and the clouds..."
"...are all the same?"
Yûta...
Where have you gone to...?
"That's right!"
"They may take different forms, but they're all the same."
The river, maybe?
The sea?
The rain?

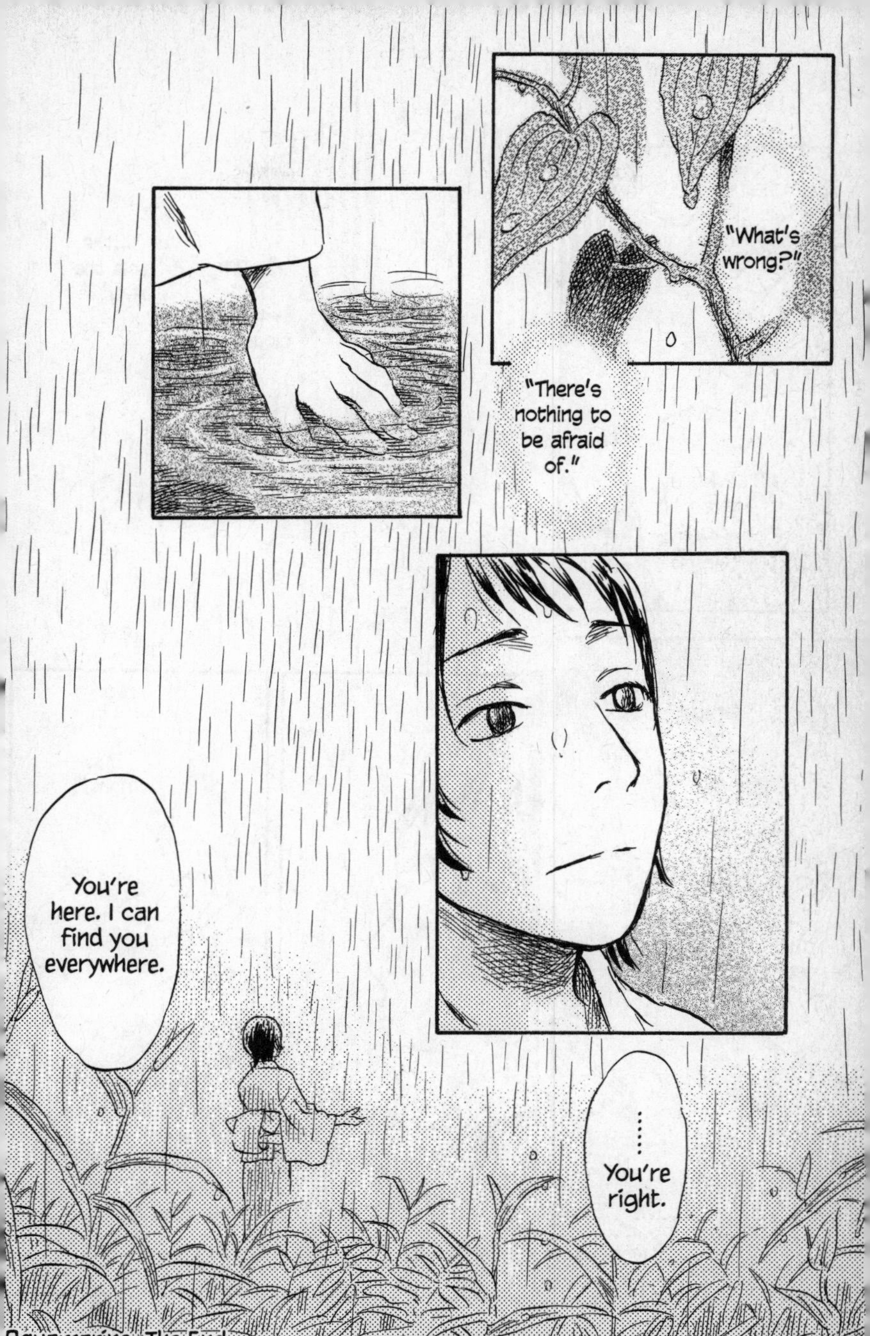
"What's wrong?"
"There's nothing to be afraid of."
You're here. I can find you everywhere.
...... You're right.

Aquamarine The End

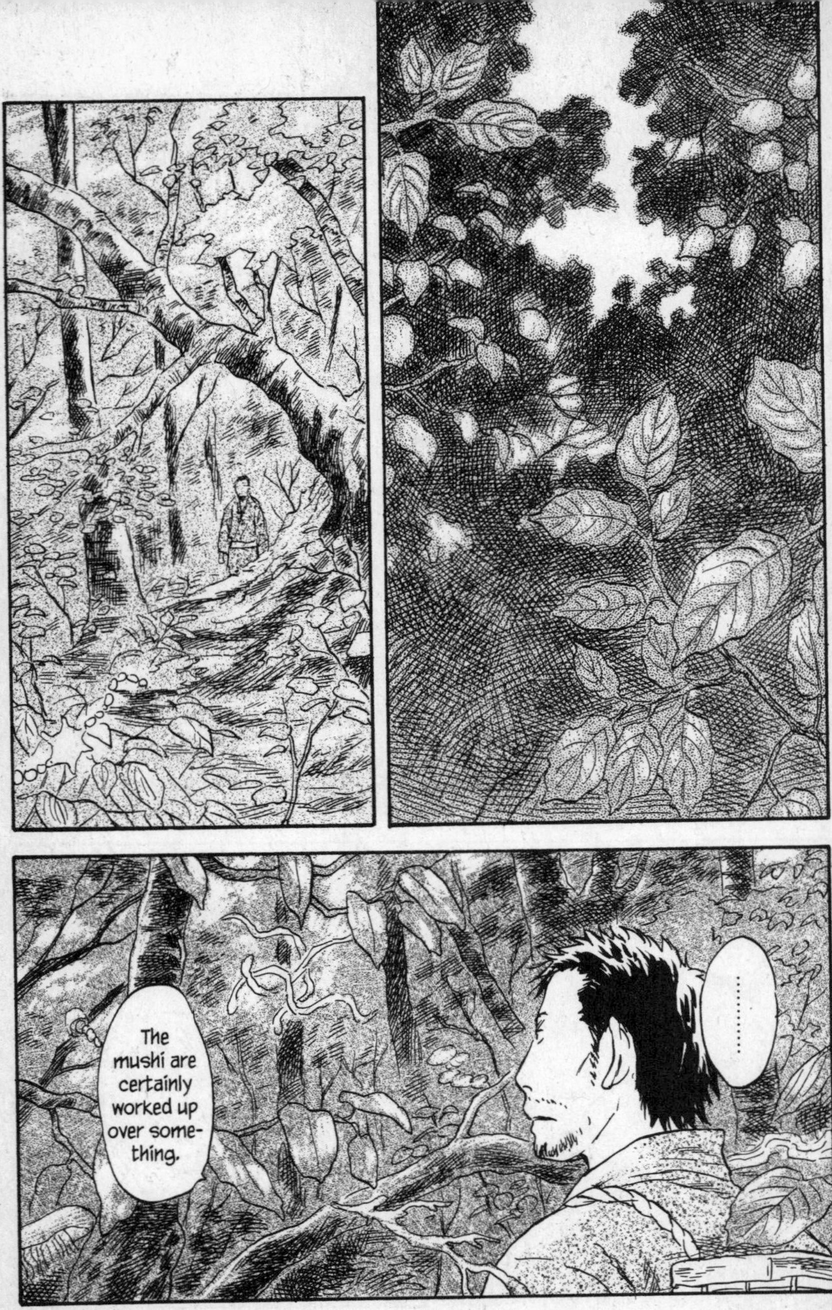
......
The mushi are certainly worked up over some-thing.

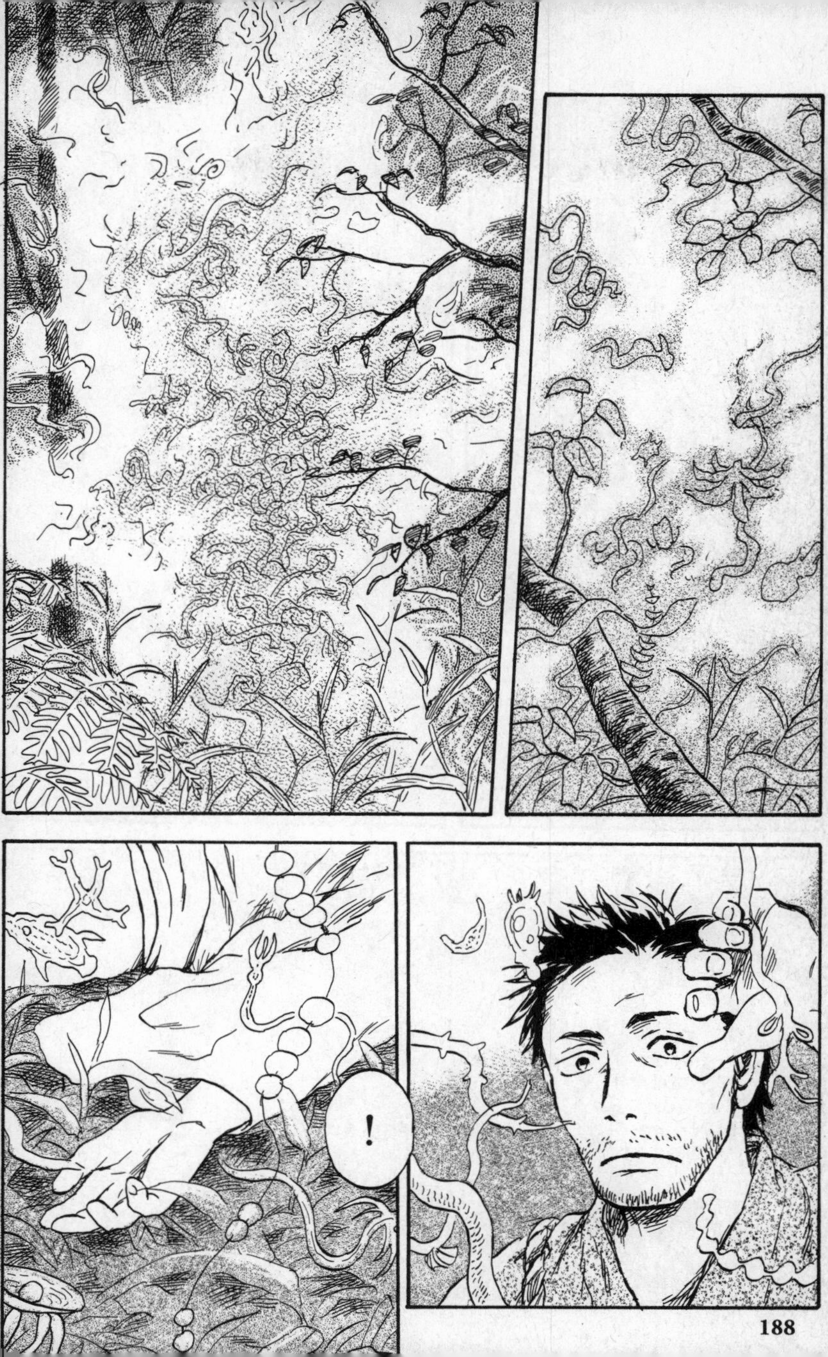
!

The Bed of Grass

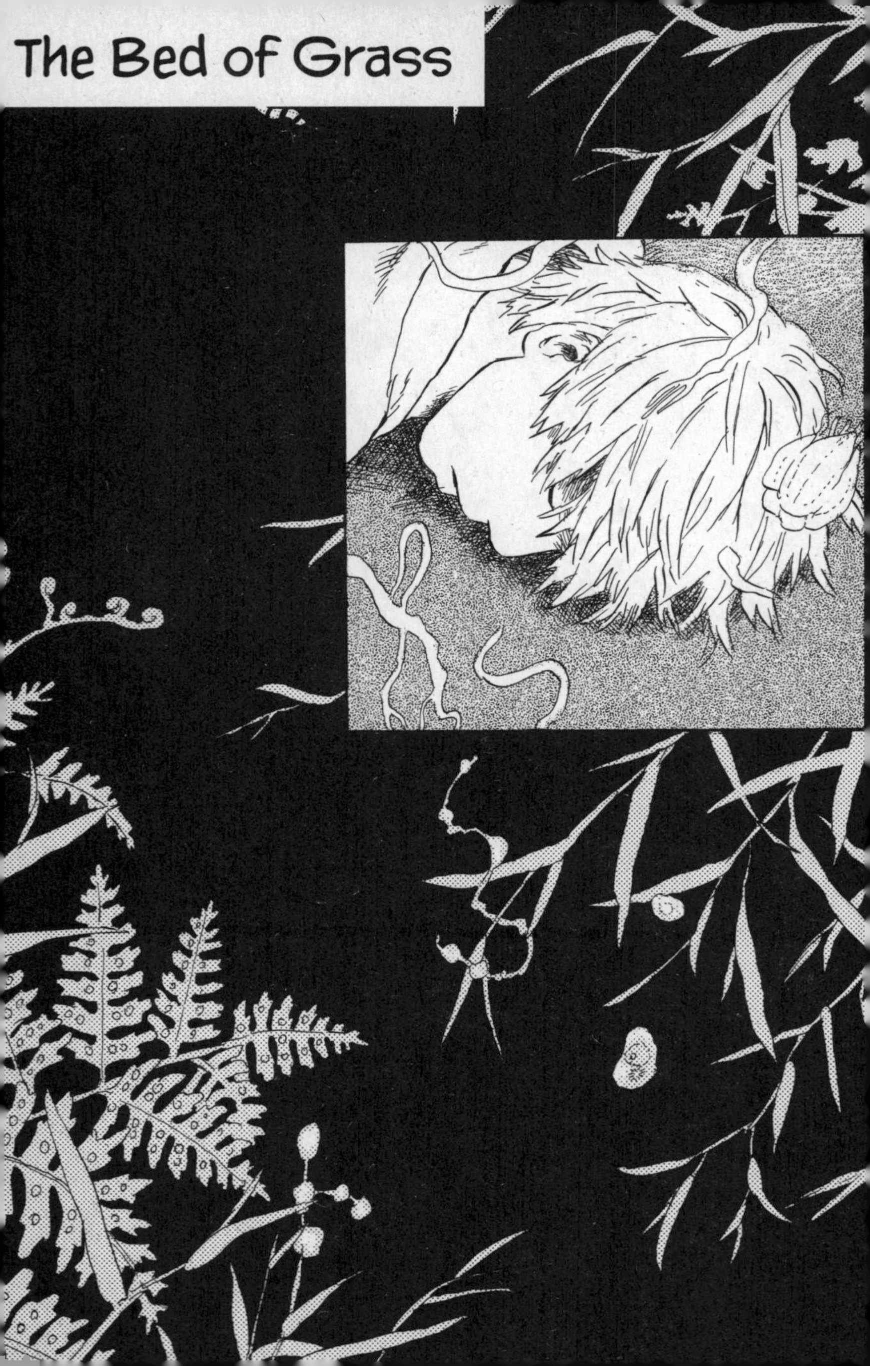

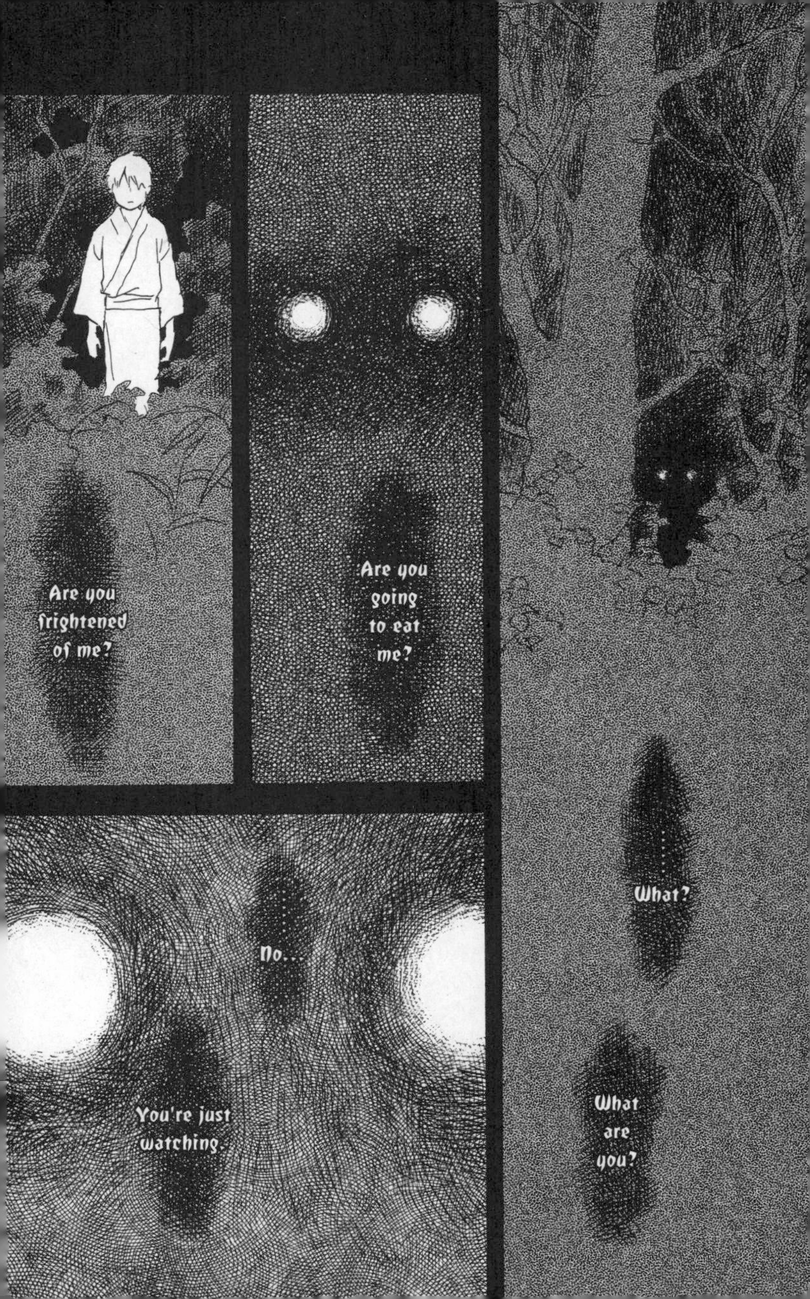
What?
What are you?
Are you going to eat me?
Are you frightened of me?
No...
You're just watching.

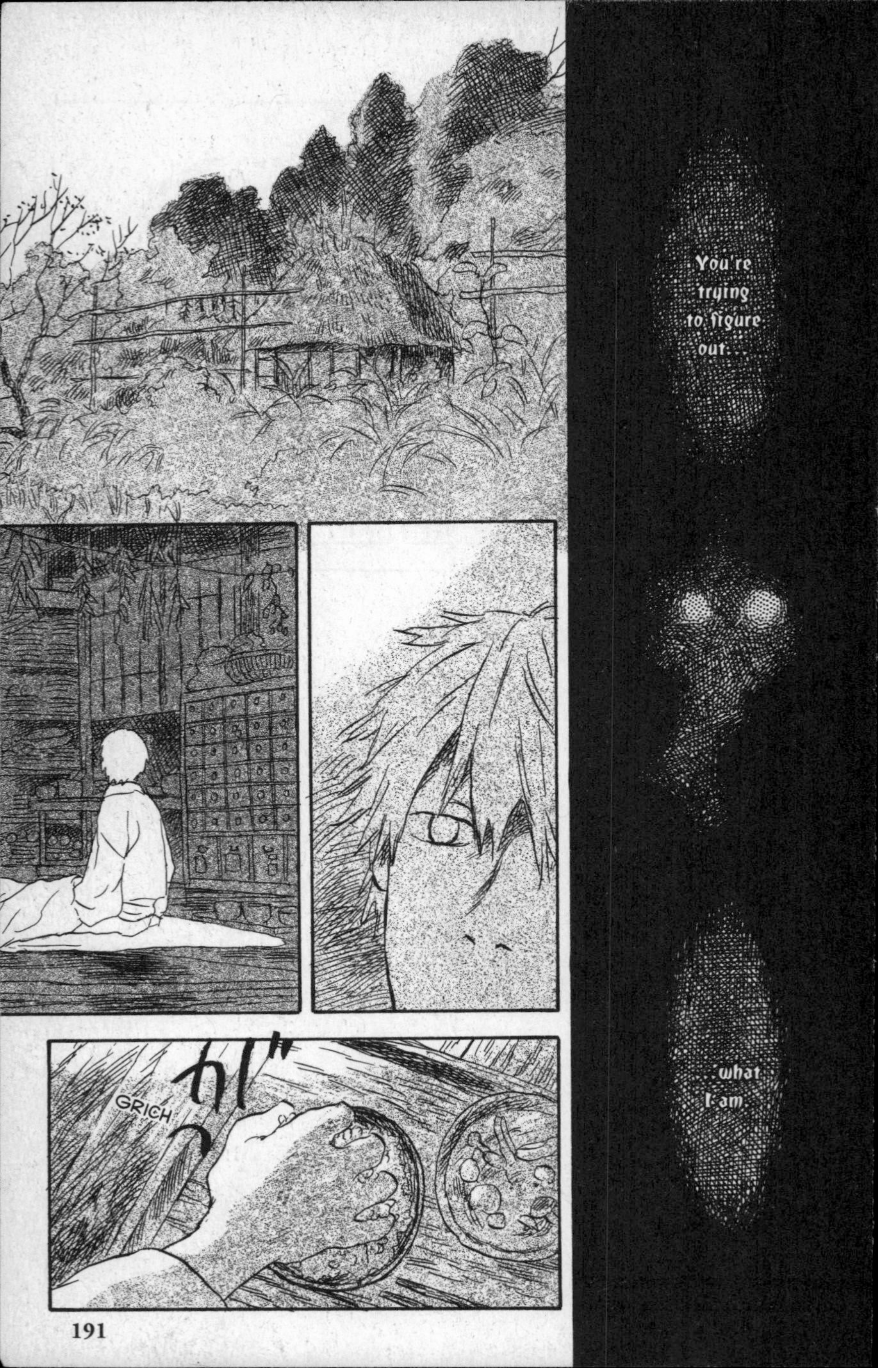

You're trying to figure out...
...what I am.
ガリっ
GRICH

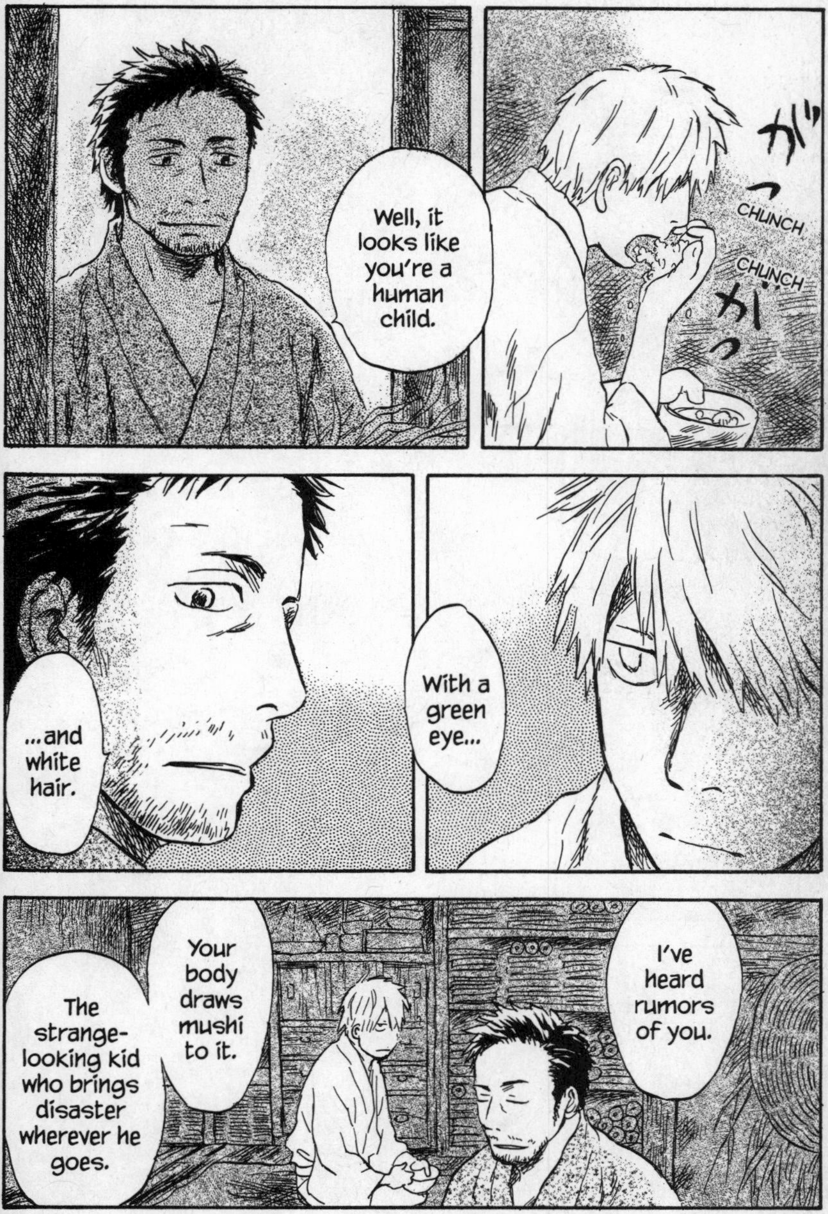
がっ
CHUNCH
CHUNCH
かっ
Well, it looks like you're a human child.
With a green eye...
...and white hair.
I've heard rumors of you.
Your body draws mushi to it.
The strange-looking kid who brings disaster wherever he goes.

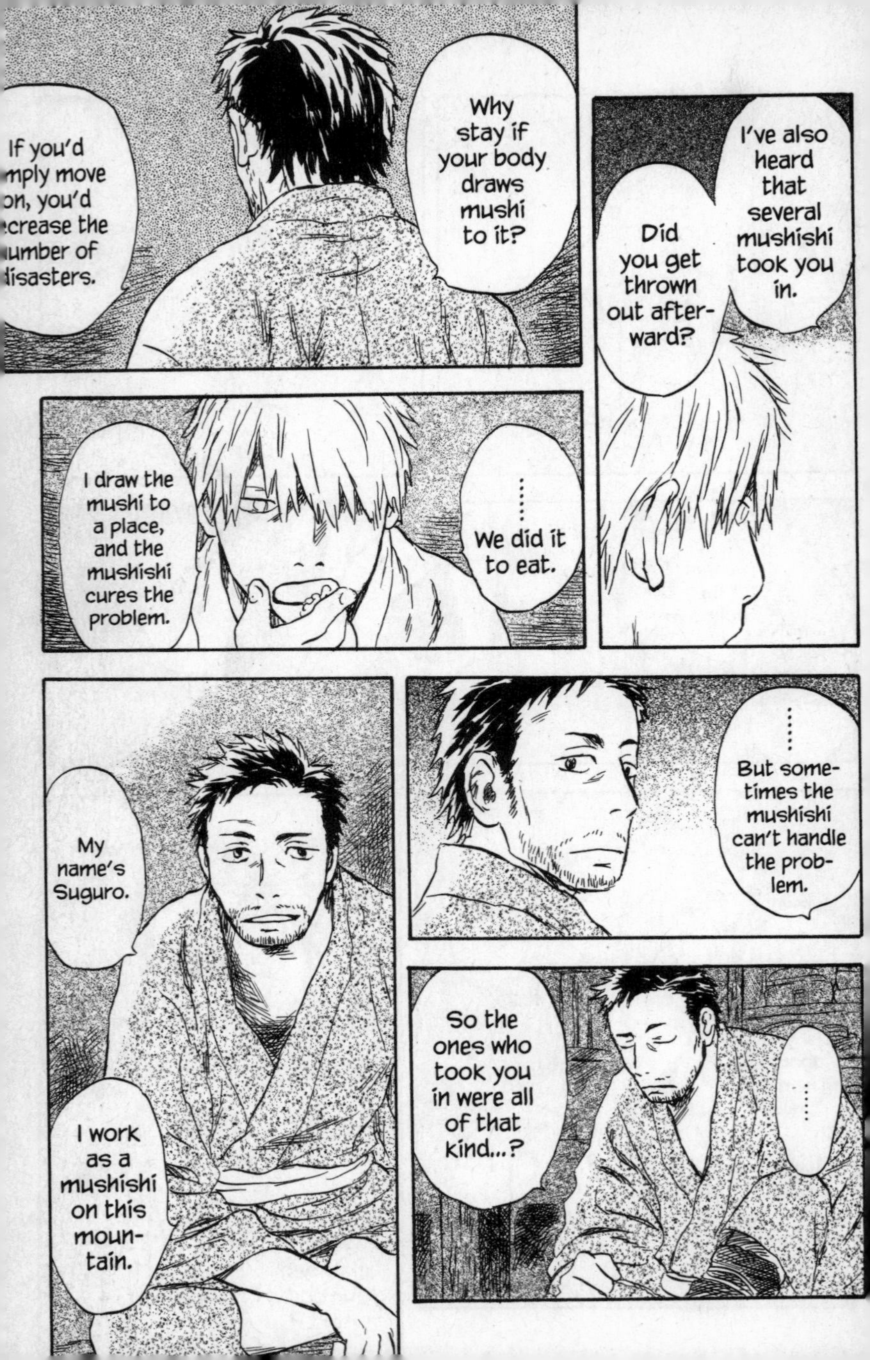

I've also heard that several mushishi took you in.
Did you get thrown out afterward?
Why stay if your body draws mushi to it?
If you'd mply move on, you'd crease the umber of isasters.
......
We did it to eat.
I draw the mushi to a place, and the mushishi cures the problem.
......
But sometimes the mushishi can't handle the problem.
So the ones who took you in were all of that kind...?
......
My name's Suguro.
I work as a mushishi on this mountain.

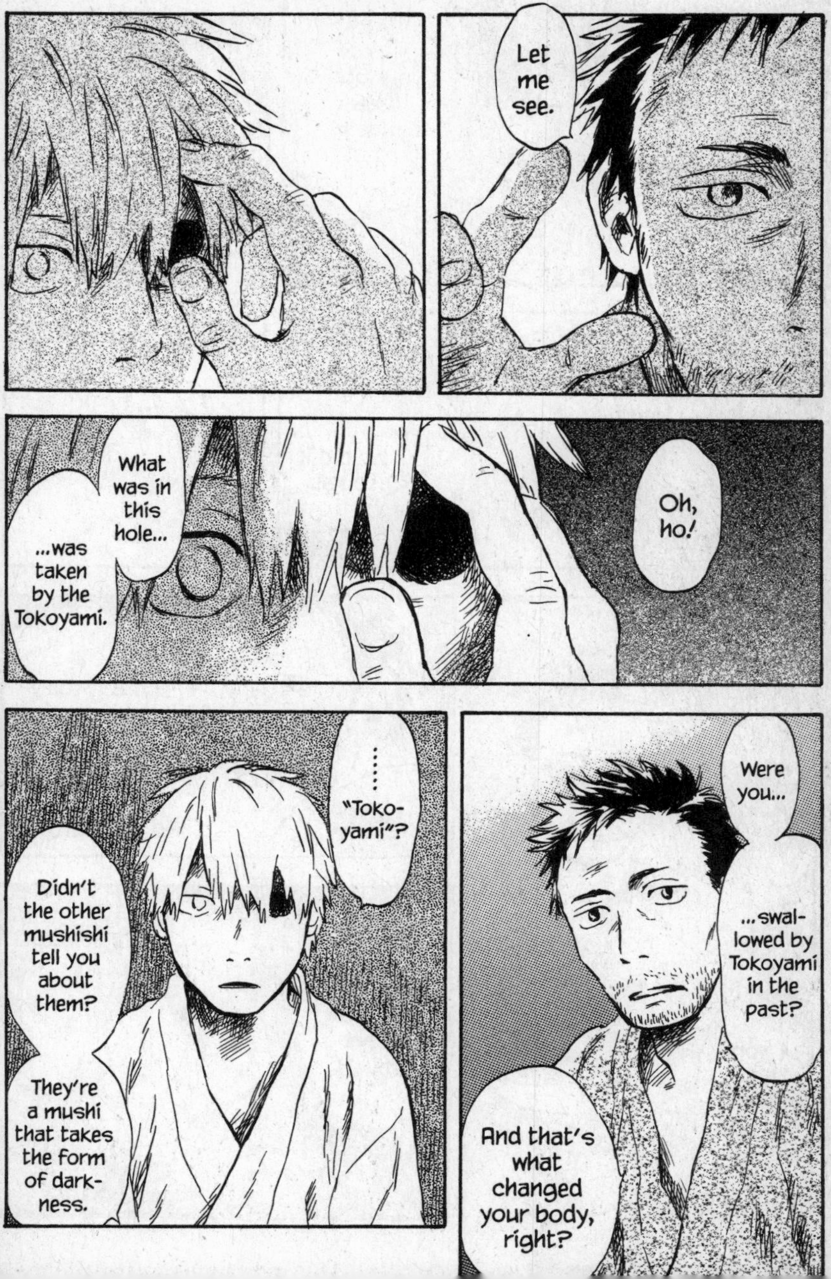
Let me see.
Oh, ho!
What was in this hole...
...was taken by the Tokoyami.
Were you...
...swallowed by Tokoyami in the past?
And that's what changed your body, right?
......
"Toko-yami"?
Didn't the other mushishi tell you about them?
They're a mushi that takes the form of dark-ness.

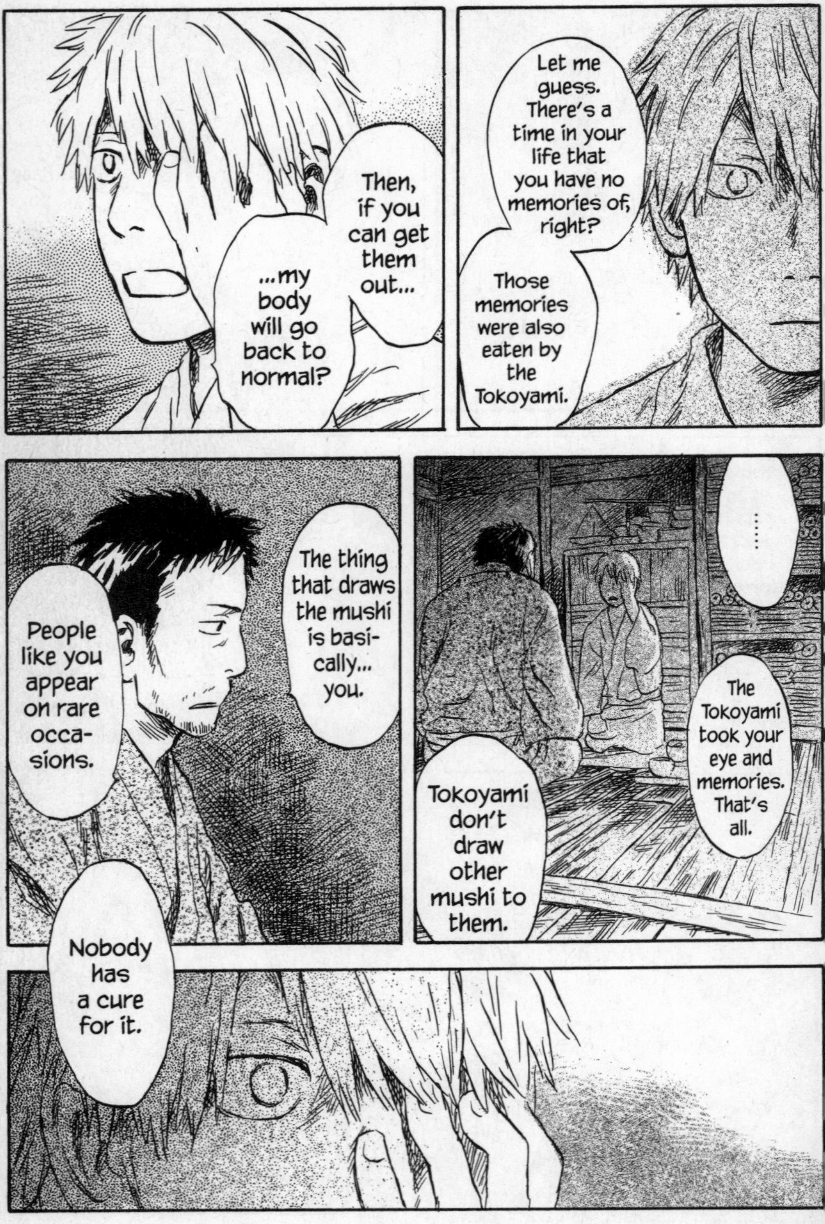
Let me guess. There's a time in your life that you have no memories of, right?
Those memories were also eaten by the Tokoyami.
Then, if you can get them out...
...my body will go back to normal?
......
The Tokoyami took your eye and memories. That's all.
Tokoyami don't draw other mushi to them.
The thing that draws the mushi is basically... you.
People like you appear on rare occasions.
Nobody has a cure for it.

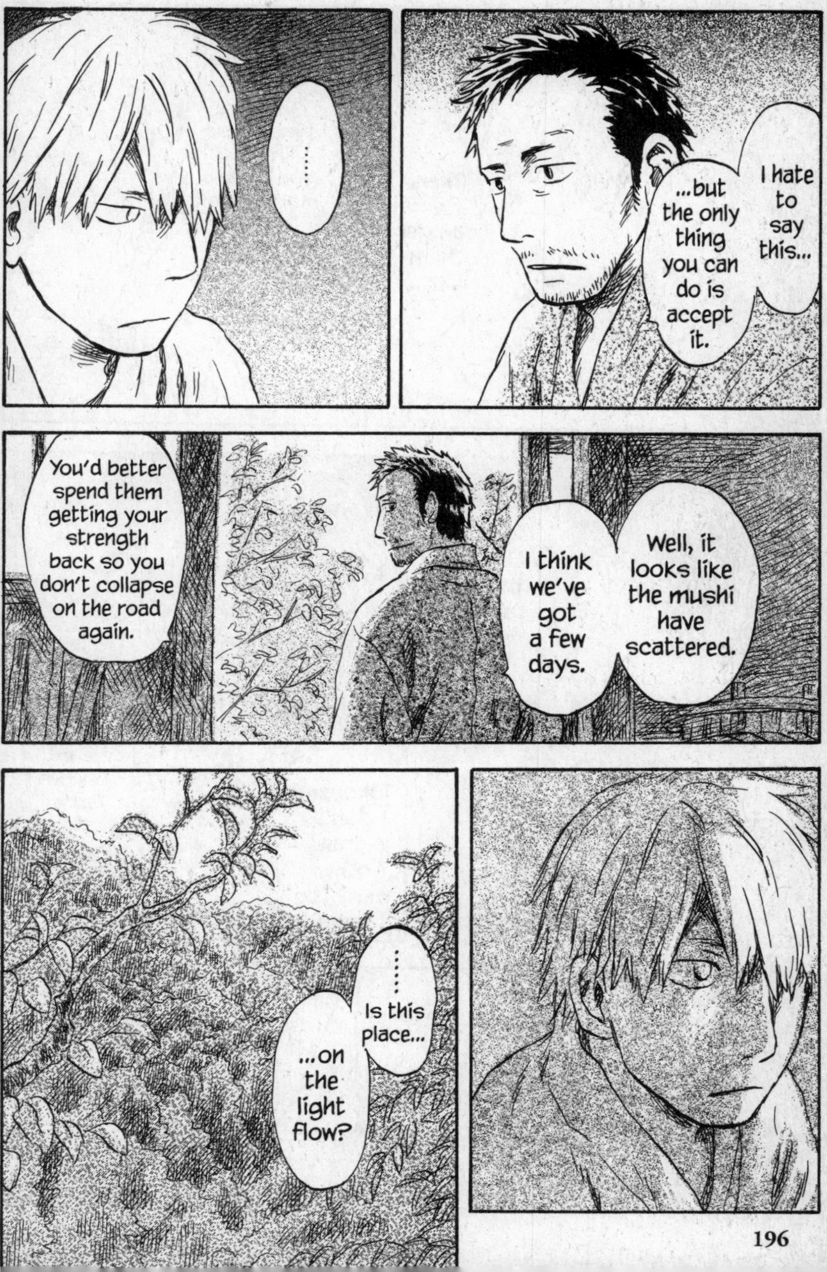
I hate to say this...
...but the only thing you can do is accept it.
......
Well, it looks like the mushi have scattered.
I think we've got a few days.
You'd better spend them getting your strength back so you don't collapse on the road again.
......
Is this place...
...on the light flow?

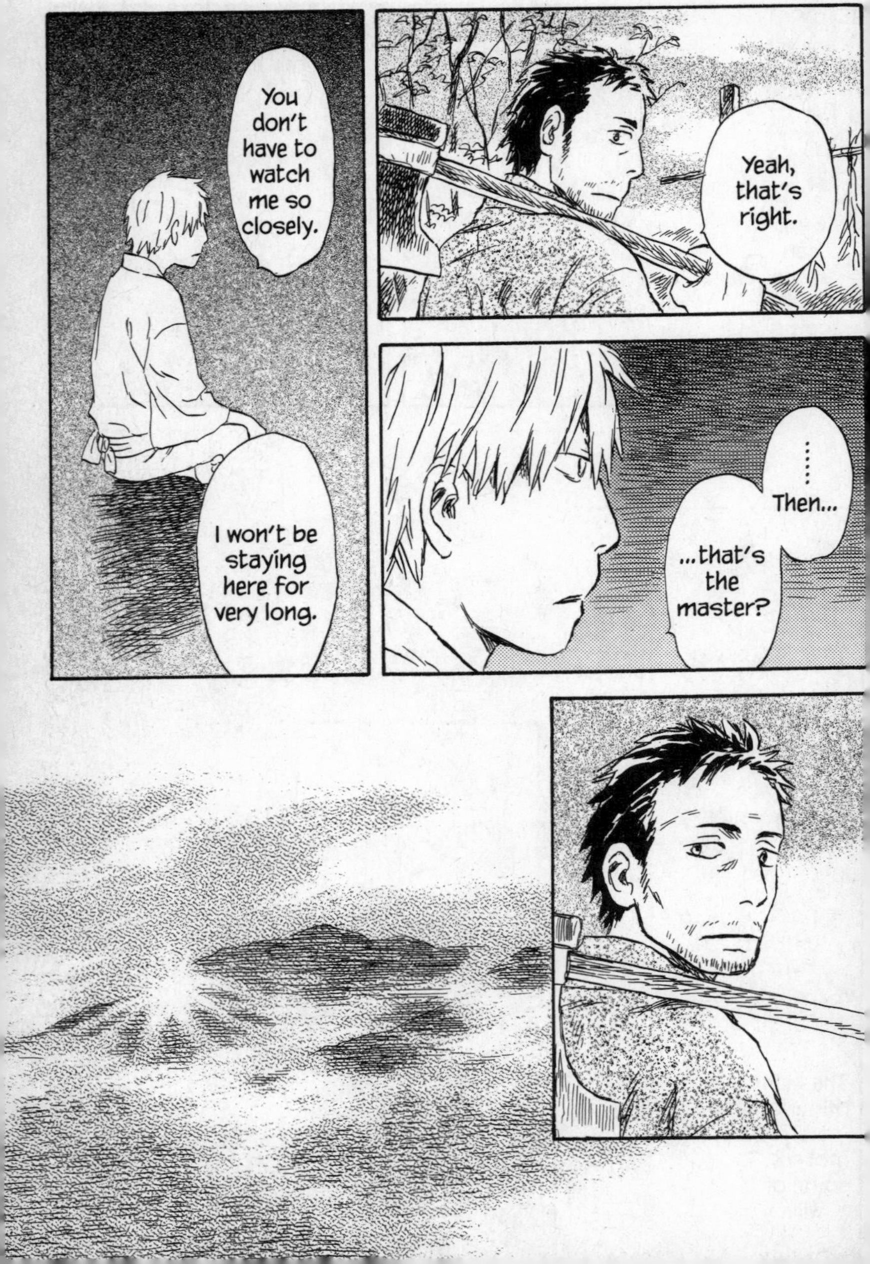
Yeah, that's right.
......
Then...
...that's the master?
You don't have to watch me so closely.
I won't be staying here for very long.

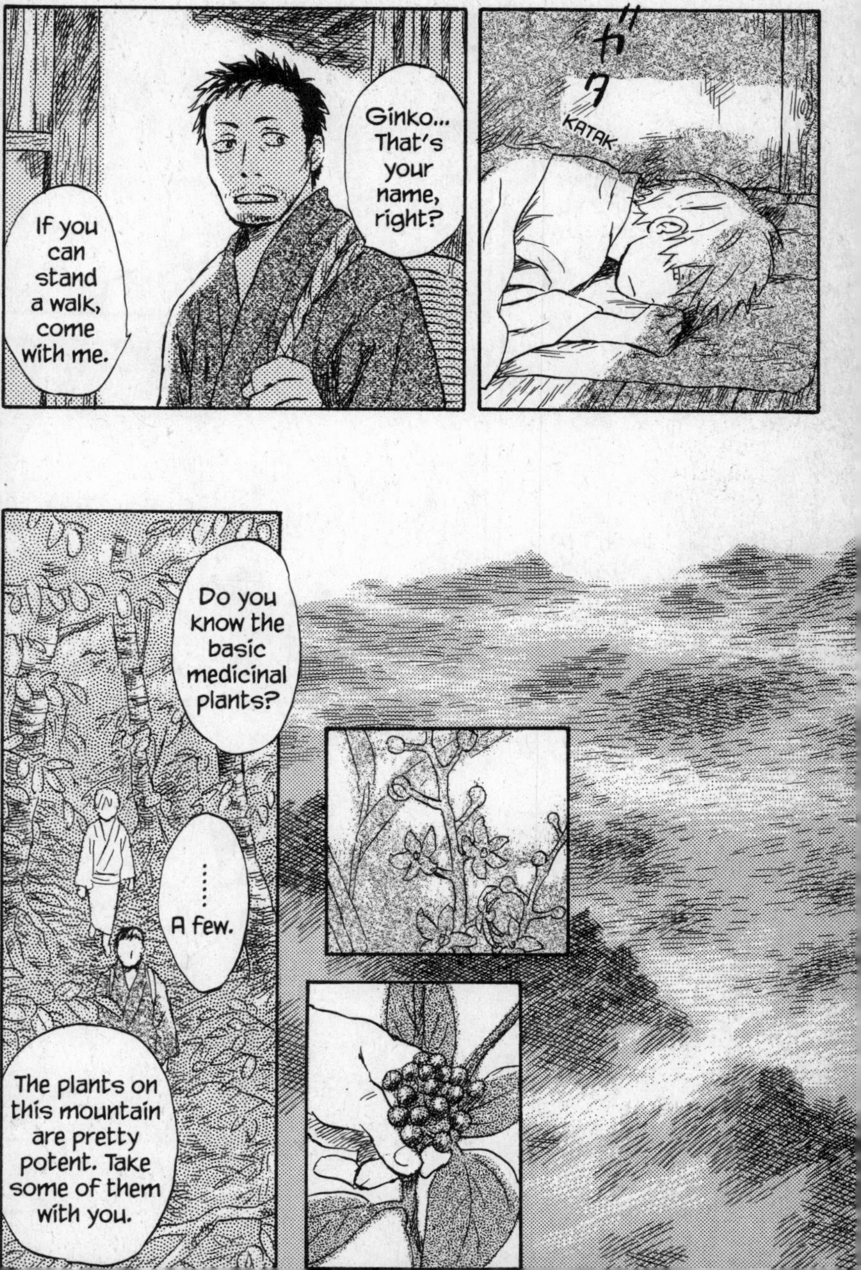
ガタ
KATAK
Ginko... That's your name, right?
If you can stand a walk, come with me.
Do you know the basic medicinal plants?
......
A few.
The plants on this mountain are pretty potent. Take some of them with you.

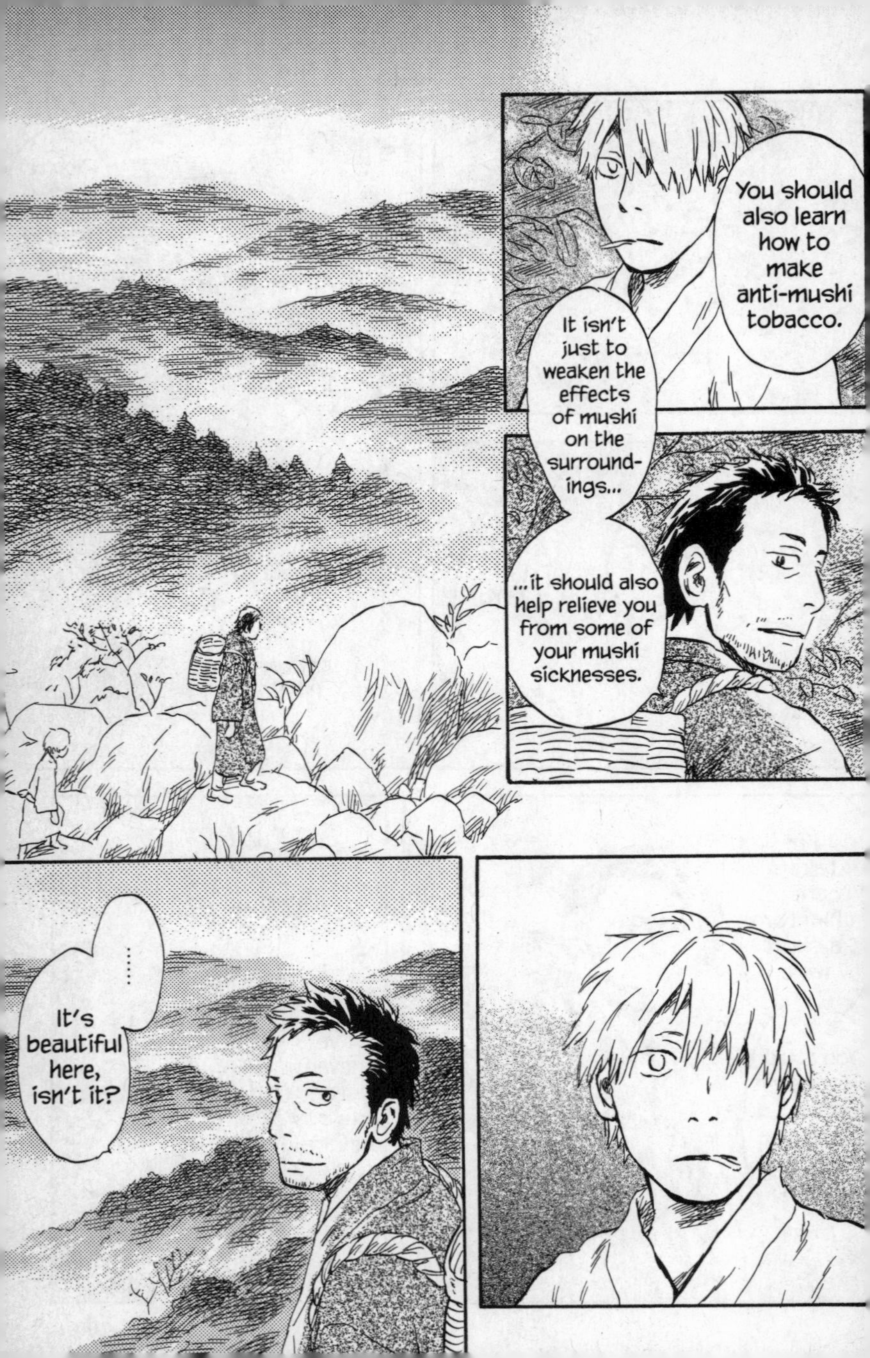
You should also learn how to make anti-mushi tobacco.
It isn't just to weaken the effects of mushi on the surround-ings...
...it should also help relieve you from some of your mushi sicknesses.
......
It's beautiful here, isn't it?

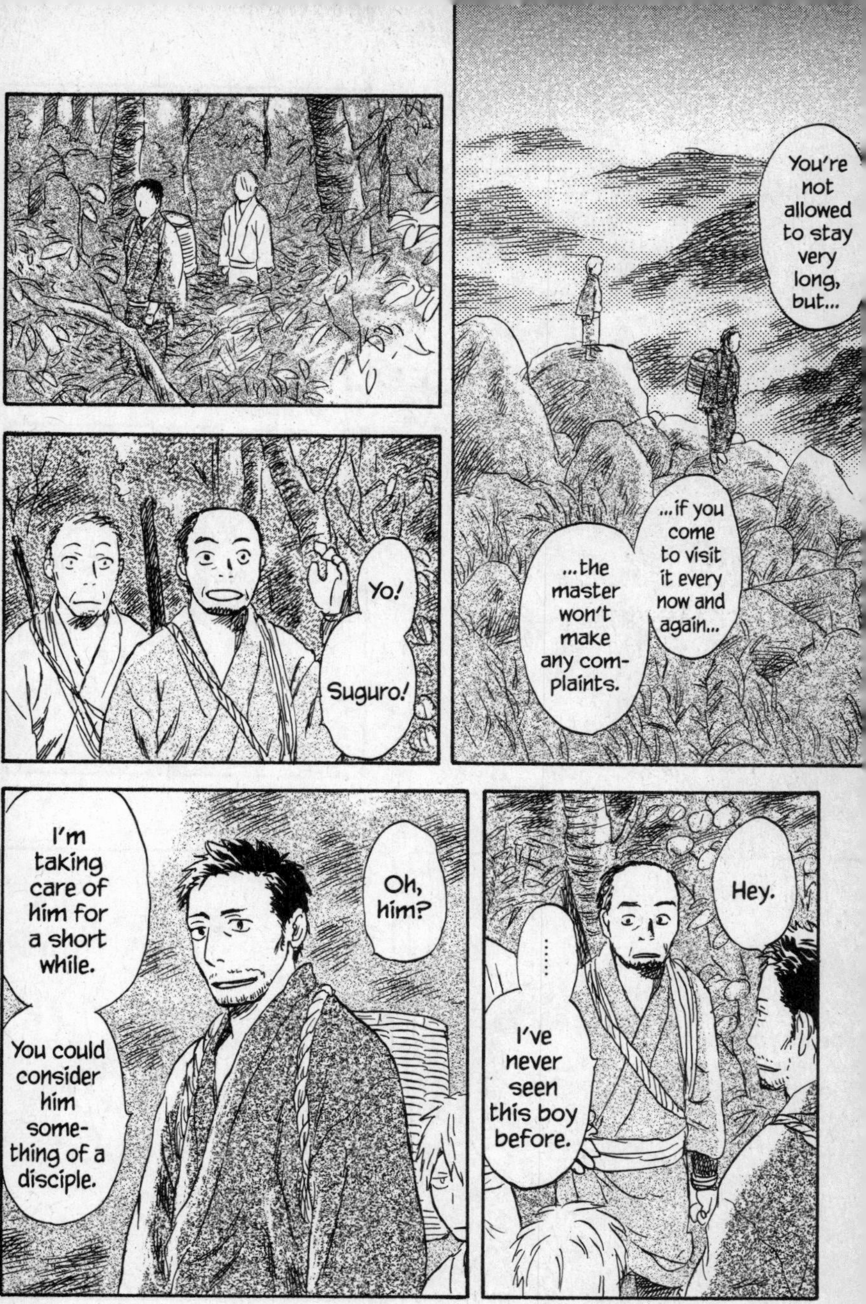
You're not allowed to stay very long, but...
...if you come to visit it every now and again...
...the master won't make any complaints.
Yo!
Suguro!
Hey.
......
I've never seen this boy before.
Oh, him?
I'm taking care of him for a short while.
You could consider him something of a disciple.

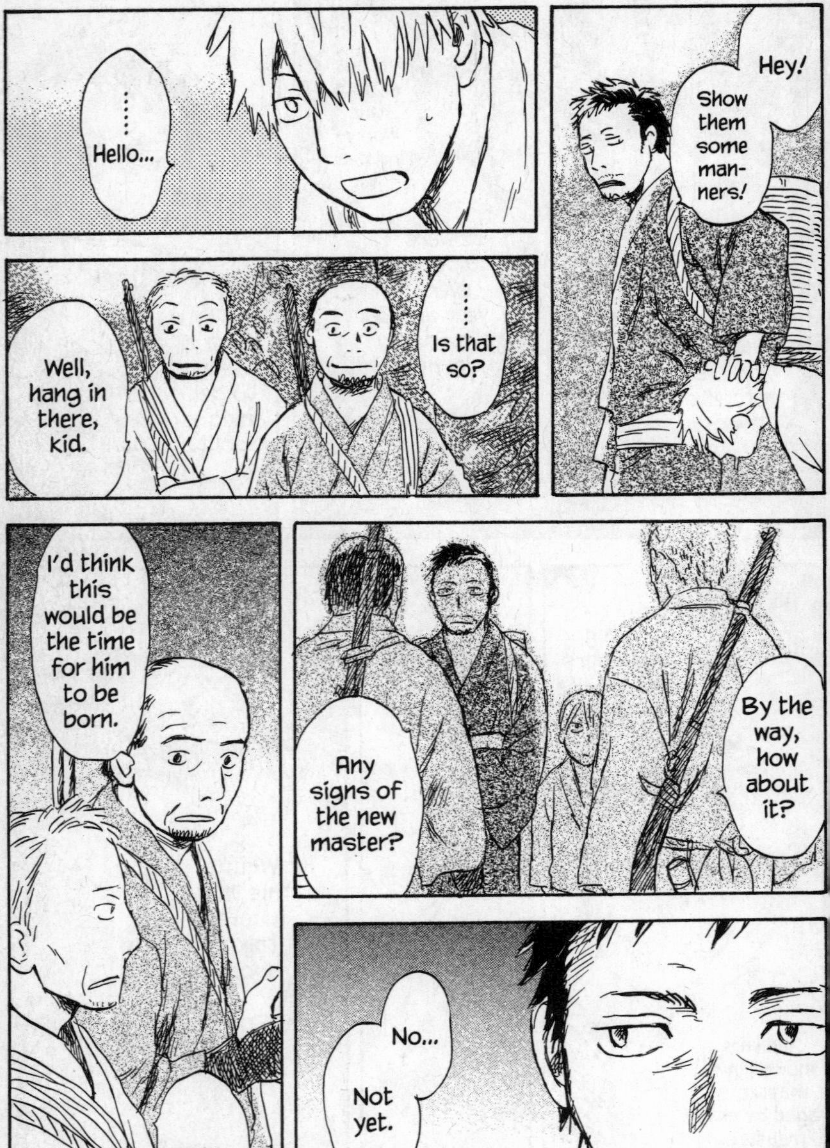
Hey! Show them some man-ners!
……
Hello...
……
Is that so?
Well, hang in there, kid.
By the way, how about it?
Any signs of the new master?
No...
Not yet.
I'd think this would be the time for him to be born.
Right...

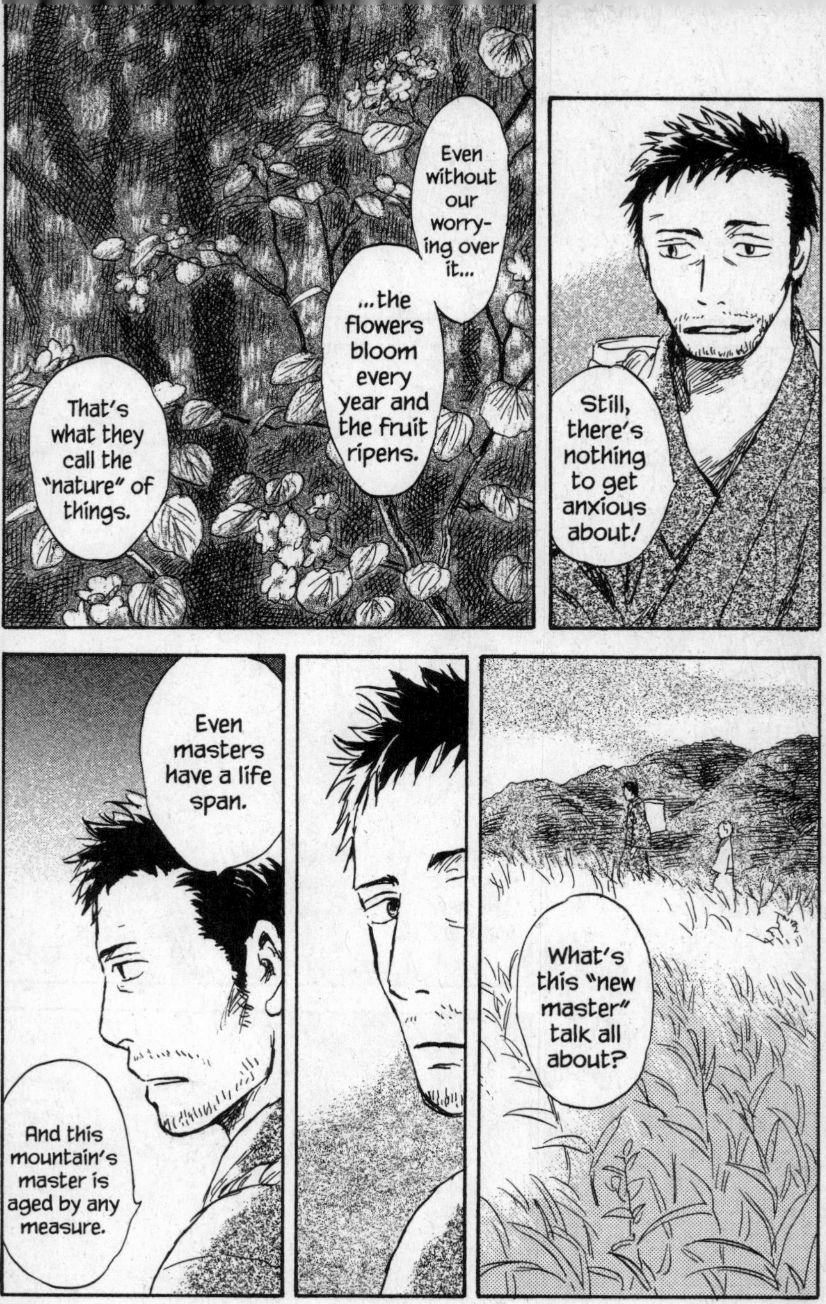
Still, there's nothing to get anxious about!
Even without our worrying over it...
...the flowers bloom every year and the fruit ripens.
That's what they call the "nature" of things.
What's this "new master" talk all about?
Even masters have a life span.
And this mountain's master is aged by any measure.

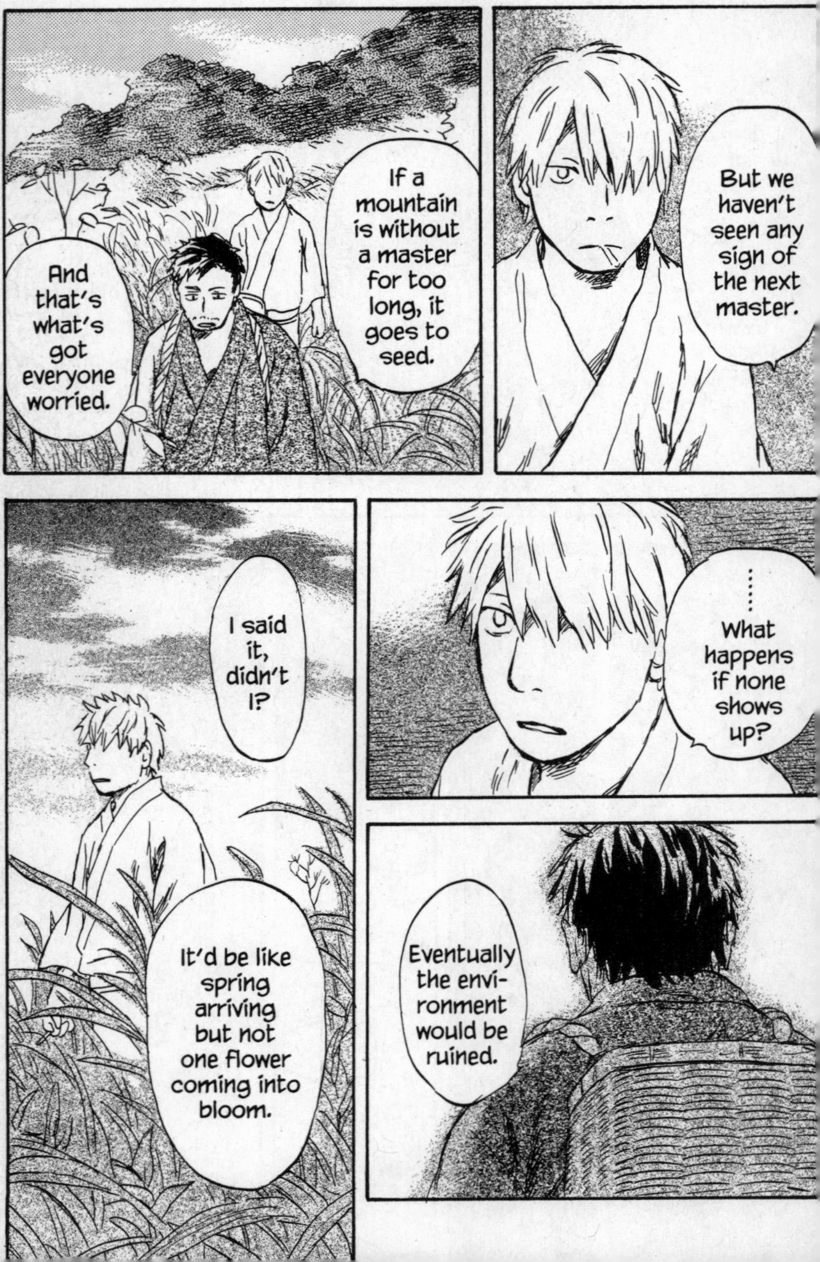
But we haven't seen any sign of the next master.
If a mountain is without a master for too long, it goes to seed.
And that's what's got everyone worried.
...... What happens if none shows up?
Eventually the envi-ronment would be ruined.
I said it, didn't I?
It'd be like spring arriving but not one flower coming into bloom.

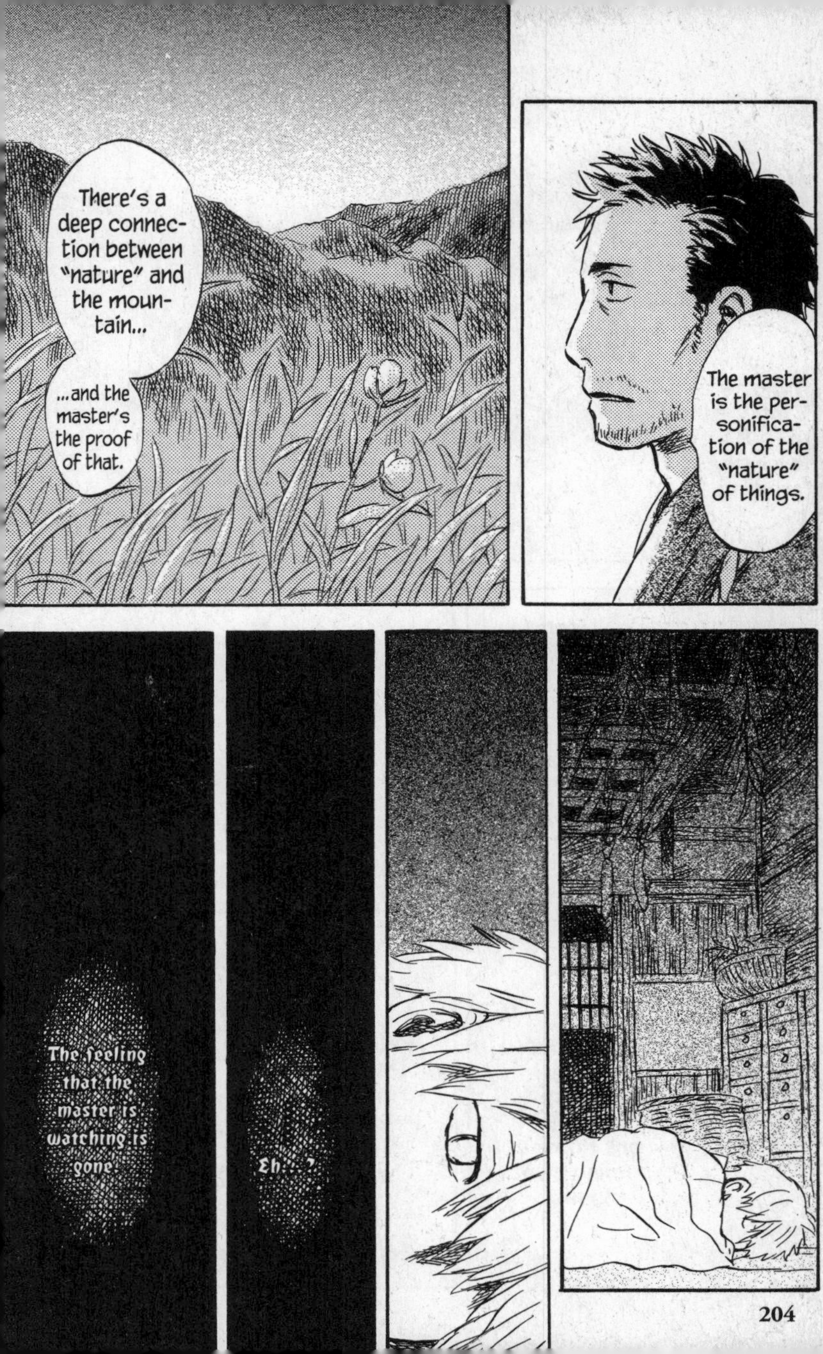
The master is the personification of the "nature" of things.
There's a deep connection between "nature" and the mountain...
...and the master's the proof of that.
Eh...?
The feeling that the master is watching is gone.

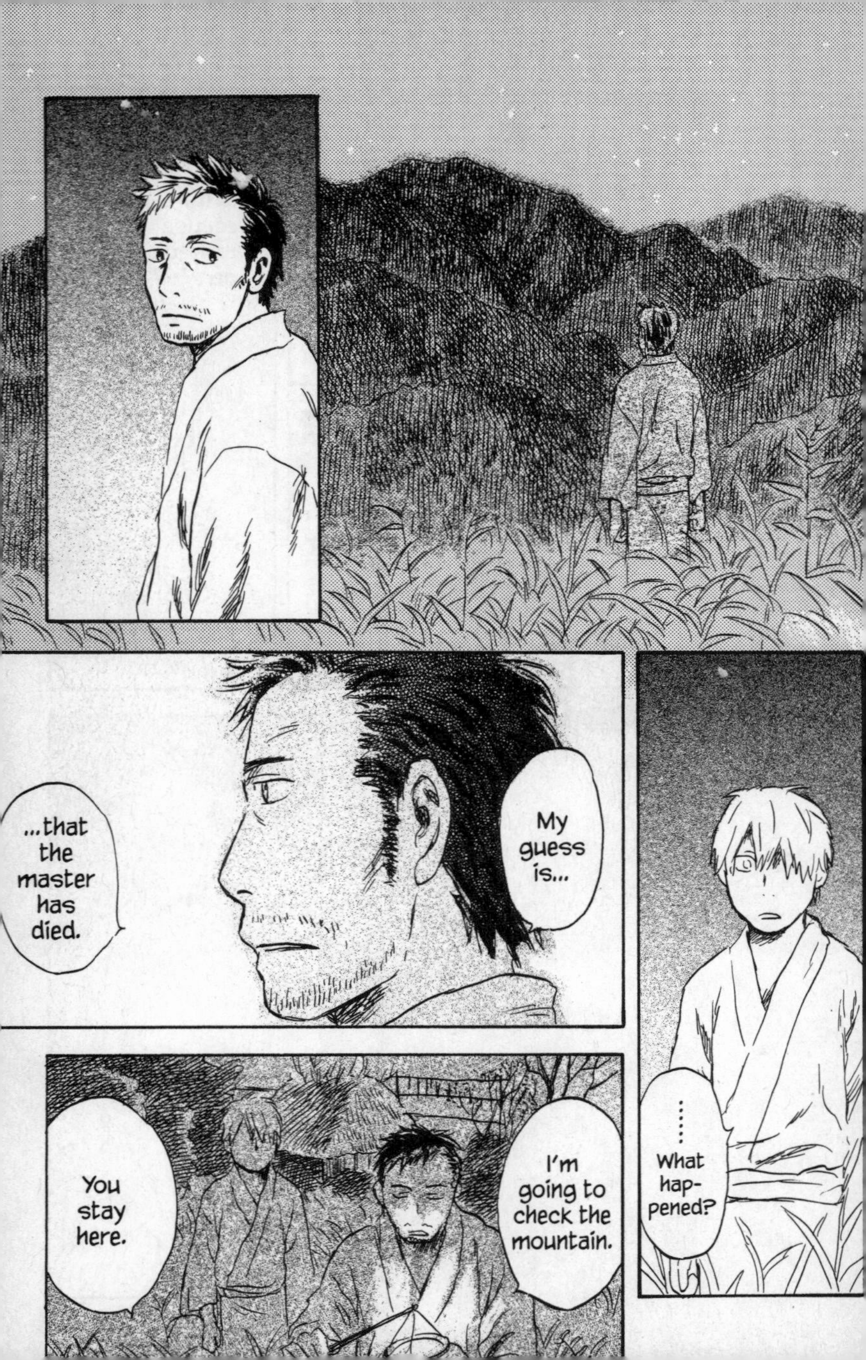
......
What hap-pened?
My guess is...
...that the master has died.
I'm going to check the mountain.
You stay here.

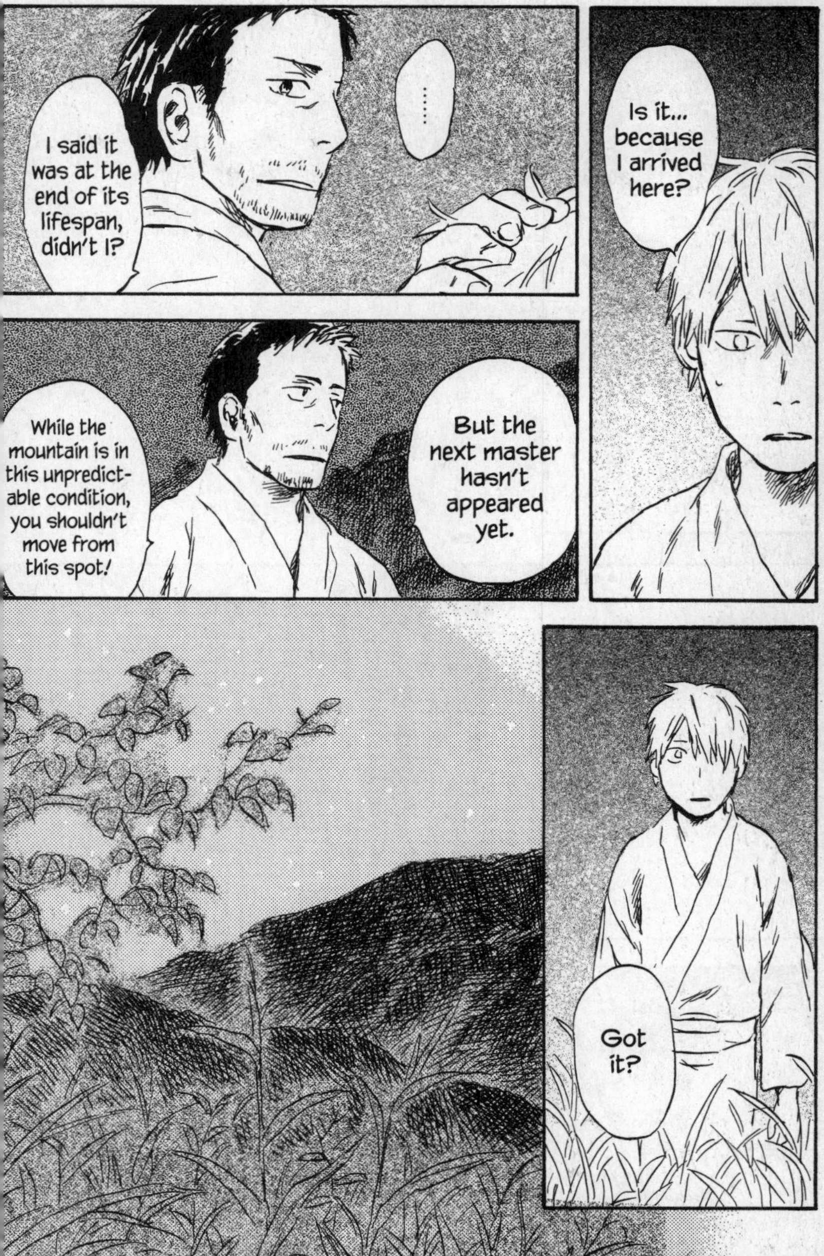
Is it... because I arrived here?
......
I said it was at the end of its lifespan, didn't I?
But the next master hasn't appeared yet.
While the mountain is in this unpredict-able condition, you shouldn't move from this spot!
Got it?

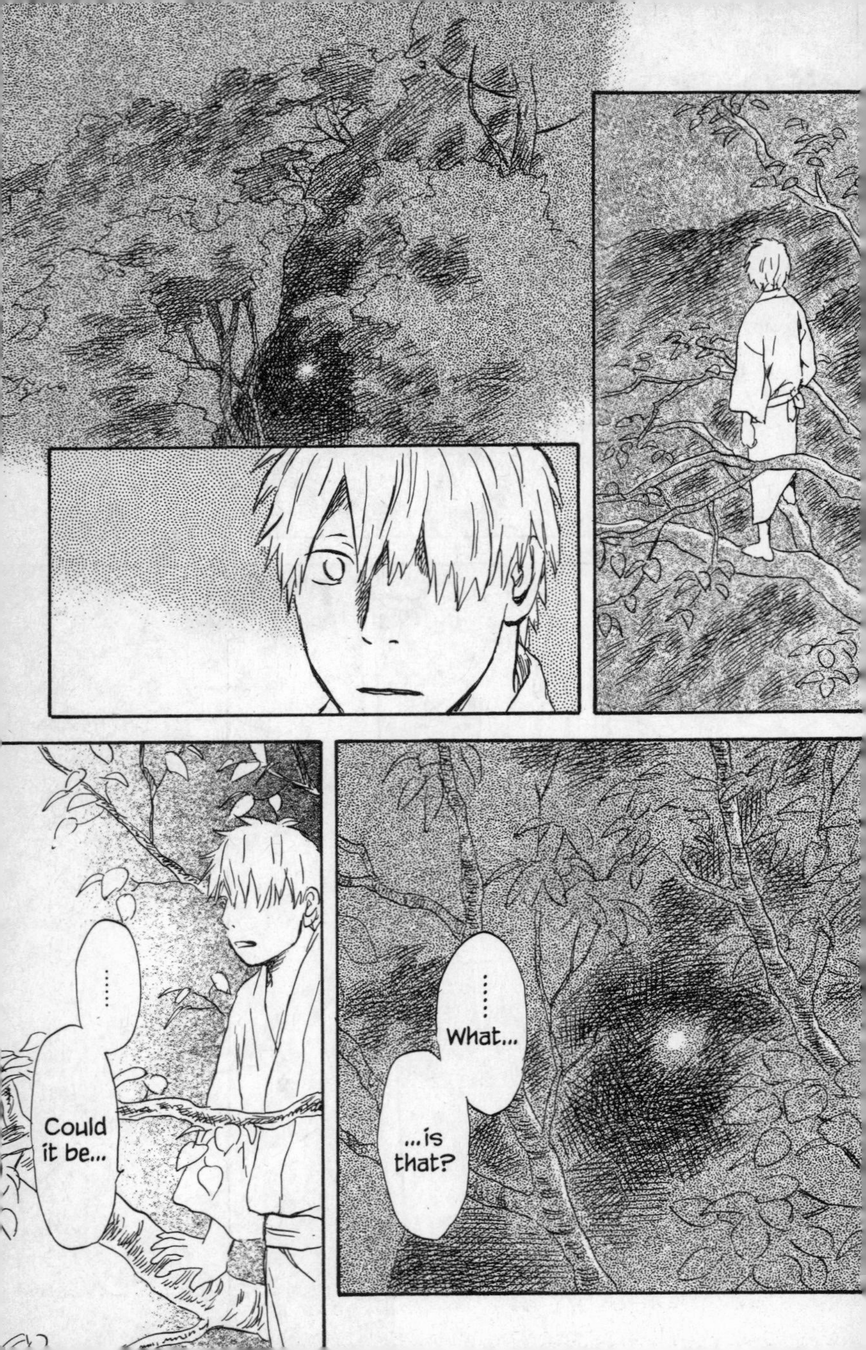
......
What...
...is that?
......
Could it be...

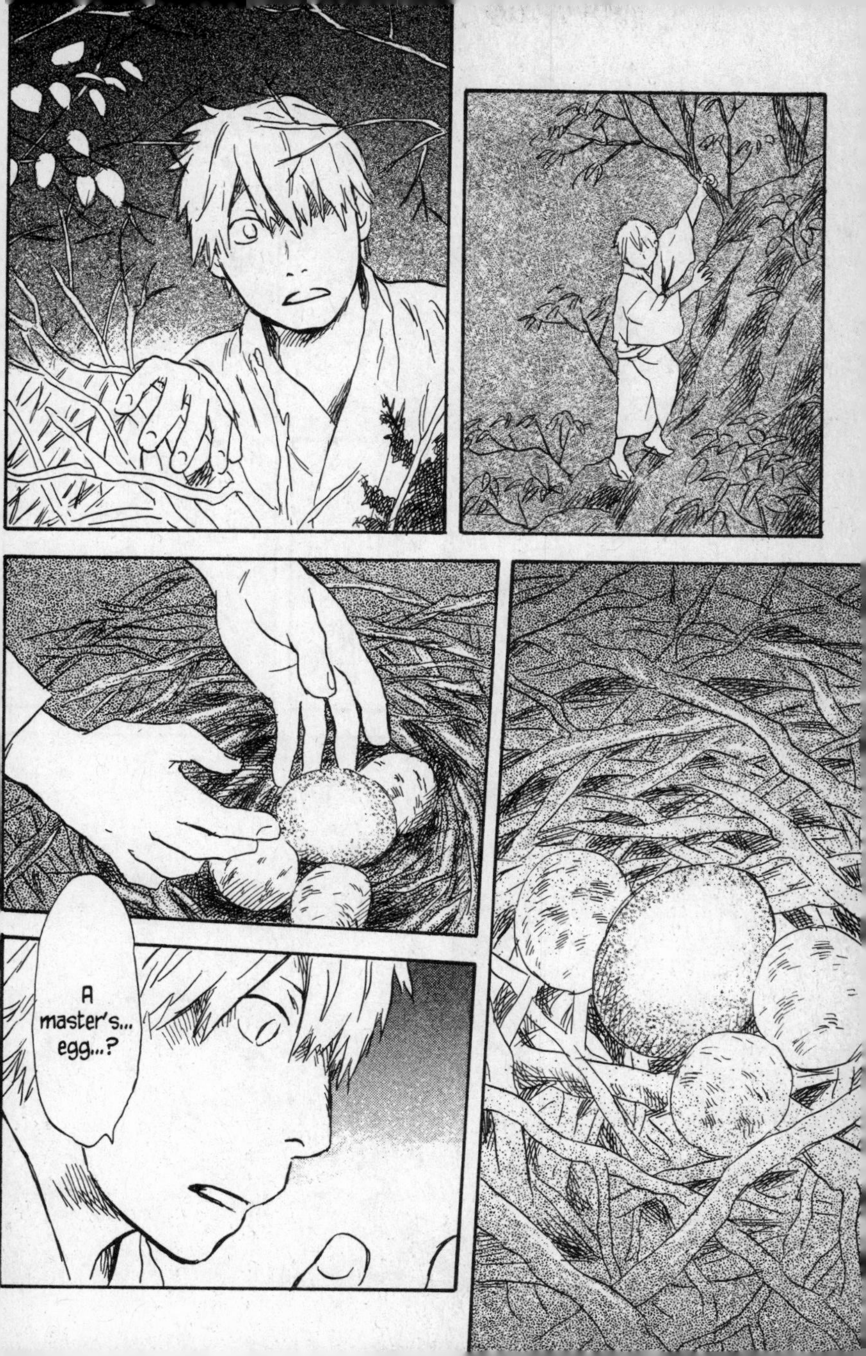
A master's... egg...?

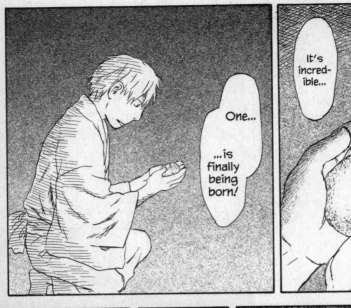

It's incred-ible...
One...
...is finally being born!
The...
...master's power I felt...
...is right inside here!

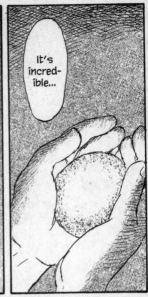

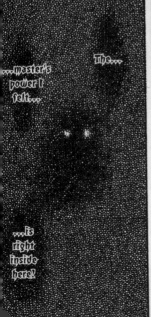

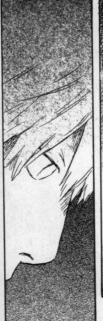

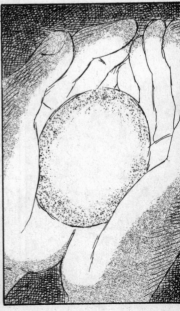

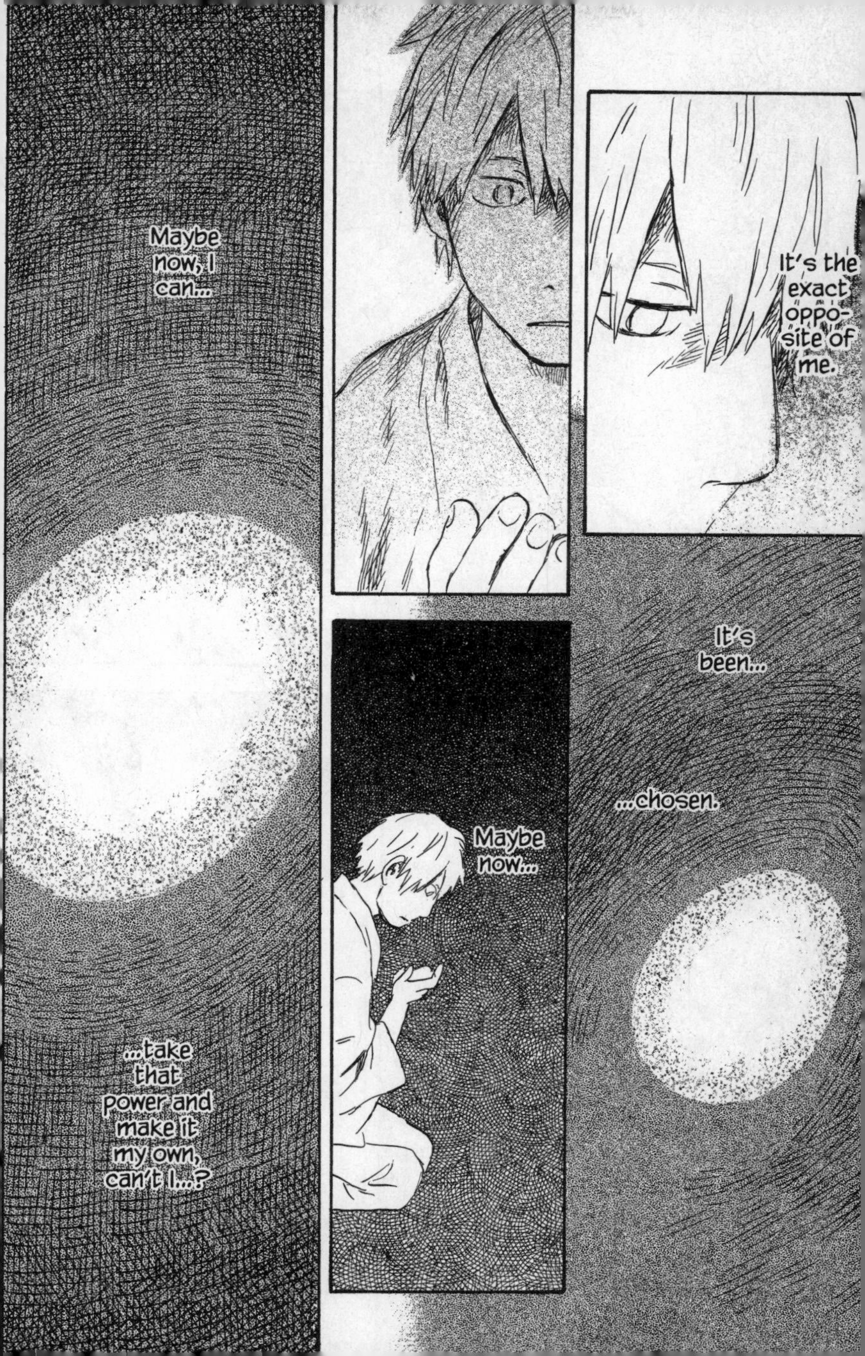
It's the exact oppo-site of me.
It's been...
...chosen.
Maybe now...
Maybe now, I can...
...take that power and make it my own, can't I...?

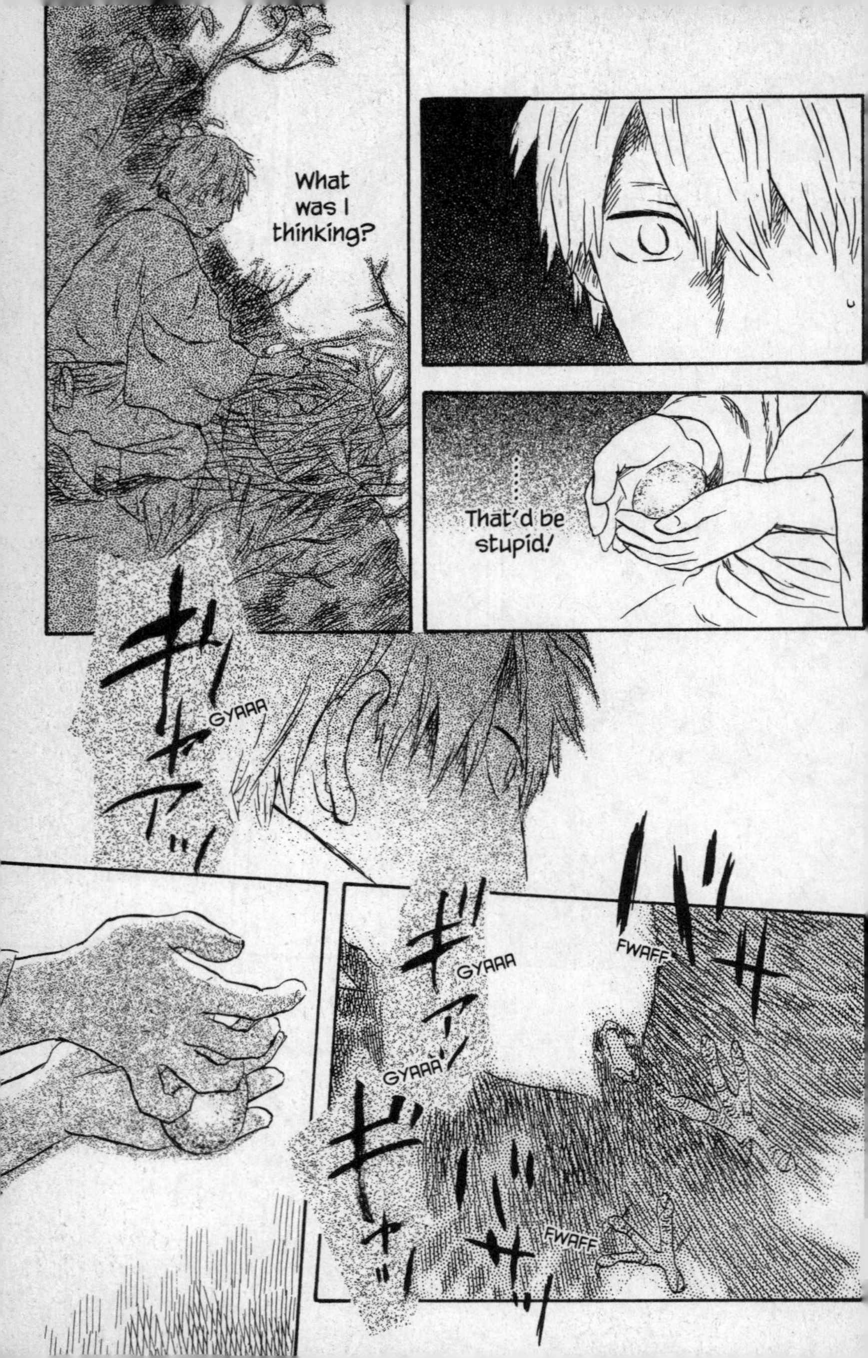
......
That'd be stupid!
What was I thinking?
GYAAA
FWAFF
GYAAA
GYAAA
FWAFF

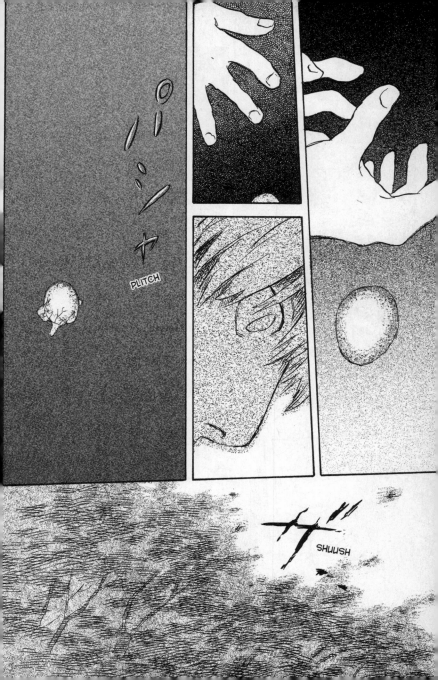

PLITCH

SHUUSH

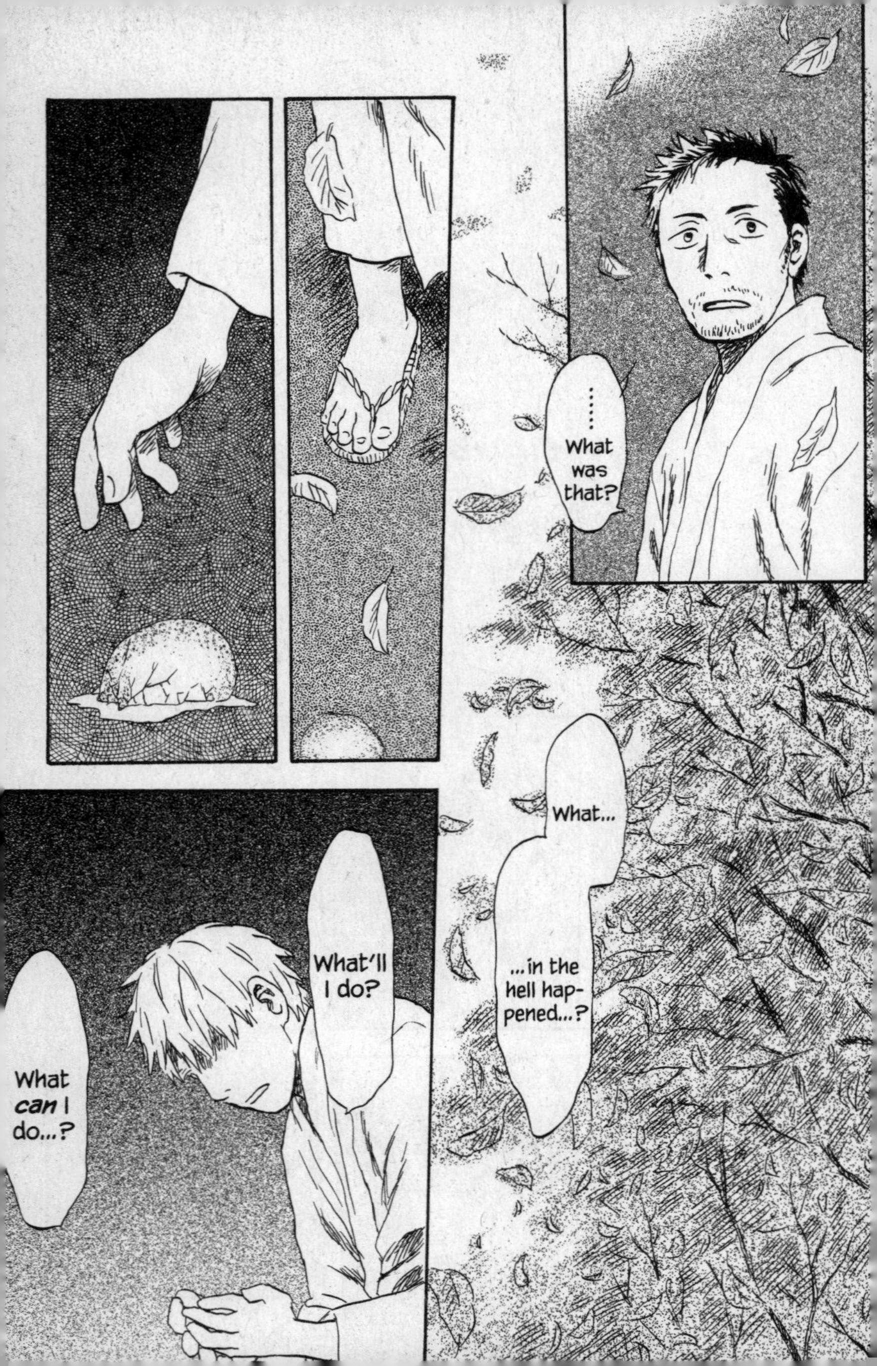
......
What was that?
What...
...in the hell hap-pened...?
What'll I do?
What *can* I do...?

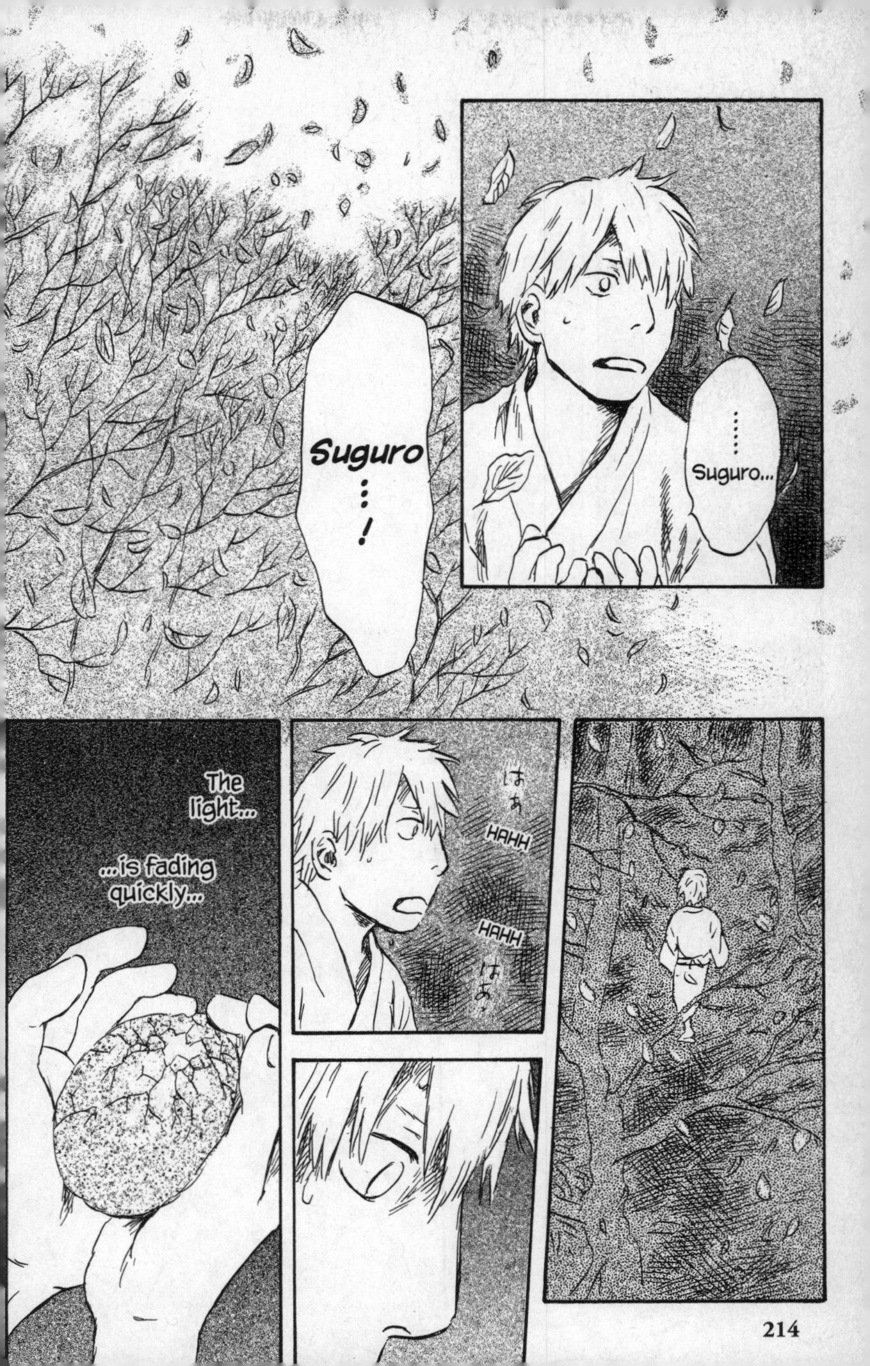
......
Suguro...
Suguro...!
はあ
HAHH
HAHH
はあ
The light...
...is fading quickly...

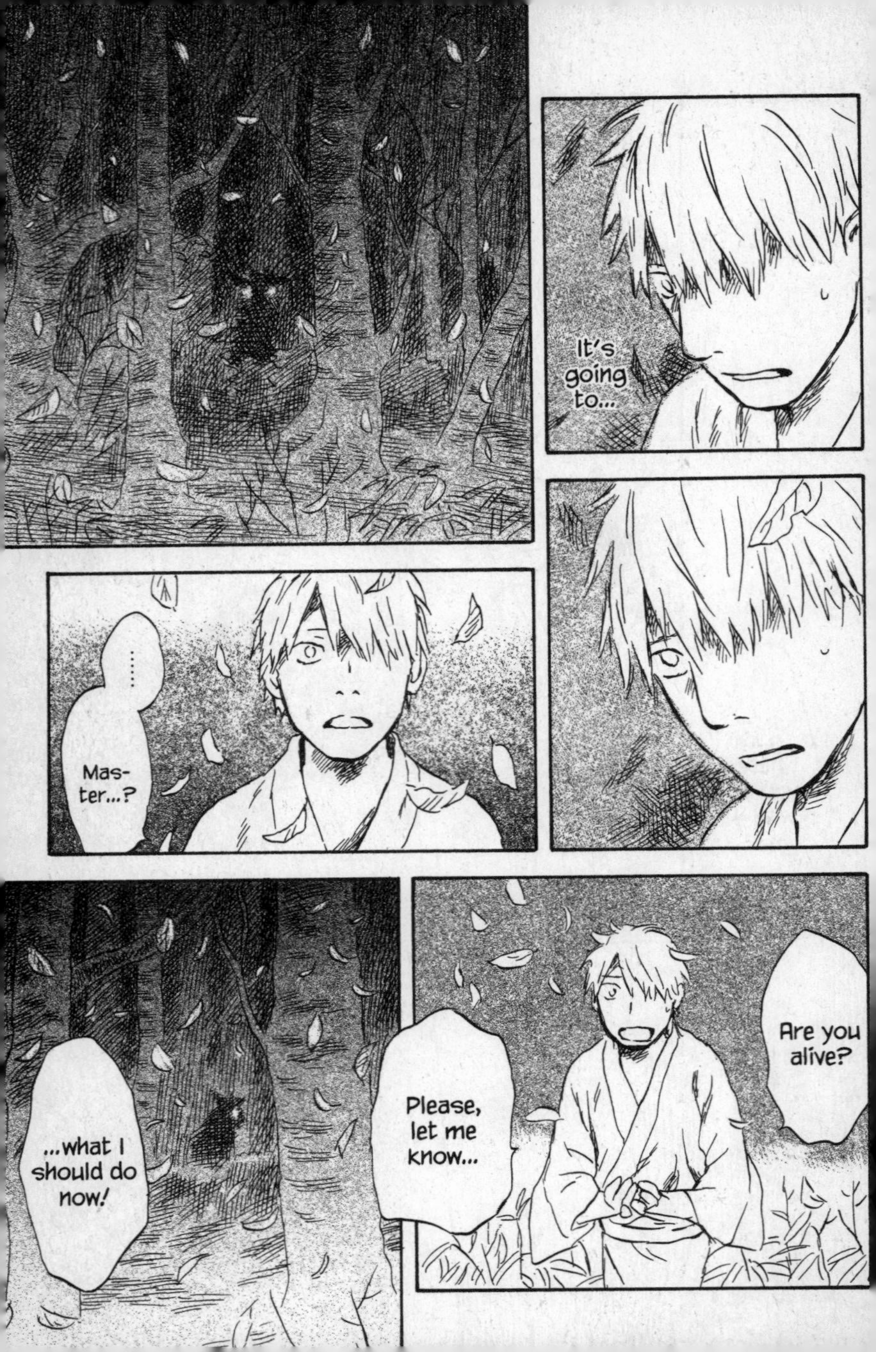
It's going to...
......
Mas-ter...?
Are you alive?
Please, let me know...
...what I should do now!

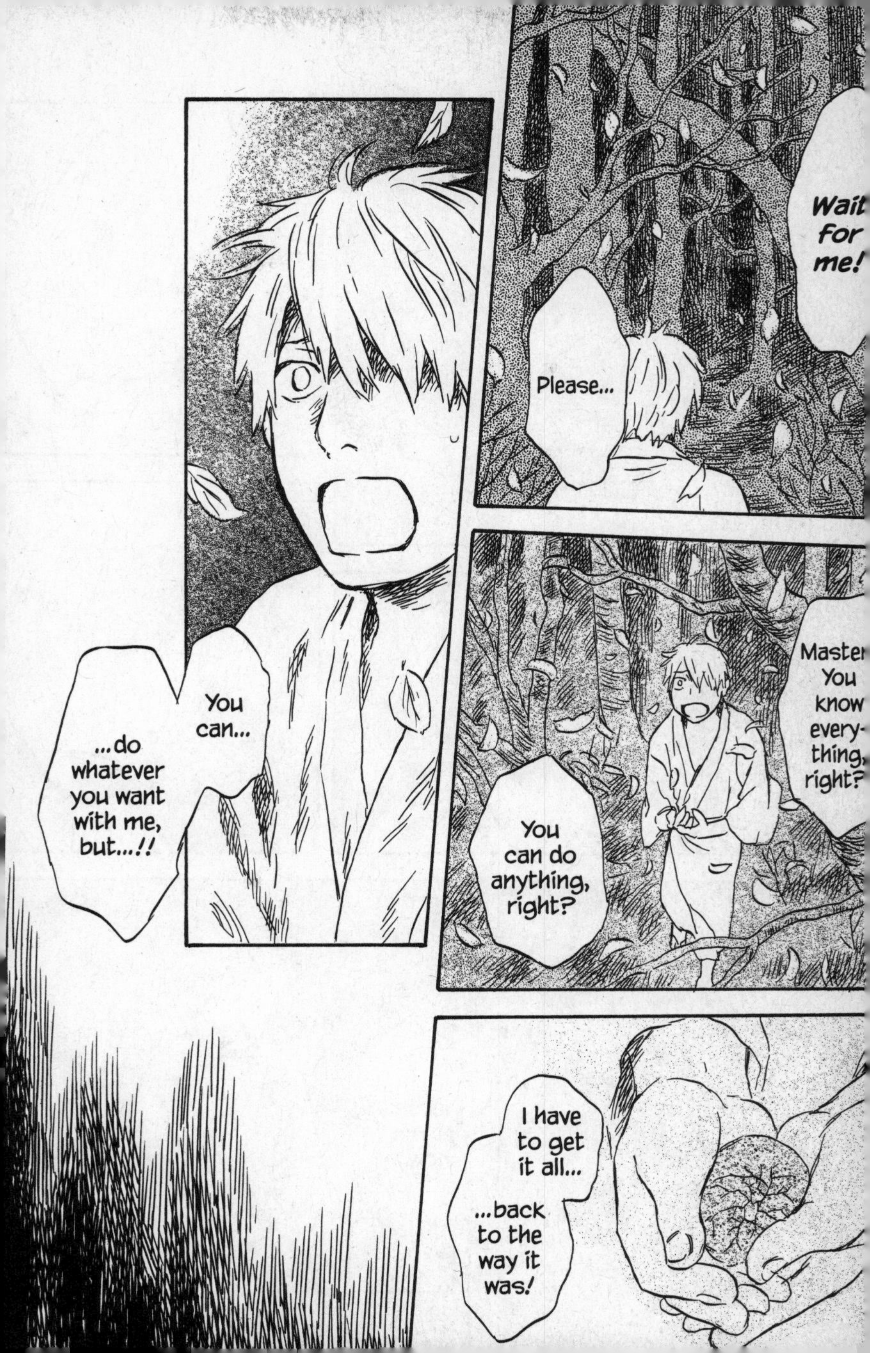
Wait for me!
Please...
Master You know every-thing, right?
You can do anything, right?
You can...
...do whatever you want with me, but...!!
I have to get it all...
...back to the way it was!

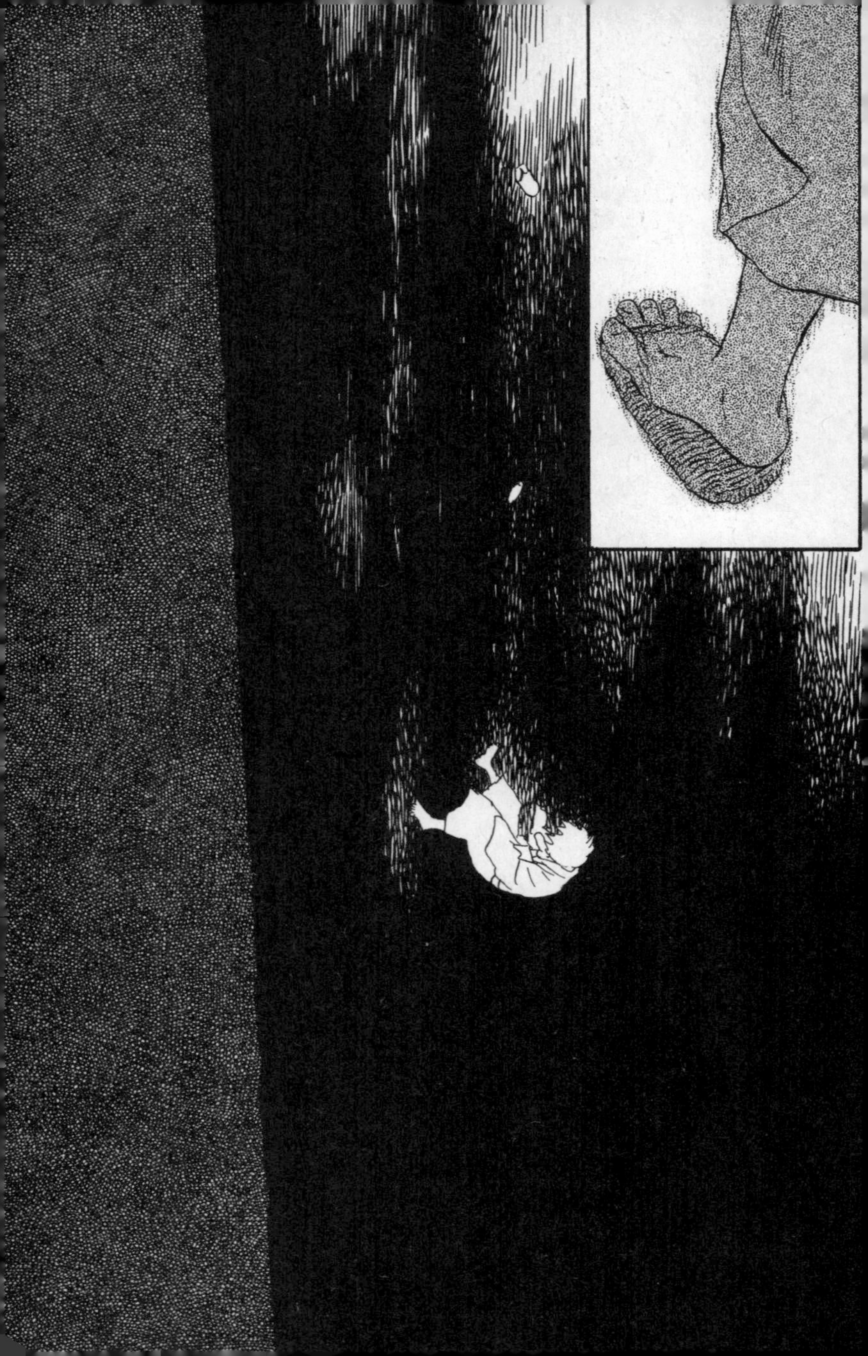

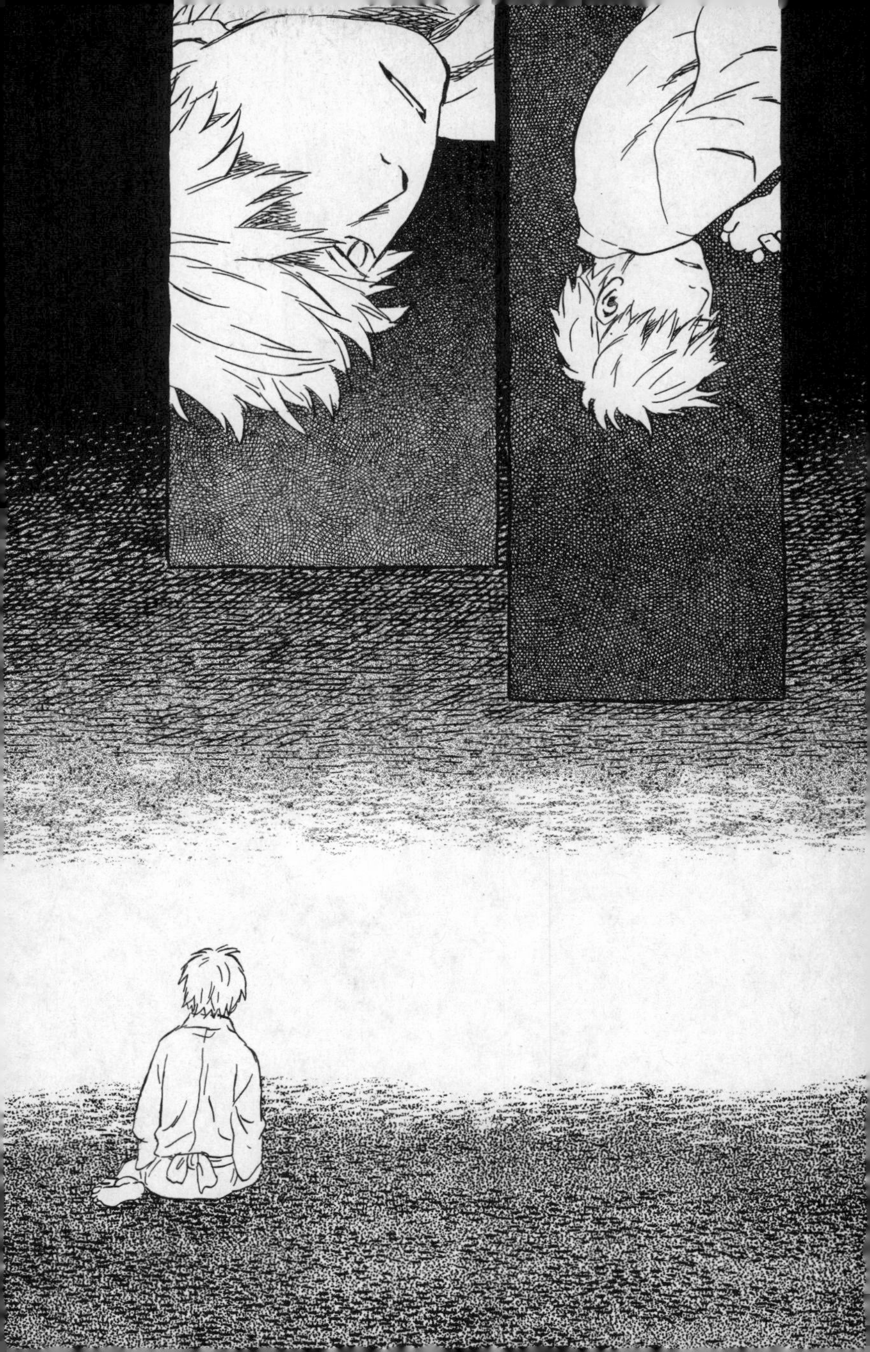

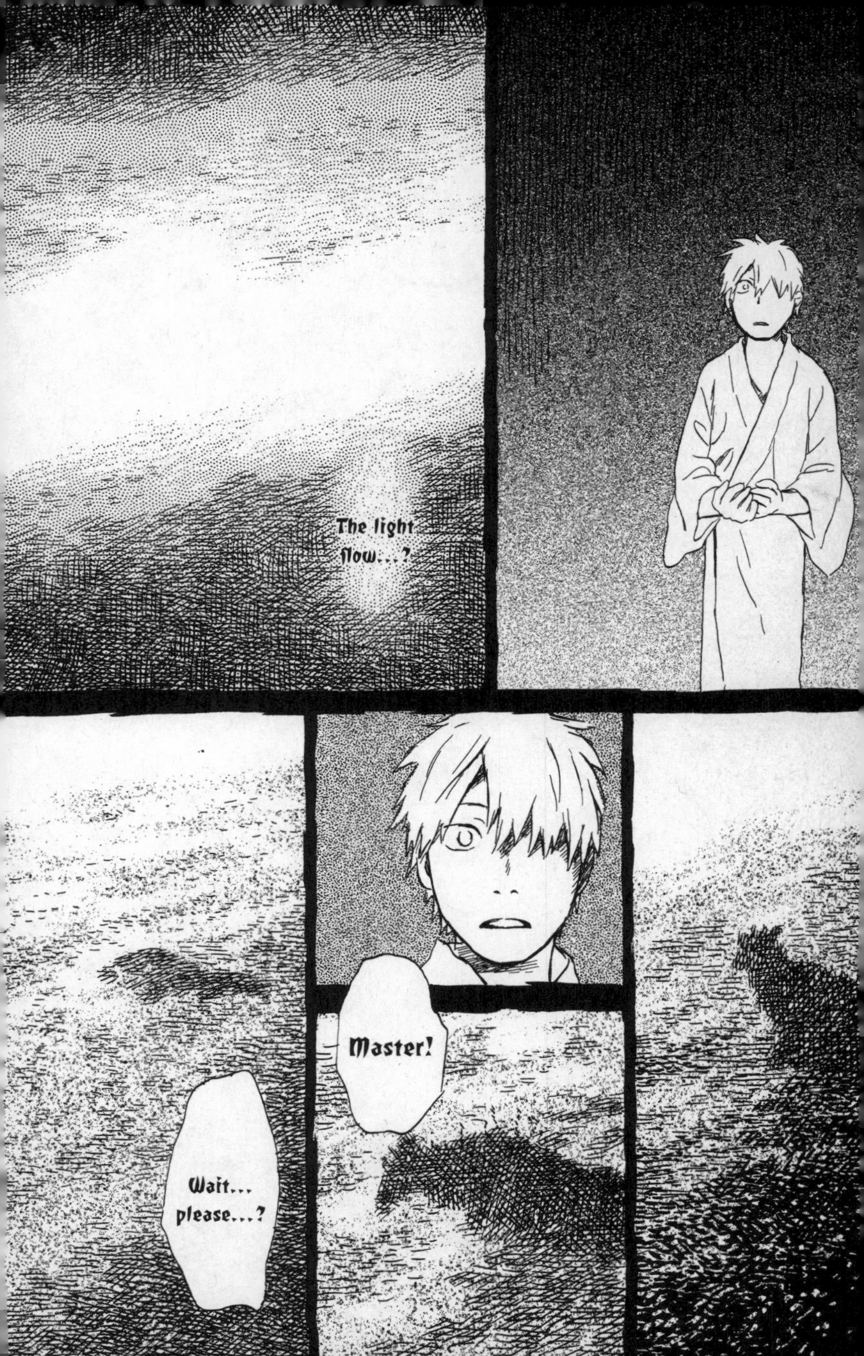
The light flow...?
Master!
Wait... please...?

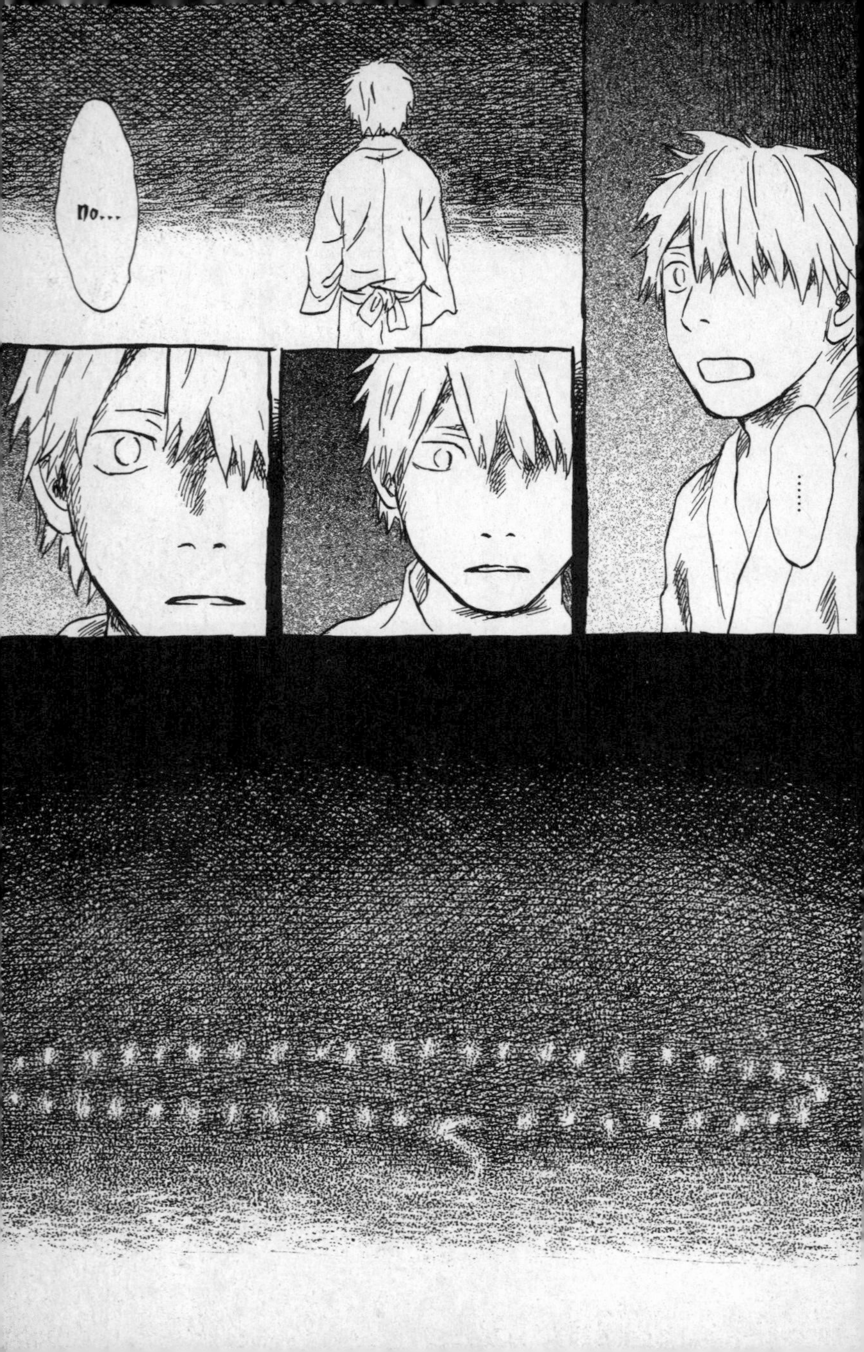
......
no...

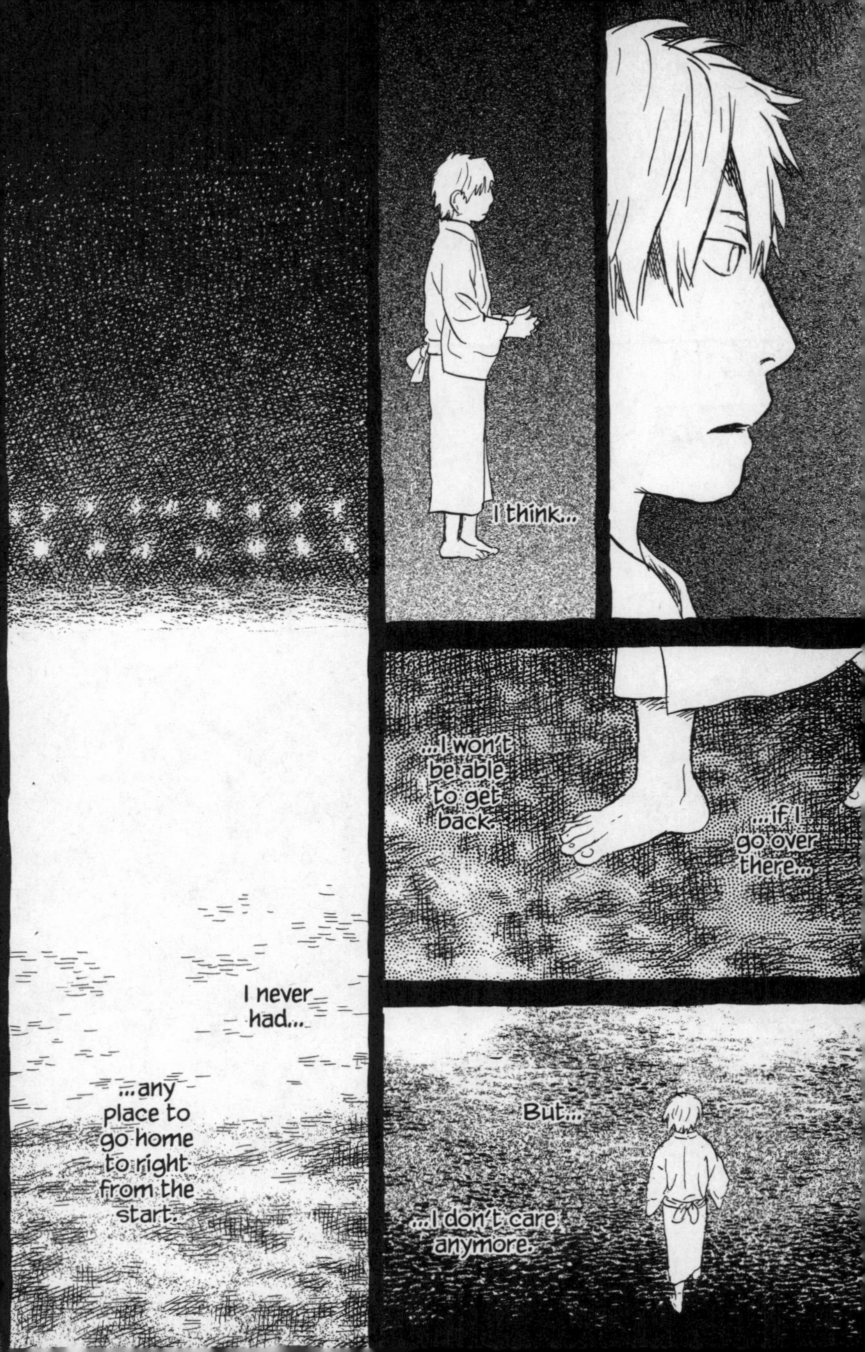
I think...
...if I go over there...
...I won't be able to get back.
But...
...I don't care anymore.
I never had...
...any place to go home to right from the start.

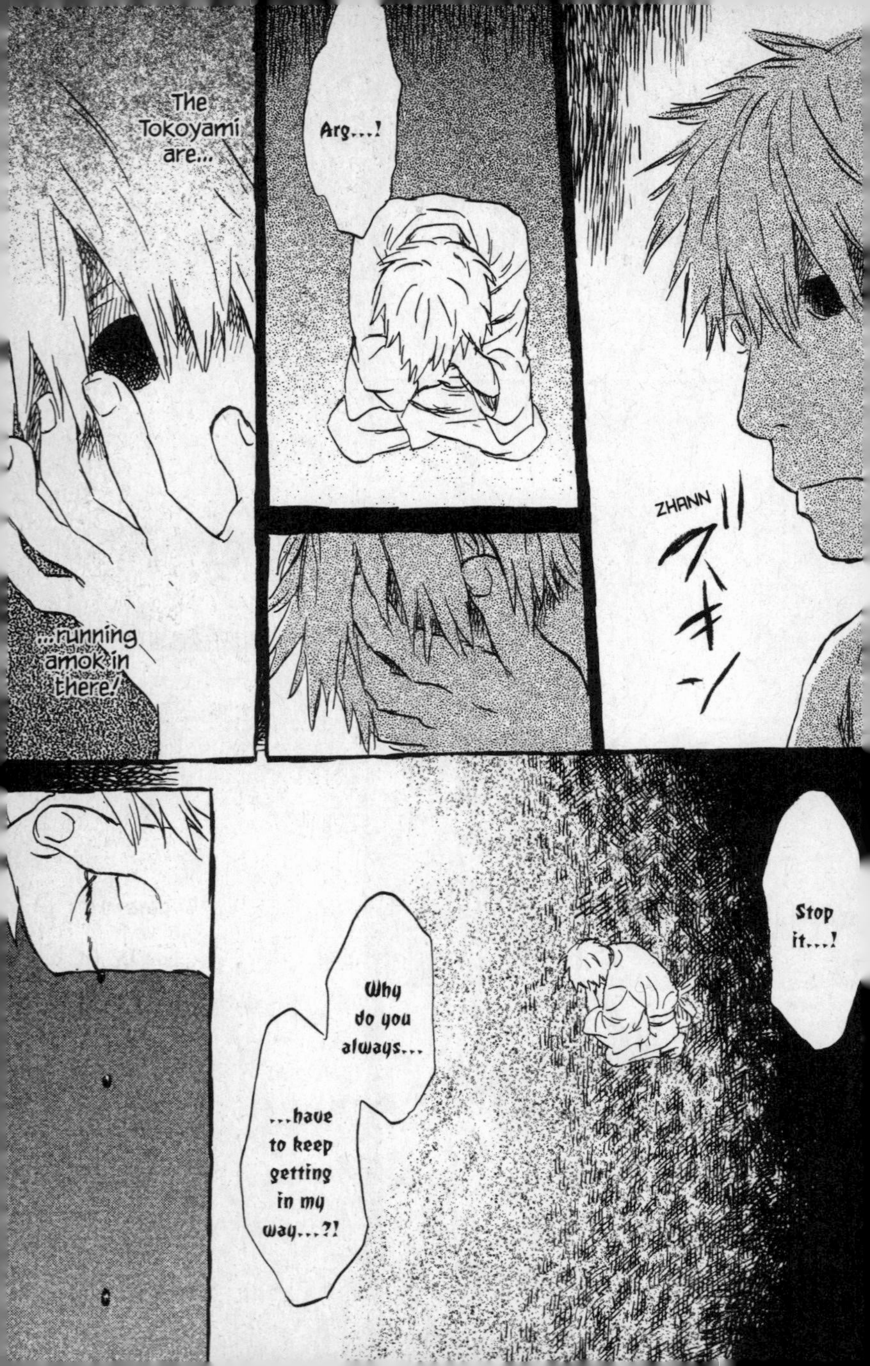
ZHANN
Arg...!
The Tokoyami are...
...running amok in there!
Stop it...!
Why do you always...
...have to keep getting in my way...?!

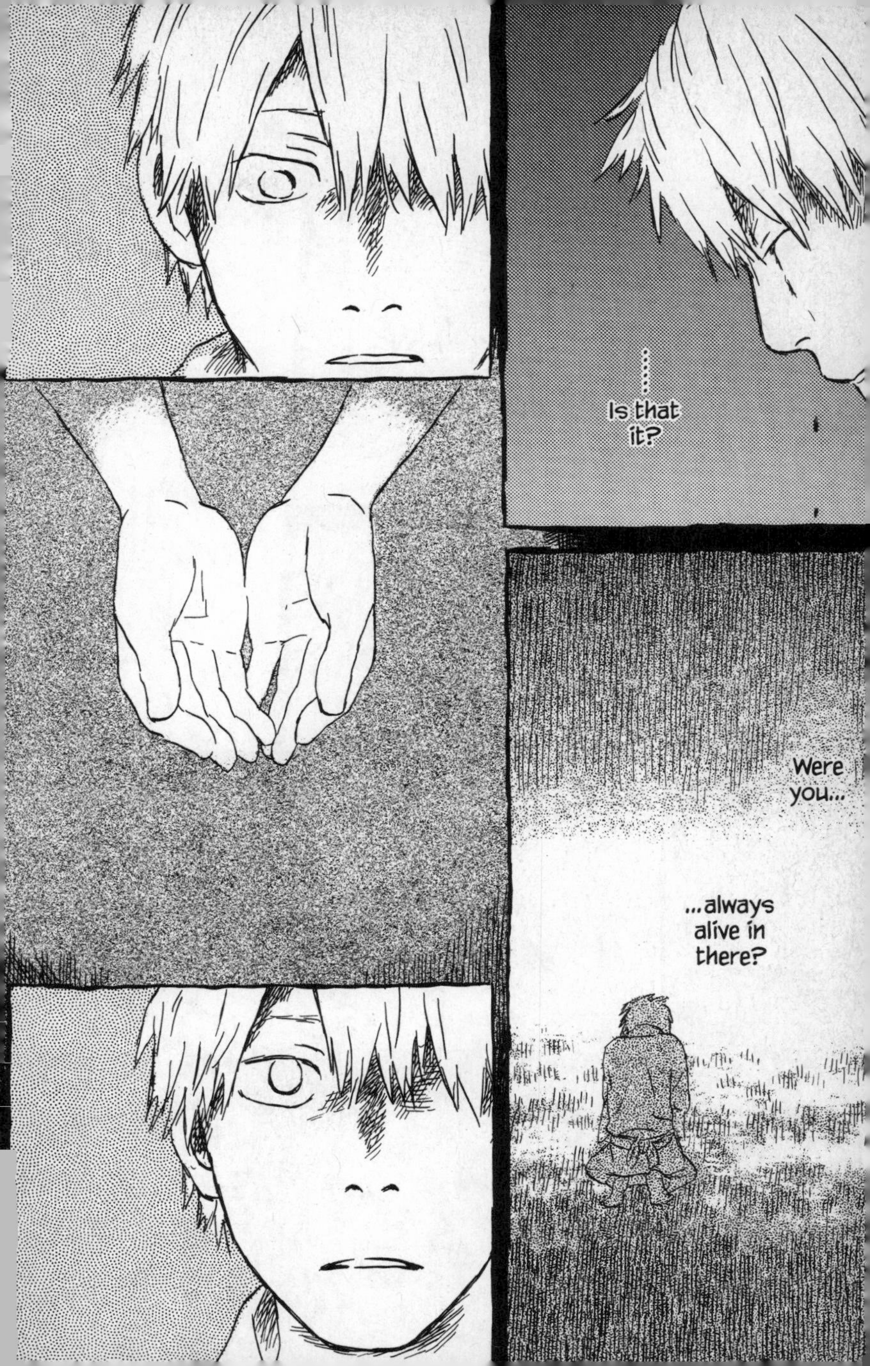
......
Is that it?
Were you...
...always alive in there?

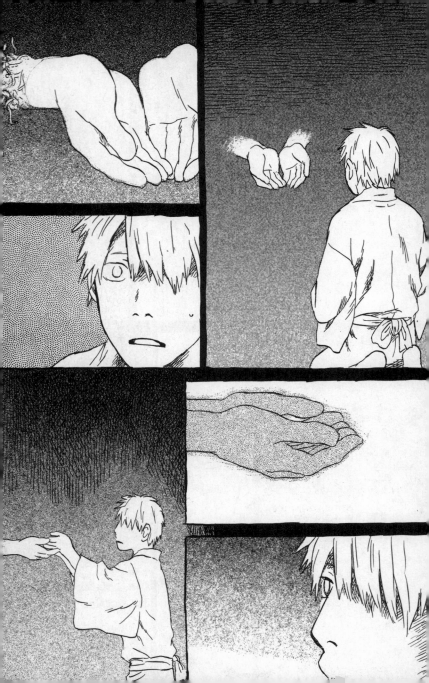

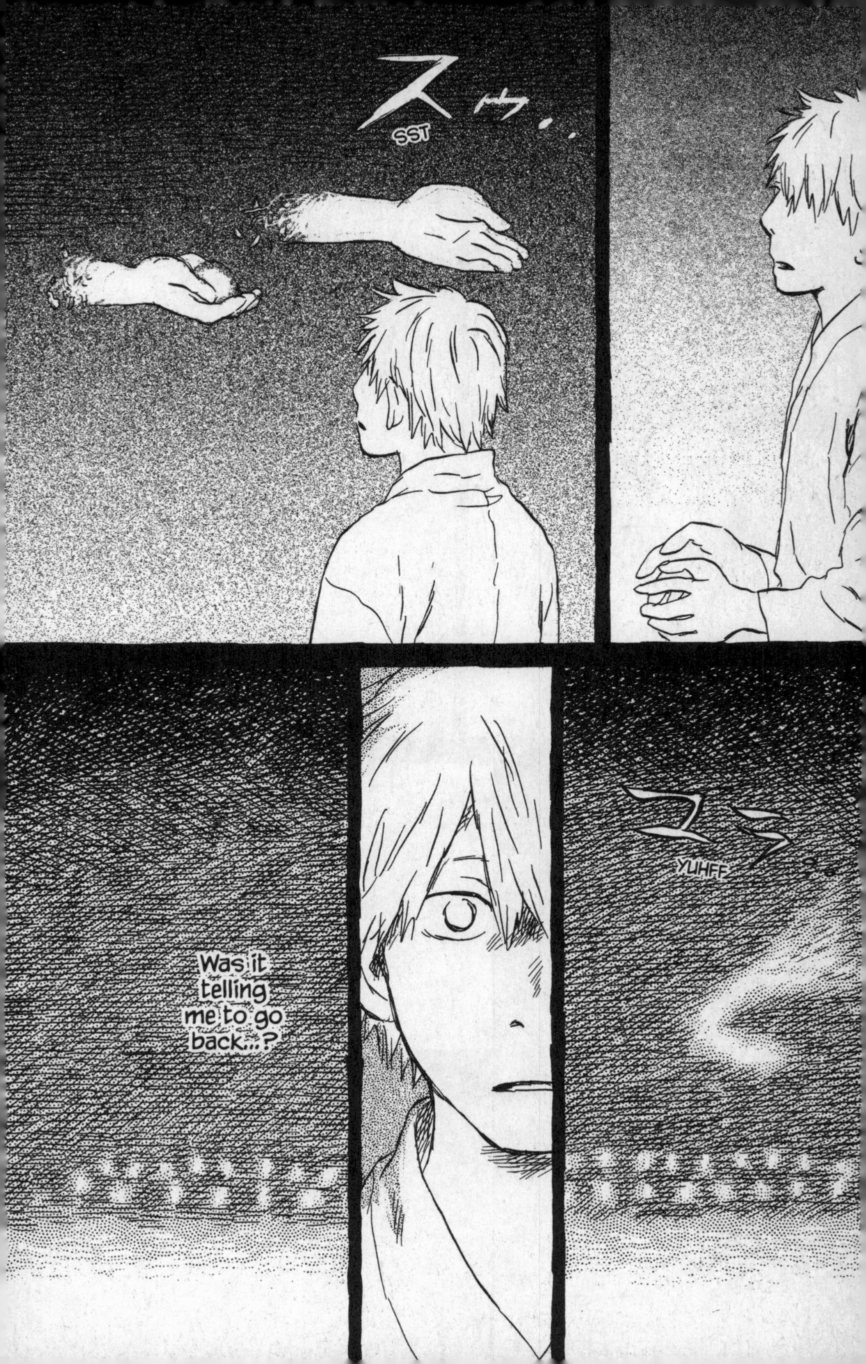
SST
YUHFF
Was it telling me to go back...?

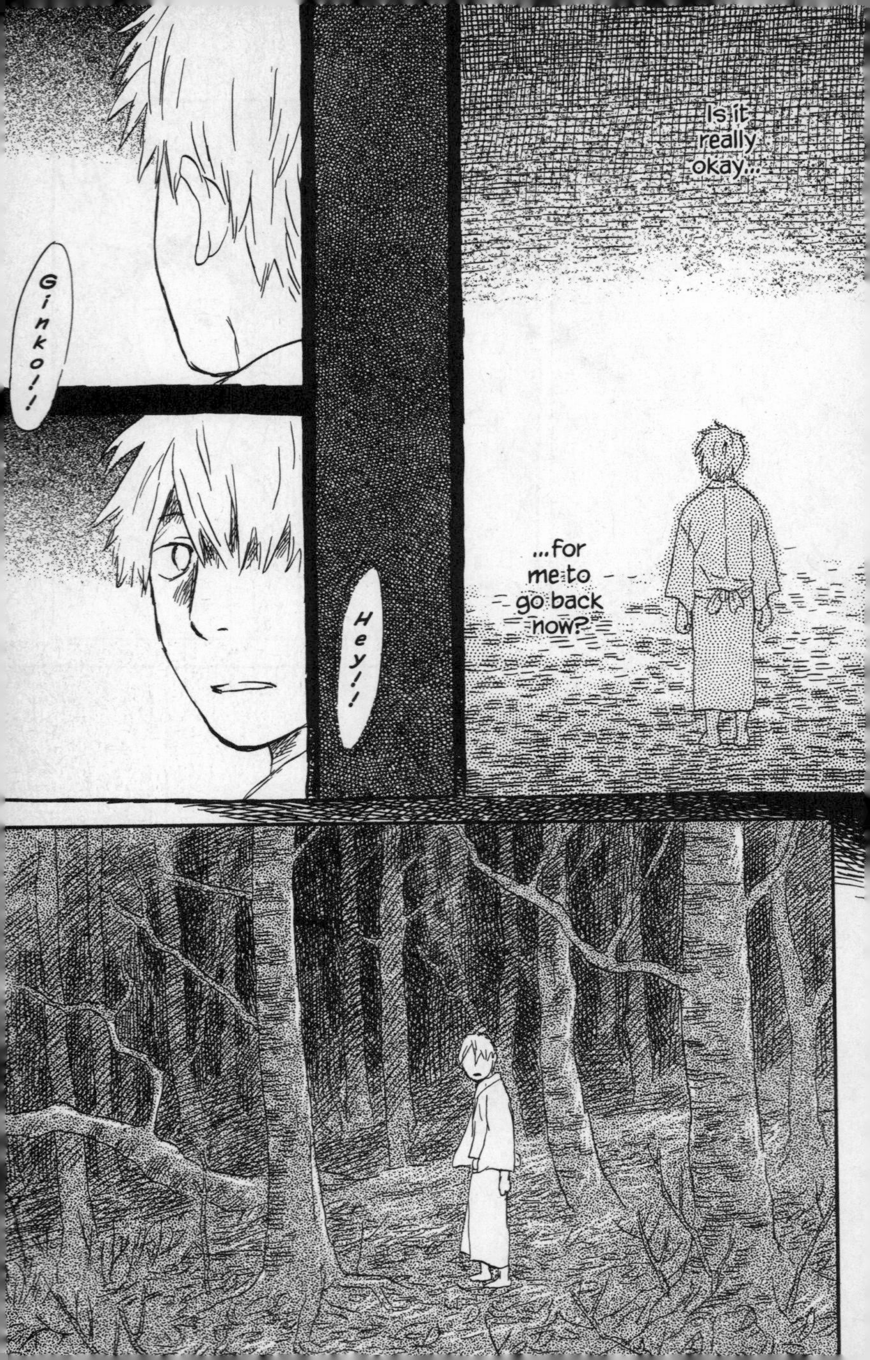
Is it really okay...
...for me to go back now?
Hey!!
Ginko!!

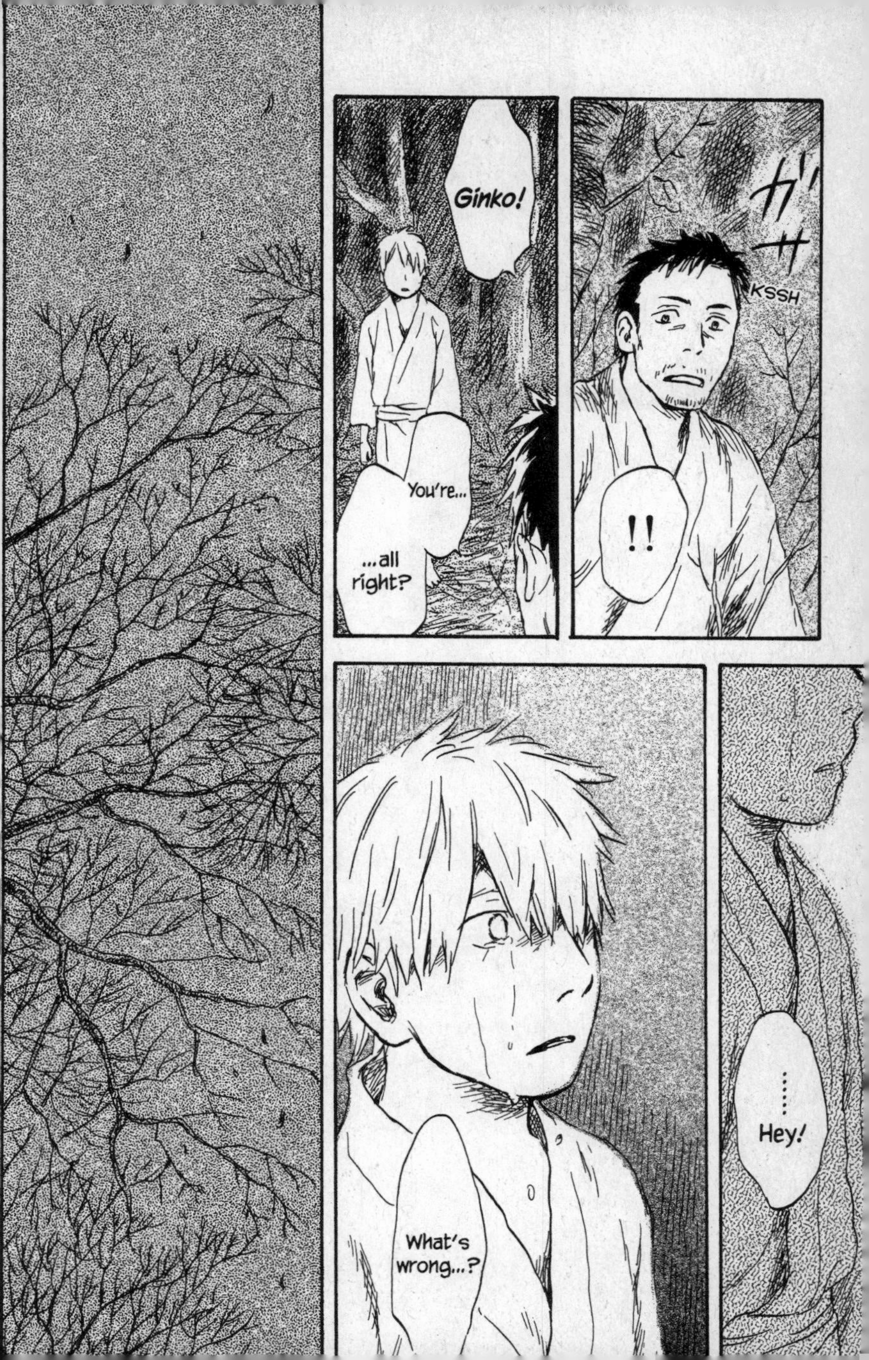
ガサ
KSSH
!!
Ginko!
You're...
...all right?
......
Hey!
What's wrong...?

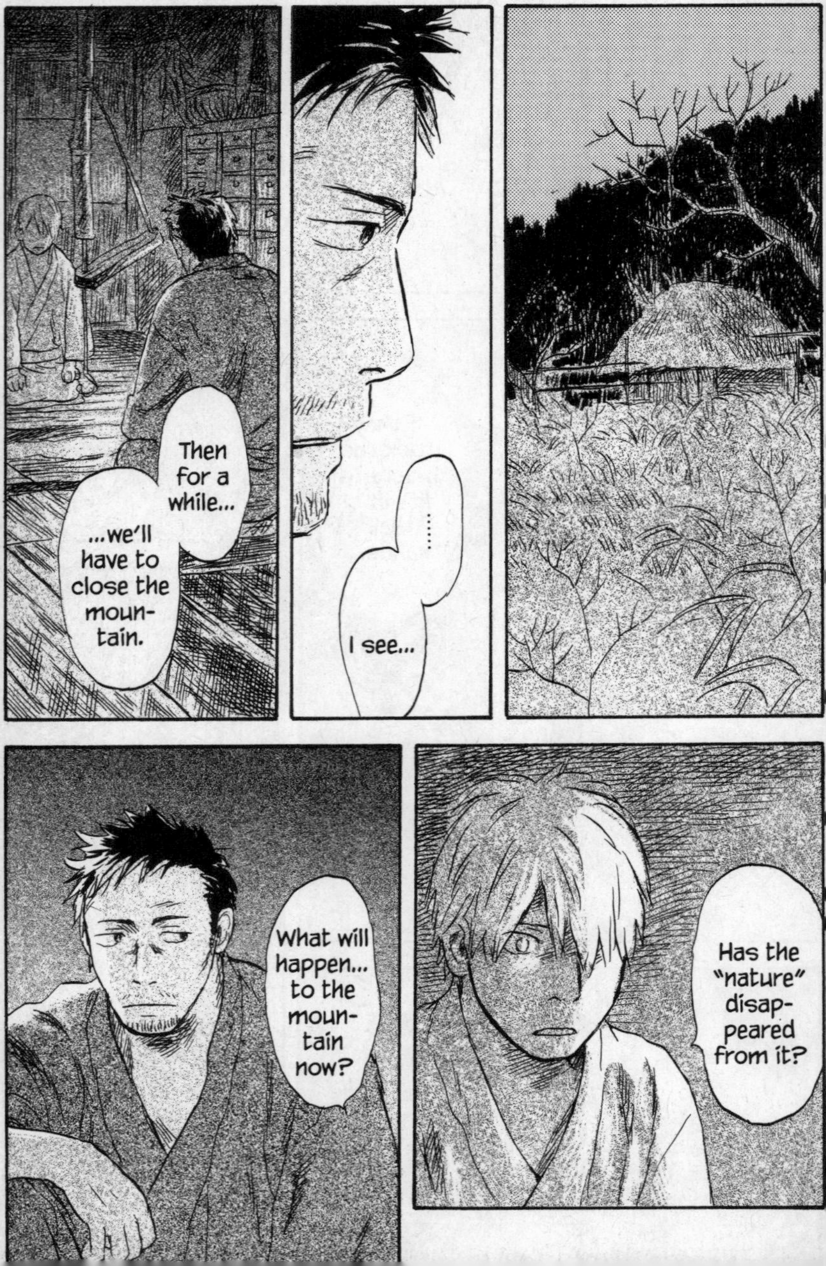
......
I see...
Then for a while...
...we'll have to close the mountain.
Has the "nature" disappeared from it?
What will happen... to the mountain now?

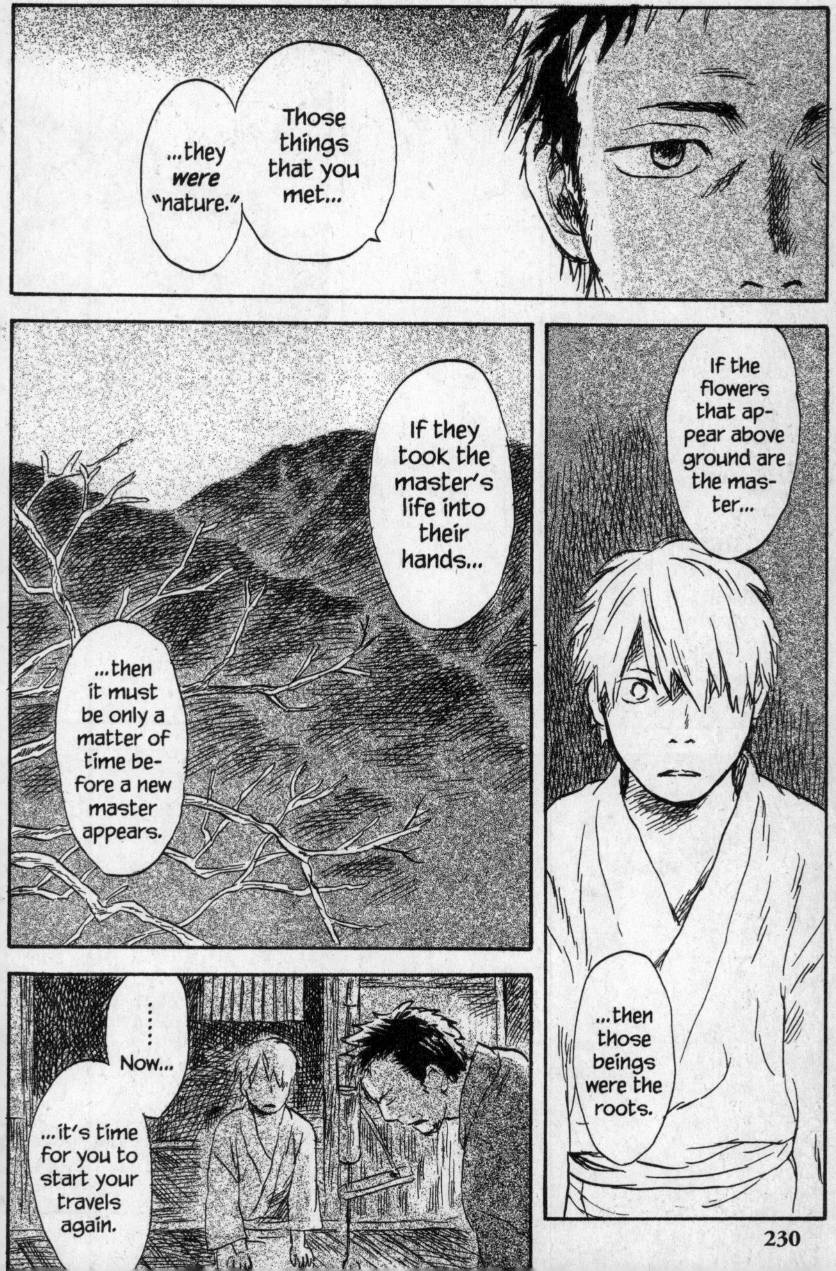
Those things that you met...
...they *were* "nature."
If the flowers that appear above ground are the master...
...then those beings were the roots.
If they took the master's life into their hands...
...then it must be only a matter of time before a new master appears.
......
Now...
...it's time for you to start your travels again.

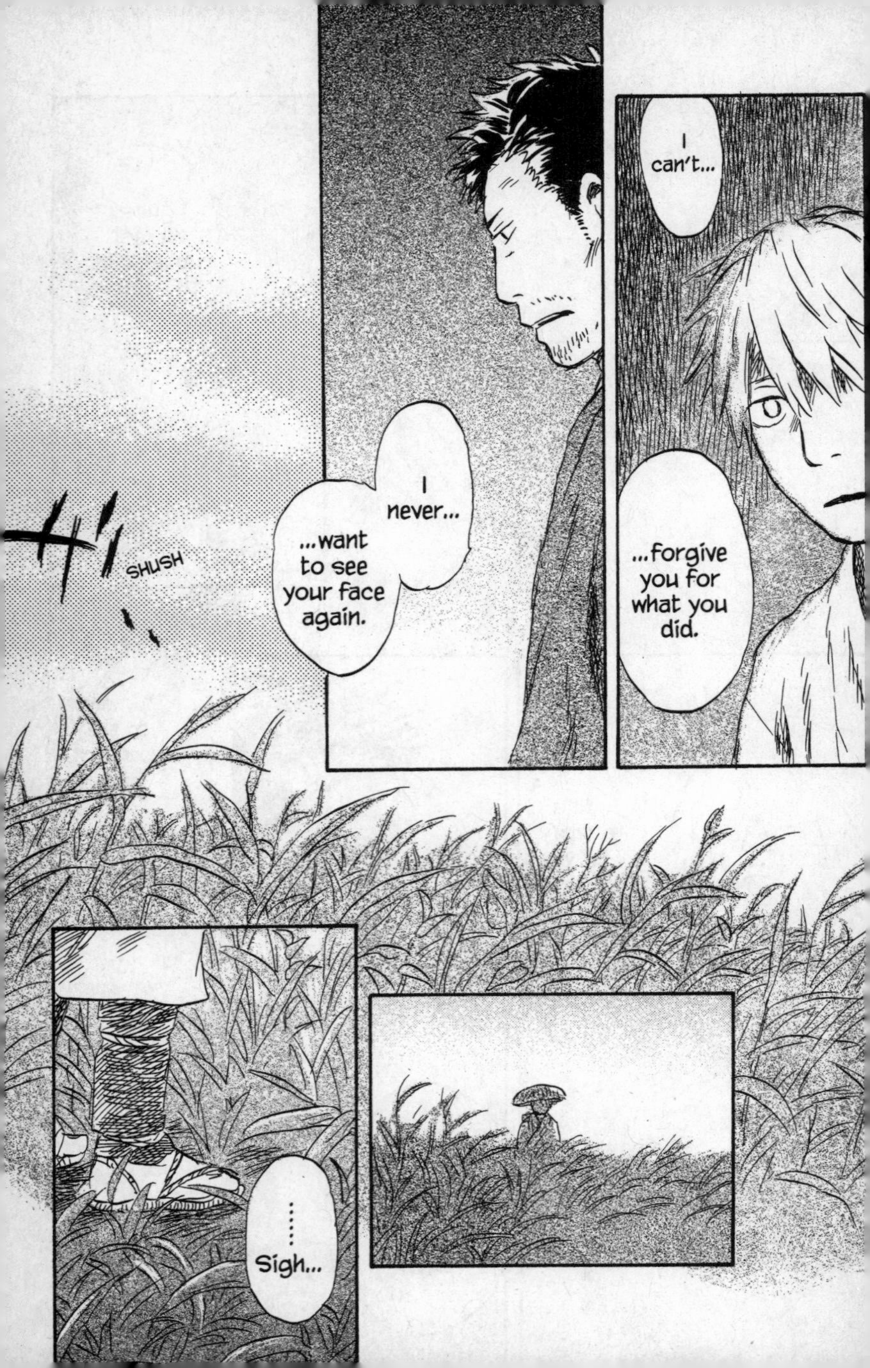

I can't...
...forgive you for what you did.
I never...
...want to see your face again.
SHUSH
......
Sigh...

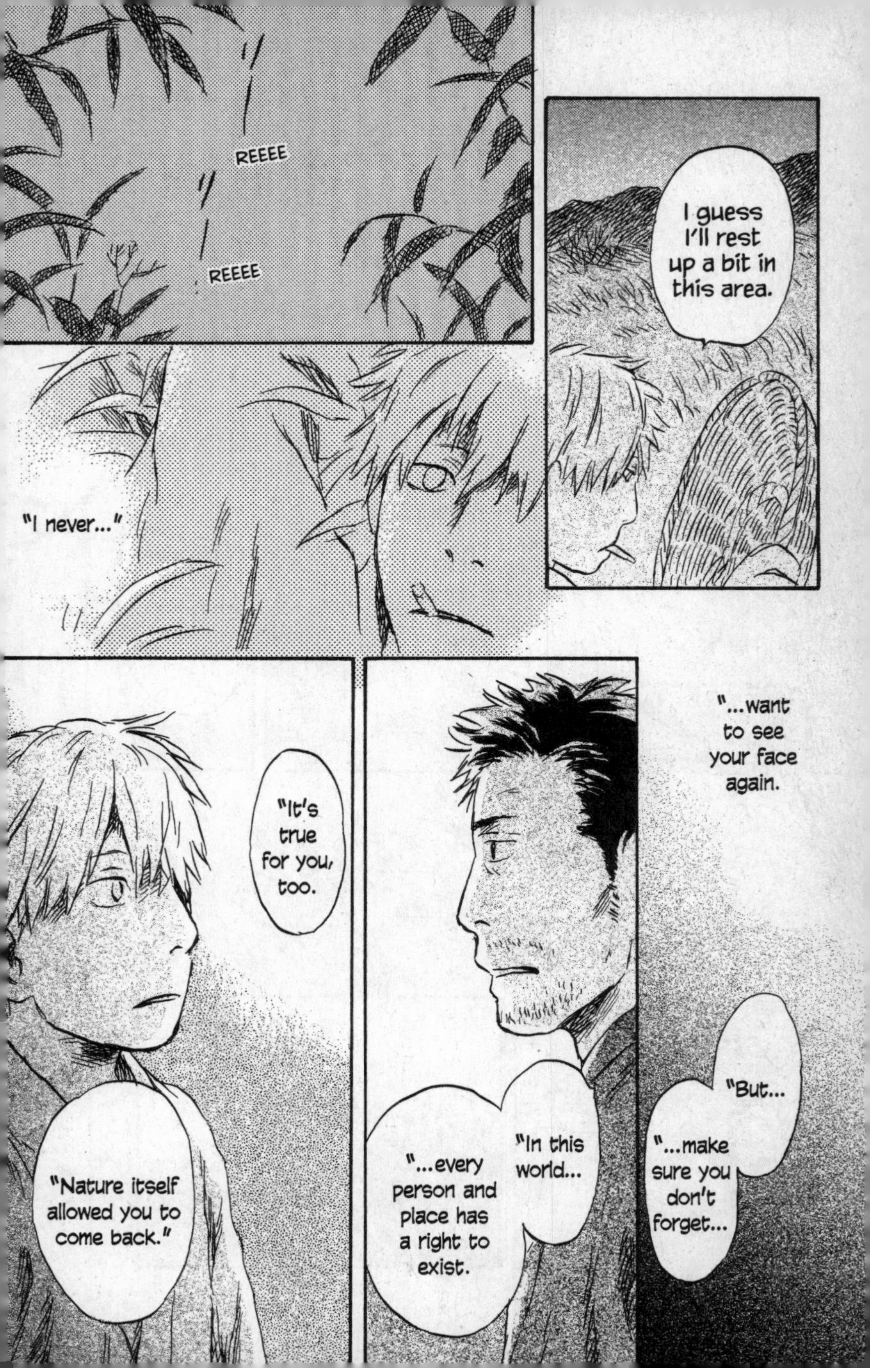
I guess I'll rest up a bit in this area.
REEEE
REEEE
"I never..."
"...want to see your face again.
"But...
"...make sure you don't forget...
"In this world...
"...every person and place has a right to exist.
"It's true for you, too.
"Nature itself allowed you to come back."

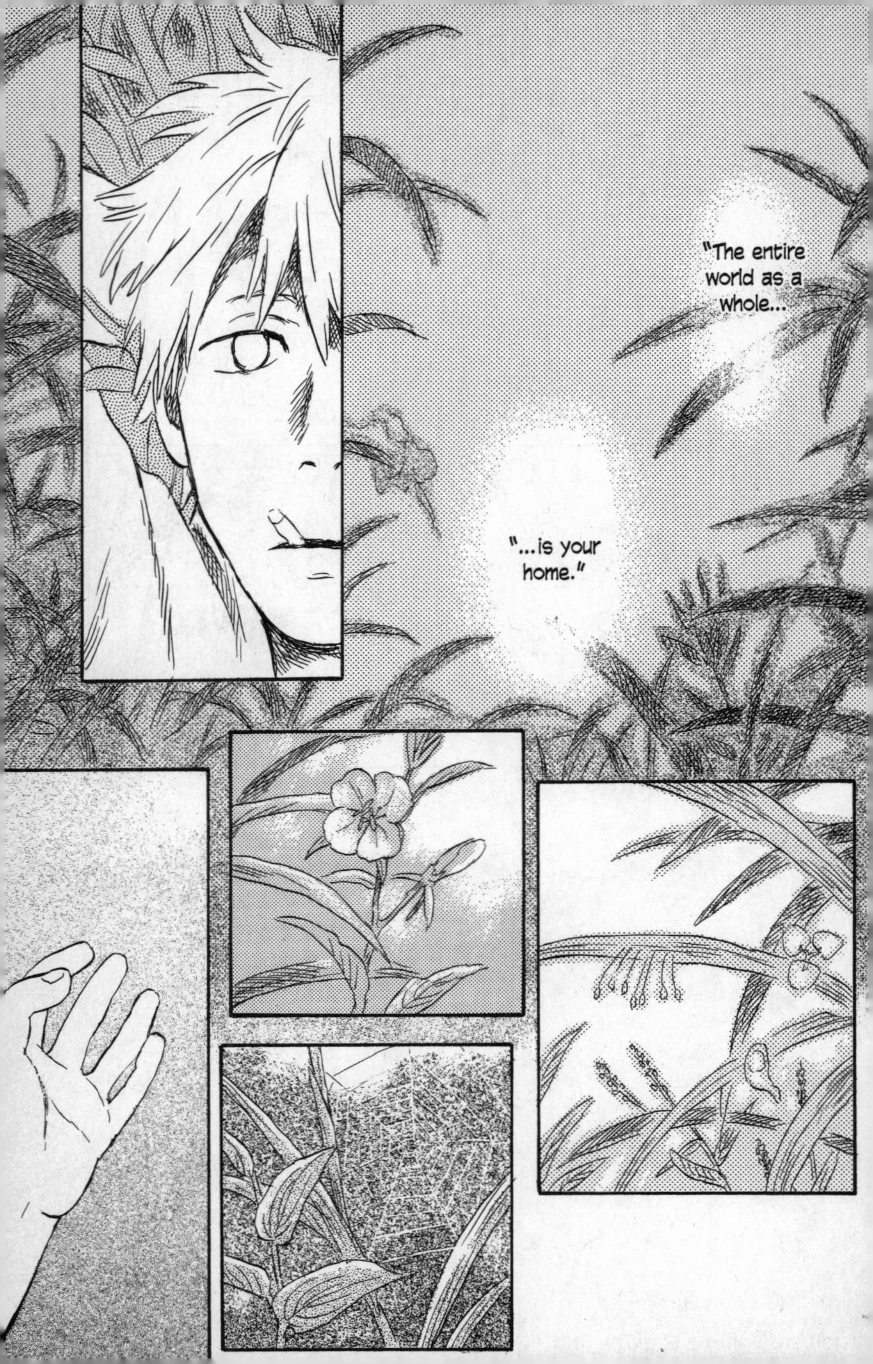
"The entire world as a whole...
"...is your home."

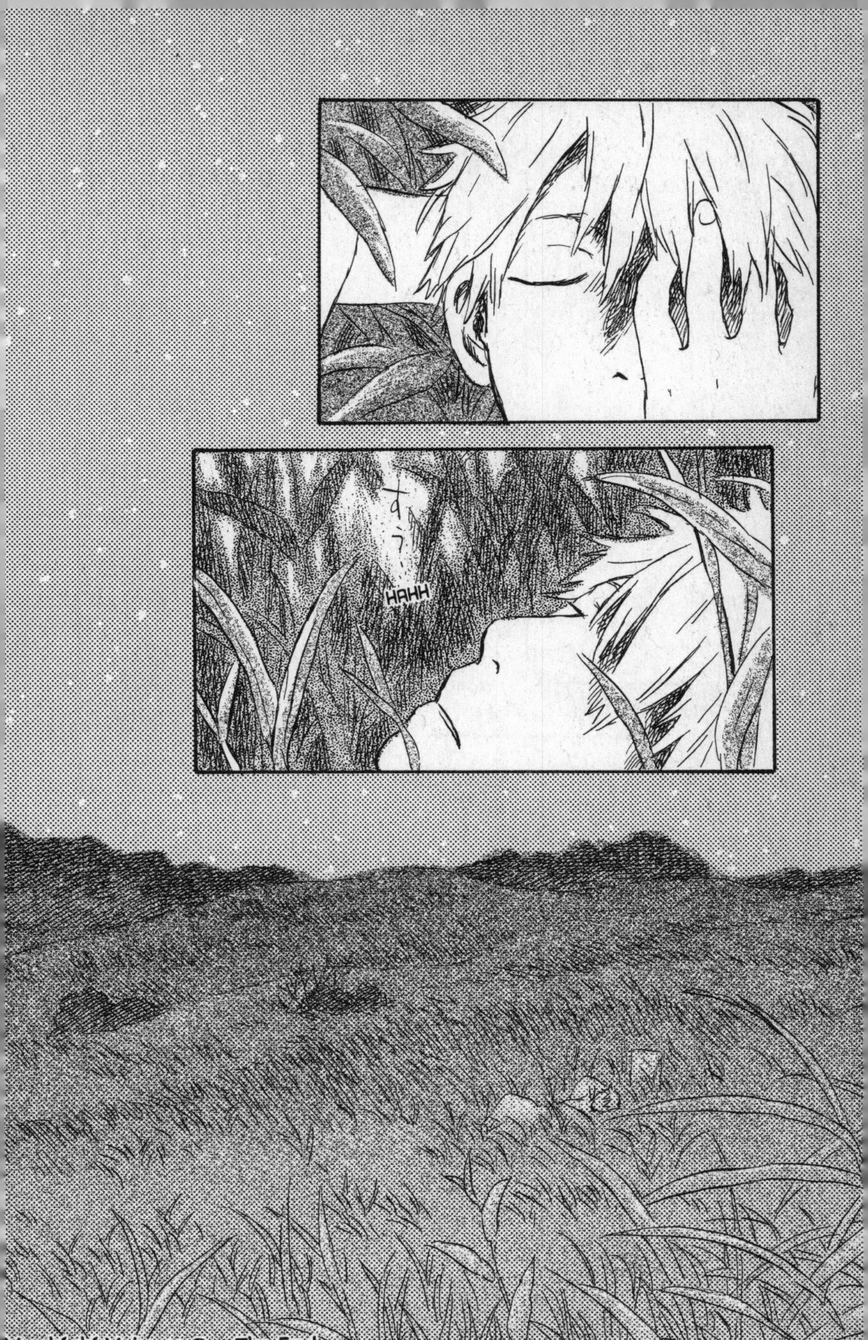
HAHH

Mushishi Volume 9 – The End

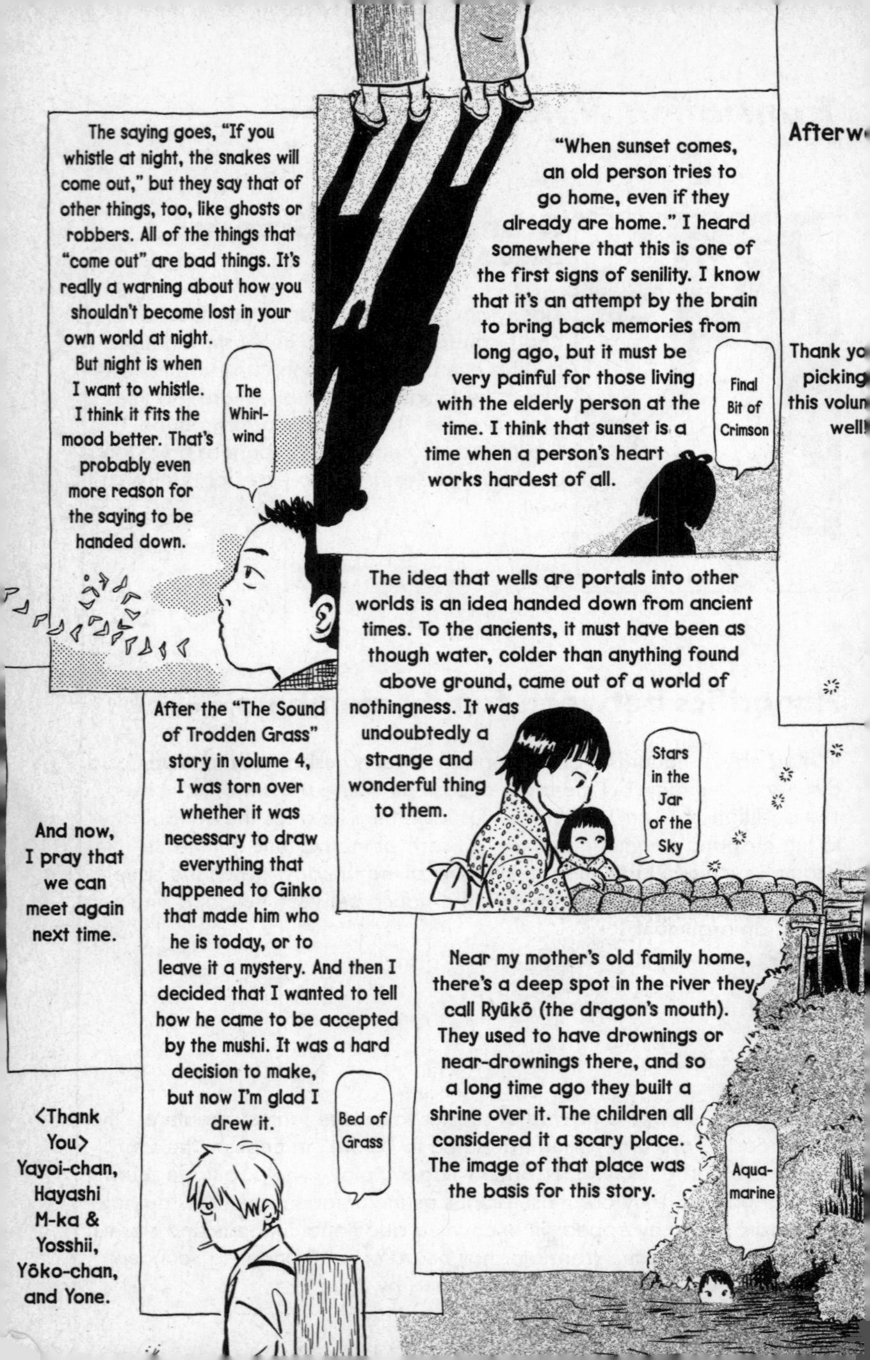
Afterw
Thank yo picking this volun well!
"When sunset comes, an old person tries to go home, even if they already are home." I heard somewhere that this is one of the first signs of senility. I know that it's an attempt by the brain to bring back memories from long ago, but it must be very painful for those living with the elderly person at the time. I think that sunset is a time when a person's heart works hardest of all.
Final Bit of Crimson
The saying goes, "If you whistle at night, the snakes will come out," but they say that of other things, too, like ghosts or robbers. All of the things that "come out" are bad things. It's really a warning about how you shouldn't become lost in your own world at night.
But night is when I want to whistle. I think it fits the mood better. That's probably even more reason for the saying to be handed down.
The Whirl-wind
The idea that wells are portals into other worlds is an idea handed down from ancient times. To the ancients, it must have been as though water, colder than anything found above ground, came out of a world of nothingness. It was undoubtedly a strange and wonderful thing to them.
Stars in the Jar of the Sky
Near my mother's old family home, there's a deep spot in the river they call Ryūkō (the dragon's mouth). They used to have drownings or near-drownings there, and so a long time ago they built a shrine over it. The children all considered it a scary place. The image of that place was the basis for this story.
Aqua-marine
After the "The Sound of Trodden Grass" story in volume 4, I was torn over whether it was necessary to draw everything that happened to Ginko that made him who he is today, or to leave it a mystery. And then I decided that I wanted to tell how he came to be accepted by the mushi. It was a hard decision to make, but now I'm glad I drew it.
Bed of Grass
And now, I pray that we can meet again next time.
<Thank You> Yayoi-chan, Hayashi M-ka & Yosshii, Yōko-chan, and Yone.

Translation Notes

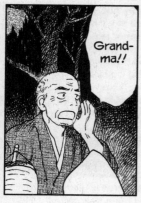

Grand-ma!!

Grandma and Grandpa, page 8

Elderly couples calling each other Grandma and Grandpa is common in Western nations, but it is even more common in Japan. Following in the Japanese tradition where job titles such as sensei (teacher or doctor) can be substituted for names, the Japanese have long used family titles as a substitute for names as well.

Honorifics between family members, page 9

In most cases, honorifics are dropped between husbands and wives as a display of intimacy, but there are occasions where the honorific is used. The addition of "-san" or "-sama" (usually the wife adds the honorific to her husband's name) may have all sorts of motivations behind it. Examples include indicating respect; recalling the days when the couple was just dating; or putting emotional distance between husband and wife during an argument.

Oni, page 20

Although there exists a myriad of sinister Japanese fantasy creatures, the main baddies are *Oni*. Often translated to "Ogre" in English, the *Oni* are brutish bad guys who terrorize villagers, play pranks, pillage, burn, and eat babies. They are most famous as the antagonists of the fairytale Momotarô, but they appear in uncounted additional legends and stories. This is the first time this translator has heard of a "changeling" concept associated with *Oni*, but I'm not surprised by it.

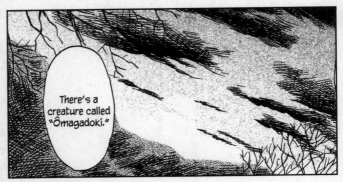

There's a creature called "Ômagadoki."

Ômagadoki, page 26

Ômagadoki is an older Japanese word for twilight. It is not often heard today, as other words such as *yûgure* are in wider use. The name of the *mushi* uses exactly the same *kanji* as in the Japanese word.

Torikaze, page 54

Like most *mushi* names, the name *Torikaze* makes perfect sense. *Tori* is the Japanese word for bird, and *kaze* means wind. So the *mushi* are given the name "wind birds."

Yobiko, page 72

Yobiko (or *yobuko*), using the kanji for *yobu* which means "to call," and the kanji for *ko* which means "child," is a word that means "police whistle." But in the case of the *mushi*, the *ko* for "child" is substituted for the *ko* for "mushi," making a *mushi* name that sounds a lot like the word for "whistle."

I'm home, page 129

The Japanese standard phrase one says when one comes home (or comes back to a place one very regularly frequents) is *tadaima*, which roughly translates to "I have just now arrived." But since coming home after a long absence is such an emotional event, the word *tadaima* can bring out powerful feelings in Japanese readers (just as the idea of "coming home" can bring out powerful emotions in English-language readers).

Isei, page 130

The *i* of the name for the *mushi*-based phenomenon *Isei* means "well," and *sei* means stars. So the name translates out logically to "well stars."

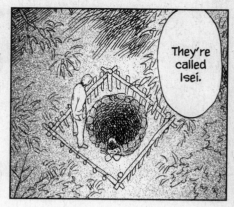

They're called Isei.

Uko, page 147

This is another straightforward *mushi* name. The *u* is the pronunciation of a kanji that means "rain," and as in *Yobiko* above, *ko* means "mushi." So this one means "rain mushi."

Nine months, page 179

The original dialog in Japanese didn't say "about nine months" before Yûta was born, it actually said, "about ten months." According to Japanese tradition, pregnancy lasts ten months and ten days. I am not quite sure what causes the discrepancy between Japanese and Western counting — possibly a difference in exactly when each culture considers to be the start of the pregnancy — but it left me with a dilemma. I had to change the number of months to the number of months that Western nations figure is a full term for a pregnancy. If I had left it ten months, readers might have concluded that she conceived Yûta after she drowned and after her husband had died.

Tokoyami, page 194

This *mushi* was first described near the end of volume 3. *Toko* means eternal and *yami* means darkness. If it seems unusual that Ginko acts as if he's hearing the name for the first time, remember that his memories of his time with Nui (as well as nearly all of his life before that) were wiped clean by the Tokoyami at the end of the chapter.

蟲

(むしし)

師

Mushishi

10

Yuki Urushibara

Contents

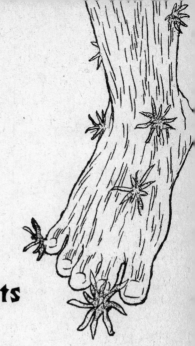

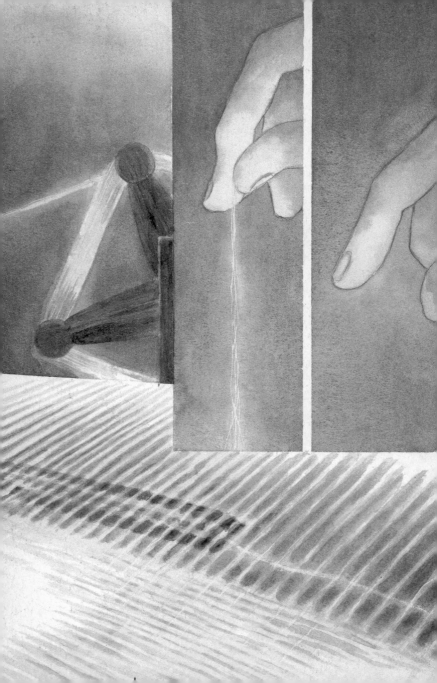

The Thread of Light

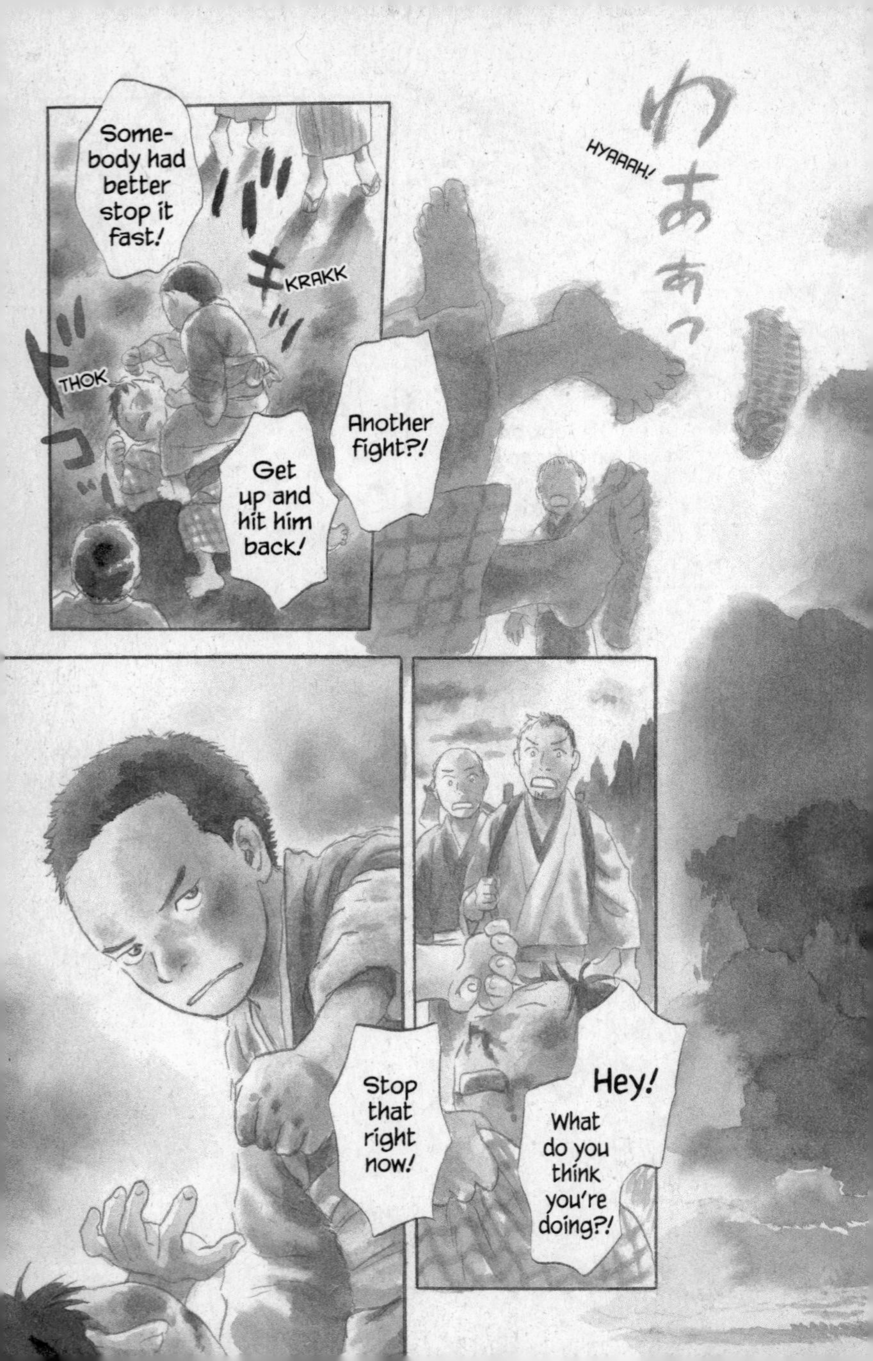

わあぁっ
HYAAAH!
Another fight?!
Some-body had better stop it fast!
KRAKK
Get up and hit him back!
THOK
Hey! What do you think you're doing?!
Stop that right now!

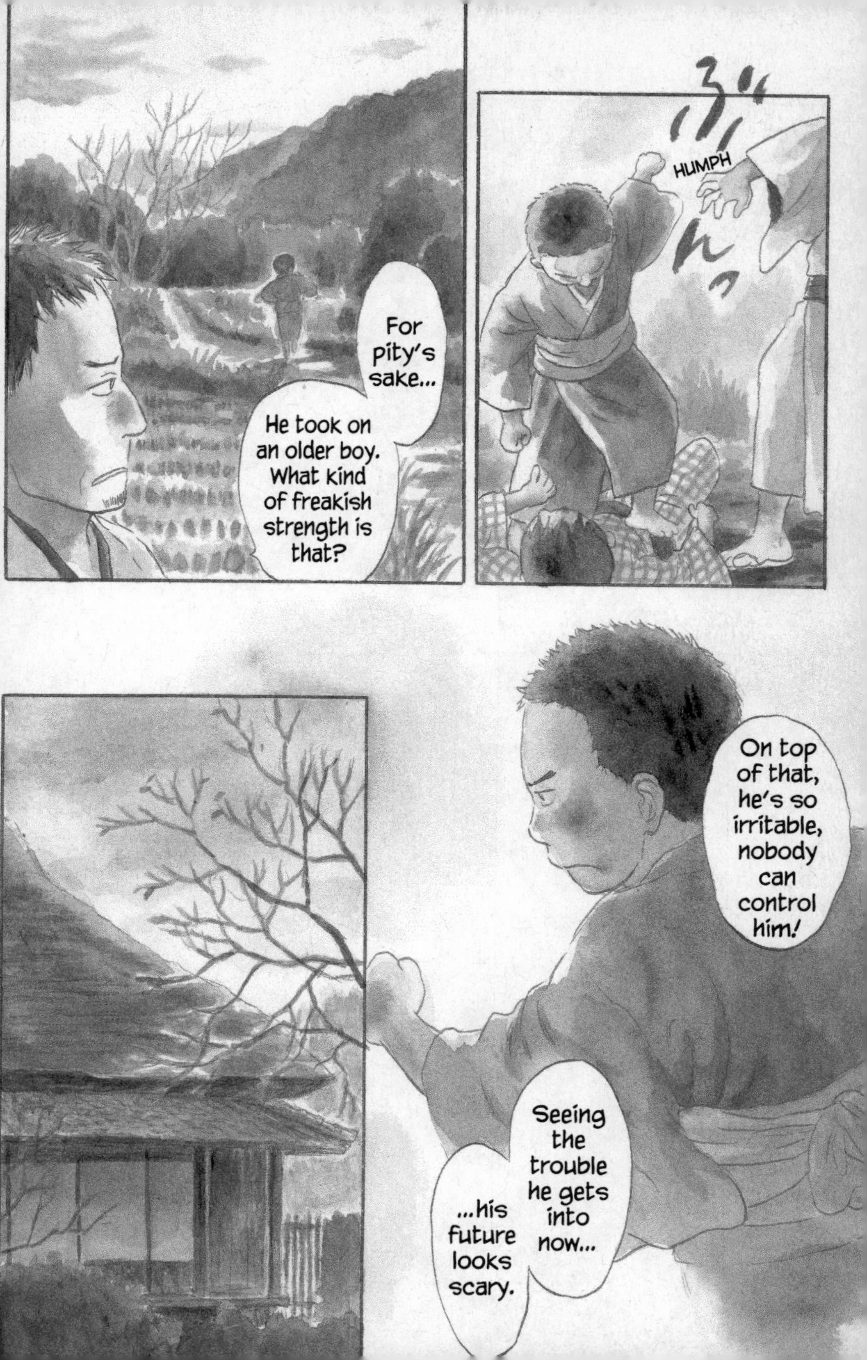
HUMPH
For pity's sake...
He took on an older boy. What kind of freakish strength is that?
On top of that, he's so irritable, nobody can control him!
Seeing the trouble he gets into now...
...his future looks scary.

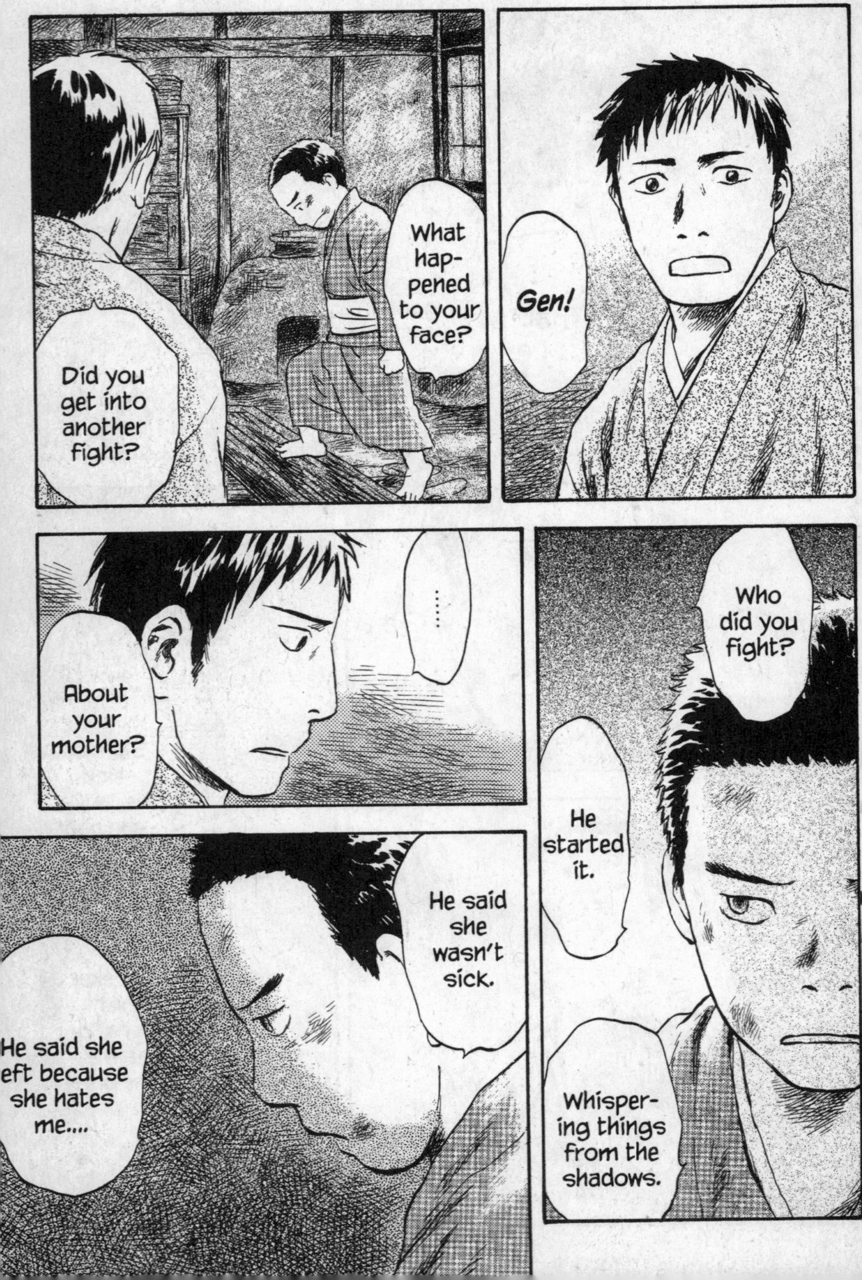
Gen!
What hap-pened to your face?
Did you get into another fight?
Who did you fight?
He started it.
Whisper-ing things from the shadows.
......
About your mother?
He said she wasn't sick.
He said she eft because she hates me....

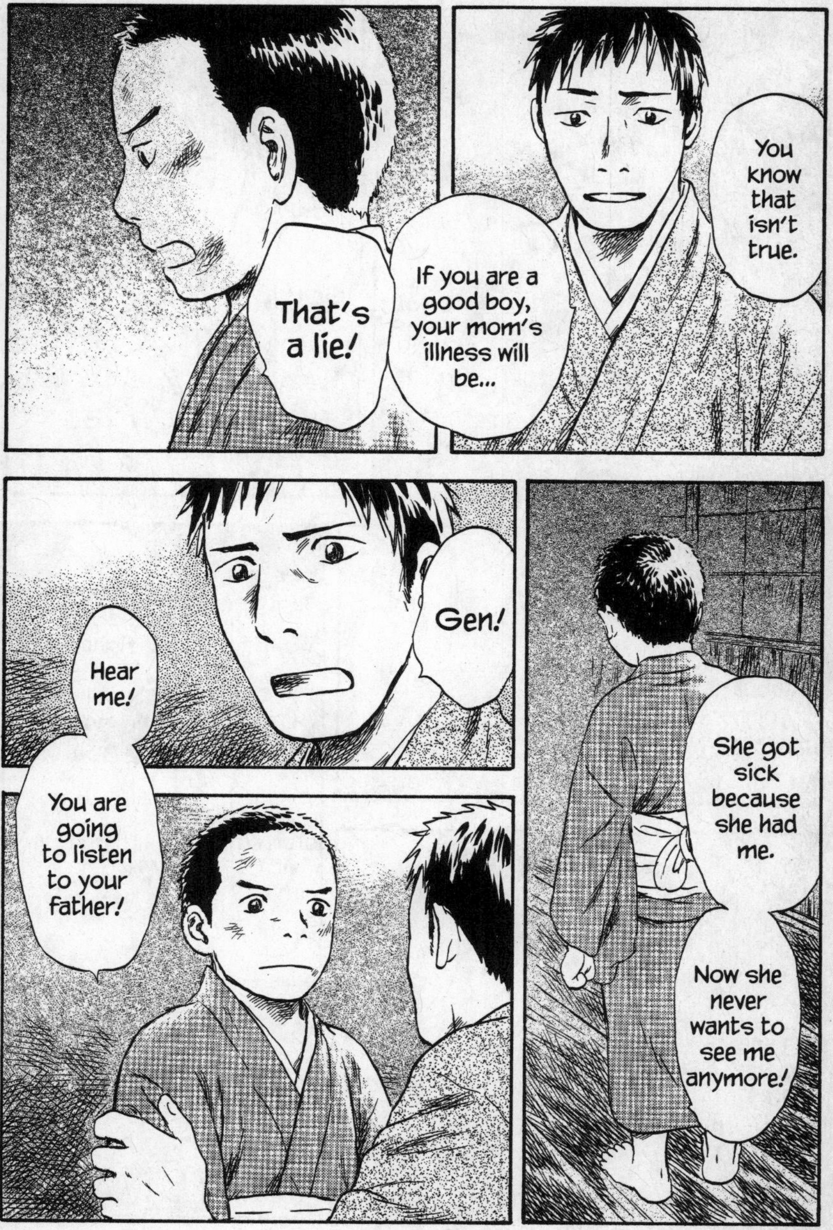
You know that isn't true.
If you are a good boy, your mom's illness will be...
That's a lie!
She got sick because she had me.
Now she never wants to see me anymore!
Gen!
Hear me!
You are going to listen to your father!

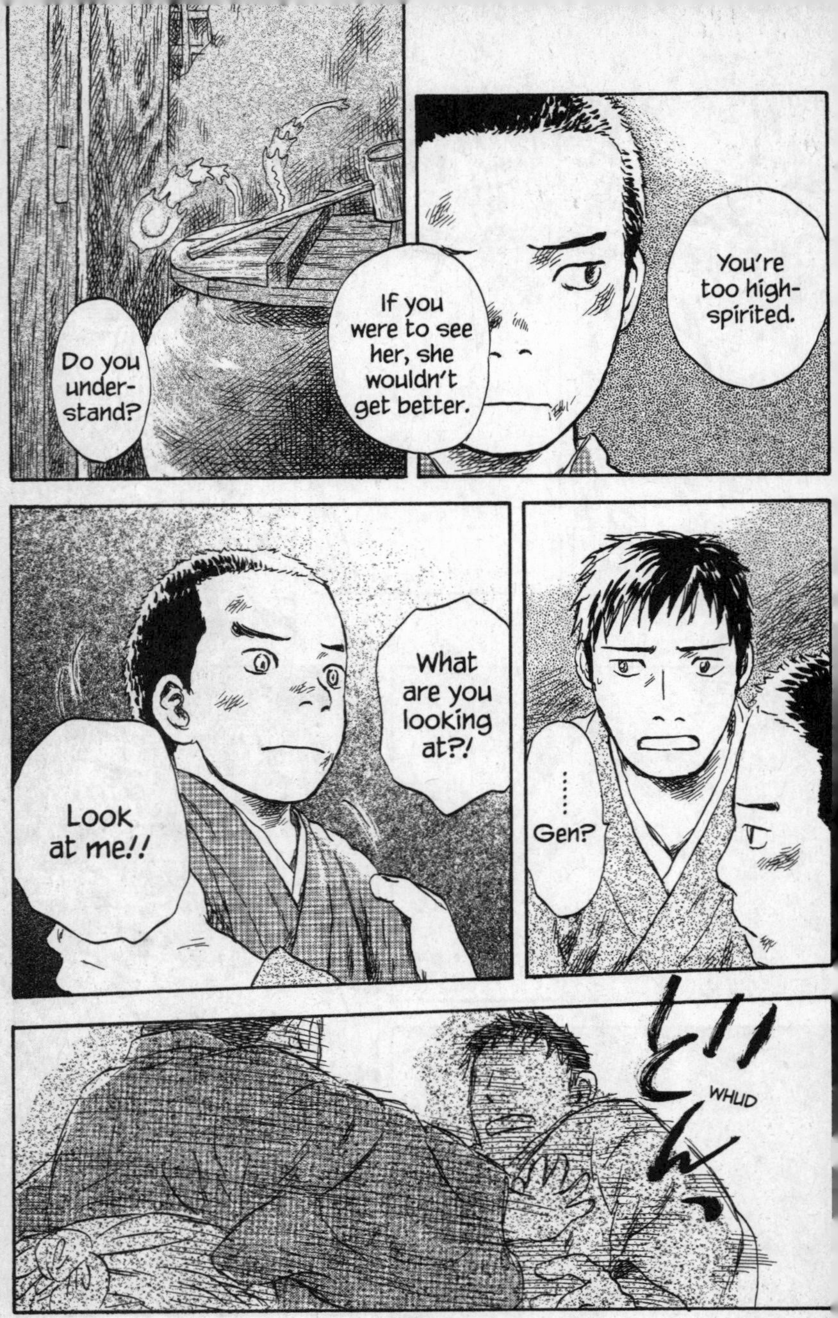
You're too high-spirited.
If you were to see her, she wouldn't get better.
Do you understand?
...... Gen?
What are you looking at?!
Look at me!!
どん
WHUD

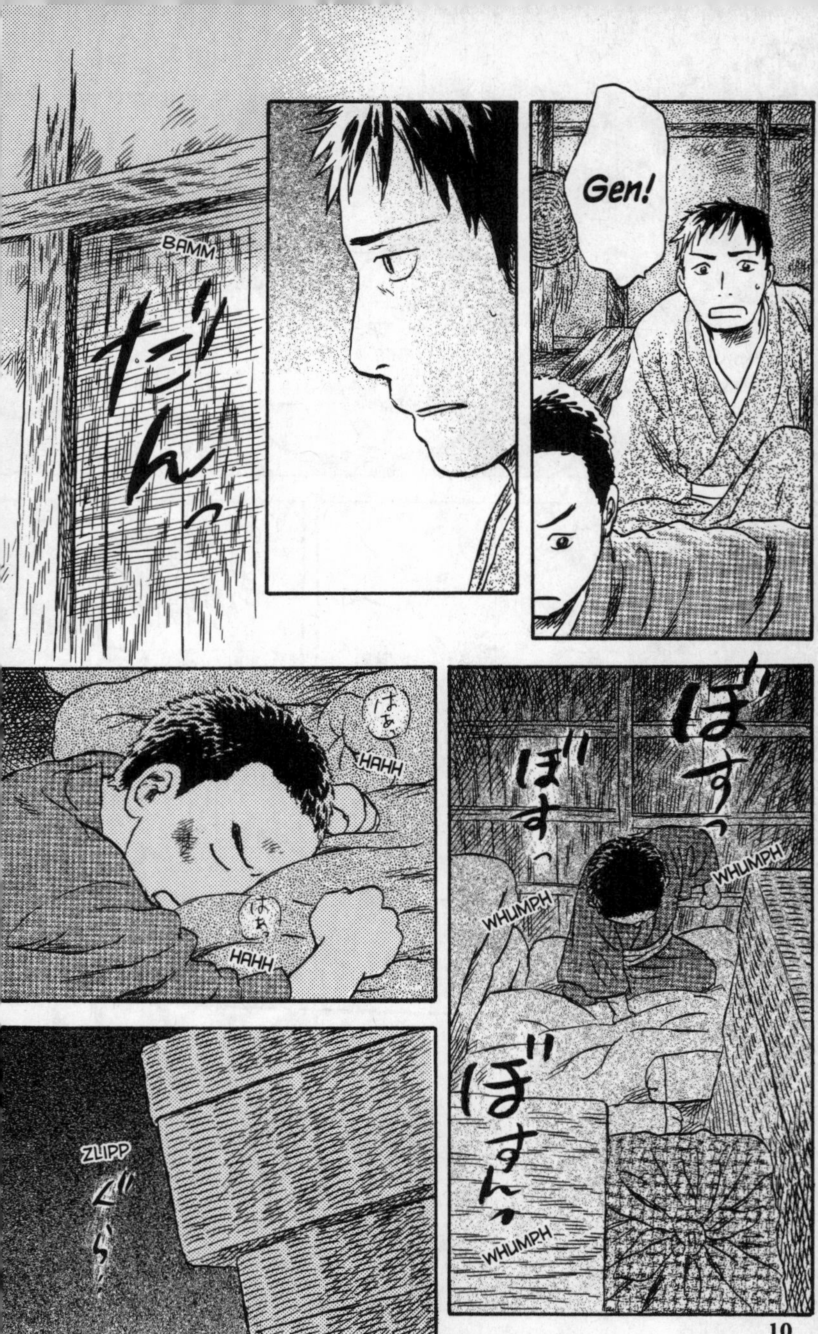
Gen!
BAMM
だん
ぼすっ
WHUMPH
ぼすっ
WHUMPH
ぼすん
WHUMPH
HAHH
HAHH
ZLIPP

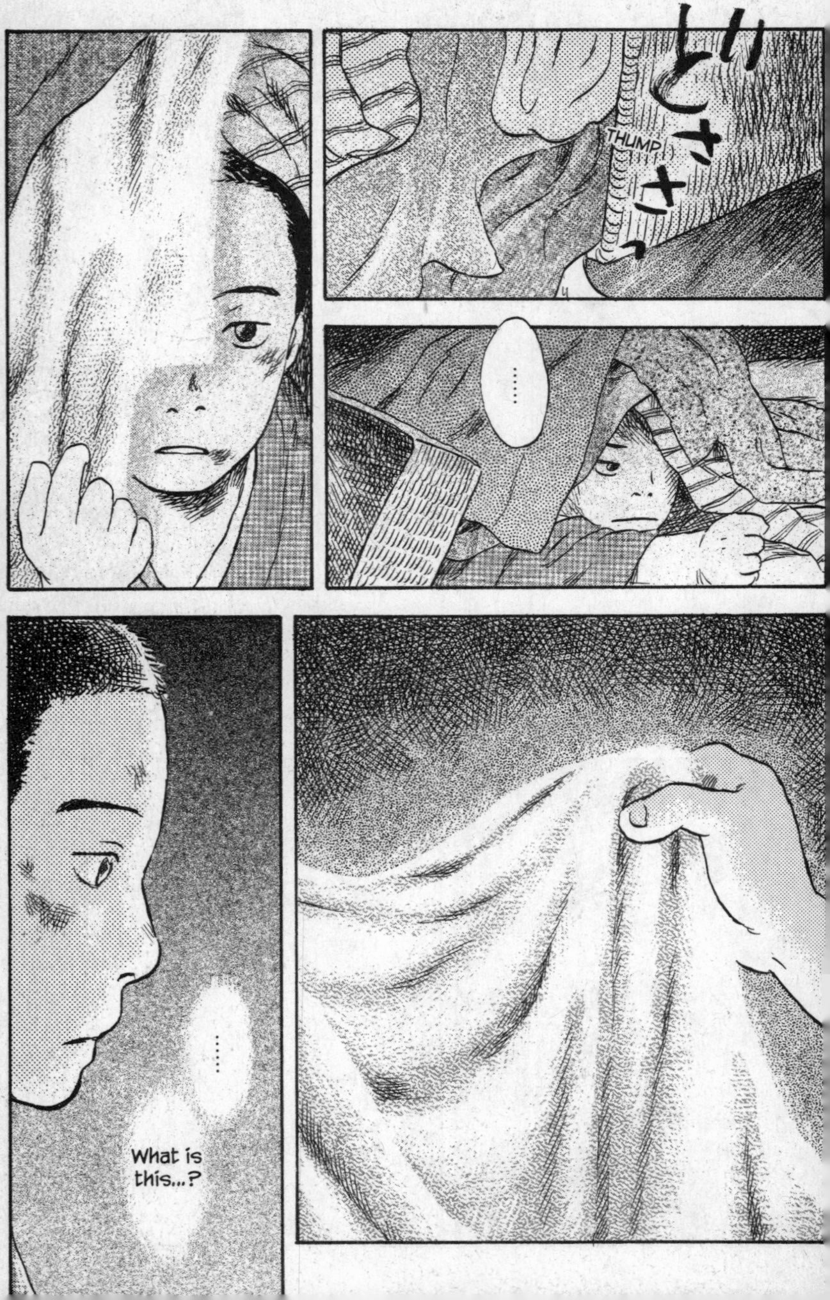
どさっ
THUMP
......
......
What is this...?

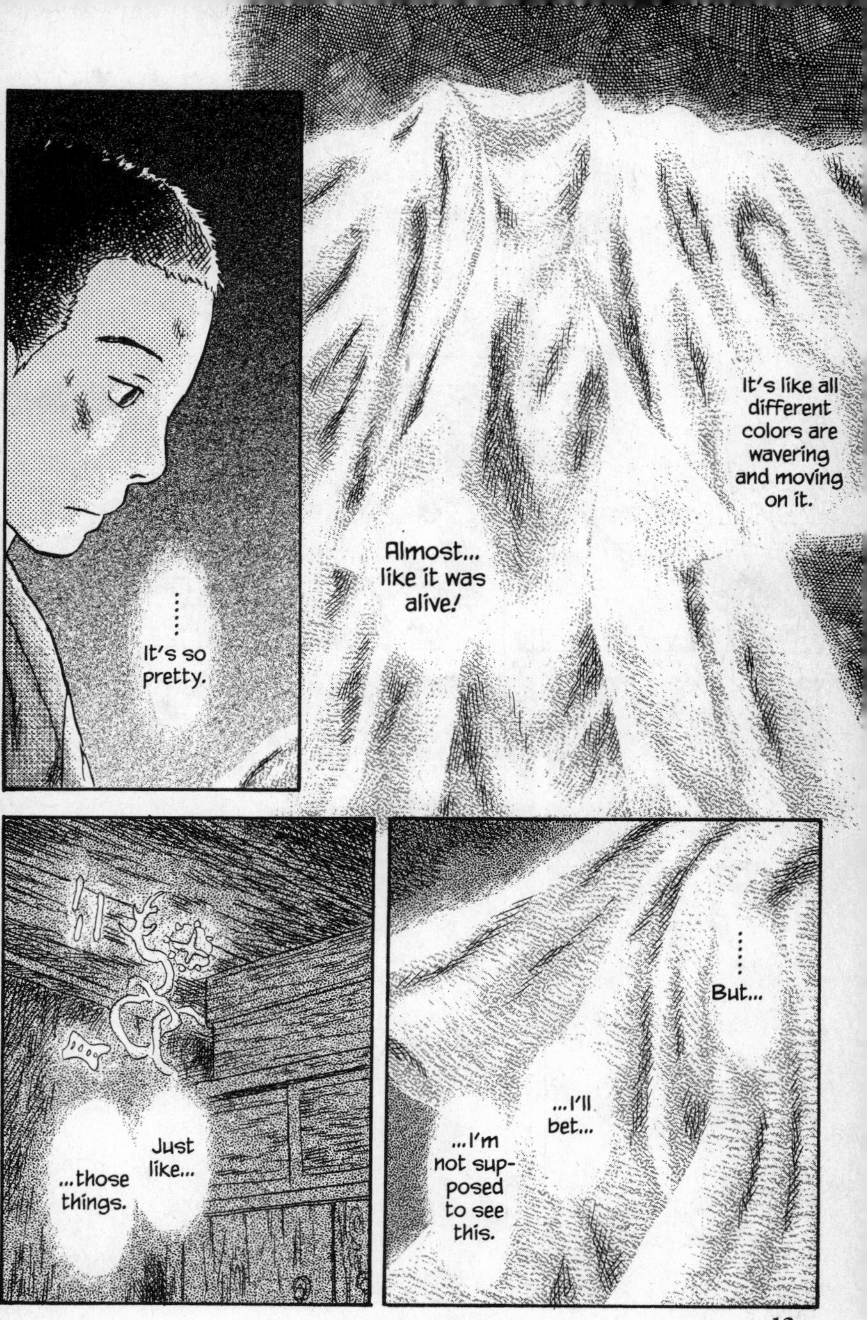
It's like all different colors are wavering and moving on it.
Almost... like it was alive!
...... It's so pretty.
...... But...
...I'll bet...
...I'm not supposed to see this.
Just like...
...those things.

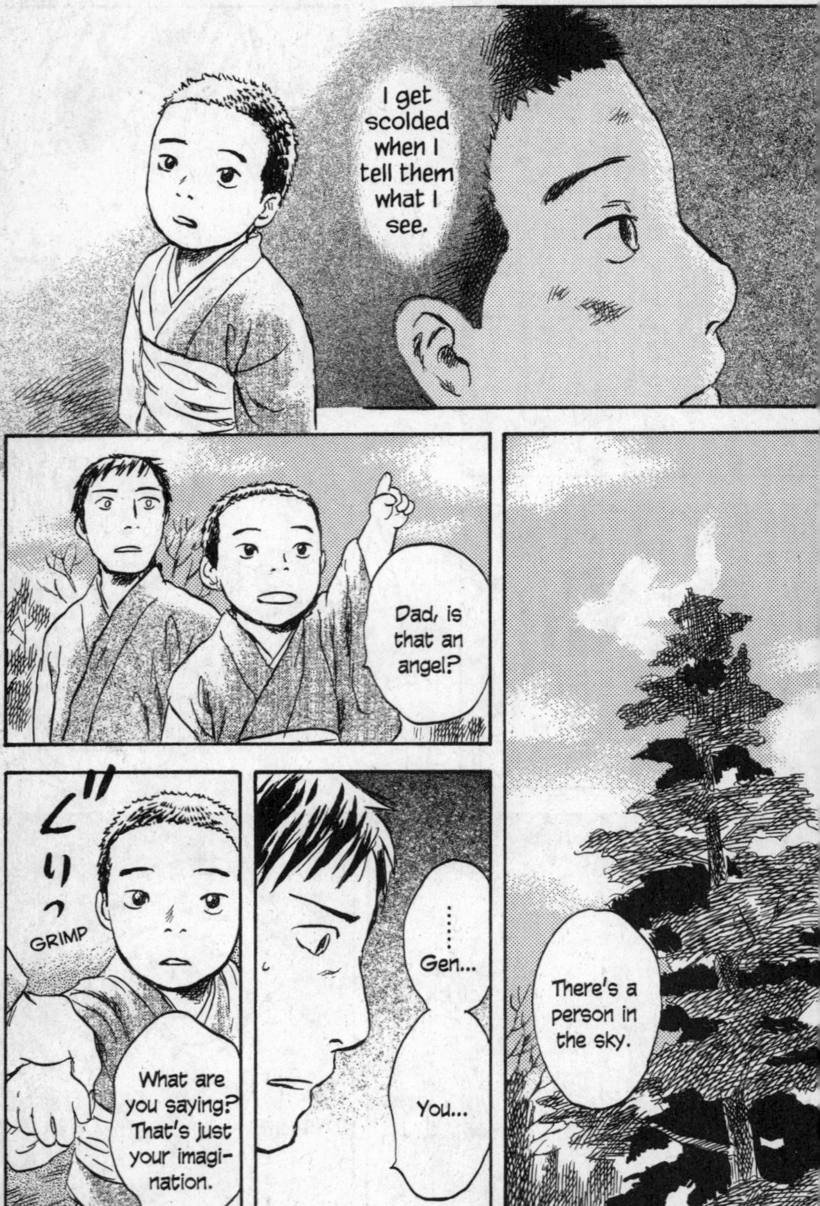
I get scolded when I tell them what I see.
There's a person in the sky.
Dad, is that an angel?
...... Gen...
You...
ぐりっ
GRIMP
What are you saying? That's just your imagination.

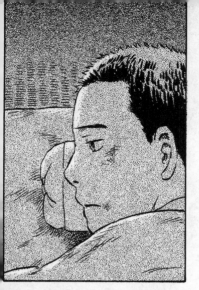

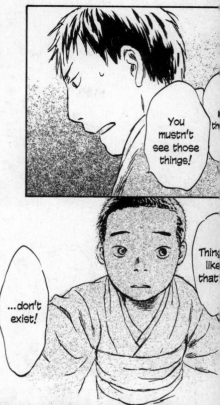

You mustn't see those things!

Thing[s] like that

...don't exist!

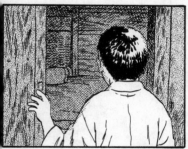

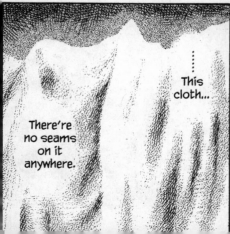

This cloth...

There're no seams on it anywhere.

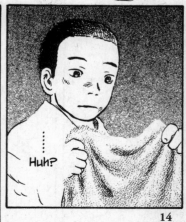

Huh?

14

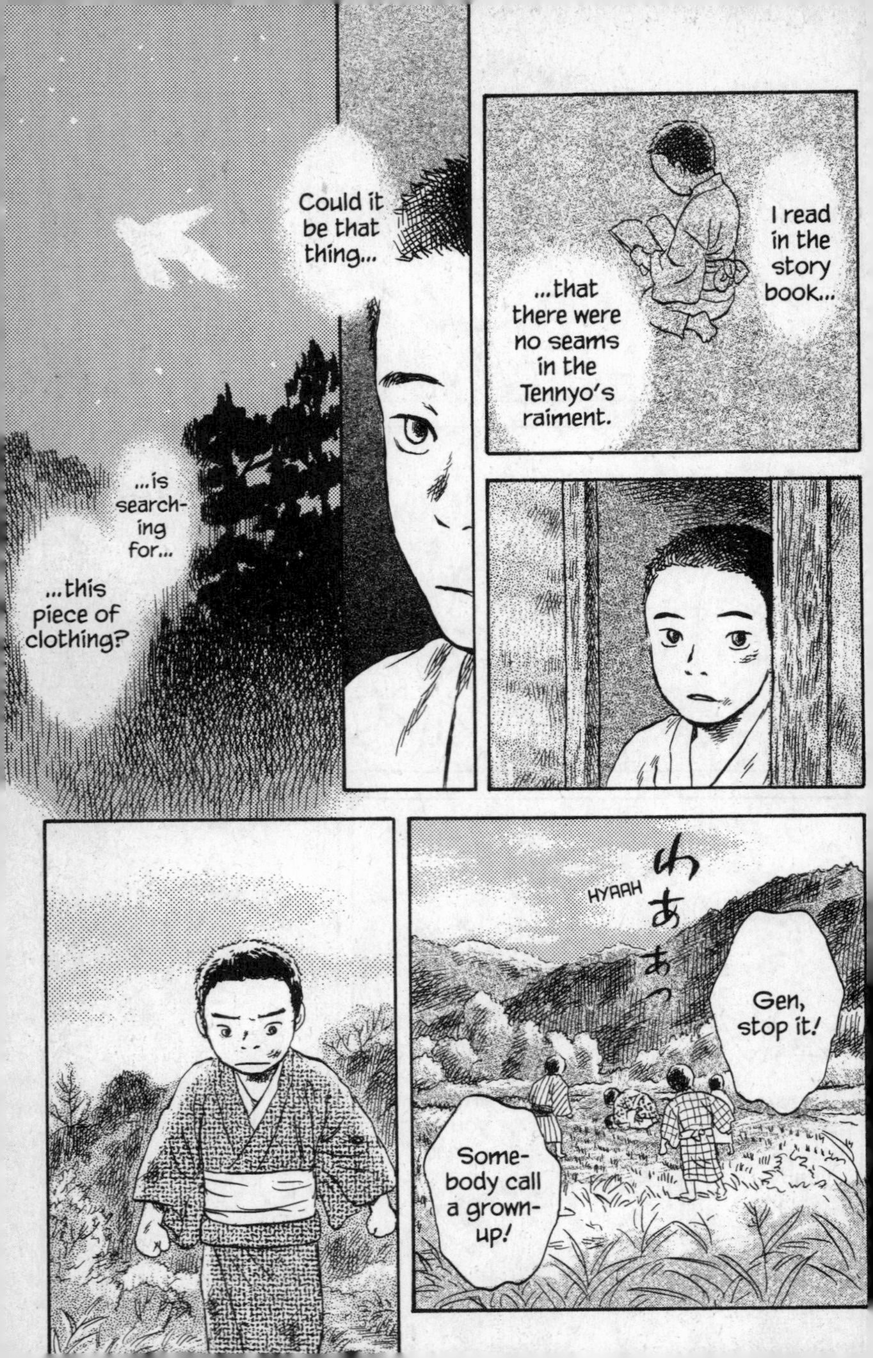
I read in the story book...
...that there were no seams in the Tennyo's raiment.
Could it be that thing...
...is searching for...
...this piece of clothing?
わあぁっ
HYAAH
Gen, stop it!
Some-body call a grown-up!

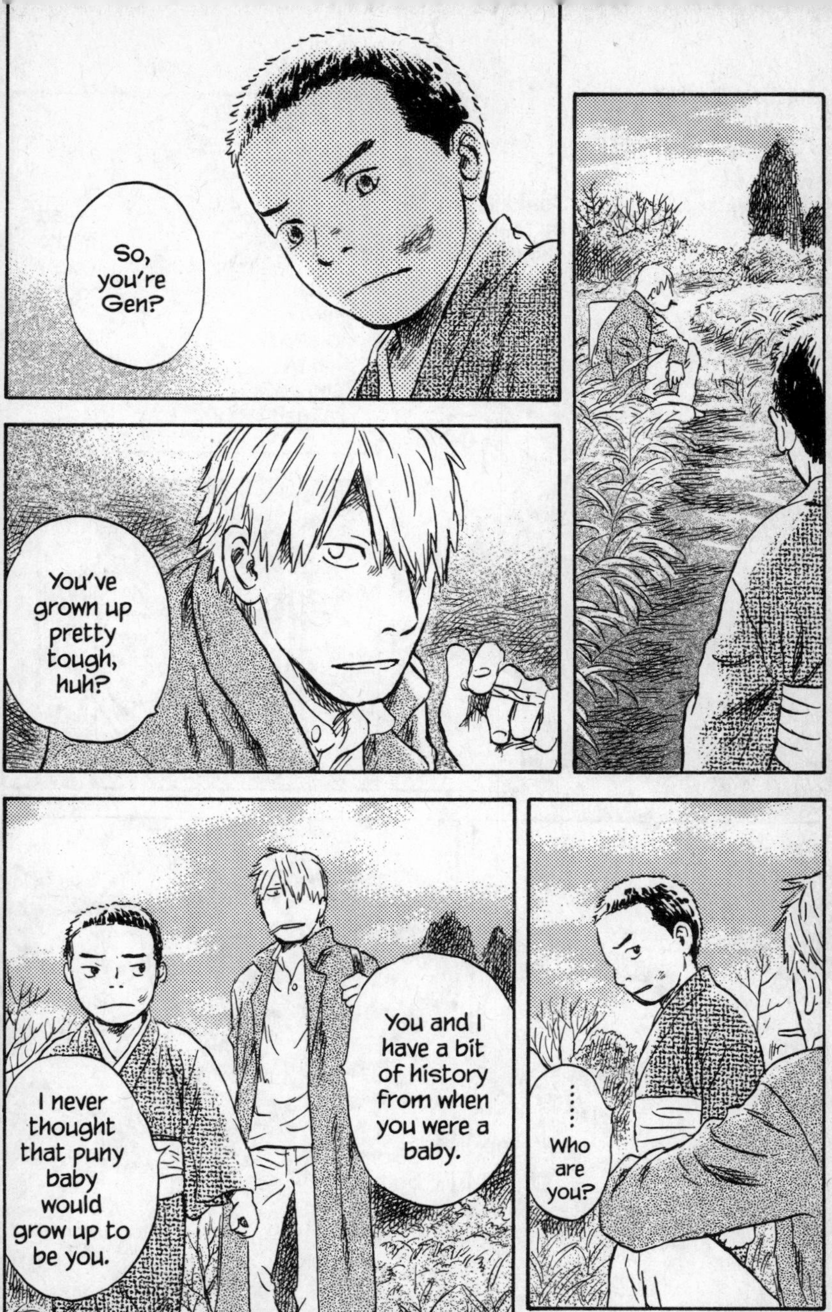
So, you're Gen?
You've grown up pretty tough, huh?
......
Who are you?
You and I have a bit of history from when you were a baby.
I never thought that puny baby would grow up to be you.

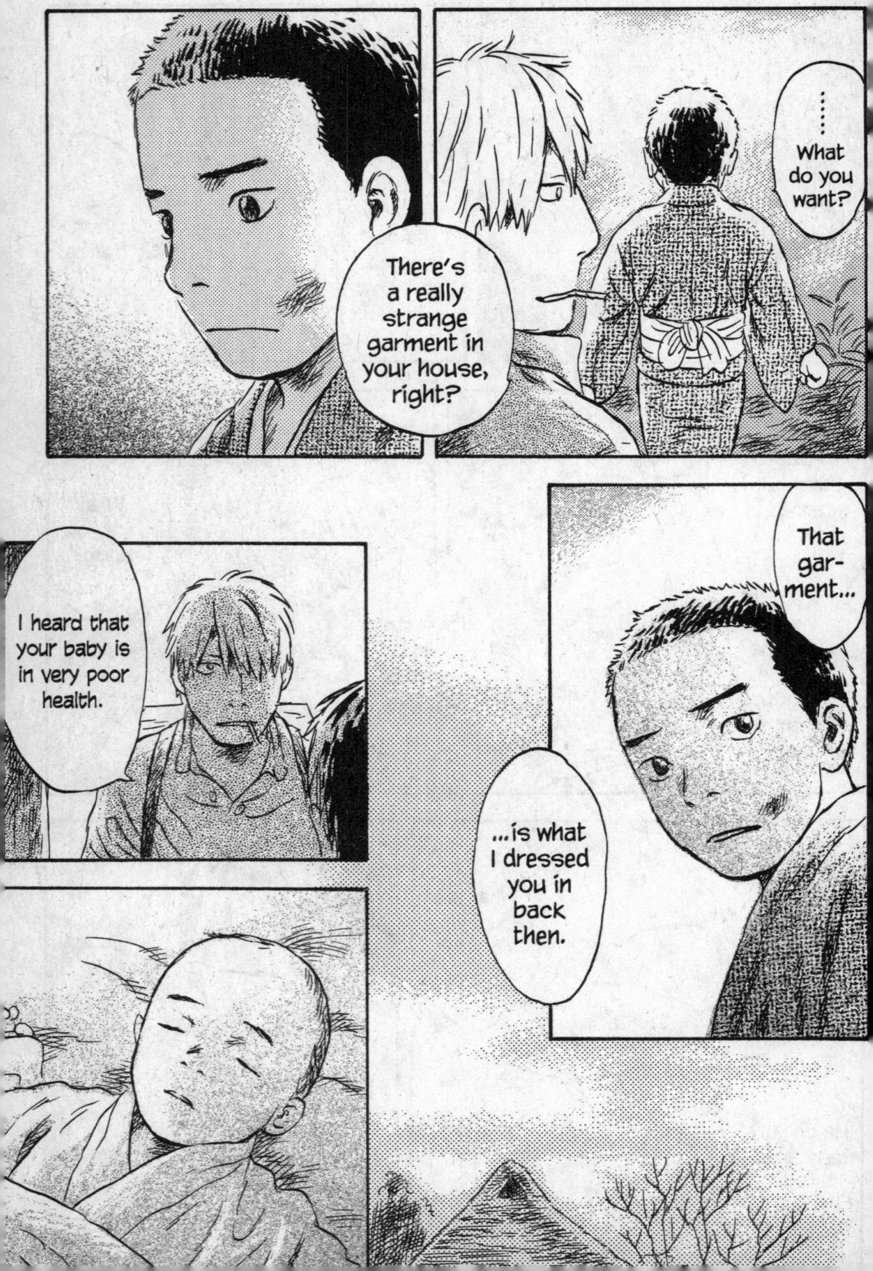
……
What do you want?
There's a really strange garment in your house, right?
That garment...
...is what I dressed you in back then.
I heard that your baby is in very poor health.

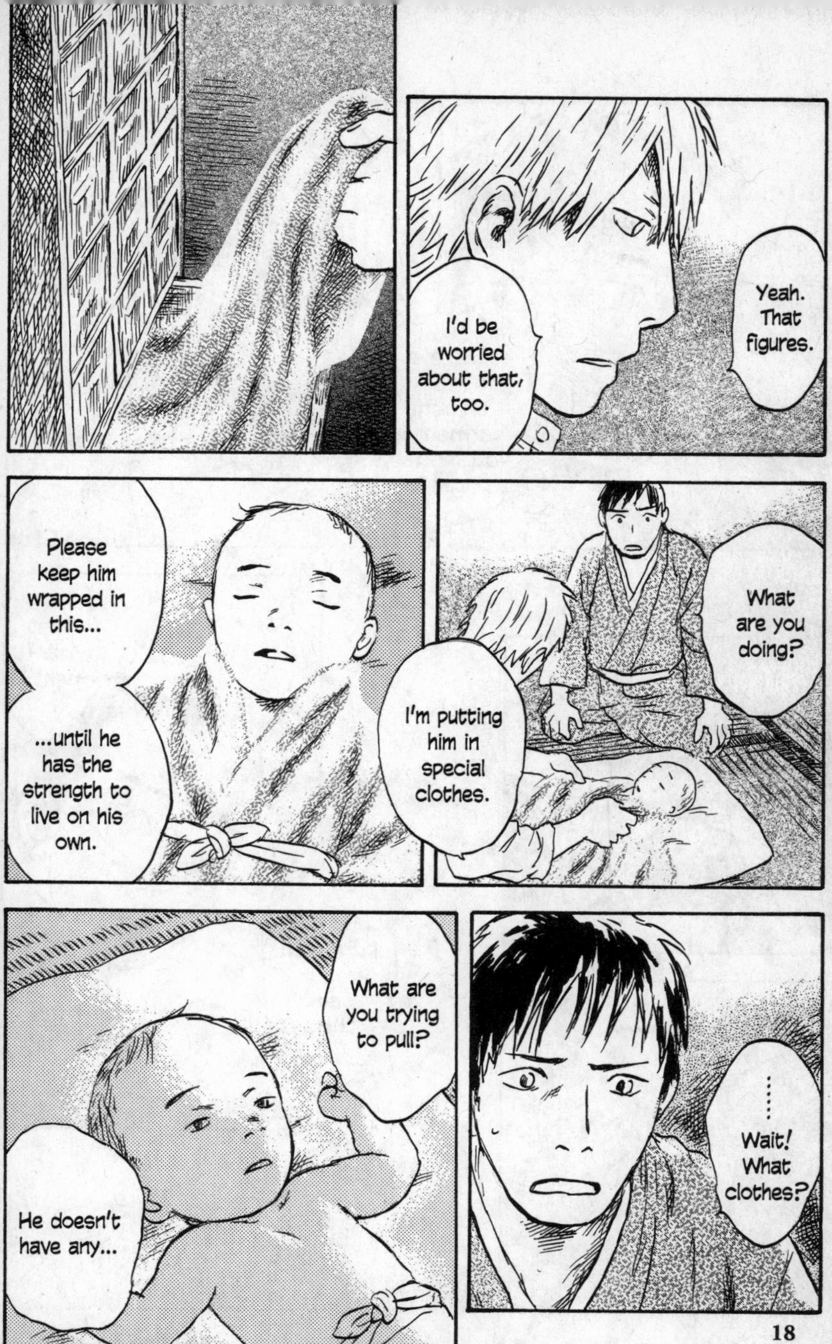
Yeah. That figures.
I'd be worried about that, too.
What are you doing?
I'm putting him in special clothes.
Please keep him wrapped in this...
...until he has the strength to live on his own.
......
Wait! What clothes?
What are you trying to pull?
He doesn't have any...

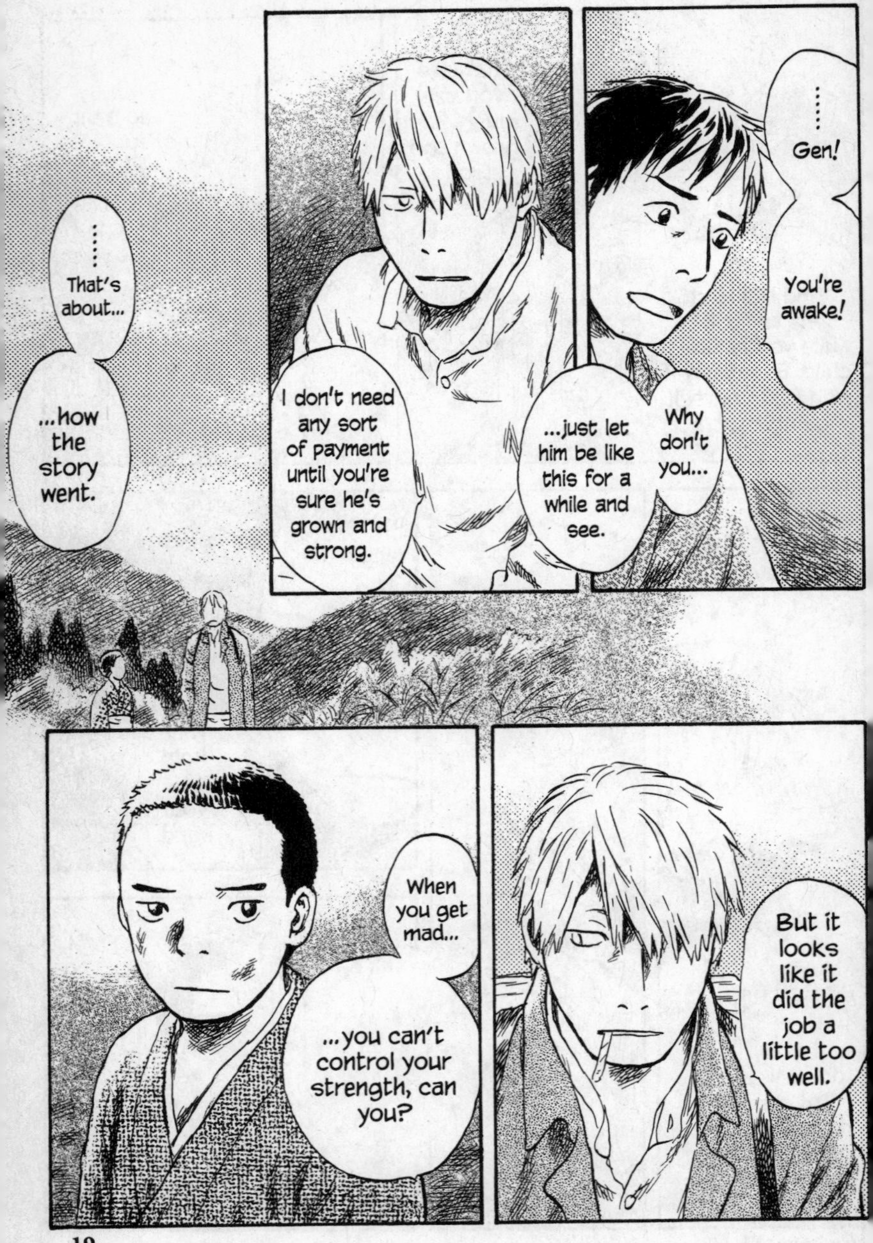

......
Gen!
You're awake!
Why don't you...
...just let him be like this for a while and see.
I don't need any sort of payment until you're sure he's grown and strong.
......
That's about...
...how the story went.
But it looks like it did the job a little too well.
When you get mad...
...you can't control your strength, can you?

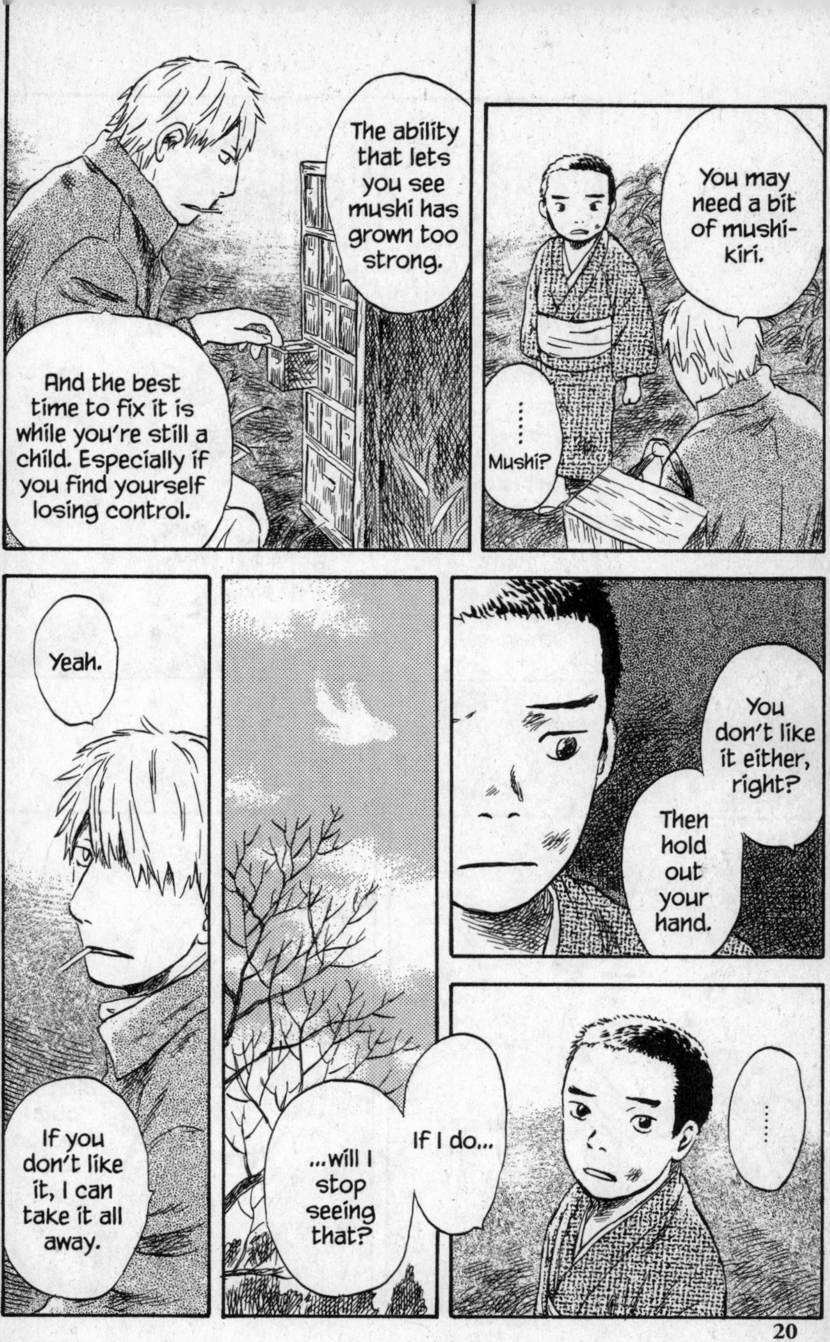
You may need a bit of mushi-kiri.
......Mushi?
The ability that lets you see mushi has grown too strong.
And the best time to fix it is while you're still a child. Especially if you find yourself losing control.
You don't like it either, right?
Then hold out your hand.
......
If I do...
...will I stop seeing that?
Yeah.
If you don't like it, I can take it all away.

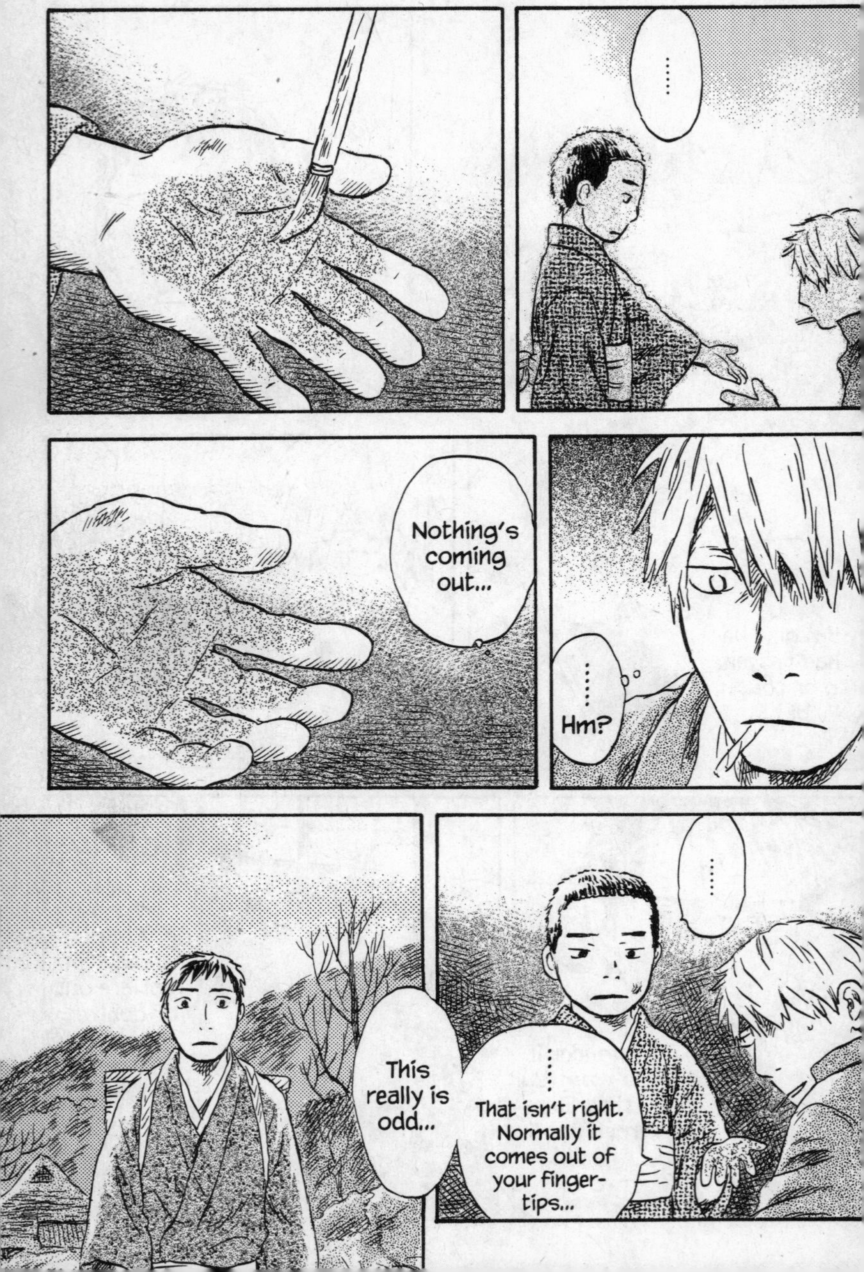
......
......
Hm?
Nothing's coming out...
......
......
That isn't right. Normally it comes out of your finger-tips...
This really is odd...

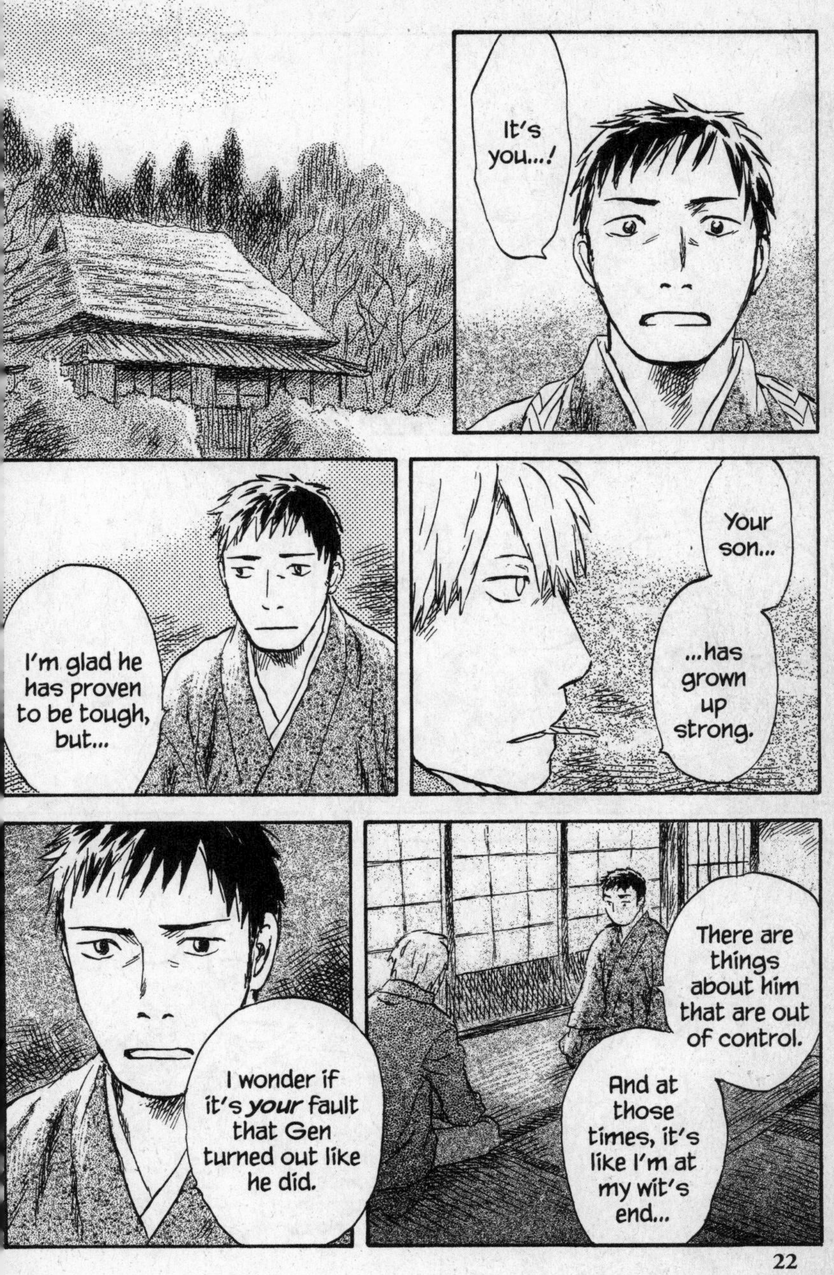
It's you...!
Your son...
...has grown up strong.
I'm glad he has proven to be tough, but...
There are things about him that are out of control.
And at those times, it's like I'm at my wit's end...
I wonder if it's *your* fault that Gen turned out like he did.

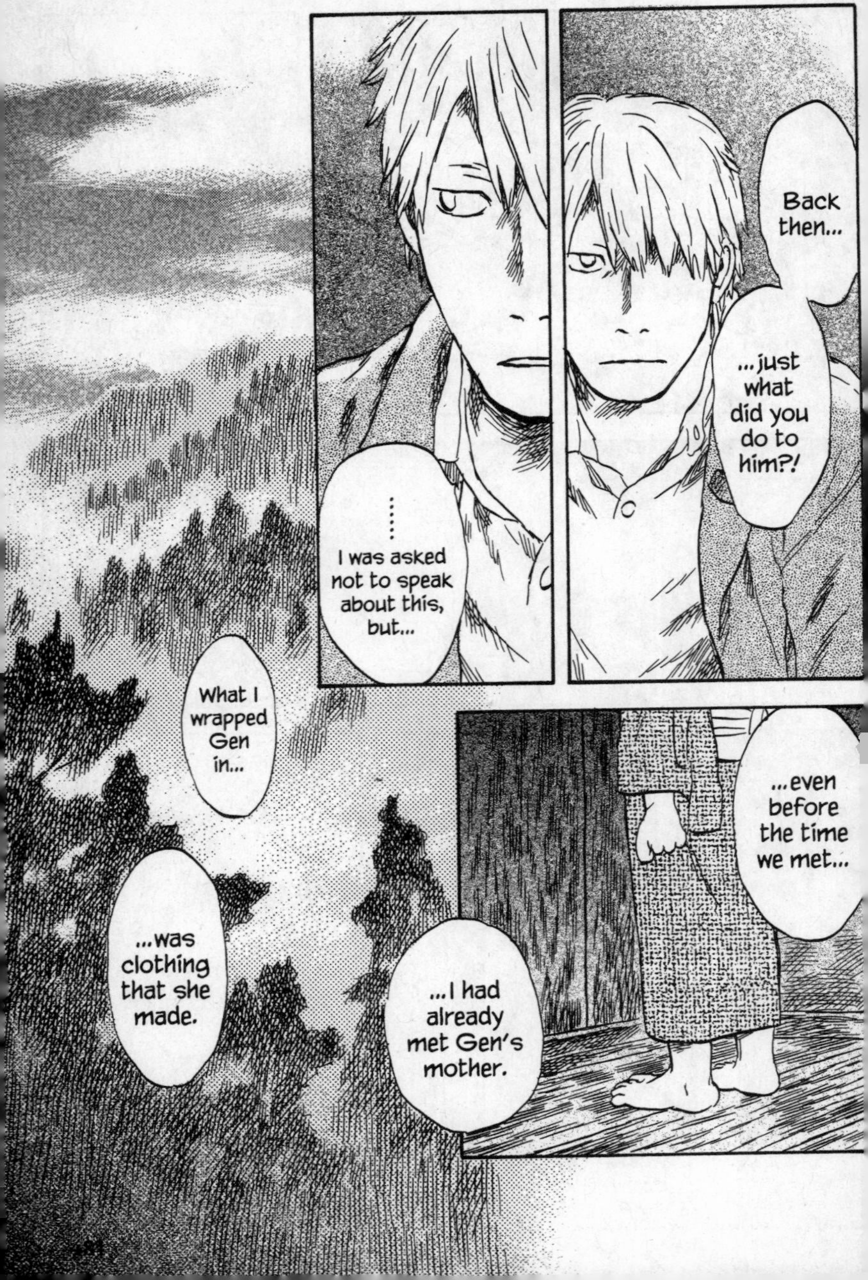
Back then...
...just what did you do to him?!
......
I was asked not to speak about this, but...
...even before the time we met...
...I had already met Gen's mother.
What I wrapped Gen in...
...was clothing that she made.

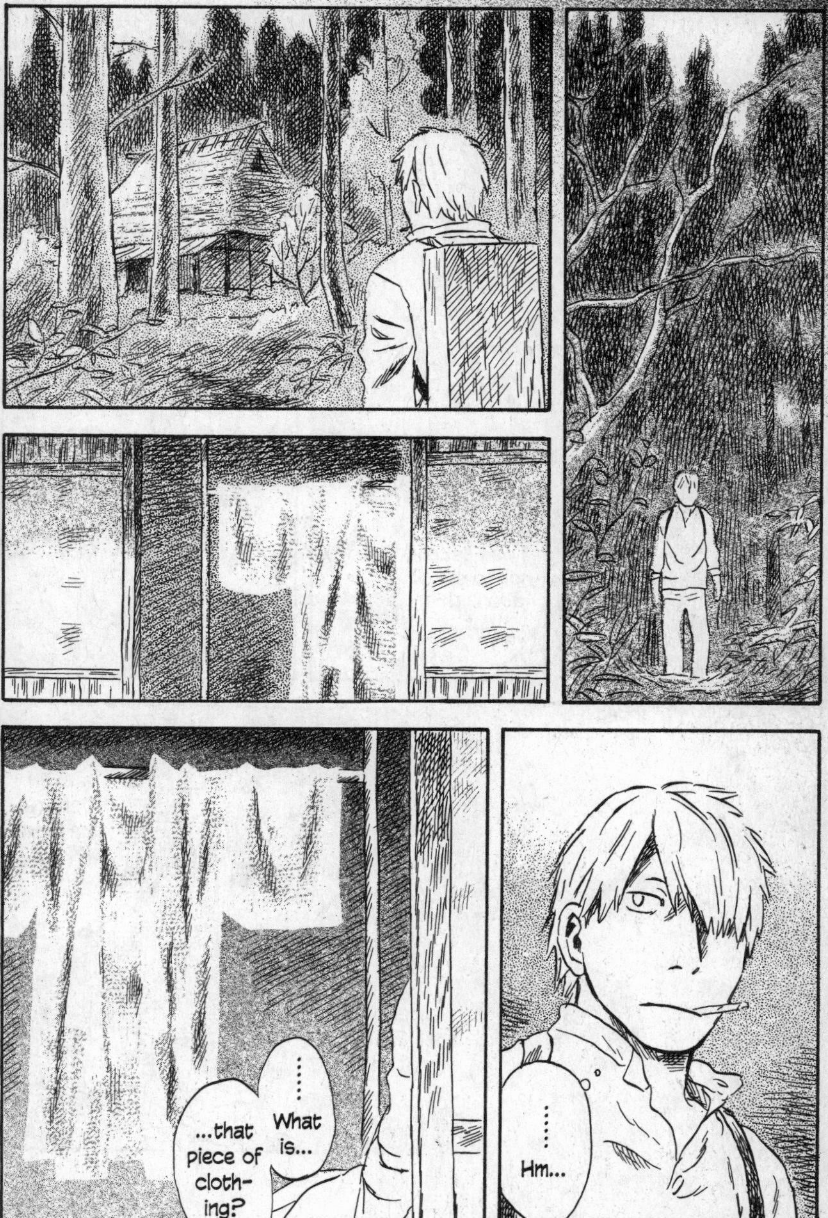
...... Hm...
...... What is...
...that piece of clothing?

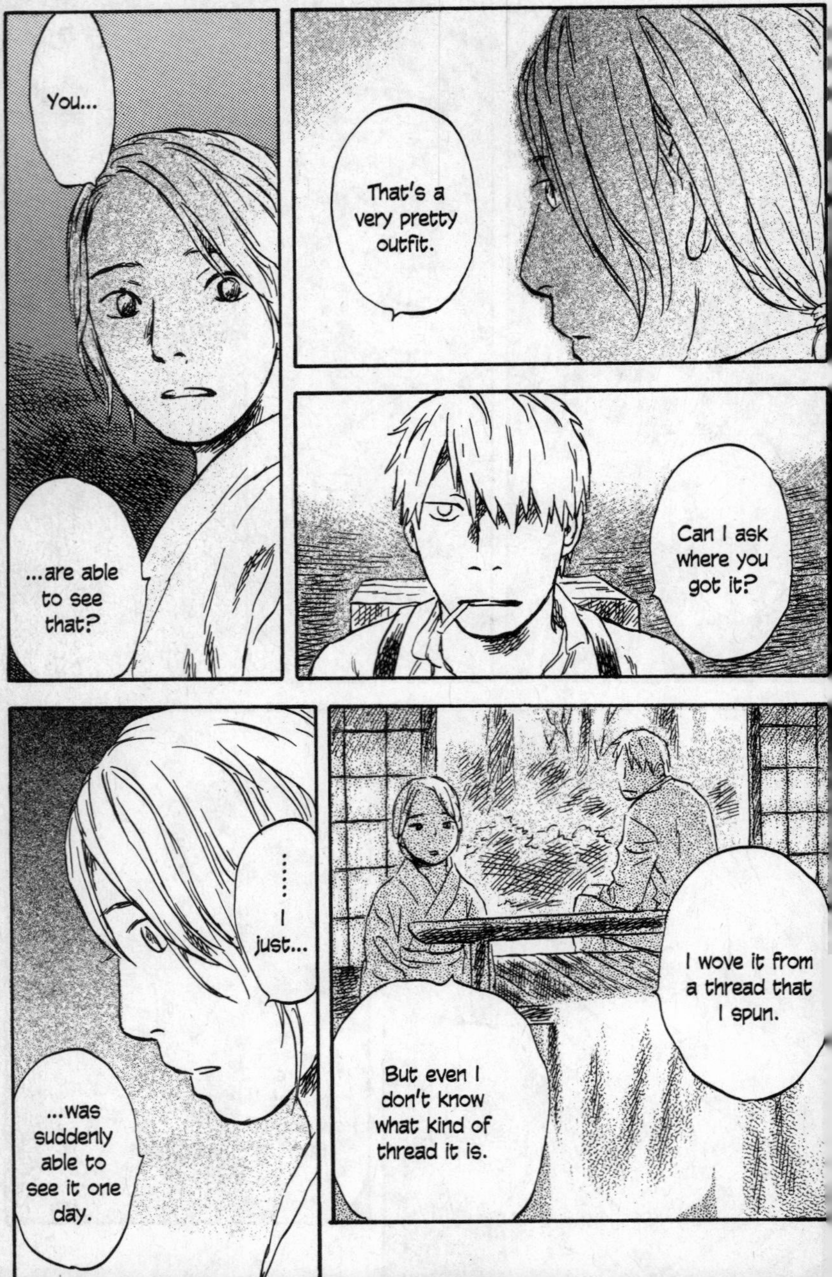
That's a very pretty outfit.
Can I ask where you got it?
You...
...are able to see that?
I wove it from a thread that I spun.
But even I don't know what kind of thread it is.
...... I just...
...was suddenly able to see it one day.

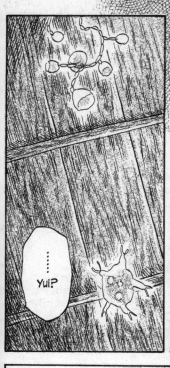

......
Yui?

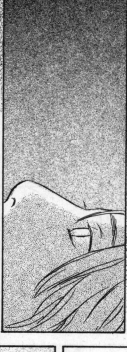

When my son was born...

...I sort of wandered between life and death.

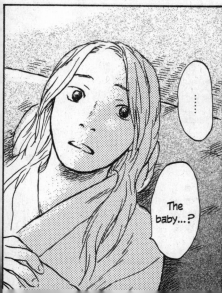

......

The baby...?

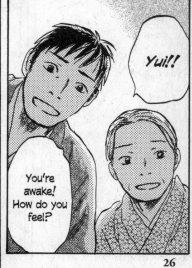

Yui!!

You're awake! How do you feel?

26

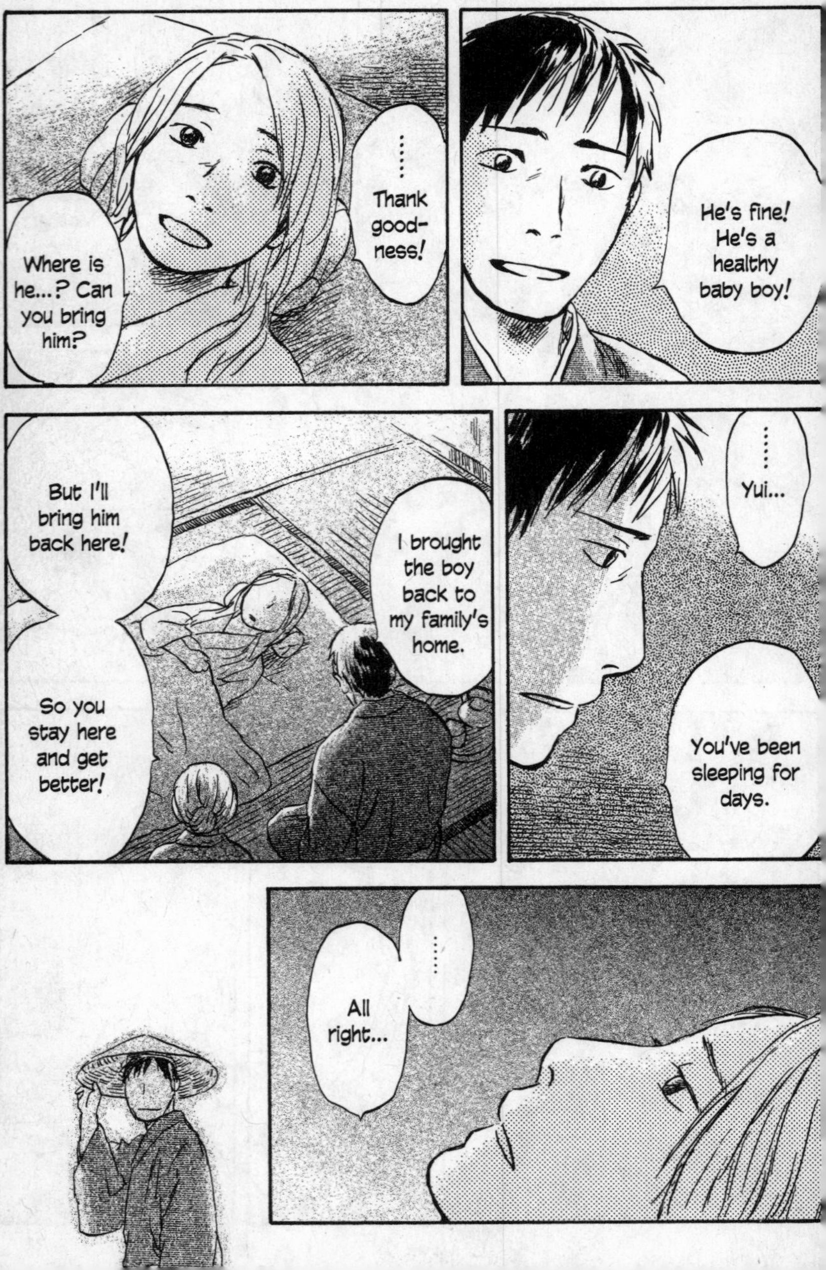
He's fine! He's a healthy baby boy!
......
Thank goodness!
Where is he...? Can you bring him?
......
Yui...
You've been sleeping for days.
I brought the boy back to my family's home.
But I'll bring him back here!
So you stay here and get better!
......
All right...

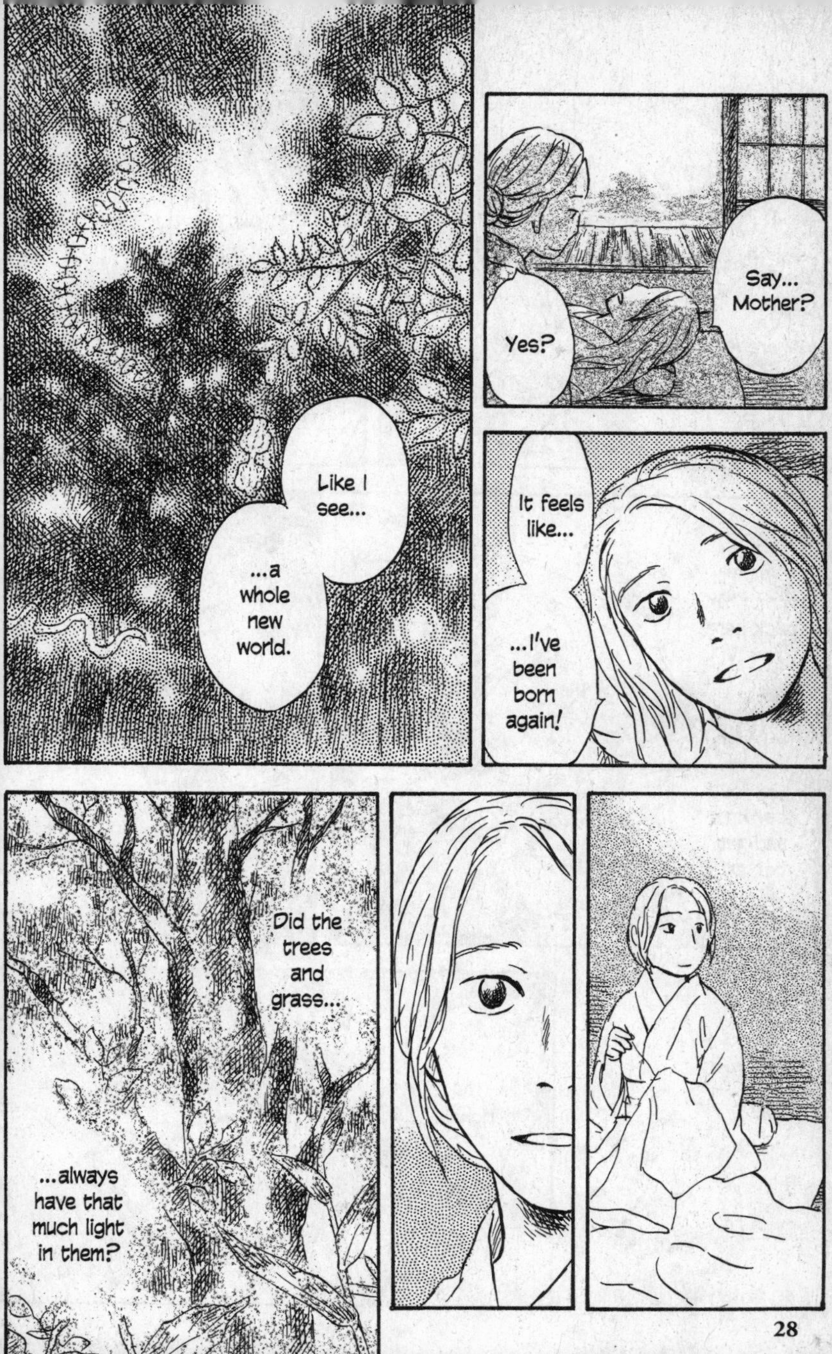
Say... Mother?
Yes?
It feels like...
...I've been born again!
Like I see...
...a whole new world.
Did the trees and grass...
...always have that much light in them?

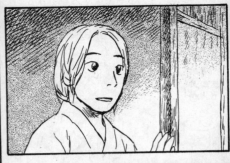

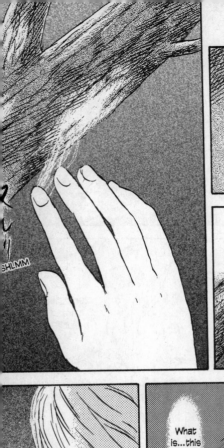

SHLMM
......
Eh?
What is...this thread?
But...it's so beautiful!

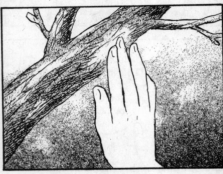

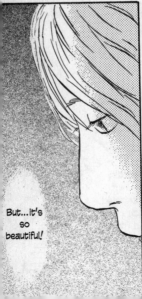

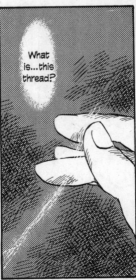

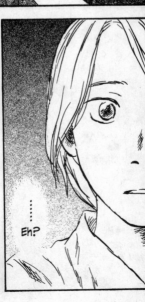

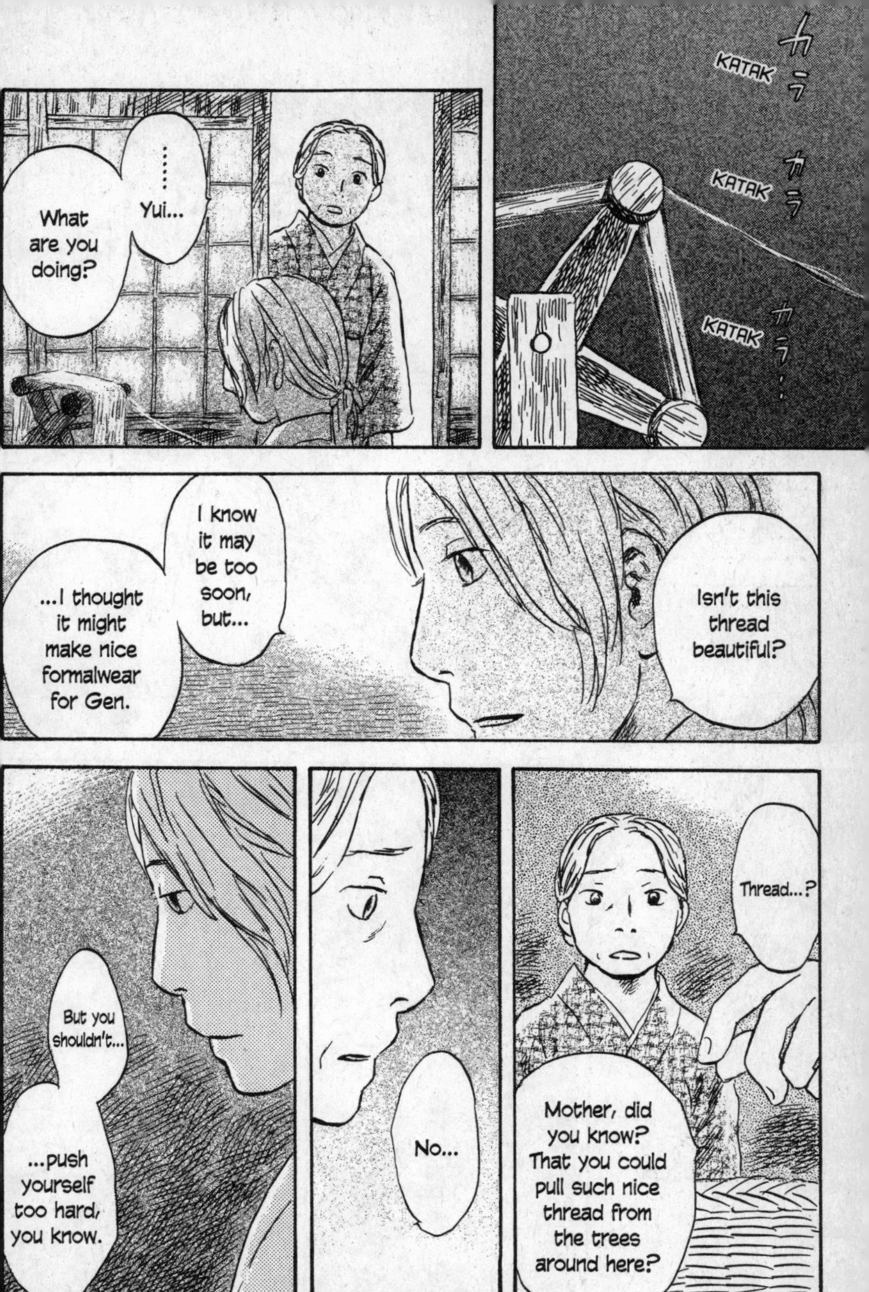
カラ
KATAK
カラ
KATAK
カラ
KATAK
……
Yui...
What are you doing?
Isn't this thread beautiful?
I know it may be too soon, but...
...I thought it might make nice formalwear for Gen.
Thread...?
Mother, did you know? That you could pull such nice thread from the trees around here?
No...
But you shouldn't...
...push yourself too hard, you know.

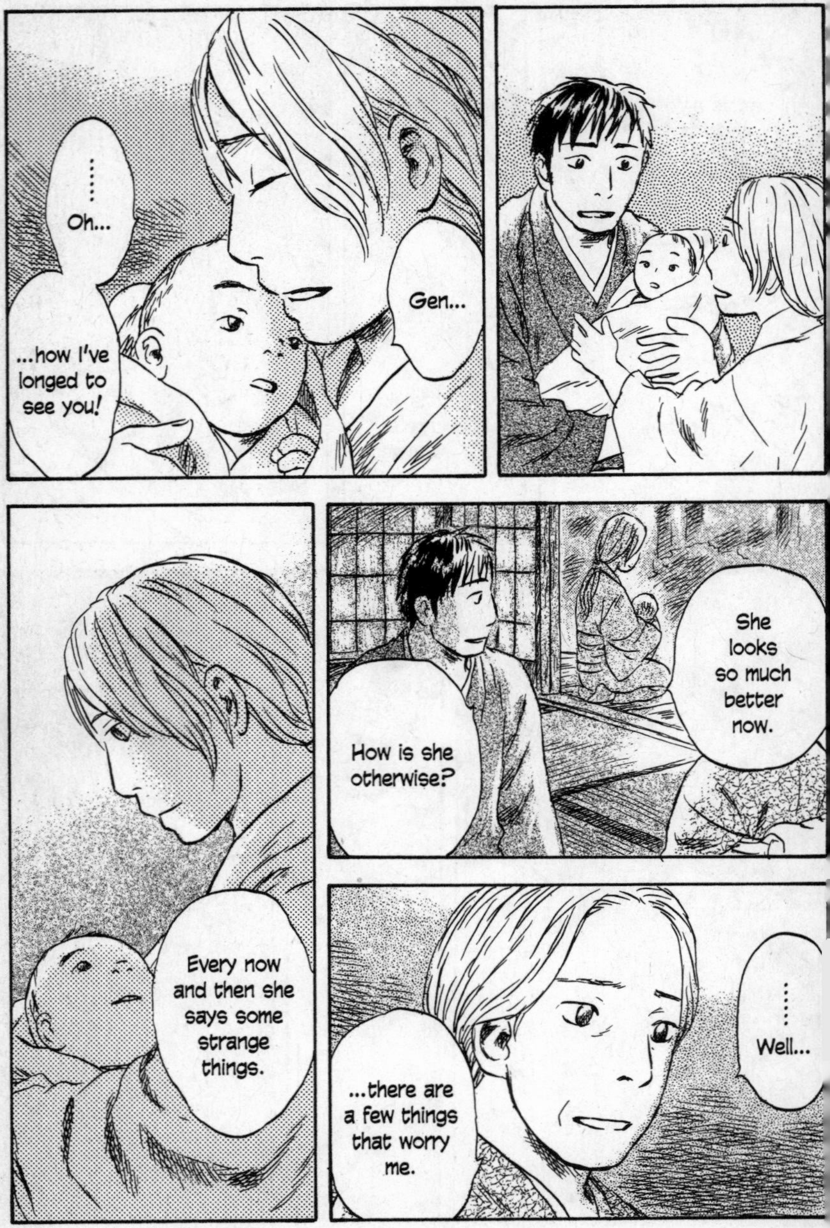
Gen...
......Oh...
...how I've longed to see you!
She looks so much better now.
How is she otherwise?
......Well...
...there are a few things that worry me.
Every now and then she says some strange things.

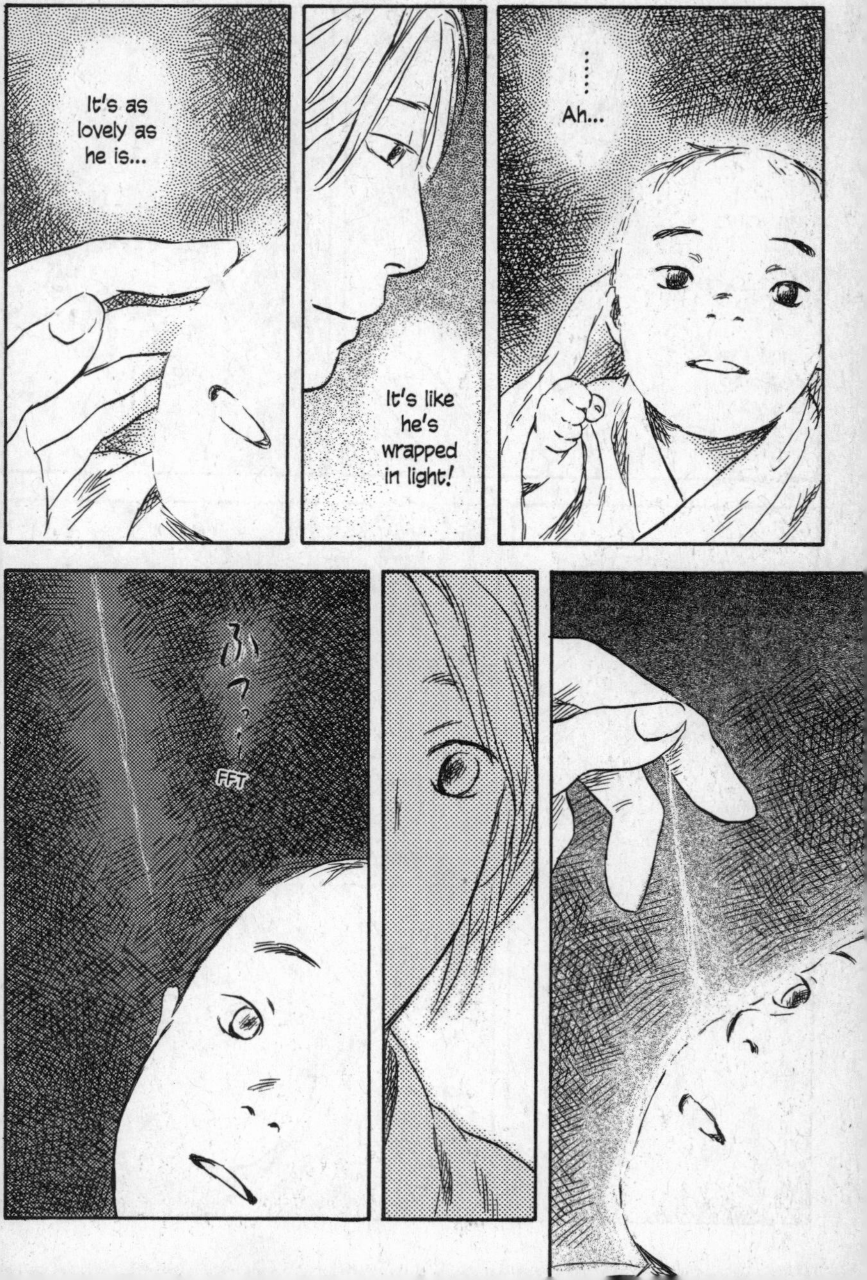
……
Ah...
It's like he's wrapped in light!
It's as lovely as he is...
ふっ…
FFT

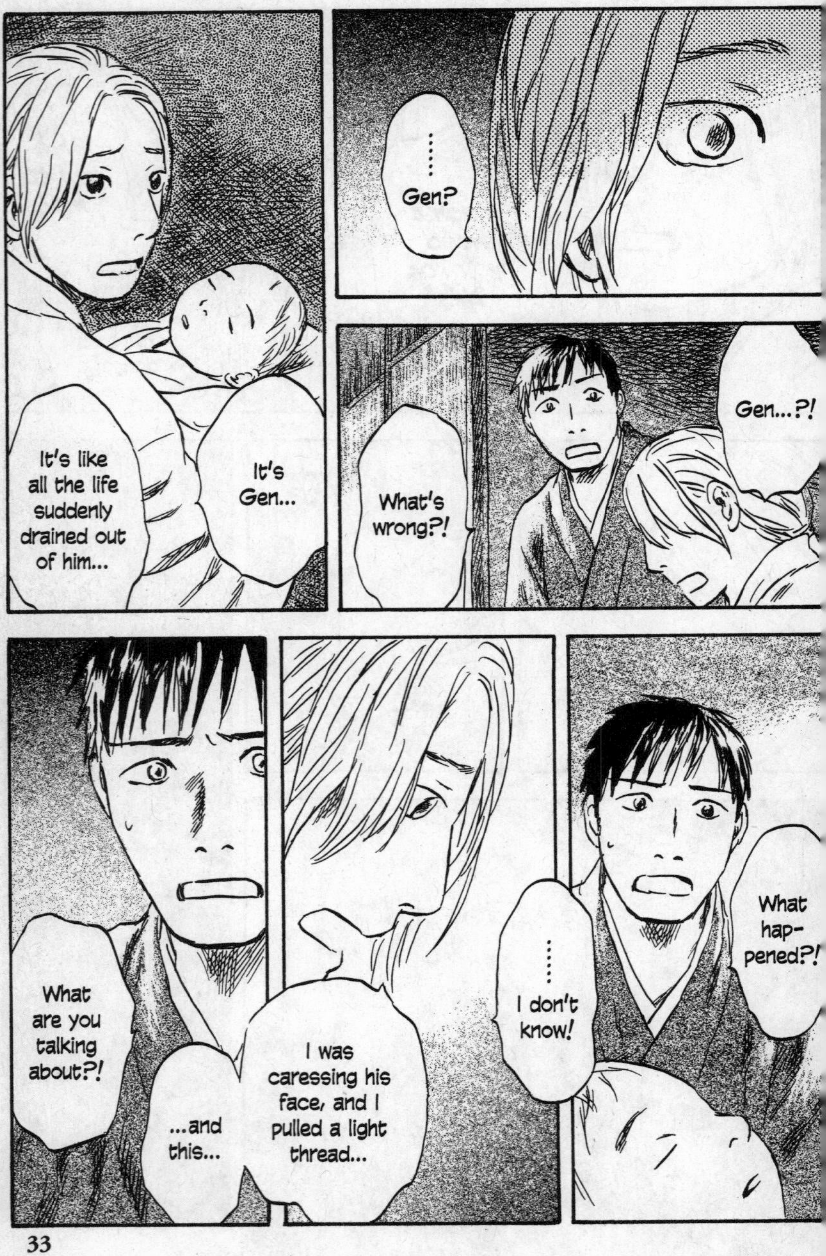

......
Gen?
Gen...?!
What's wrong?!
It's Gen...
It's like all the life suddenly drained out of him...
What hap-pened?!
......
I don't know!
I was caressing his face, and I pulled a light thread...
...and this...
What are you talking about?!

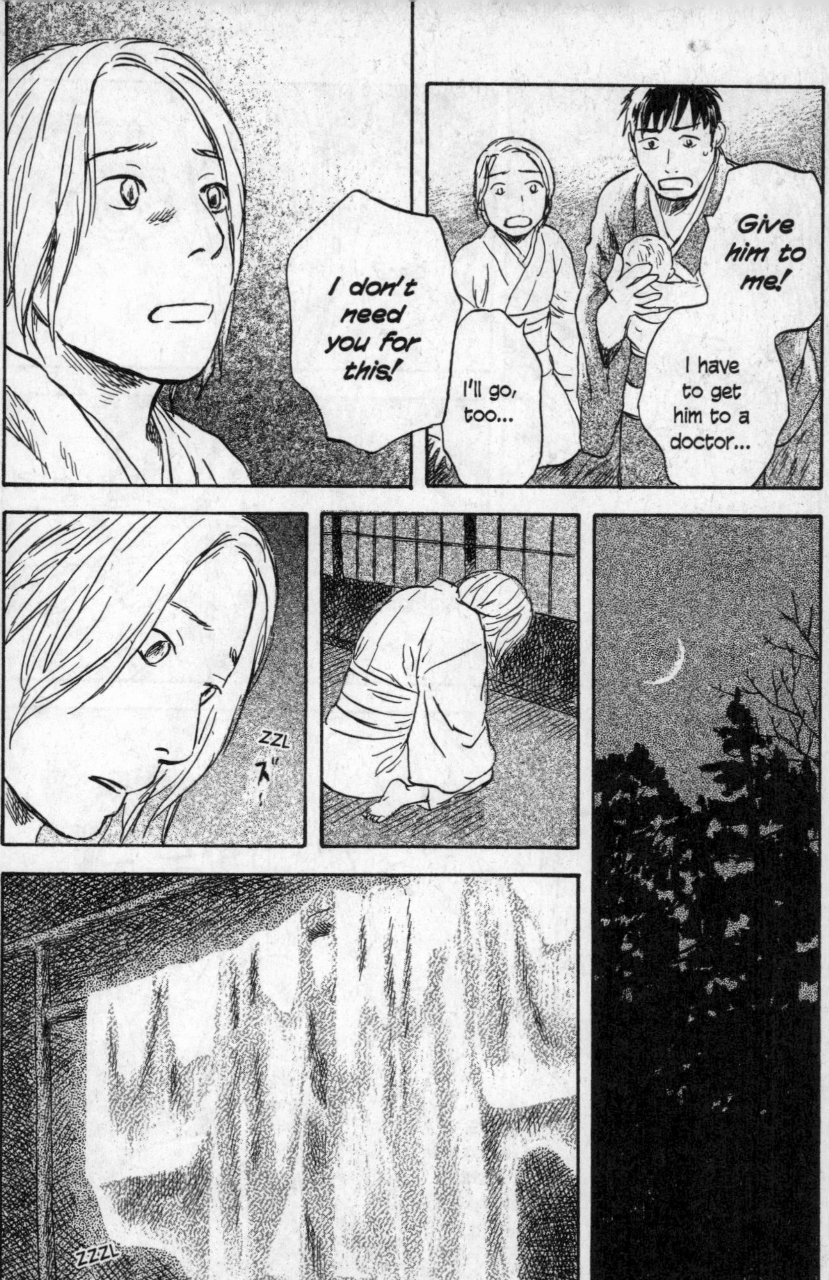
Give him to me!
I have to get him to a doctor...
I'll go, too...
I don't need you for this!
ZZL
ズ
ZZZL
ズズ

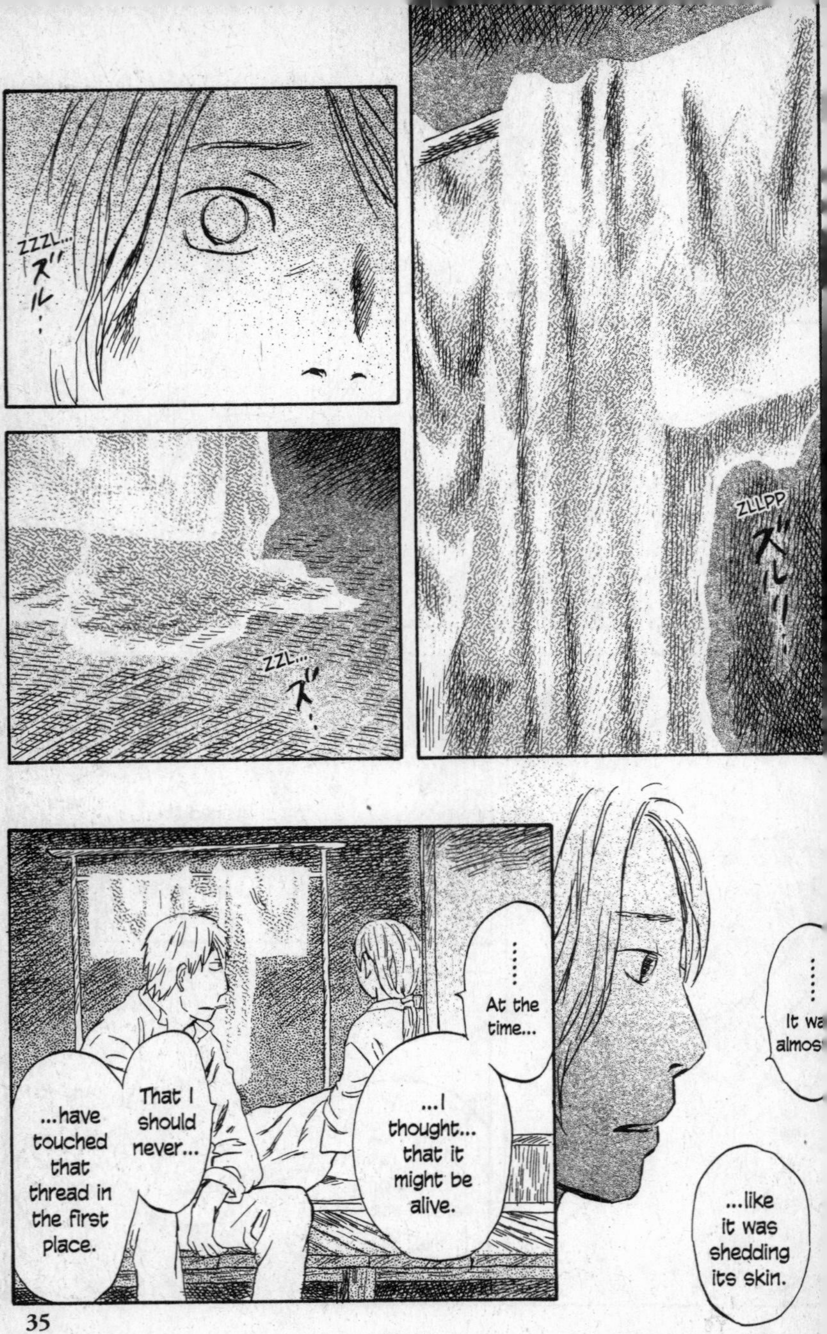

ZLLPP
ズルー…
ZZZL...
ズル…
ZZL...
ズ…
......
It wa
almos
...like it was shedding its skin.
......
At the time...
...I thought... that it might be alive.
That I should never...
...have touched that thread in the first place.

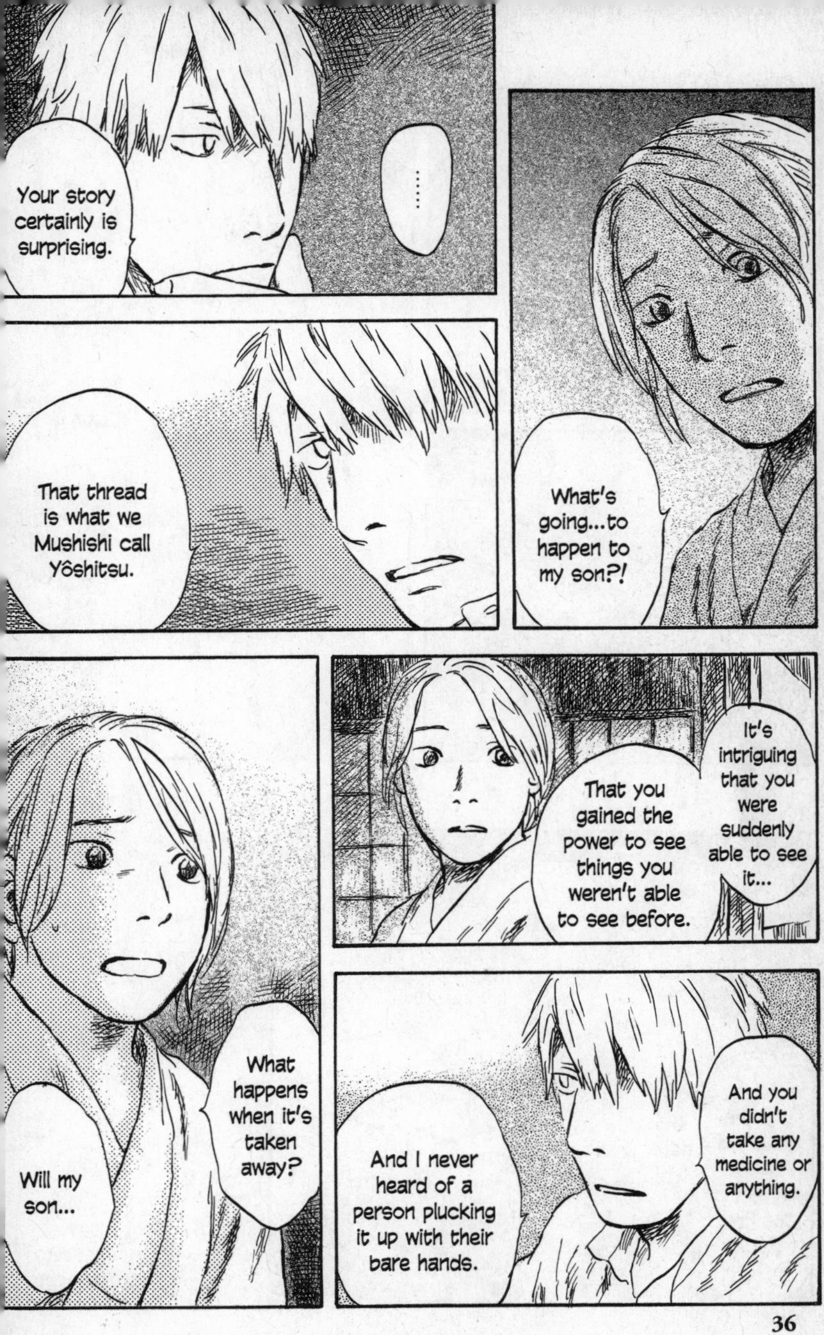
What's going...to happen to my son?!
......
Your story certainly is surprising.
That thread is what we Mushishi call Yôshitsu.
It's intriguing that you were suddenly able to see it...
That you gained the power to see things you weren't able to see before.
And you didn't take any medicine or anything.
And I never heard of a person plucking it up with their bare hands.
What happens when it's taken away?
Will my son...

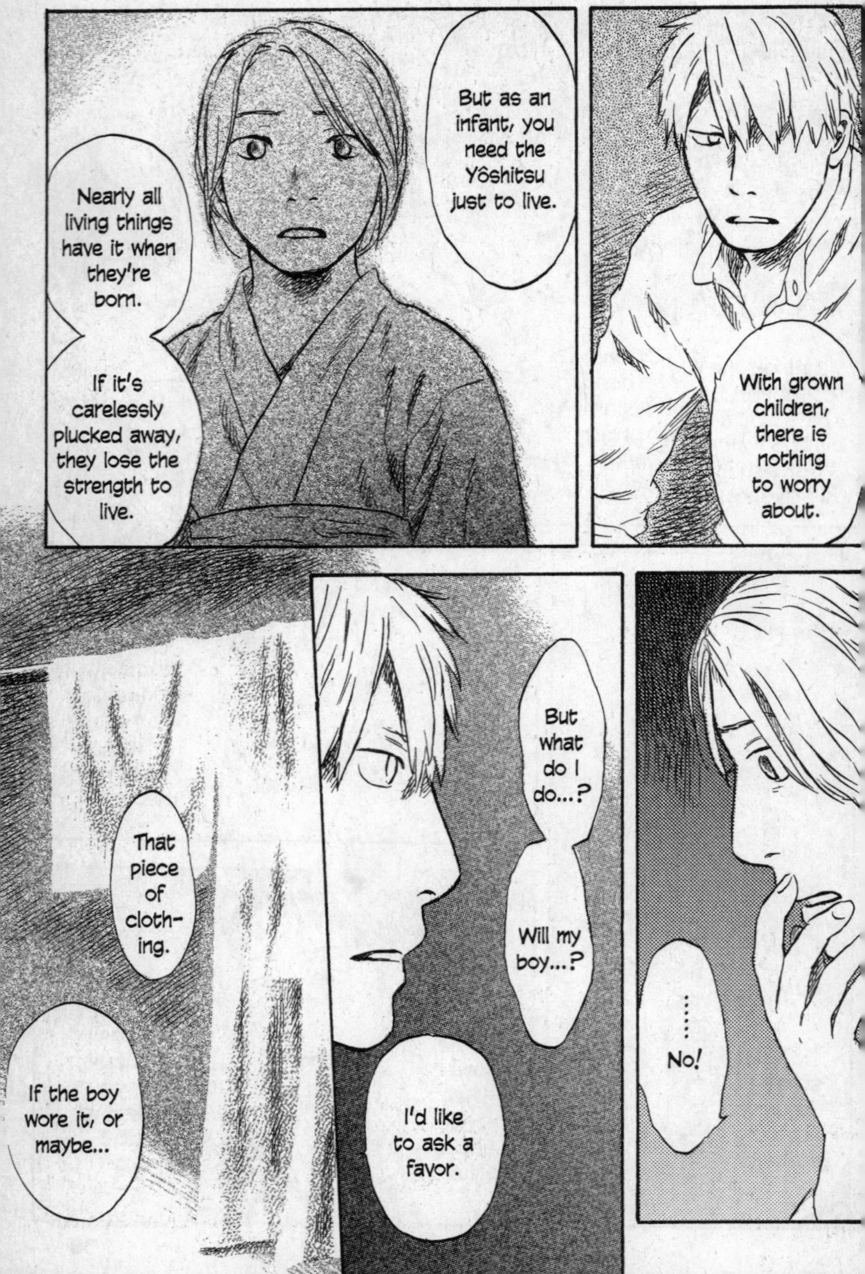
With grown children, there is nothing to worry about.
But as an infant, you need the Yôshitsu just to live.
Nearly all living things have it when they're born.
If it's carelessly plucked away, they lose the strength to live.
...... No!
But what do I do...?
Will my boy...?
I'd like to ask a favor.
That piece of cloth-ing.
If the boy wore it, or maybe...

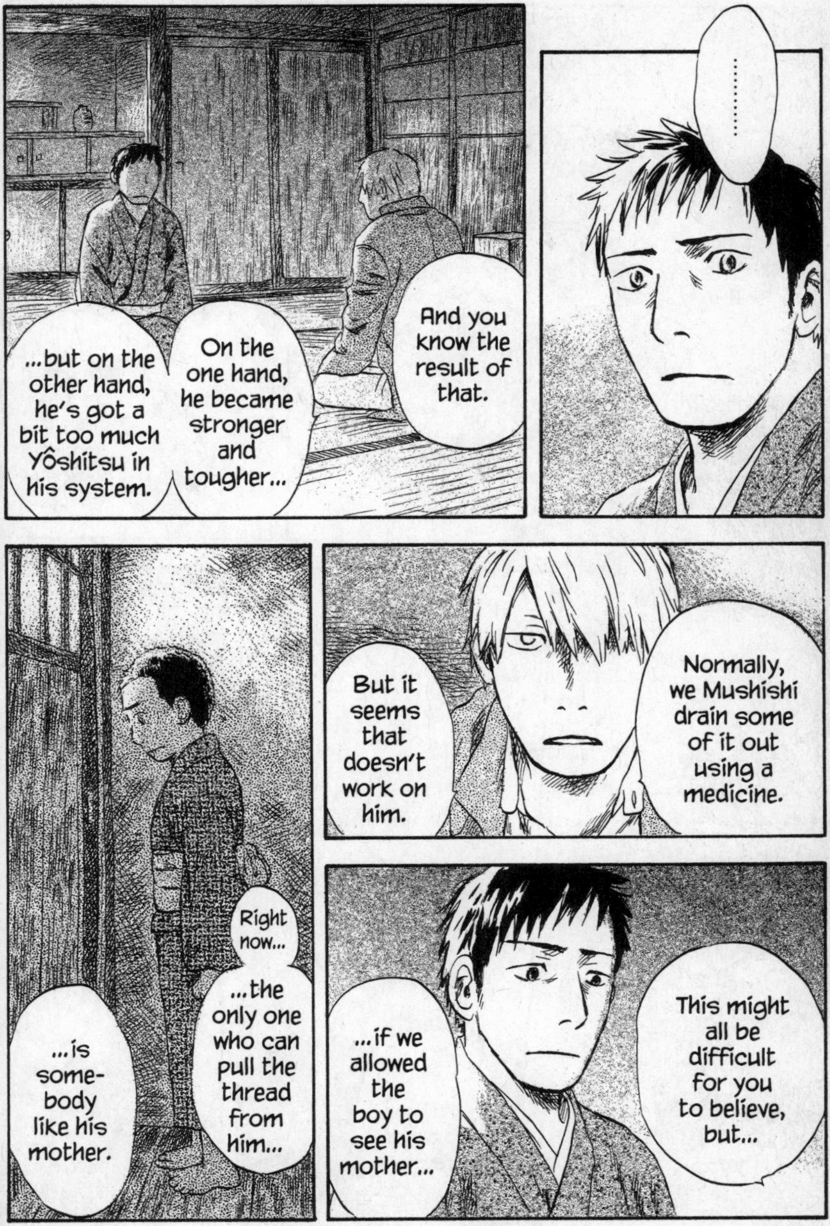
......
And you know the result of that.
On the one hand, he became stronger and tougher...
...but on the other hand, he's got a bit too much Yôshitsu in his system.
Normally, we Mushishi drain some of it out using a medicine.
But it seems that doesn't work on him.
This might all be difficult for you to believe, but...
...if we allowed the boy to see his mother...
Right now...
...the only one who can pull the thread from him...
...is somebody like his mother.

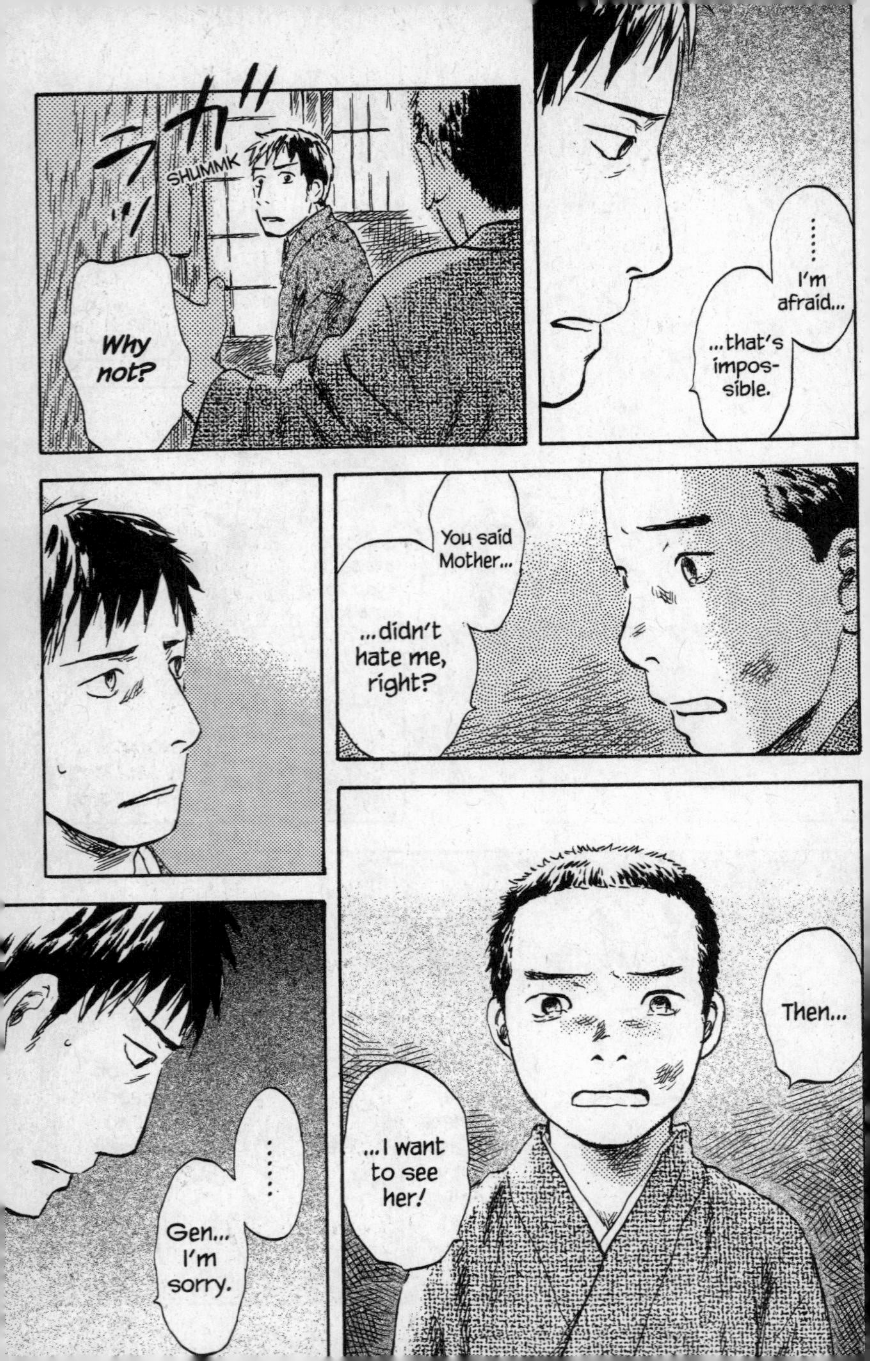

......
I'm afraid...
...that's impos-sible.
SHUMMK
Why not?
You said Mother...
...didn't hate me, right?
Then...
...I want to see her!
......
Gen... I'm sorry.

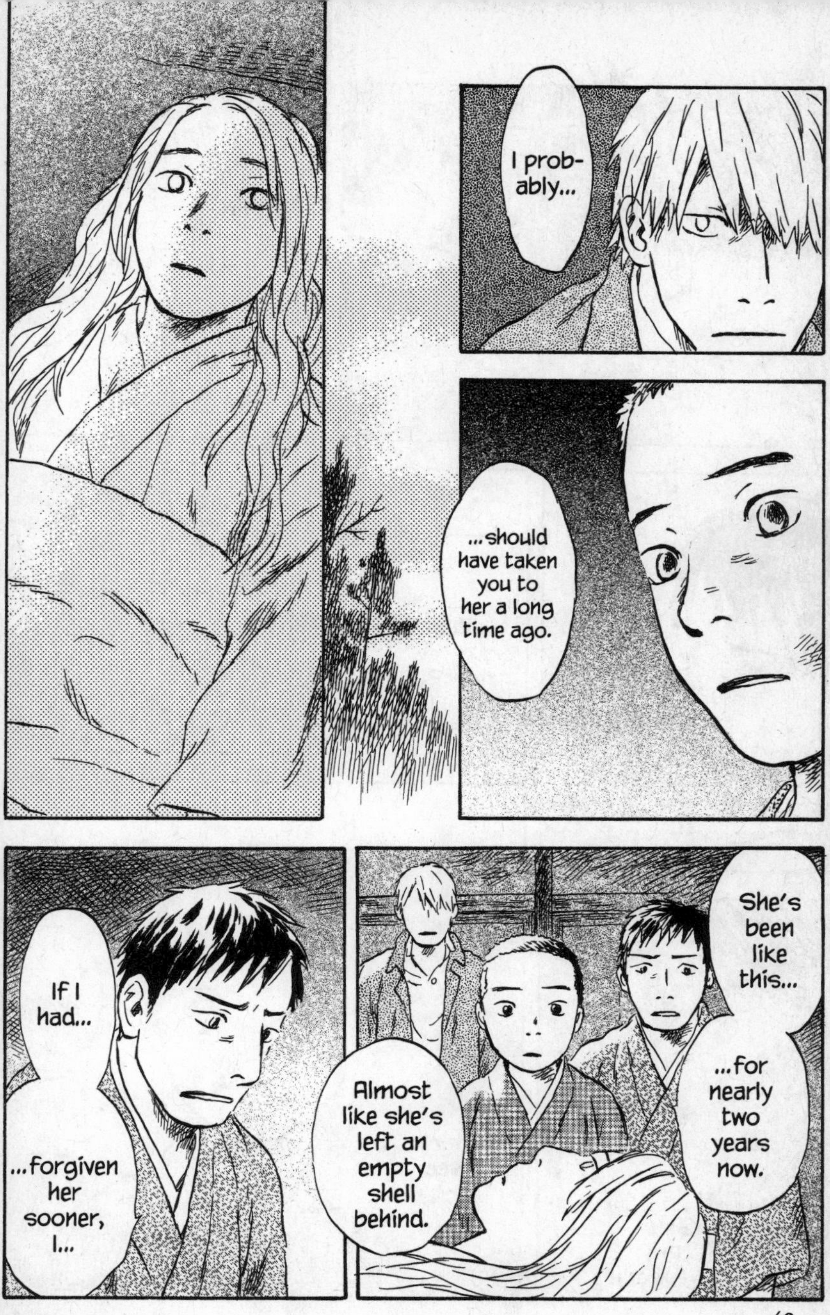

I prob-ably...
...should have taken you to her a long time ago.
She's been like this...
...for nearly two years now.
Almost like she's left an empty shell behind.
If I had...
...forgiven her sooner, I...

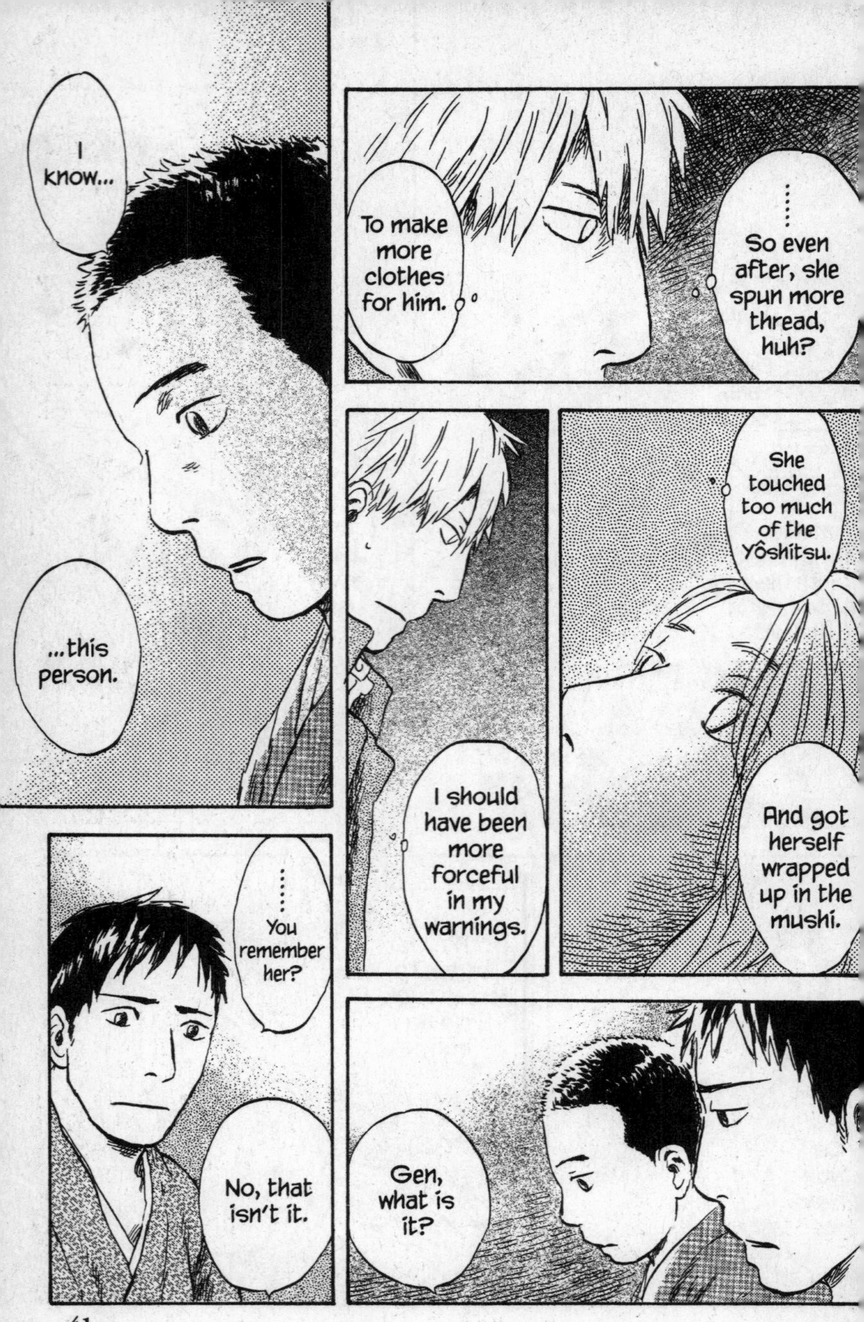
......
So even after, she spun more thread, huh?
To make more clothes for him.
She touched too much of the Yôshitsu.
And got herself wrapped up in the mushi.
I should have been more forceful in my warnings.
I know...
...this person.
Gen, what is it?
......
You remember her?
No, that isn't it.

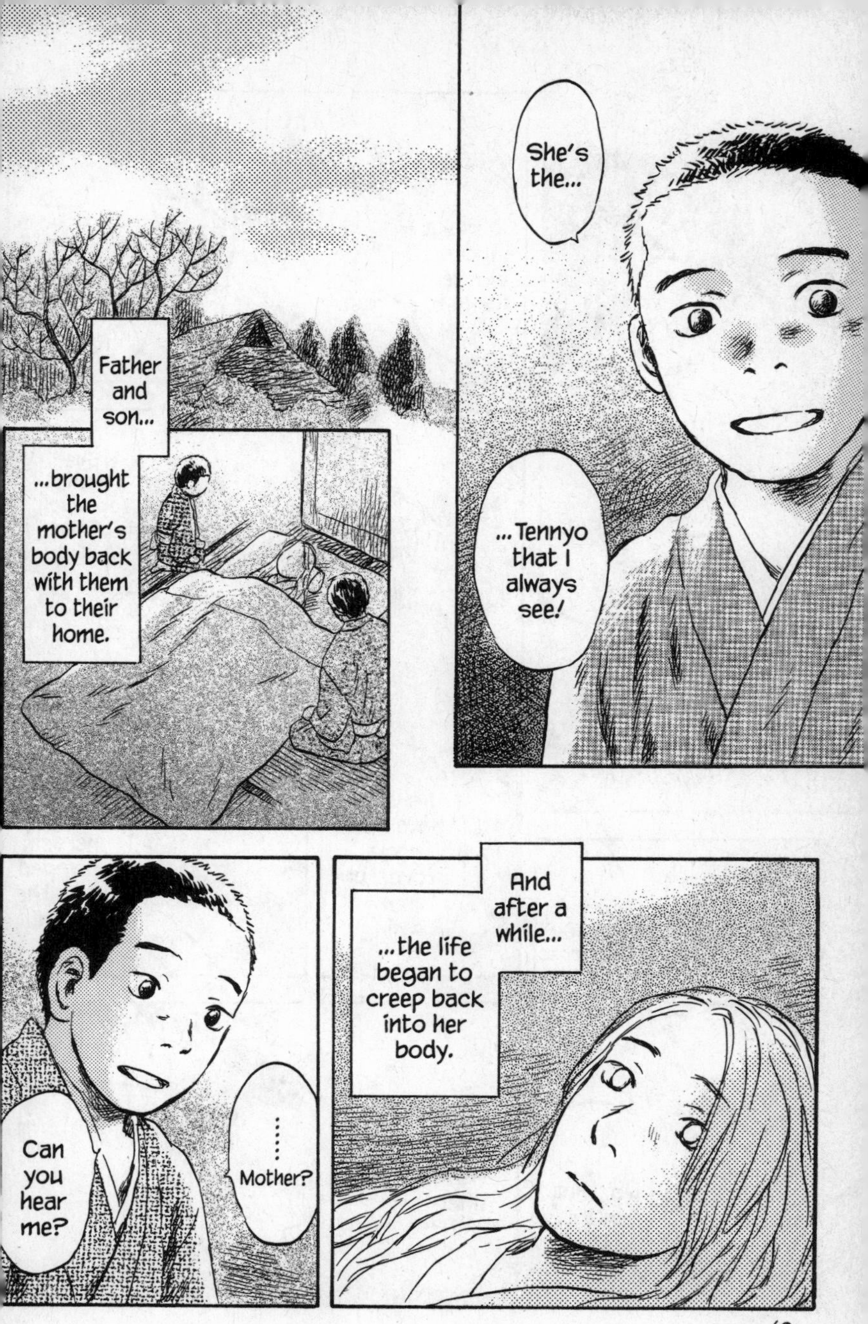
She's the...
...Tennyo that I always see!
Father and son...
...brought the mother's body back with them to their home.
And after a while...
...the life began to creep back into her body.
......Mother?
Can you hear me?

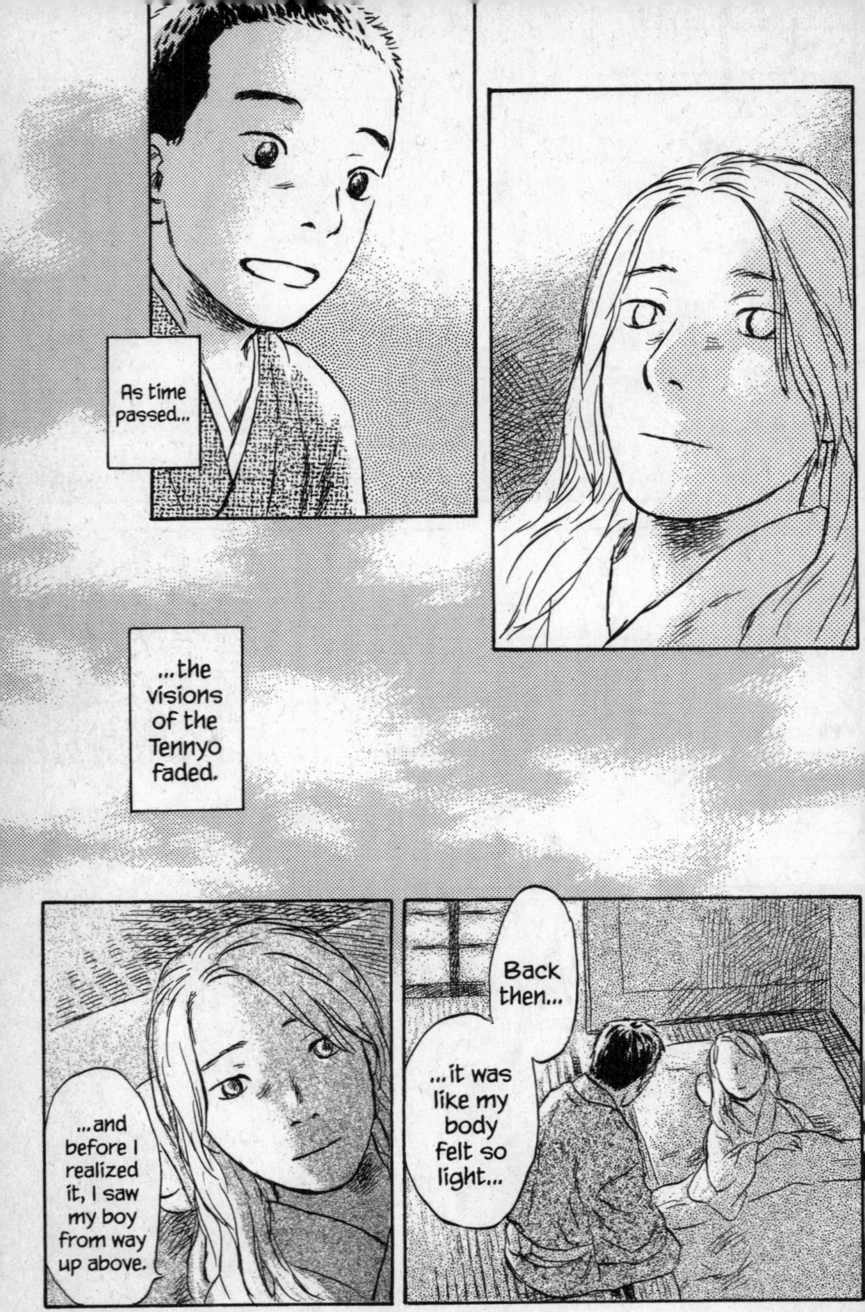
As time passed...
...the visions of the Tennyo faded.
Back then...
...it was like my body felt so light...
...and before I realized it, I saw my boy from way up above.

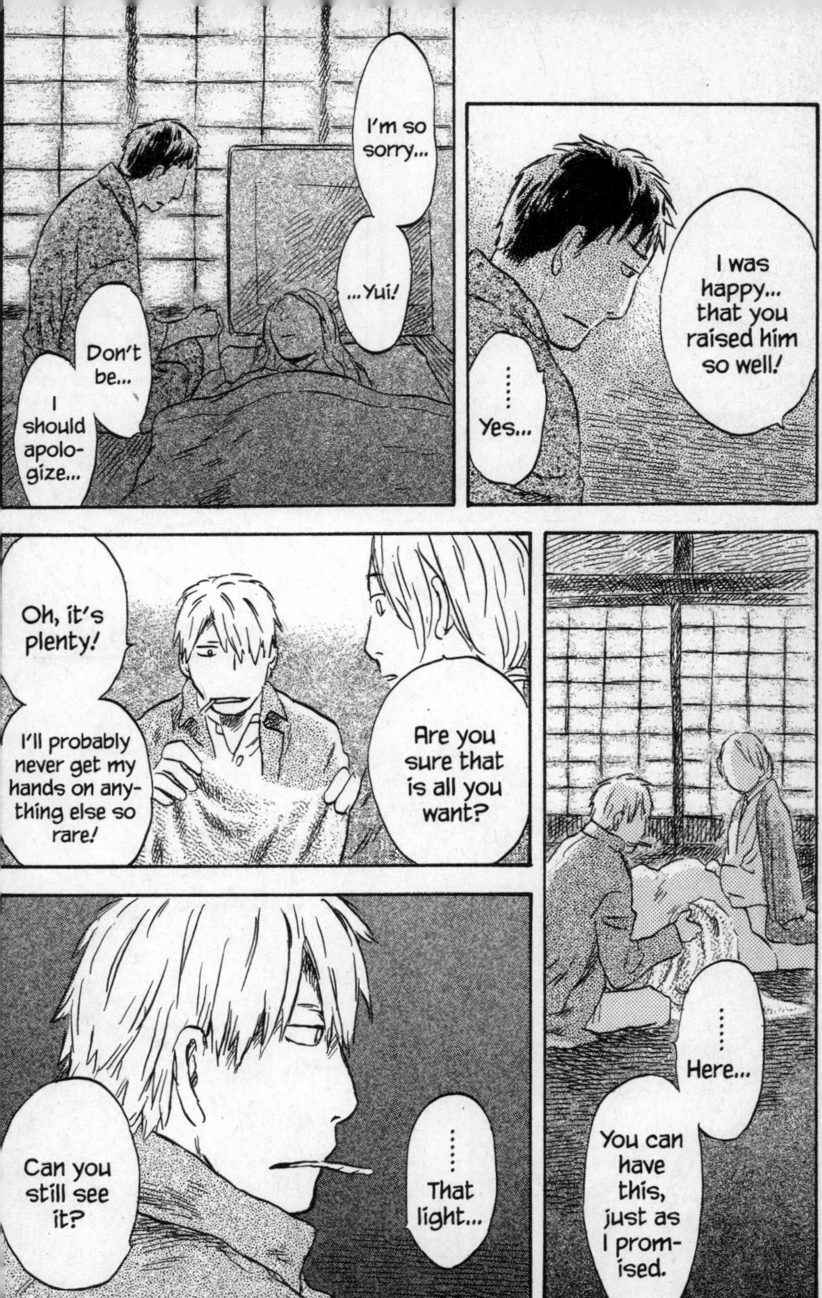
I was happy... that you raised him so well!
......
Yes...
I'm so sorry...
...Yui!
Don't be...
I should apologize...
......
Here...
You can have this, just as I promised.
Are you sure that is all you want?
Oh, it's plenty!
I'll probably never get my hands on anything else so rare!
......
That light...
Can you still see it?

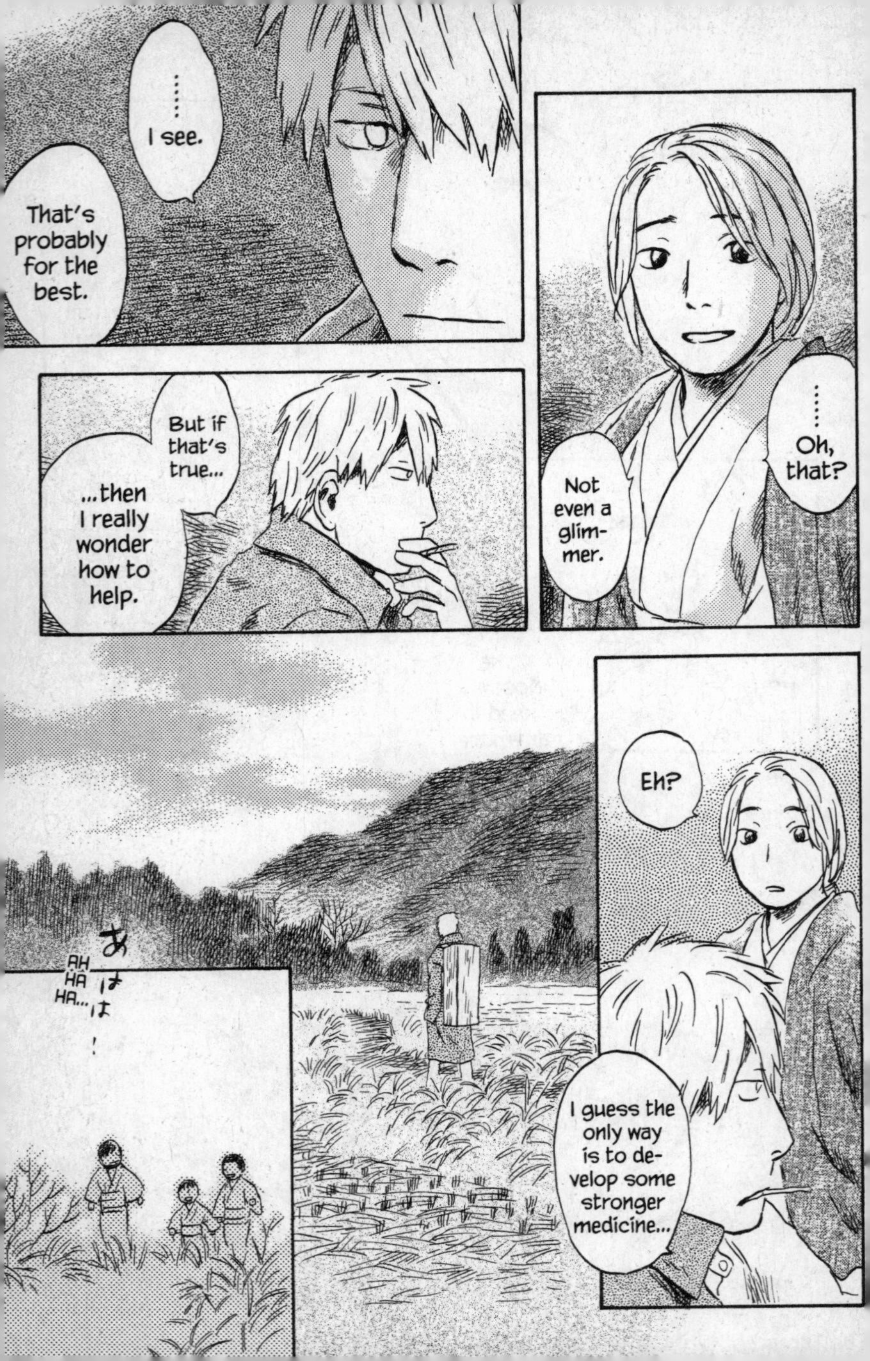
......
Oh, that?
Not even a glimmer.
......
I see.
That's probably for the best.
But if that's true...
...then I really wonder how to help.
Eh?
I guess the only way is to develop some stronger medicine...
あははは!
AH HA HA...

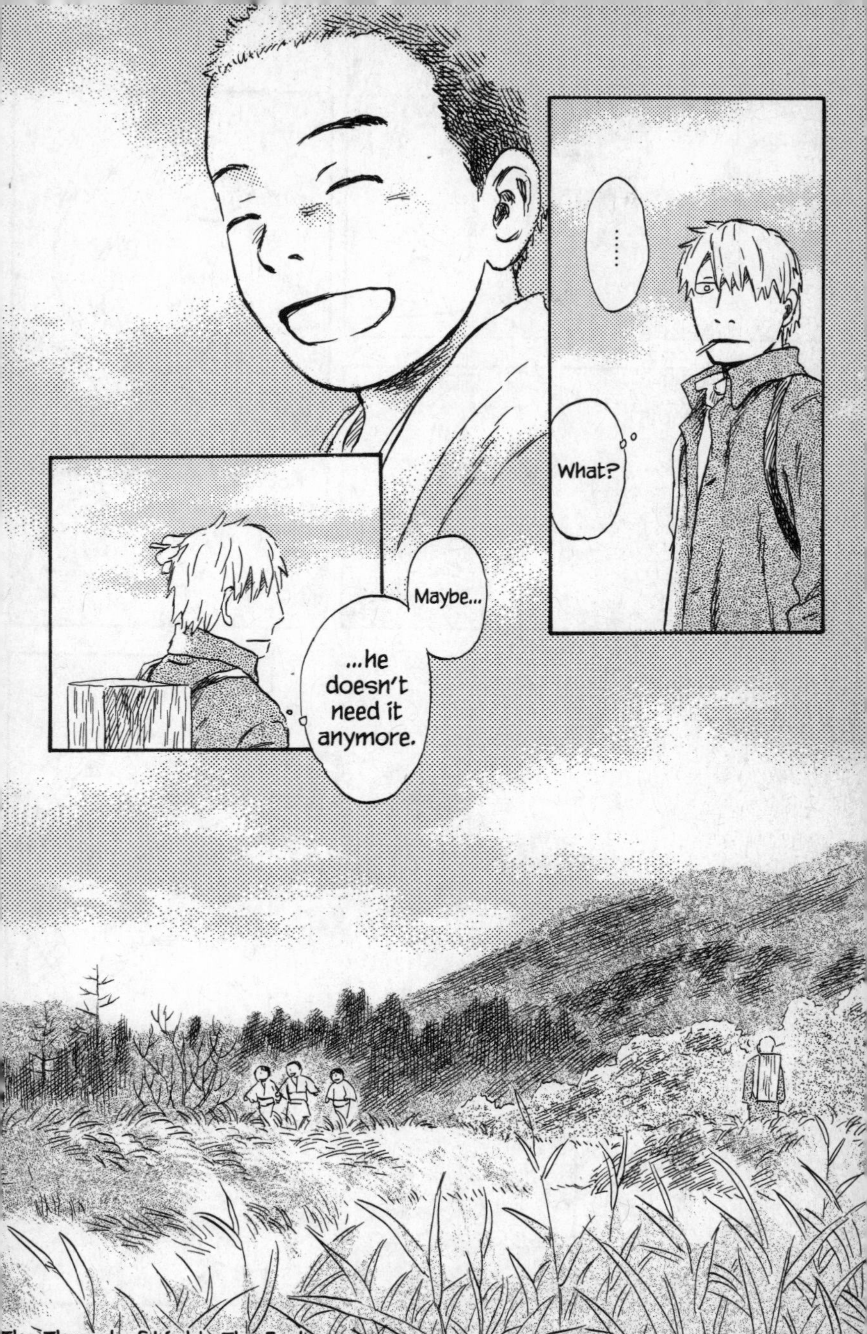
......
What?
Maybe...
...he doesn't need it anymore.
The Thread of Light The End

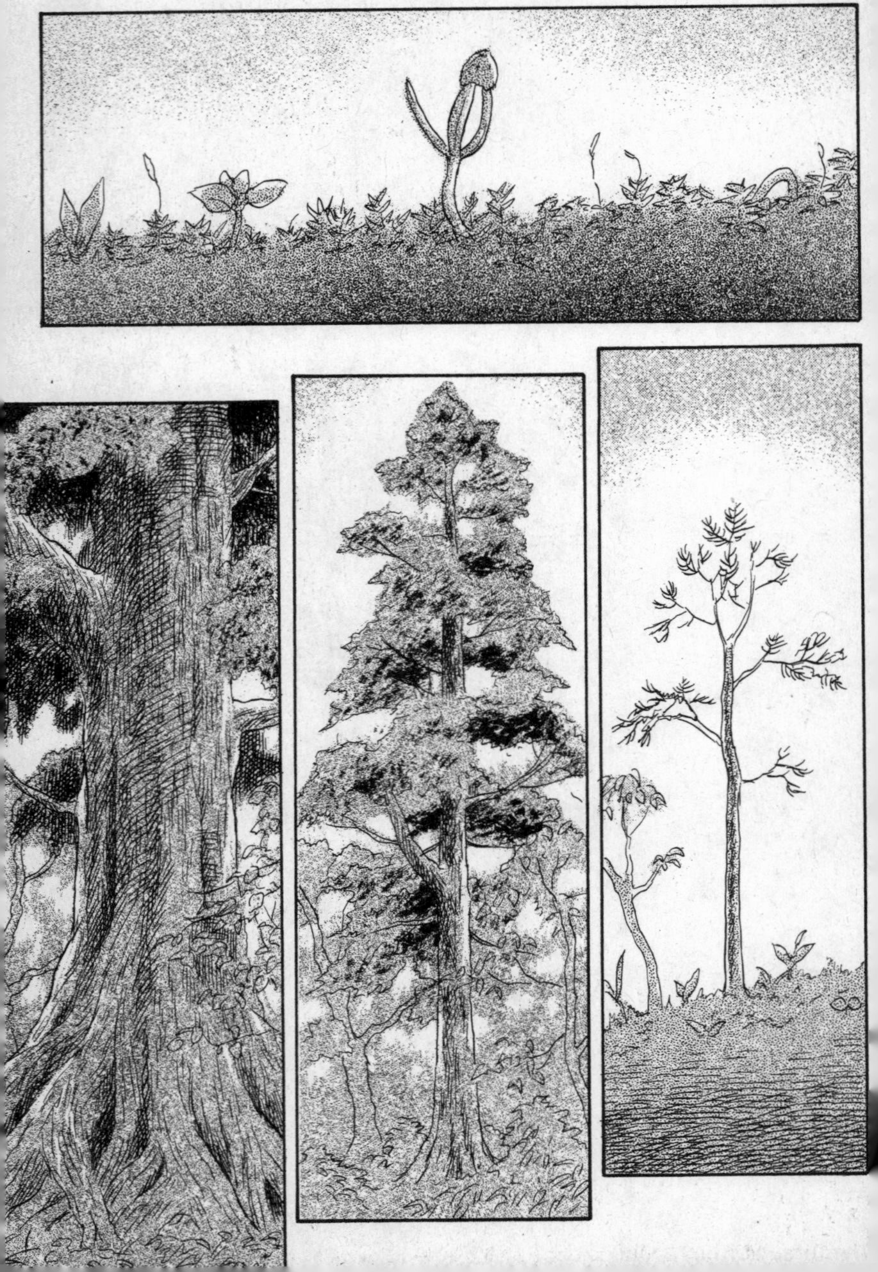

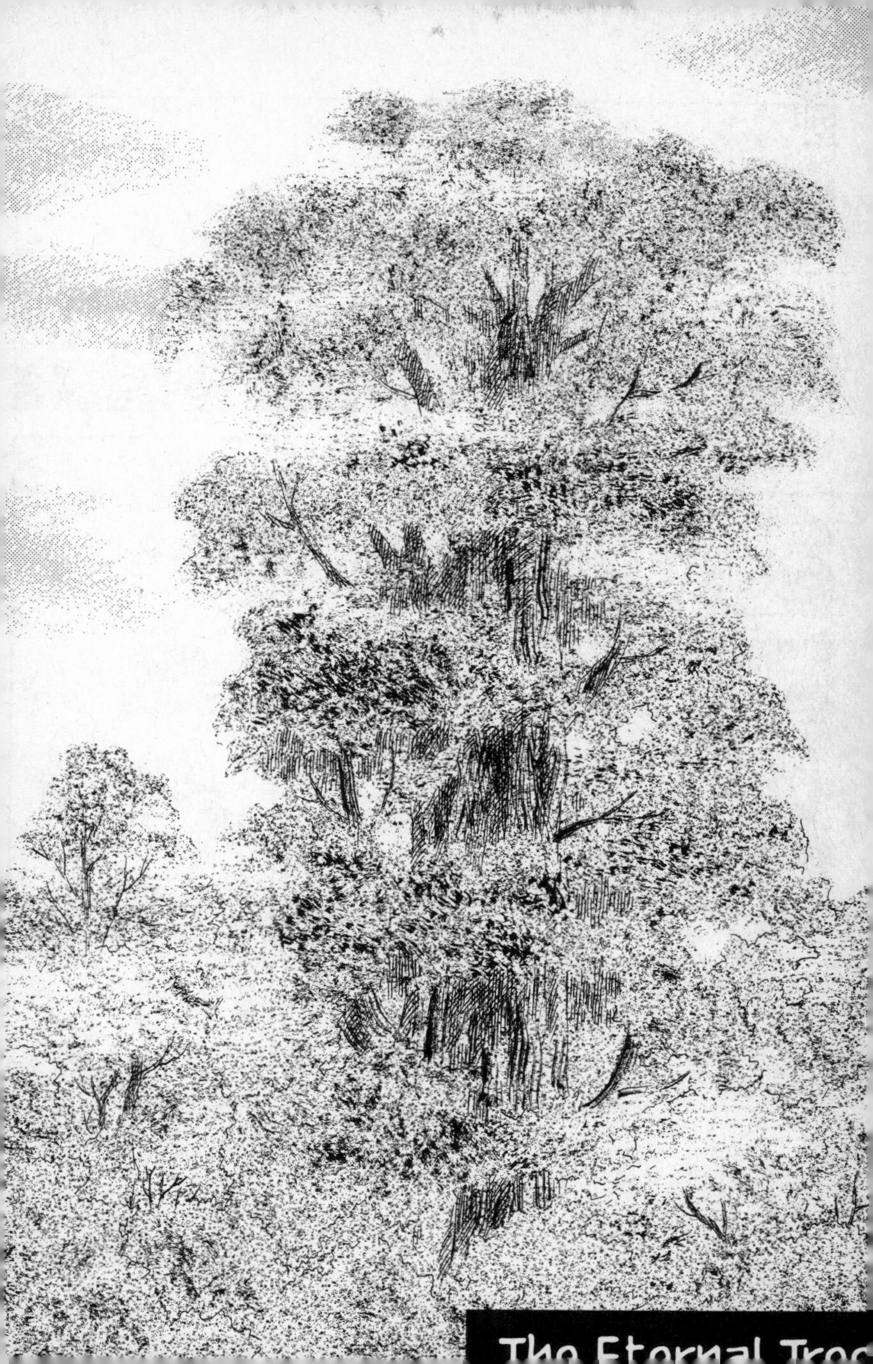

The Eternal Tree

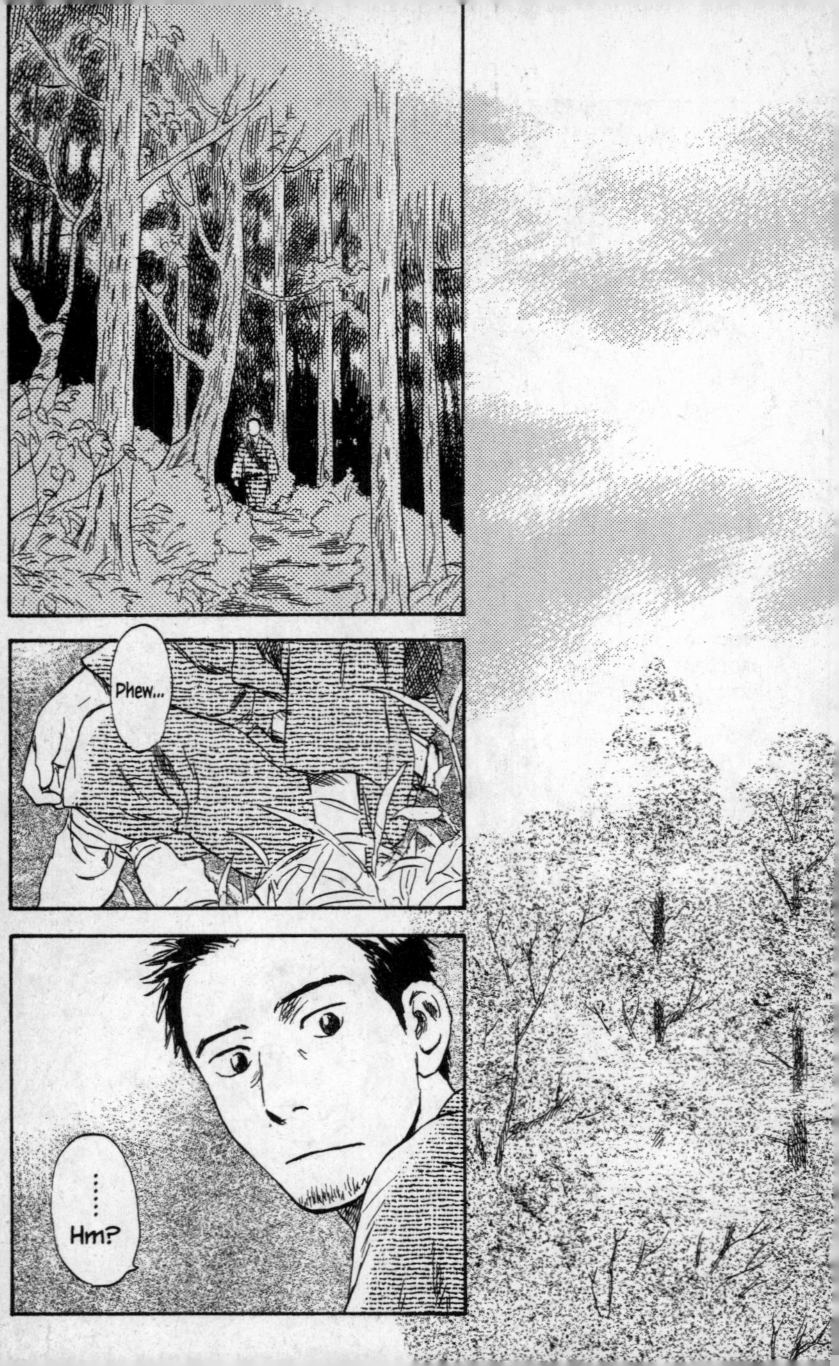
Phew...
......
Hm?

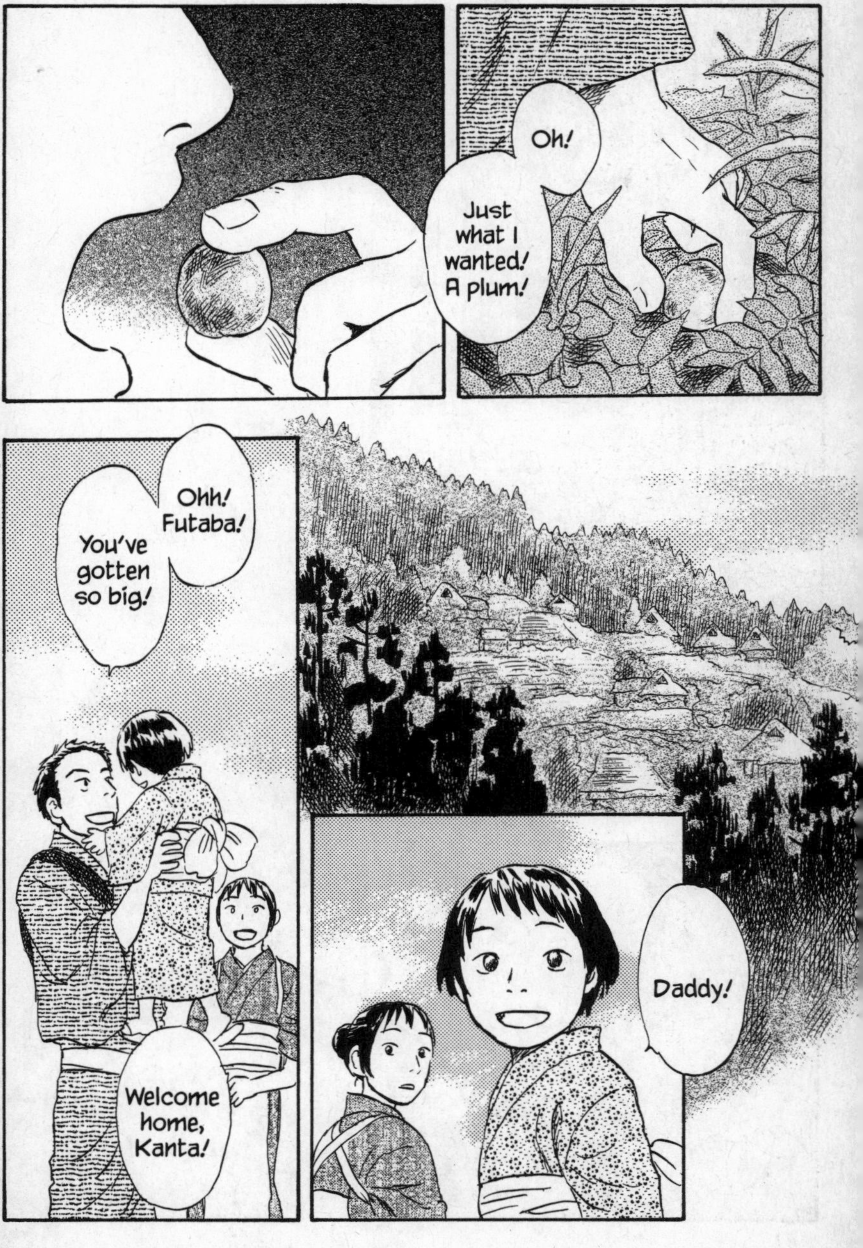
Oh!
Just what I wanted! A plum!
Daddy!
Ohh! Futaba!
You've gotten so big!
Welcome home, Kanta!

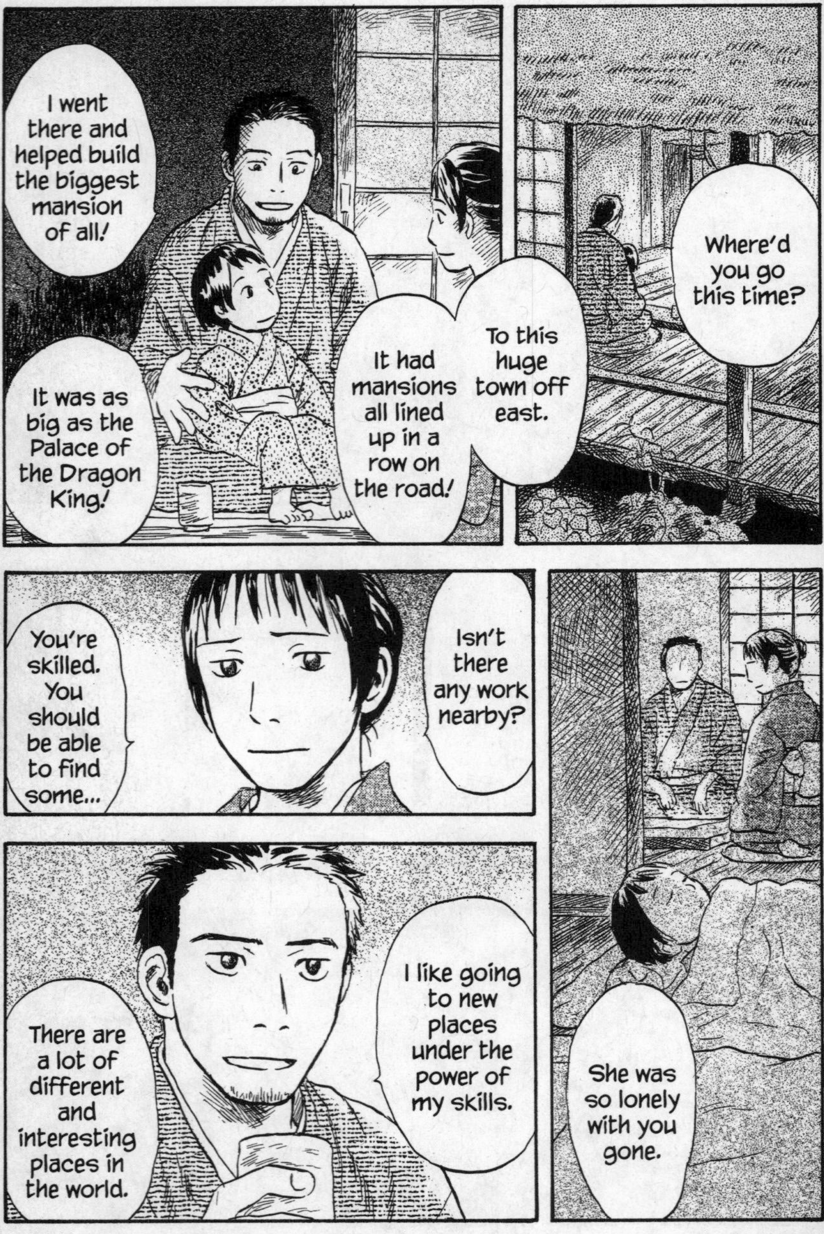
Where'd you go this time?
To this huge town off east.
It had mansions all lined up in a row on the road!
I went there and helped build the biggest mansion of all!
It was as big as the Palace of the Dragon King!
She was so lonely with you gone.
Isn't there any work nearby?
You're skilled. You should be able to find some...
I like going to new places under the power of my skills.
There are a lot of different and interesting places in the world.

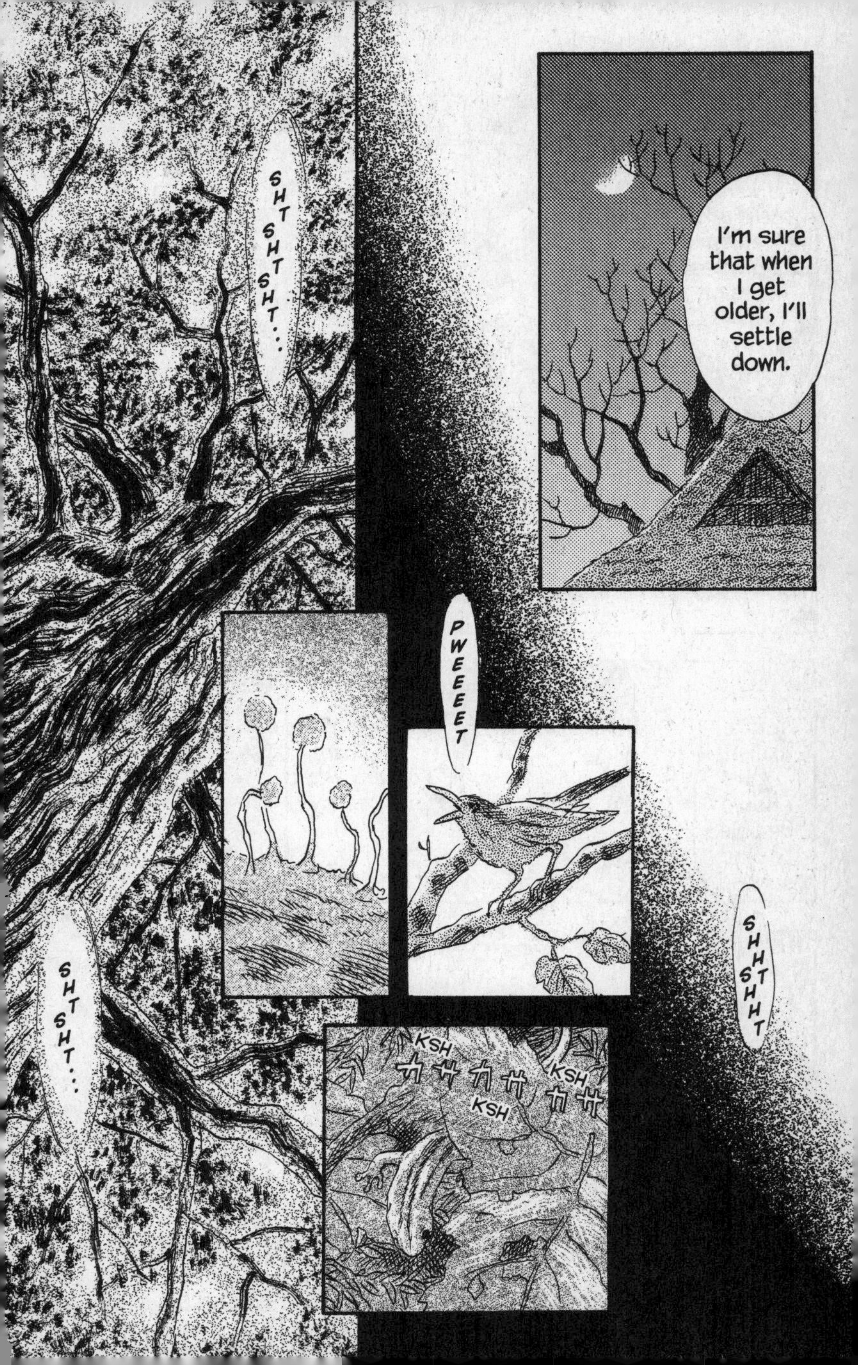
I'm sure that when I get older, I'll settle down.
PWEEEEET
SHT SHT SHT...
SHHT SHHT
KSH
KSH
KSH
SHT SHT...

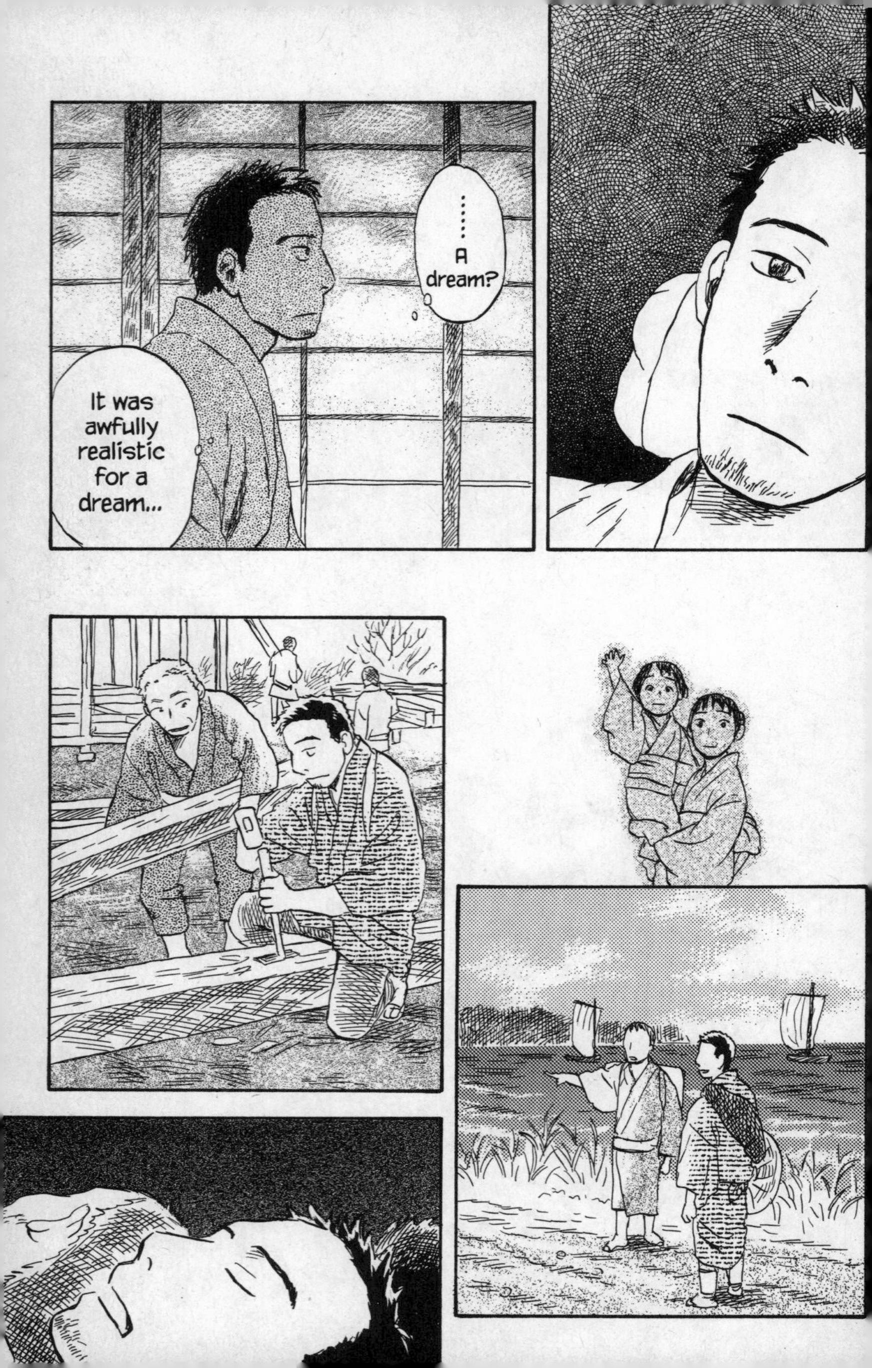
...... A dream?
It was awfully realistic for a dream...

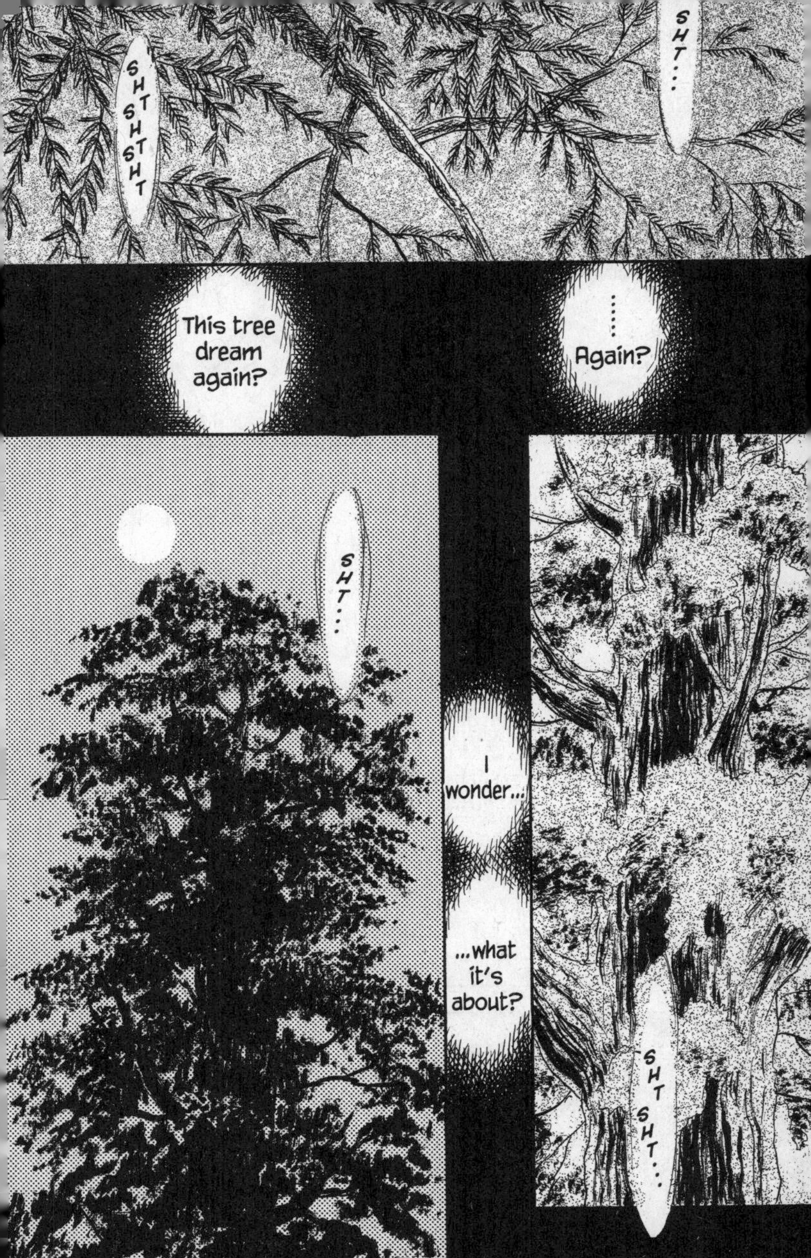
SHT...
SHT SHT SHT SHT
......
Again?
This tree dream again?
SHT SHT...
I wonder...
...what it's about?
SHT...

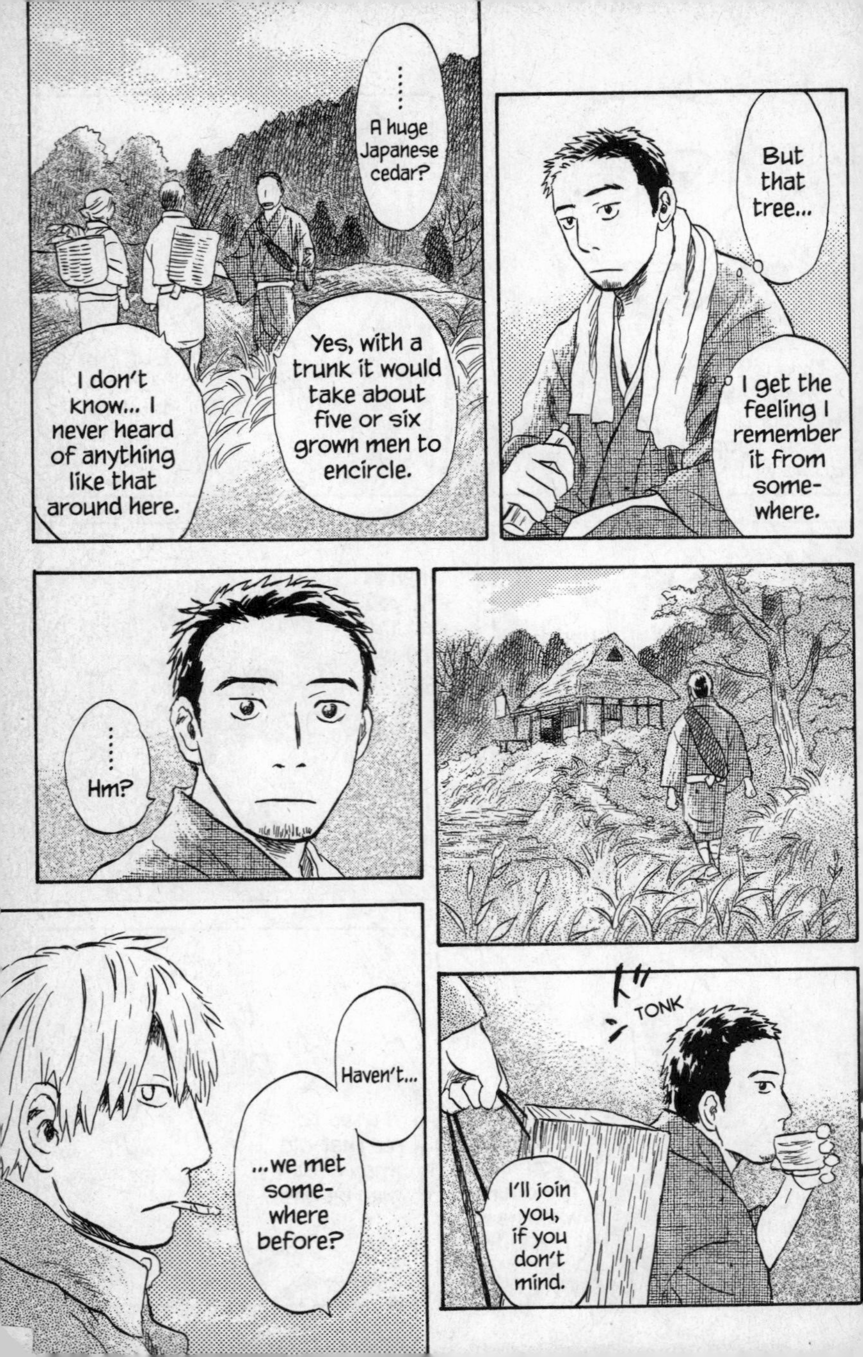

But that tree...
I get the feeling I remember it from some-where.
......
A huge Japanese cedar?
Yes, with a trunk it would take about five or six grown men to encircle.
I don't know... I never heard of anything like that around here.
......
Hm?
TONK
I'll join you, if you don't mind.
Haven't...
...we met some-where before?

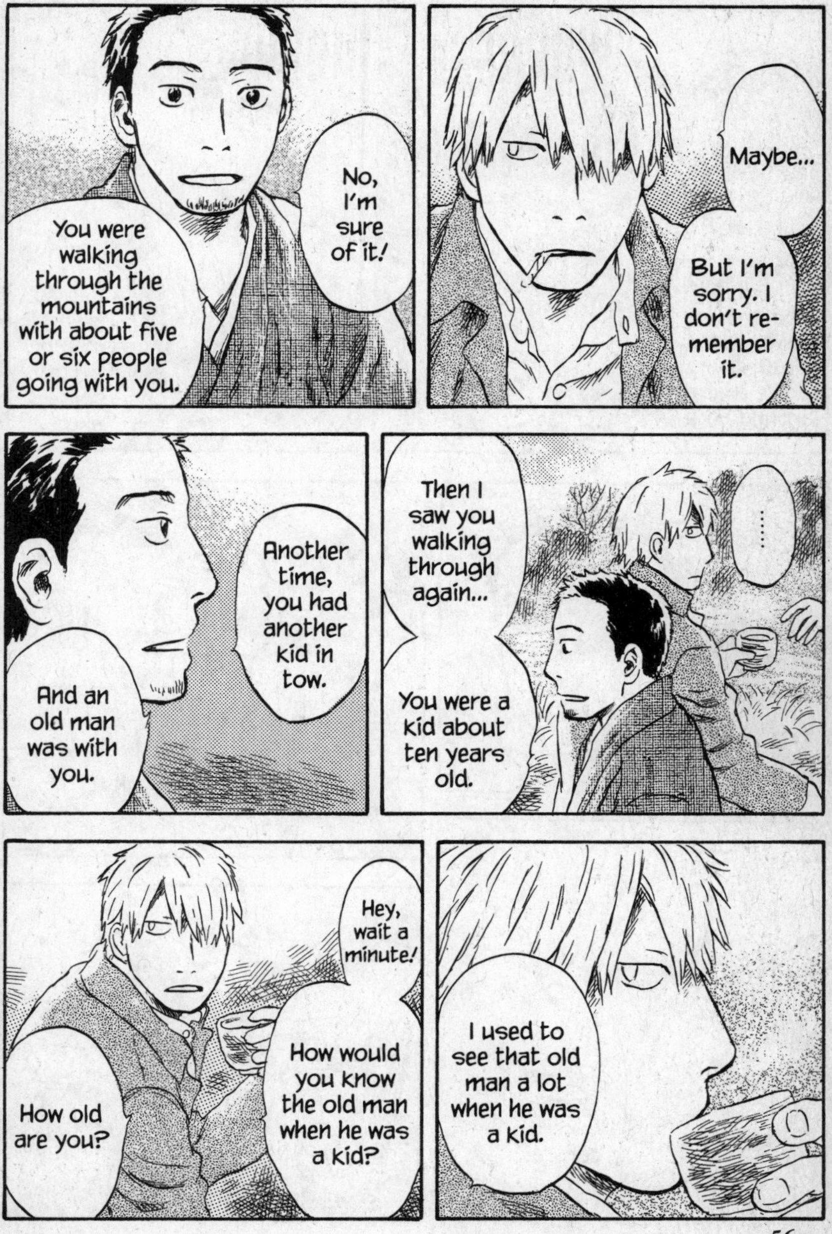
Maybe...
But I'm sorry. I don't re-member it.
No, I'm sure of it!
You were walking through the mountains with about five or six people going with you.
……
Then I saw you walking through again...
You were a kid about ten years old.
Another time, you had another kid in tow.
And an old man was with you.
I used to see that old man a lot when he was a kid.
Hey, wait a minute!
How would you know the old man when he was a kid?
How old are you?

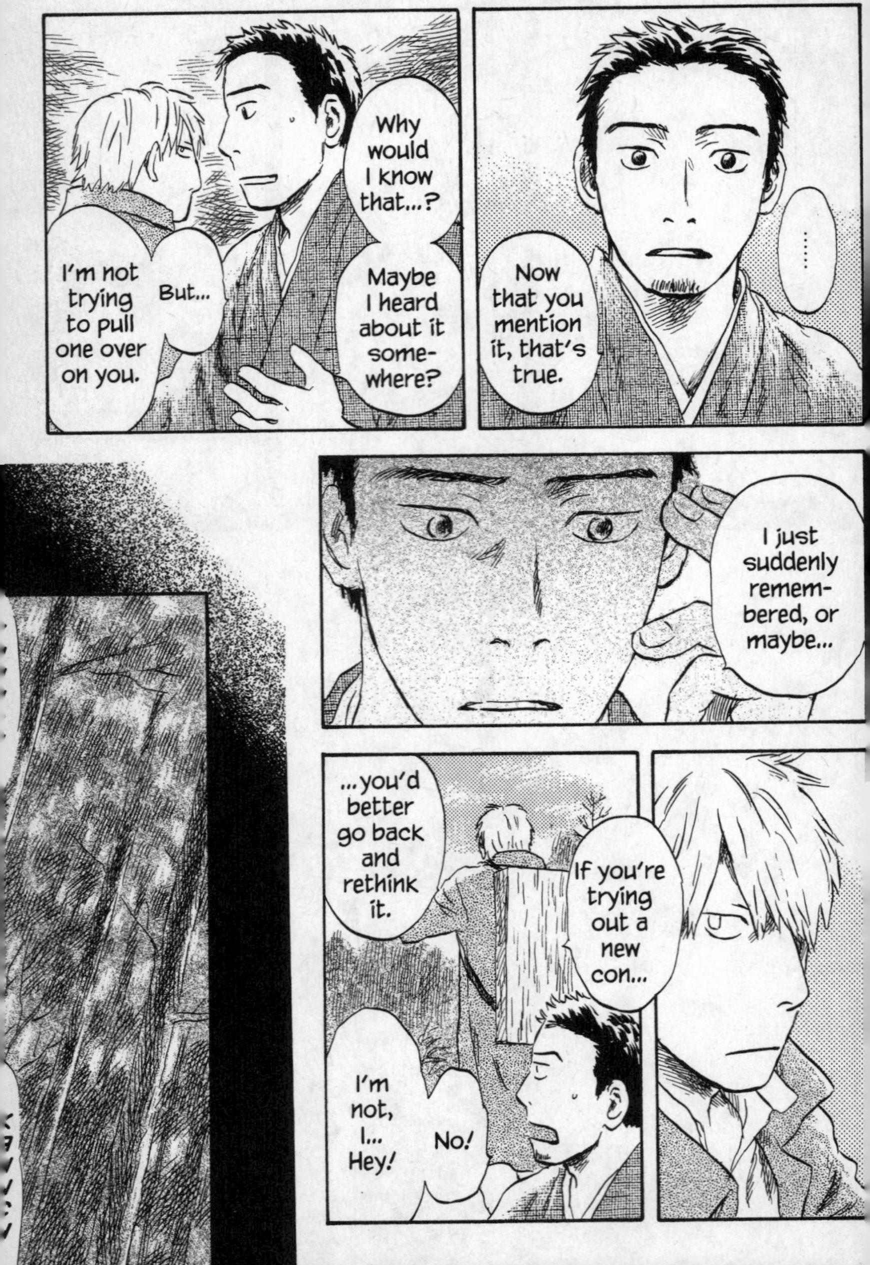
......
Now that you mention it, that's true.
Why would I know that...?
Maybe I heard about it some-where?
But...
I'm not trying to pull one over on you.
I just suddenly remem-bered, or maybe...
If you're trying out a new con...
...you'd better go back and rethink it.
No!
I'm not, I... Hey!

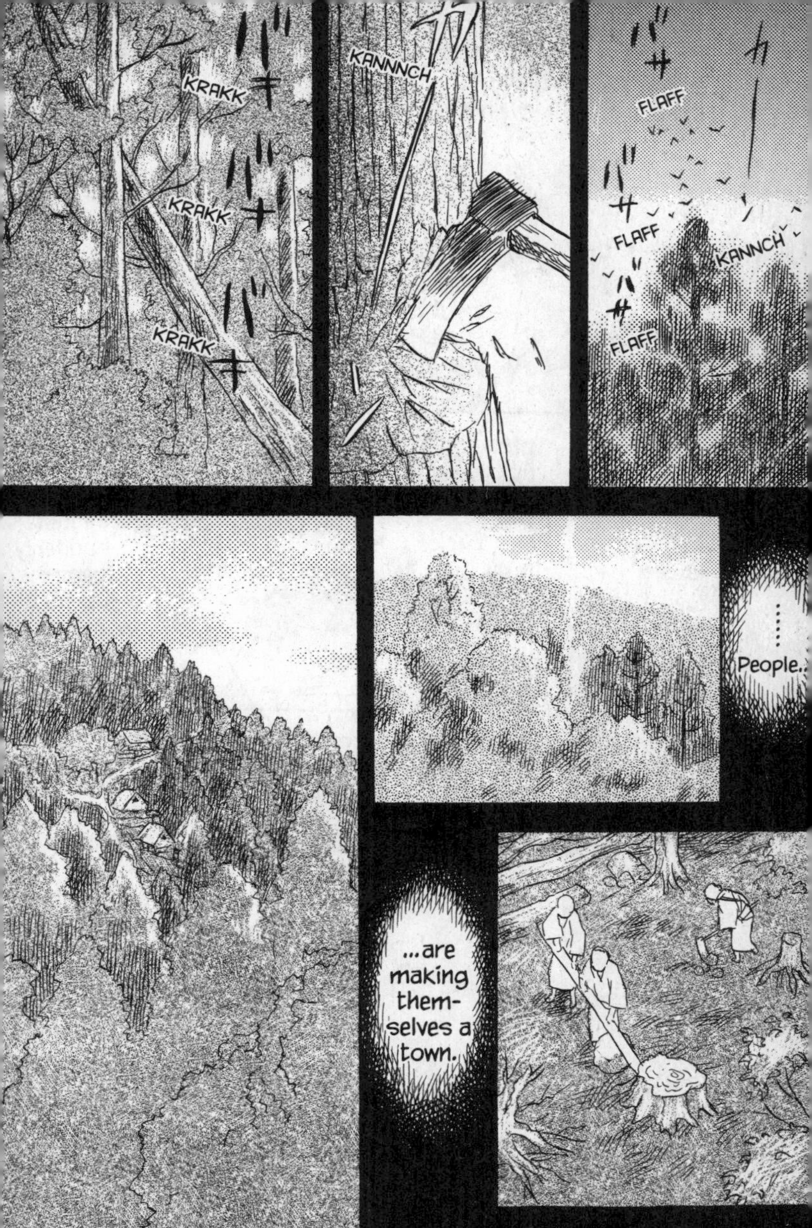
FLAFF
FLAFF
KANNCH
FLAFF
KANNNCH
KRAKK
KRAKK
KRAKK
......
People...
...are making them-selves a town.

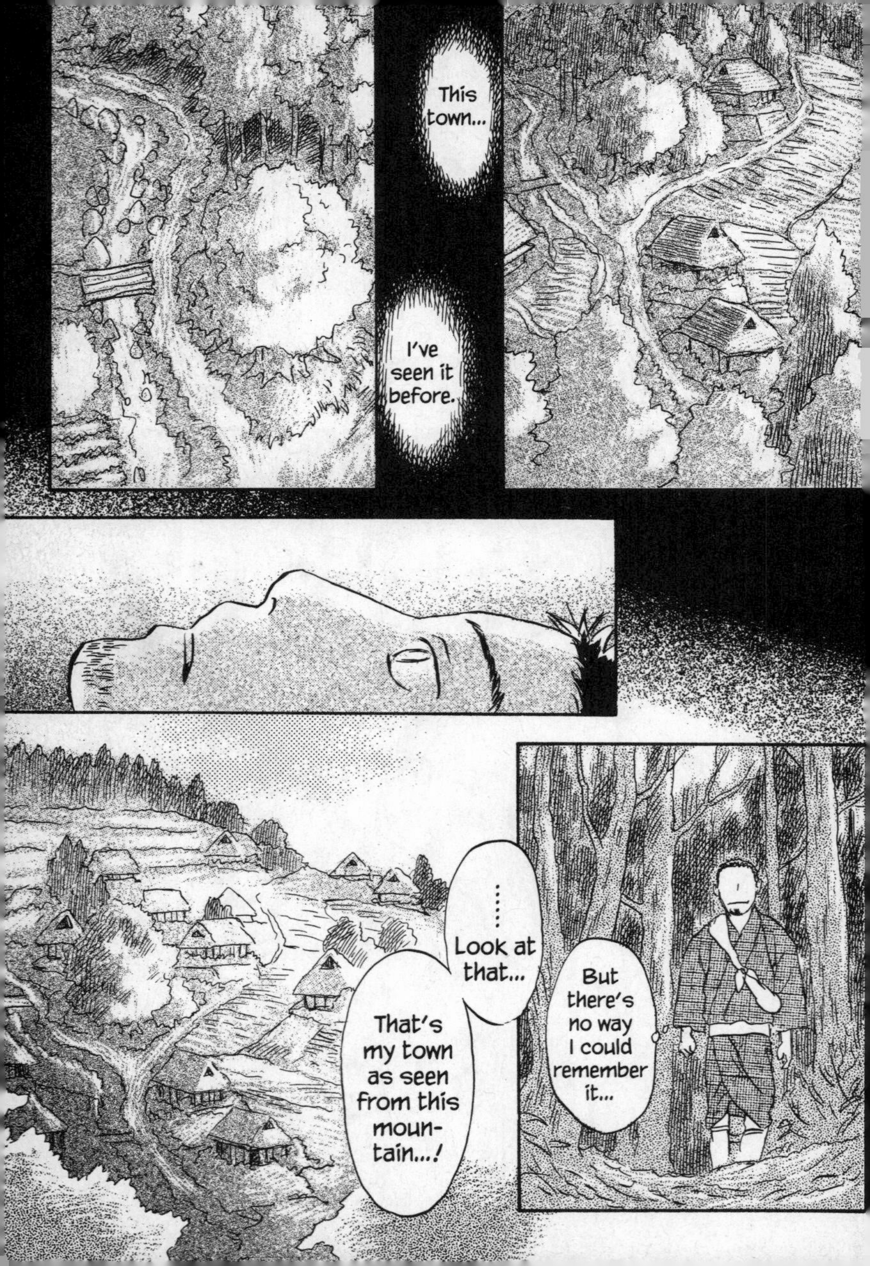
This town...
I've seen it before.
......
Look at that...
That's my town as seen from this moun-tain...!
But there's no way I could remember it...

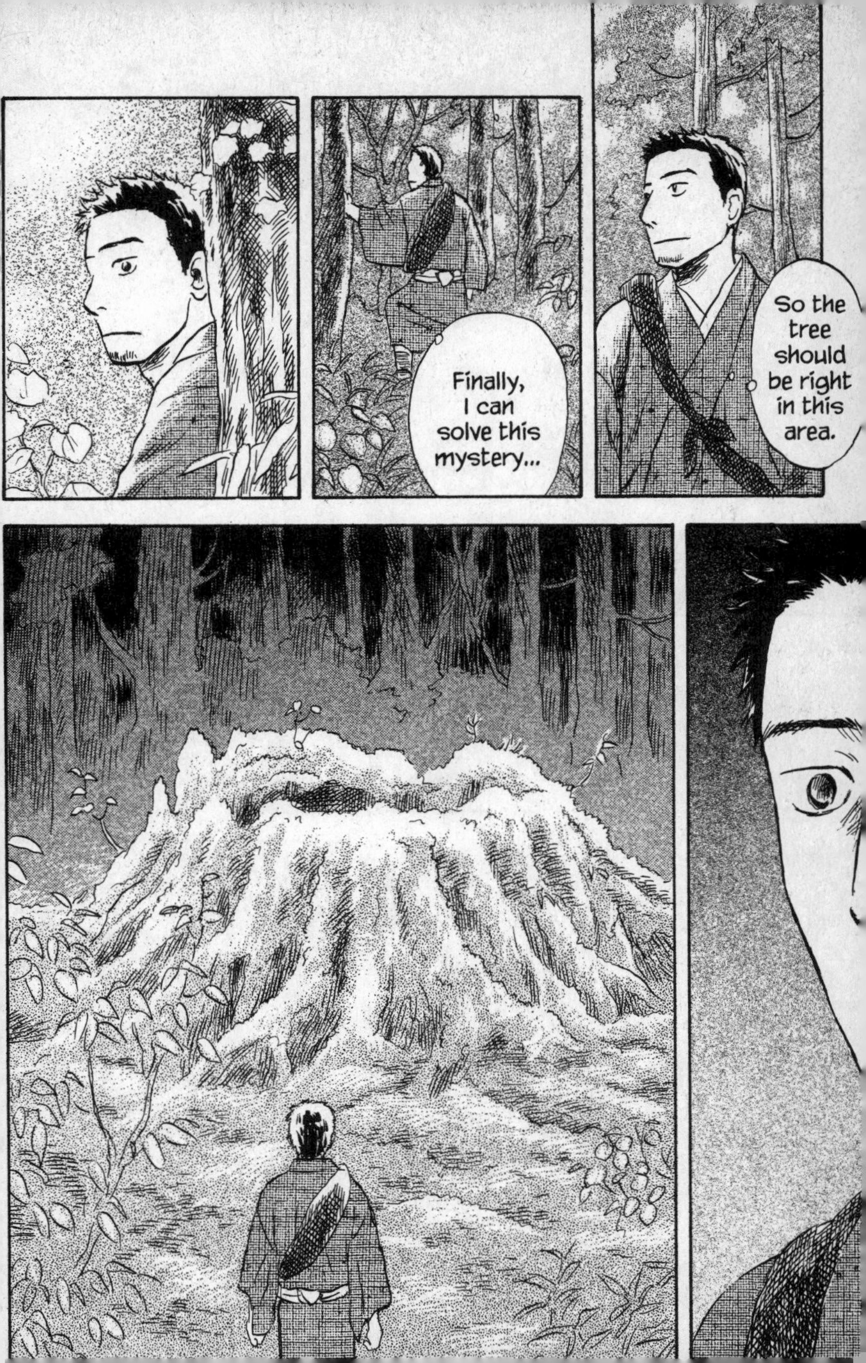
So the tree should be right in this area.
Finally, I can solve this mystery...

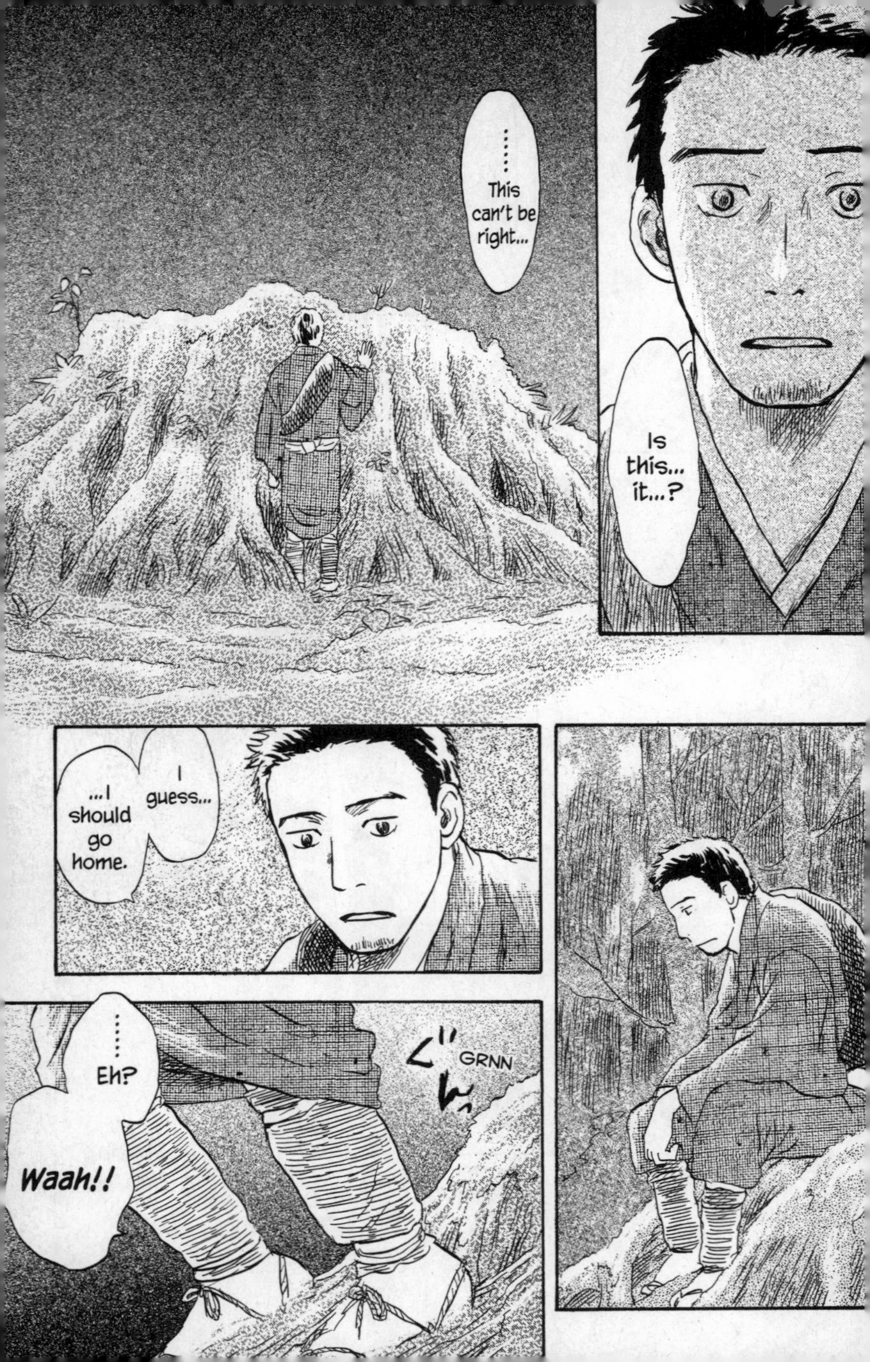
Is this... it...?
...... This can't be right...
I guess...
...I should go home.
GRNN
...... Eh?
Waah!!

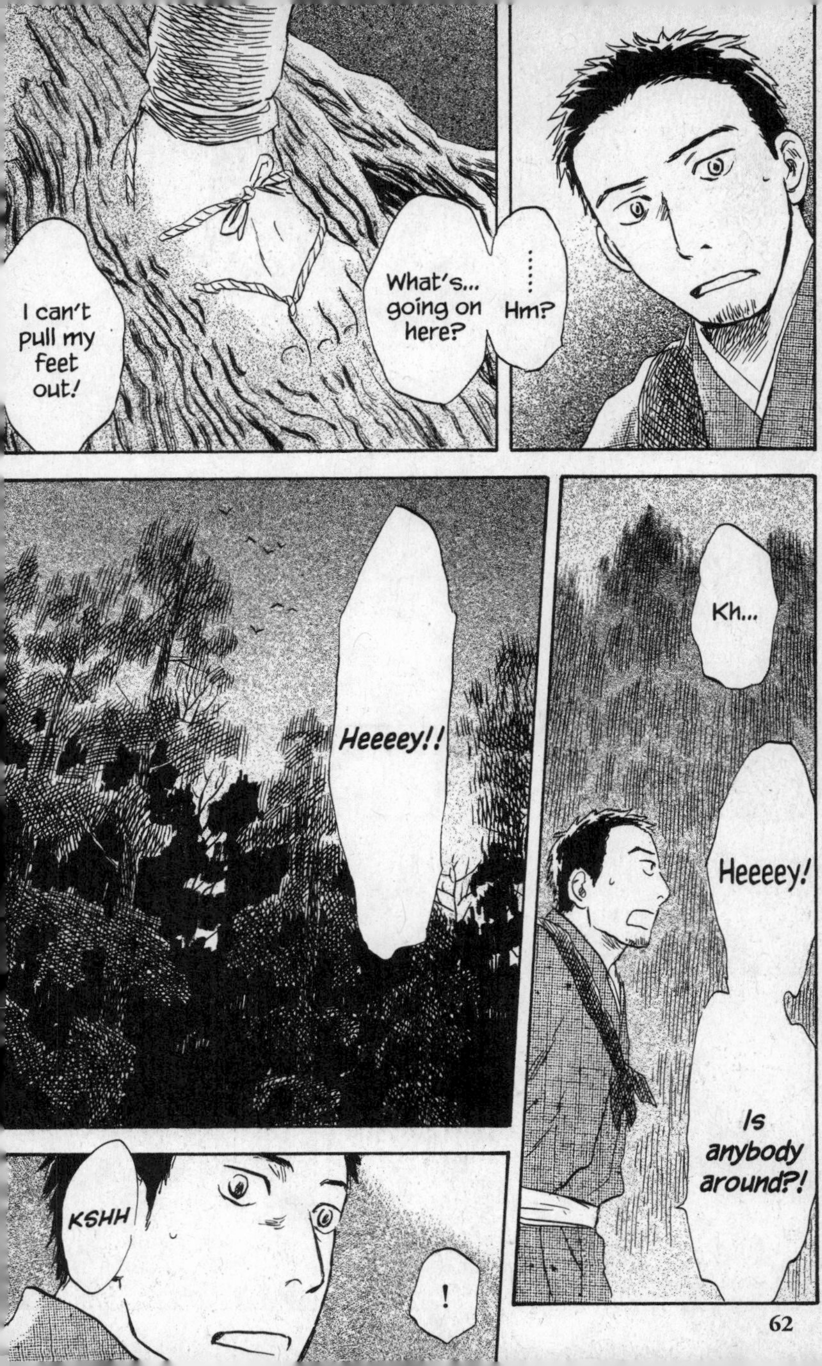
......
Hm?
What's... going on here?
I can't pull my feet out!
Kh...
Heeeey!
Is anybody around?!
Heeeey!!
KSHH
!

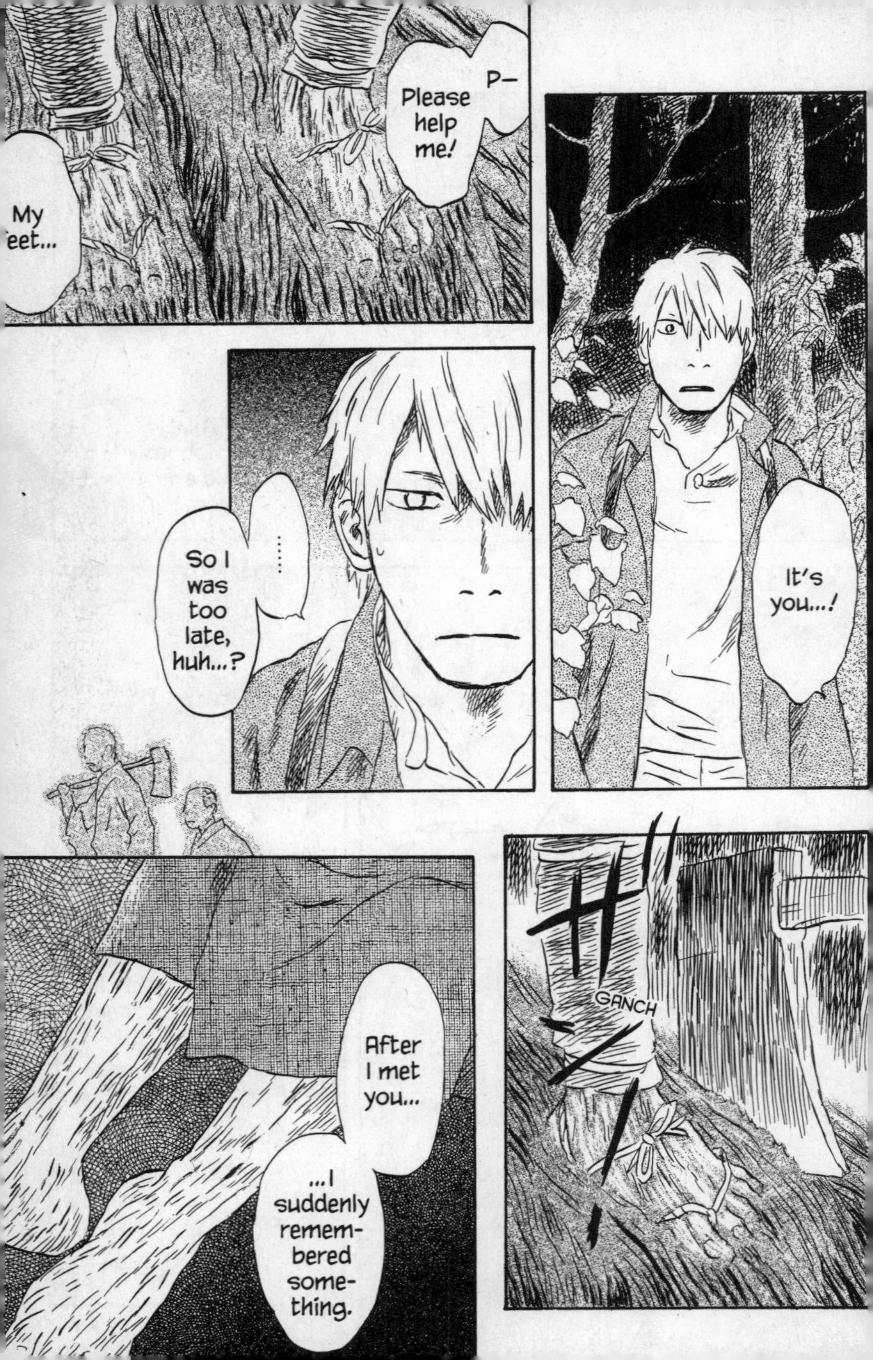
P—
Please help me!
My feet...
It's you...!
......
So I was too late, huh...?
GANCH
After I met you...
...I suddenly remem-bered some-thing.

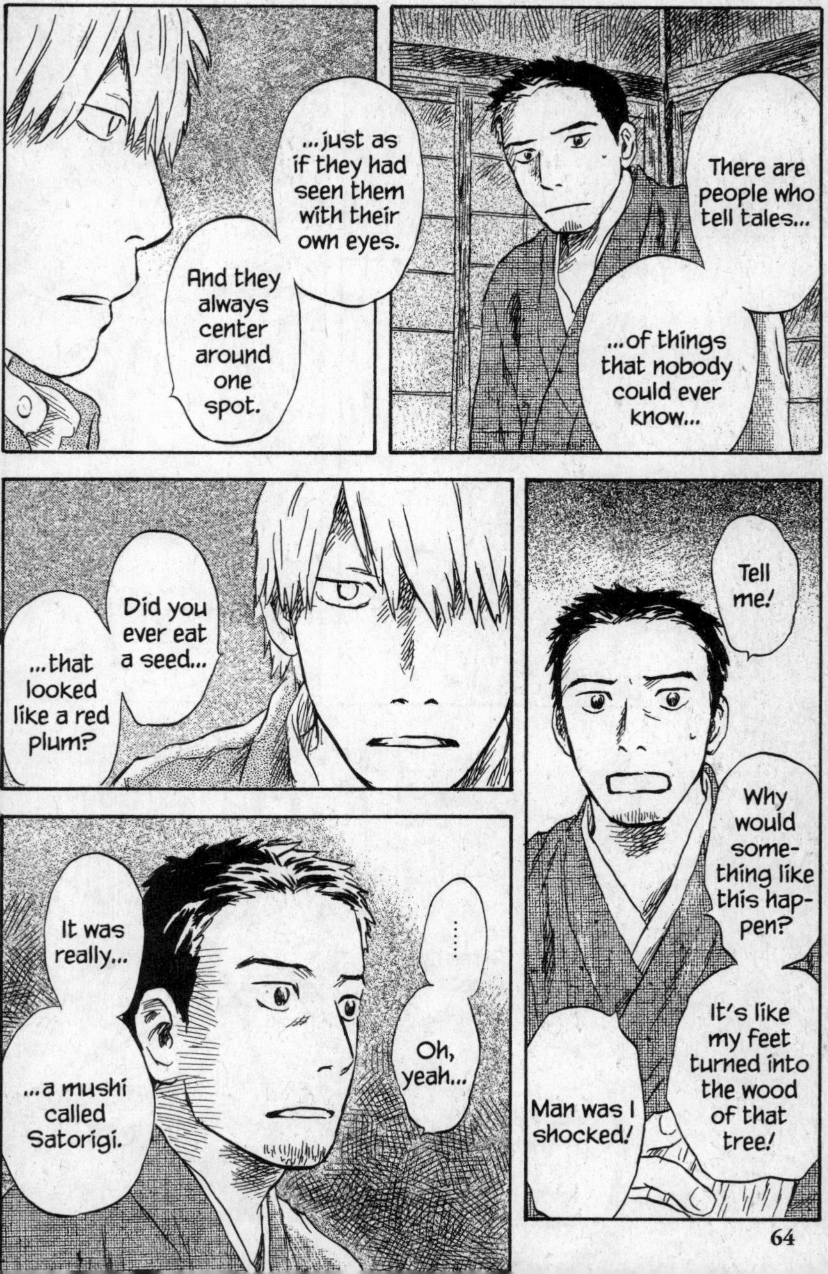
There are people who tell tales...
...of things that nobody could ever know...
...just as if they had seen them with their own eyes.
And they always center around one spot.
Tell me!
Why would some-thing like this hap-pen?
It's like my feet turned into the wood of that tree!
Man was I shocked!
Did you ever eat a seed...
...that looked like a red plum?
......
Oh, yeah...
It was really...
...a mushi called Satorigi.

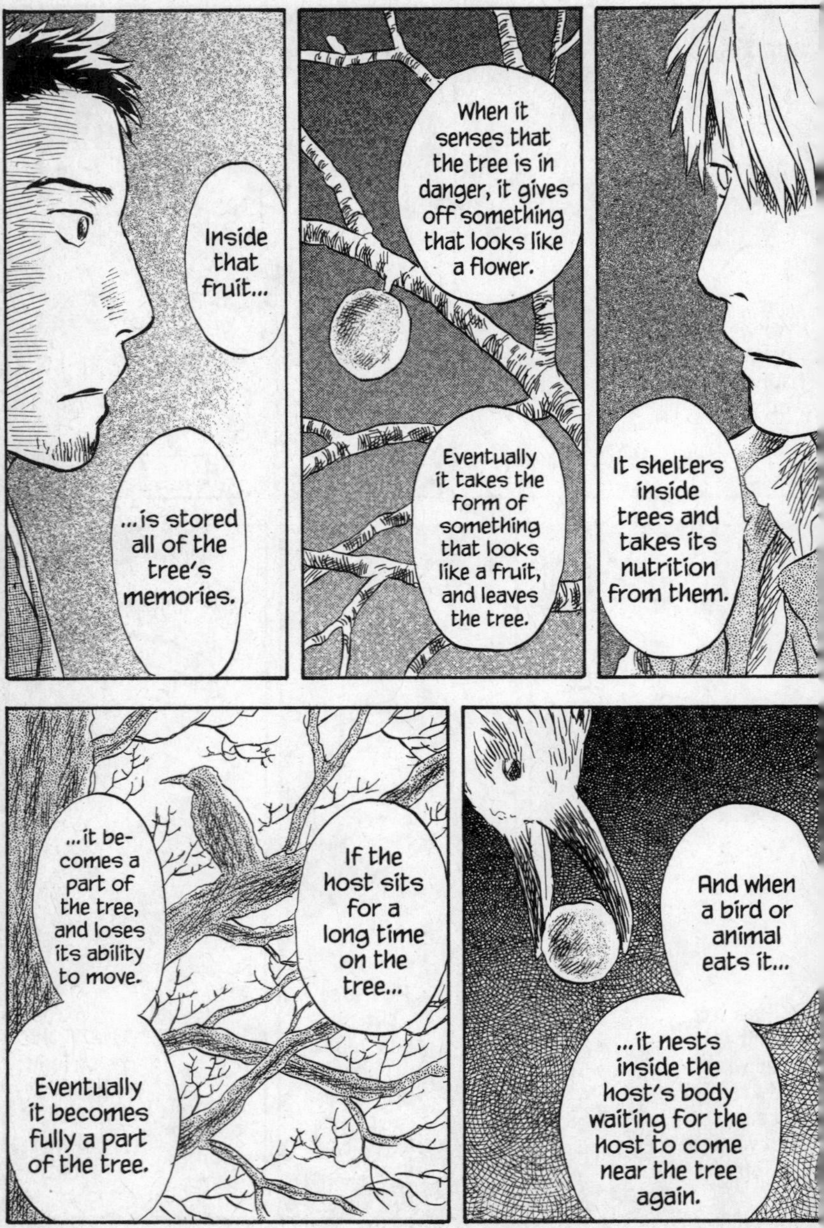
It shelters inside trees and takes its nutrition from them.
When it senses that the tree is in danger, it gives off something that looks like a flower.
Eventually it takes the form of something that looks like a fruit, and leaves the tree.
Inside that fruit...
...is stored all of the tree's memories.
And when a bird or animal eats it...
...it nests inside the host's body waiting for the host to come near the tree again.
If the host sits for a long time on the tree...
...it be-comes a part of the tree, and loses its ability to move.
Eventually it becomes fully a part of the tree.

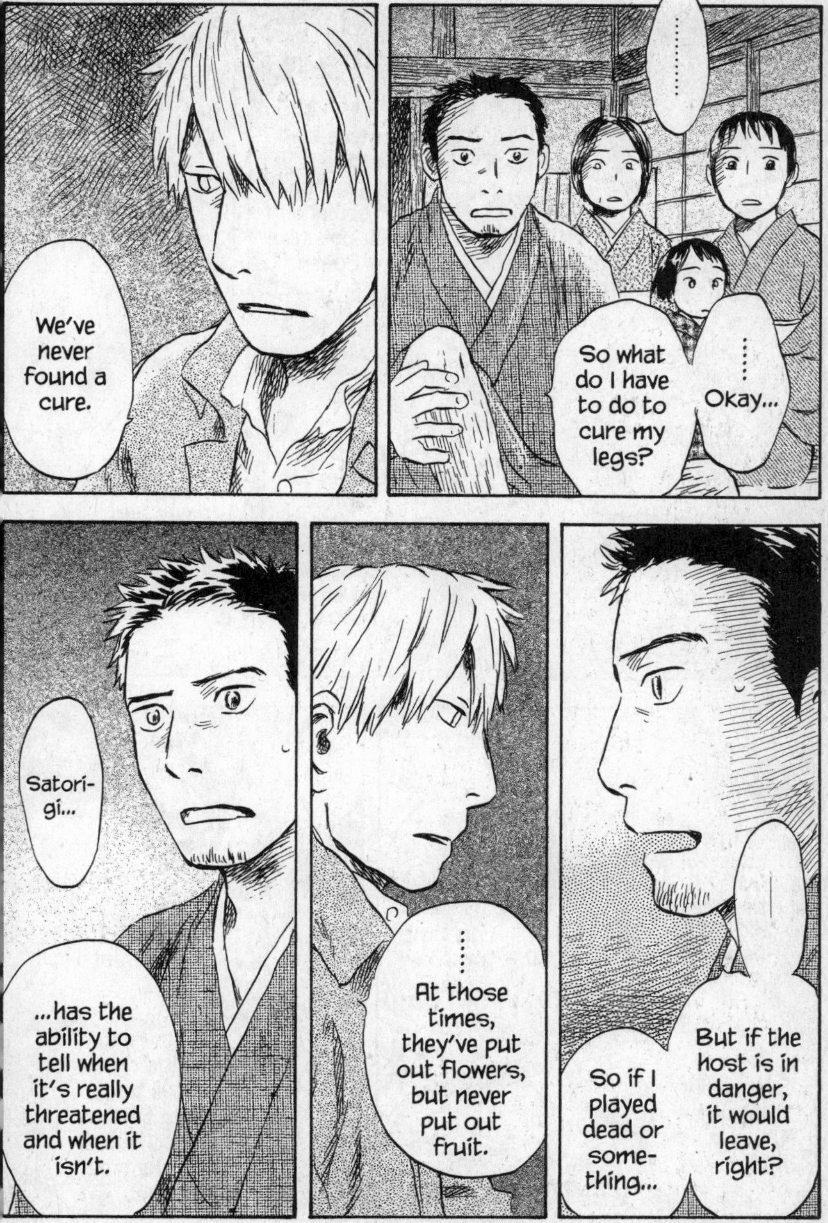
……
…… Okay...
So what do I have to do to cure my legs?
We've never found a cure.
But if the host is in danger, it would leave, right?
So if I played dead or something...
…… At those times, they've put out flowers, but never put out fruit.
Satori-gi...
...has the ability to tell when it's really threatened and when it isn't.

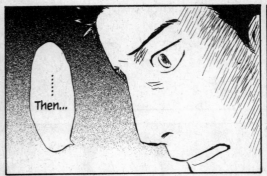

Then...

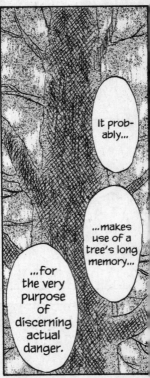

It prob-ably...

...makes use of a tree's long memory...

...for the very purpose of discerning actual danger.

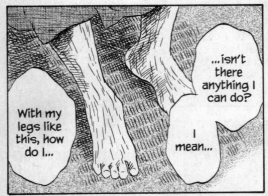

...isn't there anything I can do?

I mean...

With my legs like this, how do I...

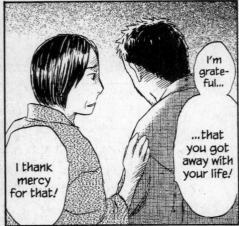

I'm grate-ful...

...that you got away with your life!

I thank mercy for that!

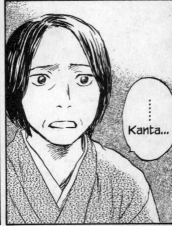

......

Kanta...

67

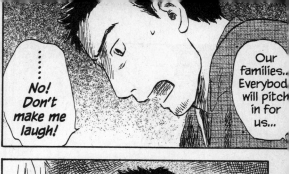

Our families.. Everybod
will pitch
in for
us...

......
No!
Don't
make me
laugh!

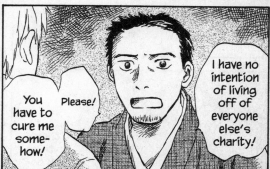

......

I have no
intention
of living
off of
everyone
else's
charity!

You
have to
cure me
some-
how!

Please!

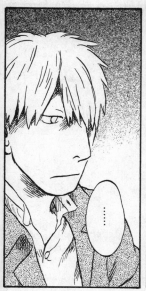

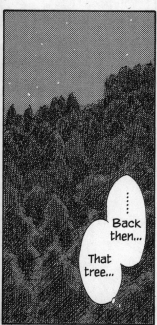

......
Back
then...
That
tree...

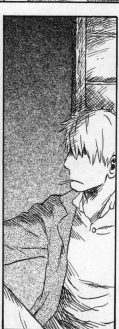

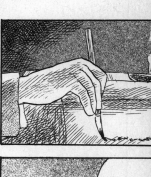

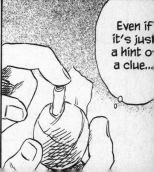

Even if
it's jus
a hint o
a clue...

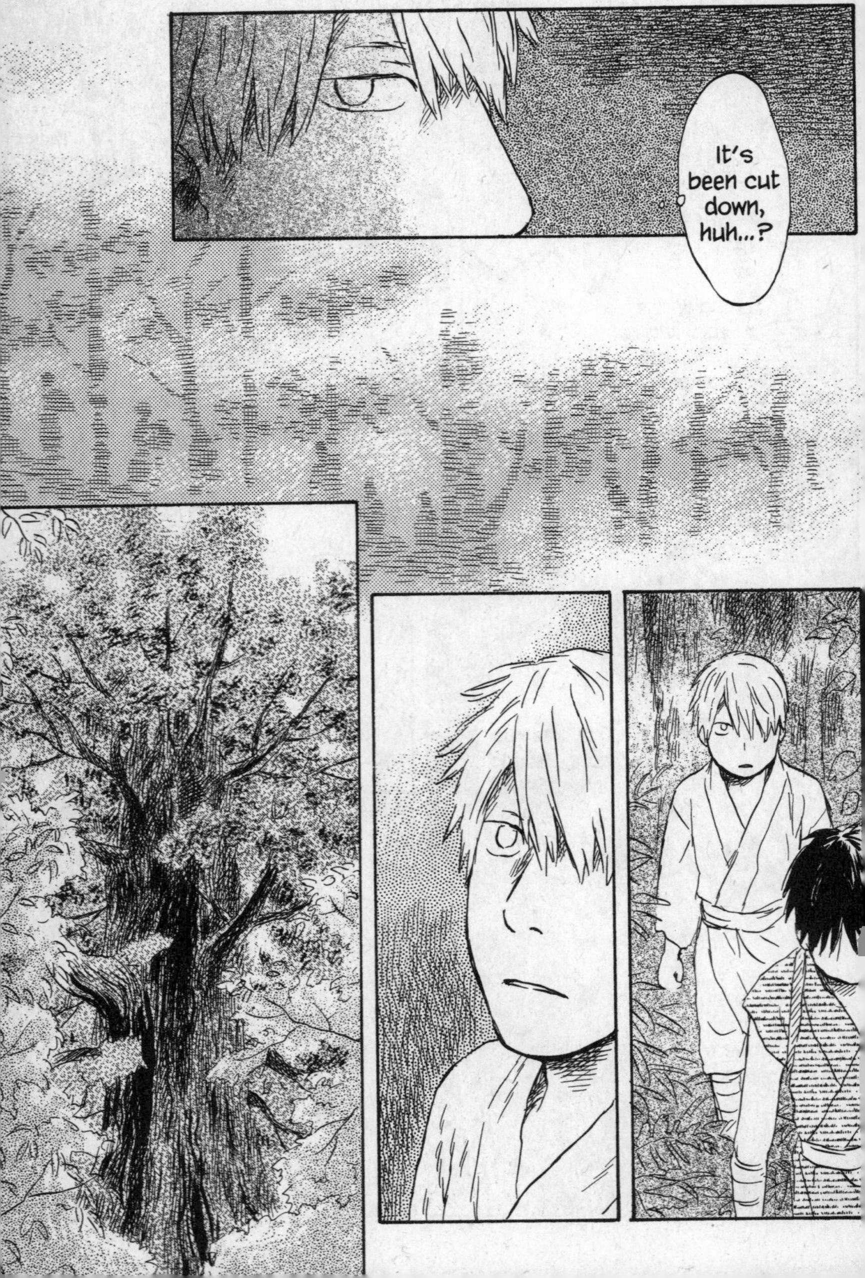
It's been cut down, huh...?

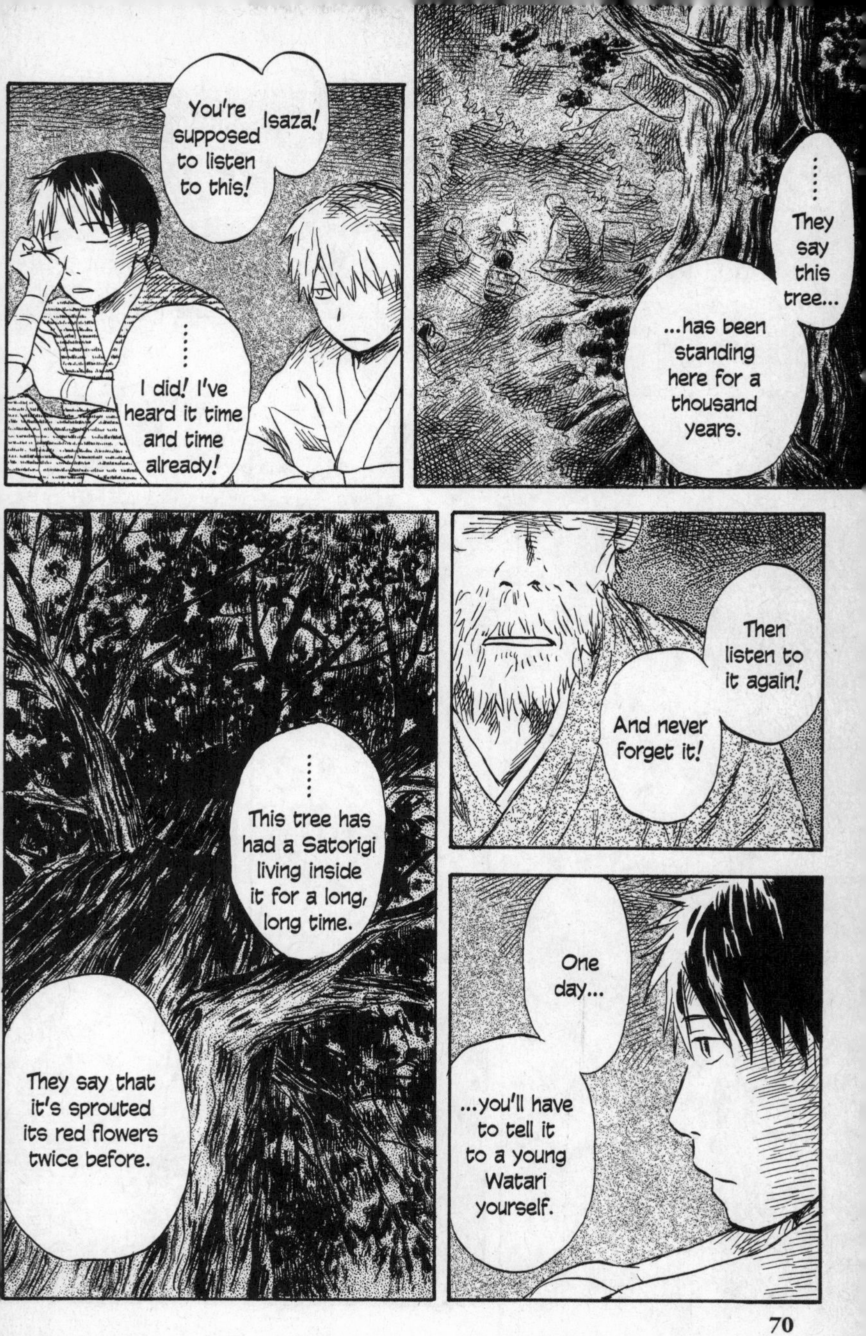
......
They say this tree...
...has been standing here for a thousand years.
Isaza!
You're supposed to listen to this!
......
I did! I've heard it time and time already!
Then listen to it again!
And never forget it!
One day...
...you'll have to tell it to a young Watari yourself.
......
This tree has had a Satorigi living inside it for a long, long time.
They say that it's sprouted its red flowers twice before.

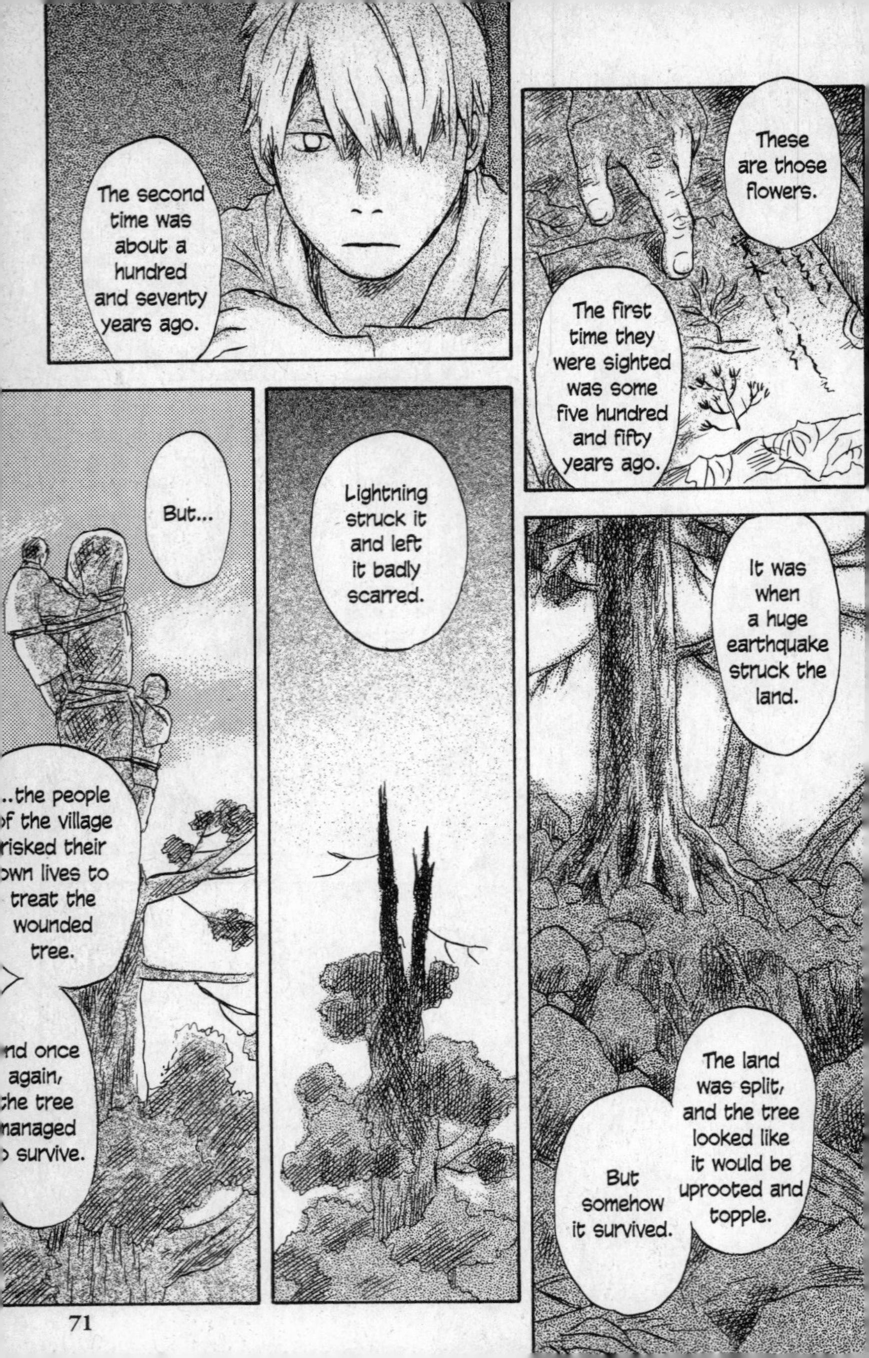
These are those flowers.
The first time they were sighted was some five hundred and fifty years ago.
It was when a huge earthquake struck the land.
The land was split, and the tree looked like it would be uprooted and topple.
But somehow it survived.
The second time was about a hundred and seventy years ago.
Lightning struck it and left it badly scarred.
But...
..the people of the village risked their own lives to treat the wounded tree.
nd once again, he tree managed o survive.

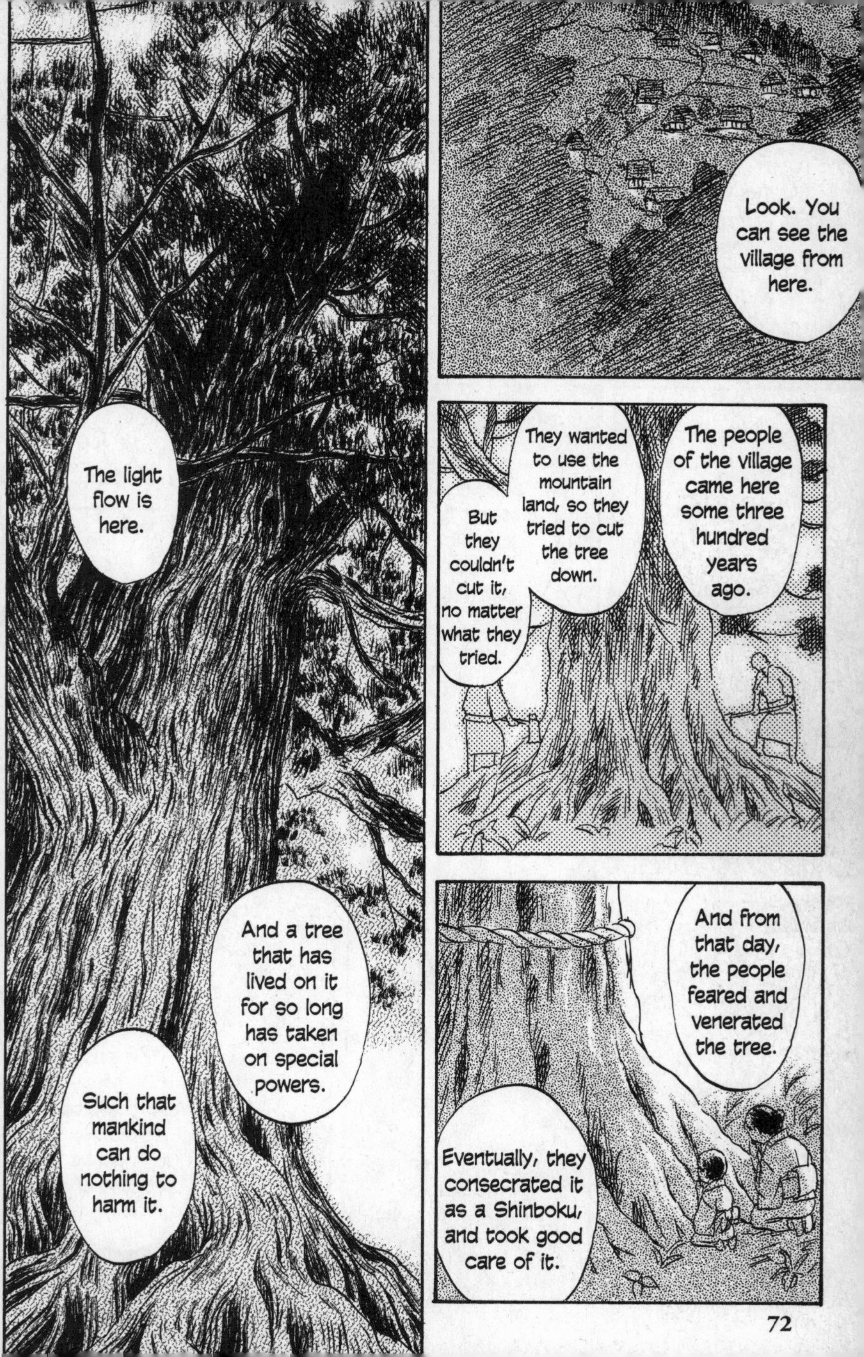
Look. You can see the village from here.
The people of the village came here some three hundred years ago.
They wanted to use the mountain land, so they tried to cut the tree down.
But they couldn't cut it, no matter what they tried.
And from that day, the people feared and venerated the tree.
Eventually, they consecrated it as a Shinboku, and took good care of it.
The light flow is here.
And a tree that has lived on it for so long has taken on special powers.
Such that mankind can do nothing to harm it.

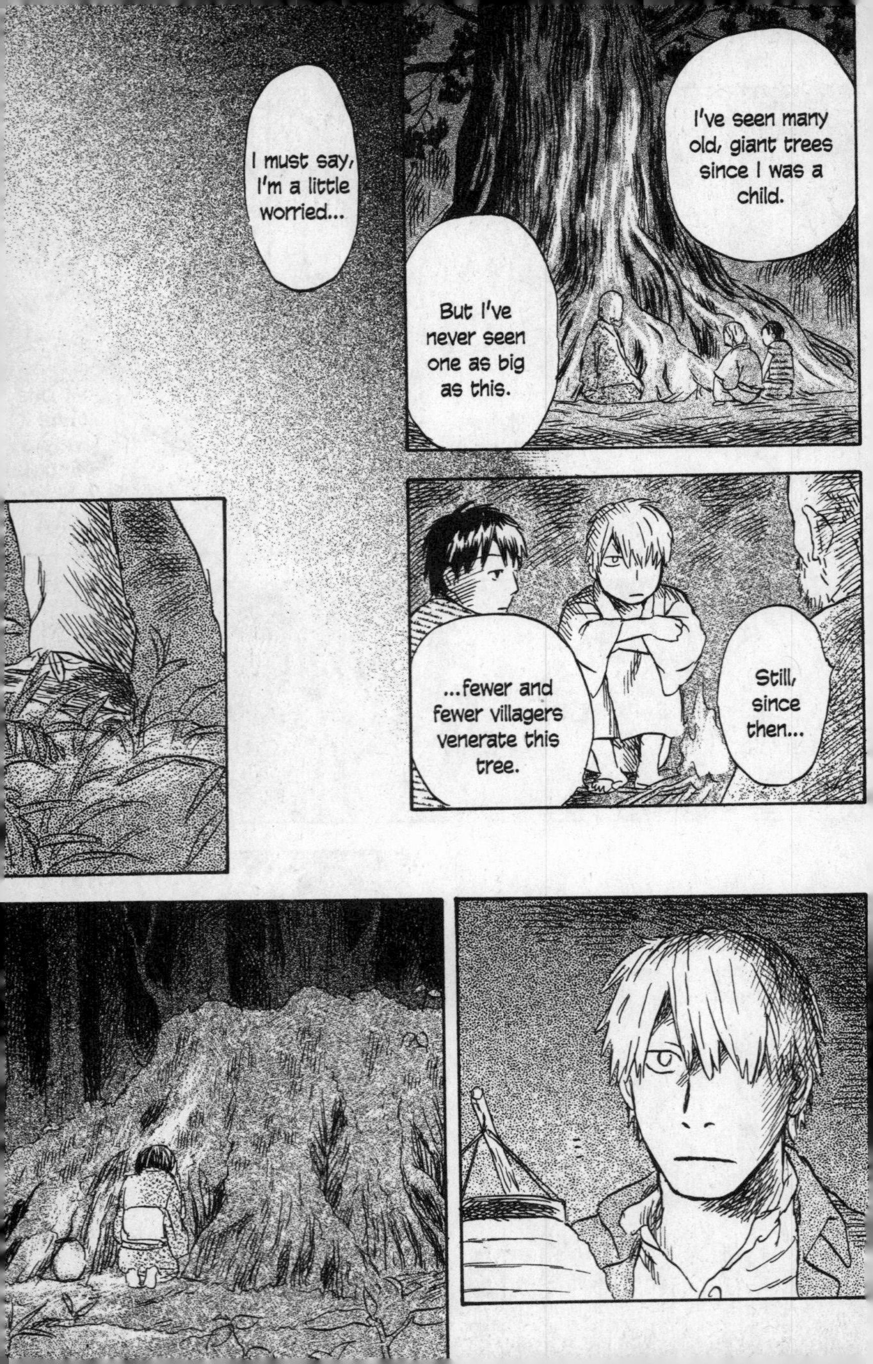
I've seen many old, giant trees since I was a child.
But I've never seen one as big as this.
I must say, I'm a little worried...
Still, since then...
...fewer and fewer villagers venerate this tree.

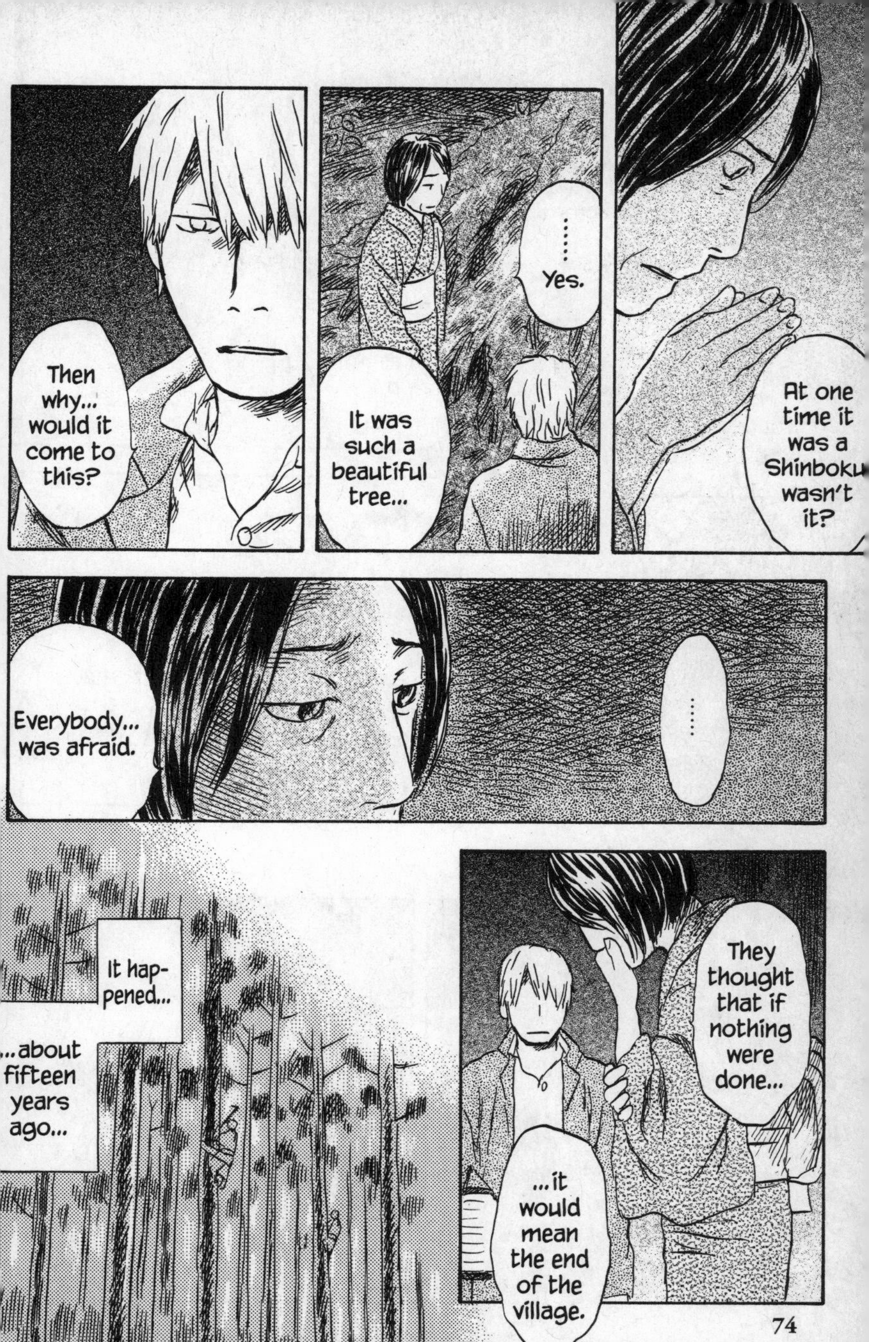
At one time it was a Shinboku wasn't it?
......Yes.
It was such a beautiful tree...
Then why... would it come to this?
......
Everybody... was afraid.
They thought that if nothing were done...
...it would mean the end of the village.
It hap-pened...
...about fifteen years ago...

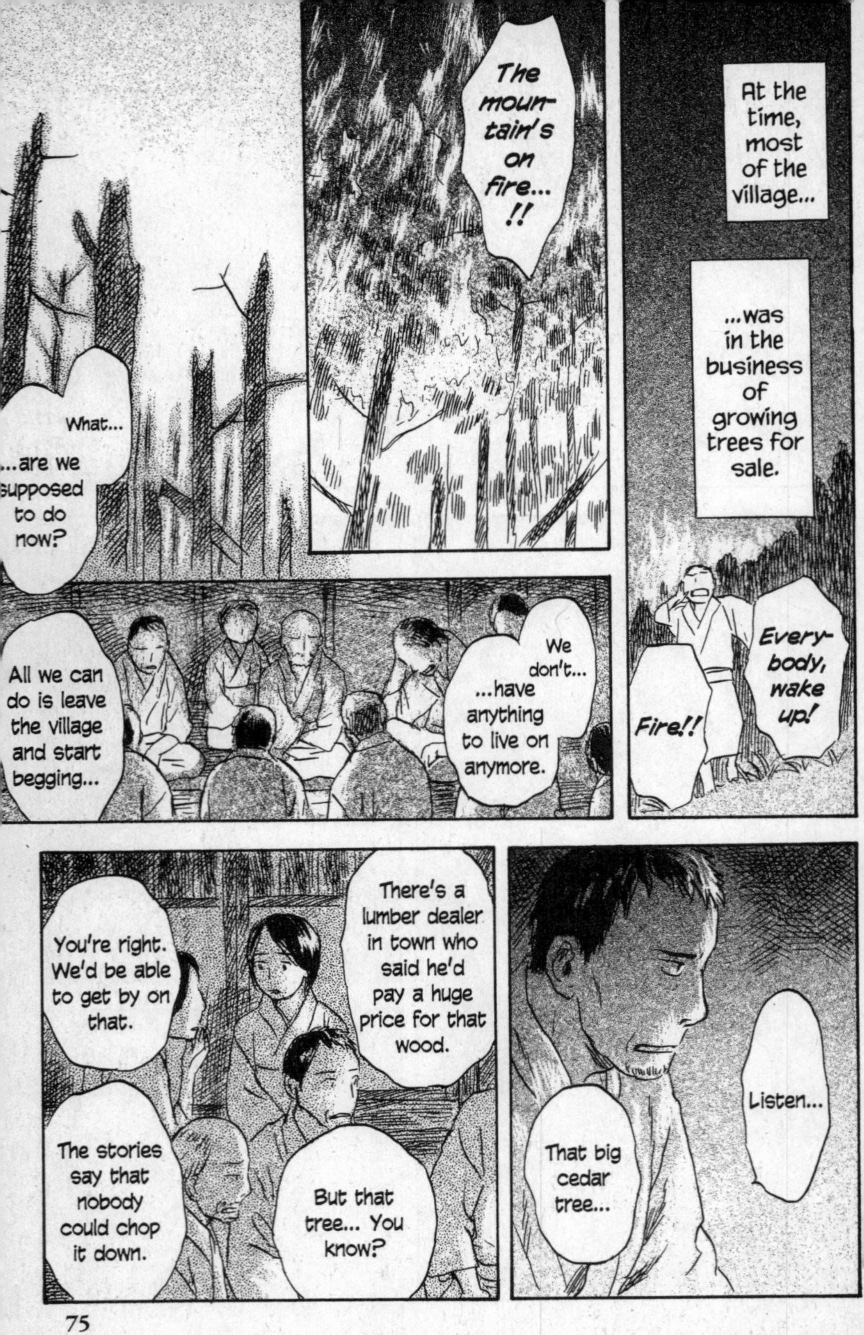
At the time, most of the village...
...was in the business of growing trees for sale.
Every-body, wake up!
Fire!!
The moun-tain's on fire... !!
What...
...are we supposed to do now?
We don't...
...have anything to live on anymore.
All we can do is leave the village and start begging...
Listen...
That big cedar tree...
There's a lumber dealer in town who said he'd pay a huge price for that wood.
You're right. We'd be able to get by on that.
But that tree... You know?
The stories say that nobody could chop it down.

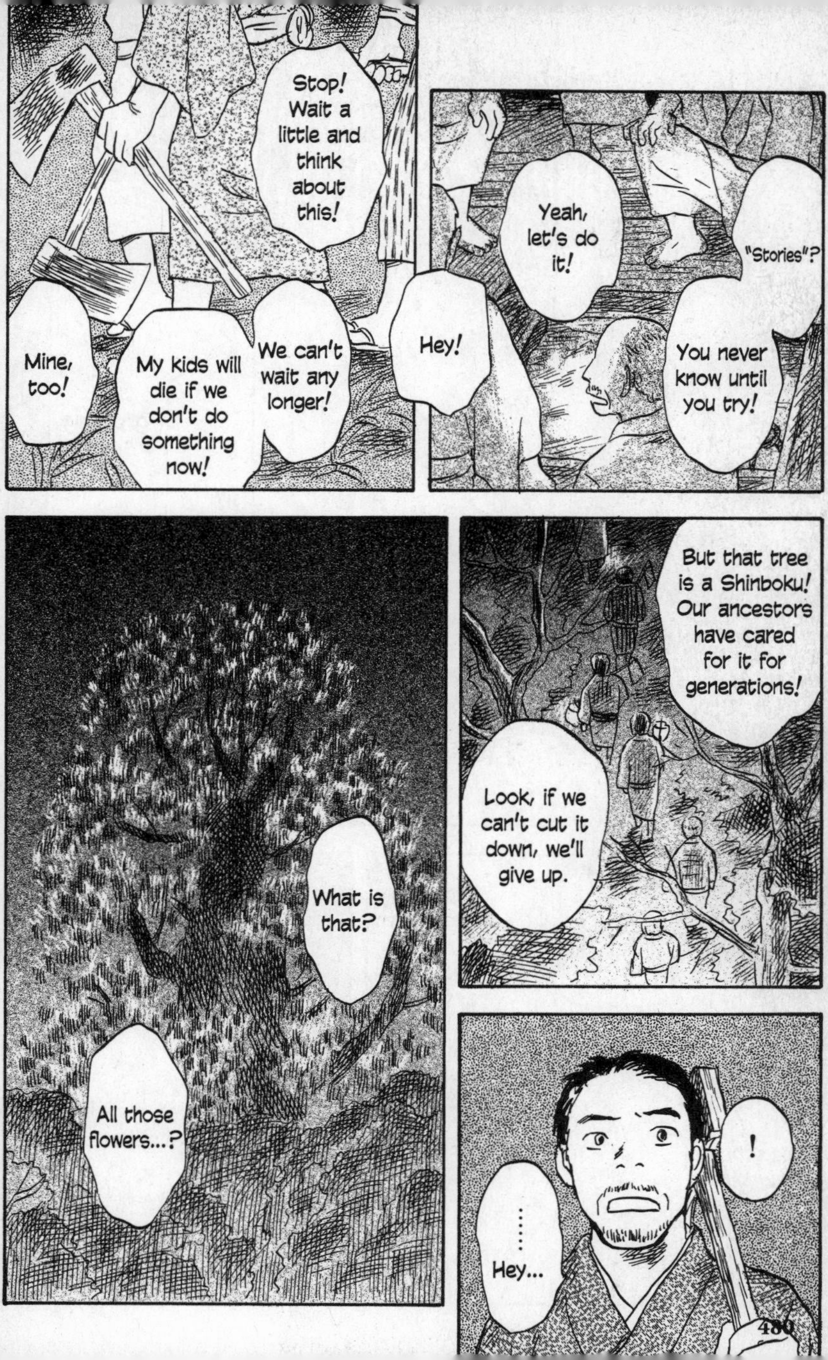
"Stories"?
Yeah, let's do it!
You never know until you try!
Hey!
Stop! Wait a little and think about this!
We can't wait any longer!
My kids will die if we don't do something now!
Mine, too!
But that tree is a Shinboku! Our ancestors have cared for it for generations!
Look, if we can't cut it down, we'll give up.
!
......Hey...
What is that?
All those flowers...?

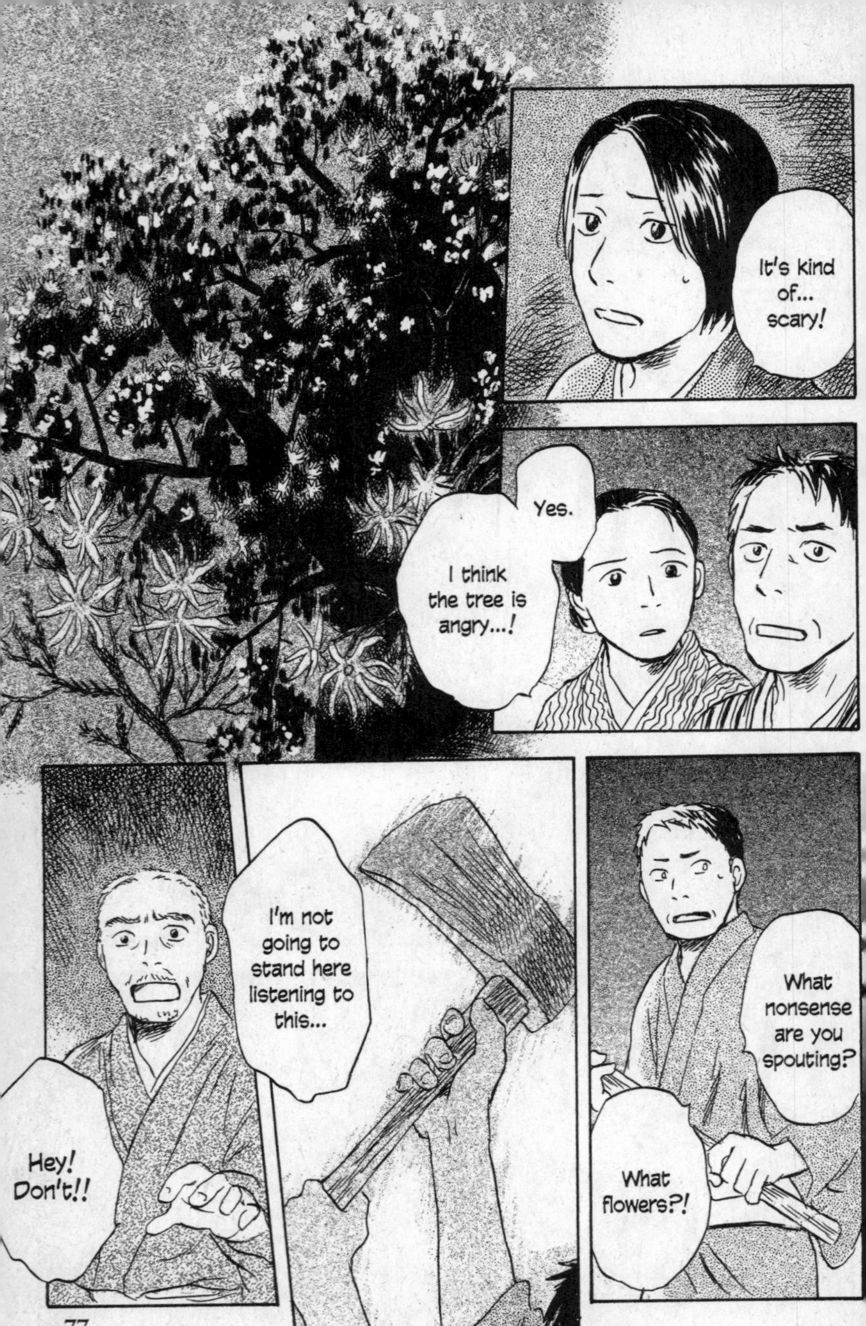
It's kind of... scary!
Yes.
I think the tree is angry...!
What nonsense are you spouting?
What flowers?!
I'm not going to stand here listening to this...
Hey! Don't!!

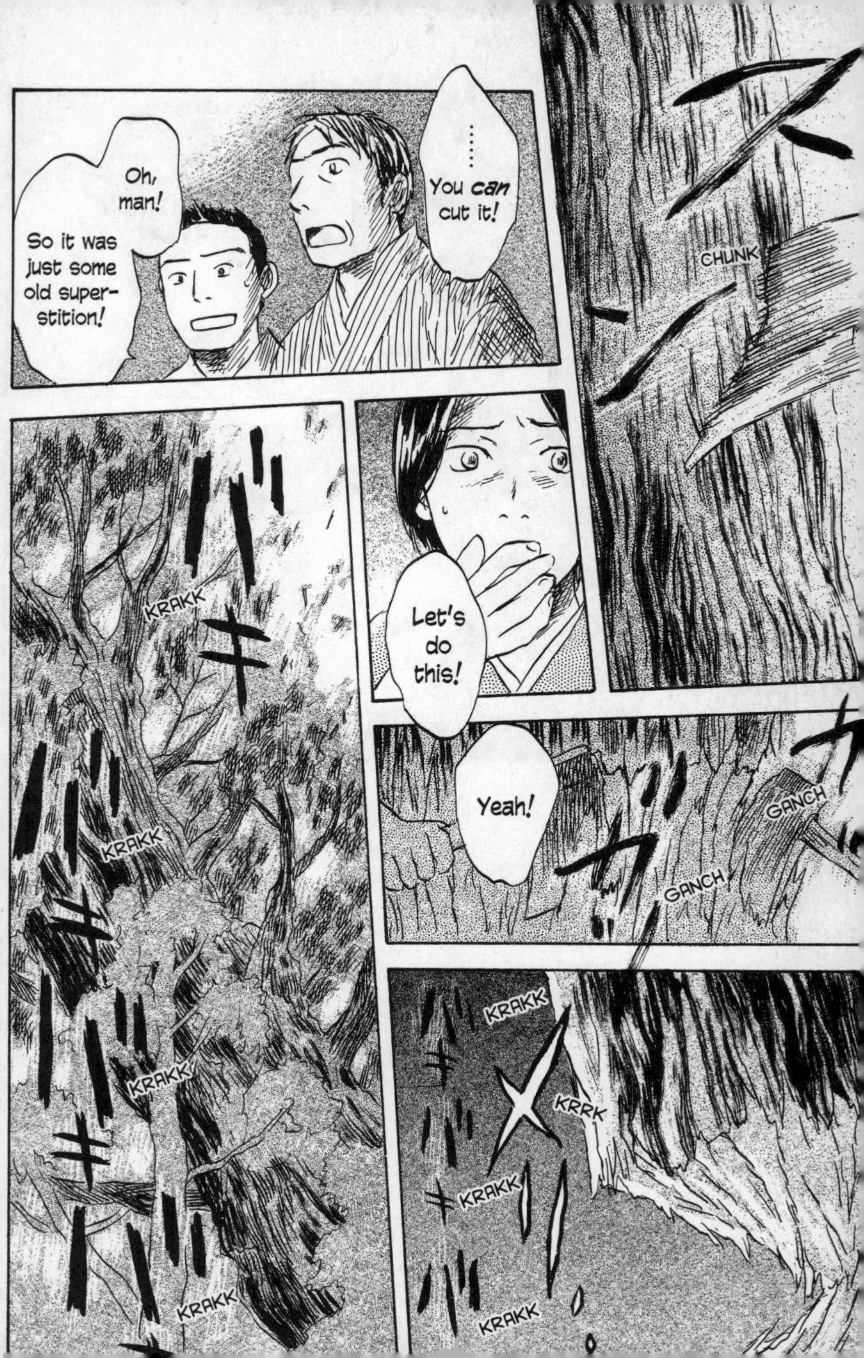
CHUNK
……
You *can* cut it!
Oh, man!
So it was just some old superstition!
Let's do this!
Yeah!
GANCH
GANCH
KRAKK
KRRK
KRAKK
KRAKK
KRAKK
KRAKK
KRAKK
KRAKK

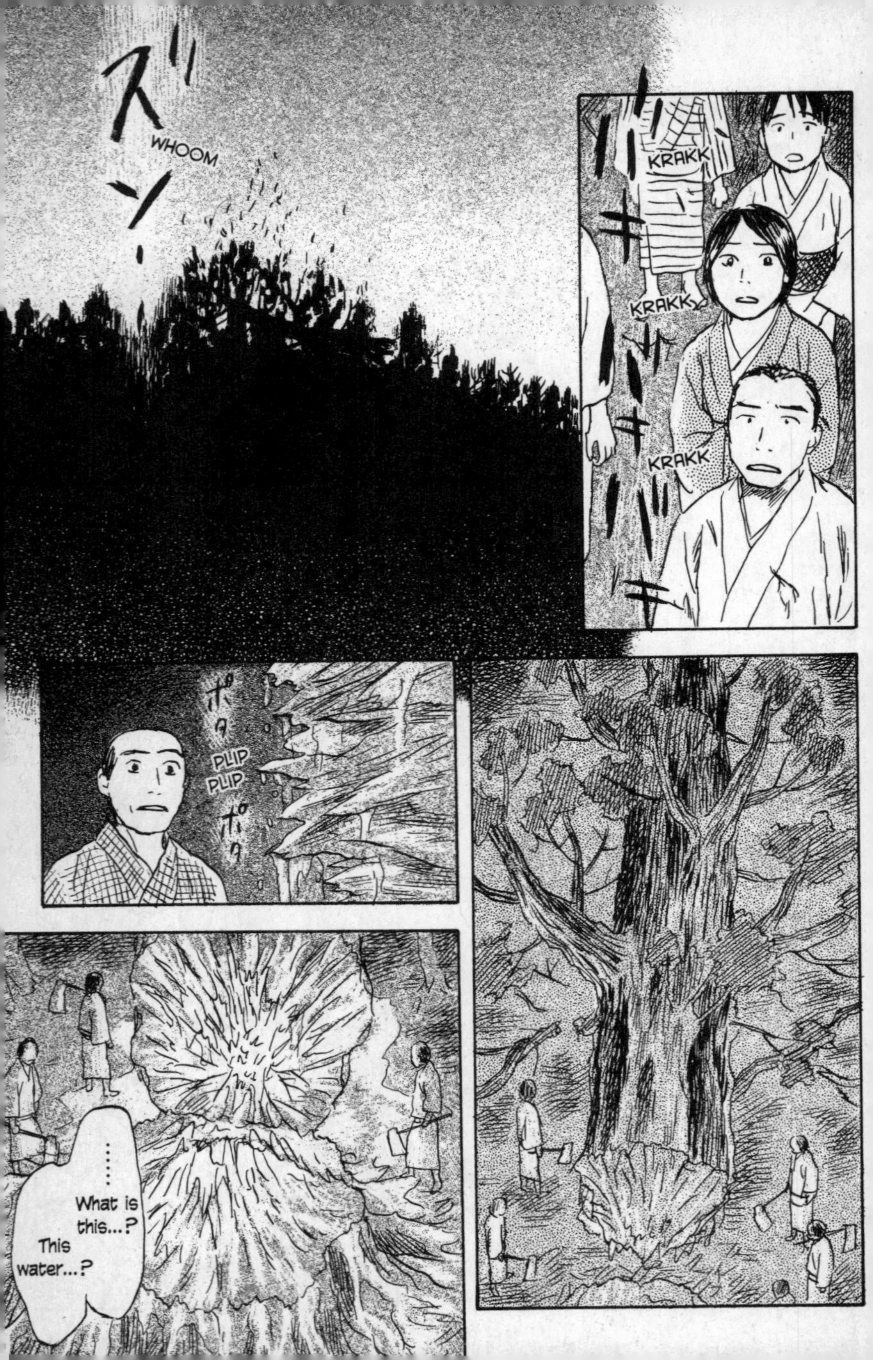
KRAKK
KRAKK
KRAKK
WHOOM
PLIP PLIP
...... What is this...? This water...?

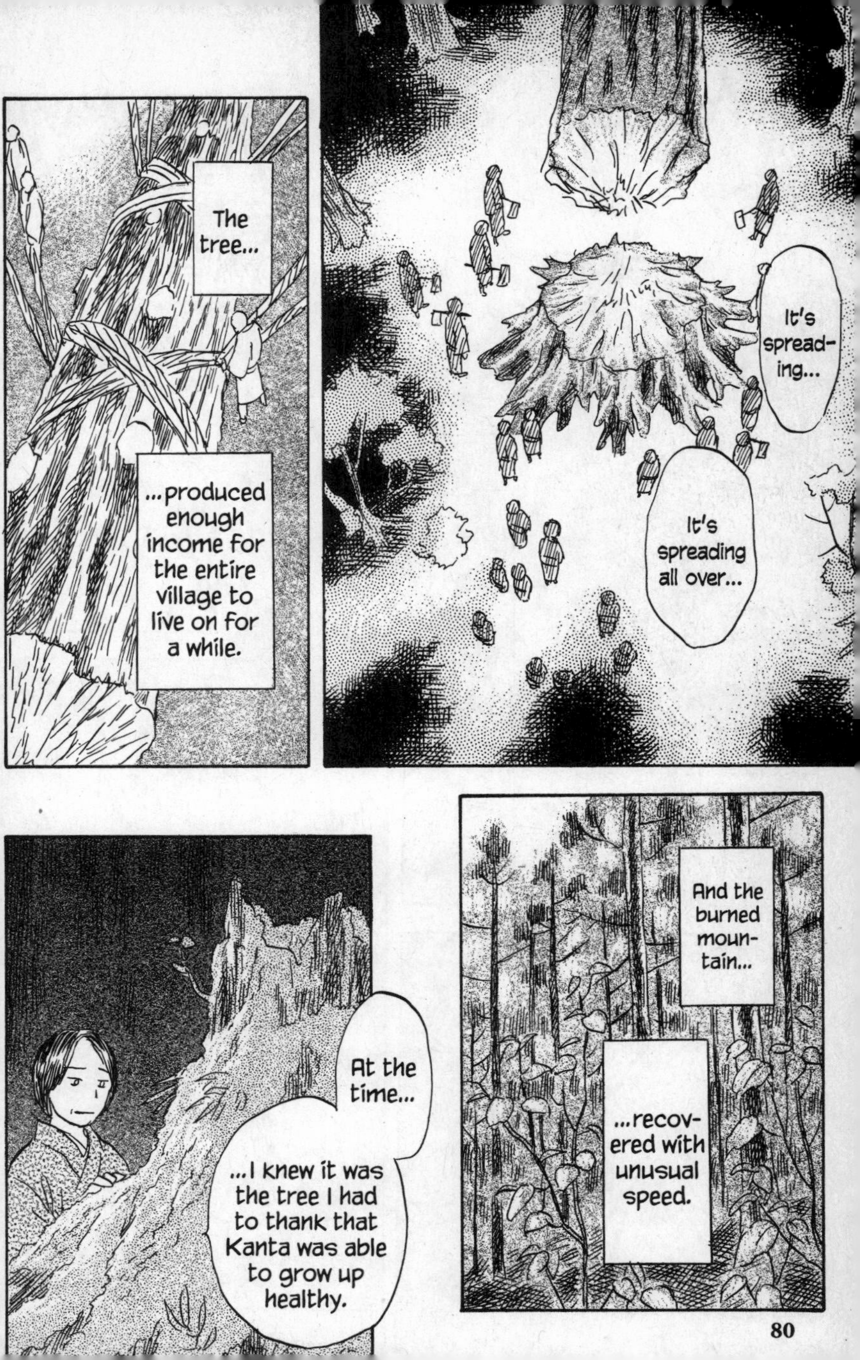
It's spreading...
It's spreading all over...
The tree...
...produced enough income for the entire village to live on for a while.
And the burned mountain...
...recovered with unusual speed.
At the time...
...I knew it was the tree I had to thank that Kanta was able to grow up healthy.

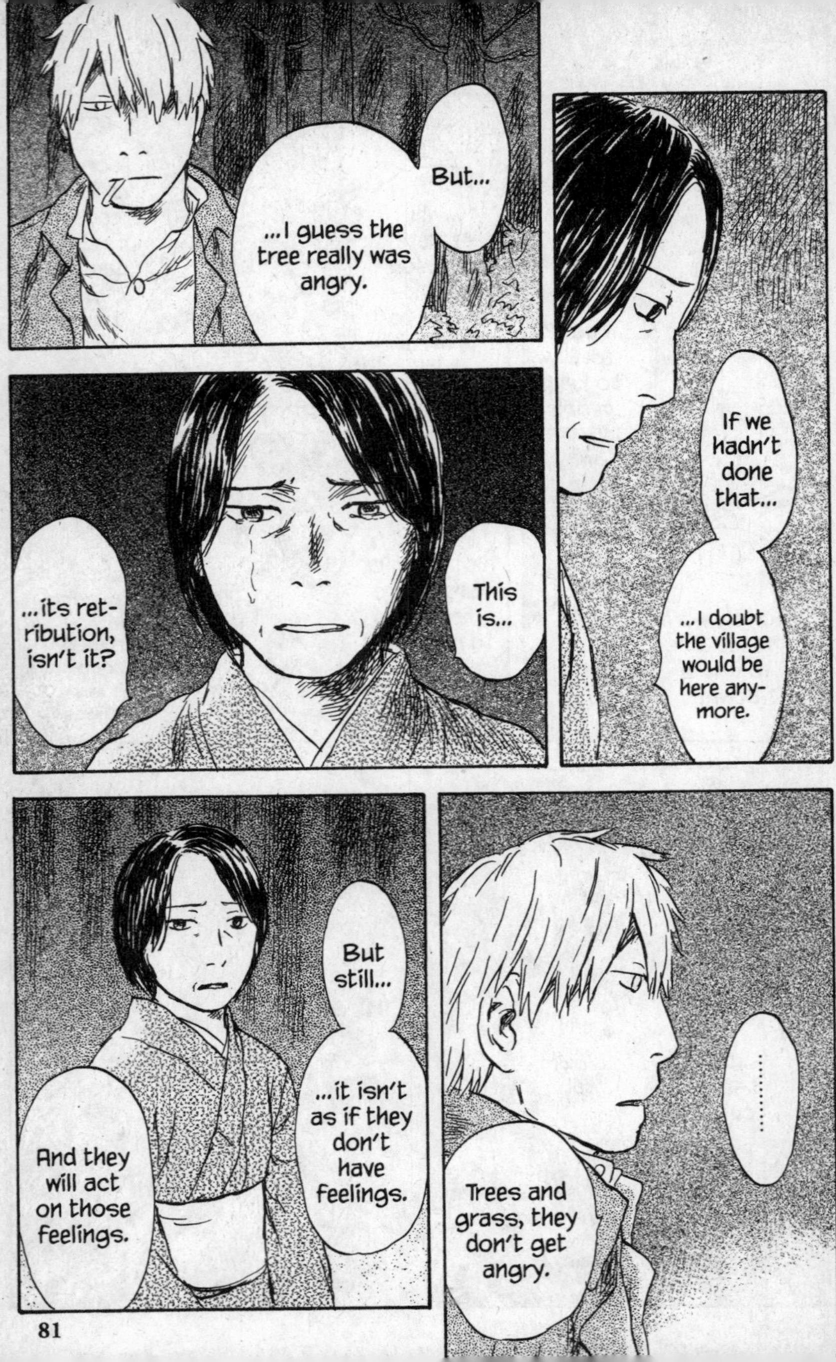
If we hadn't done that...
...I doubt the village would be here any-more.
But...
...I guess the tree really was angry.
This is...
...its ret-ribution, isn't it?
......
Trees and grass, they don't get angry.
But still...
...it isn't as if they don't have feelings.
And they will act on those feelings.

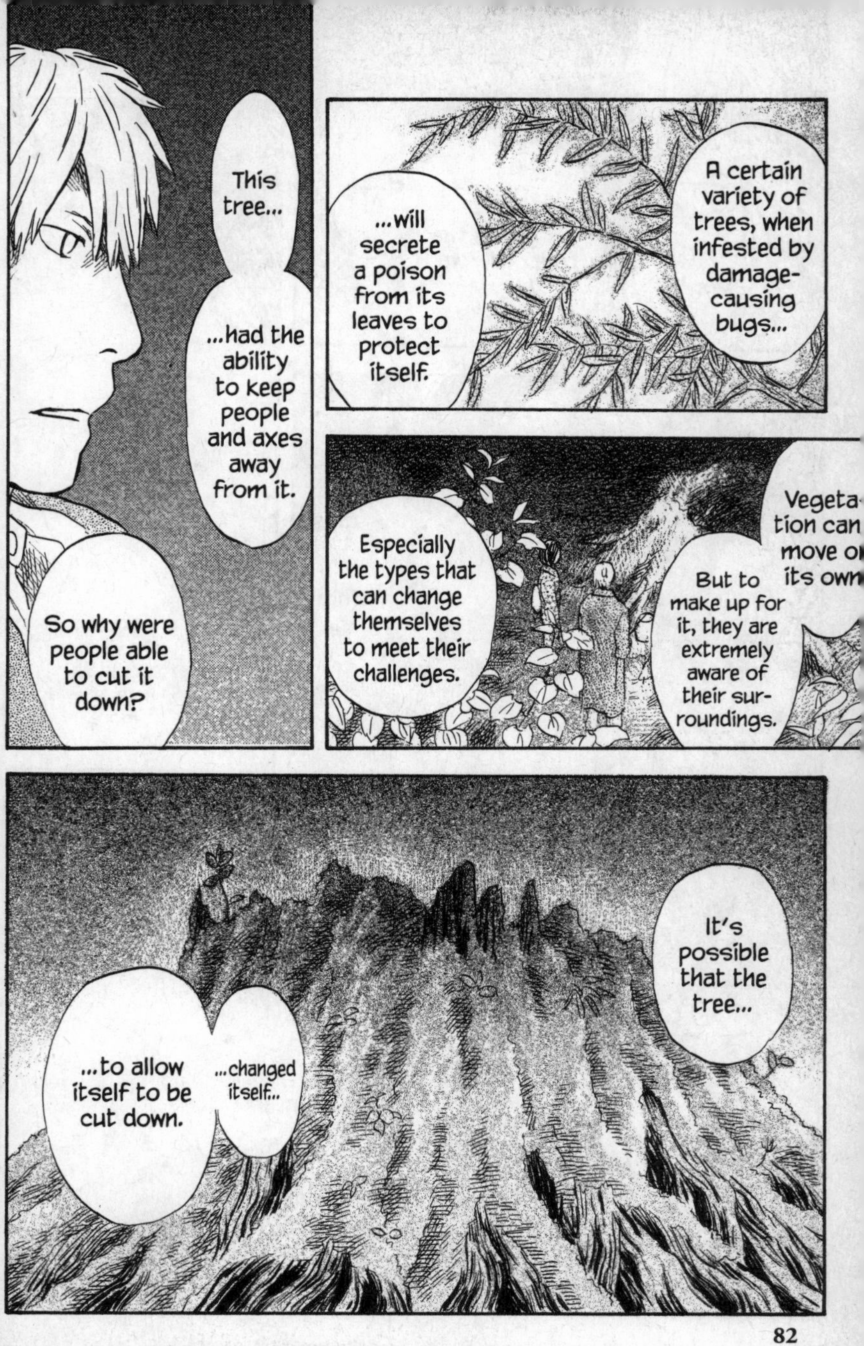
A certain variety of trees, when infested by damage-causing bugs...
...will secrete a poison from its leaves to protect itself.
Vegeta-tion can move o its own
But to make up for it, they are extremely aware of their surroundings.
Especially the types that can change themselves to meet their challenges.
This tree...
...had the ability to keep people and axes away from it.
So why were people able to cut it down?
It's possible that the tree...
...changed itself...
...to allow itself to be cut down.

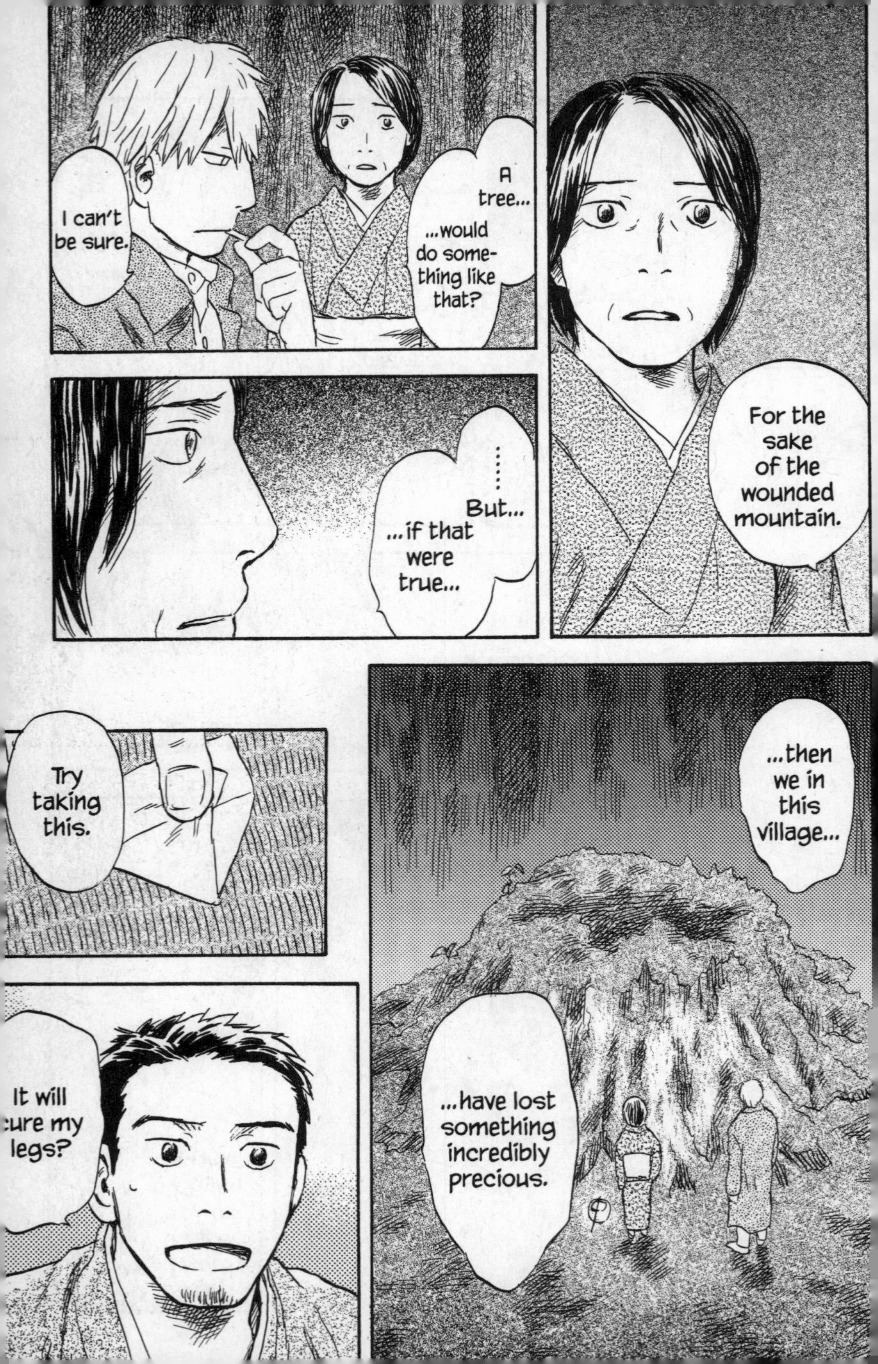
For the sake of the wounded mountain.
A tree... ...would do something like that?
I can't be sure.
......
But... ...if that were true...
...then we in this village...
...have lost something incredibly precious.
Try taking this.
It will cure my legs?

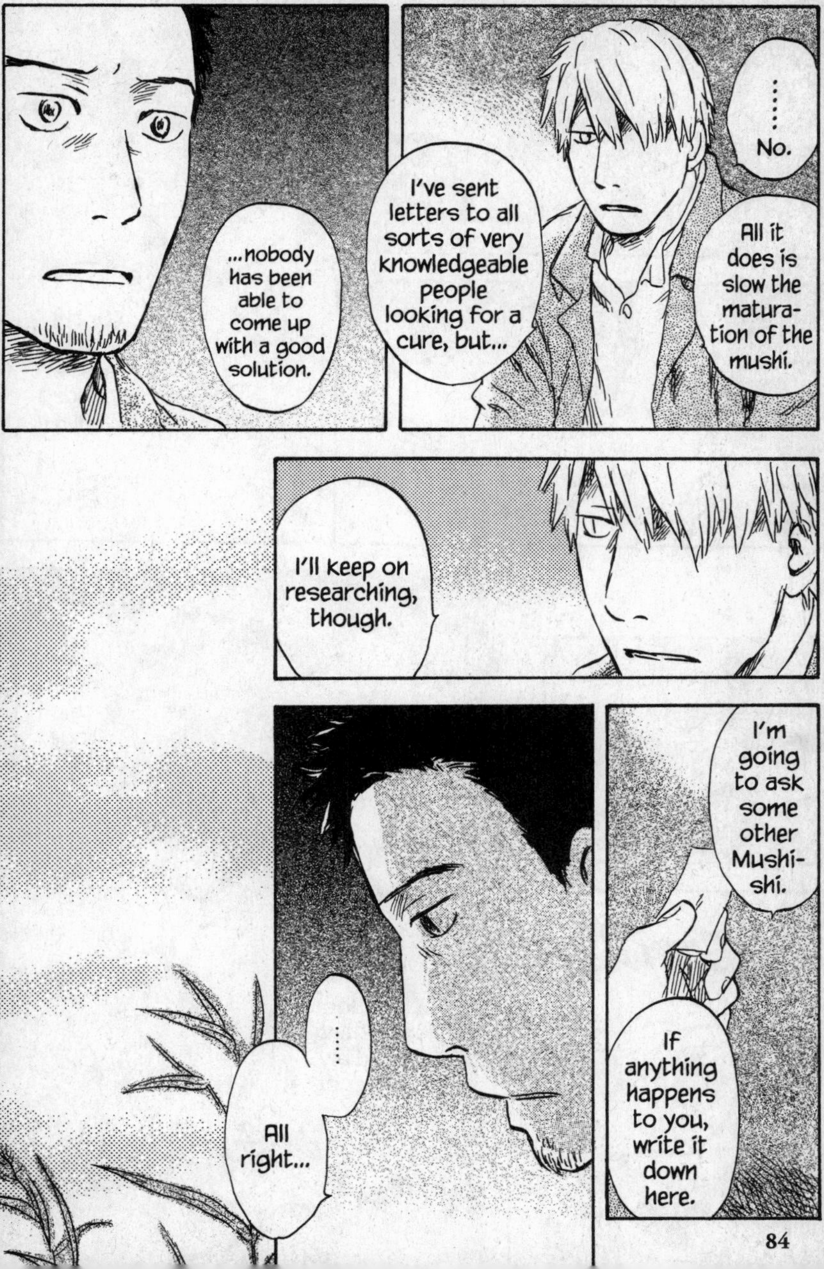
......
No.
All it does is slow the maturation of the mushi.
I've sent letters to all sorts of very knowledgeable people looking for a cure, but...
...nobody has been able to come up with a good solution.
I'll keep on researching, though.
I'm going to ask some other Mushi-shi.
If anything happens to you, write it down here.
......
All right...

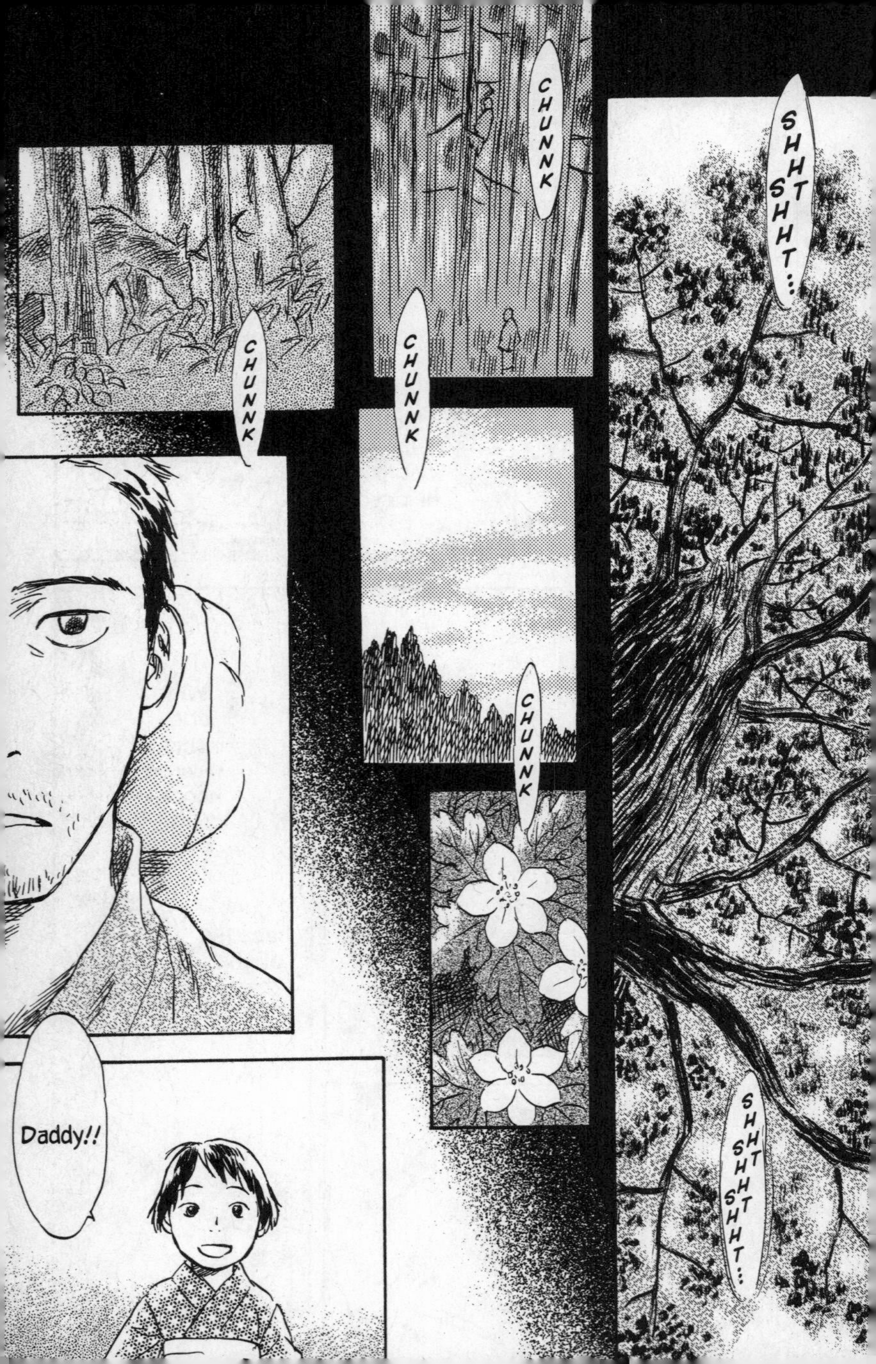
SHHT SHHT...
SHHT SHHT SHHT...
CHUNNK
CHUNNK
CHUNNK
CHUNNK
Daddy!!

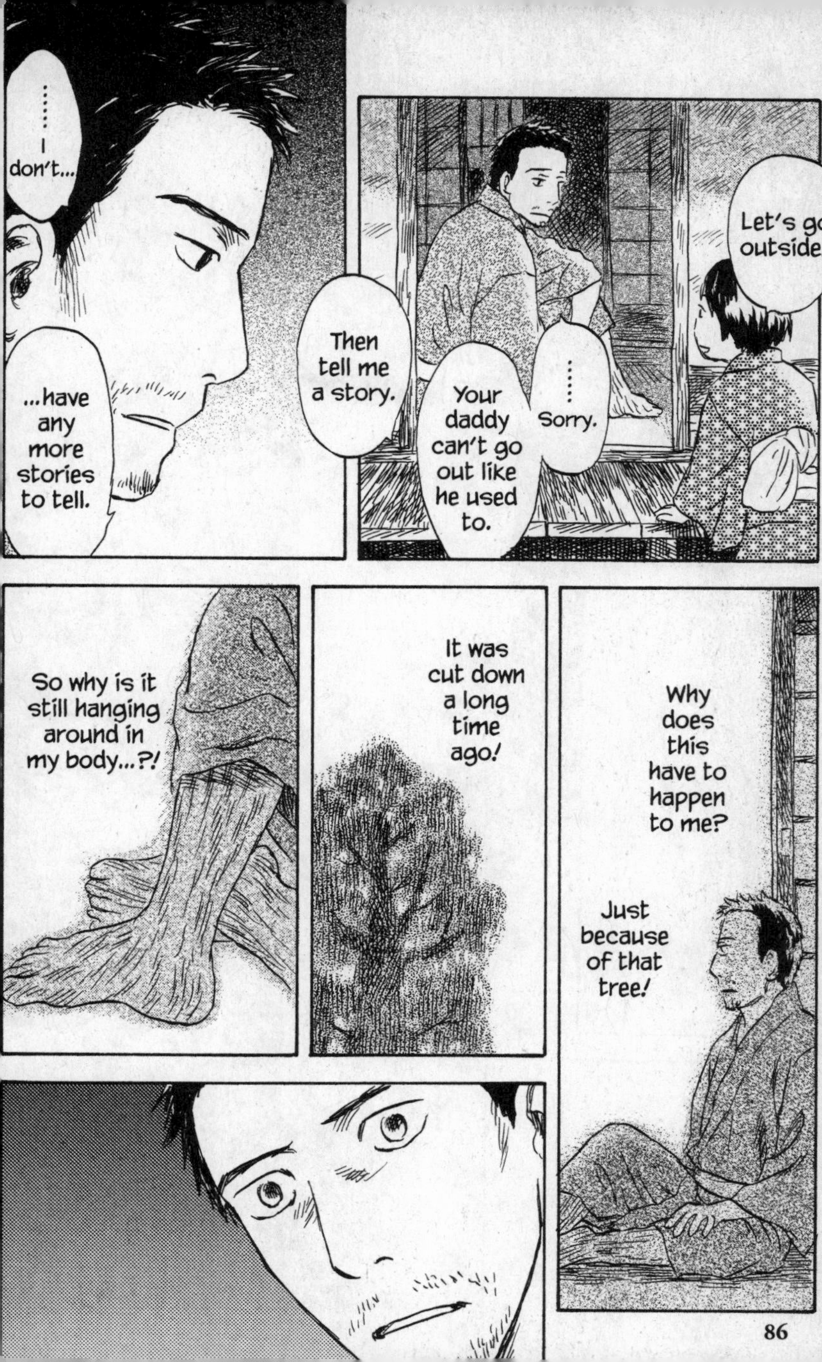
Let's go outside!
......Sorry.
Your daddy can't go out like he used to.
Then tell me a story.
......I don't...
...have any more stories to tell.
Why does this have to happen to me?
Just because of that tree!
It was cut down a long time ago!
So why is it still hanging around in my body...?!

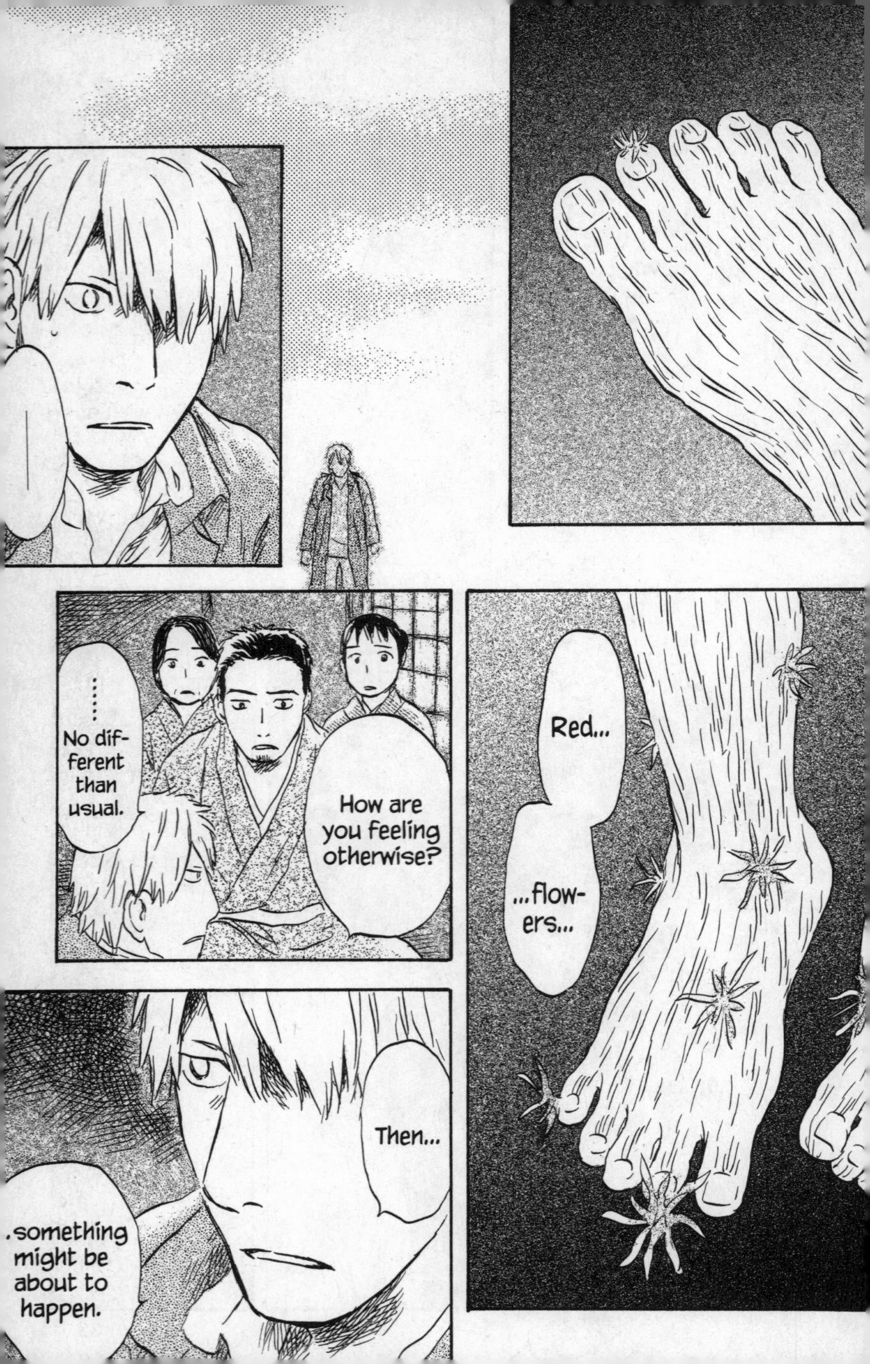
Red...
...flowers...
How are you feeling otherwise?
...... No different than usual.
Then...
.something might be about to happen.

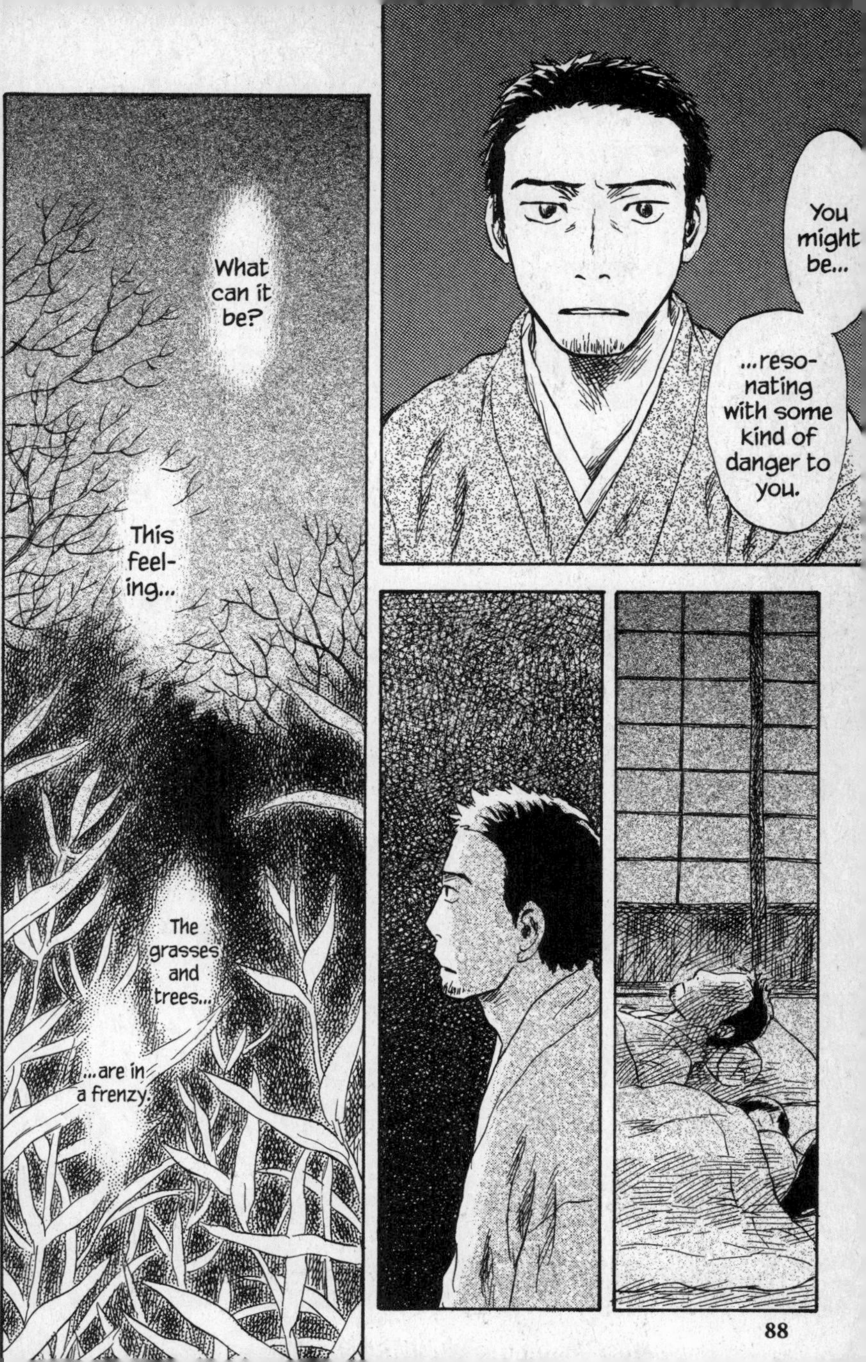
You might be...
...reso-nating with some kind of danger to you.
What can it be?
This feel-ing...
The grasses and trees...
...are in a frenzy.

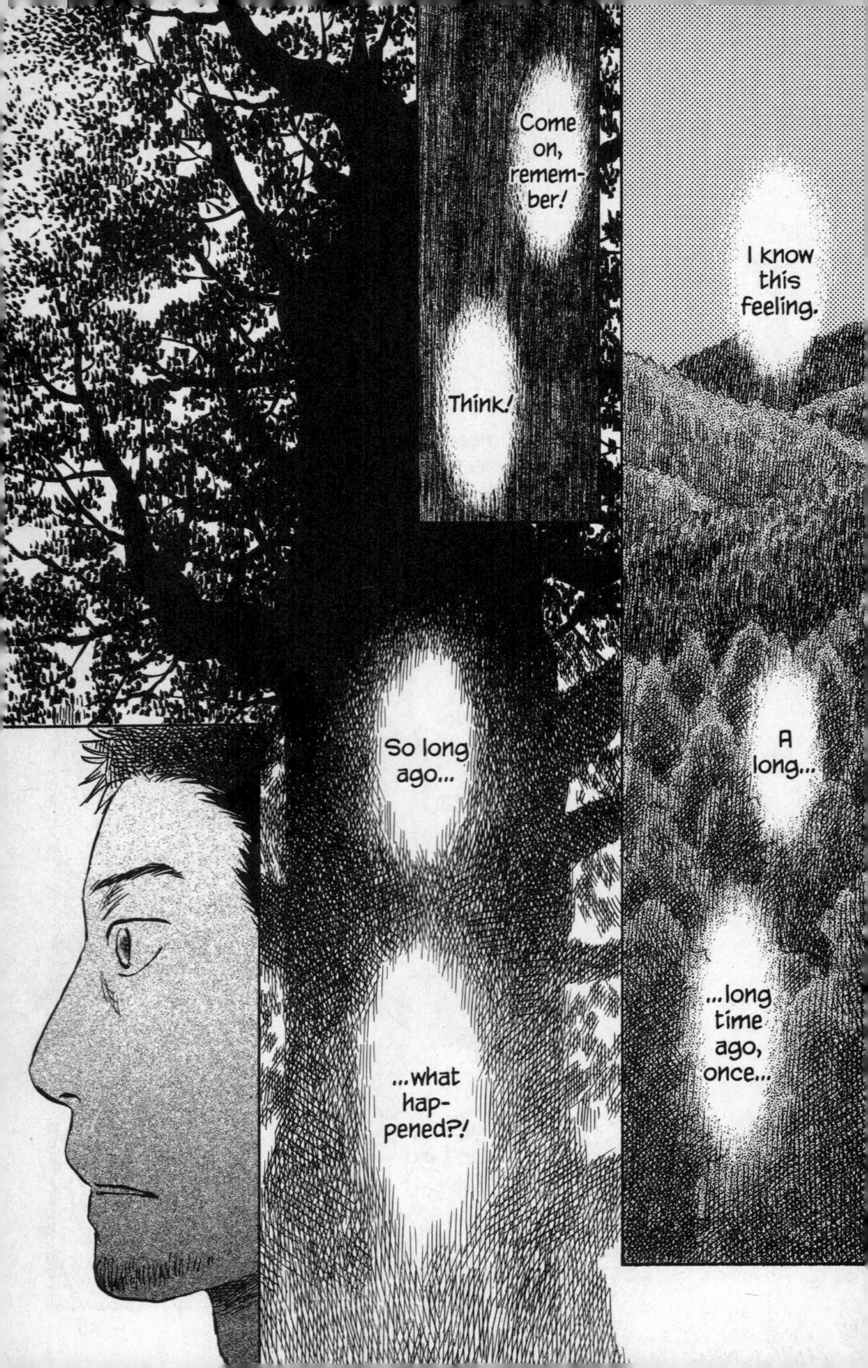
I know this feeling.
A long...
...long time ago, once...
Come on, remember!
Think!
So long ago...
...what happened?!

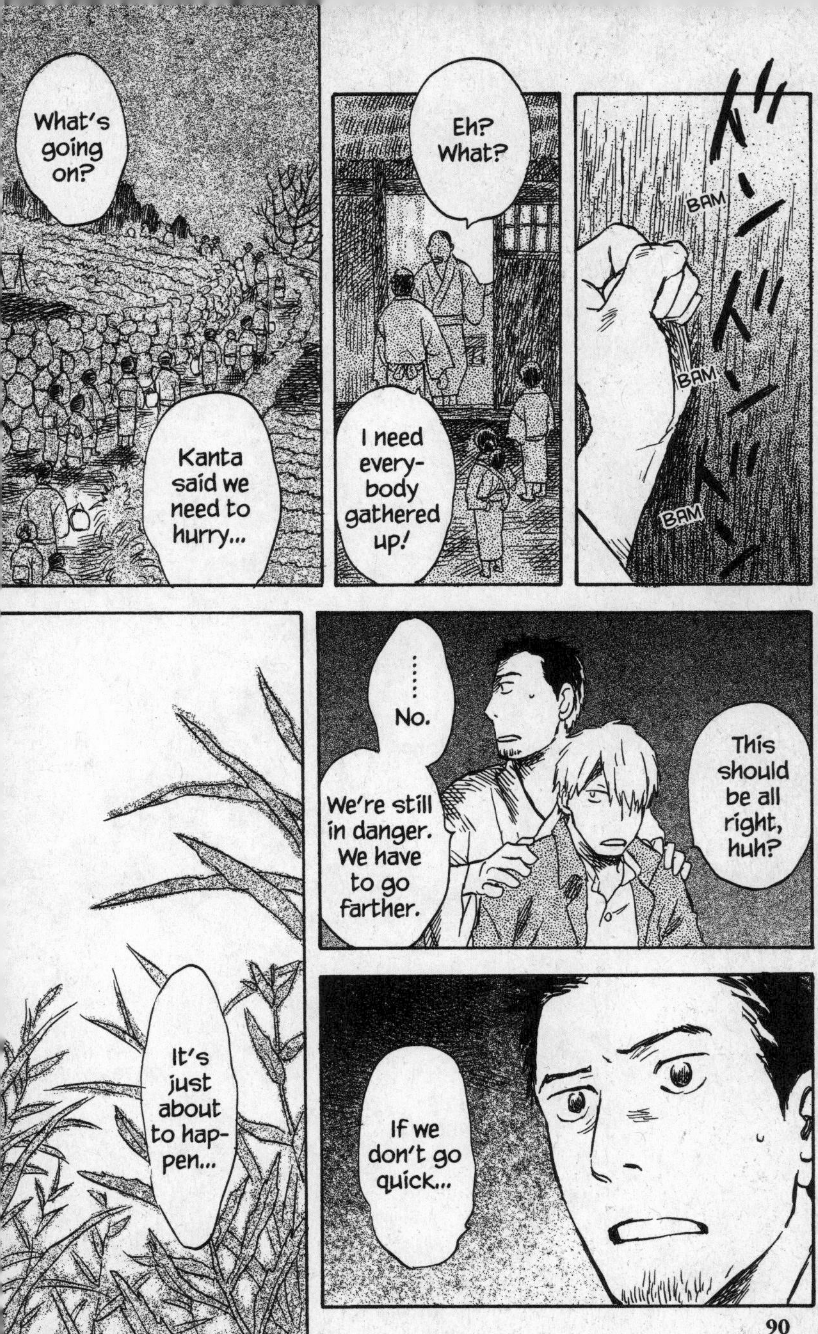
BAM
BAM
BAM
Eh? What?
I need every-body gathered up!
What's going on?
Kanta said we need to hurry...
This should be all right, huh?
...... No.
We're still in danger. We have to go farther.
If we don't go quick...
It's just about to happen...

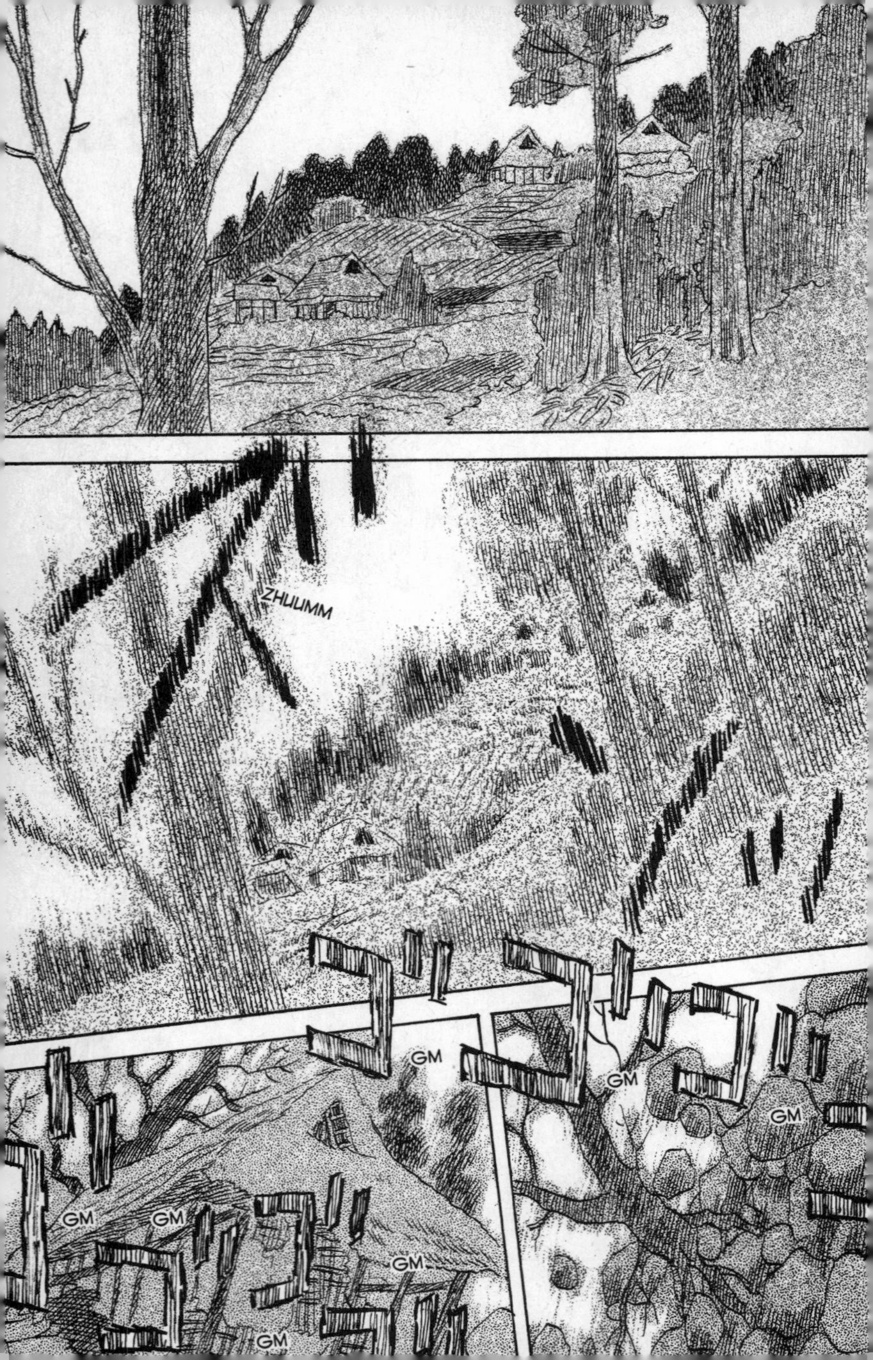
ZHUUMM
GM
GM
GM
GM
GM
GM
GM

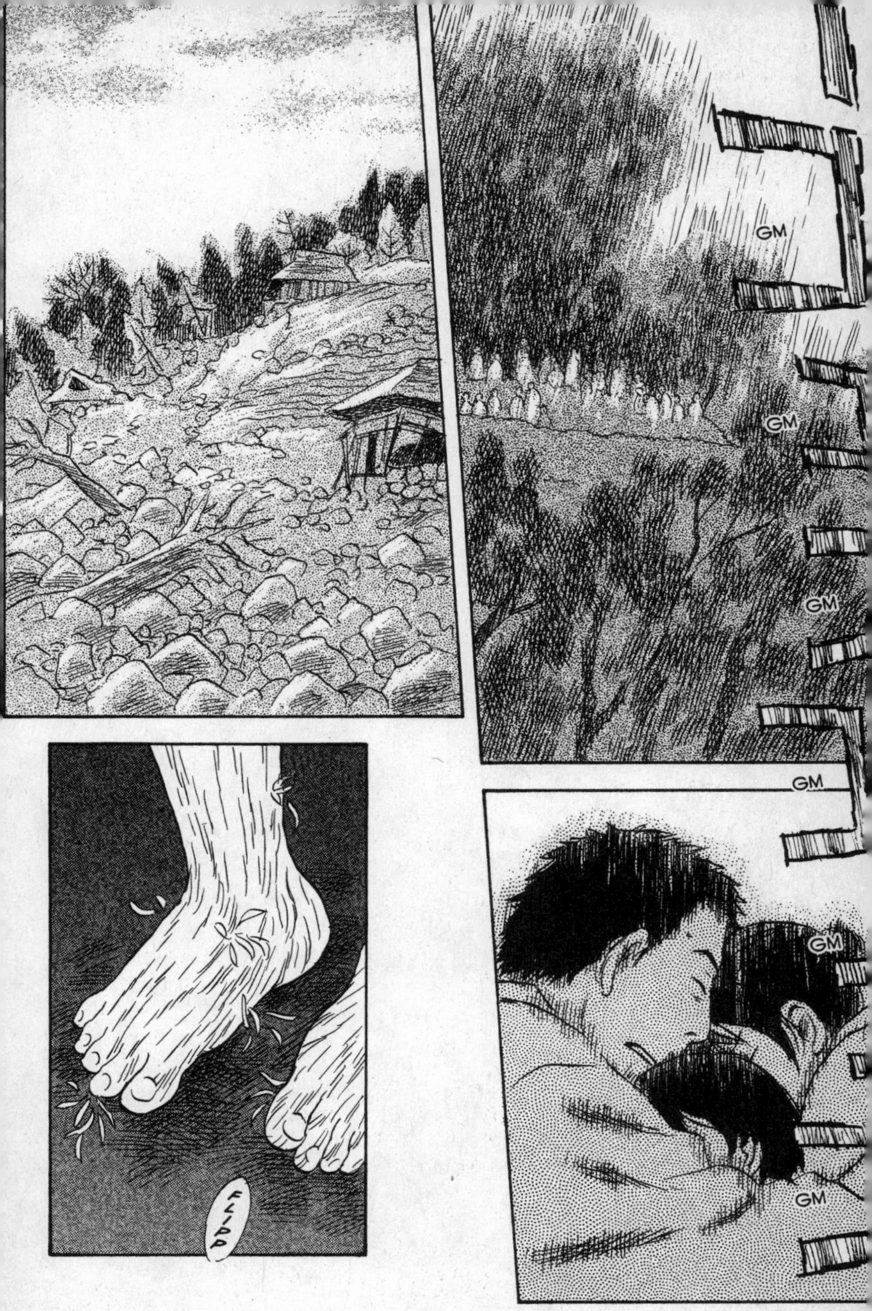
GM
GM
GM
GM
GM
GM
FLIPP

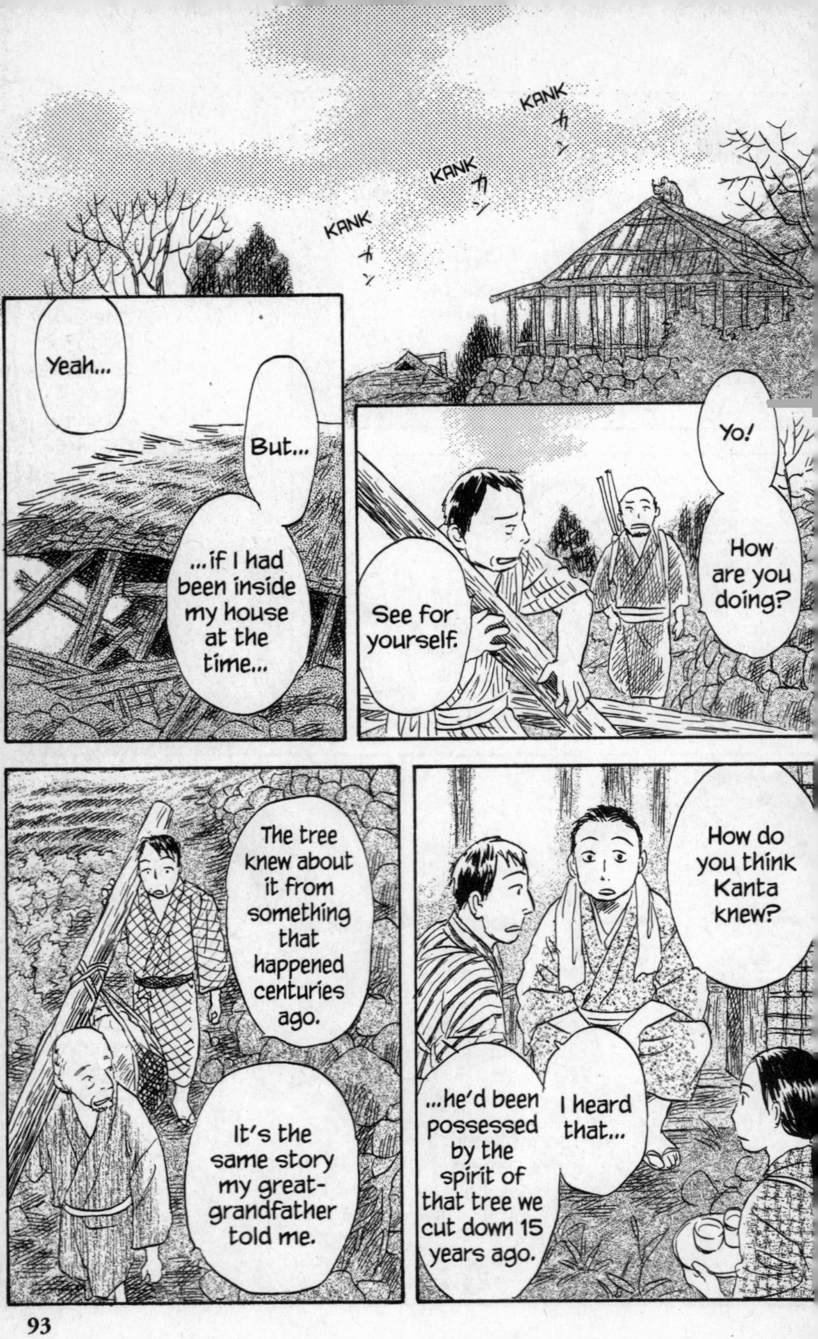
KANK
カン
KANK
カン
KANK
カン
Yo!
How are you doing?
See for yourself.
Yeah...
But...
...if I had been inside my house at the time...
How do you think Kanta knew?
I heard that...
...he'd been possessed by the spirit of that tree we cut down 15 years ago.
The tree knew about it from something that happened centuries ago.
It's the same story my great-grandfather told me.

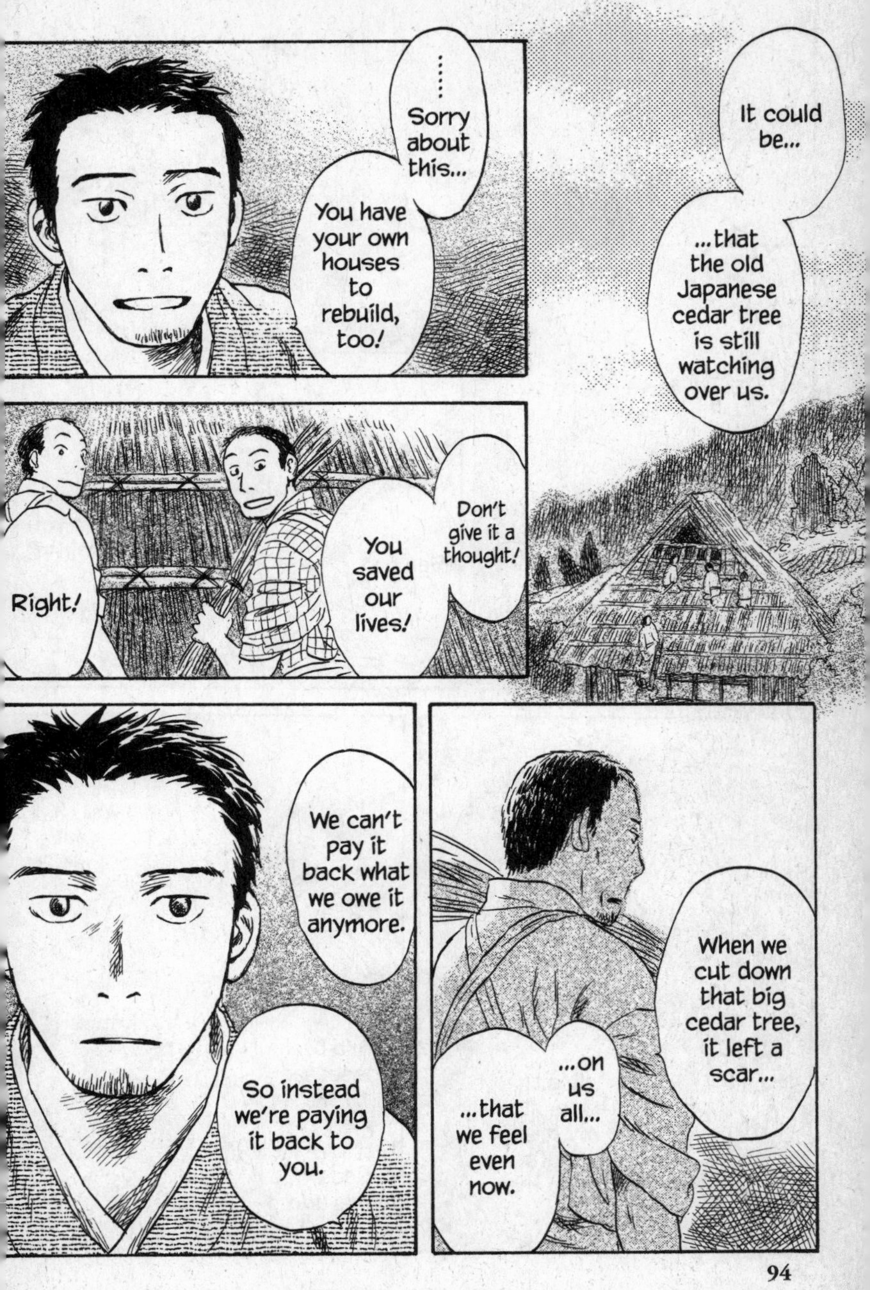
It could be...
...that the old Japanese cedar tree is still watching over us.
......
Sorry about this...
You have your own houses to rebuild, too!
Don't give it a thought!
You saved our lives!
Right!
When we cut down that big cedar tree, it left a scar...
...on us all...
...that we feel even now.
We can't pay it back what we owe it anymore.
So instead we're paying it back to you.

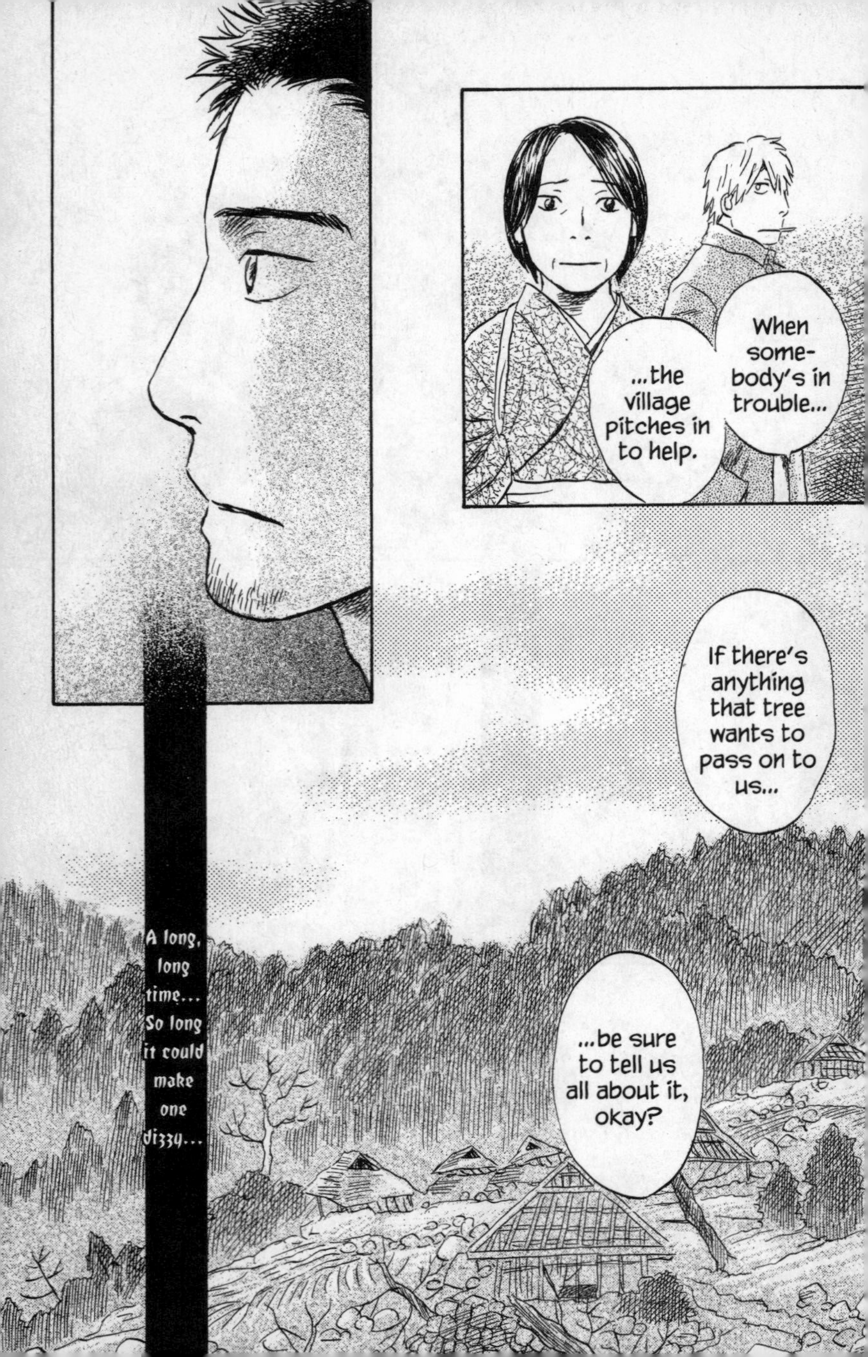
When some-body's in trouble...
...the village pitches in to help.
If there's anything that tree wants to pass on to us...
...be sure to tell us all about it, okay?
A long, long time... So long it could make one dizzy...

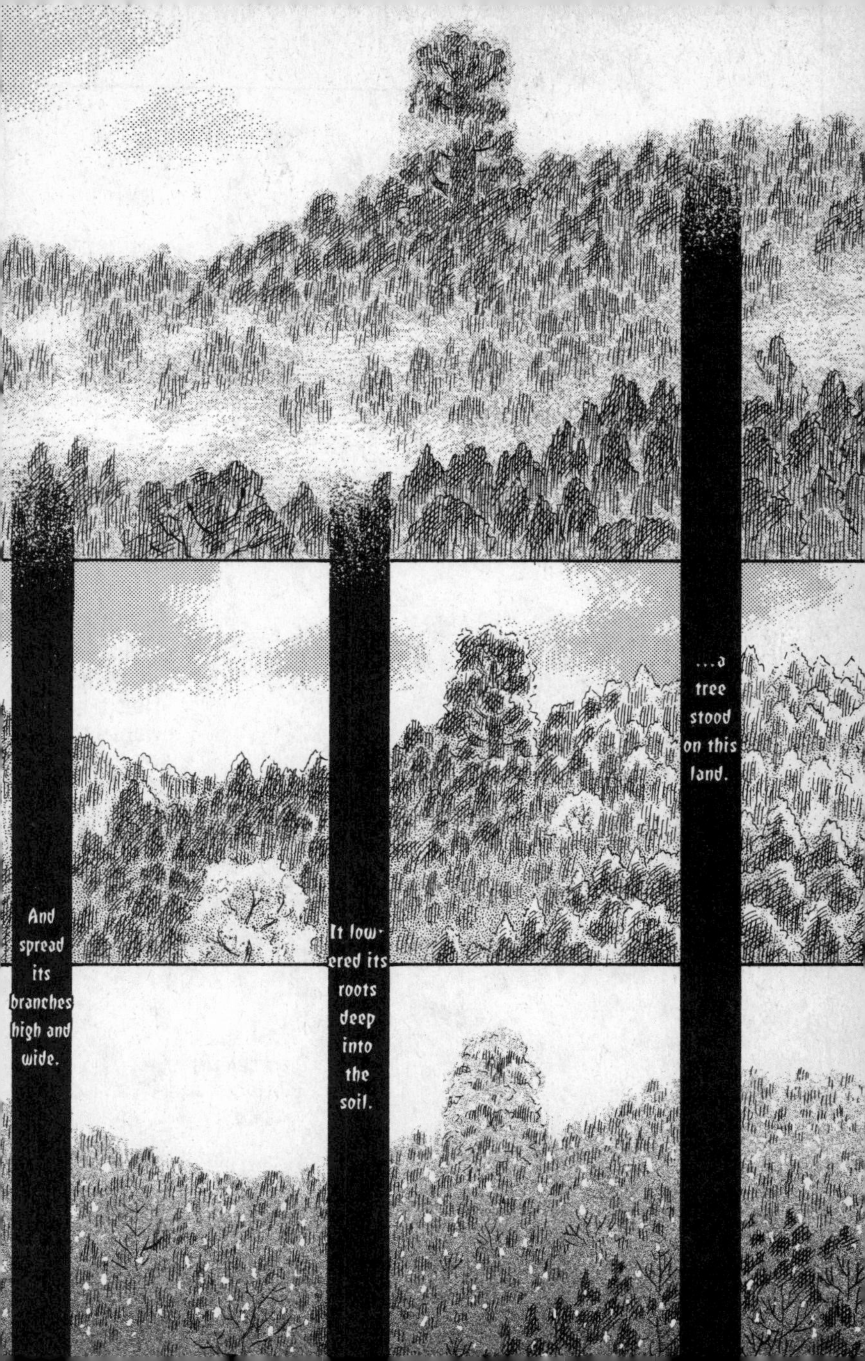
...a tree stood on this land.
It lowered its roots deep into the soil.
And spread its branches high and wide.

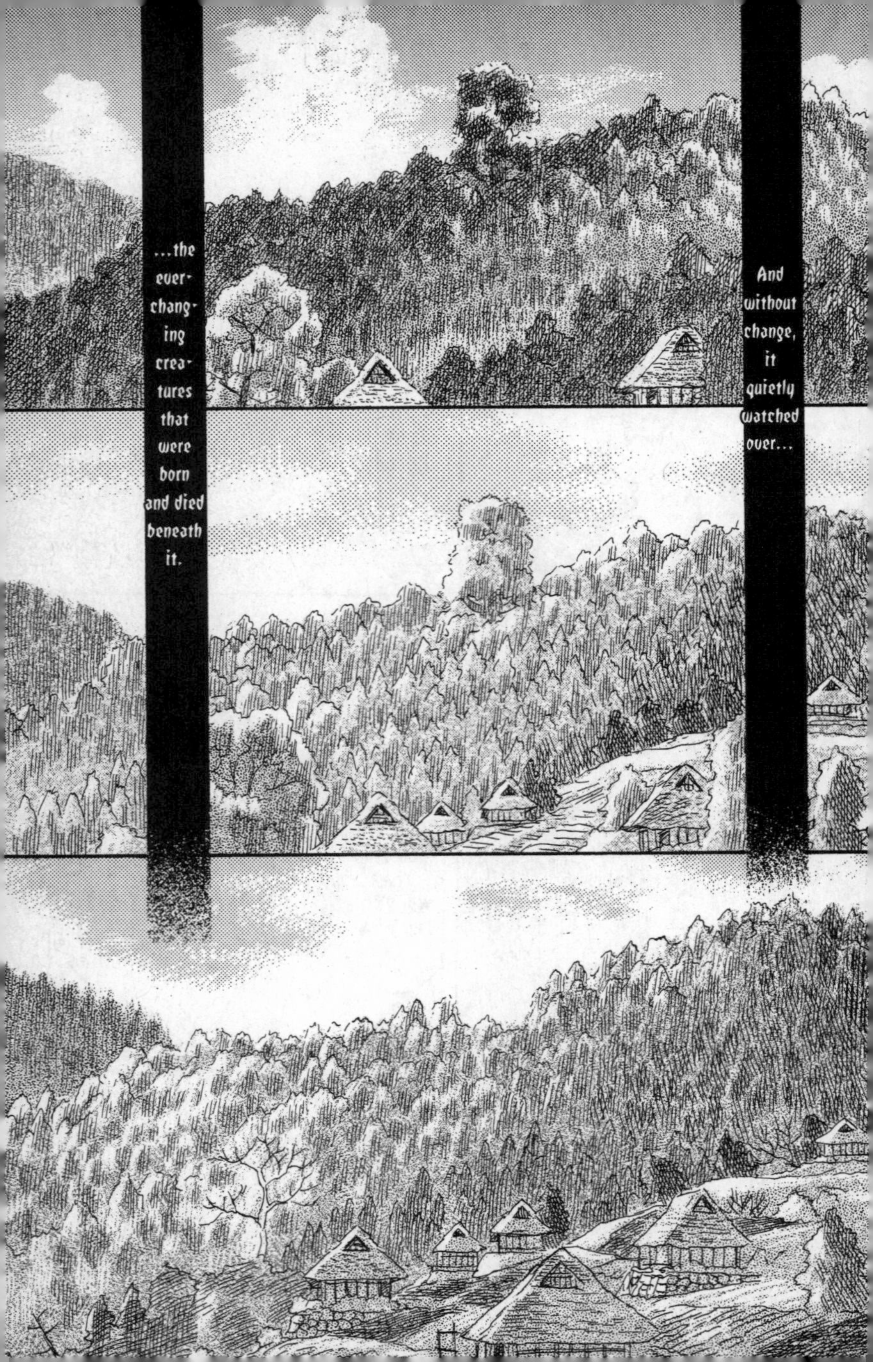
And without change, it quietly watched over...
...the ever-changing creatures that were born and died beneath it.

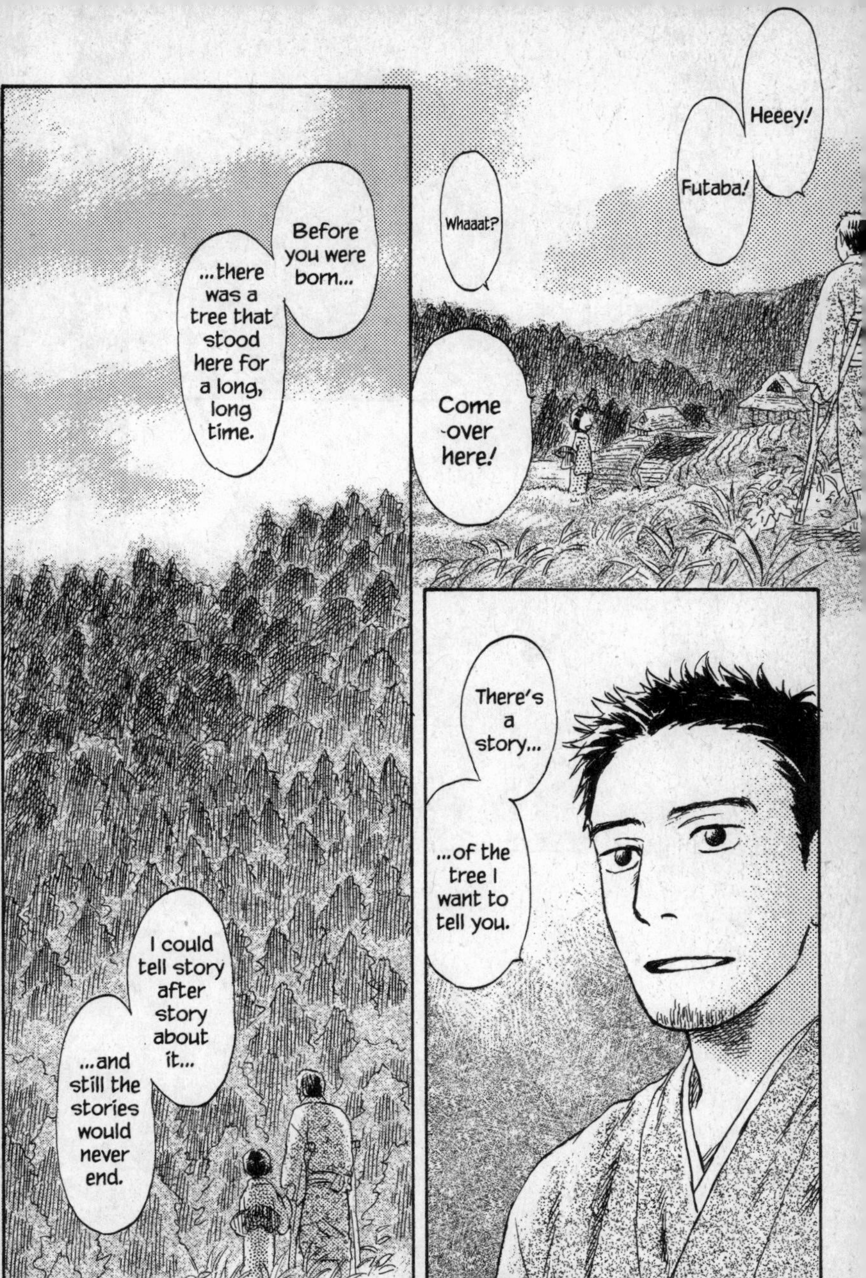
Heeey!
Futaba!
Whaaat?
Come over here!
There's a story...
...of the tree I want to tell you.
Before you were born...
...there was a tree that stood here for a long, long time.
I could tell story after story about it...
...and still the stories would never end.

The Eternal Tree The End

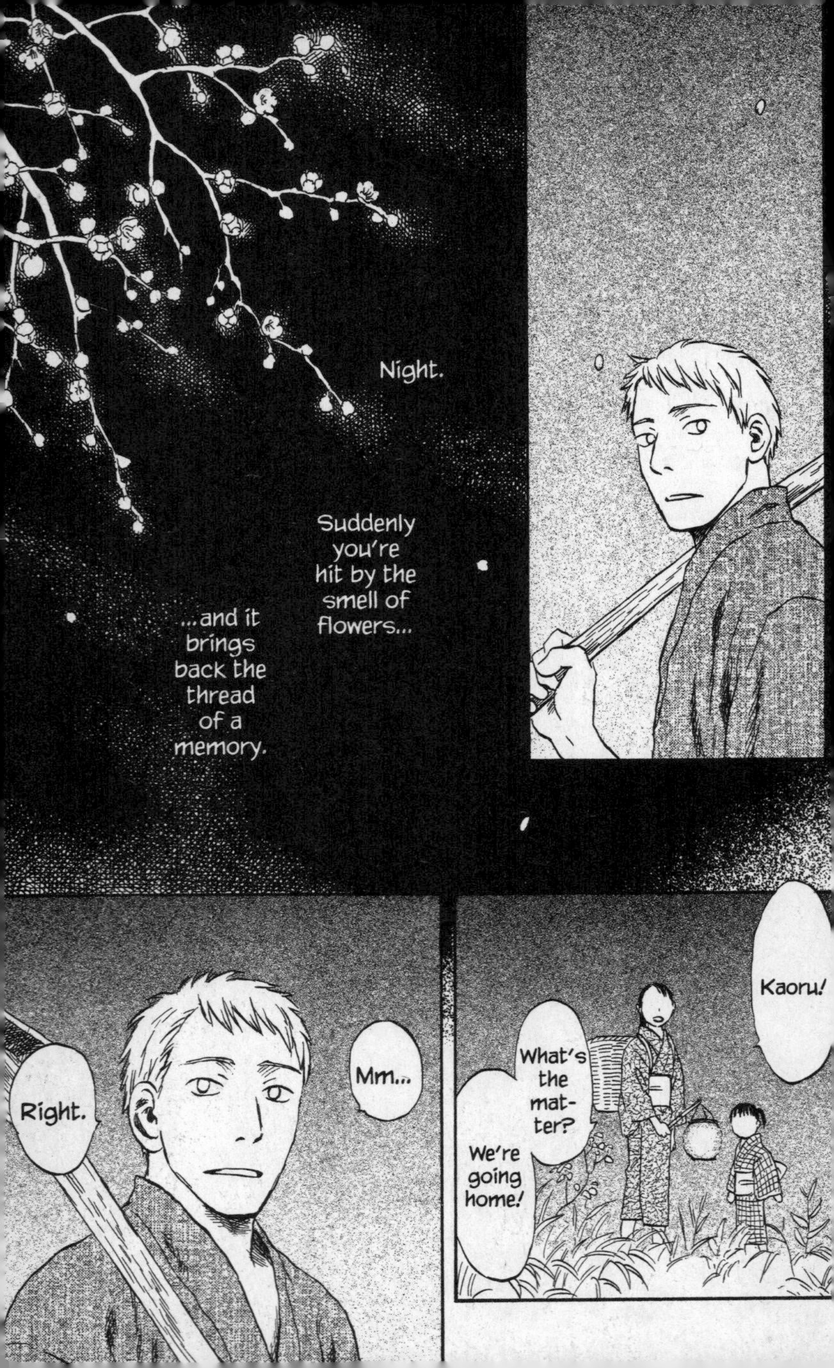
Night.
Suddenly you're hit by the smell of flowers...
...and it brings back the thread of a memory.
Kaoru!
What's the matter?
We're going home!
Mm...
Right.

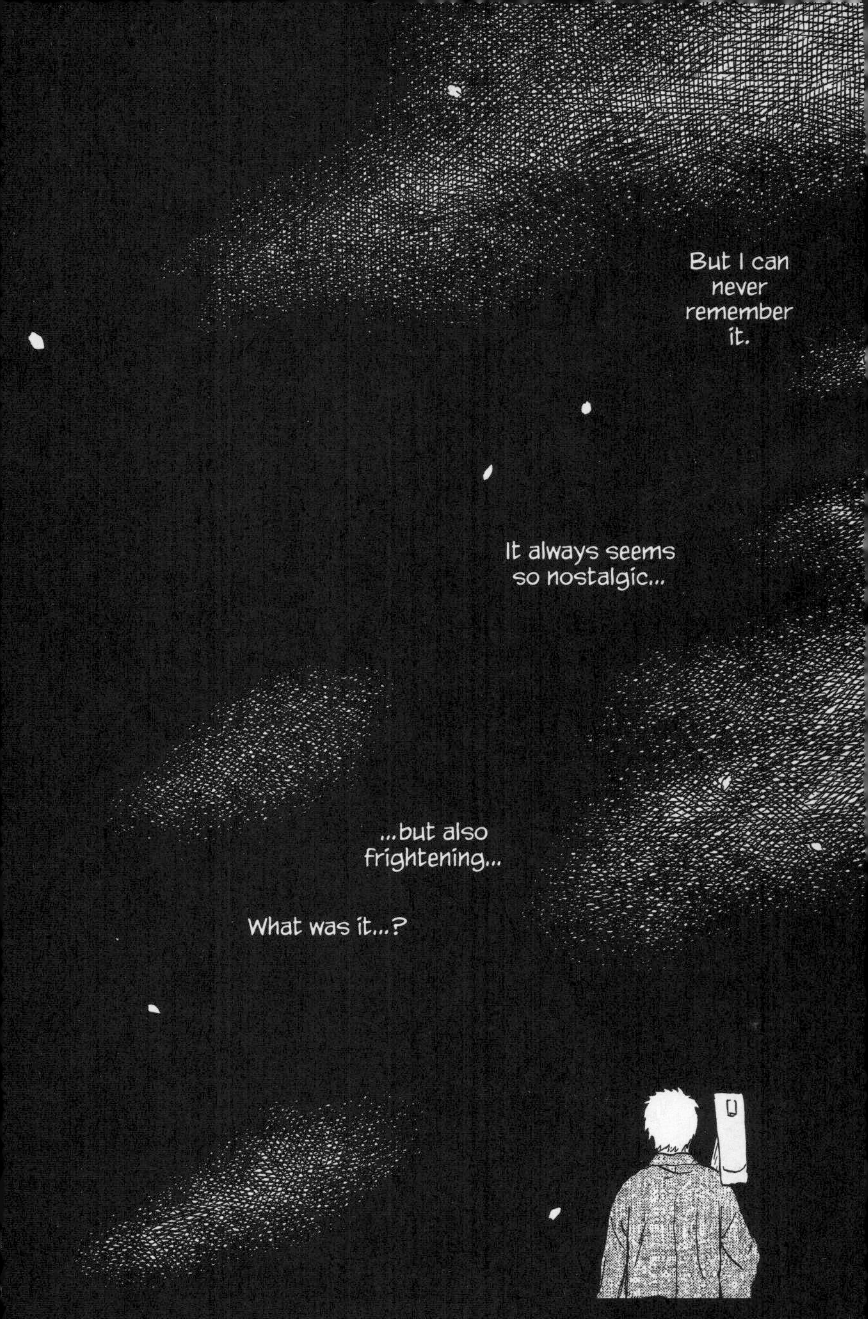
But I can never remember it.
It always seems so nostalgic...
...but also frightening...
What was it...?

The Scented Darkness

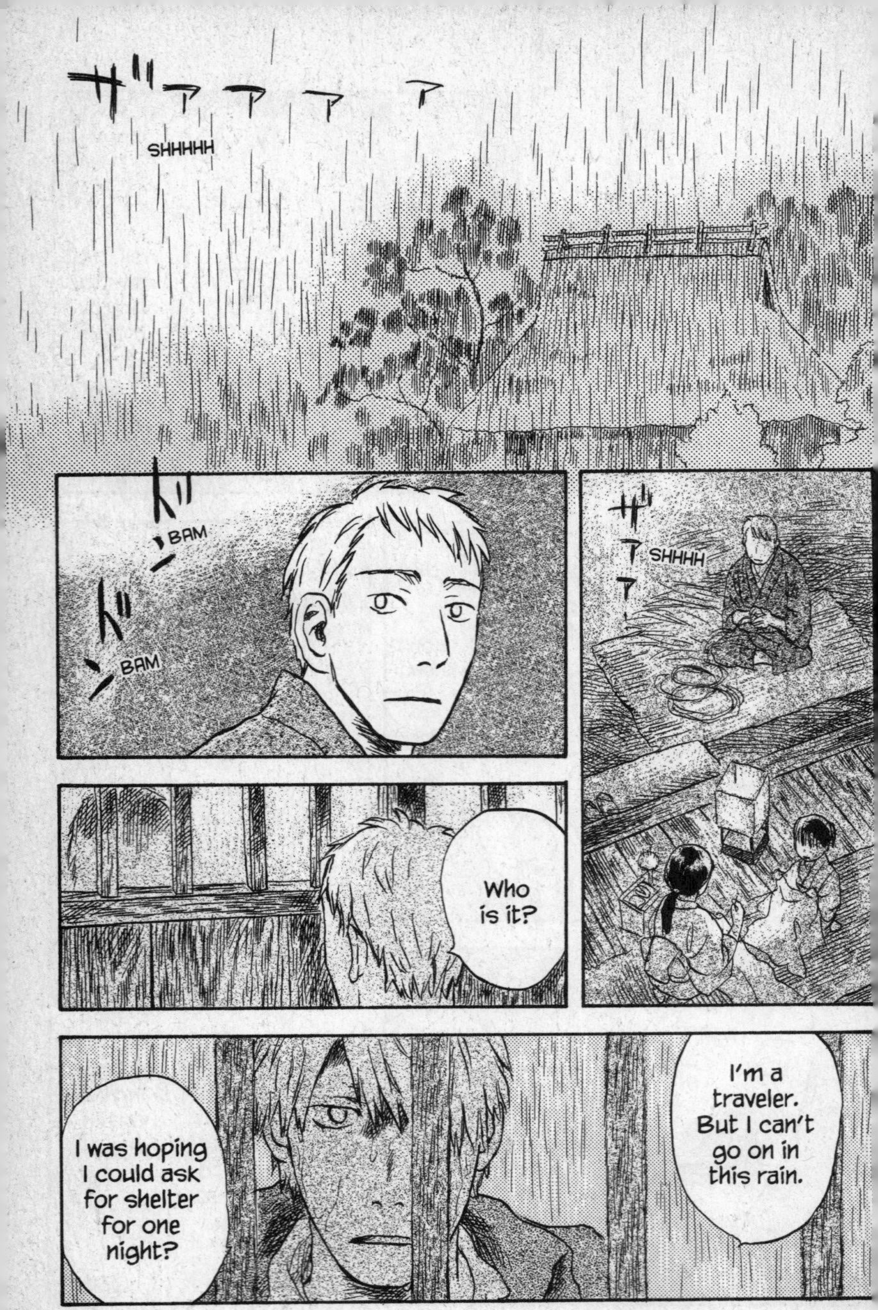
ザァァァァ
SHHHHH
ザァァ
SHHHH
ドン
BAM
ドン
BAM
Who is it?
I'm a traveler. But I can't go on in this rain.
I was hoping I could ask for shelter for one night?

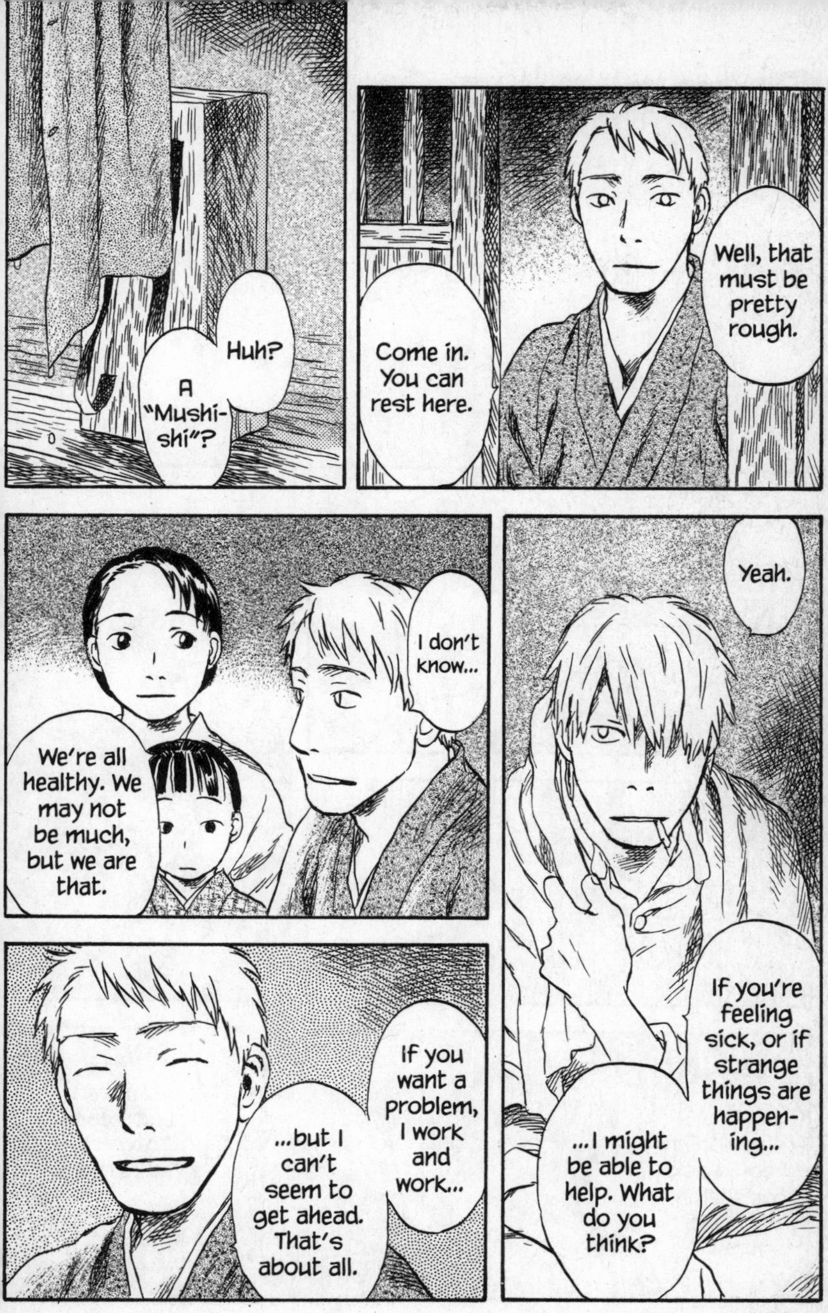
Well, that must be pretty rough.
Come in. You can rest here.
Huh?
A "Mushi-shi"?
Yeah.
If you're feeling sick, or if strange things are happening...
...I might be able to help. What do you think?
I don't know...
We're all healthy. We may not be much, but we are that.
If you want a problem, I work and work...
...but I can't seem to get ahead. That's about all.

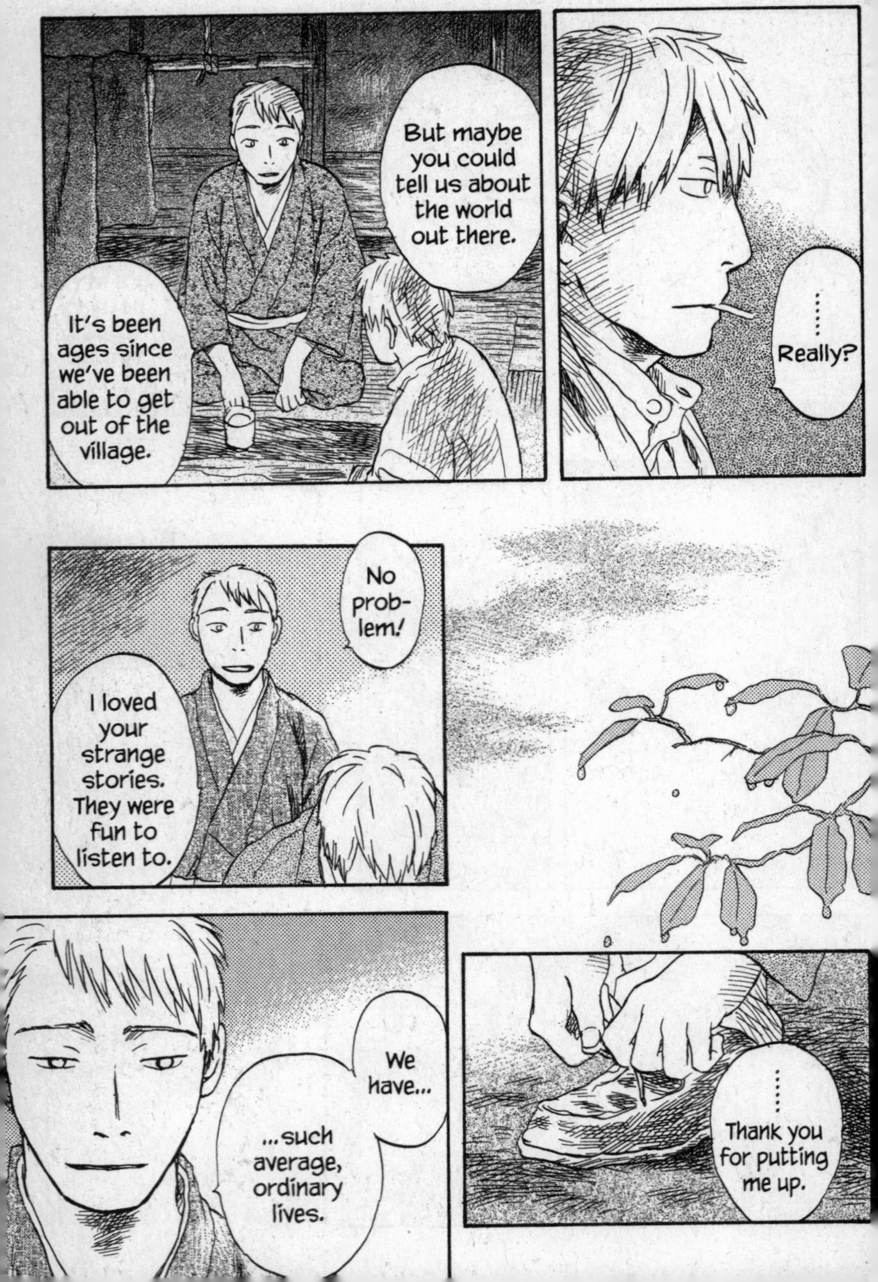
……Really?
But maybe you could tell us about the world out there.
It's been ages since we've been able to get out of the village.
No prob-lem!
I loved your strange stories. They were fun to listen to.
……Thank you for putting me up.
We have...
...such average, ordinary lives.

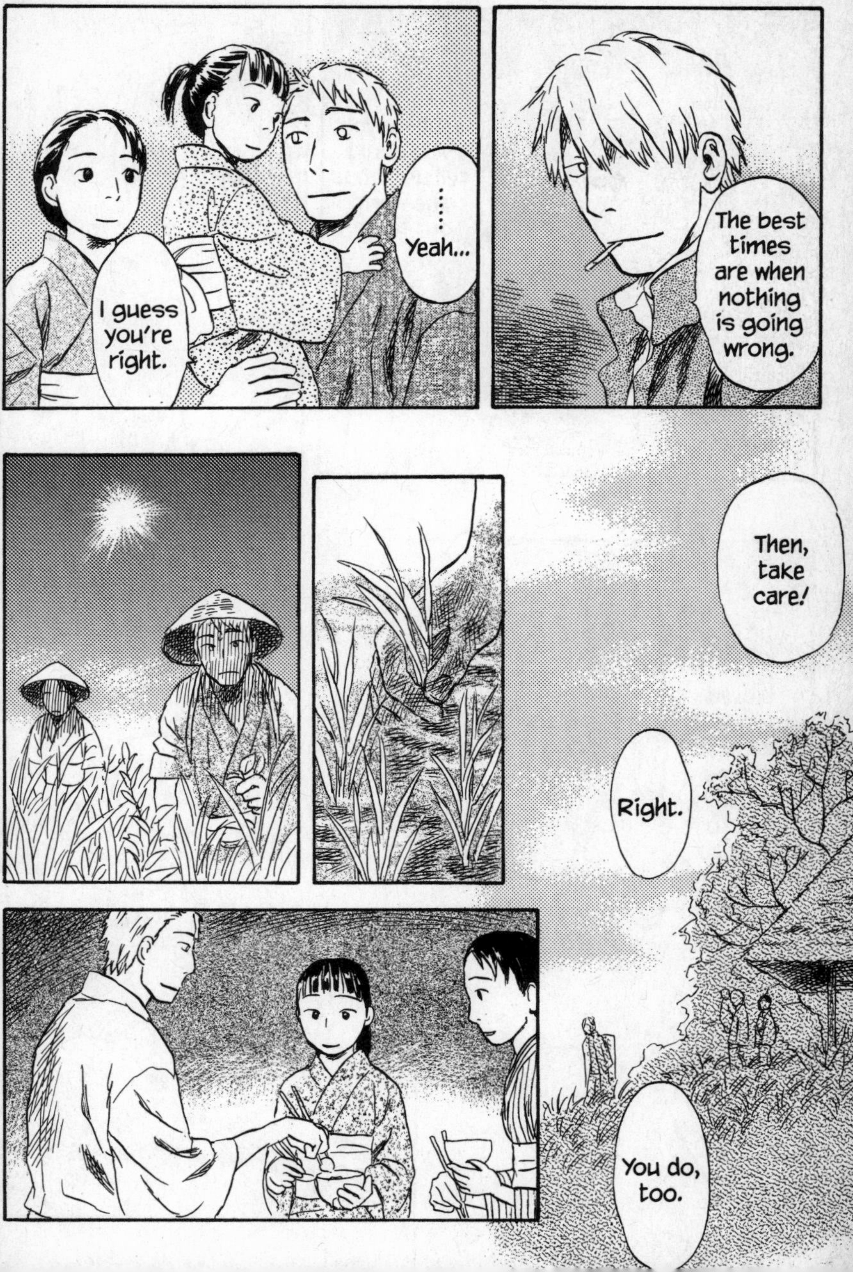
The best times are when nothing is going wrong.
......Yeah...
I guess you're right.
Then, take care!
Right.
You do, too.

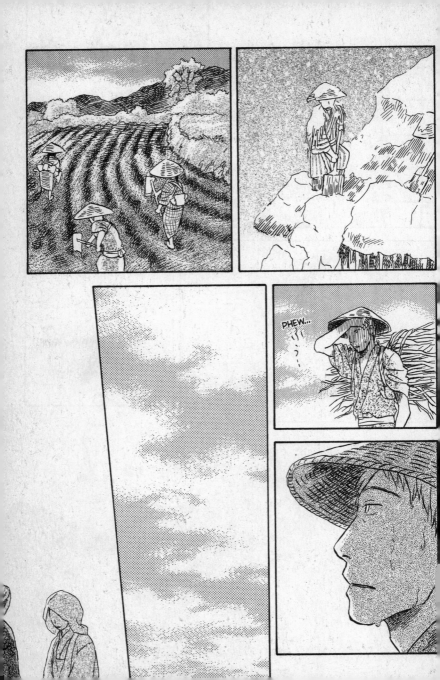

PHEW...

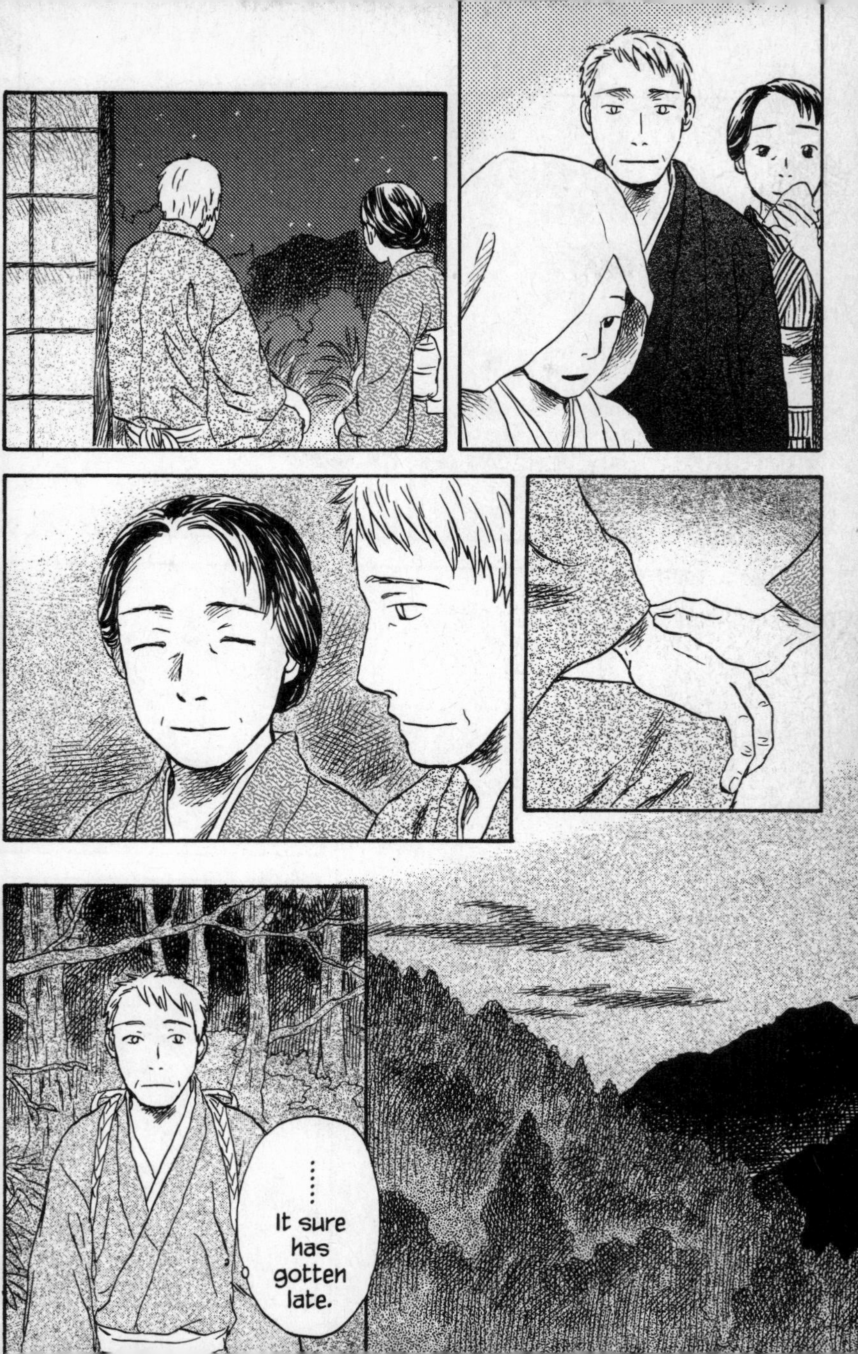
...... It sure has gotten late.

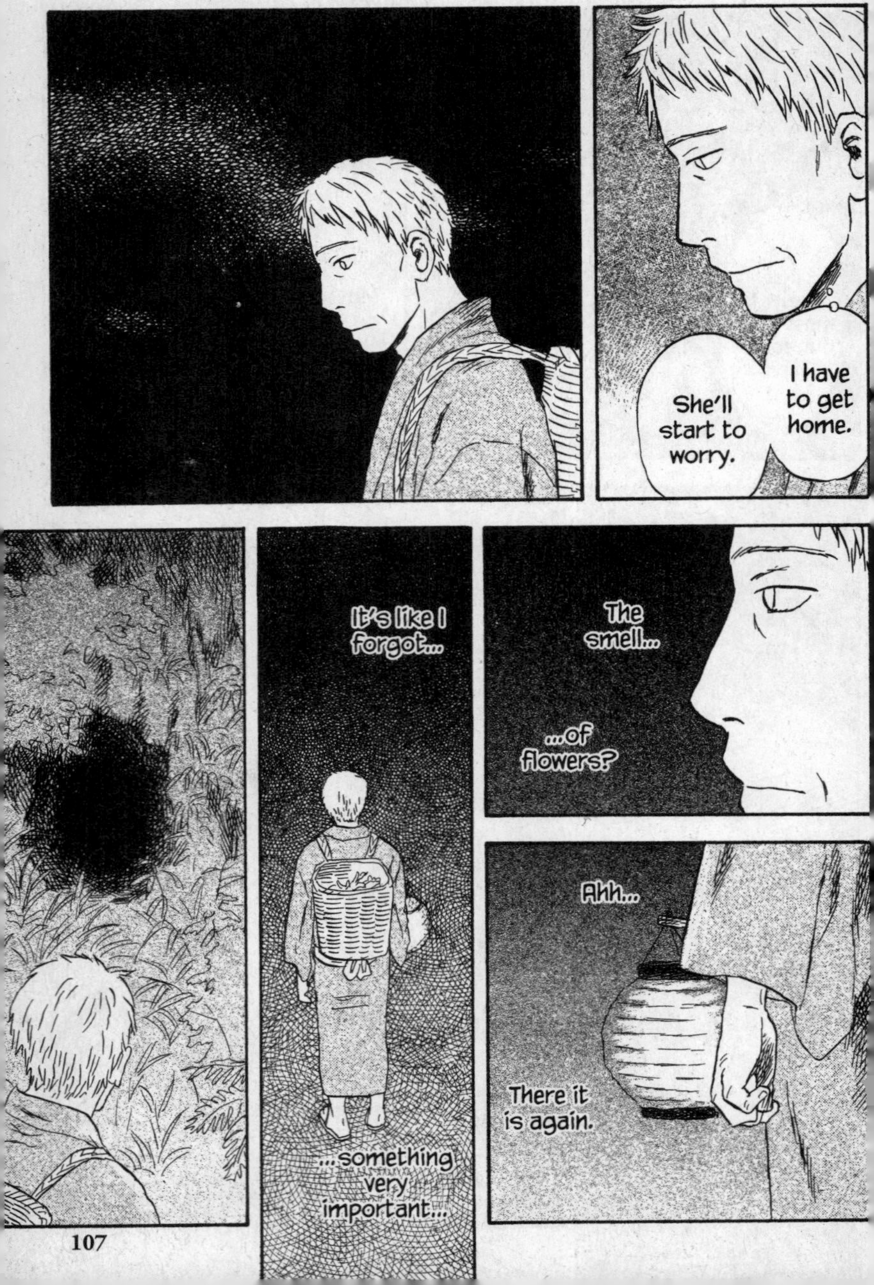
I have to get home.
She'll start to worry.
The smell...
...of flowers?
Ahh...
There it is again.
It's like I forgot...
...something very important...

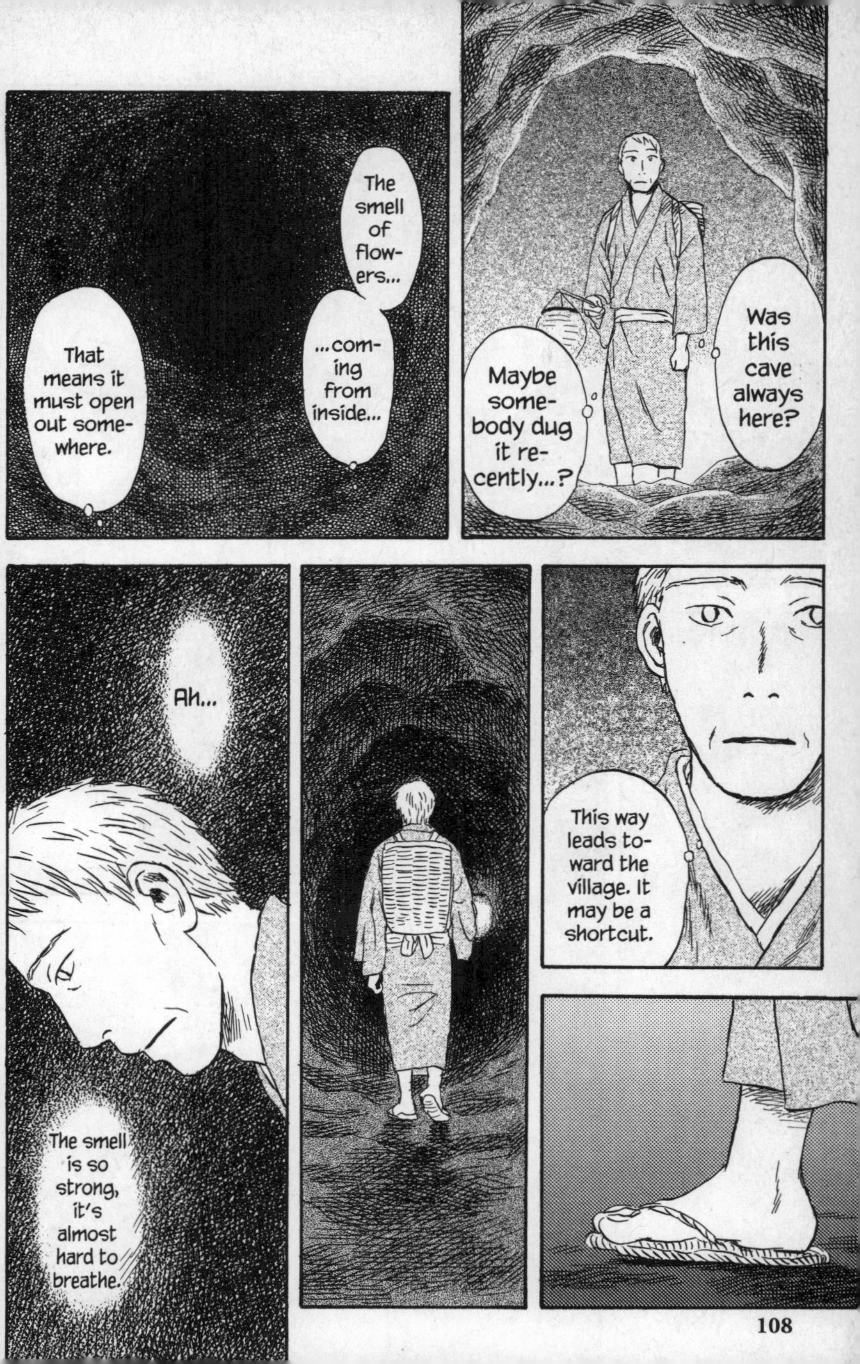
Was this cave always here?
Maybe somebody dug it recently...?
The smell of flowers...
...coming from inside...
That means it must open out somewhere.
This way leads toward the village. It may be a shortcut.
Ah...
The smell is so strong, it's almost hard to breathe.

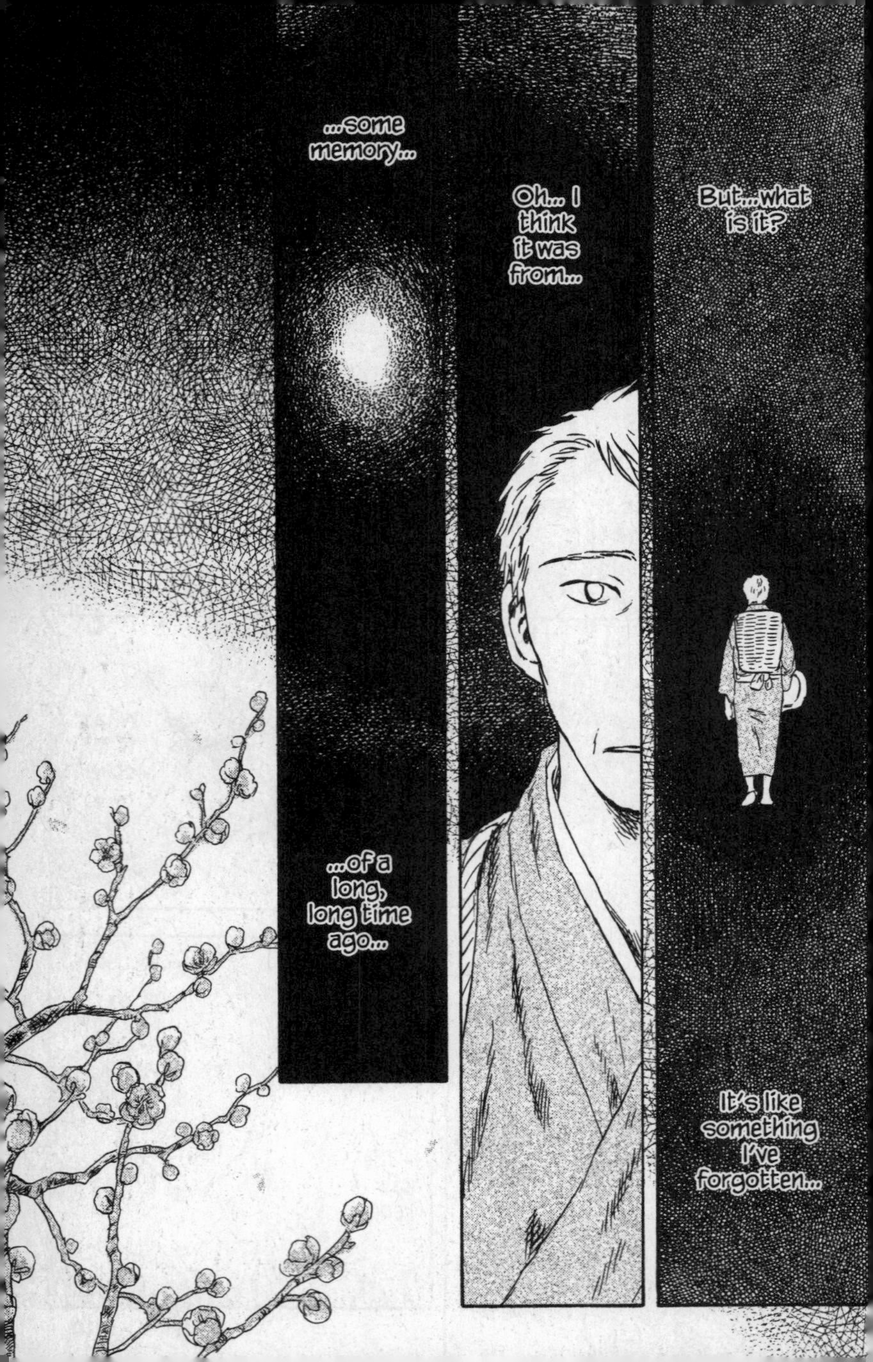
But...what is it?
It's like something I've forgotten...
Oh... I think it was from...
...some memory...
...of a long, long time ago...

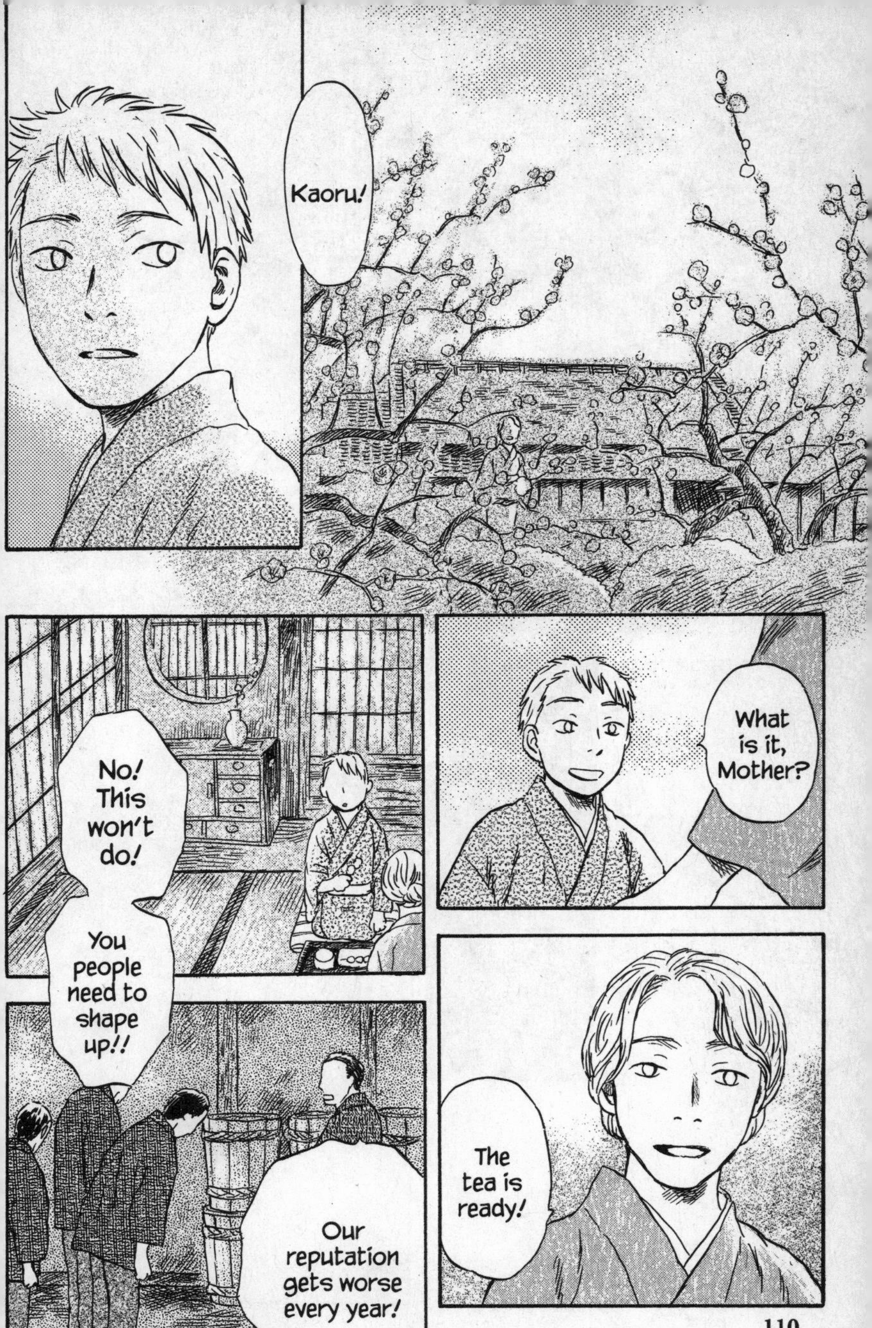
Kaoru!
What is it, Mother?
No! This won't do!
The tea is ready!
You people need to shape up!!
Our reputation gets worse every year!

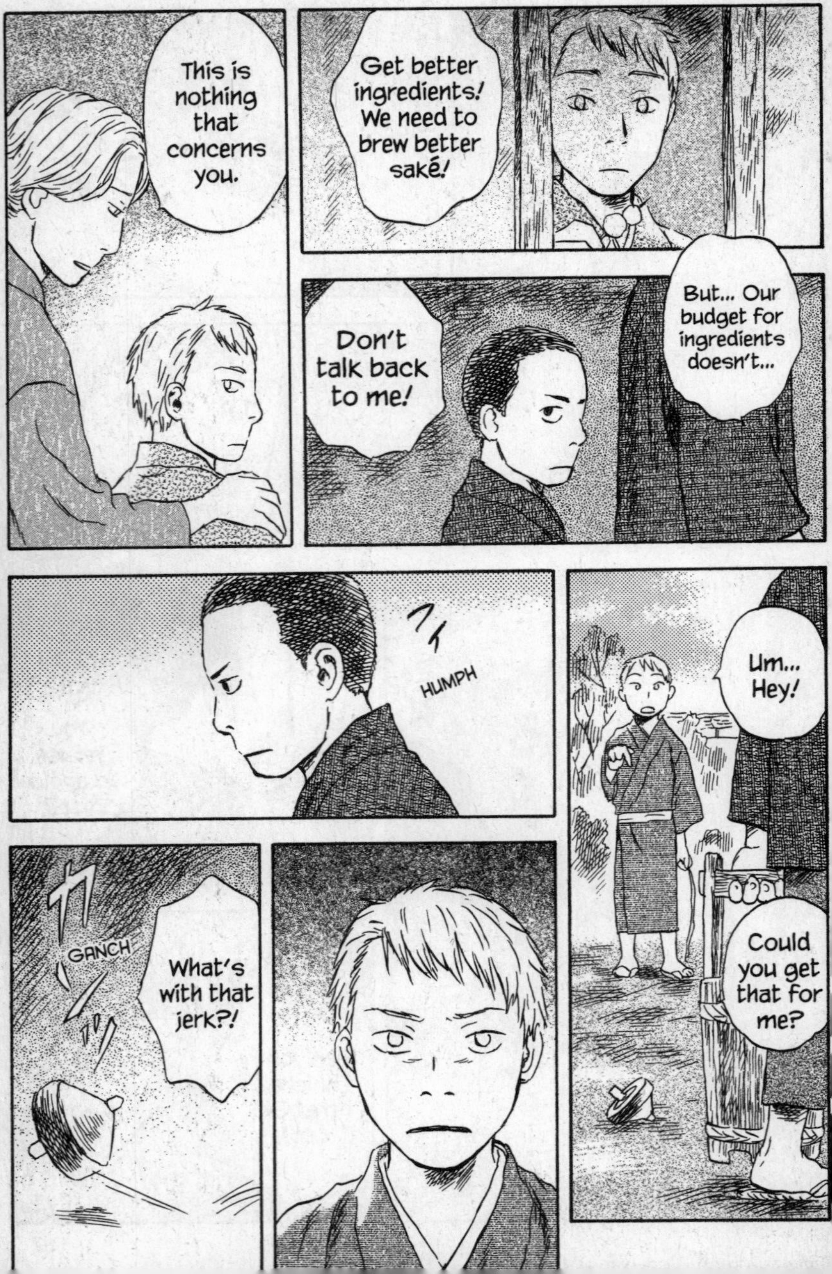
Get better ingredients! We need to brew better saké!
But... Our budget for ingredients doesn't...
Don't talk back to me!
This is nothing that concerns you.
Um... Hey!
Could you get that for me?
HUMPH
GANCH
What's with that jerk?!

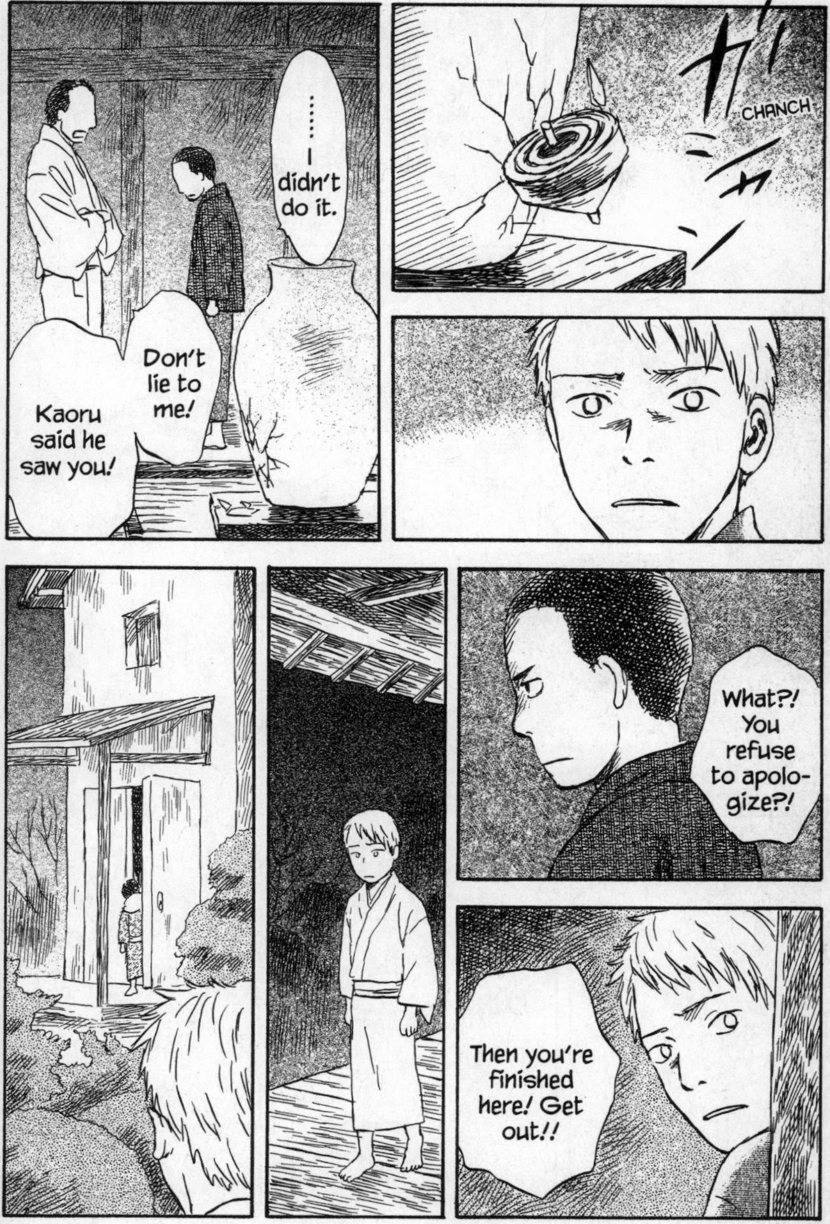
CHANCH
……I didn't do it.
Don't lie to me!
Kaoru said he saw you!
What?! You refuse to apolo-gize?!
Then you're finished here! Get out!!

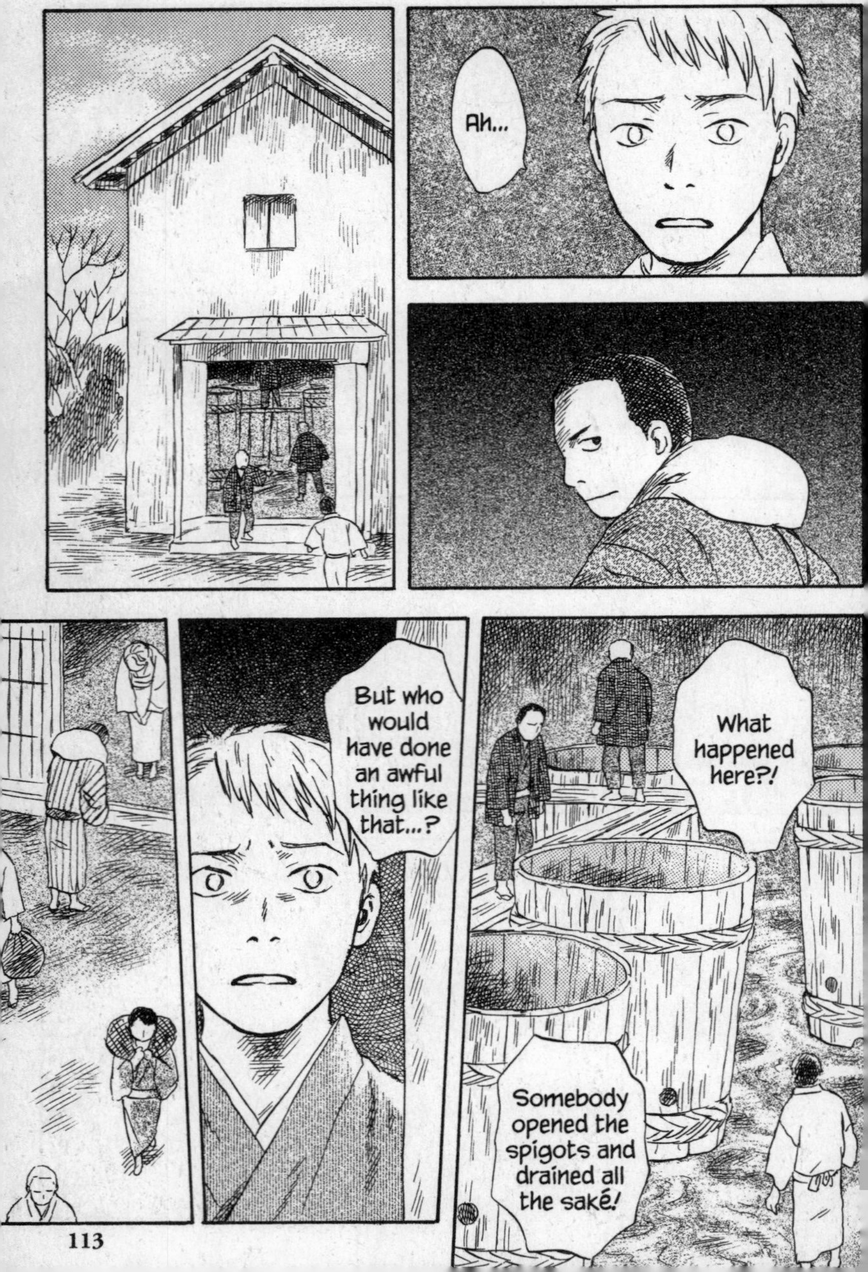
Ah...
What happened here?!
Somebody opened the spigots and drained all the saké!
But who would have done an awful thing like that...?

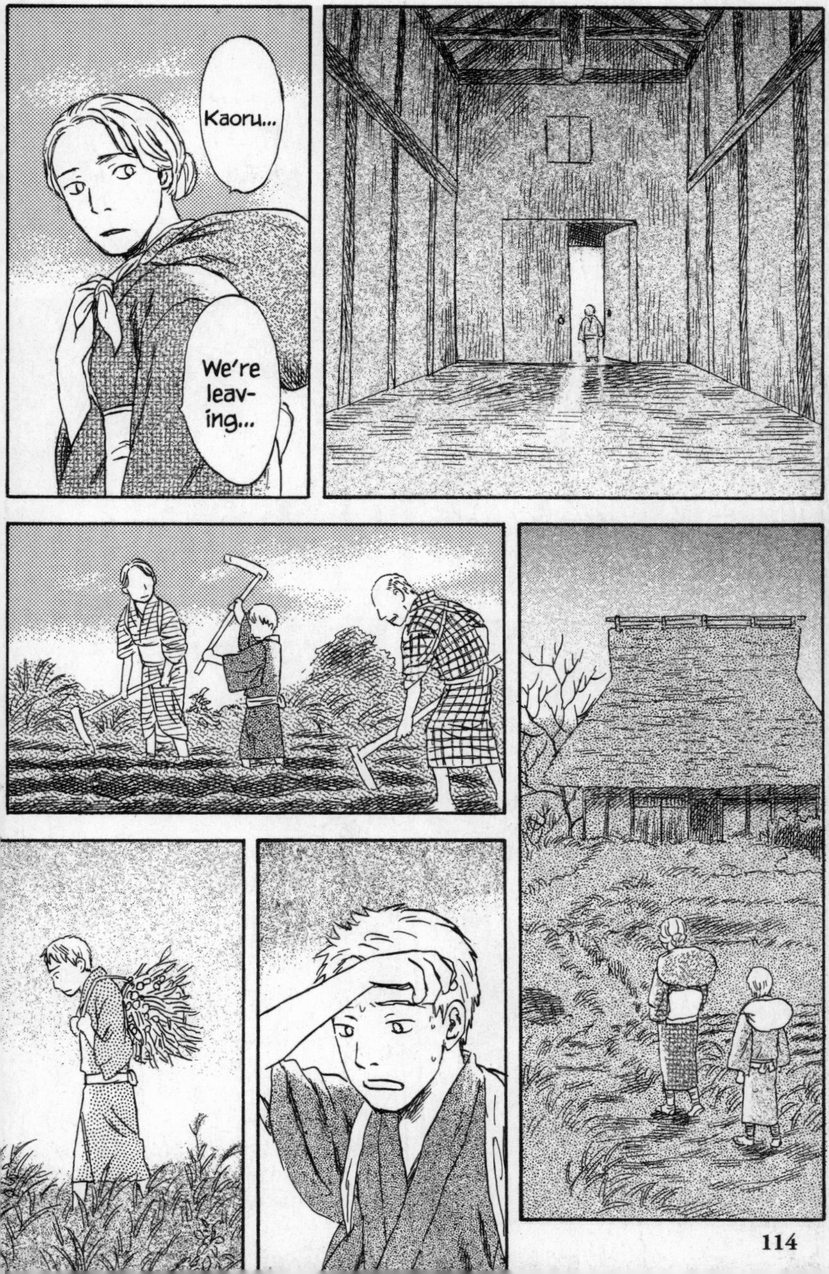
Kaoru...
We're leaving...

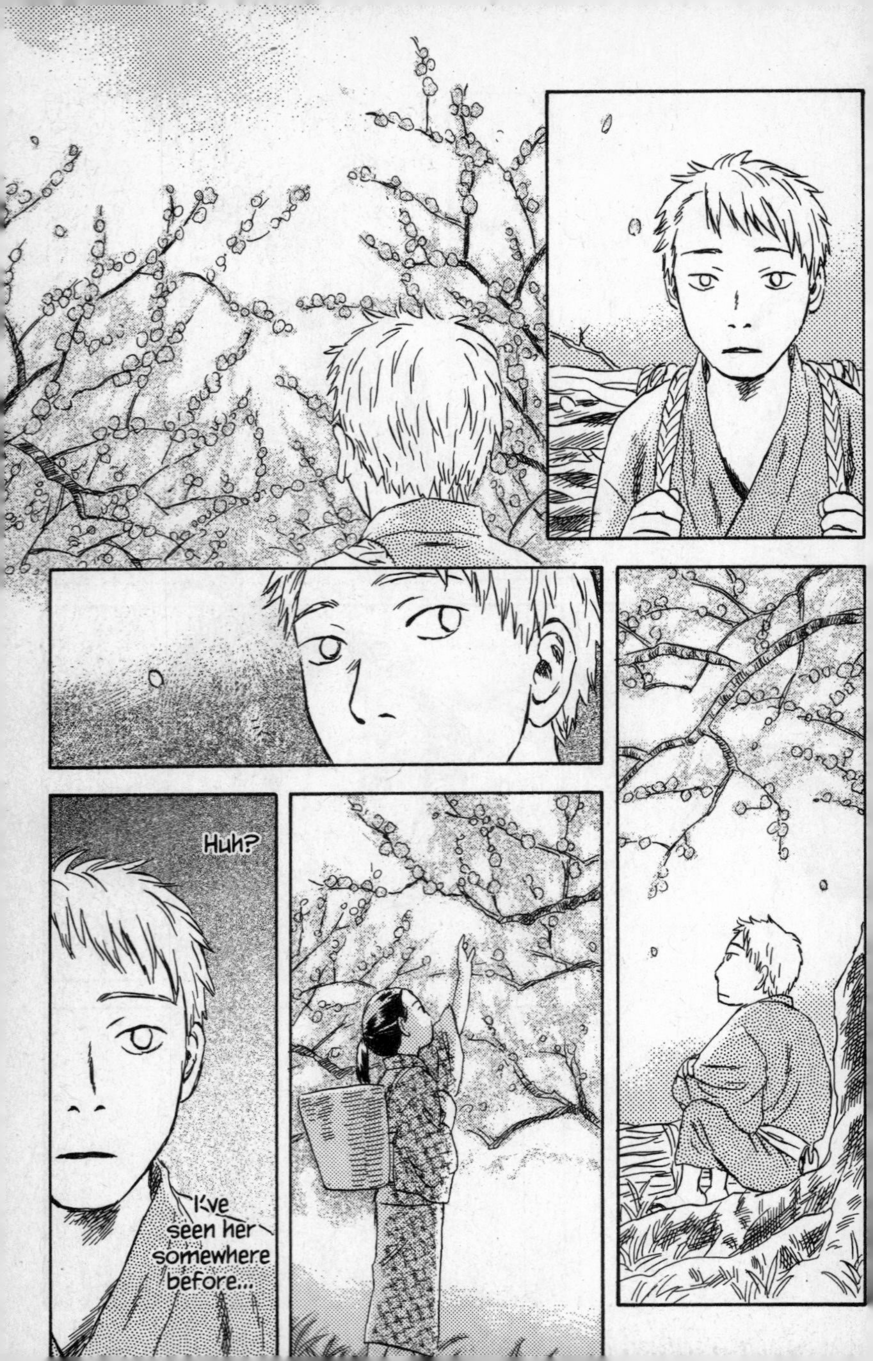
Huh?
I've seen her somewhere before...

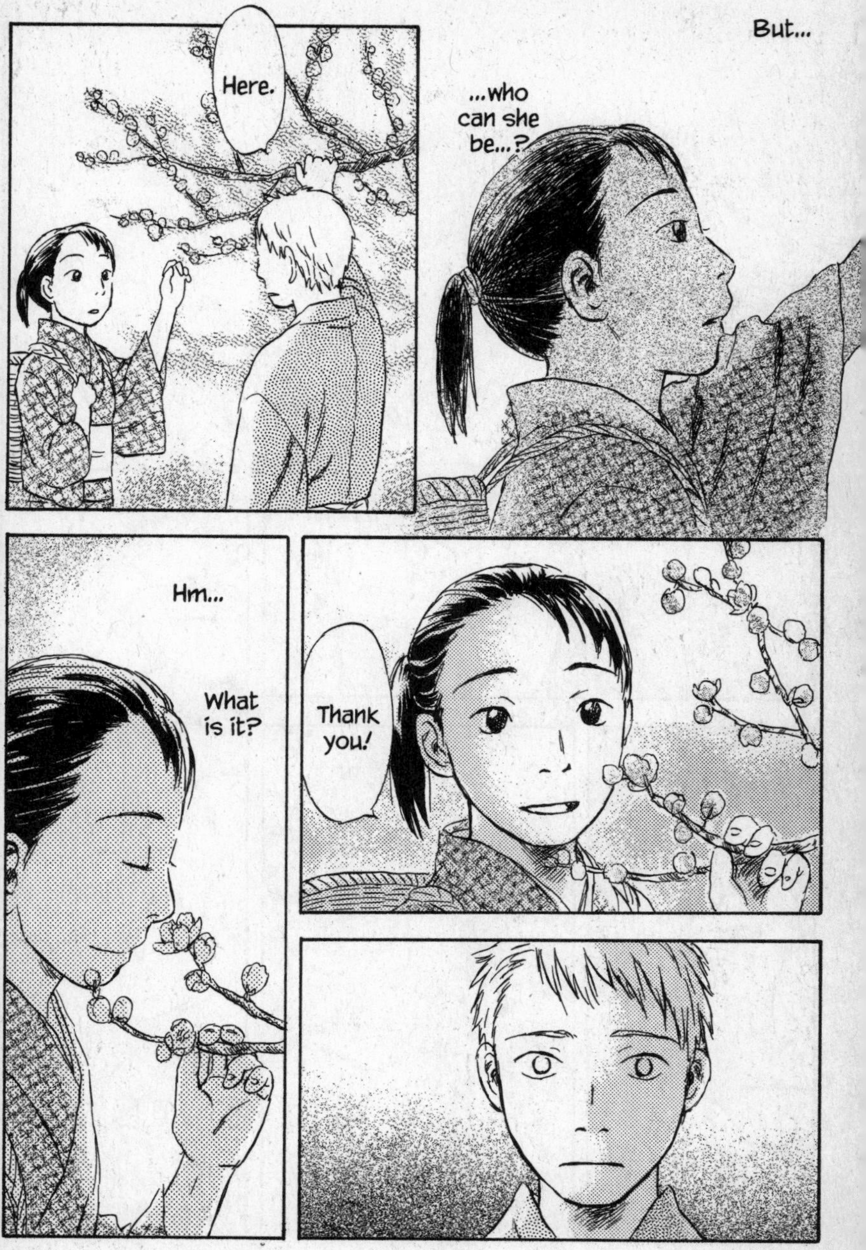
But...
...who can she be...?
Here.
Thank you!
Hm...
What is it?

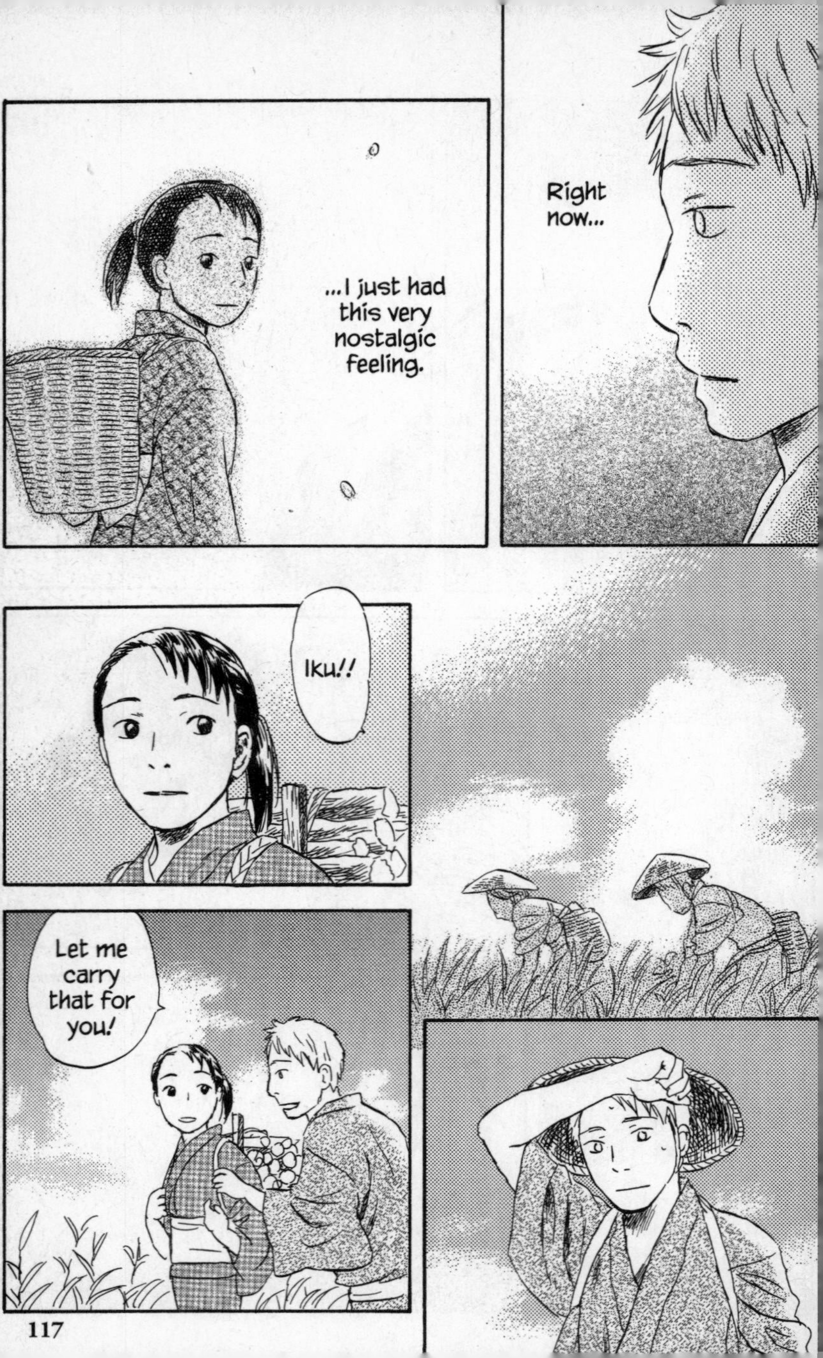
Right now...
...I just had this very nostalgic feeling.
Iku!!
Let me carry that for you!

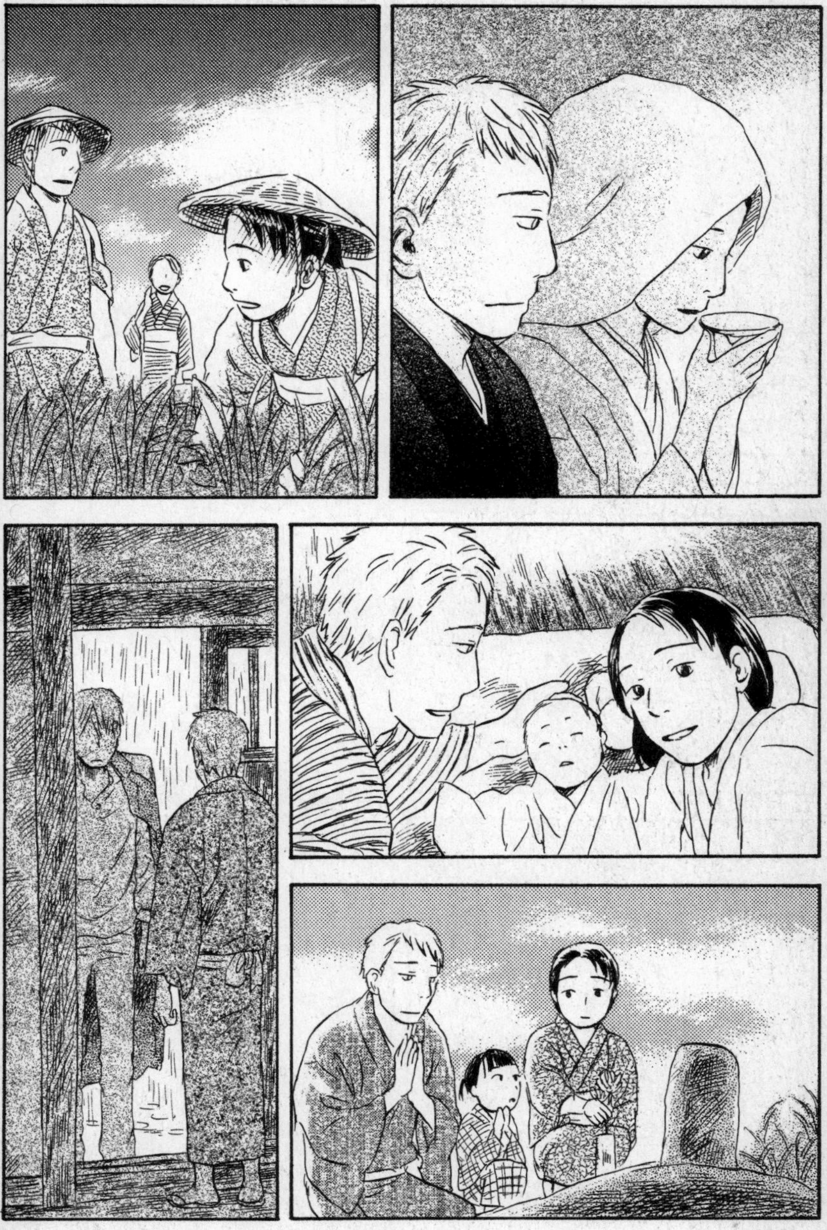

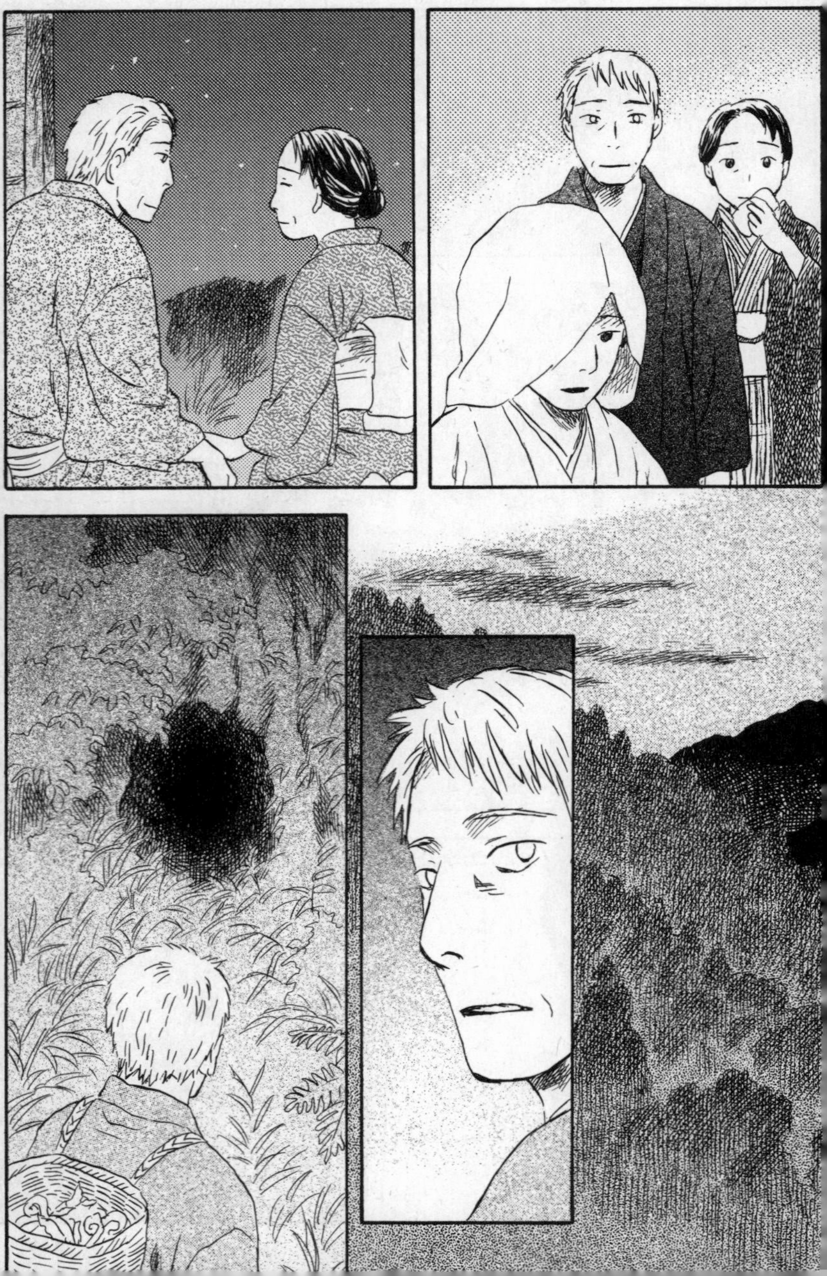

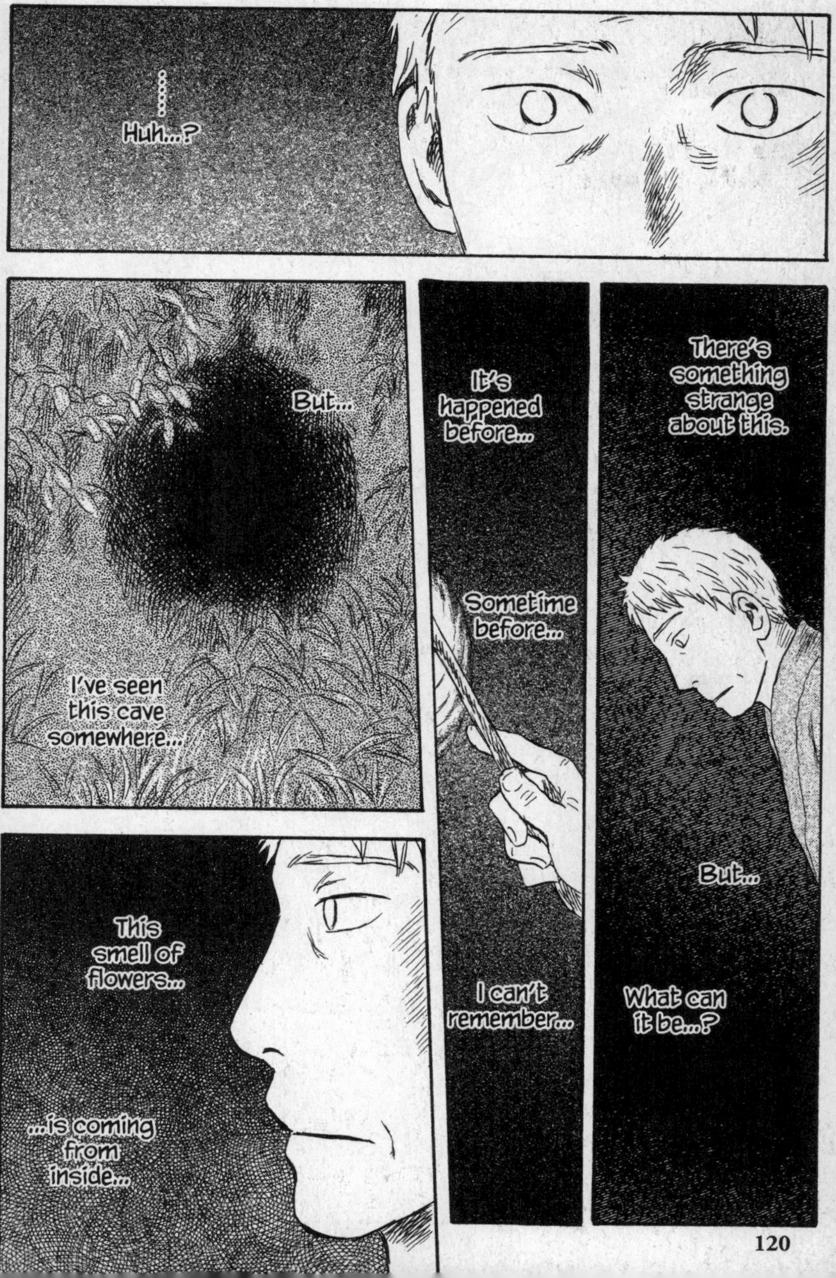
......
Huh...?
There's something strange about this.
But...
What can it be...?
It's happened before...
Sometime before...
I can't remember...
But...
I've seen this cave somewhere...
This smell of flowers...
...is coming from inside...

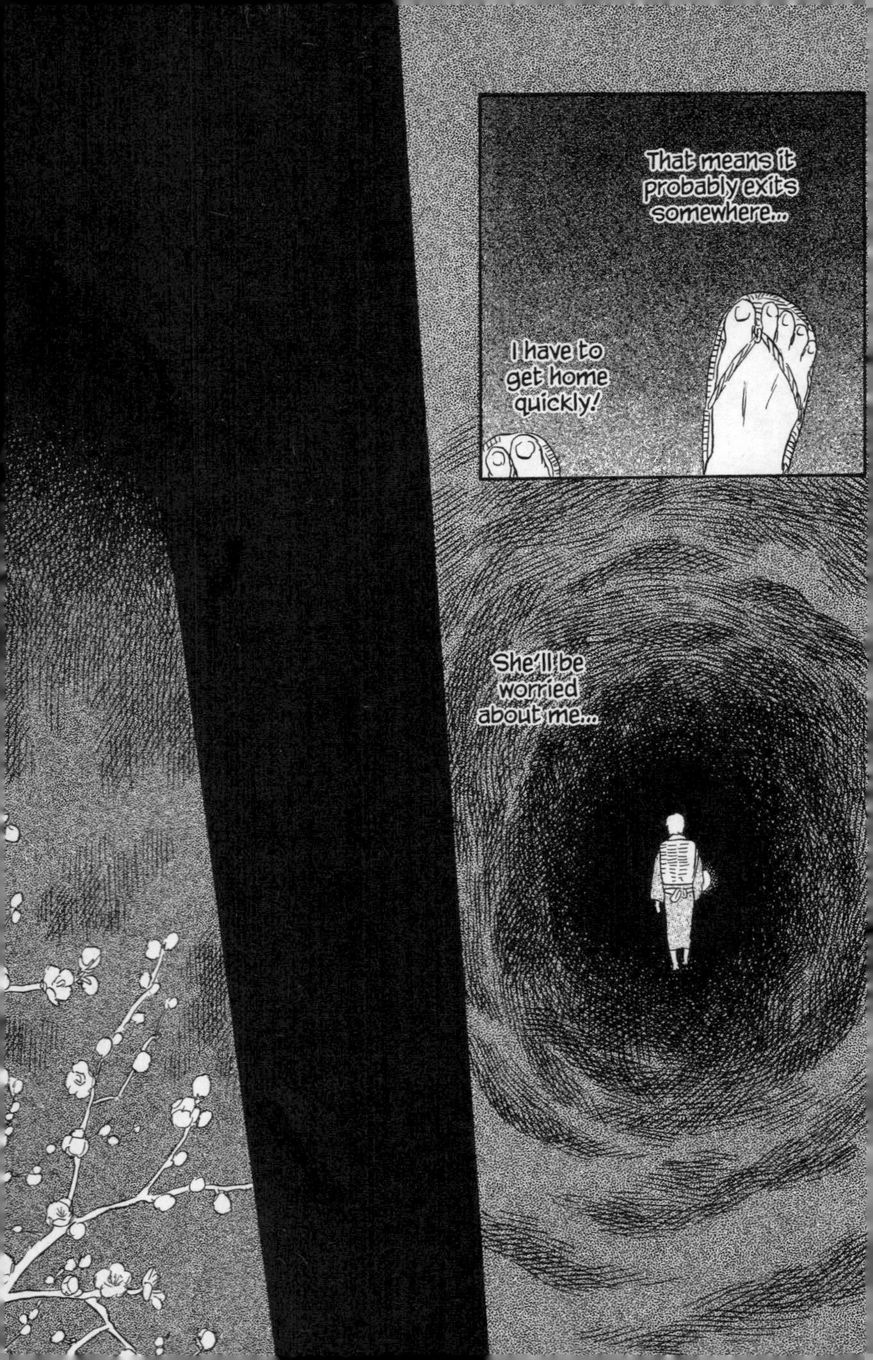
That means it probably exits somewhere...
I have to get home quickly!
She'll be worried about me...

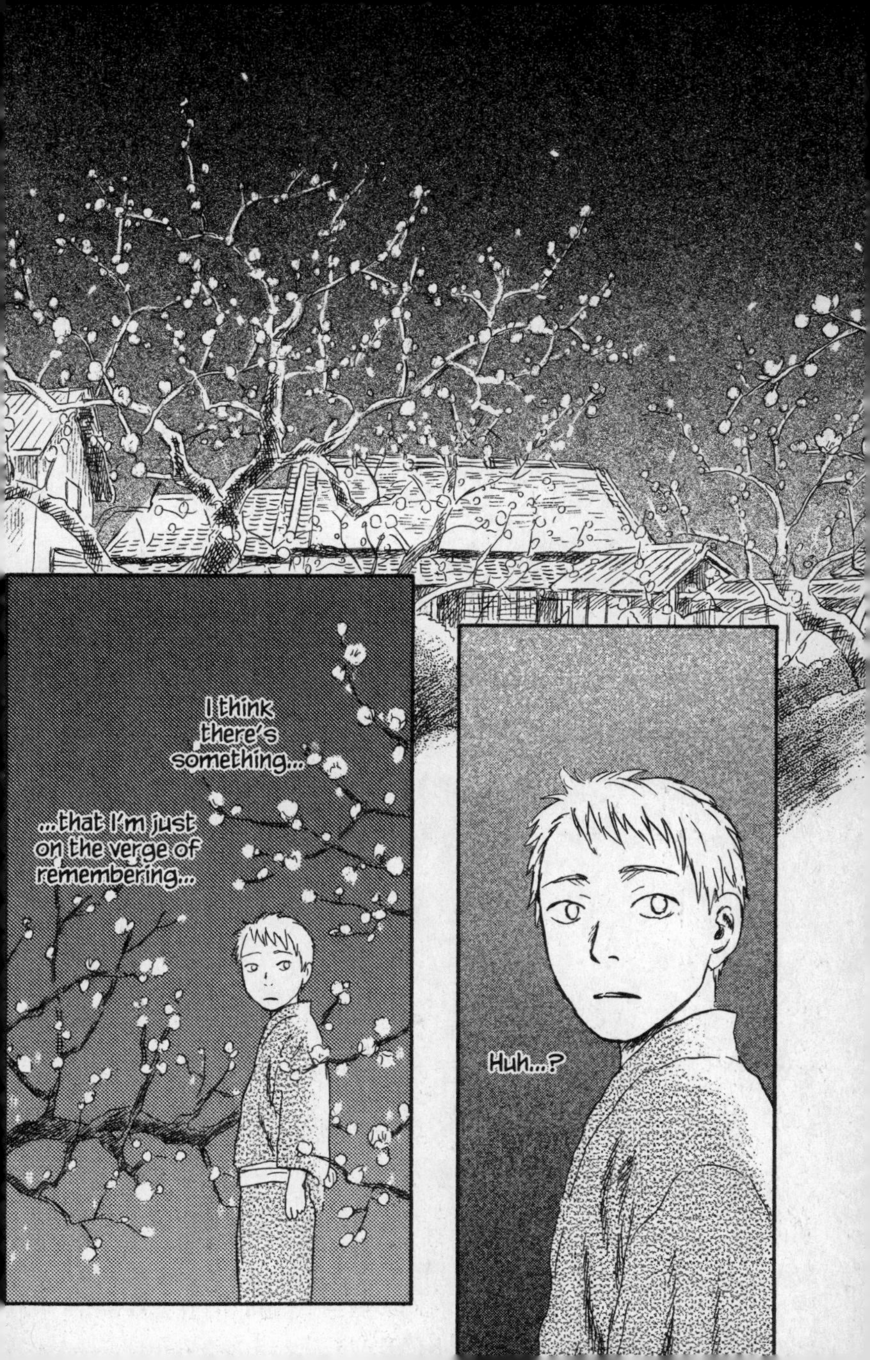
Huh...?
I think there's something...
...that I'm just on the verge of remembering...

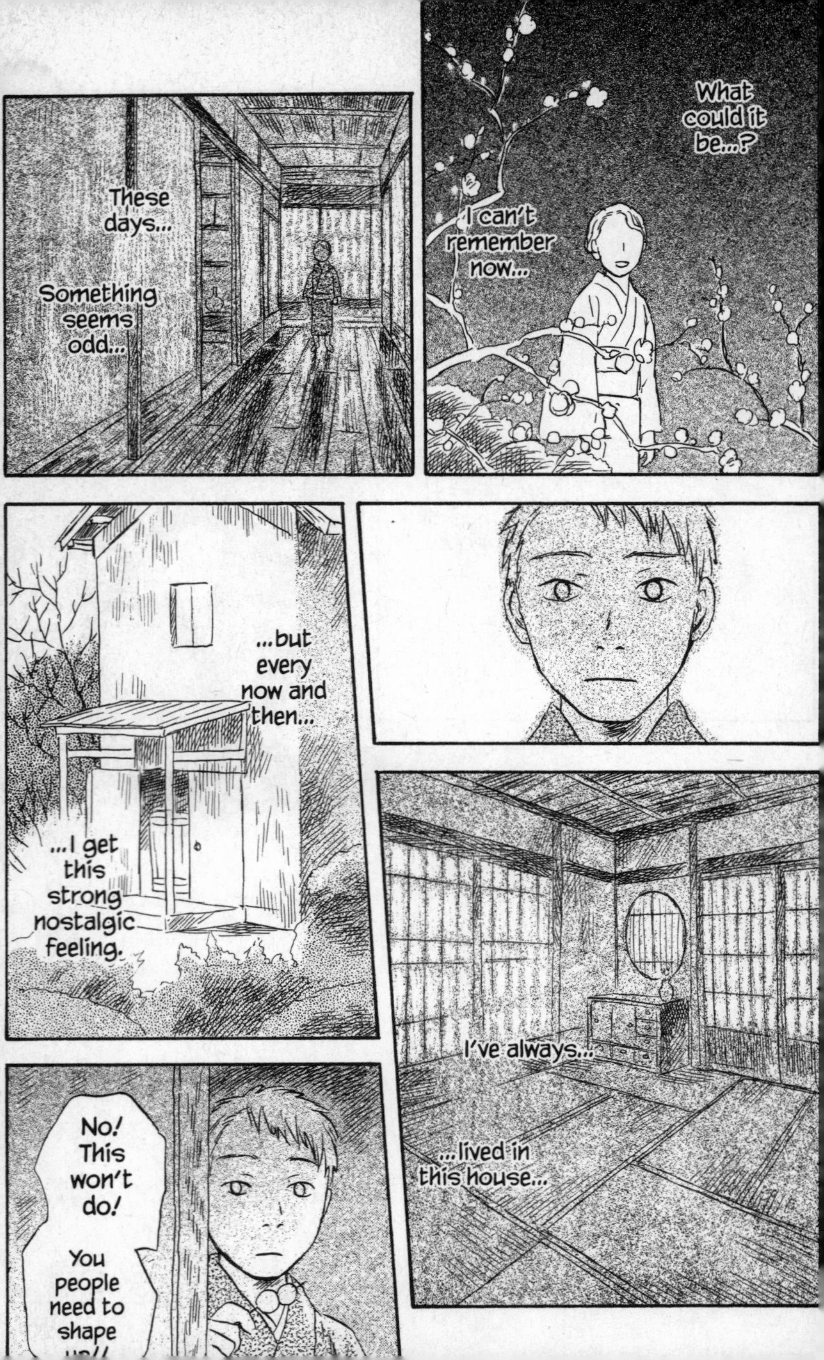
What could it be...?
I can't remember now...
These days...
Something seems odd...
I've always...
...lived in this house...
...but every now and then...
...I get this strong nostalgic feeling.
No! This won't do!
You people need to shape

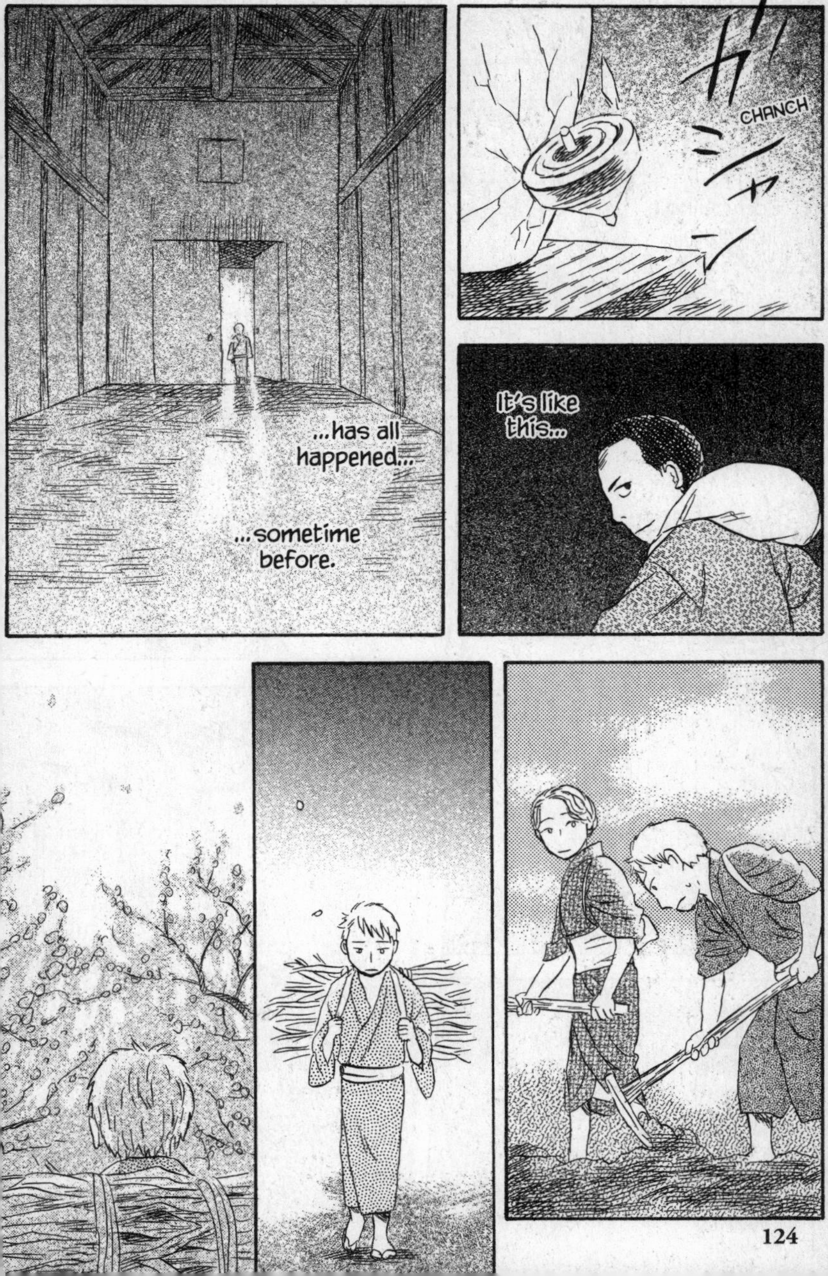
ガシャン
CHANCH
It's like this...
...has all happened...
...sometime before.

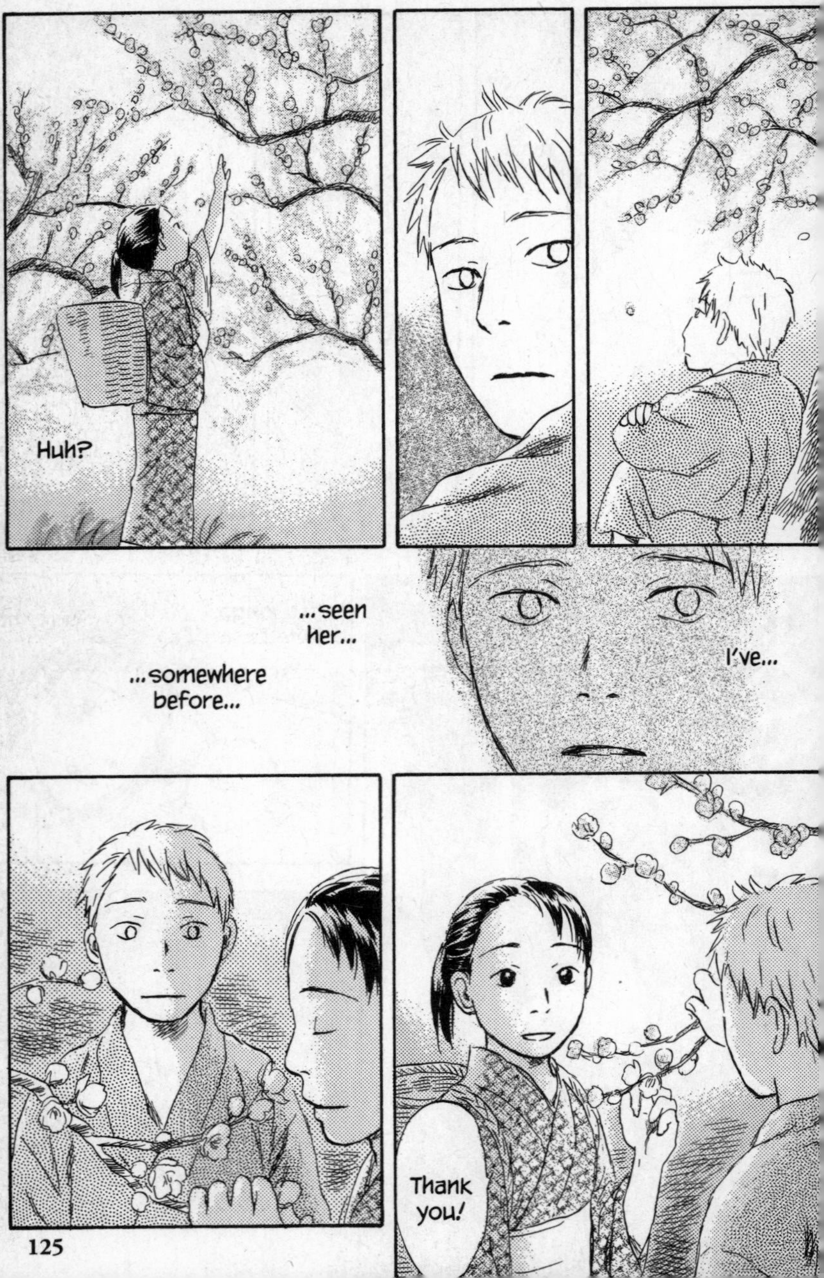
Huh?
I've...
...seen her...
...somewhere before...
Thank you!

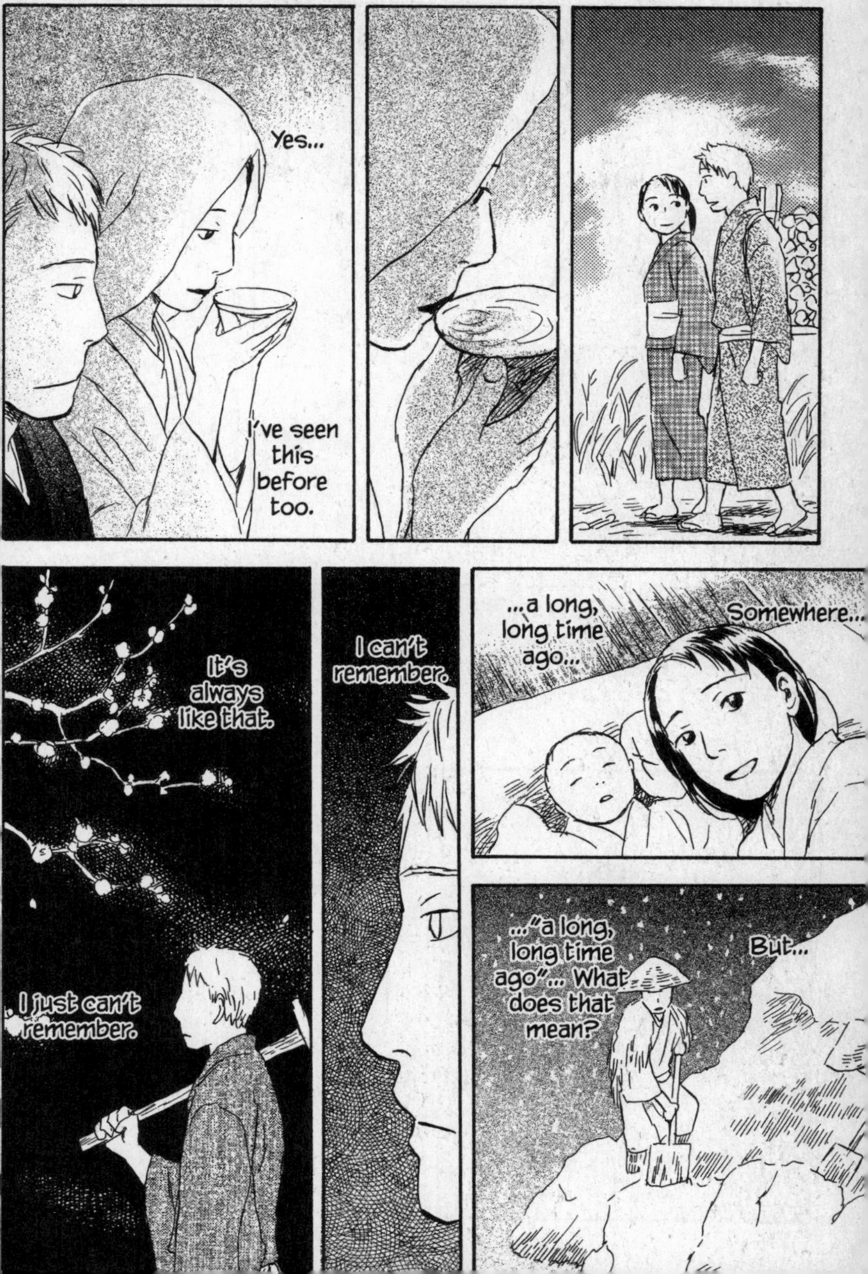
Yes...
I've seen this before too.
Somewhere...
...a long, long time ago...
But...
..."a long, long time ago"... What does that mean?
I can't remember.
It's always like that.
I just can't remember.

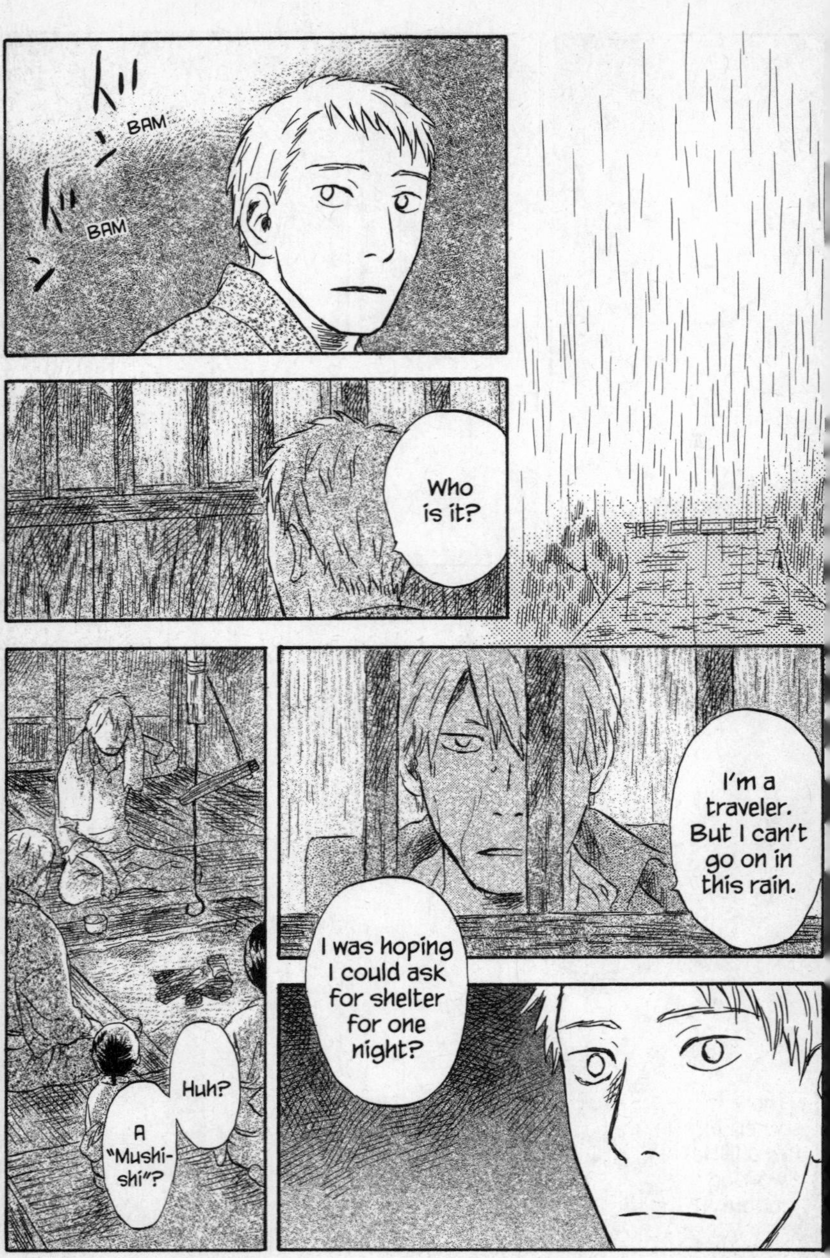
BAM
BAM
Who is it?
I'm a traveler. But I can't go on in this rain.
I was hoping I could ask for shelter for one night?
Huh?
A "Mushi-shi"?

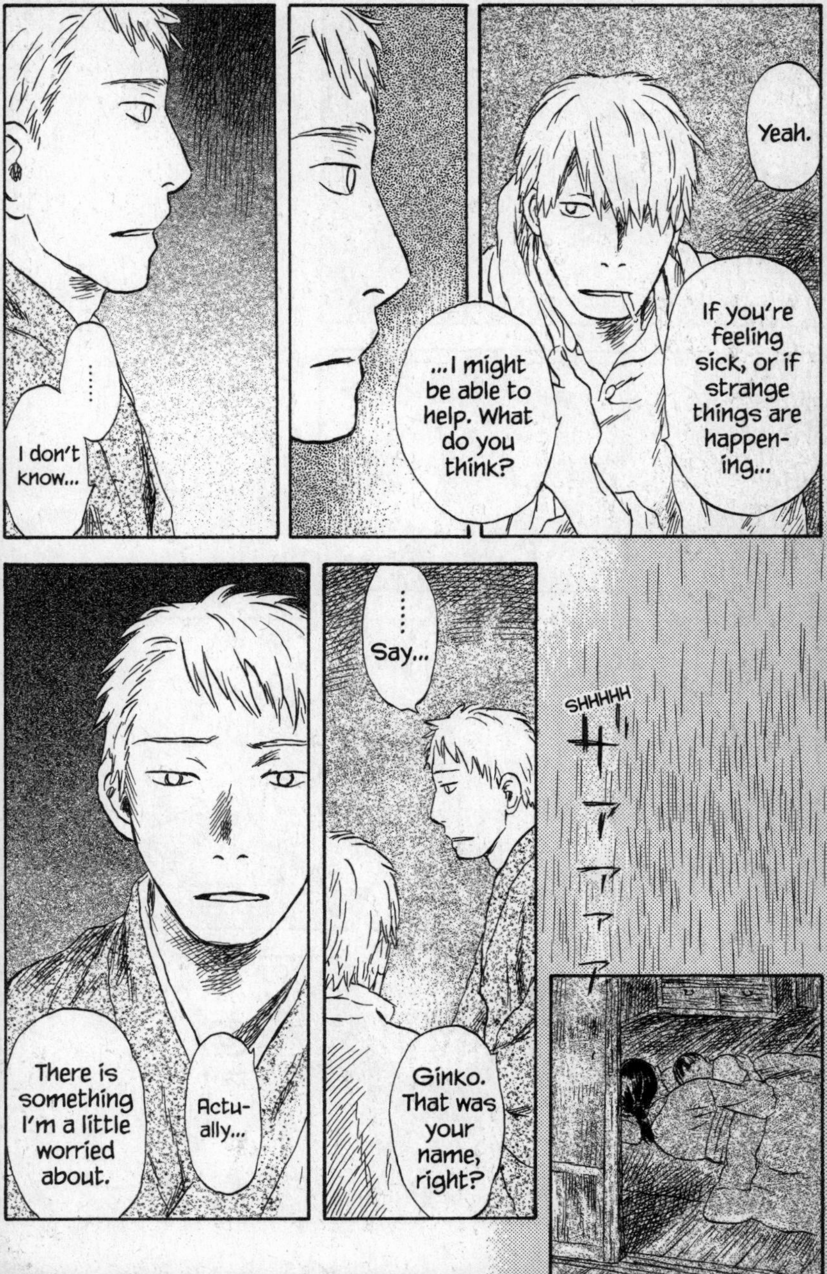
Yeah.
If you're feeling sick, or if strange things are happen-ing...
...I might be able to help. What do you think?
......
I don't know...
SHHHHH
......
Say...
Ginko. That was your name, right?
Actu-ally...
There is something I'm a little worried about.

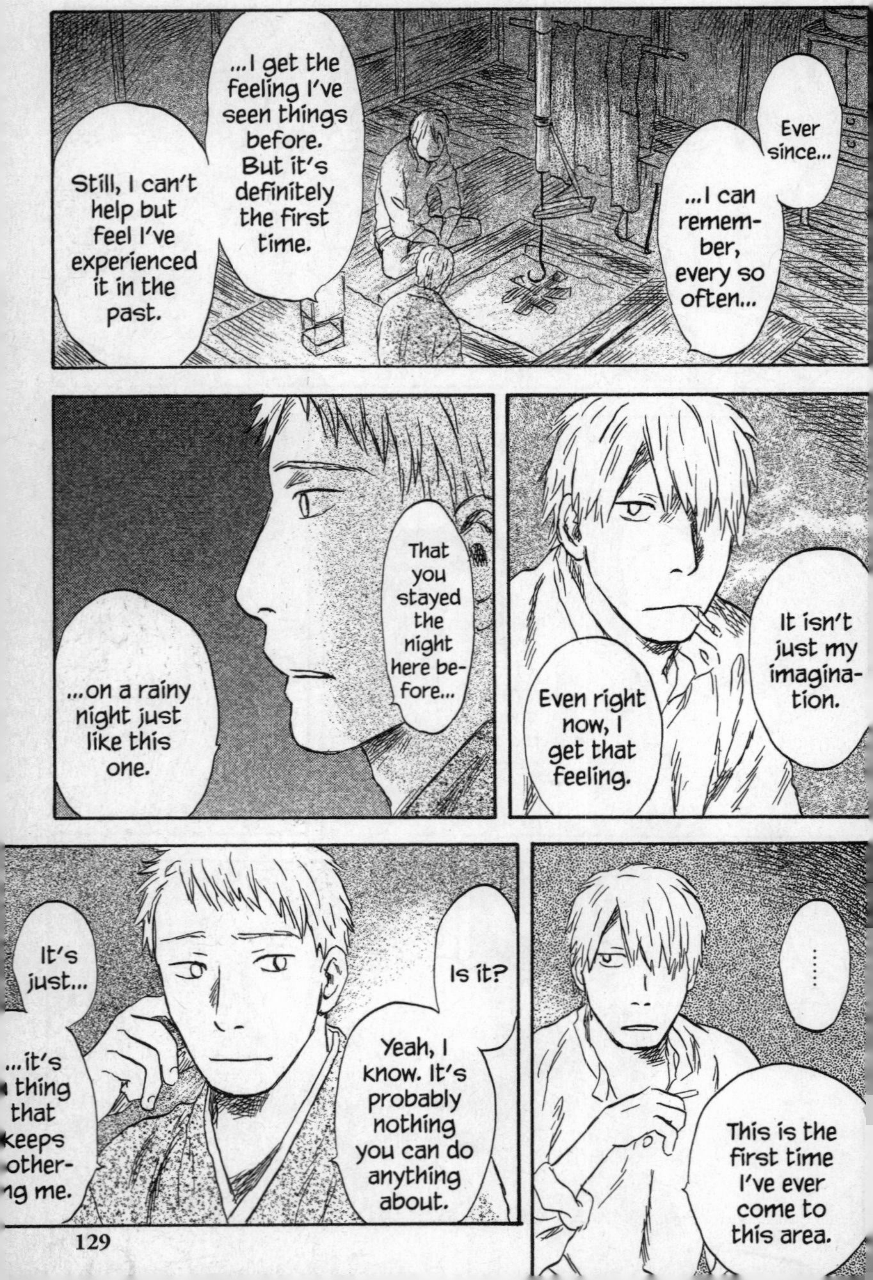
Ever since...
...I can remember, every so often...
...I get the feeling I've seen things before. But it's definitely the first time.
Still, I can't help but feel I've experienced it in the past.
It isn't just my imagination.
Even right now, I get that feeling.
That you stayed the night here before...
...on a rainy night just like this one.
......
This is the first time I've ever come to this area.
Is it?
Yeah, I know. It's probably nothing you can do anything about.
It's just...
...it's thing that keeps other- ng me.

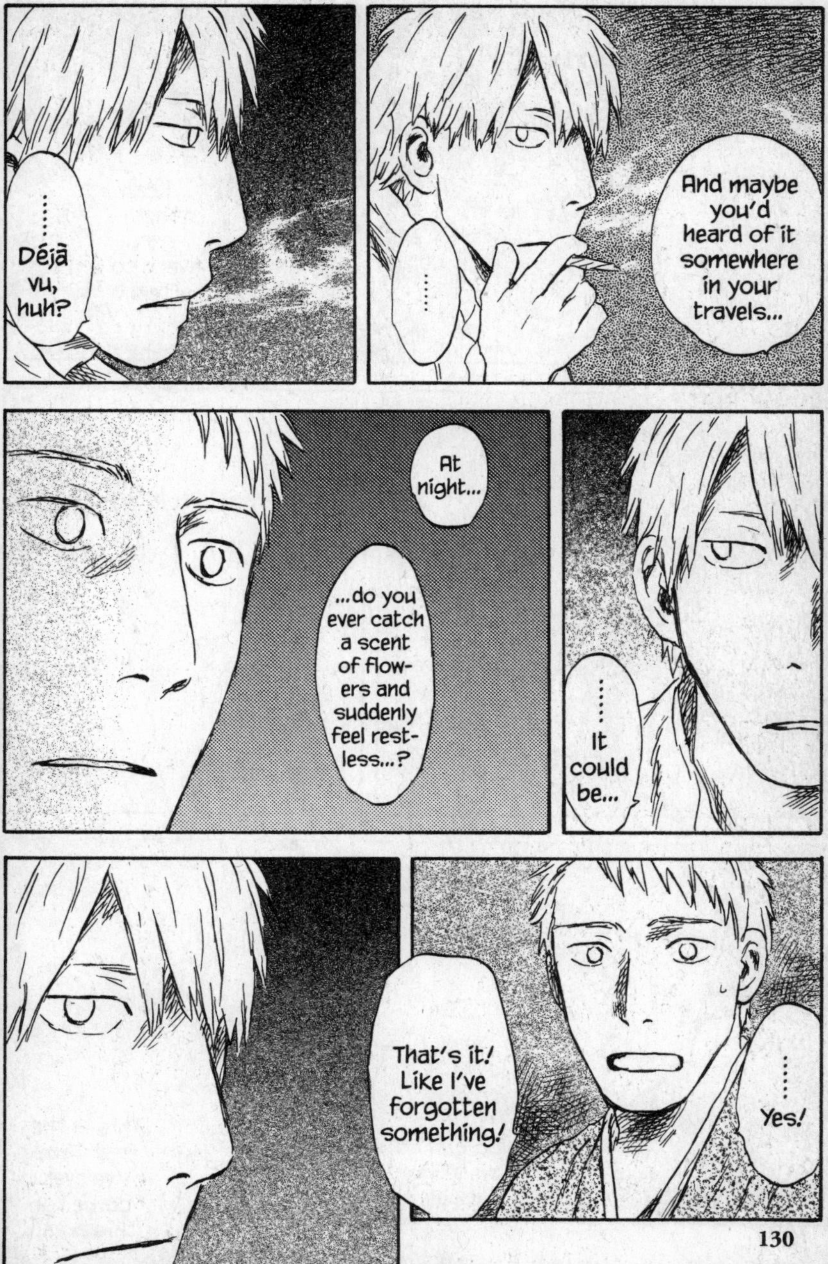
And maybe you'd heard of it somewhere in your travels...
......
...... Déjà vu, huh?
...... It could be...
At night...
...do you ever catch a scent of flowers and suddenly feel rest-less...?
...... Yes!
That's it! Like I've forgotten something!

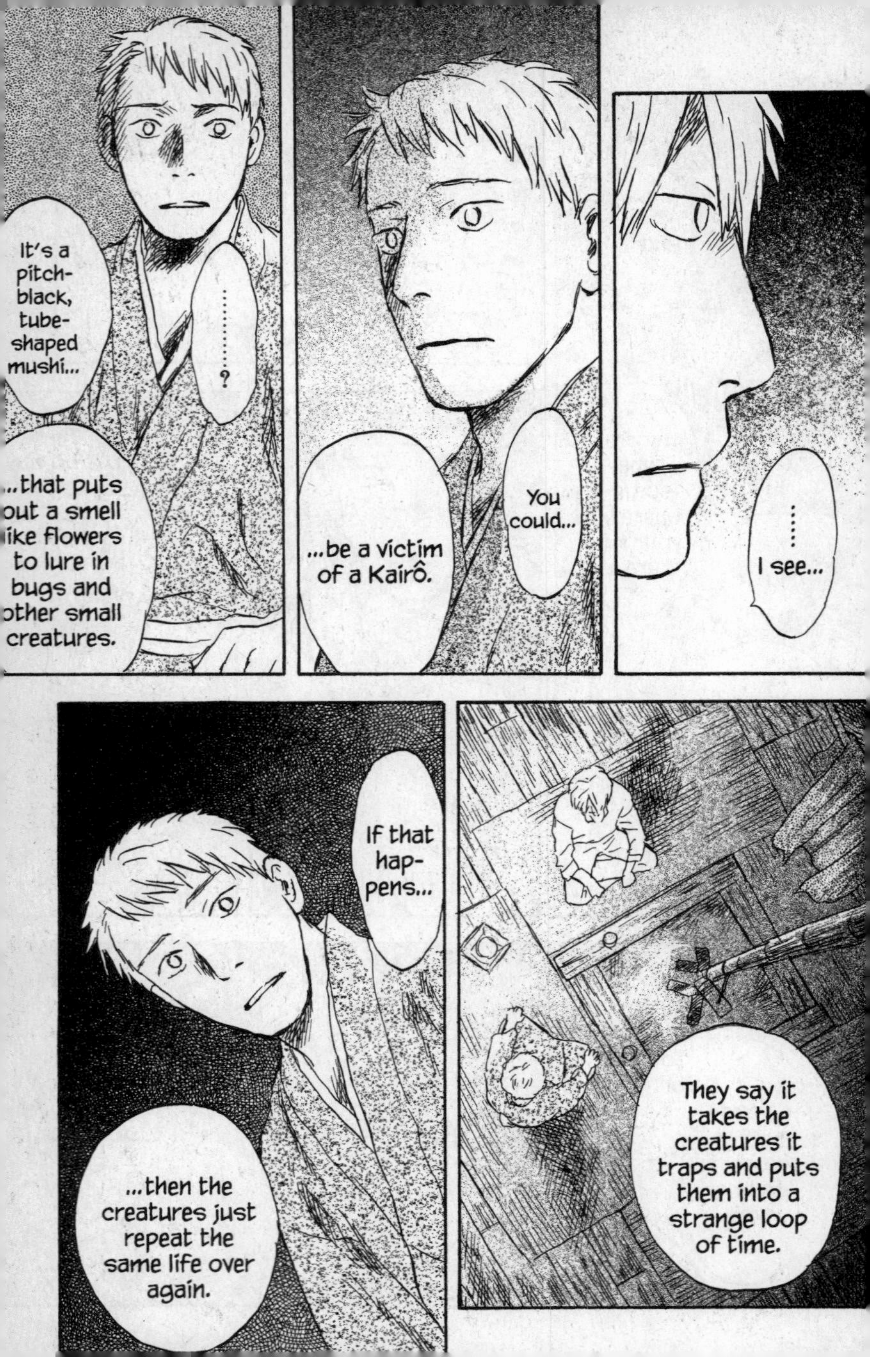
......
I see...
You could...
...be a victim of a Kairô.
It's a pitch-black, tube-shaped mushi...
......?
...that puts out a smell ike flowers to lure in bugs and other small creatures.
They say it takes the creatures it traps and puts them into a strange loop of time.
If that happens...
...then the creatures just repeat the same life over again.

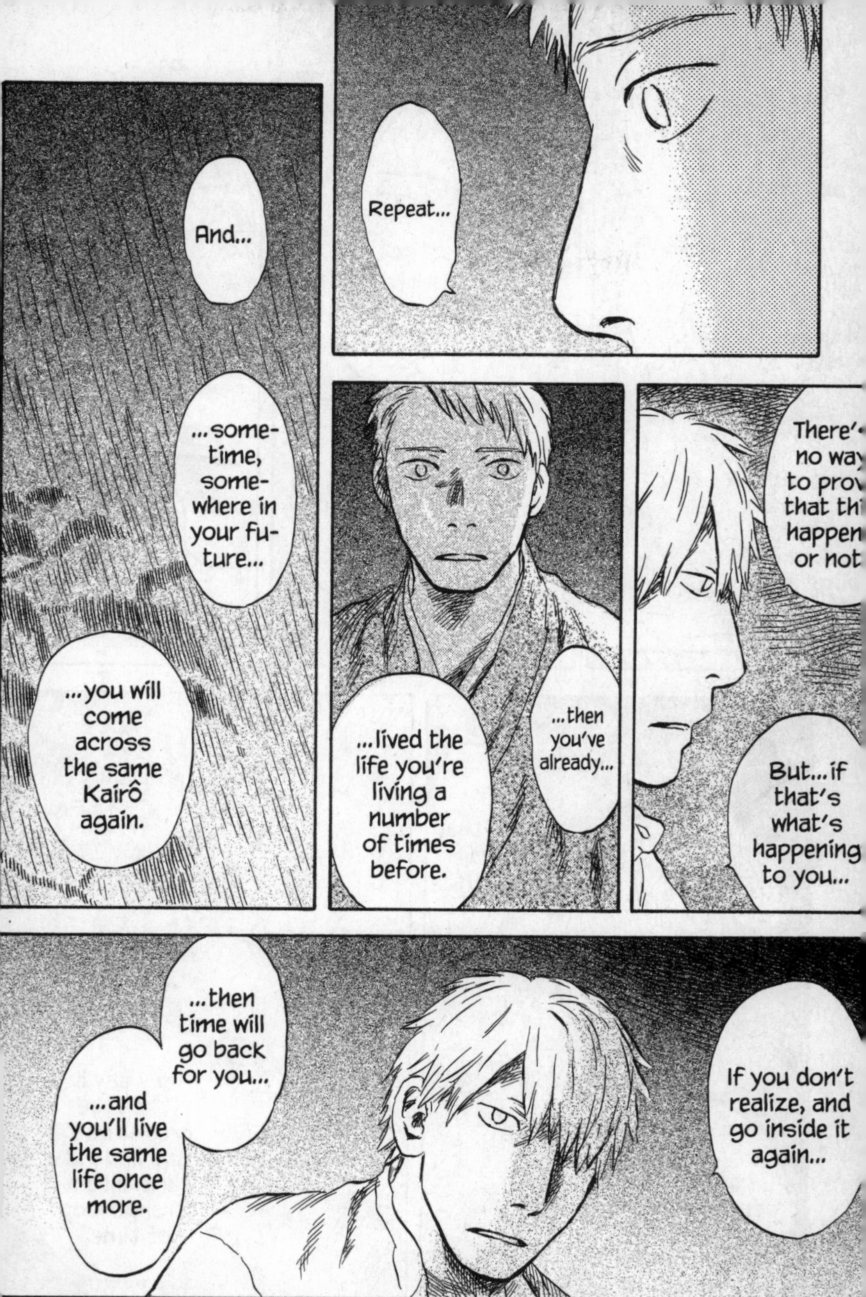
Repeat...
There' no way to prov that thi happen or not
But...if that's what's happening to you...
...then you've already...
...lived the life you're living a number of times before.
And...
...some-time, some-where in your fu-ture...
...you will come across the same Kairô again.
If you don't realize, and go inside it again...
...then time will go back for you...
...and you'll live the same life once more.

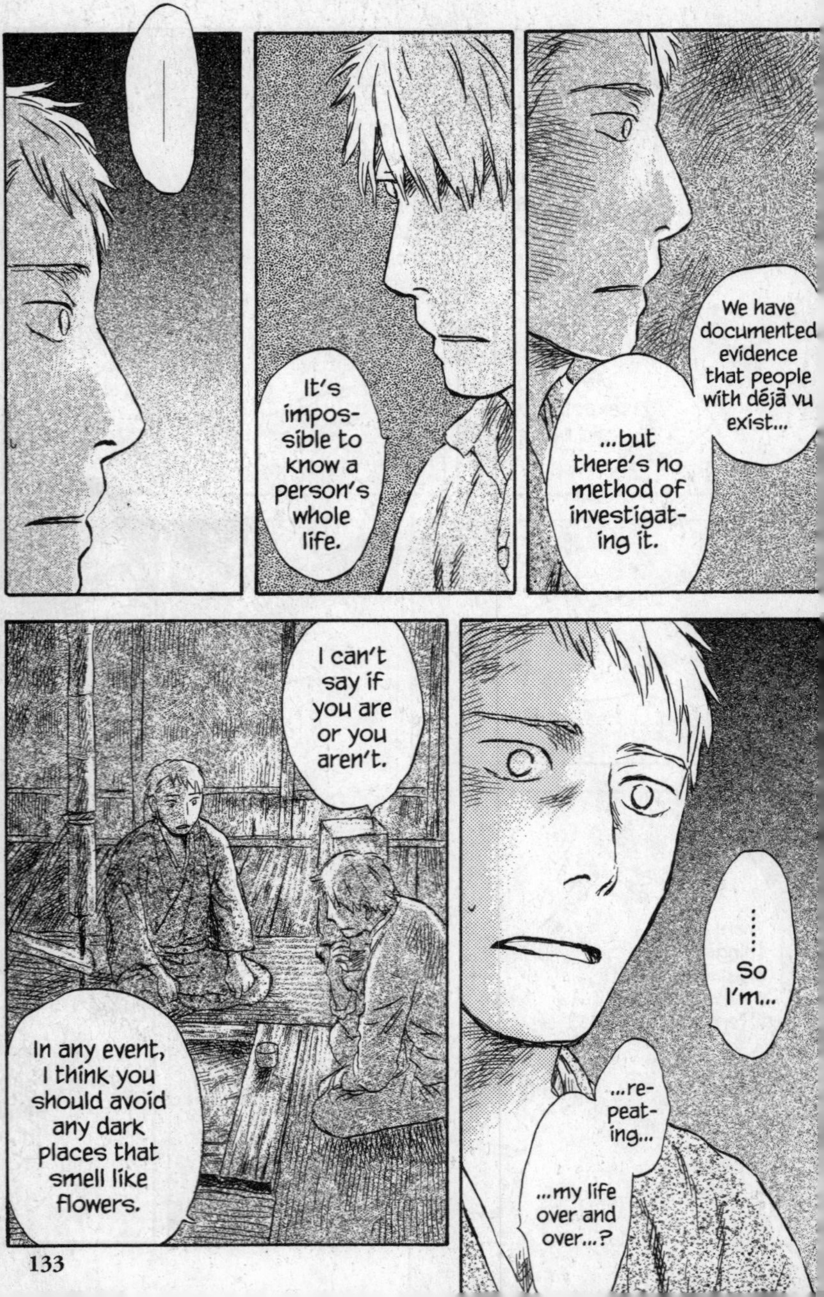
We have documented evidence that people with déjà vu exist...
...but there's no method of investigat-ing it.
It's impos-sible to know a person's whole life.
—
......
So I'm...
...re-peat-ing...
...my life over and over...?
I can't say if you are or you aren't.
In any event, I think you should avoid any dark places that smell like flowers.

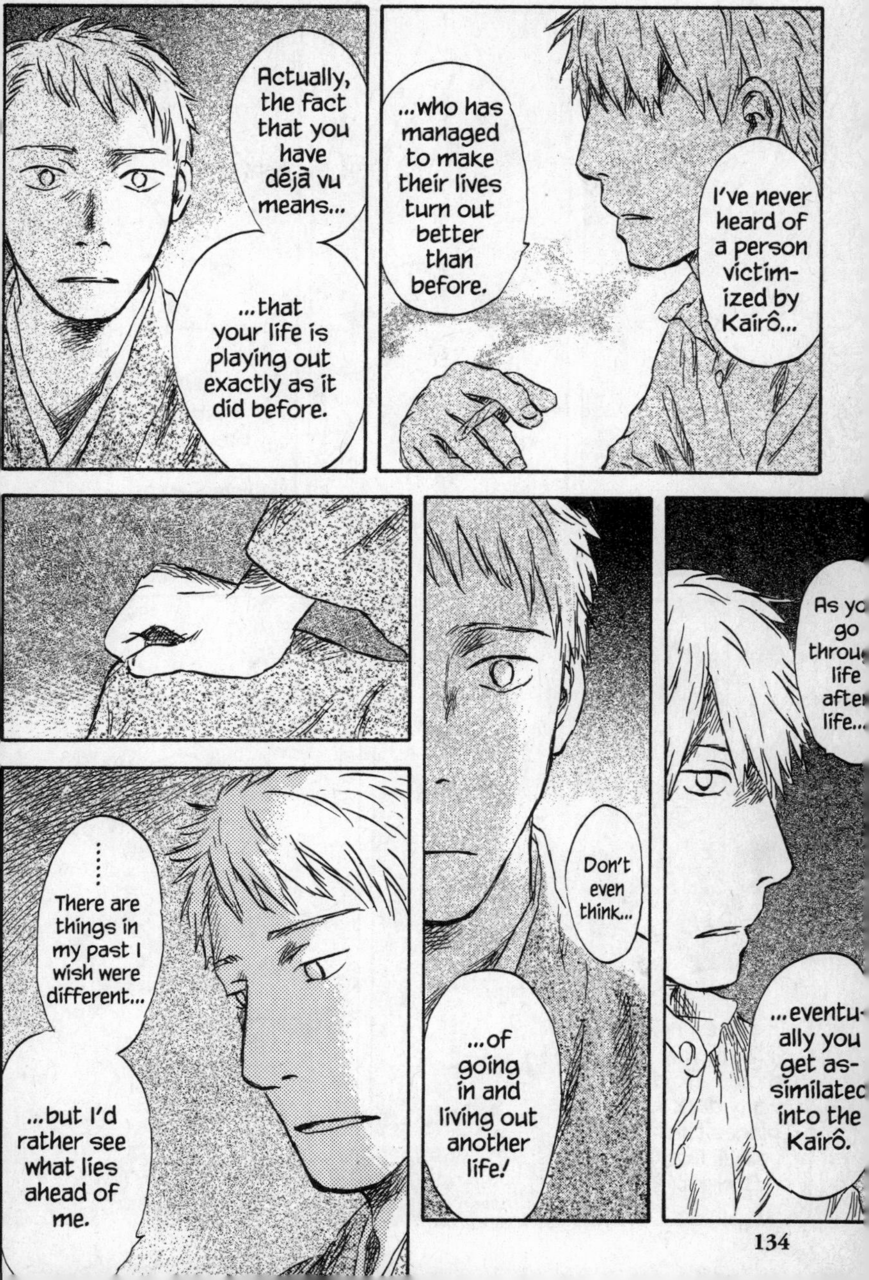
I've never heard of a person victimized by Kairô...
...who has managed to make their lives turn out better than before.
Actually, the fact that you have déjà vu means...
...that your life is playing out exactly as it did before.
As yo go throu life afte life...
...eventually you get as-similated into the Kairô.
Don't even think...
...of going in and living out another life!
......
There are things in my past I wish were different...
...but I'd rather see what lies ahead of me.

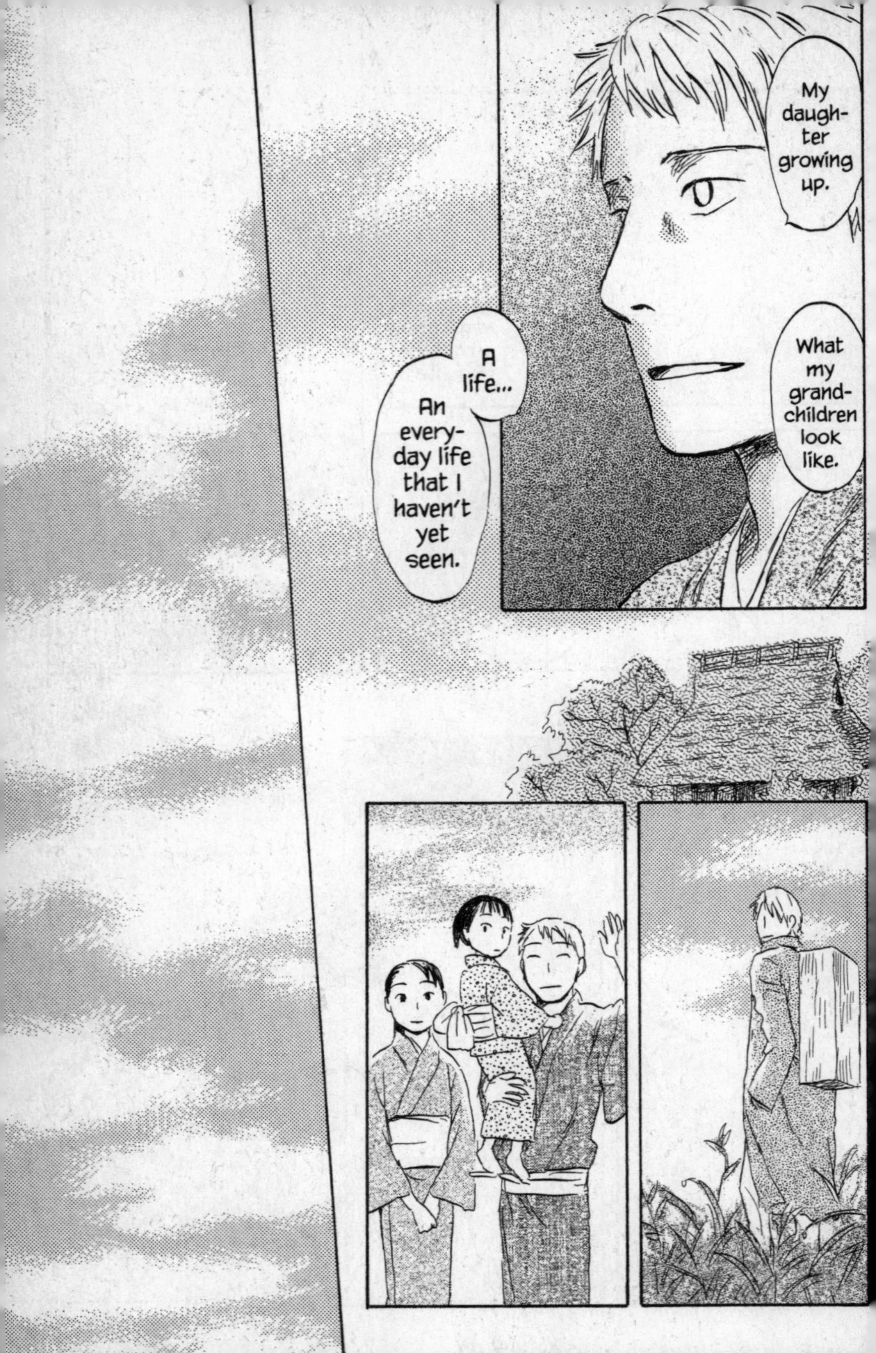
My daughter growing up.
What my grandchildren look like.
A life...
An everyday life that I haven't yet seen.

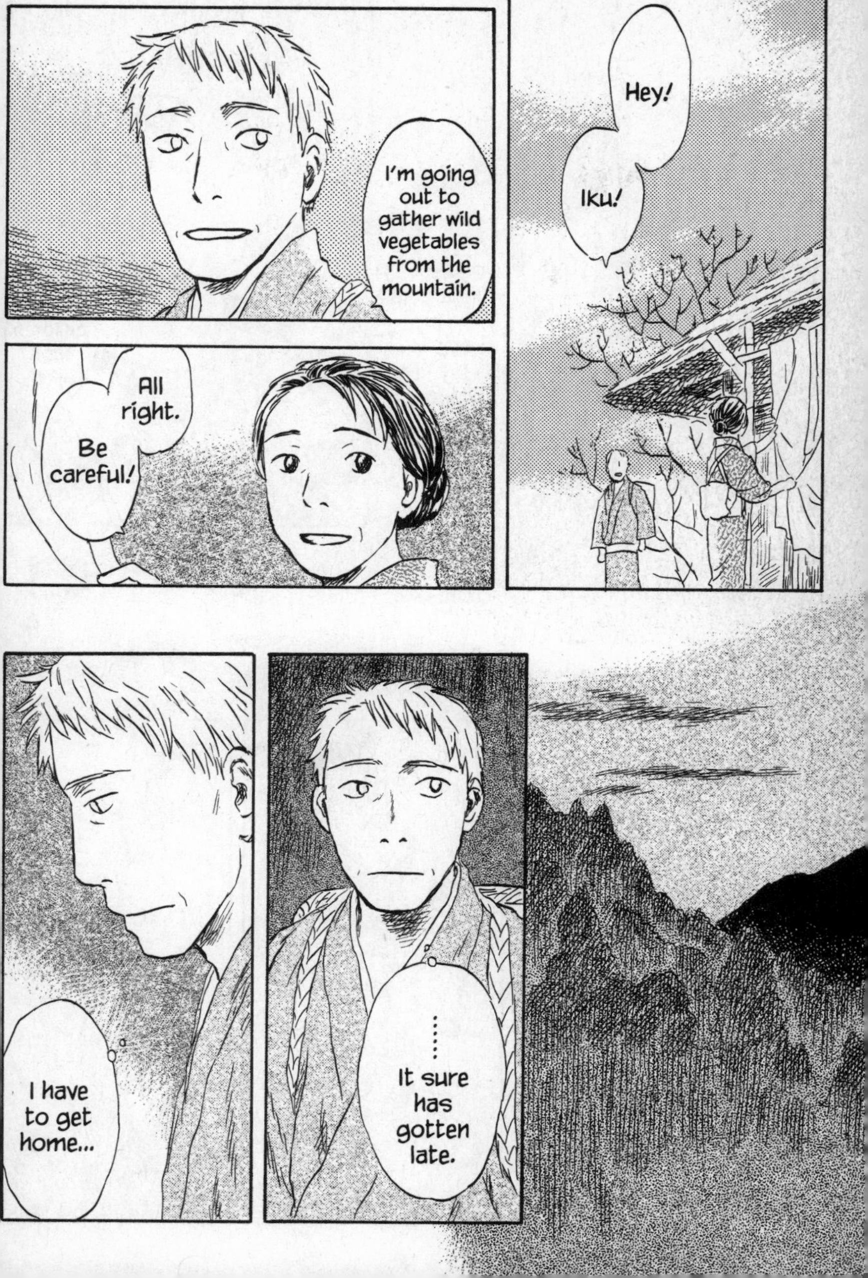

Hey!
Iku!
I'm going out to gather wild vegetables from the mountain.
All right.
Be careful!
......
It sure has gotten late.
I have to get home...

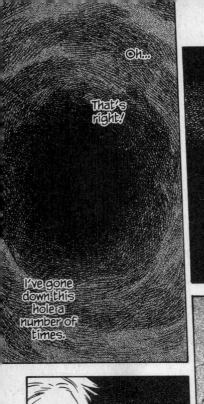

Oh...

That's right!

I've gone down this hole a number of times.

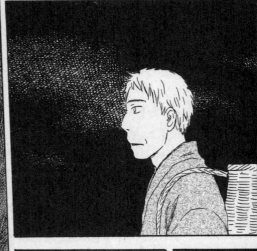

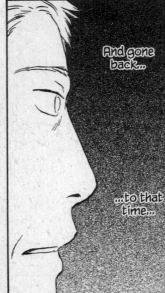

And gone back...

...to that time...

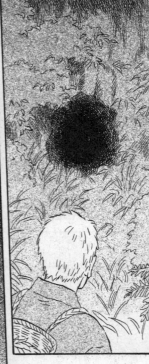

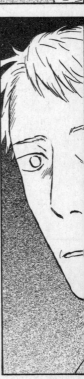

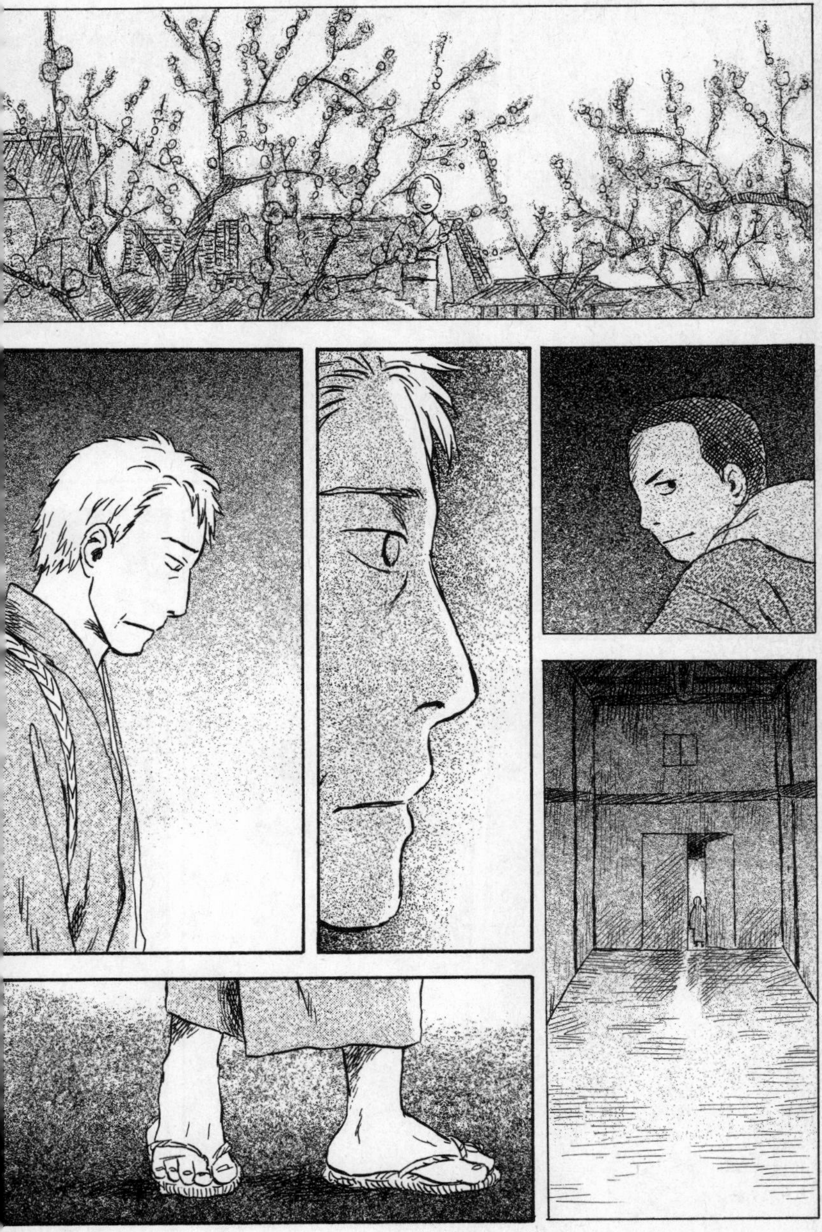

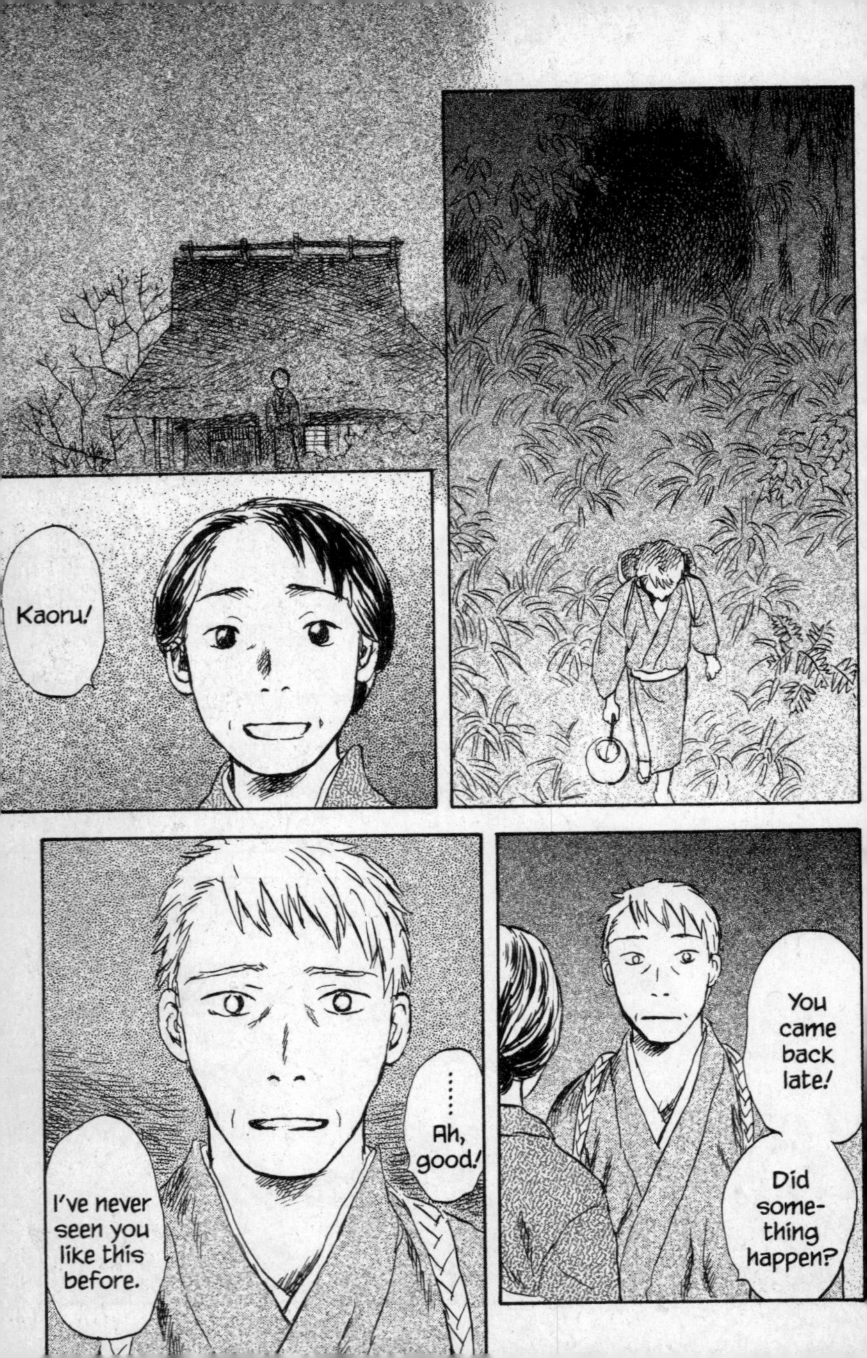
Kaoru!
You came back late!
Did something happen?
......Ah, good!
I've never seen you like this before.

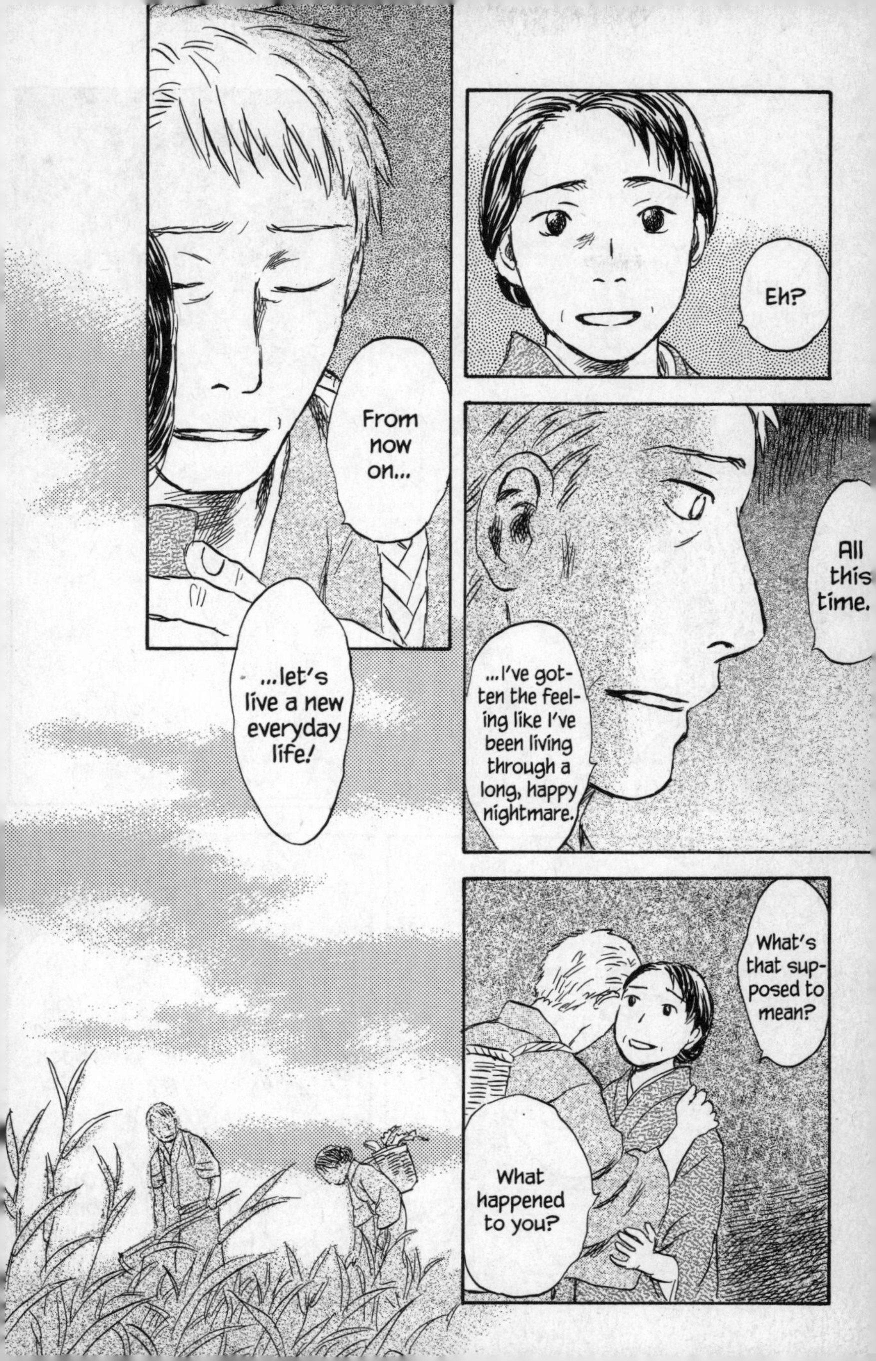
From now on...
...let's live a new everyday life!
Eh?
All this time.
...I've gotten the feeling like I've been living through a long, happy nightmare.
What's that supposed to mean?
What happened to you?

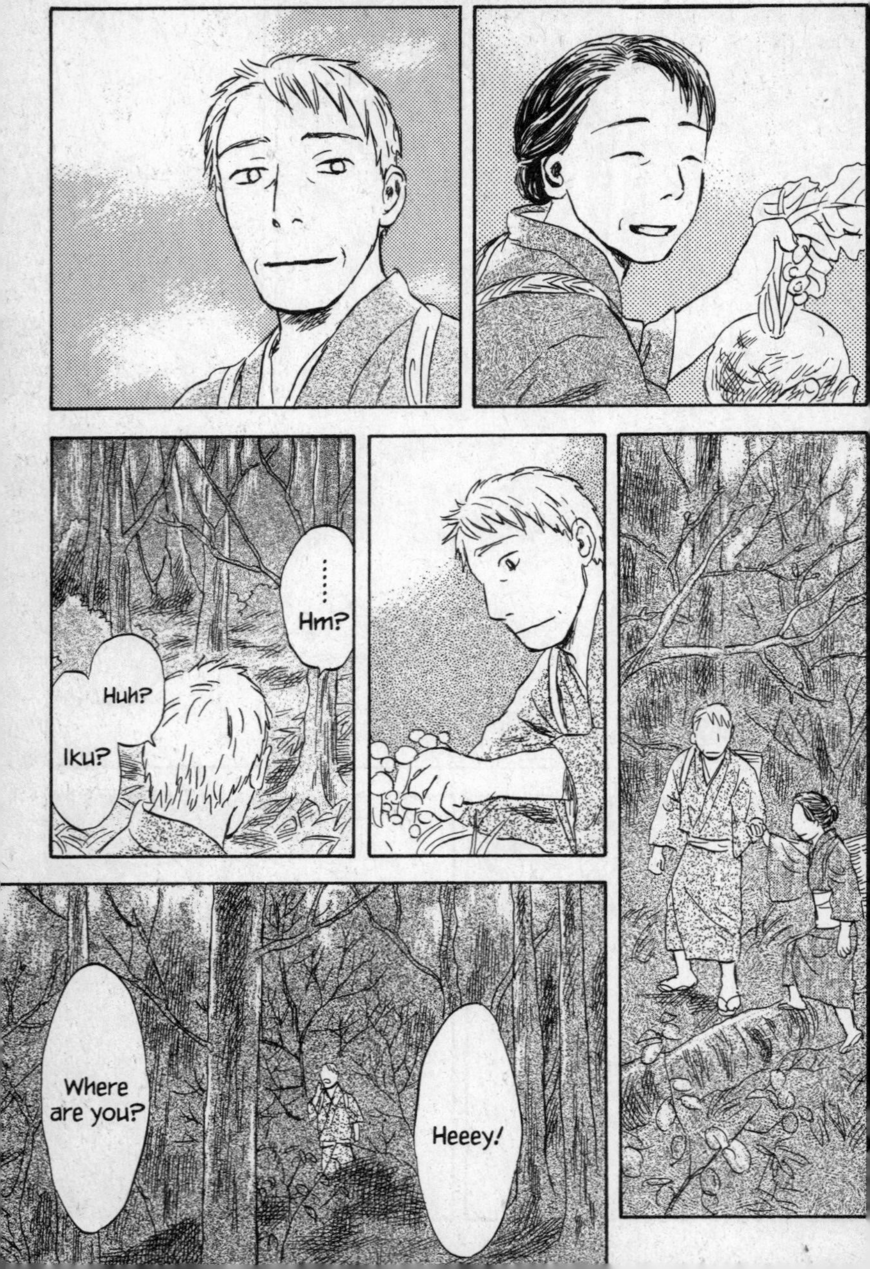

...... Hm?
Huh? Iku?
Heeey!
Where are you?

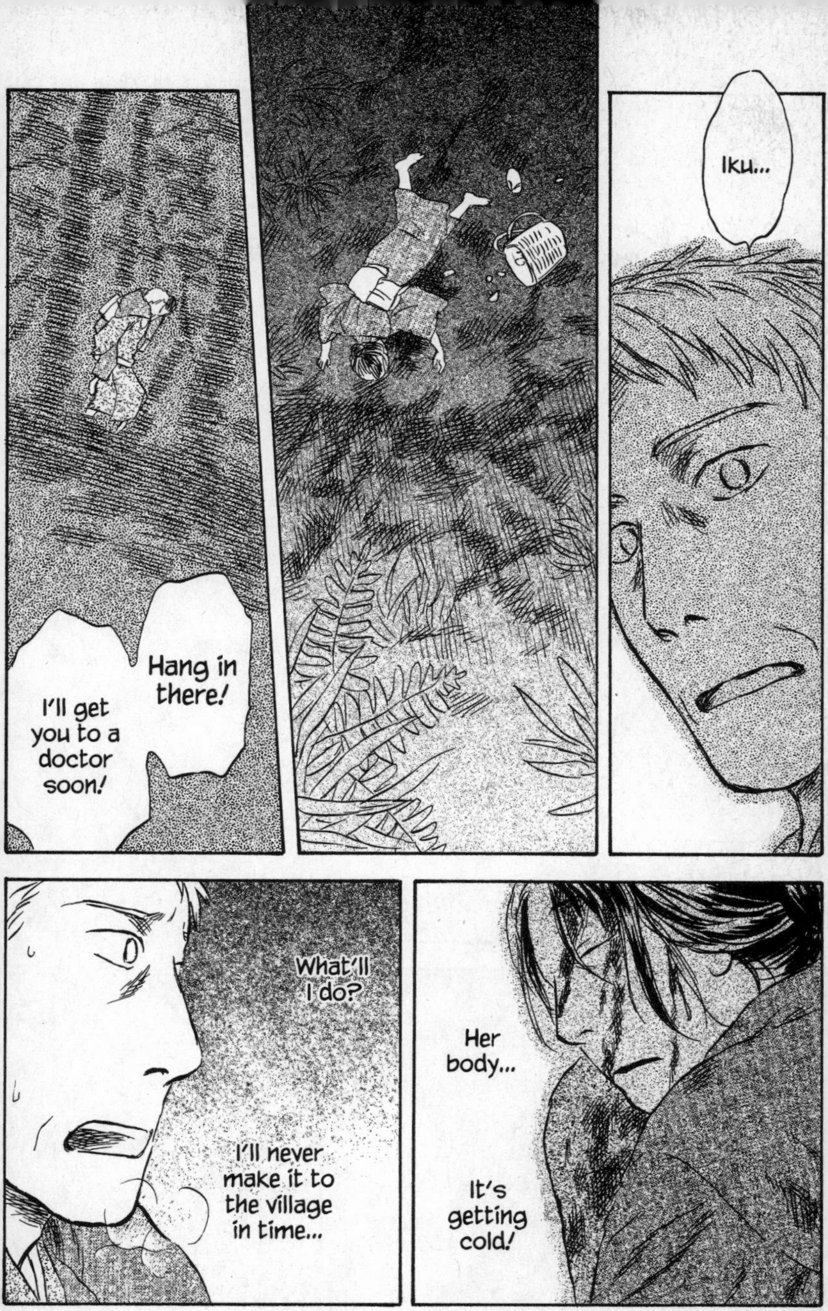
Iku...
Hang in there!
I'll get you to a doctor soon!
Her body...
It's getting cold!
What'll I do?
I'll never make it to the village in time...

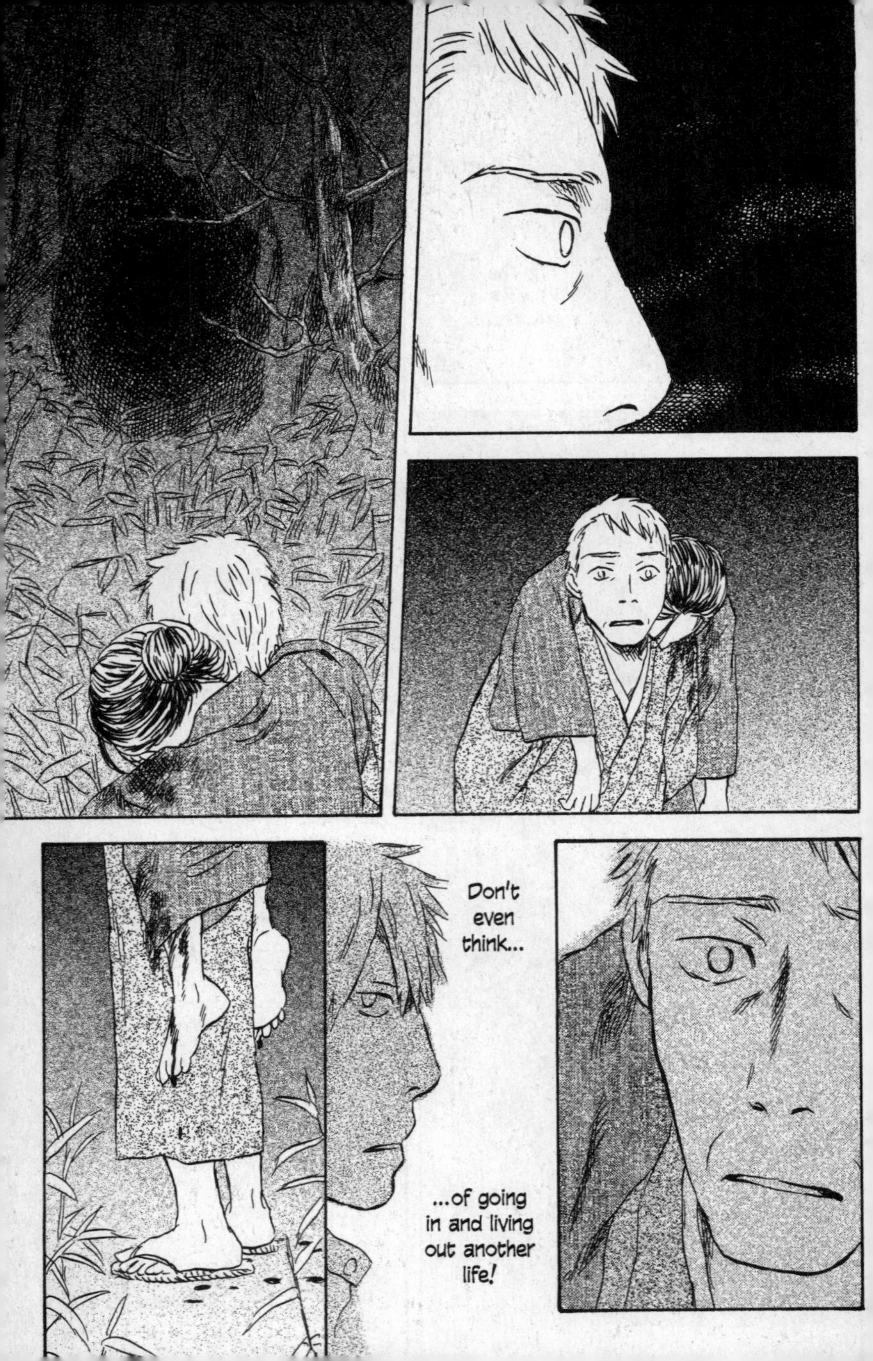
Don't even think...
...of going in and living out another life!

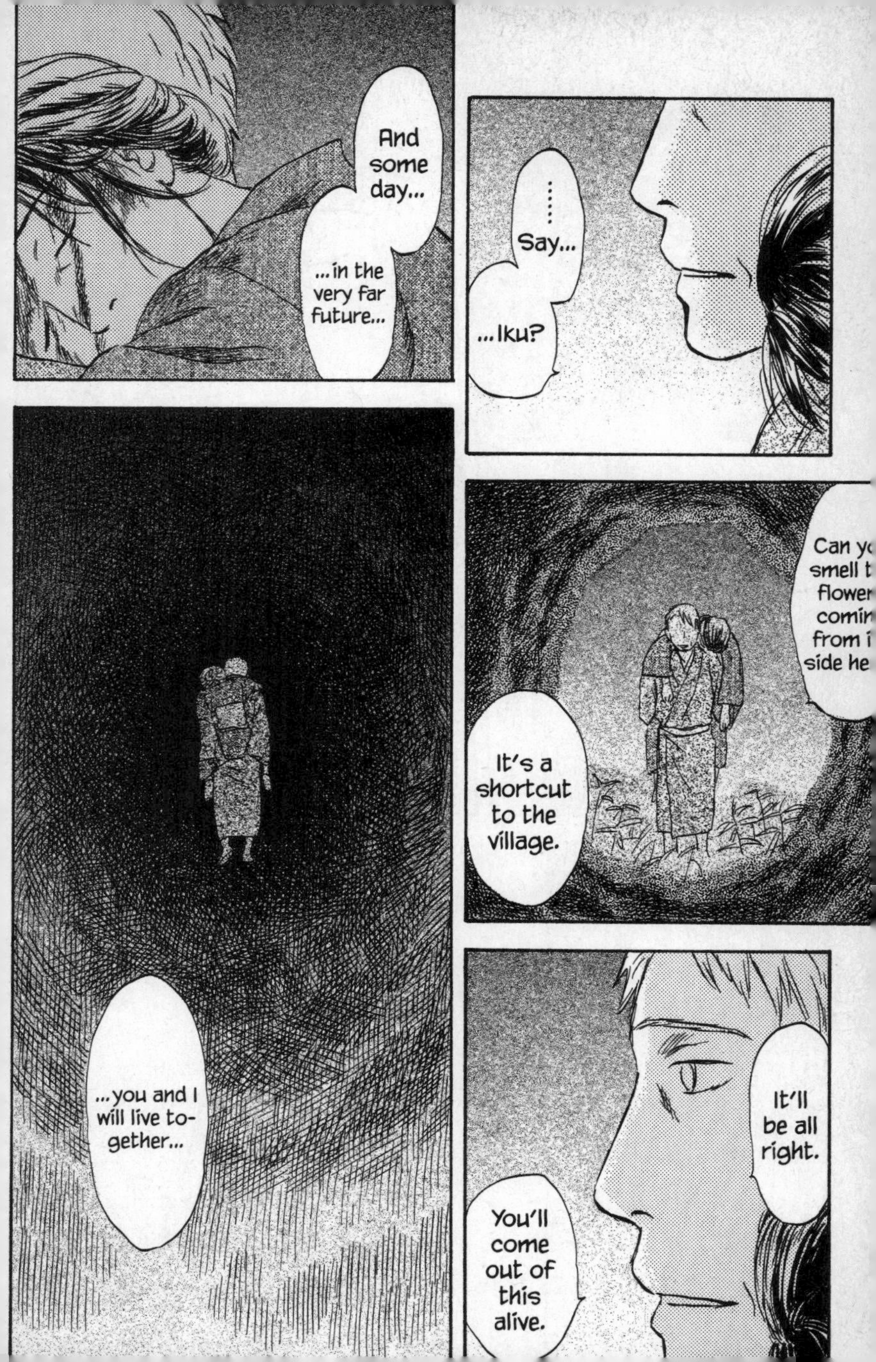
......
Say...
...Iku?
And some day...
...in the very far future...
Can yo smell t flower comin from i side he
It's a shortcut to the village.
It'll be all right.
You'll come out of this alive.
...you and I will live to-gether...

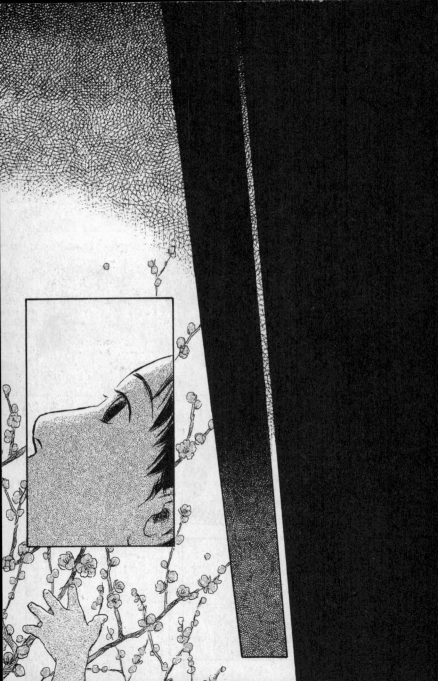

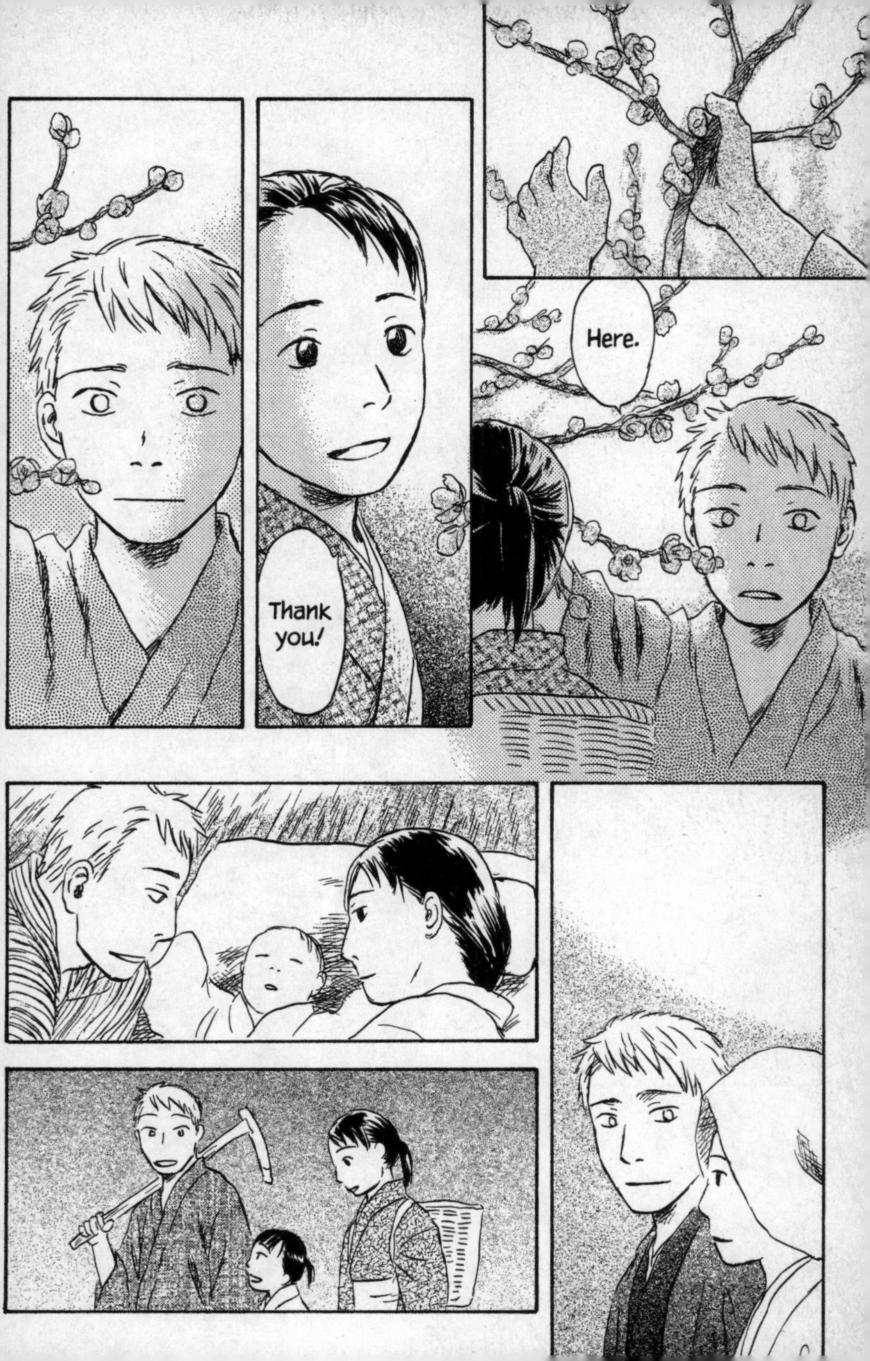
Here.
Thank you!

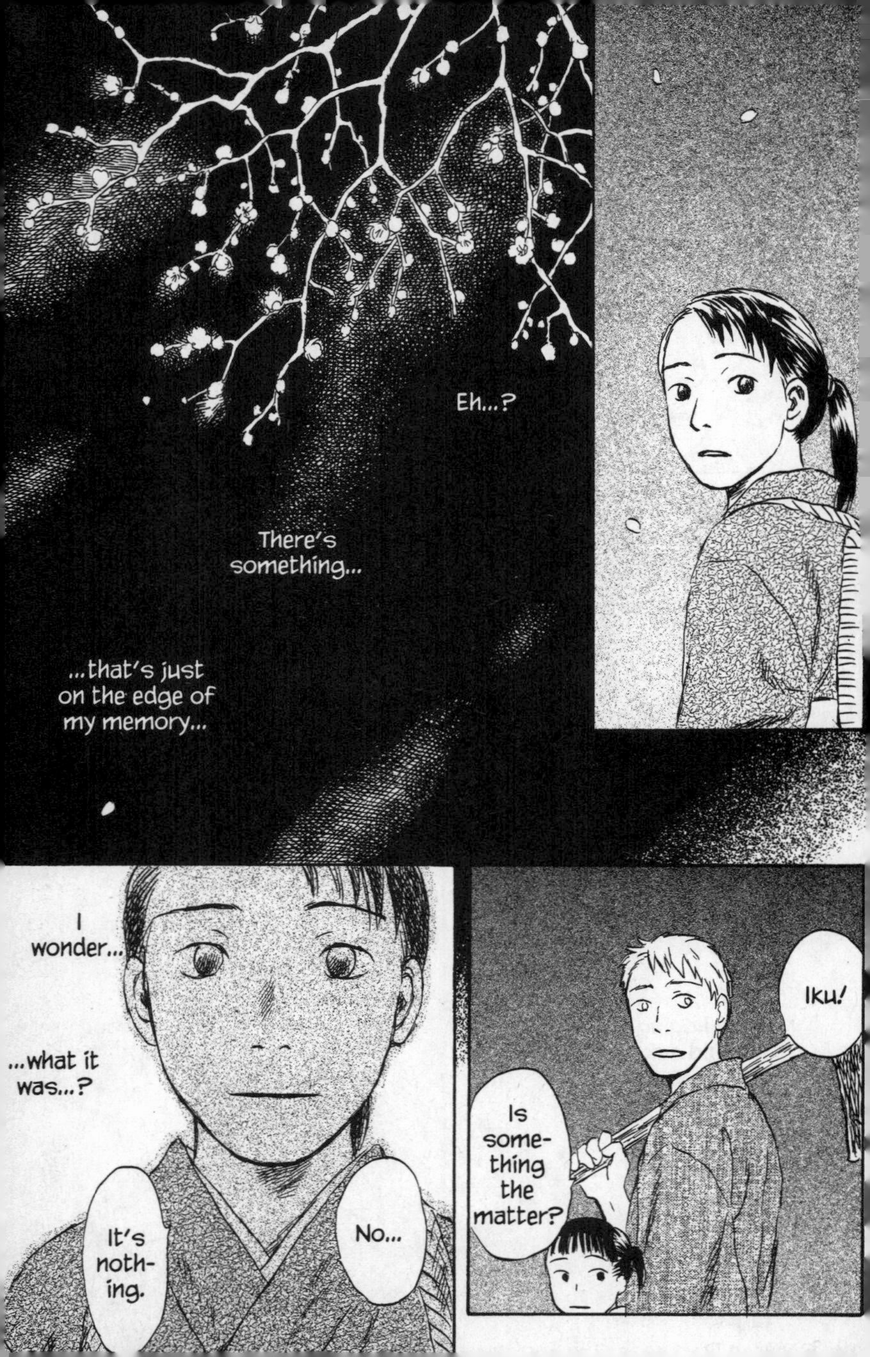
Eh...?
There's something...
...that's just on the edge of my memory...
Iku!
Is something the matter?
No...
It's nothing.
I wonder...
...what it was...?

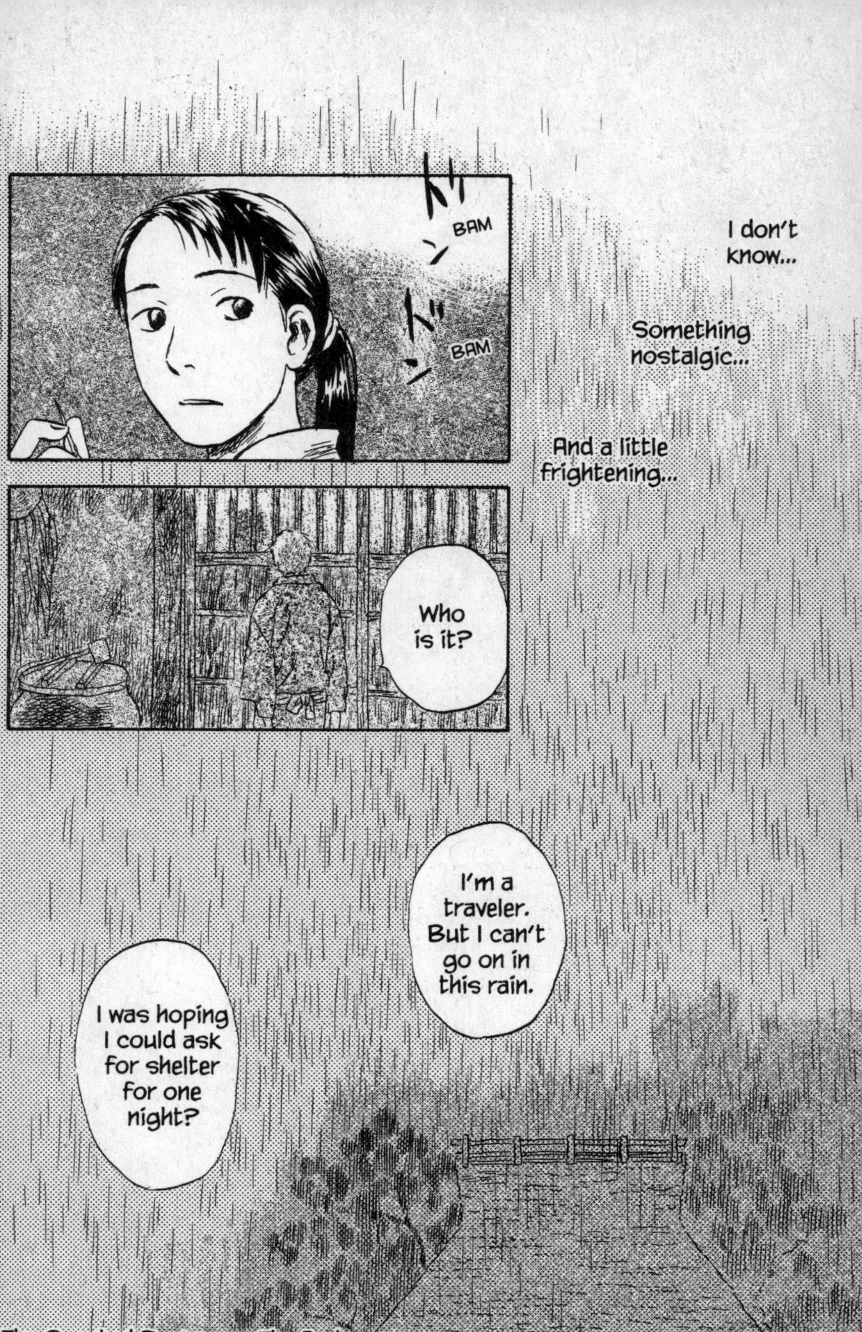
I don't know...
Something nostalgic...
And a little frightening...
ドン BAM
ドン BAM
Who is it?
I'm a traveler. But I can't go on in this rain.
I was hoping I could ask for shelter for one night?

The Scented Darkness The End

Bonus Manga

A Tale of a Very Long Time Ago
Inside the Hole Chapter

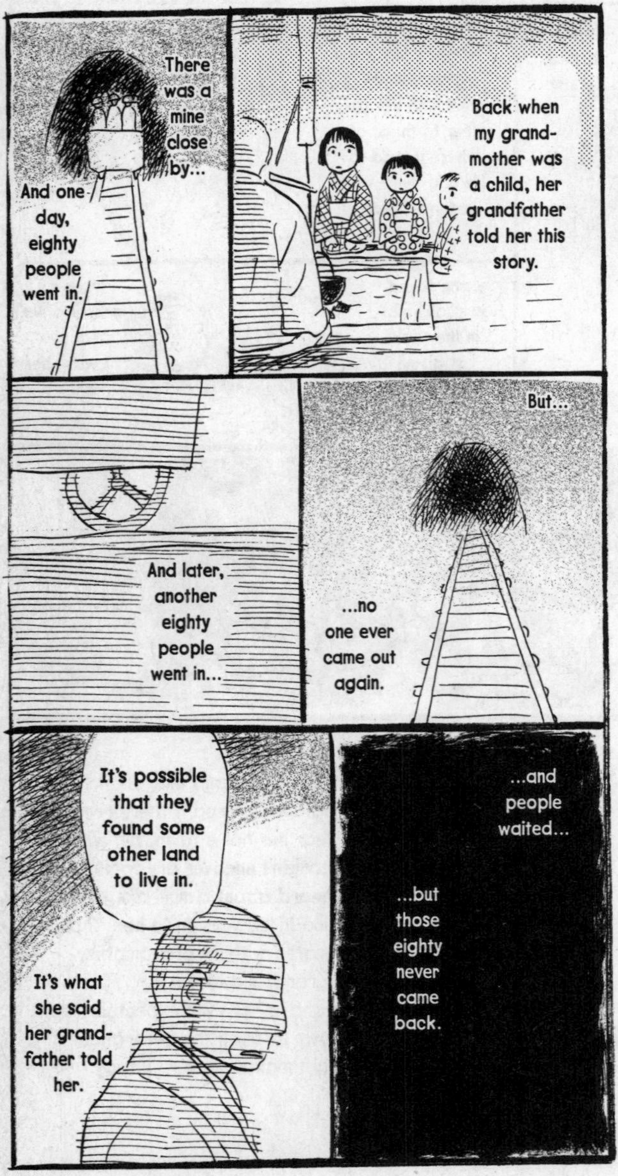
Back when my grand-mother was a child, her grandfather told her this story.
There was a mine close by...
And one day, eighty people went in.
But...
...no one ever came out again.
And later, another eighty people went in...
...and people waited...
...but those eighty never came back.
It's possible that they found some other land to live in.
It's what she said her grand-father told her.

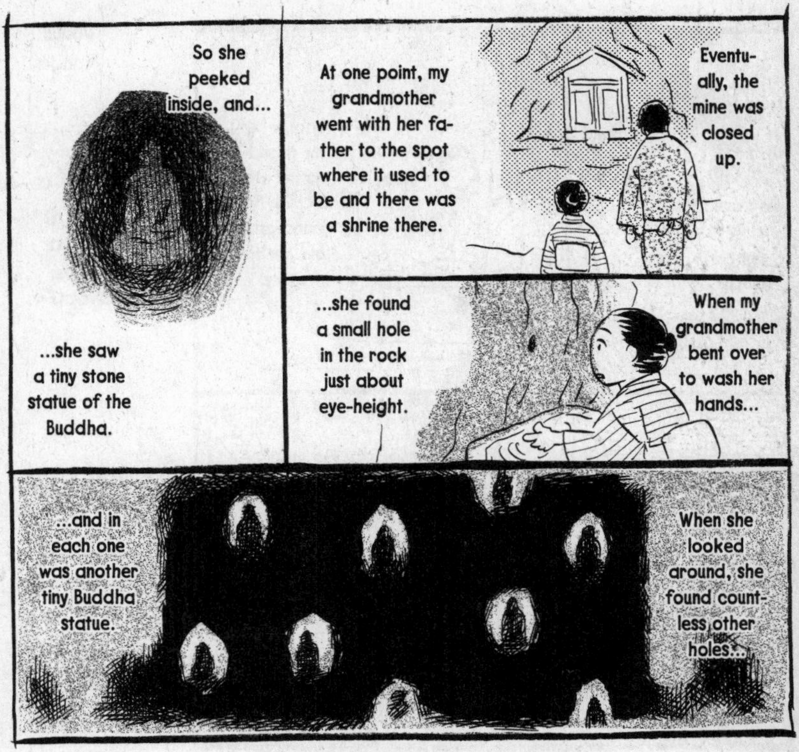
Eventually, the mine was closed up.
At one point, my grandmother went with her father to the spot where it used to be and there was a shrine there.
When my grandmother bent over to wash her hands...
...she found a small hole in the rock just about eye-height.
So she peeked inside, and...
...she saw a tiny stone statue of the Buddha.
When she looked around, she found countless other holes...
...and in each one was another tiny Buddha statue.

My grandmother will soon turn 100 years old, and her memory is gradually dimming. I wondered if there really was such a huge disaster near her home town, but when I tried to investigate, I couldn't uncover any facts.
I'm sure her grandfather heard about a mine disaster, and passed along his own modified version to her. That version must have so resonated with my grandmother that she told her grandchild about it.
I doubt my great, great grandfather ever expected his little story to be passed down through the generations.
But now that I think of it, it makes me very happy.

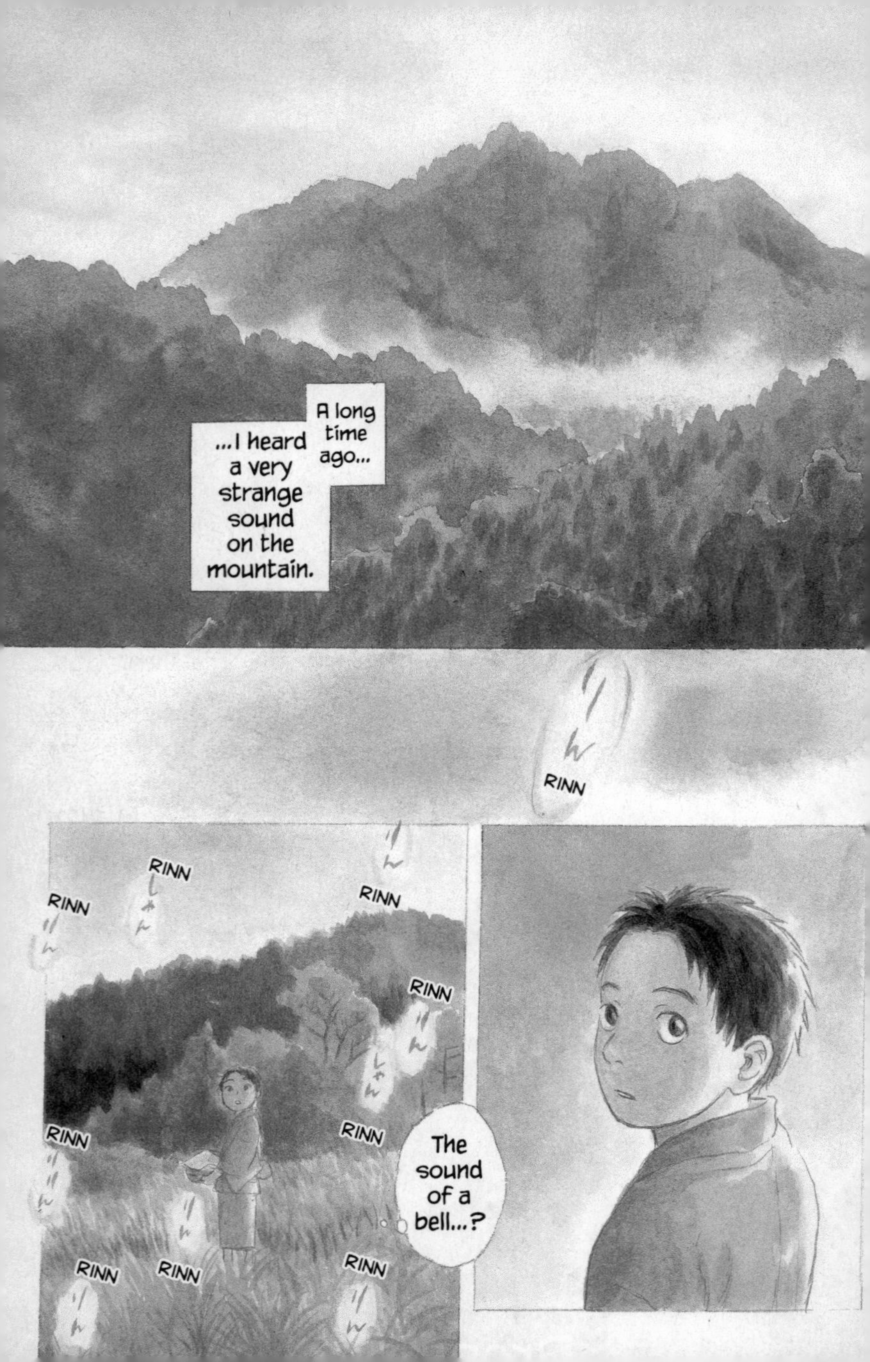
A long time ago...
...I heard a very strange sound on the mountain.
RINN
RINN
RINN
RINN
RINN
The sound of a bell...?
RINN
RINN
RINN
RINN
RINN

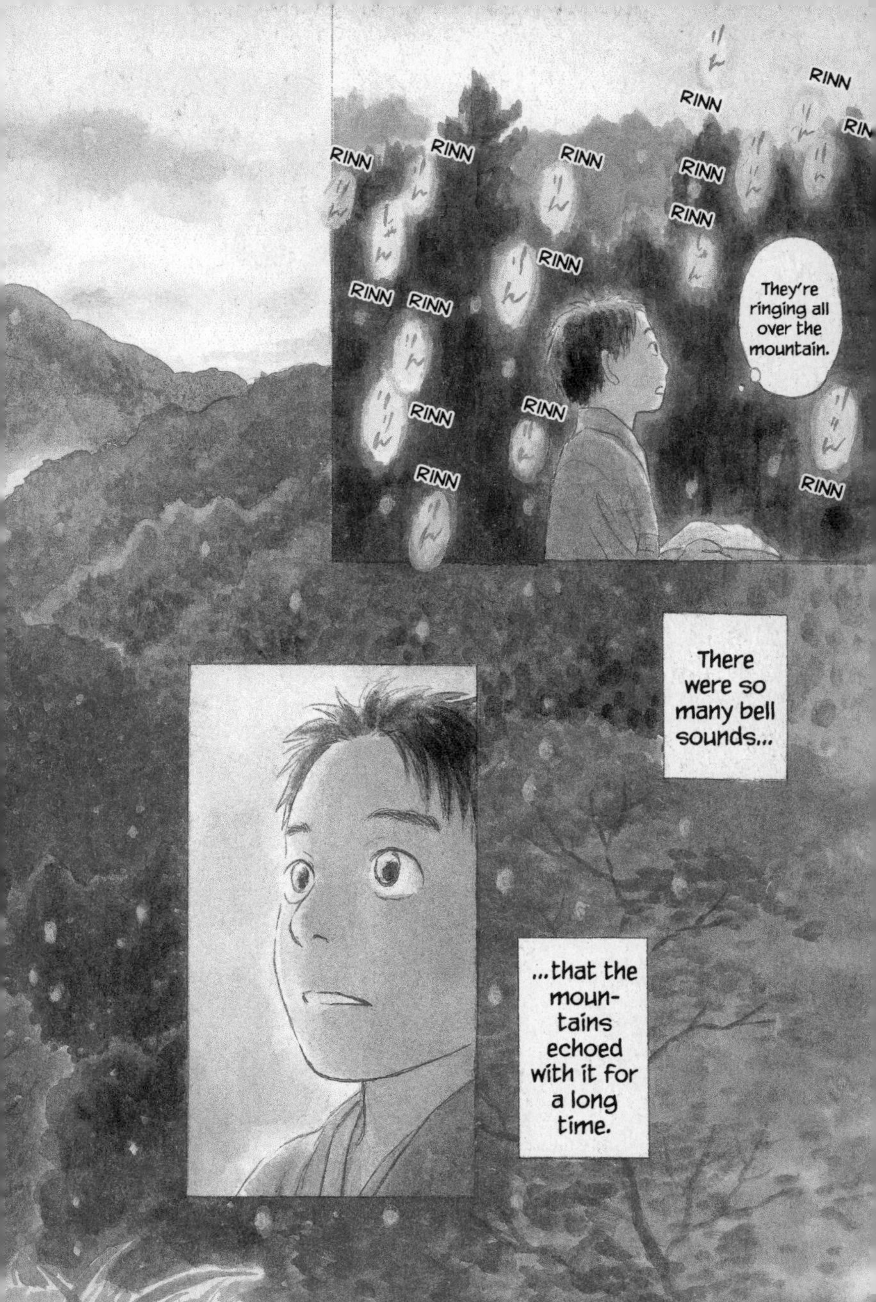
RINN
RIN
RINN
RINN
RINN
RINN
RINN
RINN
RINN
They're ringing all over the mountain.
RINN
RINN
RINN
RINN
RINN
RINN
There were so many bell sounds...
...that the mountains echoed with it for a long time.

Drops of Bells (Part 1)

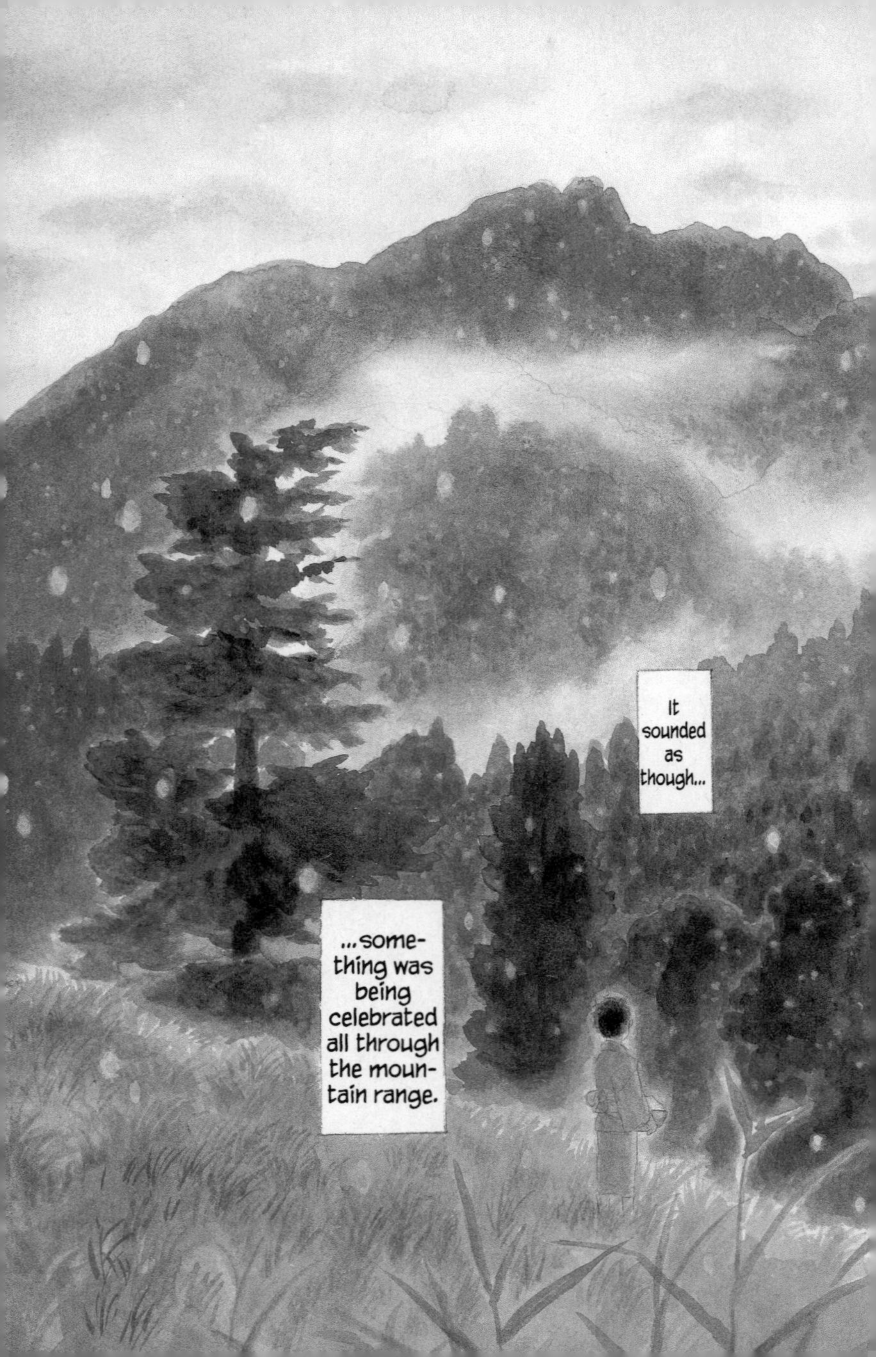
It sounded as though...
...some-thing was being celebrated all through the moun-tain range.

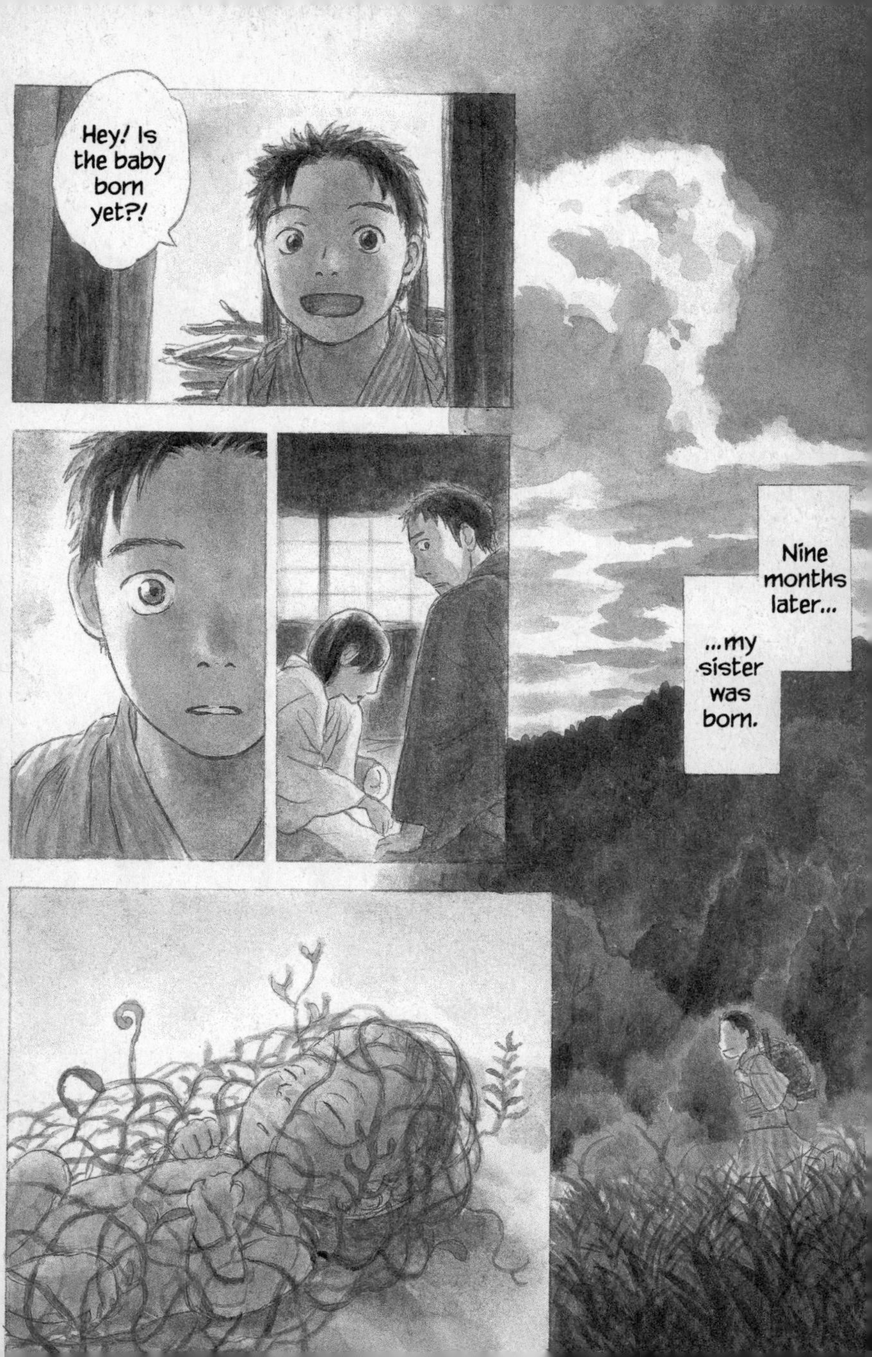
Nine months later...
...my sister was born.
Hey! Is the baby born yet?!

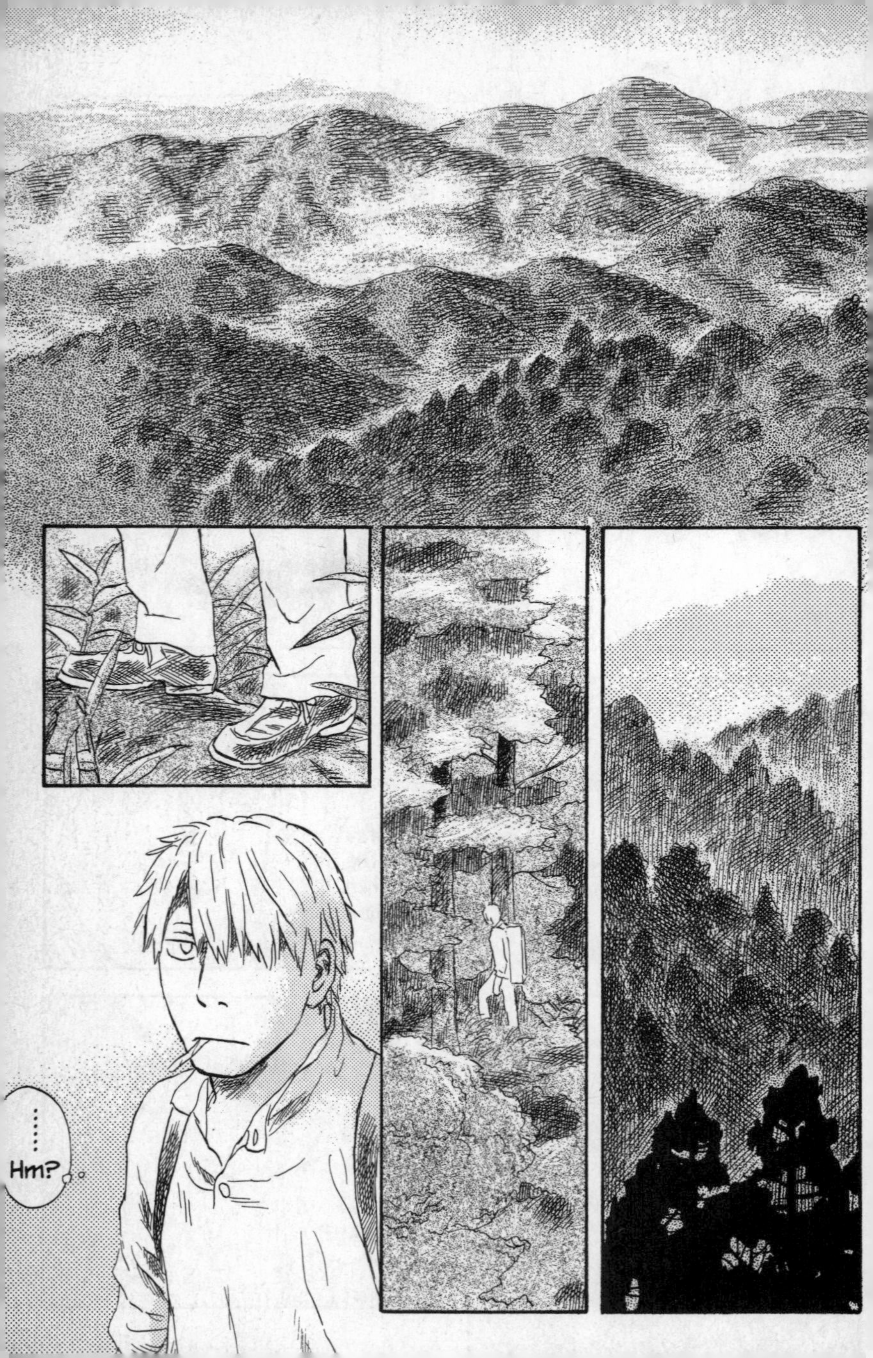

...... Hm?

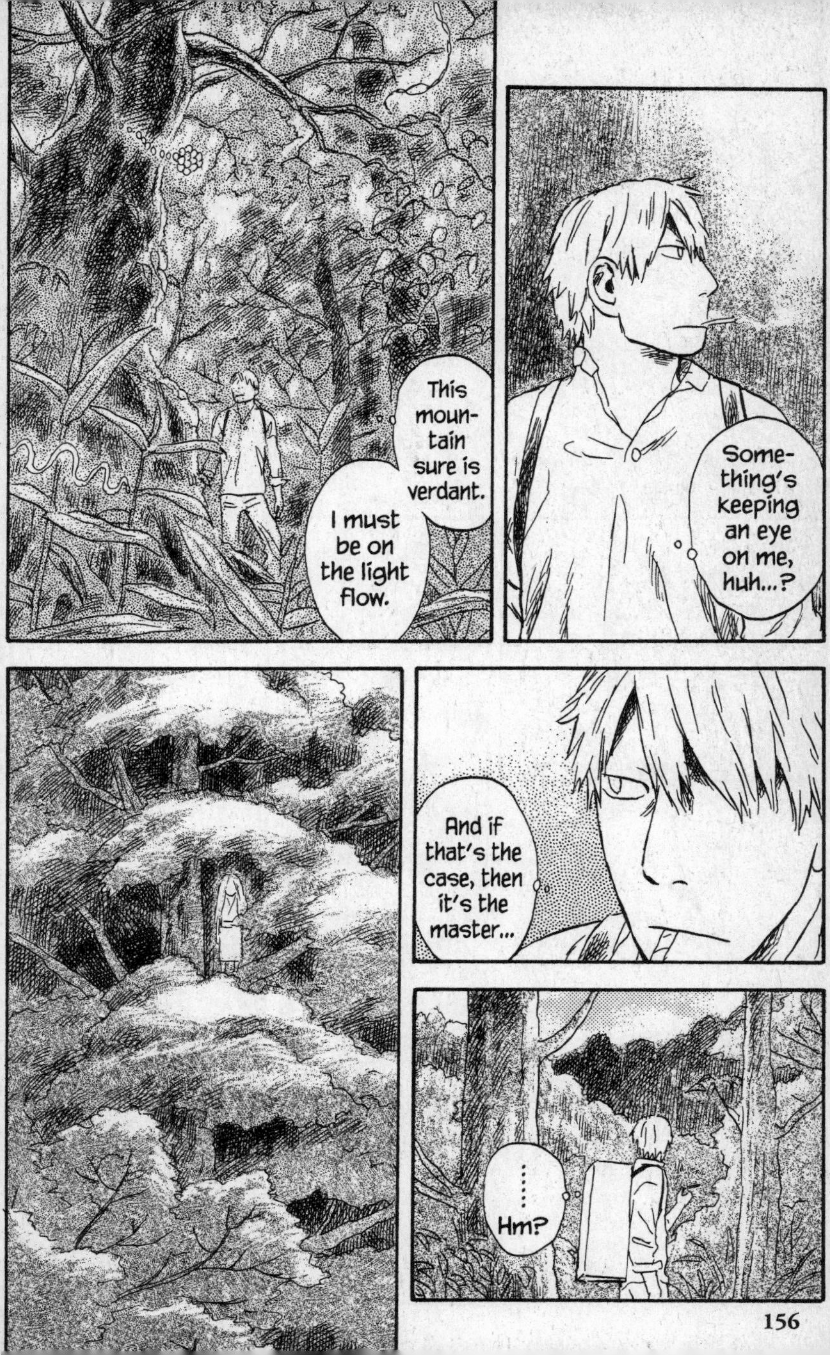
Something's keeping an eye on me, huh...?
This mountain sure is verdant.
I must be on the light flow.
And if that's the case, then it's the master...
...... Hm?

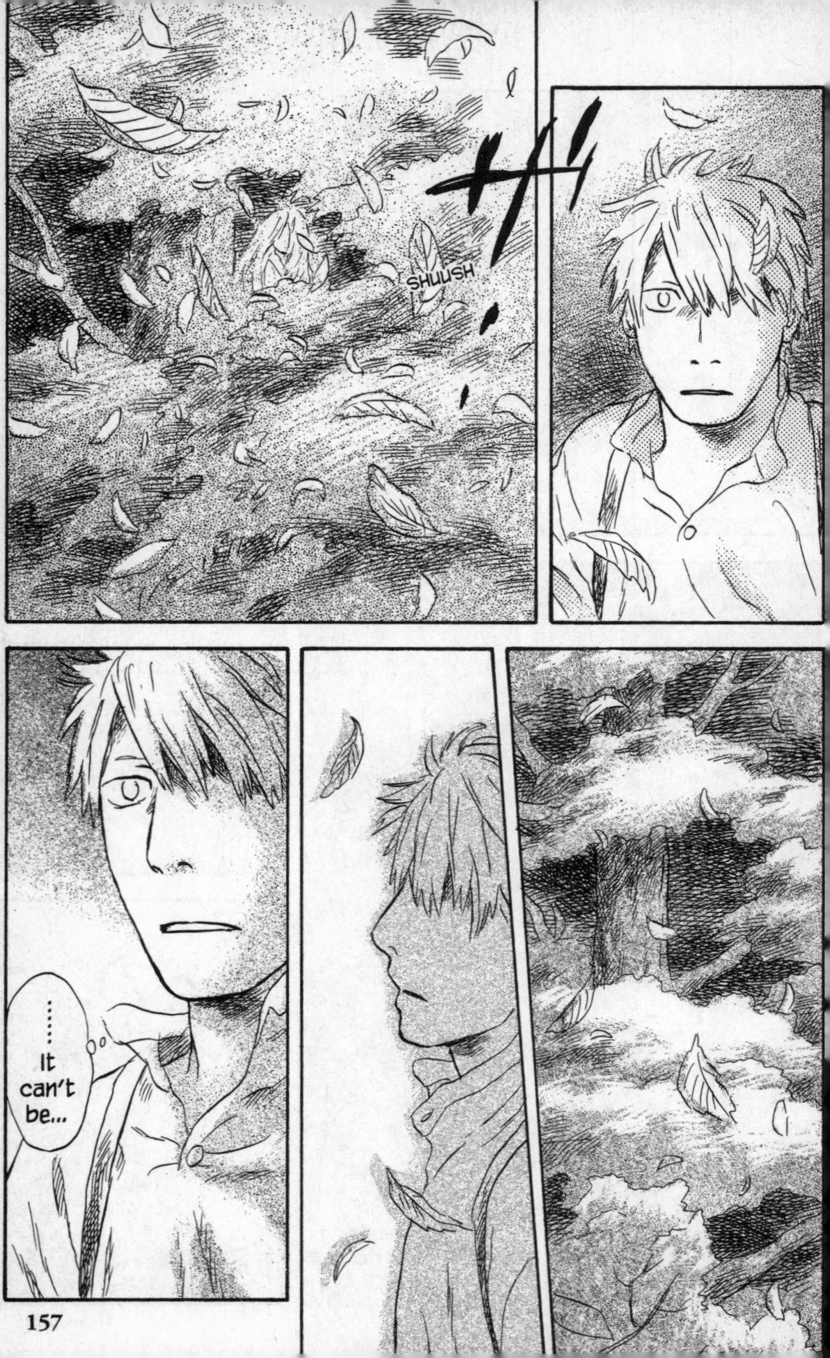
SHUUSH
...... It can't be...

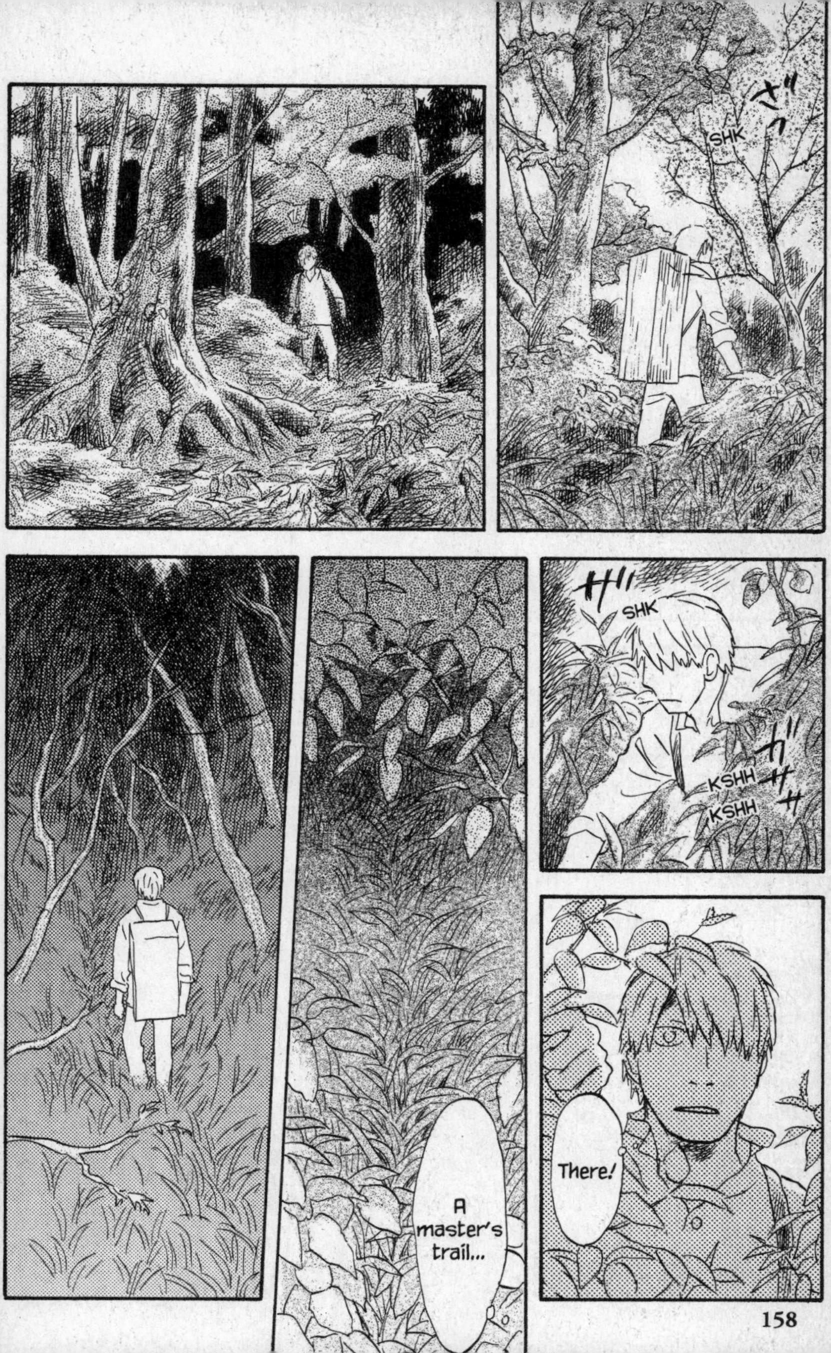
SHK
SHK
KSHH
KSHH
There!
A master's trail...

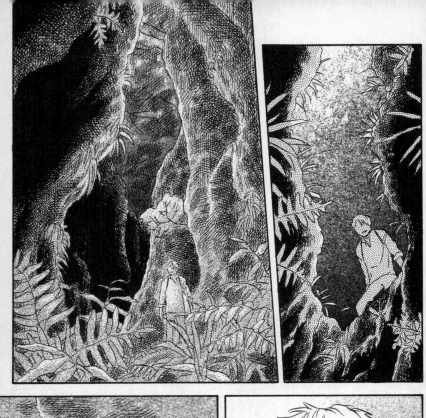

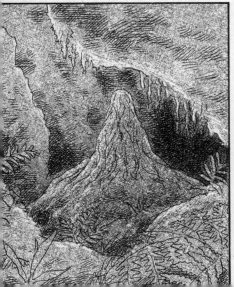

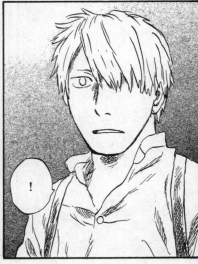

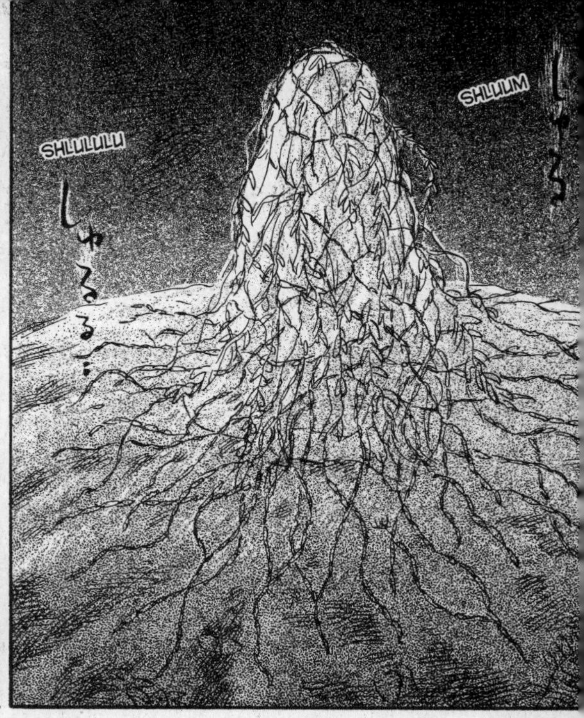
SHLUUM
しゃる
SHLULULU
しゃるる…
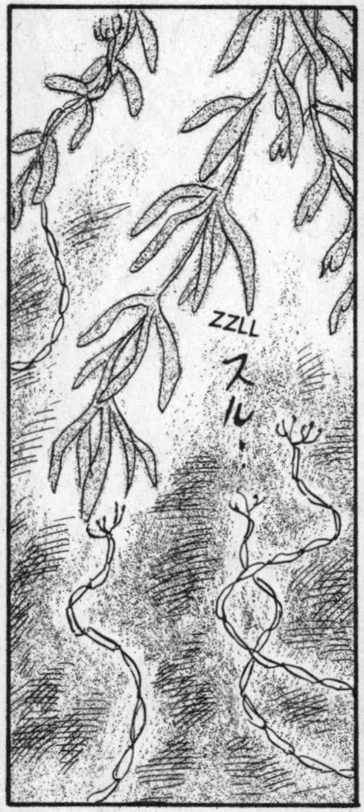
ZZLL
スル…
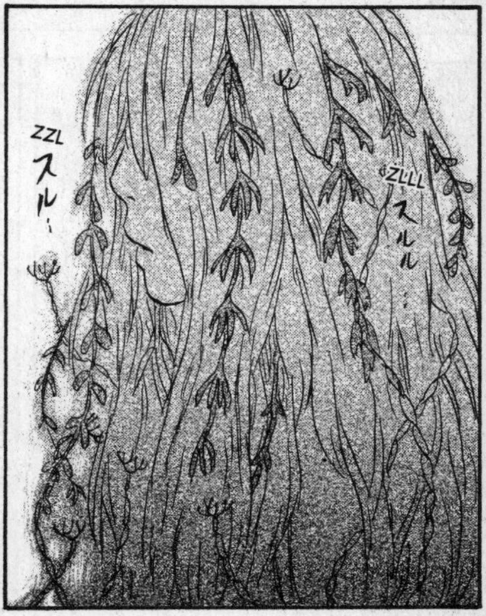
ZZL
スル…
ZZLL
スルル…
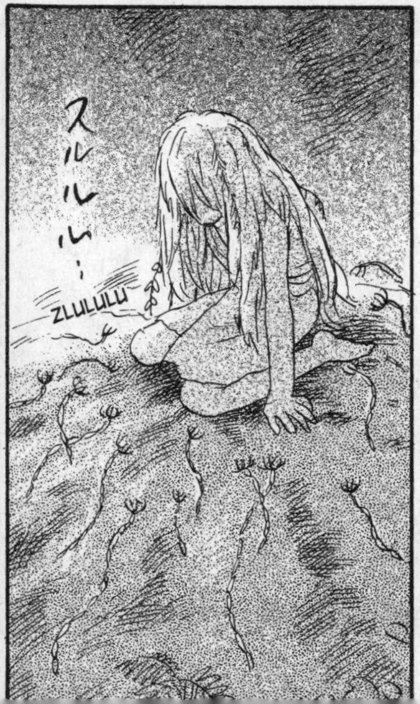
スルルル…
ZLULULU

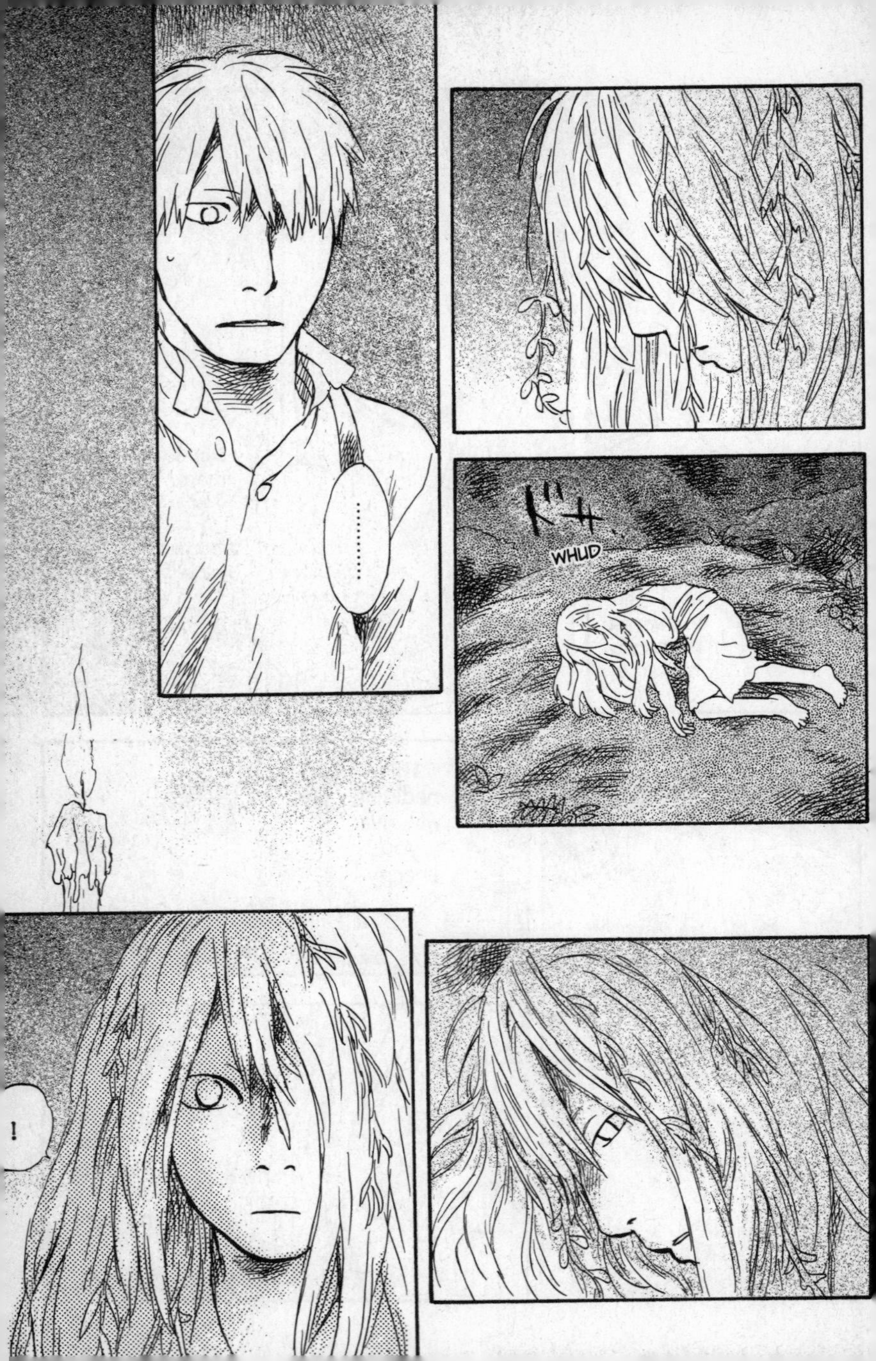
WHUD
……
!

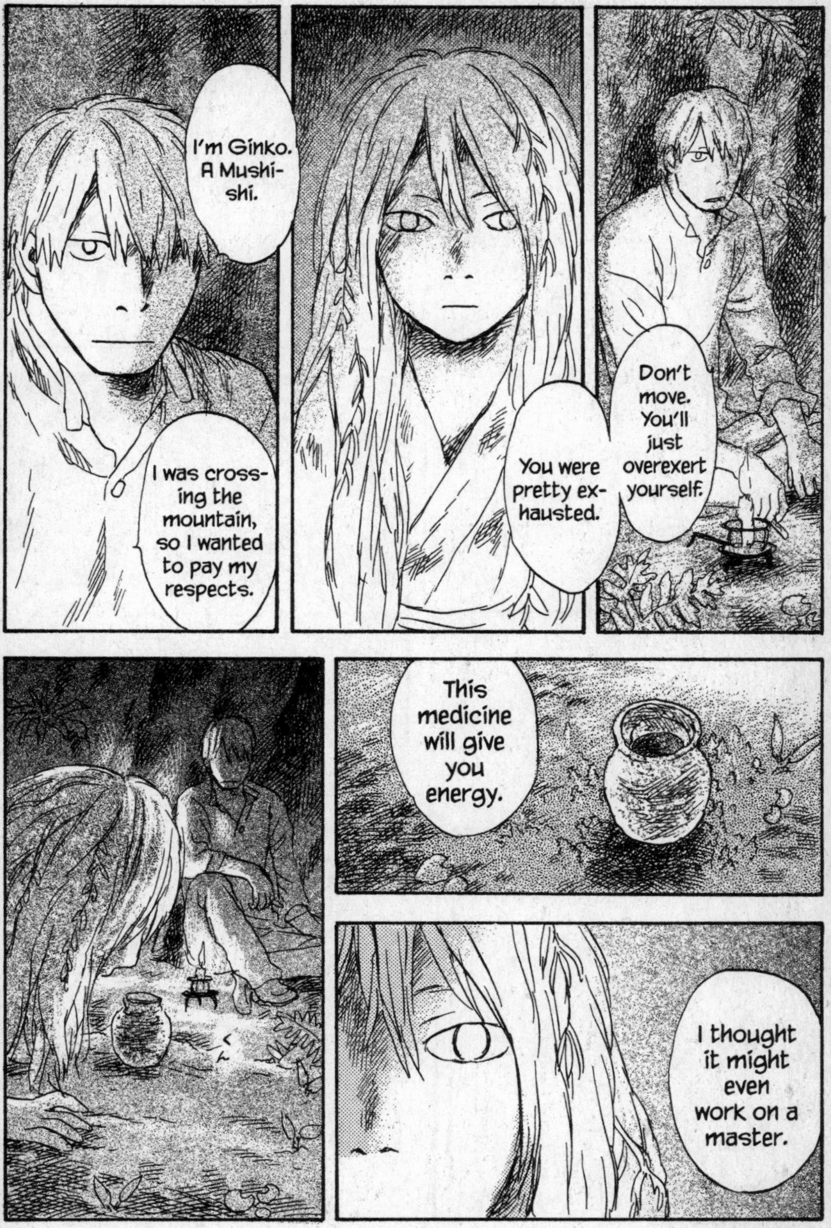
Don't move. You'll just overexert yourself.
You were pretty exhausted.
I'm Ginko. A Mushi-shi.
I was crossing the mountain, so I wanted to pay my respects.
This medicine will give you energy.
I thought it might even work on a master.

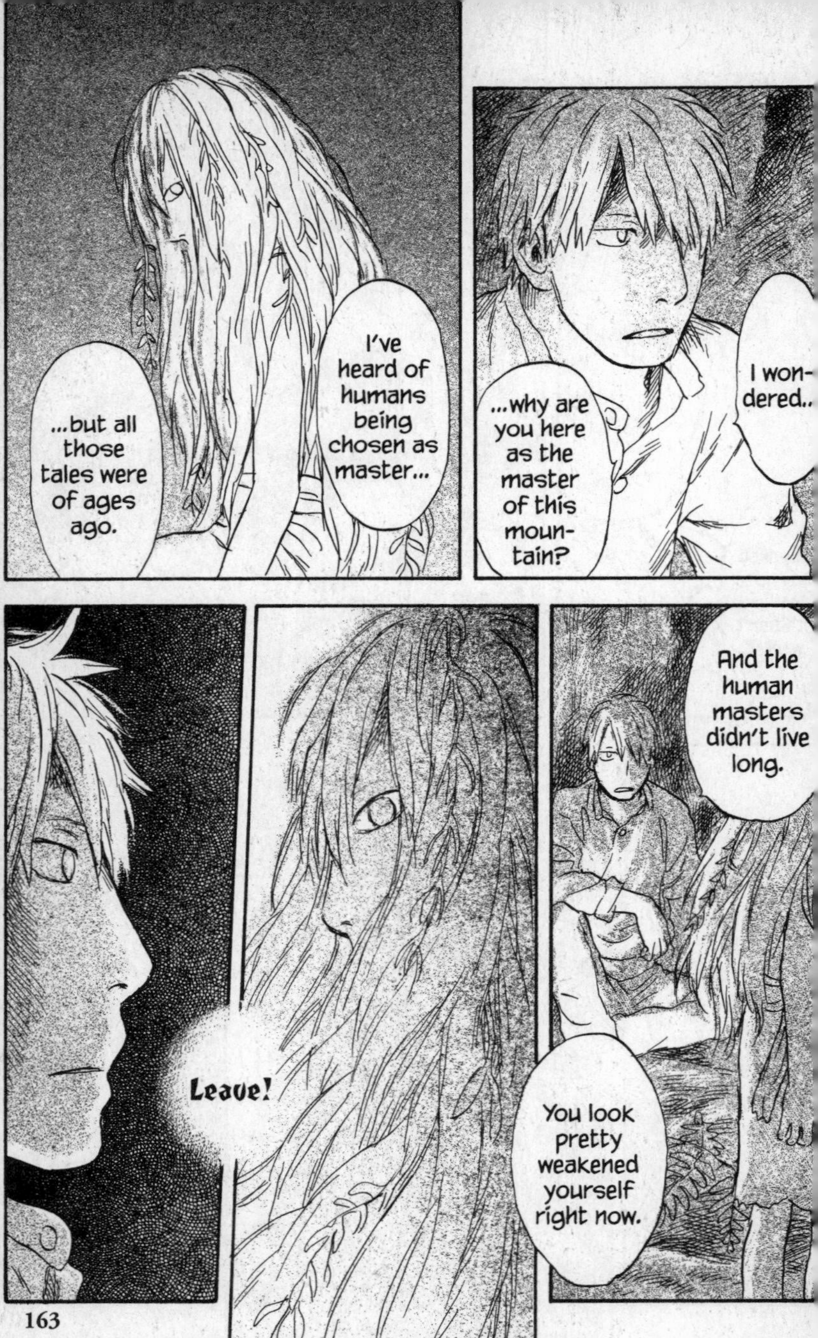
I wondered...
...why are you here as the master of this mountain?
I've heard of humans being chosen as master...
...but all those tales were of ages ago.
And the human masters didn't live long.
You look pretty weakened yourself right now.
Leave!

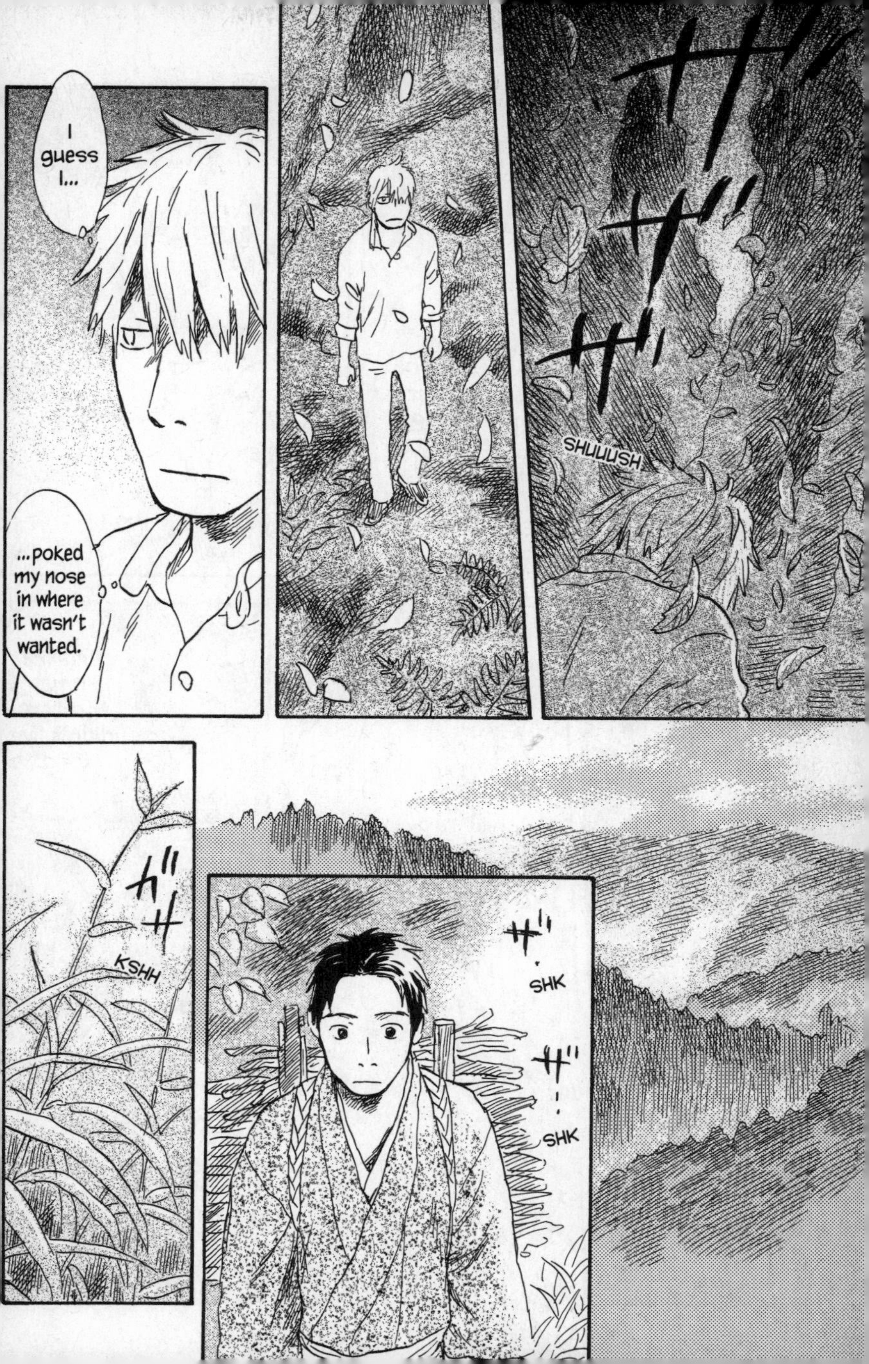
SHUUUSH
I guess I...
...poked my nose in where it wasn't wanted.
SHK
SHK
KSHH

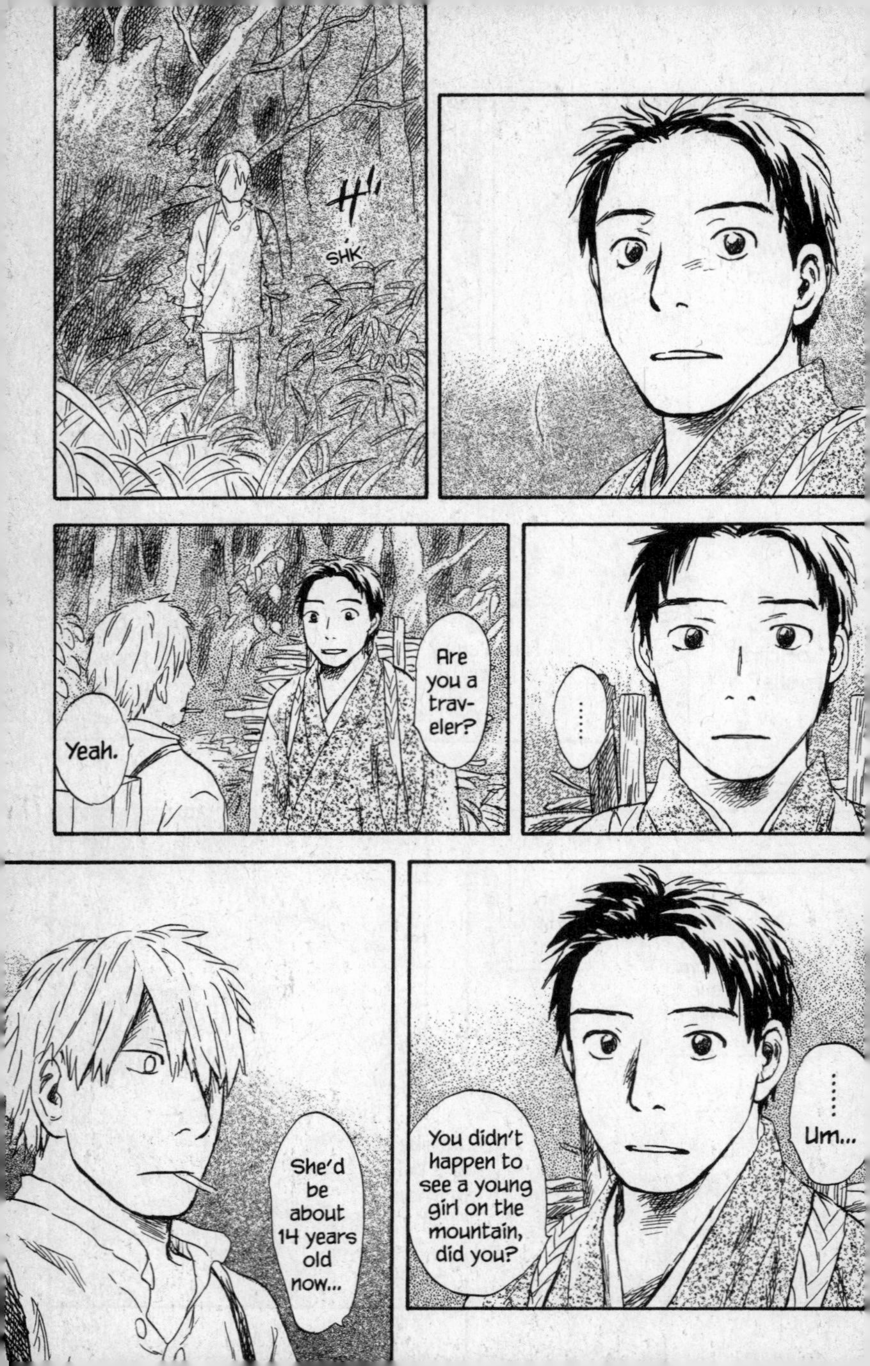
SHK
......
Are you a traveler?
Yeah.
......
Um...
You didn't happen to see a young girl on the mountain, did you?
She'd be about 14 years old now...

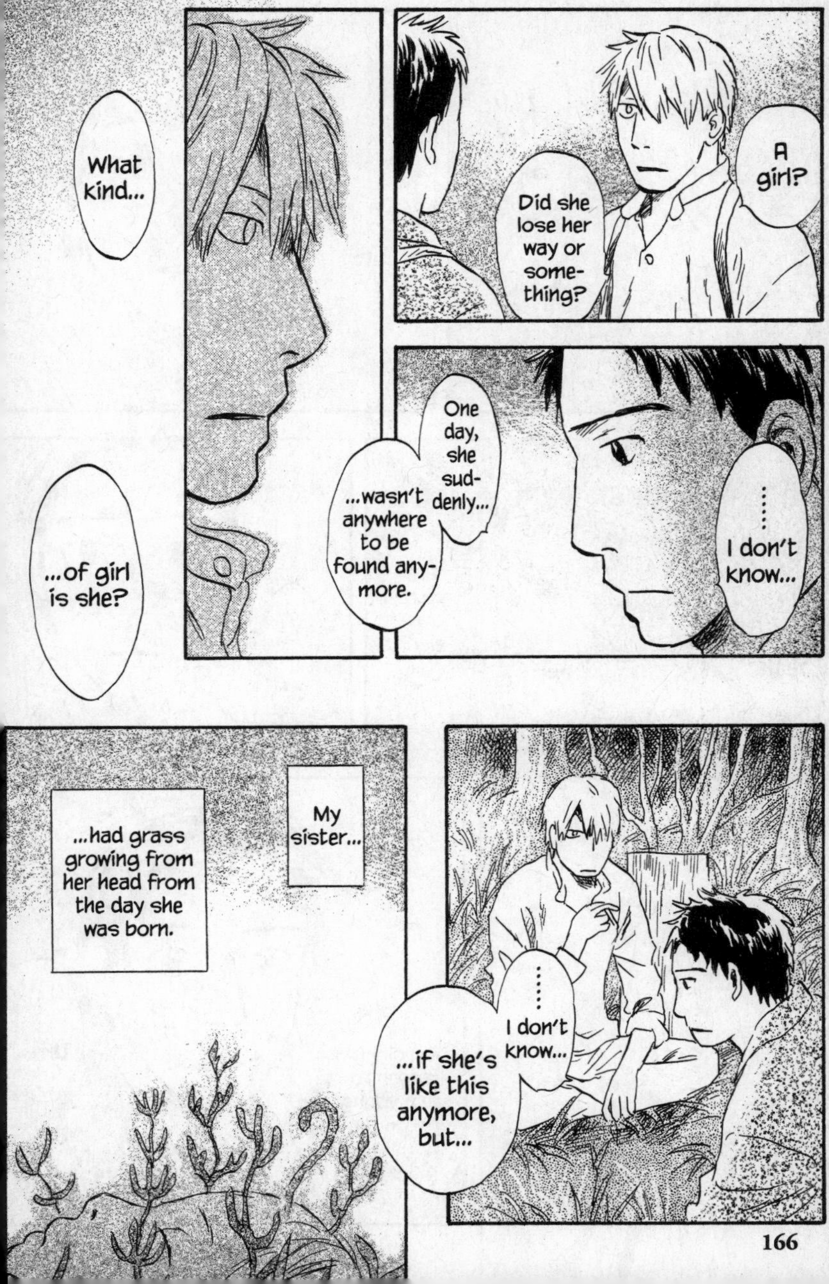
A girl?
Did she lose her way or some-thing?
...... I don't know...
One day, she sud-denly...
...wasn't anywhere to be found any-more.
What kind...
...of girl is she?
...... I don't know...
...if she's like this anymore, but...
My sister...
...had grass growing from her head from the day she was born.

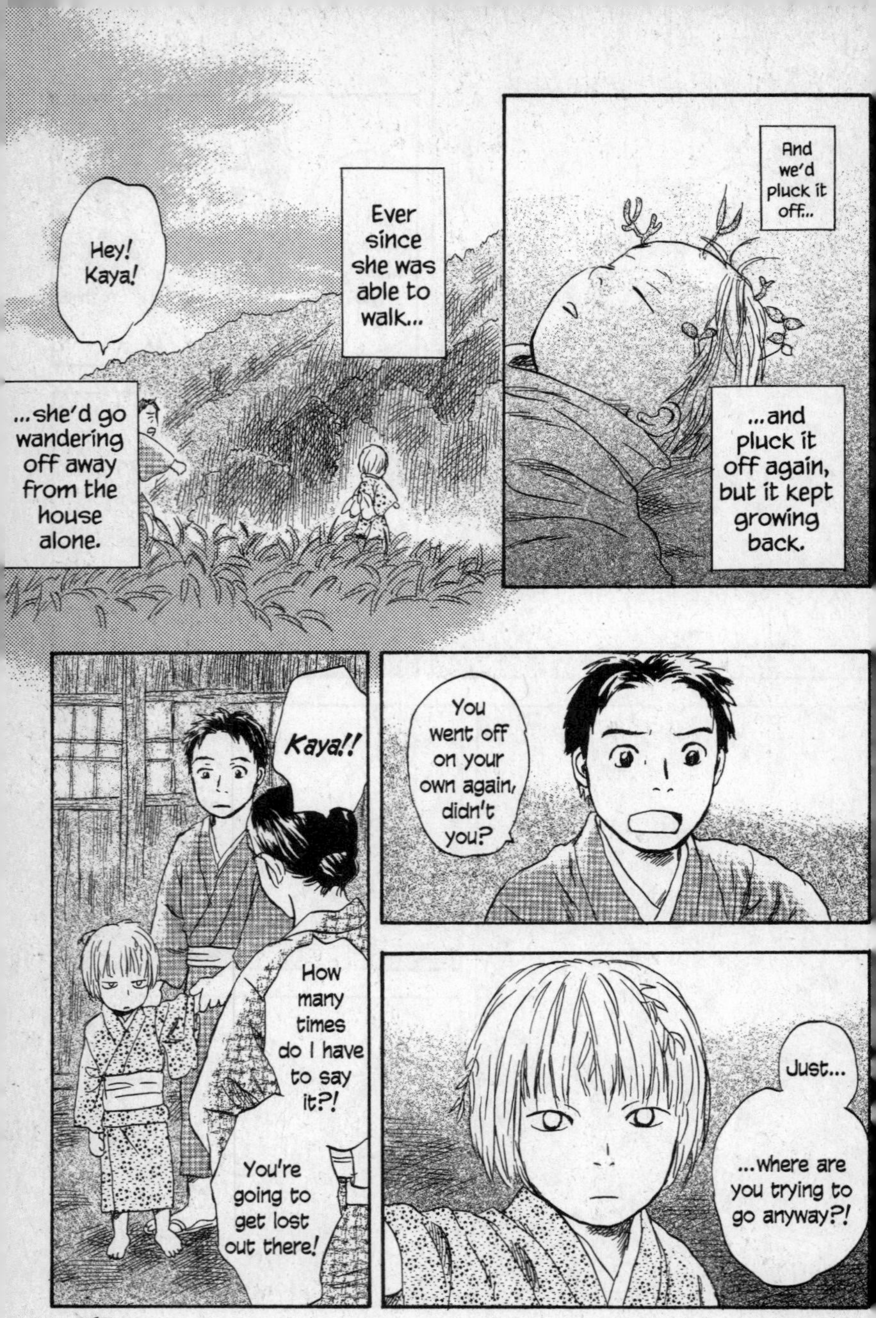
And we'd pluck it off...
...and pluck it off again, but it kept growing back.
Ever since she was able to walk...
Hey! Kaya!
...she'd go wandering off away from the house alone.
You went off on your own again, didn't you?
Just...
...where are you trying to go anyway?!
Kaya!!
How many times do I have to say it?!
You're going to get lost out there!

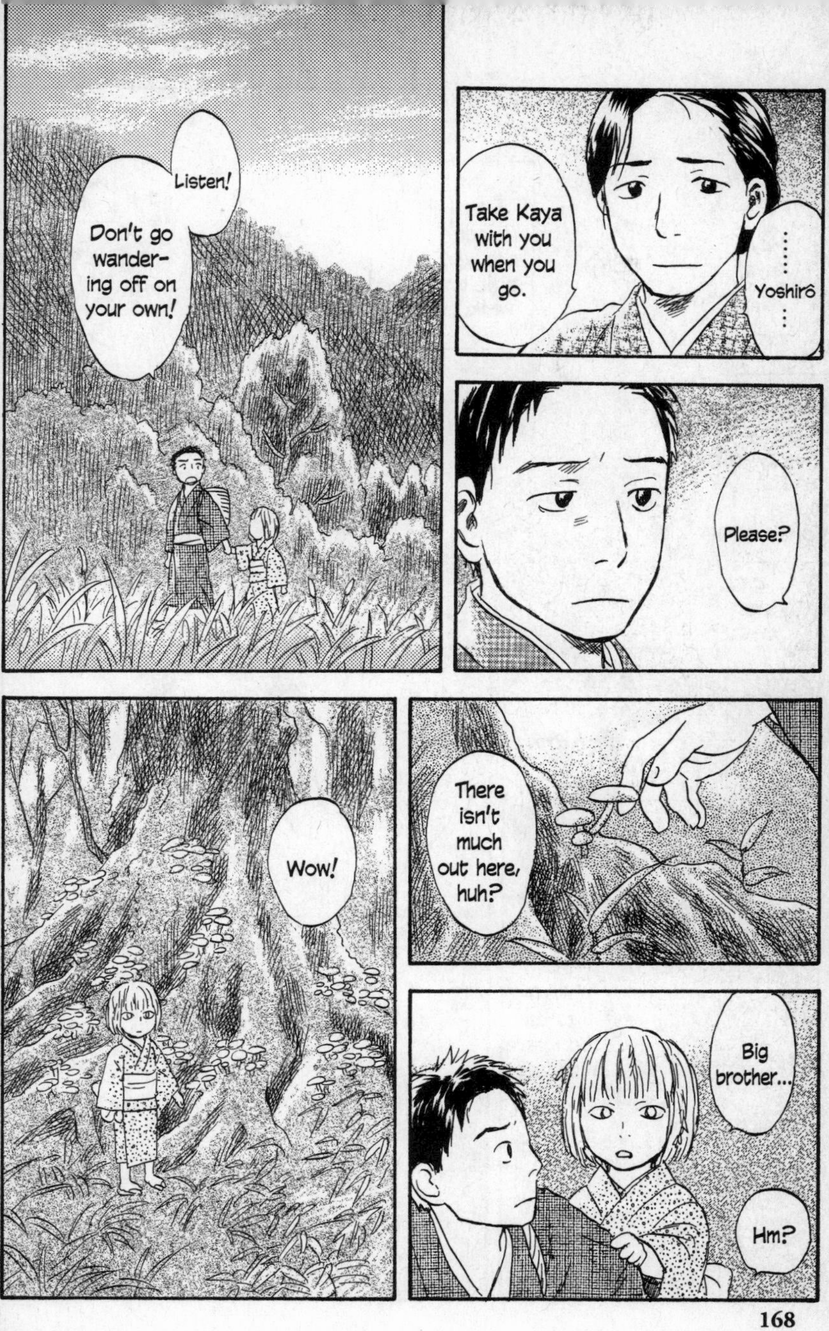

......Yoshirô......
Take Kaya with you when you go.
Please?
Listen!
Don't go wandering off on your own!
There isn't much out here, huh?
Big brother...
Hm?
Wow!

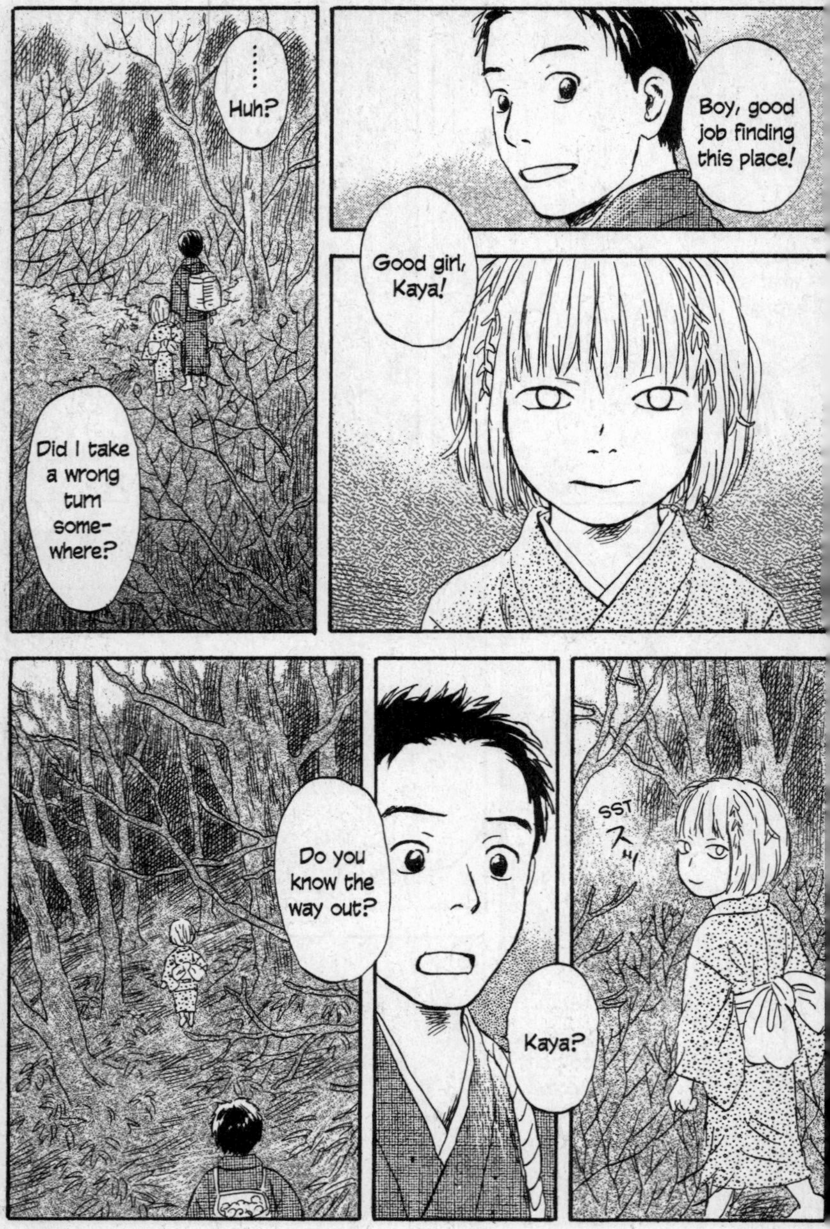
Boy, good job finding this place!
Good girl, Kaya!
......
Huh?
Did I take a wrong turn some-where?
SST
Do you know the way out?
Kaya?

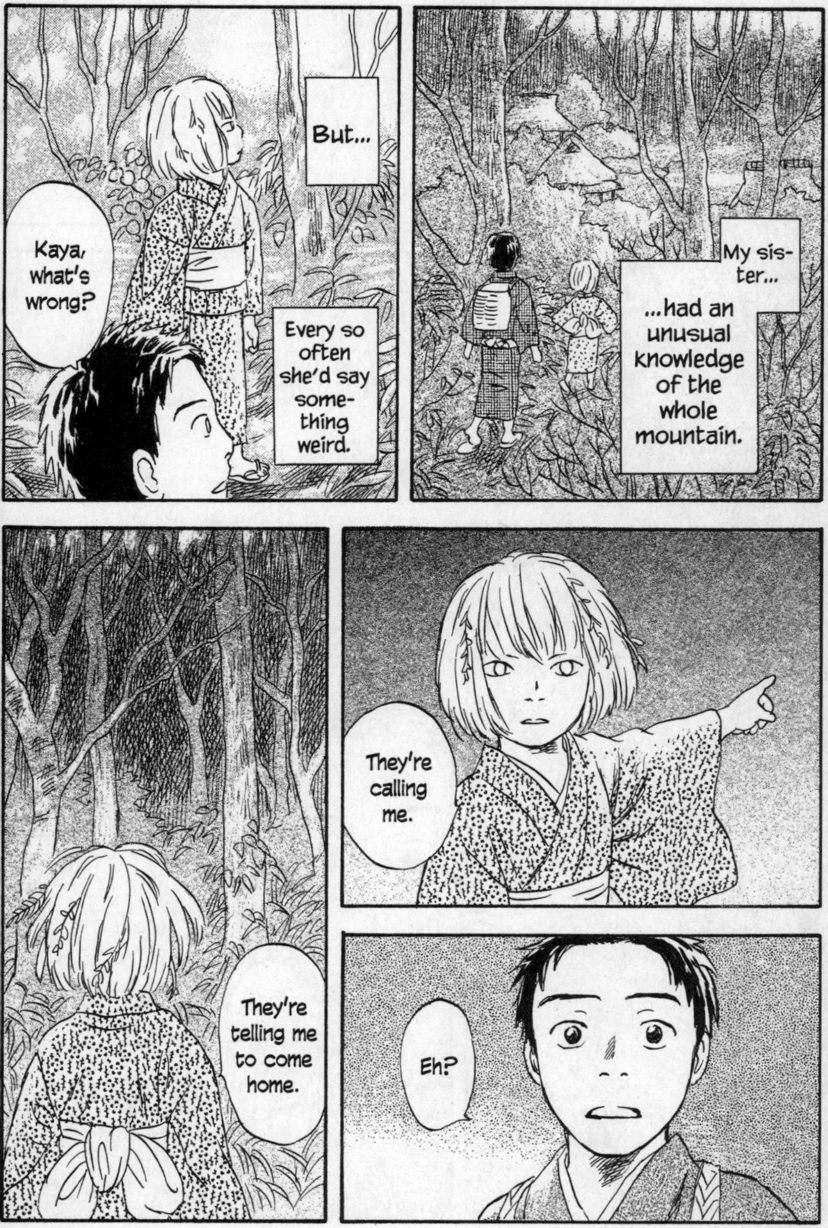
My sister...
...had an unusual knowledge of the whole mountain.
But...
Every so often she'd say something weird.
Kaya, what's wrong?
They're calling me.
Eh?
They're telling me to come home.

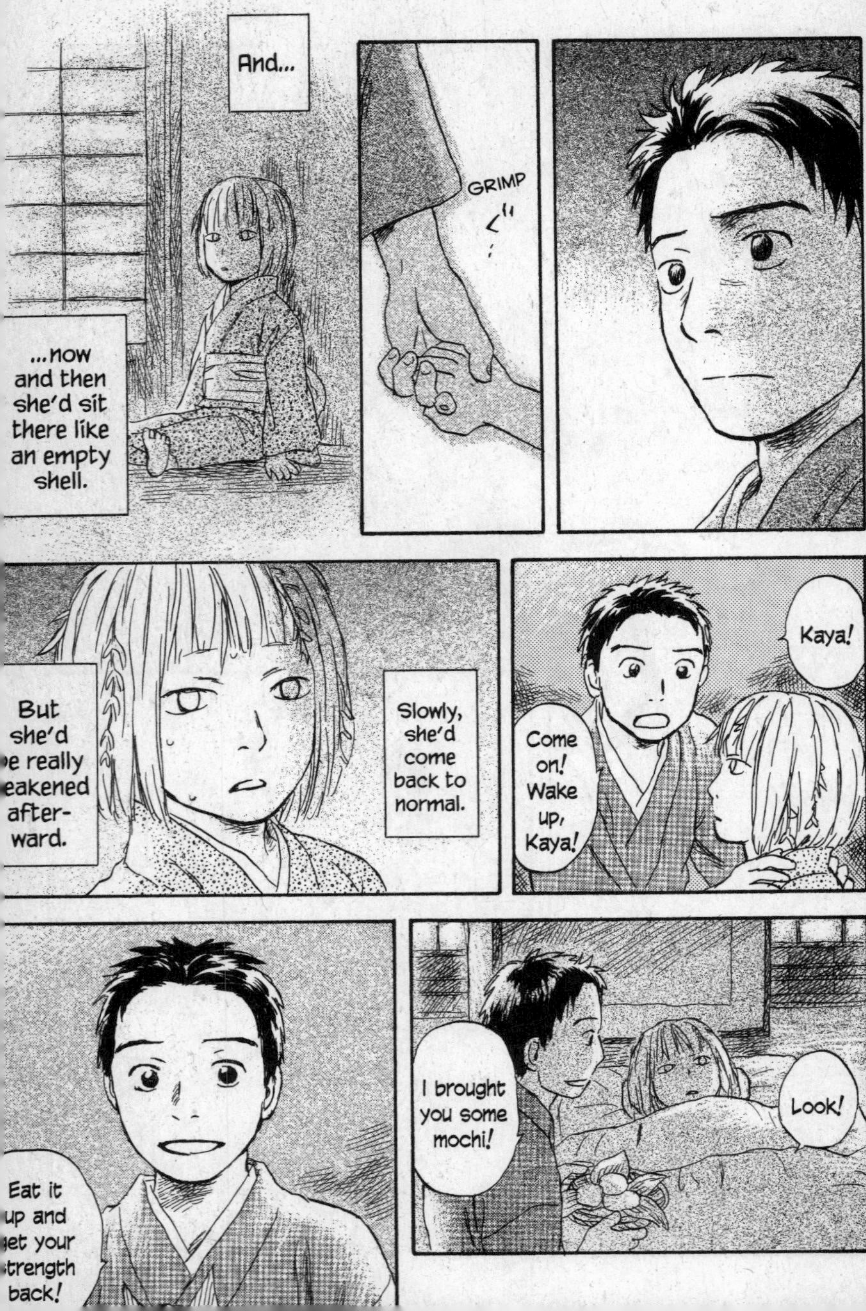
GRIMP
And...
...now and then she'd sit there like an empty shell.
Kaya!
Come on! Wake up, Kaya!
Slowly, she'd come back to normal.
But she'd e really eakened after-ward.
Look!
I brought you some mochi!
Eat it up and et your trength back!

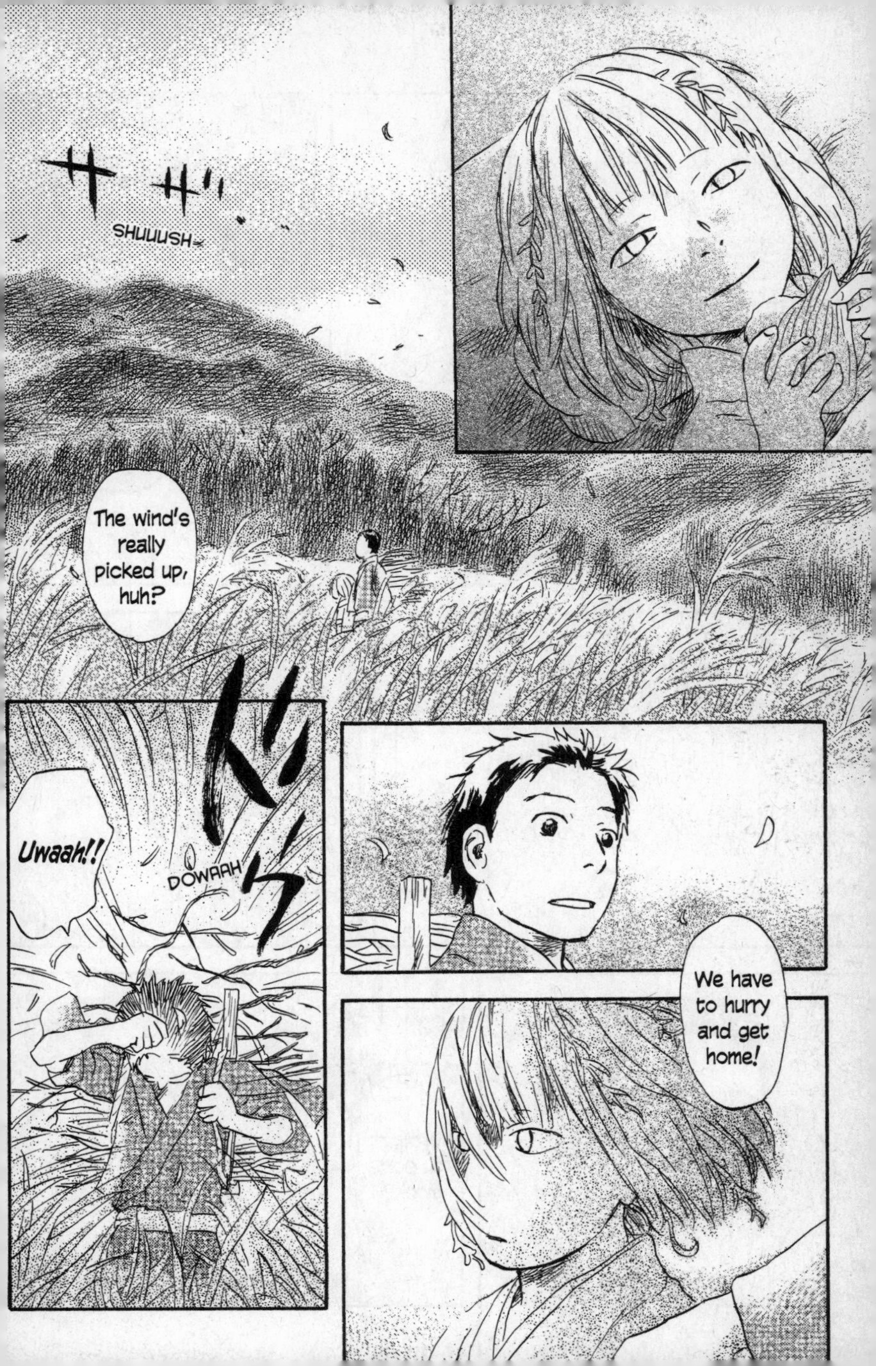
SHUUUSH
The wind's really picked up, huh?
We have to hurry and get home!
DOWAAH
Uwaah!!

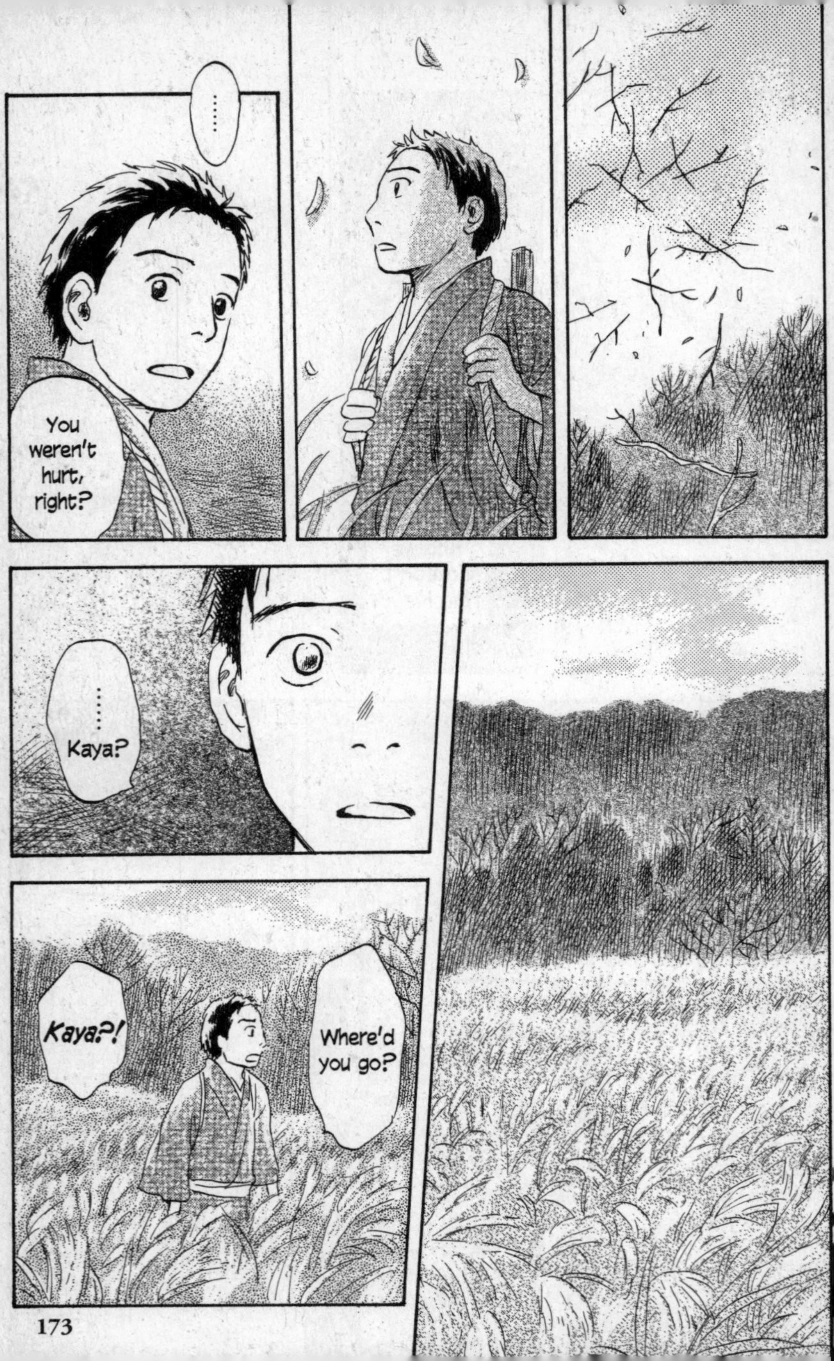
……
You weren't hurt, right?
……
Kaya?
Where'd you go?
Kaya?!

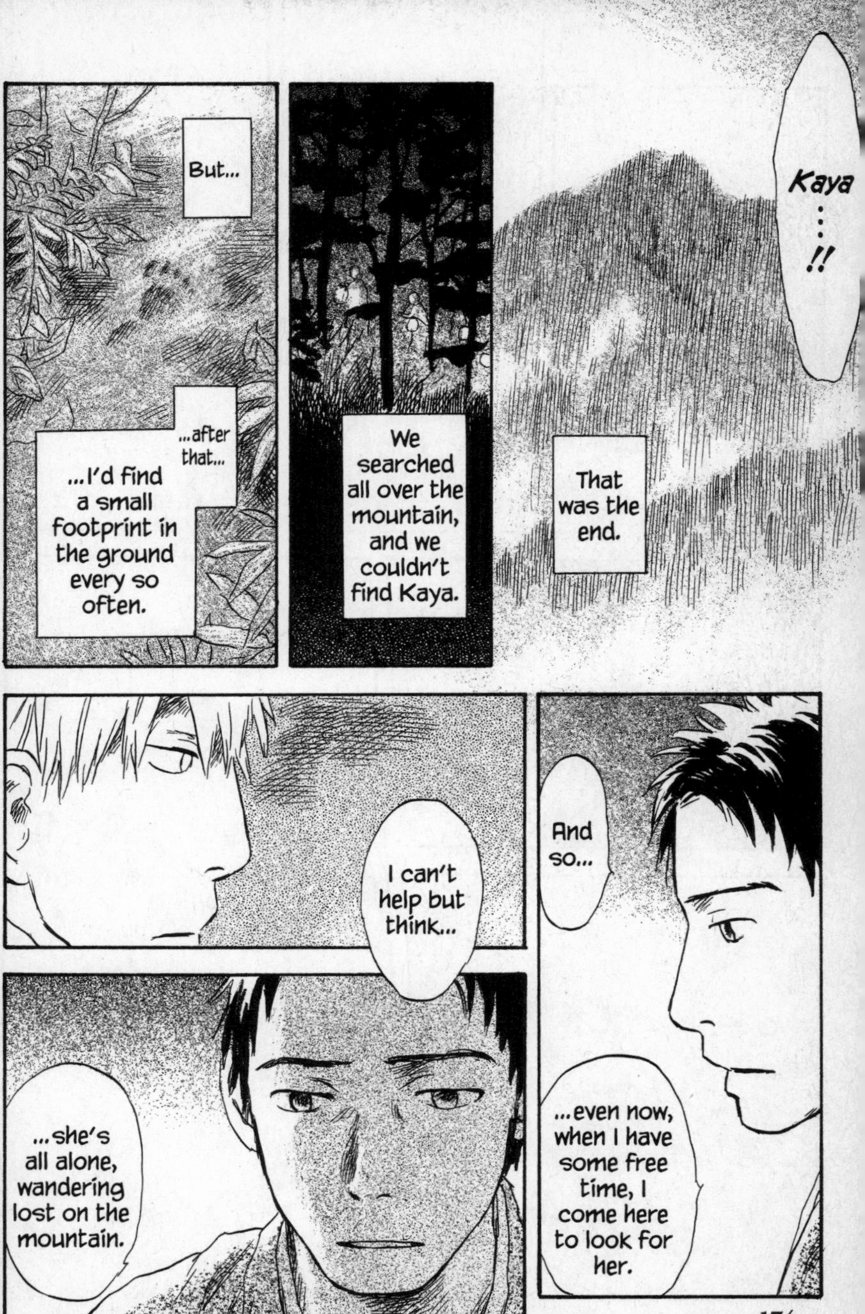
Kaya...!!
That was the end.
We searched all over the mountain, and we couldn't find Kaya.
But...
...after that...
...I'd find a small footprint in the ground every so often.
And so...
...even now, when I have some free time, I come here to look for her.
I can't help but think...
...she's all alone, wandering lost on the mountain.

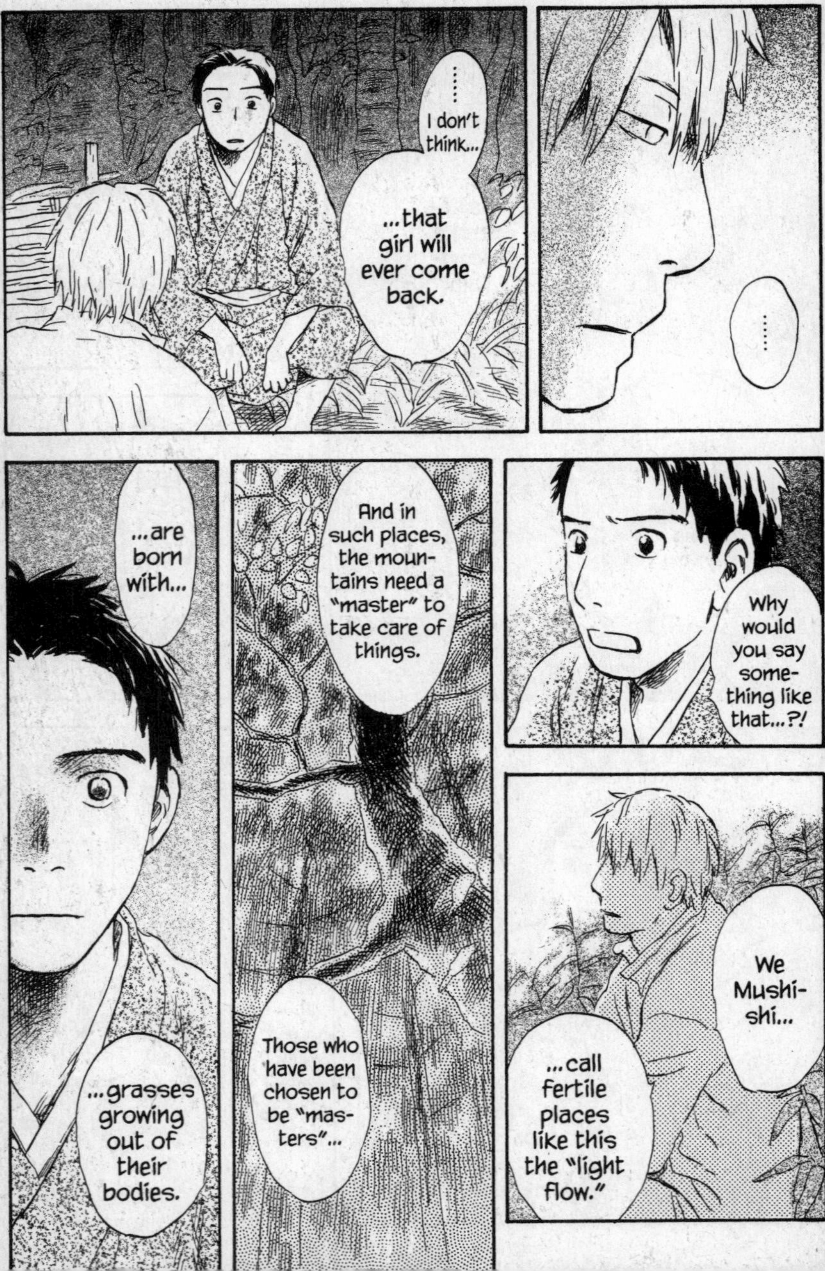
......
......
I don't think...
...that girl will ever come back.
Why would you say something like that...?!
We Mushi-shi...
...call fertile places like this the "light flow."
And in such places, the mountains need a "master" to take care of things.
Those who have been chosen to be "masters"...
...are born with...
...grasses growing out of their bodies.

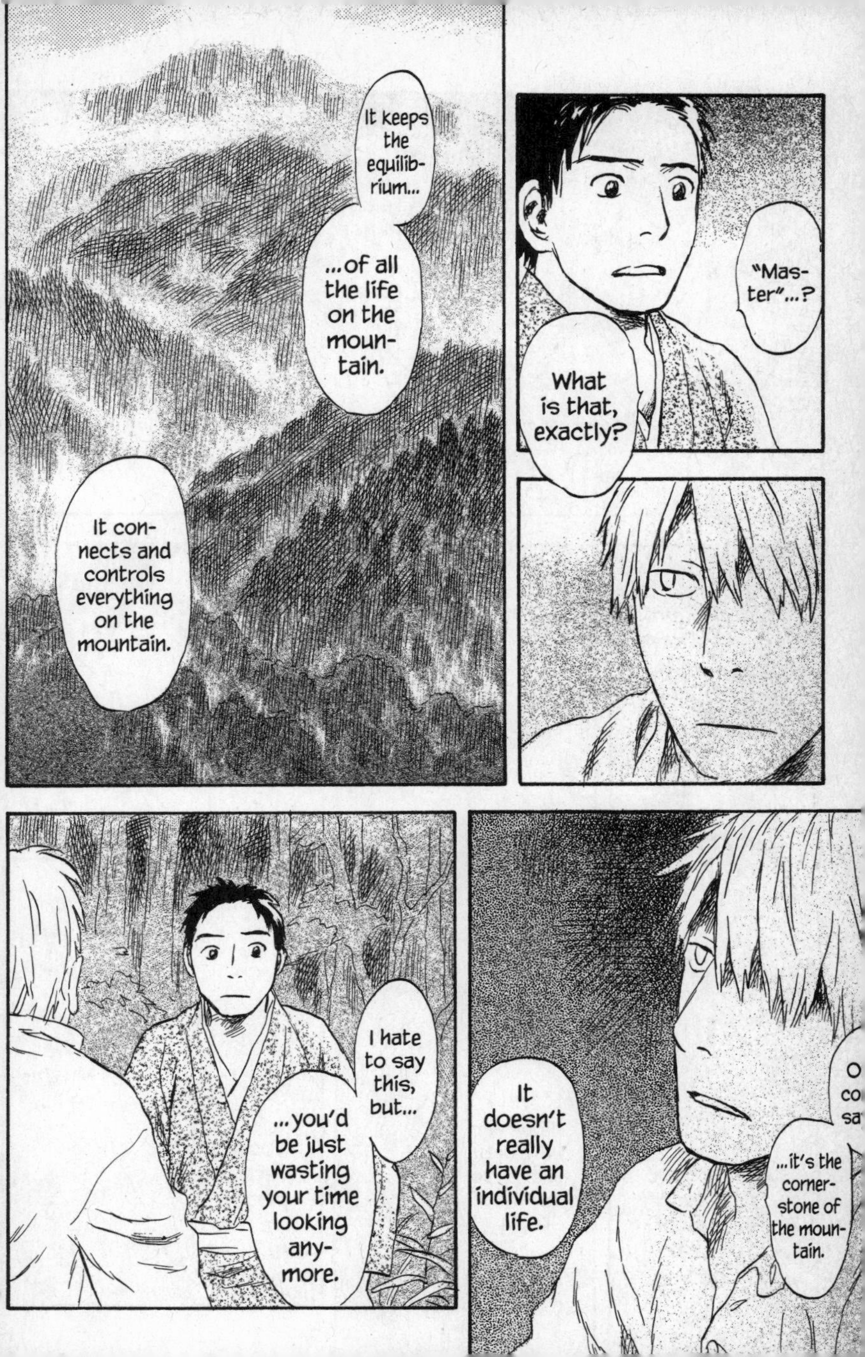
"Master"...?
What is that, exactly?
It keeps the equilibrium...
...of all the life on the mountain.
It connects and controls everything on the mountain.
...it's the cornerstone of the mountain.
It doesn't really have an individual life.
I hate to say this, but...
...you'd be just wasting your time looking anymore.

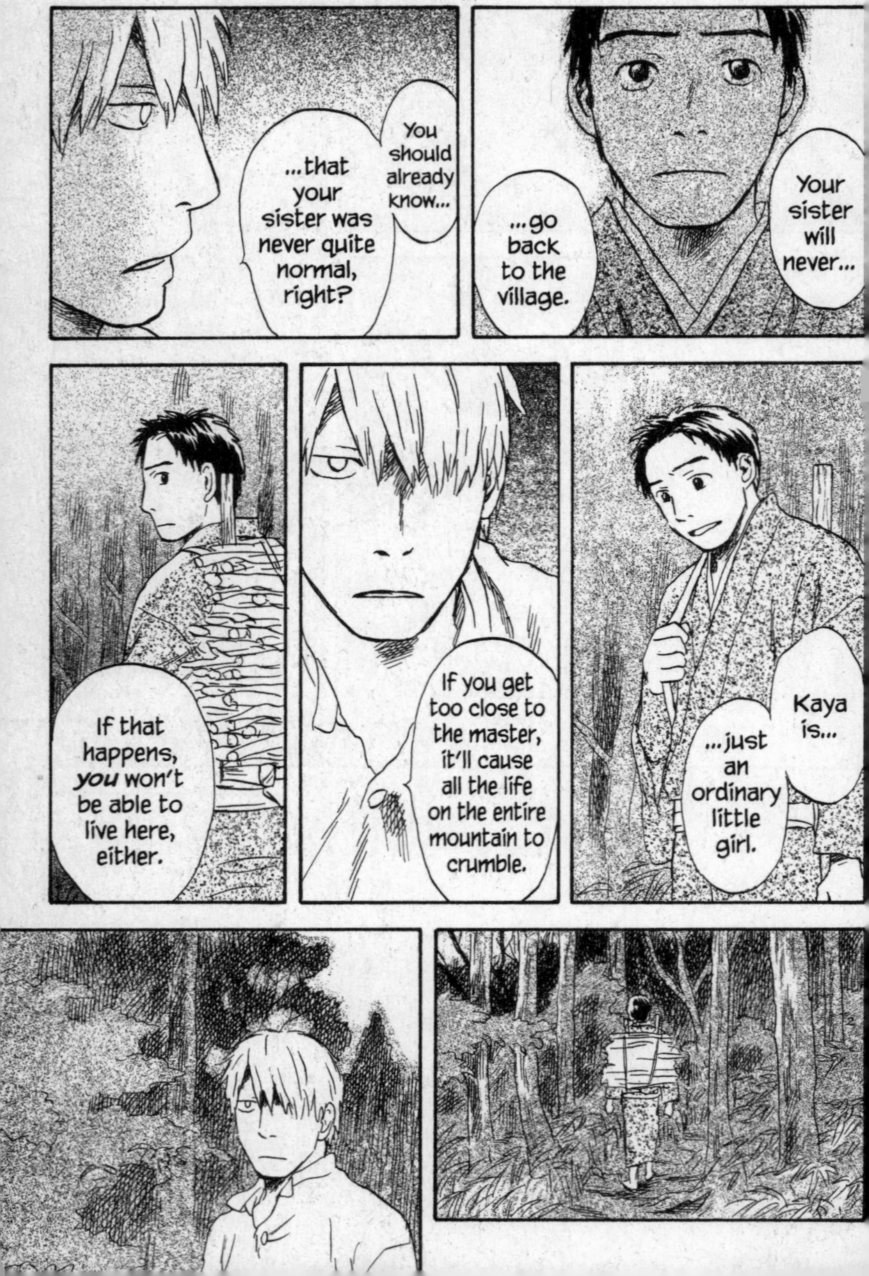
Your sister will never...
...go back to the village.
You should already know...
...that your sister was never quite normal, right?
Kaya is...
...just an ordinary little girl.
If you get too close to the master, it'll cause all the life on the entire mountain to crumble.
If that happens, *you* won't be able to live here, either.

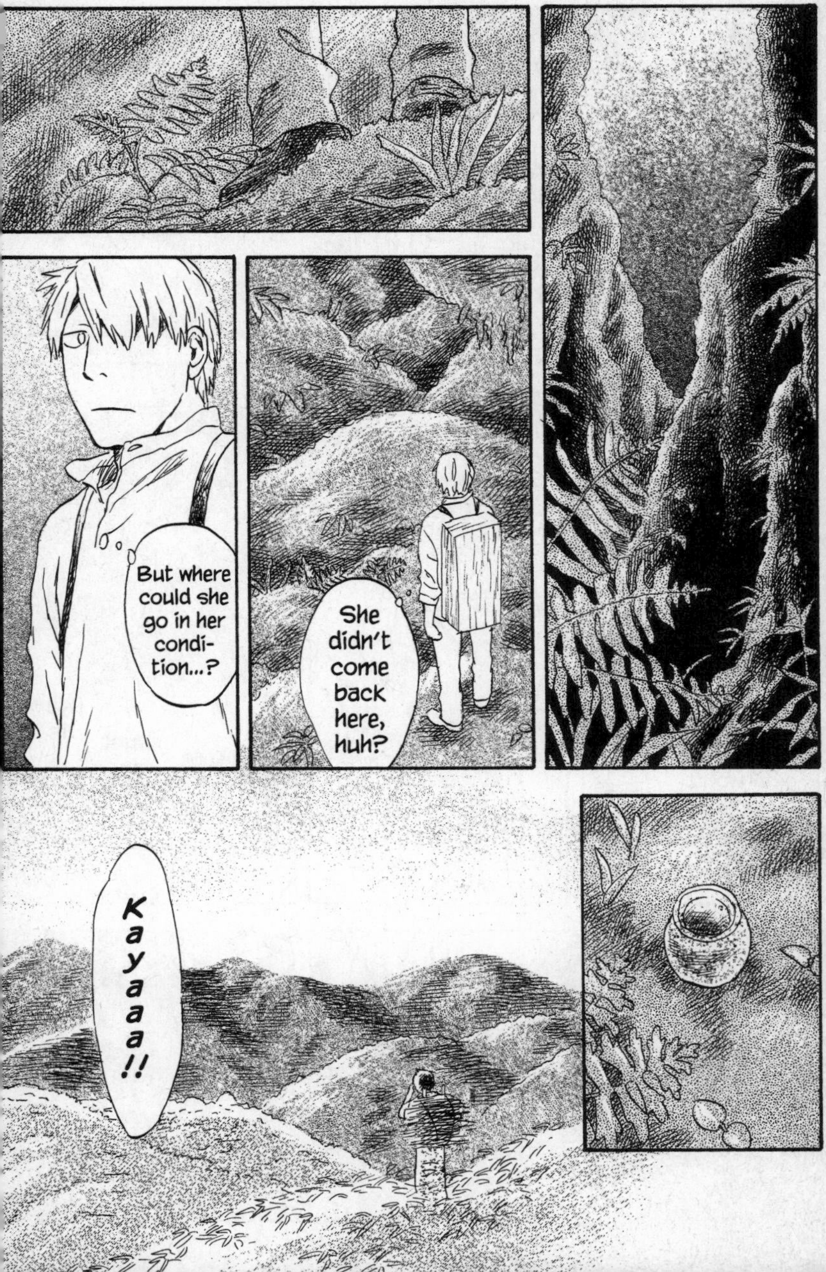
She didn't come back here, huh?
But where could she go in her condi-tion...?
Kayaaa!!

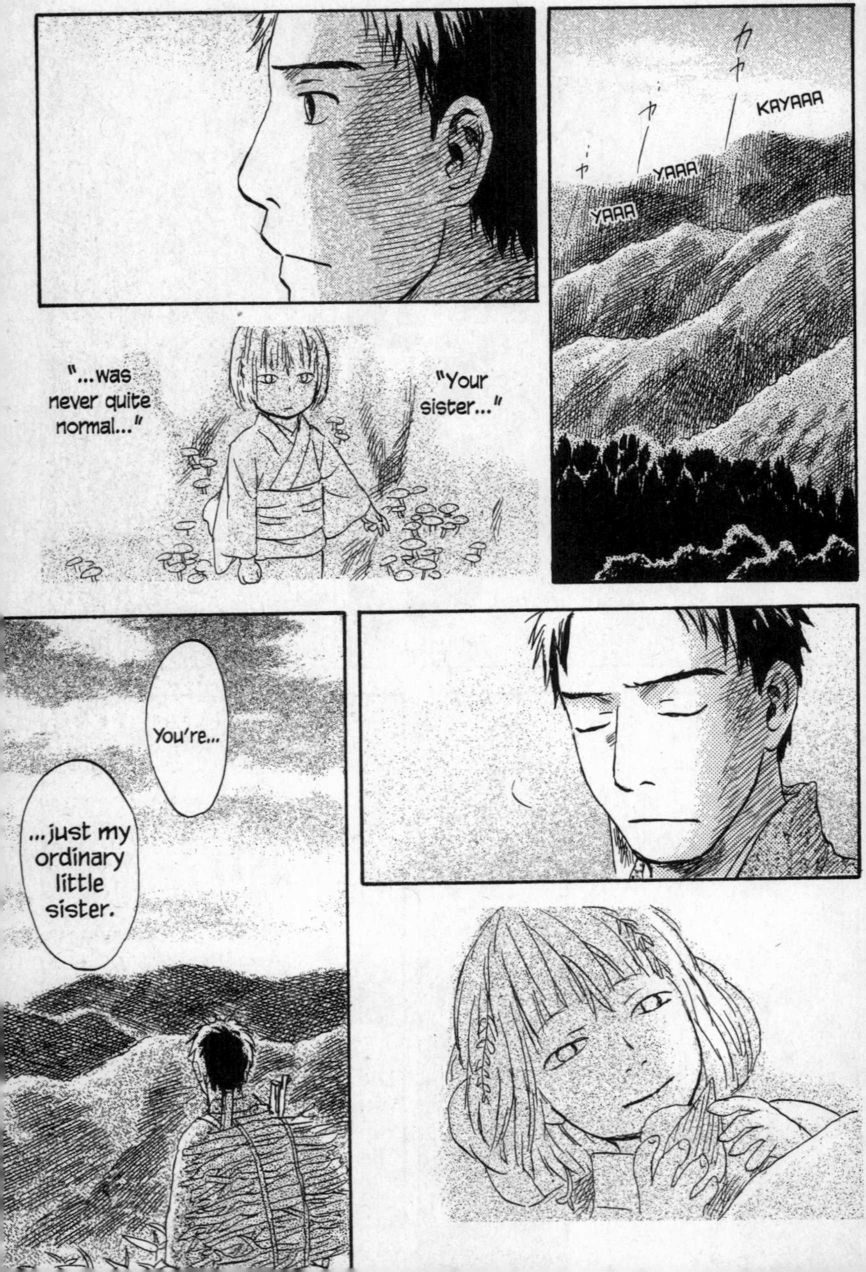
KAYAAA
YAAA
YAAA
"Your sister..."
"...was never quite normal..."
You're...
...just my ordinary little sister.

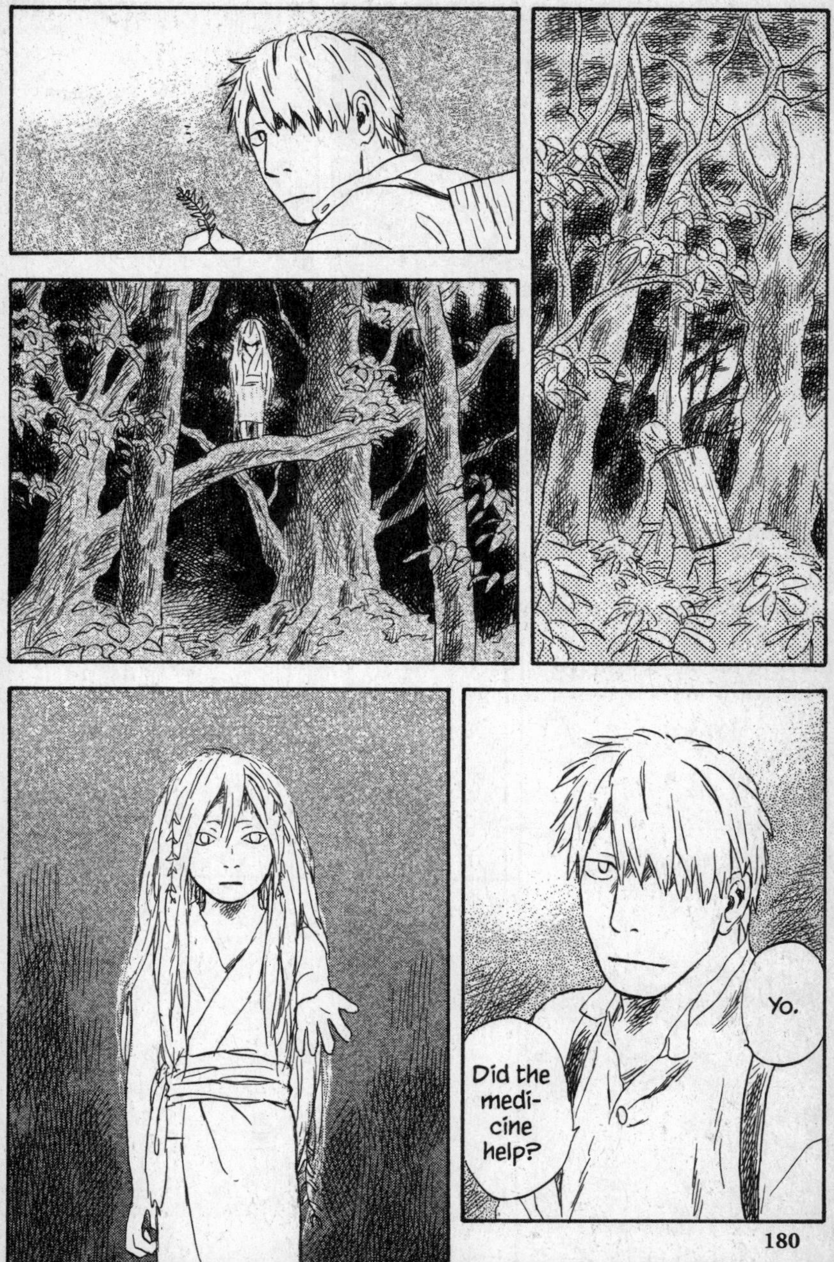
Yo.
Did the medicine help?

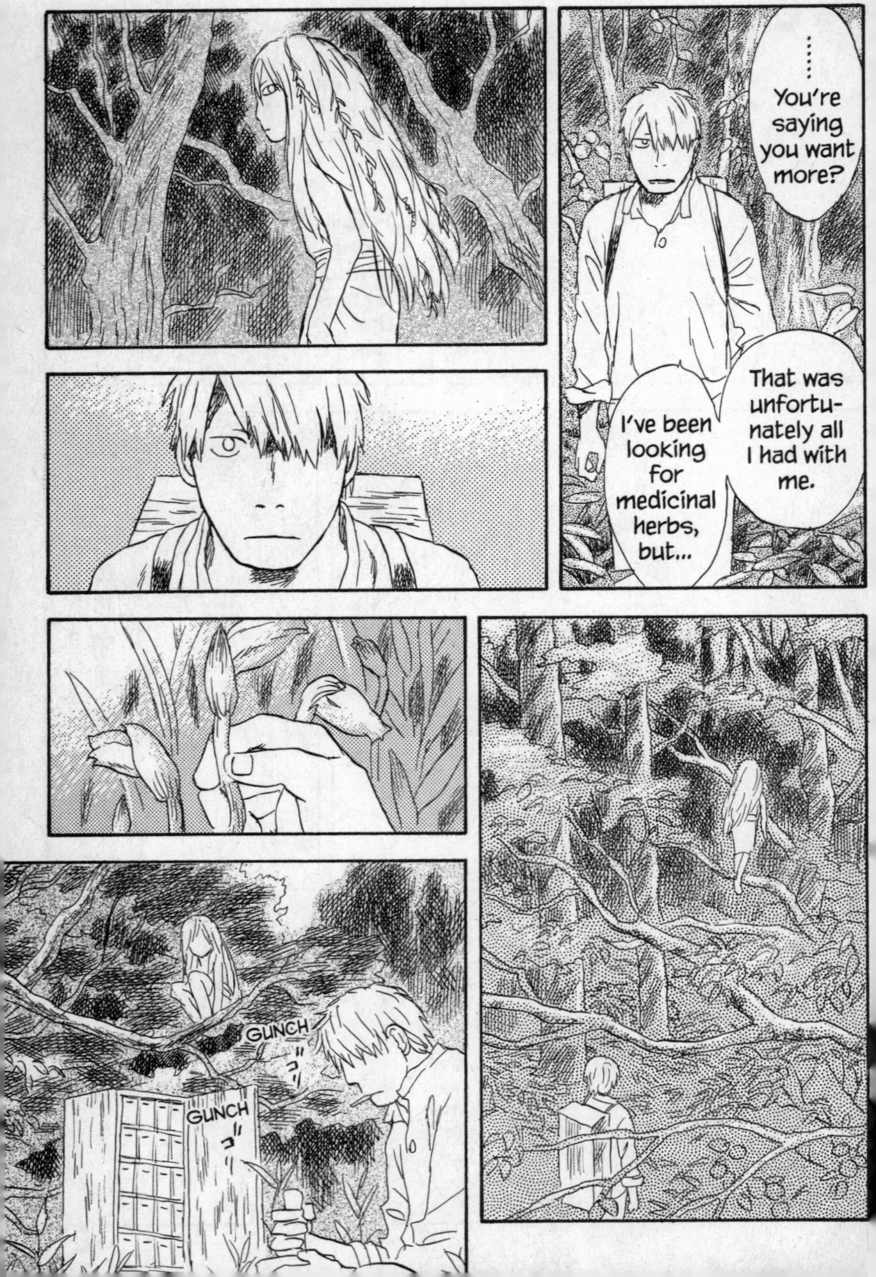
......
You're saying you want more?
That was unfortunately all I had with me.
I've been looking for medicinal herbs, but...
GUNCH
GUNCH

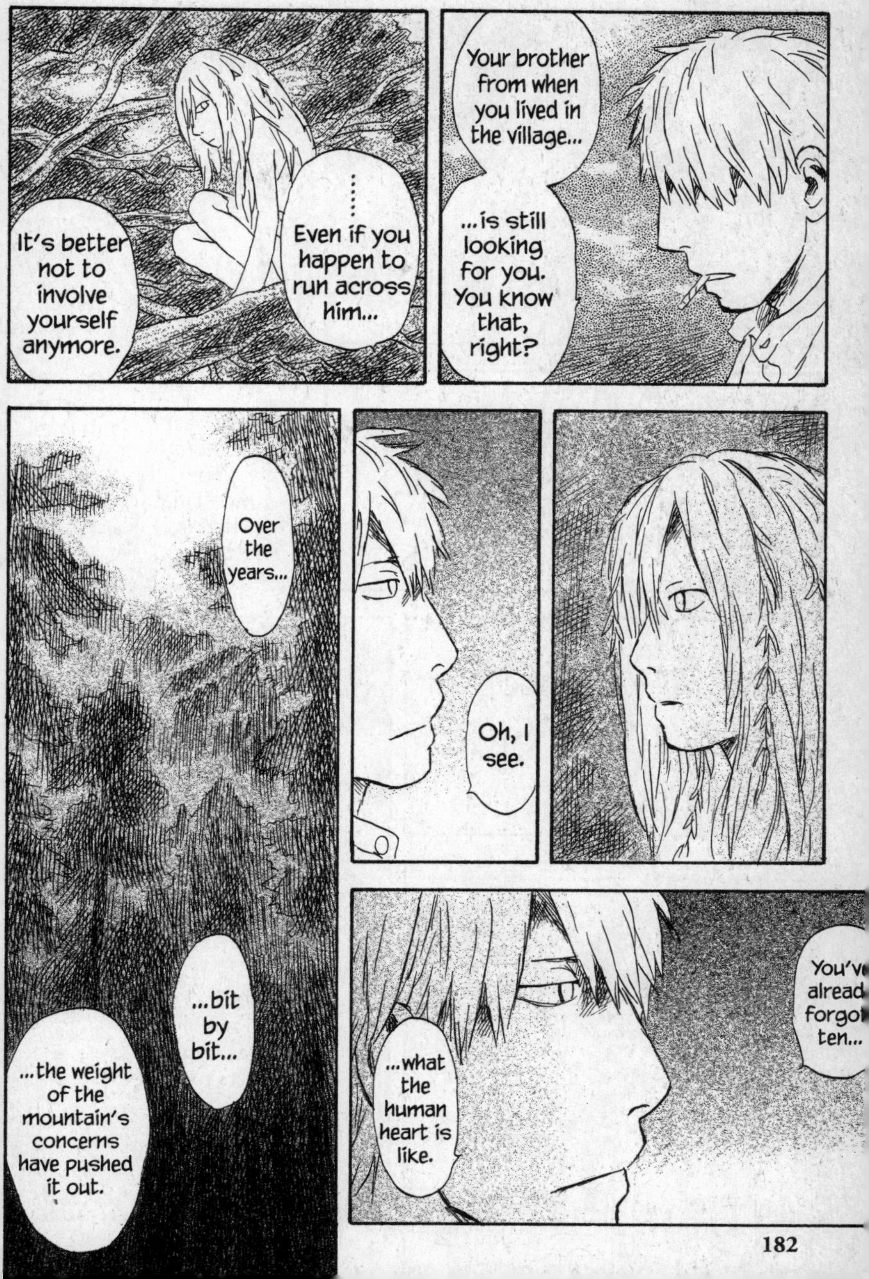
Your brother from when you lived in the village...
...is still looking for you. You know that, right?
......
Even if you happen to run across him...
It's better not to involve yourself anymore.
Oh, I see.
You'v alread forgot ten...
...what the human heart is like.
Over the years...
...bit by bit...
...the weight of the mountain's concerns have pushed it out.

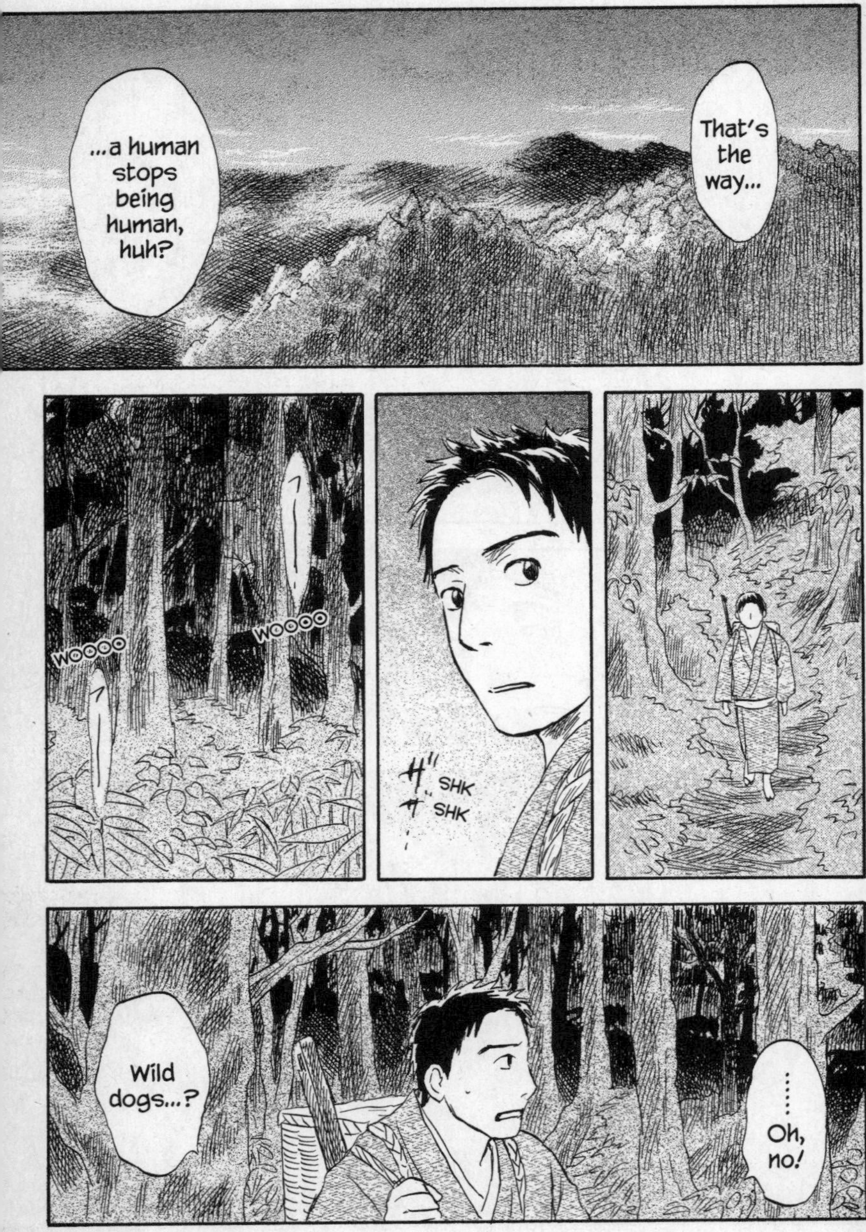
That's the way...
...a human stops being human, huh?
SHK
SHK
WOOOO
WOOOO
...... Oh, no!
Wild dogs...?

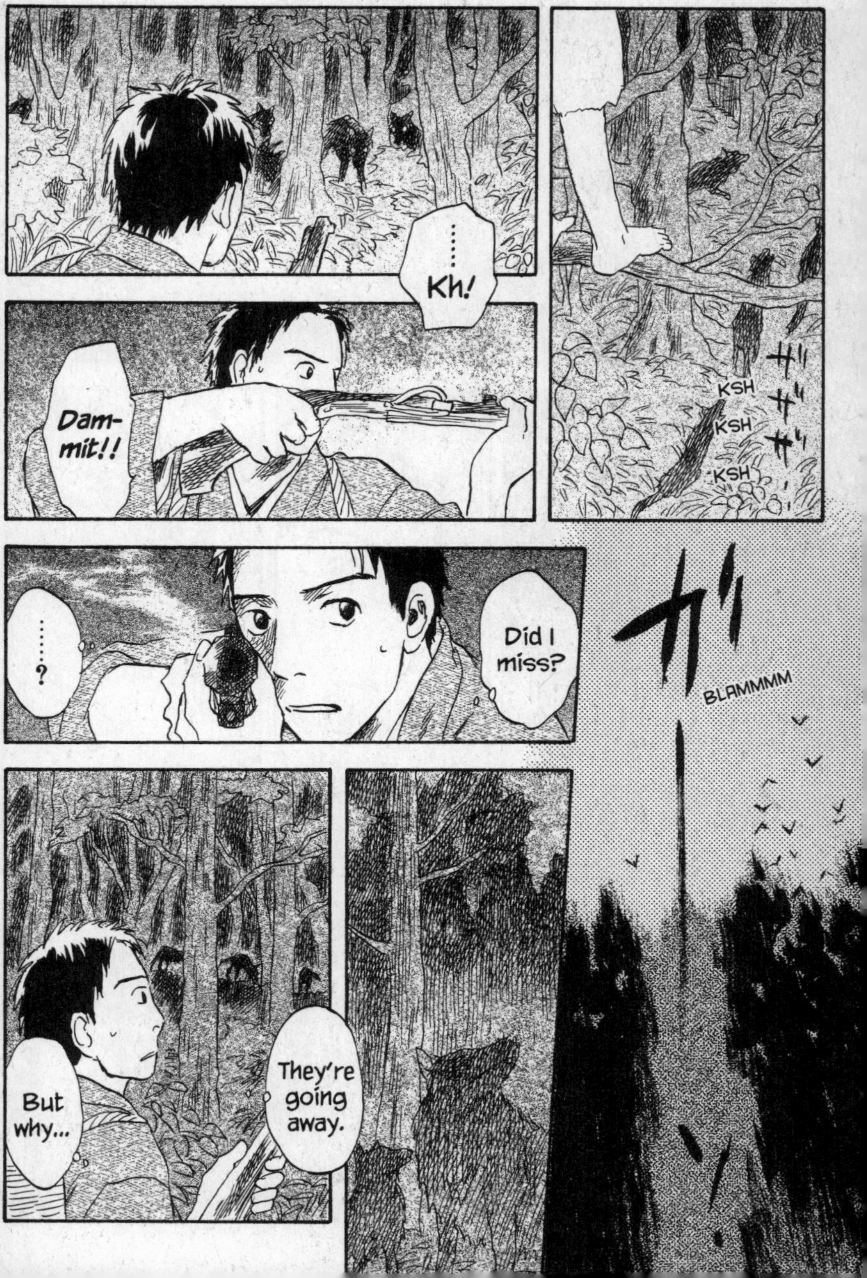
KSH
KSH
KSH
...... Kh!
Dam-mit!!
BLAMMMM
Did I miss?
......?
They're going away.
But why...

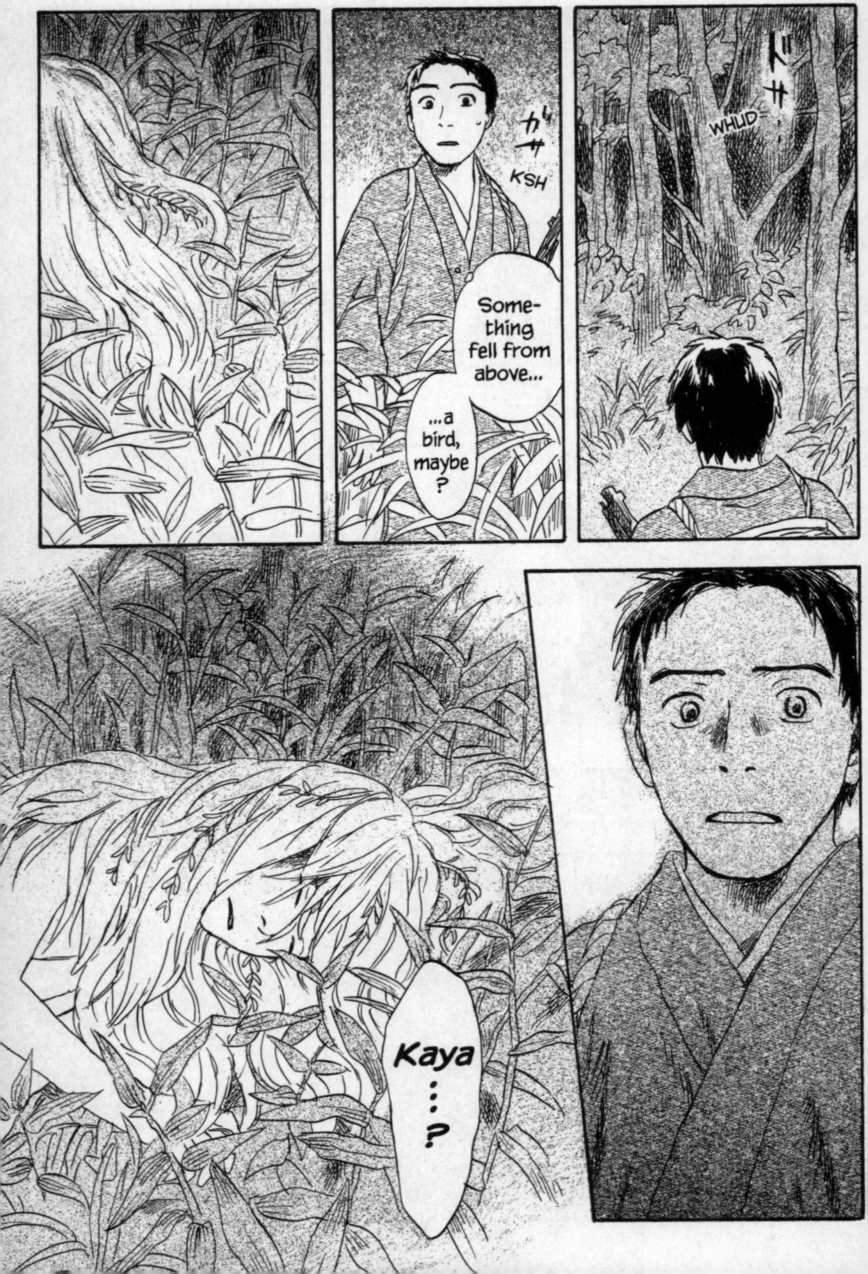
WHUD
KSH
Something fell from above...
...a bird, maybe?
Kaya...?

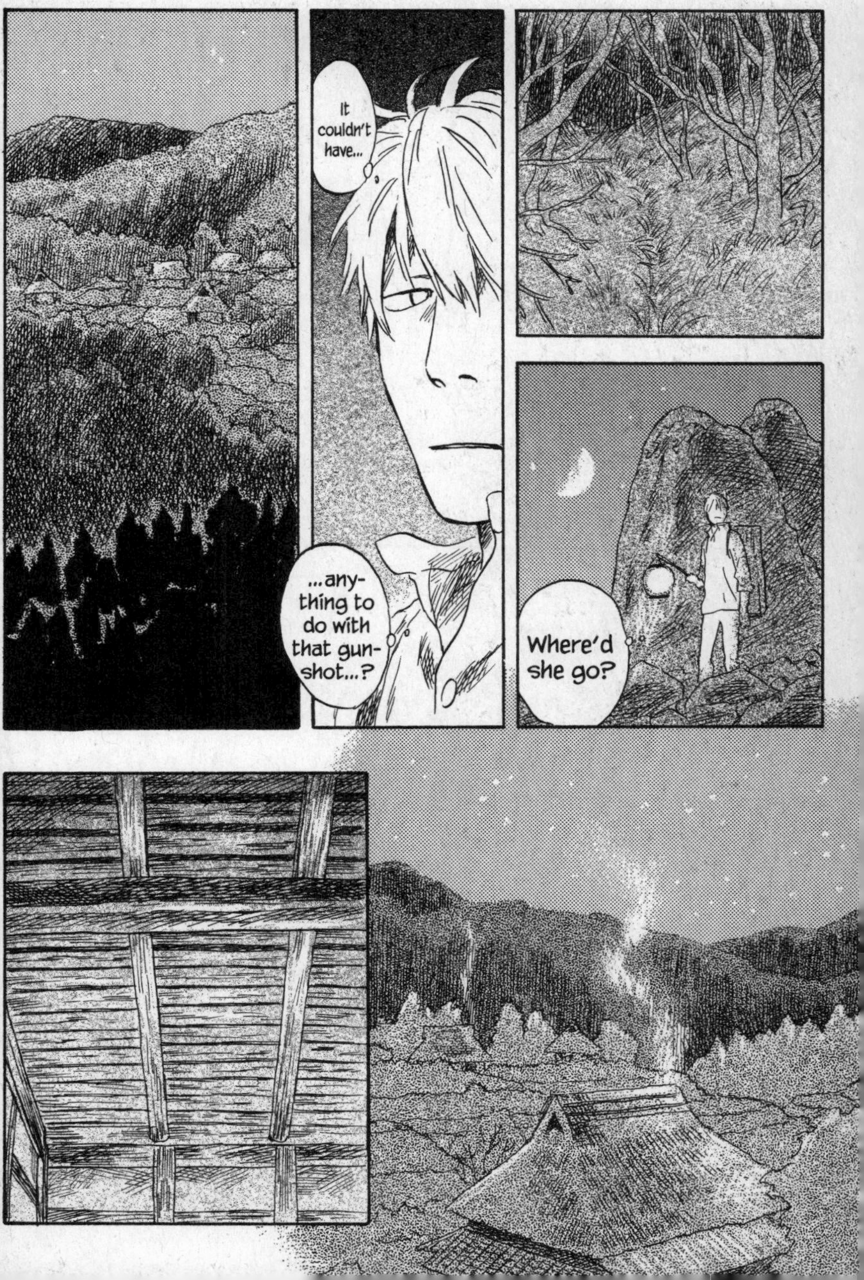
Where'd she go?
It couldn't have...
...anything to do with that gunshot...?

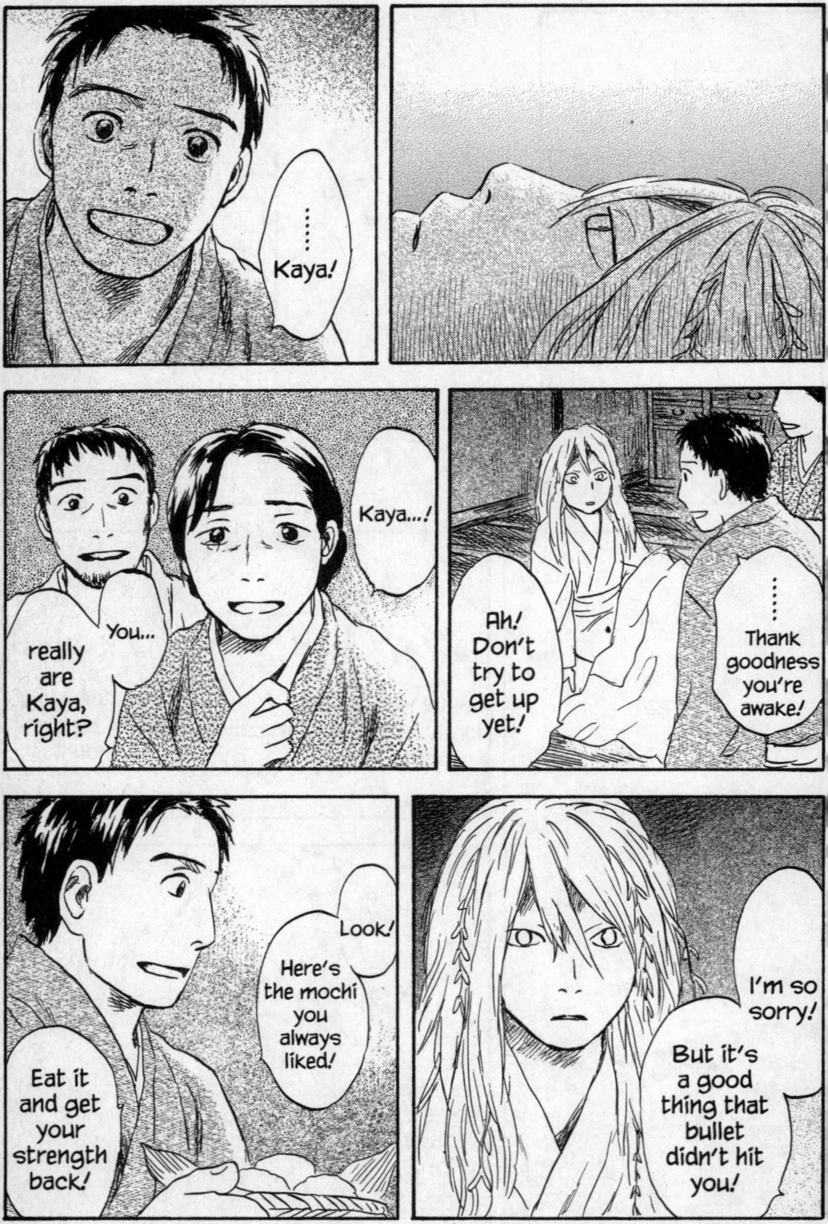
......Kaya!
...... Thank goodness you're awake!
Ah! Don't try to get up yet!
Kaya...!
You...
really are Kaya, right?
I'm so sorry!
But it's a good thing that bullet didn't hit you!
Look!
Here's the mochi you always liked!
Eat it and get your strength back!

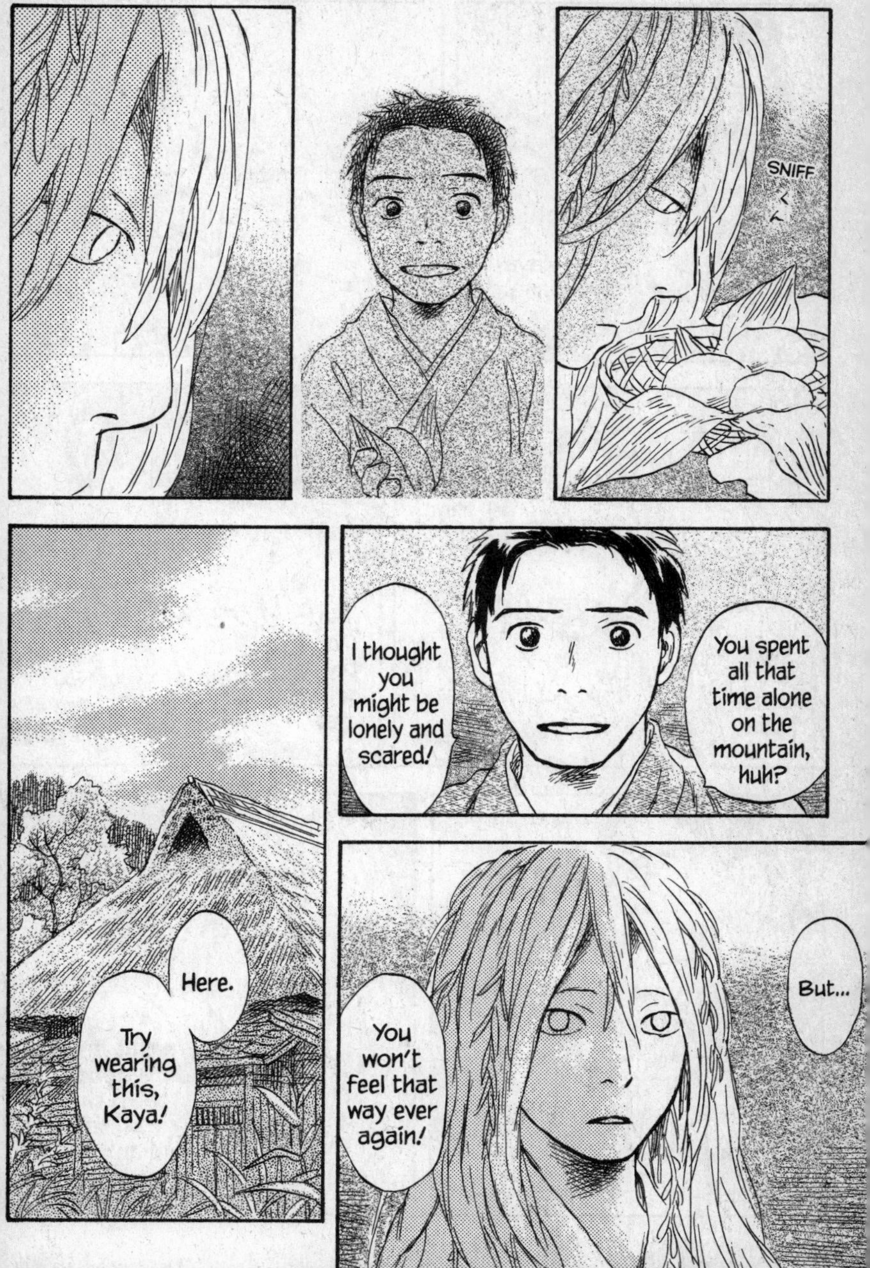
SNIFF
くん
You spent all that time alone on the mountain, huh?
I thought you might be lonely and scared!
But...
You won't feel that way ever again!
Here.
Try wearing this, Kaya!

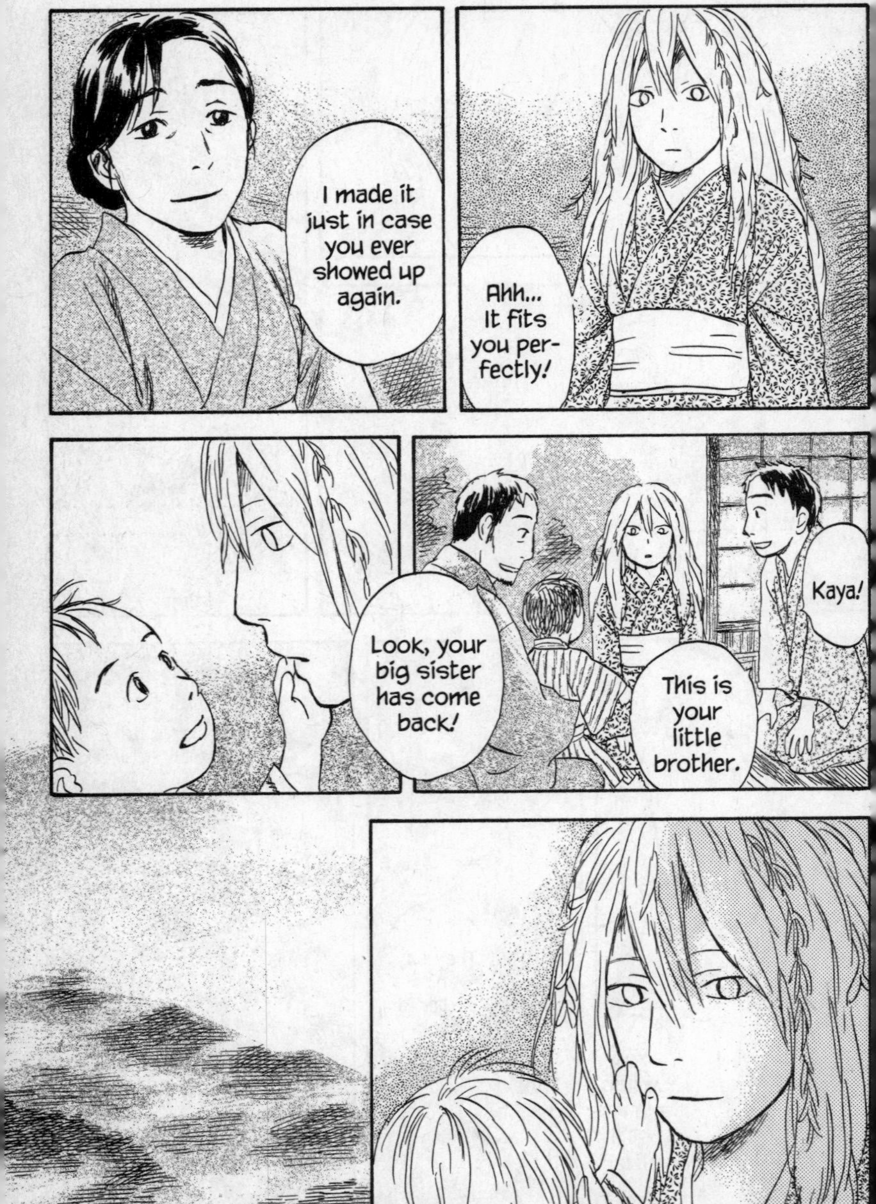
Ahh... It fits you per-fectly!
I made it just in case you ever showed up again.
Kaya!
This is your little brother.
Look, your big sister has come back!

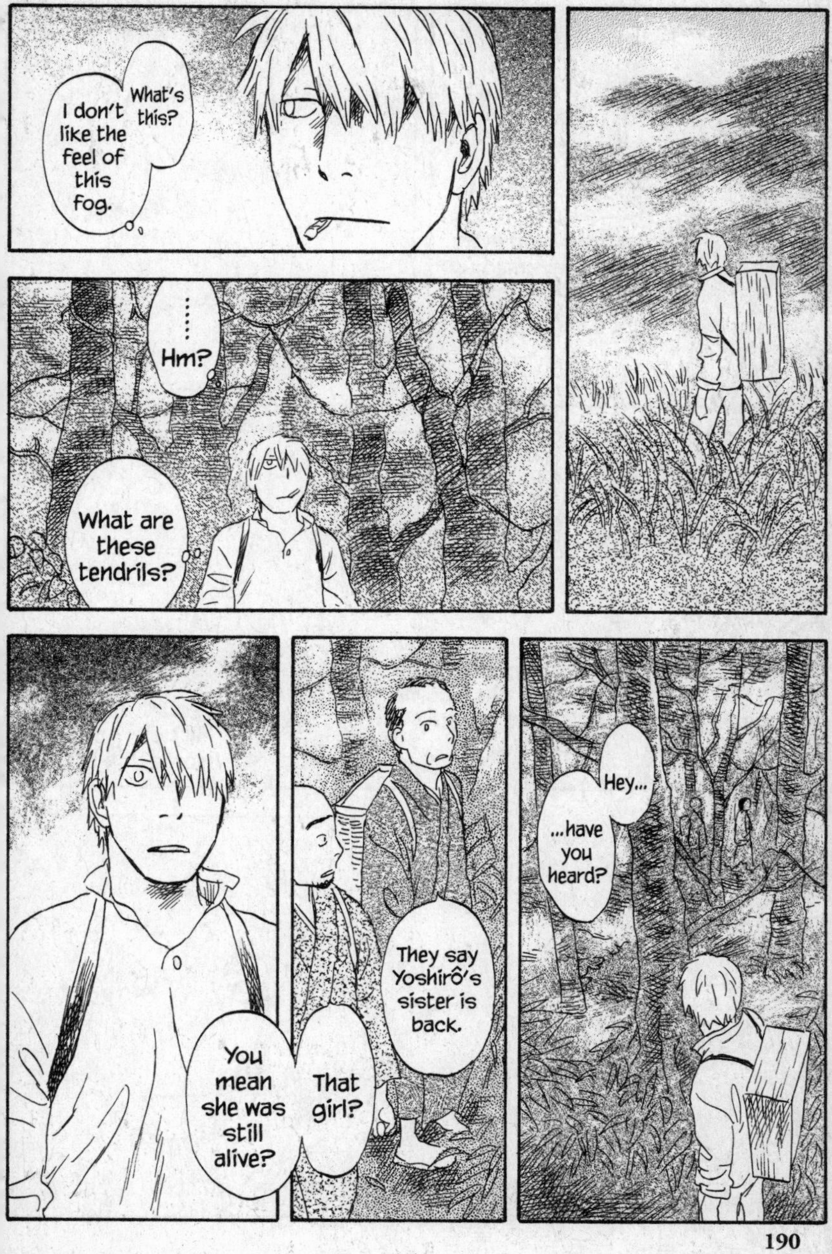
What's this?
I don't like the feel of this fog.
......
Hm?
What are these tendrils?
Hey...
...have you heard?
They say Yoshirô's sister is back.
That girl?
You mean she was still alive?

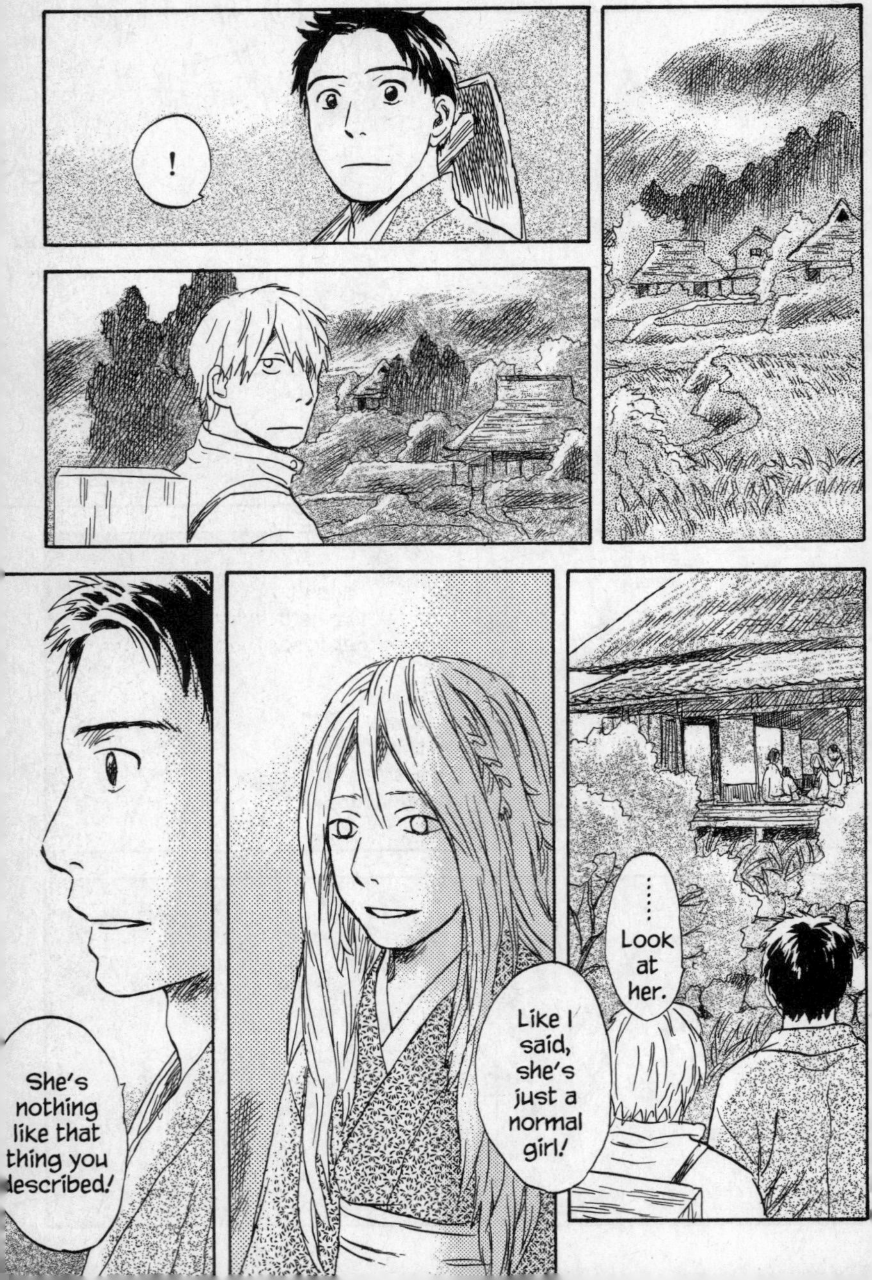
!
......
Look at her.
Like I said, she's just a normal girl!
She's nothing like that thing you described!

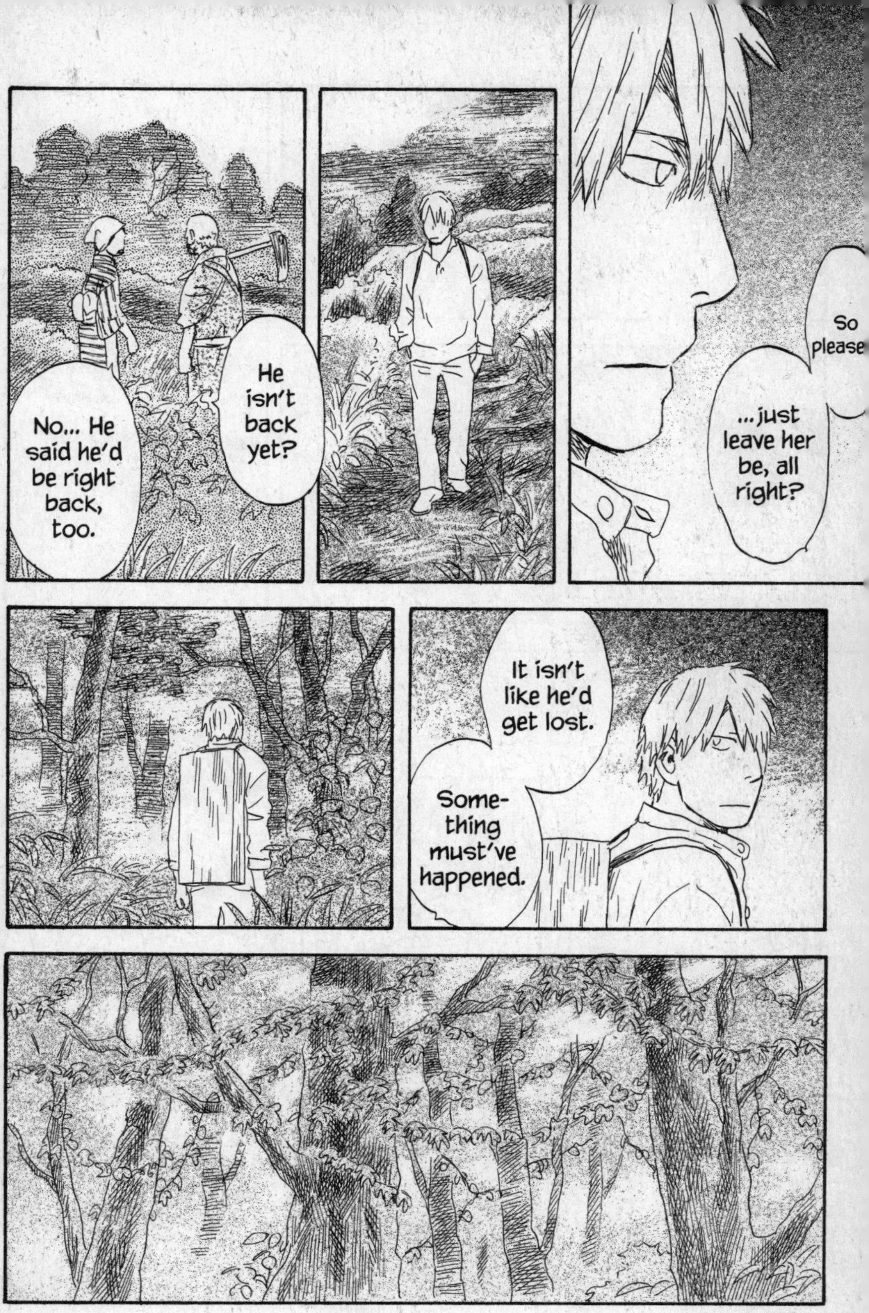
So please
...just leave her be, all right?
He isn't back yet?
No... He said he'd be right back, too.
It isn't like he'd get lost.
Some-thing must've happened.

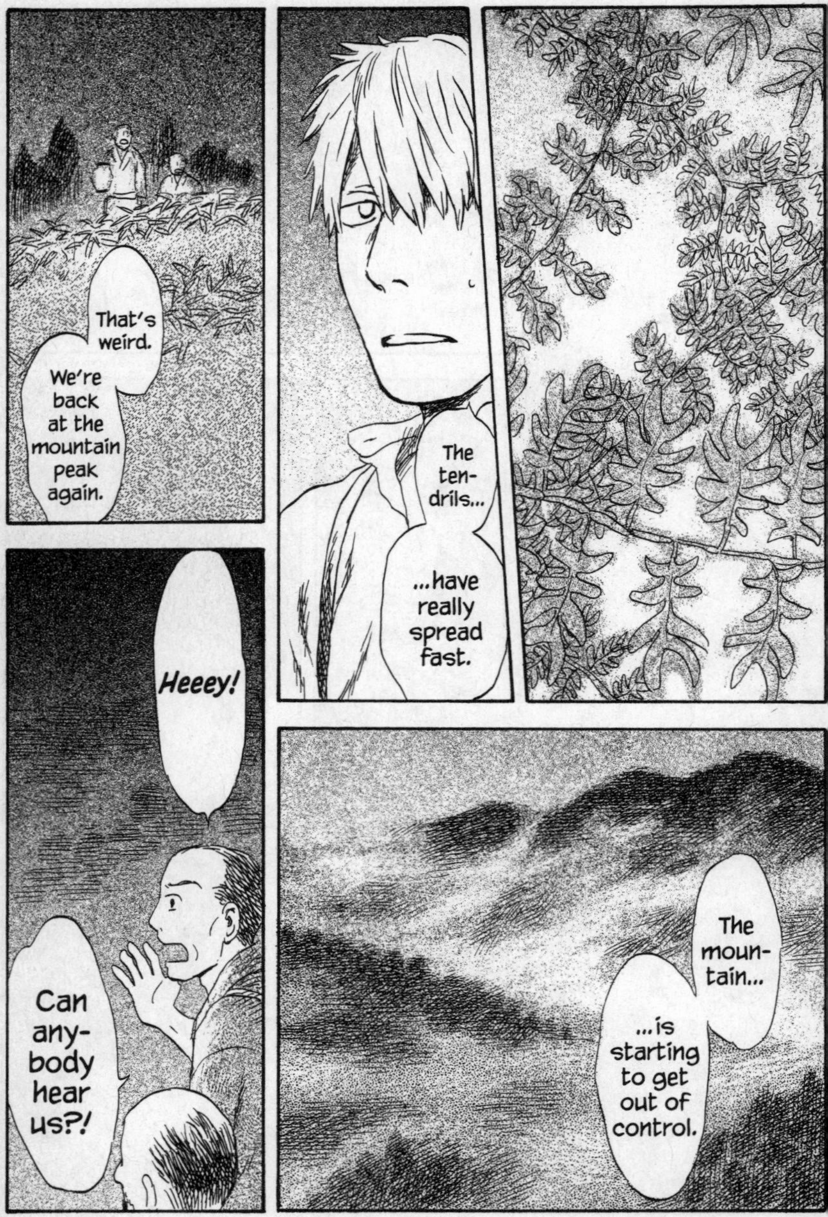
The ten-drils...
...have really spread fast.
That's weird.
We're back at the mountain peak again.
The moun-tain...
...is starting to get out of control.
Heeey!
Can any-body hear us?!

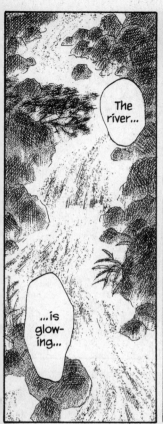

The river...

...is glow-ing...

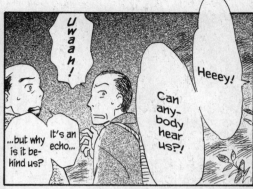

Uwaah!

Heeey!

Can any-body hear us?!

...but why is it be-hind us?

It's an echo...

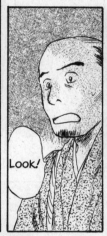

Look!

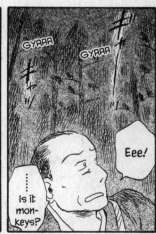

GYAAA

GYAAA

Eee!

...... Is it mon-keys?

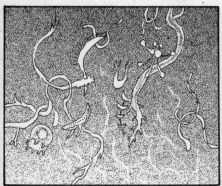

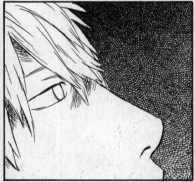

194

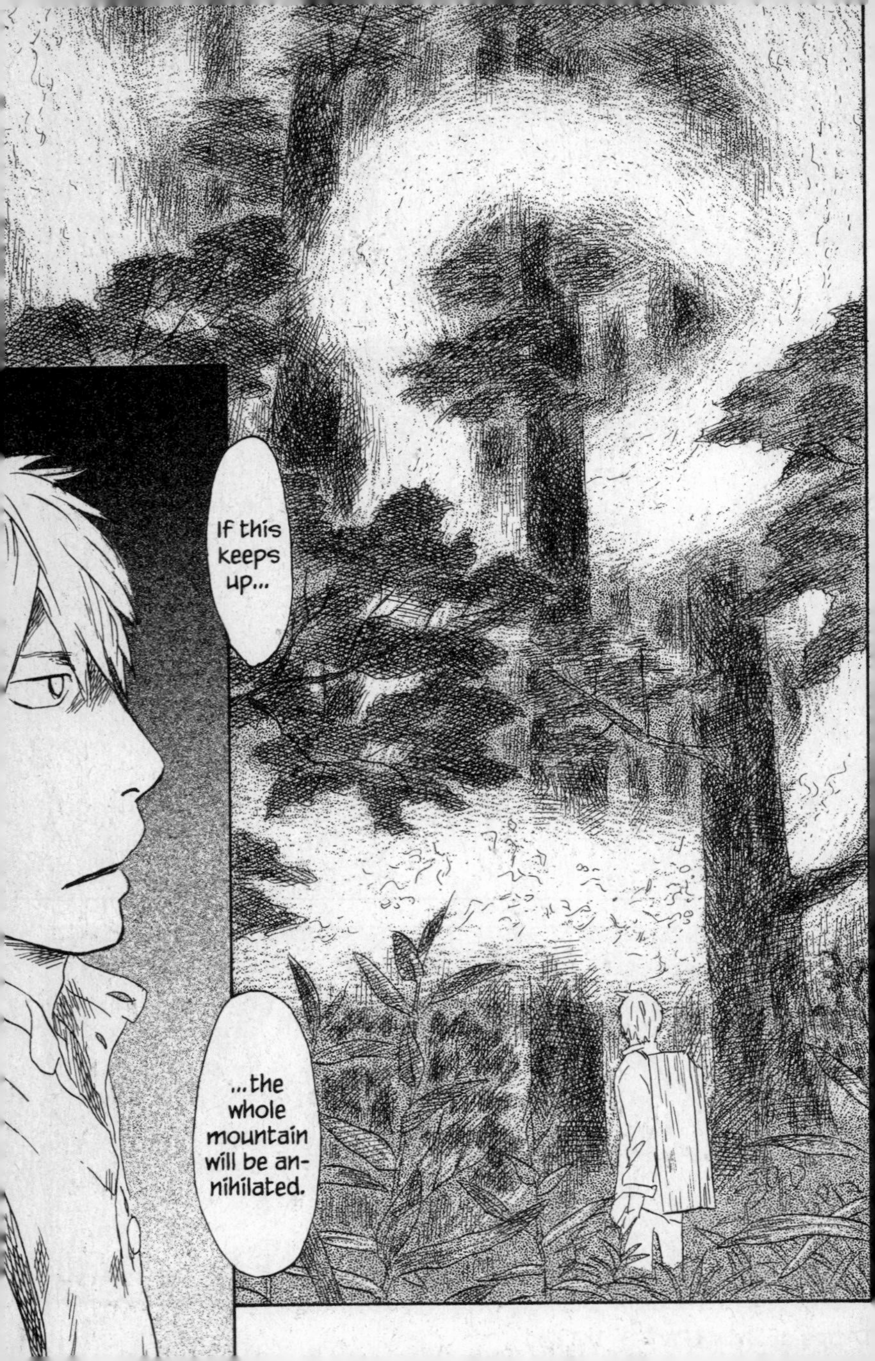
If this keeps up...
...the whole mountain will be an-nihilated.

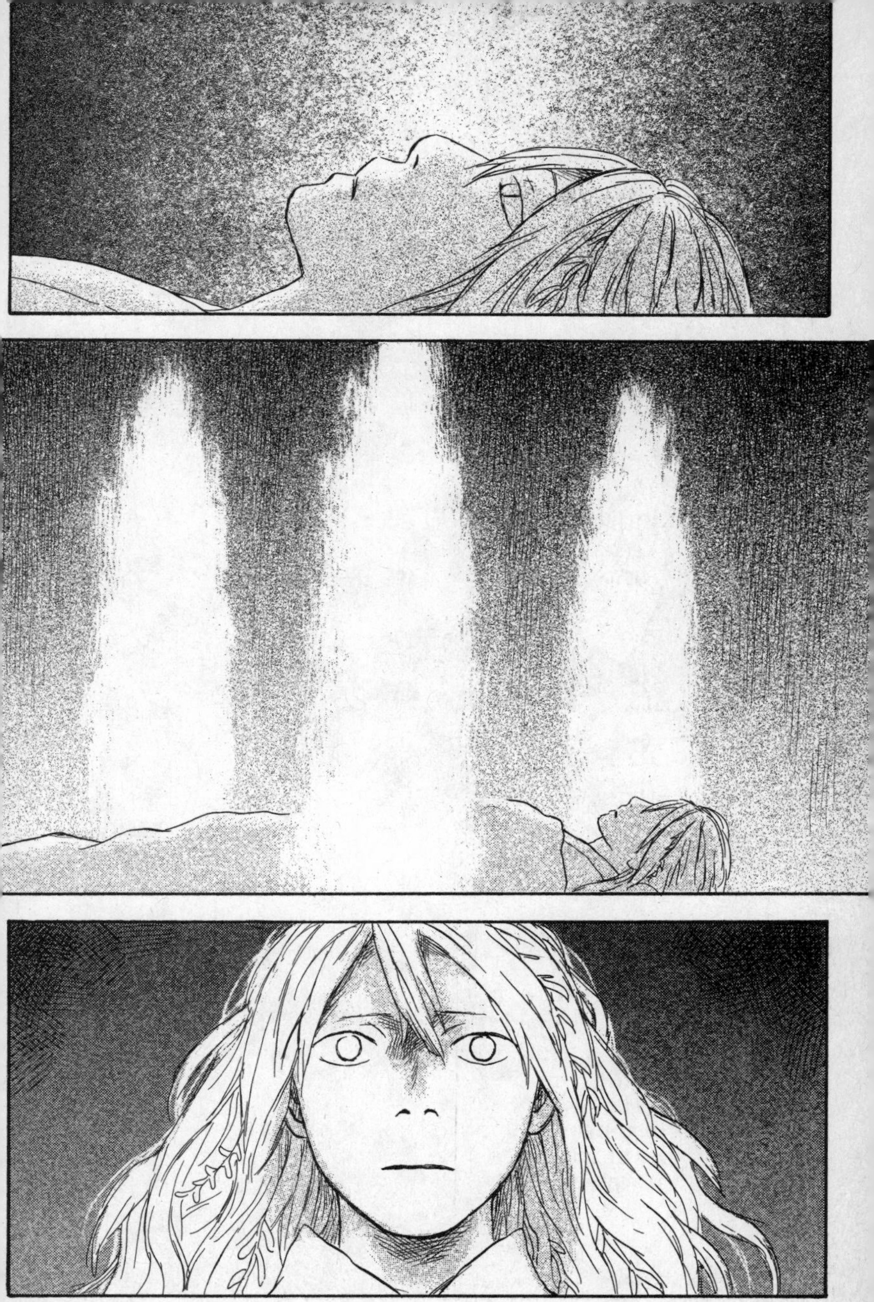

Drops of Bells (Part 1) The End

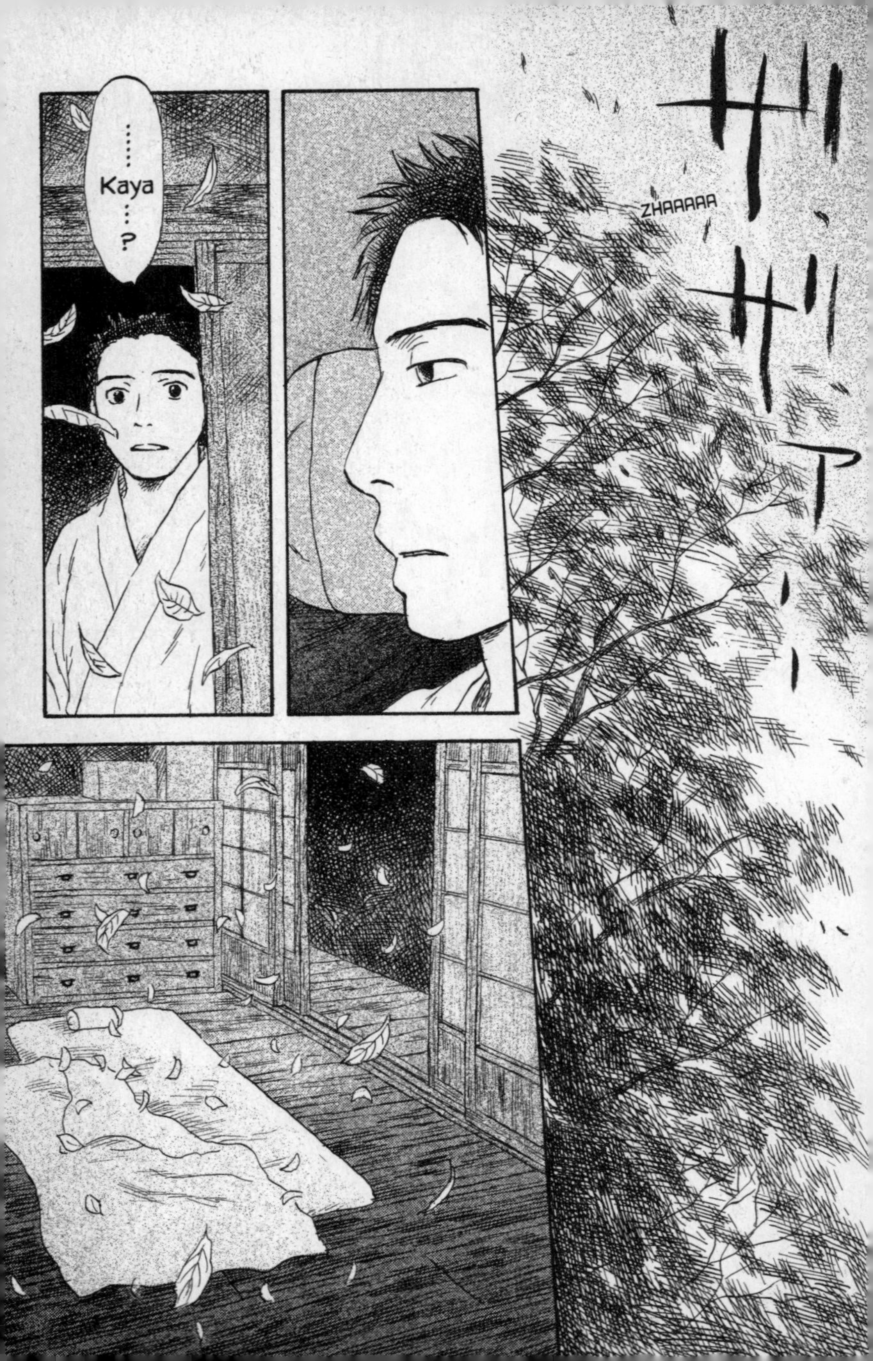
ザリザリア
ZHAAAAA
......Kaya...?

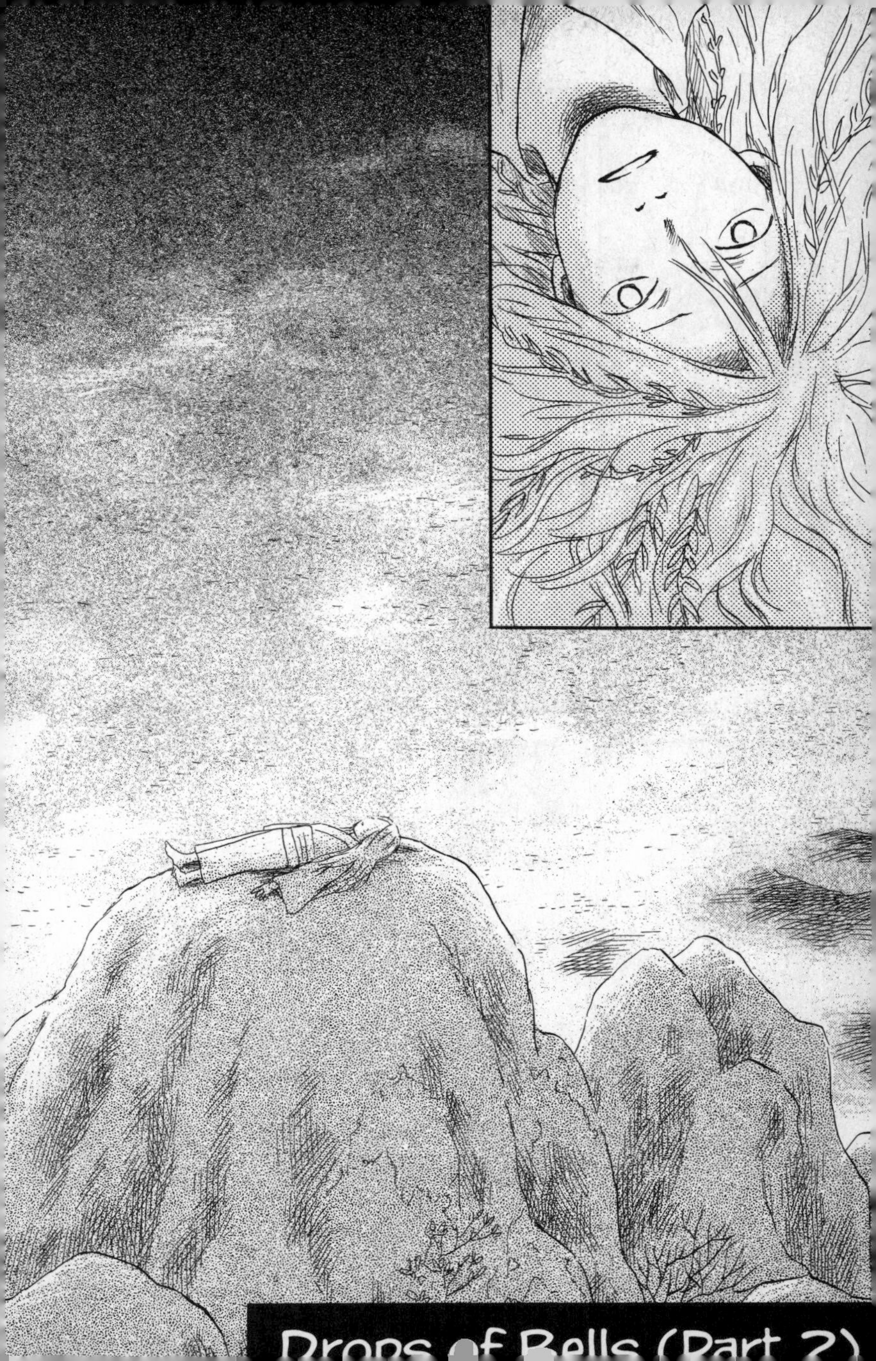
Drops of Bells (Part 2)

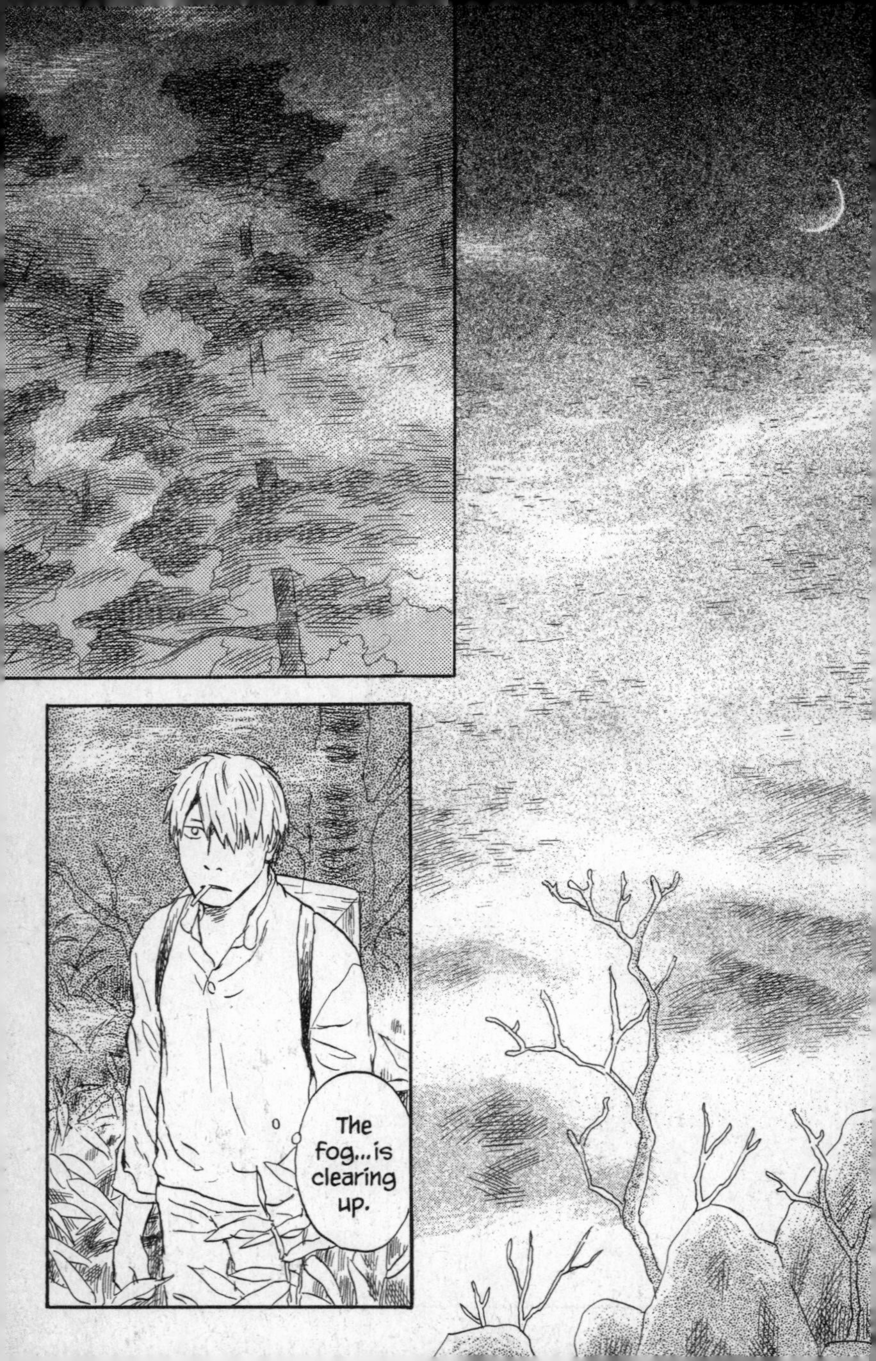
The fog...is clearing up.

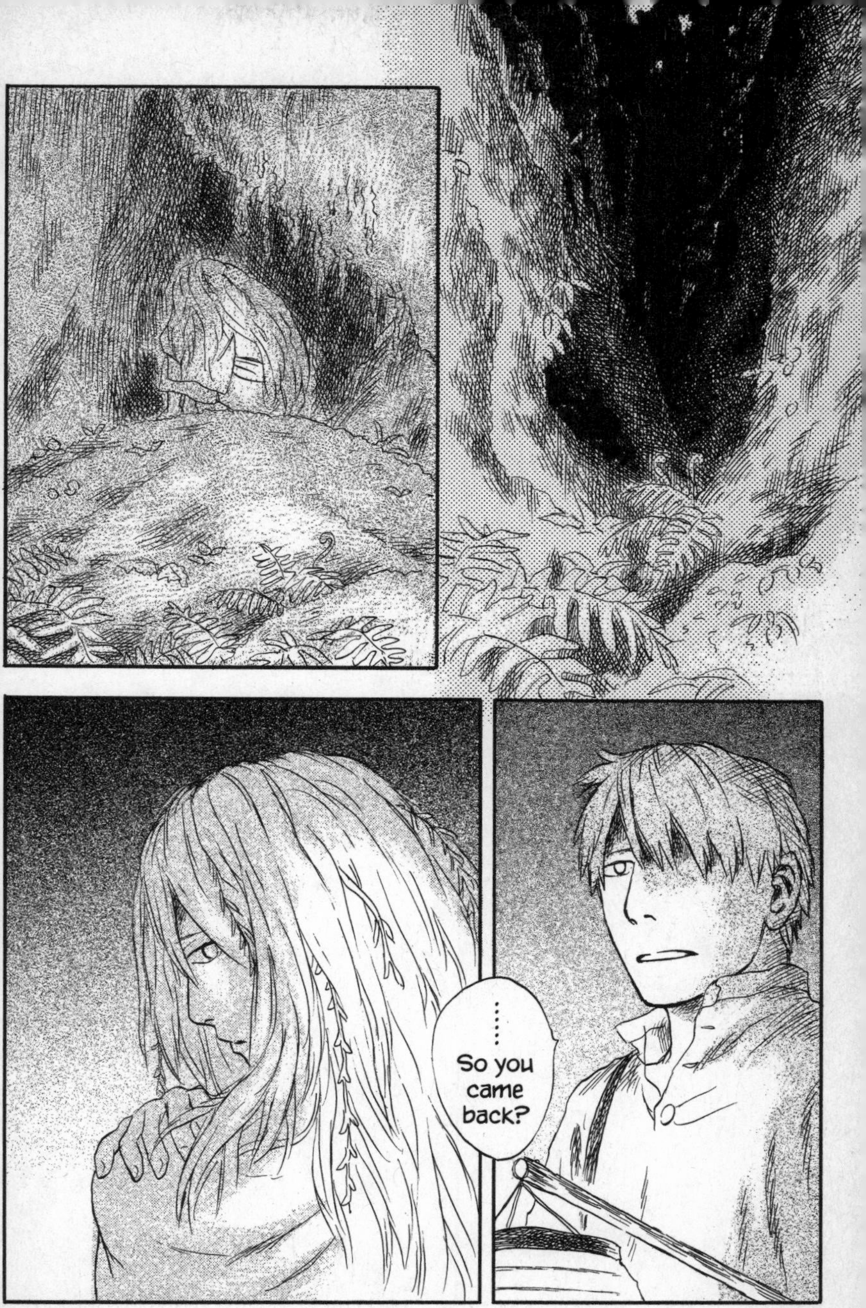
......
So you came back?

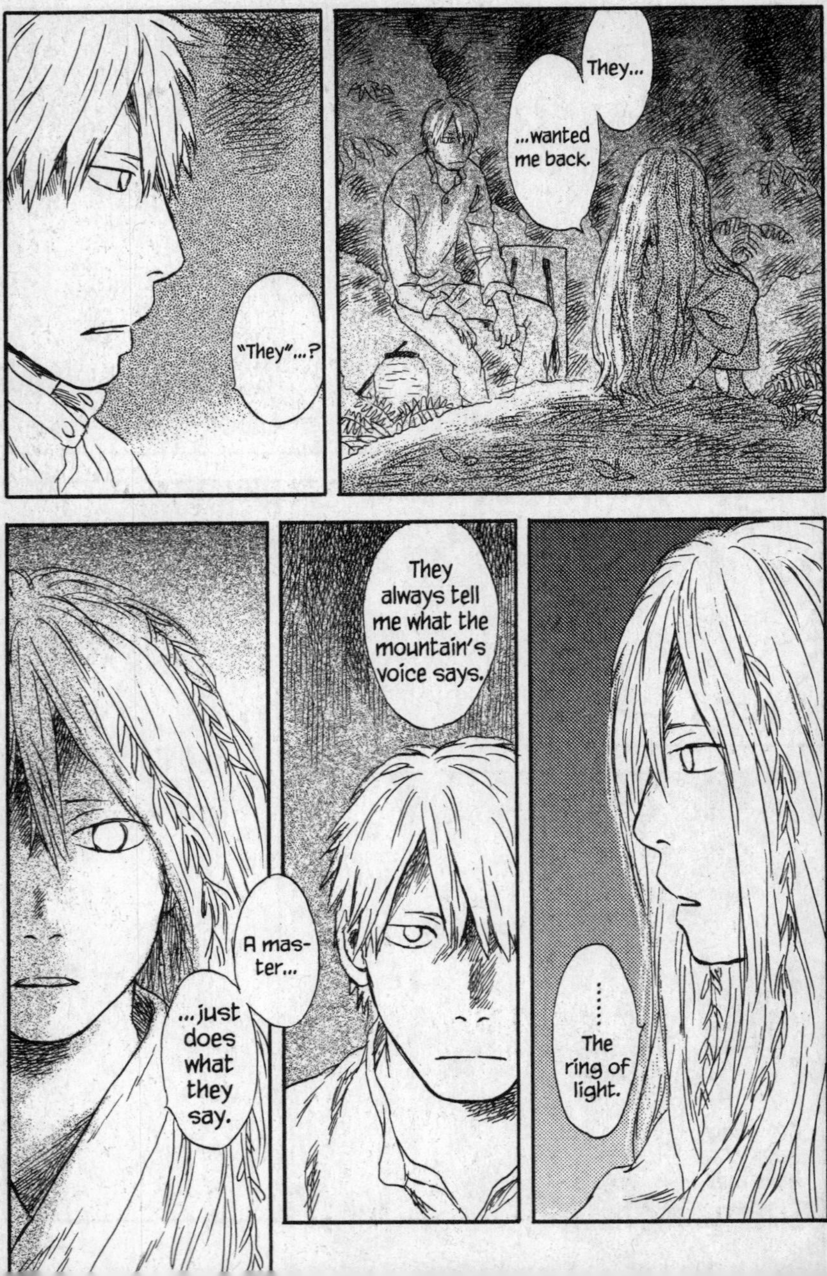
They...
...wanted me back.
"They"...?
......
The ring of light.
They always tell me what the mountain's voice says.
A mas-ter...
...just does what they say.

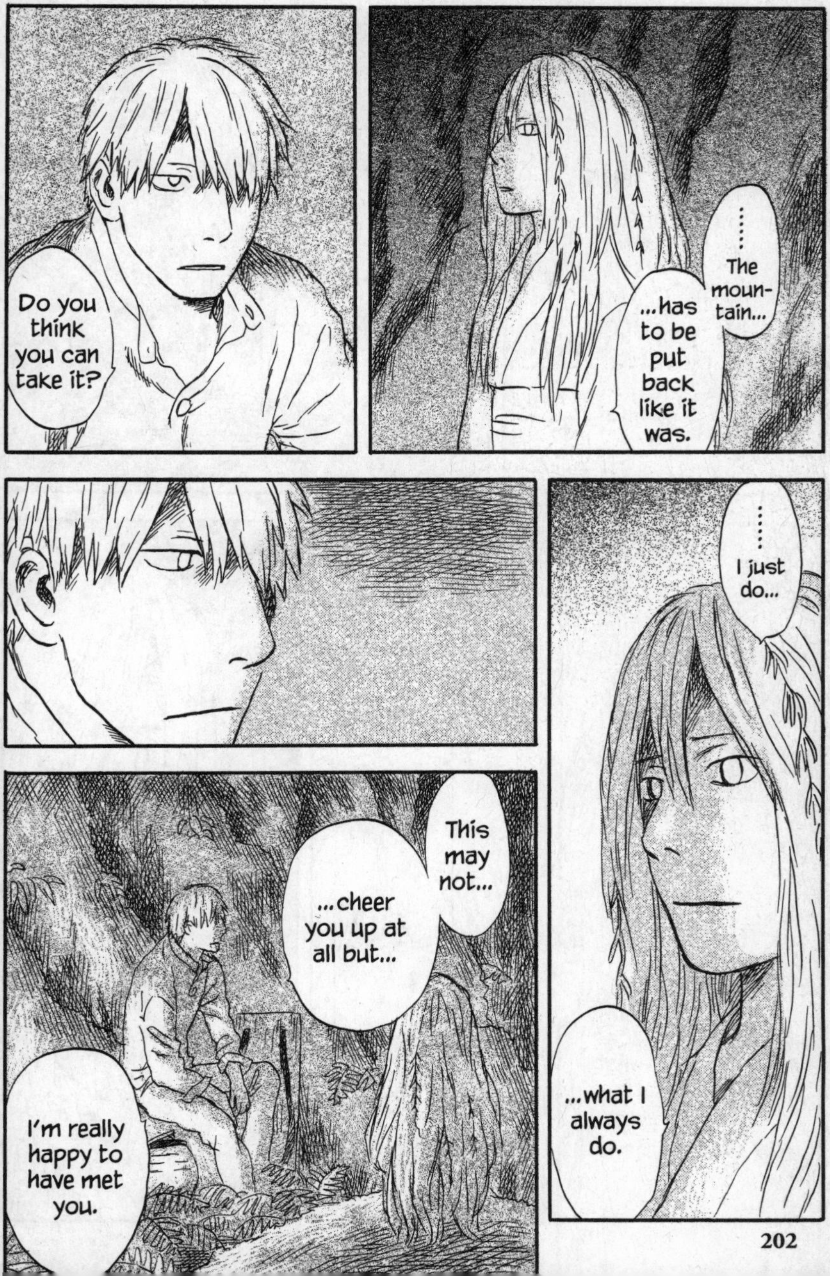
......
The mountain...
...has to be put back like it was.
Do you think you can take it?
......
I just do...
...what I always do.
This may not...
...cheer you up at all but...
I'm really happy to have met you.

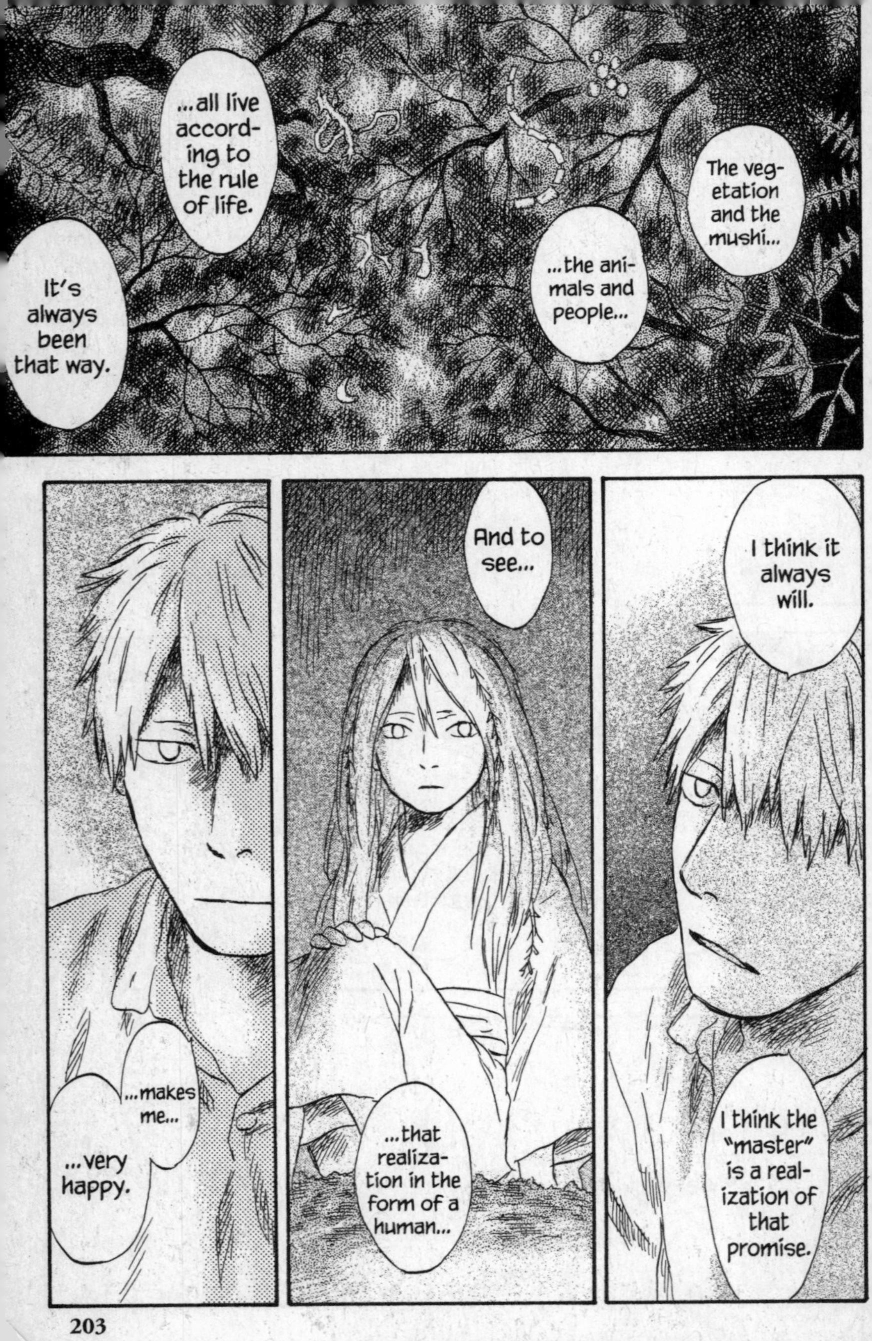
The vegetation and the mushi...
...the animals and people...
...all live according to the rule of life.
It's always been that way.
I think it always will.
I think the "master" is a realization of that promise.
And to see...
...that realization in the form of a human...
...makes me...
...very happy.

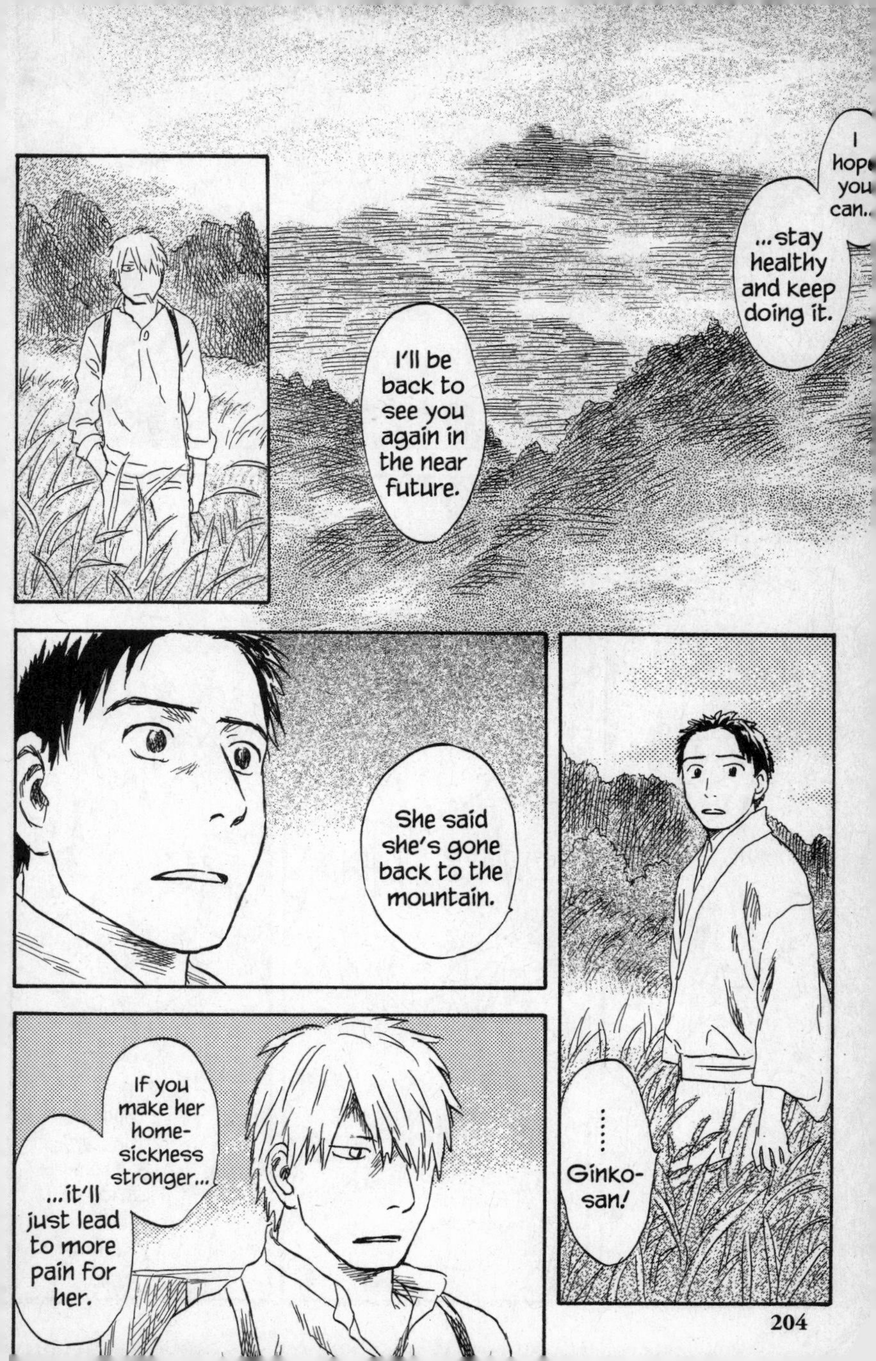
I hope you can..
...stay healthy and keep doing it.
I'll be back to see you again in the near future.
......
Ginko-san!
She said she's gone back to the mountain.
If you make her home-sickness stronger...
...it'll just lead to more pain for her.

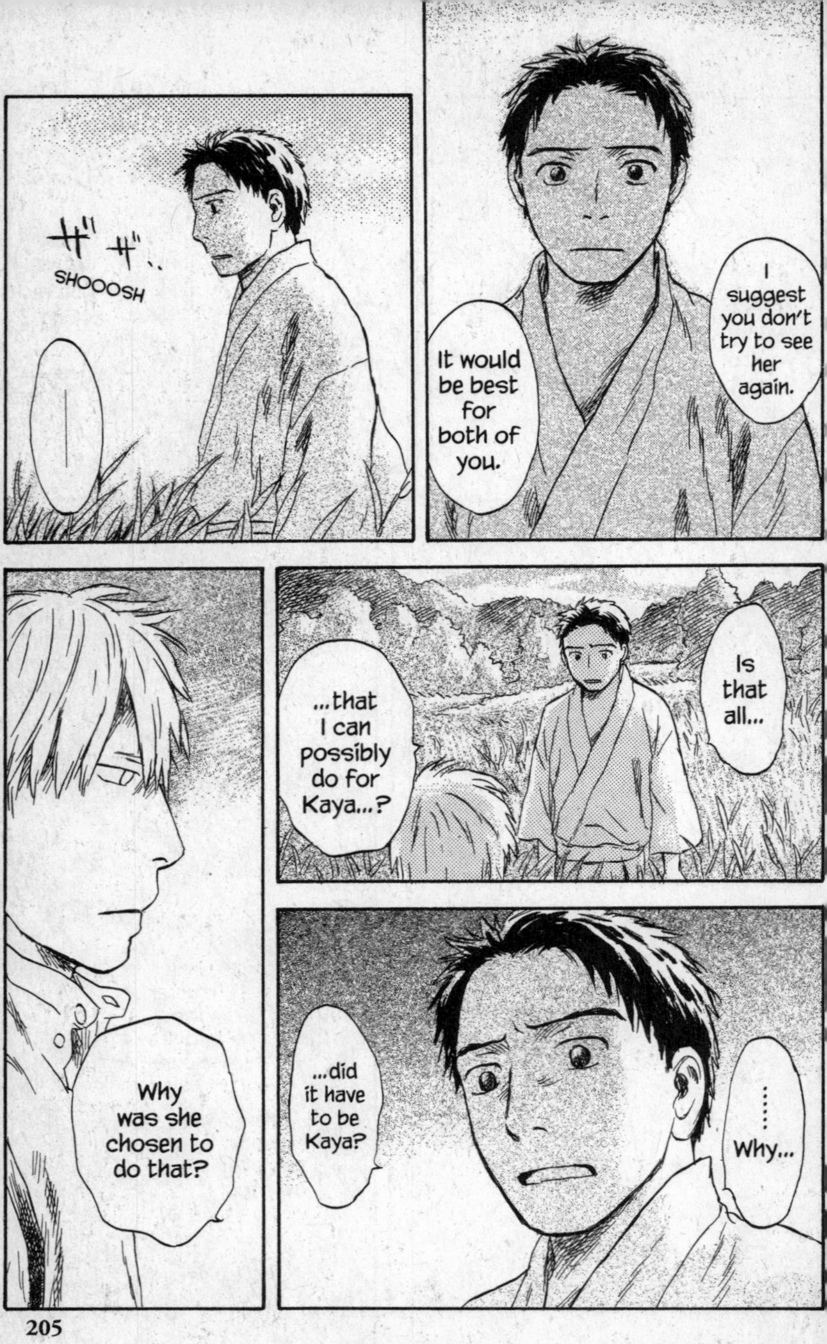
I suggest you don't try to see her again.
It would be best for both of you.
ザザ..
SHOOOSH
Is that all...
...that I can possibly do for Kaya...?
......Why...
...did it have to be Kaya?
Why was she chosen to do that?

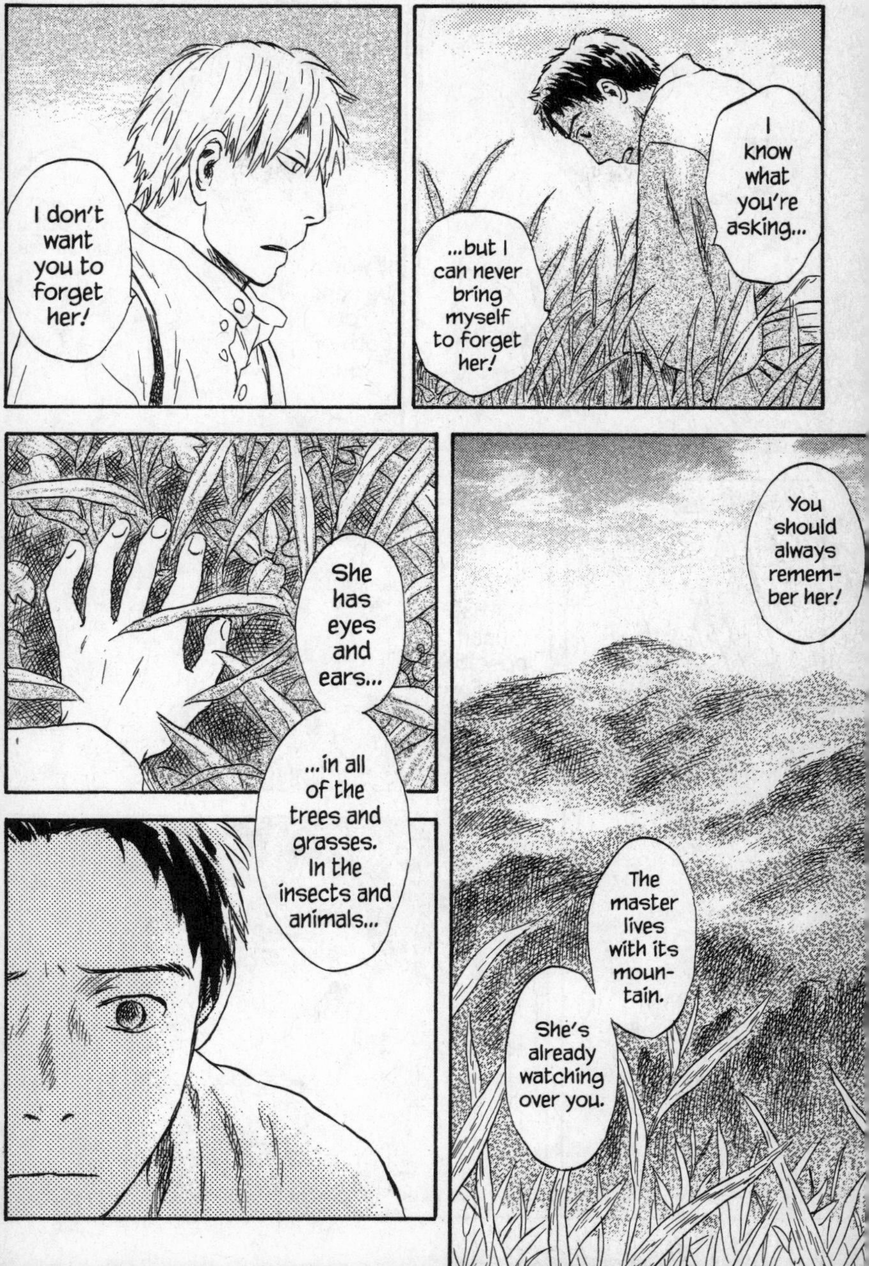
I know what you're asking...
...but I can never bring myself to forget her!
I don't want you to forget her!
You should always remember her!
The master lives with its mountain.
She's already watching over you.
She has eyes and ears...
...in all of the trees and grasses. In the insects and animals...

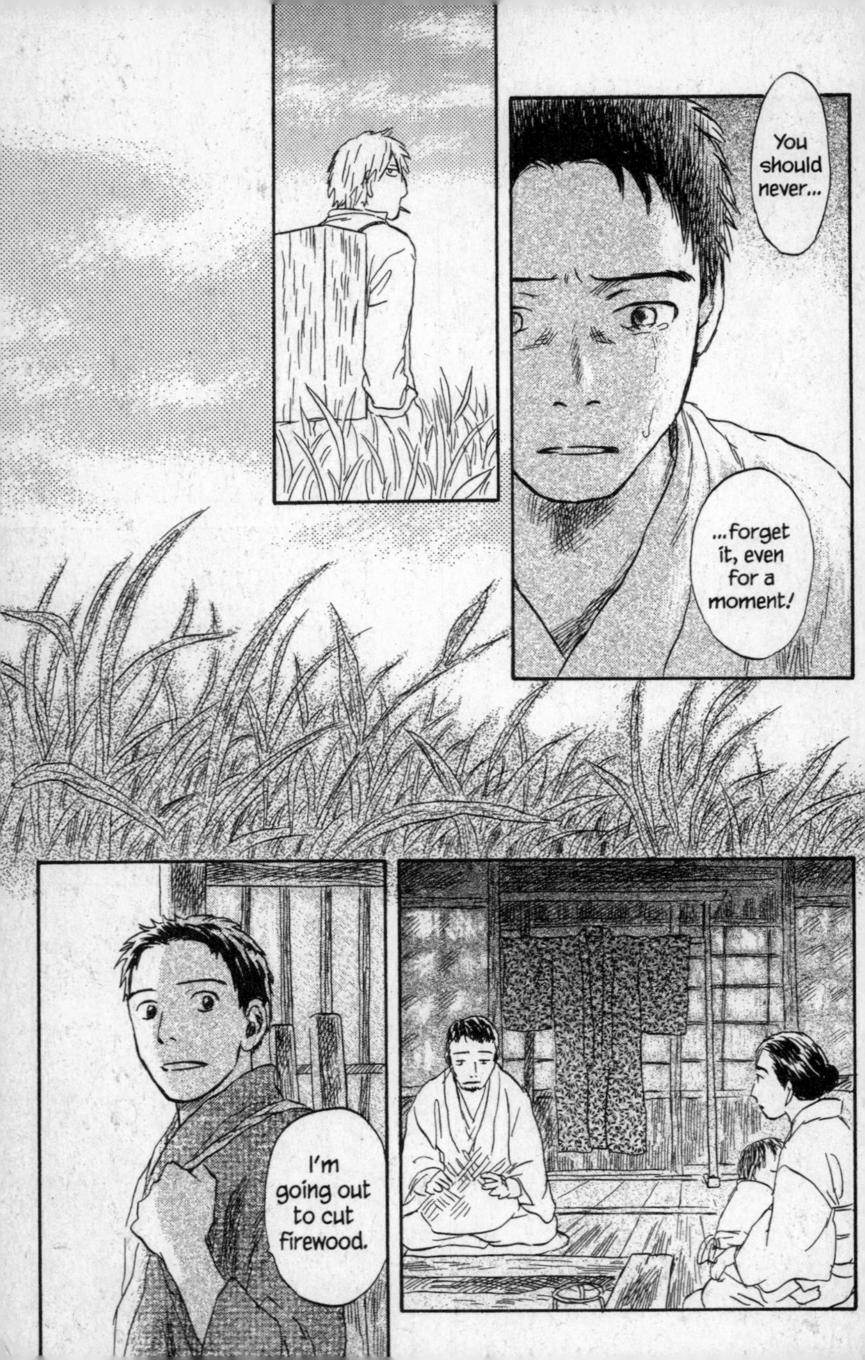
You should never...
...forget it, even for a moment!
I'm going out to cut firewood.

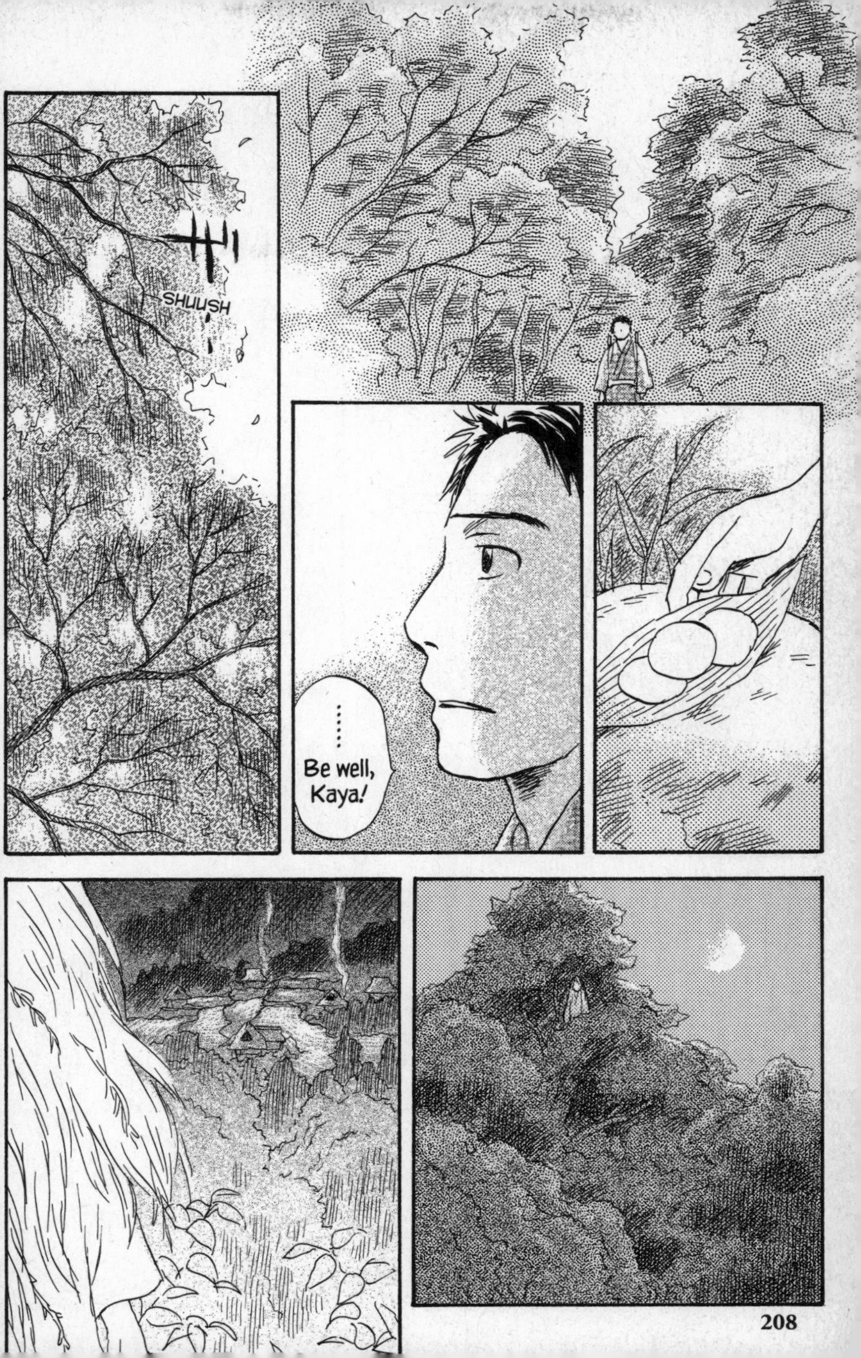

......
Be well, Kaya!
SHUUSH

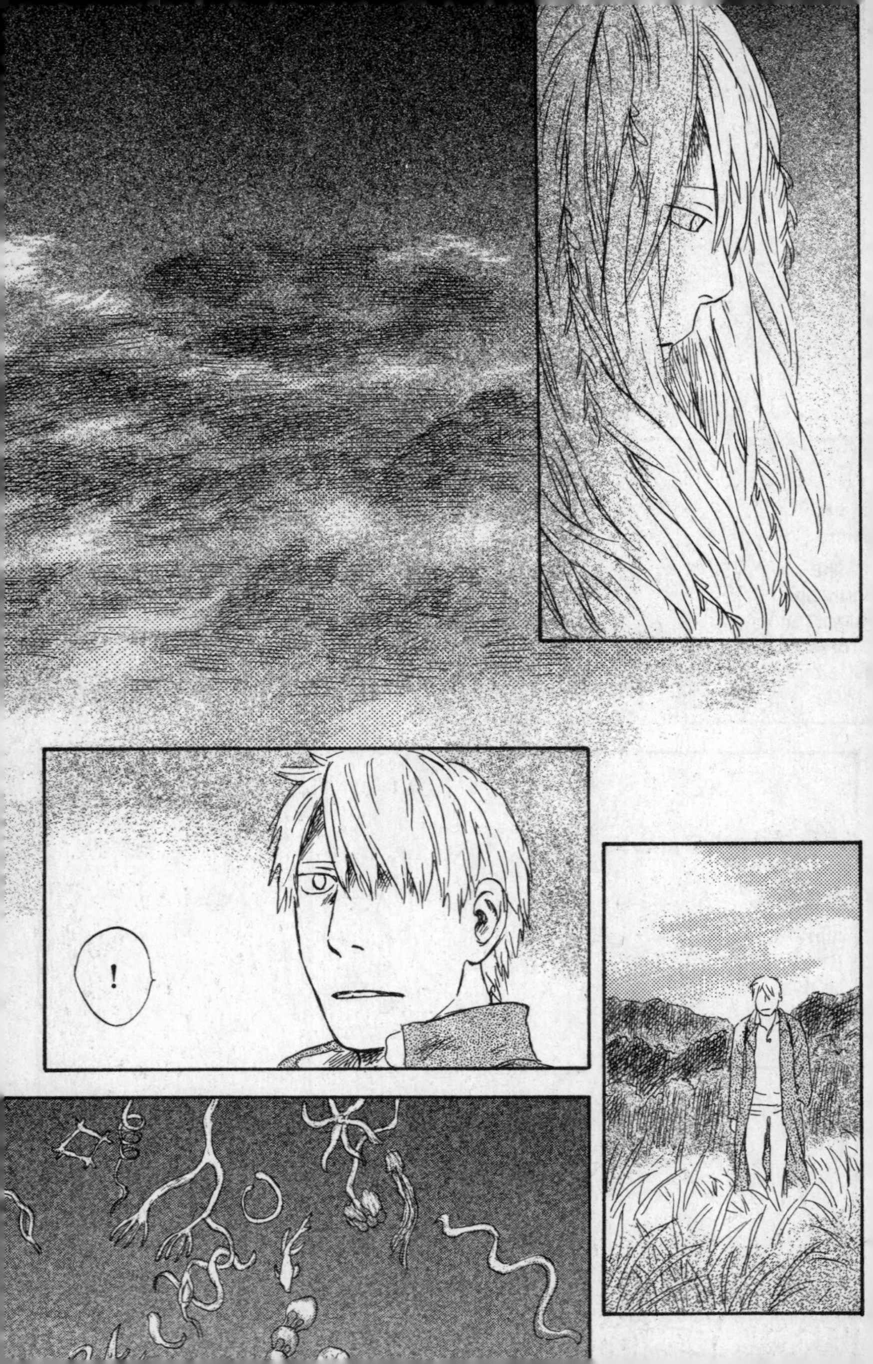
!

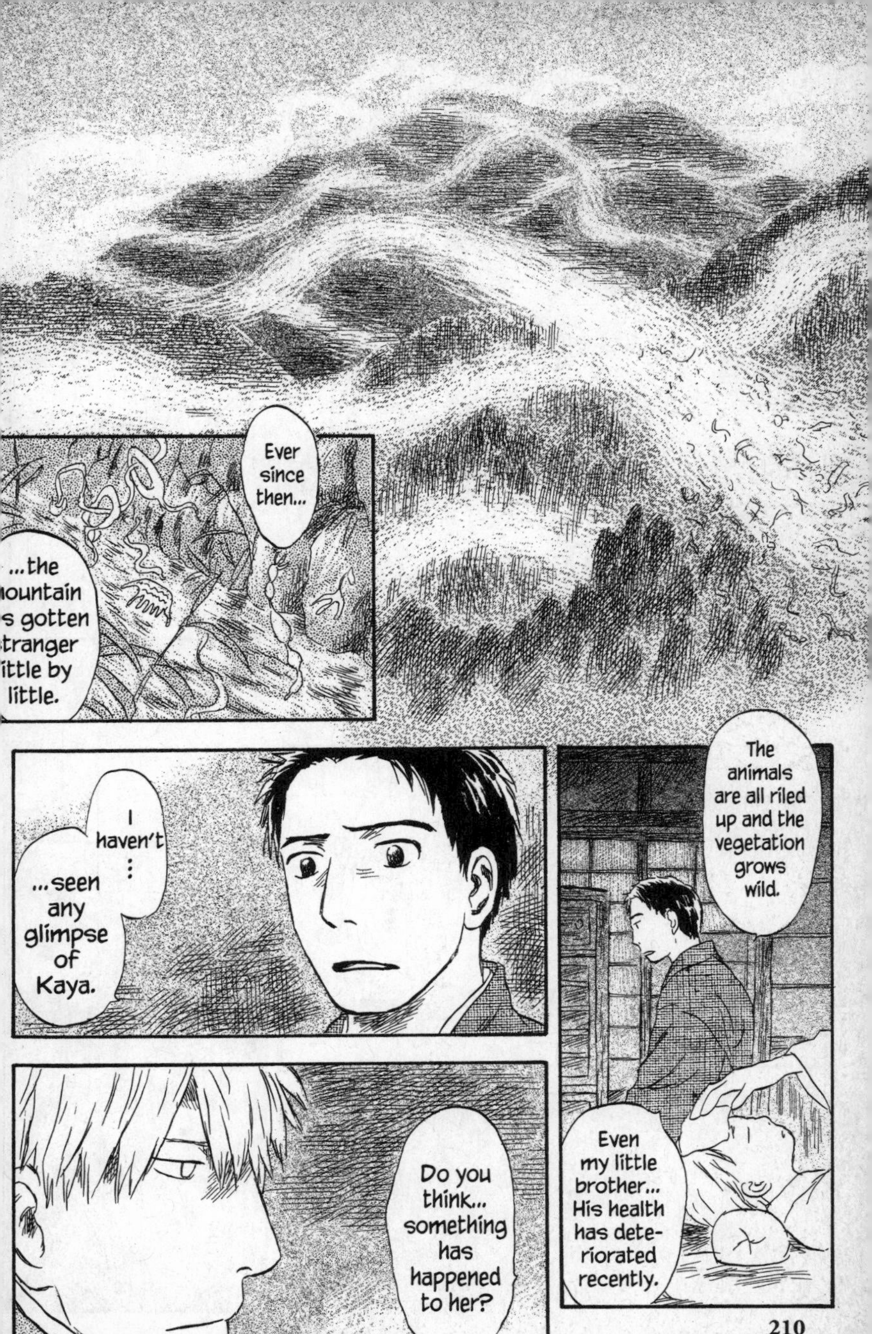
Ever since then...
...the ountain s gotten tranger ittle by little.
The animals are all riled up and the vegetation grows wild.
Even my little brother... His health has dete-riorated recently.
I haven't...
...seen any glimpse of Kaya.
Do you think... something has happened to her?

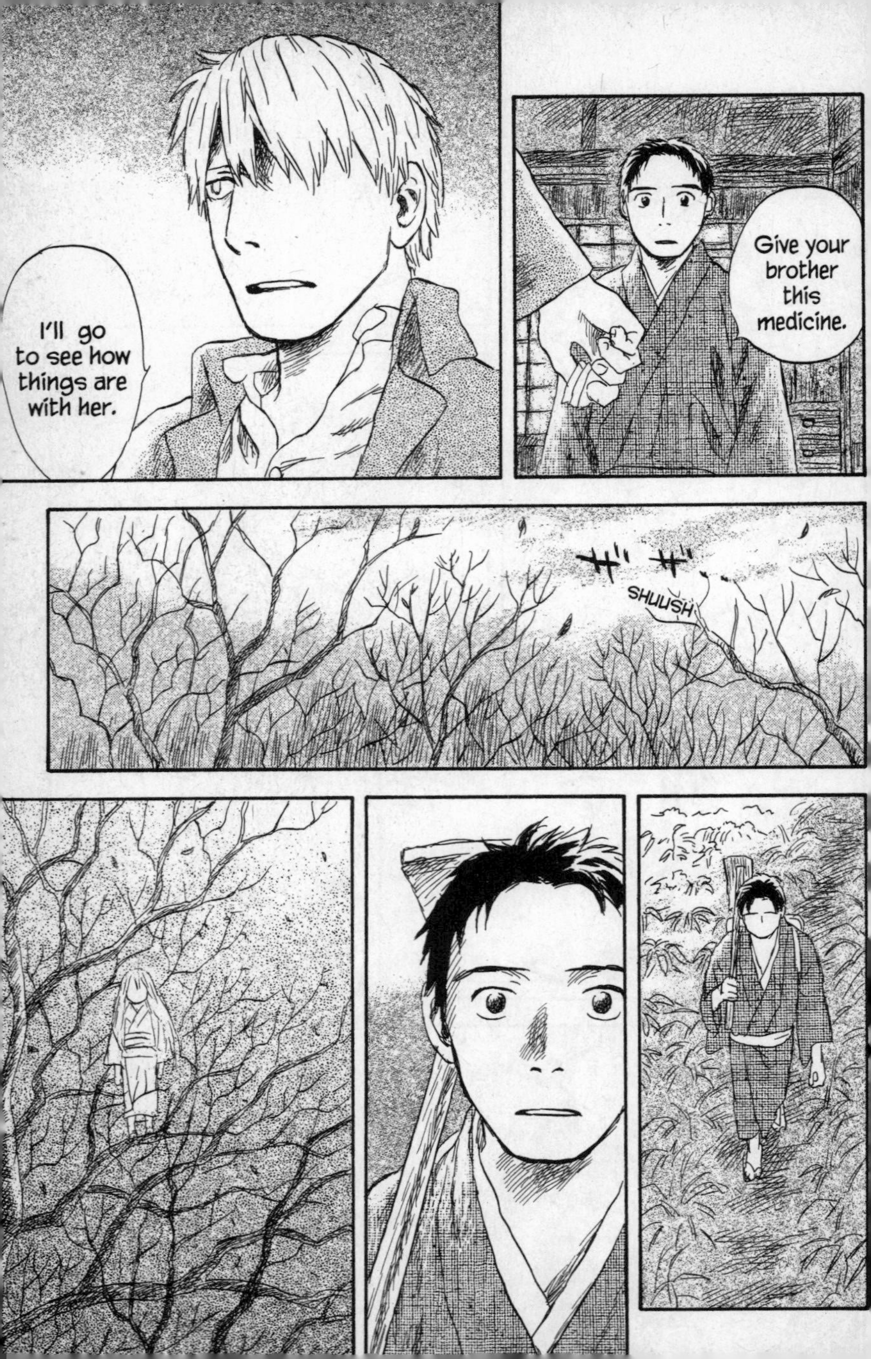
Give your brother this medicine.
I'll go to see how things are with her.
ザ ザ…
SHUUSH

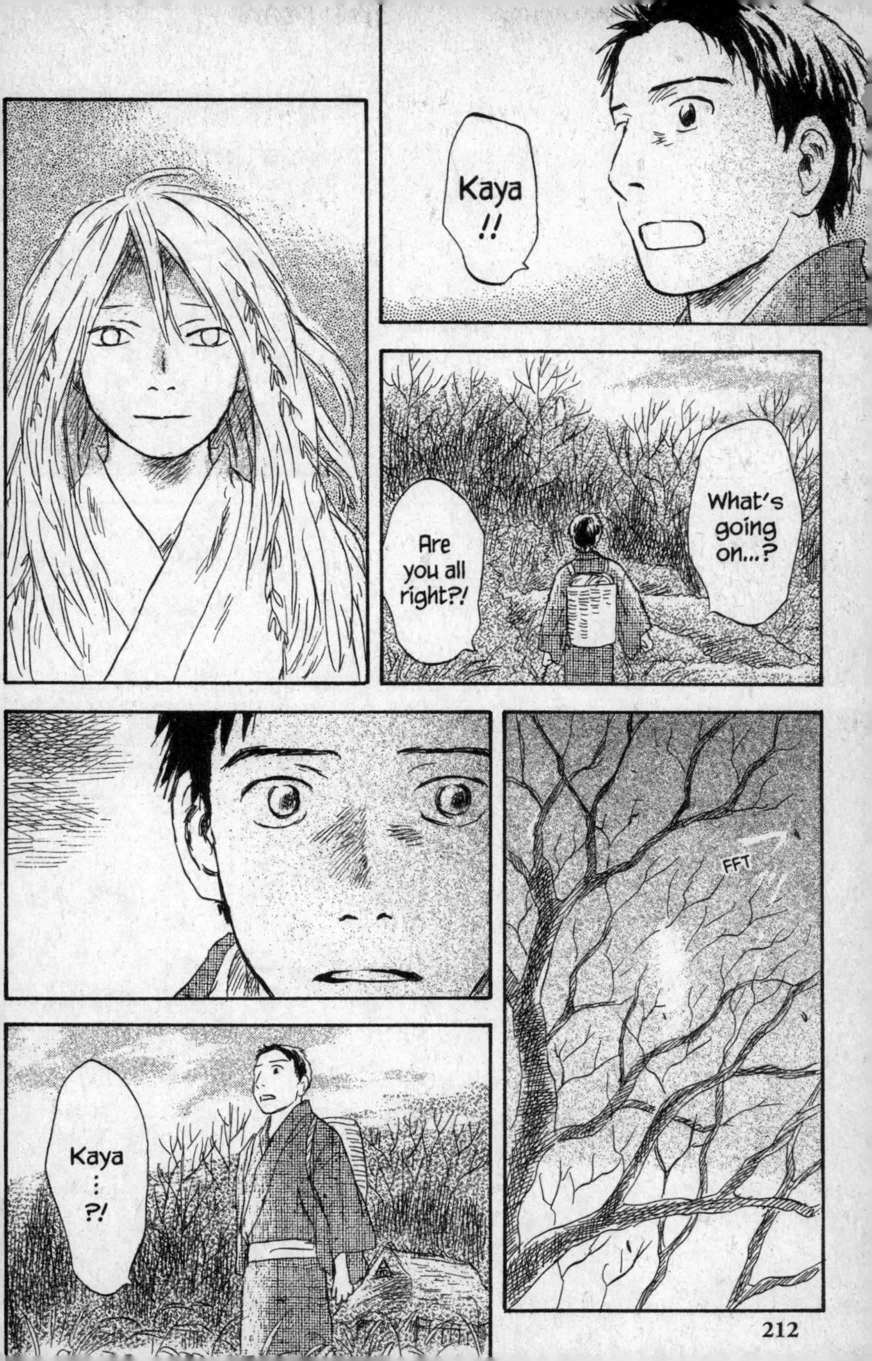
Kaya !!
What's going on...?
Are you all right?!
FFT
Kaya ... ?!

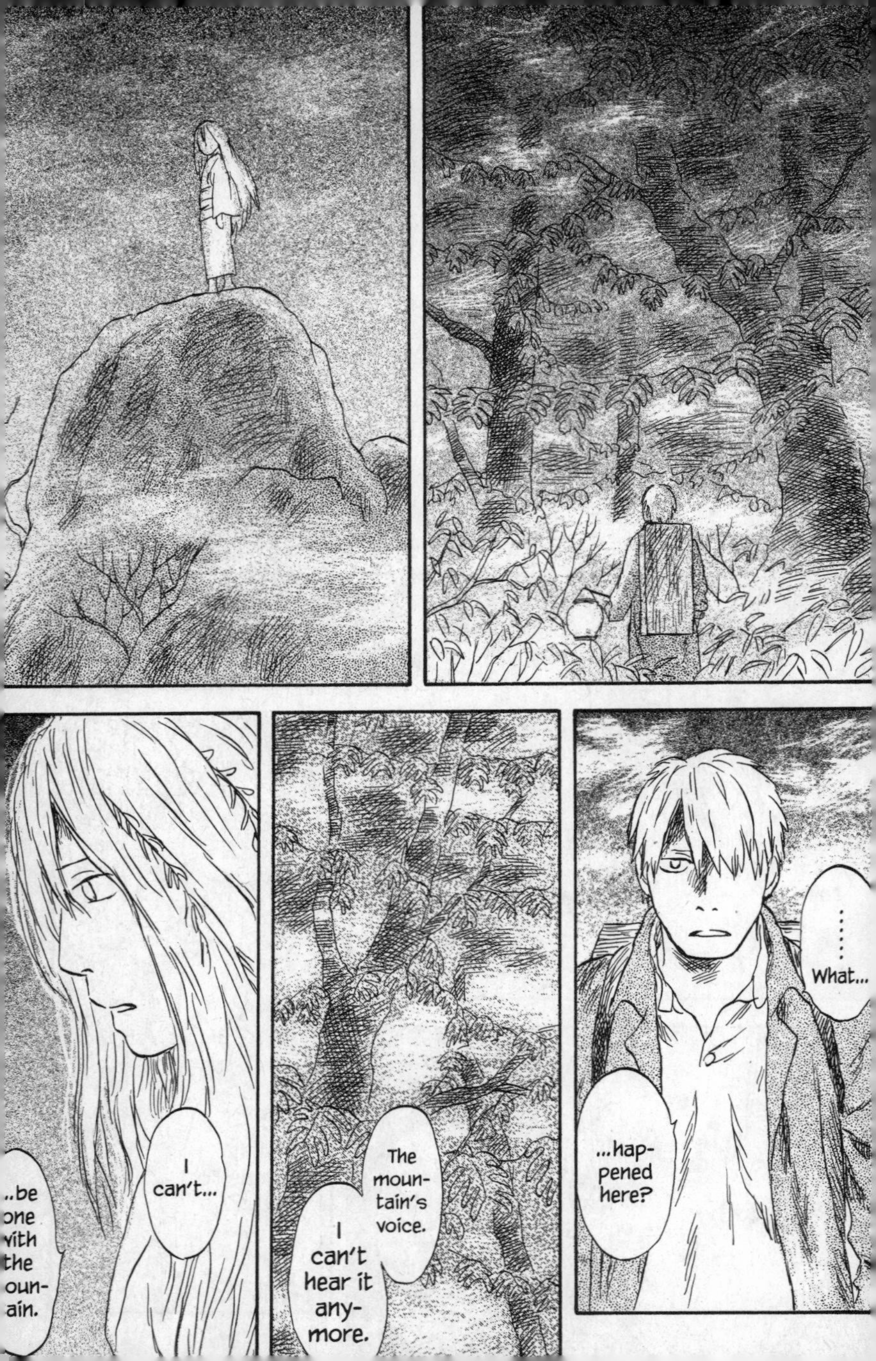

......
What...
...hap-pened here?
The moun-tain's voice.
I can't hear it any-more.
I can't...
..be one with the oun-ain.

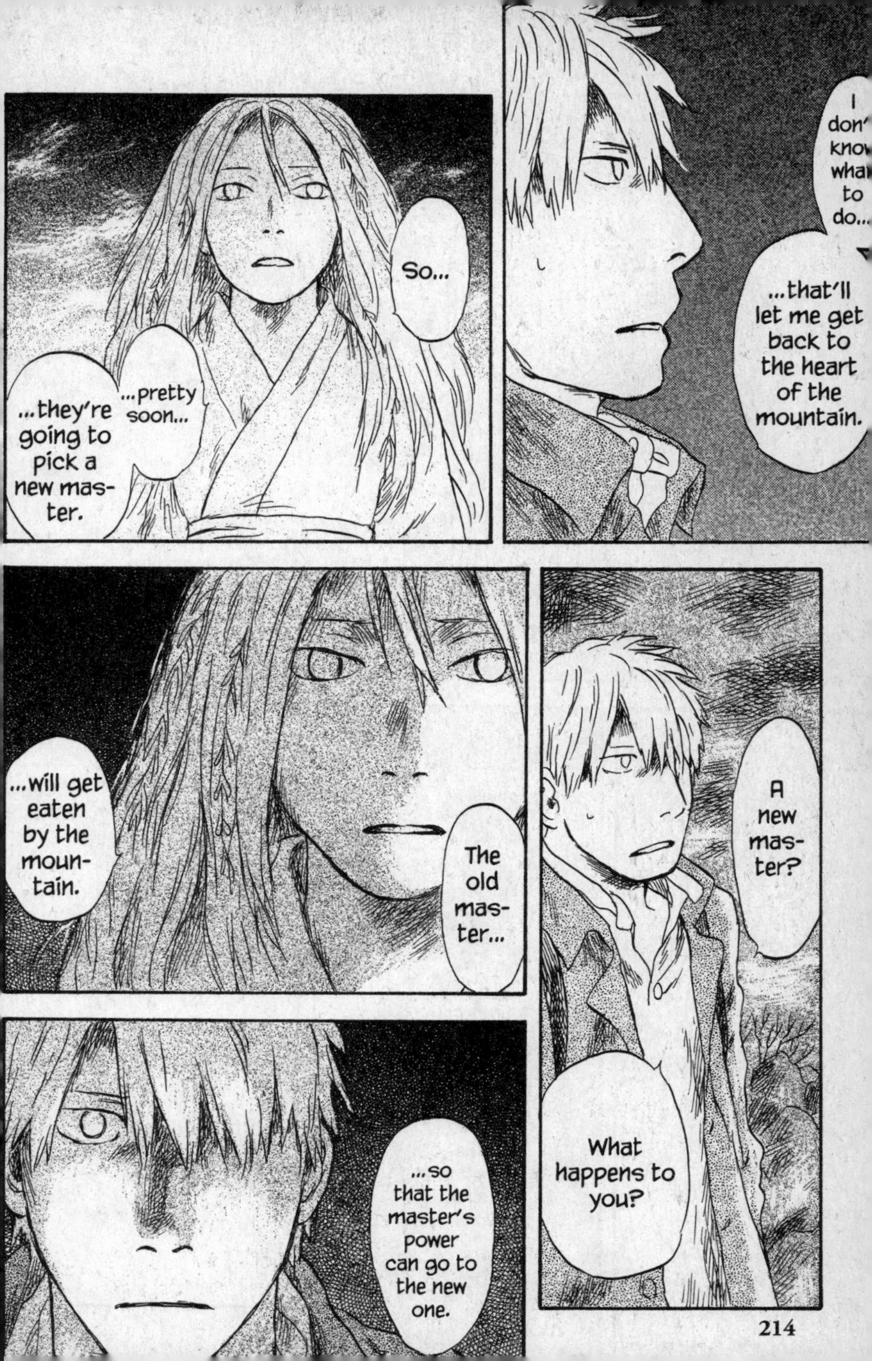
I don' kno wha to do...
...that'll let me get back to the heart of the mountain.
So...
...pretty soon...
...they're going to pick a new master.
A new master?
What happens to you?
The old master...
...will get eaten by the mountain.
...so that the master's power can go to the new one.

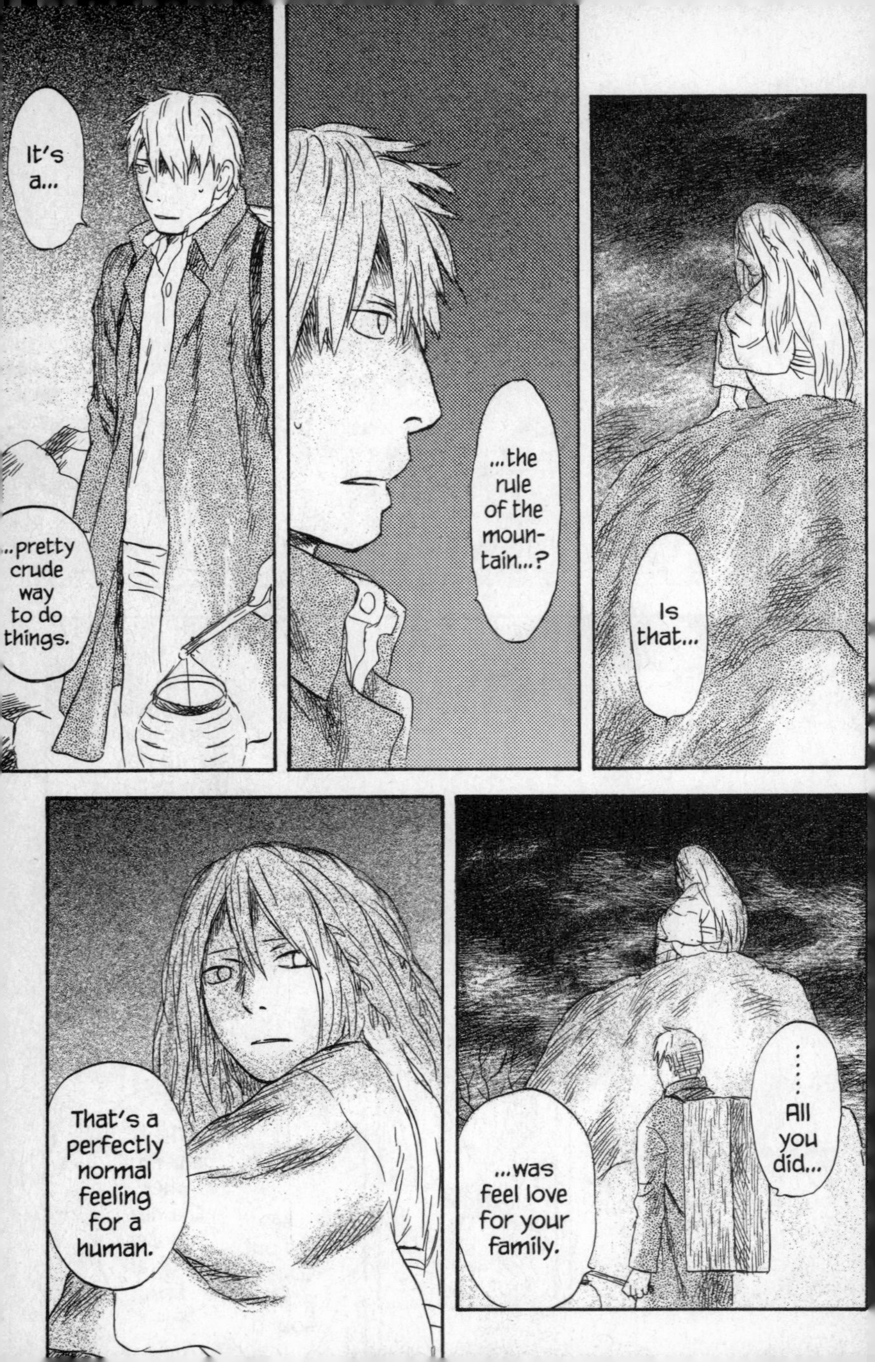
Is that...
...the rule of the mountain...?
It's a...
...pretty crude way to do things.
......
All you did...
...was feel love for your family.
That's a perfectly normal feeling for a human.

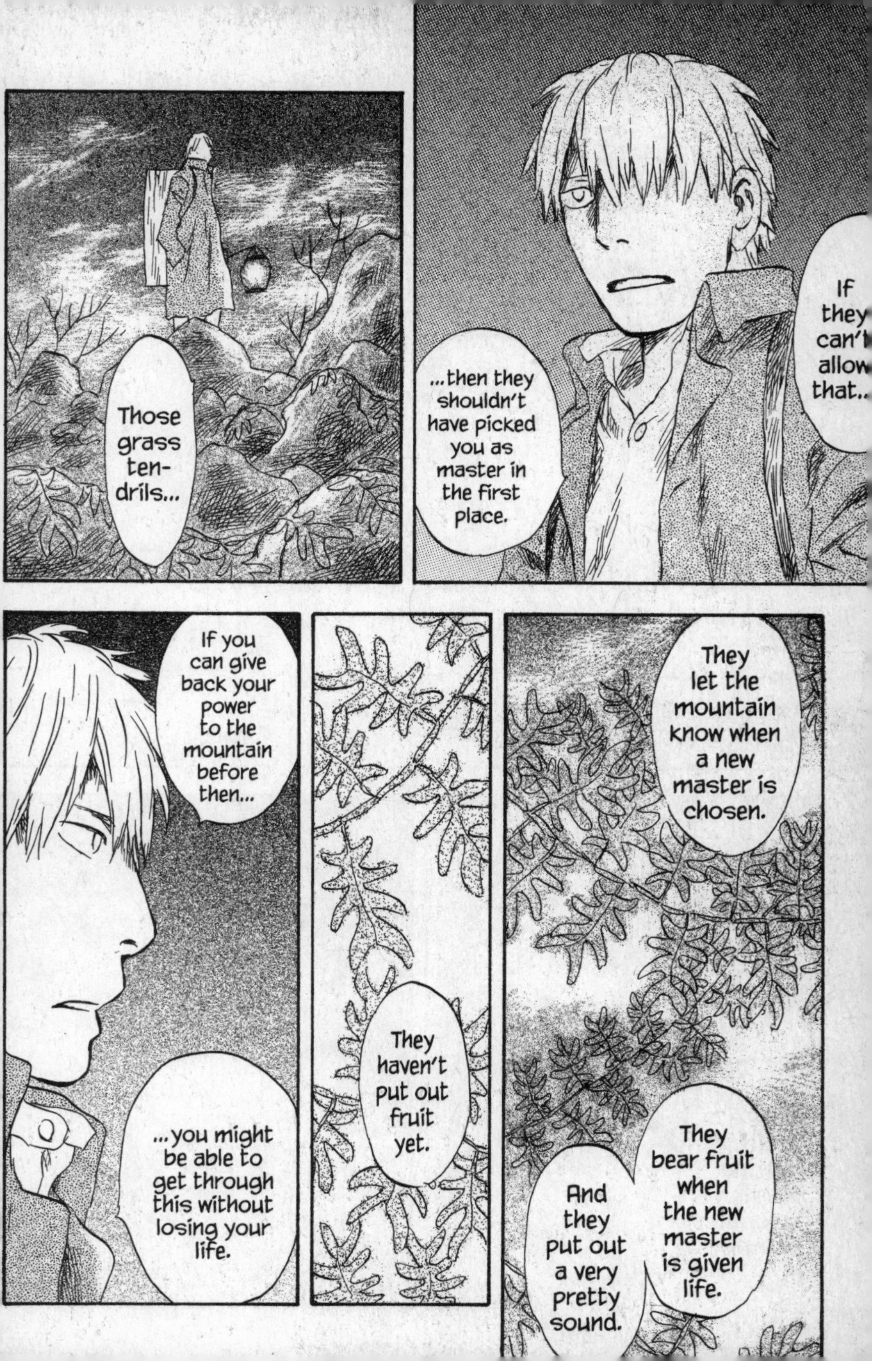
If they can' allow that..
...then they shouldn't have picked you as master in the first place.
Those grass ten-drils...
They let the mountain know when a new master is chosen.
They bear fruit when the new master is given life.
And they put out a very pretty sound.
They haven't put out fruit yet.
If you can give back your power to the mountain before then...
...you might be able to get through this without losing your life.

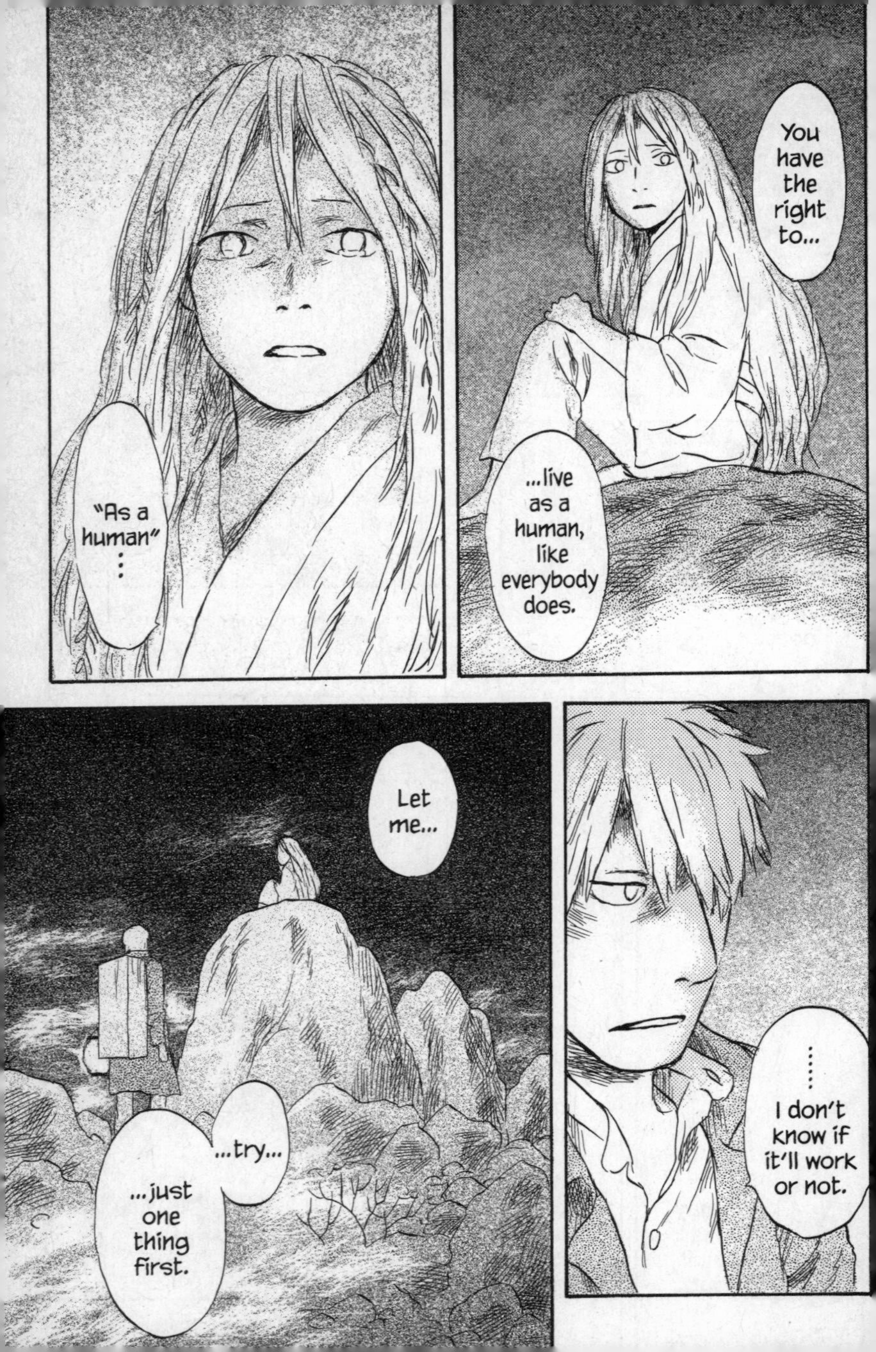
You have the right to...
...live as a human, like everybody does.
"As a human" ...
...... I don't know if it'll work or not.
Let me...
...try...
...just one thing first.

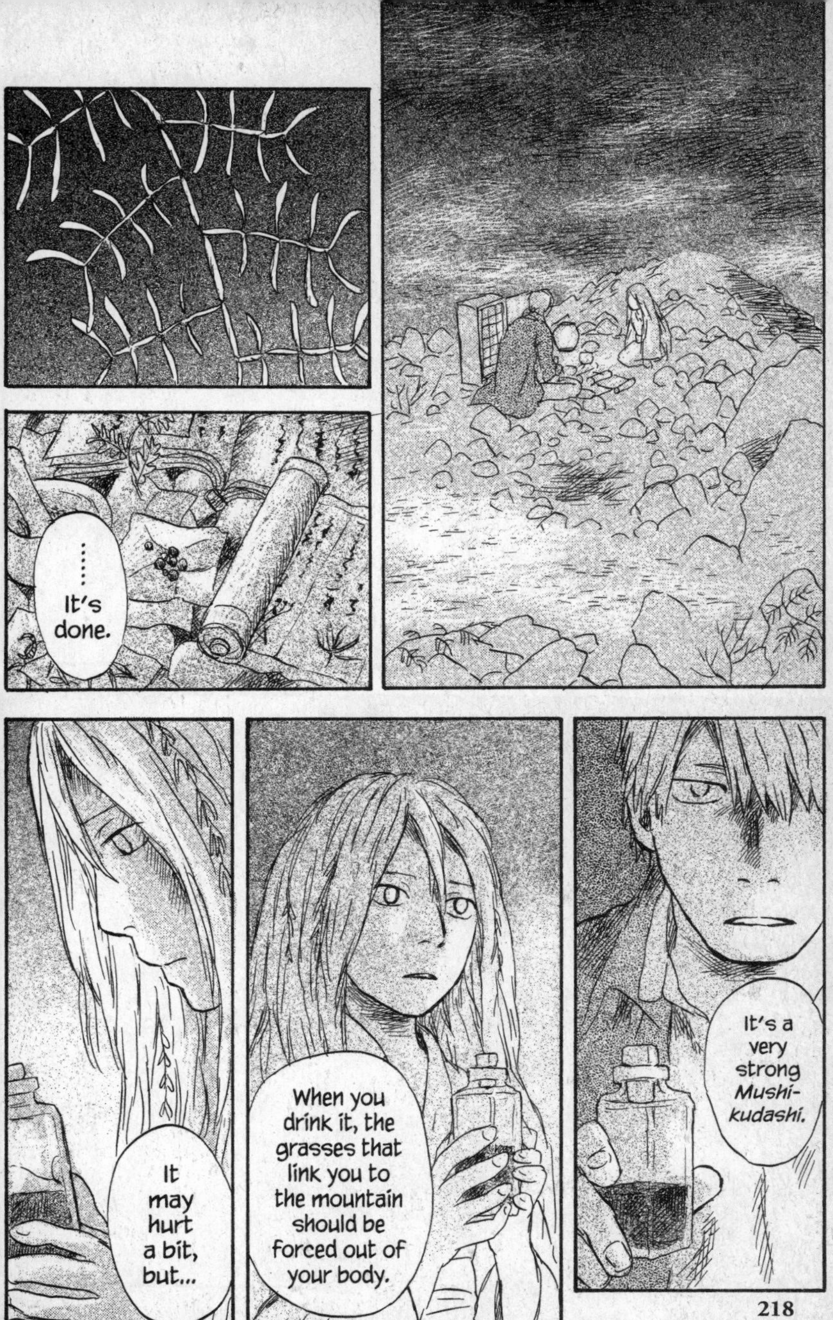
...... It's done.
It's a very strong *Mushi-kudashi.*
When you drink it, the grasses that link you to the mountain should be forced out of your body.
It may hurt a bit, but...

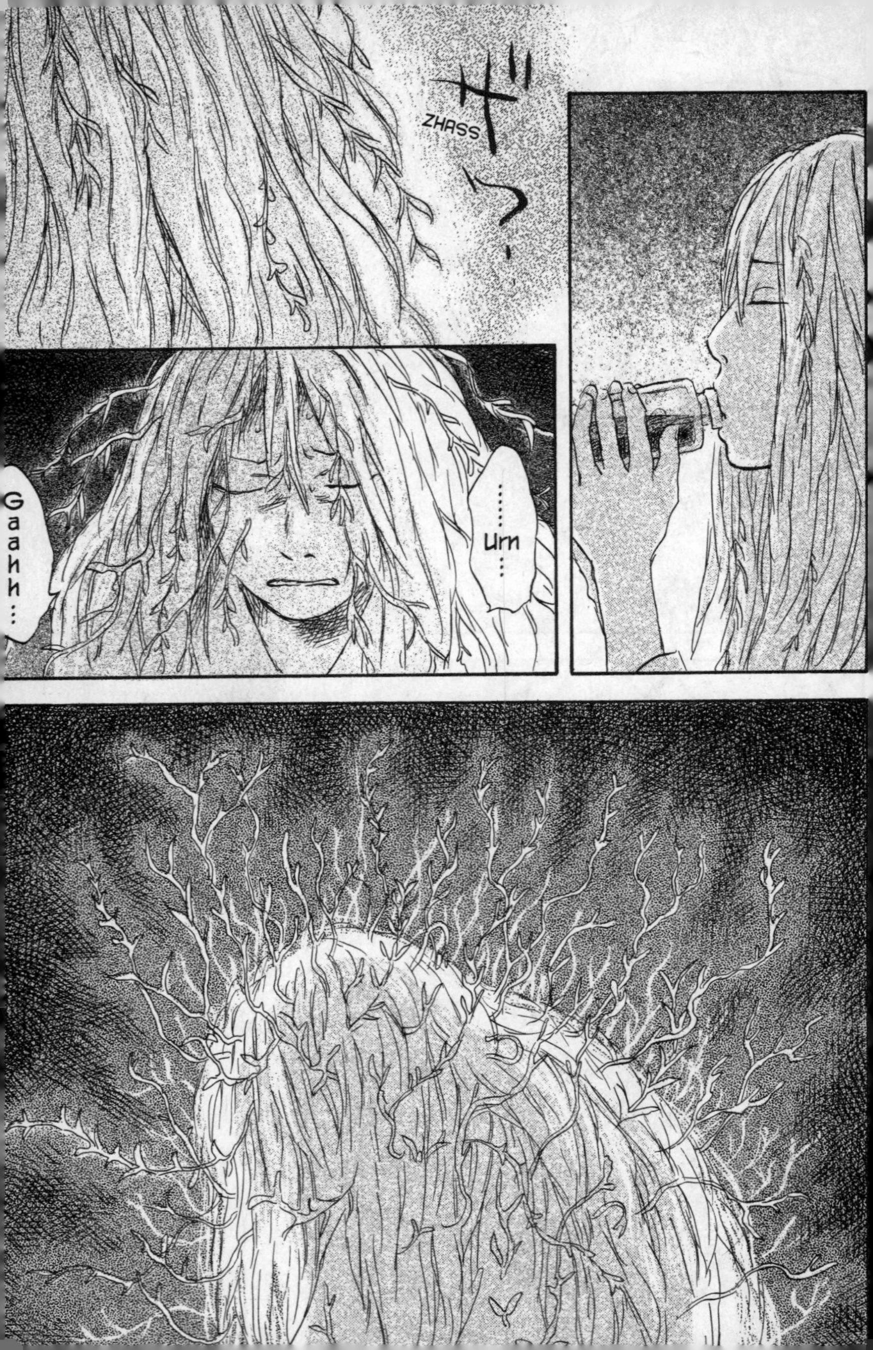
ザッ
ZHASS
......Urn......
Gaahh...

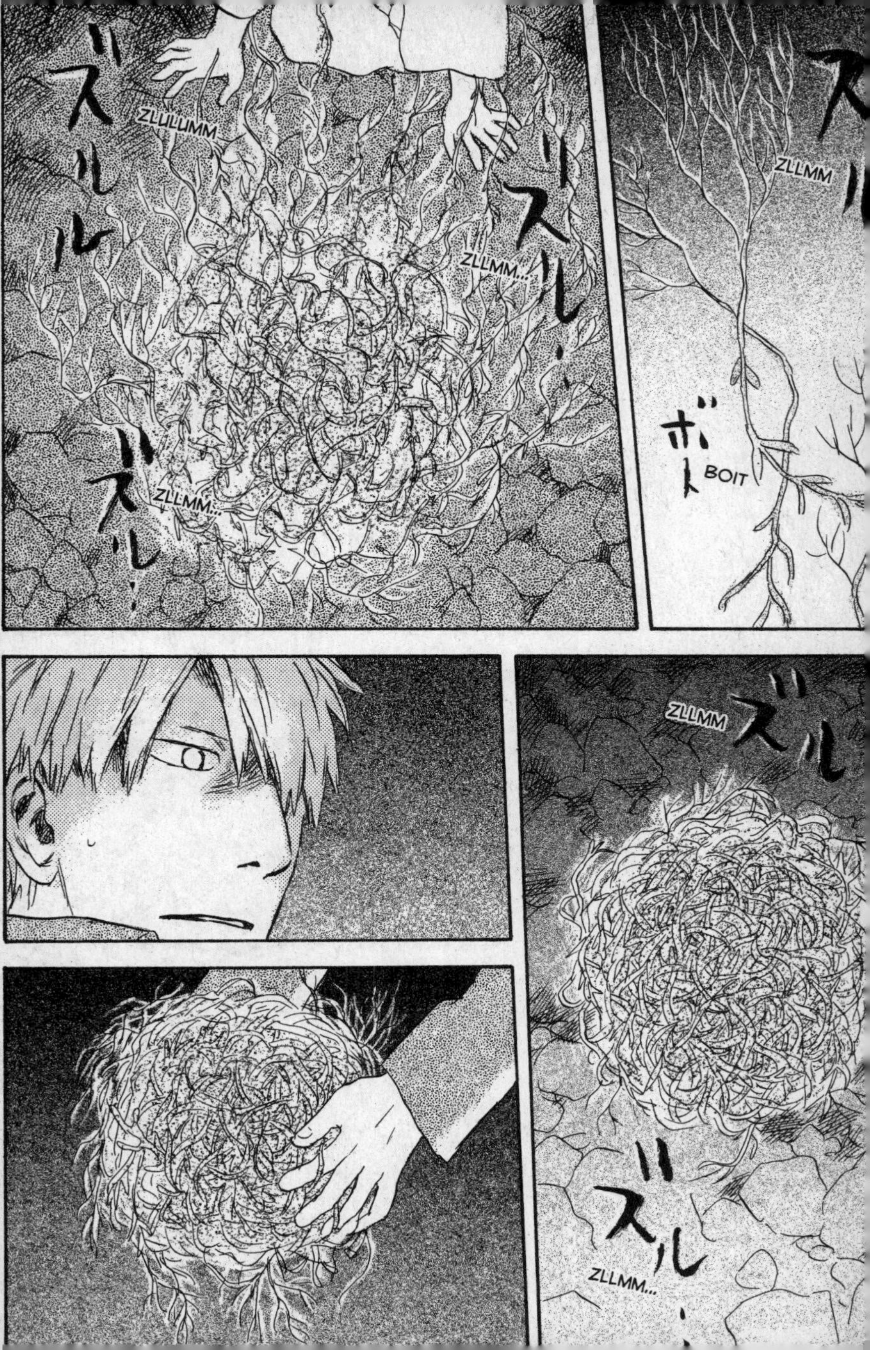

スル
ZLLMM
ボト
BOIT
ズルル…
ZLLMM...
ズルル
ZLULUMM
ズル…
ZLLMM...
ズル
ZLLMM
ズル…
ZLLMM...

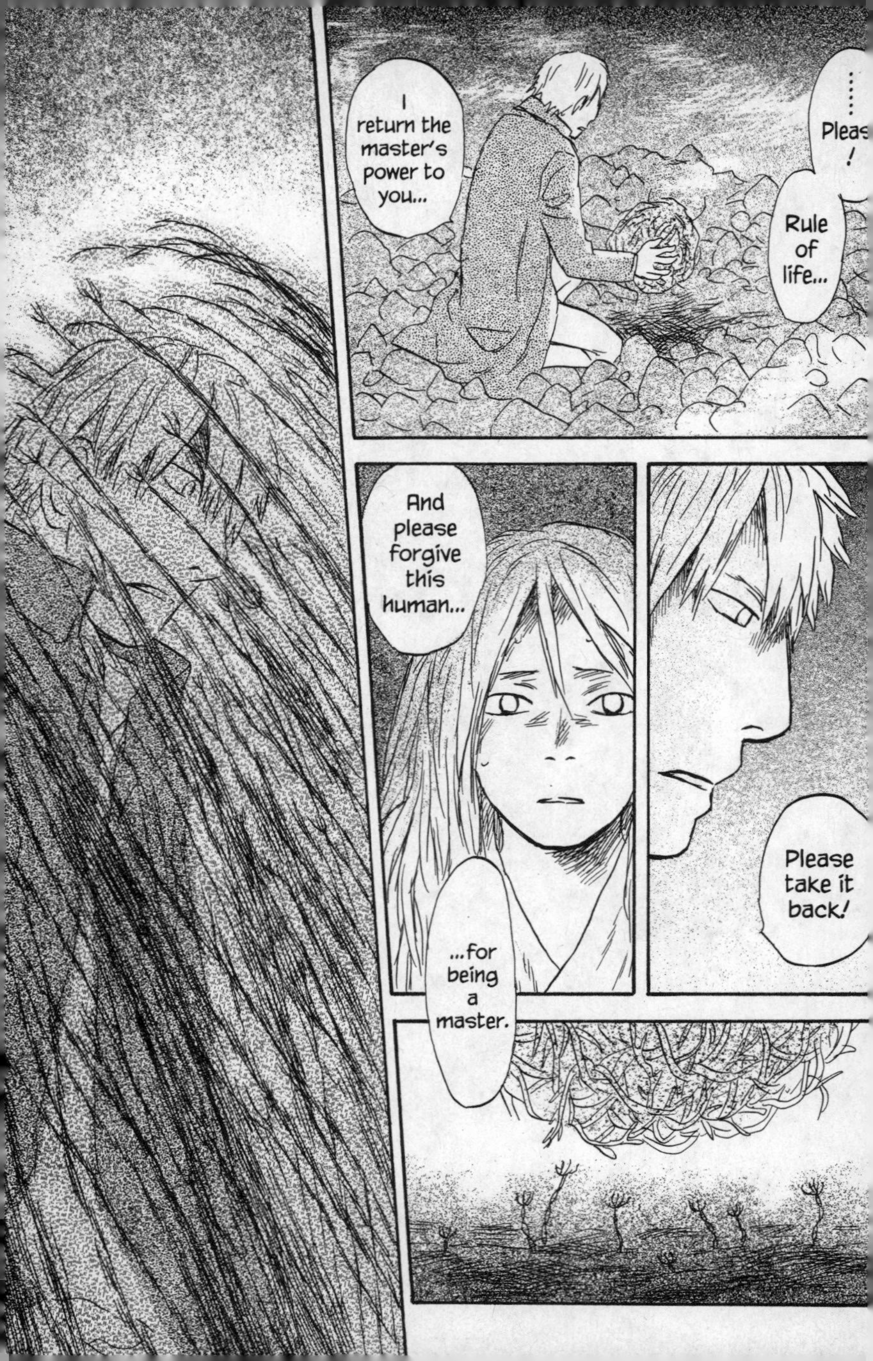
......Pleas!
Rule of life...
I return the master's power to you...
Please take it back!
And please forgive this human...
...for being a master.

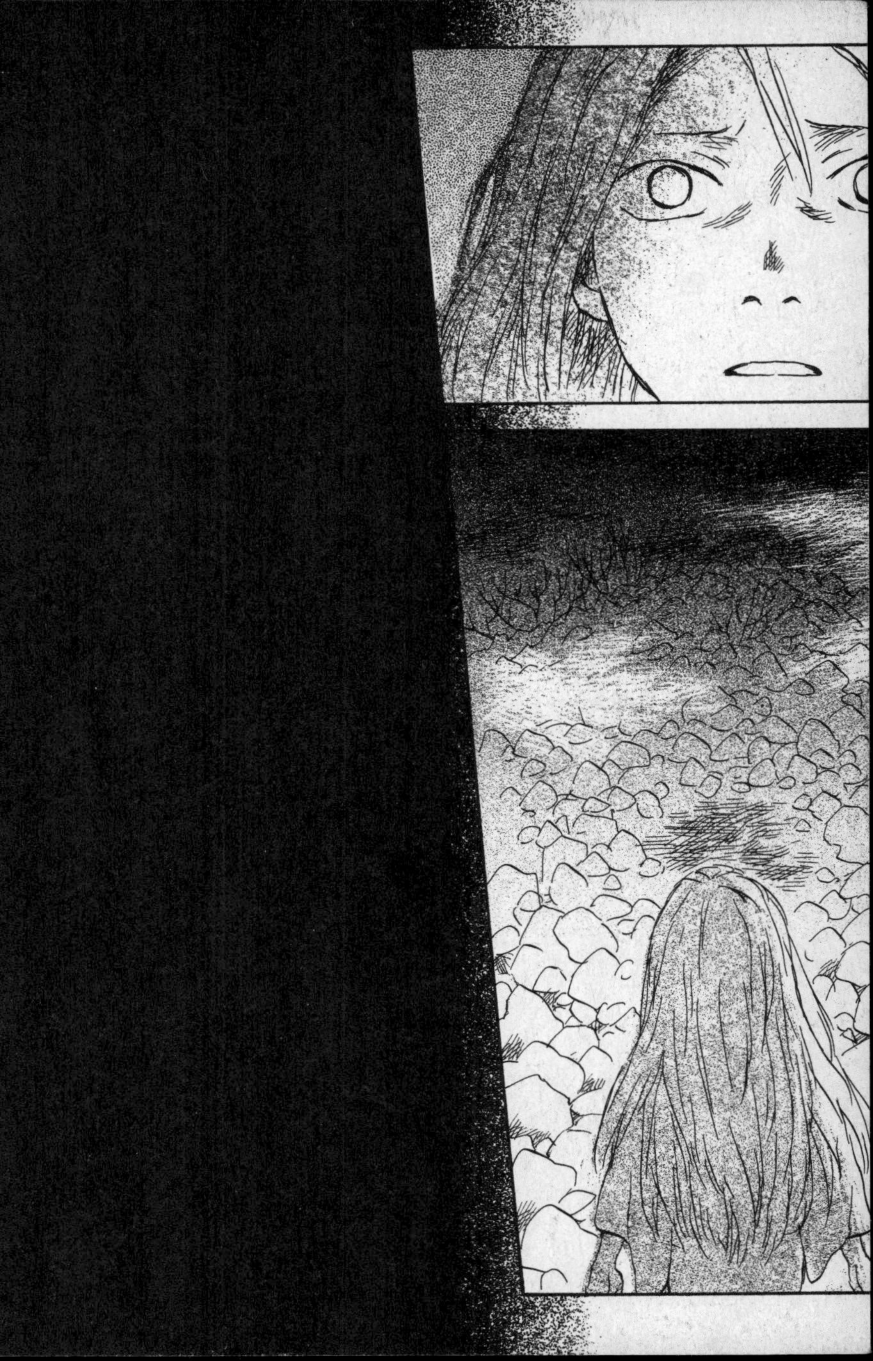

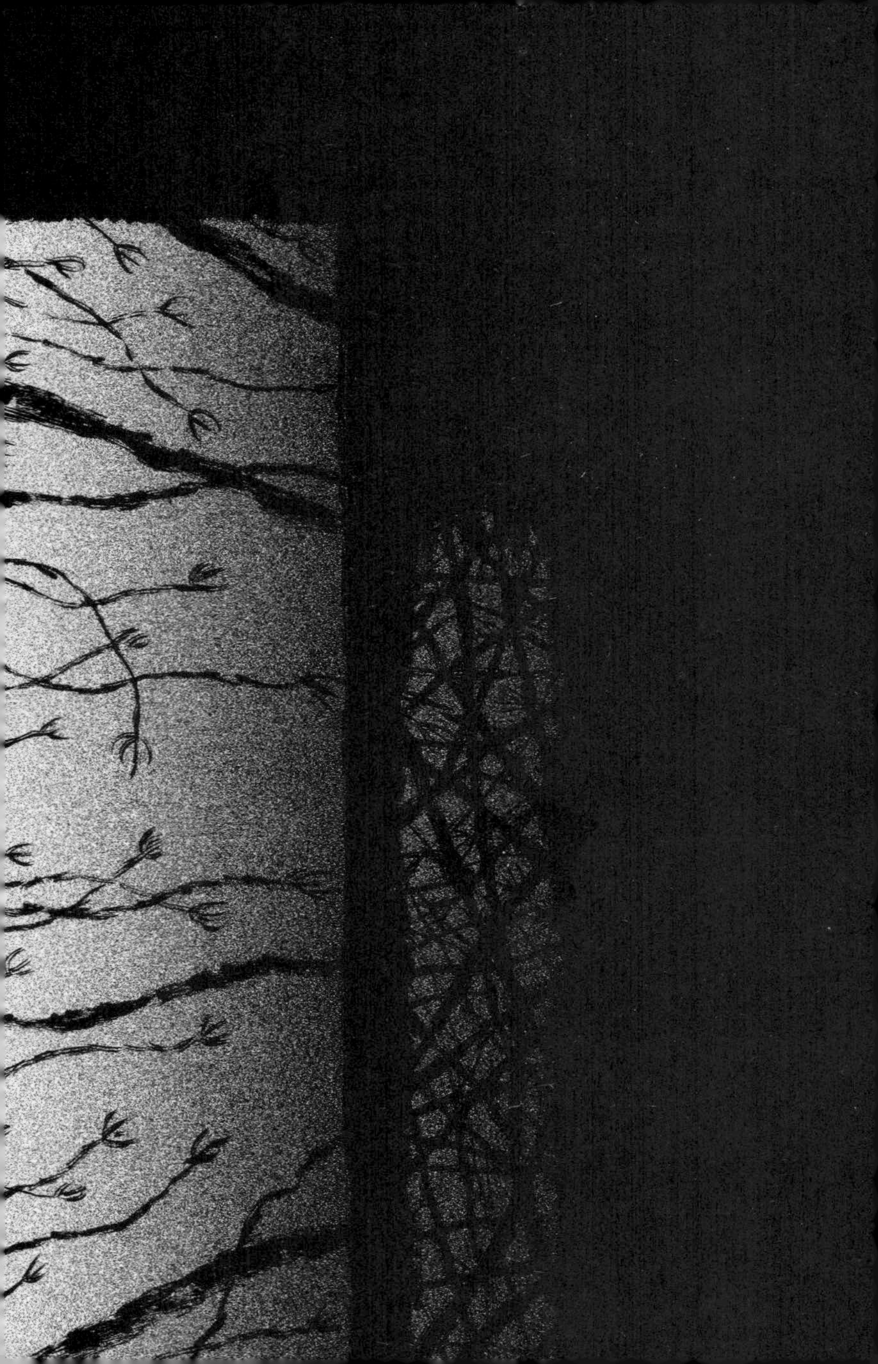

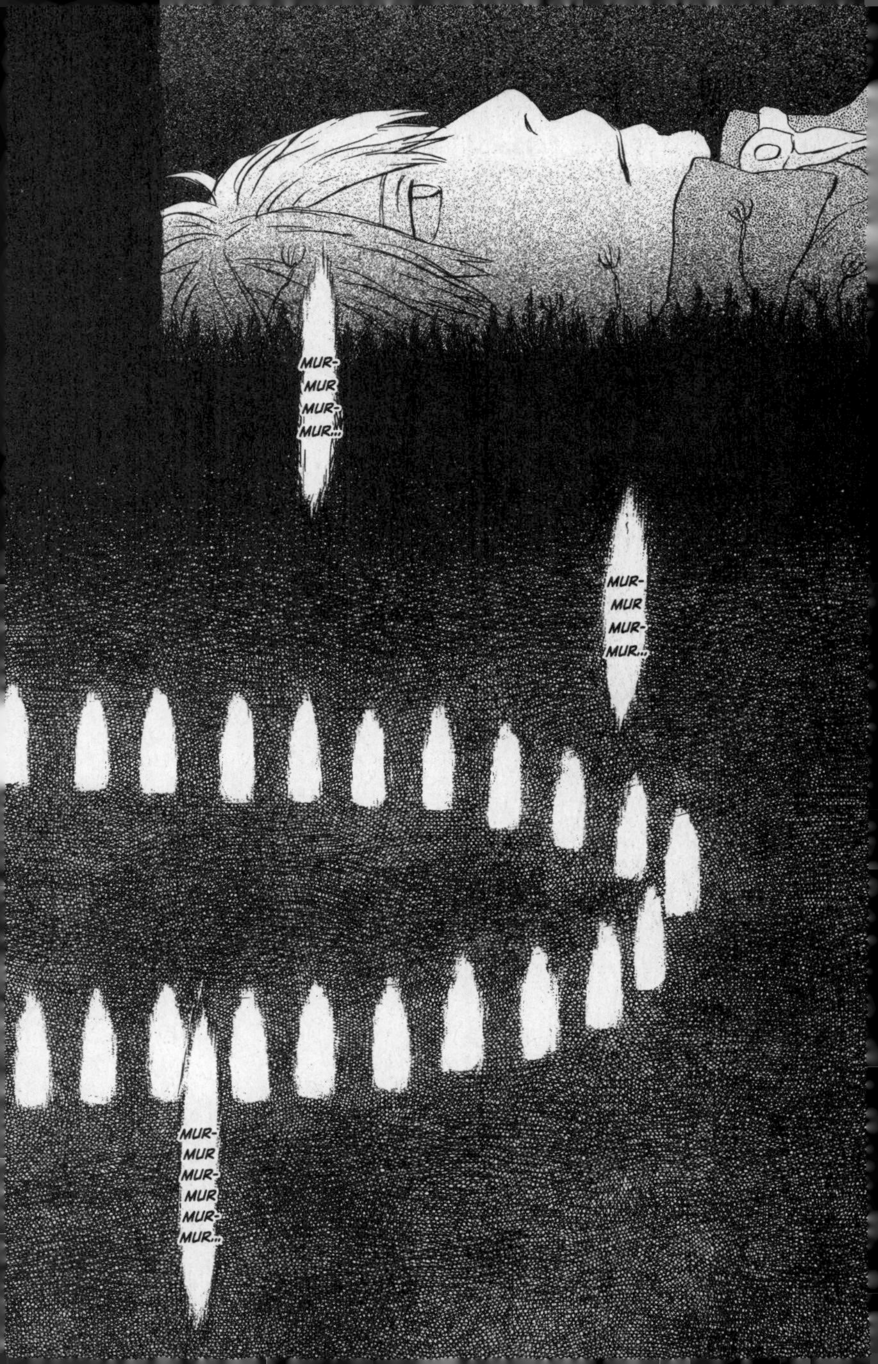
MUR-
MUR
MUR-
MUR...
MUR-
MUR
MUR-
MUR...
MUR-
MUR
MUR-
MUR
MUR-
MUR...

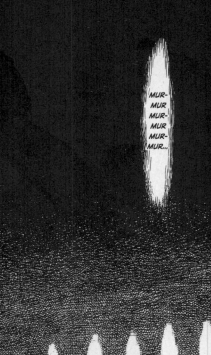

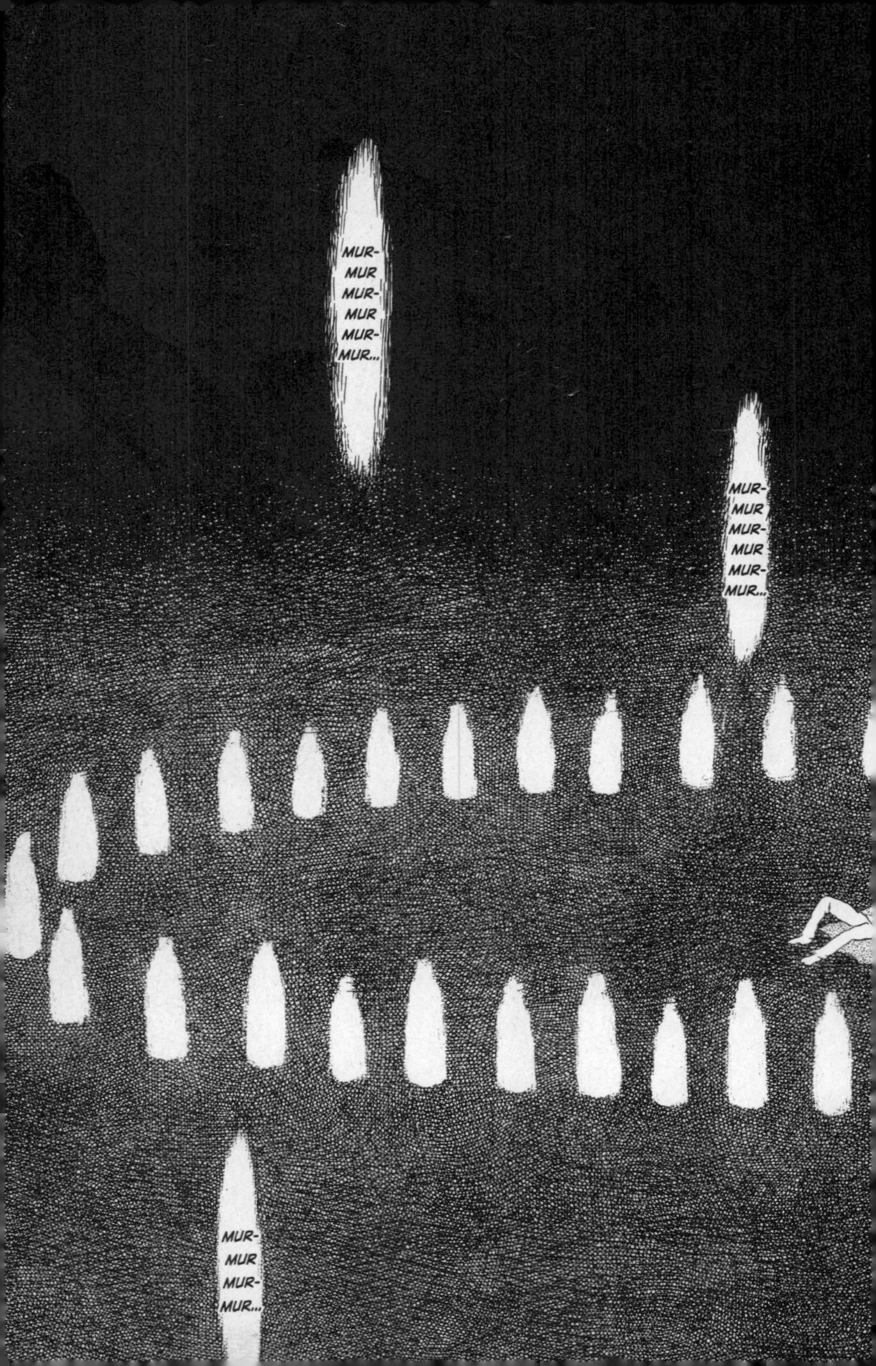

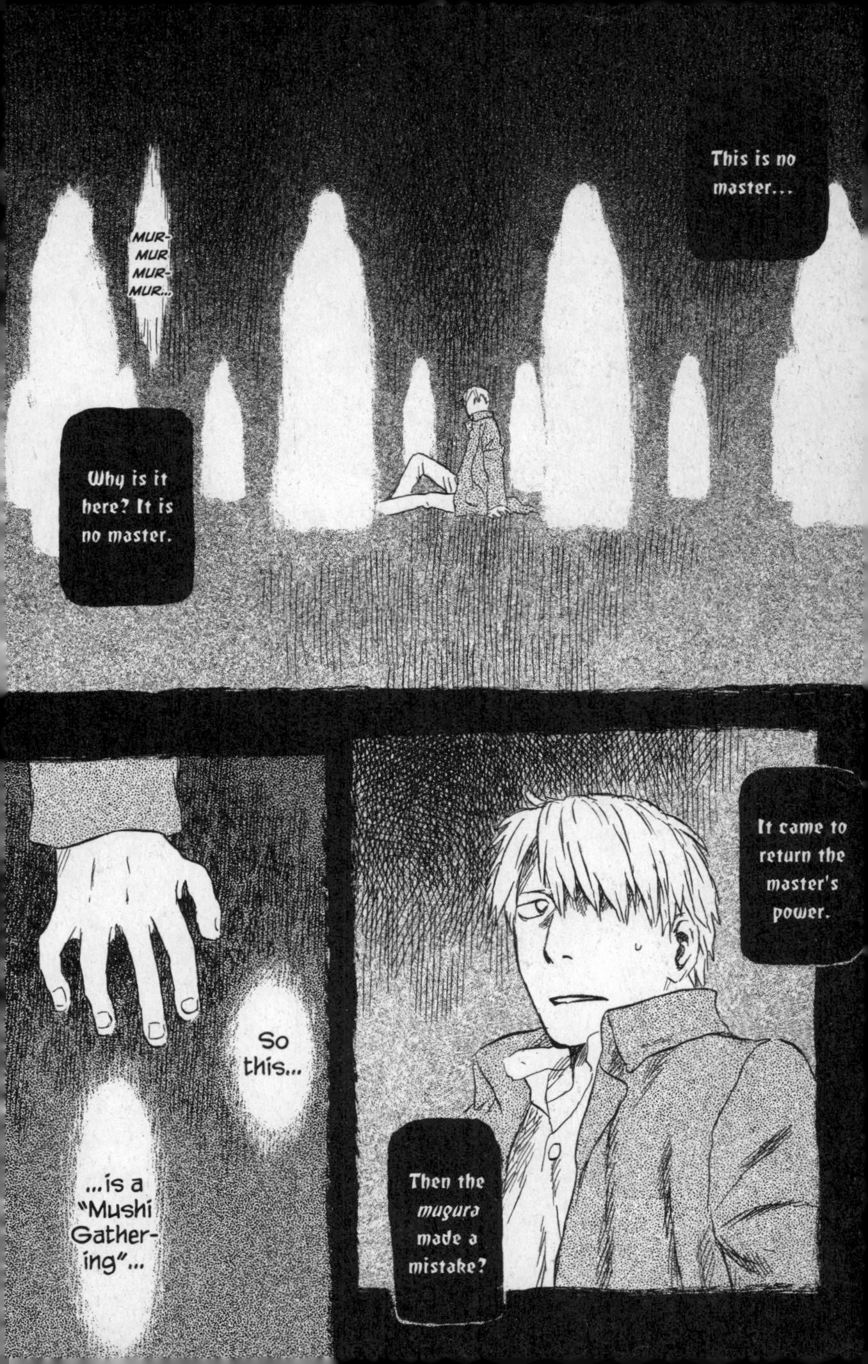
This is no master...
MUR-MUR MUR-MUR...
Why is it here? It is no master.
It came to return the master's power.
Then the *mugura* made a mistake?
So this...
...is a "Mushi Gathering"...

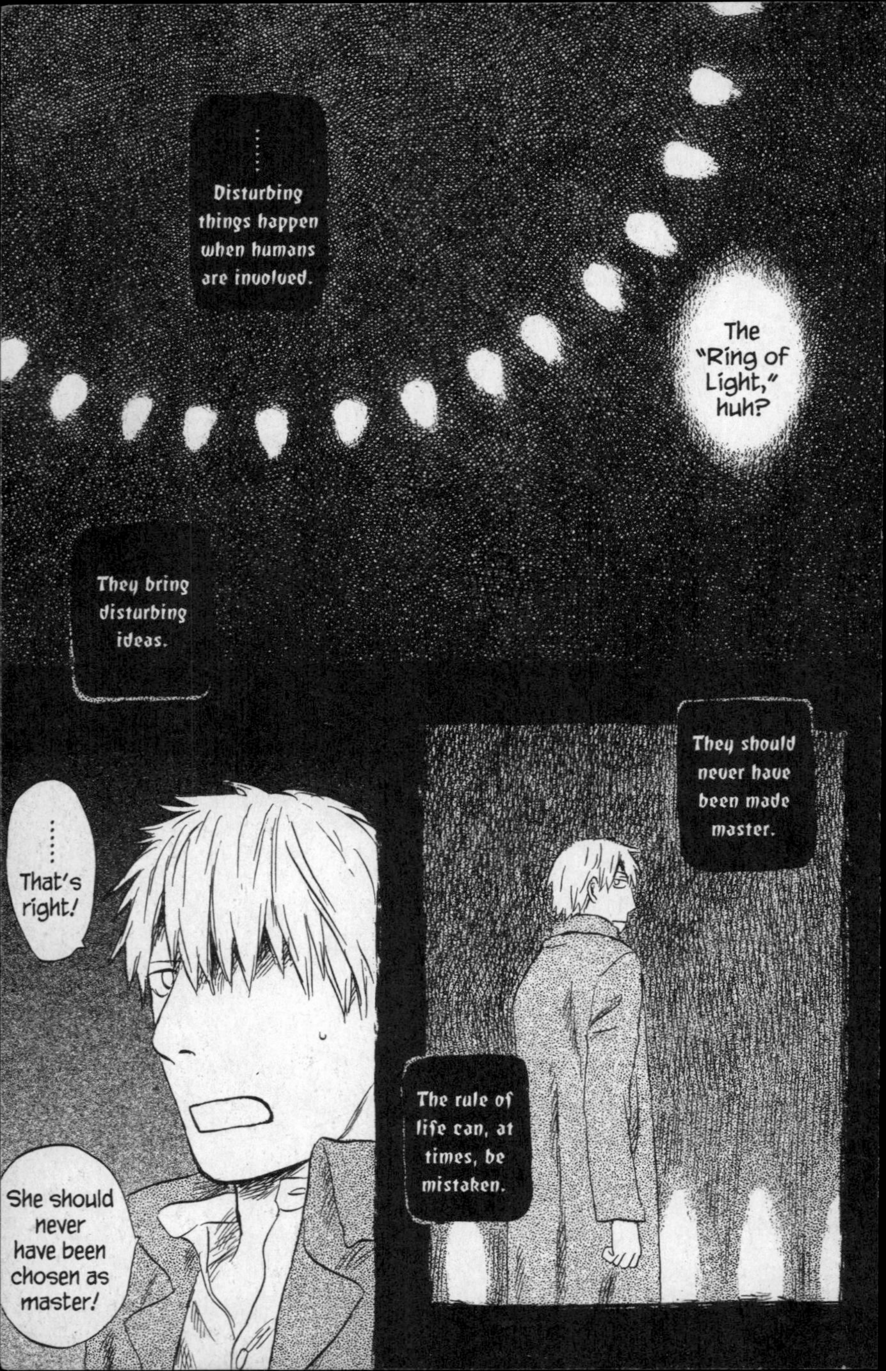
The "Ring of Light," huh?
...... Disturbing things happen when humans are involved.
They bring disturbing ideas.
They should never have been made master.
The rule of life can, at times, be mistaken.
...... That's right!
She should never have been chosen as master!

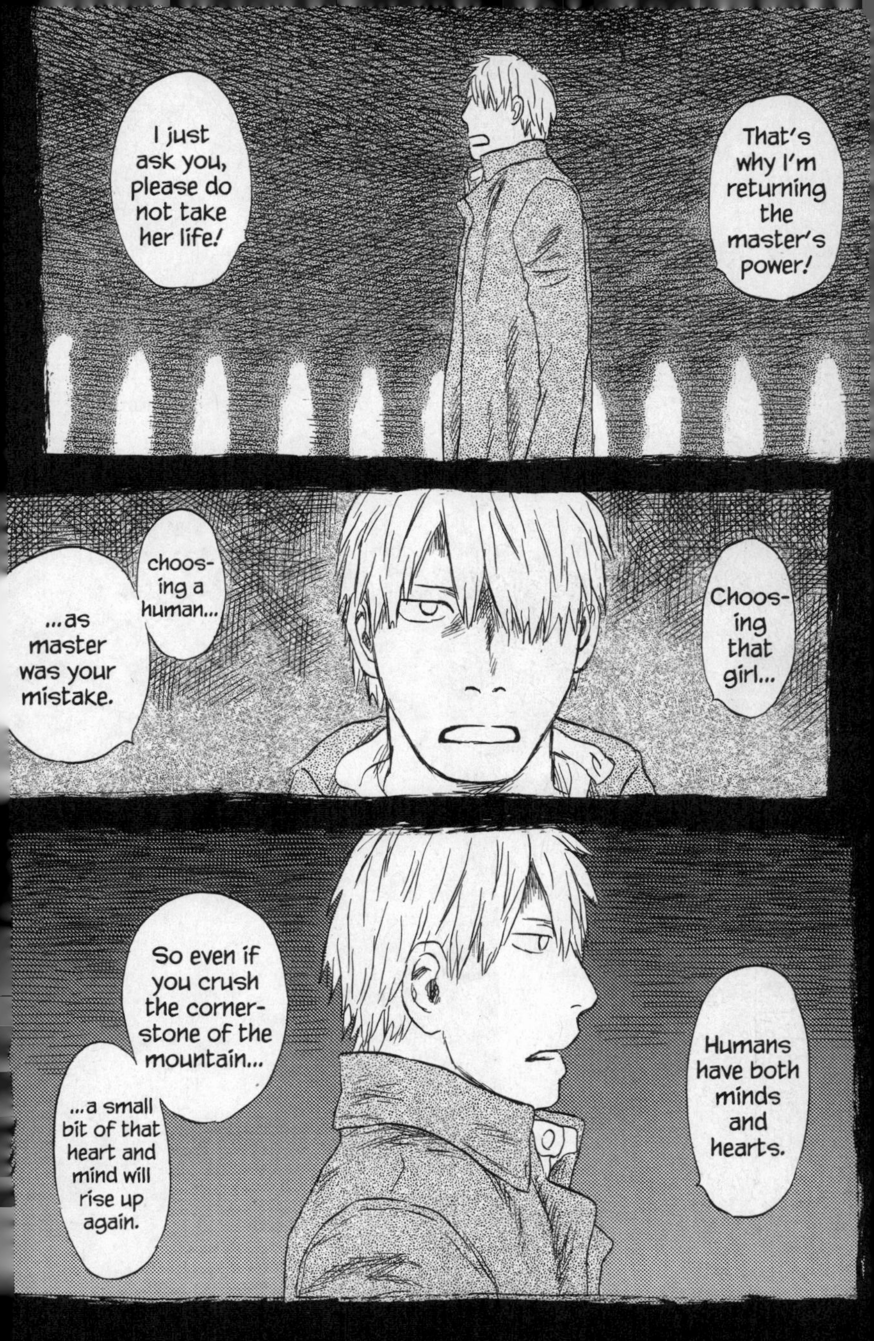
That's why I'm returning the master's power!
I just ask you, please do not take her life!
Choosing that girl...
choosing a human...
...as master was your mistake.
Humans have both minds and hearts.
So even if you crush the cornerstone of the mountain...
...a small bit of that heart and mind will rise up again.

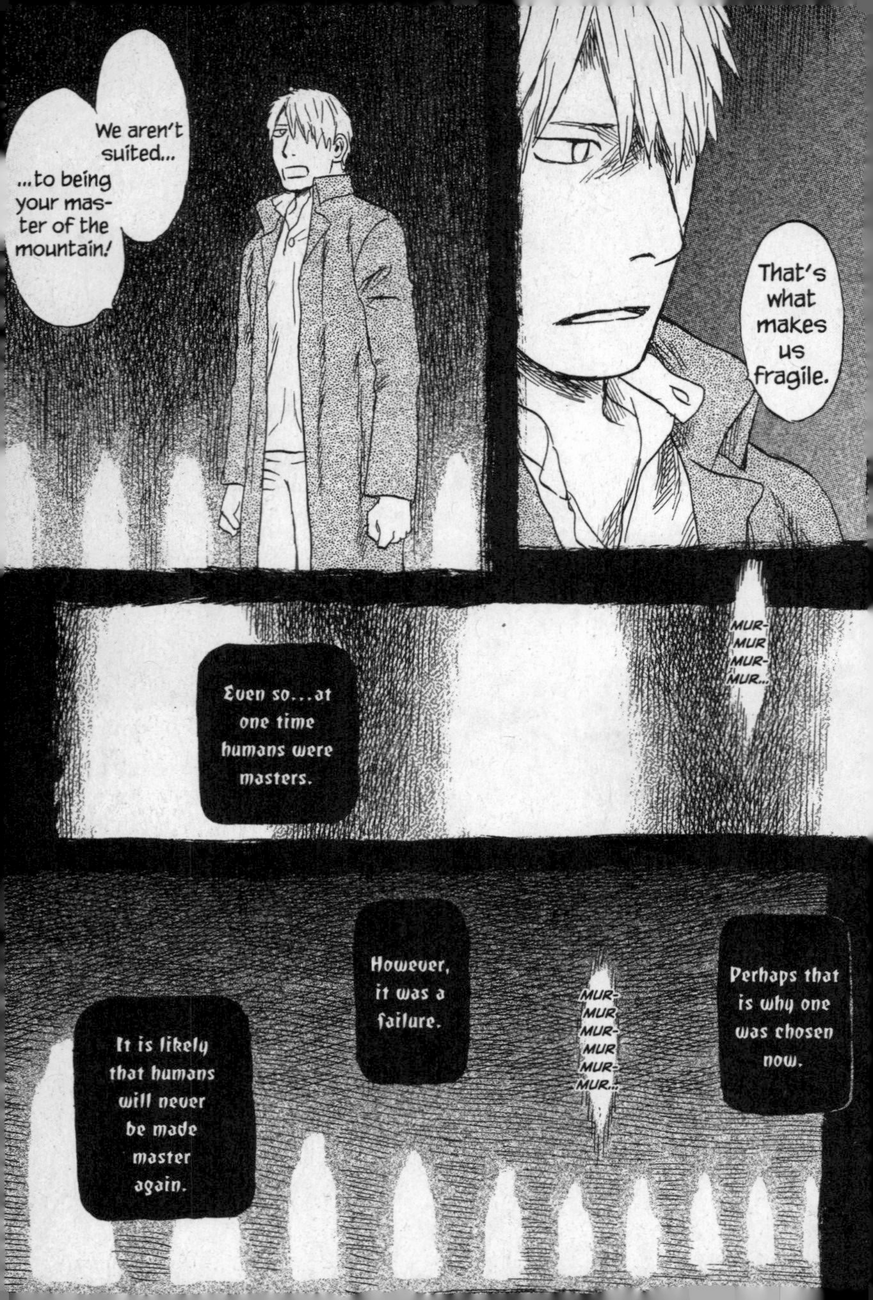
That's what makes us fragile.
We aren't suited...
...to being your master of the mountain!
MUR-MUR MUR-MUR...
Even so...at one time humans were masters.
Perhaps that is why one was chosen now.
MUR-MUR MUR-MUR MUR-MUR...
However, it was a failure.
It is likely that humans will never be made master again.

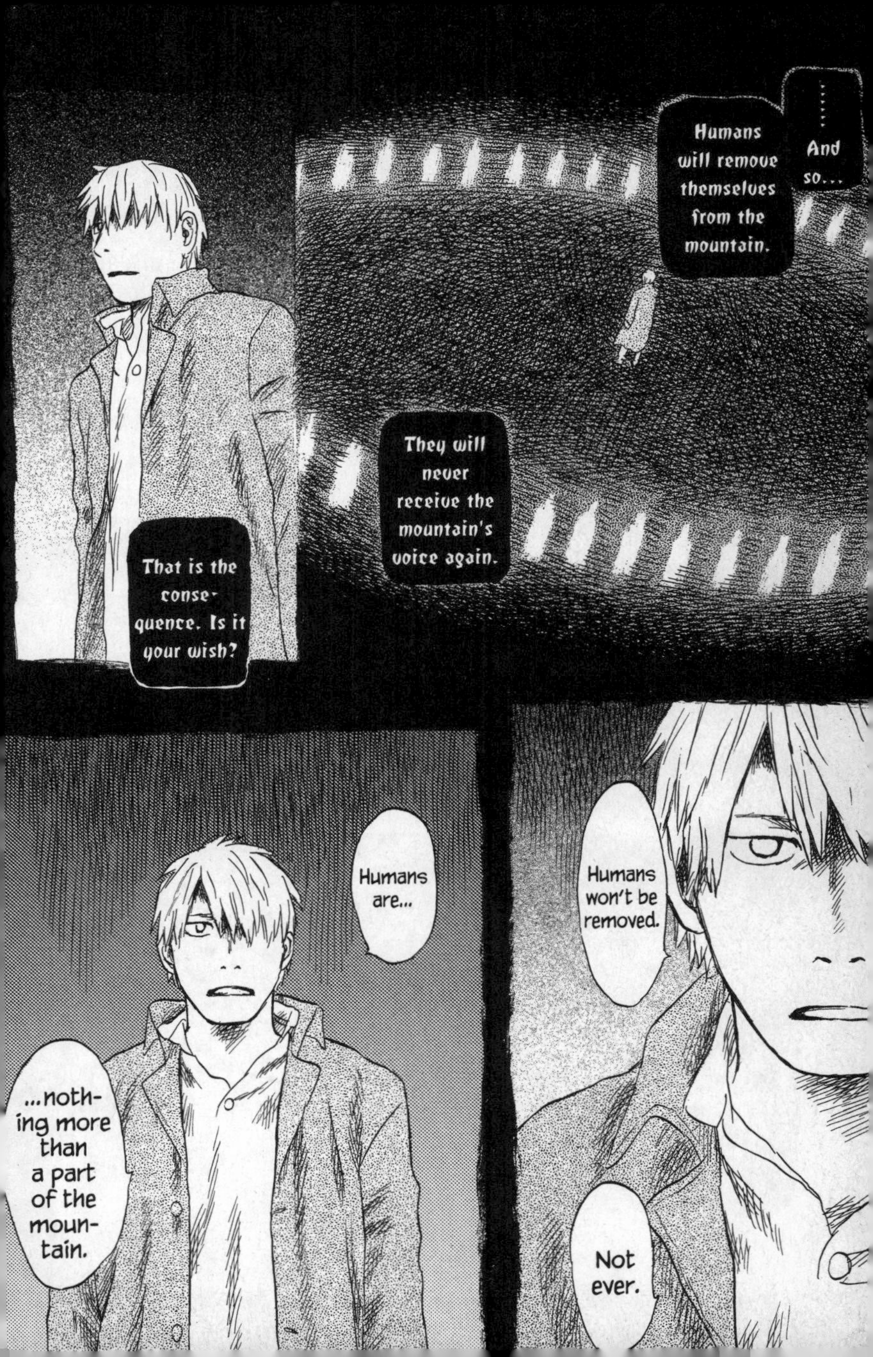
......
And so...
Humans will remove themselves from the mountain.
They will never receive the mountain's voice again.
That is the conse-quence. Is it your wish?
Humans won't be removed.
Not ever.
Humans are...
...noth-ing more than a part of the mountain.

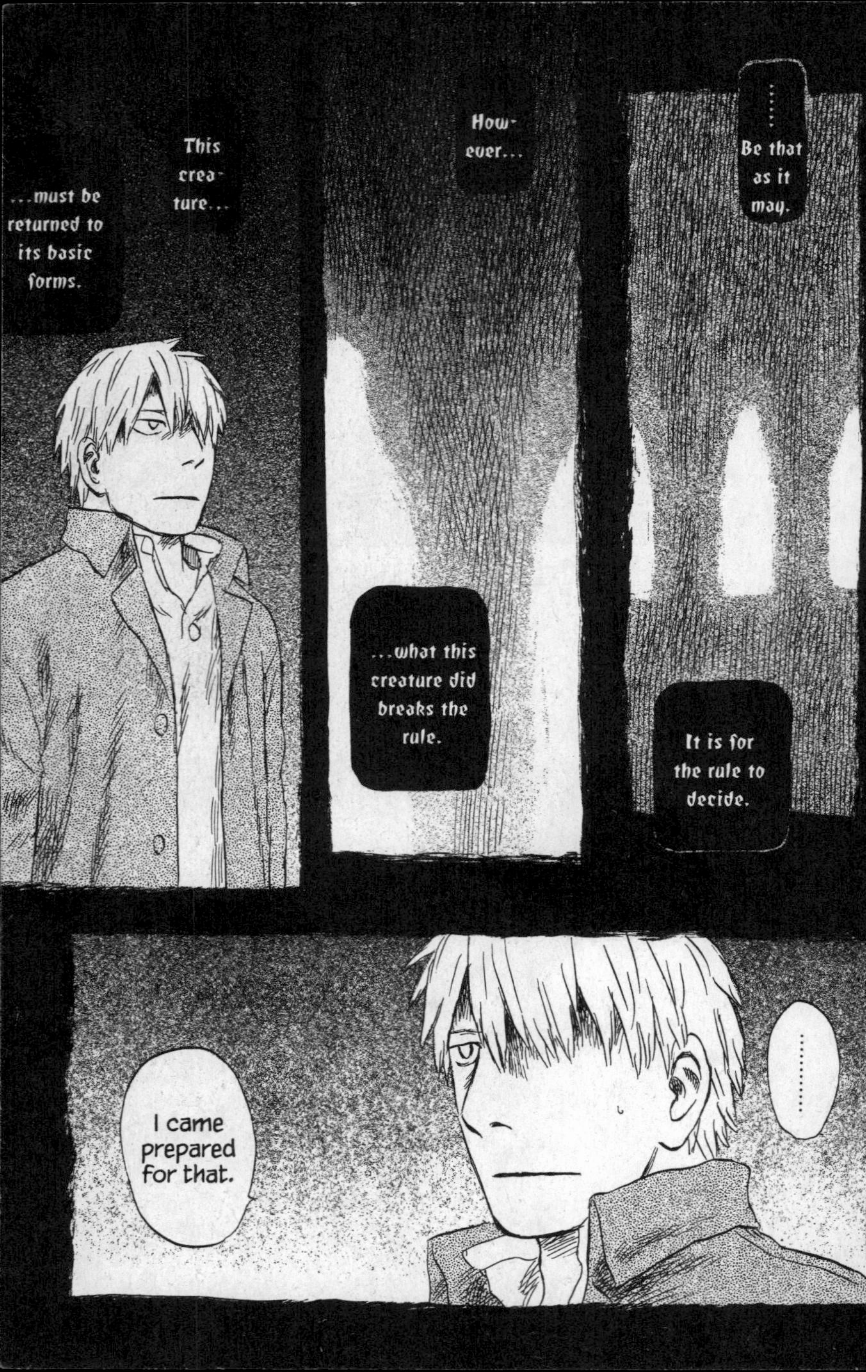
......
Be that as it may.
It is for the rule to decide.
However...
...what this creature did breaks the rule.
This creature...
...must be returned to its basic forms.
......
I came prepared for that.

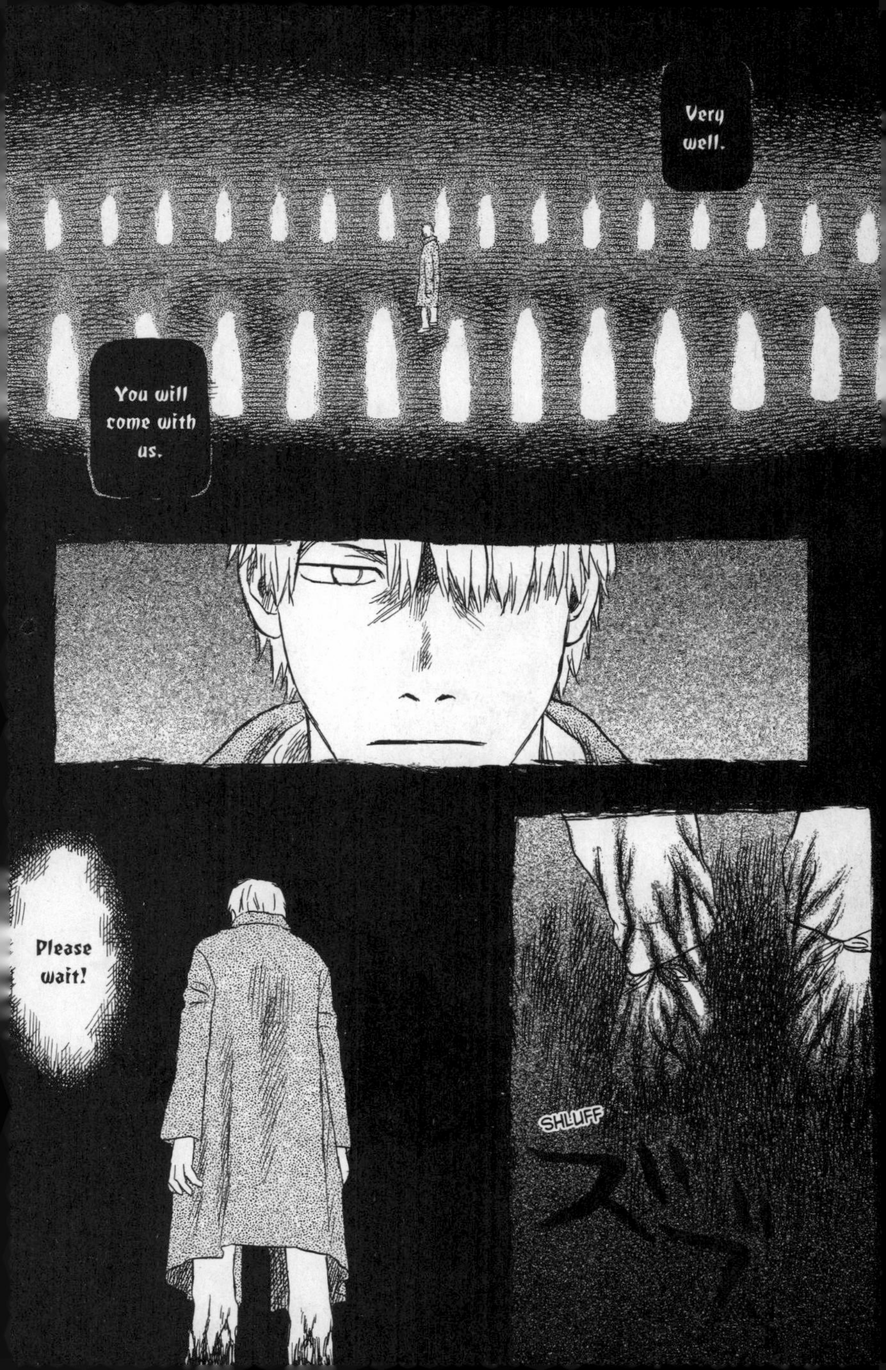
Very well.
You will come with us.
SHLUFF
Please wait!

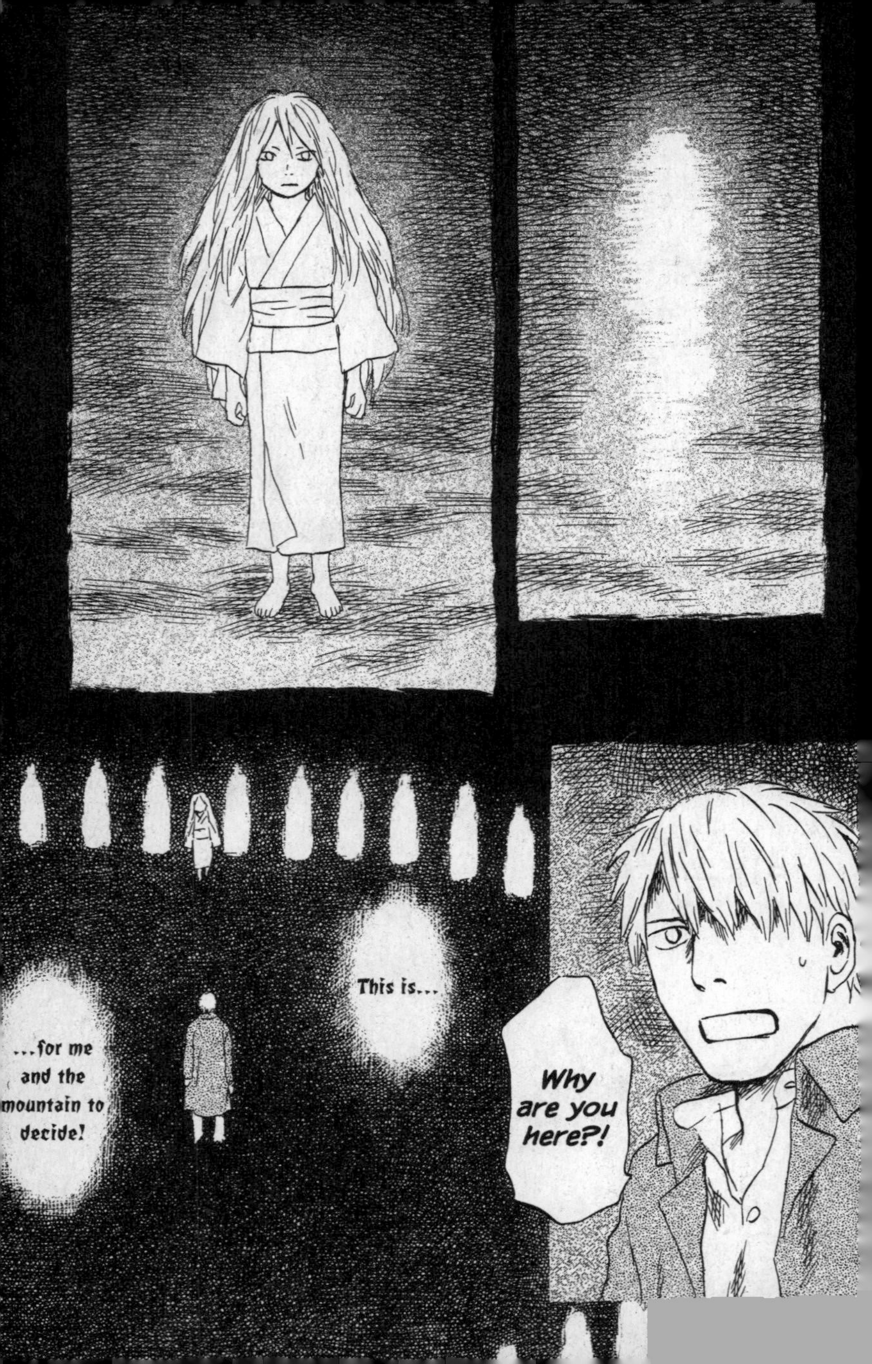
Why are you here?!
This is...
...for me and the mountain to decide!

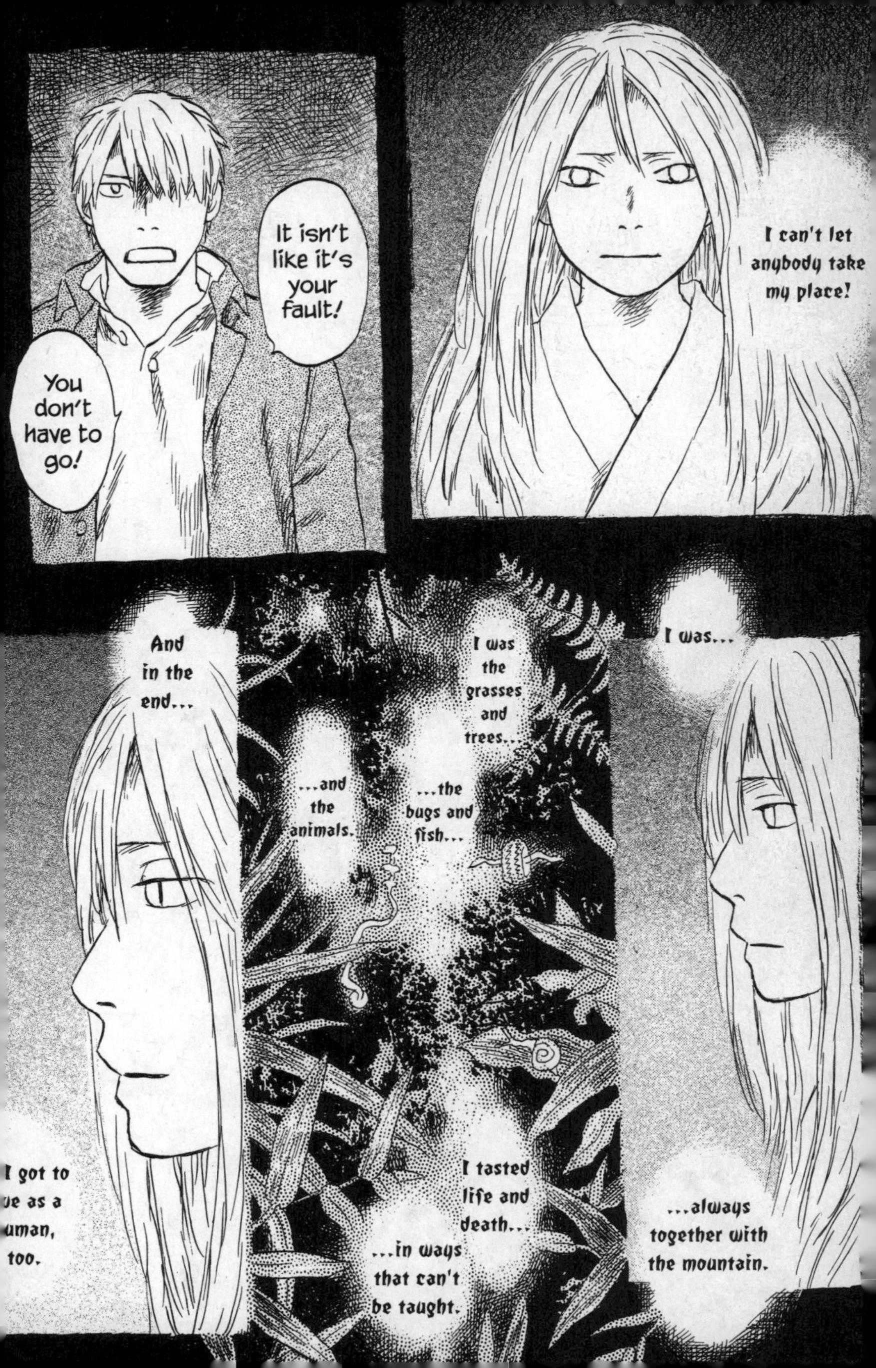
I can't let anybody take my place!
It isn't like it's your fault!
You don't have to go!
I was...
...always together with the mountain.
I was the grasses and trees...
...the bugs and fish...
...and the animals.
I tasted life and death...
...in ways that can't be taught.
And in the end...
I got to ve as a uman, too.

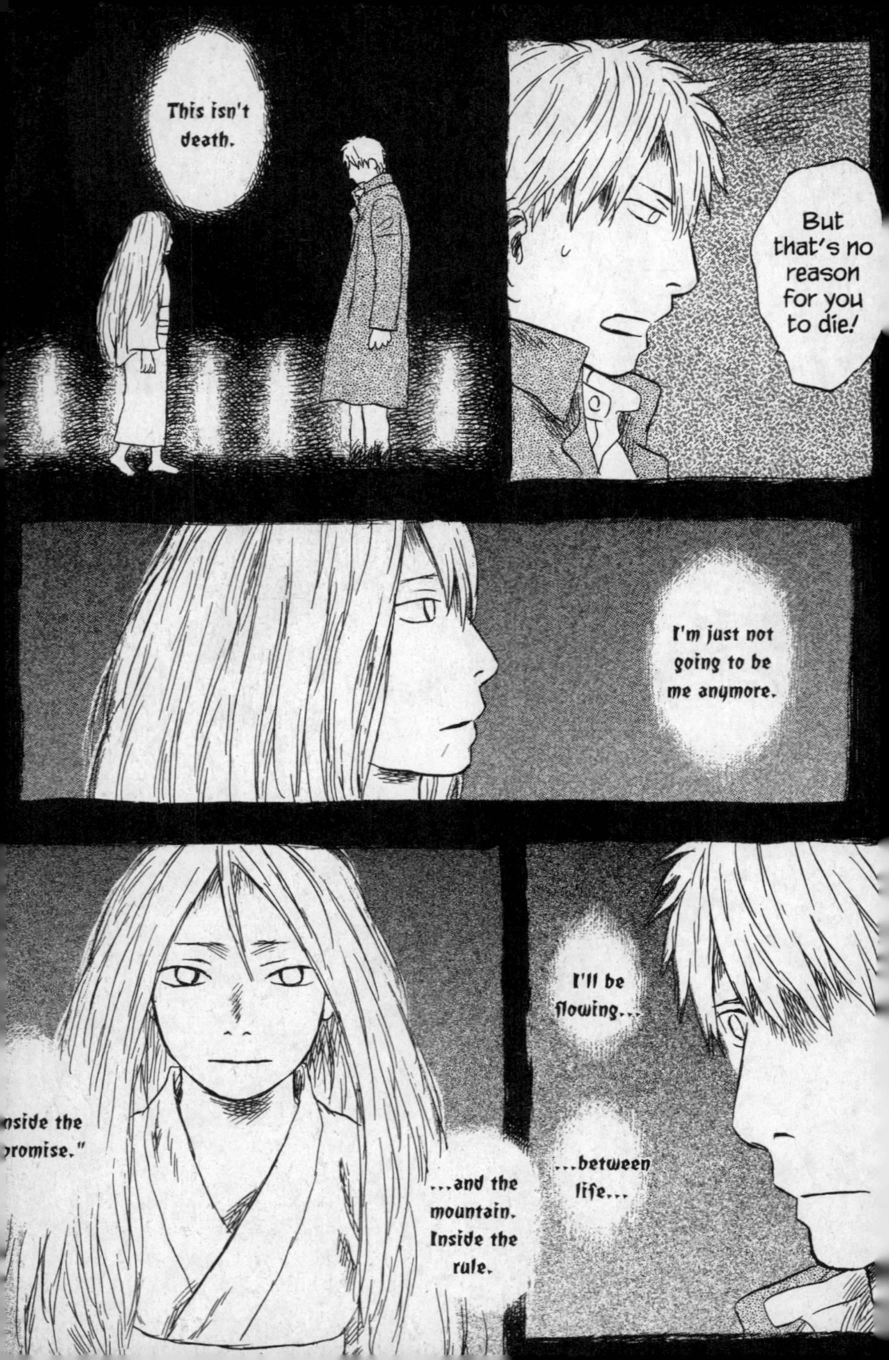
But that's no reason for you to die!
This isn't death.
I'm just not going to be me anymore.
I'll be flowing...
...between life...
...and the mountain. Inside the rule.
nside the romise."

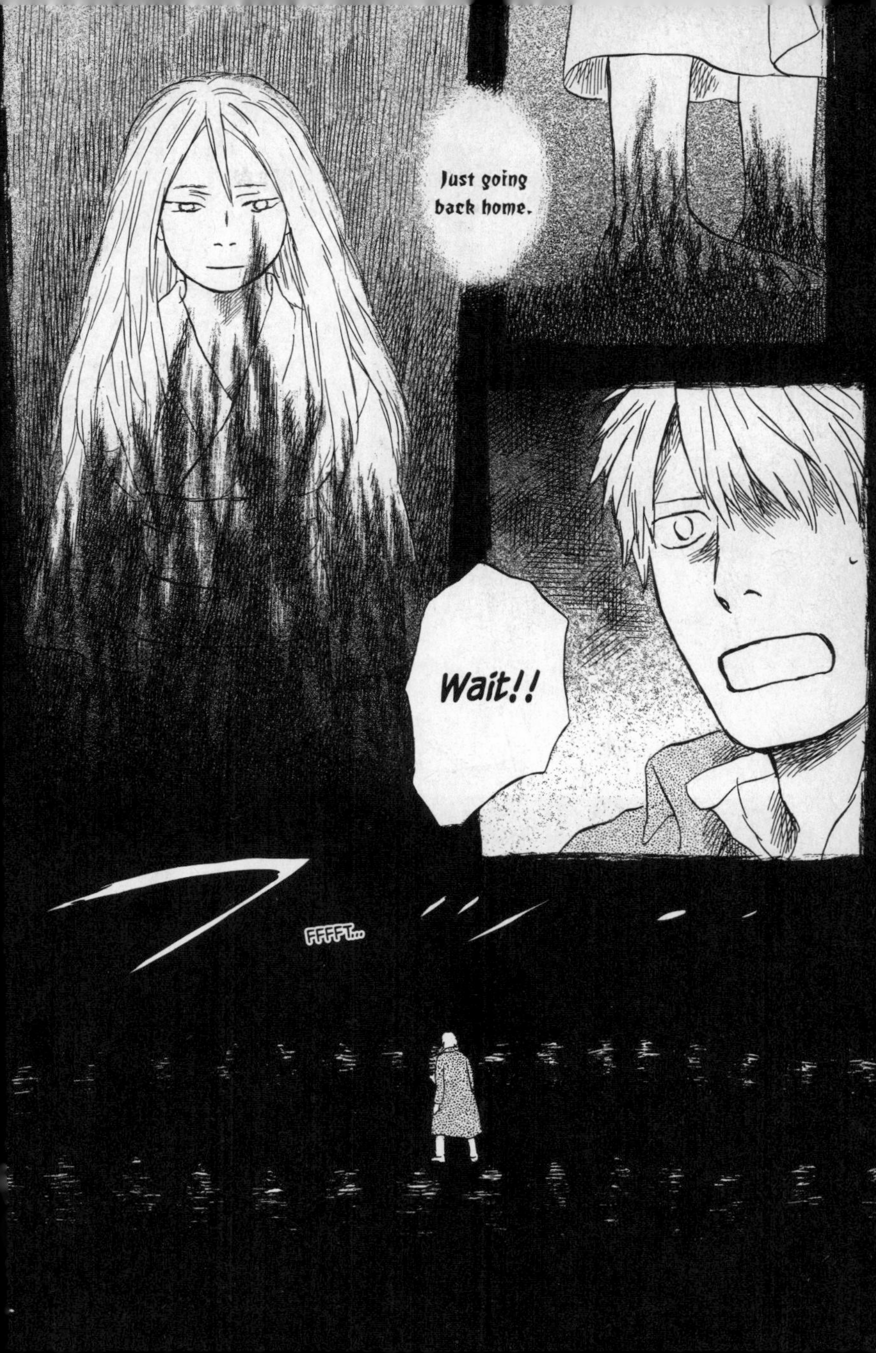
Just going back home.
Wait!!
FFFFT...

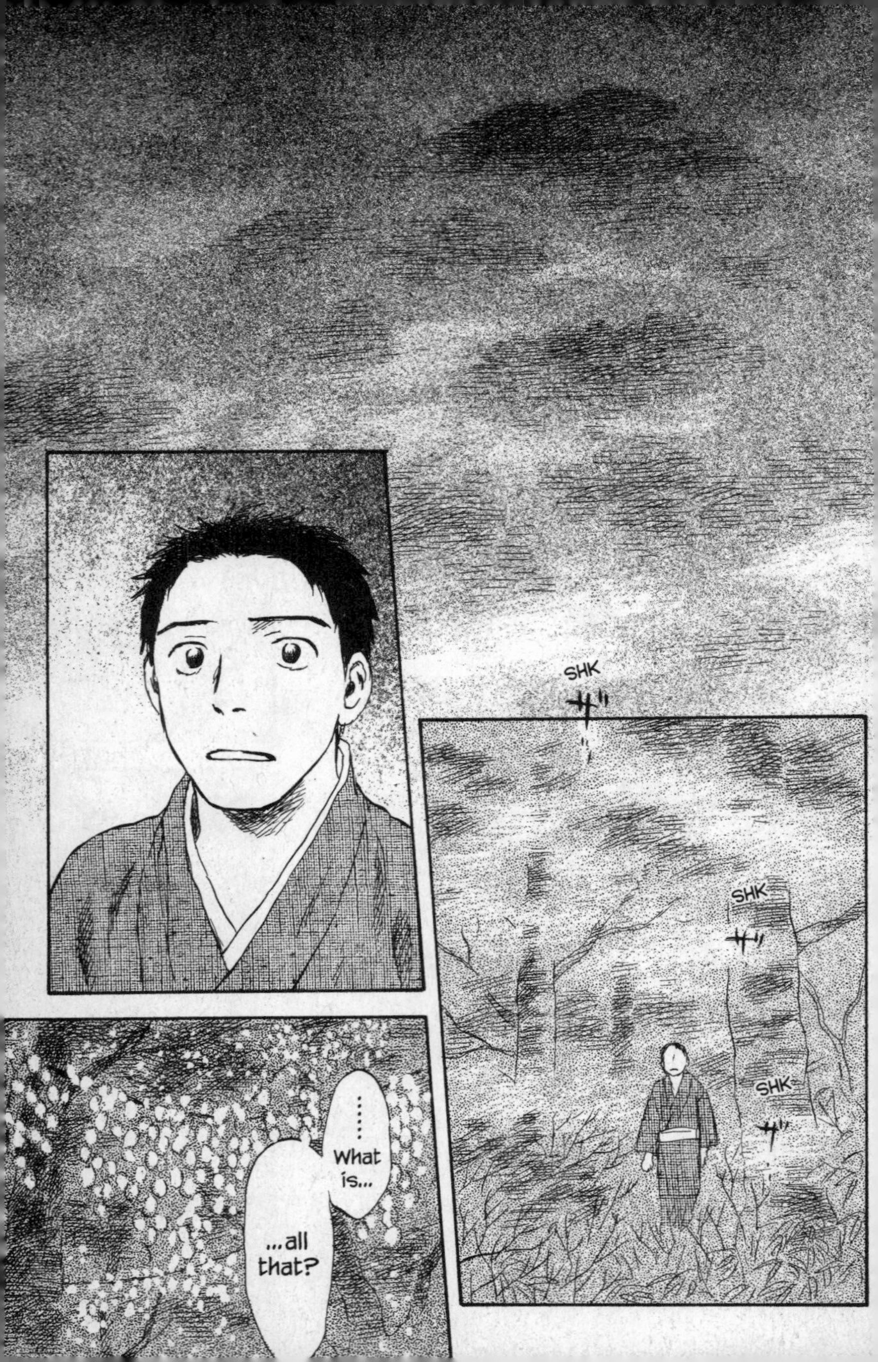
SHK
SHK
SHK
......what is...
...all that?

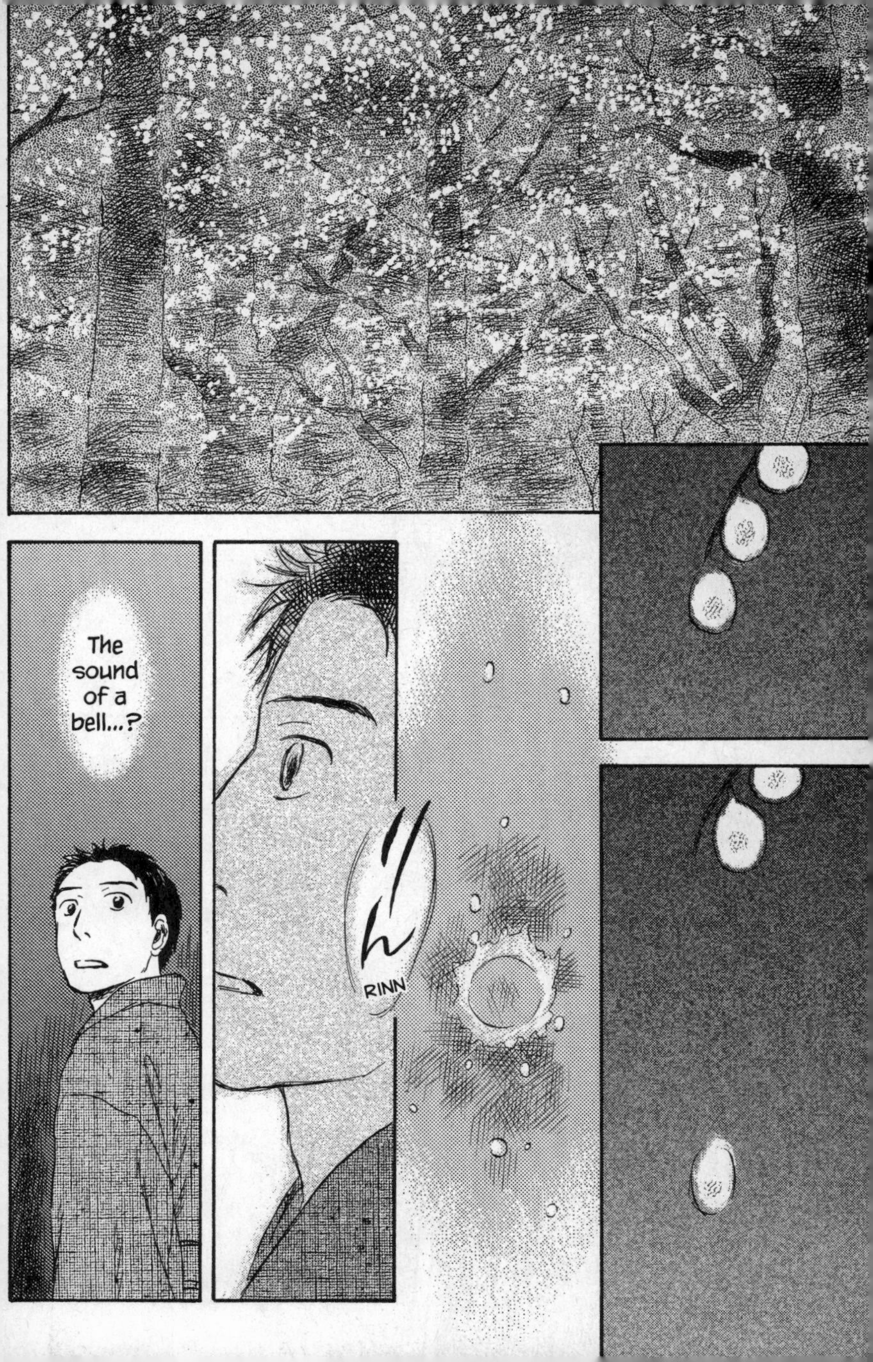
RINN
The sound of a bell...?

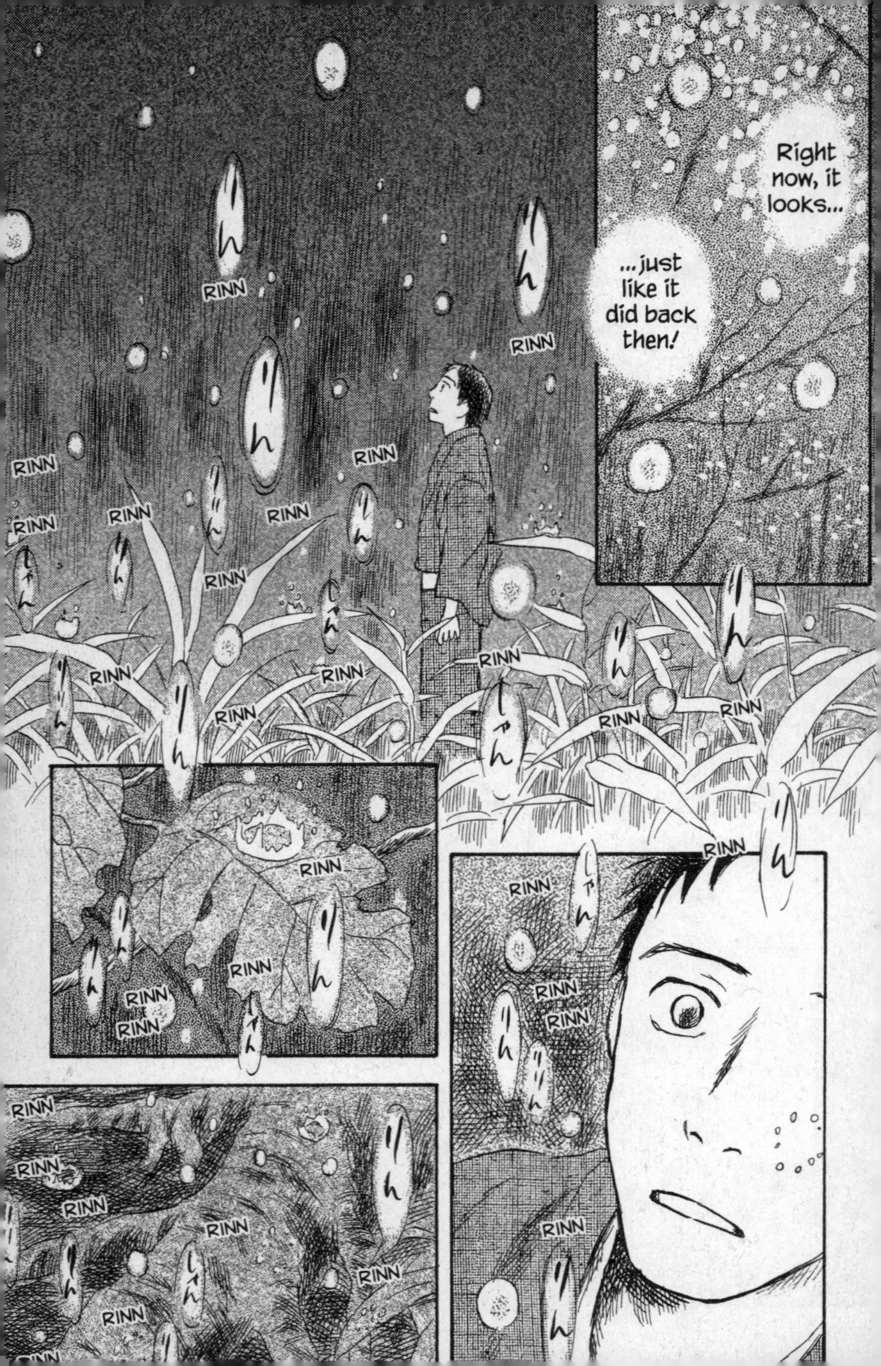
Right now, it looks...
...just like it did back then!
RINN
RINN
RINN
RINN
RINN
RINN
RINN
RINN
RINN
RINN
RINN
RINN
RINN
RINN
RINN
RINN
RINN
RINN
RINN
RINN
RINN
RINN
RINN
RINN
RINN
RINN
RINN
RINN
RINN
RINN

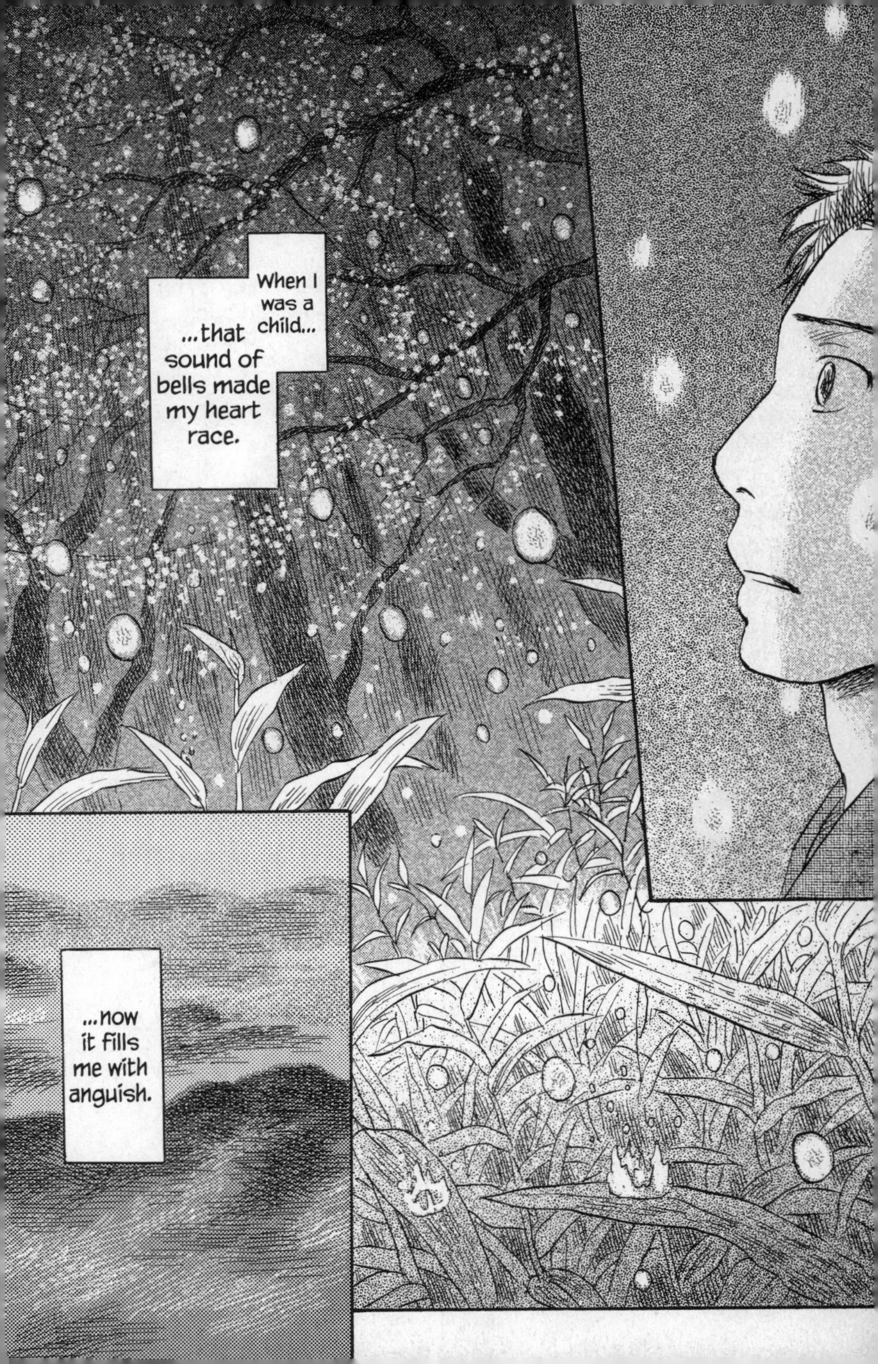
When I was a child...
...that sound of bells made my heart race.
...now it fills me with anguish.

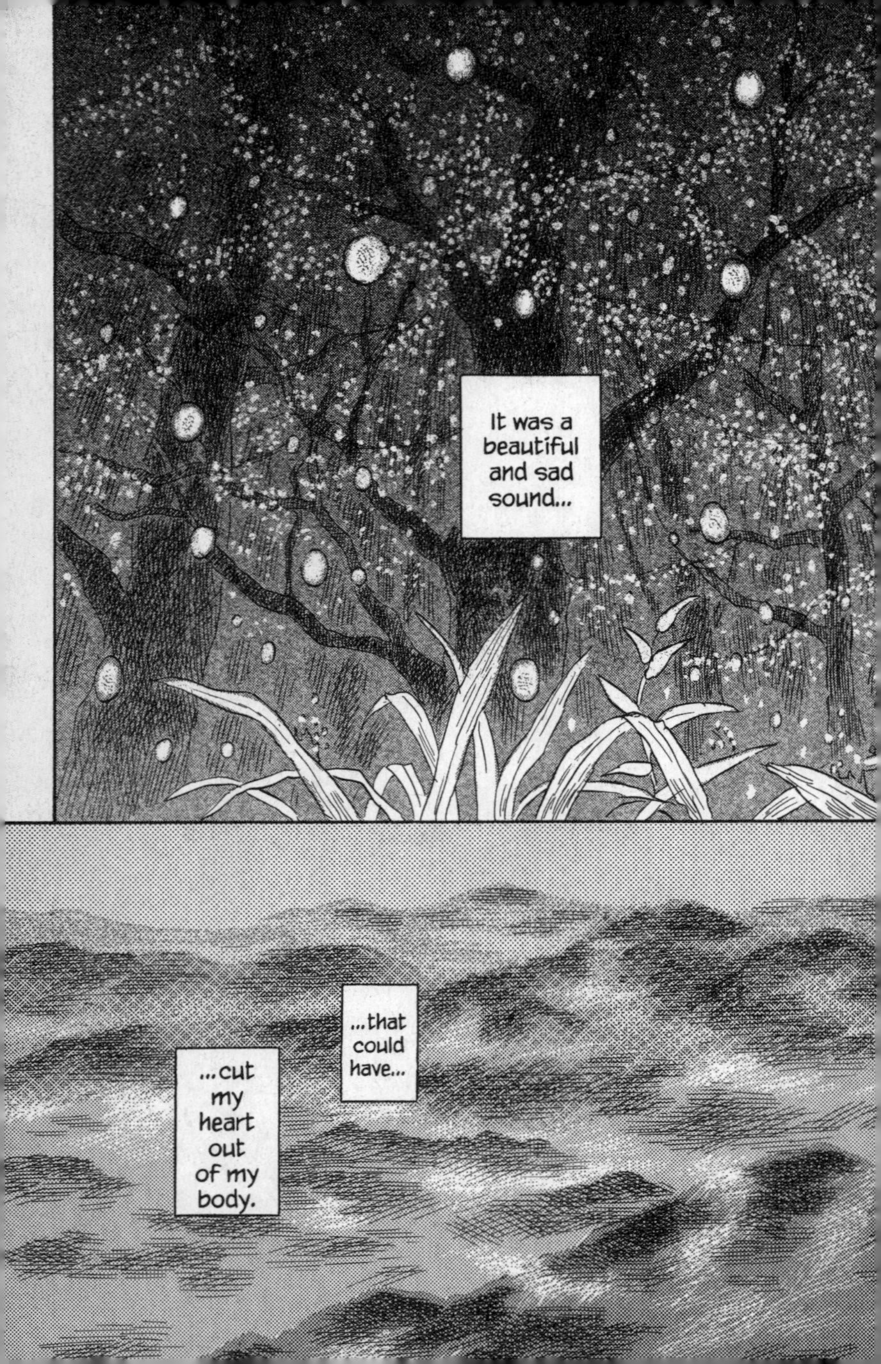
It was a beautiful and sad sound...
...that could have...
...cut my heart out of my body.

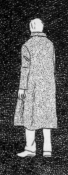

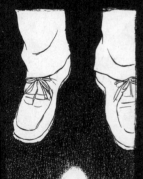

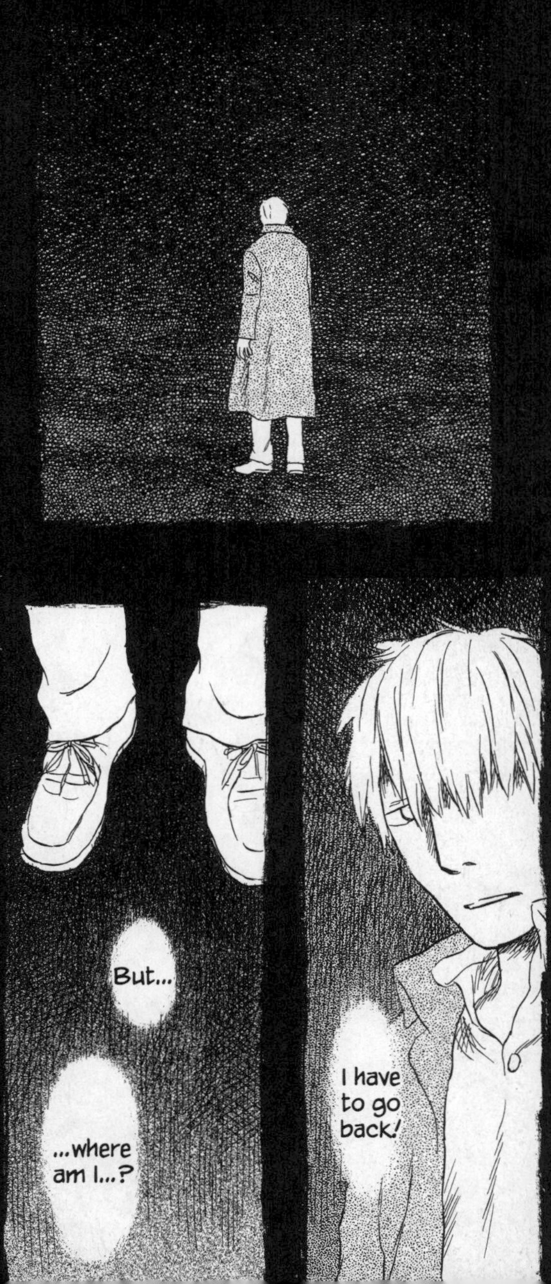

But...

...where
am I...?

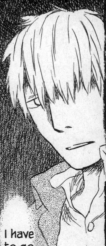

I have
to go
back!

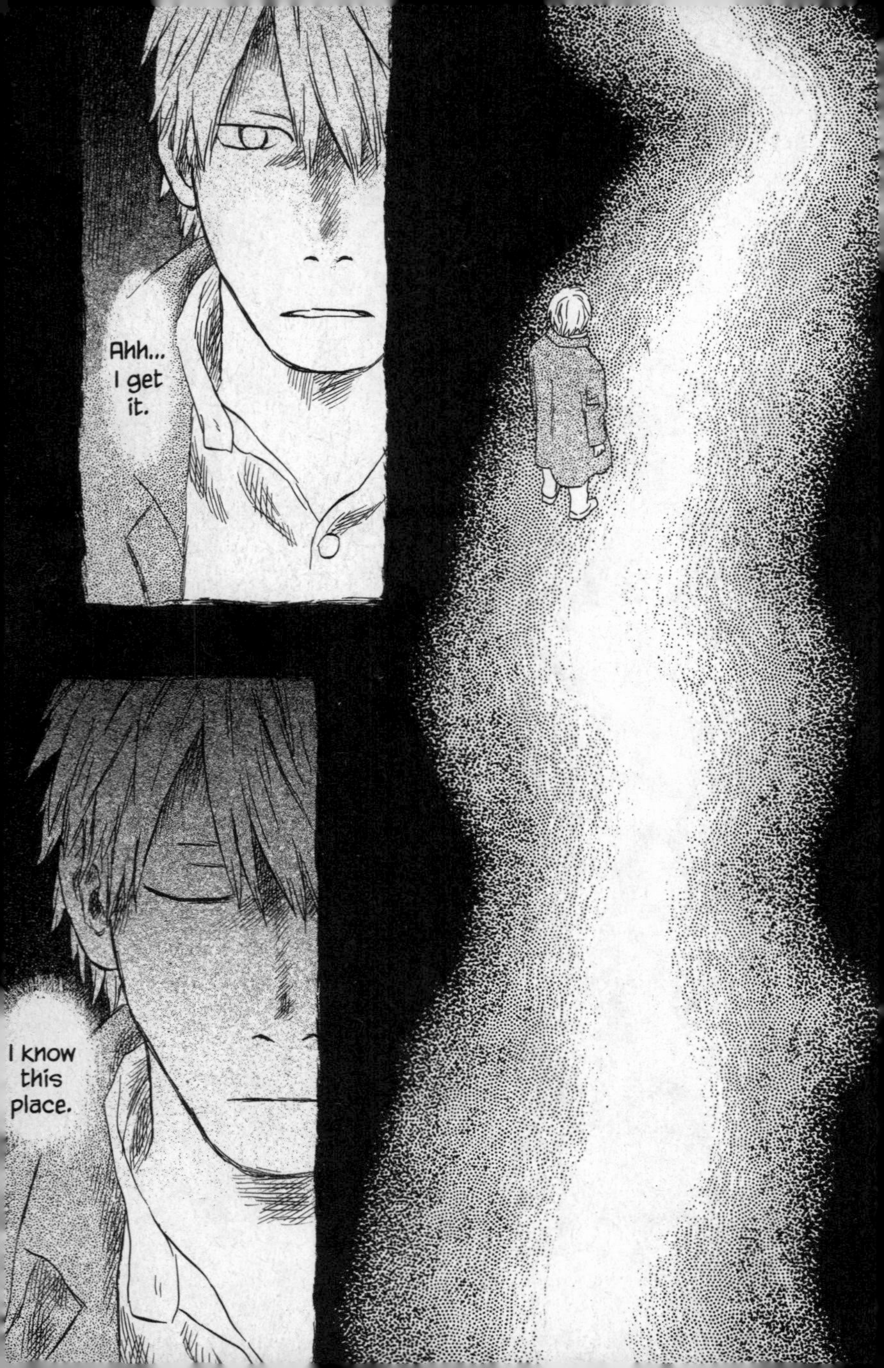
Ahh... I get it.
I know this place.

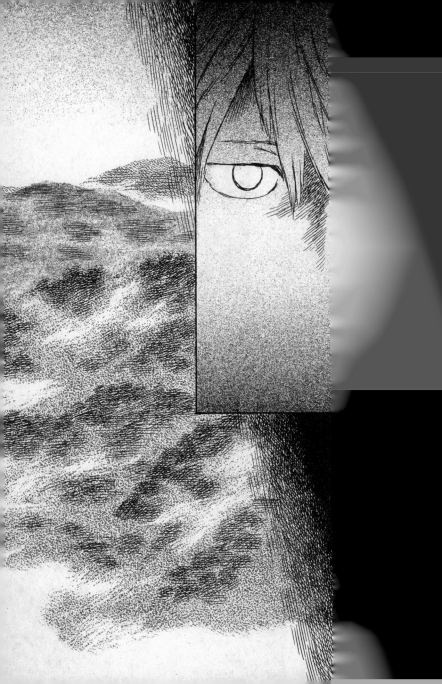

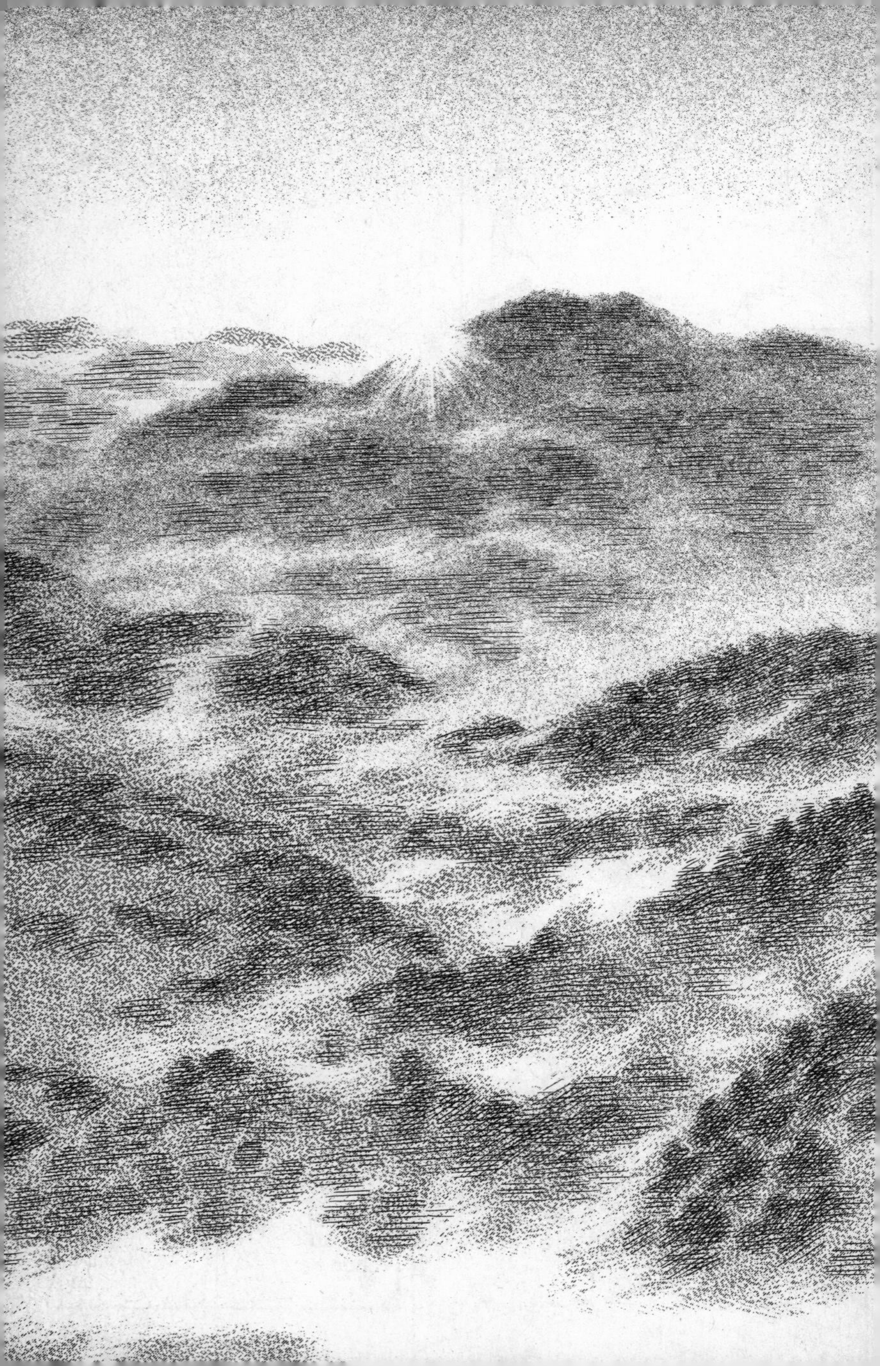

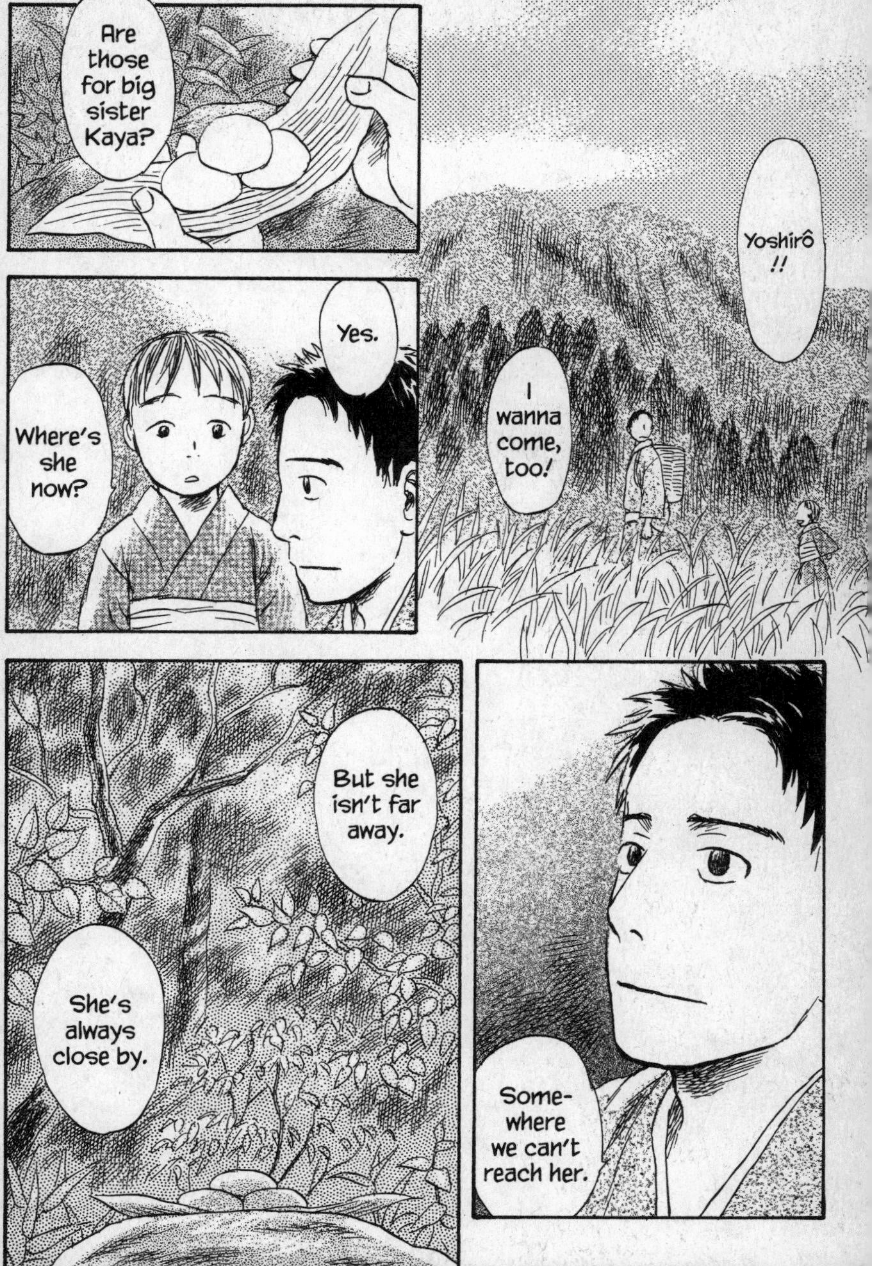
Yoshirô !!
I wanna come, too!
Are those for big sister Kaya?
Yes.
Where's she now?
Some-where we can't reach her.
But she isn't far away.
She's always close by.

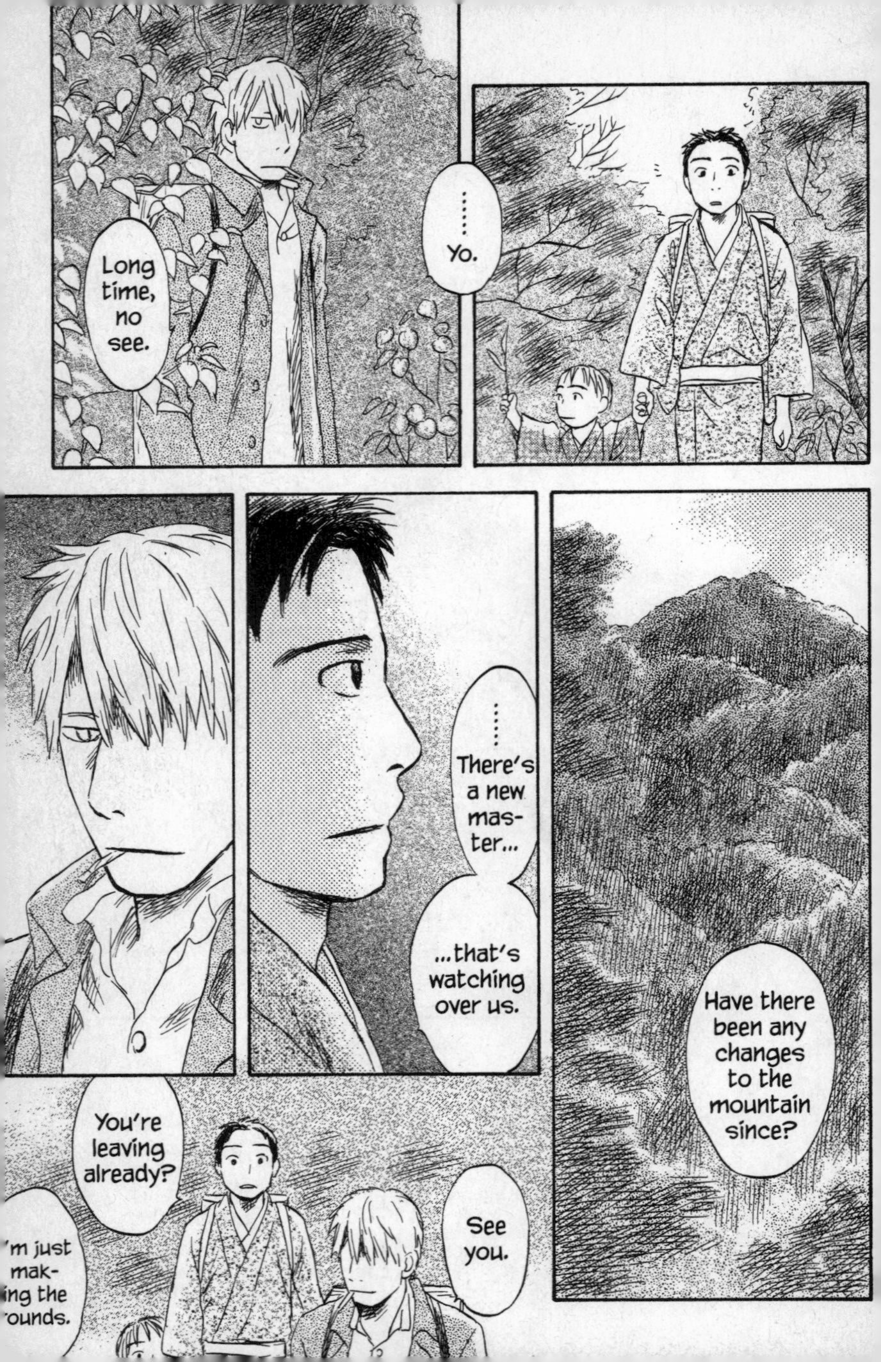
……Yo.
Long time, no see.
Have there been any changes to the mountain since?
……There's a new mas- ter...
...that's watching over us.
See you.
You're leaving already?
'm just mak- ing the ounds.

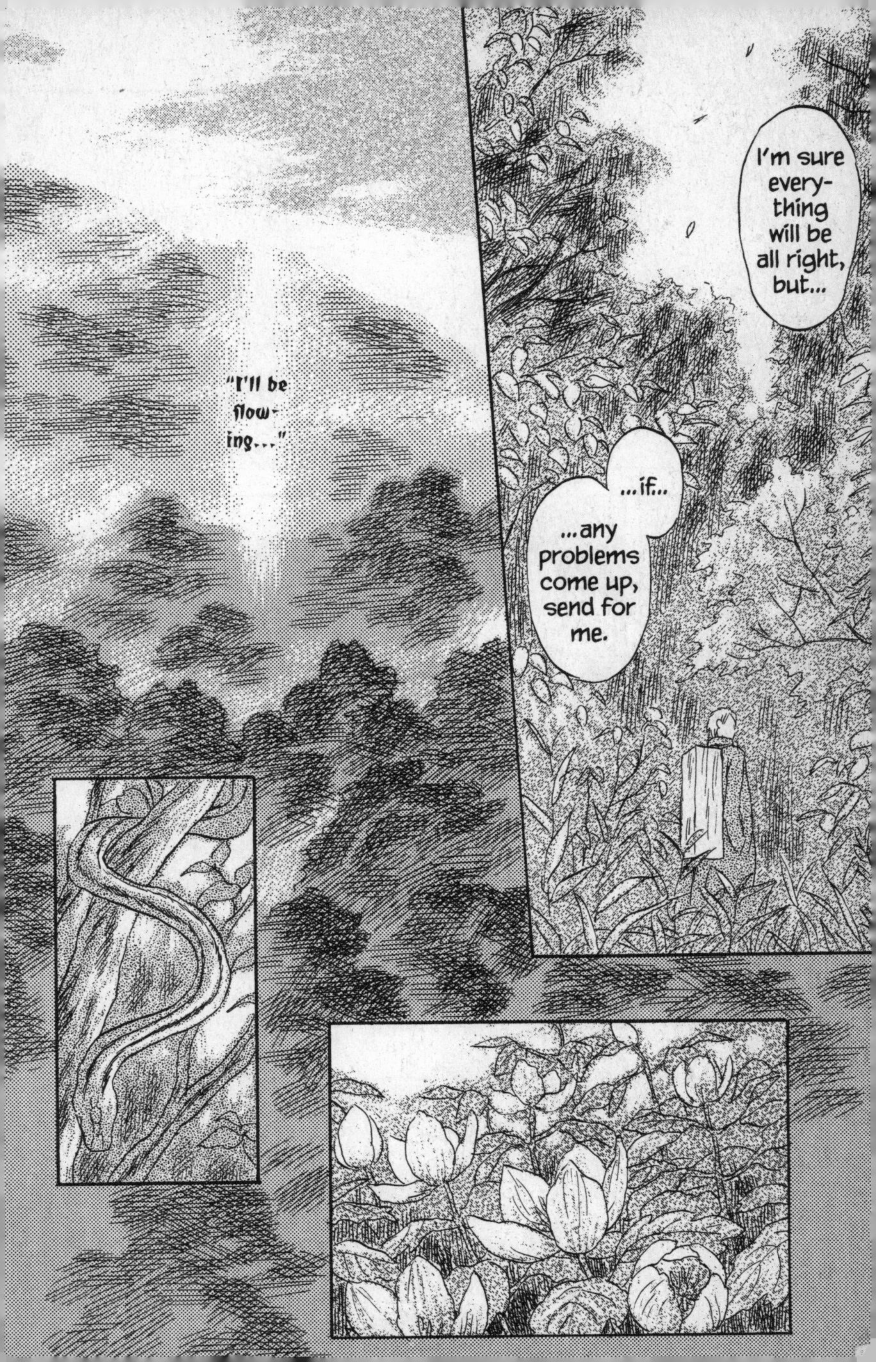
I'm sure every-thing will be all right, but...
...if...
...any problems come up, send for me.
"I'll be flow-ing..."

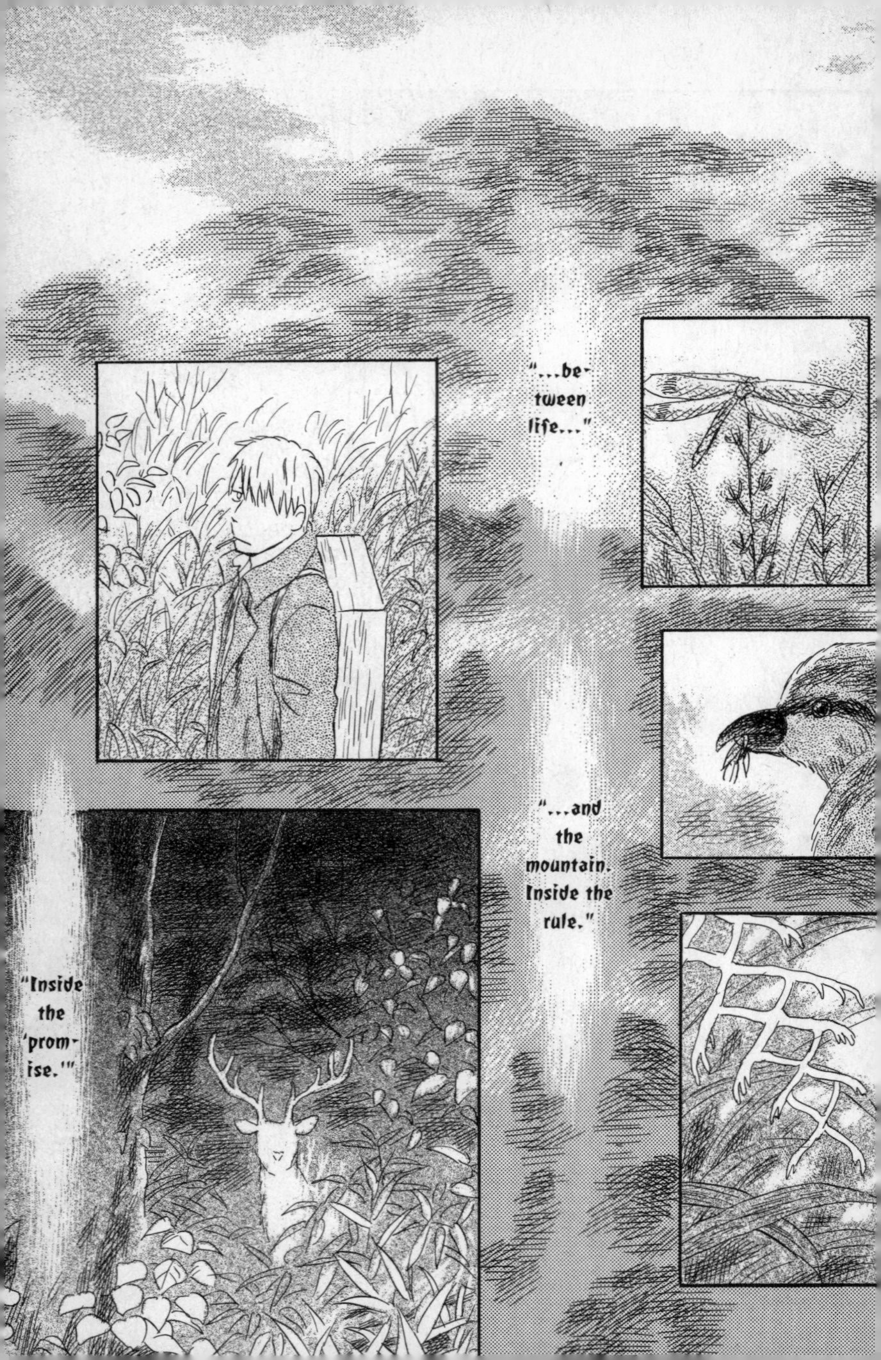
"...be-tween life..."
"...and the mountain. Inside the rule."
"Inside the 'promise.'"

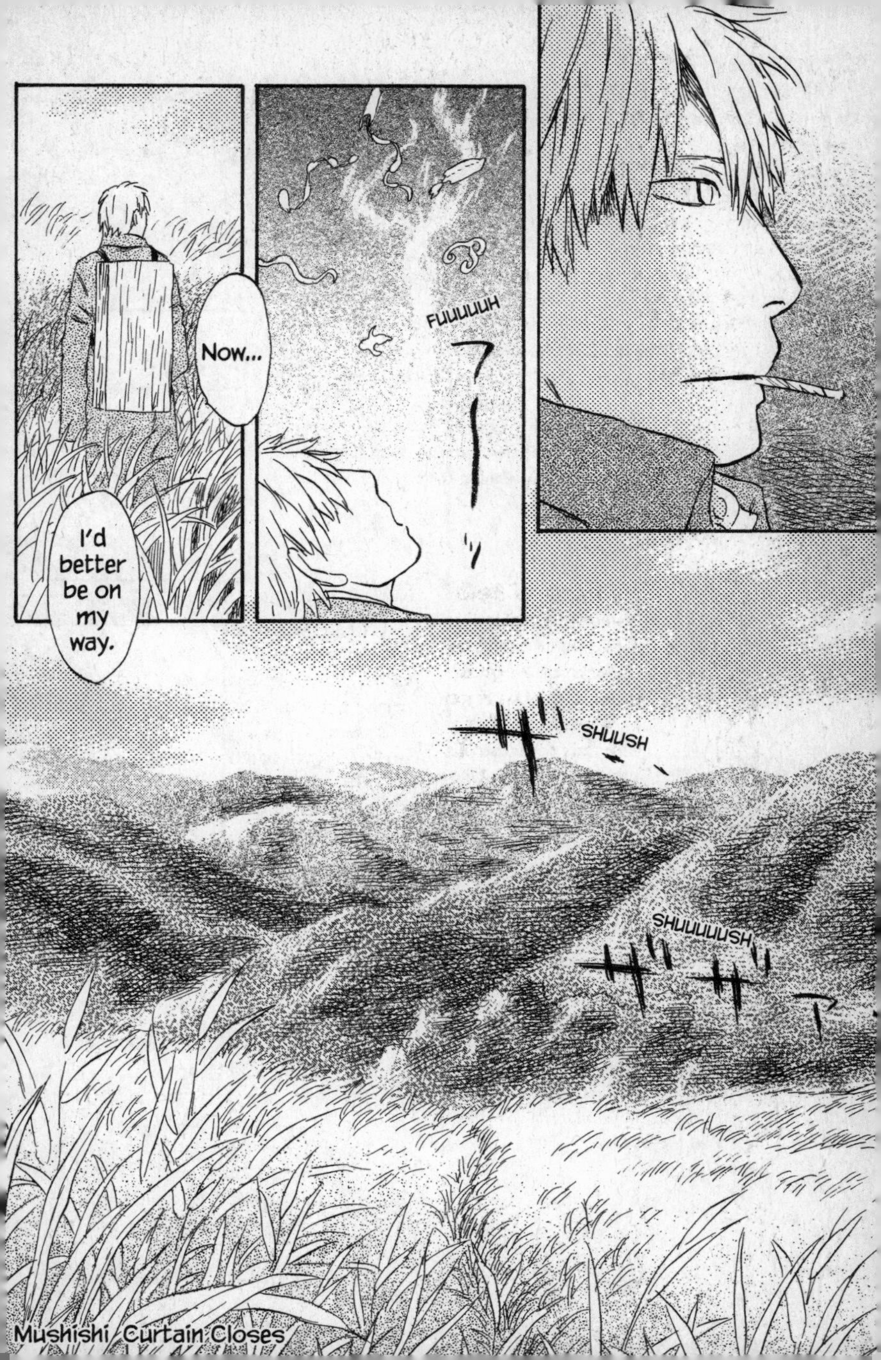
FUUUUUH
Now...
I'd better be on my way.
SHUUSH
SHUUUUUSH
Mushishi Curtain Closes

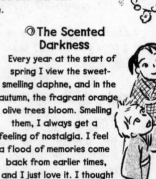

Afterword

Thanks to you, we made it to Volume 10 to close the curtain on the series.

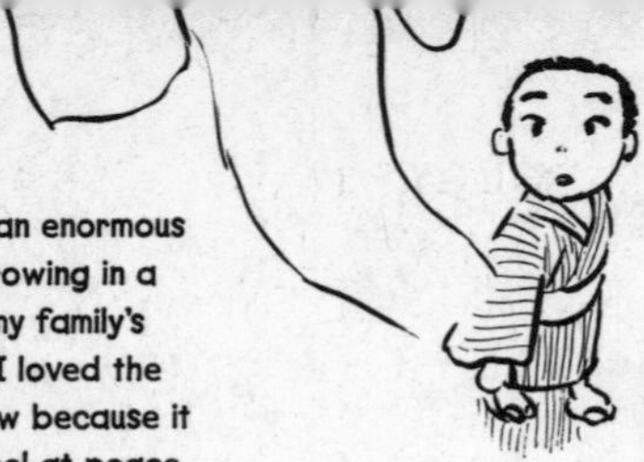

◎The Thread of Light

I love the phrase "Teni-muhô," and that's how I thought up this story. I heard from my mother how having children can change a woman's body. You're not only giving away a share of your blood, but you are also sheltering a different individual's life within you, and I couldn't help but think what a huge burden that must be.

◎The Eternal Tree

There used to be an enormous camphor tree growing in a place close to my family's ancestral home. I loved the place where it grew because it always made me feel at peace. But one year, a typhoon came in and toppled it. I remember looking at the broken trunk and thinking how it must've hurt.

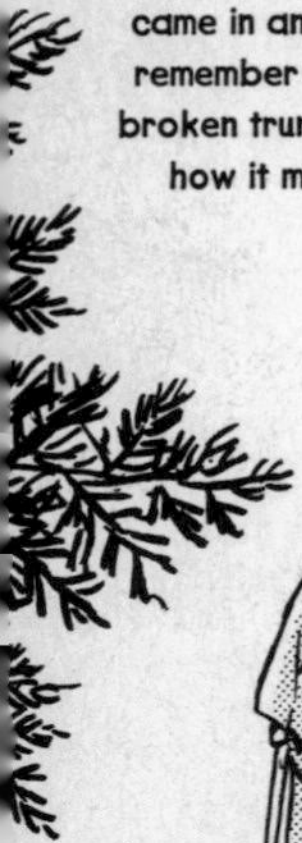

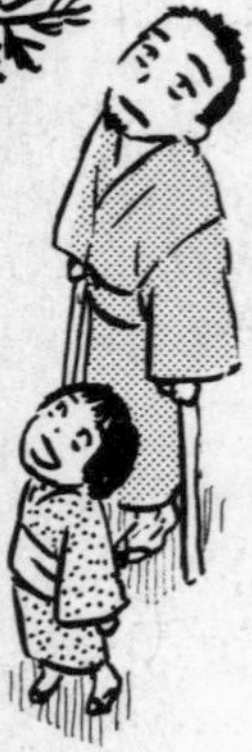

◎The Scented Darkness

Every year at the start of spring I view the sweet-smelling daphne, and in the autumn, the fragrant orange olive trees bloom. Smelling them, I always get a feeling of nostalgia. I feel a flood of memories come back from earlier times, and I just love it. I thought that feeling would be even stronger at night.

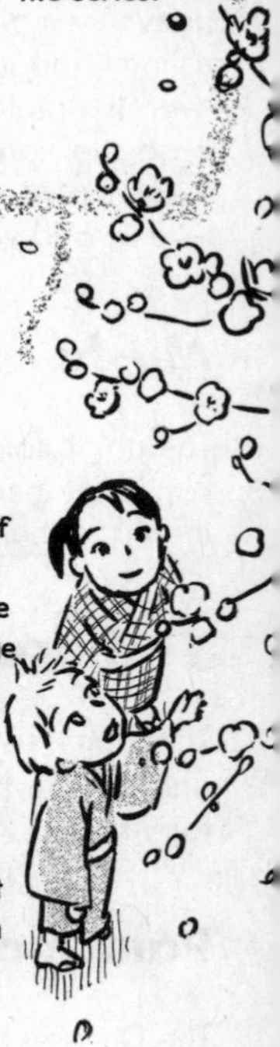

◎Drops of Bells

I've heard a saying that the sound of bells is an imitation of the gods' voices. The sound is just so beautiful! But I also think that somewhere in the sound is something very sad.

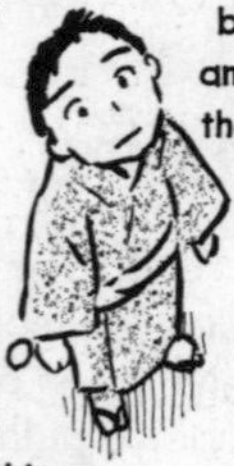

To everyone who helped support Mushishi!
My Editor from Afternoon, Takashi Miyazaki-sama.
The designer, Fake Graphics-sama.
My assistants!
Hayashi M-ka & Mami Yosshii-chan.
Yayoi Miyake-chan!
Yôko-chan! Yone!
Thank you so much!

Thanks to you all for following along on Ginko's journeys. Truly, thank you very much! Now we will be parting ways with him, but we'll be happy if he continues his travels in much the same way he always has.

And here's hoping I can meet up with you in some new place.

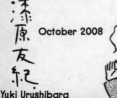

October 2008

漆原友紀

Yuki Urushibara

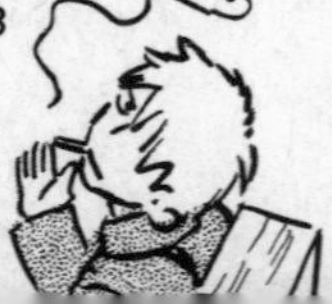

Translation Notes

Tennyo's raiment, page 15

"Hagoromo" is a Noh play about a fisherman who discovers some heavenly maidens (*Tennyo*) bathing. Lying by the pool are their heavenly raiment (*hagoromo*). Wanting a garment as a trophy, he steals one. However, the maiden whose robe was stolen cannot return to heaven without it, so she agrees to dance for him in exchange for its return. The play is taken from Japanese mythology, but similar legends appear in China and Korea, and variations are found in India and in the Arabian Nights tales.

Mushi-kiri, page 20

The name for this medication is made up of the kanji for *mushi* and the kanji that means cut. It refers to cutting the connection between the human and the *mushi*.

Yôshitsu, page 36

The name Yôshitsu is made up of *yô*, which means fairy or supernatural, and *shitsu* which means matter or substance. So it could be interpreted as fairy-stuff.

Palace of the Dragon King, page 51

The Dragon King (or Dragon God's) palace is featured in several Japanese myths, legends, and fairy tales, the most popular of which is the tale of Urashima Taro, who rescues a turtle. As a reward, a turtle messenger brings him to the Dragon God's palace at the bottom of the sea.

Satorigi, page 64

The word *satori* has found its way into the English language as a small or sudden enlightenment. In Japanese it means that as well, but its more down-to-Earth interpretation is simply "understanding." The kanji for *ki* means tree.

Shinboku, page 72

Shinboku are trees that have been venerated as housing *kami*, the Shintô religion's animist deities, usually translated as "gods." Trees that are so designated are particularly long lived, unusually large, have survived disasters when most other trees didn't, or have had some other distinguishing attribute. Their trunks are often decorated with folded strips of white paper, a Shintô indicator of a sacred site.

The Scented Darkness, page 100

The word *kaoru* means a scent, as in something pleasant. (Bad smells get other words.) Note that the character's name is also Kaoru, so this could also be interpreted as Kaoru's darkness.

Kairô, page 132

The *mushi* name Kairô is made up of the kanji pronounced *kai*, which means to go through a cycle, and *rô*, which means narrow.

Mushi-kudashi, page 218

There are actual medicines that go by the Japanese name of *mushi-kudashi*. They are medicines for purging parasites found within the body such as tapeworms and the like. In present-day Japan the kanji for *mushi* is the one meaning bug, whereas the *mushi-kudashi* that Ginko mentioned used the kanji for the *mushi* of the Mushishi world.

Teni-muhô, page 251

Teni-muhô is a Japanese term meaning flawless, but it is made up of kanji that mean heaven, cloth, no, and seam. In other words, this word denoting perfection has a literal meaning of heavenly raiment with no seams.

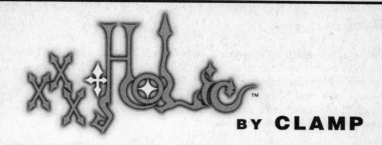

BY **CLAMP**

Watanuki Kimihiro is haunted by visions. When he finds himself irresistibly drawn into a shop owned by Yûko, a mysterious witch, he is offered the chance to rid himself of the spirits that plague him. He accepts, but soon realizes that he's just been tricked into working for the shop to pay off the cost of Yûko's services! But this isn't any ordinary kind of shop . . . In this shop, Yûko grants wishes to those in need. But they must have the strength of will not only to truly understand their need, but to give up something incredibly precious in return.

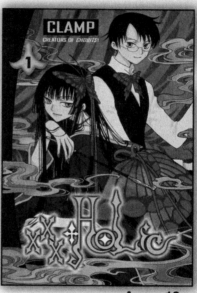

Ages: 13+

Special extras in each volume! Read them all!

VISIT WWW.DELREYMANGA.COM TO:
• View release date calendars for upcoming volumes
• Sign up for Del Rey's free manga e-newsletter
• Find out the latest about new Del Rey Manga series

SAYONARA, ZETSUBOU-SENSEI

BY KOJI KUMETA

THE POWER OF NEGATIVE THINKING
VOLUME 1

Nozomu Itoshiki is depressed. Very depressed. He's certifiably suicidal, but he's also the beloved schoolteacher of a class of unique students, each charming in her own way. For all of them, it's a special time, when the right teacher can have a lasting positive effect on their lives. But is that teacher Itoshiki, a.k.a. Zetsubou-sensei, who just wants to find the perfect place to die?

SAYONARA, ZETSUBOU-SENSEI
THE POWER OF NEGATIVE THINKING VOLUME 1
KOJI KUMETA

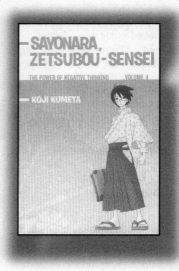

Available anywhere books or comics are sold!

VISIT WWW.DELREYMANGA.COM TO:
- Read sample pages
- View release date calendars for upcoming volumes
- Sign up for Del Rey's free manga e-newsletter
- Find out the latest about new Del Rey Manga series

RATING OT AGES 16+

DEL REY MANGA デルレイ
www.delreymanga.com

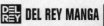

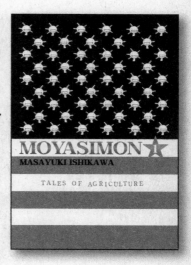
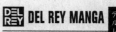

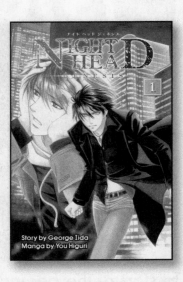
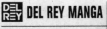
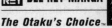

[STOP!]

You are going the wrong way!

Manga is a completely different
type of reading experience.

To start at the *beginning*, go to the *end*!

That's right! Authentic manga is read the traditional Japanese
way—from right to left, exactly the *opposite* of how American
books are read. It's easy to follow: Just go to the other end of
the book, and read each page—and each panel—from right side
to left side, starting at the top right. Now you're experiencing
manga as it was meant to be.